W9-CDC-118

MAN AND HIS MEASURE

FRANCIS CONNOLLY
FORDHAM UNIVERSITY

MAN *and* HIS MEASURE

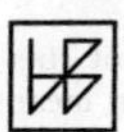

HARCOURT, BRACE & WORLD, INC.

NEW YORK BURLINGAME

Library of Congress Catalog Card Number: 64-13284

PRINTED IN THE UNITED STATES OF AMERICA

TO THE

STUDENTS OF THIS GENERATION

FOR WHOM

JOHN F. KENNEDY

ASSAYED THE MEASURE OF MAN

IN THESE WORDS FROM HIS INAUGURAL ADDRESS

The torch has been passed to a new generation . . . born in this century, tempered by war, disciplined by a hard and bitter peace, proud of our ancient heritage—and unwilling to witness or permit the slow undoing of those human rights to which this nation has always been committed . . . .

With a good conscience our only sure reward, with history the final judge of our deeds, let us go forth to lead the land we love, asking His blessing and His help, but knowing that here on earth God's work must truly be our own.

CONTENTS

PART ONE
What Is Man?

I
THE BEGINNING OF AWARENESS
Experience and Language

II
THE HEROIC IMAGE
Who Am I? Whom Ought I to Become?

DRAMA

III
THE TRAGIC EXPERIENCE
Out of Passion—Perception

STORIES

ESSAYS

POETRY

DRAMA

V
THOUGHT AND LANGUAGE
The Modes of Science and the Modes of Art

PART TWO

What is Man's Measure?

VI

THE MEASURE OF EXCELLENCE

The Habitual Vision of Greatness

ESSAYS

POETRY

VIII
THE MEASURE OF JUSTICE
The Passionate Will to Give Each Man What is Rightfully His

STORIES

POETRY

ANALYTIC TABLE OF CONTENTS

PROSE FICTION:

Short Stories

PROSE FICTION:

Long Stories and Novellas

ESSAYS:

Autobiography, Narration, and Description

ESSAYS:

Biography, History, Exposition, and Narration

ESSAYS:

Literary Criticism

ESSAYS:

Analysis, Argument, and Persuasion

ANALYSIS BY DEFINITION AND CLASSIFICATION

ANALYSIS BY COMPARISON AND CONTRAST

ANALYSIS BY CAUSAL ANALYSIS AND PROCESS

ESSAYS:
Argument and Persuasion

ESSAYS:
Research Paper

POETRY:

Lyrical

POETRY:
Narrative and Dramatic

POETRY:
Satirical, Humorous, and Didactic

DRAMA

PREFACE

THE AIM of this book is to offer some representative writings that, taken individually, will provide genuine enjoyment and, taken together, will direct the reader's attention to the perennial questions: What is man? What is his measure? This aim presupposes that literary achievement consists in good part of an imaginative realization of what these questions imply. It presupposes, too, that the surest way to excite interest in literary technique and scholarship is to exhibit the permanent concern of literature for man's permanent questions.

The design of this anthology is thematic. The theme is "man and his measure." Part One, "What Is Man?" shows how literature, in various forms (drama, essay, short story, and poem) and in its full range from the classical period to the present, explores the question: What does it mean to be a man? The selections in Section I, "The Beginning of Awareness," demonstrate that man is intellectually aware; he sees, feels, thinks, and responds to his experiences. The selections in Section II, "The Heroic Image," show how this awareness gives rise to aspiration: man hopes to achieve his full human destiny, and thus he models himself according to various heroic, or anti-heroic, patterns. Some inevitable consequences of his aspirations are defeat, fear, and suffering. The tragic experiences from which he may derive a purer sense of his selfhood and of his common humanity are described in the selections in Section III, "The Tragic Experience." Other consequences of his aspirations are a sharper intellectual grasp of the absurdities of human life and the development of a comic sense that helps man to enjoy, or at least to endure, his unpredictable human predicament. Selections that illustrate these consequences appear in Section IV, "The Comic Experience." Man's personal maturity as well as the maturity of the race as a whole results in a progressive refinement of human powers of thought and expression, as we see in Section V, "Thought and Language."

In Part One, then, the reader may trace man's development as it is reflected in and through literature from an initial awareness of experience and language to an awareness of his own awareness—that is, to a fuller consciousness of his many powers of sensation, feeling, thought, and expression. Man is aware, man hopes and aspires. Man weeps, he laughs, he reflects upon, and words his experiences. But this paradigm hardly exhausts the mystery of man. Nor does it supply the measure according to which we may estimate the value of his experiences.

As Ruth Nanda Anshen observes, "The naturalist principle that man is the measure of all things has been shattered more than ever in our age by the question, 'What is the measure of man?'" She goes on to say, "Contemporary man is more profoundly perplexed about the nature of man than his ancestors were . . . . And having lost the sense of who and what he is, he fails to grasp the meaning of his fellow man, of his vocation, and of the nature and purpose of knowledge itself."[1] Man needs to transcend his singular experiences, in Miss Anshen's words, to point toward "a morality of aspiration to spiritual experience," to discover another dimension of the human spirit.

Part Two, "What Is Man's Measure?" focuses on literature that embodies a "morality of aspiration," that searches for measures of intellectual excellence, moral integrity, and happiness. The selections in Section VI, "The Measure of Excellence," are particularly relevant for contemporary students. They demonstrate the ideal of intellectual excellence in thought and in the arts of expression—an ideal measured not only by the best achievements of the past but also by the needs of the present and the opportunities of the future. Literature also discovers how love encompasses more than the craving for affection, emotional satisfaction, and self-expression, and the selections in Section VII, "The Measure of Love," describe the various ways man loves. Section VIII, "The Measure of Justice," records man's struggle to be just in his relations with society, with the state, with governments, with his fellow man, and, above all, with his own conscience. Finally, in Section IX, "The Measure of Wisdom," we see how literature is forever in search of that harmony between true knowledge and prudent action that guides man toward happiness.

In addition to its focus on various interrelated themes, *Man and His Measure* is also designed to present the characteristic achievements of literary forms and genres: of the short story and novella; of the drama, both tragic and comic; of poems lyric, narrative and dramatic, satirical and didactic; of essays both formal and informal. Thus the selections may be read not only in the light of a theme but also in the light of their formal and stylistic qualities. Sophocles's *Oedipus Rex*, for instance, illustrates the Greek view of the meaning of tragic experience and, simultaneously, the artistic structure of Attic tragedy. Similarly, Cervantes's "The Captive's Story" embodies Renaissance ideals of the military hero and demonstrates, especially in the perspective of the succeeding stories by Muriel Spark and Katherine Anne Porter, the technical characteristics of earlier narrative fiction. We should mention, too, that the more detailed questions on the particular structure and style of the selections, as well as

1 In the Introduction to *A Quest for Life's Meaning* by F. S. C. Northrop (Simon and Schuster, 1962), pp. xiv and xix.

explanatory notes on the more demanding selections, like those of Plato, St. Augustine, Molière, Hopkins, Yeats, and Eliot, are provided in the *Instructor's Manual* prepared to accompany this book.

Some of the teachers who use this book will want to stress the relevance of literature to human needs; still others the importance of understanding that literature as a whole is a continuous dialogue between past and present—that, for instance, John Henry Newman and T. S. Eliot converse with Virgil and Dante as Dante once conversed with Virgil and Virgil with Homer. Many teachers will prefer to concentrate on the formal literary perfections of a single great work of a Sophocles, a Shakespeare, a Molière. In pursuing one or several of these time-tested and useful ends, the teacher may be tempted to overlook a simple bread-and-butter objective: the development of the student's writing ability.

A central purpose of *Man and His Measure* is to challenge the student to think in a personal way about the most important problems of human existence, to provide a context within which he can develop his thoughts, and, above all, to encourage him to write, and thus to enter, however modestly, into that continuous civilized conversation we call humane literature. If it be objected that the student needs first to learn how to write plain prose before he enters a civilized conversation, the reply might be that he can learn to write more effectively by accepting the challenge of excellence than he can by avoiding it. Hence, in drawing up writing assignments for the *Instructor's Manual,* this editor has assumed that, while the student writer is limited, he is also perfectible, and that, while he needs the discipline of many short exercises in the usual rhetorical manner, he benefits too by more extended and more original assignments.

For the basic ideas of this anthology I acknowledge my prolonged indebtedness to many authors, past and present. Some are represented in these pages, others are cited in the introductory sections and in the *Instructor's Manual.* I am particularly indebted to the authors whose words I quoted or paraphrased in the epigraphs. They are, in the order of their appearance, W. H. Auden (II), Francis Fergusson (III), Alfred North Whitehead (VI), Guillem de Montanhagol (VII), St. Thomas Aquinas (VIII), and St. Augustine (IX). Each of these writers suggested important insights into themes presented in *Man and His Measure.*

I was encouraged to stress, once again, the role of literature as a humane as well as a formal and historical study by my younger colleagues and students. They have persistently reminded me that the most enduring and exciting element of literature is its unending search for the meaning of man. The key word here is *search.* Search implies that we approach literature with questions like Who am I? Whom ought I to become? What do I know? What ought I to know? It may be that many readers will find some of the answers they seek. It is certain, however, that all readers will discover that seeking is finding, especially when their seeking advances in depth and perspective. To ask questions is to foreshadow answers. For we cannot seek, we cannot question without first possessing, however obscurely, some intuition into the meanings that are both the incentives and the goals of our study.

Above all, in thanking those who have helped me, I wish to acknowledge the unfailing generosity of Mary K. Connolly, who prepared the manuscript for the press and assisted in reading proof.

August 1963 FRANCIS CONNOLLY

PART ONE

What Is Man?

I

THE BEGINNING OF AWARENESS

Experience and Language

INTRODUCTION

I

WHEN we speak of awareness, what do we mean? The word itself means to be wary, to be awake, to recognize what may easily be overlooked. It implies a state of heightened consciousness in which we respond to individual sights and sounds and, more importantly, to the meanings of our perceptions, our feelings, our thoughts, our actions, and our resolutions. In short, to be aware is to be alive to ourselves, to our personal being.

In literature awareness goes by other names. A writer is said to be aware when he responds to experience with understanding, imagination, sympathy. All these terms imply that the writer has seen vividly, has felt intensely, has recorded exactly memorable impressions that, by virtue of his literary skill, come into our possession. Henry James summed up his advice to young writers in two principles. The first was: "Write from experience only." But then James hastened to add: "Try to be one of the people on whom nothing is lost!" Thus the writer is one who benefits by experience; what he receives from life he gives to his readers. Awareness, then, is a combination of the power to receive from life and the power to communicate what one has received.

Perhaps the writer's greatest gift to us is his communication of his own creative power. He does this by inducing us to become, in a sense, cocreators in his own work. To know him we must read his work warily, alert not only to the literal *what* of his language, but to its nuanced and modifying *how*. The writer's *how* is the particular form and convention in which he chooses to express himself and the tone of voice that he employs directly in his own address, as in the essay, or obliquely through fictitious persons, as in the story, poem, or drama. A vigilant reader re-creates what the author has written in the total sense of *what* and *how*.

The reader can advance to a higher degree of awareness, one that involves creative activity of his own. This activity is simply his response to a work of literature. True, one cannot talk back to a book as one can to a living person. Nevertheless, all literature is a kind of dialogue in which the reader takes an active part by questioning, interpreting, comparing, contrasting, and judging the author's work. Where the reader approves, he tends to expand and apply the insights of the writer to his own experience. Where he disapproves, he tends to develop the points of difference by proposing other points of view or opposite assumptions. Live literature provokes creative thinking, blessing, in Portia's phrase, him that takes as well as him that gives.

While all literature, whatever its theme, stimulates our awareness, the literature centering on the theme of self-knowledge touches us to the quick; it compels us to look first at the experiences of others, then to discover and examine experiences of our own. In the selections that follow, you will find a common concern with the theme of self-knowledge, of initial moral awareness. Most of the stories, essays, and poems are directly concerned with youth; all deal with some aspect of "growing up."

II

IN WILLIAM FAULKNER'S "The Bear" young Isaac McCaslin goes on a hunt. The hunt is exciting in itself; but "The Bear" is more importantly the story of young McCaslin's growing awareness of his heritage and his personal destiny. At the end, his father's words render the theme explicitly:

> "Courage, and honor, and pride," his father said, "and pity, and love of justice and liberty. They all touch the heart, and what the heart holds to becomes truth, as far as we know the truth. Do you see now?" . . .
>
> "Yes, sir," he said.

The boy in "Sled" also comes to his moment of awareness when, after gratuitously and maliciously deceiving his sister, he tastes the misery of remorse. "He was wishing that he were some time a long time away from now and somewhere a long way away from here." Like Isaac, he *sees,* once his heart is touched.

In "The Rocking-Horse Winner" poor Paul, obsessed by the unspoken phrase *"There must be more money,"* does not fully realize that his mother's failure to love him drives him to his death. But the reader is aware of it. D. H. Lawrence's sustained irony, through which the fascinated spectator sees more than the characters see, relentlessly presses home the effects, social as well as personal, of perverted values. "But, poor devil, poor devil, he's best gone out of a life where he rides his rocking-horse to find a winner." This final remark of Paul's uncle speaks our own awareness of the tragedy implicit in the loveless love of money.

III

THESE three stories are dramatic presentations of impressions derived from experience. In fiction we witness the illusion of action; characters act and speak in the theater of the imagination and the author is only indirectly present in the voice of the narrator. Different, but no less valuable, is the direct presentation of moments of awareness in the personal essay. Here the writer, speaking in his own voice, recalls moments of intense joy or sorrow that are unforgettable for their own sake, or moments of special insight that, upon reflection, seem to have shaped his life.

The range of the personal essay is varied in subject and perspective. Thus, in "A Winter Treat," Laurie Lee, the British poet, recaptures the hilarity of childhood in his account of the annual church tea and entertainment. If one asked the poet his reasons for writing the essay, his answer might be: "The event lives with me as one of the great moments of my childhood, and I must tell you about it—as I remember it." The style—simple, unpretentious, effervescent—reflects the happiness of youthful experience.

On the other hand, while James Agee's "Knoxville: Summer 1915" and John Updike's "Boyhood in the 1940's" also focus on childhood and youth and maintain points of view consonant with youthful speakers, their tone is subtly blended with the attitudes of maturity. Agee's recollections are in the historical present. The action takes place directly before our eyes, but we know it as a past action reborn in his imagination. "It is not of the games children play in the evening that I want to speak now, it is of a contemporaneous atmosphere that has little to do with them: that of the fathers of families. . . ." This sentence creates a double vision: that of the young boy and that of the man remembering his boyhood.

Similarly, John Updike's boyhood impressions mesh with subsequent knowledge. "It has taken me the shock of many returnings," he writes, ". . . to learn . . . that change is the order of things." Here too we are reminded that the writer's perspective combines the past and the present, that the incident, however faithfully recorded, is suspended in a delicately strong web of reflection. These essays are, in short, more complex in subject, tone, and perspective than Lee's "A Winter Treat."

There are still higher degrees of complication in our awareness. If, as Henry James remarked, the true writer is one on whom nothing is lost, one can readily understand how much those writers are aware of who fuse their own direct impressions of life with the impressions they have received from books.

In "Out of a Book" Elizabeth Bowen reminds us how deeply the imagination, the faculty of awareness, "is rooted in the compost of forgotten books." For her, as for most creative readers and writers, it is almost impossible to discriminate among impressions received through experience and those first grasped through reading. And Graham Greene tells us unequivocally that for him the reading of a book in youth could mark a crisis, "the moment when life took a new slant in its journey towards death."

Elizabeth Bowen and Graham Greene are gifted writers who needed no invitation to adventure alone among books. Their childhood desire to read was as compelling as their mature impulse to write. They are both exceptional cases. The great majority of readers become aware of literature through the stimulation of the classroom. Francis Townsend's "A Freshman in Lilliput" tells us how his encounter with a great teacher first opened his eyes to the value of "the strictest fidelity to one's thoughts," then to an awareness of the complicated simplicity of Jonathan Swift's style, and ultimately to a fruitful career as a scholarly man of letters.

Essays such as those by Elizabeth Bowen, Greene, and Townsend show how our moments of awareness, whether derived from life or from literature, are directly relevant to our own creative life—that is, to all our awarenesses taken together, connected, examined, assessed, and finally made articulate.

That memory is an agent of intellect, however deeply rooted in sense, is partly the theme of the selection from Book X of St. Augustine's *Confessions.* St. Augustine finds memory to be one great answer to the riddling question of personal identity. When he asks himself "Who art thou?" he searches for the answer in his awarenesses, in his memory. For him memory is far more comprehensive than it is for those who restrict it to the facts of consciousness. Memory is infinitely enriched by its possession of wisdom. It is a manifold awareness. St. Augustine describes it thus:

> Behold in the plains, and caves, and caverns of my memory, innumerable and innumerably full of innumerable kinds of things . . . over all these do I run, I fly; I dive on this side and on that, as far as I can, and there is no end. So great is the force of memory, so great the force of life, even in the mortal life of man.

IV

IF PROSE literature is the artistic record of those luminous moments in which sense is radiant with intelligence and feeling, then what is poetry? Poetry too is just such a record. But it speaks a special language—one that is necessarily more concentrated, more selective in its diction, more intensely expressed, and hence more tightly organized in a structure of words and sounds. Prose is recitation; poetry is song, chant, evocation. Poetry conveys meanings far beyond those contained in its explicit statements. Like music, it vibrates in the memory, echoing with a different resonance in different souls.

The vigilant reader will attempt to receive each resonance—not necessarily to agree with it, for the resonance of poetry is not arguable—but to recognize it as a particular sensibility responding to a particular human predicament. The poem is the meeting ground of two souls, not merely of two intellects.

This description of the awareness found in a poem implies that poetry is intensely personal. So it is. The five poems in Section I all deal with revelations derived by observation and reflection on some aspect of childhood. They all express some feeling about childhood, yet all take different points of view. Walt Whitman's lyric "Beginning My Studies" conveys a note of wonder in a brief soliloquy. John Crowe Ransom warns his school girls that their beauty is perishable. For Francis Thompson childhood is a mingling of sadness in the sweet and sweetness in the sad. For William Butler Yeats the presence of the school children is an occasion for meditative vision about the mystery of human nature. Gerard Manley Hopkins fuses youth, spring, and grace in his prayerful sonnet. In his elaborate "Ode: Intimations of Immortality," William Wordsworth speculates on the presence of the divine in the child and in nature. One man carols joyfully; another laments; a third, trembling, prays; a fourth dreams; a fifth weaves a dream into a philosophy. Each one puts us in possession of the poet's experience in language that is at once recognizable yet strange. Each man, by recording his personal history, awakens our own conscious personality.

For a measure of man, as of literature, is the quality of awareness; we achieve a human size when we are one of those on whom "nothing is lost."

STORIES

William Faulkner

THE BEAR

HE WAS ten. But it had already begun, long before that day when at last he wrote his age in two figures and he saw for the first time the camp where his father and Major de Spain and old General Compson and the others spent two weeks each November and two weeks again each June. He had already inherited then, without ever having seen it, the tremendous bear with one trap-ruined foot which, in an area almost a hundred miles deep, had earned itself a name, a definite designation like a living man.

He had listened to it for years: the long legend of corncribs rifled, of shotes and grown pigs and even calves carried bodily into the woods and devoured, of traps and deadfalls overthrown and dogs mangled and slain, and shotgun and even rifle charges delivered at point-blank range and with no more effect than so many peas blown through a tube by a boy—a corridor of wreckage and destruction beginning back before he was born, through which sped, not fast but rather with the ruthless and irresistible deliberation of a locomotive, the shaggy tremendous shape.

It ran in his knowledge before he ever saw it. It looked and towered in his dreams before he even saw the unaxed woods where it left its crooked print, shaggy, huge, red-eyed, not malevolent but just big—too big for the dogs which tried to bay it, for the horses which tried to ride it down, for the men and the bullets they fired into it, too big for the very country which was its constricting scope. He seemed to see it entire with a child's complete divination before he ever laid eyes on either—the doomed wilderness whose edges were being constantly and punily gnawed at by men with axes and plows who feared it because it was wilderness, men myriad and nameless even to one another in the land where the old bear had earned a name, through which ran not even a mortal animal but an anachronism, indomitable and invincible, out of an old dead time, a phantom, epitome and apotheosis of the old wild life at which the puny humans swarmed and hacked in a fury of abhorrence and fear, like pgymies about the ankles of a drowsing elephant: the old bear solitary, indomitable and alone, widowered, childless, and absolved of mortality—old Priam reft of his old wife and having outlived all his sons.

Until he was ten, each November he would watch the wagon containing the dogs and the bedding and food and guns and his father and Tennie's Jim, the Negro, and Sam Fathers, the Indian, son of a slave woman and a Chickasaw chief, depart on the road to town, to Jefferson, where Major de Spain and the others would join them. To the boy, at seven, eight, and nine, they were not going into the Big Bottom to hunt bear and deer, but to keep yearly rendezvous with the bear which they did not even intend to kill. Two weeks later they would return, with no trophy, no head and skin. He had not expected it. He had not even been afraid it would be in the wagon. He believed that even after he was ten and his father would let him go too, for those two weeks in November, he would merely make another one, along with his father and Major de Spain and General Compson and the others, the dogs which feared to bay at it and the rifles and shotguns which failed even to bleed it, in the yearly pageant of the old bear's furious immortality.

Then he heard the dogs. It was in the second week of his first time in the camp. He stood with Sam Fathers against a big oak beside the faint crossing where they had stood each dawn for nine days now, hearing the dogs. He had heard them once before, one morning last week—a murmur, sourceless, echoing through the wet woods, swelling presently into separate voices which he could recognize and call by name. He had raised and cocked the gun as Sam told him and stood motionless again while the uproar, the invisible course, swept up and past and faded; it seemed to him that he could actually see the deer, the buck, blond, smoke-colored, elongated with speed, fleeing, vanishing, the woods, the gray solitude, still ringing even when the cries of the dogs had died away.

"Now let the hammers down," Sam said.

"You knew they were not coming here too," he said

"Yes," Sam said. "I want you to learn how to do when you didn't shoot. It's after the chance for the bear or the deer has done already come and gone that men and dogs get killed."

"Anyway," he said, "it was just a deer."

Then on the tenth morning he heard the dogs again. And he readied the too-long, too-heavy gun as Sam had taught him, before Sam even spoke. But this time it was no deer, no ringing chorus of dogs running strong on a free scent, but a moiling yapping an octave too high, with something more than indecision and even abjectness in it, not even moving very fast, taking a long time to pass completely out of hearing, leaving then somewhere in the air that echo, thin, slightly hysterical, abject, almost grieving, with no sense of a fleeing, unseen, smoke-colored, grass-eating shape ahead of it, and Sam, who had taught him first of all to cock the gun and take position where he could see everywhere and then never move again, had himself moved up beside him; he could hear Sam breathing at his shoulder, and he could see the arched curve of the old man's inhaling nostrils.

"Hah," Sam said. "Not even running. Walking."

"Old Ben!" the boy said. "But up here!" he cried. "Way up here!"

"He do it every year," Sam said. "Once. Maybe to see who in camp this time, if he can shoot or not. Whether we got the dog yet that can bay and hold him. He'll take them to the river, then he'll send them back home. We may as well go back too; see how they look when they come back to camp."

When they reached the camp the hounds were already there, ten of them crouching back under the kitchen, the boy and Sam squatting to peer back into the obscurity where they had huddled, quiet, the eyes luminous, glowing at them and vanishing, and no sound, only that effluvium of something more than dog, stronger than dog and not just animal, just beast, because still there had been nothing in front of that abject and almost painful yapping save the solitude, the wilderness, so that when the eleventh hound came in at noon and with all the others watching—even old Uncle Ash, who called himself first a cook—Sam daubed the tattered ear and the raked shoulder with turpentine and axle grease, to the boy it was still no living creature, but the wilderness which, leaning for the moment down, had patted lightly once the hound's temerity.

"Just like a man," Sam said. "Just like folks. Put off as long as she could having to be brave, knowing all the time that sooner or later she would have to be brave to keep on living with herself, and knowing all the time beforehand what was going to happen to her when she done it."

That afternoon, himself on the one-eyed wagon mule which did not mind the smell of blood nor, as they told him, of bear, and with Sam on the other one, they rode for more than three hours through the rapid, shortening winter day. They followed no path, no trail even that he could see; almost at once they were in a country which he had never seen before. Then he knew why Sam had made him ride the mule which would not spook. The sound one stopped short and tried to whirl and bolt even as Sam got down, blowing its breath, jerking and wrenching at the rein, while Sam held it, coaxing it forward with his voice, since he could not risk tying it, drawing it forward while the boy got down from the marred one.

Then, standing beside Sam in the gloom of the dying afternoon, he looked down at the rotted over-turned log, gutted and scored with claw marks and, in the wet earth beside it, the print of the enormous warped two-toed foot. He knew now what he had smelled when he peered under the kitchen where the dogs huddled. He realized for the first time that the bear which had run in his listening and loomed in his dreams since before he could remember to the contrary, and which, therefore, must have existed in the listening and dreams of his father and Major de Spain and even old General Compson, too, before they began to remember in their turn, was a mortal animal, and that if they had departed for the camp each November without any actual hope of bringing its trophy back, it was not because it could not be slain, but because so far they had had no actual hope to.

"Tomorrow," he said.

"We'll try tomorrow," Sam said. "We ain't got the dog yet."

"We've got eleven. They ran him this morning."

"It won't need but one," Sam said. "He ain't here. Maybe he ain't nowhere. The only other way will be for him to run by accident over somebody that has a gun."

"That wouldn't be me," the boy said. "It will be Walter or Major or—"

"It might," Sam said. "You watch close in the morning. Because he's smart. That's how come he has lived this long. If he gets hemmed up and has to pick out somebody to run over, he will pick out you."

"How?" the boy said. "How will he know—" He ceased. "You mean he already knows me, that I ain't never been here before, ain't had time to find out yet whether I—" He ceased again, looking at Sam, the old man whose face revealed nothing until it smiled. He said humbly, not even amazed, "It was me he was watching. I don't reckon he did need to come but once."

The next morning they left the camp three hours before daylight. They rode this time because it was too far to walk, even the dogs in the wagon; again the first gray light found him in a place which he had never seen before, where Sam had placed him and told him to stay and then departed. With the gun which was too big for him, which did not even belong to him, but to Major de Spain, and which he had fired only once—at a stump on the first day, to learn the recoil and how to reload it—he stood against a gum tree beside a little bayou whose black still water crept without movement out of a canebrake and crossed a small clearing and into cane again, where, invisible, a bird—the big woodpecker called Lord-to-God by Negroes—clattered at a dead limb.

It was a stand like any other, dissimilar only in incidentals to the one where he had stood each morning for ten days; a territory new to him, yet no less familiar than that other one which, after almost two weeks, he had come to believe he knew a little—the same solitude, the same loneliness through which human beings had merely passed without altering it, leaving no mark, no scar, which looked exactly as it must have looked when the first ancestor of Sam Fathers' Chickasaw predecessors crept into it and looked about, club or stone ax or bone arrow drawn and poised; different only because, squatting at the edge of the kitchen, he smelled the hounds huddled and cringing beneath it and saw the raked ear and shoulder of the one who, Sam said, had had to be brave once in order to live with herself, and saw yesterday in the earth beside the gutted log the print of the living foot.

He heard no dogs at all. He never did hear them. He only heard the drumming of the woodpecker stop short off and knew that the bear was looking at him. He never saw it. He did not know whether it was in front of him or behind him. He did not move, holding the useless gun, which he had not even had warning to cock and which even now he did not cock, tasting in his saliva that taint as of brass which he knew now because he had smelled it when he peered under the kitchen at the huddled dogs.

Then it was gone. As abruptly as it had ceased, the woodpecker's dry, monotonous clatter set up again, and after a while he even believed he could hear the dogs—a murmur, scarce a sound even, which he had probably been hearing for some time before he even remarked it, drifting into hearing and then out again, dying away. They came nowhere near him. If it was a bear they ran, it was another bear. It was Sam himself who came out of the cane and crossed the bayou, followed by the injured bitch of yesterday. She was almost at heel, like a bird dog, making no sound. She came and crouched against his leg, trembling, staring off into the cane.

"I didn't see him," he said. "I didn't, Sam!"

"I know it," Sam said. "He done the looking. You didn't hear him neither, did you?"

"No," the boy said. "I—"

"He's smart," Sam said. "Too smart." He looked down at the hound, trembling faintly and steadily against the boy's knee. From the raked shoulder a few drops of fresh blood oozed and clung. "Too big. We ain't got the dog yet. But maybe someday. Maybe not next time. But someday."

So I must see him, he thought. *I must look at him.* Otherwise, it seemed to him that it would go on like this forever, as it had gone on with his father and Major de Spain, who was older than his father, and even with old General Compson, who had been old enough to be a brigade commander in 1865. Otherwise, it would go on so forever, next time and next time, after and after and after. It seemed to him that he could never see the two of them, himself and the bear, shadowy in the limbo from which time emerged, becoming time; the old bear absolved of mortality and himself partaking, sharing a little of it, enough of it. And he knew now what he had smelled in the huddled dogs and tasted in his saliva. He recognized fear. *So I will have to see him,* he thought, without dread or even hope. *I will have to look at him.*

It was in June of the next year. He was eleven. They were in camp again, celebrating Major de Spain's and General Compson's birthdays. Although the one had been born in September and the other in the depth of winter and in another decade, they had met for two weeks to fish and shoot squirrels and turkeys and run coons and wildcats with the dogs at night. That is, he and Boon Hoggenbeck and the Negroes fished and shot squirrels and ran the coons and cats, because the proved hunters, not only Major de Spain and old General Compson, who spent those two weeks sitting in a rocking chair before a tremendous iron pot of Brunswick stew, stirring and tasting, with old Ash to quarrel with about how he was making it and Tennie's Jim to pour whiskey from the demijohn into the tin dipper from which he drank it, but even the boy's father and Walter Ewell, who were still young enough, scorned such, other than shooting the wild gobblers with pistols for wagers on their marksmanship.

Or, that is, his father and the others believed he was hunting squirrels. Until the third day, he thought that Sam Fathers believed that too. Each morning he would leave the camp right after breakfast. He had his own gun now, a Christmas present. He went back to the tree beside the bayou where he had stood that morning. Using the compass which old General Compson had given him, he ranged from that point; he was teaching himself to be a better-than-fair woodsman without knowing he was doing it. On the second day he even found the gutted log where he had first seen the crooked print. It was almost completely crumbled now, healing with unbelievable speed, a passionate and almost visible relinquishment, back into the earth from which the tree had grown.

He ranged the summer woods now, green with gloom; if anything, actually dimmer than in November's gray dissolution, where, even at noon, the sun fell only in intermittent dappling upon the earth, which never completely dried out and which crawled with snakes—moccasins and water snakes and rattlers, themselves the color of the dappling gloom, so that he would not always see them until they moved, returning later and later, first day, second day, passing in the twilight of the third evening the little log pen enclosing the log stable where Sam was putting up the horses for the night.

"You ain't looked right yet," Sam said.

He stopped. For a moment he didn't answer. Then he said peacefully, in a peaceful rushing burst as when a boy's miniature dam in a little brook gives way, "All right. But how? I went to the bayou. I even found that log again. I—"

"I reckon that was all right. Likely he's been watching you. You never saw his foot?"

"I," the boy said—"I didn't—I never thought—"

"It's the gun," Sam said. He stood beside the fence motionless—the old man, the Indian, in the battered faded overalls and the five-cent straw hat which in the Negro's race had been the badge of his enslavement and was now the regalia of his freedom. The camp—the clearing, the house, the barn and its tiny lot with which Major de Spain in his turn had scratched punily and evanescently at the wilderness—faded in the dusk, back into the immemorial darkness of the woods. *The gun*, the boy thought. *The gun.*

"Be scared," Sam said. "You can't help that. But don't be afraid. Ain't nothing in the woods going to hurt you unless you corner it, or it smells that you are afraid. A bear or a deer, too, has got to be scared of a coward the same as a brave man has got to be."

The gun, the boy thought.

"You will have to choose," Sam said.

He left the camp before daylight, long before Uncle Ash would wake in his quilts on the kitchen floor and start the fire for breakfast. He had only the compass and a stick for snakes. He could go almost a mile before he would begin to need the compass. He sat on a log, the invisible compass in his invisible hand, while the secret night sounds, fallen still at his movements, scurried again and then ceased for good, and the owls ceased and gave over to the waking of day birds, and he could see the compass. Then he went fast yet still quietly; he was becoming better and better as a woodsman, still without having yet realized it.

He jumped a doe and a fawn at sunrise, walked them out of the bed, close enough to see them—the crash of undergrowth, the white scut, the fawn scudding behind her faster than he had believed it could run. He was hunting right, upwind, as Sam had taught him; not that it mattered now. He had left the gun; of his own will and relinquishment he had accepted not a gambit, not a choice, but a condition in which not only the bear's heretofore inviolable anonymity but all the old rules and balances of hunter and hunted had been abrogated. He would not even be afraid, not even in the moment when the fear would take him completely—blood, skin, bowels, bones, memory from the long time before it became his memory—all save that thin, clear, immortal lucidity which alone differed him from this bear and from all the other bear and deer he would ever kill in the humility and pride of his skill and endurance, to which Sam had spoken when he leaned in the twilight on the lot fence yesterday.

By noon he was far beyond the little bayou, farther into the new and alien country than he had ever been. He was traveling now not only by the old, heavy, biscuit-thick silver watch which had belonged to his grandfather. When he stopped at last, it was for the first time since he had risen from the log at dawn when he could see the compass. It was far enough. He had left the camp nine hours ago; nine hours from now, dark would have already been an hour old. But he didn't think that. He thought, *All right. Yes. But what?* and stood for a moment, alien and small in the green and topless solitude, answering his own question before it had formed and ceased. It was the watch, the compass, the stick—the three lifeless mechanicals with which for nine hours he had fended the wilderness off; he hung the watch and compass carefully on a bush and leaned the stick beside them and relinquished completely to it.

He had not been going very fast for the last two or three hours. He went no faster now, since distance would not matter even if he could have gone fast. And he was trying to keep a bearing on the tree where he had left the compass, trying to complete a circle which would bring him back to it or at least intersect itself, since direction would not matter now either. But the tree was not there, and he did as Sam had schooled him—made the next circle in the opposite direction, so that the two patterns would bisect somewhere, but crossing no print of his own feet, finding the tree as last, but in the wrong place—no bush, no compass, no watch—and the tree not even the tree, because there was a down log beside it and he did what Sam Fathers had told him was the next thing and the last.

As he sat down on the log he saw the crooked print—the warped, tremendous, two-toed indentation which, even as he watched it, filled with water. As he looked up, the wilderness coalesced, solidified—the glade, the tree he sought, the bush, the watch and the compass glinting where a ray of sunshine touched them. Then he saw the bear. It did not emerge, appear; it was just there, immobile, solid, fixed in the hot dappling of the green and windless noon, not as big as he had dreamed it, but as big as he had expected it, bigger, dimensionless against the dappled obscurity, looking at him where he sat quietly on the log and looked back at it.

Then it moved. It made no sound. It did not hurry. It crossed the glade, walking for an instant into the full glare of the sun; when it reached the other side it stopped again and looked back at him across one shoulder while his quiet breathing inhaled and exhaled three times.

Then it was gone. It didn't walk into the woods, the undergrowth.

It faded, sank back into the wilderness as he had watched a fish, a huge old bass, sink and vanish into the dark depths of its pool without even any movement of its fins.

He thought, *It will be next fall.* But it was not next fall, nor the next nor the next. He was fourteen then. He had killed his buck, and Sam Fathers had marked his face with the hot blood, and in the next year he killed a bear. But even before that accolade he had become as competent in the woods as many grown men with the same experience; by his fourteenth year he was a better woodsman than most grown men with more. There was no territory within thirty miles of the camp that he did not know—bayou, ridge, brake, landmark, tree and path. He could have led anyone to any point in it without deviation, and brought them out again. He knew the game trails that even Sam Fathers did not know; in his thirteenth year he found a buck's bedding place, and unbeknown to his father he borrowed Walter Ewell's rifle and lay in wait at dawn and killed the buck when it walked back to the bed, as Sam had told him how the old Chickasaw fathers did.

But not the old bear, although by now he knew its footprints better than he did his own, and not only the crooked one. He could see any one of the three sound ones and distinguish it from any other, and not only by its size. There were other bears within these thirty miles which left tracks almost as large, but this was more than that. If Sam Fathers had been his mentor and the back-yard rabbits and squirrels at home his kindergarten, then the wilderness the old bear ran was his college, the old male bear itself, so long unwifed and childless as to have become its own ungendered progenitor, was his alma mater. But he never saw it.

He could find the crooked print now almost whenever he liked, fifteen or ten or five miles, or sometimes nearer the camp than that. Twice while on stand during the three years he heard the dogs strike its trail by accident; on the second time they jumped it seemingly, the voices high, abject, almost human in hysteria, as on that first morning two years ago. But not the bear itself. He would remember that noon three years ago, the glade, himself and the bear fixed during that moment in the windless and dappled blaze, and it would seem to him that it had never happened, that he had dreamed that too. But it had happened. They had looked at each other, they had emerged from the wilderness old as earth, synchronized to the instant by something more than the blood that moved the flesh and bones which bore them, and touched, pledged something, affirmed, something more lasting than the frail web of bones and flesh which any accident could obliterate.

Then he saw it again. Because of the very fact that he thought of nothing else, he had forgotten to look for it. He was still hunting with Walter Ewell's rifle. He saw it cross the end of a long blow-down, a corridor where a tornado had swept, rushing through rather than over the tangle of trunks and branches as a locomotive would have, faster than he had ever believed it could move, almost as fast as a deer even, because a deer would have spent most of that time in the air, faster than he could bring the rifle sights up with it. And now he knew what had been wrong during all the three years. He sat on a log, shaking and trembling as if he had never seen the woods before nor anything that ran them, wondering with incredulous amazement how he could have forgotten the very thing which Sam Fathers had told him and which the bear itself had proved the next day and had now returned after three years to reaffirm.

And now he knew what Sam Fathers had meant about the right dog, a dog in which size would mean less than nothing. So when he returned alone in April—school was out then, so that the sons of farmers could help with the land's planting, and at last his father had granted him permission, on his promise to be back in four days—he had the dog. It was his own, a mongrel of the sort called by Negroes a fyce, a ratter, itself not much bigger than a rat and possessing that bravery which had long since stopped being courage and had become foolhardiness.

It did not take four days. Alone again, he found the trail on the first morning. It was not a stalk; it was an ambush. He timed the meeting almost as if it were an appointment with a human being. Himself holding the fyce muffled in a feed sack and Sam Fathers with two of the hounds on a piece of a plowline rope, they lay down wind of the trail at dawn of the second morning. They were so close that the bear turned without even running, as if in surprised amazement at the shrill and frantic uproar of the released fyce, turning at bay against the trunk of a tree, on its hind feet; it seemed to the boy that it would never stop rising, taller and taller, and even the two hounds seemed to take a desperate and despairing courage from the fyce, following it as it went in.

Then he realized that the fyce was actually not going to stop. He flung, threw the gun away, and ran; when he overtook and grasped the frantically pin-wheeling little dog, it seemed to him that he was directly under the bear.

He could smell it, strong and hot and rank. Sprawling, he looked up to where it loomed and towered over him like a cloudburst and colored like a thunderclap, quite familiar, peacefully and even lucidly familiar, until he remembered: This was the way he had used to dream about it. Then it was gone. He didn't see it go. He knelt, holding the frantic fyce with both hands, hearing the abashed wailing of the hounds drawing farther and farther away, until Sam came up. He carried the gun. He laid it down quietly beside the boy and stood looking down at him.

"You've done seed him twice now with a gun in your hands," he said. "This time you couldn't have missed him."

The boy rose. He still held the fyce. Even in his arms and clear of the ground, it yapped frantically, straining and surging after the fading uproar of the two hounds like a tangle of wire springs. He was panting a little, but he was neither shaking nor trembling now.

"Neither could you!" he said. "You had the gun! Neither did you!"

"And you didn't shoot," his father said. "How close were you?"

"I don't know, sir," he said. "There was a big wood tick inside his right hind leg. I saw that. But I didn't have the gun then."

"But you didn't shoot when you had the gun," his father said. "Why?"

But he didn't answer, and his father didn't wait for him to, rising and crossing the room, across the pelt of the bear which the boy had killed two years ago and the larger one which his father had killed before he was born, to the bookcase beneath the mounted head of the boy's first buck. It was the room which his father called the office, from which all the plantation business was transacted; in it for the fourteen years of his life he had heard the best of all talking. Major de Spain would be there and sometimes old General Compson, and Walter Ewell and Boon Hoggenback and Sam Fathers and Tennie's Jim, too, were hunters, knew the woods and what ran them.

He would hear it, not talking himself but listening—the wilderness, the big woods, bigger and older than any recorded document of white man fatuous enough to believe he had bought any fragment of it or Indian ruthless enough to pretend that any fragment of it had been his to convey. It was of the men, not white nor black nor red, but men, hunters with the will and hardihood to endure and the humility and skill to survive, and the dogs and the bear and deer juxtaposed and reliefed against it, ordered and compelled by and within the wilderness in the ancient and unremitting contest by the ancient and immitigable rules which voided all regrets and brooked no quarter, the voices quiet and weighty and deliberate for retrospection and recollection and exact remembering, while he squatted in the blazing firelight as Tennie's Jim squatted, who stirred only to put more wood on the fire and to pass the bottle from one glass to another. Because the bottle was always present, so that after a while it seemed to him that those fierce instants of heart and brain and courage and wiliness and speed were concentrated and distilled into that brown liquor which not women, not boys and children, but only hunters drank, drinking not of the blood they had spilled but some condensation of the wild immortal spirit, drinking it moderately, humbly even, not with the pagan's base hope of acquiring the virtues of cunning and strength and speed, but in salute to them.

His father returned with the book and sat down again and opened it. "Listen," he said. He read the five stanzas aloud, his voice quiet and deliberate in the room where there was no fire now because it was already spring. Then he looked up. The boy watched him. "All right," his father said. "Listen." He read again, but only the second stanza this time, to the end of it, the last two lines, and closed the book and put it on the table beside him. "She cannot fade, though thou hast not thy bliss, forever wilt thou love, and she be fair," he said.

"He's talking about a girl," the boy said.

"He had to talk about something," his father said. Then he said, "He was talking about truth. Truth doesn't change. Truth is one thing. It covers all things which touch the heart—honor and pride and pity and justice and courage and love. Do you see now?"

He didn't know. Somehow it was simpler than that. There was an old bear, fierce and ruthless, not merely just to stay alive, but with the fierce pride of liberty and freedom, proud enough of the liberty and freedom to see it threatened without fear or even alarm; nay, who at times even seemed deliberately to put that freedom and liberty in jeopardy in order to savor them, to remind his old strong bones and flesh to keep supple and quick to defend and preserve them. There was an old man, son of a Negro slave and an Indian king, inheritor on the one side of the long chronicle of a people who had learned humility through suffering, and pride through the endurance which survived the suffering and injustice, and on the other side, the chronicle of a people even longer in the land than the first, yet who no longer existed in the land at all save in the solitary brotherhood of an old Negro's alien blood and the wild and invincible spirit of an old bear. There was a boy who wished to learn humility and pride in order to become skillful and worthy in the woods, who suddenly found himself becoming so skillful so rapidly that he feared he would never become worthy because he had not learned humility and pride, although he had tried to, until one day and as suddenly he discovered that an old man who could not have defined either had led him, as though by the hand, to that point where an old bear and a little mongrel of a dog showed him that, by possessing one thing other, he would possess them both.

And a little dog, nameless and mongrel and many-fathered, grown, yet weighing less than six pounds, saying as if to itself, "I can't be dangerous, because there's nothing much smaller than I am; I can't be fierce, because they would call it just a noise; I can't be humble, because I'm already too close to the ground to genuflect; I can't be proud, because I wouldn't be near enough to it for anyone to know who was casting the shadow, and I don't even know that I'm not going to heaven, because they have already decided that I don't possess an immortal soul. So all I can be is brave. But it's all right. I can be that, even if they still call it just noise."

That was all. It was simple, much simpler than somebody talking in a book about youth and a girl he would never need to grieve over, because he could never approach any nearer her and would never have to get any farther away. He had heard about a bear, and finally got big enough to trail it, and he trailed it four years and at last met it with a gun in his hands and he didn't shoot. Because a little dog— But he could have shot long before the little dog covered the twenty yards to where the bear waited, and Sam Fathers could have shot at any time during that interminable minute while Old Ben stood on his hind feet over them. He stopped. His father was watching him gravely across the spring-rife twilight of the room; when he spoke, his words were as quiet as the twilight, too, not loud, because they did not need to be because they would last. "Courage, and honor, and pride," his father said, "and pity, and love of justice and of liberty. They all touch the heart, and what the heart holds to becomes truth, as far as we know the truth. Do you see now?"

Sam, and Old Ben, and Nip, he thought. And himself too. He had been all right too. His father had said so. "Yes, sir," he said.

Thomas E. Adams

SLED

ALL THE adventure of the night and snow lay before him: if only he could get out of the house.

"You can't go out," his mother said, "until you learn how to act like a gentleman. Now apologize to your sister."

He stared across the table at his sister.

"Go on," his mother said.

His sister was watching her plate. He could detect the trace of a smile at the corners of her mouth.

"I won't! She's laughing at me!" He saw the smile grow more pronounced. "Besides, she *is* a liar!"

His sister did not even bother to look up, and he felt from looking

---

at her that he had said exactly what she had wanted him to say. He grew irritated at his stupidity.

"That settles it," his mother said calmly, without turning from the stove. "No outs for you."

He stared at his hands, his mind in a panic. He could feel the smile on his sister's face. His hand fumbled with the fork on his plate. "No," he said meekly, prodding a piece of meat with the fork. "I'll apologize."

His sister looked up at him innocently.

"Well?" said his mother. "Go on."

He took a deep breath. "I'm . . ." He met his sister's gaze. "I'm sorry!" But it came out too loudly, he knew.

"He is not," his sister said.

He clenched his teeth and pinched his legs with his fingers. "I am too," he said. It sounded good, he knew; and it was half over. He had control now, and he relaxed a bit and even said further: "I'm sorry I called you a liar."

"That's better," his mother said. "You two should love each other. Not always be fighting."

He paused strategically for a long moment.

"Can I go out now?"

"Yes," his mother said.

He rose from the table, glaring at his sister with a broad grin, calling her a liar with his eyes.

His hand plucked his jacket from the couch and swirled it around his back. The buttons refused to fit through the holes, so he let them go in despair. He sat down just long enough to pull on his shiny black rubbers. Finally he put on his gloves. Then with four proud strides he arrived at the door and reached for the knob.

"Put your hat on," his mother said without looking at him.

His face, toward the door, screwed and tightened with disgust. "Aw Ma."

"Put it on."

"Aw Ma, it's not that cold out."

"Put it on."

"Honest Ma, it's not that cold out."

"Are you going to put your hat on, or are you going to stay and help with the dishes?"

He sighed. "All right," he said. "I'll put it on."

The door to the kitchen closed on his back and he was alone in the cold gloom of the shed. Pale light streamed through the frosted window and fell against the wall where the sled stood. The dark cold room was silent, and he was free. He moved into the shaft of light and stopped when from the kitchen he heard the muffled murmur of his mother's voice, as if she were far away. He listened. The murmuring hushed and he was alone again.

The sled. It was leaning against the wall, its varnished wood glistening in the moonlight. He moved closer to it and he saw his shadow block the light, and he heard the cold cracking of the loose linoleum beneath his feet.

He picked it up. He felt the smooth wood slippery in his gloved hands. The thin steel runners shone blue in the light, as he moved one finger along the polished surface to erase any dust. He shifted the sled in his hands and stood getting the feel of its weight the way he had seen his brother hold a rifle. He gripped the sled tightly, aware of the strength in his arms; and he felt proud to be strong and alone and far away with the sled in the dark cold silent room.

The sled was small and light. But strong. And when he ran with it, he ran very quickly, quicker than anyone, because it was very light and small and not bulky like other sleds. And when he ran with it, he carried it as if it were a part of him, as if he carried nothing in his arms. He set the rear end on the floor and let the sled lean against him, his hands on the steering bar. He pushed down on the bar and the thin runners curved gracefully because they were made of shiny blue flexible steel; and with them he could turn sharply in the snow, sharper than anyone. It was the best sled. It was his.

He felt a slight chill in the cold room, and in the moonlight he saw his breath in vapor rising like cigarette smoke before his eyes. His body shivered with excitement as he moved hurriedly but noiselessly to the door. He flung it open; and the snow blue and sparkling, and the shadows deep and mysterious, and the air silent and cold: all awaited him.

"Joey!" From the kitchen came his mother's voice. He turned toward the kitchen door and refused to answer.

"Joseph!"

"What!" His tone was arrogant, and a chill of fear rushed through his mind.

There was a long awful silence.

"Don't you forget to be home by seven o'clock." She hadn't noticed, and his fear was gone.

"All right!" He answered, ashamed of his fear. He stepped across the threshold and closed the door. Then he removed the hat and dropped it in the snow beside the porch.

He plodded down the alley, thrilling in the cold white silence—the snow was thick. The gate creaked as he pushed it open, holding and guiding the sled through the portal. The street was white, and shiny were the icy tracks of automobiles in the lamplight above. While between him and the light the black branches of trees ticked softly in the slight wind. In the gutters stood enormous heaps of snow, pale and dark in the shadows, stretching away from him like a string of mountains. He moved out of the shadows, between two piles of snow, and into the center of the street; where he stood for a moment gazing down the white road that gradually grew darker until it melted into the gloom at the far end.

Then he started to trot slowly down the street. Slowly, slowly gaining speed without losing balance. Faster he went now, watching the snow glide beneath his shiny black rubbers. Faster and faster, but stiffly, don't slip. Don't fall, don't fall: now! And his body plunged downward, and the sled whacked in the quiet and the white close to his eyes was flying beneath him as he felt the thrill of gliding alone along a shadowy street, with only the ski-sound of the sled in the packed snow. Then before his eyes the moving snow gradually slowed. And stopped. And he heard only the low sound of the wind and his breath.

Up again and start the trot. He moved to the beating sound of his feet along the ground. His breath came heavily and quickly, and matched the rhythm of his pumping legs, straining to carry the weight of his body without the balance of his arms. He reached a wild dangerous breakneck speed, and his leg muscles swelled and ached from the tension, and the fear of falling too early filled his mind; and down he let his body go. The white road rushed to meet him; he was off again, guiding the sled obliquely across the street toward a huge pile of snow near a driveway.

Squinting his eyes into the biting wind, he calculated when he would turn to avoid crashing. The pile, framed against the darkness of the sky, glistened white and shiny. It loomed larger and larger before him. He steered the sled sharply, bending the bar; and the snow flew as the sled churned sideways, and he heard suddenly a cold metallic snap. He and the sled went tumbling over in the hard wet snow. He rolled with it and the steering bar jarred his forehead. Then the dark sky and snow stopped turning, and all he felt was the cold air stinging the bump on his forehead.

The runner had snapped; the sled was broken. He stared at the shiny smooth runner and touched the jagged edge with his fingers. He sat in the middle of the driveway, the sled cradled in his lap, running his fingers up and down the thin runner until he came to the jagged edge where it had broken.

With his fingers he took the two broken edges and fitted them back into place. They stuck together with only a thin crooked line to indicate the split. But it was like putting a broken cup together. He stared at it, and wished it would be all right and felt like crying.

He got up and walked slowly back down the street to his house. He sat down between the back bumper of a parked car and a pile of snow. Cradling the sled across his legs, he put the two edges together again and stared at them. He felt a thickness in his throat, and he swallowed hard to remove it, but it did not go away.

He leaned back, resting his head against the snowpile. Through his wet eyelids he saw the lamplight shimmering brightly against the sky. He closed his eyes and saw again the shiny graceful curve of the runner. But it was broken now. He had bent it too far; too far. With his hand he rubbed his neck, then his eyes, then his neck again. And he felt the snow coming wet through his pants. As he shifted to a new position, he heard the creaking of a gate. He turned toward the sound.

His sister was walking away from his house. He watched her move slowly across the street and into the grocery store. Through the plate-glass window he saw her talking with the storekeeper. He stared down at the runner. With his gloves off, he ran his fingers along the cold smooth surface and felt the thin breakline. He got up, brushed the snow off the seat of his pants, and walked to the gate to wait for his sister.

He saw her take a package from the man and come out of the store. She walked carefully on the smooth white, her figure dark in its own shadow as she passed beneath the streetlight, the package in her arm. When she reached the curb on his side, he rested his arms on the nose of the sled and exhaled a deep breath nervously. He pretended to be staring in the opposite direction.

When he heard her feet crunching softly in the snow, he turned: "Hi," he said.

"Hi," she said, and she paused for a moment. "Good sledding?"

"Uhuh," he said. "Just right. Snow's packed nice and hard. Hardly any slush at all." He paused. "I'm just resting a bit now."

She nodded. "I just went for some milk."

His fingers moved slowly down the runner and touched the joined edges.

"Well . . ." she said, about to leave.

His fingers trembled slightly, and he felt his heart begin to beat rapidly: "Do you want to take a flop?" In the still night air he heard with surprise the calm sound of his voice.

Her face came suddenly alive. "Can I? I mean, will you let me? Really?"

"Sure," he said. "Go ahead," and he handed her the sled very carefully. She gave him the package.

He put the bag under his arm and watched her move out of the shadows of the trees and into the light. She started to trot slowly, awkwardly, bearing the sled. She passed directly beneath the light and then she slipped and slowed to regain her balance. The sled looked large and heavy in her arms, and seeing her awkwardness, he realized she would be hurt badly in the fall. She was moving away again, out of the reach of the streetlight, and into the gray haze farther down the road.

He moved to the curb, holding the bag tightly under his arm, hearing his heart pounding in his ears. He wanted to stop her, and he opened his mouth as if to call to her; but no sound came. It was too late: her dark figure was already starting the fall, putting the sled beneath her. Whack! And her head dipped with the front end jutting the ground, and the back of the sled and her legs rose like a seesaw and down they came with another muffled sound. The street was quiet, except for a low whimper that filled his ears.

He saw her figure rise slowly and move toward him. He walked out to meet her beneath the light. She held the sled loosely in one hand, the broken runner dangling, reflecting light as she moved.

She sobbed and looking up he saw bright tears falling down her cheeks, and a thin line of blood trickling down her chin. In the corner of her mouth near the red swelling on her lip, a little bubble of spit shone with the blood in the light.

He felt that he should say something but he did not speak.

"I'm . . . I'm sorry," she said and the bubble broke. "I'm sorry I . . . your sled." She looked down at the sled. "It'll never be the same."

"It'll be all right," he said. He felt that he ought to do something but he did not move. "I can get it soldered. Don't worry about it." But he saw from her expression that she thought he was only trying to make her feel better.

"No," she said, shaking her head emphatically. "No it won't! It'll always have that weak spot now." She began to cry very hard. "I'm sorry."

He made an awkward gesture of forgiveness with his hand. "Don't cry," he said.

She kept crying.

"It wasn't your fault," he said.

"Yes it was," she said. "Oh, yes it was."

"No!" he said. "No it wasn't!" But she didn't seem to hear him, and he felt his words were useless. He sighed wearily with defeat, not knowing what to say next. He saw her glance up at him as if to see whether he were still watching her, then she quickly lowered her gaze and said with despair and anguish: "Oh . . . girls are so stupid!"

There was no sound. She was no longer crying. She was looking at the ground: waiting. His ears heard nothing; they felt only the cold silent air.

"No they aren't," he said halfheartedly. And he heard her breathing again. He felt he had been forced to say that. In her shining eyes he saw an expression he did not understand. He wished she would go in the house. But seeing the tears on her cheeks and the blood on her chin, he immediately regretted the thought.

She wiped her chin with her sleeve, and he winced, feeling rough cloth on an open cut. "Don't do that," his hand moved to his back pocket, "use my handkerchief."

She waited.

The pocket was empty. "I haven't got one," he said.

Staring directly at him, she patted gingerly the swollen part of her lip with the tips of her fingers.

He moved closer to her. "Let me see," he said. With his hands he grasped her head and tilted it so that the light fell directly on the cut.

"It's not too bad," she said calmly. And as she said it she looked straight into his eyes, and he felt she was perfectly at ease; while standing that close to her, he felt clumsy and out of place.

In his hands her head was small and fragile, and her hair was soft and warm; he felt the rapid pulsing of the vein in her temple: his ears grew hot with shame.

"Maybe I better go inside and wash it off?" she asked.

With his finger he wiped the blood from her chin. "Yes," he said, feeling relieved. "You go inside and wash it off." He took the sled and gave her the package.

He stared at the ground as they walked to the gate in silence. When they reached the curb he became aware that she was watching him.

"You've got a nasty bump on your forehead," she said.

"Yes," he said. "I fell."

"Let me put some snow on it," she said, reaching to the ground.

He caught her wrist and held it gently. "No," he said.

He saw her about to object: "It's all right. You go inside and take care of your lip." He said it softly but with his grip and his eyes he told her more firmly.

"All right," she said after a moment, and he released his hold. "But don't forget to put your hat on."

He stared at her.

"I mean, *before* you go back in the house."

They both smiled.

"Thanks for reminding me," he said, and he dropped the sled in the snow and hurried to hold the gate open for her.

She hesitated, then smiled proudly as he beckoned her into the alley.

He watched her walk away from him down the dark alley in the gray snow. Her small figure swayed awkwardly as she stepped carefully in the deep snow, so as not to get her feet too wet. Her head was bowed and her shoulders hunched and he humbly felt her weakness. And he felt her cold. And he felt the snow running cold down her boots around her ankles. And though she wasn't crying now, he could still hear her low sobbing, and he saw her shining eyes and the tears falling and she trying to stop them and they falling even faster. And he wished he had never gone sledding. He wished that he had never even come out of the house tonight.

The back door closed. He turned and moved about nervously kicking at the ground. At the edge of the curb he dug his hands deep into the cold wet snow. He came up with a handful and absently began shaping and smoothing it. He stopped abruptly and dropped it at his feet.

He did not hear it fall. He was looking up at the dark sky but he did not see it. He put his cold hands in his back pockets but he did not feel them. He was wishing that he were some time a long time away from now and somewhere a long way away from here.

In the corner of his eye something suddenly dimmed. Across the street in the grocery store the light was out: it was seven o'clock.

D. H. Lawrence

THE ROCKING-HORSE WINNER

THERE was a woman who was beautiful, who started with all the advantages, yet she had no luck. She married for love, and the love turned to dust. She had bonny children, yet she felt they had been thrust upon her, and she could not love them. They looked at her coldly, as if they were finding fault with her. And hurriedly she felt she must cover up some fault in herself. Yet what it was that she must cover up she never knew. Nevertheless, when her children were present, she always felt the centre of her heart go hard. This troubled her, and in her manner she was all the more gentle and anxious for her children, as if she loved them very much. Only she herself knew that at the centre of her heart was a hard little place that could not feel love, no, not for anybody. Everybody else said of her: "She is such a good mother. She adores her children." Only she herself, and her children themselves, knew it was not so. They read it in each other's eyes.

There were a boy and two little girls. They lived in a pleasant house, with a garden, and they had discreet servants, and felt themselves superior to anyone in the neighbourhood.

Although they lived in style, they felt always an anxiety in the house. There was never enough money. The mother had a small income, and the father had a small income, but not nearly enough for the social position which they had to keep up. The father went in to town to some office. But though he had good prospects, these prospects never materialized. There was always the grinding sense of the shortage of money, though the style was always kept up.

At last the mother said: "I will see if *I* can't make something." But she did not know where to begin. She racked her brains, and tried this thing and the other, but could not find anything successful. The failure made deep lines come into her face. Her children were growing up, they would have to go to school. There must be more money, there must be more money. The father, who was always very handsome and expensive in his tastes, seemed as if he never *would* be able to do anything worth doing. And the mother, who had a great belief in herself, did not succeed any better, and her tastes were just as expensive.

And so the house came to be haunted by the unspoken phrase: *There must be more money! There must be more money!* The children could hear it all the time, though nobody said it aloud. They heard it at Christmas, when the expensive and splendid toys filled the nursery. Behind the shining modern rocking-horse, behind the smart doll's-house, a voice would start whispering: "There *must* be more money! There *must* be more money!" And the children would stop playing, to listen for a moment. They would look into each other's eyes, to see if they had all heard. And each one saw in the eyes of the other two that they too had heard. "There *must* be more money! There *must* be more money!"

It came whispering from the springs of the still-swaying rocking-horse, and even the horse, bending his wooden, champing head, heard it. The big doll, sitting so pink and smirking in her new pram, could hear it quite plainly, and seemed to be smirking all the more self-consciously because of it. The foolish puppy, too, that took the place of the teddy-bear, he was looking so extraordinarily foolish for no other reason but that he heard the secret whisper all over the house: "There *must* be more money!"

Yet nobody ever said it aloud. The whisper was everywhere, and therefore no one spoke it. Just as no one ever says: "We are breathing!" in spite of the fact that breath is coming and going all the time.

"Mother," said the boy Paul one day, "why don't we keep a car of our own? Why do we always use uncle's, or else a taxi?"

"Because we're the poor members of the family," said the mother.

"But why *are* we, mother?"

"Well—I suppose," she said slowly and bitterly, "it's because your father has no luck."

The boy was silent for some time.

"Is luck money, mother?" he asked rather timidly.

"No, Paul. Not quite. It's what causes you to have money."

"Oh!" said Paul vaguely. "I thought when Uncle Oscar said *filthy lucker*, it meant money."

"*Filthy* lucre does mean money," said the mother. "But it's lucre, not luck."

"Oh!" said the boy. "Then what *is* luck, mother?"

"It's what causes you to have money. If you're lucky you have money. That's why it's better to be born lucky than rich. If you're rich, you may lose your money. But if you're lucky, you will always get more money."

"Oh! Will you? And is father not lucky?"

"Very unlucky, I should say," she said bitterly.

The boy watched her with unsure eyes.

"Why?" he asked.

"I don't know. Nobody ever knows why one person is lucky and another unlucky."

"Don't they? Nobody at all? Does *nobody* know?"

"Perhaps God. But He never tells."

"He ought to, then. And aren't you lucky either, mother?"

"I can't be, if I married an unlucky husband."

"But by yourself, aren't you?"

"I used to think I was, before I married. Now I think I am very unlucky indeed."

"Why?"

"Well—never mind! Perhaps I'm not really," she said.

The child looked at her, to see if she meant it. But he saw, by the lines of her mouth, that she was only trying to hide something from him.

"Well, anyhow," he said stoutly, "I'm a lucky person."

"Why?" said his mother, with a sudden laugh.

He stared at her. He didn't even know why he had said it.

"God told me," he asserted, brazening it out.

"I hope He did, dear!" she said, again with a laugh, but rather bitter.

"He did, mother!"

"Excellent!" said the mother, using one of her husband's exclamations.

The boy saw she did not believe him; or, rather, that she paid no attention to his assertion. This angered him somewhat, and made him want to compel her attention.

He went off by himself, vaguely, in a childish way, seeking for the clue to "luck." Absorbed, taking no heed of other people, he went about with a sort of stealth, seeking inwardly for luck. He wanted luck, he wanted it, he wanted it. When the two girls were playing dolls in the nursery, he would sit on his big rocking-horse, charging madly into space, with a frenzy that made the little girls peer at him uneasily. Wildly the horse careered, the waving dark hair of the boy tossed, his eyes had a strange glare in them. The little girls dared not speak to him.

When he had ridden to the end of his mad little journey, he climbed down and stood in front of his rocking-horse, staring fixedly into its lowered face. Its red mouth was slightly open, its big eye was wide and glassy-bright.

"Now!" he would silently command the snorting steed. "Now, take me to where there is luck! Now take me!"

And he would slash the horse on the neck with the little whip he had asked Uncle Oscar for. He *knew* the horse could take him to where there was luck, if only he forced it. So he would mount again, and start on his furious ride, hoping at last to get there. He knew he could get there.

"You'll break your horse, Paul!" said the nurse.

"He's always riding like that! I wish he'd leave off!" said his elder sister Joan.

But he only glared down on them in silence. Nurse gave him up. She could make nothing of him. Anyhow he was growing beyond her.

One day his mother and his Uncle Oscar came in when he was on one of his furious rides. He did not speak to them.

"Hallo, you young jockey! Riding a winner?" said his uncle.

"Aren't you growing too big for a rocking-horse? You're not a very little boy any longer, you know," said his mother.

But Paul only gave a blue glare from his big, rather close-set eyes. He would speak to nobody when he was in full tilt. His mother watched him with an anxious expression on her face.

At last he suddenly stopped forcing his horse into the mechanical gallop, and slid down.

"Well, I got there!" he announced fiercely, his blue eyes still flaring, and his sturdy long legs straddling apart.

"Where did you get to?" asked his mother.

"Where I wanted to go," he flared back at her.

"That's right, son!" said Uncle Oscar. "Don't you stop till you get there. What's the horse's name?"

"He doesn't have a name," said the boy.

"Gets on without all right?" asked the uncle.

"Well, he has different names. He was called Sansovino last week."

"Sansovino, eh? Won the Ascot. How did you know his name?"

"He always talks about horse-races with Bassett," said Joan.

The uncle was delighted to find that his small nephew was posted with all the racing news. Bassett, the young gardener, who had been wounded in the left foot in the war and had got his present job through Oscar Cresswell, whose batman he had been, was a perfect blade of the "turf." He lived in the racing events, and the small boy lived with him.

Oscar Cresswell got it all from Bassett.

"Master Paul comes and asks me, so I can't do more than tell him, sir," said Bassett, his face terribly serious, as if he were speaking of religious matters.

"And does he ever put anything on a horse he fancies?"

"Well—I don't want to give him away—he's a young sport, a fine sport, sir. Would you mind asking him himself? He sort of takes a pleasure in it, and perhaps he'd feel I was giving him away, sir, if you don't mind."

Bassett was serious as a church.

The uncle went back to his nephew and took him off for a ride in the car.

"Say, Paul, old man, do you ever put anything on a horse?" the uncle asked.

The boy watched the handsome man closely.

"Why, do you think I oughtn't to?" he parried.

"Not a bit of it! I thought perhaps you might give me a tip for the Lincoln."

The car sped on into the country, going down to Uncle Oscar's place in Hampshire.

"Honour bright?" said the nephew.

"Honour bright, son!" said the uncle.

"Well, then, Daffodil."

"Daffodil! I doubt it, sonny. What about Mirza?"

"I only know the winner," said the boy. "That's Daffodil."

"Daffodil, eh?"

There was a pause. Daffodil was an obscure horse comparatively.

"Uncle!"

"Yes, son?"

"You won't let it go any further, will you? I promised Bassett."

"Bassett be damned, old man! What's he got to do with it?"

"We're partners. We've been partners from the first. Uncle, he lent me my first five shillings, which I lost. I promised him, honour bright, it was only between me and him; only you gave me that ten-shilling note I started winning with, so I thought you were lucky. You won't let it go any further, will you?"

The boy gazed at his uncle from those big, hot, blue eyes, set rather close together. The uncle stirred and laughed uneasily.

"Right you are, son! I'll keep your tip private. Daffodil, eh? How much are you putting on him?"

"All except twenty pounds," said the boy. "I keep that in reserve."

The uncle thought it a good joke.

"You keep twenty pounds in reserve, do you, you young romancer? What are you betting, then?"

"I'm betting three hundred," said the boy gravely. "But it's between you and me, Uncle Oscar! Honour bright?"

The uncle burst into a roar of laughter.

"It's between you and me all right, you young Nat Gould," he said, laughing. "But where's your three hundred?"

"Bassett keeps it for me. We're partners."

"You are, are you! And what is Bassett putting on Daffodil?"

"He won't go quite as high as I do, I expect. Perhaps he'll go a hundred and fifty."

"What, pennies?" laughed the uncle.

"Pounds," said the child, with a surprised look at his uncle. "Bassett keeps a bigger reserve than I do."

Between wonder and amusement Uncle Oscar was silent. He pursued the matter no further, but he determined to take his nephew with him to the Lincoln races.

"Now, son," he said, "I'm putting twenty on Mirza, and I'll put five for you on any horse you fancy. What's your pick?"

"Daffodil, uncle."

"No, not the fiver on Daffodil!"

"I should if it was my own fiver," said the child.

"Good! Good! Right you are! A fiver for me and a fiver for you on Daffodil."

The child had never been to a race-meeting before, and his eyes were blue fire. He pursed his mouth tight, and watched. A Frenchman just in front had put his money on Lancelot. Wild with excitement, he flayed his arms up and down, yelling "*Lancelot! Lancelot!*" in his French accent.

Daffodil came in first, Lancelot second, Mirza third. The child, flushed and with eyes blazing, was curiously serene. His uncle brought him four five-pound notes, four to one.

"What am I to do with these?" he cried, waving them before the boy's eyes.

"I suppose we'll talk to Bassett," said the boy. "I expect I have fifteen hundred now; and twenty in reserve; and this twenty."

His uncle studied him for some moments.

"Look here, son!" he said. "You're not serious about Bassett and that fifteen hundred, are you?"

"Yes, I am. But it's between you and me, uncle. Honour bright!"

"Honour bright all right, son! But I must talk to Bassett."

"If you'd like to be a partner, uncle, with Bassett and me, we could all be partners. Only, you'd have to promise, honour bright, uncle, not to let it go beyond us three. Bassett and I are lucky, and you must be lucky, because it was your ten shillings I started winning with. . . ."

Uncle Oscar took both Bassett and Paul into Richmond Park for an afternoon, and there they talked.

"It's like this, you see, sir," Bassett said. "Master Paul would get me talking about racing events, spinning yarns, you know, sir. And he was always keen on knowing if I'd made or if I'd lost. It's about a year since, now, that I put five shilling on Blush of Dawn for him—and we lost. Then the luck turned, with that ten shillings he had from you, that we put on Singhalese. And since that time, it's been pretty steady, all things considering. What do you say, Master Paul?"

"We're all right when we're sure," said Paul. "It's when we're not quite sure that we go down."

"Oh, but we're careful then," said Bassett.

"But when are you *sure?*" smiled Uncle Oscar.

"It's Master Paul, sir," said Bassett, in a secret, religious voice. "It's as if he had it from heaven. Like Daffodil, now, for the Lincoln. That was as sure as eggs."

"Did you put anything on Daffodil?" asked Oscar Cresswell.

"Yes, sir, I made my bit."

"And my nephew?"

Bassett was obstinately silent, looking at Paul.

"I made twelve hundred, didn't I, Bassett? I told uncle I was putting three hundred on Daffodil."

"That's right," said Bassett, nodding.

"But where's the money?" asked the uncle.

"I keep it safe locked up, sir. Master Paul he can have it any minute he likes to ask for it."

"What, fifteen hundred pounds?"

"And twenty! And *forty,* that is, with the twenty he made on the course."

"It's amazing!" said the uncle.

"If Master Paul offers you to be partners, sir, I would, if I were you; if you'll excuse me," said Bassett.

Oscar Cresswell thought about it.

"I'll see the money," he said.

They drove home again, and sure enough, Bassett came round to the garden-house with fifteen hundred pounds in notes. The twenty pounds reserve was left with Joe Glee, in the Turf Commission deposit.

"You see, it's all right, uncle, when I'm *sure!* Then we go strong, for all we're worth. Don't we, Bassett?"

"We do that, Master Paul."

"And when are you sure?" said the uncle, laughing.

"Oh, well, sometimes I'm *absolutely* sure, like about Daffodil," said the boy; "and sometimes I have an idea; and sometimes I haven't even an idea, have I, Bassett? Then we're careful, because we mostly go down."

"You do, do you! And when you're sure, like about Daffodil, what makes you sure, sonny?"

"Oh, well, I don't know," said the boy uneasily. "I'm sure, you know, uncle; that's all."

"It's as if he had it from heaven, sir," Bassett reiterated.

"I should say so!" said the uncle.

But he became a partner. And when the Leger was coming on, Paul was "sure" about Lively Spark, which was a quite inconsiderable horse. The boy insisted on putting a thousand on the horse. Bassett went for five hundred, and Oscar Cresswell two hundred. Lively Spark came in first, and the betting had been ten to one against him. Paul had made ten thousand.

"You see," he said, "I was absolutely sure of him."

Even Oscar Cresswell had cleared two thousand.

"Look here, son," he said, "this sort of thing makes me nervous."

"It needn't, uncle! Perhaps I shan't be sure again for a long time."

"But what are you going to do with your money?" asked the uncle.

"Of course," said the boy, "I started it for mother. She said she had no luck, because father is unlucky, so I thought if *I* was lucky, it might stop whispering."

"What might stop whispering?"

"Our house. I *hate* our house for whispering."

"What does it whisper?"

"Why—why"—the boy fidgeted—"why, I don't know. But it's always short of money, you know, uncle."

"I know it, son, I know it."

"You know people send mother writs, don't you uncle?"

"I'm afraid I do," said the uncle.

"And then the house whispers, like people laughing at you behind your back. It's awful, that is! I thought if I was lucky . . ."

"You might stop it," added the uncle.

The boy watched him with big blue eyes, that had an uncanny cold fire in them, and he said never a word.

"Well, then!" said the uncle. "What are we doing?"

"I shouldn't like mother to know I was lucky," said the boy.

"Why not, son?"

"She'd stop me."

"I don't think she would."

"Oh!"—and the boy writhed in an odd way—"I *don't* want her to know, uncle."

"All right, son! We'll manage it without her knowing."

They managed it very easily. Paul, at the other's suggestion, handed over five thousand pounds to his uncle, who deposited it with the family lawyer, who was then to notify Paul's mother that a relative had put five thousand pounds into his hands, which sum was to be paid out a thousand pounds at a time, on the mother's birthday, for the next five years.

"So she'll have a birthday present of a thousand pounds for five successive years," said Uncle Oscar. "I hope it won't make it all the harder for her later."

Paul's mother had her birthday in November. The house had been "whispering" worse than ever lately, and, even in spite of his luck, Paul could not bear up against it. He was very anxious to see the effect of the birthday letter, telling his mother about the thousand pounds.

When there were no visitors, Paul now took his meal with his parents, as he was beyond the nursery control. His mother went into town nearly every day. She had discovered that she had an odd knack of sketching furs and dress materials, so she worked secretly in the studio of a friend who was the chief "artist" for the leading drapers. She drew the figures of ladies in furs and ladies in silk and sequins for the newspaper advertisements. This young woman artist earned several thousand pounds a year, but Paul's mother only made several hundreds, and she was again dissatisfied. She so wanted to be first in something, and she did not succeed, even in making sketches for drapery advertisements.

She was down to breakfast on the morning of her birthday. Paul watched her face as she read her letters. He knew the lawyer's letter. As his mother read it, her face hardened and became more expressionless. Then a cold, determined look came on her mouth. She hid the letter under the pile of others, and said not a word about it.

"Didn't you have anything nice in the post for your birthday, mother?" said Paul.

"Quite moderately nice," she said, her voice cold and absent.

She went away to town without saying more.

But in the afternoon Uncle Oscar appeared. He said Paul's mother had had a long interview with the lawyer, asking if the whole five thousand could not be advanced at once, as she was in debt.

"What do you think, uncle?" said the boy.

"I leave it to you, son."

"Oh, let her have it, then! We can get some more with the other," said the boy.

"A bird in the hand is worth two in the bush, laddie!" said Uncle Oscar.

"But I'm sure to *know* for the Grand National; or the Lincolnshire; or else the Derby. I'm sure to know for *one* of them," said Paul.

So Uncle Oscar signed the agreement, and Paul's mother touched the whole five thousand. Then something very curious happened. The voices in the house suddenly went mad, like a chorus of frogs on a spring evening. There were certain new furnishings, and Paul had a tutor. He was *really* going to Eton, his father's school, in the following autumn. There were flowers in the winter, and a blossoming of the luxury Paul's mother had been used to. And yet the voices in the house, behind the sprays of mimosa and almond blossom, and from under the piles of iridescent cushions, simply trilled and screamed in a sort of ecstasy: "There *must* be more money! Oh-h-h; there *must* be more money. Oh, now, now-w! Now-w-w—there *must* be more money!—more than ever! More than ever!"

It frightened Paul terribly. He studied away at his Latin and Greek with his tutors. But his intense hours were spent with Bassett. The Grand National had gone by: he had not "known," and had lost a hundred pounds. Summer was at hand. He was in agony for the Lincoln. But even for the Lincoln he didn't "know," and he lost fifty pounds. He became wild-eyed and strange, as if something were going to explode in him.

"Let it alone, son! Don't you bother about it!" urged Uncle Oscar. But it was as if the boy couldn't really hear what his uncle was saying.

"I've got to know for the Derby! I've got to know for the Derby!" the child reiterated, his big blue eyes blazing with a sort of madness.

His mother noticed how overwrought he was.

"You'd better go to the seaside. Wouldn't you like to go now to the seaside, instead of waiting? I think you'd better," she said, looking down at him anxiously, her heart curiously heavy because of him.

But the child lifted his uncanny blue eyes.

"I couldn't possibly go before the Derby, mother!" he said. "I couldn't possibly!"

"Why not?" she said, her voice becoming heavy when she was opposed. "Why not? You can still go from the seaside to see the Derby with your Uncle Oscar, if that's what you wish. No need for you to wait here. Besides, I think you care too much about these races. It's a bad sign. My family has been a gambling family, and you won't know till you grow up how much damage it has done. But it has done damage. I shall have to send Bassett away, and ask Uncle Oscar not to talk racing to you, unless you promise to be reasonable about it; go away to the seaside and forget it. You're all nerves!"

"I'll do what you like, mother, so long as you don't send me away till after the Derby," the boy said.

"Send you away from where? Just from this house?"

"Yes," he said, gazing at her.

"Why, you curious child, what makes you care about this house so much, suddenly? I never knew you loved it."

He gazed at her without speaking. He had a secret within a secret, something he had not divulged, even to Bassett or to his Uncle Oscar.

But his mother, after standing undecided and a little bit sullen for some moments, said:

"Very well, then! Don't go to the seaside till after the Derby, if you don't wish it. But promise me you won't let your nerves go to pieces. Promise you won't think so much about horse-racing and *events,* as you call them!"

"Oh, no," said the boy casually. "I won't think much about them, mother. You needn't worry. I wouldn't worry, mother, if I were you."

"If you were me and I were you," said his mother, "I wonder what we *should* do!"

"But you know you needn't worry, mother, don't you?" the boy repeated.

"I should be awfully glad to know it," she said wearily.

"Oh, well, you *can,* you know. I mean you *ought* to know you needn't worry," he insisted.

"Ought I? Then I'll see about it," she said.

Paul's secret of secrets was his wooden horse, that which had no name. Since he was emancipated from a nurse and a nursery-governess, he had had his rocking-horse removed to his own bedroom at the top of the house.

"Surely, you're too big for a rocking-horse!" his mother had remonstrated.

"Well, you see, mother, till I can have a *real* horse, I like to have *some* sort of animal about," had been his quaint answer.

"Do you feel he keeps you company?" she laughed.

"Oh, yes! He's very good, he always keeps me company, when I'm there," said Paul.

So the horse, rather shabby, stood in an arrested prance in the boy's bedroom.

The Derby was drawing near, and the boy grew more and more tense. He hardly heard what was spoken to him, he was very frail, and his eyes were really uncanny. His mother had sudden strange seizures of uneasiness about him. Sometimes, for half-an-hour, she would feel a sudden anxiety about him that was almost anguish. She wanted to rush to him at once, and know he was safe.

Two nights before the Derby, she was at a big party in town, when one of her rushes of anxiety about her boy, her first-born, gripped her heart till she could hardly speak. She fought with the feeling, might and main, for she believed in common-sense. But it was too strong. She had to leave the dance and go downstairs to telephone to the country. The children's nursery-governess was terribly surprised and startled at being rung up in the night.

"Are the children all right, Miss Wilmot?"

"Oh, yes, they are quite all right."

"Master Paul? Is he all right?

"He went to bed as right as a trivet. Shall I run up and look at him?"

"No," said Paul's mother reluctantly. "No! Don't trouble. It's all right. Don't sit up. We shall be home fairly soon." She did not want her son's privacy intruded upon.

"Very good," said the governess.

It was about one o'clock when Paul's mother and father drove up to their house. All was still. Paul's mother went to her room and slipped off her white fur cloak. She had told her maid not to wait up for her. She heard her husband downstairs, mixing a whisky-and-soda.

And then, because of the strange anxiety at her heart, she stole upstairs to her son's room. Noiselessly she went along the upper corridor. Was there a faint noise? What was it?

She stood, with arrested muscles, outside his door, listening. There was a strange, heavy, and yet not loud noise. Her heart stood still. It was a soundless noise, yet rushing and powerful. Something huge, in violent, hushed motion. What was it? What in God's name was it? She ought to know. She felt that she knew the noise. She knew what it was.

Yet she could not place it. She couldn't say what it was. And on and on it went, like a madness.

Softly, frozen with anxiety and fear, she turned the door-handle.

The room was dark. Yet in the space near the window, she heard and saw something plunging to and fro. She gazed in fear and amazement.

Then suddenly she switched on the light, and saw her son, in his green pyjamas madly surging on the rocking-horse. The blaze of light suddenly lit him up, as he urged the wooden horse, and lit her up, as she stood, blonde, in her dress of pale green and crystal, in the doorway.

"Paul!" she cried. "Whatever are you doing?"

"It's Malabar!" he screamed, in a powerful strange voice. "It's Malabar!"

His eyes blazed at her for one strange and senseless second, as he ceased urging his wooden horse. Then he fell with a crash to the ground, and she, all her tormented motherhood flooding upon her, rushed to gather him up.

But he was unconscious, and unconscious he remained, with some brain-fever. He talked and tossed, and his mother sat stonily by his side.

"Malabar! It's Malabar! Bassett, Bassett, I *know!* It's Malabar!"

So the child cried, trying to get up and urge the rocking-horse that gave him his inspiration.

"What does he mean by Malabar?" asked the heart-frozen mother.

"I don't know," said the father stonily.

"What does he mean by Malabar?" she asked her brother Oscar.

"It's one of the horses running for the Derby," was the answer.

And, in spite of himself, Oscar Cresswell spoke to Bassett, and himself put a thousand on Malabar: at fourteen to one.

The third day of the illness was critical: they were waiting for a change. The boy, with his rather long, curly hair, was tossing ceaselessly on the pillow. He neither slept nor regained consciousness, and his eyes were like blue stones. His mother sat, feeling her heart had gone, turned actually into a stone.

In the evening, Oscar Cresswell did not come, but Bassett sent a message, saying could he come up for one moment, just one moment? Paul's mother was very angry at the intrusion, but on second thought she agreed. The boy was the same. Perhaps Bassett might bring him to consciousness.

The gardener, a shortish fellow with a little brown mustache, and sharp little brown eyes, tip-toed into the room, touched his imaginary cap to Paul's mother, and stole to the bedside, staring with glittering, smallish eyes, at the tossing, dying child.

"Master Paul!" he whispered. "Master Paul! Malabar came in first all right, a clean win. I did as you told me. You've made over seventy thousand pounds, you have; you've got over eighty thousand. Malabar came in all right, Master Paul."

"Malabar! Malabar! Did I say Malabar, mother? Did I say Malabar? Do you think I'm lucky, mother? I knew Malabar, didn't I? Over eighty thousand pounds. I call that lucky, don't you, mother? Over eighty thousand pounds! I knew, didn't I know I knew? Malabar came in all right. If I ride my horse till I'm sure, then I tell you, Bassett, you can go as high as you like. Did you go for all you were worth, Bassett?"

"I went a thousand on it, Master Paul."

"I never told you, mother, that if I can ride my horse, and *get there,* then I'm absolutely sure—oh, absolutely! Mother, did I ever tell you? I *am* lucky!"

"No, you never did," said the mother.

But the boy died in the night.

And even as he lay dead, his mother heard her brother's voice saying to her: "My God, Hester, you're eighty-odd thousand to the good, and a poor devil of a son to the bad. But, poor devil, poor devil, he's best gone out of a life where he rides his rocking-horse to find a winner."

ESSAYS

Laurie Lee

A WINTER TREAT

THE PAROCHIAL Church Tea and Annual Entertainment was the village's winter treat. It took place in the schoolroom, round about Twelfth Night, and cost us a shilling to go. The Tea was an orgy of communal gluttony, in which everyone took pains to eat more than his money's worth and the helpers ate more than the customers. The Entertainment which followed, home-produced and by lamplight, provided us with sufficient catch phrases for a year.

Regularly, for a few weeks before the night, one witnessed the same scenes in our kitchen, the sisters sitting in various corners of the room, muttering secretly to themselves, smiling, nodding, and making lah-di-dah gestures with a kind of intent and solitary madness. They were rehearsing their sketches for the Entertainment, which I found impossible not to learn, too, so that I would be haunted for days by three nightmare monologues full of one-sided unanswered questions.

On the morning of the feast we got the school ready. We built a stage out of trestles and planks. Mr. Robinson was in the cloakroom slicing boiled ham, where he'd been for the last three days, and three giggling helpers were now forking the meat and slapping it into sandwiches. Outside in the yard John Barraclough had arrived and set up his old field kitchen, had broken six hurdles across his knee and filled up the boiler with water. Laid out on the wall were thirty-five teapots, freshly washed and drying in the wind. The feast was preparing; and by carrying chairs, helping with the stage, and fetching water from the spring, Jack and I made ourselves sufficiently noticeable to earn a free ticket each.

Punctually at six, with big eating to be done, we returned to the lighted school. Villagers with lanterns streamed in from all quarters. We heard the bubbling of water in Barraclough's boiler, smelt the sweet woodsmoke from his fire, saw his red face lit like a turnip lamp as he crouched to stoke up the flames.

We lined up in the cold, not noticing the cold, waiting for the doors to open. When they did, it was chins and boots and elbows, no queues; we just fought our way in. Lamplight and decorations had transformed the schoolroom from a prison into a banqueting hall. The long trestle-tables were patterned with food: fly-cake, brown buns, ham sandwiches. The two stoves were roaring, reeking of coke. The helpers had their teapots charged. We sat down stiffly and gazed at the food; fidgeted, coughed and waited. . . .

The stage curtains parted to reveal the Squire, wearing a cloak and a deer-stalking hat. He cast his dim, wet eyes round the crowded room, then sighed and turned to go. Somebody whispered from behind the curtain. "Bless me!" said the Squire, and came back.

"The Parochial Church Tea!" he began, then paused. "Is with us again . . . I suggest. And Entertainment. Another year! Another year comes round! . . . When I see you all gathered together here—once more—when I see—when I think . . . And here you all are! When I see you here—as I'm sure you all are—once again . . . It comes to me, friends!—how time—how you—how all of us here—as it were . . ." His moustache was quivering, tears ran down his face, he groped for the curtains and left.

His place was taken by the snow-haired Vicar, who beamed weakly upon us all.

"What is the smallest room in the world?" he asked.

"A mushroom!" we bawled, without hesitation.

"And the largest, may I ask?"

"ROOM FOR IMPROVEMENT!"

"You know it," he muttered crossly. Recovering himself, he folded his hands: "And now, O bountiful Father . . ."

We barked through grace and got our hands on the food and began to eat it in any old order. Cakes, buns, ham, it didn't matter at all, we just worked from one plate to the next. Folk by the fires fanned themselves with sandwiches, a joker fried ham on the stove, steaming brown teapots passed up and down, and we were so busy there was small conversation. Through the lighted windows we could see snow falling, huge feathers against the dark. "It's old Mother Hawkins a-plucking her geese!" cried someone; an excellent omen. Twelfth Night, and old Mother Hawkins at work, up in the sky with her birds; we loosened our belts and began to nod at each other; it was going to be a year of fat.

We had littered the tables with our messy leavings of cake crumbs and broken meat; some hands still went through the motions of eating, but clearly we'd had enough. The Vicar rose to his feet again, and again we thanked the Lord. "And now, my friends, comes the—er—feast for the soul. If you would care to—ah—take the air a moment, willing hands are waiting to clear the hall and prepare for the—um—Entertainment. . . ."

We crowded outside and huddled in the snow while the tables were taken away. Inside, behind curtains, the actors were making up—and my moment, too, was approaching. The snow whirled about me and I began to sweat; I wanted to run off home. Then the doors reopened and I crouched by the stove, shivering and chattering with nerves. The curtains parted and the Entertainment began, with a comic I neither saw nor heard. . . .

"For the next item, ladies and gentlemen, we have an instrumental duet, by Miss Brown and—er—young Laurie Lee."

Smirking with misery I walked to the stage. Eileen's face was as white as a minim. She sat at the piano, placed the music crooked, I straightened it, it fell to the ground. I groped to retrieve it; we looked at one another with hatred; the audience was still as death. Eileen tried to give me an A, but struck B instead, and I tuned up like an ape threading needles. At last we were ready, I raised my fiddle; and Eileen was off like a bolting horse. I caught her up in the middle of the piece—which I believe was a lullaby—and after playing the repeats, only twice as fast, we just stopped, frozen motionless, spent.

Some hearty stamping and whistling followed, and a shout of "Give us another!" Eileen and I didn't exchange a glance, but we loved each other now. We found the music of "Danny Boy" and began to give it all our emotion, dawdling dreamily among the fruitier chords and scampering over the high bits; till the audience joined in, using their hymn-singing voices, which showed us the utmost respect. When it was over I returned to my seat by the stove, my body feeling smooth and beautiful. Eileen's mother was weeping into her hat, and so was mine, I think. . . .

Now I was free to become one of the audience, and the Entertainment burgeoned before me. What had seemed to me earlier as the capering of demons now became a spectacle of human genius. Turn followed turn in variety and splendor. Mr. Crosby, the organist, told jokes and stories as though his very life depended on them, trembling, sweating, never pausing for a laugh, and rolling his eyes at the wings for rescue. We loved him, however, and wouldn't let him go, while he grew more and more hysterical, racing through monologues, gabbling songs about shrimps, skipping, mopping, and jumping up and down, as though humoring a tribe of savages.

Major Doveton came next, with his Indian banjo, which was even harder to tune than my fiddle. He straddled a chair and began wrestling with the keys, cursing us in English and Urdu. Then all the strings broke, and he snarled off the stage and started kicking the banjo round the cloakroom. He was followed by a play in which Marjorie, as Cinderella, sat in a goose-feathered dress in a castle. While waiting for the pumpkin to turn into a coach, she sang "All alone by the telephone."

Two ballads came next, and Mrs. Pimbury, a widow, sang them

both with astonishing spirit. The first invited us to go with her to Canada; the second was addressed to a mushroom:

Grow! Grow! Grow! Little mushroom, grow!
Somebody wants you soon.
I'll call again tomorrow morning—
 See!
And if you've grown bigger you will just suit ME!
So Grow! Grow! Grow! little mushroom—Grow!

Though we'd not heard this before, it soon became part of our heritage, as did the song of a later lady. This last—the Baroness von Hodenburg—sealed our entertainment with almost professional distinction. She was a guest star from Sheepscombe and her appearance was striking; it enshrined all the mystery of art. She wore a loose green gown like a hospital patient's, and her hair was red and long. "She writes," whispered Mother. "Poems and booklets and that."

"I am going to sink you," announced this lady, "a little ditty I convected myself. Bose vords und music, I may say, is mine—und zey refer to ziss pleasant valleys."

With that she sat down, arched her beautiful back, raised her bangled wrists over the keyboard, then ripped off some startling runs and trills, and sang with a ringing laugh:

Elfin volk come over the hill!
Come und dance, just vere you vill!
Brink your pipes, und brink your flutes,
Brink your sveetly-soundink notes!
Come avay-hay! Life is gay-hay!
Life—is—Gay!

We thought this song soppy, but we never forgot it. From then on, whenever we saw the Baroness in the lanes we used to bowl the song at her through the hedges. But she would only stop, and cock her head, and smile dreamily to herself. . . .

After these songs the night ended with slapstick; rough stuff about babies, chaps dressed as women, broad Gloucester exchanges between yokels and toffs, with the yokels coming off best. We ached with joy, and kicked at the chairs; but we knew the end was coming. The Vicar got up, proposed a vote of thanks, and said oranges would be distributed at the gate. The National Anthem was romped through, we all began coughing, then streamed outdoors through the snow.

Back home our sisters discussed their performances till the tears dripped off their noses. But to us boys it was not over, not till tomorrow; there was still one squeeze left in the lemon. Tomorrow, very early, we'd go back to the schoolroom, find the baskets of broken food—half-eaten buns, ham coated with cake crumbs—and together we'd finish the lot.

James Agee

KNOXVILLE: SUMMER 1915

WE ARE talking now of summer evenings in Knoxville, Tennessee in the time that I lived there so successfully disguised to myself as a child. It was a little bit mixed sort of block, fairly solidly lower middle class, with one or two juts apiece on either side of that. The houses corresponded: middle-sized gracefully fretted wood houses built in the late nineties and early nineteen hundreds, with small front and side and more spacious back yards, and trees in the yards, and porches. These were softwooded trees, poplars, tulip trees, cottonwoods. There were fences around one or two of the houses, but mainly the yards ran into each other with only now and then a low hedge that wasn't doing very well. There were few good friends among the grown people, and they were not poor enough for the other sort of intimate acquaintance, but everyone nodded and spoke, and even might talk short times, trivially, and at the two extremes of the general or the particular, and ordinarily nextdoor neighbors talked quite a bit when they happened to run into each other, and never paid calls. The men were mostly small businessmen, one or two very modestly executives, one or two worked with their hands, most of them clerical, and most of them between thirty and forty-five.

But it is of these evenings, I speak.

Supper was at six and was over by half past. There was still daylight, shining softly and with a tarnish, like the lining of a shell; and the carbon lamps lifted at the corners were on in the light, and the locusts were started, and the fire flies were out, and a few frogs were flopping in the dewy grass, by the time the fathers and the children came out. The children ran out first hell bent and yelling those names by which they were known; then the fathers sank out leisurely in crossed suspenders, their collars removed and their necks looking tall and shy. The mothers stayed back in the kitchen washing and drying, putting things away, recrossing their traceless footsteps like the lifetime journeys of bees, measuring out the dry cocoa for breakfast. When they

KNOXVILLE: SUMMER 1915: From *A Death in the Family* by James Agee. Reprinted by permission of Ivan Obolensky, Inc.

came out they had taken off their aprons and their skirts were dampened and they sat in rockers on their porches quietly.

It is not of the games children played in the evening that I want to speak now, it is of a contemporaneous atmosphere that has little to do with them: that of the fathers of families, each in his space of lawn, his shirt fishlike pale in the unnatural light and his face nearly anonymous, hosing their lawns. The hoses were attached at spigots that stood out of the brick foundations of the houses. The nozzles were variously set but usually so there was a long sweet stream of spray, the nozzle wet in the hand, the water trickling the right forearm and the peeled-back cuff, and the water whishing out a long loose and low-curved cone, and so gentle a sound. First an insane noise of violence in the nozzle, then the still irregular sound of adjustment, then the smoothing into steadiness and a pitch as accurately tuned to the size and style of stream as any violin. So many qualities of sound out of one hose: so many choral differences out of those several hoses that were in earshot. Out of any one hose, the almost dead silence of the release, and the short still arch of the separate big drops, silent as a held breath, and the only noise the flattering noise on leaves and the slapped grass at the fall of each big drop. That, and the intense hiss with the intense stream; that, and that same intensity not growing less but growing more quiet and delicate with the turn of the nozzle, up to that extreme tender whisper when the water was just a wide bell of film. Chiefly, though, the hoses were set much alike, in a compromise between distance and tenderness of spray (and quite surely a sense of art behind this compromise, and a quiet deep joy, too real to recognize itself), and the sounds therefore were pitched much alike; pointed by the snorting start of a new hose; decorated by some man playful with the nozzle; left empty, like God by the sparrow's fall, when any single one of them desists: and all, though near alike, of various pitch; and in this unison. These sweet pale streamings in the light lift out their pallors and their voices all together, mothers hushing their children, the hushing unnaturally prolonged, the men gentle and silent and each snail-like withdrawn into the quietude of what he singly is doing, the urination of huge children stood loosely military against an invisible wall, and gentle happy and peaceful, tasting the mean goodness of their living like the last of their suppers in their mouths; while the locusts carry on this noise of hoses on their much higher and sharper key. The noise of the locust is dry, and it seems not to be rasped or vibrated but urged from him as if through a small orifice by breath that can never give out. Also there is never one locust but an illusion of at least a thousand. The noise of each locust is pitched in some classic locust range out of which none of them varies more than two full tones: and yet you seem to hear each locust discrete from all the rest, and there is a long, slow, pulse in their noise, like the scarcely defined arch of a long and high set bridge. They are all around in every tree, so that the noise seems to come from nowhere and everywhere at once, from the whole shell heaven, shivering in your flesh and teasing your eardrums, the boldest of all the sounds of night. And yet it is habitual to summer nights, and is of the great order of noises, like the noises of the sea and of the blood her precocious grandchild, which you realize you are hearing only when you catch yourself listening. Meantime from low in the dark, just outside the swaying horizons of the hoses, conveying always grass in the damp of dew and its strong green-black smear of smell, the regular yet spaced noises of the crickets, each a sweet cold silver noise threenoted, like the slipping each time of three matched links of a small chain.

But the men by now, one by one, have silenced their hoses and drained and coiled them. Now only two, and now only one, is left, and you see only ghostlike shirt with the sleeve garters, and sober mystery of his mild face like the lifted face of large cattle enquiring of your presence in a pitchdark pool of meadow; and now he too is gone; and it has become that time of evening when people sit on their porches, rocking gently and talking gently and watching the street and the standing up into their sphere of possession of the trees, of birds hung havens, hangars. People go by; things go by. A horse, drawing a buggy, breaking his hollow iron music on the asphalt; a loud auto; a quiet auto; people in pairs, not in a hurry, scuffling, switching their weight of aestival body, talking casually, the taste hovering over them of vanilla, strawberry, pasteboard and starched milk, the image upon them of lovers and horsemen, squared with clowns in hueless amber. A street car raising its iron moan; stopping, belling and starting; stertorous; rousing and raising again its iron increasing moan and swimming its gold windows and straw seats on past and past and past, the bleak spark crackling and cursing above it like a small malignant spirit set to dog its tracks; the iron whine rises on rising speed; still risen, faints; halts; the faint stinging bell; rises again, still fainter; fainting, lifting, lifts, faints forgone: forgotten. Now is the night one blue dew.

Now is the night one blue dew, my father has drained, he has coiled the hose.
Low on the length of lawns, a frailing of fire who breathes.
Content, silver, like peeps of light, each cricket makes his comment over and over in the drowned grass.
A cold toad thumpily flounders.
Within the edges of damp shadows of side yards are hovering children nearly sick with joy of fear, who watch the unguarding of a telephone pole.
Around white carbon corner lamps bugs of all sizes are lifted elliptic,

solar systems. Big hardshells bruise themselves, assailant: he is fallen on his back, legs squiggling.
Parents on porches: rock and rock: From damp strings morning glories: hang their ancient faces.
The dry and exalted noise of the locusts from all the air at once enchants my eardrums.

On the rough wet grass of the back yard my father and mother have spread quilts. We all lie there, my mother, my father, my uncle, my aunt, and I too am lying there. First we were sitting up, then one of us lay down, and then we all lay down, on our stomachs, or on our sides, or on our backs, and they have kept on talking. They are not talking much, and the talk is quiet, of nothing in particular, of nothing at all in particular, of nothing at all. The stars are wide and alive, they seem each like a smile of great sweetness, and they seem very near. All my people are larger bodies than mine, quiet, with voices gentle and meaningless like the voices of sleeping birds. One is an artist, he is living at home. One is a musician, she is living at home. One is my mother who is good to me. One is my father who is good to me. By some chance, here they are, all on this earth; and who shall ever tell the sorrow of being on this earth, lying, on quilts, on the grass, in a summer evening, among the sounds of the night. May God bless my people, my uncle, my aunt, my mother, my good father, oh, remember them kindly in their time of trouble; and in the hour of their taking away.

After a little I am taken in and put to bed. Sleep, soft smiling, draws me unto her: and those receive me, who quietly treat me, as one familiar and well beloved in that home: but will not, oh, will not, not now, not ever; but will not ever tell me who I am.

John Updike

BOYHOOD IN THE 1940'S

WHEN I was born, my parents and my mother's parents planted a dogwood tree in the side yard of the large white house in which we lived throughout my boyhood. This tree, I learned quite early, was exactly my age; was, in a sense, me. But I never observed it closely, am not now sure what color its petals were; its presence was no more distinct than that of my shadow. The tree was my shadow, and had it died, had it ceased to occupy, each year with increasing volume and

---

brilliance, its place in the side yard, I would have felt that a blessing like the blessing of light had been withdrawn from my life.

Though I cannot ask you to see it more clearly than I myself saw it, yet mentioning it seems to open the possibility of my boyhood home coming again to life. With a sweet damp rush the grass of our yard seems to breathe again on me. It is just cut. My mother is pushing the mower, to which a canvas catch is attached. My grandmother is raking up the loose grass in thick heaps, small green haystacks impregnated with dew, and my grandfather stands off to one side, smoking a cigar, elegantly holding the elbow of his right arm in the palm of his left hand while the blue smoke twists from under his mustache and dissolves in the heavy evening air, that misted, too-rich Pennsylvania air. My father is off, doing some duty in the town; he is a conscientious man, a schoolteacher and deacon, and also, somehow, a man of the streets. . . .

HISTORY

MY BOYHOOD was spent in a world made tranquil by two invisible catastrophes: the Depression and World War II. Between 1932, when I was born, and 1945, when we moved away, the town of Shillington changed, as far as I could see, very little. The vacant lot beside our home on Philadelphia Avenue remained vacant. The houses along the street were neither altered nor replaced. The high-school grounds, season after season, continued to make a placid plain visible from our rear windows. The softball field, with its triptych backstop, was nearest us. A little beyond, on the left, were the school and its boiler house, built in the late 1920's of the same ochre brick. In the center a cinder track circumscribed the football field. At a greater distance there were the tennis courts and the poor farm fields and the tall double rows of trees marking the Poorhouse Lane. The horizon was the blue cloud, scarred by a gravel pit's orange slash, of Mount Penn, which overlooked the city of Reading.

A little gravel alley, too small to be marked with a street sign but known in the neighborhood as Shilling Alley, wound hazardously around our property and on down, past an untidy sequence of back buildings—chicken houses, barns out of plumb, a gunshop, a small lumber mill, a shack where a blind man lived, and the enchanted grotto of a garage whose cement floors had been waxed to the luster of ebony by oil drippings and in whose greasy-black depths a silver drinking fountain spurted the coldest water in the world, silver water so cold it made your front teeth throb—on down to Lancaster Avenue, the main street, where the trolley cars ran. All through those years, the trolley cars ran. All through those years Pappy Shilling, the surviving son of the landowner after whom the town was named, walked up and down Philadelphia Avenue with his thin cane and his snow-white bangs; a vibrating chain of perfect-Sunday-school-attendance pins dangled from his lapel. Each autumn the horse-chestnut trees dropped their useless, treasurable nuts; each spring the dogwood tree put forth a slightly larger spread of blossoms; always the leaning walnut tree in our back yard fretted with the same black branches the view we had.

Within our house, too, there was little change. My grandparents did not die, though they seemed very old. My father continued to teach at the high school; he had secured the job shortly after I was born. No one else was born. I was an only child. A great many only children were born in 1932. I make no apologies. I do not remember ever feeling the space for a competitor within the house. The five of us already there locked into a star that would have shattered like crystal at the admission of a sixth. We had no pets. We fed Tommy on the porch, but he was too wild to set foot in the kitchen, and only my grandmother, in a way wild herself, could touch him. Tommy came to us increasingly battered and once did not come at all. As if he had never existed: that was death. And then there was a squirrel, Tilly, that we fed peanuts to; she became very tame, and under the grape arbor would take them from our hands—the excitement of those tiny brown teeth shivering against my fingertips: life. But she, too, came from the outside, and returned to her tree, and did not dare intrude in our house.

The arrangement inside, which seemed to me so absolute, had been achieved, beyond the peripheries of my vision, drastically and accidentally. It may, at first, have been meant to be temporary. My father and grandfather were casualties of the early thirties. My father lost his job as a cable splicer with the telephone company; he and my mother had been living—for how long I have never understood—in boardinghouses and hotels throughout western Pennsylvania, in towns whose names (Hazelton, Altoona) even now make their faces light up with youth, a glow flowing out of the darkness preceding my birth. They lived through this darkness, and the details of the adventure that my mother recalls—her lonely closeted days, the games of solitaire, the novels by Turgenev, the prostitutes downstairs, the men sleeping and starving in the parks of Pittsburgh—seem to waken in her an unjust and unreasonable happiness that used to rouse jealousy in my childish heart. I remember waiting with her by a window for my father to return from weeks on the road. It is in the Shillington living room. My hands are on the radiator ridges, I can see my father striding through the hedge toward the grape arbor, I feel my mother's excitement beside me mingle with mine. But she says this cannot be; he had lost his job before I was born.

My grandfather came from farming people in the south of the

county. He prospered, and prematurely retired; the large suburban house he bought to house his good fortune became his fortune's shell, the one fragment of it left him. The two men pooled their diminished resources of strength and property and, with their women, came to live together. I do not believe they expected this arrangement to last long. For all of them—for all four of my adult guardians—Shillington was a snag, a halt in a journey that had begun elsewhere. Only I belonged to the town. The accidents that had planted me here made uneasy echoes in the house, but, like Tilly and Tommy, their source was beyond my vision. . . .

I moved upward from grade to grade and birthday to birthday on a notched stick that itself was held perfectly steady. There was the movie house, and the playground, and the schools, and the grocery stores, and our yard, and my friends, and the horse-chestnut trees. My geography went like this: in the center of the world lay our neighborhood of Shillington. Around it there was greater Shillington, and around that, Berks County. Around Berks County there was the State of Pennsylvania, the best, the least eccentric, state in the Union. Around Pennsylvania, there was the United States, with a greater weight of people on the right and a greater weight of land on the left. For clear geometrical reasons, not all children could be born, like me, at the center of the nation. But that some children chose to be born in other countries and even continents seemed sad and fantastic. There was only one possible nation: mine. Above this vast, rectangular, slightly (the schoolteachers insisted) curved field of the blessed, there was the sky, and the flag, and, mixed up with both, Roosevelt.

DEMOCRATS

WE WERE Democrats. My grandfather lived for ninety years, and always voted, and always voted straight Democrat. A marvelous chain of votes, as marvelous as the chain of Sunday-school attendance pins that vibrated from Pappy Shilling's lapel. The political tradition that shaped his so incorruptible prejudice I am not historian enough to understand; it had something to do with Lincoln's determination to drive all the cattle out of this section of Pennsylvania if Lee won the Battle of Gettysburg.

My parents are close to me. The events that shaped their views touched my bones. At the time when I was conceived and born, they felt in themselves a whole nation stunned, frightened, despairing. With Roosevelt, hope returned. This simple impression of salvation is my political inheritance. That this impression is not universally shared amazes me. It is as if there existed a class of people who deny that the sun is bright. To me as a child Republicans seemed blind dragons; their prototype was my barber—an artist, a charmer, the only man, my mother insists, who ever cut my hair properly. Nimble and bald, he used to execute little tap-dance figures on the linoleum floor of his shop, and with engaging loyalty he always had the games of Philadelphia's two eighth-place teams tuned in on the radio. But on one subject he was rabid; the last time he cut my hair he positively asserted that our President had died of syphilis. I cannot to this day hear a Republican put forth his philosophy without hearing the snip of scissors above my ears and feeling the little ends of hair crawling across my hot face, reddened by shame and the choking pressure of the paper collar.

NOW

ROOSEVELT was for me the cap on a steadfast world, its emblem and crown. He was always there. Now he is a weakening memory, a semi-myth; it has begun to seem fabulous—like an episode in a medieval chronicle—that the greatest nation in the world was led through the world's greatest war by a man who could not walk. Now, my barber has retired, my hair is a wretched thatch grizzled with gray, and, of the two Philadelphia ball clubs, one has left Philadelphia and one is not always in last place. Now the brick home of my boyhood is owned by a doctor, who has added an annex to the front, to contain his offices. The house was too narrow for its lot and its height; it had a pinched look from the front that used to annoy my mother. But that thin white front with its eyes of green window sash and its mouth of striped awning had been a face to me; it has vanished. My dogwood tree still stands in the side yard, taller than ever, but the walnut tree out back has been cut down. My grandparents are dead. Pappy Shilling is dead. Shilling Alley has been straightened, and hardtopped, and rechristened Brobst Street. The trolley cars no longer run. The vacant lots across the town have been filled with new houses and stores. New homes have been built far out Philadelphia Avenue and all over the poorhouse property. The poorhouse has been demolished. The poorhouse dam and its aphrodisiac groves have been trimmed into a town park. If I could go again into 117 Philadelphia Avenue, and look out the rear windows, I would see, beyond the football field and the cinder track, a new, two-million-dollar high school, and beyond it, where still stands one row of the double line of trees that marked the Poorhouse Lane, a gaudy depth of postwar housing and a Food Fair like a hideous ark breasting an ocean of parked cars. Here, where wheat grew, loudspeakers unremittingly vomit commercials. It has taken me the shocks of many returnings, more and more widely spaced now, to learn, what seems simple enough, that change is the order of things. The immutability, the steadfastness, of the site of my boyhood was an exceptional effect, purchased for me at unimaginable cost by the paralyzing calamity of the Depression and the heroic external effort of the Second World War.

ENVIRONMENT

THE DIFFERENCE between a childhood and a boyhood must be this: our childhood is what we alone have had; our boyhood is what any boy in our environment would have had. My environment was a straight street about three city blocks long, with a slight slope that was most noticeable when you were on a bicycle. Though many of its residents commuted to Reading factories and offices, the neighborhood retained a rural flavor. Corn grew in the strip of land between the alley and the school grounds. We ourselves had a large vegetable garden, which we tended not as a hobby but in earnest, to get food to eat. We sold asparagus and eggs to our neighbors. Our peddling things humiliated me, but then I was a new generation. The bulk of the people in the neighborhood were not long off the farm. One old lady down the street, with an immense throat goiter, still wore a bonnet. The most aristocratic people in the block were the full-fashioned knitters; Reading's textile industry prospered in the Depression. I felt neither prosperous nor poor. We kept the food money in a little recipe box on top of the icebox, and there were nearly always a few bills and coins in it. My father's job paid him poorly but me well; it gave me a sense of, not prestige, but *place*. As a schoolteacher's son, I was assigned a role; people knew me. When I walked down the street to school, the houses called, "Chonny."

SCHOOLS

THE ELEMENTARY school was a big brick cube set in a square of black surfacing chalked and painted with the diagrams and runes of children's games. Wire fences guarded the neighboring homes from the playground. Whoever, at soccer, kicked the ball over the fence into Snitzy's yard had to bring it back. It was very terrible to have to go into Snitzy's yard, but there was only one ball for each grade. Snitzy was a large dark old German who might give you the ball or lock you up in his garage, depending upon his mood. He did not move like other men; suddenly the air near you condensed, and his huge black hands were around your head.

On the way to school, walking down Lancaster Avenue, we passed Henry's, a variety store, where we bought punch-out licorice belts and tablets with Edward G. Robinson and Hedy Lamarr smiling on the cover. In October, Hallowe'en masks appeared, hung on wire clotheslines. Hanging limp, these faces of Chinamen and pirates and witches were distorted, and, thickly clustered and rustling against each other, they seemed more frightening masking empty air than they did mounted on the heads of my friends—which was frightening enough. It is strange how fear resists the attacks of reason, how you can know with absolute certainty that is is only Mark Wenrich or Jimmy Trexler whose eyes are moving so weirdly in those almond-shaped holes, and yet still be frightened. I abhorred that effect of double eyes a mask gives; it was as bad as seeing a person's mouth move upside down.

I was a Crow. That is my chief memory of what went on inside the elementary school. In music class the singers were divided into three groups: Nightingales, Robins, and Crows. From year to year the names changed. Sometimes the Crows were Parrots. When visitors from the high school, or elsewhere "outside," came to hear us sing, the Crows were taken out of the room and sent upstairs to watch with the fifth grade an educational film about salmon fishing in the Columbia River. Usually there were only two of us, me and a girl from Philadelphia Avenue whose voice was in truth very husky. I never understood why I was a Crow, though it gave me a certain derisive distinction. As I heard it, I sang rather well, and my singing gives me pleasure still.

The other Crow was the first girl I kissed. I just did it, one day, walking back from school along the gutter where the water from the ice plant ran down, because somebody dared me to. And I continued to do it every day, when we reached that spot on the pavement, until a neighbor told my mother, and she, with a solemn weight that seemed unrelated to the airy act, forbade it.

I walked to school mostly with girls. It happened that the mothers of Philadelphia Avenue and, a block up, of Second Street, had borne female babies in 1932. These babies now teased me, the lone boy in their pack, by singing the new song, "Oh, Johnny, oh Johnny, how you can love!" and stealing my precious rubber-lined bookbag. The queen of these girls later became the May Queen of our senior class. She had freckles and thick pigtails and green eyes and her mother made her wear high-top shoes long after the rest of us had stopped. She had so much vitality that on the way back from school her nose would start bleeding for no reason. We would be walking along over the wings of the maple seeds and suddenly she would tip her head back and rest it on a wall while someone ran and soaked a handkerchief in the ice-plant water and applied it to her streaming, narrow, crimson-shining nostrils. She was a Nightingale. I loved her deeply, and ineffectually.

My love for that girl carries through all those elementary-school cloakrooms; they always smelled of wet raincoats and rubbers. That tangy, thinly resonant, lonely smell: can love have a better envelope? Everything I did in grammar school was meant to catch her attention.

I had a daydream wherein the stars of the music class were asked to pick partners and she, a Nightingale, picked me, a Crow. The teacher was shocked; the class buzzed. To their amazement I sang superbly; my voice, thought to be so ugly, in duet with hers was beautiful. Still singing, we led some sort of parade. In the world of reality, my triumph was getting her to slap me once. In the third grade. She was always slapping boys in those years; I could not quite figure out what they did. Pull her pigtails, untie her shoes, snatch at her dress, tease her (they called her "Pug")—this much I could see. But somehow there seemed to be under these offensive acts a current running the opposite way; for it was precisely the boys who were most hateful to her that she talked to solemnly at recess, and walked with after school, and whose names she wrote on the sides of her books. Without seeing this current, but deducing its presence, I tried to jump in; I entered a tussle she was having with a boy in homeroom before the bell. I pulled the bow at the back of her dress, and was slapped so hard that children at the other end of the hall heard the crack. I was overjoyed; the stain and pain on my face seemed a badge of initiation. But it was not; the distance between us remained as it was; I did not really want to tease her, I wanted to rescue her, and to be rescued by her. I lacked—and perhaps here the only child suffers a certain deprivation—that kink in the instincts on which childish courtship turns. He lacks a certain easy roughness with other children.

All the years I was at the elementary school the high school loomed large in my mind. Its students, tall, hairy, smoke-breathing, paced the streets seemingly equal with adults. I could see part of its immensity from our rear windows. It was there that my father performed his mysteries every day, striding off from breakfast, down through the grape arbor, his coat pocket bristling with defective pens. He now and then took me over there; the incorruptible smell of varnish and red sweeping wax, the size of the desks, the height of the drinking fountains, the fantastic dimensions of the combination gymnasium-auditorium made me feel that these were halls in which a race of giants had ages ago labored through lives of colossal bliss. At the end of each summer, usually on Labor Day Monday, he and I went into his classroom, Room 201, and unpacked the books and arranged the tablets and the pencils on the desks of his homeroom pupils. Sharpening forty pencils was a chore; sharing it with him, a solemn pleasure. To this day I look up at my father through the cedar smell of pencil shavings. To see his key open the front portals of oak, to share alone with him for an hour the pirate hoard of uncracked books and golden pencils, to switch off the lights and leave the room and walk down the darkly lustrous perspective of the corridor and perhaps halt for a few words by an open door that revealed another teacher, like a sorcerer in his sanctum, inscribing forms beside a huge polished globe of the earth—such territories of wonder boyhood alone can acquire.

THE PLAYGROUND

UP FROM the hardball diamond, on a plateau bounded on three sides by cornfields, a pavilion contained some tables and a shed for equipment. I spent my summer weekdays there from the age I was so small that the dust stirred by the feet of roof-ball players got into my eyes. Roof ball was the favorite game. It was played with a red rubber ball smaller than a basketball. The object was to hit it back up on the roof of the pavilion, the whole line of children in succession. Those who failed dropped out. When there was just one person left, a new game began with the cry "*Noo*-oo *gay*-ame," and we lined up in the order in which we had gone out, so that the lines began with the strongest and tallest and ended with the weakest and youngest. But there was never any doubt that everybody could play; it was perfect democracy. Often the line contained as many as thirty pairs of legs, arranged chronologically. By the time we moved away, I had become a regular front-runner; I knew how to flick the ball to give it spin, how to leap up and send the ball skimming the length of the roof edge, how to plump it with my knuckles when there was a high bounce. Somehow the game never palled; the sight of the ball bouncing along the tar-paper of the foreshortened roof was always important. Many days I was at the playground from nine o'clock, when they ran up the American flag, until four, when they called the equipment in, and played nothing else. . . .

Reality seemed slightly more intense at the playground. There was a dust, a daring. It was a children's world; nowhere else did we gather in such numbers with so few adults over us. The playground occupied a platform of earth; we were exposed, it seems now, to the sun and sky. Witness

THE ENORMOUS CLOUD

IT WAS a strange glimpse. One day, playing roof ball, and I could be six, nine, or twelve when it happened, I looked up and overhead there was an enormous cloud. Someone, maybe I, even called, "Look at the cloud!" It was a bright day; out of nowhere had materialized a cloud, roughly circular in shape, as big as a continent, leaden-blue in the mass, radiant silver along the edges. Its size seemed overwhelming; it was more than a portent, it was the fulfillment of one. I had never seen, and never saw again, such a big cloud.

For of course what is strange is that clouds have no size. Moving in an immaterial medium at an indeterminate distance, they offer no hold for measurement, and we do not even judge them relative to each other. Even, as on a rainy day, when the sky is filled from horizon to horizon, we do not think, "What an enormous cloud." It is as if the soul is a camera shutter customarily set at "ordinary"; but now and then, through some inadvertence, it is tripped wide open and the film is flooded with an enigmatic image.

Another time the sky spoke at the playground, telling me that treachery can come from above. It was our Field Day. One of the events was a race in which we put our shoes in a heap, lined up at a distance, ran to the heap, found our shoes, put them on, and raced back. The winner got a ticket to the Shillington movie theater. I was the first to find my shoes, and was tying my laces when, out of the ring of adults and older children who had collected to watch, a voice urged, "Hurry! Don't tie the laces." I didn't, and ran back, and was disqualified. The world reeled at the treachery of that unseen high voice: I loved the movies.

THE MOVIE HOUSE

IT WAS two blocks from my home; I began to go alone from the age of six. My mother, so strict about my kissing girls, was strangely indulgent about this. The theater ran three shows a week, for two days each, and was closed on Sundays. Many weeks I went three times. I remember a summer evening in our yard. Supper is over, the walnut tree throws a heavy shadow. The fireflies are not out yet. My father is off, my mother and her parents are turning the earth in our garden. Some burning sticks and paper on our ash heap fill the damp air with low smoke; I express a wish to go to the movies, expecting to be told no. Instead, my mother tells me to go into the house and clean up; I come into the yard again in clean shorts, the shadows slightly heavier, the dew a little wetter; I am given eleven cents and run down Philadelphia Avenue in my ironed shorts and fresh shirt, down past the running ice-plant water, the dime and the penny in my hand. I always ran to the movies. If it was not a movie with Adolphe Menjou, it was a horror picture. People turning into cats—fingers going stubby into paws and hair being blurred in with double exposure—and Egyptian tombs and English houses where doors creak and wind disturbs the curtains and dogs refuse to go into certain rooms because they sense something supersensory. I used to crouch down into the seat and hold my coat in front of my face when I sensed a frightening scene coming, peeking through the buttonhole to find out when it was over. Through the buttonhole Frankenstein's monster glowered; lightning flashed; sweat poured over the bolts that held his face together. On the way home, I ran again, in terror now. Darkness had come, the first show was from seven to nine, by nine even the longest summer day was ending. Each porch along the street seemed to be a tomb crammed with shadows, each shrub seemed to shelter a grasping arm. I ran with a frantic high step, trying to keep my ankles away from the reaching hands. The last and worst terror was our own porch; low brick walls on either side concealed possible cat people. Leaping high, I launched myself at the door and, if no one was in the front of the house, fled through suffocating halls past gaping doorways to the kitchen, where there was always someone working, and a light bulb burning. The icebox. The rickety worn table, oilcloth-covered, where we ate. The windows solid black and fortified by the interior brightness. But even then I kept my legs away from the dark space beneath the table.

These were Hollywood's comfortable years. The theater—a shallowly sloped hall, too narrow to have a central aisle—was usually crowded, though I liked it most on Monday nights, when it was emptiest. It seemed most mine then. I had a favorite seat—rear row, extreme left—and my favorite moment was the instant when the orange side lights, Babylonian in design, were still lit, and the curtain was closed but there was obviously somebody up in the projection room, for the camera had started to whir. In the next instant I knew a broad dusty beam of light would fill the air above me, and the titles of the travelogue would appear on the curtains, their projected steadiness undulating as with an unhurried, composed screech the curtains were drawn back, revealing the screen alive with images that then would pass through a few focal adjustments. In that delicate, promissory whir was my favorite moment.

On Saturday afternoons the owner gave us all Hershey bars as we came out of the matinee. On Christmas morning he showed a free hour of cartoons and the superintendent of the Lutheran Sunday school led us in singing carols, gesticulating in front of the high blank screen, no bigger than the shadow of the moth that sometimes landed on the lens. His booming voice would echo curiously on the bare walls, usually so dark and muffling but that on this one morning, containing a loud sea of Christmas children, had a bare, clean, morning quality that echoed. After this special show we all went down to the Town Hall, where the plumpest borough employee, disguised as Santa Claus, gave us each a green box of chocolates. Shillington was small enough to support such traditions.

THREE BOYS

A, *B*, and *C*, I'll say, in case they care. *A* lived next door; he *loomed* next door, rather. He seemed immense—a great wallowing fatso stuffed with possessions; he was the son of a full-fashioned knitter. He seemed to have a beer-belly—solid, portentous, proud. After several generations beer-bellies may become congenital. Also his face had no features; it was just a blank ball on his shoulders. He used to call me "Ostrich," after Disney's Ollie Ostrich. My neck was not very long; the name seemed horribly unfair; it was its injustice that made me cry. But nothing I could say, or scream, would make him stop. And I still, now and then sometimes—in reading, say, a book review by one of the apple-cheeked savants of the quarterlies or one of the pious gremlins who manufacture puns for *Time*—get the old sensations: my ears close up, my eyes go warm, my chest feels thin as an eggshell, my voice churns silently in my stomach. From A I received my first impression of the smug, chinkless, irresistible *power* of stupidity; it is the most powerful force on earth. It says "Ostrich" often enough, and the universe crumbles.

A was more than a boy, he was a force-field that could manifest itself in many forms, that could take the wiry, disconsolate shape of wide-mouthed, tiny-eared boys who would now and then beat me up on the way back from school. I did not greatly mind being beaten up, though I resisted it. For one thing, it firmly involved me, at least during the beating, with the circumambient humanity that so often seemed evasive. Also, the boys who applied the beating were misfits, periodic flunkers, who wore knickers whose knees had lost the corduroy ribbing and men's shirts with the top button buttoned—this last an infallible sign of deep poverty. So that I felt there was some justice, some condonable revenge, being applied with their fists to this little teacher's son. And then there was the delicious alarm of my mother and grandmother when I returned home bloody, bruised, and torn. My father took the attitude that it was making a boy of me, an attitude I dimly shared. He and I both were afraid of me becoming a sissy—he perhaps more afraid than I.

When I was eleven or so I met *B*. It was summer and I was down at the playground. He was pushing a little tank with moving rubber treads up and down the hills in the sandbox. It was a beautiful little toy, mottled with camouflage green; patriotic manufacturers produced throughout the war millions of such authentic miniatures which we maneuvered with authentic, if miniature, hate. Drawn by the toy, I spoke to him; though taller and a little older than I, he had my dull straight brown hair and a look of being also alone. We became fast friends. He lived just up the street—toward the poorhouse, the east part of the street, from which the little winds of tragedy blew. He had just moved from the Midwest, and his mother was a widow. Besides wage war, we did many things together. We played marbles for days at a time, until one of us had won the other's entire coffee-canful. With jigsaws we cut out of plywood animals copied from comic books. We made movies by tearing the pages out of Big Little Books and coloring the drawings and pasting them in a strip, and winding them on toilet-paper spools, and making a cardboard carton a theater. We rigged up telephones, and racing wagons, and miniature cities, using orange crates and cigar boxes and peanut-butter jars and such potent debris. We loved Smokey Stover and were always saying "Foo." We had an intense spell of Monopoly. He called me "Uppy"—the only person who ever did so. I remember once, knowing he was coming down that afternoon to my house to play Monopoly, in order to show my joy I set up the board elaborately, with the Chance and Community Chest cards fanned painstakingly, like spiral staircases. He came into the room, groaned, "Uppy, what are you doing?" and impatiently scrabbled the cards together in a sensible pile. The older we got, the more the year between us told, and the more my friendship embarrassed him. We fought. Once, to my horror, I heard myself taunting him with the fact that he had no father. The unmentionable, the unforgivable. I suppose we patched things up, children do, but nothing was quite right after that. He had a long, pale, serious face, with buck teeth, and is probably an electronics engineer somewhere now, doing secret government work.

So through *B* I first experienced the pattern of friendship. There are three stages. First, acquaintance: we are new to each other, make each other laugh in surprise, and demand nothing beyond politeness. The death of the one would startle the other, no more. It is a pleasant stage, a stable stage; on austere rations of exposure it can live a lifetime, and the two parties to it always feel a slight gratification upon meeting, will feel vaguely confirmed in their human state. Then comes intimacy: now we laugh before two words of the joke are out of the other's mouth, because we know what he will say. Our whole two beings seem marvelously joined, from our toes to our heads, along tingling points of agreement; everything we venture is right, everything we put forth lodges in a corresponding socket in the frame of the other. The death of the one would grieve the other. To be together is to enjoy a mounting excitement, a constant echo and amplification. It is an ecstatic and unstable stage, bound of its own agitation to tip into the third: revulsion. One or the other makes a misjudgment; presumes; puts forth that which does not meet agreement. Sometimes there is an explosion; more often the moment is swallowed in silence, and months pass before its nature dawns. Instead of dissolving, it grows. The mind, the throat, are clogged; forgiveness, forgetfulness, that have arrived so often, fail. Now everything jars and is distasteful; the betrayal, perhaps a tiny fraction in itself, has inverted the tingling column of agreement, made all pluses minuses. Everything about the other is hateful, despicable; yet he cannot be dismissed. We have confided in him too many minutes, too many words; he has those minutes and words as hostages, and his confidences are embedded in us where they cannot be scraped away, and even rivers of time cannot erode them completely, for there are indelible stains. Now—though the friends may continue to meet, and smile, as if they had never trespassed beyond acquaintance—the death of the one would please the other.

An unhappy pattern to which C is an exception. He was my friend before kindergarten, he is my friend still. I go to his home now, and he and his wife serve me and my wife with alcoholic drinks and slices of excellent cheese on crisp crackers, just as twenty years ago he served me with treats from his mother's refrigerator. He was a born host, and I a born guest. Also, he was intelligent. If my childhood's brain, when I look back at it, seems a primitive mammal, a lemur or shrew, his brain was an angel whose visitation was widely hailed as wonderful. When in school he stood to recite, his cool rectangular forehead glowed. He tucked his right hand into his left armpit and with his left hand mechanically tapped a pencil against his thigh. His answers were always correct. He beat me at spelling bees and, in another sort of competition, when we both collected Big Little Books, he outbid me for my supreme find (in the attic of a third boy), the first Mickey Mouse. I can still see that book, I wanted it so badly, its paper tan with age and its drawings done in Disney's primitive style, when Mickey's black chest is naked like a child's and his eyes are two nicked oblongs. Losing it was perhaps a lucky blow; it began to wean me away from any hope of ever having possessions.

C was fearless. He deliberately set fields on fire; he engaged in rock-throwing duels with tough boys. One afternoon he persisted in playing quoits with me although—as the hospital discovered that night—his appendix was nearly bursting. He was enterprising. He peddled magazine subscriptions door-to-door; he mowed neighbors' lawns; he struck financial bargains with his father. He collected stamps so well his collection blossomed into a stamp company that filled his room with steel cabinets and mimeograph machinery. He collected money—every time I went over to his house he would get out a little tin box and count the money in it for me: $27.50 one week, $29.95 the next, $30.90 the next—all changed into new bills nicely folded together. It was a strange ritual, whose meaning for me was: since he was doing it, I didn't have to. His money made me richer. We read Ellery Queen and played chess and invented board games and discussed infinity together. In later adolescence, he collected records. He liked the Goodman quintets but loved Fats Waller. Sitting there in that room so familiar to me, where the machinery of the Shilco Stamp Company still crowded the walls and for that matter the tin box of money might still be hiding, while my pale friend grunted softly along with that dead dark angel on "You're Not the Only Oyster in the Stew," I felt, in the best sense, patronized. The perfect guest of the perfect host. What made it perfect was that we had both spent our entire lives in Shillington. . . .

THE NIGHT-BLOOMING CEREUS

IT WAS during the war; early in the war, 1942. *Collier's* had printed a cover showing Hirohito, splendidly costumed and fanged, standing malevolently in front of a bedraggled, bewildered Hitler and an even more decrepit and craven Mussolini. Our troops in the Pacific were reeling from island to island; the Japanese seemed a race of demons capable of anything. The night-blooming cereus was the property of a family who lived down the street in a stucco house that on the inside was narrow and dark in the way that houses in the middle of the country sometimes are. The parlor was crowded with obscure furniture decked out with antimacassars and porcelain doodads. At Christmas a splendiferous tree bloomed in that parlor, hung with pounds of tinsel and strung popcorn and paper chains and pretzels and balls and intricate, figurative ornaments that must have been rescued from the previous century.

The blooming of the cereus was to be an event in the neighborhood; for days we had been waiting. This night—a clear warm night, in August or September—word came, somehow. My mother and grandmother and I rushed down Philadelphia Avenue in the dark. It was late; I should have been in bed. The plant stood at the side of the house, in a narrow space between the stucco wall and the hedge. A knot of neighborhood women had already gathered; heavy shoulders and hair buns were silhouetted in an indeterminate light. On its twisted, unreal stem the flow had opened its unnaturally brilliant petals. But no one was looking at it. For overhead, in the north of a black sky strewn with stars like thrown salt, the wandering fingers of an aurora borealis gestured, now lengthening and brightening so that shades of blue and green could be distinguished, now ebbing until it seemed there was nothing there at all. It was a rare sight this far south. The women muttered, sighed, and, as if involuntarily, out of the friction of their bodies, moaned. Standing among their legs and skirts, I was slapped by a sudden cold wave of fear that made my skin burn. "Is it the end of the world?" one of the women asked. There was no answer. And then a plane went over, its red lights blinking, its motors no louder than the drone of a wasp. Japanese. The Japanese were going to bomb Shillington, the center of the nation. I waited for the bomb, and without words prayed, expecting a miracle, for the appearance of angels and Japanese in the sky was restrained by the same impossibility, an impossibility that the swollen waxy brilliant white of the flower by my knees had sucked from the night.

The plane of course passed; it was one of ours; my prayer was answered with the usual appearance of absence. We went home, and the world reconstituted its veneer of reason, but the moans of the women had rubbed something in me bare.

ART

LEAFING through a scrapbook my mother long ago made of my childhood drawings, I was greeted by one I had titled "Mr. Sun talking to Old Man Winter in his Office." Old Man Winter, a cloud with stick legs, and his host, a radiant ball with similar legs, sit at ease, both smiling, on two chairs that are the only furniture of the solar office. That the source of all light should have, somewhere, an office, suited my conception of an artist, who was someone who lived in a small town like Shillington, and who, equipped with pencils and paper, practiced his solitary trade as methodically as the dentist practiced his. And indeed, that is how it is at present with me.

Goethe—probably among others—says to be wary of our youthful wishes, for in maturity we are apt to get them. I go back, now, to Pennsylvania, and on one of the walls of the house in which my parents now live there hangs a photograph of myself as a boy. I am smiling, and staring with clear eyes at something in the corner of the room. I stand before that photograph, and am disappointed to receive no flicker, not the shadow of a flicker, of approval, of gratitude. The boy continues to smile at the corner of the room, beyond me. That boy is not a ghost to me, he is real to me; it is I who am a ghost to him. I, in my present state, was one of the ghosts that haunted his childhood. Like some phantom conjured by this child from a glue bottle, I have executed his commands; acquired pencils, paper, and an office. Now I wait apprehensively for his next command, or at least a nod of appreciation, and he smiles through me, as if I am already transparent with failure.

He saw art—between drawing and writing he ignorantly made no distinction—as a method of riding a thin pencil line out of Shillington, out of time altogether, into an infinity of unseen and even unborn hearts. He pictured this infinity as radiant. How innocent! But his assumption here, like his assumptions on religion and politics, is one for which I had found no certain substitute. He loved blank paper and obedience to this love led me to a difficult artistic attempt. I reasoned thus: just as the paper is the basis for the marks upon it, might not events be contingent upon a never-expressed (because featureless) ground? Is the true marvel of Sunday skaters the pattern of their pirouettes or the fact that they are silently upheld? Blankness is not emptiness; we may skate upon an intense radiance we do not see because we see nothing else. And in fact there is a color, a quiet but tireless goodness that things at rest, like a brick wall or a small stone, seem to affirm. A wordless reassurance these things are pressing to give. An hallucination? To transcribe middleness with all its grits, bumps, and anonymities, in its fullness of satisfaction and mystery: is it possible or, in view of the suffering that violently colors the periphery and that at all moments threatens to move into the center, worth doing? Possibly not; but the horse-chestnut trees, the telephone poles, the porches, the green hedges recede to a calm point that in my subjective geography is still the center of the world.

END

I WAS walking down this Philadelphia Avenue one April and was just stepping over the shallow little rain gutter in the pavement that could throw you if you were on roller skates—though it had been years since I had been on roller skates—when from the semidetached house across the street a boy broke and ran. He was the youngest of six sons. All of his brothers were in the armed services, and five blue stars hung in his home's front window. He was several years older than I was, and used to annoy my grandparents by walking through our yard, down past the grape arbor, on his way to high school. On his long legs he was now running diagonally across the high-crowned street. I was the only other person out in the air. "Chonny!" he called. I was flattered to have him, so tall and grown, speak to me. "Did you hear?"

"No. What?"

"On the radio. The President is dead."

That summer the war ended, and that fall, suddenly mobile, we moved away from the big white house. We moved on Hallowe'en night. As the movers were fitting the last pieces of our furniture, furniture that had not moved since I was born, into their truck, little figures dressed as ghosts and cats flitted in and out of the shadows of the street. A few rang our bell, and when my mother opened the door they were frightened by the empty rooms they saw behind her, and went away without begging. When the last things had been packed, and the kitchen light turned off, and the doors locked, the three of us—my grandparents were already at the new house—got into the old Buick my father had bought—in Shillington we had never had a car, for we could walk everywhere—and drove up the street, east, toward the poorhouse and beyond. Somewhat self-consciously and cruelly dramatizing my grief, for I was thirteen and beginning to be cunning, I twisted and watched our house recede through the rear window. Moonlight momentarily caught in an upper pane; then the reflection passed, and the brightest thing was the white brick wall itself. Against the broad part where I used to play tennis with myself, the silhouette of the dogwood tree stood, confused with the shapes of the other bushes in our side yard but taller. I turned away before it would have disappeared from sight, and so it is that my shadow has always remained in one place.

Francis G. Townsend

A FRESHMAN IN LILLIPUT

WHEN I was a freshman, *Gulliver's Travels* taught me more about writing than any other book. Other freshmen might find little to learn from it, but that is because they do not have Craig LaDrière for a teacher.

LaDrière spent one year at St. Louis University as a graduate assistant. Perhaps that was just as well, since most institutions are not built to withstand such powerful forces! Yet we students were almost contemptuous on the first day of class, when he walked into the room, the picture of patrician splendor. He wore pince-nez glasses which were secured from absent-minded disaster by a thin black ribbon about his neck. The razor sharp creases in his trousers led the eye downward to his spotless gray spats. We recalled later how we groaned inwardly at his appearance, but we discovered shortly that his mind was as precise and elegant as his attire.

Our textbook claimed to teach writing. Aside from his horror at such presumption, LaDrière was shocked by the first paragraph, which said that men must write from birth to grave. When he came to the phrase "from birth to grave," he threw the book forward on the desk, disengaged his pince-nez, and launched into a discourse on abstraction, concretion, and metaphor. He explained how one might say "from birth to death," or "from cradle to grave," but never could one combine the two without violence. How account for phrasing like "from birth to grave"? Possibly a writer feels the need of sprightliness, and "birth to death" is not sprightly, whereas "cradle to grave" would be, except for the unfortunate fact that it is a cliché. So the writer tries for the best of both possible worlds, thereby confessing that he wants color but can't find it outside of clichés; at one and the same time he displays his fear of clichés, and his inability to dispense with them.

It took LaDrière an hour to complete his exposition. By the end of that time we had an idea that we had better use words carefully if at all, and the next few weeks left some of us wondering if the latter alternative was not the better. He never missed the slightest imperfec-

---

A FRESHMAN IN LILLIPUT: From the *Journal of Conference on College Composition and Communication,* May 1962. Reprinted with the permission of the National Council of Teachers of English and Francis G. Townsend.

tion in our themes and his grades were discouraging. I remember sweating out three hundred of the most judiciously chosen words I have ever strung together, without a single mechanical error and with not a single superfluous word, with not even a single word used in anything but its primary meaning. The paper was graded A- with the comment that it seemed dull.

In the meantime class periods droned on, with LaDrière indulging in protracted explanations of the finest distinctions between alternate words or alternate constructions. Our teacher was a considerate man. When students began falling asleep, he lowered his voice so that he would not disturb them. He was never bothered by lack of attention, but if there was any disturbance, his astonishment at such rudeness was enough to quell it. So we sweated and slumbered through the first semester, and by the end of it most of us had discovered that we had learned a great deal about this business of writing.

We carefully signed up for LaDrière's section in the second semester. Some innocent recruits joined our number, and it was great sport to watch them squirming through LaDrière's lectures and chafing under his picayunish theme correcting. "You'll learn," we wiser freshmen told them, and they did. Three Ph.D.'s came from that one section of freshman English.

What did he teach? He taught the strictest fidelity to one's own thoughts. There is probably no one whose experience, whose beliefs would not be intensely interesting, if he could find the verbal symbols which give them external form. The high school boy is content with an approximation of what he really means. Hence he will begin a paragraph with a vague "this," referring indiscriminately to any or all of what has gone before, but usually to nothing in particular. He dotes on words like "type," because nearly everything can be called some sort of a type without mental effort. He leans heavily on the verb "to be," because it applies equally well to every last thing, concrete or abstract, in God's whole universe, and the noumenal world beyond.

When a man attains his majority, he is responsible for more than his own acts. He has to accept responsibility for his own words and his own ideas. He must choose the exact word and the exact construction to convey exactly what he has in mind. For the college man, precision takes precedence over all other qualities in writing—it might even be said that mature writing consists of nothing else whatsoever.

In our early days with LaDrière we quarreled with his screwy theories. "If you pick exactly the right word the first time, that's the right word from then on?"

"Correct."

"So every time you mean the same thing, you use the same word?"

"Correct."

"Then you use the same word over and over, and that's awkward!"

"Correct. Does the awkwardness lie in the word or in your way of thinking?"

A great light began to dawn on us. To write honestly is to discover certain horrifying things about yourself. For example, you don't know anything, or your highly original thought turns out to be a commonplace or, worse still, a transparent piece of idiocy. Writing is a process of self-criticism. The better you write, the less chance of concealing your weaknesses from others, not to mention yourself.

That last phrase would have amused LaDrière. Why would anyone use it unless he wanted to mention a thing without seeming to? Of course, the phrase sounds gracefully off-handed despite its absurdity, but LaDrière taught us that precision creates a grace of its own. Arrange thoughts in natural sequence and gracefulness will appear, like the figure hidden in Michelangelo's marble.

One day he told us that in his opinion the greatest stylist in our language was Jonathan Swift, the author of *Gulliver's Travels*. Like many before and since, I was startled to hear a children's book called a major work of art. I got a copy and read it.

At that time I was overawed by the gravity of Swift scholarship, and I argued in coffee house sessions that Swift was a philosopher. I have since come to feel that Dr. Johnson's comments were justified: think of big men and little men and you have it all. In many passages, especially in Book III, *Gulliver's Travels* remains childish, and even the brilliance of Book IV does not make it a model of good sense. The book lives because it is a work of art, and not the least of its art is the perfect modeling of its sentences and paragraphs.

The hallmark of Swift's style is its complete subordination of words to thoughts, so that the verbal symbols disappear, leaving only the ideas they represent. It is almost as if he scorned words as impediments to the motion of thought. Because he eschews the petty graces of rhetoric, he achieves the ultimate grace of absolute clarity.

Consider the problem he faced in describing how Gulliver awoke in Lilliput, and how he solved it.

> I lay down on the grass, which was very soft, where I slept sounder than ever I remember to have done in my life, and, as I reckoned, above nine hours; for when I awaked, it was just daylight. I attempted to rise, but was not able to stir: for as I happened to lie on my back, I found my arms and legs were strongly fastened on each side to the ground; and my hair, which was long and thick, tied down in the same manner. I likewise felt several slender ligatures across my body, from my armpits to my thighs. I could only look upwards, the sun began to grow hot, and the light offended my eyes. I heard a confused noise about me, but, in the posture I lay, could see nothing except the sky. In a little time

> I felt something alive moving on my left leg, which advancing gently forward over my breast, came almost up to my chin; when, bending my eyes downwards as much as I could, I perceived it to be a human creature not six inches high, with a bow and arrow in his hands, and a quiver at his back.

Sequence of time and progression in space govern the organization of this passage to the last detail, yet every modifier is inserted next to the word it modifies, with one exception, the "which" referring to "something alive." A lesser writer would have been disturbed by the proximity of "leg" to "which," but here the context is so firm that no false reference is possible; consequently Swift completes his main clause instead of pausing for a parenthesis, as he usually does. And since matter of factness is the dominant key in the whole composition, note the effect of slipping "a human creature not six inches high" into the second of two parallel subordinate clauses, each interrupted by a leisurely participial construction. Now, having casually introduced his climactic detail, he tails off into two apparently unimportant bits of description, "with a bow and arrow in his hands, and a quiver at his back." The little something alive has his counterparts in other unimportant constructs!

Whether or not Swift would be good medicine for the average freshman I do not know, but the disease that ails most freshmen is the uncontrolled growth of clauses and phrases. Too often freshman English is taught as a stimulant instead of as surgery. It is true that you can get a class all worked up about ideas, and the dean will hear what a fascinating teacher you are, but the students wind up like their elders, using words like "meaningful," which means that a thing has meaning, but exactly what is not at all clear. In a little while, freshmen will have small need for exuberant rhetorical effects. When their ideas come to mean something, rather than to be meaningful, they will need the hard outlines of the Swiftian sentence, stripped of excrescences, reduced to essential subordinating words like "which" and "when" with lean participial phrases inserted where they belong.

To learn to appreciate the prose style of Jonathan Swift is to learn more about practical literary criticism than Brooks and Warren can teach. It seldom fails. In the middle of a disquisition on Swift's ideas, ask a class abruptly what they think of his prose, and you will be told he has no style. Neither does Dickens. But Henry James, there was a stylist. See how his language attracts attention to itself.

Freshman English is not supposed to be a source of innocent merriment. Its object all sublime is to make thought yield to words. Nobody quite learns how, but I went farther with Jonathan Swift and Craig LaDrière than ever before or since.

Elizabeth Bowen

OUT OF A BOOK

I KNOW that I have in my make-up layers of synthetic experience, and that the most powerful of my memories are only half true.

Reduced to the minimum, to the what did happen, my life would be unrecognizable by me. Those layers of fictitious memory densify as they go deeper down. And this surely must be the case with everyone else who reads deeply, ravenously, unthinkingly, sensuously, as a child. The overlapping and haunting of life by fiction began, of course, before there was anything to be got from the printed page; it began from the day one was old enough to be told a story or shown a picture book. It went on up to the age when a bookish attitude towards books began to be inculcated by education. The young person is then thrown out of Eden; for evermore his brain is to stand posted between his self and the story. Appreciation of literature is the end of magic: in place of the virgin susceptibility to what is written he is given taste, something to be refined and trained.

Happily, the Eden, like a natal climate, can be unconsciously remembered, and the magic stored up in those years goes on secreting under to-day's chosen sensations and calculated thoughts. What entered the system during childhood remains; and remains indistinguishable from the life of those years because it was the greater part of the life. Probably children, if they said what they thought, would be much franker about the insufficiency of so-called real life to the requirements of those who demand to be really alive. Nothing but the story can meet the untried nature's need and capacity for the whole. Of course one cannot narrow down children to the reading child; but I could not as a child, and I cannot now, conceive what the non-reading child must be like inside. Outdoor children were incomprehensible to me when I was their age, and I still find them dull; I could not, and cannot, find out what makes them do what they do, or why they like what they like; and of such children now they are grown up I can only say that I cannot conceive what they remember, if they do remember—for how can even the senses carry imprints when there was no story? The non-reading active children were not stupid; they had their senses. Nor was it the clever children who read most, or who were at any rate the ones who inhaled fiction—quite apart there were always the horrible little students, future grown-ups, who pursued

OUT OF A BOOK: Reprinted from *Collected Impressions* by Elizabeth Bowen by permission of Alfred A. Knopf, Inc. Published 1950 by Alfred A. Knopf, Inc.

knowledge. The light-headed reading child and the outdoor child had more in common (in fact, the life of sensation) than either had with the student. Readers of my kind were the heady ones, the sensationalists—recognizing one another at sight we were banded together inside a climate of our own. Landscapes or insides of houses or streets or gardens, outings or even fatigue duties all took the cast of the book we were circulating at the time; and the reading made of us an electric ring. Books were story or story-poetry books: we were unaware that there could be any others.

Some of the heady group remained wonderfully proof against education: having never graduated these are the disreputable grown-ups who snap up shiny magazines and garner and carry home from libraries fiction that the critics ignore. They read as we all once read—because they must: without fiction, either life would be insufficient or the winds from the north would blow too cold. They read as we all read when we were twelve; but unfortunately the magic has been adulterated; the dependence has become ignominious—it becomes an enormity, inside the full-sized body, to read without the brain. Now the stories they seek go on being children's stories, only with sex added to the formula; and somehow the addition queers everything. These readers, all the same, are the great malleable bulk, the majority, the greater public—hence best-sellers, with their partly artful, partly unconscious play on a magic that has gone stale. The only above-board grown-up children's stories are detective stories.

No, it is not only our fate but our business to lose innocence, and once we have lost that it is futile to attempt a picnic in Eden. One kind of power to read, or power that reading had over us, is gone. And not only that: it is a mistake to as much as re-open the books of childhood—they are bare ruined choirs. Everything has evaporated from those words, leaving them meaningless on the page. This is the case, for me, even with Dickens—I cannot read him now because I read him exhaustively as a child. Though I did not in those years read all his books, I cannot now read any that I did not read then—there is no more oxygen left, for me, anywhere in the atmosphere of his writing. The boredom I seem to feel as I pursue the plots is, really, a flagging of my intellect in this (by me) forever used up and devitalized air. I came to an end with Dickens when I had absorbed him into myself.

Yes, one stripped bare the books of one's childhood to make oneself—it is inevitable that there should be nothing left when one goes back to them. The fickleness of children and very young persons shocks their elders—children abandon people, for instance, without a flicker, with a simplicity that really ought not to be hurting: the abandoned one has been either a 'best" friend or an object of hero-worship, and the more emotionally fruitful and fanciful the relationship, the more complete the break. "Where is So-and-so these days? I don't seem to have heard anything about him (or her) for a long time. Haven't you two got any more plans?"—"Oh, I can't be bothered." What applies to people applies to books, and for the same reason: everything that was wanted has been taken; only the husk or, still worse, mortifying repetition remains. The child is on the make—rapacious, mobile and single-minded. If the exhausted book survives physical abandonment—being given away or left out in the garden in the rain—it languishes on in its owner's indifferent keeping; however, once memory and sentiment have had time to set in and gather about it, it is safe. I still keep a row of books I loved as a child—but I neither wish nor dare to touch them.

What do I mean by those books making myself? In the first place, they were power-testing athletics for my imagination—cross-country runs into strange country, sprints, long and high jumps. It was exhilarating to discover what one could feel: the discovery itself was an advance. Then, by successively "being" a character in every book I read, I doubled the meaning of everything that happened in my otherwise constricted life. Books introduced me to, and magnified, desire and danger. They represented life, with a conclusiveness I had no reason to challenge, as an affair of mysteries and attractions, in which each object or place or face was in itself a volume of promises and deceptions, and in which nothing was impossible. Books made me see everything that I saw either as a symbol or as having its place in a mythology—in fact, reading gave bias to my observations of everything in the between-times when I was not reading. And obviously, the characters in the books gave prototypes under which, for evermore, to assemble all living people. This did not by any means simplify people for me; it had the reverse effect, and I was glad that it should—the characters who came out of my childish reading to obsess me were the incalculable ones, who always moved in a blur of potentialities. It appeared that nobody who mattered was capable of being explained. Thus was inculcated a feeling for the dark horse. I can trace in all people whom I have loved a succession from book characters—not from one only, from a fusion of many. "Millions of strange shadows on you tend."[1]

Also the expectation, the search, was geographic. I was and I am still on the look out for places where something happened: the quivering needle swings in turn to a prospect of country, a town unwrapping itself from folds of landscape or seen across water, or a significant house. Such places are haunted—scenes of acute sensation for someone, vicariously me. My identity, so far as I can pin it down at all, resides among these implacable likes or dislikes, these subjections to

1 [Shakespeare, Sonnet 53.]

magnetism spaced out between ever-widening lacunae of indifference. I feel certain that if I *could* read my way back, analytically, through the books of my childhood, the clues to everything could be found.

The child lives in the book; but just as much the book lives in the child. I mean that, admittedly, the process of reading is reciprocal; the book is no more than a formula, to be furnished out with images out of the reader's mind. At any age, the reader must come across: the child reader is the most eager and quick to do so; he not only lends to the story, he flings into the story the whole of his sensuous experience which from being limited is the more intense. Book dishes draw saliva to the mouth; book fears raise gooseflesh and make the palms clammy; book suspense makes the cheeks burn and the heart thump. Still more, at the very touch of a phrase there is a surge of brilliant visual images: the child rushes up the scenery for the story. When the story, as so often happens, demands what has not yet come into stock, indefatigable makeshifts are arrived at—as when a play that calls for elaborate staging is performed by an enterprising little company with scanty equipment and few drop-scenes. Extension (to draw an iceberg out of a fishmonger's iceblook) or multiplication (to make a thin, known wood into a trackless forest) goes on. For castles, gorges, or anything else spectacular out of art or nature, recollections of picture postcards, posters or travel albums are drawn on; and, of course, the child to-day has amassed a whole further scenic stock from the cinema. This provision of a convincing *where* for the story is a reflex.

For the child, any real-life scene that has once been sucked into the ambience of the story is affected, or infected, forever. The road, cross-roads, corner of a wood, cliff, flight of steps, town square, quayside or door in a wall keeps a transmuted existence: it has not only given body to fiction, it has partaken of fiction's body. Such a thing, place or scene cannot again be walked past indifferently; it exerts a pull and sets up a tremor; and it is to indent the memory for life. It is at these points, indeed, that what I have called synthetic experience has its sources. Into that experience come relationships, involving valid emotion, between the child reader and book characters; a residuum of the book will be in all other emotions that are to follow.

In reverse, there are the real-life places—towns, seaports, suburbs of London—unknown to the child, though heard of, which become "real" through being also in books. For instance, after *David Copperfield* I could not hear either Dover or Yarmouth mentioned, in the most ordinary context, without excitement: I had a line on them. Towns that were in books, and the routes between them travelled by characters, stood out in relief on the neutral map of England. Not a

Londoner, I was continuously filling in and starring my map of the environs—at Richmond lived Sir Percy, the Scarlet Pimpernel, and his wife Marguerite, who fainted into a bed of heliotrope in her riverside garden; at Highgate, the Steerforths and Rosa Dartle, at Blackheath and Lewisham, the E. Nesbit children. When I came to read *Kipps*,[2] I was made dizzy by the discovery that I had, for years, been living in two places, Hythe and Folkestone, that were in a book. Historic places one was taken to see meant no more and no less to me than this; history was fiction—it took me a long time to be able to see that it gained anything further from being "true."

Though not all reading children grow up to be writers, I take it that most creative writers must in their day have been reading children. All through creative writing there must run a sense of dishonesty and of debt. In fact, is there such a thing, any more, as creative writing? The imagination, which may appear to bear such individual fruit, is rooted in a compost of forgotten books. The apparent choices of art are nothing but addictions, pre-dispositions: where did these come from, how were they formed? The aesthetic is nothing but a return to images that will allow nothing to take their place; the aesthetic is nothing but an attempt to disguise and glorify the enforced return. All susceptibility belongs to the age of magic, the Eden where fact and fiction were the same; the imaginative writer was the imaginative child, who relied for life upon being lied to—and how, now, is he to separate the lies from his consciousness of life? If he be a novelist, all his psychology is merely a new parade of the old mythology. We have relied on our childhoods, on the sensations of childhood, because we mistake vividness for purity; actually, the story was there first—one is forced to see that it was the story that apparelled everything in celestial light. It could lead to madness to look back and back for the true primary impression or sensation; those we did ever experience we have forgotten—we only remember that to which something was added. Almost no experience, however much simplified by the distance of time, is to be vouched for as being wholly my own—*did* I live through that, or was I told that it happened, or did I read it? When I write, I am re-creating what was created for me. The gladness of vision, in writing, is my own gladness, but not at my own vision. I may see, for instance, a road running uphill, a skyline, a figure coming slowly over the hill—the approach of the figure is momentous, accompanied by fear or rapture or fear of rapture or a rapture of fear. But who and how is this? Am I sure this is not a figure out of a book?

2 [Sir Percy is the Scarlet Pimpernel in Baroness Orczy's novel of the same name. The Steerforths and Rosa Dartle occur in Charles Dickens' *David Copperfield*. The Nesbit children are the creation of Edith Nesbit Bland, a writer of children's stories. *Kipps* is a novel by H. G. Wells.]

Graham Greene

THE LOST CHILDHOOD

PERHAPS it is only in childhood that books have any deep influence on our lives. In later life we admire, we are entertained, we may modify some views we already hold, but we are more likely to find in books merely a confirmation of what is in our minds already: as in a love affair it is our own features that we see reflected flatteringly back.

But in childhood all books are books of divination, telling us about the future, and like the fortune teller who sees a long journey in the cards or death by water they influence the future. I suppose that is why books excited us so much. What do we ever get nowadays from reading to equal the excitement and the revelation in those first fourteen years? Of course I should be interested to hear that a new novel by Mr. E. M. Forster was going to appear this spring, but I could never compare that mild expectation of civilized pleasure with the missed heartbeat, the appalled glee I felt when I found on a library shelf a novel by Rider Haggard, Percy Westerman, Captain Brereton or Stanley Weyman which I had not read before. No, it is in those early years that I would look for the crisis, the moment when life took a new slant in its journey towards death.

I remember distinctly the suddenness with which a key turned in a lock and I found I could read—not just the sentences in a reading book with the syllables coupled like railway carriages, but a real book. It was paper-covered with the picture of a boy, bound and gagged, dangling at the end of a rope inside a well with the water rising above his waist—an adventure of Dixon Brett, detective. All a long summer holiday I kept my secret, as I believed: I did not want anybody to know that I could read. I suppose I half consciously realized even then that this was the dangerous moment. I was safe so long as I could not read—the wheels had not begun to turn, but now the future stood around on bookshelves everywhere waiting for the child to choose—the life of a chartered accountant perhaps, a colonial civil servant, a planter in China, a steady job in a bank, happiness and misery, eventually one particular form of death, for surely we choose our death much as we choose our job. It grows out of our acts and our evasions, out of our fears and out of our moments of courage. I suppose my mother must have discovered my secret, for on the jour-

---

ney home I was presented for the train with another real book, a copy of Ballantyne's *Coral Island* with only a single picture to look at, a coloured frontispiece. But I would admit nothing. All the long journey I stared at the one picture and never opened the book.

But there on the shelves at home (so many shelves for we were a large family) the books waited—one book in particular, but before I reach that one down let me take a few others at random from the shelf. Each was a crystal in which the child dreamed that he saw life moving. Here in a cover stamped dramatically in several colours was Captain Gilson's *The Pirate Aeroplane*. I must have read that book six times at least—the story of a lost civilization in the Sahara and of a villainous Yankee pirate with an aeroplane like a box kite and bombs the size of tennis balls who held the golden city to ransom. It was saved by the hero, a young subaltern who crept up to the pirate camp to put the aeroplane out of action. He was captured and watched his enemies dig his grave. He was to be shot at dawn, and to pass the time and keep his mind from uncomfortable thoughts the amiable Yankee pirate played cards with him—the mild nursery game of Kuhn Kan. The memory of that nocturnal game on the edge of life haunted me for years, until I set it to rest at last in one of my own novels with a game of poker played in remotely similar circumstances.

And here is *Sophy of Kravonia* by Anthony Hope—the story of a kitchen-maid who became a queen. One of the first films I ever saw, about 1911, was made from that book, and I can hear still the rumble of the Queen's guns crossing the high Kravonian pass beaten hollowly out on a single piano. Then there was Stanley Weyman's *The Story of Francis Cludde*, and above all other books at that time of my life, *King Solomon's Mines*.

This book did not perhaps provide the crisis, but it certainly influenced the future. If it had not been for that romantic tale of Allan Quatermain, Sir Henry Curtis, Captain Good, and, above all, the ancient witch Gagool, would I at nineteen have studied the appointments list of the Colonial Office and very nearly picked on the Nigerian Navy for a career? And later, when surely I ought to have known better, the odd African fixation remained. In 1935 I found myself sick with fever on a camp bed in a Liberian native's hut with a candle going out in an empty whiskey bottle and a rat moving in the shadows. Wasn't it the incurable fascination of Gagool with her bare yellow skull, the wrinkled scalp that moved and contracted like the hood of a cobra, that led me to work all through 1942 in a little stuffy office in Freetown, Sierra Leone? There is not much in common between the land of the Kukuanas, behind the desert and the mountain range of Sheba's Breast, and a tin-roofed house on a bit of swamp where the vultures moved like domestic trukeys and the pi-dogs kept me awake on moonlight nights with their wailing, and the white women yellowed by atebrin drove by to the club; but the two belonged at any rate to the same continent, and, however distantly, to the same region of the imagination—the region of uncertainty, of not knowing the way about. Once I came a little nearer to Gagool and her witch-hunters, one night in Zigita on the Liberian side of the French Guinea border, when my servants sat in their shuttered hut with their hands over their eyes and someone beat a drum and a whole town stayed behind closed doors while the big bush devil—whom it would mean blindness to see—moved between the huts.

But *King Solomon's Mines* could not finally satisfy. It was not the right answer. The key did not quite fit. Gagool I could recognize—didn't she wait for me in dreams every night in the passage by the linen cupboard, near the nursery door? and she continues to wait, when the mind is sick or tired, though now she is dressed in the theological garments of Despair and speaks in Spenser's accents:

> The longer life, I wote the greater sin,
> The greater sin, the greater punishment.

Yes, Gagool has remained a permanent part of the imagination, but Quatermain and Curtis—weren't they, even when I was only ten years old, a little too good to be true? They were men of such unyielding integrity (they would only admit a fault in order to show how it might be overcome) that the wavering personality of a child could not rest for long against those monumental shoulders. A child, after all, knows most of the game—it is only an attitude to it that he lacks. He is quite well aware of cowardice, shame, deception, disappointment. Sir Henry Curtis perched upon a rock bleeding from a dozen wounds but fighting on with the remnant of the Greys against the hordes of Twala was too heroic. These men were like Platonic ideas: they were not life as one had already begun to know it.

But when—perhaps I was fourteen by that time—I took Miss Marjorie Bowen's *The Viper of Milan* from the library shelf, the future for better or worse really struck. From that moment I began to write. All the other possible futures slid away: the potential civil servant, the don, the clerk had to look for other incarnations. Imitation after imitation of Miss Bowen's magnificent novel went into exercise books—stories of sixteenth-century Italy or twelfth-century England marked with enormous brutality and a despairing romanticism. It was as if I had been supplied once and for all with subject.

Why? On the surface *The Viper of Milan* is only the story of a war between Gian Galeazzo Visconti, Duke of Milan, and Mastino della Scala, Duke of Verona, told with zest and cunning and an amazing pictorial sense. Why did it creep in and colour and explain the terrible living world of the stone stairs and the never quiet dormitory? It was no good in that real world to dream that one would ever be a Sir Henry Curtis, but della Scala who at last turned from an honesty that never paid and betrayed his friends and died dishonoured and a failure even at treachery—it was easier for a child to escape behind his mask. As for Visconti, with his beauty, his patience and his genius for evil, I had watched him pass by many a time in his black Sunday suit smelling of mothballs. His name was Carter. He exercised terror from a distance like a snowcloud over the young fields. Goodness has only once found a perfect incarnation in a human body and never will again, but evil can always find a home there. Human nature is not black and white but black and grey. I read all that in *The Viper of Milan* and I looked round and I saw that it was so.

There was another theme I found there. At the end of *The Viper of Milan*—you will remember if you have once read it—comes the great scene of complete success—della Scala is dead, Ferrara, Verona, Novara, Mantua, have all fallen, the messengers pour in with news of fresh victories, the whole world outside is cracking up, and Visconti sits and jokes in the wine light. I was not on the classical side or I would have discovered, I suppose, in Greek literature instead of in Miss Bowen's novel a sense of doom that lies over success—the feeling that the pendulum is about to swing. That too made sense; one looked around and saw the doomed everywhere—the champion runner who one day would sag over the tape; the head of the school who would atone, poor devil, during forty dreary undistinguished years; the scholar . . . and when success began to touch oneself too, however mildly, one could only pray that failure would not be held off for too long.

One had lived for fourteen years in a wild jungle country without a map, but now the paths had been traced and naturally one had to follow them. But I think it was Miss Bowen's apparent zest that made me want to write. One could not read her without believing that to write was to live and to enjoy, and before one had discovered one's mistake it was too late—the first book one does enjoy. Anyway she had given me my pattern—religion might later explain it to me in other terms, but the pattern was already there—perfect evil walking the world where perfect good can never walk again, and only the pendulum ensures that after all in the end justice is done. Man is never satisfied, and often I have wished that my hand had not moved further than [Haggard's] *King Solomon's Mines,* and that the future I had taken down from the nursery shelf had been a district office in Sierra Leone and twelve tours of malarial duty and a finishing dose of blackwater fever when the danger of retirement approached. What is the good of wishing? The books are always there, the moment of crisis waits, and now our children in their turn are taking down the future and opening the pages. In his poem "Germinal" A. E. wrote:

> In ancient shadows and twilights
> Where childhood had stayed,
> The world's great sorrows were born
> And its heroes were made.
> In the lost boyhood of Judas
> Christ was betrayed.

St. Augustine

THE POWER OF MEMORY

AND I TURNED myself unto myself, and said to myself, "Who art thou?" And I answered, "A man." And behold, in me there present themselves to me soul, and body, one without, the other within. By which of these ought I to seek my God? I had sought Him in the body from earth to heaven, so far as I could send messengers, the beams of mine eyes. But the better is the inner, for to it as presiding and judging, all the bodily messengers reported the answers of heaven and earth, and all things therein, who said, "We are not God, but He made us." These things did my inner man know by the ministry of the outer: I the inner knew them; I, the mind, through the senses of my body. I asked the whole frame of the world about my God; and it answered me, "I am not He, but He made me."

Is not this corporeal figure apparent to all whose senses are perfect? why then speaks it not the same to all? Animals small and great see it, but they cannot ask it: because no reason is set over their senses to judge on what they report. But men can ask, so that the invisible things of God are clearly seen, being understood by the things that are made; but by love of them, they are made subject unto them: and subjects cannot judge. Nor yet do the creatures answer such as ask, unless they can judge; nor yet do they change their voice (i.e., their appearance), if one man only sees, another seeing asks, so as to appear one way to this man, another way to that, but appearing the same way to both, it is dumb to this, speaks to that; yea rather it speaks to all; but they only understand, who compare its voice received from without, with the truth within. For truth saith unto me, "Neither heaven, nor earth, nor any other body is thy God." This, their very nature saith to him that seeth them: "They are a mass; a mass is less in a part thereof than in the whole." Now

---

THE POWER OF MEMORY: From *The Confessions of St. Augustine,* translated by Edward B. Pusey, D.D.

to thee I speak, O my soul, thou art my better part: for thou quickenest the mass of my body, giving it life, which no body can give to a body: but thy God is even unto thee the Life of thy life.

What then do I love, when I love my God? who is He above the head of my soul? By my very soul will I ascend to Him. I will pass beyond that power whereby I am united to my body, and fill its whole frame with life. Nor can I by that power find my God; for so horse and mule that have no understanding might find Him; seeing it is the same power, whereby even their bodies live. But another power there is, not that only whereby I animate, but that too whereby I imbue with sense my flesh, which the Lord hath framed for me: commanding the eye not to hear, and the ear not to see; but the eye, that through it I should see, and the ear, that through it I should hear; and to the other senses severally, what is to each their own peculiar seats and offices; which, being divers, I the one mind, do through them enact. I will pass beyond this power of mine also; for this also have the horse, and mule, for they also perceive through the body.

I will pass then beyond this power of my nature also, rising by degrees unto Him Who made me. And I come to the fields and spacious palaces of my memory, where are the treasures of innumerable images, brought into it from things of all sorts perceived by the senses. There is stored up, whatsoever besides we think, either by enlarging or diminishing, or any other way varying those things which the sense hath come to; and whatever else hath been committed and laid up, which forgetfulness hath not yet swallowed up and buried. When I enter there, I require what I will to be brought forth, and something instantly comes; others must be longer sought after, which are fetched, as it were, out of some inner receptacle; others rush out in troops, and while one thing is desired and required, they start forth, as who should say, "Is it perchance I?" These I drive away with the hand of my heart, from the face of my remembrance; until what I wish for be unveiled, and appear in sight, out of its secret place. Other things come up readily, in unbroken order, as they are called for; those in front making way for the following; and as they make way, they are hidden from sight, ready to come when I will. All which takes place when I repeat a thing by heart.

There are all things preserved distinctly and under general heads, each having entered by its own avenue: as light, and all colours and forms of bodies by the eyes; by the ears all sorts of sounds; all smells by the avenue of the nostrils; all tastes by the mouth; and by the sensation of the whole body, what is hard or soft; hot or cold; smooth or rugged; heavy or light; either outwardly or inwardly to the body. All these doth that great harbour of the memory receive in her numberless secret and inexpressible windings, to be forthcoming, and brought out at need; each entering in by his own gate, and there laid up. Nor yet do the things themselves enter in; only the images of the things perceived are there in readiness, for thought to recall. Which images, how they are formed, who can tell, though it doth plainly appear by which sense each hath been brought in and stored up? For even while I dwell in darkness and silence, in my memory I can produce colours, if I will, and discern betwixt black and white, and what others I will: nor yet do sounds break in and disturb the image drawn in by my eyes, which I am reviewing, though they also are there, lying dormant, and laid up, as it were, apart. For these too I call forth, and forthwith they appear. And though my tongue be still, and my throat mute, so can I sing as much as I will; nor do those images of colours, which notwithstanding be there, intrude themselves and interrupt, when another store is called for, which flowed in by the ears. So the other things, piled in and up by the other senses, I recall at my pleasure. Yea, I discern the breath of lilies from violets, though smelling nothing; and I prefer honey to sweet wine, smooth before rugged, at the time neither tasting nor handling, but remembering only.

These things do I within, in that vast court of my memory. For there are present with me, heaven, earth, sea, and whatever I could think on therein, besides what I have forgotten. There also meet I with myself, and recall myself, and when, where, and what I have done, and under what feelings. There be all which I remember, either on my own experience, or other's credit. Out of the same store do I myself with the past continually combine fresh and fresh likenesses of things which I have experienced, or, from what I have experienced, have believed: and thence again infer future actions, events and hopes, and all these again I reflect on, as present. "I will do this or that," say I to myself, in that great receptacle of my mind, stored with the images of things so many and so great, "and this or that will follow." "O that this or that might be!" "God avert this or that!" So speak I to myself: and when I speak, the images of all I speak of are present, out of the same treasury of memory; nor would I speak of any thereof, were the images wanting.

Great is this force of memory, excessive great, O my God; a large and boundless chamber! who ever sounded the bottom thereof? yet is this a power of mine, and belongs unto my nature; nor do I myself comprehend all that I am. Therefore is the mind too strait to contain itself. And where should that be, which it containeth not of itself? Is it without it, and not within? how then doth it not comprehend itself? A wonderful admiration surprises me, amazement seizes me upon this. And men go abroad to admire the heights of mountains, the mighty billows of the sea, the broad tides of rivers, the compass of the ocean, and the circuits of the stars, and pass themselves by; nor wonder that when I spake of all these things, I did not see them with mine eyes, yet could not have spoken of them, unless I then actually saw the mountains, billows, rivers, stars which I had seen, and that ocean which I believe to be, inwardly in my memory, and that, with the same vast spaces between, as if I saw them abroad. Yet did not I by seeing draw them into myself, when with mine eyes I beheld them; nor are they themselves with me, but their images only. And I know by what sense of the body each was impressed upon me.

Yet not these alone does the unmeasurable capacity of my memory retain. Here also is all, learnt of the liberal sciences and as yet unforgotten; removed as it were to some inner place, which is yet no place: nor are they the images thereof, but the things themselves. For, what is literature, what the art of disputing, how many kinds of questions there be, whatsoever of these I know, in such manner exists in my memory, as that I have not taken in the image, and left out the thing, or that it should have sounded and passed away like a voice fixed on the ear by that impress, whereby it might be recalled, as if it sounded, when it no longer sounded; or as a smell while it passes and evaporates into air affects the sense of smell, whence it conveys into the memory an image of itself, which remembering, we renew, or as meat, which verily in the belly hath now no taste, and yet in the memory still in a manner tasteth; or as any thing which the body by touch perceiveth, and which when removed from us, the memory still conceives. For those things are not transmitted into the memory, but their images only are with an admirable swiftness caught up, and stored as it were in wondrous cabinets, and thence wonderfully by the act of remembering, brought forth.

But now when I hear that there be three kinds of questions, "Whether the thing be? what it is? of what kind it is?" I do indeed hold the images of the sounds of which those words be composed, and that those sounds, with a noise passed through the air, and now are not. But the things themselves which are signified by those sounds, I never reached with any sense of my body, nor ever discerned them otherwise than in my mind; yet in my memory have I laid up not their images, but themselves. Which how they entered into me, let them say if they can; for I have gone over all the avenues of my flesh, but cannot find by which they entered. For the eyes say, "If those images were coloured, we reported of them." The ears say, "If they sound, we gave knowledge of them." The nostrils say, "If they smell, they passed by us." The taste says, "Unless they have a savour, ask me not." The touch says, "If it have not size, I handled it not; if I handled it not, I gave no notice of it." Whence and how entered these things into my memory? I know not how. For when I learned them, I gave not credit to another man's mind, but recognised them in mine; and approving them for true, I commended them to it, laying them up as it were, whence I might bring them forth when I willed. In my heart then they were, even before I learned them, but in my memory they were not. Where then? or wherefore, when they were spoken, did I acknowledge them, and said, "So is it, it is true," unless that they were already in the memory, but so thrown back and buried as it were in deeper recesses, that had not suggestion of another drawn them forth I had perchance been unable to conceive of them?

Wherefore we find, that to learn these things whereof we imbibe not the images by our senses, but perceive within by themselves, without images, as they are, is nothing else, but by conception, to receive, and by marking to take heed that those things, which the memory did before contain at random and unarranged, be laid up at hand as it were in that same memory where before they lay unknown, scattered and neglected, and so readily occur to the mind familiarised to them. And how many things of this kind does my memory bear which have been already found out, and as I said, placed as it were at hand, which we are said to have learned and come to know which were I for some short space of time to cease to call to mind, they are again so buried, and glide back, as it were, into the deeper recesses, that they must again, as if new, be thought out thence, for other abode they have none; but they must be drawn together again, that they may be known; that is to say, they must as it were be collected together from their dispersion: whence the word "cogitation" is derived. For cogo (collect) and cogito (re-collect) have the same relation to each other as ago and agito, facio and factito. But the mind hath appropriated to itself this word (cogitation), so that, not what is "collected" any how, but what is "re-collected," i.e., brought together, in the mind, is properly said to be cogitated, or thought upon.

The memory containeth also reasons and laws innumerable of numbers and dimensions, none of which hath any bodily sense impressed; seeing they have neither colour, nor sound, nor taste, nor smell, nor touch. I have heard the sound of the words whereby when discussed they are denoted: but the sounds are other than the things. For the sounds are other in Greek than in Latin; but the things are neither Greek, nor Latin, nor any other language. I have seen the lines of architects, the very finest, like a spider's thread; but those are still different, they are not the images of those lines which the eye of flesh showed me: he knoweth them, whosoever without any conception whatsoever of a body, recognizes them within himself. I have perceived also the numbers of the things with which we number all the senses of my body; but those numbers wherewith we number are different, nor are they the images of these, and therefore they indeed are. Let him who seeth them not, deride me for saying these things, and I will pity him, while he derides me.

All these things I remember, and how I learnt them I remember. Many things also most falsely objected against them have I heard, and remember; which though they be false, yet is it not false that I remember them; and I remember also that I have discerned betwixt those truths and these falsehoods objected to them. And I perceive that the present discerning of these things is different from remembering that I oftentimes discerned them, when I often thought upon them. I both remember then to have often understood these things; and what I now discern and understand, I lay up in my memory, that hereafter I may remember that I understand it now. So then I remember also to have remembered; as if hereafter I shall call to remembrance, that I have now been able to remember these things, by the force of memory shall I call it to remembrance.

The same memory contains also the affections of my mind, not in the same manner that my mind itself contains them, when it feels them; but far otherwise, according to a power of its own. For without rejoicing I remember myself to have joyed; and without sorrow do I recollect my past sorrow. And that I once feared, I review without fear; and without desire call to mind a past desire. Sometimes, on the contrary, with joy do I remember my fore-past sorrow, and with sorrow, joy. Which is not wonderful, as to the body; for mind is one thing, body another. If I therefore with joy remember some past pain of body, it is not so wonderful. But now seeing this very memory itself is mind (for when we give a thing in charge, to be kept to memory, we say, "See that you keep it in mind"; and when we forget, we say, "It did not come to my mind," and, "It slipped out of my mind," calling the memory itself the mind); this being so, how is it that when with joy I remember my past sorrow, the mind hath joy, the memory hath sorrow; the mind upon the joyfulness which is in it, is joyful, yet the memory upon the sadness which is in it, is not sad? Does the memory perchance not belong to the mind? Who will say so? The memory then is, as it were, the belly of the mind, and joy and sadness, like sweet and bitter food; which, when committed to the memory, are as it were, passed into the belly, where they may be stowed, but cannot taste. Ridiculous it is to imagine these to be alike; and yet are they not utterly unlike.

But, behold, out of my memory I bring it, when I say there be four perturbations of the mind, desire, joy, fear, sorrow; and whatsoever I can dispute thereon, by dividing each into its subordinate species, and by defining it, in my memory find I what to say, and thence do I bring it: yet am I not disturbed by any of these perturbations, when by calling them to mind, I remember them; yea, and before I recalled and brought them back, they were there; and therefore could they, by recollection, thence be brought. Perchance, then, as meat is by chewing the cud brought up out of the belly, so by recollection these out of the memory. Why then does not the disputer, thus recollecting, taste in the mouth of his musing the sweetness of joy, or the bitterness of sorrow? Is the comparison unlike in this, because not in all respects like? For who would willingly speak thereof, if so oft as we name grief or fear, we should be compelled to be sad or fearful? And yet could we not speak of them, did we not find in our memory, not only the sounds of the names according to the images impressed by the senses of the body, but notions of the very things themselves which we never received by any avenue of the body, but which the mind itself perceiving by the experience of its own passions, committed to the memory, or the memory of itself retained, without being committed unto it.

But whether by images or no, who can readily say? Thus, I name a stone, I name the sun, the things themselves not being present to my senses, but their images to my memory. I name a bodily pain, yet it is not present with me, when nothing aches: yet unless its image were present to my memory, I should not know what to say thereof, nor in discoursing discern pain from pleasure. I name bodily health; being sound in body, the thing itself is present with me; yet, unless its image also were present in my memory, I could by no means recall what the sound of this name should signify. Nor would the sick, when health were named, recognise what were spoken, unless the same image were by the force of memory retained, although the thing itself were absent from the body. I name numbers whereby we number; and not their images, but themselves are present in my memory. I name the image of the sun, and that image is present in my memory. For I recall not the image of its image, but the image itself is present to me, calling it to mind. I name memory, and I recognise what I name. And where do I recognise it, but in the memory itself? Is it also present to itself by its image, and not by itself?

What, when I name forgetfulness, and withal recognise what I name? whence should I recognise it, did I not remember it? I speak not of the sound of the name, but of the thing which it signifies: which if I had forgotten, I could not recognise what that sound signifies. When then I remember memory, memory itself is, through itself, present with itself: but when I remember forgetfulness, there are present both memory and forgetfulness; memory whereby I remember, forgetfulness which I remember. But what is forgetfulness, but the privation of memory? How then is it present that I remember it, since when present I cannot remember? But if what we remember we hold it in memory, yet, unless we did remember forgetfulness, we could never at the hearing of the name recognise the thing thereby signified, then forgetfulness is retained by memory. Present then it is, that we forget not, and being so, we forget. It is to be understood from this that forgetfulness when we remember it, is not present to the memory by itself but by its image; because if it were present by itself, it would not cause us to remember, but to forget. Who now shall search out this? who shall comprehend how it is?

Lord, I, truly, toil therein, yea and toil in myself; I am become a heavy soil requiring over much sweat of the brow. For we are not now searching out the regions of heaven, or measuring the distances of the stars, or enquiring the balancings of the earth. It is I myself who remember, I the mind. It is not so wonderful, if what I myself am not, be far from me. But what is nearer to me than myself? And lo, the force of mine own memory is not understood by me; though I cannot so much as name myself without it. For what shall I say, when it is clear to me that I remember forgetfulness? Shall I say that that is not in my memory, which I remember? or shall I say that forgetfulness is for this purpose in my memory, that I might not forget? Both were most absurd. What third way is there? How can I say that the image of forgetfulness is retained by my memory, not forgetfulness itself, when I remember it? How could I say this either, seeing that when the image of any thing is impressed on the memory, the thing itself must needs be first present, whence that image may be impressed? For thus do I remember Carthage, thus all places where I have been, thus men's faces whom I have seen, and things reported by the other senses; thus the health or sickness of the body. For when these things were present, my memory received from them images, which being present with me, I might look on and bring back in my mind, when I remembered them in their absence. If then this forgetfulness is retained in the memory through its image, not through itself, then plainly itself was once present, that its image might be taken. But when it was present, how did it write its image in the memory, seeing that forgetfulness by its presence effaces even what it finds already noted? And yet, in whatever way, although that way be past conceiving and explaining, yet certain am I that I remember forgetfulness itself also, whereby what we remember is effaced.

Great is the power of memory, a fearful thing, O my God, a deep and boundless manifoldness; and this thing is the mind, and this am I myself. What am I then, O my God? What nature am I? A life various and manifold, and exceeding immense. Behold in the plains, and caves, and caverns of my memory, innumerable and innumerably full of innumerable kinds of things, either through images, as all bodies; or by actual presence, as the arts; or by certain notions or impressions, as the affections of the mind, which, even when the mind doth not feel, the memory retaineth, while yet whatsoever is in the memory is also in the mind—over all these do I run, I fly; I dive on this side and on that, as far as I can, and there is no end. So great is the force of memory, so great the force of life, even in the mortal life of man. What shall I do then, O Thou my true life, my God? I will pass even beyond this power of mine which is called memory: yea, I will pass beyond it, that I may approach unto Thee, O sweet Light. What sayest Thou to me? See, I am mounting up through my mind towards Thee who abidest above me. Yea, I now will pass beyond this power of mine which is called memory, desirous to arrive at Thee, whence Thou mayest be arrived at; and to cleave unto Thee, whence one may cleave unto Thee. For even beasts and birds have memory; else could they not return to their dens and nests, nor many other things they are used unto: nor indeed could they be used to anything, but by memory. I will pass then beyond memory also, that I may arrive at Him who hath separated me from the four-footed beasts and made me wiser than the fowls of the air, I will pass beyond memory also, and where shall I find Thee, Thou truly good and certain sweetness? And where shall I find Thee? If I find Thee without my memory, then do I not retain Thee in my memory. And how shall I find Thee, if I remember Thee not?

For the woman that had lost her groat, and sought it with a light; unless she had remembered it, she had never found it. For when it was found, whence should she know whether it were the same, unless she remembered it? I remember to have sought and found many a thing; and this I thereby know, that when I was seeking any of them, and was asked, "Is this it?" "Is that it?" so long said I "No," until that were offered me which I sought. Which had I not remembered (whatever it were) though it were offered me, yet should I not find it, because I could not recognise it. And so it ever is, when we seek and find any lost thing. Notwithstanding, when any thing is by chance lost from the sight, not from the memory (as any visible body), yet its image is still retained within, and it is sought until it be restored to sight; and when it is found, it is recognised by the image which is within: nor do we say that we have found what was lost, unless we recognise it; nor can we recognise it, unless we remember it. But this was lost to the eyes, but retained in the memory.

But what when the memory itself loses any thing, as falls out when we forget and seek that we may recollect? Where in the end do we search, but in the memory itself? and there, if one thing be perchance offered instead of another, we reject it, until what we seek meets us; and when it doth, we say, "This is it"; which we should not unless we recognised it, nor recognise it unless we remembered it. Certainly then we had forgotten it. Or, had not the whole escaped us, but by the part whereof we had hold, was the lost part sought for; in that the memory felt that it did not carry on together all which it was wont, and maimed, as it were, by the curtailment of its ancient habit, demanded the restoration of what it missed? For instance, if we see or think of some one known to us, and having forgotten his name, try to recover it; whatever else occurs, connects itself not therewith; because it was not wont to be thought upon together with him, and therefore is rejected, until that present itself, whereon the knowledge reposes equably as its wonted object. And whence does that present itself, but out of the memory itself? for even when we recognise it, on being reminded by another, it is thence it comes. For we do not believe it as something new, but, upon recollection, allow what was named to be right. But were it utterly blotted out of the mind, we should not remember it, even when reminded. For we have not as yet utterly forgotten that, which we remember ourselves to have forgotten. What then we have utterly forgotten, though lost, we cannot even seek after.

How then do I seek Thee, O Lord? For when I seek Thee, my God, I seek a happy life. I will seek Thee, that my soul may live. For my body liveth by my soul; and my soul by Thee. How then do I seek a happy life, seeing I have it not, until I can say, where I ought to say it, "It is enough"? How seek I it? By remembrance, as though I had forgotten it, remembering that I had forgotten it? Or, desiring to learn it as a thing unknown, either never having known, or so forgotten it, as not even to remember that I had forgotten it? is not a happy life what all will, and no one altogether wills it not? where have they known it, that they so will it? where seen it, that they so love it? Truly we have it, how, I know not. Yea, there is another way, wherein when one hath it, then is he happy; and there are, who are blessed, in hope. These have it in a lower kind, than they who have it in very deed; yet are they better off than such as are happy neither in deed nor in hope. Yet even these, had they it not in some sort, would not so will to be happy, which that they do will, is most certain. They have known it then, I know not how, and so have it by some sort of knowledge, what, I know not, and am perplexed whether it be in the memory, which if it be, then we have been happy once; whether all severally, or in that man who first sinned, in whom also we all died, and from whom we are all born with misery, I now enquire not; but only, whether the happy life be in the memory? For neither should we love it, did we not know it. We hear the name, and we all confess that we desire the things; for we are not delighted with the mere sound. For when a Greek hears it in Latin, he is not delighted, not knowing what is spoken; but we Latins are delighted, as would he too, if he heard it in Greek; because the thing itself is neither Greek nor Latin, which Greeks and Latins, and men of all other tongues, long for so earnestly. Known therefore it is to all, for could they with one voice be asked, "would they be happy?" they would answer without doubt, "they would." And this could not be, unless the thing itself whereof it is the name were retained in their memory.

But is it so, as one remembers Carthage who hath seen it? No. For a happy life is not seen with the eye, because it is not a body. As we remember numbers then? No. For these, he that hath in his knowledge, seeks not further to attain unto; but a happy life we have in our knowledge, and therefore love it, and yet still desire to attain it, that we may be happy. As we remember eloquence then? No. For although upon hearing this name also, some call to mind the thing, who still are not yet eloquent, and many who desire to be so, whence it appears that it is in their knowledge; yet these have by their bodily senses observed others to be eloquent, and been delighted, and desire to be the like (though indeed they would not be delighted but for some inward knowledge thereof, nor wish to be the like, unless they were thus delighted); whereas a happy life, we do by no bodily sense experience in others. As then we remember joy? Perchance; for my joy I remember, even when sad, as a happy life, when unhappy; nor did I ever with bodily sense see, hear, smell, taste, or touch my joy; but I experienced it in my mind, when I rejoiced; and the knowledge of it clave to my memory, so that I can recall it with disgust sometimes, at others with longing, according to the nature of the things, wherein I remember myself to have joyed. For even from foul things have I been immersed in a sort of joy; which now recalling, I detest and execrate; otherwhiles in good and honest things, which I recall with longing, although perchance no longer present; and therefore with sadness I recall former joy.

Where then and when did I experience my happy life, that I should remember, and love, and long for it? Nor is it I alone, or some few besides, but we all would fain be happy; which, unless by some certain knowledge we knew, we should not with so certain a will desire. But how is this, that if two men be asked whether they would go to the wars, one, perchance would answer that he would, the other, that he would not; but if they were asked whether they would be happy, both would instantly without any doubting say they would; and for no other reason would the one go to the wars, and the other not, but to be happy. Is it perchance that as one looks for his joy in this thing, another in that, all agree in their desire of being happy, as they would (if they were asked) that they wished to have joy, and this joy they call a happy life? Although then one obtains this joy by one means, another by another, all have one end, which they strive to attain, namely, joy. Which being a thing which all must say they have experienced, it is therefore found in the memory, and recognised whenever the name of a happy life is mentioned.

Far be it, Lord, far be it from the heart of Thy servant who here confesseth unto Thee, far be it, that, be the joy what it may, I should therefore think myself happy. For there is a joy which is not given to the ungodly, but to those who love Thee for Thine own sake, whose joy Thou Thyself art. And this is the happy life, to rejoice to Thee, of Thee, for Thee; this is it, and there is no other. For they who think there is another, pursue some other and not the true joy. Yet is not their will turned away from some semblance of joy.

It is not certain then that all wish to be happy, inasmuch as they who wish not to joy in Thee, which is the only happy life, do not truly desire the happy life. Or do all men desire this, but because the flesh lusteth against the Spirit, and the Spirit against the flesh, that they cannot do what they would, they fall upon that which they can, and are content therewith; because, what they are not able to do, they do not will so strongly as would suffice to make them able? For I ask any one, had he rather joy in truth, or in falsehood? They will as little hesitate to say "in the truth," as to say "that they desire to be happy," for a happy life is joy in the truth: for this is a joying in Thee, Who art the Truth, O God my light, health of my countenance, my God. This is the happy life which all desire; this life which alone is happy, all desire; to joy in the truth all desire. I have met with many that would deceive; who would be deceived, no one. Where then did they know this happy life, save where they know the truth also? For they love it also, since they would not be deceived. And when they love a happy life, which is no other than joying in the truth, then also do they love the truth; which yet they would not love, were there not some notice of it in their memory. Why then joy they not in it? why are they not happy? because they are more strongly taken up with other things which have more power to make them miserable, than that which they so faintly remember to make them happy. For there is yet a little light in men; let them walk, let them walk, that the darkness overtake them not.

But why doth "truth generate hatred," and the man of Thine, preaching the truth, become an enemy to them? whereas a happy life is loved, which is nothing else but joying in the truth; unless that truth is in that kind loved, that they who love anything else would gladly have that which they love to be the truth: and because they would not be deceived, would not be convinced that they are so? Therefore do they hate the truth for that thing's sake which they love instead of the truth. They love truth when she enlightens, they hate her when she reproves. For since they would not be deceived, and would deceive, they love her when she discovers herself unto them, and hate her when she discovers them. Whence she shall so repay them, that they who would not be made manifest by her, she both against their will makes manifest, and herself becometh not manifest unto them. Thus, thus, yea thus doth the mind of man, thus blind and sick, foul and ill-favoured, wish to be hidden, but that aught should be hidden from it, it wills not. But the contrary is requited it, that itself should not be hidden from the Truth; but the Truth is hid from it. Yet even thus miserable, it had rather joy in truths than in falsehoods. Happy then will it be, when, no distraction interposing, it shall joy in that only Truth, by Whom all things are true.

See what a space I have gone over in my memory seeking Thee, O Lord; and I have not found Thee, without it. Nor have I found any thing concerning Thee, but what I have kept in memory, ever since I learnt Thee. For since I learnt Thee, I have not forgotten Thee. For where I found Truth, there found I my God, the Truth itself; which since I learnt, I have not forgotten. Since then I learnt Thee, Thou residest in my memory; and there do I find Thee, when I call Thee to remembrance, and delight in Thee. These be my holy delights, which Thou hast given me in Thy mercy, having regard to my poverty.

But where in my memory residest Thou, O Lord, where residest Thou there? what manner of lodging hast Thou framed for Thee? what manner of sanctuary hast Thou builded for Thee? Thou hast given this honour to my memory, to reside in it; but in what quarter of it Thou residest, that am I considering. For in thinking on Thee, I passed beyond such parts of it as the beasts also have, for I found Thee not there among the images of corporeal things: and I came to those parts to which I committed the affections of my mind, nor found Thee there. And I entered into the very seat of my mind (which it hath in my memory, inasmuch as the mind remembers itself also), neither wert Thou there: for as Thou art not a corporeal image, nor the affection of a living being (as when we rejoice, condole, desire, fear, remember, forget; or the like); so neither art Thou the mind itself; because Thou art the Lord God of the mind; and all these are changed, but Thou remainest unchangeable over all, and yet hast vouchsafed to dwell in my memory, since I learnt Thee. And why seek I now in what place thereof Thou dwellest, as if there were places therein? Sure I am, that in it Thou dwellest, since I have remembered Thee ever since I learnt Thee, and there I find Thee, when I call Thee to remembrance.

Where then did I find Thee, that I might learn Thee? For in my memory Thou wert not, before I learned Thee. Where then did I find Thee, that I might learn Thee, but in Thee above me? Place there is none; we go backward and forward, and there is no place. Every where, O Truth, dost Thou give audience to all who ask counsel of Thee, and at once answerest all, though on manifold matters they ask Thy counsel. Clearly dost Thou answer, though all do not clearly hear. All consult Thee on what they will, though they hear not always what they will. He is Thy best servant who looks not so much to hear that from Thee which himself willeth, as rather to will that, which from Thee he heareth.

Too late loved I Thee, O Thou Beauty of ancient days, yet ever new! too late I loved Thee! And behold, Thou wert within, and I abroad, and there I searched for Thee; deformed I, plunging amid those fair forms which Thou hadst made. Thou wert with me, but I was not with Thee. Things held me far from Thee, which, unless they were in Thee, were not at all. Thou calledst, and shoutedst, and burstest my deafness. Thou flashedst, shonest, and scatteredst my blindness. Thou breathedst odours, and I drew in breath and pant for Thee. I tasted, and hunger and thirst. Thou touchedst me, and I burned for Thy peace.

When I shall with my whole self cleave to Thee, I shall no where have sorrow or labour; and my life shall wholly live, as wholly full of Thee. But now since whom Thou fillest, Thou liftest up, because I am not full of Thee I am a burden to myself. Lamentable joys strive with joyous sorrows: and on which side is the victory, I know not. Woe is me! Lord, have pity on me. My evil sorrows strive with my good joys; and on which side is the victory, I know not. Woe is me! Lord, have pity on me. Woe is me! lo! I hide not my wounds; Thou art the Physician, I the sick; Thou merciful, I miserable. Is not the life of man upon earth all trial? Who wishes for troubles and difficulties? Thou commandest them to be endured, not to be loved. No man loves what he endures, though he love to endure. For though he rejoices that he endures, he had rather there were nothing for him to endure. In adversity I long for prosperity, in prosperity I fear adversity. What middle place is there betwixt these two, where the life of man is not all trial? Woe to the prosperities of the world, once and again, through fear of adversity, and corruption of joy! Woe to the adversities of the world, once and again, and the third time, from the longing for prosperity, and because adversity itself is a hard thing, and lest it shatter endurance. Is not the life of man upon earth all trial: without any interval?

And all my hope is no where but in Thy exceeding great mercy. Give what Thou enjoinest, and enjoin what Thou wilt. Thou enjoinest us continency; and when I knew, saith one, that no man can be continent, unless God give it, this also was a part of wisdom to know whose gift she is. By continency verily are we bound up and brought back into One, whence we were dissipated into many. For too little doth he love Thee, who loves any thing with Thee, which he loveth not for Thee. O love, who ever burnest and never consumest! O charity, my God, kindle me. Thou enjoinest continency: give me what Thou enjoinest, and enjoin what Thou wilt.

POETRY

Walt Whitman

BEGINNING MY STUDIES

BEGINNING my studies the first step pleas'd me so much,
The mere fact consciousness, these forms, the power of motion,
The least insect or animal, the senses, eyesight, love,
The first step I say awed me and pleas'd me so much,
I have hardly gone and hardly wish'd to go any farther,
But stop and loiter all the time to sing it in ecstatic songs.

John Crowe Ransom

BLUE GIRLS

TWIRLING your blue skirts, traveling the sward
Under the towers of your seminary,
Go listen to your teachers old and contrary
Without believing a word.

Tie the white fillets then about your lustrous hair
And think no more of what will come to pass
Than bluebirds that go walking on the grass
And chattering on the air.

Practice your beauty, blue girls, before it fail;
And I will cry with my loud lips and publish
Beauty which all our power shall never establish,
It is so frail.

For I could tell you a story which is true:
I know a lady with a terrible tongue,
Blear eyes fallen from blue,
All her perfections tarnished—yet it is not long
Since she was lovelier than any of you.

Francis Thompson

DAISY

WHERE THE thistle lifts a purple crown
Six foot out of the turf,
And the harebell shakes on the windy hill—
O breath of the distant surf!—

The hills look over on the South,
And southward dreams the sea;
And with the sea-breeze hand in hand
Came innocence and she.

Where 'mid the gorse the raspberry
Red for the gatherer springs;
Two children did we stray and talk
Wise, idle, childish things.

She listened with big-lipped surprise,
Breast-deep 'mid flower and spine:
Her skin was like a grape whose veins
Run snow instead of wine.

She knew not those sweet words she spake,
Nor knew her own sweet way;
But there's never a bird, so sweet a song
Thronged in whose throat all day.

Oh, there were flowers in Storrington
On the turf and on the spray;
But the sweetest flower on Sussex hills
Was the Daisy-flower that day!

Her beauty smoothed earth's furrowed face.
She gave me tokens three:—
A look, a word of her winsome mouth,
And a wild raspberry.

A berry red, a guileless look,
A still word,—strings of sand!
And yet they made my wild, wild heart
Fly down to her little hand.

For standing artless as the air
And candid as the skies,
She took the berries with her hand
And the love with her sweet eyes.

The fairest things have fleetest end,
Their scent survives their close:
But the rose's scent is bitterness
To him that loved the rose.

She looked a little wistfully,
Then went her sunshine way:—
The sea's eye had a mist on it,
And the leaves fell from the day.

She went her unremembering way,
She went and left in me
The pang of all the partings gone,
And partings yet to be.

She left me marveling why my soul
Was sad that she was glad;
At all the sadness in the sweet,
The sweetness in the sad.

Still, still I seemed to see her, still
Look up with soft replies,
And take the berries with her hand,
And the love with her lovely eyes.

Nothing begins, and nothing ends,
That is not paid with moan,
For we are born in other's pain,
And perish in our own.

William Butler Yeats

AMONG SCHOOL CHILDREN

1

I WALK through the long schoolroom questioning;
A kind old nun in a white hood replies;
The children learn to cipher and to sing,
To study reading-books and histories,
To cut and sew, be neat in everything
In the best modern way—the children's eyes
In momentary wonder stare upon
A sixty-year-old smiling public man.

2

I dream of a Ledaean body, bent
Above a sinking fire, a tale that she
Told of a harsh reproof, or trivial event
That changed some childish day to tragedy—
Told, and it seemed that our two natures blent
Into a sphere from youthful sympathy,
Or else, to alter Plato's parable,
Into the yolk and white of the one shell.

3

And thinking of that fit of grief or rage
I look upon one child or t'other there
And wonder if she stood so at that age—
For even daughters of the swan can share
Something of every paddler's heritage—
And had that color upon cheek or hair,
And thereupon my heart is driven wild:
She stands before me as a living child.

4

Her present image floats into the mind—
Did Quattrocento finger fashion it
Hollow of cheek as though it drank the wind
And took a mess of shadows for its meat?
And I though never of Ledaean kind
Had pretty plumage once—enough of that,
Better to smile on all that smile, and show
There is a comfortable kind of old scarecrow.

5

What youthful mother, a shape upon her lap
Honey of generation had betrayed,
And that must sleep, shriek, struggle to escape
As recollection or the drug decide,
Would think her son, did she but see that shape
With sixty or more winters on its head,
A compensation for the pang of his birth,
Or the uncertainty of his setting forth?

6

Plato thought nature but a spume that plays
Upon a ghostly paradigm of things;
Solider Aristotle played the taws
Upon the bottom of a king of kings;
World-famous golden-thighed Pythagoras
Fingered upon a fiddle-stick or strings
What a star sang and careless Muses heard:
Old clothes upon old sticks to scare a bird.

7

Both nuns and mothers worship images,
But those the candles light are not as those
That animate a mother's reveries,
But keep a marble or a bronze repose.
And yet they too break hearts—O Presences
That passion, piety or affection knows,
And that all heavenly glory symbolise—
O self-born mockers of man's enterprise;

8

Labour is blossoming or dancing where
The body is not bruised to pleasure soul,
Nor beauty born out of its own despair,
Nor blear-eyed wisdom out of midnight oil.
O chestnut-tree, great-rooted blossomer,
Are you the leaf, the blossom or the bole?
O body swayed to music, O brightening glance,
How can we know the dancer from the dance?

Gerard Manley Hopkins

SPRING

NOTHING is so beautiful as spring—
When weeds, in wheels, shoot long and lovely and lush;
 Thrush's eggs look little low heavens, and thrush
Through the echoing timber does so rinse and wring
The ear, it strikes like lightnings to hear him sing;
 The glassy peartree leaves and blooms, they brush
 The descending blue; that blue is all in a rush
With richness; the racing lambs too have fair their fling.

What is all this juice and all this joy?
 A strain of the earth's sweet being in the beginning
In Eden garden.—Have, get, before it cloy,
 Before it cloud, Christ, lord, and sour with sinning,
Innocent mind and Mayday in girl and boy,
 Most, O maid's child, thy choice and worthy the winning.

William Wordsworth

ODE: INTIMATIONS OF IMMORTALITY FROM RECOLLECTIONS OF EARLY CHILDHOOD

1

THERE was a time when meadow, grove, and stream,
The earth, and every common sight,
To me did seem
Apparelled in celestial light,
The glory and the freshness of a dream.
It is not now as it hath been of yore;—
Turn wheresoe'er I may,
By night or day,
The things which I have seen I now can see no more.

2

The Rainbow comes and goes,
And lovely is the Rose,
The Moon doth with delight
Look round her when the heavens are bare,
Waters on a starry night
Are beautiful and fair;
The sunshine is a glorious birth;
But yet I know, where'er I go,
That there hath past away a glory from the earth.

3

Now, while the birds thus sing a joyous song,
And while the young lambs bound
As to the tabor's sound,
To me alone there came a thought of grief:
A timely utterance gave that thought relief,
And I again am strong:
The cataracts blow their trumpets from the steep;
No more shall grief of mine the season wrong;
I hear the Echoes through the mountains throng,
The Winds come to me from the fields of sleep,
And all the earth is gay;
Land and sea
Give themselves up to jollity,
And with the heart of May
Doth every Beast keep holiday;—
Thou Child of Joy,
Shout round me, let me hear thy shouts, thou happy Shepherd-boy!

4

Ye blessèd Creatures, I have heard the call
Ye to each other make; I see
The heavens laugh with you in your jubilee;
My heart is at your festival,
My head hath its coronal,
The fulness of your bliss, I feel — I feel it all.
Oh evil day! If I were sullen
While Earth herself is adorning,
This sweet May-morning,
And the Children are culling
On every side,
In a thousand valleys far and wide,
Fresh flowers; while the sun shines warm,
And the Babe leaps up on his Mother's arm: —
I hear, I hear, with joy I hear!
— But there's a Tree, of many, one,
A single Field which I have looked upon,
Both of them speak of something that is gone:
The Pansy at my feet
Doth the same tale repeat:
Whither is fled the visionary gleam?
Where is it now, the glory and the dream?

5

Our birth is but a sleep and a forgetting;
The Soul that rises with us, our life's Star,
Hath had elsewhere its setting,
And cometh from afar:
Not in entire forgetfulness,
And not in utter nakedness,
But trailing clouds of glory do we come
From God, who is our home:
Heaven lies about us in our infancy!
Shades of the prison-house begin to close
Upon the growing Boy,
But He beholds the light, and whence it flows,
He sees it in his joy;
The Youth, who daily farther from the east
Must travel, still is Nature's Priest,
And by the vision splendid
Is on his way attended;
At length the Man perceives it die away,
And fade into the light of common day.

6

Earth fills her lap with pleasures of her own;
Yearnings she hath in her own natural kind,

And, even with something of a Mother's mind,
And no unworthy aim,
The homely Nurse doth all she can
To make her Foster-child, her Inmate Man,
Forget the glories he hath known,
And that imperial palace whence he came.

7

Behold the Child among his new-born blisses,
A six years' Darling of a pigmy size!
See, where 'mid work of his own hand he lies,
Fretted by sallies of his mother's kisses,
With light upon him from his father's eyes!
See, at his feet, some little plan or chart,
Some fragment from his dream of human life,
Shaped by himself with newly-learned art;
A wedding or a festival,
A mourning or a funeral;
And this hath now his heart,
And unto this he frames his song:
Then will be fit his tongue
To dialogues of business, love, or strife;
But it will not be long
Ere this be thrown aside,
And with new joy and pride
The little Actor cons another part;
Filling from time to time his "humorous stage"
With all the Persons, down to palsied Age,
That Life brings with her in her equipage;
As if his whole vocation
Were endless imitation.

8

Thou, whose exterior semblance doth belie
Thy Soul's immensity;
Thou best Philosopher, who yet dost keep
Thy heritage, thou Eye among the blind,
That, deaf and silent, read'st the eternal deep,
Haunted for ever by the eternal mind,—
Mighty Prophet! Seer blest!
On whom those truths do rest,
Which we were toiling all our lives to find,
In darkness lost, the darkness of the grave;
Thou, over whom thy Immortality
Broods like the Day, a Master o'er a Slave,
A Presence which is not to be put by;
Thou little Child, yet glorious in the might
Of heaven-born freedom on thy being's height,

Why with such earnest pains dost thou provoke
The years to bring the inevitable yoke,
Thus blindly with thy blessedness at strife?
Full soon thy Soul shall have her earthly freight,
And custom lie upon thee with a weight,
Heavy as frost, and deep almost as life!

9

O joy! that in our embers
Is something that doth live,
That nature yet remembers
What was so fugitive!
The thought of our past years in me doth breed
Perpetual benediction: not indeed
For that which is most worthy to be blest—
Delight and liberty, the simple creed
Of Childhood, whether busy or at rest,
With new-fledged hope still fluttering in his breast:—
Not for these I raise
The song of thanks and praise;
But for those obstinate questionings
Of sense and outward things,
Fallings from us, vanishings;
Blank misgivings of a Creature
Moving about in worlds not realised,
High instincts before which our mortal Nature
Did tremble like a guilty Thing surprised:
But for those first affections,
Those shadowy recollections,
Which, be they what they may,
Are yet the fountain light of all our day,
Are yet a master light of all our seeing;
Uphold us, cherish, and have power to make
Our noisy years seem moments in the being
Of the eternal Silence: truths that wake,
To perish never;
Which neither listlessness, nor mad endeavour,
Nor Man nor Boy,
Nor all that is at enmity with joy,
Can utterly abolish or destroy!
Hence in a season of calm weather
Though inland far we be,
Our Souls have sight of that immortal sea
Which brought us hither,
Can in a moment travel thither,
And see the Children sport upon the shore,
And hear the mighty waters rolling evermore.

10

Then sing, ye Birds, sing, sing a joyous song!
　　And let the young Lambs bound
　　As to the tabor's sound!
We in thought will join your throng,
　　Ye that pipe and ye that play,
　　Ye that through your hearts to-day
　　Feel the gladness of the May!
What though the radiance which was once so bright
Be now for ever taken from my sight,
　　Though nothing can bring back the hour
Of splendour in the grass, of glory in the flower;
　　We will grieve not, rather find
　　Strength in what remains behind;
　　In the primal sympathy
　　Which having been must ever be;
　　In the soothing thoughts that spring
　　Out of human suffering;
　　In the faith that looks through death,
In years that bring the philosophic mind.

11

And O, ye Fountains, Meadows, Hills, and Groves,
Forebode not any severing of our loves!
Yet in my heart of hearts I feel your might;
I only have relinquished one delight
To live beneath your more habitual sway.
I love the Brooks which down their channels fret,
Even more than when I tripped lightly as they;
The innocent brightness of a new-born Day
　　　　Is lovely yet;
The Clouds that gather round the setting sun
Do take a sober colouring from an eye
That hath kept watch o'er man's mortality;
Another race hath been, and other palms are won.
Thanks to the human heart by which we live,
Thanks to its tenderness, its joys, and fears,
To me the meanest flower that blows can give
Thoughts that do often lie too deep for tears.

II

THE HEROIC IMAGE
Who Am I? Whom Ought I To Become?

INTRODUCTION

I

AWARENESS comes first. Aspiration, man's desire to rise to his own possibilities, is the first fruit of that awareness. No one has stated this relation between awareness and aspiration, or the search for the heroic image, better than W. H. Auden. All men, he writes, whether they be readers or not, seek the clarification of two questions:

> 1) *Who am I?* What is the difference between man and all other creatures? What relations are possible between them? What is man's status in the universe? What are the conditions of his existence which he must accept as his fate which no wishing can alter?
>
> 2) *Whom ought I to become?* What are the characteristics of the hero, the authentic man whom everybody should admire and try to become? Vice versa, what are the characteristics of the churl, the unauthentic man whom everybody should try to avoid becoming?[1]

Hence, it is not surprising that literature, in its first stirrings, is chiefly concerned with the celebration of the deeds of its heroes, those who reveal most vividly man's sense of honor, loyalty, courage, intelligence. Heroes are the men other men measure themselves by. Whether they are bigger than life, as the godlike figures of classical mythology, or merely life-sized men and women struggling to do their best in a workaday world, as the characters in a Charles Dickens novel, heroes show us a way to meet life, to come to grips with it, to understand it better, to accept it with courage, even with joy.

This is not to say that heroic literature always celebrates the triumphs of the hero and always evokes a feeling of optimism. Not at

1 From the essay "Robert Frost" in *The Dyer's Hand and Other Essays* by W. H. Auden, Random House, 1962, 344–45.

all. Often, as in *The Odyssey* and *The Aeneid*, it reveals the triumph of the hero only after describing his long and arduous effort and great suffering. More often than not, it tells us how the hero meets his death. The hero's rewards are seldom riches, comfort, or any of the compensations of an affluent life. His rewards are, rather, honor, esteem, glory, or the privilege of having achieved the full measure of his humanity, of having achieved perfection within the limits of human imperfection.

Homer, the first great poet in Western literature, created an heroic type that still captures the contemporary imagination despite a widespread sympathy for his opposite, the anti-hero of the modern novel, who sinks hopelessly in his sea of troubles. Achilles, the hero of *The Iliad*, is a warrior-prince whose wrath ("Sing, muse, the wrath of Achilles") inspired the main action of Homer's epic. In many ways Achilles is, by modern standards, a regrettably violent figure. He is often egotistic, vain, arrogant, and cruel, and some readers prefer to admire his victim, Hector, the chief of the Trojans. Yet Achilles, for all his defects, lived by an heroic code. Offered the choice of a short life with glory or a long one without it, he chose the former. He pursued consciously, and with unwavering fortitude, an ideal of excellence in war and in peace. In battle he was first among the Greeks, and his withdrawal from the battle resulted in a temporary Trojan victory. In peace, he was an accomplished and vigorous orator, the peer of wise Nestor and wily Ulysses. He aspired not only to be the first among men in fact, but to be known for his excellence among men who came after him. Excellence, in a sense, meant immortality.

How the ideal of excellence inspired the Greek sense of the hero is clearer to modern eyes in *The Odyssey*. In the opening scene of Homer's second great epic, the goddess Athene, appearing in human form, approaches Telemachus, the son of Ulysses. Athene's purpose is to pave the way for Ulysses' return. She wants Telemachus to search for his father. Note how her arguments stir him by proposing an heroic action that will guarantee him glory among men:

> "You must not hold to childish ways, because you are now no longer the child you were. Have you not heard what fame royal Orestes gained with all mankind, because he slew the slayer, wily Aegisthus, who had slain his famous father [Agamemnon]? You, too, my friend—for certainly I find you fair and tall—be strong, that men hereafter born may speak your praise. . . ."
>
> Saying this, clear-eyed Athene passed away, even as a bird—a sea-hawk—takes its flight. Into his heart she had brought strength and courage, turning his thoughts upon his father even more than before.

As he marked this in his mind, an awe came on his heart; he knew a god was with him. Straightway he sought the suitors, godlike himself.

Godlike. The word implies excellence of body, mind, and spirit, a supreme courage such as that displayed by Achilles in the Trojan War, by Ulysses in his voyage home, by Aeneas in his struggle to establish Rome. Godlike, to the Ancients, did not mean that Achilles, Ulysses, and Aeneas were above the human plane, but rather that they were at the top of it, so that the gods, who were presented as human themselves, favored them, fostered their plans, predestined them to greatness.

If Homer and Virgil created heroes who embodied Greco-Roman ideals of human greatness, their successors created heroes who also pursued, and achieved, excellence. But for later poets, excellence had new dimensions. Excellence still meant feats of physical prowess, as the deeds of Charlemagne and Roland and the Cid Campeador attest. It still meant intellectual skill or wisdom, as the characters of King Arthur in the Arthurian legends and Vasco da Gama in Camoëns' *Lusiads* make clear. But later poets saw the true hero as one who possessed a *moral* grandeur that Homer and Virgil had merely prefigured. Thus Tasso's Godfrey in *Jerusalem Delivered* and Spenser's Gloriana in *The Faerie Queene*, Adam and Eve in Milton's *Paradise Lost* and *Paradise Regained*—all these heroes and heroines embody ideals far more sophisticated than those of Achilles, Ulysses, and Aeneas. They reflect more elaborate systems of ethics, a greater refinement of conscience, a greater range of moral experience.

The heroic tradition did not end with John Milton. Man continued to aspire and new heroes were created, or rather recognized, as generation succeeded generation. New nations, formed by new cultures, demanded heroes who imaged their own sense of excellence and their own national identity. New generations of men also search for heroes to succeed if not to replace those of the past. In our own times, our heroes—Hemingway's soldiers, writers, bullfighters, and fishermen, Faulkner's men of conscience, Steinbeck's scientific humanists—are more realistic than the heroes of an older tradition. But they represent a similar search for excellence, now called integrity, or humanity, or grace under pressure, or simply honesty. Even our anti-heroes, the defeated men and women of existentialist or "beat" literature, testify indirectly to the drive for excellence. The bitter rejection of mediocrity is often the greatest testimony to the desire for excellence; the protest of despair is sometimes a way of asserting our aspirations.

Aspiration, then, is not only a permanent theme of literature; it is also a theme of compelling interest today. In our complex age where many ideals compete for our attention, we feel the need to discriminate among ideals. We are invited to pursue individual excellence, particularly along intellectual or aesthetic lines. We are urged to become expert in one or another art or science. We are asked to merge, if not submerge, personal ideals with those of the community, the nation, or the one world of united nations. We must choose among many ideals, most, if not all of them, excellent, but some of them clearly incompatible with others. Our personal choice of an ideal, or of several compatible ideals, will be based on judgments that are derived from other sources besides literature. But literature can help us to understand just what human ideals imply. Properly read, literature disposes us to see our own situation more clearly and thus readies us, so to speak, to choose our ideals wisely.

II

JUST how literature disposes us to see our human situation more clearly may be best illustrated by the stories, essays, poems, and the drama in this section. The selections are meant to be enjoyed because they are interesting in themselves, as literature, and because, ranged side by side, each one comments on the other, provoking comparison and contrast that help us form our own judgments.

The first selection, "The Captive's Story," is a romantic tale that Cervantes inserted in Part I of his *Don Quixote*. Based partly on the author's own experiences as a prisoner of war, "The Captive's Story" sets forth one phase of the Renaissance ideal of chivalry. Captain Ruy Perez de Viedma, as he is subsequently identified, chooses to serve his God and King as a soldier instead of following the profession of letters or of government service as did his brothers. In modest, soldierly language, he offers a straightforward account of extraordinary adventures—courageous fighting, romance, intrigue, escape.

Both the Captain and his beloved Zoraida, despite their courtly manners and literary turn of speech, are essentially simple. They know what they want; they have resolved their doubts. They aspire to be among those best souls who trust in noble exploits to win for them, in the conventional language of the first sonnet, "a better home there in the skies." For Zoraida and the Captain to fall in death is no defeat, provided they have lived to the end according to their moral code.

Muriel Spark's "You Should Have Seen the Mess" is sharply antithetical in tone and method to Cervantes' heroic romance. Lorna Merrifield, the narrator, is a consciously up-to-date spokesman for the well-adjusted membership of the new welfare state. Like the Captain, she too has her code. But, whereas the Captain admired heroism, fidelity, and honor, Lorna is attracted to hygiene, gadgets, and respectability. Her aspirations are limited to a "comfy" apartment in a housing project. Totally beyond her range of response are the dusty treasures of the grammar school and the solicitor's office, and the disorderly human excellence of the Darbys and Willy Morley. Lorna is happy only at a place like the Lewis Chemical Company, where neatness, efficiency, and respectability minister to her sense of the fitness of things.

We should not regard Lorna Merrifield, however, as totally representative of our contemporary civilization. True, her unconscious mouthings of the materialistic clichés of commercial advertising and demagogic politics make her a plausible symbol of what is called mass culture. But, as the author's ironical tone informs us, Lorna's idea of the good life is distressingly, if amusingly, superficial. Far more representative of modern hope and fear is Laura, the anguished heroine of Katherine Anne Porter's "Flowering Judas."

Miss Porter's Laura is an opposite of Muriel Spark's stenographer. She is deeply sensitive, intelligent, and committed, a secular nun, so to speak, idealistically serving a revolutionary cause in Mexico. Her devotion both to humanity and to her fellow human beings is mocked by the venality and violence of her associates, particularly Braggioni. "He has the malice, the cleverness, the wickedness, the sharpness of wit, the hardness of heart, stipulated for loving the world profitably." Braggioni makes Laura doubt her calling. Alive to tenderness, her instinct tells her she must cultivate a stoicism "against that disaster she fears, though she cannot name it." That disaster, made evident in the short but poignant dream with which the story ends, is Laura's feeling that she has confused "love with revolution, night with day, life with death." And in her confusion she has, culpably or not, implicated herself in a horrifying betrayal. She is a victim "betrayed irreparably by the disunion between her way of life and her feeling of what life should be." She is a victim too in that she feels she has betrayed herself. "Murderer!" cries Eugenio in her dream. "Laura cried No! and at the sound of her own voice, she awoke trembling, and was afraid to sleep again."

III

THE essays of C. M. Bowra, Iris Origo, and Thomas Carlyle, in addition to their helpful explanations of specific heroic poems represented or alluded to in Section II, describe the heroic ideal as it developed in the classical, medieval, and Renaissance periods. Their common concern is with an idea of man that would serve as a measure of man.

Thus Bowra describes Aeneas as Virgil's attempt to create an image of "his own reformed and Roman ideal of manhood," an ideal that, when realized in the poem, served as a model for future poets: "Once Virgil had opened up a new vision of human worth and recast the heroic ideal in a new mould, he set an example which later poets could not but follow . . . any new heroic ideal must take account of what he said."

That Dante owed much to Virgil, his admired guide and master, is common knowledge. But Dante's measure of man goes beyond the Stoic ideal, however much that ideal was embellished by Virgil. Dante added the ideal of spiritual love that, in the thousand years since Virgil's death, had assimilated and transformed the Roman ideals of justice and duty. As Carlyle writes, "These sublime ideas of his, terrible and beautiful, are the fruit of the Christian Meditation of all the good men who have gone before him."

In her profile of the Renaissance scholar Vittorino de Feltre, Iris Origo shows how the ideals of the classical and Christian ages were applied to education. Where Virgil sowed and Dante reaped, Vittorino gathered up the harvest and prepared food to nourish minds and form tastes. The result of Vittorino's training was the perfect prince: sober and chaste in his personal conduct, a patron if not a practitioner of the arts, a wise and just ruler, an efficient man of action. He is the prototype of innumerable Renaissance portraits of the nobleman that appear in conduct books and educational manuals and in stories and dramas. Cervantes depicts him in the figure of Don Juan Perez de Viedma in *Don Quixote*. Shakespeare extols him in Ophelia's description of Hamlet as courtier, soldier, scholar: "The expectancy and rose of the fair state/ The glass of fashion and the mold of form."

In later times the Renaissance image of the ideal courtier gave way to that of the gentleman. The true gentleman, urbane in manner, liberally educated, trained to take a leading role in any society, was the admired figure of eighteenth- and nineteenth-century novelists like Samuel Richardson and Jane Austen. He also provided the pattern of education in the eighteenth and nineteenth centuries. J. H. Newman, no worshiper of worldly rank or social snobbery, in his classic *The Idea of a University* recognizes the gentleman as the "beau ideal" of a university education.

Each age, then, inherits an heroic image from the past, and remodels that image to express its own aspirations. In twentieth-century America we may admire the models of the Renaissance courtier and the gentleman, but the temper of the times and the pressure of social change actively discourage our imitating them. Indeed, Emmet John Hughes in his "The Notion of an American Gentleman" asks whether, "in a climate so mockingly inhospitable as American society," the gentleman as a species can survive. To answer this question he describes the essential characteristics of a gentleman, identifies a score of representative gentlemen, and then shows what it is that makes them gentlemen. Despite the leveling tendency of huge democratic societies, the heroic image not only survives, but also takes on a new distinction. The American gentleman, Hughes tells us, "possesses, in his national temper, one of the most elemental, as well as the most rare, requisites for being a gentleman: he does not fret and strive too much over being one."

IV

WHILE the essays by Bowra, Carlyle, Origo, and Hughes center on general ideals, the poems of this section have their own special emphasis, even when they reflect well-defined ideals. The genius of the writer modifies the heroic tradition. Virgil's story of Dido is notable for its delicate poise between an admiration for the heroism of Aeneas, who placed duty to the gods before his love for Dido, and pity for the Carthaginian queen, who is his heroic antitype. Thus classic poise and romantic pathos coexist side by side. Tennyson's Ulysses bears a close resemblance to his Homeric prototype but he often speaks like a nineteenth-century philosopher. Similarly, Tennyson's King Arthur in "Morte d'Arthur" is partly an historical reconstruction of Sir Thomas Malory's legendary King of the Britons, but he is also a man of Tennyson's own times who reluctantly bids farewell to the noble past and counsels acceptance of the new.

At times, then, the poet's admiration for his hero reflects his own individual sensibility even more than it does the ideal of his age. Often, however, the poem expresses a conviction, a commitment, a belief. Thus, in Dante's Canto III of the *Paradiso* we read of Dante's first encounter with the blessed in heaven. He first addresses Piccarda Donati, who was compelled by her fierce brother Corso to leave her convent and to marry the violent Rosselinno della Tosa. Because of her broken vow she is in the lowest sphere in heaven. Is she therefore less happy than those in the higher spheres? Dante's inquiry elicits a long explanation (ll. 70–120) on the nature of human happiness. Happiness consists in love and in conformity to God's will. Line 85, "And in His will is perfected our peace" (*e la sua voluntate è nostra pace*), is perhaps one of the most quoted lines of all poetry.

In these passages Dante clearly expresses his view that heroism and aspiration are linked to a divine order. Conversely, Byron employs the myth of Prometheus to glorify man's absolute independence and defiance of the gods. In "Prometheus" man's sole happiness appears to be a rebellion which makes his spirit "an equal to all woes . . ./ Triumphant where it dares defy/ And making Death a Victory."

Both views, that of Dante, who finds the measure of man in God's will, and that of Byron, who finds it in rebellion, are represented in Christopher Marlowe's Doctor Faustus. Mephistophilis, a devil, testifies to Dante's thesis. He describes himself as an unhappy spirit who fell, with Lucifer, because of pride and insolence. When Faustus asks him why he is on earth and not in hell, Mephistophilis replies:

> Why this is hell, nor am I out of it:
> Think'st thou that I who saw the face of God,
> And tasted the eternal joys of heaven,
> Am not tormented with ten tousand hells,
> In being deprived of everlasting bliss?

Faustus, swollen with pride, answers with a kind of Byronic defiance.

> What, is great Mephistophilis so passionate
> For being deprivèd of the joys of heaven?
> Learn thou of Faustus manly fortitude,
> And scorn those joys thou never shalt possess.
> Go bear these tidings to great Lucifer:
> Seeing Faustus hath incurred eternal death
> By desperate thoughts against Jove's deity,
> Say he surrenders up to him his soul. . . .

Faustus' defiance crumbles at the end of the play, when he too testifies to Dante's view of the measure of man.

These examples suggest that in most serious poetry an heroic figure is proposed as the paradigm, the exemplary case, that can be taken, at least implicitly, as the measure of man.

What, then, can be said of the modern "hero," such as the unknown citizen of W. H. Auden's poem? The speaker in the poem says that "in the modern sense of an old-fashioned word, [the unknown citizen] was a saint." But his sanctity consists in perfect obedience to an omnipotent scientific state, a conformity to a law of statistical averages. Or what can be said of the currently popular image of the organization man who shapes his life according to the demands of the bureau, company, or group that secures his prosperity at the price of his liberty? These questions point up the problems that literature perpetually forces us to consider: Who am I? Whom ought I to become? Literature, as Lionel Trilling has reminded us, presents us with an inescapable moral challenge that can be met only by a personal repsonse. This personal response can only be the search for, and the aspiration to achieve, the measure of man.

Perfect achievement may not be possible. Yet the effort alone contributes to the making of a civilized man. Robert Browning puts it this way in "Rabbi Ben Ezra":

> Shall life succeed in that it seems to fail:
> What I aspired to be,
> And was not, comforts me;
> A brute I might have been, but would not sink i' the scale.

STORIES

Miguel de Cervantes Saavedra

THE CAPTIVE'S STORY

"IT WAS in a village in the mountains of León that the line of which I come had its beginnings, a family more favored by nature than by fortune, although amid the poverty that prevailed in that region my father had the reputation of being a rich man and indeed might have been one, had he displayed the same skill in conserving his property that he did in squandering it. His inclination to liberal spending came from his having been a soldier in his youth, for that is a school in which the miser becomes generous and the generous becomes prodigal; if there are some soldiers that are parsimonious, they may be said to be freaks such as are rarely to be met with.

"My father went beyond the bounds of liberality and came close to prodigality, which is not a profitable thing for a married man with children to bring up who are to succeed him and carry on his name. He had three of them, all of them males and of an age to decide upon their calling in life. Accordingly, when he saw that, as he put it, there was no use in his trying to overcome his natural propensity, he made up his mind to rid himself of the instrument and cause of his lavish spending; in other words, he would get rid of his property, for without his fortune Alexander himself would have appeared in straitened circumstances. And so, calling the three of us together one day and closeting himself alone with us, he proceeded to address us somewhat in the following manner:

" 'My sons, there is no need of my telling you that I have your welfare at heart; it is enough to know and state that you are my sons. On the other hand, the fact that I am unable to control myself when it comes to preserving your estate may well give you a contrary impression. For this reason, in order that you may be assured from now on that I love you as a father should and have no desire to ruin you as a stepfather might, I have decided to do for you something that I have long had in mind and to which I have given the most mature consideration. You are of an age to enter upon your professions in life, or at least to choose the ones which, when you are older, will bring you profit and honor.

" 'What I have thought of doing is to divide my estate into four parts, three of which I will turn over to you so that each has that which is his by right, while the fourth part I will retain for my own livelihood and support for the rest of the time that Heaven shall be pleased to grant me. But after each of you has had his due share of the property, I would have you follow one of the courses that I shall indicate. We have here in Spain a proverb which to my mind is a very true one, as indeed they all are, being wise maxims drawn from long experience. This one runs, "The Church, the sea, or the Royal Household," which in plainer language is equivalent to saying, "He who would make the most of himself and become a rich man, let him become a churchman, or go to sea and be a merchant, or enter the service of kings in their palaces." For there is another saying, "Better a king's crumb than a lord's favor."

" 'I tell you this because it is my wish that one of you follow the profession of letters, that another go into trade, and that the third serve his king as a soldier, seeing that it is a difficult thing to obtain service in his household; for if the military life does not bring much wealth, it does confer fame and high esteem. Within a week, I will give you your shares in money, without defrauding you of a single penny, as you shall see in due course. Tell me, then, if you feel inclined to follow my advice and precepts in relation to what I have suggested.'

"He then called upon me as the eldest to answer; and after having told him that he ought not to rid himself of his property in that manner but should spend as much of it as he wished, since we were young and able to make our own way, I ended by assuring him that I would do as he desired, my own choice being to follow the profession of arms and thus serve God and my king. My second brother, having made a similar declaration, announced his intention of going to the Indies and investing his share in commerce. The youngest one, and in my opinion the wisest, said that he preferred to enter the Church or to go to Salamanca to complete the course of study that he had already begun.

"When we had made our choice of callings, my father embraced us all, and within the brief space of time mentioned he carried out his promise by giving each of us his share, which as I remember amounted to three thousand ducats in currency; for an uncle of ours had purchased the estate and paid for it in cash in order to keep it in the family. On that same day the three of us took leave of our good-hearted father; but inasmuch as it seemed to me an inhuman thing for him to be left with so little money in his old age, I prevailed upon him to take two of my three thousand ducats, since the remainder would be sufficient to meet my wants as a soldier. Moved by my example, my two brothers each gave him a thousand, so that he had in all four thousand, plus the three thousand which, as it appeared, his share of the estate was worth; for he did not care to dispose of his portion but preferred to keep it in land.

"And so, then, as I was saying, we took our leave of him and of our uncle, not without much feeling and many tears on the part of all. They charged us to let them know, whenever it was possible for us to do so, as to how we were faring and whether we were meeting with prosperity or adversity, and we promised them that we would. When he had embraced us and given us his benediction, we all departed, one setting out for Salamanca, another for Seville, while I made for Alicante, where I had heard there was a Genoese craft taking on a cargo of wool for that city.

"It is now twenty-two years since I left my father's house, and although in the course of that time I have written a number of letters, I have had no word either of him or of my brothers. As to my own experiences during those years, I shall relate them for you briefly. Embarking at Alicante, I had a fair voyage to Genoa, and from there I went on to Milan, where I fitted myself out with arms and a few accessories. For it was my intention to take service in the Piedmont, and I was already on my way to Alessandria della Paglia when I heard that the great Duke of Alva was starting for Flanders. I then changed my plan and, joining his army, served with him in the three campaigns that he waged. I was present at the deaths of the Counts of Egmont and Hoorne and rose to the rank of ensign under a famous captain of Guadalajara, Diego de Urbina by name. After I had been in Flanders for some while, news came of the league which his Holiness, Pope Pius V of blessed memory, had formed with Venice and Spain against the common enemy, the Turk, who about that time had taken, with his fleet, the famous island of Cyprus, which was then under the rule of the Venetians. This was a serious loss and one truly to be deplored.

"It was known for a fact that the commanding general of this league was to be his Most Serene Highness, John of Austria, brother of our good King Philip, and there was much talk of the great and warlike preparations that he was making. I was deeply stirred by all this and felt a desire to take part in the coming campaign; and although I had prospects and almost certain promises of being promoted to captain where I then served, on the first occasion that offered, I chose to leave all this and return to Italy. And as it happened, John of Austria had just arrived in Genoa on his way to Naples to join the Venetian fleet, as he afterward did as Messina.

"In short, I may tell you that I was soon taking part in that most fortunate campaign, having already been made a captain of infantry, an honor that I owed to my good fortune rather than to my merits. And on that day that was so happy a one for all Christendom, since it revealed to all the nations of the world the error under which they had been laboring in believing that the Turks were invincible at sea—on that day, I repeat, in which the haughty Ottoman pride was shattered, among all the happy ones that were there (and those Christians that died were even happier than those that remained alive and victorious), I alone was wretched; for in place of a naval crown such as I might have hoped for had it been in Roman times, I found myself on the night that followed that famous day with chains on my feet and manacles on my hands.

"The way in which it came about was this: El Uchali, King of Algiers, a bold and successful corsair, had attacked and captured the flagship of Malta, on which only three knights were left alive and those three badly wounded; whereupon the ship of Giovanni Andrea, on which I and my company were stationed, came to its assistance. Doing what was customary under the circumstances, I leaped aboard the enemy galley, which, by veering off from the attacking vessel, prevented my men from following me. Thus I was alone among the enemy, who so greatly outnumbered me that any hope of resistance was vain; and the short of it is, after I had been badly wounded, they captured me. As you know, gentlemen, El Uchali and all his fleet made their escape, so that I was left a prisoner in his hands; and that is the reason why it was that only I was miserable among so many who were happy, and a captive among so many who were free. For there were fifteen thousand Christians slaving at the oars in the Turkish fleet who that day obtained their liberty.

"They took me to Constantinople, where the Grand Turk Selim made my master commander at sea for having done his duty in battle so well and displayed his bravery by carrying off the standard of the Order of Malta. The following year, which was '72, I was in Navarino, rowing in the flagship with the three lanterns, and there I saw and noted how the opportunity was lost for capturing the entire Turkish fleet in the harbor; for all the sailors and Janizaries were convinced that they would be attacked while in port and had their clothing and their *passamaques,* or shoes, in readiness in order that they might be able to flee overland without waiting to give combat, so great was the fear that our fleet had inspired in them. But Heaven ordained otherwise, not because of any fault or carelessness on the part of our commander, but as a punishment for the sins of Christendom, since it is God's will that we should have with us always the agents of his wrath.

"The upshot of it was, El Uchali withdrew to Modon, which is an island near Navarino, and there, disembarking his men, he proceeded to fortify the mouth of the harbor, after which he waited quietly until John retired. On this voyage one of the galleys, called the *Prize,* whose captain was a son of the famous corsair Barbarossa, was captured by the Neapolitan craft known as the *She-Wolf,* commanded by that thunder-bolt of war, that father to his men, the fortunate and never-vanquished captain, Don Alvaro de Bazán, Marquis of Santa Cruz.

"I must not omit telling you what took place in connection with this capture. Barbarossa's son was so cruel and treated his captives so badly that the moment the rowers saw the *She-Wolf* bearing down and gaining upon them, they all at one and the same time dropped their oars and seized the captain, who was standing upon the gangway platform, urging them to row faster. Laying hold of him, they passed him on from bench to bench and from poop to prow, and so bit and chewed him that before he had gone much farther than the ship's mast his soul had already gone to Hell. Such, as I have said, was the cruelty with which he treated them and the hatred that they had for him.

"We then returned to Constantinople, and the next year, which was '73, we learned how John had captured Tunis, driven the Turks out of that kingdom, and placed Muley Hamet on the throne, thus cutting short the hopes that Muley Hamida, bravest and cruelest Moor in all the world, had of returning to rule there. The Great Turk felt this loss very keenly and, having resort to the cunning which all those of his line possess, he made peace with the Venetians, who desired it much more than he did; and the following year, in '74, he attacked the Goleta[1] and the Fort near Tunis which John had left in a state of semi-completion.

"During all this time I was at the oar, with no hope whatever of gaining my freedom. At least I had no hope of ransom, for I was determined not to write the news of my misfortune to my father. Both the Goleta and the Fort finally fell, for in front of them were massed seventy-five thousand Turkish regulars, while the number of Moors and Arabs from all over Africa was in excess of four hundred thousand; and this enormous force was equipped with so many munitions and engines of war and accompanied by so many sappers that the latter might readily have buried both their objectives under handfuls of earth.

"The Goleta, which had previously been looked upon as inexpugnable, was the first to succumb; and if it was lost, this was not the fault of its defenders, who did all that they should and could have done. It was rather due to the fact that, as experience showed, it was easy to throw up entrenchments in the desert sand; for water was commonly found there at a depth of two palms, but the Turks went down for a depth of two varas without striking any, and as a result, piling their sandbags one on top of another, they were able to raise ramparts so high that they could command the walls of the fort and fire upon them as from a bastion, so that it was impossible to make a stand or put up a defense.

"It was the common opinion that our men did wrong in shutting

1 [A fort.]

themselves up in the Goleta instead of waiting for the enemy in the open, along the landing place; but those who say this speak from a distance and with little experience in such matters. If in the Goleta and the Fort there were barely seven thousand soldiers in all, how could so small a force, no matter how courageous, hope to sally forth onto the open plain and hold its own against so numerous an opposing one? And how could such a force fail to be lost unless reinforcements were sent to it, especially when surrounded by enemies that were not only so many in number and so determined, but that were fighting on their own soil?

"It seemed to many, and to me as well, that Heaven was doing Spain a special favor by mercifully permitting the destruction of that source and lair of so many woes, that glutton, sponge, and waster responsible for the profitless spending of an infinite amount of money which served no other cause than that of preserving the memory of its capture by the invincible Charles V—as if, to sustain that memory, which is and shall be eternal, those stones were necessary. The Fort likewise fell, but the Turks had to win it inch by inch, for the soldiers who defended it fought so stoutly and bravely that they slew more than twenty-five thousand of the enemy in the course of twenty-two general assaults. Of the three hundred of them that were taken prisoners, not one was without a wound, which is clear proof of their valor and determination and the ability with which they had defended and held their posts.

"A small fort or tower that stood in the middle of the lagoon also conditionally surrendered. It was under the command of a gentleman and famous soldier of Valencia, Don Juan Zanoguerra. Among those captured was Don Pedro Puertocarrero, commandant of the Goleta, who had done all that he could to defend his fort and felt the loss of it so keenly that he died of grief on the way to Constantinople, where his captors were taking him. Yet another was Gabriele Serbelloni, a Milanese gentleman, a great engineer and a very brave soldier.

"In the defense of these two strongholds there died many noteworthy persons, among whom was Pagano Doria, a knight of the Order of St. John, a man of generous disposition as was shown by the extreme liberality with which he treated his brother, the famous Giovanni Andrea Doria; and the saddest part of it all was that he died at the hands of some Arabs to whom, when he saw that the Fort was lost, he had entrusted himself when they offered to conduct him, disguised in Moorish costume, to Tabarca, a small coastal fort or station held by the Genoese, who there ply the trade of coral fishing. The Arabs cut off his head and took it to the commander of the Turkish fleet, who thereupon proved the truth of our Castilian proverb that asserts that 'although the treason may be acceptable, the traitor is abhorred'; for it is said that the general in question ordered those who brought him this present to be hanged because they had not delivered their victim alive.

"Among the Christians in the Fort was one named Don Pedro de Aguilar, a native of some village in Andalusia, I cannot tell you which one; he had been an ensign and was looked upon as a most capable soldier, and in addition, he was a man of rare intellectual attainments, being especially gifted in what is known as poetry. I speak of him for the reason that fate brought him to my galley and my bench, since we were both slaves to the same master; and before we left port this gentleman composed two sonnets in the manner of epitaphs, one to the Goleta and the other to the Fort. As a matter of fact, I mean to recite them for you, for I know them by heart, and I do not think they will bore you, but quite the reverse."

When the captive mentioned Don Pedro de Aguilar's name, Don Fernando glanced at his companions and all three of them smiled; and when he came to read the sonnets, one of them interrupted him.

"Before your grace goes any further," he said, "I beg you to tell me what became of that Pedro de Aguilar of whom you speak."

"All I know," replied the captive, "is that at the end of the two years he spent in Constantinople he disguised himself as an Albanian and made his escape in the company of a Greek spy. I cannot tell you if he succeeded in regaining his liberty or not, but it is my belief that he did, for a year later I saw the Greek in Constantinople but was unable to ask him what the outcome of their journey had been."

"I can tell you that," replied the gentleman, "for this Don Pedro is my brother and at this moment is in our village, in sound health, rich, married, and the father of three children."

"Thanks be to God." said the captive, "for all His mercies; for in my opinion there is no happiness on earth that can equal that of recovering one's lost liberty."

"What is more," the gentleman went on, "I am familiar with those sonnets that my brother composed."

"Recite them, then, your Grace," said the captive, "for you will be able to do so better than I."

"With pleasure," said the gentleman; and he proceeded to recite the one on the Goleta, which was as follows:

SONNET

Blest souls that have been freed of mortal guise
And by reason of your good deeds here below,
The Noble exploits that ye have to show,
Have gone to a better home there in the skies,
How often 'mid the heat of battle cries
Have ye spilt the blood of many a doughty foe

As, staining sand and sea, ye did overthrow
The wicked in their pride, O high emprise!
'Twas life not valor failed the weary arm,
And even as ye died ye well might claim
The victory, thus wrested from defeat.
Ye fell, 'tis true, and suffered mortal harm
Between the blade and wall, yet still your fame
Lives on and rises to the glory seat.

"That is the way I remember it also," remarked the captive.

"And the one on the Fort," said the gentleman, "runs like this, if I am not mistaken."

SONNET

Out of the sterile earth, this rubble heap,
These tumbled ruins that now strew the ground,
Three thousand souls a better home have found;
Three thousand soldiers that once here did sleep
Have gone above, their guerdon fair to reap.
It was in vain their valor did abound;
Few and exhausted, suffering many a wound,
They gave their lives their honor bright to keep.
This bit of earth has ever been the haunt
Of mournful memories beyond man's count,
Both now and in the ages long since past;
But no more worthy souls can Heaven vaunt
Amongst the many that from this spot did mount
Than these brave ones that are Heaven's own at last.

The sonnets were not displeasing, and the captive was happy over the news of his comrade which he had received. He then went on with his story.

"Well, then, the Goleta and the Fort having fallen, the Turks ordered the former stronghold dismantled, there being nothing left of the Fort to raze; and in order to accomplish the task more speedily and with less labor, they mined three-quarters of it, but by no device could they succeed in blowing up what appeared to be the weakest part, namely the old walls. On the other hand, all that remained of the new fortifications that the Little Friar had built was brought to the ground with the greatest of ease.

"Finally, the victorious fleet returned in triumph to Constantinople, and a few months afterwards my master, El Uchali, died, the one who was known as 'Uchali Fartax,' which in the Turkish tongue means 'scurvy renegade'; for that is what he was, and it is the custom of the Turks to bestow names that signify some fault or virtue. This is for the reason that they have only four surnames altogether, which apply to those descended from the Ottoman line; the others, as I started to say, take their names and surnames from bodily defects or moral characteristics. And this Scurvy One, being a slave of the Grand Seignior's, had slaved at the oar for fourteen years, being then more than thirty-four years of age when he turned renegade. The way it came about was this: as he was rowing one day a Turk had dealt him a blow, and in order to be revenged on the fellow he renounced his faith. After that, his valor proved to be so outstanding that he did not have to resort to the usual underhanded ways and means by which the Great Turk's favorites rise at court, but was made king of Algiers and later commander at sea, which is the office that is third in rank in that seigniory.

"El Uchali was a Calabrian by birth and a man of moral principle who treated his captives with great humanity. He came to have three thousand of them, and after his death they were divided in accordance with the provisions of his will between the Grand Seignior (who is heir to all who die and who shares with the offspring left by the deceased) and his renegades. I fell to a Venetian renegade who, as a cabin boy aboard a ship, had been captured by Uchali. His master grew so fond of him that the youth became his prime favorite, and he also came to be the cruelest one of his kind that was ever seen. His name was Hassan Aga, and, amassing great wealth, he rose to be king of Algiers. I accompanied him there from Constantinople and was somewhat pleased at being so near to Spain. Not that I intended to write to anyone there concerning my misfortunes; but I wished to see if fortune would be more favorable to me here than it had been in Turkey, where I had unsuccessfully essayed a thousand different means of escape. In Algiers I thought to find other ways of attaining what I desired; for never once did the hope leave me of achieving my freedom; and when my plottings and schemings did not come up to expectations and my attempts were unsuccessful, I did not at once abandon myself to despair but began to look for or invent some fresh hope to sustain me, however faint and weak it might be.

"In this way I managed to keep myself alive, shut up in a prison or house which the Turks call a bagnio, in which they confine their Christian captives, both those of the king and those belonging to certain private individuals, and also those that are referred to as being *del Almacen,*[2] that is to say, captives that belong to the Council and serve the city in public works and other employment. It is very difficult for these last to obtain their freedom, for inasmuch as they are held in common and have no individual for a master, there is no one with whom to treat regarding their ransom even where they have the

2 [Of the Council; in this context, of warehouse workers.]

means for purchasing their liberation. In these bagnios, as I have said, they are accustomed to place captives belonging to certain private citizens of the town, chiefly the ones that are to be ransomed, since there they may keep them in safety and leisure. For the king's captives do not go out to labor with the rest of the galley crew, unless their ransom be late in coming, in which case, by way of inducing them to write for it more urgently, they put them to work and send them to gather wood with the others, which is no small task.

"I, then, was one of this group; for when they discovered that I was a captain, although I told them that I had no fortune and few prospects, they nevertheless insisted upon placing me among those gentlemen and others who were waiting for ransom. They put a chain upon me, but more as a mark of my status than in order to keep me from escaping; and thus I spent my days in that bagnio along with many important personages who had been designated and were being held for the purpose I have mentioned. And although we were at times harassed by hunger and the want of clothing, nothing distressed us so much as what we almost constantly saw and heard of the cruelties, such as never before were heard of or seen, which my master practised upon the Christians. Each day he hanged his man, impaled one, cut off the ear of another; and all this with so little excuse, or with none at all, that the Turks had to admit he did it simply to be doing it, inasmuch as their natural bent toward the entire human race is a homicidal one.

"The only person who made out well with him was a Spanish soldier by the name of Saavedra, for although this man had done things which will remain in the memory of that people for years to come, and all by way of obtaining his liberty, yet the Moor never dealt him a blow nor ordered him flogged; as a matter of fact, he never even gave him so much as a harsh word. And for the least of the many things that Saavedra did, we were all afraid that he would be impaled, and he himself feared it more than once. If time permitted, which unfortunately it does not, I could tell you here and now something of that soldier's exploits which would interest and amaze you much more than my own story.

"To continue: Overlooking the courtyard of our prison were the windows of a wealthy Moor of high rank. These, as is usually the case, more nearly resembled peepholes and were, moreover, covered with very thick and tightly drawn blinds. It happened, then, that one day I and three companions were on the prison terrace, amusing ourselves by seeing how far we could leap with our chains on; and, since we were alone, all the rest of the Christians having gone out to labor, I chanced to raise my eyes, when through one of those closed windows I saw a reed appear with a piece of linen cloth attached to the end of it, and it was moving and waving as if signaling for us to come and take it. As we stood gazing up at it, one of those who was with me went over and placed himself directly beneath the reed to see if it would be released or what would happen; but the moment he did so, it was raised and moved from side to side as if someone were saying no by shaking the head. The Christian then came back, and at once it was lowered again and the person above began making exactly the same motions with it as before. Another of my companions repeated the performance, and the same thing happened with him. And a third man had a similar experience.

"Seeing this, I could not resist the temptation to try my luck, and as soon as I was beneath the reed, it was dropped. It fell at my feet there in the bagnio, and I immediately hastened to untie the linen cloth, whereupon I found knotted in it ten cianis, which are gold coins of base alloy in use among the Moors, each being worth ten reales in our money. I need not tell you how happy I was over this windfall, and my happiness was equaled by my wonder as to how it had come to us, and to me in particular, since the unwillingness of the donor to release the reed to anyone other than me showed clearly that I was the one for whom the favor was intended. Taking the welcome money, I broke the reed and went back to the terrace, where I once more gazed up at the window. Then it was I saw a very white hand emerge, which opened and closed very quickly; and by this we understood or were led to imagine that it was some woman who lived in that house who had shown us this act of kindness. By way of thanking her, we salaamed after the fashion of the Moors, which is done by bowing the head, bending the body at the waist, and crossing the arms upon the bosom.

"Shortly afterward, through the same window, there came a little cross made of reeds, only to be at once withdrawn. This strengthened us in the belief that some Christian woman must be a captive in that house, and that it was she who had done us the favor; but the whiteness of the hand and the Moorish bracelets of which we had caught a glimpse inclined us to think otherwise, although we fancied that it might be some fair renegade, for such women are commonly taken as lawful wives by their masters, who are glad to do this, since they esteem them more highly than those of their own race.

"In all our discussions about the matter, however, we were very far from the truth; but from that time forth we were solely concerned with looking up at that window from which the reed had appeared, as if it had been our north star. Two weeks went by in which we had no further sight of it, nor of the hand, nor any signal whatsoever. And although during that time we did our best to find out who lived in the house and if there was any renegade Christian woman in it, we found no one who could tell us any more about the matter than that the house belonged to a rich and prominent Moor by the name of Hadji Morato, a former alcaide of La Pata, which is a very important office with them.

"But just as we had given up hope of a second rain of cianis, we unexpectedly saw the reed appear again with another knotted cloth on the end of it, a thicker one this time. This happened at an hour when the bagnio was all but deserted, as it had been on the previous occasion, and we made the same test, each of the others in turn going to stand beneath the window before I did, but it was only when I came up that the reed was released and dropped. I undid the knot and found forty Spanish gold crowns and a message written in Arabic with the sign of the cross beneath it. I kissed the cross, took the crowns, and returned to the terrace, where we all again salaamed. Then the hand appeared once more, and I made signs that we would read the message, after which the window was closed. We were at once pleased and bewildered by what had occurred, and as none of us understood Arabic, great was our curiosity to know what the message contained, and greater still our difficulty in finding someone who could read it for us.

"Finally, I decided to take a certain renegade into my confidence. He was a native of Murcia who professed to be a good friend of mine and who had promised to keep any secret that I might entrust to him; for it is the custom of some renegades, when they intend to return to Christian territory, to carry about with them testimonials of one sort or another from important captives to the effect that So-and-So is a good man, has always shown kindness to Christians, and is anxious to flee at the first opportunity that offers. There are those who procure these certificates with a proper object in mind, and there are others who cunningly misemploy them in case of need. The latter, when they go to commit depredations on Christian soil, if perchance they are lost or captured, will produce their affidavits as evidence of the purpose for which they came: namely, that of remaining in a Christian land; and they will assert that it was for this reason they joined the Turks. In such a manner they escape the immediate consequences of their act and are reconciled with the Church before it can punish them; and then, as soon as they are able to do so, they return to Barbary to become what they were before. But, as has been said, there are others who make honest use of these certificates and actually do remain with their coreligionists.

"It was one of these renegades who was my friend. He had testimonials from all of us in which we expressed our confidence in him as forcefully as we could, and if the Moors had found him with these papers on his person, they would have burned him alive. He was known to be well versed in Arabic, being able not only to speak it but to write it as well. And so, before I unbosomed myself to him, I asked him to read the message for me, telling him that I had accidently come upon it in a hole in my cell. He opened it and studied it for some little time, muttering to himself all the while. I asked him if he understood it, and he assured me that he did, very well, and that if I wished him to give it to me word for word, I should provide him with pen and ink, as he could do it better that way. We gave him what he asked for, and he tranlsated the message little by little. When he had finished he said, 'You will find set down here in Spanish absolutely everything that is written on this paper; and you are to remember that where it says Lela Marien, that means Our Lady the Virgin Mary.'

"Following is the message as he had transcribed it:

> When I was young, my father had a slave girl who taught me the Christian *zala*[3] in my language, and she also told me many things about Lela Marien. The Christain woman died, and I know that she did not go to the fire but is with Allah, for twice afterward I saw her and she told me to make my way to the land of the Christians to see Lela Marien, who loved me a great deal. I do not know how to do so. I have seen many Christians from this window, and only you have seemed to me to be a gentleman. I am very young and beautiful and have much money to take with me. See if you can arrange for us to go, and there you may be my husband if you wish. If you do not wish it so, it will not matter to me, for Lela Marien will provide someone to marry me. I myself have written this; have a care as to whom you give it to read; do not trust any Moor, for they are all treacherous. I am deeply concerned lest you show this to someone, for if my father knew of it, he would cast me into a well and cover me with stones. On the reed I shall put a thread. Attach your reply to it, and in case you have no one who can write Arabic for you, tell me by means of signs and Lela Marien will make me understand. May She and Allah and this cross protect you. The cross I kiss many times, as the Christian slave woman bade me.

"You can imagine, gentle folk, how astonished and pleased we were by the contents of this message. Indeed, we showed our feelings so openly that the renegade realized it was not by chance that this paper had been found but that it was in reality addressed to one of our number. He accordingly now asked us if his suspicions were true, telling us that we should confide everything to him, as he would be willing to risk his life for our freedom. Saying this, he brought forth from his bosom a metal crucifix and with many tears swore by the God whom that image represented and in whom he, though a wicked

3 [Worship.]

sinner, still fully and faithfully believed, that he would loyally guard all the secrets we might see fit to reveal to him; for he felt—indeed, he was almost certain—that through the one who had written that message he and all of us would be able to gain our freedom and it would be possible for him to fulfill his dearest wish, that of returning to the bosom of Holy Mother Church, from which like a rotten limb he had been severed and separated through ignorance and sin.

"So many tears did the renegade shed, and so many signs of repentance did he show, that we all of us unanimously consented and agreed to tell him the truth of the matter; and so we proceeded to give him an account of everything, keeping nothing hidden. We pointed out to him the little window through which the reed had appeared, and he then and there made note of the house and announced his intention of taking special pains to find out who lived in it. We also decided that it would be well to reply to the Moorish damsel's note, and, seeing that we had someone there who was capable of doing this, the renegade at once wrote out the words that I dictated to him, which were exactly as I shall give them to you; for nothing of any importance that happened to me in the course of this adventure has slipped my memory, nor shall it escape me as long as I live. This was the reply that we sent to the Moorish lady:

> May the true Allah protect you, my lady, and that blessed Mary who is the true Mother of God and who has put it in your heart to go to the land of the Christians, because she loves you well. Pray to her to show you how you may carry out her command, for she is well disposed and will assuredly do so. Do not fail to write and advise me of your plans, and I will always let you have an answer. The great Allah has given us a Christian captive who knows how to read and write your language, as you can plainly see from this message. Thus, with nothing to fear, we shall be able to know your wishes. You say that if you go to the land of the Christians, you will be my wife, and I as a good Christian promise you that you shall be, and you know that Christians keep their promises better than Moors. May Allah and Mary His Mother watch over you, my lady.

"Having written and sealed this message, I waited two days until the bagnio was deserted as usual, and then I went out to my accustomed place on the terrace to see if the reed would appear, which it did very shortly. As soon as I caught sight of it, although I could not see who was letting it down, I held up the paper as a sign the person above should attach the thread. This had already been done, however, and I now fastened the paper to it, and shortly thereafter our star once more made its appearance with the white banner of peace in the form of a little bundle. It fell at my feet, and, upon picking it up, I found in the the cloth all sorts of gold and silver coins, more than fifty crowns, which more than fifty times doubled our happiness and strengthened our hope of obtaining our liberty.

"That same night our renegade came back and told us what he had learned. The one who lived in that house was the same Moor whose name, Hadji Morato, had been mentioned to us. He was enormously rich and had one daughter, the only heir to all his wealth; and it was the general opinion in the city that she was the most beautiful woman in Barbary. Many of the viceroys who came here had sought her hand in marriage, but she had been unwilling to wed; and it was also known that she had had a female slave who was a Christian and who was now dead. All of which bore out what was said in the note. We then took counsel with the renegade as to what we should do in order to rescue the Moorish damsel and make our escape to the land of Christians, and it was finally agreed that we should wait until we had further word from Zoraida, which was the name of the one who now wishes to be known as Maria. For we saw plainly enough that she and no other would be able to provide a way out of all these difficulties. When we had reached this decision, the renegade told us not to worry, that he would set us at liberty or lose his life in the attempt.

"For four days the bagnio was full of people, and as a result the reed did not appear, but at the end of that period, when the place was once more empty, the bundle was again let down, so pregnant-looking as to promise a very happy birth. The reed and the cloth descended to me, and I found in the latter a message and a hundred gold crowns, with no other money whatsoever. The renegade being present, we gave him the note to read inside our cell, and he translated it for us as follows:

> Sir, I do not know how to arrange for us to go to Spain, nor has Lela Marien told me, although I have asked it of her. The thing that can be done is for me to give you for this venture much money in gold. Ransom yourself and your friends with it, and let one of you go ahead to the land of the Christians, purchase a boat there, and return for the others. He will find me in my father's garden, which is at the Babazón gate, near the seashore. I expect to be there all this summer with my father and my servants. You will be able to take me away from there by night and carry me to the boat with nothing to fear. And remember that you are to be my husband, or I shall ask Mary to punish you. If you can trust no one to go for the boat, ransom yourself and go; for I know that you are more trustworthy than any other, being a gentleman and a Christian. Make it a point to become familiar with the garden; and, meanwhile, when I see you out for a stroll, I shall know that the bagnio is empty and will give you much money. Allah protect you, my lord.

"Such were the contents of the second note; and when all had heard it read, each offered to be the ransomed one, promising to go and return with all haste; and I myself made the same offer. But the renegade opposed all this, saying he would by no means consent for anyone to go free until we all went together; for experience had taught him that men when freed were lax about keeping the word they had given in captivity. He added that many times certain important captives had had recourse to this expedient and had ransomed one of their number to go to Valencia or Majorca, providing him with sufficient money to fit out a boat and return for them, but he had never come back. For, the renegade observed, liberty recovered and the dread of losing it again would erase from their memories all the obligations that there are. By way of showing us the truth of this statement, he briefly related for us what had recently happened to some Christian gentlemen, one of the strangest cases that had ever been heard of in those parts where the most astonishing and terrifying things are all the time occurring.

"In short, he told us that what we could and should do was to give him the ransom money intended for one of us Christians, and he would buy a boat there in Algiers under pretext of turning merchant and trading with Tetuan and along the coast in that region. Being a ship's master, it would be easy for him to hit upon a way of rescuing us from the bagnio and putting us all aboard, especially if the Moorish lady, as she said, was to provide the money for ransoming the entire lot of us. As free men, it would be the easiest thing in the world to embark, even at midday. The greatest obstacle lay in the fact that the Moors would not permit any renegade to buy or own a boat, unless it was a vessel to go on pillaging expeditions; for they feared that if he purchased a small one, especially if he was a Spaniard, he merely wanted it for the purpose of escaping to Christian territory. He, our friend, could readily overcome this difficulty, however, by taking a Tagarin Moor into partnership with him in the purchase of the boat and the profits to be derived from it, and under cover of this arrangement he could become master of the craft; and with that he regarded the rest of it as something already accomplished.

"Although it seemed to me and to my comrades that it would have been better to send to Majorca for the boat as the Moorish lady had suggested, we did not dare oppose him, being fearful that if we did not do as he said he would reveal our plans and put us in danger of losing our lives when our dealings with Zoraida were discovered, for whose life we would all have given our own. We accordingly determined to leave the matter in the hands of God and in those of the renegade, and we therewith replied to Zoraida that we would do all that she had counseled us, since the advice she had given us was as good as if it had come from Lela Marien herself, adding that it remained for her to decide as to whether the project was to be postponed or put into execution at once. I also, once more, made an offer to marry her. And so it came about that the next day, when there was no one in the bagnio, she on various occasions by means of the reed and the cloth conveyed to us two thousand gold crowns and a message in which she informed us that on the next *Jumá*, that is to say, Friday, she was leaving for her father's summer place and that before she left she would give us more money. In case this was not enough, we were to let her know and we might have anything we asked for; for her father had so much that he would never miss it, and, what was more, she held the keys to everything.

"We at once gave the renegade fifteen hundred crowns with which to buy the boat, while I took eight hundred to procure my own ransom, giving the money to a merchant of Valencia who was in Algiers at the time and who had the king release me on the promise that, when the next boat arrived from home, he would pay the ransom fee; for if he were to pay it at once, the king might suspect that the funds had been in Algiers for some time and that the merchant for his own profit had kept the matter secret. Moreover, my master was so captious that I on no account dared pay him immediately. And so, on the Thursday before the Friday that the beauteous Zoraida had fixed as the day for going to her father's summer place, she gave us another thousand crowns, at the same time advising us of her departure and requesting me, in case I was ransomed, to make myself acquainted with the site or, in any event, to seek to procure an opportunity for going there to see her. I replied in a few words that I would do this, urging her to be sure and commend us to Lela Marien by making use of all those prayers that the slave woman had taught her.

"When this had been done, it was arranged that my three companions likewise should be ransomed, so that they would be able to leave the bagnio; since if they saw me set at liberty while they remained behind, despite the fact that there was sufficient money to ransom them, they might create a disturbance and the devil might put it into their heads to do something that would injure Zoraida. It was true that, in view of their rank, I could feel reasonably safe in this regard, but, nevertheless, I did not wish to imperil the undertaking, and so I had them released at the same time as myself, paying over all the money to the merchant in order that he might with confidence and security pledge his word, although we never once divulged to him our secret plan, as there would have been too much danger in doing so.

"A fortnight had not gone by before our renegade had bought a boat capable of carrying more than thirty persons; and by way of rendering the project safer and allaying suspicion, he made a voyage, as he had suggested, to a place called Shershel which is thirty leagues from Algiers in the direction of Oran and which does a large trade in dried figs. Two or three times he did this in the company of the Tagarin Moor I have mentioned; for *Tagarinos* is the name given in Barbary to the Moors of Aragon, while those of Granada are called *Mudéjares;* but in the kingdom of Fez the *Mudéjares* are termed *Elches,* and they are the ones whom that king chiefly employs in war.

"To go on with my story, then: Each time that he passed with his boat he anchored in a cove that was not two crossbow shots from the house where Zoraida was waiting, and there, with the two little Moors that served him as oarsmen, he would deliberately station himself, either to say his prayers or by way of acting out the part he was later to perform in earnest. Thus, he would go to Zoraida's garden and beg fruit, and her father would give it to him without recognizing him. As he told me afterward, he would have liked to have a word with Zoraida herself so he could tell her he was there on my orders to bear her off to the land of the Christians and at the same time urge her to feel safe and happy.

"This, however, was impossible, for Moorish ladies do not permit themselves to be seen by any of their own race or by any Turk unless their husband or father so commands them. With Christian captives, on the other hand, they are allowed to converse and have dealings to a rather surprising extent. For my part, I was just as glad that he had not spoken to her, for she might have been disturbed to find her plan being discussed by renegades.

"But God in any case had ordained otherwise, and our renegade did not have an opportunity of gratifying his laudable desire. Seeing how safely he was able to go to Shershel and return and anchor where he chose, and perceiving that the Tagarin, his companion, was wholly compliant with his wishes and that all that was needed now was a few Christians to man the oars, he told me to look about for some that I might take with me in addition to those that were being ransomed and to engage them for the following Friday, which was the date he had set for our departure. I accordingly spoke to a dozen Spaniards, all of them powerful rowers. They were chosen from among those that were best in a position to leave the city, and it was no small task finding so many of them at that particular moment, since there were then twenty ships at sea and they had taken all the available oarsmen.

"I should not have been able to find them if it had not been that their master that summer was not going on a cruise but was occupied with completing the construction of a galiot which he had on the stocks. All that I told these men was that the next Friday afternoon they should steal out one by one and wait for me in the vicinity of Hadji Morato's garden. I gave these directions to each one separately, instructing them that if they saw any other Christians in the neighborhood, all they were to say to them was that I had ordered them to stay there until I came.

"Having attended to this, I had something else to do that was still more important, and that was to let Zoraida know how far our plans had progressed in order that she might be forewarned and not be caught off guard if we suddenly decided to abduct her before, as she would think, the Christian's boat would have had time to return. I therefore resolved to go to the garden and see if I could speak with her; so on a day before my departure I went there under pretense of gathering a few herbs, and the first person I encountered was her father, who addressed me in the language that throughout Barbary and even in Constantinople is in use between captives and Moors, and which is neither Moorish nor Castilian nor the tongue of any other nation, but a mixture of all of them by means of which we manage to understand one another. It was in this language that he asked me who I was and what I was doing in his garden. I replied that I was Arnaut Mami's slave—because I knew for a certainty that Arnaut Mami was a very great friend of his—and that I was looking for herbs to make him a salad. He then inquired as to whether I was a ransomed man or not and what price my master wanted for me.

"As I was thus engaged in answering his questionings, the lovely Zoraida came out of the garden house. She had caught sight of me some while before; and since Moorish women, as I have said, are not at all prudish about showing themselves to Christians and do not avoid their company, she thought nothing of coming up to where her father stood conversing with me. In fact, when her father saw her slowly approaching, he called to her to come. It would be too much for me to undertake to describe for you now the great beauty, the air of gentle breeding, the rich and elegant attire with which my beloved Zoraida presented herself to my gaze. I shall merely tell you that more pearls hung from her comely throat, her ears, her hair than she has hairs on her head. On her feet, which, as is the custom, were bare, she wore two *carcajes*—for that is what they call bracelets for the ankles in the Moorish tongue—made of purest gold and set with many diamonds whose value, as she told me afterward, her father estimated at ten thousand doblas, while those upon her wrist were worth fully as much as the others.

"The pearls also were numerous, for the way that Moorish women have of displaying their magnificence is by decking themselves out in this manner. And so it is you find more pearls of one kind or another among the Moors than all the other nations combined have to show, and Zoraida's father was reputed to have an abundance of them and the best that there were in Algiers. In addition, he had more than two hundred thousand Spanish crowns, and the fair one I now call mine was mistress of all this wealth.

"If you would form an idea of how beautiful she was in her prosperous days and when so adorned, you have but to observe how much of beauty is left her now after all that she has suffered. For it is a well-known fact that the beauty of some women has its day and season and is diminished or heightened by accidental causes. It is, moreover, a natural thing that the passions of the mind should add to or detract from it, and most often they destroy it utterly. What I am trying to say is that, as she came toward me that day, she impressed me as being, both in herself and in her adornments, the most dazzling creature that I had ever seen, and when I thought of all that I owed to her, it seemed to me that I had before me a goddess from Heaven who had come to earth for my delight and comfort.

"As she came up, her father told her in their language that I was the captive of his friend, Arnaut Mami, and that I had come to look for a salad. She gave me her hand and, in that admixture of tongues that I have described, asked me if I was a gentleman and why it was I had not been ransomed. I replied that I already had been, and that from the price paid she could see the esteem in which my master held me, for the sum of one thousand five hundred soltanis had been put up for me. To which she answered, 'In truth, had you been my father's slave, I would not have permitted him to let you go for twice as much, for you Christians always lie in everything you say and make yourselves out to be poor in order to cheat the Moors.'

" 'That may be, lady,' I said, 'but I dealt truthfully with my master, as I do and shall do with everybody in this world.'

" 'And when are you going?' Zoraida asked.

" 'Tomorrow, I expect; for there is a vessel here from France that sets sail then and I intend to go on it.'

" 'Would it not be better,' said Zoraida, 'to wait for one from Spain, seeing that the French are not your friends?'

" 'No,' I told her, 'although if I were certain that a ship from Spain was on the way, I would wait for it. It is more likely, however, that I shall go tomorrow, for the desire I have to see my native land and my loved ones is such that I cannot bear to wait for another opportunity, even though a better one, if it be late in coming.'

" 'You no doubt have a wife in your own country,' she said, 'and I suppose you are anxious to see her.'

" 'No,' I assured her, 'I am not married, but I have promised to wed as soon as I return.'

" 'And is the lady to whom you have given this promise beautiful?'

" 'She is so beautiful,' I replied, 'that by way of praising her and telling the simple truth, I will say that she very much resembles you.'

"Her father laughed heartily at this. 'In Allah's name, Christian,' he said, 'she must be beautiful indeed if she is like my daughter, who is the most beautiful in all this realm. If you do not believe me, look at her well and tell me if I do not speak the truth.'

"Throughout the greater part of this conversation, Zoraida's father acted as our interpreter, being the more adept at languages; for while she spoke the bastard tongue that, as I have said, is in use there, she expressed her meaning by signs rather than by words.

"As we were discussing these and other subjects, a Moor came running up, crying in a loud voice that four Turks had leaped the garden railing or wall and were picking the fruit although it was not yet ripe. Both the old man and Zoraida were alarmed at this; for the fear that the Moors have of the Turks is a common and, so to speak, an instinctive thing. They are especially afraid of Turkish soldiers, who treat their Moorish subjects more haughtily, insolently, and cruelly than if the latter were their slaves.

"Zoraida's father then said to her, 'Daughter, retire to the house and shut yourself in while I speak to these dogs. As for you, Christian, gather your herbs and go in peace, and may Allah bring you safely to your own country.'

"I bowed, and he went away to look for the Turks, leaving me alone with Zoraida, who made as if to go back into the house as her father had commanded her. He had no sooner disappeared among the garden trees, however, then she, her eyes brimming with tears, turned to me and said, '*Tamejí*, Christian, *tamejí*?' Which means 'Are you going, Christian, are you going?'

"And I answered her, 'Yes, lady, but under no condition without you. Wait for me next *Jumá*, and do not be frightened when you see us, for we are surely going to the land of the Christians.'

"I said this in such a way that she understood everything very well; and, throwing her arm about my neck, she began with faltering step to walk toward the house. But as luck would have it—and it would have been very unlucky indeed for us if Heaven had not ordered it otherwise—as we were going along in this manner, her father, who was coming back from his encounter with the Turks, caught sight of us, and we knew that he had seen us and had seen her arm about me. But Zoraida, cleverly on her guard, did not remove her arm; instead, she clung to me more than ever and laid her head upon my bosom, swaying at the knees a little and giving every evidence of having fainted, while I pretended to be supporting her against my will. The old man ran up to us and, seeing his daughter in this condition, asked her what the matter was.

" 'Undoubtedly,' he said, when he received no reply. 'it was those dogs coming into the garden that did this to her.' And, taking her off my bosom, he pressed her to his own, as she, her eyes not yet dry from her tears, sighed deeply and said, '*Amejí*,[4] Christian, *amejí!*'

" 'It is not necessary, my daughter, for the Christian to go,' her father said. 'He has done you no harm, and the Turks have left. There is no cause for you to be frightened, for nothing is going to hurt you, since the Turks at my request have gone back to where they belong.'

" 'It is true, sir, as you have said,' I told him, 'that they have given her a fright; but since she says for me to go, I would not cause her any annoyance; and so, peace be with you, and with your permission I will return to this garden for herbs, if I find it necessary, for my master says there are no better ones for salad than those that grow here.'

" 'Come back for all that you need,' replied Hadji Morato. 'My daughter does not say this because you or any of the other Christians annoy her. She either meant that the Turks should go, not you, or else that it was time you were looking for your herbs.'

"With this, I at once took my leave of both of them, and Zoraida, who appeared to be suffering deeply, went away with her father, while I, under pretense of gathering my salad, was able to roam the garden at will. I carefully noted the entrances and exits, the means they used to secure the house, and everything that might facilitate our plan; after which, I went to give an account of what had happened to the renegade and my companions. In the meanwhile, I looked forward to the time when I should be able to enjoy undisturbed the boon which fate had bestowed upon me in the person of the beauteous and charming Zoraida.

"Time went by, and at length the day came that meant so much to us. With all of us following the plan which, after many long discussions and the most careful consideration, we had decided upon, we met with the success that we longed for. On the next Friday after the day on which I had spoken to Zoraida in the garden, our renegade at nightfall anchored his boat almost directly opposite the house where she was, the Christians who were to man the oars having been notified in advance that they might hide themselves in various places round about. As they waited for me, they were all of them anxious and elated, eager to board the vessel on which their gaze was fixed; for they were unaware of the arrangement with the renegade and thought that they would have to gain their freedom by force of arm, through slaying the Moors who were on the boat.

"Accordingly, as soon as I and my companions showed ourselves, those who were in hiding sighted us and came up. This was at an hour when the gates of the city were closed, and in the whole of the coun-

4 [Go.]

tryside not a soul was to be seen. When we were all together, we discussed the question as to whether it would be better to go first for Zoraida or to make prisoners of the Moorish oarsmen. Before we had reached a decision, our renegade arrived and asked us what was the cause of our delay, for it was now time, all the Moors being off guard and most of them asleep. I told him why we were hesitating, and he replied that the most important thing was to capture the vessel first of all, which could be done very easily and with no danger whatever, and after that we could go for Zoraida. We all agreed with him, and so, without waiting any longer and with him as our guide, we went to the vessel, where he was the first to leap aboard. Laying a hand on his cutlass, he cried in the Moorish tongue. 'None of you stir from here or it will cost you your lives!'

"By this time nearly all the Christians were aboard; and the Moors, who were possessed of little courage, upon hearing their captain address them in this manner, were thoroughly terrified. None of them dared reach for his weapons, and for that matter, they had few if any; and so, without saying a word, they let themselves be shackled by the Christians, who accomplished this very quickly, threatening them that if they raised any kind of outcry they would all die by the knife.

"When this had been achieved, with half our number remaining behind to guard the prisoners, the rest of us, again with the renegade as our guide, made our way to Hadji Morato's garden; and it was our good fortune that, as we went to try the gate, it swung open as readily as if it had not been locked. We then, very quietly and saying nothing, went on to the house without our presence being discovered by anyone. Zoraida, fairest of the fair, was waiting for us at a window, and as soon as she heard the sound of people below, she asked in a low voice if we were *Nizarani*, that is to say, Christians. I answered in the affirmative, saying that she should come down. Recognizing me, she did not hesitate for a moment, but without a word she came down instantly and, opening the door, appeared there in the sight of all, so beautiful and so richly clad that I cannot possibly tell you how she looked.

"As soon as I saw her, I took one of her hands and began kissing it, and the renegade and my two comrades did the same, while the others, being unacquainted with the circumstances, followed our example, since it seemed to them that we were merely recognizing and thanking her as the lady who was responsible for our going free. The renegade asked in Moorish if her father was in the house, and she replied that he was sleeping.

" 'Then it will be necessary to wake him,' he said, 'for we must take him with us and everything of value that there is in this beautiful summer place.'

"'No,' she answered, 'you must by no means lay hands on my father. In this house there is nothing for you save that which I bring with me, and it is enough to make you all rich and happy. Wait a moment and you will see.'

"She then went back into the house, saying she would return at once and bidding us meanwhile not to make any noise. I took this opportunity of asking the renegade what had passed between them, and when he told me, I made it clear to him that under no condition was he to go beyond Zoraida's wishes. She now reappeared with a small trunk filled with gold crowns, so heavy that she could hardly carry it. At that instant, unfortunately, her father awoke and, hearing a noise in the garden, came to the window and looked out. Recognizing us all as Christians, he began bawling at the top of his lungs in Arabic, 'Christians! Christians! Thieves! Thieves!' This frightened us very much and threw us into confusion; but the renegade, perceiving the danger we were in and how important it was to go through with our undertaking before being detected, ran up as fast as he could to where Hadji Morato was, being accompanied by some of the rest of us. As for myself I did not dare leave Zoraida unprotected, for she, half fainting, had fallen in my arms.

"In brief, those who went up handled the matter so expeditiously that in a moment they were back, bringing with them Hadji Morato, his hands bound and with a napkin over his mouth so that he could not speak a word—and they threatened him that if he tried to speak it would cost him his life. When his daughter saw him, she put her hands over her eyes, and her father in turn was horrified at sight of her, not knowing that she had placed herself in our hands of her own free will. But it was essential now for us to be on our way, and so we hastily but with due care boarded the ship, where those that we had left behind were waiting for us, fearful that some untoward accident had befallen us.

"It was a little after two in the morning by the time we were all on the vessel. They then untied Hadji Morato's hands and removed the napkin from his mouth, but the renegade again warned him not to say anything or they would kill him. As the old man looked at his daughter, he began sighing mournfully, especially when he saw her held tightly in my embrace, and when he observed that she did not struggle, protest, or attempt to escape me; but he nonetheless remained silent lest they carry out the renegade's threat.

"Finding herself on the boat now and perceiving that we were about to row away while her father and the other Moors remained bound, Zoraida spoke to the renegade, requesting him to do her the favor of releasing the prisoners, particularly her father, as she would rather cast herself into the sea than have a parent who loved her so dearly carried away captive in front of her eyes and through her fault. The renegade repeated to me what she had said, and, for my part, I was quite willing. He, however, replied that this was not the wise thing to do, for the reason that, if they were left behind, they would alarm the entire city and countryside, whereupon some fast-sailing craft would put out in pursuit of us and so comb the sea and land that there would be no possibility of our escaping. What we might do, he added, was to give them their freedom as soon as we set foot on Christian soil. We all agreed to this, and when the matter was explained to Zoraida, along with the reasons why we could not comply with her wishes, she also was satisfied. And then, gladly and silently, cheerfully and with alacrity, each one of our powerful rowers took up his oar, as, commending ourselves with all our hearts to God, we set out on our voyage to the island of Majorca, which is the nearest Christian territory.

"However, inasmuch as the tramontane wind was blowing a little and the sea was a bit rough, it was impossible for us to follow the route to Majorca, and we were compelled to hug the coast in the direction of Oran. This worried us considerably, for we feared that we would be discovered from the town of Shershel, which is about seventy miles from Algiers. And we also were afraid that we might encounter in those waters one of the galiots that commonly ply the coast with merchandise of Tetuán, although each of us secretly felt that if we did meet with a merchant vessel of that sort, providing it was not a cruiser, we not only should not be captured but, rather, should be able to come into possession of a craft in which we could more safely complete our voyage. In the meantime, as we were sailing along, Zoraida buried her face in my hands in order not to see her father, and I could hear her calling on Lela Marien to come to our aid.

"We must have gone a good thirty miles when dawn came, and we found ourselves at a distance of something like three musket shots off land. The shore was deserted, and we saw no one who might descry us, but, nevertheless, by rowing as hard as we could we put out a little more to the open sea, which was now somewhat calmer. When we were about two leagues from the coast, the order was given to row by turns so that we could have a bite to eat, the ship being well stocked with food; but those at the oars said it was not yet time for them to take a rest—the others might eat, but they themselves did not wish on any account to relax their efforts. We were starting to do as they had suggested when a strong wind came up, which obliged us to leave off rowing and set sail at once for Oran, that being the only course left us. All this was done very quickly, and with the sail we made more than eight miles an hour, with no fear other than that of falling in with a vessel that was out cruising.

"We gave the Moorish rowers some food, and the renegade consoled them by telling them they were not captives but would be given their freedom at the first opportunity. He said the same to Zoraida's father, who replied, 'If you promised me anything else, O Christian, I might believe it and hope for it by reason of the generous treatment you have accorded me, but when it comes to setting me free, do not think that I am so simple-minded as to put any credence in that; for you would never have incurred the risk of depriving me of my liberty only to restore it to me so freely, especially since you know who I am and the profit you may derive from releasing me. Indeed, if you wish to name the sum, I hereby offer you whatever you ask for me and for this unfortunate daughter of mine, or for her alone, for she is the greater and better part of my soul.'

"As he said this, he began weeping so bitterly that we were all moved to compassion, and Zoraida could not resist stealing a glance at him. When she saw him weeping, she was so touched that she rose from my feet and went over to embrace him, and as she laid her cheek against his the two of them shed so many tears that a number of us could not but join them in their weeping. But when her father perceived that she was in festive attire and decked out in all her jewels, he spoke to her in their own language.

" 'How does it come, my daughter,' he said, 'that last night, at dusk, before this terrible thing happened to us, I saw you clad in ordinary household garb; and now, without your having had time to dress, and without my having brought you any good news to celebrate by thus adorning and bedecking your person, I nonetheless behold you wearing the best garments with which I was able to provide you when fortune smiled upon us? Answer me this, for I am even more astonished and bewildered by it than I am by this misfortune that has come to us.'

"The renegade informed us of all that the Moor had said to his daughter, who did not utter a word in reply. And when the old man saw, over at one side of the boat, the small trunk in which she was in the habit of keeping her jewels, he was more bewildered than ever; for he knew very well that he had not brought it to the summer place but had left it in Algiers. He thereupon asked her how the trunk had come into our hands and what was inside it; and then the renegade, without giving Zoraida time to answer, spoke up.

" 'You need not trouble, sir, to ask your daughter Zoraida so many questions, for I can give you one answer that will serve for all. I would have you know that she is a Christian, and that it is she who has filed our chains for us and set us free from our captivity. She goes of her own free will and, I fancy, is as happy about it as one who emerges from darkness into light, from death into life, or from the pains of hell into glory everlasting.'

" 'Is it true, my daughter, what this man says?' asked the Moor.

" 'It is,' said Zoraida.

" 'So you are a Christian,' said the old man, 'and it is you who have placed your father in the hands of his enemies?'

" 'As to my being a Christian,' she told him, 'that is true enough, but it is not true that I am responsible for your being in this situation; for I never had any desire to leave you or to do you harm, but only to do good to myself.'

" 'And what good have you done yourself, daughter?'

" 'Put that question,' she said, 'to Lela Marien, for she can tell you better than I.'

"No sooner had he heard this than the Moor, with an incredibly swift movement, hurled himself head foremost into the sea; and he would undoubtedly have drowned if the long and cumbersome robe that he wore had not tended to bear him up. Zoraida screamed for someone to rescue him, whereupon we all ran forward and, seizing him by his robe, hauled him in, half drowned and unconscious, at which his daughter was so distressed that she wept over him as bitterly and mournfully as if he were already dead. We turned him face downward and he disgorged much water, and after a couple of hours he was himself once more.

"Meanwhile, the wind had changed and we had to make for land, exerting all our strength at the oars in order not to be driven ashore. Luck was with us, and we were able to put into a cove alongside a promontory or cape which the Moors call *Cava Rumia,* signifying in our language 'the wicked Christian woman'; for it is a tradition among them that La Cava, through whom Spain was lost, is buried in that spot, '*cava*' in their tongue meaning 'bad woman,' while '*rumia*' is 'Christian.' They regard it as bad luck to be compelled to drop anchor there, and they never do so unless it is absolutely necessary. But for us it was not the 'bad woman's' shelter; rather, it was a haven in distress, as the sea was now raging.

"Stationing our sentinels on land and never once relinquishing the oars, we ate what the renegade had provided and prayed to God and Our Lady with all our hearts that they would favor and aid us in order that we might bring to a happy conclusion an undertaking that had begun so propitiously. Upon Zoraida's request, the order was given to set her father and all the other Moors ashore, for her tender heart could not bear to see her father thus bound and her fellow countrymen held prisoners in front of her very eyes. We promised her that this should be done as soon as it came time for us to depart; for we ran no risk by leaving them in this deserted place. Our prayers were not in vain; for, Heaven favoring us, the wind changed and the sea grew calm, inviting us to resume with cheerful hearts the voyage that we had begun.

"We then unbound the Moors and, one by one, set them on land, at which they were greatly astonished; but when it came to disembarking Zoraida's father, who had by now completely recovered his senses, he gave us a piece of his mind.

" 'Why do you think, Christians,' he said, 'that this wicked female is happy at your giving me my liberty? Do you imagine that it is out of filial affection? Assuredly not. It is only because my presence is an impediment to the carrying out of her base designs. And do not think that what has led her to change her religion is a belief that yours is better than ours; it is because she knows that in your country immodesty is more freely practiced than in ours.'

"As her father spoke, another Christian and I held Zoraida's arms that she might not be tempted to some foolish act. The old man now turned upon her.

" 'O infamous and ill-advised maiden! Where do you think you are going, so blindly and foolishly, with these dogs, our natural enemies? Cursed be the hour in which I begot you, and cursed all the luxury in which I have reared you!'

"Seeing that he was likely to go on in this way for some while, I hastened to put him ashore; and from there he kept on shouting at us, pursuing us with his curses and lamentations as he implored Mohammed to pray to Allah that we be destroyed, confounded, and brought to an end. And when, having set sail, we could no longer hear his words, we could still see his gestures, could see him plucking out his beard, tearing his hair, and rolling on the ground. At one point he raised his voice to such a pitch that we could make out what he said.

" 'Return, my beloved daughter, return to land, and I will forgive you everything. Give those men the money that is yours and come back to comfort your brokenhearted father, who, if you leave him now, will leave his bones on these deserted sands.'

"Zoraida heard all this and was deeply grieved by it. Weeping, she could only say to him in reply, 'O my father, may it please Allah that Lela Marien, who has been the cause of my turning Christian, console you in your sorrow! Allah well knows that I could have done nothing other than what I did. These Christians are in no wise to blame, for even had I not wished to come with them, even had I chosen to remain at home, it would have been impossible, so eagerly did my soul urge me to do that which to me seems as good, my dear father, as it seems evil to you.'

"When she said this, her father could no longer hear her, for we had lost him from view; and so, while I comforted Zoraida, we all of us turned our attention to the voyage, as we now had a wind so favorable that we firmly expected to be off the coast of Spain by dawn the next day.

"Blessings, however, are almost never unmixed with some evil that, without our having foreseen it, comes to disturb them. It may have been simply our misfortune, or it may have been those curses that the Moor had heaped upon his daughter (for a curse of that kind is always to be dreaded, whatever the father may be like), but, in any event, our luck now changed. We were on the high seas, and the night was a little more than three hours gone. We were proceeding at full sail with the oars lashed, since the wind had relieved us of the necessity of using them, when by the light of the moon, which was shining brightly, we sighted alongside us a square-rigged vessel with all sails set that was luffing a little and standing across our course. It was so close upon us that we had to strike sail in order not to run foul of her, while they swung their prow about to give us room to pass.

"They now came to the ship's rail to ask us who we were, from where we came, and where we were going. When these questions were put to us in French, our renegade said, 'Let no one answer, for they are undoubtedly French pirates who plunder everything in sight.' As a result of this warning, no one said a word in reply. We were a little ahead, and the other vessel was lying to leeward, when suddenly they fired two pieces of artillery, both of them, as it seemed, loaded with chain-shot; for with one they cut our mast in half and brought both mast and sail down into the sea, while the other cannon, discharged at the same moment, sent a shot into the middle of our craft, laying it wide open but doing no further damage to it. As we saw ourselves sinking, we began crying out for help, imploring those on the other ship to come to our aid as we were filling with water. They then struck their own sails, and lowering a skiff or boat, as many as a dozen Frenchmen, all well armed, with matchlocks and matches lighted, came alongside us. When they saw how few we were and how our craft was going down, they took us in, telling us that this had come about through our discourtesy in not answering them.

"Our renegade, then, without anyone's seeing what he did, took the trunk containing Zoraida's wealth and dumped it into the sea. To make a long story short, we all went aboard with the Frenchmen, who, after they had learned everything they wished to know about us, proceeded to despoil us of all that we possessed as if we had been their deadly enemies. They even took Zoraida's anklets, but this did not grieve me as much as it did her. What I feared more was that, having deprived her of her exceedingly rich and precious gems, they would go on to steal that jewel that was worth more than all the others and which she most esteemed. Their desires, however, did not go beyond money, in which regard they were insatiable in their covetousness. They would even have taken the garments their captives wore if these had been of any use to them. Some of them were for wrapping us all in a sail and tossing us into the sea; for it was their intention, by passing themselves off as Bretons, to put in at certain Spanish ports, and if they brought us in alive they would be punished when the theft was discovered.

"But the captain, who was the one who had despoiled my beloved Zoraida, said that he was content with the prize that he had and did not wish to stop at any port in Spain. Instead, he preferred to slip through the Strait of Gibraltar at night, or any way he could, and go on to La Rochelle, the port from which he had put out. Accordingly, they agreed to let us take their small boat and all that we needed for the brief voyage that remained for us. This they did the next day, within sight of the Spanish coast, a sight that caused us wholly to forget all our sufferings and hardships, which were as if they had never been, so great is the joy that comes from recovering one's lost freedom.

"It may have been around midday when they put us in the boat, giving us two kegs of water and some biscuit. And as the lovely Zoraida went to embark, the captain, moved by some sympathetic impulse or other, gave her as many as twenty gold crowns and would not permit his men to take from her those same garments that she is now wearing. As we entered the small boat, we thanked them for their kindness, our manner being one of gratitude rather than indignation, and they then put out to sea, making for the Strait, while we, needing no other compass than the land that lay ahead of us, bent to the oars so lustily that by sundown we were, as we thought, near enough to be able to reach it before the night was far gone.

"But as there was no moon and the sky was darkened over and we were ignorant of our exact whereabouts, it did not seem wise to attempt a landing, although many of us thought that we should do so, saying that it would be better to run ashore even if it were on some rocks, far from any inhabited place, since in that way we would assure ourselves against the very likely danger of Tetuán corsairs, who at night are in Barbary and by morning off the coast of Spain, where they commonly take some prize and then return to sleep in their own houses. There were a number of conflicting suggestions, but the one that was finally adopted was that we should gradually draw near the shore and, if the sea was calm enough to permit it, land wherever we were able.

"This was the plan followed, and shortly before midnight we came to the foot of an enormous and very high mountain that was not so near the sea but that it afforded a convenient space for a landing. We ran up on the sand and leaped ashore, kissing the ground on which we stood and shedding many joyful tears as we gave thanks to God, Our Lord, for the incomparable blessing that He had conferred upon us. Removing the provisions from the boat, we drew it ashore and then went a long way up the mountain; for even here we could not feel in our hearts or bring ourselves to believe that the land beneath our feet was Christian soil. The sun, it seemed to me, came up more slowly than we could have wished, and in the meanwhile we had climbed the entire mountainside in an effort to see if we could discover any village or even a few shepherds' huts; but however much we strained our eyes, we were able to descry no village, no human being, no path, no road.

"Nevertheless, we determined to keep on and go farther inland, since surely we could not fail to come upon someone who could give us our bearings. What distressed me more than anything else was seeing Zoraida go on foot over this rough country; for though I once tried carrying her on my shoulders, my weariness wearied her more than she was rested by her repose, and so she would not again consent to my making the exertion but went along very cheerfully and patiently, her hand in mine. We had gone, I imagine, a little less than a quarter of a league when there reached our ears the sound of a little bell, which showed plainly that we must be near some flock or herd, and as we all gazed about us attentively to see if we could discern any, we saw at the foot of a cork tree a young shepherd who very calmly and unconcernedly was engaged in whittling a stick with his knife.

"We called to him, and he, raising his head, got to his feet very nimbly. As we afterward learned, the first persons that he caught sight of among us were the renegade and Zoraida, and seeing them in Moorish costume, he thought that all Barbary must have descended upon him. Dashing with amazing swiftness into a near-by wood, he began raising a terrible din as he shouted, 'Moors! Moors! The Moors have landed! Moors! Moors! To arms! To arms!'

"We were quite perplexed by all this, not knowing what to do; but, reflecting that the shepherd's cries would arouse the countryside and that the mounted coast guard would soon be along to find out what the trouble was, we decided that the renegade should take off his Turkish clothes and put on a captive's jacket, which one of us now gave him though he himself was left with only his shirt. And then, commending ourselves to God, we proceeded along the same path that the shepherd had taken, expecting that the guard would be upon us at any moment. In this we were not wrong, for two hours had not gone by when, as we were coming out of a thicket onto a plain, we caught sight of all of fifty horsemen coming toward us at top speed.

"As soon as we saw them, we stopped and watched them, and they, when they came up and found, in place of the Moors they were seeking, a handful of poor Christians, were very much surprised. One of them asked if it was we who had caused the shepherd to sound the call to arms. 'Yes,' I replied, and was about to go on and tell him our story, who we were and from whence we came, when one of our number happened to recognize the horseman who had put the question and, without giving me a chance to reply, spoke up and said, 'Thanks be to God, sirs, for having brought us into such good hands; for unless I am mistaken, this region where we now are is in the neighborhood of Vélez Málaga—unless all the years of my captivity have so deprived me of my memory that I cannot recall that you, sir, who have just asked us our names, are Pedro de Bustamente, my uncle.'

"The Christian captive had no sooner said this than the horseman dismounted and came up to embrace the young fellow. 'My dearest nephew!' he cried. 'I recognize you now. I and my sister—your mother—and all your relatives who are still alive have wept for you as dead, and now it appears that God has been pleased to prolong their lives that they might have the pleasure of seeing you again. We had heard that you were in Algiers, but from the look of your garments and those of all this company I realize that you have been miraculously liberated.'

"'That,' replied the young man, 'is the truth, and there will be time to tell you all about it.'

"As soon as the guardsmen realized that we were Christian captives, they dismounted, and each then offered us his own horse to carry us to the city of Vélez Málaga, which was a league and a half from there. We told them where we had left the boat, and some of them went back to get it and take it to the town. Others mounted behind us on the cruppers, Zoraida going with the young man's uncle.

"The entire town came out to receive us, for someone had ridden ahead and told them of our coming. They were not the kind of folk to be astonished at seeing captives free or Moors held prisoner, being quite accustomed to such a sight. What they rather marveled at was Zoraida's beauty. Despite the fact that she was weary from the journey, she looked her loveliest at that moment, so joyful was she at finding herself on Christian soil with nothing to fear any longer. Happiness had put so much color into her face that—unless it can be that my love for her deceived me—I shall venture to say that there never was a more beautiful creature in all this world, none that I have ever seen, at any rate.

"We went directly to the church to thank God for his mercy; and as soon as Zoraida entered the portals, she remarked that there were faces there that resembled that of Lela Marien. We informed her that these were images of the Virgin, and the renegade to the best of his ability then went on to explain what their meaning was and how she might worship them as if each were the same Lela Marien who had spoken to her. Being possessed of a good, clear mind, she understood all this very readily. After that, they took us to various houses in the town, and the Christian who had come with us brought the renegade, Zoraida, and me to the home of his parents, who were people in moderately comfortable circumstances and who entertained us with as great a show of affection as they did their own son.

"We were in Vélez for six days, at the end of which time the renegade, having ascertained what he had to do, departed for Granada in order that, through the mediation of the Holy Inquisition, he might be restored to the sacred bosom of the Church. Each of the other liberated Christians went his own way, Zoraida and I being left with no other means than the crowns which the French captain had courteously given her. With them I purchased the beast on which she now rides; and with me serving her up to now as father and squire, not as husband, we are at present on our way to see if my own father is still alive or if one of my brothers has prospered to a greater extent than I.

"Seeing that Heaven has seen fit to give her to me as my companion, I can imagine no other fortune, however good, that might come to me which I should hold to be of greater worth. The patience with which she endures the hardships that poverty brings with it, and her desire to become a Christian, are such as to fill me with admiration and induce me to serve her all my life long. My happiness, however, at knowing that I am hers and she is mine is marred by the fact that I am at a loss where to find a nook in my own country in which to shelter her. For it may be that time and death have wrought such changes in the life and fortunes of my father and my brothers that, if they should not be there, I shall hardly find anyone who is acquainted with me.

"Gentle folk, that is all there is to my story. As to whether it be a pleasing and a curious one, that is for you in your good judgment to decide. For my own part, I may say that I should like to have told it more briefly, although, as it is, the fear of tiring you has led me to omit a number of incidents."

Muriel Spark

YOU SHOULD HAVE SEEN THE MESS

I AM NOW more than glad that I did not pass into the Grammar School five years ago, although it was a disappointment at the time. I was always good at English, but not so good at the other subjects!!

I am glad that I went to the Secondary Modern School, because it was only constructed the year before. Therefore, it was much more hygienic than the Grammar School. The Secondary Modern was light and airy, and the walls were painted with a bright, washable, gloss. One day, I was sent over to the Grammar School, with a note for one of the teachers, and you should have seen the mess! The corridors were dusty, and I saw dust on the window ledges, which were chipped. I saw into one of the classrooms. It was very untidy in there.

I am also glad that I did not go to the Grammar School, because of what it does to one's habits. This may appear to be a strange remark, at first sight. It is a good thing to have an education behind you, and I do not believe in ignorance, but I have had certain experiences, with educated people, since going out into the world.

I am seventeen years of age, and left school two years ago last month. I had my A certificate for typing, so got my first job, as a junior, in a solicitor's office. Mum was pleased at this, and Dad said it was a first-class start, as it was an old established firm. I must say that when I went for the interview, I was surprised at the windows, and the stairs up to the offices were also far from clean. There was a little waiting room, where some of the elements were missing from the gas fire, and the carpet on the floor was worn. However, Mr. Heygate's office, into which I was shown for the interview, was better. The furniture was old, but it was polished, and there was a good carpet, I will say that. The glass of the bookcase was very clean.

I was to start on the Monday, so along I went. They took me to the general office, where there were two senior shorthand-typists, and a clerk, Mr. Gresham, who was far from smart in appearance. You should have seen the mess!! There was no floor covering whatsoever, and so dusty everywhere. There were shelves all round the room, with old box files on them. The box files were falling to pieces, and all the old papers inside them were crumpled. The worst shock of all was the tea cups. It was my duty to make tea, mornings and afternoons. Miss Bewlay showed me where everything was kept. It was kept in an old orange box, and the cups were all cracked. There were not enough

---

saucers to go round, etc. I will not go into the facilities, but they were also far from hygienic. After three days, I told Mum, and she was upset, most of all about the cracked cups. We never keep a cracked cup, but throw it out, because those cracks can harbour germs. So Mum gave me my own cup to take to the office.

Then at the end of the week, when I got my salary, Mr. Heygate said, "Well, Lorna, what are you going to do with your first pay?" I did not like him saying this, and I nearly passed a comment, but I said, "I don't know." He said, "What do you do in the evenings, Lorna? Do you watch Telly?" I did take this as an insult, because we call it TV, and his remark made me out to be uneducated. I just stood, and did not answer, and he looked surprised. Next day, Saturday, I told Mum and Dad about the facilities, and we decided I should not go back to that job. Also, the desks in the general office were rickety. Dad was indignant, because Mr. Heygate's concern was flourishing, and he had letters after his name.

Everyone admires our flat, because Mum keeps it spotless, and Dad keeps doing things to it. He had done it up all over, and got permission from the Council to re-modernise the kitchen. I well recall the Health Visitor, remarking to Mum, "You could eat off your floor, Mrs. Merrifield." It is true that you could eat your lunch off Mum's floors, and any hour of the day or night you will find every corner spick and span.

Next, I was sent by the agency to a Publisher's for an interview, because of being good at English. One look was enough!! My next interview was a success, and I am still at Low's Chemical Co. It is a modern block, with a quarter of an hour rest period, morning and afternoon. Mr. Marwood is very smart in appearance. He is well spoken, although he has not got a university education behind him. There is special lighting over the desks, and the typewriters are latest models.

So I am happy at Low's. But I have met other people, of an educated type, in the past year, and it has opened my eyes. It so happened that I had to go to the Doctor's house, to fetch a prescription for my young brother, Trevor, when the epidemic was on. I rang the bell, and Mrs. Darby came to the door. She was small, with fair hair, but too long, and a green maternity dress. But she was very nice to me. I had to wait in their living-room, and you should have seen the state it was in! There were broken toys on the carpet, and the ash trays were full up. There were contemporary pictures on the walls, but the furniture was not contemporary, but old-fashioned, with covers which were past standing up to another wash, I should say. To cut a long story short, Dr. Darby and Mrs. Darby have always been very kind to me, and they meant everything for the best. Dr. Darby is also short and fair, and they have three children, a girl and a boy, and now a baby boy.

When I went that day for the prescription, Dr. Darby said to me, "You look pale, Lorna. It's the London atmosphere. Come on a picnic with us, in the car, on Saturday." After that I went with the Darbys more and more. I liked them, but I did not like the mess, and it was a surprise. But I also kept in with them for the opportunity of meeting people, and Mum and Dad were pleased that I had made nice friends. So I did not say anything about the cracked lino, and the paintwork all chipped. The children's clothes were very shabby for a Doctor, and she changed them out of their school clothes when they came home from school, into those worn-out garments. Mum always kept us spotless to go out to play, and I do not like to say it, but those Darby children frequently looked like the Leary family, which the Council evicted from our block, as they were far from houseproud.

One day, when I was there, Mavis (as I called Mrs. Darby by then) put her head out of the window, and shouted to the boy, "John, stop peeing over the cabbages at once. Pee on the lawn." I did not know which way to look. Mum would never say a word like that from the window, and I know for a fact that Trevor would never pass water outside, not even bathing in the sea.

I went there usually at the weekends, but sometimes on weekdays, after supper. They had an idea to make a match for me with a chemist's assistant, whom they had taken up too. He was an orphan, and I do not say there was anything wrong with that. But he was not accustomed to those little extras that I was. He was a good-looking boy, I will say that. So I went once to a dance, and twice to the films with him. To look at, he was quite clean in appearance. But there was only hot water at the weekend at his place, and he said that a bath once a week was sufficient. Jim (as I called Dr. Darby by then) said it was sufficient also, and surprised me. He did not have much money, and I do not hold that against him. But there was no hurry for me, and I could wait for a man in a better position, so that I would not miss those little extras. So he started going out with a girl from the coffee bar, and did not come to the Darbys very much then.

There were plenty of boys at the office, but I will say this for the Darbys, they had lots of friends coming and going, and they had interesting conversation, although sometimes it gave me a surprise, and I did not know where to look. And sometimes they had people who were very down and out, although there is no need to be. But most of the guests were different, so it made a comparison with the boys at the office, who were not so educated in their conversation.

Now it was near the time for Mavis to have her baby, and I was to come in at the weekend, to keep an eye on the children, while the help had her day off. Mavis did not go away to have her baby, but would have it at home, in their double bed, as they did not have twin beds, although he was a Doctor. A girl I knew, in our block, was engaged, but was let down, and even she had her baby in the labour ward. I was sure the bedroom was not hygienic for having a baby, but I did not mention it.

One day, after the baby boy came along, they took me in the car to the country, to see Jim's mother. The baby was put in a carry-cot at the back of the car. He began to cry, and without a word of a lie, Jim said to him over his shoulder, 'Oh shut your gob, you little bastard.' I did not know what to do, and Mavis was smoking a cigarette. Dad would not dream of saying such a thing to Trevor or I. When we arrived at Jim's mother's place, Jim said, "It's a fourteenth-century cottage, Lorna." I could well believe it. It was very cracked and old, and it made one wonder how Jim could let his old mother live in this tumble-down cottage, as he was so good to everyone else. So Mavis knocked at the door, and the old lady came. There was not much anyone could do to the inside. Mavis said, "Isn't it charming, Lorna?" If that was a joke, it was going too far. I said to the old Mrs. Darby, "Are you going to be re-housed?" but she did not understand this, and I explained how you have to apply to the Council, and keep at them. But it was funny that the Council had not done something already, when they go round condemning. Then old Mrs. Darby said, "My dear, I shall be re-housed in the Grave." I did not know where to look.

There was a carpet hanging on the wall, which I think was there to hide a damp spot. She had a good TV set, I will say that. But some of the walls were bare brick, and the facilities were outside, through the garden. The furniture was far from new.

One Saturday afternoon, as I happened to go to the Darbys, they were just going off to a film, and they took me too. It was the Curzon, and afterwards we went to a flat in Curzon Street. It was a very clean block, I will say that, and there were good carpets at the entrance. The couple there had contemporary furniture, and they also spoke about music. It was a nice place, but there was no Welfare Centre to the flats, where people could go for social intercourse, advice and guidance. But they were well-spoken, and I met Willy Morley, who was an artist. Willy sat beside me, and we had a drink. He was young, dark, with a dark shirt, so one could not see right away if he was clean. Soon after this, Jim said to me, "Willy wants to paint you, Lorna. But you'd better ask your Mum." Mum said it was all right if he was a friend of the Darbys.

I can honestly say that Willy's place was the most unhygienic place

I have seen in my life. He said I had an unusual type of beauty, which he must capture. This was when we came back to his place from the restaurant. The light was very dim, but I could see the bed had not been made, and the sheets were far from clean. He said he must paint me, but I told Mavis I did not like to go back there. "Don't you like Willy?" she asked. I could not deny that I liked Willy, in a way. There was something about him, I will say that. Mavis said, "I hope he hasn't been making a pass at you, Lorna." I said he had not done so, which was almost true, because he did not attempt to go to the full extent. It was always unhygienic when I went to Willy's place, and I told him so once, but he said, "Lorna, you are a joy." He had a nice way, and he took me out in his car, which was a good one, but dirty inside, like his place. Jim said one day, "He has pots of money, Lorna," and Mavis said, "You might make a man of him, as he is keen on you." They always said Willy came from a good family.

But I saw that one could not do anything with him. He would not change his shirt very often, or get clothes, but he went round like a tramp, lending people money, as I have seen with my own eyes. His place was in a terrible mess, with the empty bottles, and laundry in the corner. He gave me several gifts over the period, which I took, as he would have only given them away, but he never tried to go to the full extent. He never painted my portrait, as he was painting fruit on a table all that time, and they said his pictures were marvellous, and thought Willy and I were getting married.

One night, when I went home, I was upset as usual, after Willy's place. Mum and Dad had gone to bed, and I looked round our kitchen which is done in primrose and white. Then I went into the living-room, where Dad has done one wall in a patterned paper, deep rose and white, and the other walls pale rose, with white wood-work. The suite is new, and Mum keeps everything beautiful. So it came to me, all of a sudden, what a fool I was, going with Willy. I agree to equality, but as to me marrying Willy, as I said to Mavis, when I recall his place, and the good carpet gone greasy, not to mention the paint oozing out of the tubes, I think it would break my heart to sink so low.

Katherine Anne Porter

FLOWERING JUDAS

BRAGGIONI sits heaped upon the edge of a straight-backed chair much too small for him, and sings to Laura in a furry, mournful voice. Laura has begun to find reasons for avoiding her own house until the latest possible moment, for Braggioni is there almost every night. No matter how late she is, he will be sitting there with a surly, waiting expression, pulling at his kinky yellow hair, thumbing the strings of his guitar, snarling a tune under his breath. Lupe the Indian maid meets Laura at the door, and says with a flicker of a glance towards the upper room, "He waits."

Laura wishes to lie down, she is tired of her hairpins and the feel of her long tight sleeves, but she says to him, "Have you a new song for me this evening?" If he says yes, she asks him to sing it. If he says no, she remembers his favorite one, and asks him to sing it again. Lupe brings her a cup of chocolate and plate of rice, and Laura eats at the small table under the lamp, first inviting Braggioni, whose answer is always the same: "I have eaten, and besides, chocolate thickens the voice."

Laura says, "Sing, then," and Braggioni heaves himself into song. He scratches the guitar familiarly as though it were a pet animal, and sings passionately off key, taking the high notes in a prolonged painful squeal. Laura, who haunts the markets listening to the ballad singers, and stops every day to hear the blind boy playing his reed-flute in Sixteenth of September Street, listens to Braggioni with pitiless courtesy, because she dares not smile at his miserable performance. Nobody dares to smile at him. Braggioni is cruel to everyone, with a kind of specialized insolence, but he is so vain of his talents, and so sensitive to slights, it would require a cruelty and vanity greater than his own to lay a finger on the vast cureless wound of his self-esteem. It would require courage, too, for it is dangerous to offend him, and nobody has this courage.

Braggioni loves himself with such tenderness and amplitude and eternal charity that his followers—for he is a leader of men, a skilled revolutionist, and his skin has been punctured in honorable warfare—warm themselves in the reflected glow, and say to each other: "He has a real nobility, a love of humanity raised above mere personal affections." The excess of this self-love has flowed out, inconveniently for her, over Laura, who, with so many others, owes her comfortable situation and her salary to him. When he is in a very good humor, he tells her, "I am tempted to forgive you for being a *gringa, Gringita!*"[1] and Laura, burning, imagines herself leaning forward suddenly, and with a sound back-handed slap wiping the suety smile from his face. If he notices her eyes at these moments he gives no sign.

She knows what Braggioni would offer her, and she must resist tenaciously without appearing to resist, and if she could avoid it she would not admit even to herself the slow drift of his intention. During these long evenings which have spoiled a long month for her, she sits in her deep chair with an open book on her knees, resting her eyes on the consoling rigidity of the printed page when the sight and sound of Braggioni singing threaten to identify themselves with all her remembered afflictions and to add their weight to her uneasy premonitions of the future. The gluttonous bulk of Braggioni has become a symbol of her many disillusions, for a revolutionist should be lean, animated by heroic faith, a vessel of abstract virtues. This is nonsense, she knows it now and is ashamed of it. Revolution must have leaders, and leadership is a career for energetic men. She is, her comrades tell her, full of romantic error, for what she defines as cynicism in them is merely "a developed sense of reality." She is almost too willing to say, "I am wrong, I suppose I don't really understand the principles," and afterward she makes a secret truce with herself, determined not to surrender her will to such expedient logic. But she cannot help feeling that she has been betrayed irreparably by the disunion between her way of living and her feeling of what life should be, and at times she is almost contented to rest in this sense of grievance as a private store of consolation. Sometimes she wishes to run away, but she stays. Now she longs to fly out of this room, down the narrow stairs, and into the street where the houses lean together like conspirators under a single mottled lamp, and leave Braggioni singing to himself.

Instead she looks at Braggioni, frankly and clearly, like a good child who understands the rules of behavior. Her knees cling together under sound blue serge, and her round white collar is not purposely nun-like. She wears the uniform of an idea, and has renounced vanities. She was born Roman Catholic, and in spite of her fear of being seen by someone who might make a scandal of it, she slips now and again into some crumbling little church, kneels on the chilly stone, and says a Hail Mary on the gold rosary she bought in Tehuantepec. It is no good and she ends by examining the altar with its tinsel flowers and ragged brocades, and feels tender about the battered doll-shape of some male saint whose white, lace-trimmed drawers hang limply around his ankles below the hieratic dignity of his velvet robe.

1 [Foreign woman; little foreign woman.]

She has encased herself in a set of principles derived from her early training, leaving no detail of gesture or of personal taste untouched, and for this reason she will not wear lace made on machines. This is her private heresy, for in her special group the machine is sacred, and will be the salvation of the workers. She loves fine lace, and there is a tiny edge of fluted cobweb on this collar, which is one of twenty precisely alike, folded in blue tissue paper in the upper drawer of her clothes chest.

Braggioni catches her glance solidly as if he had been waiting for it, leans forward, balancing his paunch between his spread knees, and sings with tremendous emphasis, weighing his words. He has, the song relates, no father and no mother, nor even a friend to console him; lonely as a wave of the sea he comes and goes, lonely as a wave. His mouth opens round and yearns sideways, his balloon cheeks grow oily with the labor of song. He bulges marvelously in his expensive garments. Over his lavender collar, crushed upon a purple necktie, held by a diamond hoop: over his ammunition belt of tooled leather worked in silver, buckled cruelly around his gasping middle: over the tops of his glossy yellow shoes Braggioni swells with ominous ripeness, his mauve silk hose stretched taut, his ankles bound with the stout leather thongs of his shoes.

When he stretches his eyelids at Laura she notes again that his eyes are the true tawny yellow cat's eyes. He is rich, not in money, he tells her, but in power, and this power brings with it the blameless ownership of things, and the right to indulge his love of small luxuries. "I have a taste for the elegant refinements," he said once, flourishing a yellow silk handkerchief before her nose. "Smell that? It is Jockey Club, imported from New York." Nonetheless he is wounded by life. He will say so presently. "It is true everything turns to dust in the hand, to gall on the tongue." He sighs and his leather belt creaks like a saddle girth. "I am disappointed in everything as it comes. Everything." He shakes his head. "You, poor thing, you will be disappointed too. You are born for it. We are more alike than you realize in some things. Wait and see. Some day you will remember what I have told you, you will know that Braggioni was your friend."

Laura feels a slow chill, a purely physical sense of danger, a warning in her blood that violence, mutilation, a shocking death, wait for her with lessening patience. She has translated this fear into something homely, immediate, and sometimes hesitates before crossing the street. "My personal fate is nothing, except as the testimony of a mental attitude," she reminds herself, quoting from some forgotten philosophical primer, and is sensible enough to add, "Anyhow, I shall not be killed by an automobile if I can help it."

"It may be true I am as corrupt, in another way, as Braggioni," she thinks in spite of herself, "as callous, as incomplete," and if this is so, any kind of death seems preferable. Still she sits quietly, she does not run. Where could she go? Uninvited she has promised herself to this place; she can no longer imagine herself as living in another country, and there is no pleasure in remembering her life before she came here.

Precisely what is the nature of this devotion, its true motives, and what are its obligations? Laura cannot say. She spends part of her days in Xochimilco, near by, teaching Indian children to say in English, "The cat is on the mat." When she appears in the classroom they crowd about her with smiles on their wise, innocent, clay-colored faces, crying, "Good morning, my titcher!" in immaculate voices, and they make of her desk a fresh garden of flowers every day.

During her leisure she goes to union meetings and listens to busy important voices quarreling over tactics, methods, internal politics. She visits the prisoners of her own political faith in their cells, where they entertain themselves with counting cockroaches, repenting of their indiscretions, composing their memoirs, writing out manifestoes and plans for their comrades who are still walking about free, hands in pockets, sniffing fresh air. Laura brings them food and cigarettes and a little money, and she brings messages disguised in equivocal phrases from the men outside who dare not set foot in the prison for fear of disappearing into the cells kept empty for them. If the prisoners confuse night and day, and complain, "Dear little Laura, time doesn't pass in this infernal hole, and I won't know when it is time to sleep unless I have a reminder," she brings them their favorite narcotics, and says in a tone that does not wound them with pity, "Tonight will really be night for you," and though her Spanish amuses them, they find her comforting, useful. If they lose patience and all faith, and curse the slowness of their friends in coming to their rescue with money and influence, they trust her not to repeat everything, and if she inquires, "Where do you think we can find money, or influence?" they are certain to answer, "Well, there is Braggioni, why doesn't he do something?"

She smuggles letters from headquarters to men hiding from firing squads in back streets in mildewed houses, where they sit in tumbled beds and talk bitterly as if all Mexico were at their heels, when Laura knows positively they might appear at the band concert in the Alameda on Sunday morning, and no one would notice them. But Braggioni says, "Let them sweat a little. The next time they may be careful. It is very restful to have them out of the way for a while." She is not afraid to knock on any door in any street after midnight, and enter in the darkness, and say to one of these men who is really in danger: "They will be looking for you—seriously—tomorrow morning after six. Here is some money from Vicente. Go to Vera Cruz and wait."

She borrows money from the Roumanian agitator to give to his bitter enemy the Polish agitator. The favor of Braggioni is their disputed territory, and Braggioni holds the balance nicely, for he can use them both. The Polish agitator talks love to her over café tables, hoping to exploit what he believes is her secret sentimental preference for him, and he gives her misinformation which he begs her to repeat as the solemn truth to certain persons. The Roumanian is more adroit. He is generous with his money in all good causes, and lies to her with an air of ingenuous candor, as if he were her good friend and confidant. She never repeats anything they may say. Braggioni never asks questions. He has other ways to discover all that he wishes to know about them.

Nobody touches her, but all praise her gray eyes, and the soft, round under lip which promises gayety, yet is always grave, nearly always firmly closed: and they cannot understand why she is in Mexico. She walks back and forth on her errands, with puzzled eyebrows, carrying her little folder of drawings and music and school papers. No dancer dances more beautifully than Laura walks, and she inspires some amusing, unexpected ardors, which cause little gossip, because nothing comes of them. A young captain who had been a soldier in Zapata's army attempted, during a horseback ride near Cuernavaca, to express his desire for her with the noble simplicity befitting a rude folk-hero: but gently, because he was gentle. This gentleness was his defeat, for when he alighted, and removed her foot from the stirrup, and essayed to draw her down into his arms, her horse, ordinarily a tame one, shied fiercely, reared and plunged away. The young hero's horse careered blindly after his stable-mate, and the hero did not return to the hotel until rather late that evening. At breakfast he came to her table in full charro dress, gray buckskin jacket and trousers with strings of silver buttons down the leg, and he was in a humorous, careless mood. "May I sit with you?" and "You are a wonderful rider. I was terrified that you might be thrown and dragged. I should never have forgiven myself. But I cannot admire you enough for your riding!"

"I learned to ride in Arizona," said Laura.

"If you will ride with me again this morning, I promise you a horse that will not shy with you," he said. But Laura remembered that she must return to Mexico City at noon.

Next morning the children made a celebration and spent their playtime writing on the blackboard, "We lov ar ticher," and with tinted chalks they drew wreaths of flowers around the words. The young hero wrote her a letter: "I am a very foolish, wasteful, impulsive man. I should have first said I love you, and then you would not have run away. But you shall see me again." Laura thought, "I must send him a box of colored crayons," but she was trying to forgive herself for having spurred her horse at the wrong moment.

A brown, shock-haired youth came and stood in her patio one night and sang like a lost soul for two hours, but Laura could think of nothing to do about it. The moonlight spread a wash of gauzy silver over the clear spaces of the garden, and the shadows were cobalt blue. The scarlet blossoms of the Judas tree were dull purple, and the names of the colors repeated themselves automatically in her mind, while she watched not the boy, but his shadow, fallen like a dark garment across the fountain rim, trailing in the water. Lupe came silently and whispered expert counsel in her ear: "If you will throw him one little flower, he will sing another song or two and go away." Laura threw the flower, and he sang a last song and went away with the flower tucked in the band of his hat. Lupe said, "He is one of the organizers of the Typographers Union, and before that he sold corridos in the Merced market, and before that, he came from Guanajuato, where I was born, I would not trust any man, but I trust least those from Guanajuato."

She did not tell Laura that he would be back again the next night, and the next, nor that he would follow her at a certain fixed distance around the Merced market, through the Zócolo, up Francisco I. Madero Avenue, and so along the Paseo de la Reforma to Chapultepec Park, and into the Philosopher's Footpath, still with that flower withering in his hat, and an indivisible attention in his eyes.

Now Laura is accustomed to him, it means nothing except that he is nineteen years old and is observing a convention with all propriety, as though it were founded on a law of nature, which in the end it might well prove to be. He is beginning to write poems which he prints on a wooden press, and he leaves them stuck like handbills in her door. She is pleasantly disturbed by the abstract, unhurried watchfulness of his black eyes which will in time turn easily towards another object. She tells herself that throwing the flower was a mistake, for she is twenty-two years old and knows better; but she refuses to regret it, and persuades herself that her negation of all external events as they occur is a sign that she is gradually perfecting herself in the stoicism she strives to cultivate against that disaster she fears, though she cannot name it.

She is not at home in the world. Every day she teaches children who remain strangers to her, though she loves their tender round hands and their charming opportunist savagery. She knocks at unfamiliar doors not knowing whether a friend or a stranger shall answer, and even if a known face emerges from the sour gloom of that unknown interior, still it is the face of a stranger. No matter what this stranger says to her, nor what her message to him, the very cells of her flesh reject knowledge and kinship in one monotonous word. No. No. No. She draws her strength from this one holy talismanic word which does not suffer her to be led into evil. Denying everything, she may walk anywhere in safety, she looks at everything without amazement.

No, repeats this firm unchanging voice of her blood; and she looks at Braggioni without amazement. He is a great man, he wishes to impress this simple girl who covers her great round breasts with thick dark cloth, and who hides long, invaluably beautiful legs under a heavy skirt. She is almost thin except for the incomprehensible fullness of her breasts, like a nursing mother's, and Braggioni, who considers himself a judge of women, speculates again on the puzzle of her notorious virginity, and takes the liberty of speech which she permits without a sign of modesty, indeed, without any sort of sign, which is disconcerting.

"You think you are so cold, *gringita!* Wait and see. You will surprise yourself some day! May I be there to advise you!" He stretches his eyelids at her, and his ill-humored cat's eyes waver in separate glance for the two points of light marking the opposite ends of a smoothly drawn path between the swollen curve of her breasts. He is not put off by that blue serge, nor by her resolutely fixed gaze. There is all the time in the world. His cheeks are bellying with the wind of song. "O girl with the dark eyes," he sings, and reconsiders. "But yours are not dark. I can change all that. O girl with the green eyes, you have stolen my heart away!" Then his mind wanders to the song, and Laura feels the weight of his attention being shifted elsewhere. Singing thus, he seems harmless, he is quite harmless, there is nothing to do but sit patiently and say "No," when the moment comes. She draws a full breath, and her mind wanders also, but not far. She dares not wander too far.

Not for nothing has Braggioni taken pains to be a good revolutionist and a professional lover of humanity. He will never die of it. He has the malice, the cleverness, the wickedness, the sharpness of wit, the hardness of heart, stipulated for loving the world profitably. *He will never die of it.* He will live to see himself kicked out from his feeding trough by other hungry world-saviors. Traditionally he must sing in spite of his life which drives him to bloodshed, he tells Laura, for his father was a Tuscany peasant who drifted to Yucatan and married a Maya woman: a woman of race, an aristocrat. They gave him the love and knowledge of music, thus: and under the rip of this thumbnail, the strings of the instrument complain like exposed nerves.

Once he was called Delgadito by all the girls and married women who ran after him; he was so scrawny all his bones showed under his thin cotton clothing, and he could squeeze his emptiness to the very backbone with his two hands. He was a poet and the revolution was only a dream then; too many women loved him and sapped away his youth, and he could never find enough to eat anywhere, anywhere! Now he is a leader of men, crafty men who whisper in his ear, hungry men who wait for hours outside his office for a word with him, emaciated men with wild faces who waylay him at the street gate with a timid, "Comrade, let me tell you . . ." and they blow the foul breath from their empty stomachs in his face.

He is always sympathetic. He gives them handfuls of small coins from his own pocket, he promises them work, there will be demonstrations, they must join the unions and attend the meetings, above all they must be on the watch for spies. They are closer to him than his own brothers, without them he can do nothing—until tomorrow, comrade!

Until tomorrow. "They are stupid, they are lazy, they are treacherous, they would cut my throat for nothing," he says to Laura. He has good food and abundant drink, he hires an automobile and drives in the Paseo on Sunday morning, and enjoys plenty of sleep in a soft bed beside a wife who dares not disturb him; and he sits pampering his bones in easy billows of fat, singing to Laura, who knows and thinks these things about him. When he was fifteen, he tried to drown himself because he loved a girl, his first love, and she laughed at him. "A thousand women have paid for that," and his tight little mouth turns down at the corners. Now he perfumes his hair with Jockey Club, and confides to Laura: "One woman is really as good as another for me, in the dark. I prefer them all."

His wife organizes unions among the girls in the cigarette factories, and walks in picket lines, and even speaks at meetings in the evening. But she cannot be brought to acknowledge the benefits of true liberty. "I tell her I must have my freedom, net. She does not understand my point of view." Laura has heard this many times. Braggioni scratches the guitar and meditates. "She is an instinctively virtuous woman, pure gold, no doubt of that. If she were not, I should lock her up, and she knows it."

His wife, who works so hard for the good of the factory girls, employs part of her leisure lying on the floor weeping because there are so many women in the world, and only one husband for her, and she never knows where nor when to look for him. He told her: "Unless you can learn to cry when I am not here, I must go away for good." That day he went away and took a room at the Hotel Madrid.

It is this month of separation for the sake of higher principles that has been spoiled not only for Mrs. Braggioni, whose sense of reality is beyond criticism, but for Laura, who feels herself bogged in a nightmare. Tonight Laura envies Mrs. Braggioni, who is alone, and free to weep as much as she pleases about a concrete wrong. Laura has just come from a visit to the prison, and she is waiting for tomorrow with a bitter anxiety as if tomorrow may not come, but time may be caught immovably in this hour, with herself transfixed, Braggioni singing on forever, and Eugenio's body not yet discovered by the guard.

Braggioni says: "Are you going to sleep?" Almost before she can shake her head, he begins telling her about the May-day disturbances coming on in Morelia, for the Catholics hold a festival in honor of the Blessed Virgin, and the Socialists celebrate their martyrs on that day. "There will be two independent processions, starting from either end of town, and they will march until they meet, and the rest depends . . ." He asks her to oil and load his pistols. Standing up, he unbuckles his ammunition belt, and spreads it laden across her knees. Laura sits with the shells slipping through the cleaning cloth dipped in oil, and he says again he cannot understand why she works so hard for the revolutionary idea unless she loves some man who is in it. "Are you not in love with someone?" "No," says Laura. "And no one is in love with you?" "No." "Then it is your own fault. No woman need go begging. Why, what is the matter with you? The legless beggar woman in the Alameda has a perfectly faithful lover. Did you know that?"

Laura peers down the pistol barrel and says nothing, but a long, slow faintness rises and subsides in her; Braggioni curves his swollen fingers around the throat of the guitar and softly smothers the music out of it, and when she hears him again he seems to have forgotten her, and is speaking in the hypnotic voice he uses when talking in small rooms to a listening, close-gathered crowd. Some day this world, now seemingly so composed and eternal, to the edges of every sea shall be merely a tangle of gaping trenches, of crashing walls and broken bodies. Everything must be torn from its accustomed place where it has rotted for centuries, hurled skyward and distributed, cast down again clean as rain, without separate identity. Nothing shall survive that the stiffened hands of poverty have created for the rich and no one shall be left alive except the elect spirits destined to procreate a new world cleansed of cruelty and injustice, ruled by benevolent anarchy: "Pistols are good, I love them, cannon are even better, but in the end I pin my faith to good dynamite," he concludes, and strokes the pistol lying in her hands. "Once I dreamed of destroying this city, in case it offered resistance to General Ortíz, but it fell into his hands like an overripe pear."

He is made restless by his own words, rises and stands waiting. Laura holds up the belt to him: "Put that on, and go kill somebody in Morelia, and you will be happier," she says softly. The presence of death in the room makes her bold. "Today, I found Eugenio going into a stupor. He refused to allow me to call the prison doctor. He had taken all the tablets I brought him yesterday. He said he took them because he was bored."

"He is a fool, and his death is his own business," says Braggioni, fastening his belt carefully.

"I told him if he had waited only a little while longer, you would have got him set free," says Laura. "He said he did not want to wait."

"He is a fool and we are well rid of him," says Braggioni, reaching for his hat.

He goes away. Laura knows his mood has changed, she will not see him any more for awhile. He will send word when he needs her to go on errands into strange streets, to speak to the strange faces that will appear, like clay masks with the power of human speech, to mutter their thanks to Braggioni for his help. Now she is free, and she thinks, I must run while there is time. But she does not go.

Braggioni enters his own house where for a month his wife has spent many hours every night weeping and tangling her hair upon her pillow. She is weeping now, and she weeps more at the sight of him, the cause of all her sorrows. He looks about the room. Nothing is changed, the smells are good and familiar, he is well acquainted with the woman who comes toward him with no reproach except grief on her face. He says to her tenderly: "You are so good, please don't cry any more, you dear good creature." She says, "Are you tired, my angel? Sit here and I will wash your feet." She brings a bowl of water, and kneeling, unlaces his shoes, and when from her knees she raises her sad eyes under her blackened lids, he is sorry for everything, and bursts into tears. "Ah, yes, I am hungry, I am tired, let us eat something together," he says, between sobs. His wife leans her head on his arm and says, "Forgive me!" and this time he is refreshed by the solemn, endless rain of her tears.

Laura takes off her serge dress and puts on a white linen nightgown and goes to bed. She turns her head a little to one side, and lying still, reminds herself that it is time to sleep. Numbers tick in her brain like little clocks, soundless doors close of themselves around her. If you would sleep, you must not remember anything, the children will say tomorrow, good morning, my teacher, the poor prisoners who come every day bringing flowers to their jailor. 1-2-3-4-5—it is monstrous to confuse love with revolution, night with day, life with death—ah, Eugenio!

The tolling of the midnight bell is a signal, but what does it mean? Get up, Laura, and follow me: come out of your sleep, out of your bed, out of this strange house. What are you doing in this house? Without a word, without fear she rose and reached for Eugenio's hand, but he eluded her with a sharp, sly smile and drifted away. This is not all, you shall see—Murderer, he said, follow me, I will show you a new country, but it is far away and we must hurry. No, said Laura, not unless you take my hand, no; and she clung first to the stair rail, and then to the topmost branch of the Judas tree that bent down slowly and set her upon the earth, and then to the rocky ledge of a cliff, and then to the jagged wave of a sea that was not water but a desert of crumbling stone. Where are you taking me, she asked in wonder but without fear. To death, and it is a long way off, and we must hurry, said Eugenio. No, said Laura, not unless you take my hand. Then eat these flowers, poor prisoner, said Eugenio in a voice of pity, take and eat: and from the Judas tree he stripped the warm bleeding flowers, and held them to her lips. She saw that his hand was fleshless, a cluster of small white petrified branches, and his eye sockets were without light, but she ate the flowers greedily for they satisfied both hunger and thirst. Murderer! said Eugenio, and Cannibal! This is my body and my blood. Laura cried No! and at the sound of her own voice, she awoke trembling, and was afraid to sleep again.

ESSAYS

C. M. Bowra

AENEAS: THE ROMAN HERO

VIRGIL was not the first to write the epic of Rome. In the third century B.C. Naevius had used the old Saturnian measure for his *Punic War* and in the next century Ennius' *Annals* traced the Roman story from Romulus to his own day. The first of these poems must have had many similarities to oral epic or even to ballad; the second, despite its use of the hexameter and many effective adaptations of the Homeric manner, was built on the annalistic plan which is always liable to appear when poetry annexes history. Virgil knew both works, and his own poem must have been meant to supersede them and to give in a more satisfactory form the truth about Rome as it had been revealed to his own generation. To do this he adopted a remarkable method. He abandoned the annalistic scheme and instead of versifying history presented the Roman character and destiny through a poem about a legendary and largely imaginary past. His concern was less with historical events than with their meaning, less with Rome at this or that time than as it was from the beginning and forever, less with individual Romans than with a single, symbolical hero who stands for the qualities and the experience which are typically Roman. By skilful literary devices, such as prophecies spoken by gods or visions seen in Elysium or scenes depicted on works of art, Virgil links up the mythical past with recorded history and his own time. But such excursions are exceptional and take up less than 300 lines in a total of nearly 10,000. The main action of the *Aeneid* takes place some three hundred years before the foundation of Rome; the leading hero and his followers are not Romans nor even Italians but Trojans whose ancestral connection with Italy is dim and remote; much of the action takes place outside Italy, and when it moves there, is confined to a small area around the Tiber; Aeneas himself is a homeless wanderer who asks for no more than a few acres for himself and his company. This remote past is connected with the present by many ingenious ties. The Trojan heroes are the ancestors of famous Roman families and bear names honoured in Roman history; their ceremonies, their habits, their games, forecast what are later to be characteristic of Rome; they touch at places familiar to every

---

AENEAS: THE ROMAN HERO: From *From Virgil to Milton* by C. M. Bowra. Used by permission of Macmillan & Company, Ltd., London.

Roman; into their story local legends and traditions are woven; the gods who support and sustain them are those whose cults formed the official religion of the Roman people. And more significant than these external connections are the Roman spirit, virtues, and outlook which the Trojans display. The difficulties encountered by these first ancestors, their relations to the gods, their emotions and their ideals, their family loyalties, their behaviour in peace and war, their attitude to the divine task laid upon them, are somehow typical and representative of the Romans as they were believed to have always been. Virgil is less concerned with origins than with a permanent reality as it was displayed from the first and is still being displayed in his own time.

Such a plan and such a purpose demanded a new kind of poetry, and when we turn from the *Iliad* to the *Aeneid*, it is clear that the whole outlook is different and that Virgil has a new vision of human nature and of heroic virtue. Homer concentrates on individuals and their destinies. The dooms of Achilles and Hector dominate his design; their characters determine the action. But from the start Virgil shows that his special concern is the destiny not of a man but of a nation, not of Aeneas but of Rome. Though he opens with "Arms and the man" and suggests that his hero is another Achilles or Odysseus, he has, before his first paragraph is finished, shown that he reaches beyond Aeneas to the long history that followed from him:

> whence came the Latin race,
> The Alban sires and lofty walls of Rome.

Soon afterwards, when he has noted the obstacles which the Trojans meet in their wanderings, he again ends a period on a similar note:

> So vast a task to found the Roman race.

Then, when Venus complains that her son, Aeneas, is unjustly treated, Jupiter replies not only by promising that all will be well with Aeneas but by giving a prophetic sketch of Roman history to Julius Caesar. The reward which the ancestor of the Roman race is to receive is much more than his own success or glory, more even than his settlement in Italy; it is the assurance of Rome's destiny, of universal and unending dominion:

> To them I give no bounds in space or time
> But empire without end.

At the outset Virgil shows what kind of destiny is the subject of his poem. The wanderings and sufferings and ultimate success of Aeneas and his followers are but a preliminary and a preparation for a much vaster theme. It was with reason that Petronius, like Tennyson, called the poet "Roman Virgil."

The fundamental theme of the *Aeneid* is the destiny of Rome as it was revealed in this mythical dawn of history before Rome itself existed. This destiny is presented in the person of Aeneas who not only struggles and suffers for the Rome that is to be but is already a typical Roman. If his individual fortune is subordinate to the fortune of Rome, his character shows what Romans are. He is Virgil's hero in a new kind of heroic poem, and in him we see how different Virgil's epic vision is from Homer's. Aeneas is Virgil's own creation, conceived with the special purpose of showing what a Roman hero is. Unlike Homer, Virgil owes little in his hero's character to tradition. Whereas Homer had to conform to established notions and make his Achilles "swift of foot," his Agamemnon "king of men" and his Odysseus "of many wiles," Virgil was bound by no such obligations. He could find his characters where he chose and shape them to suit his own purpose. His Aeneas owes something to Homeric precedent in being a great warrior and a devout servant of the gods, but he has taken on a new personality and is the true child of Virgil's brooding meditation and imaginative vision. The persons of the *Aeneid* are created and fashioned for a special purpose. They contribute to the main design, and everything that they say or do may be considered in the light of Rome's destiny. For this reason it is wrong to treat them as if they were dramatic characters like Homer's. They are more, and they are less. They are more, because they stand for something outside themselves, for something typically and essentially Roman; they are types, examples, symbols. And they are less, because any typical character will lack the lineaments and idiosyncrasies, the personal appeal and the intimate claims, of a character who is created for his own sake and for the poet's pleasure in him. . . .

Against the imperfect types of Turnus and Dido Virgil had to set his own reformed and Roman ideal of manhood. His task was indeed difficult. He had to create a man who should on the one hand be comparable to the noblest Homeric heroes in such universally honoured qualities as courage and endurance and on the other hand should present in himself the qualities which the Augustan age admired beyond all others but which had meant nothing to Homer. Virgil's treatment of Dido and Turnus shows that his new hero could not be ruled by the self-assertive spirit and cult of honour which inspired the heroic outlook; he must be based on some other principle more suited to an age of peace and order. But if he was to rival Achilles and Odysseus, he must be a great man and a ruler of men. Virgil had to present a hero who appealed both by his greatness and by his goodness, by his superior gifts and by his Roman *virtus*.[1] On the one hand he must be a fitting member of the heroic age to which legend assigned him, and on the other he must represent in its fullness and variety the new idea of manhood which Augustus advocated and proclaimed as characteristically Roman. The result was Aeneas, a character so compounded of different elements that he has often been derided even by those who love Virgil. Yet to him Virgil gave his deepest meditations and some of his finest poetry. To understand him we must try to recapture some of the ideas and sentiments of the Augustan age.

Aeneas comes from Homer, and in the *Aeneid* he is presented as a great warrior who is almost the equal of Hector. To him Hector appears after death, as to his legitimate successor in the defence of Troy. Andromache associates him with Hector when she asks if the boy Ascanius has the courage and spirit of his father Aeneas and his uncle Hector. Aeneas' fame has spread through the whole world, and Dido knows all about him before she sees him, while in Italy Pallas is amazed that so renowned a man should appear before him on the Tiber. He has the heroic qualities of divine blood, prowess in war, personal beauty, and power to command men. But he has something more than this. His essential quality, as his distinguishing epithet of *pius* shows, is his *pietas,* his devotion to the gods and to all their demands. When Iloneus speaks of him to Dido, he shows the combination of qualities in Aeneas:

> A king we had, Aeneas: none more just,
> More righteous, more renowned in war and arms.

Aeneas is not only a great soldier; he is a good man. So to some degree, Homer had made him when he told of his many sacrifices to Poseidon, but Virgil enlarges the concept of this goodness until it covers much more than the performance of religious rites. Aeneas' *pietas*[2] is shown in his devotion to his country, to his father, to his wife, to his child, to his followers and above all to the many duties and the special task which the gods lay on him. He is *pius* because he does what a good man should. The epithet which Virgil gives him is unlike the epithets which Homer gives to his heroes. For while these denote physical characteristics or qualities useful in war, *pius* indicates a spiritual quality which has nothing to do with war and is specially concerned with the relations between Aeneas and the gods. Thus at the start Virgil's hero is set in a different order of things and claims a different kind of attention. In this unprecedented epithet for an epic hero and in all that it implies is the clue to Virgil's conception of Aeneas.

1 [Virtue or power.]

2 [Piety or fidelity.]

Aeneas is *pius*, but he is not a perfect and ideal man throughout the poem. The indignation which he has excited in more than one critic for his obvious faults shows not that Virgil's idea of goodness was singularly unlike our own but that he chose to show a good man in the making and the means by which he is made. To understand Aeneas we must understand the scheme by which Virgil presents him, a scheme based on the moral views of the Augustan age but modified by Virgil's own beliefs and admirations. The clue to Aeneas is that he is built on a Stoic plan. St. Augustine hints at this when he touches on Aeneas' treatment of Dido and treats it as being typically Stoic because while he sheds tears for her, his purpose is not shaken by her sufferings:

> His mind unmoved, his tears fall down in vain.

It is not certain that St. Augustine interprets the line correctly, but his main conclusion is right. Aeneas has undeniably something Stoic about him which accounts for the alleged paradoxes and contradictions of his character. There is nothing strange in this. In the moral reforms which Augustus preached and planned a revived Stoicism took a prominent place. It breathes through the patriotic odes of Horace, and it survived through the first two centuries A.D. Originally Stoicism was a creed to meet the horrors of an age in which there was no political or personal security. Against this disorder it set the citadel of a man's soul in which he could live at peace with himself and with the universe and by subduing his emotions be undismayed at whatever might happen. The Augustan Romans took over this creed and gave it a new reference. It suited them because it disapproved of self-assertion and ambition and laid great emphasis on social duties. It was well suited to an age which hoped to recover from the excesses of unfettered individualism. The quiet, self-denying, self-sacrificing citizen who was prepared to do what he was told was a type dear to Augustus. Virgil knew the theory and the doctrine, and though in his youth he had leaned towards Epicurus, he was deeply affected by them. . . .

In his relations with Dido Aeneas fails though not quite in the way that modern critics find so deplorable. What is wrong is not his desertion of her, which is ordered by the gods and necessary for the fulfilment of his task in Italy, but his surrender in the first place to her love and his subsequent neglect of his real duty which lies away from Carthage. Virgil does not show clearly what Aeneas' motives are; they seem at least not to be love for Dido, for whom he shows little more than grateful affection. But of his fault there is no question; it is neglect and forgetfulness of duty. Mercury, sent by Jupiter, makes it quite clear:

Forgetful of thy realm and fate!

This forgetfulness, due perhaps to sloth and love of ease, is a kind of intemperance, a failure in moderation, a state of false pleasure in which a temporary advantage is mistaken for a real good. Aeneas' duty, as Mercury tells him, is owed to his son, and he must do it. This is precisely what he tells Dido, and though her furious reception of his defence makes it look feeble, it is all that he can say, and it is right. Nor would it perhaps have seemed so weak to a Roman. For his duty is concerned with the foundation of Rome, and it cannot be right to set a woman's feelings before that destiny. Aeneas is fond of Dido and he feels pity for her, but his conscience is stronger than his emotions and wins in the end. When he leaves her, he acts as a Stoic should, and undoes, so far as he can, the evil which he has committed by allowing himself to forget his task in her company.

In Book V Aeneas is faced with another crisis. During the Funeral Games of his father, the women of his company, stirred up by Juno's agent, begin to burn his ships with the purpose of keeping him in Sicily. Aeneas sees the havoc that they have started and prays to Jupiter to stop it. Jupiter sends rain and the fire is quenched. But even after this display of divine help, Aeneas is full of misgivings:

But prince Aeneas, by that sad mischance
Sore stricken, rolls the burden of his thoughts
This way and that. There should he make his home,
Heedless of fate, or grasp Italian shores?

It seems almost incredible that Aeneas should at this juncture think of abandoning his quest. Yet he does, and it shows how deeply his emotions still rule him. The catastrophe of the burned ships has filled him with such despair that for the moment he ceases to believe in his destiny. Fortunately he is saved by the old sailor Nautes, who not only gives him sensible advice about leaving the women in Sicily and sailing with the rest of his company, but sums up the situation in a way that must have appealed to every Roman conscience:

Go, goddess' son, where fate drives—back or on.
Endurance conquers fortune, come what may.

The fate which Aeneas should follow is the destiny which the gods have given him, and he should be master enough of himself to know this. Nautes brings him to his senses, and when this advice is fortified by words from the spirit of Anchises, Aeneas recovers his confidence and sets sail for Italy. He never again allows his feelings to *obscure* his knowledge of his duty.

Once he lands in Italy Aeneas is a new man. He makes no more mistakes, and always does what is right in the circumstances. He is never again assailed by doubt or despair; his only hesitations are about the right means to the known end, and these after due consideration he finds. . . . When Aeneas touches the fated soil of Italy, he has learned his lessons and found that self-control and wisdom which the Stoics regarded as the mark of a good man. His earlier adventures and mistakes have not been in vain. For they have made him surer of himself and more confident of the divine destiny which leads him.

The Stoic ideas which inform Virgil's conception of Aeneas' ordeal and development persist to some degree in the later books of the *Aeneid,* but with a different purpose. Aeneas is the just and wise prince, and he must not act unjustly, particularly in such important matters as peace and war, about which the Augustan age had been taught by bitter experience to hold strong views. Aeneas is very like an invader, and he lives in a heroic past, but he must not be allowed to make war as Homer's heroes make it, simply to indulge his own desire for glory. For this reason Virgil makes Aeneas face war with a consciousness of grave responsibilities and of nice distinctions between moral issues. Just as Cicero says that the only right reason for declaring war is that "life may be lived in peace without wrong," so Virgil is careful to put Aeneas in the right when war is forced upon him by the Latins. Earlier versions of the story said that the Trojans began the attack and were resisted by the Latins; Virgil reverses the situation and makes Aeneas do everything to secure his aims by peaceful negotiations. His envoy makes the most modest demands of King Latinus, and the king is perfectly willing to accede to them. When war is begun by the Latins, Aeneas conducts it in the spirit which Cicero advocates, "that nothing should be sought but peace." Even after the aggression of the Latins, Aeneas tells their envoys, who ask for leave to bury the dead, that he is willing to grant much more than that:

> Peace for the dead and slain in war you ask.
> I'd grant it gladly to the living too.

When the truce is broken, his chief thought is to have it restored. He tries to avert a general slaughter and offers to settle the issue by a single combat between himself and Turnus. He cries out to the excited armies:

> Oh stay your wrath! The pact is made, and all
> The rules are fixt. My right to fight alone!

In this we hear the spirit of the Augustan age as its master proclaimed it when he said that he himself had never made war "without just and necessary reasons" and that he always pardoned his enemies when the general safety allowed. Such an attitude towards war bears no resemblance to anything heroic or Homeric. War had become an evil which may be undertaken only when there is no alternative, and it must be conducted in a spirit of chivalry and clemency.

Though Aeneas is built largely on a Stoic plan and conforms in some important respects to the Stoic ideal of the wise man, he is not only this. He has other qualities which lie outside the Stoic purview and are even hostile to it. This is not hard to understand. The Stoic ideal, interesting though it is as an attempt to set a man above his troubles and his failings and to provide him with a feeling of security in a disordered society, failed to conquer mankind because it denied the worth of much that the human heart thinks holy and will not willingly forgo. St. Augustine was not alone in feeling that the Stoics were inhuman in their attempt to suppress all emotions, no matter how reputable. Many other men felt that such an exaltation of reason is wrong in so far as it dries up the natural springs of many excellent actions. Though Virgil used Stoic conceptions for the development of Aeneas' character, his warm-hearted, compassionate temperament was not satisfied with an ordeal so cold and so remote. If Stoicism provides a scheme by which Aeneas is tested and matured, it does not explain much else in him. Aeneas, with all his faults and contradictions, is essentially a creature of emotions. It is true that at first these are the cause of his failures and may be condemned, but Virgil did not believe that his ideal Roman should lack emotions altogether. His confident Aeneas of the later books is still highly emotional, but his emotions are now in harmony with his appointed purpose and help in his pursuit of it.

The most important of these divagations from the Stoic norm is the part played by pity in the character of Aeneas. For many readers this is the most Virgilian of all qualities, the most typical and most essential feature of the *Aeneid*. When Aeneas sees the episodes of the Trojan War depicted in stone at Carthage, he utters the famous words which have so often been quoted as the centre of Virgil's outlook and message:

> Here praise has its rewards,
> Fortune its tears, and man's fate stirs the heart.

The words do not mean all that is sometimes claimed for them; they are certainly not a declaration that human life is nothing but tears. But they show that Aeneas on arriving in a strange land feels that here too is not only the glory but the pathos of life. In his mind the two are equally important, and such a view is far removed from Stoic detachment. The same quality comes out when Aeneas sees the ghosts of the unburied dead wandering in the underworld and halts his steps:

> With thought and pity for their unjust lot.

He allows his compassion here to assert itself at the expense of a divine ordinance and to criticize the government of the universe. No correct Stoic would dream of doing such a thing, and it shows how strong pity is in Aeneas and what importance Virgil attaches to it. . . .

More surprising than Aeneas' outbursts of pity are his outbursts of anger and fury, which continue after he has arrived in Italy and are evidently essential to his mature personality. The Stoics would have disapproved of them without qualification. They defined anger as the desire for revenge and thought it odious because it makes deliberate and considered action impossible. Seneca says that it is the result not of goodness but of weakness, often frivolous or flippant, and that any good it may do in the way of punishment or correction can be better done from a sense of duty. Even Marcus Aurelius, who in many ways resembles Aeneas and seems to embody the ideal Roman in his historical self, condemns anger with majestic austerity. In anger, he says, the soul wrongs itself; it is senseless against wrongdoers because they act unwillingly through ignorance, and it is not a proper function of man. Yet Virgil made anger part of Aeneas' character and a potent force in his warlike doings. It rises at the death of Pallas and takes the form of a violent desire to punish Turnus, though for a time it is exercised at the expense of others like Magus, Tarquitus and Lucagus, who do not share Turnus' responsibility for killing Pallas. In the second part of Book X Aeneas is driven by wild fury against all his opponents. He takes the four sons of Sulmo to be a human sacrifice at Pallas' pyre, and not all the admiration of Donatus—"how great Aeneas' virtue is shown to be, how great his devotion in honouring the memory of the dead"—can make us feel that he is acting humanly or even rationally. When Magus makes a pitiful appeal for mercy, Aeneas refuses with heartless irony and tells him that his death is demanded by the dead Anchises and the boy Iulus. He throws Tarquitus to the fishes and denies him the decencies of burial with the derisive taunt that his mother will not bury him nor lay his limbs in the ancestral tomb. . . .

The combination of such qualities in a single hero demands some explanation. It is sometimes said that in it Virgil modelled Aeneas on Achilles and did not reconcile the obvious discords. It is true that these episodes have their parallels in the furious revenge which Achilles exacts for the death of Patroclus. But if so, Virgil has failed to make his hero convincing or consistent. These outbursts of heroic fury ill suit the exponent of Roman virtues with his strong distaste for war. But another explanation is possible. Virgil liked and admired Augustus, and at the same time knew that Augustus' dominion was based on force. In his youth he had risen to power by a series of violent acts, which he justified as the vengeance for the death of Julius. Legends had gathered round this vengeance and portrayed Augustus as moved by violent and angry feelings. They may not be true, but they were circulated and known and had become part of Augustus' myth. After Philippi Augustus was said to have behaved much as Aeneas behaves after the death of Pallas. Aeneas refuses burial to Tarquitus and tells him that the birds and fishes will lick his wounds; when a dying man asked Augustus for burial, he said that the birds would soon settle that question. Aeneas is so angry that no appeal to the names of his father and his son moves him to spare Lucagus; Augustus is said to have made a father play a game with his sons to decide which should live and then looked on while both were killed. Aeneas sacrifices the sons of Sulmo at Pallas' pyre; Augustus was said to have sacrificed three hundred prisoners of war after Perusia on the Ides of March at the altar of Julius. Whether these tales are true or not, Augustus undoubtedly took a fierce revenge for the murder of his adopted father, and it is possible that Virgil modelled Aeneas' revenge for Pallas on it. He seems to have felt that there are times when it is right even for a compassionate man like Aeneas to lose control of himself and to be carried away by anger. This anger is thought to be good not only in its cause but in its results. It helps Aeneas to secure his destiny and to overcome those who resist it. Normally considerate and compassionate, he is slow to anger, but some things so shock him that they awake it, and, when it comes, it is terrible. At the back of his mind Virgil seems to have had a conception of a great man whose natural instincts are all for reason and agreement, but who, when he finds that these are useless, shows how powerful his passions can be. Aeneas, who has to subdue so much of himself, has also at times to subdue his gentler feelings and to allow full liberty to more primitive elements which are normally alien to him.

Virgil has put so much into Aeneas that he has hardly made him a living man. But though he lacks human solidity, he is important as an ideal and a symbol. So far from acting for his own pleasure or glory, he does what the gods demand of him. In the performance of this duty he finds little happiness. He would rather at times give up his task, and he envies the Trojans who have settled in Sicily and have no such labours as his. His stay in Carthage shows how easily his natural instincts can conquer his sense of duty, and there is a pathetic sincerity in his words to Dido:

> I seek not Italy by choice.

He takes no pride in his adventures, no satisfaction in their successful conclusion. His whole life is dictated by the gods. They tell him what to do and make him do it, and he obeys in an uncomplaining but certainly not a joyful spirit of acceptance. He is aptly symbolised by Virgil's picture of him shouldering the great shield on which Vulcan has depicted the deeds of his descendents:

> His shoulder bears his grandson's fame and fate.

On Aeneas the whole burden of Rome seems to lie, and it is not surprising that he lacks the instinctive vigour and vitality of Homer's heroes. The new world which Virgil sought to interpret needed men like this, not heroes like Turnus whose individual ambitions lead to destruction. . . .

In the *Aeneid* Virgil presented a new ideal of heroism and showed in what fields it could be exercised. The essence of his conception is that a man's *virtus* is shown less in battle and physical danger than in the defeat of his own weaknesses. The chief obstacles which Aeneas finds are in himself, and his greatest victories are when he triumphs over them. Even in battle his highest moments are when he sees past the fury of the fight to some higher end of unity and harmony. Conversely, Dido and Turnus fail because, despite their innate nobility and strength of will, they give in to their passions and desires. Virgil's idea of heroism is quite different from Homer's because it depends much less on physical gifts than on moral strength and is displayed not merely in battle but in many departments of life. Moreover, Homer's heroes never question the worth of the glory which they seek, but Aeneas, hampered by doubts and misgivings, is unsure not only about his glory but about his whole destiny. This uncertainty is one of his greatest trials, and he shows his worth by pursuing his task despite all his doubts about it. His success is all the greater because it is won largely in spite of his own human feelings. In him Virgil displays what man really is, a creature uncertain of his place in the universe and of the goal to which he moves. To the distrustful and uncertain Augustan age this conception came with the urgency of truth, and Virgil's immediate and lasting success was due to his having found an answer to the spiritual needs of his time. In the vision of Rome he presented an ideal strong enough to win the devotion of his contemporaries, and in his belief in sacrifice and suffering he prepared the way across the centuries to those like Marcus Aurelius and St. Augustine who asked that men should live and die for an ideal city greater and more truly universal than Rome. Once Virgil had opened up a new vision of human worth and recast the heroic ideal in a new mould, he set an example which later poets could not but follow. They might not accept his interpretation of human destiny in all its details, but they felt that he had marked out the main lines for epic poetry and that any new heroic ideal must take account of what he said.

Iris Origo

LA GIOCOSA: A SCHOOL FOR FREE MEN

IN THE little dominion of Mantua, in the year 1423, an experiment in education began, of which the results were more far-reaching than its founder could ever, in his most hopeful moments, have foreseen. His name was Vittorino da Feltre, and his school was called La Giocosa. The pupils schooled there, and later on their children and grandchildren, grew up to form little centers of civilization as complete as the world has ever seen—the courts of Mantua and Urbino, of Ferrara and Milan—and the ideas underlying that civilization are still under active debate today. After five hundred years, the famous "Renaissance Man" still seems rather larger than life-size—not only a scholar but an athlete, a captain of armies, a wise ruler, and a patron of all the arts. Were these claims indeed justified? If they were, it is surely still pertinent to inquire by what process it was that such a man was shaped.

Let us look first at the man who founded this school and directed it for twenty-three years: Vittorino Rambaldoni, generally known, from his little native city in the Venetian Alps, as Vittorino da Feltre. His appearance, according to the two portraits remaining of him and the accounts of his contemporaries, was unimpressive—a man small and slight in stature, with an ascetic yet kindly face, a quiet voice, and a gentle and unemphatic manner, who was always dressed in a plain dark scholar's gown and rough sandals. Yet so high was this little schoolmaster's reputation that when, on a visit to Pope Eugenius IV, he knelt at the Pontiff's feet, the Pope raised him up, exclaiming, "How great a soul is lodged in this little body! Had my position allowed it, it is I who would have liked to rise, as he came in."

When Gianfrancesco Gonzaga, Marquis of Mantua, invited Vittorino to his court as preceptor to his sons, the teacher—who had had schools of his own in Padua and Venice—hesitated greatly before accepting, and then did so on two conditions: that his employer should never require anything of him "unworthy of either of us," and that, in the management of the boys and the household, he should be given as free a hand "as if he were the boys' own

---

father." Gianfrancesco agreed; and Vittorino, without even inquiring what his salary was to be, took up his new post.

The house which was assigned to him and his pupils was a fine villa on the outskirts of Mantua. Built in 1388 by Gianfrancesco's predecessor as a pleasure house, it stood in the midst of wide meadows sloping down to the river Mincio and was bordered by broad, shady avenues, while the interior was decorated with frescoes of beasts, birds, and children at play. Vittorino started by stripping it of every luxury: fine hangings and draperies, silver and gold plates and ornaments. Then he turned to the daily life of his pupils. The young Gonzagas—of whom the two elder, Ludovico and Carlo, at once came into his charge, the younger children later on—were not at first sight prepossessing pupils. Ludovico was a fat, phlegmatic boy with a great belly and dragging steps, who spent his days in eating, drinking, and sleeping; Carlo, while tall and active, was rickety and nervous. (Both boys were soon restored to health by their preceptor's wise diet.) Their companions, the sons of the Mantuan nobles, were a set of spoiled and lawless boys dressed in fine silks and brocades adorned with jewels, heavily scented and pomaded, who came to school whenever they pleased and spent much of their time there with acrobats and jesters.

To all this Vittorino put an end. After a short period of patient inaction, during which he quietly observed each pupil, he firmly dismissed a few whom he considered incorrigible, and those servants who had encouraged their bad habits. He placed a reliable porter at the gate, so that no one could come in or go out without his permission. He obtained the Marquis' permission to summon a few of his former pupils from Venice, to appoint competent teachers for every branch of learning, and to award scholarships to some poor boys of outstanding gifts, who were received at La Giocosa (as they had been in his previous school in Padua) "for the love of God." Then he set to work.

The object of his training was, in his own words, the full development of each of the principal elements of man's nature: "the mind, the body, and the heart." The first two parts of this formula were, of course, based on the familiar Platonic principle: "gymnastic for the body and music for the mind." The rest of it was based on the teachings of Christianity. And it was the combination of both, the harmonious blending of the ideals of Humanism and of Christianity, which gave to Vittorino's school its particular flavor.

In returning to the classical conception of the equal development of body and mind, Vittorino swept aside many centuries of medieval prejudice, according to which the body represented only the lower part of our nature. It is true that at the medieval courts young knights had been taught to ride, joust, and hunt, but never had it been admitted that, as Plato had taught, the perfect man could only be formed by a harmonious balance between mind and body. But now Vittorino turned La Giocosa into a true classical gymnasium. His pupils were taught to run, to wrestle, to play football, to hunt, to swim and fish in the waters of the Mincio, and to learn the arts of javelin-throwing, archery, and dancing. In summer they were even taken mountain-climbing (then a most unusual pursuit) in the Venetian Alps. And so much attention was paid to dignity of carriage that if Vittorino saw a boy standing about awkwardly or slouching, he would chalk a circle around the place where the boy stood and require him to remain there motionless for a specified time, in the presence of his companions in a correct posture.

All the sports of La Giocosa must have made the school a paradise for active boys, compared to the almost wholly sedentary lives of the pupils of the monastic orders, but for Vittorino their real purpose was training in hardihood and self-restraint. Just as he abolished any corporal punishment, so he required his pupils to show their own respect for their bodies by the greatest moderation in eating, drinking, and sleeping; by regular exercise in all seasons; and by denying themselves any self-indulgence, such as wearing gloves or furs or fine linen or sleeping in featherbeds, or even allowing themselves a small fire on the coldest, most misty days of the Mantuan winter. "Clap your hands or stamp your feet," he would say to his boys when they were cold, "or say a fine poem, to stir the sluggish blood in your veins." He himself, even when visibly numb with cold, was never seen to stand before a fire.

So much for one side of education at La Giocosa. What was the academic training? Vergerius, who taught in the University of Padua when Vittorino was there, defined "liberal studies" as "those worthy of being studied by free men, to promote virtue and knowledge." The approved subjects included first, of course, the classics; then philosophy and history, mathematics, and, with some reservations, music and dancing. Indeed the only major subjects excluded were medicine, theology, and the law, which were university subjects in any case. Vittorino, however, always maintained that it was not fair to expect every pupil to show the same tastes and talents. "Whatever our own predilections may be, we recognize that we must follow nature's lead." He declared that "everyone has some gift, if only one can discover it," and he therefore bestowed especial pains upon the dullest boys, trying to find some subject or skill to meet their needs.

Such individual attention was all the more remarkable when we consider that his school contained sixty or seventy pupils of the most various ages (the Gonzaga children entered at the age of five, but Sassuolo da Prato only at twenty-one). We are told that—in the belief that five hours of sleep were enough for a keen scholar—Vittorino would walk about the school in the dark on early winter mornings with a candle in one hand and a book in the other, rousing the ablest scholars from their sleep, to work with them for an extra hour, "and encourage them with grave and earnest words to high endeavor."

The youngest children learned to read by playing games with colored letter cards. Arithmetic, too, was at first taught as a game; for, like Quintilian, Vittorino believed that "the first thing to be avoided is, that a child should begin by feeling aversion for the studies he cannot yet love." History and mythology, too, were told as exciting and ennobling stories. By the time the child was six or seven he was ready to begin his serious studies in *grammatica*, the foundation of all knowledge, for this word comprised not only the study of Greek and Latin grammar (both languages being started together) but the reading of the great classical authors. A great deal of the teaching was oral: in the grammar lesson the master would dictate the list of words to be learned by heart and their declensions, commenting on any grammatical difficulty as it arose. When the time came for reading the Greek or Latin text itself, the master would first read a passage aloud, explaining and commenting, followed by each pupil reading the same passage in turn, until not only his translation but his enunciation and expression were considered perfect. Finally each passage was learned by heart. Every child was taught to read aloud agreeably and clearly, "not muttering in his teeth," and without uncouth gestures or making faces. And Vittorino was always especially pleased when any of them asked questions, saying that a passive acceptance of instruction was an infallible sign of an inattentive, dull, or lazy mind.

In the choice of authors, the principle was that laid down by Vergerius: "Begin with the best." Virgil, Homer, Cicero, and Demosthenes were the four authors on whom the teaching at La Giocosa was based. Only after these had been thoroughly mastered were the pupils allowed to pass on to Lucan and Ovid (in extracts, to "form an elegiac taste"), as well as to Xenophon and Herodotus. Terence, Plautus, Horace, and Juvenal were permitted only to the older boys, whose characters were considered to be already formed. In Greek the advanced students were allowed to read first Aeschylus and then Euripides and Sophocles, as well as Pindar, Theocritus, and some parts of Aristophanes. Vittorino thought it very important to learn

Greek at the same time as Latin, and, since he considered himself only a mediocre Greek scholar, he engaged two renowned Greek teachers for La Giocosa, both recommended by the great Humanist Francesco Filelfo—George of Trebizond and the celebrated grammarian Theodore Gaza.

All the pupils were expected to write Greek and Latin verses and to compose speeches in these languages, which they recited to their companions or to distinguished guests. One boy composed such an oration to thank his fellow students for having saved him from drowning. Gianlucido Gonzaga, at fourteen, recited two hundred Latin hexameters of his own composition, celebrating the arrival of the Emperor Sigismund in Mantua, to an illustrious visitor, the Abbot Ambrogio of Camaldoli, "with so much grace," according to his hearer, "that I think Virgil spoke no better when he recited the sixth book of the *Aeneid* to Augustus." And he added that on the same day Gianlucido's sister of ten, Cecilia, wrote for him in Greek and Latin "with so much elegance as to put me to shame, considering that among my own pupils I could scarcely find one capable of doing the same." In these orations Vittorino advised his pupils to use a clear, straightforward style, avoiding archaisms and any excessive display of learning; and indeed it is plain that he was well aware of the dangers, as well as the advantages, of too great a skill in rhetoric. "There is," he said, "nothing that may eventually do greater harm to a city than eloquence, for . . . when it is possessed by evil men, they may use it to stir up trouble and to corrupt public manners."

As for the other subjects, history was confined to that of Greece and Rome, ignoring both medieval and contemporary history, and was entirely uncritical. Vittorino, for instance, whose favorite historian was Livy, indignantly repudiated any suggestion that so great a man could ever have been inaccurate. Equally, the study of philosophy was limited to ethics—that is, to the study of precepts from Cicero, Aristotle, Seneca, and Boethius, with illustrations from Plutarch, and at La Giocosa (though not in most other schools), of some of the Fathers of the Church, particularly Saint Jerome. Mathematics was given an important place and included geometry and astronomy. Vittorino also added the study of natural history (in a very rudimentary form) but discarded and despised astrology, in spite of its general popularity. As to music, many Humanists still regarded it, as the Middle Ages had done, with a considerable amount of distrust, declaring that too many young men "lose all vigor of mind and of character in their absorption in unworthy harmonies." But Vittorino, like Plato, held that it was necessary to the formation of a "complete" man; at La Giocosa both singing and playing the lyre and the lute were taught, and even dancing to music was approved.

In this connection a word must be said—since it was in this, too, that Humanist education broke new ground—about Vittorino's views on the education of women. His only girl pupils were the two Gonzaga daughters, Cecilia and Margherita, but other little blue-stockings were being formed at much the same time in other parts of Italy. In Verona, Guarino's two pupils, Isotta and Ginevra Nogarola, were given a sound classical education. In Florence, when Poliziano fell in love with his beautiful pupil Alessandra Scala, it was in Greek verses that they corresponded. "You bring me, Alessandra, sweet violets—but I would taste the fruit."

There are, however, several prevalent misconceptions about the Humanist education of women. The first is that up to that time no girls had received any education at all: little Minervas, learned and wise, had sprung full-armed from the brains of Vittorino, Guarino, or Poliziano. Yet there is, for instance, the description given by the Tuscan chronicler Giovanni Morelli of his sister Mea, a whole century before the emergence of the young ladies of the Renaissance. This young lady, who had "hands of ivory, so well-shaped that they seemed to have been drawn by Giotto," was "delicate and pleasant in her speech, modest and measured in her gestures, yet a valiant, frank woman with a virile soul. She read and wrote as well as any man, she danced and sang perfectly, she was skilled in the arts of housekeeping, guiding her family with good advice and good habits, and living cheerfully and gaily." This is, surely, a woman as highly civilized (except for a knowledge of Latin and Greek) as any daughter of the Renaissance. Moreover, it is also not entirely true that Vittorino, or indeed any other Humanist, advocated the *same* education for girls as for their brothers. Cecilia and Margherita Gonzaga did indeed study the classics. They were encouraged to know something of history, to practice the arts of agreeable conversation, to ride and dance and sing and play the lute, and above all, to appreciate poetry; since, according to the first treatise on education dedicated to a woman (written by Leonardo Bruni for Battista Malatesta), "anyone ignorant of and indifferent to so valuable an aid to knowledge and so ennobling a source of pleasure can by no means be entitled to be called educated." But arithmetic and geometry were wholly omitted from their curriculum, and also rhetoric, as "absolutely outside a woman's province." And the *first* place in a woman's education (in this all teachers agreed) was to be given to "the whole field of religion and morals, as a subject peculiarly her own."

And now we come to the third and most important part of Vittorino's method: the formation of what he called "the heart" and we should call character. Since he well knew that it can be formed only by example, he spent every hour of the day with his pupils, bearing a silent witness by his own life to the virtues he most valued: self-restraint, modesty, truthfulness, and kindness. His gentle equanimity, we are told, was the result of a stern self-discipline, by which he had conquered the sensuality and quick temper of his youth—at La Giocosa he led a life as dedicated as any monk's. His generosity was as spontaneous as his gentle smile: not only did many penniless students owe him their education, but his purse was always open to the poor. At his death, in spite of the handsome yearly salary of 240 gold florins awarded him by the Gonzagas, it was found that there was nothing left for his heirs but a little farm not far from Mantua, on the very site (and this must have delighted him) which was believed to be that of Virgil's birthplace. He was generous, too, with what he valued more than money: his fine collection of books, lending them freely, but becoming so angry when they were taken without leave that a law was passed in Mantua declaring the unauthorized borrowing of a book to be a punishable misdemeanor, like any other theft.

A poet in his youth, he finally destroyed the few poems he had kept and wrote very little else; all his energy went into his studies and his teaching. A devout Christian, he never required of his boys an austerity equal to his own (he lived on the most frugal of diets and scourged himself daily), but he did demand a daily attendance at Mass, confession once a month, and, above all, a deep reverence in word and deed. The only occasion when, breaking his own rule, he inflicted a corporal punishment was when he overheard Carlo Gonzaga blaspheme in the heat of a quarrel, and gave him, in the presence of the whole school, a sound box on the ear.

But the punishment that his pupils most dreaded was merely his displeasure and, in cases of cruelty or deceit, his glance of contempt and refusal to speak for several days to the offender. This was the more marked because at all other times his relationship with the boys was easy and affectionate, sharing their sports, delighting in their successes. Abbot Ambrogio has left us a charming description of him at the Gonzaga castle of Goito in the hills, where he had taken some of his younger pupils to escape from the summer heat: the children clustering round "on the happiest terms with him" to take part in the talk and show off their accomplishments, and then, when the guest left, riding with him for some distance to speed him on his way.

It should always be remembered that Vittorino considered Humanist education to be, above all, a *practical* preparation for life. His aim, he said, was not the formation of a great scholar but of a complete citizen. "Not everyone is obliged to excel in philosophy, medicine, or the law, nor are all equally favored by nature; but all are destined to live in society and to practice virtue." (By society he meant, of course, not only the world of the courts, but the community of men.) It was for this reason that, in spite of his personal interest in the clever poor students whom he himself had brought to the school, he attached an especial importance to the training of young noblemen, realizing that it was they who would become the model for all their subjects. It is in this sense only that La Giocosa can be considered, like the public schools of England, a school for the formation of a ruling class. But it was certainly, in its emphasis on the fusion of virtue and knowledge, a school for an elite—in Vergerius' words, for "free men."

And now we may inquire, what indeed were the fruits of this education? The Milky Way that led from La Giocosa across the skies of the Renaissance is full of minor stars: grammarians and versifiers, mathematicians, learned bishops, a musician and a *condottiere*.[1] But we know that the formation of able scholars, or indeed of specialists of any kind, was not Vittorino's purpose. Did he then succeed in his ultimate aim, that of forming some "complete" human beings? The answer is, I think, both yes and no. The moral climate of the courts was a very different one from that inculcated on the playing fields of La Giocosa, and the violence, cruelty, and treachery which underlay the civilization of the Renaissance inevitably tainted the lives and characters of many of his pupils—except those who, like the brilliant and gentle Cecilia Gonzaga, forsook the life of the world for a convent. The rest had to deal with the society of their time as they found it—a world in which their old master's lessons of truthfulness, mildness, and forbearance held little place. Where Vittorino was entirely successful, however, was in the transmission of a certain fineness of taste—in life as well as in art. Ferrara under Lionello d'Este and his bride Margherita Gonzaga; Mantua under Ludovico Gonzaga and his son Federigo, and again in the next generation, under Federigo's son Francesco, who brought home Isabella d'Este as his bride; Urbino under Federigo da Montefeltro and his son Guidobaldo, who married Ludovico Gonzaga's granddaughter Elisabetta; and finally, Milan under the rule of Beatrice d'Este (Isabella's sister) and her husband Ludovico Sforza—these four courts showed, under the influence of Vittorino's pupils or their descendants, a remarkably fine flowering of the human spirit, an exquisite pattern of civilized life. If their members did not all, in Vittorino's sense, "practice virtue," they certainly had learned to perfection how "to live in society." Indeed, all other societies before and since, with perhaps the exception of

1 [A professional soldier.]

eleventh-century Japan, seem by comparison a little graceless, a little coarse.

Two men, both pupils of Vittorino's, stand out as the dominating figures of two of these courts: Ludovico Gonzaga, Marquis of Mantua, and Federigo da Montefeltro, Duke of Urbino. Both were skillful and intrepid *condottieri;* both were also wise rulers; both made their courts centers of learning and of the arts.

The temperaments of these two men, however, were widely dissimilar. From early youth Federigo (in spite of his illegitimate birth) had seemed marked for success. "*Tu quoque Caesar eris*" (You also will be Caesar), Vittorino would remind him in his school days, and it is said that his pupil's promise sometimes caused him to shed tears of joy. Ludovico, on the other hand, had so many obstacles to overcome that one may doubt whether he would ever have become a great man without the early help of his master. It was Vittorino's training that, in his boyhood, enabled him to conquer his ill-health and his tendency to corpulence and apathy; and it was also Vittorino's intercession that at last obtained his father's forgiveness when, having despaired of ever being able to rival his handsome, gifted younger brother Carlo at home, he took service under Filippo Maria Visconti in Milan and spent long, bitter years abroad in exile. Yet it may well have been these years spent earning his spurs as a *condottiere* that fortified and matured him, for when he inherited the state of Mantua, Ludovico at once showed himself a wise and provident ruler. He built dikes and banks to stem the floods of the river Po and a canal (designed by Brunelleschi) to irrigate the Mantuan plain, assigning the land to anyone who was prepared to farm it properly; he paved the city streets, built a hospital, and set up a printing press. He summoned the great architect Alberti to design two new churches, that of San Sebastiano and the Basilica of Sant' Andrea; the mathematician Bartolomeo Manfredi to make the clock for his great new belfry; and Andrea Mantegna to decorate his palace, declaring that Mantegna's little toe was dearer to him than the whole body of most of his subjects.

Under Vittorino's guidance Ludovico enriched his library with rare manuscripts. (It included not only a fine collection of Greek and Latin authors and of medieval manuscripts, but a few books in the Vulgar, among them one thus described in the inventory: "INCIPIT, *nel mezo del camin di nostra vita,* ET FINIT, *l'amor che move il sole e l'altre stelle,*" CONTINET CARTAS 74.)[2] He seized every pretext—a birth or a wedding or a foreign prince's visit—for great feasts and

2 [Beginning with "Midway the journey of this life," and ending with "The Love that moves the sun and the other stars." These are the first and last lines of Dante's *Divine Comedy*.]

banquets; he offered constant hospitality to scholars such as Filelfo and Pico della Mirandola, and such poets as Poliziano, whose *Orpheus* was written and performed in Mantua. And if at the end of all this the Mantuan coffers were empty, he was not ashamed to ask one of his artists to wait a little longer for full payment, since, he said, at the moment the Gonzaga jewels were in pawn! Yet the portraits of him that have come down to us are not those of a happy man. They show the face of a ruler who has achieved power and security, but on whom the years of struggle and anxiety have left their mark—a man always on his guard, never forgetful of the motto on the family crest, CAUTIUS, "live cautiously."

It is to the other of Vittorino's most famous pupils, Federigo da Montefeltro, that we must turn to see not only the qualities of the mind, but also of the heart, that La Giocosa sought to form; for here indeed we are close to finding Vittorino's "complete man." Although he was not entirely free, as a *condottiere*, from the cruelty of other soldiers of fortune, Federigo was almost unique in his faithfulness to his word and to his friends, in defeat as in victory. As a ruler his generosity and friendliness, and a total absence of the suspicion and arrogance of almost all other princes of his times, endeared him to all his subjects. Accounts by his contemporaries describe him as spending a part of each day, alone and unguarded, in the market place or in the shops of his artisans. "To one he would say, 'How is your old father?' to another, 'How does your trade thrive?' or 'Have you got a wife yet?' . . . One he took by the hand, he put his hand on another's shoulder, and spoke to all uncovered, so that men would say, when anyone was very busy, 'Why, you have more to do than Federigo's berretta!' "

One morning, meeting a wedding procession, Federigo dismounted to join the escort that was honoring the bride; and on a winter's day, when the monastery of San Bernardino, outside the city, was snowed in, he himself set off at the head of his men to cut a path through the snow to feed the hungry monks. In times of famine he distributed corn free from his private estate in Apulia. Whenever possible, he answered petitions on the same day he received them. It is hardly surprising that, as he walked through the streets, people would kneel down, crying, "God keep you, *signore*!"

At the same time Federigo displayed to the full, with the fruits of his successful wars, the magnificence expected of a Renaissance prince. Life in the great palace designed for him by Laurana was on a truly royal scale. His household counted "500 mouths," which included—besides knights, men-at-arms, grooms, and servants—four teachers of grammar, philosophy, and rhetoric, five architects and engineers, a German astrologer, five "readers aloud at meals," four "elderly and staid gentlemen" for his wife's court, four transcribers of manuscripts, the keeper of the bloodhounds, and the keeper of the giraffe. His stables held three hundred horses; his library, the rarest and most complete collection of manuscripts and books in Europe. His own tastes remained those formed at La Giocosa. Livy and Saint Augustine were read aloud to him at meals, and in the afternoons, if he was not watching a joust or some boys practicing gymnastics on the wide meadow of San Francisco, he would attend a classical lecture, or discuss theology, through a grating, with the learned Abbess of the Convent of Santa Chiara.

His son Guidobaldo followed in his father's footsteps. At a very early age he showed a passion for the classics and for geography and history, as well as for the gymnastics and knightly sports which greatly injured his already fragile health. After his marriage at sixteen to Ludovico Gonzaga's granddaughter Elisabetta, their court became a magnet for the best scholars and artists in Italy. The scholar Pietro Bembo came for a few days' visit, and stayed for six years; Castiglione came and wrote *Il Cortigiano* [*The Courtier*]. The artists at Guidobaldo's court were Piero della Francesca, Francesco di Giorgio, Justus van Ghent, Ambrogio da Milano, Giovanni Sanzi (who was also the court chronicler), and above all, Sanzi's son, "the divine Raphael," who later on, in his famous *School of Athens* in the Vatican, reproduced the very quintessence of the Renaissance view of the classical world.

The days were spent in hunting, jousting, and riding; the evenings in singing to the harpsichord or the lute, or in parlor games, and especially, under the guidance of the gentle Duchess and her brilliant sister-in-law, Emilia Pia, in long philosophic debates: Was it indeed true that matter was masculine and form feminine? What were the qualities required of the perfect courtier? And of the ideal woman? And what was the true nature of love? "It is," said Bembo, "nought but a desire to enjoy beauty, and since one can only desire what one knows, so knowledge must precede desire." But the highest love, he maintained, the Platonic, "is an emanation of the divine goodness . . . shining over all created things, like the sun's light." So, night after night, they talked, until the candles burned low and the ladies, in their stiff brocades and high, heavy headdresses, dispersed to bed, and the Duke went down to his great library, where the portrait of his father's old schoolmaster—placed beside the greatest classical philosophers and the Fathers of the Church—bore witness to the influence he had exerted, and to his pupil's gratitude: "Federigo to Vittorino da Feltre, his revered master, who by word and example instructed him in all human excellence."

Thomas Carlyle

THE HERO AS POET: DANTE

. . . .

IN ANCIENT and also in modern periods we find a few Poets who are accounted perfect; whom it were a kind treason to find fault with. This is noteworthy; this is right: yet in strictness it is only an illusion. At bottom, clearly enough, there is no perfect Poet! A vein of Poetry exists in the hearts of all men; no man is made altogether of Poetry. We are all poets when we read a poem well. The "imagination that shudders at the Hell of Dante," is not that the same faculty, weaker in degree, as Dante's own? No one but Shakspeare can embody, out of *Saxo Grammaticus*, the story of *Hamlet* as Shakspeare did: but every one models some kind of story out of it; every one embodies it better or worse. We need not spend time in defining. Where there is no specific difference, as between round and square, all definition must be more or less arbitrary. A man that has *so* much more of the poetic element developed in him as to have become noticeable, will be called Poet by his neighbours. World-Poets too, those whom we are to take for perfect Poets, are settled by critics in the same way. One who rises *so* far above the general level of Poets will, to such and such critics, seem a Universal Poet; as he ought to do. And yet it is, and must be, an arbitrary distinction. All Poets, all men, have some touches of the Universal; no man is wholly made of that. Most poets are very soon forgotten; but not the noblest Shakspeare or Homer of them can be remembered *forever*;—a day comes when he too is not!

Nevertheless, you will say, there must be a difference between true Poetry and true Speech not poetical: what is the difference? On this point many things have been written, especially by late German Critics, some of which are not very intelligible at first. They say, for example, that the Poet has an *infinitude* in him: communicates an Unendlichkeit,[1] a certain character of "infinitude," to whatsoever he delineates. This, though not very precise, yet on so vague a matter is worth remembering: if well meditated, some meaning will gradually be found in it. For my own part, I find considerable meaning in the old vulgar distinction of Poetry being *metrical*, having music in it, being a Song. Truly, if pressed to give a definition, one might say this as soon as anything else: If your delineation be authentically *musical*, musical, not in word only, but in heart and substance, in

1 [Eternity.]

all the thoughts and utterances of it, in the whole conception of it, then it will be poetical; if not, not.—Musical: how much lies in that! A *musical* thought is one spoken by a mind that has penetrated into the inmost heart of the thing; detected the inmost mystery of it, namely the *melody* that lies hidden in it; the inward harmony of coherence which is its soul, whereby it exists, and has a right to be, here in this world. All inmost things, we may say, are melodious; naturally utter themselves in Song. The meaning of Song goes deep. Who is there that, in logical words, can express the effect music has on us? A kind of inarticulate unfathomable speech, which leads us to the edge of the Infinite, and lets us for moments gaze into that!

Nay all speech, even the commonest speech, has something of song in it: not a parish in the world but has its parish-accent;—the rhythm or *tune* to which the people there *sing* what they have to say! Accent is a kind of chanting; all men have accent of their own,—though they only *notice* that of others. Observe too how all passionate language does of itself become musical,—with a finer music than the mere accent; the speech of a man even in zealous anger becomes a chant, a song. All deep things are Song. It seems somehow the very central essence of us, Song; as if all the rest were but wrappages and hulls! The primal element of us; of us, and of all things. The Greeks fabled of Sphere-Harmonies; it was the feeling they had of the inner structure of Nature; that the soul of all her voices and utterances was perfect music. Poetry, therefore, we will call *musical Thought.* The Poet is he who *thinks* in that manner. At bottom, it turns still on power of intellect; it is a man's sincerity and depth of vision that makes him a Poet. See deep enough, and you see musically; the heart of Nature *being* everywhere music, if you can only reach it.

The *Vates* Poet, with his melodious Apocalypse of Nature, seems to hold a poor rank among us, in comparison with the *Vates* Prophet; his function, and our esteem of him for his function alike slight. The Hero taken as Divinity; the Hero taken as Prophet; then next the Hero taken only as Poet: does it not look as if our estimate of the Great Man, epoch after epoch, were continually diminishing? We take him first for a god, then for one god-inspired; and now in the next stage of it, his most miraculous word gains from us only the recognition that he is a Poet, beautiful verse-maker, man of genius, or suchlike!—It looks so; but I persuade myself that intrinsically it is not so. If we consider well, it will perhaps appear that in man still there is the *same* altogether peculiar admiration for the Heroic Gift, by what name soever called, that there at any time was.

I should say, if we do not now reckon a Great man literally divine, it is that our notions of God, of the supreme unattainable Fountain of Splendour, Wisdom and Heroism, are ever rising *higher*; not altogether that our reverence for these qualities, as manifested in our like, is getting lower. This is worth taking thought of. Sceptical Dilettantism, the curse of these ages, a curse which will not last forever, does indeed in this the highest province of human things, as in all provinces, make sad work; and our reverence for great men, all crippled, blinded, paralytic as it is, comes out in poor plight, hardly recognisable. Men worship the shows of great men; the most disbelieve that there is any reality of great men to worship. The dreariest, fatalest faith; believing which, one would literally despair of human things. Nevertheless look, for example, at Napoleon! A Corsican lieutenant of artillery; that is the show of *him*: yet is he not obeyed, *worshipped* after his sort, as all the Tiaraed and Diademed of the world put together could not be? High Duchesses, and ostlers of inns, gather round the Scottish rustic, Burns;—a strange feeling dwelling in each that they had never heard a man like this; that, on the whole, this is the man! In the secret heart of these people it still dimly reveals itself, though there is no accredited way of uttering it at present, that this rustic, with his black brows and flashing sun-eyes, and strange words moving laughter and tears, is of a dignity far beyond all others, incommensurable with all others. Do not we feel it so? But now, were Dilettantism, Scepticism, Triviality, and all that sorrowful brood, cast-out of us,—as, by God's blessing, they shall one day be; were faith in the shows of things entirely swept-out, replaced by clear faith in the *things*, so that a man acted on the impulse of that only, and counted the other non-extant; what a new livelier feeling towards this Burns were it!

Nay here in these pages, such as they are, have we not two mere Poets, if not deified, yet we may say beatified? Shakspeare and Dante are Saints of Poetry; really, if we will think of it, *canonised*, so that it is impiety to meddle with them. The unguided instinct of the world, working across all these perverse impediments, has arrived at such result. Dante and Shakspeare are a peculiar Two. They dwell apart, in a kind of royal solitude; none equal, none second to them: in the general feeling of the world, a certain transcendentalism, a glory as of complete perfection, invests these two. They *are* canonised, though no Pope or Cardinals took hand in doing it! Such, in spite of every perverting influence, in the most unheroic times, is still our indestructible reverence for heroism. . . .

Many volumes have been written by way of commentary on Dante and his Book; yet, on the whole, with no great result. His Biography is, as it were, irrecoverably lost for us. An unimportant, wandering, sorrowstricken man, not much note was taken of him while he lived; and the most of that has vanished, in the long space that now intervenes. It is five centuries since he ceased writing and living here. After all commentaries, the Book itself is mainly what we know of him. The Book;—and one might add that Portrait commonly attributed to Giotto, which, looking on it, you cannot help inclining to think genuine, whoever did it. To me it is a most touching face; perhaps of all faces that I know, the most so. Lonely there, painted as on vacancy, with the simple laurel wound round it; the deathless sorrow and pain, the known victory which is also deathless; —significant of the whole history of Dante! I think it is the mournfulest face that ever was painted from reality; an altogether tragic, heart-affecting face. There is in it, as foundation of it, the softness, tenderness, gentle affection as of a child; but all this is as if congealed into sharp contradiction, into abnegation, isolation, proud hopeless pain. A soft ethereal soul looking-out so stern, implacable, grim-trenchant, as from imprisonment of thick-ribbed ice! Withal it is a silent pain too, a silent scornful one: the lip is curled in a kind of godlike disdain of the thing that is eating-out his heart,—as if it were withal a mean insignificant thing, as if he whom it had power to torture and strangle were greater than it. The face of one wholly in protest, and life-long unsurrendering battle, against the world. Affection all converted into indignation: an implacable indignation; slow, equable, silent, like that of a god! The eye too, it looks out as in a kind of *surprise*, a kind of inquiry, Why the world was of such a sort? This is Dante: so he looks, this "voice of ten silent centuries," and sings us "his mystic unfathomable song."

The little that we know of Dante's Life corresponds well enough with this Portrait and this Book. He was born at Florence, in the upper class of society, in the year 1265. His education was the best then going; much school-divinity, Aristotelean logic, some Latin classics,—no inconsiderable insight into certain provinces of things: and Dante, with his earnest intelligent nature, we need not doubt, learned better than most all that was learnable. He has a clear cultivated understanding, and of great subtlety; the best fruit of education he had contrived to realise from these scholastics. He knows accurately and well what lies close to him; but, in such a time, without printed books or free intercourse, he could not know well what was distant: the small clear light, most luminous for what is near, breaks itself into singular *chiaroscuro* striking on what is far off. This was Dante's learning from the schools. In life, he had gone through the usual destinies; been twice out campaigning as a soldier for the Florentine State, been on embassy; had in his thirty-fifth year, by natural gradation of talent and service, become one of the Chief Magistrates of Florence. He had met in boyhood a certain Beatrice Portinari, a beautiful little girl of his own age and rank, and grown-up thenceforth in partial sight of her, in some distant intercourse with her. All readers know his graceful affecting account of this; and then of their being parted; of her being wedded to another, and of her death soon after. She makes a great figure in Dante's Poem; seems to have made a great figure in his life. Of all beings it might seem as if she, held apart from him, far apart at last in the dim Eternity, were the only one he had ever with his whole strength of affection loved. She died: Dante himself was wedded; but it seems not happily, far from happily. I fancy, the rigorous earnest man, with his keen excitabilities, was not altogether easy to make happy.

We will not complain of Dante's miseries: had all gone right with him as he wished it, he might have been Prior, Podestà, or whatsoever they call it, of Florence, well accepted among neighbours,—and the world had wanted one of the most notable words ever spoken or sung. Florence would have had another prosperous Lord Mayor; and the ten dumb centuries continued voiceless, and the ten other listening centuries (for there will be ten of them and more) had no *Divina Commedia* to hear! We will complain of nothing. A nobler destiny was appointed for this Dante; and he, struggling like a man led towards death and crucifixion, could not help fulfilling it. Give *him* the choice of his happiness! He knew not, more than we do, what was really happy, what was really miserable.

In Dante's Priorship, the Guelf-Ghibelline, Bianchi-Neri, or some other confused disturbance rose to such a height, that Dante, whose party had seemed the stronger, was with his friends cast unexpectedly forth into banishment; doomed thenceforth to a life of woe and wandering. His property was all confiscated and more; he had the fiercest feeling that it was entirely unjust, nefarious in the sight of God and man. He tried what was in him to get reinstated; tried even by warlike surprisal, with arms in his hand: but it would not do; bad only had become worse. There is a record, I believe, still extant in the Florence Archives, dooming this Dante, wheresoever caught, to be burnt alive. Burnt alive; so it stands, they say: a very curious civic document. Another curious document, some considerable number of years later, is a Letter of Dante's to the Florentine Magistrates, written in answer to a milder proposal of theirs, that he should return on condition of apologising and paying a fine. He answers, with fixed stern pride: "If I cannot return without calling myself guilty, I will never return, *nunquam revertar*."

For Dante there was now no home in this world. He wandered from patron to patron, from place to place; proving in his own bitter words, "How hard is the path, *Come è duro calle*." The wretched are not cheerful company. Dante, poor and banished, with his proud earnest nature, with his moody humours, was not a man to conciliate men. Petrarch reports of him that being at Can della Scala's court, and blamed one day for his gloom and taciturnity, he answered in no courtier-like way. Della Scala stood among his courtiers, with mimes and buffoons (*nebulones ac histriones*) making him heartily merry; when turning to Dante, he said: "Is it not strange, now, that this poor fool should make himself so entertaining; while you, a wise man, sit there day after day, and have nothing to amuse us with at all?" Dante answered bitterly: "No, not strange; your Highness is to recollect the Proverb, *Like to Like;*"—given the amuser, the amusee must also be given! Such a man, with his proud silent ways, with his sarcasms and sorrows, was not made to succeed at court. By degrees, it came to be evident to him that he had no longer any resting-place, or hope of benefit, in this earth. The earthly world had cast him forth, to wander, wander; no living heart to love him now; for his sore miseries there was no solace here.

The deeper naturally would the Eternal World impress itself on him; that awful reality over which, after all, this Time-world, with its Florences and banishments, only flutters as an unreal shadow. Florence thou shalt never see: but Hell and Purgatory and Heaven thou shalt surely see! What is Florence, Can della Scala, and the World and Life altogether? ETERNITY: thither, of a truth, not elsewhither, art thou and all things bound! The great soul of Dante, homeless on earth, made its home more and more in that awful other world. Naturally his thoughts brooded on that, as on the one fact important for him. Bodied or bodiless, it is the one fact important for all men:—but to Dante, in that age, it was bodied in fixed certainty of scientific shape; he no more doubted of that *Malebolge*[2] Pool, that it all lay there with its gloomy circles, with its *alti guai,*[3] and that he himself should see it, than we doubt that we should see Constantinople if we went thither. Dante's heart, long filled with this, brooding over it in speechless thought and awe, bursts forth at length into "mystic unfathomable song;" and this his *Divine Comedy,* the most remarkable of all modern Books, is the result.

It must have been a great solacement to Dante, and was, as we can see, a proud thought for him at times, That he, here in exile, could do this work; that no Florence, nor no man or men, could hinder him from doing it, or even much help him in doing it. He knew too, partly, that it was great; the greatest a man could do. "If thou follow thy star, *Se tu segui tua stella,*"—so could the Hero, in his forsakenness, in his extreme need, still say to himself: "Follow thou thy star, thou shalt not fail of a glorious haven!" The labour of writing, we find, and indeed could know otherwise, was great and

2 [A place in Hell. Cf. *Inferno,* XXIV.] 3 [High-pitched wails.]

painful for him; he says, This Book, "which has made me lean for many years." Ah yes, it was won, all of it, with pain and sore toil, —not in sport, but in grim earnest. His Book, as indeed most good Books are, has been written, in many senses, with his heart's blood. It is his whole history, this Book. He died after finishing it; not yet very old, at the age of fifty-six;—broken-hearted rather, as is said. He lies buried in his death-city Ravenna: *Hic claudor Dantes patriis extorris ab oris*. The Florentines begged back his body, in a century after; the Ravenna people would not give it. "Here am I Dante laid, shut-out from my native shores."

I said, Dante's Poem was a Song: it is Tieck who calls it "a mystic unfathomable Song;" and such is literally the character of it. Coleridge remarks very pertinently somewhere, that wherever you find a sentence musically worded, of true rhythm and melody in the words, there is something deep and good in the meaning too. For body and soul, word and idea, go strangely together here as everywhere. Song: we said before, it was the Heroic of Speech! All *old* Poems, Homer's and the rest, are authentically Songs. I would say, in strictness, that all right Poems are; that whatsoever is not *sung* is properly no Poem, but a piece of Prose cramped into jingling lines, —to the great injury of the grammar, to the great grief of the reader, for most part! What we want to get at is the *thought* the man had, if he had any: why should he twist it into jingle, if he *could* speak it out plainly? It is only when the heart of him is rapt into true passion of melody, and the very tones of him, according to Coleridge's remark, become musical by the greatness, depth and music of his thoughts, that we can give him right to rhyme and sing; that we call him a Poet, and listen to him as the Heroic of Speakers,—whose speech *is* Song. Pretenders to this are many; and to an earnest reader, I doubt, it is for most part a very melancholy, not to say an insupportable business, that of reading rhyme! Rhyme that had no inward necessity to be rhymed;—it ought to have told us plainly, without any jingle, what it was aiming at. I would advise all men who *can* speak their thought, not to sing it; to understand that, in a serious time, among serious men, there is no vocation in them for singing it. Precisely as we love the true song, and are charmed by it as by something divine, so shall we hate the false song, and account it a mere wooden noise, a thing hollow, superfluous, altogether an insincere and offensive thing.

I give Dante my highest praise when I say of his *Divine Comedy* that it is, in all senses, genuinely a Song. In the very sound of it there is a *canto fermo;* it proceeds as by a chant. The language, his simple *terza rima,* doubtless helped him in this. One reads along naturally with a sort of *lilt*. But I add, that it could not be otherwise; for the essence and material of the work are themselves rhythmic. Its depth, and rapt passion and sincerity, makes it musical;—go *deep* enough, there is music everywhere. A true inward symmetry, what one calls an architectural harmony, reigns in it, proportionates it all: architectural; which also partakes of the character of music. The three kingdoms, *Inferno, Purgatorio, Paradiso,* look-out on one another like compartments of a great edifice; a great supernatural world-cathedral, piled-up there, stern, solemn, awful; Dante's World of Souls! It is, at bottom, the *sincerest* of all Poems; sincerity, here too, we find to be the measure of worth. It came deep out of the author's heart of hearts; and it goes deep, and through long generations, into ours. The people of Verona, when they saw him on the streets, used to say, "*Eccovi l' uom ch' è stato all' Inferno,* See, there is the man that was in Hell!" Ah, yes, he had been in Hell;—in Hell enough, in long severe sorrow and struggle; as the like of him is pretty sure to have been. Commedias that come-out *divine* are not accomplished otherwise. Thought, true labour of any kind, highest virtue itself, is it not the daughter of Pain? Born as out of the black whirlwind;—true *effort,* in fact, as of a captive struggling to free himself: that is Thought. In all ways we are "to become perfect through *suffering.*" —But, as I say, no work known to me is so elaborated as this of Dante's. It has all been as if molten, in the hottest furnace of his soul. It had made him "lean" for many years. Not the general whole only; every compartment of it is worked-out, with intense earnestness, into truth, into clear visuality. Each answers to the other; each fits in its place, like a marble stone accurately hewn and polished. It is the soul of Dante, and in this the soul of the Middle Ages, rendered forever rhythmically visible there. No light task; a right intense one: but a task which is *done.*

Perhaps one would say, *intensity,* with the much that depends on it, is the prevailing character of Dante's genius. Dante does not come before us as a large catholic mind; rather as a narrow and even sectarian mind: it is partly the fruit of his age and position, but partly too of his own nature. His greatness has, in all senses, concentered itself into fiery emphasis and depth. He is world-great not because he is world-wide, but because he is world-deep. Through all objects he pierces as it were down into the heart of Being. I know nothing so intense as Dante. Consider, for example, to begin with the outermost development of his intensity, consider how he paints. He has a great power of vision; seizes the very type of a thing; presents that and nothing more. You remember that first view he gets of the Hall of Dite: *red* pinnacle, redhot cone of iron glowing through the dim immensity of gloom;—so vivid, so distinct, visible at once and forever! It is as an emblem of the whole genius of Dante. There is a brevity, an abrupt precision in him: Tacitus is not briefer, more condensed; and then in Dante it seems a natural condensation, spontaneous to the man. One smiting word; and then there is silence, nothing more said. His silence is more eloquent than words. It is strange with what a sharp decisive grace he snatches the true likeness of a matter: cuts into the matter as with a pen of fire. Plutus, the blustering giant, collapses at Virgil's rebuke; it is "as the sails sink, the mast being suddenly broken." Or that poor Brunetto Latini, with the *cotto aspetto*,[4] "face baked," parched brown and lean; and the "fiery snow," that falls on them there, a "fiery snow without wind," slow, deliberate, never-ending! Or the lids of those Tombs; square sarcophaguses, in that silent dim-burning Hall, each with its Soul in torment; the lids laid open there; they are to be shut at the Day of Judgment, through Eternity. And how Farinata rises; and how Cavalcante falls—at hearing of his Son, and the past tense "fue"![5] The very movements in Dante have something brief; swift, decisive, almost military. It is of the inmost essence of his genius this sort of painting. The fiery, swift Italian nature of the man, so silent, passionate, with its quick abrupt movements, its silent "pale rages," speaks itself in these things.

For though this of painting is one of the outermost developments of a man, it comes like all else from the essential faculty of him; it is physiognomical of the whole man. Find a man whose words paint you a likeness, you have found a man worth something; mark his manner of doing it, as very characteristic of him. In the first place, he could not have discerned the object at all, or seen the vital type of it, unless he had, what we may call, *sympathised* with it,—had sympathy in him to bestow on objects. He must have been *sincere* about it too; sincere and sympathetic: a man without worth cannot give you the likeness of any object; he dwells in vague outwardness, fallacy and trivial hearsay, about all objects. And indeed may we not say that intellect altogether expresses itself in this power of discerning what an object is? Whatsoever of faculty a man's mind may have will come out here. Is it even of business, a matter to be done? The gifted man is he who *sees* the essential point, and leaves all the rest aside as surplusage: it is his faculty too, the man of business's faculty, that he discern the true *likeness*, not the false superficial one, of the thing he has got to work in. And how much of *morality* is in the kind of insight we get of anything; "the eye seeing in all things what it brought with it the faculty of seeing"! To the mean eye all things are trivial, as certainly as to the jaundiced they are yellow. Raphael, the

4 [This phrase and the subsequent Italian phrases that are translated within the text are Dante's, chiefly from the *Purgatorio*.]
5 [Went; a mistake. In Dante the word is *had*.]

Painters tell us, is the best of all Portrait-painters withal. No most gifted eye can exhaust the significance of any object. In the commonest human face there lies more than Raphael will take-away with him.

Dante's painting is not graphic only, brief, true, and of a vividness as of fire in dark night; taken on the wider scale, it is everyway noble, and the outcome of a great soul. Francesca and her Lover, what qualities in that! A thing woven as out of rainbows, on a ground of eternal black. A small flute-voice of infinite wail speaks there, into our very heart of hearts. A touch of womanhood in it too; *della bella persona, che mi fu tolta;*[6] and how, even in the Pit of woe, it is a solace that *he* will never part from her! Saddest tragedy in these *alti guai*. And the racking winds, in that *aer bruno*,[7] whirl them away again, to wail forever!—Strange to think: Dante was the friend of this poor Francesca's father; Francesca herself may have sat upon the Poet's knee, as a bright innocent little child. Infinite pity, yet also infinite rigour of law: it is so Nature is made; it is so Dante discerned that she was made. What a paltry notion is that of his *Divine Comedy's* being a poor splenetic impotent terrestial libel; putting those into Hell whom he could not be avenged-upon on earth! I suppose if ever pity, tender as a mother's, was in the heart of any man, it was in Dante's. But a man who does not know rigour cannot pity either. His very pity will be cowardly, egoistic,—sentimentality, or little better. I know not in the world an affection equal to that of Dante. It is a tenderness, a trembling, longing, pitying love: like the wail of Æolean harps, soft, soft; like a child's young heart;—and then that stern, sore-saddened heart! These longings of his towards his Beatrice; their meeting together in the *Paradiso*; his gazing in her pure transfigured eyes, her that had been purified by death so long, separated from him so far:—one likens it to the song of angels; it is among the purest utterances of affection, perhaps the very purest, that ever came out of a human soul.

For the *intense* Dante is intense in all things; he has got into the essence of all. His intellectual insight as painter, on occasion too as reasoner, is but the result of all other sorts of intensity. Morally great, above all, we must call him; it is the beginning of all. His scorn, his grief are as transcendent as his love;—as indeed, what are they but the *inverse* or *converse* of his love? "*A Dio spiacenti ed a' nemici sui*, Hateful to God and to the enemies of God:" lofty scorn, unappeasable silent reprobation and aversion; "*Non ragionam di lor*, We will not speak of *them*, look only and pass." Or think of this; "They have not the *hope* to die, *Non han speranza di morte*." One day, it had risen sternly benign on the scathed heart of Dante, that he,

6 [With the fair body of which I was bereft.]

7 [Dark air.]

wretched, never-resting, worn as he was, would full surely *die;* "that Destiny itself could not doom him not to die." Such words are in this man. For rigour, earnestness and depth, he is not to be paralleled in the modern world; to seek his parallel we must go into the Hebrew Bible, and live with the antique Prophets there.

I do not agree with much modern criticism, in greatly preferring the *Inferno* to the two other parts of the Divine *Commedia.* Such preference belongs, I imagine, to our general Byronism of taste, and is like to be a transient feeling. The *Purgatorio* and *Paradiso,* especially the former, one would almost say, is even more excellent than it. It is a noble thing that *Purgatorio,* "Mountain of Purification"; an emblem of the noblest conception of that age. If Sin is so fatal, and Hell is and must be so rigorous, awful, yet in Repentance too is man purified; Repentance is the grand Christian act. It is beautiful how Dante works it out. The *tremolar dell' onde* that "trembling" of the ocean-waves, under the first pure gleam of morning, dawning afar on the wandering Two, is as the type of an altered mood. Hope has now dawned; never-dying Hope, if in company still with heavy sorrow. The obscure sojourn of dæmons and reprobate is underfoot; a soft breathing of penitence mounts higher and higher, to the Throne of Mercy itself. "Pray for me," the denizens of that Mount of Pain all say to him. "Tell my Giovanna to pray for me," my daughter Giovanna; "I think her mother loves me no more!" They toil painfully up by that winding steep, "bent-down like corbels of a building," some of them,—crushed-together so "for the sin of pride"; yet nevertheless in years, in ages and æons, they shall have reached the top, which is Heaven's gate, and by Mercy shall have been admitted in. The joy too of all, when one has prevailed; the whole Mountain shakes with joy, and a psalm of praise rises, when one soul has perfected repentance and got its sin and misery left behind! I call all this a noble embodiment of a true noble thought.

But indeed the Three compartments mutually support one another, are indispensable to one another. The *Paradiso,* a kind of inarticulate music to me, is the redeeming side of the *Inferno;* the *Inferno* without it were untrue. All three make-up the true Unseen World, as figured in the Christianity of the Middle Ages; a thing forever memorable, forever true in the essence of it, to all men. It was perhaps delineated in no human soul with such depth of veracity as in this of Dante's; a man *sent* to sing it, to keep it long memorable. Very notable with what brief simplicity he passes out of the every-day reality, into the Invisible one; and in the second or third stanza, we find ourselves in the World of Spirits; and dwell there, as among things palpable, indubitable! To Dante they *were* so; the real world, as it is called, and its facts, was but the threshold to an infinitely higher Fact of a World. At bottom, the one was as *preter*-natural as the other. Has not each man a soul? He will not only be a spirit, but is one. To the earnest Dante it is all one visible Fact; he believes it, sees it; is the Poet of it in virtue of that. Sincerity, I say again, is the saving merit, now as always.

Dante's Hell, Purgatory, Paradise, are a symbol withal, an emblematic representation of his Belief about this Universe:—some Critic in a future age, like those Scandinavian ones the other day, who has ceased altogether to think as Dante did, may find this too all an "Allegory," perhaps an idle Allegory! "It is a sublime embodiment, or sublimest, of the soul of Christianity. It expresses, as in huge world-wide architectural emblems, how the Christian Dante felt Good and Evil to be the two polar elements of this Creation, on which it all turns; that these two differ not by *preferability* of one to the other, but by incompatibility absolute and infinite; that the one is excellent and high as light and Heaven, the other hideous, black as Gehenna and the Pit of Hell! Everlasting Justice, yet with Penitence, with everlasting Pity,—all Christianism, as Dante and the Middle Ages had it, is emblemed here. Emblemed: and yet, as I urged the other day, with what entire truth of purpose; how unconscious of any embleming! Hell, Purgatory, Paradise: these things were not fashioned as emblems; was there, in our Modern European Mind, any thought at all of their being emblems? Were they not indubitable awful facts; the whole heart of man taking them for practically true, all Nature everywhere confirming them? So is it always in these things. Men do not believe an Allegory. The future Critic, whatever his new thought may be, who considers this of Dante to have been all got-up as an Allegory, will commit one sore mistake!—Paganism we recognised as a veracious expression of the earnest awe-struck feeling of man towards the Universe; veracious, true once, and still not without worth for us. But mark here the difference of Paganism and Christianism; one great difference. Paganism emblemed chiefly the Operations of Nature; the destinies, efforts, combinations, vicissitudes of things and men in this world; Christianism emblemed the Law of Human Duty, the Moral Law of Man. One was for the sensuous nature: a rude helpless utterance of the *first* Thought of men, —the chief recognised virtue, Courage, Superiority to Fear. The other was not for the sensuous nature, but for the moral. What a progress is here, if in that one respect only!—

And so in this Dante, as we said, had ten silent centuries, in a very strange way, found a voice. The *Divina Commedia* is of Dante's writing; yet in truth *it* belongs to ten Christian centuries, only the finishing of it is Dante's. So always. The craftsman there, the smith with that metal of his, with these tools, with these cunning methods, how little of all he does is properly *his* work! All past inventive men work there with him;—as indeed with all of us, in all things. Dante is the spokesman of the Middle Ages; the Thought they lived by stands here in everlasting music. These sublime ideas of his, terrible and beautiful, are the fruit of the Christian Meditation of all the good men who had gone before him. Precious they; but also is not he precious? Much, had not he spoken, would have been dumb; not dead, yet living voiceless.

On the whole, is it not an utterance, this Mystic Song, at once of one of the greatest human souls, and of the highest thing that Europe had hitherto realised for itself? Christianism, as Dante sings it, is another than Paganism in the rude Norse mind; another than "Bastard Christianism" half-articulately spoken in the Arab Desert seven-hundred years before!—The noblest *idea* made *real* hitherto among men, is sung, and emblemed-forth abidingly, by one of the noblest men. In the one sense and in the other, are we not right glad to possess it? As I calculate, it may last yet for long thousands of years. For the thing that is uttered from the inmost parts of a man's soul, differs altogether from what is uttered by the outer part. The outer is of the day, under the empire of mode; the outer passes away, in swift endless changes; the inmost is the same yesterday, today and forever. True souls, in all generations of the world, who look in this Dante, will find a brotherhood in him; the deep sincerity of his thoughts, his woes and hopes, will speak likewise to their sincerity; they will feel that this Dante too was a brother. Napoleon in Saint-Helena is charmed with the genial veracity of old Homer. The oldest Hebrew Prophet, under a vesture the most diverse from ours, does yet, because he speaks from the heart of man, speak to all men's hearts. It is the one sole secret of continuing long memorable. Dante, for depth of sincerity, is like an antique Prophet too; his words, like theirs, come from his very heart. One need not wonder if it were predicted that his Poem might be the most enduring thing our Europe has yet made; for nothing so endures as a truly spoken word. All cathedrals, pontificalities, brass and stone, and outer arrangement never so lasting, are brief in comparison to an unfathomable heart-song like this: one feels as if it might survive, still of importance to men, when these had all sunk into new irrecognisable combinations, and had ceased individually to be. Europe has made much; great cities, great empires, encyclopædias, creeds, bodies of opinion and practice: but it has made little of the class of Dante's Thought. Homer yet *is*, veritably present face to face with every open soul of us; and Greece, where is *it*? Desolate for thousands of years; away, vanished; a bewildered heap of stones and rubbish, the life and existence of it all gone. Like a dream; like the dust of King Agamemnon! Greece was; Greece, except in the *words* it spoke, is not.

Emmet John Hughes

THE NOTION OF AN AMERICAN GENTLEMAN

A GENTLEMAN, according to so keen and authentically American a wit as Fred Allen, is any man who would not hit a woman with his hat on. And thereby hangs a tale—part historical and part moral, quite whimsical and a little serious. The tale does not concern the mythical man whose menace is as nicely mannered as Mr. Allen suggested. It concerns the question, so sharply insinuated by Mr. Allen's humor, whether *the gentleman* is a species that can survive—if indeed it ever existed except as an object of vaudevillian scorn—in a climate so mockingly inhospitable as American society. Can the creature exist? *Does* he? What does he look like?

Now a serious definition—social or semantic—poses a problem that must immediately be (a) acknowledged and (b) ignored. The problem is a most elemental proposition: by any understanding of the term "gentleman" (American or alien), he is one not given to discussing other gentlemen in public, much less writing of them, much less still propounding presumptuous definitions of their nature. Accordingly any commentary on the matter is *ipso facto* profoundly lacking in any authority whatsoever. Hence it must be arbitrary, captious, opinionated, and a little insolent. And only in this recklessly lighthearted spirit may the inquiry be pursued. Thus. . . .

All that follows is dedicated, definitely, to proving, deviously, three quite unprovable propositions. *First:* a gentleman is a quite specific, and specifically useful, member of any society. *Second:* the requisite qualities are considerably more profound than the commandment to tip one's hat before slapping a lady. And *third:* there exists an American species of gentleman rather distinct from other types in history and the world at large, and quite estimable too. As for the tenuous evidence. . .

The easiest aspect of any process of definition is the negative, so we may begin with the quickly demonstrable: the kinds of gentleman that the American is *not*. History seems generously populated with *these* gentlemen, and we need note a few such types so essentially alien to the American temper. There was, for example, the scholar-gentleman of the Renaissance, elaborately defined and exalted

THE NOTION OF AN AMERICAN GENTLEMAN: From *Esquire* magazine, May 1960. Reprinted by permission of *Esquire* magazine.

by Castiglione in his *Book of the Courtier,* thus: "Besyde goodnesse, the true and principall ornament of the mynde in everye manne (I beleave) are letters." Whatever else may be said of this noble sentiment, it can hardly be said to have an American ring to it. If Fred Allen were alive to look back upon the decade of the 1950's, with its emphatic disdain for "eggheads," he quite possibly would observe: a gentleman is a man who always murmurs some apology to his hearer before crudely alluding to the experience, pretentious and bizarre, of having lately read a serious book.

Nor does the elaborate elegance of the Chesterfieldian gentleman of the eighteenth century seem any less foreign. "Manner is all, in everything," the English Earl wrote. "It is by manner only that you can please, and consequently rise. . . . Your sole business now is to shine, not to weigh. Weight without luster is lead. You had better talk trifles elegantly to the most trifling woman, than coarse inelegant sense to the most solid man." It is true that an *American* book on manners a century ago commended highly the gentleman who, when his servant dropped a platter of boiled tongue on the floor, remarked, calmly, eruditely, and idiotically: "'Tis a mere *lapsus linguae,*[1] gentlemen." But the passion for gleam and polish in manners broadly strikes the American mind as not lustrous but just ludicrous.

What, then, of the nineteenth century's stern kind of retort to the shiny vulgarity of the Chesterfieldian gentleman—the stern evangelical gentleman sentimentalized by Samuel Richardson and loosely associated with the remembrance of things Victorian? Somehow, this, too, seems to stand equally far from an American notion of gentlemanliness. The obsessive Richardsonian concern for technical chastity ("A man who offers freedoms to his female servant, deserves not, however rich and powerful, to be called a gentleman") catches the cold flavor of American Puritanism, but that is about all. For as the fluent and facile American idiom would tend to dismiss the Castiglione ideal as a "grind" and the Chesterfieldian version as a fop, so it would largely frown upon this pietistic fellow as a prig.

What history seems to suggest, nationality strives to confirm: the American notion (still assuming its existence) seems to contrast rather explicitly with favored views in lands more old and courtly. There is the ancient but suggestive aphorism about the distinct ways in which gentlemen of different nationalities are given to enter any handsomely appointed living room: the Frenchman quickly asks who owns it all; the Englishman acts as if he owned it; and the American acts as if he gave not a damn who owned it. To most American eyes and ears, the symbols and sounds of the gentleman of England seem strange indeed: the titles and trappings of aristocracy, the

1 [Slip of the tongue.]

stiff poise disciplining and disguising emotion, the subdued conversation with its stress upon the barely audible monosyllable, the severe social accent upon accent. As for the flourishing manners of Latin men with respect to (not necessarily *toward*) the opposite sex, the American is likely to observe glumly that it seems, to him, sensible to kiss a lady almost anywhere except on the finger tips. In manners as in politics, the American seems likely to feel himself rather alone in the world.

In the doubt-shedding light of all this, from the historic to the trivial, the obvious question arises, again, whether the *genus Americanus* is not simply and plainly a contradiction in terms. There are, roughly speaking, two arrays of witnesses who rarely tire of assuring the American gentleman that he does not exist. They are: foreign gentlemen (largely self-appointed) and American women (largely self-appreciative). Their testimony can scarcely claim to be disinterested and dispassionate, but they demand hearing, if only because it is quite impossible, in any event, to silence the condescension of the one or the complaint of the other.

The truth is that there is probably a stronger case to be made for the deep doubts of these critics than is achieved by their own invective. The very vocabulary of American speech suggests a certain abiding distrust of the social sheen commonly confused with gentlemanliness. The word "genteel" itself long ago acquired a pejorative quality. Nor has any decently mannered American boy survived his school years without being flayed by his classmates for being a "sissy." Grown to burly manhood, he is likely to find himself often enough using the peculiarly American abbreviation, "gents," as if the very word, fully syllabized, would insult all within hearing. The incongruity of this is suggested by trying to imagine any such shy slurring of *señor* or *monsieur*. And it is perhaps not irrelevant that American law is heavy with provisions, notably in the anti-trust field, condemning things called "gentlemen's agreements" (quite valid, for example, in England).

The speech of the people reflects something, of course, of the history of the nation. Once the Revolutionary generation presiding over the nation's birth had disappeared, American society tended to give relatively little living space to anything smacking of aristocracy or gentry. The towering landmarks of the American historical scene —from the ragged frontier of the past to the bustling metropolis of the present—have been almost equally uncongenial to the cultivation of social conventions or graces, there being little practical occasion for them either in wagon train or in subway. And the time of the maturing of American society—the Golden Age of the late nineteenth century, so crudely conspicuous in its waste and consumption and pomp and acquisitiveness—was hardly characterized by a matching maturing in manners or tastes. This was the time when the Modern Conquerors—the generals and geniuses of American business enterprise—ransacked the castles and churches and palaces of Europe to adorn themselves and their abodes with the trappings, but not the discrimination, of a new aristocracy. Renaissance masterpieces smiled from the walls, strains of uncomprehended Mozart and Beethoven echoed through the rooms, the full armor of medieval knights attended the doorways—of the homes of men unsurpassed in appreciation of the ways to buttress fortunes by producing iron girders and tin cans, glue, cement and nails. The climate, in short, was most encouraging to the general notion, later popularized by aphorism, that it takes three generations, or one good guess in the stock market, to make a gentleman. It was that simple—and shallow.

The heritage, thus unkindly construed, has hardly been one to cultivate the idea of serious self-cultivation (which has something to do with being a gentleman). This helps explain why the species (still assuming its existence) has not seemed a fabulously common one. It was a heritage, in fact, sure to breed that most unattractive man of manners acidly etched by O. Henry: "In dress, habits, manners, provincialism, routine and narrowness, he acquired that charming insolence, that irritating completeness, that sophisticated crassness, that overbalanced poise that makes the Manhattan gentleman so delightfully small in his greatness."

And this pseudo-gentleman, of course, is precisely the chilling caricature who most exasperates the most severe of all critics of the American man, the Manhattan woman. In her eyes—cold with contempt or glazed with boredom—the man in question (in question in every sense) falls pitiably and infuriatingly short of any concept of a serious gentleman. His manners are respectable but meaningless: they speak for a pose, but not for a person. His attitudes toward women range from unpleasant extreme to unpleasant extreme: either elaborately deferential but without true respect, or masculinely brusque without true firmness. In the serious statistics of human size, he is fatefully younger than his years and smaller than his fortune. His image and profile seem forever to blur and mingle with those of all surrounding pseudo-gentlemen. All, indeed, seem essentially faceless—their assumed manners, their acquired artifices, even their gaucheries, all seem interchangeable, undistinguishing and undistinguished. And when on rare occasions, with a flourish of some manner of individual initiative, one aspires to being provocative, he generally succeeds only in being provoking.

History, O. Henry and the American woman, then, might tend to agree: the American gentleman really is nobody but that comic fellow whom Fred Allen had in mind, the man who really is not there at all.

Who says the contrary?

To begin with—and most impressively—the contrary *is* suggested by history, the muse so notoriously given to talking out of both sides of her mouth. For it is time, herewith, to get closer to the point: what *is* a gentleman anyway? And, instantly upon looking at the question, we learn that the idea of a gentleman, far from being utterly alien to American tradition, is, first, an idea essentially modern, and, secondly, an idea whose European and American versions are by no means so dissimilar as one might first suspect.

The word, and the idea, first came upon the Western scene to distinguish a man of "gentle" birth from *both* a serf and a noble: a new type of man, of a certain distinction, notably the bearing of arms. This makes him a relatively modern species, and Sir George Sitwell once remarked, for example, that no one "ever described himself or was described by others as a gentleman before the year 1413." What is more interesting is the fact that the abundant literature on the subject after the fifteenth century makes clear that views and reactions rather casually called "American" have, indeed, been voiced about gentlemen for centuries by indisputably European sources and commentators. *Thus:* no lament upon the crassness of the American gentleman in the Golden Age, and his inelegant materialism, is significantly different from the grief expressed as long ago as Chaucer's time in *Piers Plowman:* "Soap-sellers and their sons for silver are made knights." *Thus:* no American scorn for the vulgar fatuities of Chesterfieldian etiquette could surpass Dr. Johnson's snarling that the *Letters* of the fastidious Earl "teach the morals of a whore and the manners of a dancing master."

The Chesterfieldian notion of gentility, however, itself suggests something rather curious. Upon first scanning, the *Letters,* with their fierce concern for all the minutiae of personal presence, form, behavior and hygiene, seem inanely fastidious—as when the father writes his son such exquisitely refined prescriptions as: "I hope you take infinite care of your teeth; the consequences of neglecting the mouth are serious, not only to one's self but to others." But a moment's reflection suggests that, while this is hardly a common subject for paternal correspondence in America, no society has probably ever matched contemporary American society in persistent public preoccupation with cavities, falling hair, shaven legs, body odors, unsightly pimples, lip shades and hair tints. It is an incongruous suggestion, but it seems barely possible that the verbose Earl's letters may, historically speaking, have been mailed special delivery to the modern huckster, so full of commercial, if not paternal, concern for the grooming and the manicuring of his society's sons and daughters.

But—the frivolous aside—there is a certain serious substance to the oldest European idea of a gentleman that appeals, directly and forcefully, to the most modern American idea of what a man should be, in himself and to others. Consider, for example, from the early years of the seventeenth century, the observation of Thomas Gainsford: "Generositie doth not account him a gentleman which is only descended of noble bloud, in power great, in jewels rich, in furniture fine, in attendants brave. . . . But to be a perfect Gentleman is to be measured in his words, liberall in giving, sober in diet, honest in living, tender in pardoning, and valiant in fighting." The definition is good and explicit. And it is one that almost any American would both recognize and admire.

A few truths, then, slowly shape themselves from the haphazard evidence. For one thing, it seems a deceptive distinction which insists that any European idea of a gentleman must be largely a gleaming matter of surface and manner and poise—and the American idea, by contrast, a thing of baser but tougher metal, a concern with elemental character or acclaimed accomplishment, a disdain for grace or form. There are grains of truth, but no more, in such oversimplification.

And a still more serious truth would appear to be this: the *gentleman*—the word and the idea—suggests substance as well as style, meaning as well as manner. Once this is discerned, it becomes clear that the role of serious gentlemen in American history has been quite a significant one. If the Founding Fathers were not largely "gentlemen" (with a few boisterous exceptions), the word has little meaning and no nation has ever been profoundly affected, in its destiny, by gentlemen. A Jefferson stands out as example, in style as well as in serious quality, even in the weakness as well as the strength often associated with the gentleman: while writing eloquently upon the wisdom of frugality, he could speed toward bankruptcy with the full life at Monticello. And a Lincoln—so different in heritage and in bearing and in manner from a Jefferson—could hardly be denied possession of some of the profounder qualities that endow the idea of a gentleman with meaning.

Nor does the proof of the American species come only from the dusty tomes so wont to overlook the lack of grace, the gaucheries or the vulgarities of their subjects. There is plain enough proof in living examples on the contemporary American scene and precisely on that part of the scene *least* widely respected for its good manners: the arena of politics. Thus a Rockefeller and a Harriman, successive occupiers of, and contenders for, the office of Governor of the most populous State of the Union: by any standard—education, presence, sense of service, dignity of manner, awareness of propriety—surely gentlemen by any reasonable definition. Or one may consider the evident, widely appreciated qualities of the two men who have most recently, and twice, contested for the Presidency. In the popular image, the essential qualities of the person of each seem slightly different. In an Eisenhower, all see certain manifest marks of the man: integrity, honor, responsibility, graciousness, manliness. In a Stevenson, the qualities of the man seem no less clear: dedication, sobriety, intelligence, education, charm. In politics, in personalities, in capacities, the men may differ. But in *one* thing at least, they are the same: they are gentlemen.

Nor can it possibly be contended that they stand for some remarkable and obscure minority, for all serious American professions immediately suggest obvious, and impressive, figures of gentlemen. The judiciary, of course, has been abundant with them—from a Holmes or a Brandeis to a Learned Hand: men of principle to match their presence, depth to give meaning to their manner. In the arts, one may arbitrarily note such figures as those of an Oscar Hammerstein or a Paul Muni—men of plain weight and force, in countenance as much as manner, unneedful of pretense or bluster. Criticism and letters can immediately suggest such men as John Mason Brown or Brooks Atkinson or J. P. Marquand—gentle and correct and courteous, wearing their learning or distinction with the ease and lightness of great familiarity and little self-esteem. In the sphere of higher education and the great foundations, men as different in age and in interests as a Robert Hutchins, or Notre Dame's Father Theodore Hesburgh, or Princeton's Robert Goheen, are all as one in the vigor and poise of a gentleman. And far from least conspicuous, of course, are those publicly recognized products of the American military production—men of the fiber, the innate capacity for command, of a Lucius Clay or a Walter Bedell Smith. Significantly, at the death of George Marshall last year, George Kennan wrote to the New York *Times* a moving, discerning tribute to the man, ending with this salute.

> The judgment of history may, of course, modify this estimate of General Marshall's record as Secretary of State. It cannot alter the image that remains in the memory of those who were close to him in that office. It was the image of *the American gentleman at his best*—honorable, courteous, devoid of arrogance, exacting of others but even more of himself, intolerant only of cowardice, deviousness, and cynicism.

So a conclusion comes: the *genus Americanus* does indeed exist—in some ways, but far from all ways, different from that known to other societies. Quite probably, it is to be found least commonly in those spheres of society where many most commonly seek it. If so, that is the error of the seeker. It might even be that the American woman, so skeptical of the existence of the American gentleman, should first concern herself with the question of the existence of the American gentlewoman. And the commonly lamented failure—that the man neglects to make her "feel" like a woman—is *whose* failure?

And, finally, the question no longer to be evaded: if *he* does exist, *what* is he? What *makes* the man a gentleman?

So pretentious an inquiry must be pursued, thus, to its logical conclusion—the full and boundless presumption. Accordingly, let it be categorically insisted: the American Gentleman (all lingering uncertainty of his true existence banished by the use of capital letters) must respect five marks. Specifically. . . .

HE IS A MAN. The proposition, let it be quickly affirmed, is not self-evident. Not only are transvestites excluded; so are a multitude of variations and mutations, down to (or up to) fop, dandy, gigolo, or simply the socially avid escort with an unappeasable appetite to see, to be seen, but never to be seen through. To the pseudo-gentleman's misfortune, the last is inevitable, especially in the coldly discerning vision of the one whose attentive respect he most covets—a woman. In short, the essential proposition is the obvious: to be a gentle man, a man must first be a man. For, as in all human relations, gentleness is a function and a form of strength, not of weakness.

HE IS A USEFUL MAN. The adjective may seem redundant, but it is clarifying. The gentleman does not exist simply as a piece of animated decoration or ornament. He partakes of his environment, and he gives to it. He occupies *space*, serious space—something more than the night club's choice table, the theatre's house-seats, the opera's costliest circle, or the delicately cha-cha'ed edge of the most crowded dance floor. He takes up more serious *room* in his society than these pleasurable but scarcely significant spaces. The Earl of Chesterfield notwithstanding, he has *weight*—before he worries about luster.

The matter is as profound as it is old, for the need for the substance to sustain the style has been sensed by every society's understanding of the gentleman—even back to, and including, the fabulously decorous age of chivalry. Only a shallow view of the chivalric idea could dismiss its code as "a picturesque mimicry of high sentiment." For, as one English historian has observed: "Above all, it inculcated an ideal of social service . . . service, however humble its nature, free from degradation or disparagement; service of the weak by the strong; service of the poor by the wealthy; service of the lowly by the high."

In short: the gentleman *then,* and the gentleman *now,* had to be of some use—to some one and to some thing—other than himself.

HE RESPECTS WOMEN. The respect he gives is, of course, neither unctuous nor fawning. In the best sense, it is a respect that issues from a healthy and proper self-respect, for here again, as elsewhere in human relations, the person with no responsible sense of self can only be insensible to others as well. Accordingly, the gentleman dismisses as trivial feminine fancy all notion of equality between the sexes. He conducts himself with the simple awareness that nothing so infuriates a woman dedicated to the proposition of such equality as having to contend with a man who takes the proposition seriously. For almost invariably, of course, the American woman most covetous of the status of man is the same woman who complains, with appropriate sobs, that she knows no man who makes her "feel" like a woman. And from the elemental distinction between man and woman, the gentleman proceeds to make the further discrimination—*among* women. And those deserving of his respect receive the further courtesy of his withholding it from those who do not.

HE RESPECTS MEN. He respects them as individuals. He does not see or appraise them in categories—of status or race or religion or wealth or renown. He discriminates among them not in terms of how much each has accomplished, but in terms of how much has been fulfilled of what each *can* accomplish. He does and says the things that are uncontingent and unreciprocal—the deed done, the gesture extended, the word uttered, essentially always for *its own* sake, free of ulterior motive, unhopeful of any return. Accordingly, he is particularly thoughtful to those who can be of no possible service to him. For it is still exceedingly difficult to improve upon the axiom of John Henry, Cardinal Newman: "It is almost a definition of a gentleman to say he is one who never inflicts pain."

HE IS HIMSELF—AND DOES NOT TRY TO BE A GENTLEMAN. No requisite is more basic—nor more commonly ignored. The effortful striving is the sure exercise in self-frustration, not to mention the embarrassment, or distaste, of others. For the poseur gives mockery, not respect, to what he pretends to be. The acquired but alien manner, the anxiety to impress, the earnestly assumed and studiously rehearsed role, the sustained seeking to elicit response or recognition—all are marks of the cheap replica, the pathetic parody. For, while a gentleman should obviously display good manners, their proper role is not to conceal, but to reveal the true person. And this perhaps is the rule of rules: the gentleman is never trying to *prove* something—least of all himself.

These, then, are some pertinent qualities and considerations, all stated with blithe arbitrariness. They are serious qualities, in some respects, suggesting something, perhaps, of the nature of man himself. But the line between morals and manners becomes, at points, a thin one. And so one wonders: may not some signs on the simple surface of manners suggest the presence, or the lack, of the deeper qualities of a gentleman, beneath and behind the personal presence?

Since the fashion of the day places exaggerated premium on convenient check-lists in such matters, let fashion have its way—and five of the simple surface *manners* of a gentleman be briskly noted:

HE DISPLAYS SPECIAL CONCERN FOR THOSE AT HIS MERCY OR WHIM. There is, in the modern American metropolis, no more devastatingly authoritative witness to the truth or the falsity of a man's claim to be a gentleman than the secretary in his office, the waiter in his restaurant, or the servant in his home. Fortunately for many aspirants, these are rarely garrulous witnesses. But the test stands. For it takes only *politeness* for a man to be civil to his worldly equals. It takes *courtesy* for him to be respectful to all.

HE LISTENS AS WELL AS HE TALKS. In the deepest sense, the mature gentleman heeds the maxim of childhood and speaks when, and as, spoken to—addressing himself to the sense, and the sensibility, of another. His speech does not issue from a lofty summit of self. If it were as a hand, it would never be clenched or thrusting like a fist, never thumping backs and shoulders, but would find contentment and companionship in the easy and gentle touching or joining of fingers. So voices, too, can and should meet one another.

HE SHUNS DISPLAY, AS WELL AS DISCUSSION, OF SELF. The three subjects least common in his conversation are: his fortune, his possessions, and his achievements. And the discretion of his simplest actions follows the discretion of his ordinary speech. In public places, his tips are full but not lavish, his complaints fair and firm but not querulous. In his home, he does not introduce his latest guest first (and passionately) to his Impressionist paintings, then (and casually) to his waiting friends. He is remarkable for his lack of zeal in relating his prowess at skeet-shooting last Sunday, his astute manipulation of longs and shorts last week, his shrewd tacking in last summer's yacht race, his breath-taking spill last winter on the slopes of St. Moritz. The one person, in short, for whom he shows no concern and little interest is the first person singular.

HE RESPECTS CONVENTIONS. He feels no need to display what might be called conspicuous independence or license—no gnawing urge to prove his individuality, to proclaim his personal identity, by disdain for the commonplace or the accepted, especially the inherited. He has the wit to know that conventions, even conventions of mere manners, usually have had their origin in rather sensible attempts to make one person's conduct more helpful or respectful to another.

And even the observance of the trivial and the obsolete convention (such as the gentleman walking on the outside of the lady), while lacking any practical purpose, does suggest the basis of all courtesy: awareness of the presence of the other person.

HE RESPECTS PRACTICALITIES. Without this regard to balance his concern for convention, he would be not a respecter, but a prisoner, of form and fashion. It remains forever possible to be a painstaking practitioner of politeness but, at the same time, a total stranger to courtesy. And this happens when the outward form or manner is allowed to distort one's self or to disregard another. Thus the gentleman refrains from trying to impress another with extravagance beyond his means. Thus—on a trivial but practical level—he may meet the modern challenge of the low-slung taxi by entering it ahead of the lady in evening dress, if only to spare her back or gown.

Simple things, silly things, serious things; things most mundane and things most moral . . . somehow they all contrive to make a man a bit more, or a bit less, a gentleman.

While most of the matters noted are universally known, there are a few special American accents to all this, bespeaking an American Gentleman (he does exist, doesn't he?) a little distinct from all others. Indeed, the American has one notable advantage over all others, for he emphatically possesses, in his national temper, one of the most elemental, as well as the most rare, requisites for being a gentleman: he does not fret and strive too much over being one.

Least of all is he disposed to worry about anybody's definition of one.

And this is probably the brightest sign that he may be one.

POETRY

Virgil

THE AENEID: BOOK IV

BUT NOW for some while the queen had been growing more grievously love-sick,
Feeding the wound with her life-blood, the fire biting within her.
Much did she muse on the hero's nobility, and much
On his family's fame. His look, his words had gone to her heart
And lodged there: she could get no peace from love's disquiet.
The morrow's morn had chased from heaven the dewy darkness,
Was carrying the sun's torch far and wide over earth,
When, almost beside herself, she spoke to her sister, her confidante:—
Anna, sister, why do these nerve-racking dreams haunt me?
This man, this stranger I've welcomed into my house—what of him?
How gallantly he looks, how powerful in chest and shoulders!
I really do think, and have reason to think, that he is heaven-born.
Mean souls convict themselves by cowardice. Oh, imagine
The fates that have harried him, the fight to a finish he told of!
Were it not that my purpose is fixed irrevocably
Never to tie myself in wedlock again to anyone,
Since that first love of mine proved false and let death cheat me;
Had I not taken a loathing for the idea of marriage,
For him, for this one man, I could perhaps have weakened.
Anna, I will confess it, since poor Sychaeus, my husband,
Was killed and our home broken up by my brother's murderous act,
This man is the only one who has stirred my senses and sapped
My will. I feel once more the scars of the old flame.
But no, I would rather the earth should open and swallow me
Or the Father of heaven strike me with lightning down to the shades—
The pale shades and deep night of the Underworld—before
I violate or deny pure widowhood's claim upon me.
He who first wedded me took with him, when he died,
My right to love: let him keep it, there, in the tomb, for ever.
So Dido spoke, and the rising tears flooded her bosom.
Anna replied:—
You are dearer to me than the light of day.
Must you go on wasting your youth in mourning and solitude,
Never to know the blessings of love, the delight of children?
Do you think that ashes, or ghosts underground, can mind about such things?

I know that in Libya, yes, and in Tyre before it, no wooers
Could touch your atrophied heart: Iarbas was rejected
And other lords of Africa, the breeding-ground of the great.
Very well: but when love comes, and pleases, why fight against it?
Besides, you should think of the nations whose land you have settled in—
Threatening encirclement are the Gaetuli, indomitable
In war, the Numidians (no bridle for them), the unfriendly Syrtes;
On your other frontier, a waterless desert and the far-raging
Barcaei: I need not mention the prospect of Tyrian aggression,
Your brother's menacing attitude.
I hold it was providential indeed, and Juno willed it,
That hither the Trojan fleet should have made their way. Oh, sister,
Married to such a man, what a city you'll see, what a kingdom
Established here! With the Trojans as our comrades in arms,
What heights of glory will not we Carthaginians soar to!
Only solicit the gods' favour, perform the due rites,
And plying our guest with attentions, spin a web to delay him,
While out at sea the winter runs wild and Orion is stormy,
While his ships are in bad repair, while the weather is unacquiescent.
These words blew to a blaze the spark of love in the queen's heart,
Set hope to her wavering will and melted her modesty's rigour.
So first they went to the shrines, beseeching at every altar
For grace: as religion requires, they sacrificed chosen sheep to
Ceres, giver of increase, to Phoebus, and to the Wine-god;
To Juno, chief of all, for the marriage-bond is her business.
Dido herself, most beautiful, chalice in hand, would pour
Libations between the horns of a milk-white heifer, and slowly
Would pace by the dripping altars, with the gods looking on,
And daily renew her sacrifice, pouring over the victims'
Opened bodies to see what their pulsing entrails signified.
Ah, little the soothsayers know! What value have vows or shrines
For a woman wild with passion, the while love's flame eats into
Her gentle flesh and love's wound works silently in her breast?
So burns the ill-starred Dido, wandering at large through the town
In a rage of desire, like a doe pierced by an arrow—a doe which
Some hunting shepherd has hit with a long shot while unwary
She stepped through the Cretan woods, and all unknowing has left his
Winged weapon within her: the doe runs fleetly around the Dictaean
Woods and clearings, the deathly shaft stuck deep in her flank.
Now she conducts Aeneas on a tour of her city, and shows him
The vast resources of Carthage, the home there ready and waiting;
Begins to speak, then breaks off, leaving a sentence unfinished.
Now, as the day draws out, she wants to renew that first feast.
In fond distraction begs to hear once again the Trojan
Story, and hangs on his words as once again he tells it.
Then, when the company's broken up, when the moon is dimming
Her beams in turn and the dipping stars invite to sleep,

Alone she frets in the lonely house, lies down on her bed,
Then leaves it again: he's not there, not there, but she hears him and sees him.
Or charmed by his likeness to his father, she keeps Ascanius
Long in her lap to assuage the passion she must not utter.
Work on the half-built towers is closed down meanwhile; the men
Of Carthage have laid off drilling, or building the wharves and vital
Defences of their town; the unfinished works are idle—
Great frowning walls, head-in-air cranes, all at a standstill.

Now as soon as Jupiter's consort perceived that Dido was mad 90
With love and quite beyond caring about her reputation,
She, Juno, approached Venus, making these overtures:—

A praiseworthy feat, I must say, a fine achievement you've brought off,
You and your boy; it should make a great, a lasting name for you—
One woman mastered by the arts of two immortals!
It has not entirely escaped me that you were afraid of my city
And keenly suspicious of towering Carthage's hospitality.
But how will it all end? Where is our rivalry taking us?
Would it not be far better, by arranging a marriage, to seal
A lasting peace? You have got the thing you had set your heart on:
Dido's afire with love, wholly infatuated. 101
Well then, let us unite these nations and rule them with equal
Authority. Let Dido slave for a Trojan husband,
And let the Tyrians pass into your hand as her dowry.

Venus, aware that this was double-talk by which
Juno aimed at basing the future Italian empire
On Africa, countered with these words:—

Senseless indeed to reject
Such terms and prefer to settle the matter with you by hostilities,
Provided fortune favour the plan which you propose.
But I'm in two minds about destiny, I am not sure if Juppiter 110
Wishes one city formed of Tyrians and Trojan exiles,
Or would approve a pact or miscegenation between them.
You are his wife: you may ask him to make his policy clearer.
Proceed. I will support you.

Queen Juno replied thus:

That shall be my task. Now, to solve our immediate problem,
I will briefly put forward a scheme—pray give me your attention.
Aeneas and his unfortunate Dido plan to go
A-hunting in the woods to-morrow, as soon as the sun
Has risen and unshrouded the world below with his rays. 119
On these two, while the beaters are scurrying about and stopping
The coverts with cordon of nets, I shall pour down a darkling rain-storm
And hail as well, and send thunder hallooing all over the sky.
Dispersing for shelter, the rest of the hunt will be cloaked in the mirk;
But Dido and lord Aeneas, finding their way to the same cave,

Shall meet. I'll be there: and if I may rely on your goodwill,
There I shall join them in lasting marriage, and seal her his,
With Hymen present in person.
Venus made no opposition
To Juno's request, though she smiled at the ingenuity of it.
So now, as Aurora was rising out of her ocean bed
And the day-beam lofted, there sallied forth the *élite* of Carthage:
With fine-meshed nets and snares and the broad hunting lances
Massylian riders galloped behind a keen-nosed pack.
The queen dallies: the foremost Carthaginians await her
By the palace door, where stands her horse, caparisoned
In purple and gold, high-spirited, champing the foam-flecked bit.
At last she comes, with many courtiers in attendance:
She wears a Phoenician habit, piped with bright-coloured braid:
Her quiver is gold, her hair bound up with a golden clasp,
A brooch of gold fastens the waist of her brilliant dress.
Her Trojan friends were there too, and young Ascanius
In high glee. But by far the handsomest of them all
Was Aeneas, who came to her side now and joined forces with hers.
It was like when Apollo leaves Lycia, his winter palace,
And Xanthus river to visit Delos, his mother's home,
And renew the dances, while round his altar Cretans and Dryopes
And the tattooed Agathyrsi are raising a polyglot din:
The god himself steps out on the Cynthian range, a circlet
Of gold and a wreath of pliant bay on his flowing hair,
The jangling weapons slung from his shoulder. Nimble as he,
Aeneas moved, with the same fine glow on his handsome face.
When they had reached the mountains, the trackless haunt of game,
Wild goats—picture the scene!—started from crags up above there,
Ran down the slopes: from another direction stags were galloping
Over the open ground of a glen, deserting the heights—
A whole herd jostling together in flight, with a dust-cloud above it.
But young Ascanius, proud of his mettlesome horse, was riding
Along the vale, outstripping group after group of hunters,
And praying hard that, instead of such tame quarry, a frothing
Boar might come his way or a sand-coloured mountain lion.
At this stage a murmur, a growling began to be heard
In the sky: soon followed a deluge of rain and hail together.
The Trojan sportsmen, their Carthaginian friends and the grandson
Of Venus, in some alarm, scattered over the terrain
Looking for shelter. Torrents roared down from the mountain tops.
Now Dido and the prince Aeneas found themselves
In the same cave. Primordial Earth and presiding Juno
Gave the signal. The firmament flickered with fire, a witness
Of wedding. Somewhere above, the Nymphs cried out in pleasure.
That day was doom's first birthday and that first day was the cause of
Evils: Dido recked nothing for appearance or reputation:
The love she brooded on now was a secret love no longer;

Marriage, she called it, drawing the word to veil her sin.
  Straightaway went Rumour through the great cities of Libya—
Rumour, the swiftest traveller of all the ills on earth,
Thriving on movement, gathering strength as it goes; at the start
A small and cowardly thing, it soon puffs itself up,
And walking upon the ground, buries its head in the cloud base.
The legend is that, enraged with the gods, Mother Earth produced
This creature, her last child, as a sister to Enceladus
And Coeus—a swift-footed creature, a winged angel of ruin,
A terrible, grotesque monster, each feather upon whose body—
Incredible though it sounds—has a sleepless eye beneath it,
And for every eye she has also a tongue, a voice and a pricked ear.
At night she flits midway between earth and sky, through the gloom
Screeching, and never closes her eyelids in sweet slumber:
By day she is perched like a look-out either upon a roof-top
Or some high turret; so she terrorises whole cities
Loud-speaker of truth, hoarder of mischievous falsehood, equally.
This creature was now regaling the people with various scandal
In great glee, announcing fact and fiction indiscriminately:
Item, Aeneas has come here, a prince of Trojan blood,
And the beauteous Dido deigns to have her name linked with his;
The couple are spending the winter in debauchery, the whole long
Winter, forgetting their kingdoms, rapt in a trance of lust.
Such gossip did vile Rumour pepper on every mouth.
Not long before she came to the ears of king Iarbas,
Whispering inflammatory words and heaping up his resentment.
  He, the son of Amman by a ravished African nymph,
Had established a hundred shrines to Jove in his ample realm,
A hundred altars, and consecrated their quenchless flames
And vigils unceasing there; the ground was richly steeped in
Victims' blood, and bouquets of flowers adorned the portals.
He now, driven out of his mind by that bitter blast of rumour,
There at the altar, among the presences of the gods,
Prayed, it is said, to Jove, with importunate, humble entreaty:—
  Almighty Jove, whom now for the first time the Moorish people
Pledge with wine as they banquet on ornamental couches,
Do you observe these things? Or are we foolish to shudder
When you shoot fire, O Father, foolish to be dismayed
By lightning which is quite aimless and thunder which growls without
    meaning?
That woman who, wandering within our frontiers, paid to establish
Her insignificant township, permitted by us to plough up
A piece of the coast and be queen of it—that woman, rejecting my
    offer
Of marriage, has taken Aeneas as lord and master there.
And now that philanderer, with his effeminate following—
His chin and oil-sleeked hair set off by a Phrygian bonnet—
That fellow is in possession; while we bring gifts to your shrine,

If indeed you are there and we do not worship a vain myth.
  Thus did Iarbas pray, with his hands on the altar; and Jove
Omnipotent, hearing him, bent down his gaze upon Dido's
City and on those lovers lost to their higher fame.
Then he addressed Mercury, entrusting to him this errand:—
  Go quick, my son, whistle up the Zephyrs and wing your way
Down to the Trojan leader, who is dallying now in Carthage
Without one thought for the city which fate has assigned to be his.
Carry my dictate along the hastening winds and tell him,
Not for such ways did his matchless mother guarantee him
To us, nor for such ends rescue him twice from the Greeks;
Rather, that he should rule an Italy fertile in leadership
And loud with war, should hand on a line which sprang from the noble
Teucer and bring the whole world under a system of law.
If the glory of such great exploits no longer fires his heart
And for his own renown he will make no effort at all,
Does he grudge his son, Ascanius, the glory of Rome to be?
What aim, what hope does he cherish, delaying there in a hostile
Land, with no thought for posterity or his Italian kingdom?
Let him sail. That is the gist. Give him that message from me.
  Jove spake. Mercury now got ready to obey
His father's command. So first he bound on his feet the sandals,
The golden sandals whose wings waft him aloft over the sea
And land alike with the hurrying breath of the breezes. Then
He took up his magic wand (with this he summons wan ghosts
From Orcus and consigns others to dreary Tartarus,
Gives sleep or takes it away, seals up the eyes of dead men).
Now, with that trusty wand, he drove the winds and threshed through
The cloud-wrack; descried as he flew the peak and precipitous flanks of
Atlas, that dour mountain which props the sky with his summit—
Atlas, his pine-bristled head for ever enwrapped in a bandeau
Of glooming cloud, for ever beaten by wind and rain;
Snow lies deep on his shoulders, and watercourses plunge down
That ancient's chin, while his shaggy beard is stiff with ice.
Here first did Mercury pause, hovering on beautifully-balanced
Wings; then stooped, dived bodily down to the sea below,
Like a bird which along the short and around the promontories
Goes fishing, flying low, wave-hopping over the water.
Even so did Mercury skim between earth and sky
Towards the Libyan coast, cutting his path through the winds,
On his way from that mountain giant, Atlas, his mother's sire.
As soon as his winged feet had carried him to the shacks there,
He noticed Aeneas superintending the work on towers
And new buildings: he wore a sword studded with yellow
Jaspers, and a fine cloak of glowing Tyrian purple
Hung from his shoulders—the wealthy Dido had fashioned it,
Interweaving the fabric with threads of gold, as a present for him.

Mercury went for him at once:—
So now you are laying
Foundations for lofty Carthage, building a beautiful city
To please a woman, lost to the interests of your own realm?
The king of the gods, who directs heaven and earth with his deity,
Sends me to you from bright Olympus: the king of the gods
Gave me this message to carry express through the air:—What do you
Aim at or hope for, idling and fiddling here in Libya?
If you're indifferent to your own high destiny
And for your own renown you will make no effort at all,
Think of your young hopeful, Ascanius, growing to manhood,
The inheritance which you owe him—an Italian kingdom, the soil of Rome.
Such were the words which Mercury delivered;
And breaking off abruptly, was manifest no more,
But vanished into thin air, far beyond human ken.
Dazed indeed by that vision was Aeneas, and dumbfounded:
His hair stood on end with terror, the voice stuck in his throat.
Awed by this admonition from the great throne above,
He desired to fly the country, dear though it was to him.
But oh, what was he to do? What words could he find to get round
The temperamental queen? How broach the matter to her?
His mind was in feverish conflict, tossed from one side to the other,
Twisting and turning all ways to find a way past his dilemma.
So vacillating, at last he felt this the better decision:—
Sending for Mnestheus, Sergestus and brave Serestus, he bade them
Secretly get the ships ready; muster their friends on the beach,
Be prepared to fight: the cause of so drastic a change of plan
They must keep dark: in the meanwhile, assuming that generous Dido
Knew nothing and could not imagine the end of so great a love,
Aeneas would try for a way to approach her, the kindest moment
For speaking, the best way to deal with this delicate matter. His comrades
Obeyed the command and did as he told them with cheerful alacrity.
But who can ever hoodwink a woman in love? The queen,
Apprehensive even when things went well, now sensed his deception,
Got wind of what was going to happen. That mischievous Rumour,
Whispering the fleet was preparing to sail, put her in a frenzy.
Distraught, she witlessly wandered about the city, raving
Like some Bacchante driven wild, when the emblems of sanctity
Stir, by the shouts of "Hail, Bacchus!" and drawn to Cithaeron
At night by the din of revellers, at the triennial orgies.
Finding Aeneas at last, she cried, before he could speak:—
Unfaithful man, did you think you could do such a dreadful thing
And keep it dark? yes, skulk from my land without one word?
Our love, the vows you made me—do these not give you pause,
Nor even the thought of Dido meeting a painful death?

Now, in the dead of winter, to be getting your ships ready
And hurrying to set sail when northerly gales are blowing,
You heartless one! Suppose the fields were not foreign, the home was
Not strange that you are bound for, suppose Troy stood as of old,
Would you be sailing for Troy, now, in this stormy weather?
Am I your reason for going? By these tears, by the hand you gave me—
They are all I have left, to-day, in my misery—I implore you,
And by our union of hearts, by our marriage hardly begun,
If I have ever helped you at all, if anything
About me pleased you, be sad for our broken home, forgo
Your purpose, I beg you, unless it's too late for prayers of mine!
Because of you, the Libyan tribes and the Nomad chieftains
Hate me, the Tyrians are hostile: because of you I have lost
My old reputation for faithfulness—the one thing that could have made me
Immortal. Oh, I am dying! To what, my guest, are you leaving me?
"Guest"—that is all I may call you now, who have called you husband.
Why do I linger here? Shall I wait till my brother, Pygmalion,
Destroys this place, or Iarbas leads me away captive?
If even I might have conceived a child by you before
You went away, a little Aeneas to play in the palace
And, in spite of all this, to remind me of you by his looks, oh then
I should not feel so utterly finished and desolate.
  She had spoken. Aeneas, mindful of Jove's words, kept his eyes
Unyielding, and with a great effort repressed his feeling for her.
In the end he managed to answer:—
                                        Dido, I'll never pretend
You have not been good to me, deserving of everything
You can claim. I shall not regret my memories of Elissa
As long as I breathe, as long as I remember my own self.
For my conduct—this, briefly: I did not look to make off from here
In secret—do not suppose it; nor did I offer you marriage
At any time or consent to be bound by a marriage contract.
If fate allowed me to be my own master, and gave me
Free will to choose my way of life, to solve my problems,
Old Troy would be my first choice: I would restore it, and honour
My people's relics—the high halls of Priam perpetuated,
Troy given back to its conquered sons, a renaissant city,
Had been my task. But now Apollo and the Lycian
Oracle have told me that Italy is our bourne.
There lies my heart, my homeland. You, a Phoenician, are held by
These Carthaginian towers, by the charm of your Libyan city:
So can you grudge us Trojans our vision of settling down
In Italy? We too may seek a kingdom abroad.
Often as night envelops the earth in dewy darkness,
Often as star-rise, the troubled ghost of my father, Anchises,

Comes to me in my dreams, warns me and frightens me.
I am disturbed no less by the wrong I am doing Ascanius,
Defrauding him of his destined realm in Hesperia.
What's more, just now the courier of heaven, sent by Juppiter—
I swear it on your life and mine—conveyed to me, swiftly flying,
His orders: I saw the god, as clear as day, with my own eyes,
Entering the city, and these ears drank in the words he uttered.
No more reproaches, then—they only torture us both.
God's will, not mine, says "Italy".
  All the while he was speaking she gazed at him askance,
Her glances flickering over him, eyes exploring the whole man
In deadly silence. Now, furiously, she burst out:—
  Faithless and false! No goddess mothered you, no Dardanus
Your ancestor! I believe harsh Caucasus begat you
On a flint-hearted rock and Hyrcanian tigers suckled you.
Why should I hide my feelings? What worse can there be to keep them for?
Not one sigh from him when I wept! Not a softer glance!
Did he yield an inch, or a tear, in pity for her who loves him?
I don't know what to say first. It has come to this,—not Juno,
Not Jove himself can view my plight with the eye of justice.
Nowhere is it safe to be trustful. I took him, a castaway,
A pauper, and shared my kingdom with him—I must have been mad—
Rescued his lost fleet, rescued his friends from death.
Oh, I'm on fire and drifting! And now Apollo's prophecies,
Lycian oracles, couriers of heaven sent by Juppiter
With stern commands—all these order you to betray me.
Oh, of course this is just the sort of transaction that troubles the calm of
The gods. I'll not keep you, nor probe the dishonesty of your words.
Chase your Italy, then! Go, sail to your realm overseas!
I only hope that, if the just spirits have any power,
Marooned on some mid-sea rock you may drink the full cup of agony
And often cry out for Dido. I'll dog you, from far, with the death-fires;
And when cold death has parted my soul from my body, my spectre
Will be wherever you are. You shall pay for the evil you've done me.
The tale of your punishment will come to me down in the shades.
  With these words Dido suddenly ended, and sick at heart
Turned from him, tore herself away from his eyes, ran indoors,
While he hung back in dread of a still worse scene, although
He had much to say. Her maids bore up the fainting queen
Into her marble chamber and laid her down on the bed.
  But the god-fearing Aeneas, much as he longed to soothe
Her anguish with consolation, with words that would end her troubles,
Heavily sighing, his heart melting from love of her,

Nevertheless obeyed the gods and went off to his fleet.
Whereupon the Trojans redoubled their efforts, all along
The beach dragging down the tall ships, launching the well-tarred bottoms,
Fetching green wood to make oars and baulks of unfashioned timber
From the forest, so eager they were to be gone.
You could see them on the move, hurrying out of the city.
It looked like an army of ants when, provident for winter,
They're looting a great big corn-heap and storing it up in their own house;
Over a field the black file goes, as they carry the loot
On a narrow track through the grass; some are strenuously pushing
The enormous grains of corn with their shoulders, while others marshal
The traffic and keep it moving: their whole road seethes with activity.
Ah, Dido, what did you feel when you saw these things going forward?
What moans you gave when, looking forth from your high roof-top,
You beheld the whole length of the beach aswarm with men, and the sea's face
Alive with the sound and fury of preparations for sailing!
Excess of love, to what lengths you drive our human hearts!
Once again she was driven to try what tears and entreaties
Could do, and let love beggar her pride—she would leave no appeal
Untried, lest, for want of it, she should all needlessly die.
Anna, you see the bustle down there on the beach; from all sides
They have assembled; their canvas is stretched to the winds already,
And the elated mariners have garlanded their ships.
If I was able to anticipate this deep anguish,
I shall be able to bear it. But do this one thing, Anna,
For your poor sister. You were the only confidante
Of that faithless man: he told you even his secret thoughts:
You alone know the most tactful way, the best time to approach him.
Go, sister, and make this appeal to my disdainful enemy:—
Say that *I* never conspired with the Greeks at Aulis to ruin
The Trojan people, nor sent squadrons of ships against Troy;
I never desecrated the ashes of dead Anchises,
So why must Aeneas be deaf and obdurate to my pleading?
Why off so fast? Will he grant a last wish to her who unhappily
Loves him, and wait for a favouring wind, an easier voyage?
Not for our marriage that was do I plead now— he has forsworn it,
Nor that he go without his dear Latium and give up his kingdom.
I ask a mere nothing—just time to give rein to despair and thus calm it,
To learn from ill luck how to grieve for what I have lost, and to bear it.
This last favour I beg—oh, pity your sister!—and if he
Grants it, I will repay him; my death shall be his interest.

Such were her prayers, and such the tearful entreaties her agonised
Sister conveyed to Aeneas again and again. But unmoved by
Tearful entreaties he was, adamant against all pleadings:
Fate blocked them, heaven stopped his ears lest he turn complaisant.
As when some stalwart oak-tree, some veteran of the Alps,
Is assailed by a wintry wind whose veering gusts tear at it,
Trying to root it up; wildly whistle the branches,
The leaves come flocking down from aloft as the bole is battered;
But the tree stands firm on its crag, for high as its head is carried
Into the sky, so deep do its roots go down towards Hades:
Even thus was the hero belaboured for long with every kind of
Pleading, and his great heart thrilled through and through with the
pain of it;
Resolute, though, was his mind; unavailingly rolled her tears.
But hapless Dido, frightened out of her wits by her destiny,
Prayed for death: she would gaze no more on the dome of daylight.
And now, strengthening her resolve to act and to leave this world,
She saw, as she laid gifts on the incense-burning altars—
Horrible to relate—the holy water turn black
And the wine she poured changing uncannily to blood.
She told no one, even her sister, of this phenomenon.
Again, she had dedicated a chantry of marble within
The palace to her first husband; held it in highest reverence;
Hung it with snow-white fleeces and with festoons of greenery:
Well, from this shrine, when night covered the earth, she seemed
To be hearing words—the voice of that husband calling upon her.
There was something dirge-like, too, in the tones of the owl on the
roof-top
Whose lonely, repeated cries were drawn out to a long keening.
Besides, she recalled with horror presages, dread forewarnings
Of the prophets of old. Aeneas himself pursued her remorselessly
In dreams, driving her mad; or else she dreamed of unending
Solitude and desertion, of walking alone and eternally
Down a long road, through an empty land, in search of her Tyrians.
Just so does the raving Pentheus see covens of Furies and has the
Delusion of seeing two suns in the sky and a double Thebes:
Just so on the stage does Orestes, the son of Agamemnon,
Move wildly about while his mother pursues him with torches and
black snakes,
And at the door the avenging Furies cut off his retreat.
So when, overmastered by grief, she conceived a criminal madness
And doomed herself to death, she worked out the time and method
In secret; then, putting on an expression of calm hopefulness
To hide her resolve, she approached her sorrowing sister with these
words:—
I have found out a way, Anna—oh, wish me joy of it—
To get him back or else get free of my love for him.
Near Ocean's furthest bound and the sunset is Aethiopia,

The very last place on earth, where giant Atlas pivots
The wheeling sky, embossed with fiery stars, on his shoulders.
I have been in touch with a priestess from there, a Massylian, who once,
As warden of the Hesperides' sacred close, was used to
Feed the dragon which guarded their orchard of golden apples,
Sprinkling its food with moist honey and sedative poppy-seeds.
Now this enchantress claims that her spells can liberate
One's heart, or can inject love-pangs, just as she wishes;
Can stop the flow of rivers, send the stars flying backwards,
Conjure ghosts in the night: she can make the earth cry out
Under one's feet, and elm trees come trooping down from the mountains.
Dear sister, I solemnly call to witness the gods and you whom
I love, that I do not willingly resort to her magic arts.
You must build up a funeral pyre high in the inner courtyard,
And keep it dark: lay on it the arms which that godless man
Has left on the pegs in our bedroom, all relics of him, and the marriage-bed
That was the ruin of me. To blot out all that reminds me
Of that vile man is my pleasure and what the enchantress directs.
So Dido spoke, and fell silent, her face going deadly white.
Yet Anna never suspected that Dido was planning her own death
Through these queer rites, nor imagined how frantic a madness possessed her,
Nor feared any worse would happen than when Sychaeus had died.
So she made the arrangements required of her.
When in the innermost court of the palace the pyre had been built up
To a great height with pinewood and logs of ilex, the queen
Festooned the place with garlands and wreathed it with funereal
Foliage: then she laid on it the clothes, the sword which Aeneas
Had left, and an effigy of him; she well knew what was to happen.
Altars are set up all round. Her hair unloosed, the enchantress
Loudly invokes three hundred deities—Erebus, Chaos,
Hecate, three in one, and three-faced Diana, the virgin.
She had sprinkled water which came, she pretended, from Lake Avernus;
Herbs she had gathered, cut by moonlight with a bronze knife—
Poisonous herbs all rank with juices of black venom;
She has found a love charm, a gland torn from the forehead of a new-born
Foal before its mother could get it.
Dido, the sacramental grain in her purified hands,
One foot unsandalled, her dress uncinctured, stood by the altars
Calling upon the gods and the stars that know fate's secrets,
Death at her heart, and prayed to whatever power it is
Holds unrequited lovers in its fair, faithful keeping.

Was night. All over the earth, creatures were plucking the flower
Of soothing sleep, the woods and the wild seas fallen quiet—
A time when constellations have reached their mid-career,
When the countryside is all still, the beasts and the brilliant birds
That haunt the lakes' wide waters or the tangled undergrowth
Of the champain, stilled in sleep under the quiet night—
Cares are lulled and hearts can forget for a while their travails.
Not so the Phoenician queen: death at her heart, she could not
Ever relax in sleep, let the night in to her eyes
Or mind: her agonies mounted, her love reared up again
And savaged her, till she writhed in a boiling sea of passion.
So thus she began, her thoughts whirling round in a vicious circle:—
What shall I do? Shall I, who've been jilted, return to my former
Suitors? go down on my knees for marriage to one of the Nomads
Although, time and again, I once rejected their offers?
Well then, am I to follow the Trojan's fleet and bow to
Their lightest word? I helped them once. Will that help me now?
Dare I think they remember with gratitude my old kindness?
But even if I wished it, who would suffer me, welcome me
Aboard those arrogant ships? They hate me. Ah, duped and ruined!—
Surely by now I should know the ill faith of Laomedon's people?
So then? Shall I sail, by myself, with those exulting mariners,
Or sail against them with all my Tyrian folk about me—
My people, whom once I could hardly persuade to depart from
Sidon—
Bidding them man their ships and driving them out to sea again?
Better die—I deserve it—end my pain with the sword.
Sister, you started it all: overborne by my tears, you laid up
These evils to drive me mad, put me at the mercy of a foe.
Oh, that I could have been some child of nature and lived
An innocent life, untouched by marriage and all its troubles!
I have broken the faith I vowed to the memory of Sichaeus.
Such were the reproaches she could not refrain from uttering.
High on the poop of his ship, resolute now for departure,
Aeneas slept; preparations for sailing were fully completed.
To him in a dream there appeared the shape of the god, returning
Just as he'd looked before, as if giving the same admonitions—
Mercury's very image, the voice, the complexion, the yellow
Hair and the handsome youthful body identical:—
Goddess-born, can you go on sleeping at such a crisis?
Are you out of your mind, not to see what dangers are brewing up
Around you, and not to hear the favouring breath of the West wind?
Being set upon death, her heart is aswirl with conflicting passions,
Aye, she is brooding now some trick, some desperate deed.
Why are you not going, all speed, while the going is good?
If dawn find you still here, delaying by these shores,
You'll have the whole sea swarming with hostile ships, there will be
Firebrands coming against you, you'll see this beach ablaze.

Up and away, then! No more lingering! Woman was ever
A veering, weathercock creature.
He spoke, and vanished in the darkness.
Then, startled by the shock of the apparition, Aeneas
Snatched himself out of sleep and urgently stirred up his
comrades:—
Jump to it, men! To your watch! Get to the rowing benches!
Smartly! Hoist the sails! A god from heaven above
Spurs me to cut the cables, make off and lose not a moment:
This was his second warning. O blessed god, we follow you,
God indeed, and once more we obey the command joyfully!
Be with us! Look kindly upon us! Grant us good sailing weather!
Thus did Aeneas cry, and flashing his sword from its scabbard,
With the drawn blade he servered the moorings. The same sense of
Urgency fired his comrades all; they cut and ran for it.
The shore lay empty, The ships covered the open sea.
The oarsmen swept the blue and sent the foam flying with hard
strokes.
And now was Aurora, leaving the saffron bed of Tithonus,
Beginning to shower upon earth the light of another day.
The queen, looking forth from her roof-top, as soon as she saw the
sky
Grow pale and the Trojan fleet running before the wind,
Aware that the beach and the roadstead were empty, the sailors gone,
Struck herself three times, four times, upon her lovely breast,
Tore at her yellow hair, and exclaimed:—
In god's name! shall that foreigner
Scuttle away and make a laughing-stock of my country?
Will not my people stand to arms for a mass pursuit?
Will some not rush the warships out of the docks? Move, then!
Bring firebrands apace, issue the weapons, pull on the oars!
What am I saying? Where am I? What madness veers my mind?
Poor Dido, the wrong you have done—is it only now coming home
to you?
You should have thought of that when you gave him your sceptre.
So this is
The word of honour of one who, men say, totes round his home-gods
Everywhere, and bore on his back a doddering father!
Why could I not have seized him, torn up his body and littered
The sea with it? finished his friends with the sword, finished his own
Ascanius and served him up for his father to banquet on?
The outcome of battle had been uncertain?—Let it have been so:
Since I was to die, whom had I to fear? I should have stormed
Their bulwarks with fire, set alight their gangways, gutted the whole
lot—
Folk, father and child—then flung myself on the conflagration.
O sun, with your beams surveying all that is done on earth!
Juno, the mediator and witness of my tragedy!

Hecate, whose name is howled by night at the city crossroads!
Avenging Furies, and you, the patrons of dying Elissa!—
Hear me! Incline your godheads to note this wickedness
So worthy of your wrath! And hear my prayer! If he,
That damned soul, must make port and get to land, if thus
Jove destines it, if that bourne is fixed for him irrevocably,
May he be harried in war by adventurous tribes, and exiled
From his own land; may Ascanius be torn from his arms; may he have to
Sue for aid, and see his own friends squalidly dying.
Yes, and when he's accepted the terms of a harsh peace,
Let him never enjoy his realm or the allotted span,
But fall before his time and lie on the sands, unburied.
That is my last prayer. I pour it out, with my lifeblood.
Let you, my Tyrians, sharpen your hatred upon his children
And all their seed for ever: send this as a present to
My ghost. Between my people and his, no love, no alliance!
Rise up from my dead bones, avenger! Rise up, one
To hound the Trojan settlers with fire and steel remorselessly,
Now, some day, whenever the strength for it shall be granted!
Shore to shore, sea to sea, weapon to weapon opposed—
I call down a feud between them and us to the last generation!
These things she said; then tried to think of every expedient,
Seeking the quickest way out of the life she hated.
Briefly now she addressed Barce, the nurse of Sychaeus,
Her own being dust and ashes, interred in her native land:—
Dear nurse, please will you get my sister, Anna. She must
Hasten to purify herself with living water, and fetch
The cattle, tell her—the atonement offerings, as directed;
Then let her come. And do you go and put on the holy headband.
These rites of Jove of the Underworld, duly made ready and started,
I mean to go through with now, and put an end to my troubles,
Committing to the flames the funeral pyre of that Trojan.
She spoke. The nurse hurried off with senile officiousness.
But Dido, trembling, distraught by the terrible thing she was doing,
Her bloodshot eyes all restless, with hectic blotches upon
Her quivering cheeks, yet pale with the shade of advancing death,
Ran to the innermost court of the palace, climbed the lofty
Pyre, frantic at heart, and drew Aeneas' sword—
Her present to him, procured once for a far different purpose.
Then, after eyeing the clothes he had left behind, and the memoried
Bed, pausing to weep and brood on him for a little,
She lay down on the bed and spoke her very last words:—
O relics of him, things dear to me while fate, while heaven allowed it,
Receive this life of mine, release me from my troubles!
I have lived, I have run to the finish the course which fortune gave me:

And now, a queenly shade, I shall pass to the world below.
I built a famous city, saw my own place established,
Avenged a husband, exacted a price for a brother's enmity.
Happy I would have been, ah, beyond words happy,
If only the Trojan ships had never come to my shore!
These words; then, burying her face in the bed:—
Shall I die unavenged?
At least let me die. Thus, thus! I go to the dark, go gladly. 660
May he look long, from out there on the deep, at my flaming pyre,
The heartless! And may my death-fires signal bad luck for his voyage!
She had spoken; and with these words, her attendants saw her falling
Upon the sword, they could see the blood spouting up over
The blade, and her hands spattered. Their screams rang to the roofs of
The palace; then rumour ran amok through the shocked city.
All was weeping and wailing, the streets were filled with a keening
Of women, the air resounded with terrible lamentations.
It was as if Carthage or ancient Tyre should be falling,
With enemy troops breaking into the town and a conflagration
Furiously sweeping over the abodes of men and of gods. 671
Anna heard it: half dead from extreme fear, she ran through
The crowd, tearing her cheeks with her nails, beating her breast
With her fists, and called aloud by name on the dying woman:—
So this was your purpose, Dido? You were making a dupe of me?
That pyre, those lighted altars—for me, they were leading to this?
How shall I chide you for leaving me? Were you too proud to let your
Sister die with you? You should have called me to share your end:
One hour, one pang of the sword could have carried us both away.
Did I build this pyre with my own hands, invoking our family gods,
So that you might lie on it, and I, the cause of your troubles, not be there? 681
You have destroyed more than your self—me, and the lords
And commons and city of Sidon. Quick! Water for her wounds!
Let me bathe them, and if any last breath is fluttering from her mouth,
Catch it in mine!
So saying, she had scaled the towering pyre,
Taken the dying woman into her lap, was caressing her,
Sobbing, trying to staunch the dark blood with her own dress.
Dido made an effort to raise her heavy eyes,
Then gave it up: the sword-blade grated against her breast bone.
Three times she struggled to rise, to lift herself on an elbow, 690
Three times rolled back on the bed. Her wandering gaze went up
To the sky, looking for light: she gave a moan when she saw it.
Then did almighty Juno take pity on her long-drawn-out
Sufferings and hard going, sent Iris down from Olympus

To part the agonised soul from the body that still clung to it.
Since she was dying neither a natural death nor from others'
Violence, but desperate and untimely, driven to it
By a crazed impulse, not yet had Proserpine clipped from her head
The golden tress, or consigned her soul to the Underworld.
So now, all dewy, her pinions the colour of yellow crocus,
Her wake a thousand rainbow hues refracting the sunlight,
Iris flew down, and over Dido hovering, said:—
  As I was bidden, I take this sacred thing, the Death-god's
Due: and you I release from your body.
                                        She snipped the tress.
Then all warmth went at once, the life was lost in air.

Alfred, Lord Tennyson

ULYSSES

IT LITTLE profits that an idle king,
By this still hearth, among these barren crags,
Matched with an aged wife, I mete and dole
Unequal laws unto a savage race,
That hoard, and sleep, and feed, and know not me.
I cannot rest from travel; I will drink
Life to the lees. All times I have enjoyed
Greatly, have suffered greatly, both with those
That loved me, and alone; on shore, and when
Through scudding drifts the rainy Hyades
Vexed the dim sea. I am become a name;
For always roaming with a hungry heart
Much have I seen and known—cities of men
And manners, climates, councils, governments,
Myself not least, but honored of them all—
And drunk delight of battle with my peers,
Far on the ringing plains of windy Troy.
I am a part of all that I have met;
Yet all experience is an arch wherethrough
Gleams that untraveled world whose margin fades
Forever and forever when I move.
How dull it is to pause, to make an end,
To rust unburnished, not to shine in use!
As though to breathe were life! Life piled on life
Were all too little, and of one to me
Little remains; but every hour is saved
From that eternal silence, something more,
A bringer of new things; and vile it were
For some three suns to store and hoard myself,
And this gray spirit yearning in desire

To follow knowledge like a sinking star,
Beyond the utmost bound of human thought.
  This is my son, mine own Telemachus,
To whom I leave the scepter and the isle—
Well-loved of me, discerning to fulfill
This labor, by slow prudence to make mild
A rugged people, and through soft degrees
Subdue them to the useful and the good.
Most blameless is he, centered in the sphere
Of common duties, decent not to fail
In offices of tenderness, and pay
Meet adoration to my household gods,
When I am gone. He works his work, I mine.
  There lies the port; the vessel puffs her sail;
There gloom the dark, broad seas. My mariners,
Souls that have toiled, and wrought, and thought with me—
That ever with a frolic welcome took
The thunder and the sunshine, and opposed
Free hearts, free foreheads—you and I are old;
Old age hath yet his honor and his toil.
Death closes all; but something ere the end,
Some work of noble note, may yet be done,
Not unbecoming men that strove with gods.
The lights begin to twinkle from the rocks;
The long day wanes; the slow moon climbs; the deep
Moans round with many voices. Come, my friends.
'Tis not too late to seek a newer world.
Push off, and sitting well in order smite
The sounding furrows; for my purpose holds
To sail beyond the sunset, and the baths
Of all the western stars, until I die.
It may be that the gulfs will wash us down;
It may be we shall touch the Happy Isles,
And see the great Achilles, whom we knew.
Though much is taken, much abides; and though
We are not now that strength which in old days
Moved earth and heaven, that which we are, we are—
One equal temper of heroic hearts,
Made weak by time and fate, but strong in will
To strive, to seek, to find, and not to yield.

Alfred, Lord Tennyson

MORTE D'ARTHUR

So all day long the noise of battle roll'd
Among the mountains by the winter sea,
Until King Arthur's table, man by man,
Had fallen in Lyonnesse about their lord,
King Arthur; then, because his wound was deep,
The bold Sir Bedivere uplifted him,
Sir Bedivere, the last of all his knights,
And bore him to a chapel nigh the field,
A broken chancel with a broken cross,
That stood on a dark strait of barren land.
On one side lay the ocean, and on one
Lay a great water, and the moon was full.
  Then spake King Arthur to Sir Bedivere:
"The sequel of to-day unsolders all
The goodliest fellowship of famous knights
Whereof this world holds record. Such a sleep
They sleep—the men I loved. I think that we
Shall never more, at any future time,
Delight our souls with talk of knightly deeds,
Walking about the gardens and the halls
Of Camelot, as in the days that were.
I perish by this people which I made,—
Tho' Merlin sware that I should come again
To rule once more—but let what will be be,
I am so deeply smitten thro' the helm
That without help I cannot last till morn.
Thou therefore take my brand Excalibur,
Which was my pride, for thou rememberest how
In those old days, one summer noon, an arm
Rose up from out the bosom of the lake,
Clothed in white samite, mystic, wonderful,
Holding the sword—and how I row'd across
And took it, and have worn it, like a king;
And, wheresoever I am sung or told
In aftertime, this also shall be known.
But now delay not; take Excalibur,
And fling him far into the middle mere;
Watch what thou seest, and lightly bring me word."
  To him replied the bold Sir Bedivere:
"It is not meet, Sir King, to leave thee thus,
Aidless, alone, and smitten thro' the helm.
A little thing may harm a wounded man.
Yet I thy hest will all perform at full,

Watch what I see, and lightly bring thee word."
  So saying, from the ruin'd shrine he stept
And in the moon athwart the place of tombs,
Where lay the mighty bones of ancient men,
Old knights, and over them the sea-wind sang
Shrill, chill, with flakes of foam. He, stepping down
By zigzag paths and juts of pointed rock,
Came on the shining levels of the lake.
  There drew he forth the brand Excalibur,
And o'er him, drawing it, the winter moon,
Brightening the skirts of a long cloud, ran forth
And sparkled keen with frost against the hilt;
For all the haft twinkled with diamond sparks,
Myriads of topaz-lights, and jacinth-work
Of subtlest jewellery. He gazed so long
That both his eyes were dazzled, as he stood,
This way and that dividing the swift mind,
In act to throw; but at the last it seem'd
Better to leave Excalibur conceal'd
There in the many-knotted water-flags,
That whistled stiff and dry about the marge.
So strode he back slow to the wounded king.
  Then spake King Arthur to Sir Bedivere:
"Hast thou perform'd my mission which I gave?
What is it thou hast seen, or what hast heard?"
  And answer made the bold Sir Bedivere:
"I heard the ripple washing in the reeds,
And the wild water lapping on the crag."
  To whom replied King Arthur, faint and pale:
"Thou hast betray'd thy nature and thy name,
Not rendering true answer, as beseem'd
Thy fealty, nor like a noble knight;
For surer sign had follow'd, either hand,
Or voice, or else a motion of the mere.
This is a shameful thing for men to lie.
Yet now, I charge thee, quickly go again
As thou art lief and dear, and do the thing
I bade thee, watch, and lightly bring me word."
  Then went Sir Bedivere the second time
Across the ridge, and paced beside the mere,
Counting the dewy pebbles, fix'd in thought;
But when he saw the wonder of the hilt,
How curiously and strangely chased, he smote
His palms together, and he cried aloud:
  "And if indeed I cast the brand away,
Surely a precious thing, one worthy note,
Should thus be lost forever from the earth,
Which might have pleased the eyes of many men.

What good should follow this, if this were done?
What harm, undone? deep harm to disobey,
Seeing obedience is the bond of rule.
Were it well to obey then, if a king demand
An act unprofitable, against himself?
The king is sick, and knows not what he does.
What record, or what relic of my lord
Should be to aftertime, but empty breath
And rumors of a doubt? but were this kept,
Stored in some treasure-house of mighty kings,
Some one might show it at a joust of arms,
Saying, 'King Arthur's sword, Excalibur,
Wrought by the lonely maiden of the lake;
Nine years she wrought it, sitting in the deeps
Upon the hidden bases of the hills.'
So might some old man speak in the aftertime
To all the people, winning reverence;
But now much honor and much fame were lost."
So spake he, clouded with his own conceit,
And hid Excalibur the second time,
And so strode back slow to the wounded king.
Then spoke King Arthur, breathing heavily:
"What is it thou hast seen, or what hast heard?"
And answer made the bold Sir Bedivere:
"I heard the water lapping on the crag,
And the long ripple washing in the reeds."
To whom replied King Arthur, much in wrath:
"Ah, miserable and unkind, untrue,
Unknightly, traitor-hearted! Woe is me!
Authority forgets a dying king,
Laid widow'd of the power in his eye
That bow'd the will. I see thee what thou art,
For thou, the latest-left of all my knights,
In whom should meet the offices of all,
Thou wouldst betray me for the precious hilt;
Either from lust of gold, or like a girl
Valuing the giddy pleasure of the eyes.
Yet, for a man may fail in duty twice,
And the third time may prosper, get thee hence;
But, if thou spare to fling Excalibur,
I will arise and slay thee with my hands."
Then quickly rose Sir Bedivere, and ran,
And, leaping down the ridges lightly, plunged
Among the bulrush-beds, and clutch'd the sword,
And strongly wheel'd and threw it. The great brand
Made lightnings in the splendor of the moon,
And flashing round and round, and whirl'd in an arch,
Shot like a streamer of the northern morn,

Seen where the moving isles of winter shock
By night, with noises of the northern sea.
So flash'd and fell the brand Excalibur;
But ere he dipt the surface, rose an arm
Cloth'd in white samite, mystic, wonderful,
And caught him by the hilt, and brandish'd him
Three times, and drew him under in the mere.
And lightly went the other to the king.
  Then spoke King Arthur, drawing thicker breath:
"Now see I by thine eyes that this is done.
Speak out; what is it thou hast heard, or seen?"
  And answer made the bold Sir Bedivere:
"Sir King, I closed mine eyelids, lest the gems
Should blind my purpose, for I never saw,
Nor shall see, here or elsewhere, till I die,
Not tho' I live three lives of mortal men,
So great a miracle as yonder hilt.
Then with both hands I flung him, wheeling him;
But when I look'd again, behold an arm,
Clothed in white samite, mystic, wonderful,
That caught him by the hilt, and brandish'd him
Three times, and drew him under in the mere."
  And answer made King Arthur, breathing hard:
"My end draws nigh; 'tis time that I were gone.
Make broad thy shoulders to receive my weight,
And bear me to the margin; yet I fear
My wound hath taken cold, and I shall die."
  So saying, from the pavement he half rose,
Slowly, with pain, reclining on his arm,
And looking wistfully with wide blue eyes
As in a picture. Him Sir Bedivere
Remorsefully regarded thro' his tears,
And would have spoken, but he found not words,
Then took with care, and kneeling on one knee,
O'er both his shoulders drew the languid hands,
And rising bore him thro' the place of tombs.
  But, as he walk'd, King Arthur panted hard,
Like one that feels a nightmare on his bed
When all the house is mute. So sigh'd the king,
Muttering and murmuring at his ear, "Quick, quick!
I fear it is too late, and I shall die."
But the other swiftly strode from ridge to ridge,
Clothed with his breath, and looking, as he walk'd,
Larger than human on the frozen hills.
He heard the deep behind him, and a cry
Before. His own thought drove him like a goad.
Dry clash'd his harness in the icy caves
And barren chasms, and all to left and right

The bare black cliff clang'd round him, as he based
His feet on juts of slippery crag that rang
Sharp-smitten with the dint of armed heels—
And on a sudden, lo! the level lake,
And the long glories of the winter moon.
  Then saw they how there hove a dusky barge,
Dark as a funeral scarf from stem to stern,
Beneath them; and descending they were ware
That all the decks were dense with stately forms
Black-stoled, black-hooded, like a dream—by these
Three queens with crowns of gold—and from them rose
A cry that shiver'd to the tingling stars,
And, as it were one voice, an agony
Of lamentation, like a wind that shrills
All night in a waste land, where no one comes,
Or hath come, since the making of the world.
  Then murmur'd Arthur, "Place me in the barge,"
And to the barge they came. There those three queens
Put forth their hands, and took the king, and wept.
But she that rose the tallest of them all
And fairest laid his head upon her lap,
And loosed the shatter'd casque, and chafed his hands,
And call'd him by his name, complaining loud,
And dropping bitter tears against his brow
Striped with dark blood; for all his face was white
And colorless, and like the wither'd moon
Smote by the fresh beam of the springing east;
And all his greaves and cuisses dash'd with drops
Of onset; and the light and lustrous curls—
That made his forehead like a rising sun
High from the dais-throne—were parch'd with dust;
Or, clotted into points and hanging loose,
Mix'd with the knightly growth that fringed his lips.
So like a shatter'd column lay the king;
Not like that Arthur who, with lance in rest,
From spur to plume a star of tournament,
Shot thro' the lists at Camelot, and charged
Before the eyes of ladies and of kings.
  Then loudly cried the bold Sir Bedivere:
"Ah! my Lord Arthur, whither shall I go?
Where shall I hide my forehead and my eyes?
For now I see the true old times are dead,
When every morning brought a noble chance,
And every chance brought out a noble knight.
Such times have been not since the light that led
The holy Elders with the gift of myrrh.
But now the whole ROUND TABLE is dissolved
Which was an image of the mighty world;

And I, the last, go forth companionless,
And the days darken round me, and the years,
Among new men, strange faces, other minds."
And slowly answer'd Arthur from the barge:
"The old order changeth, yielding place to new,
And God fulfils himself in many ways,
Lest one good custom should corrupt the world.
Comfort thyself: what comfort is in me?
I have lived my life, and that which I have done
May He within himself make pure! but thou,
If thou shouldst never see my face again,
Pray for my soul. More things are wrought by prayer
Than this world dreams of. Wherefore, let thy voice
Rise like a fountain for me night and day.
For what are men better than sheep or goats
That nourish a blind life within the brain,
If, knowing God, they lift not hands of prayer
Both for themselves and those who call them friend?
For so the whole round earth is every way
Bound by gold chains about the feet of God.
But now farewell. I am going a long way
With these thou seest—if indeed I go—
For all my mind is clouded with a doubt—
To the island-valley of Avilion;
Where falls not hail, or rain, or any snow,
Nor ever wind blows loudly, but it lies
Deep-meadow'd, happy, fair with orchard lawns
And bowery hollows crown'd with summer sea,
Where I will heal me of my grievous wound."
So said he, and the barge with oar and sail
Moved from the brink, like some full-breasted swan
That, fluting a wild carol ere her death,
Ruffles her pure cold plume, and takes the flood
With swarthy webs. Long stood Sir Bedivere
Revolving many memories, till the hull
Look'd one black dot against the verge of dawn,
And on the mere the wailing died away.

Here ended Hall, and our last light, that long
Had wink'd and threaten'd darkness, flared and fell;
At which the parson, sent to sleep with sound,
And waked with silence, grunted "Good!" but we
Sat rapt: it was the tone with which he read—
Perhaps some modern touches here and there
Redeem'd it from the charge of nothingness—
Or else we loved the man, and prized his work;
I know not; but we sitting, as I said,
The cock crew loud, as at that time of year

The lusty bird takes every hour for dawn.
Then Francis, muttering, like a man ill-used,
"There now—that's nothing!" drew a little back,
And drove his heel into the smoulder'd log,
That sent a blast of sparkles up the flue.
And so to bed, where yet in sleep I seem'd
To sail with Arthur under looming shores,
Point after point; till on to dawn, when dreams
Begin to feel the truth and stir of day,
To me, methought, who waited with the crowd,
There came a bark that, blowing forward, bore
King Arthur, like a modern gentleman
Of stateliest port; and all the people cried,
"Arthur is come again: he cannot die."
Then those that stood upon the hills behind
Repeated—"Come again, and thrice as fair;"
And, further inland, voices echoed—"Come
With all good things, and war shall be no more."
At this a hundred bells began to peal,
That with the sound I woke, and heard indeed
The clear church-bells ring in the Christmas morn.

Sir Walter Scott

LOCHINVAR

O YOUNG Lochinvar is come out of the west,
Through all the wide Border his steed was the best;
And, save his good broadsword, he weapons had none,
He rode all unarmed, and he rode all alone.
So faithful in love, and so dauntless in war,
There never was knight like the young Lochinvar.

He stayed not for brake, and he stopped not for stone,
He swam the Eske River where ford there was none;
But ere he alighted at Netherby gate,
The bride had consented, the gallant came late:
For a laggard in love, and a dastard in war,
Was to wed the fair Ellen of brave Lochinvar.

So boldly he entered the Netherby Hall,
Among bridesmen, and kinsmen, and brothers, and all.
Then spoke the bride's father, his hand on his sword
(For the poor craven bridegroom said never a word),
"O, come ye in peace here, or come ye in war,
Or to dance at our bridal, young Lord Lochinvar?"

"I long wooed your daughter, my suit you denied;—
Love swells like the Solway, but ebbs like its tide,—
And now I am come, with this lost love of mine,
To lead but one measure, drink one cup of wine.
There are maidens in Scotland more lovely by far,
That would gladly be bride to the young Lochinvar."

The bride kissed the goblet; the knight took it up,
He quaffed off the wine, and he threw down the cup.
She looked down to blush, and she looked up to sigh,
With a smile on her lips, and a tear in her eye.
He took her soft hand, ere her mother could bar,—
"Now tread we a measure," said young Lochinvar.

So stately his form, and so lovely her face,
That never a hall such a galliard did grace;
While her mother did fret, and her father did fume,
And the bridegroom stood dangling his bonnet and plume;
And the bridemaidens whispered, " 'Twere better by far
To have matched our fair cousin with young Lochinvar."

One touch to her hand, and one word in her ear,
When they reached the hall-door, and the charger stood near;
So light to the croup the fair lady he swung,
So light to the saddle before her he sprung;
"She is won! we are gone! over band, bush, and scaur;
They'll have fleet steeds that follow," quoth young Lochinvar.

There was mounting 'mong Graemes of the Netherby clan;
Forsters, Fenwicks, and Musgraves, they rode and they ran:
There was racing and chasing on Canobie Lee,
But the lost bride of Netherby ne'er did they see.
So daring in love, and so dauntless in war,
Have ye e'er heard of gallant like young Lochinvar?

Michael Drayton

AGINCOURT

FAIR STOOD the wind for France,
When we our sails advance,
Nor now to prove our chance,
Longer will tarry;
But putting to the main
At Kaux, the mouth of Seine,
With all his martial train,
Landed King Harry.

And taking many a fort,
Furnished in warlike sort,
Marcheth towards Agincourt,
  In happy hour;
Skirmishing day by day
With those that stopped his way,
Where the French gen'ral lay
  With all his power.

Which in his height of pride,
King Henry to deride,
His ransom to provide
  To the King sending;
Which he neglects the while
As from a nation vile,
Yet with an angry smile
  Their fall portending.

And turning to his men,
Quoth our brave Henry then:
Though they to one be ten,
  Be not amazèd.
Yet have we well begun,
Battles so bravely won
Have ever to the sun
  By fame been raisèd.

And for myself, quoth he,
This my full rest shall be,
England ne'er mourn for me,
  Nor more esteem me;
Victor I will remain,
Or on this earth lie slain,
Never shall she sustain
  Loss to redeem me.

Poitiers and Crécy tell,
When most their pride did swell,
Under our swords they fell;
  No less our skill is
Than when our grandsire great,
Claiming the regal seat
By many a warlike feat,
  Lopped the French lilies.

The Duke of York so dread
The eager vaward led;
With the main Henry sped
  Amongst his henchmen.

Excester had the rear,
O braver man not there,
O Lord, how hot they were
  On the false Frenchmen!

They now to fight are gone,
Armour on armour shone,
Drum now to drum did groan,
  To hear was wonder,
That with cries they make
The very earth did shake,
Trumpet to trumpet spake,
  Thunder to thunder.

Well it thine age became,
O noble Erpingham,
Which didst the signal aim
  To our hid forces;
When from a meadow by,
Like a storm suddenly,
The English archery
  Stuck the French horses.

With Spanish yew so strong,
Arrows a cloth-yard long,
That like to serpents stung,
  Piercing the weather;
None from his fellow starts,
But playing manly parts,
And like true English hearts,
  Stuck close together.

When down their bows they threw,
And forth their bilboes drew,
And on the French they flew,
  Not one was tardy;
Arms were from shoulders sent,
Scalps to the teeth were rent,
Down the French peasants went;
  Our men were hardy.

This while our noble King,
His broad sword brandishing,
Down the French host did ding,
  As to o'erwhelm it;
And many a deep wound lent,
His arms with blood besprent,
And many a cruel dent
  Bruisèd his helmet.

Gloster, that Duke so good,
Next of the royal blood,
For famous England stood
With his brave brother;
Clarence, in steel so bright,
Though but a maiden knight,
Yet in that furious fight,
Scarce such another.

Warwick in blood did wade,
Oxford the foe invade,
And cruel slaughter made,
Still as they ran up;
Suffolk his axe did ply,
Beaumont and Willoughby
Bare them right doughtily,
Ferrers and Fanhope.

Upon Saint Crispin's day
Fought was this noble fray,
Which fame did not delay
To England to carry;
Oh, when shall English men
With such acts fill a pen,
Or England breed again
Such a King Harry?

Walt Whitman

ARE YOU THE NEW PERSON DRAWN TOWARD ME?

ARE YOU the new person drawn toward me?
To begin with take warning, I am surely far different from what you suppose;
Do you suppose you will find in me your ideal?
Do you think it is so easy to have me become your lover?
Do you think the friendship of me would be unalloy'd satisfaction?
Do you think I am trusty and faithful?
Do you see no further than this façade, this smooth and tolerant manner of me?
Do you suppose yourself advancing on real ground toward a real heroic man?
Have you no thought O dreamer that it may be all maya, illusion?

George Gordon, Lord Byron

PROMETHEUS

1

TITAN! to whose immortal eyes
The sufferings of mortality,
Seen in their sad reality,
Were not as things that gods despise;
What was thy pity's recompense?
A silent suffering, and intense;
The rock, the vulture, and the chain,
All that the proud can feel of pain,
The agony they do not show,
The suffocating sense of woe,
Which speaks but in its loneliness,
And then is jealous lest the sky
Should have a listener, nor will sigh
Until its voice is echoless.

2

Titan! to thee the strife was given
Between the suffering and the will,
Which torture where they cannot kill;
And the inexorable Heaven,
And the deaf tyranny of Fate,
The ruling principle of Hate,
Which for its pleasure doth create
The things it may annihilate,
Refused thee even the boon to die:
The wretched gift eternity
Was thine—and thou hast borne it well.
All that the Thunderer wrung from thee
Was but the menace which flung back
On him the torments of thy rack;
The fate thou didst so well foresee,
But would not to appease him tell;
And in thy Silence was his Sentence,
And in his Soul a vain repentance,
And evil dread so ill dissembled,
That in his hand the lightnings trembled.

3

Thy Godlike crime was to be kind,
To render with thy precepts less
The sum of human wretchedness,
And strengthen Man with his own mind;

But baffled as thou wert from high,
Still in thy patient energy,
In the endurance, and repulse
  Of thine impenetrable Spirit,
Which Earth and Heaven could not convulse,
  A mighty lesson we inherit:
Thou art a symbol and a sign
  To Mortals of their fate and force;
Like thee, Man is in part divine,
  A troubled stream from a pure source;
And Man in portions can foresee
His own funereal destiny;
His wretchedness, and his resistance,
And his sad unallied existence:
To which his Spirit may oppose
Itself—an equal to all woes,
  And a firm will, and a deep sense,
Which even in torture can descry
  Its own concenter'd recompense,
Triumphant where it dares defy,
And making Death a Victory.

Dante

PARADISO: CANTO III

THAT Sun[1] which fired my bosom of old with love
  Had thus bared for me in beauty the aspect sweet
  Of truth, expert to prove as to disprove;
And I, to avow me of all error quit,
  Confident and assured, lifted my head
  More upright, in such measure as was fit.
But now appeared a sight that riveted
  Me to itself with such compulsion keen
  That my confession from my memory fled.
As from transparent glasses polished clean,
  Or water shining smooth up to its rim,
  Yet not so that the bottom is unseen,
Our faces' lineaments return so dim
  That pearl upon white forehead not more slow
  Would on our pupils its pale image limn;
So I beheld faces that seemed aglow
  To speak, and fell into the counter-snare
  From what made love 'twixt man[2] and pool to grow.

1 [Beatrice.]　　2 [Narcissus.]

PARADISO, CANTO III: From *The Divine Comedy*. Translated and edited by Laurence Binyon. Used by permission of The Society of Authors and Mrs. Cicely Binyon.

No sooner had I marked those faces there,
Than, thinking them reflections, with swift eyes
I turned about to see of whom they were,
And saw nothing: again, in my surprise,
I turned straight to the light of my sweet Guide,
Who smiling, burned within her sainted eyes.
"Marvel not at my smiling," she replied
"To contemplate thy childlike thought revealed
Which cannot yet its foot to truth confide,
But moves thee, as ever, on emptiness to build.
True substances are these thine eyes perceive,
Remitted here for vows not all fulfilled.
Speak with them therefore, hearken and believe,
For the true light which is their happiness
Lets them not swerve, but to it they must cleave."
And I to the shade that seemed most near to press
For converse, turned me and began, as one
Who is overwrought through longing in excess:
"O spirit made for bliss, who from the sun
Of life eternal feelest the sweet ray
Which, save 'tis tasted, is conceived by none,
It will be gracious to me, if I may
Be gladdened with thy name and all your fate."
And she, with laughing eyes and no delay:
"Our charity no more locks up the gate
Against a just wish than that Charity
Which would have all its court in like estate.
On earth I was a Virgin Sister: see
What memory yields thee, and my being now
More beautiful will hide me not from thee,
But that I am Piccarda thou wilt know,
Who with these other blessed ones placed here
Am blessed in the sphere that moves most slow;
For our desires, which kindle and flame clear
Only in the pleasure of the Holy Ghost,
To what he appointeth joyfully adhere;
And this which seems to thee so lowly a post
Is given to us because the vows we made
Were broken, or complete observance lost."
Then I to her: "Something divinely glad
Shines in your marvellous aspect, to replace
In you the old conceptions that I had;
I was slow therefore to recall thy face:
But what thou tell'st me helpeth now to clear
My sight, and thee more easily to retrace.
But tell me: you that are made happy here,
Do ye to a more exalted place aspire,
To see more, or to make yourselves more dear?"

She smiled a little, and with her smiled that choir
Of spirits; then so joyous she replied
That she appeared to burn in love's first fire:
"Brother, the virtue of love hath pacified
Our will; we long for what we have alone,
Nor any craving stirs in us beside.
If we desired to reach a loftier zone,
Our longings would be all out of accord
With His will who disposeth here His own.
For that, these circles, thou wilt see, afford
No room, if love be our whole being's root
And thou ponder the meaning of that word.
Nay, 'tis of the essence of our blessed lot
In the divine will to be cloistered still
Through which our own wills into one are wrought,
As we from step to step our stations fill
Throughout this realm, to all the realm 'tis bliss
As to its King, who wills us into His will;
And in His will is perfected our peace.
It is the sea whereunto moveth all
That it creates and nature makes increase."
Then saw I how each heaven for every soul
Is paradise, though from the Supreme Good
The dews of grace not in one measure fall.
But as may hap, when sated with one food
Still for another we have appetite,
We ask for this, and that with thanks elude,
Such words and gesture used I that I might
Learn from her what that web was where she plied
The shuttle and yet drew not the head outright.
"Perfect life and high merit have enskied
A Lady above,"[3] she said, "whose rule they take
In your world who in robe and veil abide,
That they till death may, sleeping and awake,
Be with that Spouse who giveth welcome free
To all vows love may for His pleasure make.
To follow her, a young girl, did I flee
The world and, closed within her habit, vowed
Myself to the pathway of her company.
Afterwards men, used to evil more than good,
Tore me away, out of the sweet cloister;
And God knows then what way of life I trod.
This other splendour whom thou see'st appear
To thee on my right side, who, glowing pale,
Kindles with all the radiance of our sphere,
Can of herself tell also the same tale.
She was a Sister; from her head they tore

3 [St. Clare.]

Likewise the shadow of the sacred veil.
She was turned back into the world once more
Against her will, against good usage too;
Yet still upon her heart the veil she wore.
This is the light of the great Constance, who
From Suabia's second whirlwind was to bring
To birth the third Power, and the last ye knew."
Thus spoke she to me, and then began to sing
Ave Maria, and singing disappeared,
As through deep water sinks a heavy thing.
My sight, which followed far as it was powered,
When it had lost her, turned and straightway shot
To the other mark, more ardently desired,
And Beatrice, only Beatrice, it sought.
But she upon my look was flaming so
That at the first my sight endured it not;
And this made me for questioning more slow.

W. H. Auden

THE UNKNOWN CITIZEN

(TO JS/07/M/378
THIS MARBLE MONUMENT
IS ERECTED BY THE STATE)

HE WAS found by the Bureau of Statistics to be
One against whom there was no official complaint,
And all the reports on his conduct agree
That, in the modern sense of an old-fashioned word, he was a saint,
For in everything he did he served the Greater Community.
Except for the War till the day he retired
He worked in a factory and never got fired,
But satisfied his employers, Fudge Motors Inc.
Yet he wasn't a scab or odd in his views,
For his Union reports that he paid his dues,
(Our report on his Union shows it was sound)
And our Social Psychology workers found
That he was popular with his mates and liked a drink.
The Press are convinced that he bought a paper every day
And that his reactions to advertisements were normal in every way.
Policies taken out in his name prove that he was fully insured,
And his Health-card shows he was once in hospital but left it cured.
Both Producers Research and High-Grade Living declare
He was fully sensible to the advantages of the Installment Plan

And had everything necessary to the Modern Man,
A phonograph, a radio, a car and a frigidaire.
Our researchers into Public Opinion are content
That he held the proper opinions for the time of year;
When there was peace, he was for peace; when there was war, he went.
He was married and added five children to the population,
Which our Eugenist says was the right number for a parent of his generation,
And our teachers report that he never interfered with their education.
Was he free? Was he happy? The question is absurd:
Had anything been wrong, we should certainly have heard.

William Ernest Henley

INVICTUS

OUT OF the night that covers me,
   Black as the Pit from pole to pole,
I thank whatever gods may be
   For my unconquerable soul.

In the fell clutch of circumstance
   I have not winced nor cried aloud.
Under the bludgeonings of chance
   My head is bloody, but unbowed.

Beyond this place of wrath and tears
   Looms but the horror of the shade,
And yet the menace of the years
   Finds, and shall find me, unafraid.

It matters not how strait the gate,
   How charged with punishments the scroll,
I am the master of my fate:
   I am the captain of my soul.

Witter Bynner

HEROES

SHALL I ever believe again, having once believed
In fugitive heroes and the words they say?
How often from worship have I looked away
And wept I was a simpleton, deceived
By the captains of power and glory. I was a child bereaved
Of childhood. Even my closest, even they
Who loved me, had lessened into faulty clay:
And I was the one hero, I who grieved. . . .

A simpleton, indeed, choosing despair:
Either great heroes and myself a child,
Or else myself the only faultless one!
I beg you, anybody, have a care
Not to be like me—though at last I smiled . . .
We are all such little heroes in the sun.

HEROES: From *The Commonweal,* February 20, 1929. Reprinted by permission of the editor of *The Commonweal.*

DRAMA

Christopher Marlowe

THE TRAGICAL HISTORY OF DOCTOR FAUSTUS

PERSONS IN THE PLAY

CHORUS
DOCTOR FAUSTUS
WAGNER, *his Servant*
GOOD, *and* EVIL ANGEL
VALDES *and* CORNELIUS, *Conjurors*
Three Scholars
MEPHISTOPHILIS, *a Devil*
THE CLOWN
BALIOL, BELCHER, LUCIFER, BELZEBUB *and Other Devils*
THE SEVEN DEADLY SINS
THE POPE
CARDINAL OF LORRAIN
FRIARS
ROBIN, *the Ostler*
RAFE
A VINTNER
THE EMPEROR
A KNIGHT *and Attendants*
SPIRITS OF ALEXANDER *and his* PARAMOUR
A HORSE-COURSER
THE DUKE *of* VANHOLT *and his* DUCHESS
AN OLD MAN
The Spirit of HELEN OF TROY

SCENE: Mainly the Study of Doctor Faustus; otherwise a Grove, the Pope's Privy-Chamber at Rome, the Courts of the Emperor and the Duke of Vanholt and elsewhere.

[*Enter* CHORUS.]

CHORUS. Not marching now in fields of Trasimene,
Where Mars did mate the Carthaginians;
Nor sporting in the dalliance of love,
In courts of kings where state is overturned;
Nor in the pomp of proud audacious deeds,
Intends our Muse to vaunt his heavenly verse:
Only this, gentlemen—we must perform
The form of Faustus' fortunes, good or bad;
To patient judgments we appeal our plaud,
And speak for Faustus in his infancy.
Now is he born, his parents base of stock,
In Germany, within a town called Rhodes;
Of riper years to Wittenberg he went,
Whereas his kinsmen chiefly brought him up.
So soon he profits in divinity,
The fruitful plot of scholarism graced,
That shortly he was graced with doctor's name,

Excelling all whose sweet delight disputes
In heavenly matters of theology;
Till swollen with cunning, of a self-conceit,
His waxen wings did mount above his reach,
And, melting, heavens conspired his overthrow;
For, falling to a devilish exercise,
And glutted now with learning's golden gifts,
He surfeits upon cursèd necromancy.
Nothing so sweet as magic is to him,
Which he prefers before his chiefest bliss.
And this the man that in his study sits! [*Exit.*]

SCENE I.

[*Enter* FAUSTUS *in his study.*]

FAUST. Settle thy studies, Faustus, and begin
To sound the depth of that thou wilt profess;
Having commenced, be a divine in show,
Yet level at the end of every art,
And live and die in Aristotle's works.
Sweet Analytics, 'tis thou hast ravished me— [*Reads.*]
Bene dissere est finis logices.[1]
Is to dispute well logic's chiefest end?
Affords this art no greater miracle?
Then read no more, thou hast attained the end;
A greater subject fitteth Faustus' wit:
Bid ὄν χαὶ μὴ ὄν[2] farewell; Galen come,
Seeing *Ubi desinit philosophus ibi incipit medicus,*[3]
Be a physician, Faustus, heap up gold,
And be eternized for some wondrous cure. [*Reads.*]
Summum bonum medicinœ sanitas,[4]
The end of physic is our body's health.
Why, Faustus, hast thou not attained that end?
Is not thy common talk sound aphorisms?
Are not thy bills hung up as monuments,
Whereby whole cities have escaped the plague,
And thousand desperate maladies been eased?
Yet art thou still but Faustus and a man.
Wouldst thou make men to live eternally,
Or, being dead, raise them to life again,
Then this profession were to be esteemed.
Physic, farewell.—Where is Justinian? [*Reads.*]

1 [To dispute well is the end of logic.]
2 [Being and nonbeing.]
3 [Where the philosopher ends there begins the physician.]
4 [Health is the highest good of medicine.]

Si una eademque res legatur duobus, alter rem, alter valorem rei,
etc.[5]
A pretty case of paltry legacies! [*Reads.*]
Exhœreditare filium non potest pater nisi, etc.[6]
Such is the subject of the Institute
And universal body of the law.
His study fits a mercenary drudge,
Who aims at nothing but external trash;
Too servile and illiberal for me.
When all is done divinity is best;
Jerome's Bible, Faustus, view it well. [*Reads.*]
Stipendium peccati mors est.[7] Ha! *Stipendium,* etc.
The reward of sin is death. That's hard. [*Reads.*]
Si peccasse negamus, fallimur, et nulla est in nobis veritas.[8]
If we say that we have no sin we deceive ourselves, and there's no
truth in us. Why, then, belike we must sin, and so consequently die.
Ay, we must die an everlasting death.
What doctrine call you this, *Che sera sera,*
What will be, shall be? Divinity, adieu!
These metaphysics of magicians
And necromantic books are heavenly:
Lines, circles, scenes, letters, and characters:
Ay, these are those that Faustus most desires.
O, what a world of profit and delight,
Of power, of honor, of omnipotence
Is promised to the studious artisan!
All things that move between the quiet poles
Shall be at my command: emperors and kings
Are but obeyèd in their several provinces,
Nor can they raise the wind or rend the clouds;
But his dominion that exceeds in this
Stretcheth as far as doth the mind of man,
A sound magician is a mighty god:
Here, Faustus, try thy brains to gain a deity.
Wagner!

[*Enter* WAGNER.]

Commend me to my dearest friends,
The German Valdes and Cornelius;
Request them earnestly to visit me.

WAG. I will, sir. [*Exit.*]

FAUST. Their conference will be a greater help to me
Than all my labors, plod I ne'er so fast.

5 [If one and the same thing be willed to two people, one is given the thing and the other the value of the thing.]
6 [A father cannot disinherit a son unless . . .]
7 [The wages of sin is death.]
8 [If we deny we have sinned we err, and the truth is not in us.]

[*Enter* GOOD ANGEL *and* EVIL ANGEL.]

G. ANG. O Faustus! lay that damnèd book aside,
And gaze not on it lest it tempt thy soul,
And heap God's heavy wrath upon thy head.
Read, read the Scriptures: that is blasphemy.
E. ANG. Go forward, Faustus, in that famous art,
Wherein all Nature's treasure is contained:
Be thou on earth as Jove is in the sky,
Lord and commander of these elements. [*Exeunt* ANGELS.]
FAUST. How am I glutted with conceit of this!
Shall I make spirits fetch me what I please,
Resolve me of all ambiguities,
Perform what desperate enterprise I will?
I'll have them fly to India for gold,
Ransack the ocean for orient pearl,
And search all corners of the new-found world
For pleasant fruits and princely delicates;
I'll have them read me strange philosophy
And tell the secrets of all foreign kings;
I'll have them wall all Germany with brass,
And make swift Rhine circle fair Wittenberg,
I'll have them fill the public schools with silk,
Wherewith the students shall be bravely clad;
I'll levy soldiers with the coin they bring,
And chase the Prince of Parma from our land,
And reign sole king of all the provinces;
Yea, stranger engines for the brunt of war
Than was the fiery keel at Antwerp's bridge,
I'll make my servile spirits to invent.

[*Enter* VALDES *and* CORNELIUS.]

Come, German Valdes and Cornelius,
And make me blest with your sage conference.
Valdes, sweet Valdes, and Cornelius,
Know that your words have won me at the last
To practise magic and concealed arts:
Yet not your words only, but mine own fantasy
That will receive no object; for my head
But ruminates on necromantic skill.
Philosophy is odious and obscure,
Both law and physic are for petty wits;
Divinity is basest of the three,
Unpleasant, harsh, contemptible, and vile:
'Tis magic, magic that hath ravished me.
Then, gentle friends, aid me in this attempt;
And I that have with concise syllogisms

Gravelled the pastors of the German church,
And made the flowering pride of Wittenberg
Swarm to my problems, as the infernal spirits
On sweet Musæus, when he came to hell,
Will be as cunning as Agrippa was,
Whose shadows made all Europe honor him.

VALD. Faustus, these books, thy wit, and our experience
Shall make all nations to canònize us.
As Indian Moors obey their Spanish lords,
So shall the spirits of every element
Be always serviceable to us three;
Like lions shall they guard us when we please;
Like Almain rutters with their horsemen's staves
Or Lapland giants, trotting by our sides;
Sometimes like women or unwedded maids,
Shadowing more beauty in their airy brows
Than have the white breasts of the queen of love
From Venice shall they drag huge argosies,
And from America the golden fleece
That yearly stuffs old Philip's treasury;
If learnèd Faustus will be resolute.

FAUST. Waldes, as resolute am I in this
As thou to live; therefore object it not.

CORN. The miracles that magic will perform
Will make thee vow to study nothing else.
He that is grounded in astrology,
Enriched with tongues, well seen in minerals,
Hath all the principles magic doth require.
Then doubt not, Faustus, but to be renowned,
And more frequented for this mystery
Than heretofore the Delphian Oracle.
The spirits tell me they can dry the sea,
And fetch the treasure of all foreign wracks,
Ay, all the wealth that our forefathers hid
Within the massy entrails of the earth;
Then tell me, Faustus, what shall we three want?

FAUST. Nothing, Cornelius! O, this cheers my soul!
Come show me some demonstrations magical,
That I may conjure in some lusty grove,
And have these joys in full possession.

VALD. Then haste thee to some solitary grove,
And bear wise Bacon's and Albanus' works,
The Hebrew Psalter and New Testament!
And whatsoever else is requisite
We will inform thee ere our conference cease.

CORN. Valdes, first let him know the words of art;
And then, all other ceremonies learned,

Faustus may try his cunning by himself.
VALD. First I'll instruct thee in the rudiments,
And then wilt thou be perfecter than I.
FAUST. Then come and dine with me, and after meat,
We'll canvass every quiddity thereof;
For ere I sleep I'll try what I can do:
This night I'll conjure tho' I die therefore. [*Exeunt.*]

SCENE II.

Before FAUSTUS' *house.*

[*Enter two* SCHOLARS.]

1 SCHOL. I wonder what's become of Faustus that was wont to make our schools ring with *sic probo*?[9]

2 SCHOL. That shall we know, for see here comes his boy.

[*Enter* WAGNER.]

1 SCHOL. How now, sirrah! Where's thy master?
WAG. God in heaven knows!
2 SCHOL. Why, dost not thou know?
WAG. Yes, I know. But that follows not.
1 SCHOL. Go to, sirrah! leave your jesting, and tell us where he is.
WAG. That follows not necessary by force of argument, that you, being licentiate, should stand upon't: therefore acknowledge your error and be attentive.
2 SCHOL. Why, didst thou not say thou knewest?
WAG. Have you any witness on't?
1 SCHOL. Yes, sirrah, I heard you.
WAG. Ask my fellow if I be a thief.
2 SCHOL. Well, you will not tell us?
WAG. Yes, sir, I will tell you; yet if you were not dunces, you would never ask me such a question; for is not he *corpus naturale?*[10] and is not that *mobile?*[11] Then wherefore should you ask me such a question? But that I am by nature phlegmatic, slow to wrath, and prone to lechery (to love, I would say), it were not for you to come within forty feet of the place of execution, although I do not doubt to see you both hanged the next sessions. Thus having triumphed over you, I will set my countenance like a precisian, and begin to speak thus: Truly, my dear brethren, my master is within at dinner, with Valdes and Cornelius, as this wine, if it could speak, would inform your worships; and so the Lord bless you, preserve you, and keep you, my dear brethren, my dear brethren. [*Exit.*]
1 SCHOL. Nay, then. I fear he has fallen into that damned art, for which they two are infamous through the world.
2 SCHOL. Were he a stranger, and not allied to me, yet should I

9 [Thus I prove.] 10 [Natural body.] 11 [Moving.]

grieve for him. But come, let us go and inform the rector, and see if he by his grave counsel can reclaim him.

1 SCHOL. O, but I fear me nothing can reclaim him.
2 SCHOL. Yet let us try what we can do. [*Exeunt.*]

SCENE III.

[*Enter* FAUSTUS *to conjure in a grove.*]

FAUST. Now that the gloomy shadow of the earth
Longing to view Orion's drizzling look,
Leaps from the antarctic world unto the sky,
And dims the welkin with her pitchy breath,
Faustus, begin thine incantations,
And try if devils will obey thy hest,
Seeing thou hast prayed and sacrificed to them.
Within this circle is Jehovah's name,
Forward and backward anagrammatized,
The breviated names of holy saints,
Figures of every adjunct to the heavens,
And characters of signs and erring stars,
By which the spirits are enforced to rise:
Then fear not, Faustus, but be resolute,
And try the uttermost magic can perform.
Sint mihi dei Acherontis propitii! Valeat numen triplex Jehovœ! Ignei, aerii, aquatani spiritus, salvete! Orientis princeps Belzebub, inferni ardentis monarcha, et Demogorgon, propitiamus vos, ut appareat et surgate Mephistophilis. Quid tu moraris? per Jehovam, Gehennam, et consecratam aquam quam nunc spargo, signumque crucis quod nunc facio, et per vota nostra, ipse nunc surgat nobis dicatus Mephistophilis![12]

[*Enter* MEPHISTOPHILIS, *a Devil.*]

I charge thee to return and change thy shape;
Thou art too ugly to attend on me.
Go, and return an old Franciscan friar;
That holy shape becomes a devil best. [*Exit* DEVIL.]
I see there's virtue in my heavenly words;
Who would not be proficient in this art?
How pliant is this Mephistophilis,
Full of obedience and humility!
Such is the force of magic and my spells:
Now, Faustus, thou are conjurer laureat,

12 [May the gods of Acheron (Hell) be propitious! May the triple might of Jehovah prevail! Hail spirits of fire, air, water! We pay homage to you, Belzebub, prince of the east and king of burning Hell, and you, Demogorgon, in order that Mephistophilis may rise and appear. Why do you delay? By Jehovah, Gehenna, and the holy water I now sprinkle, and the sign of the cross I now do make, and by our prayers, let the said Mephistophilis now rise before us.]

That canst command great Mephistophilis:
Quin regis Mephistophilis fratris imagine.[13]

[*Enter* MEPHISTOPHILIS, *like a Franciscan friar.*]

MEPH. Now, Faustus, what would'st thou have me to do?
FAUST. I charge thee wait upon me whilst I live,
To do whatever Faustus shall command,
Be it to make the moon drop from her sphere,
Or the ocean to overwhelm the world.
MEPH. I am a servant to great Lucifer,
And may not follow thee without his leave:
No more than he commands must we perform.
FAUST. Did not he charge thee to appear to me?
MEPH. No, I came hither of mine own accord.
FAUST. Did not my conjuring speeches raise thee? Speak.
MEPH. That was the cause, but yet *per accidens,*[14]
For when we hear one rack the name of God,
Abjure the Scriptures and his Saviour Christ,
We fly in hope to get his glorious soul;
Nor will we come, unless he use such means
Whereby he is in danger to be damned:
Therefore the shortest cut for conjuring
Is stoutly to abjure the Trinity,
And pray devoutly to the Prince of Hell.
FAUST. So Faustus hath
Already done; and holds this principle,
There is no chief, but only Belzebub,
To whom Faustus doth dedicate himself.
This word "damnation" terrifies not him,
For he confounds hell in Elysium;
His ghost be with the old philosophers!
But, leaving these vain trifles of men's souls,
Tell me what is that Lucifer thy lord?
MEPH. Arch-regent and commander of all spirits.
FAUST. Was not that Lucifer an angel once?
MEPH. Yes, Faustus, and most dearly loved of God.
FAUST. How comes it then that he is prince of devils?
MEPH. O, by aspiring pride and insolence;
For which God threw him from the face of heaven.
FAUST. And what are you that live with Lucifer?
MEPH. Unhappy spirits that fell with Lucifer,
Conspired against our God with Lucifer,
And are for ever damned with Lucifer.
FAUST. Where are you damned?
MEPH. In hell.
FAUST. How comes it then that thou art out of hell?

13 [Yea, rather rule thou in the image of the brother, Mephistophilis.]
14 [By accident, that is, not essentially.]

MEPH. Why this is hell, nor am I out of it:
Think'st thou that I who saw the face of God,
And tasted the eternal joys of heaven,
Am not tormented with ten thousand hells,
In being deprived of everlasting bliss?
O Faustus! leave these frivolous demands,
Which strike a terror to my fainting soul.

FAUST. What, is great Mephistophilis so passionate
For being deprivèd of the joys of heaven?
Learn thou of Faustus manly fortitude,
And scorn those joys thou never shalt possess.
Go bear these tidings to great Lucifer:
Seeing Faustus hath incurred eternal death.
By desperate thoughts against Jove's deity,
Say he surrenders up to him his soul,
So he will spare him four and twenty years,
Letting him live in all voluptuousness;
Having thee ever to attend on me;
To give me whatsoever I shall ask,
To tell me whatsoever I demand,
To slay mine enemies, and aid my friends,
And always be obedient to my will.
Go and return to mighty Lucifer,
And meet me in my study at midnight,
And then resolve me of thy master's mind.

MEPH. I will, Faustus. [*Exit.*]

FAUST. Had I as many souls as there be stars,
I'd give them all for Mephistophilis.
By him I'll be great Emperor of the world,
And make a bridge thorough the moving air,
To pass the ocean with a band of men:
I'll join the hills that bind the Afric shore,
And make that country continent to Spain,
And both contributory to my crown.
The Emperor shall not live but by my leave,
Nor any potentate of Germany.
Now that I have obtained what I desire,
I'll live in speculation of this art
Till Mephistophilis return again. [*Exit.*]

SCENE IV.

Before FAUSTUS' *house.*

[*Enter* WAGNER *and* CLOWN.]

WAG. Sirrah, boy, come hither.

CLOWN. How, boy! Swowns, boy! I hope you have seen many boys with such pickadevaunts as I have; boy, quotha.

WAG. Tell me, sirrah, hast thou any comings in?

CLOWN. Ay, and goings out too. You may see else.

WAG. Alas, poor slave! see how poverty jesteth in his nakedness! The villain is bare and out of service, and so hungry that I know he would give his soul to the Devil for a shoulder of mutton though 'twere blood-raw.

CLOWN. How? My soul to the Devil for a shoulder of mutton, though 'twere blood-raw! Not so, good friend. By'r-lady, I had need have it well roasted and good sauce to it, if I pay so dear.

WAG. Well, wilt thou serve me, and I'll make thee go like *Qui mihi discipulus?*[15]

CLOWN. How, in verse?

WAG. No, sirrah; in beaten silk and stavesacre.

CLOWN. How, how, Knave's acre! Ay, I thought that was all the land his father left him. Do you hear? I would be sorry to rob you of your living.

WAG. Sirrah, I say in stavesacre.

CLOWN. Oho! Oho! Stavesacre! Why then belike if I were your man I should be full of vermin.

WAG. So thou shalt, whether thou beest with me or no. But, sirrah, leave your jesting, and bind yourself presently unto me for seven years, or I'll turn all the lice about thee into familiars, and they shall tear thee in pieces.

CLOWN. Do you hear, sir? You may save that labor: they are too familiar with me already: swowns! they are as bold with my flesh as if they had paid for their meat and drink.

WAG. Well, do you hear, sirrah? Hold, take these guilders.

[*Gives money.*]

CLOWN. Gridirons! what be they?

WAG. Why, French crowns.

CLOWN. Mass, but in the name of French crowns, a man were as good have as many English counters. And what should I do with these?

WAG. Why, now, sirrah, thou art at an hour's warning, whensoever and wheresoever the Devil shall fetch thee.

CLOWN. No, no. Here, take your gridirons again.

WAG. Truly I'll none of them.

CLOWN. Truly but you shall.

WAG. Bear witness I gave them him.

CLOWN. Bear witness I give them you again.

WAG. Well, I will cause two devils presently to fetch thee away—Baliol and Belcher!

CLOWN. Let your Baliol and your Belcher come here, and I'll knock them, they were never so knocked since they were devils! Say I should kill one of them, what would folks say? "Do you see yonder tall fellow in the round slop—he has killed the devil." So I should be called Kill-devil all the parish over.

15 [Who is my disciple?]

[*Enter two* DEVILS: *the* CLOWN *runs up and down crying.*]

WAG. Baliol and Belcher! Spirits, away! [*Exeunt* DEVILS.]

CLOWN. What, are they gone? A vengeance on them, they have vile long nails! There was a he-devil, and a she-devil. I'll tell you how you shall know them; all he-devils has horns, and all she-devils has clifts and cloven feet.

WAG. Well, sirrah, follow me.

CLOWN. But, do you hear—if I should serve you, would you teach me to raise up Banios and Belcheos?

WAG. I will teach thee to turn thyself to anything; to a dog, or a cat, or a mouse, or a rat, or anything.

CLOWN. How! a Christian fellow to a dog or a cat, a mouse or a rat! No, no, sir. If you turn me into anything, let it be in the likeness of a little pretty frisking flea, that I may be here and there and everywhere. O, I'll tickle the pretty wenches' plackets; I'll be amongst them, i' faith.

WAG. Well, sirrah, come.

CLOWN. But, do you hear, Wagner?

WAG. How! Baliol and Belcher!

CLOWN. O Lord! I pray, sir, let Banio and Belcher go sleep.

WAG. Villain—call me Master Wagner, and let thy eye be diametarily fixed upon my right heel, with *quasi vestigiis nostris insistere.*[16] [*Exit.*]

CLOWN. God forgive me, he speaks Dutch fustian. Well, I'll follow him: I'll serve him, that's flat. [*Exit.*]

SCENE V.

[*Enter* FAUSTUS *in his study.*]

FAUST. Now, Faustus, must
Thou needs be damned, and canst thou not be saved:
What boots it then to think of God or heaven?
Away with such vain fancies, and despair:
Despair in God, and trust in Belzebub;
Now go not backward: no, Faustus, be resolute:
Why waver'st thou? O, something soundeth in mine ears
"Abjure this magic, turn to God again!"
Ay, and Faustus will turn to God again.
To God?—He loves thee not—
The God thou serv'st is thine own appetite,
Wherein is fixed the love of Belzebub;
To him I'll build an altar and a church,
And offer lukewarm blood of new-born babes.

[*Enter* GOOD ANGEL *and* EVIL ANGEL.]

16 [As if to tread in our footsteps.]

mood of depression

G. ANG. Sweet Faustus, leave that execrable art.
FAUST. Contrition, prayer, repentance! What of them?
G. ANG. O, they are means to bring thee unto heaven.
E. ANG. Rather, illusions—fruits of lunacy,
That makes men foolish that do trust them most.
G. ANG. Sweet Faustus, think of heaven and heavenly things.
E. ANG. No, Faustus, think of honor and of wealth. [*Exeunt* ANGELS.]
FAUST. Of wealth!
Why the signiory of Embden shall be mine.
When Mephistophilis shall stand by me,
What God can hurt thee? Faustus, thou are safe:
Cast no more doubts. Come, Mephistophilis,
And bring glad tidings from great Lucifer;
Is't not midnight? Come, Mephistophilis;
Veni, veni, Mephistophile!

[*Enter* MEPHISTOPHILIS.]

Now tell me, what says Lucifer, thy lord?
MEPH. That I shall wait on Faustus whilst he lives,
So he will buy my service with his soul.
FAUST. Already Faustus hath hazarded that for thee.
MEPH. But, Faustus, thou must bequeath it solemnly,
And write a deed of gift with thine own blood,
For that security craves great Lucifer.
If thou deny it, I will back to hell.
FAUST. Stay, Mephistophilis! and tell me what good
Will my soul do thy lord.
MEPH. Enlarge his kingdom.
FAUST. Is that the reason why he tempts us thus?
MEPH. *Solamen miseris socios habuisse doloris* [17]
FAUST. Why, have you any pain that tortures others?
MEPH. As great as have the human souls of men.
But tell me, Faustus, shall I have thy soul?
And I will be thy slave, and wait on thee,
And give thee more than thou hast wit to ask.
FAUST. Ay, Mephistophilis, I give it thee.
MEPH. Then, Faustus, stab thine arm courageously,
And bind thy soul that at some certain day
Great Lucifer may claim it as his own;
And then be thou as great as Lucifer.
FAUST. [*stabbing his arm*] Lo, Mephistophilis, for love of thee,
I cut mine arm, and with my proper blood
Assure my soul to be great Lucifer's,
Chief lord and regent of perpetual night!
View here the blood that trickles from mine arm,
And let it be propitious for my wish.

17 [It is a comfort to have companions in misery.]

MEPH. But, Faustus, thou must
Write it in manner of a deed of gift.
FAUST. Ay, so I will. [*Writes*] But, Mephistophilis,
My blood congeals, and I can write no more.
MEPH. I'll fetch thee fire to dissolve it straight. [*Exit.*]
FAUST. What might the staying of my blood portend?
Is it unwilling I should write this bill?
Why streams it not that I may write afresh?
Faustus gives to thee his soul. Ah, there it stayed.
Why should'st thou not? Is not thy soul thine own?
Then write again, *Faustus gives to thee his soul.*

[*Enter* MESPHISTOPHILIS *with a chafer of coals.*]

MEPH. Here's fire. Come, Faustus, set it on.
FAUST. So now the blood begins to clear again;
Now will I make an end immediately. [*Writes.*]
MEPH. O, what will not I do to obtain his soul. [*Aside.*]
FAUST. *Consummatum est:*[18] this bill is ended.
And Faustus hath bequeathed his soul to Lucifer.
But what is this inscription on mine arm?
Homo, fuge![19] Whither should I fly?
If unto God, he'll throw me down to hell.
My senses are deceived; here's nothing writ—
I see it plain; here in this place is writ
Homo, fuge! Yet shall not Faustus fly.
MEPH. I'll fetch him somewhat to delight his mind. [*Exit.*]

[*Enter* MEPHISTOPHILIS *with* DEVILS, *giving crowns and rich apparel to* FAUSTUS, *and dance, and then depart.*]

FAUST. Speak, Mephistophilis, what means this show?
MEPH. Nothing, Faustus, but to delight thy mind withal,
And to show thee what magic can perform.
FAUST. But may I raise up spirits when I please?
MEPH. Ay, Faustus, and do greater things than these.
FAUST. Then there's enough for a thousand souls.
Here, Mephistophilis, receive this scroll,
A deed of gift of body and of soul:
But yet conditionally that thou perform
All articles prescribed between us both.
MEPH. Faustus, I swear by hell and Lucifer
To effect all promises between us made.
FAUST. Then hear me read them: *On these conditions following. First, that Faustus may be a spirit in form and substance. Secondly, that Mephistophilis shall be his servant, and at his command. Thirdly, that Mephistophilis shall do for him and bring him whatsoever. Fourthly, that he shall be in his chamber or house invisible. Lastly that he shall appear to the said John Faustus, at all times, in*

18 [It is consummated.]

19 [Flee, man!]

what form or shape soever he please. I, John Faustus, of Wittenberg, Doctor, by these presents do give both body and soul to Lucifer, Prince of the East, and his minister, Mephistophilis: and furthermore grant unto them, that twenty-four years being expired, the articles above written inviolate, full power to fetch or carry the said John Faustus, body and soul, flesh, blood, or goods, into their habitation wheresoever. By me. John Faustus.

MEPH. Speak, Faustus, do you deliver this as your deed?
FAUST. Ay, take it, and the Devil give thee good on't!
MEPH. Now, Faustus, ask what thou wilt.
FAUST. First will I question with thee about hell.
Tell me where is the place that men call hell?
MEPH. Under the heavens.
FAUST. Ay, but whereabout?
MEPH. Within the bowels of these elements,
Where we are tortured and remain for ever;
Hell hath no limits, nor is circumscibed
In one self place; for where we are is hell,
And where hell is there must we ever be:
And, to conclude, when all the world dissolves,
And every creature shall be purified,
All places shall be hell that is not heaven.
FAUST. Come, I think hell's a fable.
MEPH. Ay, think so still, till experience change thy mind.
FAUST. Why, think'st thou then that Faustus shall be damned?
MEPH. Ay, of necessity, for here's the scroll
Wherein thou hast given thy soul to Lucifer.
FAUST. Ay, and body too; but what of that?
Think'st thou that Faustus is so fond to imagine
That, after this life, there is any pain?
Tush; these are trifles, and mere old wives' tales.
MEPH. But, Faustus, I am an instance to prove the contrary.
For I am damnèd, and am now in hell.
FAUST. How! now in hell?
Nay, an this be hell, I'll willingly be damnèd here;
What? walking, disputing, etc.?
But, leaving off this, let me have a wife,
The fairest maid in Germany;
For I am wanton and lascivious,
And cannot live without a wife.
MEPH. How—a wife?
I prithee, Faustus, talk not of a wife.
FAUST. Nay, sweet Mephistophilis, fetch me one, for I will have one.
MEPH. Well—thou wilt have one. Sit there till I come:
I'll fetch thee a wife in the Devil's name. [*Exit.*]

[*Re-enter* MEPHISTOPHILIS *with a* DEVIL *dressed like a woman, with fireworks.*]

MEPH. Tell me, Faustus, how dost thou like my wife?

FAUST. A plague on her for a hot whore!

MEPH. Tut, Faustus,
Marriage is but a ceremonial toy;
And if thou lovest me, think no more of it.
I'll cull thee out the fairest courtesans.
And bring them every morning to thy bed;
She whom thine eye shall like, thy heart shall have,
Be she as chaste as was Penelope,
And as wise as Saba, or as beautiful
As was bright Lucifer before his fall.
Here, take this book, peruse it thoroughly: [*Gives a book.*]
The iterating of these lines brings gold;
The framing of this circle on the ground
Brings whirlwinds, tempests, thunder and lightning;
Pronounce this thrice devoutly to thyself,
And men in armor shall appear to thee,
Ready to execute what thou desir'st.

FAUST. Thanks, Mephistophilis; yet fain would I have a book wherein I might behold all spells and incantations, that I might raise up spirits when I please.

MEPH. Here they are, in this book. [*There turn to them.*]

FAUST. Now would I have a book where I might see all characters and planets of the heavens, that I might know their motions and dispositions.

MEPH. Here they are too. [*Turn to them.*]

FAUST. Nay, let me have one book more—and then I have done—wherein I might see all plants, herbs, and trees that grow upon the earth.

MEPH. Here they be.

FAUST. O, thou art deceived.

MEPH. Tut, I warrant thee. [*Turn to them. Exeunt.*]

SCENE VI.

[*Enter* FAUSTUS *in his study, and* MEPHISTOPHILIS.]

FAUST. When I behold the heavens, then I repent,
And curse thee, wicked Mephistophilis,
Because thou hast deprived me of those joys.

MEPH. Why, Faustus,
Think'st thou heaven is such a glorious thing?
I tell thee 'tis not half so fair as thou,
Or any man that breathes on earth.

FAUST. How prov'st thou that?

MEPH. 'Twas made for man, therefore is man more excellent.

FAUST. If it were made for man, 'twas made for me; I will renounce this magic and repent.

[*Enter* GOOD ANGEL *and* EVIL ANGEL.]

G. ANG. Faustus, repent; yet God will pity thee.
E. ANG. Thou art a spirit; God cannot pity thee.
FAUST. Who buzzeth in my ears I am a spirit?
Be I a devil, yet God may pity me;
Ay, God will pity me if I repent.
E. ANG. Ay, but Faustus never shall repent. [*Exeunt* ANGELS.]
FAUST. My heart's so hardened I cannot repent.
Scarce can I name salvation, faith, or heaven,
But fearful echoes thunder in mine ears
"Faustus, thou are damned!" Then swords and knives,
Poison, gun, halters, and envenomed steel
Are laid before me to dispatch myself,
And long ere this I should have slain myself,
Had not sweet pleasure conquered deep despair.
Have not I made blind Homer sing to me
Of Alexander's love and Œnon's death?
And hath not he that built the walls of Thebes
With ravishing sound of his melodious harp,
Made music with my Mephistophilis?
Why should I die then, or basely despair?
I am resolved: Faustus shall ne'er repent—
Come, Mephistophilis, let us dispute again,
And argue of divine astrology.
Tell me, are there many heavens above the moon?
Are all celestial bodies but one globe,
As is the substance of this centric earth?
MEPH. As are the elements, such are the spheres
Mutually folded in each other's orb,
And, Faustus,
All jointly move upon one axle-tree
Whose terminine is termed the world's wide pole;
Nor are the names of Saturn, Mars, or Jupiter
Feigned, but are erring stars.
FAUST. But tell me, have they all one motion both, *situ et tempore?*[20]
MEPH. All jointly move from east to west in twenty-four hours upon the poles of the world; but differ in their motion upon the poles of the zodiac.
FAUST. Tush!
These slender trifles Wagner can decide;
Hath Mephistophilis no greater skill?
Who knows not the double motion of the planets?
The first is finished in a natural day;
The second thus: as Saturn in thirty years;
Jupiter in twelve; Mars in four; the Sun, Venus, and Mercury in a year; the moon in twenty-eight days. Tush, these are freshmen's

20 [In place and time?]

suppositions. But tell me, hath every sphere a dominion or *intelligentia?*[21]

MEPH. Ay.

FAUST. How many heavens, or spheres, are there?

MEPH. Nine: the seven planets, the firmament, and the empyreal heaven.

FAUST. Well, resolve me in this question: Why have we not conjunctions, oppositions, aspects, eclipses, all at one time, but in some years we have more, in some less?

MEPH. *Per inœqualem motum respectu totius.*[22]

FAUST. Well, I am answered. Tell me who made the world.

MEPH. I will not.

FAUST. Sweet Mephistophilis, tell me.

MEPH. Move me not, for I will not tell thee.

FAUST. Villain, have I not bound thee to tell me anything?

MEPH. Ay, that is not against our kingdom; but this is. Think thou on hell, Faustus, for thou art damned.

FAUST. Think, Faustus, upon God that made the world.

MEPH. Remember this. [*Exit.*]

FAUST. Ay, go, accursèd spirit, to ugly hell.
'Tis thou hast damned distressèd Faustus' soul.
Is't not too late?

[*Enter* GOOD ANGEL *and* EVIL ANGEL.]

E. ANG. Too late.

G. ANG. Never too late, if Faustus can repent.

E. ANG. If thou repent, devils shall tear thee in pieces.

G. ANG. Repent, and they shall never raze thy skin. [*Exeunt* ANGELS.]

FAUST. Ah, Christ my Saviour,
Seek to save distressèd Faustus' soul!

[*Enter* LUCIFER, BELZEBUB, *and* MEPHISTOPHILIS.]

LUC. Christ cannot save thy soul, for he is just;
There's none but I have interest in the same.

FAUST. O, who art thou that look'st so terrible?

LUC. I am Lucifer,
And this is my companion-prince in hell.

FAUST. O Faustus! they are come to fetch away thy soul!

LUC. We come to tell thee thou dost injure us;
Thou talk'st of Christ contrary to thy promise;
Thou should'st not think of God: think of the Devil.

BELZ. And his dam, too.

FAUST. Nor will I henceforth: pardon me in this,
And Faustus vows never to look to heaven,
Never to name God, or to pray to him,

21 [Intelligence or spirit.]
22 [Through unequal motion in respect to the whole.]

To burn his Scriptures, slay his ministers,
And make my spirits pull his churches down.

LUC. Do so and we will highly gratify thee. Faustus, we are come from hell to show thee some pastime: sit down, and thou shalt see all the Seven Deadly Sins appear in their proper shapes.

FAUST. That sight will be as pleasing unto me,
As Paradise was to Adam the first day
Of his creation.

LUC. Talk not of Paradise nor creation, but mark this show: talk of the Devil, and nothing else: come away!

[*Enter the* SEVEN DEADLY SINS.]

Now, Faustus, examine them of their several names and dispositions.

FAUST. What art thou—the first?

PRIDE. I am Pride. I disdain to have any parents. I am like to Ovid's flea: I can creep into every corner of a wench; sometimes, like a periwig, I sit upon her brow; or like a fan of feathers, I kiss her lips; indeed I do—what do I not? But, fie, what a scent is here! I'll not speak another word, except the ground were perfumed, and covered with cloth of arras.

FAUST. What art thou—the second?

COVET. I am Covetousness, begotten of an old churl in an old leathern bag; and, might I have my wish, I would desire that this house and all the people in it were turned to gold, that I might lock you up in my good chest. O, my sweet gold!

FAUST. What art thou—the third?

WRATH. I am Wrath. I had neither father nor mother; I leapt out of a lion's mouth when I was scarce half an hour old; and ever since I have run up and down the world with this case of rapiers, wounding myself when I had nobody to fight withal. I was born in hell; and look to it, for some of you shall be my father.

FAUST. What art thou—the fourth?

ENVY. I am Envy, begotten of a chimney-sweeper and an oyster-wife. I cannot read, and therefore wish all books were burnt. I am lean with seeing others eat. O, that there would come a famine through all the world, that all might die, and I live alone! then thou should'st see how fat I would be. But must thou sit and I stand! Come down with a vengeance!

FAUST. Away, envious rascal! What art thou—the fifth?

GLUT. Who, I, sir? I am Gluttony. My parents are all dead, and the devil a penny they have left me, but a bare pension, and that is thirty meals a day and ten bevers—a small trifle to suffice nature. O, I come of a royal parentage! My grandfather was a Gammon of Bacon, my grandmother was a Hogshead of Claret wine; my godfathers were these, Peter Pickle-herring, and Martin Martlemas-beef; O, but my godmother, she was a jolly gentlewoman, and well beloved in every good town and city; her name was Mistress Margery March-bee. Now, Faustus, thou hast heard all my progeny, wilt thou bid me to supper?

FAUST. No, I'll see thee hanged: thou wilt eat up all my victuals.

GLUT. Then the Devil choke thee!

FAUST. Choke thyself, glutton! Who are thou—the sixth?

SLOTH. I am Sloth. I was begotten on a sunny bank, where I have lain ever since; and you have done me great injury to bring me from thence: let me be carried thither again by Gluttony and Lechery. I'll not speak another word for a king's ransom.

FAUST. What are you, Mistress Minx, the seventh and last?

LECHERY. Who, I, sir? I am the one that loves an inch of raw mutton better than an ell of fried stock-fish; and the first letter of my name begins with L. [*Exeunt the Sins.*]

LUC. Away to hell, to hell!
Now, Faustus, how dost thou like this?

FAUST. O, this feeds my soul!

LUC. Tut, Faustus, in hell is all manner of delight.

FAUST. O, might I see hell, and return again,
How happy were I then!

LUC. Thou shalt; I will send for thee at midnight.
In meantime take this book; peruse it thoroughly,
And thou shalt turn thyself into what shape thou wilt.

FAUST. Great thanks, mighty Lucifer!
This will I keep as chary as my life.

LUC. Farewell, Faustus, and think on the Devil.

FAUST. Farewell, great Lucifer! Come, Mephistophilis.
[*Exeunt omnes.*]

[*Enter* WAGNER *solus.*]

WAG. Learned Faustus,
To know the secrets of astronomy,
Graven in the book of Jove's high firmament,
Did mount himself to scale Olympus' top,
Being seated in a chariot burning bright,
Drawn by the strength of yoky dragons' necks.
He now is gone to prove cosmography,
And, as I guess, will first arrive at Rome,
To see the Pope the manner of his court,
And take some part of holy Peter's feast,
That to this day is highly solemnized. [*Exit* WAGNER.]

SCENE VII.

The Privy-Chamber of the POPE.

[*Enter* FAUSTUS *and* MEPHISTOPHILIS.]

FAUST. Having now, my good Mephistophilis,
Passed with delight the stately town of Trier,

Environed round with airy mountain tops,
With walls of flint, and deep entrenchèd lakes,
Not to be won by any conquering prince;
From Paris next, coasting the realm of France,
We saw the river Maine fall into Rhine,
Whose banks are set with groves of fruitful vines;
Then up to Naples, rich Campania,
Whose buildings fair and gorgeous to the eye,
The streets straight forth, and paved with finest brick,
Quarter the town in four equivalents:
There saw we learned Maro's golden tomb,
The way he cut, an English mile in length,
Thorough a rock of stone in one night's space;
From thence to Venice, Padua, and the rest,
In one of which a sumptuous temple stands,
That threats the stars with her aspiring top.
Thus hitherto has Faustus spent his time:
But tell me, now, what resting-place is this?
Hast thou, as erst I did command,
Conducted me within the walls of Rome?

MEPH. Faustus, I have; and because we will not be unprovided, I have taken up his Holiness' privy chamber for our use.

FAUST. I hope his Holiness will bid us welcome.

MEPH. Tut, 'tis no matter, man, we'll be bold with his good cheer.
And now, my Faustus, that thou may'st perceive
What Rome containeth to delight thee with,
Know that this city stands upon seven hills
That underprop the groundwork of the same:
Just through the midst runs flowing Tiber's stream,
With winding banks that cut it in two parts:
Over the which four stately bridges lean,
That make safe passage to each part of Rome:
Upon the bridge called Ponte Angelo
Erected is a castle passing strong,
Within whose walls such store of ordnance are,
And double cannons framed of carved brass,
As match the days within one complete year;
Besides the gates, and high pyramides,
Which Julius Cæsar brought from Africa.

FAUST. Now, by the kingdoms of infernal rule,
Of Styx, of Acheron, and the fiery lake
Of ever-burning Phlegethon, I swear
That I do long to see the monuments
And situation of bright-splendent Rome:
Come, therefore, let's away.

MEPH. Nay, Faustus, stay; I know you'd fain see the Pope,
And take some part of holy Peter's feast,

Where thou shalt see a troop of bald-pate friars,
Whose *summum bonum*[23] is in belly-cheer.

FAUST. Well, I'm content to compass them some sport,
And by their folly make us merriment.
Then charm me, Mephistophilis, that I
May be invisible, to do what I please
Unseen of any whilst I stay in Rome.
[MEPHISTOPHILIS *charms him.*]

MEPH. So, Faustus, now
Do what thou wilt, thou shalt not be discerned.

[*Sound a sennet. Enter the* POPE *and the* CARDINAL OF LORRAIN *to the banquet, with* FRIARS *attending.*]

POPE. My Lord of Lorrain, wilt please you draw near?

FAUST. Fall to, and the devil choke you an you spare!

POPE. How now! Who's that which spake?—Friars, look about.

FRIAR. Here's nobody, if it like your Holiness.

POPE. My lord, here is a dainty dish was sent me from the Bishop of Milan.

FAUST. I thank you, sir. [*Snatches it.*]

POPE. How now! Who's that which snatched the meat from me? Will no man look? My Lord, this dish was sent me from the Cardinal of Florence.

FAUST. You say true; I'll ha't. [*Snatches the dish.*]

POPE. What, again! My lord, I'll drink to your grace.

FAUST. I'll pledge your grace. [*Snatches the cup.*]

C. OF LOR. My Lord, it may be some ghost newly crept out of purgatory, come to beg a pardon of your Holiness.

POPE. It may be so. Friars, prepare a dirge to lay the fury of this ghost. Once again, my lord, fall to. [*The* POPE *crosseth himself.*]

FAUST. What, are you crossing of yourself?
Well, use that trick no more I would advise you. [*Cross again.*]
Well, there's the second time. Aware the third,
I give you fair warning.

[*Cross again, and* FAUSTUS *hits him a box of the ear; they all run away.*]

Come on, Mephistophilis, what shall we do?

MEPH. Nay, I know not. We shall be cursed with bell, book, and candle.

FAUST. How! bell, book, and candle—candle, book, and bell,
Forward and backward to curse Faustus to hell!
Anon you shall hear a hog grunt, a calf bleat, and an ass bray,
Because it is Saint Peter's holiday.

[*Enter all the* FRIARS *to sing the dirge.*]

FRIAR. Come, brethren, let's about our business with good devotion. [*Sing this.*]

23 [Highest good.]

Cursed be he that stole away his Holiness' meat from the table! *Maledicat Dominus!*[24]
Cursed be he that struck his Holiness a blow on the face! *Maledicat Dominus!*
Cursed be he that took Friar Sandelo a blow on the pate! *Maledicat Dominus!*
Cursed be he that disturbeth our holy dirge! *Maledicat Dominus!*
Cursed be he that took away his Holiness' wine! *Maledicat Dominus! Et omnes sancti!*[25] *Amen!*

[MEPHISTOPHILIS *and* FAUSTUS *beat the* FRIARS, *and fling fireworks among them: and so exeunt.*]

[*Enter* CHORUS.]

CHORUS. When Faustus had with pleasure ta'en the view
Of rarest things, and royal courts of kings,
He stayed his course, and so returnèd home;
Where such as bear his absence but with grief,
I mean his friends, and near'st companions,
Did gratulate his safety with kind words,
And in their conference of what befell,
Touching his journey through the world and air,
They put forth questions of astrology,
Which Faustus answered with such learnèd skill,
As they admired and wondered at his wit.
Now is his fame spread forth in every land;
Amongst the rest the Emperor is one,
Carolus the Fifth, at whose palace now
Faustus is feasted 'mongst his noblemen.
What there he did in trial of his art,
I leave untold—your eyes shall see performed. [*Exit.*]

SCENE VIII.

An Inn-yard.

[*Enter* ROBIN *the ostler with a book in his hand.*]

ROBIN. Oh, this is admirable! here I ha' stolen one of Doctor Faustus' conjuring books, and i' faith I mean to search some circles for my own use. Now will I make all the maidens in our parish dance at my pleasure, stark-naked before me; and so by that means I shall see more than e'er I felt or saw yet.

[*Enter* RAFE *calling* ROBIN.]

RAFE. Robin, prithee, come away; there's a gentleman tarries to have his horse, and he would have his things rubbed and made clean; he

24 [May God curse.]

25 [And all the saints!]

keeps such a chafing with my mistress about it; and she has sent me to look thee out prithee, come away.

ROBIN. Keep out, keep out, or else you are blown up; you are dismembered, Rafe: keep out, for I am about a roaring piece of work.

RAFE. Come, what dost thou with that same book? Thou can'st not read.

ROBIN. Yes, my master and mistress shall find that I can read, he for his forehead, she for her private study; she's born to bear with me, or else my art fails.

RAFE. Why, Robin, what book is that?

ROBIN. What book! Why, the most intolerable book for conjuring that e'er was invented by any brimstone devil.

RAFE. Can'st thou conjure with it?

ROBIN. I can do all these things easily with it; first, I can make thee drunk with ippocras at any tabern in Europe for nothing; that's one of my conjuring works.

RAFE. Our Master Parson says that's nothing.

ROBIN. True, Rafe; and more, Rafe, if thou hast any mind to Nan Spit, our kitchen-maid, then turn her and wind her to thy own use as often as thou wilt, and at midnight.

RAFE. O brave Robin, shall I have Nan Spit, and to mine own use? On that condition I'd feed thy devil with horsebread as long as he lives, of free cost.

ROBIN. No more, sweet Rafe: let's go and make clean our boots, which lie foul upon our hands, and then to our conjuring in the devil's name. [*Exeunt.*]

SCENE IX.

The same.

[*Enter* ROBIN *and* RAFE *with a silver goblet.*]

ROBIN. Come, Rafe, did not I tell thee we were for ever made by this Doctor Faustus' book? *ecce signum,*[26] here's a simple purchase for horse-keepers; our horses shall eat no hay as long as this lasts.

RAFE. But, Robin, here comes the Vintner.

ROBIN. Hush! I'll gull him supernaturally.

[*Enter* VINTNER.]

Drawer, I hope all is paid: God be with you; come, Rafe.

VINT. Soft, sir; a word with you. I must yet have a goblet paid from you, ere you go.

ROBIN. I, a goblet, Rafe; I, a goblet! I scorn you, and you are but a, etc. I, a goblet! search me.

VINT. I mean so, sir, with your favor. [*Searches him.*]

ROBIN. How say you now?

26 [Behold the sign.]

VINT. I must say somewhat to your fellow. You, sir!

RAFE. Me, sir! me, sir! search your fill. [*Vintner searches him.*] Now, sir, you may be ashamed to burden honest men with a matter of truth.

VINT. Well, t'one of you hath this goblet about you.

ROBIN. You lie, drawer, 'tis afore me. [*Aside*]—Sirrah you, I'll teach you to impeach honest men—stand by—I'll scour you for a goblet! —stand aside you had best, I charge you in the name of Belzebub. —Look to the goblet, Rafe. [*Aside to* RAFE.]

VINT. What mean you, sirrah?

ROBIN. I'll tell you what I mean. [*Reads from a book.*] *Sanctobulorum Periphrasticon*[27]—nay, I'll tickle you, Vintner. Look to the goblet, Rafe. [*Aside to* RAFE.]

[*Reads.*] *Polypragmos Belseborams framanto pacostiphos tostu, Mephistophilis,* etc.

[*Enter* MEPHISTOPHILIS, *sets squibs at their backs, and then exits. They run about.*]

VINT. *O nomine Domini!*[28] what meanest thou, Robin? thou hast no goblet.

RAFE. *Peccatum peccatorum.*[29] There's thy goblet, good Vintner. [*Gives the goblet to Vintner, who exits.*]

ROBIN. *Misericordia pro nobis!*[30] What shall I do? Good Devil, forgive me now, and I'll never rob thy library more.

[*Enter to them* MEPHISTOPHILIS.]

MEPH. Monarch of hell, under whose black survey
Great potentates do kneel with awful fear,
Upon whose altars thousand souls do lie,
How am I vexed with these villains' charms!
From Constantinople am I hither come
Only for pleasure of these damnèd slaves.

ROBIN. How, from Constantinople! You have had a great journey: will you take six-pence in your purse to pay for your supper, and begone?

MEPH. Well, villains, for your presumption I transform thee into an ape, and thee into a dog and so begone. [*Exit.*]

ROBIN. How, into an ape; that's brave! I'll have fine sport with the boys. I'll get nuts and apples enow.

RAFE. And I must be a dog.

ROBIN. I'faith thy head will never be out of the pottage pot. [*Exeunt.*]

27 [Nonsense, as is the next pseudo-Latin phrase.]
28 [Oh in God's name!] 29 [Sin of sins.] 30 [Mercy upon us!]

SCENE X.

The court.

[*Enter* EMPEROR, FAUSTUS, *and a* KNIGHT *with* ATTENDANTS.]

EMP. Master Doctor Faustus, I have heard strange report of thy knowledge in the black art, how that none in my empire nor in the whole world can compare with thee for the rare effects of magic; they say thou hast a familiar spirit, by whom thou canst accomplish what thou list. This, therefore, is my request, that thou let me see some proof of thy skill, that mine eyes may be witnesses to confirm what mine ears have heard reported; and here I swear to thee by the honor of mine imperial crown, that, whatever thou doest, thou shalt be no ways prejudiced or endamaged.

KNIGHT. I'faith he looks much like a conjuror. [*Aside.*]

FAUST. My gracious sovereign, though I must confess myself far inferior to the report men have published, and nothing answerable to the honor of your imperial majesty, yet for that love and duty binds me thereunto, I am content to do whatsoever your majesty shall command me.

EMP. Then, Doctor Faustus, mark what I shall say.
As I was sometimes solitary set
Within my closet, sundry thoughts arose
About the honor of mine ancestors,
How they had won by prowess such exploits,
Got such riches, subdued so many kingdoms
As we that do succeed, or they that shall
Hereafter possess our throne, shall
(I fear me) ne'er attain to that degree
Of high renown and great authority;
Amongst which kings is Alexander the Great,
Chief spectacle of the world's pre-eminence,
The bright shining of whose glorious acts
Lightens the world with his reflecting beams,
As when I hear but motion made of him
It grieves my soul I never saw the man.
If therefore thou by cunning of thine art
Canst raise this man from hollow vaults below,
Where lies entombed this famous conqueror,
And bring with him his beauteous paramour,
Both in their right shapes, gesture, and attire
They used to wear during their time of life,
Thou shalt both satisfy my just desire,
And give me cause to praise thee whilst I live.

FAUST. My gracious lord, I am ready to accomplish your request so far forth as by art, and power of my spirit, I am able to perform.

KNIGHT. I'faith that's just nothing at all. [*Aside.*]

FAUST. But, if it like your grace, it is not in my ability to present before your eyes the true substantial bodies of those two deceased princes, which long since are consumed to dust.

KNIGHT. Ay, marry, Master Doctor, now there's a sign of grace in you, when you will confess the truth. [*Aside.*]

FAUST. But such spirits as can lively resemble Alexander and his paramour shall appear before your grace in that manner that they best lived in, in their most flourishing estate; which I doubt not shall sufficiently content your imperial majesty.

EMP. Go to, Master Doctor, let me see them presently.

KNIGHT. Do you hear, Master Doctor? You bring Alexander and his paramour before the Emperor!

FAUST. How then, sir?

KNIGHT. I'faith that's as true as Diana turned me to a stag!

FAUST. No, sir, but when Actæon died, he left the horns for you. Mephistophilis, begone. [*Exit* MEPH.]

KNIGHT. Nay an you go to conjuring, I'll begone. [*Exit* KNIGHT.]

FAUST. I'll meet with you anon for interrupting me so. Here they are, my gracious lord.

[*Enter* MEPHISTOPHILIS *with* SPIRITS *in the shape of* ALEXANDER *and his* PARAMOUR.]

EMP. Master Doctor, I heard this lady while she lived had a wart or mole in her neck: how shall I know whether it be so or no?

FAUST. Your highness may boldly go and see.

EMP. Sure these are no spirits, but the true substantial bodies of those two deceased princes. [*Exeunt* SPIRITS.]

FAUST. Will't please your highness now to send for the knight that was so pleasant with me here of late?

EMP. One of you call him forth! [*Exit* ATTENDANT.]

[*Enter the* KNIGHT *with a pair of horns on his head.*]

How now, sir Knight! why I had thought thou had'st been a bachelor, but now I see thou hast a wife, that not only gives thee horns, but makes thee wear them. Feel on thy head.

KNIGHT. Thou damnèd wretch and execrable dog,
Bred in the concave of some monstrous rock,
How darest thou thus abuse a gentleman?
Villain, I say, undo what thou hast done!

FAUST. O, not so fast, sir; there's no haste; but, good, are you rememered how you crossed me in my conference with the Emperor? I think I have met with you for it.

EMP. Good Master Doctor, at my entreaty release him; he hath done penance sufficient.

FAUST. My gracious lord, not so much for the injury he offered me here in your presence, as to delight you with some mirth, hath Faustus worthily requited this injurious knight; which, being all I desire, I am content to release him of his horns: and, sir knight, hereafter speak well of scholars. Mephistophilis, transform him straight. [MEPHISTOPHILIS *removes the horns.*] Now, my good lord, having done my duty I humbly take my leave.

EMP. Farewell, Master Doctor; yet, ere you go,
Expect from me a bounteous reward. [*Exit* EMPEROR.]

SCENE XI.

A Green, then FAUSTUS' *house.*

[*Enter* FAUSTUS *and* MEPHISTOPHILIS.]

FAUST. Now, Mephistophilis, the restless course
That Time doth run with calm and silent foot,
Shortening my days and thread of vital life,
Calls for the payment of my latest years:
Therefore, sweet Mephistophilis, let us
Make haste to Wittenberg.

MEPH. What, will you go on horse-back or on foot?

FAUST. Nay, till I'm past this fair and pleasant green, I'll walk on foot.

[*Enter a* HORSE-COURSER.]

HORSE-C. I have been all this day seeking one Master Fustian: mass, see where he is! God save you, Master Doctor!

FAUST. What, Horse-Courser! You are well met.

HORSE-C. Do you hear, sir? I have brought you forty dollars for your horse.

FAUST. I cannot sell him so: if thou likest him for fifty, take him.

HORSE-C. Alas, sir, I have no more.—I pray you speak for me.

MEPH. I pray you let him have him: he is an honest fellow, and he has a great charge, neither wife nor child.

FAUST. Well, come, give me your money. [HORSE-COURSER *gives* FAUSTUS *the money.*] My boy will deliver him to you. But I must tell you one thing before you have him; ride him not into the water at any hand.

HORSE-C. Why, sir, will he not drink of all waters?

FAUST. O, yes, he will drink of all waters, but ride him not into the water: ride him over hedge or ditch, or where thou wilt, but not into the water.

HORSE-C. Well, sir.—Now am I made man for ever: I'll not leave my horse for twice forty: if he had but the quality of hey-ding-ding, hey-ding-ding, I'd make a brave living on him: he has a buttock as slick as an eel. [*Aside.*] Well, God buy, sir, your boy will deliver him me: but hark you, sir; if my horse be sick or ill at ease, if I bring his water to you, you'll tell me what it is?

FAUST. Away, you villain; what, dost think I am a horse-doctor?
[*Exit* HORSE-COURSER.]

What are thou, Faustus, but a man condemned to die?
Thy fatal time doth draw to final end:

Despair doth drive distrust unto my thoughts:
Confound these passions with a quiet sleep:
Tush, Christ did call the thief upon the cross;
Then rest thee, Faustus, quiet in conceit. [*Sleeps in his chair.*]

[*Re-enter* HORSE-COURSER, *all wet, crying.*]

HORSE-C. Alas, alas! Doctor Fustian quotha? Mass, Doctor Lopus was never such a doctor. Has given me a purgation has purged me of forty dollars; I shall never see them more. But yet, like an ass as I was, I would not be ruled by him, for he bade me I should ride him into no water. Now I, thinking my horse had had some rare quality that he would not have had me known of, I, like a venturous youth, rid him into the deep pond at the town's end. I was no sooner in the middle of the pond, but my horse vanished away, and I sat upon a bottle of hay, never so near drowning in my life. But I'll seek out my Doctor, and have my forty dollars again, or I'll make it the dearest horse!—O, yonder is his snipper-snapper.—Do you hear? you hey-pass, where's your master?

MEPH. Why, sir, what would you? You cannot speak with him.

HORSE-C. But I will speak with him.

MEPH. Why, he's fast asleep. Come some other time.

HORSE-C. I'll speak with him now, or I'll break his glass windows about his ears.

MEPH. I tell thee he has not slept this eight nights.

HORSE-C. An he have not slept this eight weeks I'll speak with him.

MEPH. See where he is, fast asleep.

HORSE-C. Ay, this is he. God save you, Master Doctor, Master Doctor, Master Doctor Fustian!—Forty dollars, forty dollars for a bottle of hay!

MEPH. Why, thou seest he hears thee not.

HORSE-C. So-ho, ho!—so-ho ho! (*Hollas in his ear.*) No, will you not wake? I'll make you wake ere I go. (*Pulls him by the leg, and pulls it away.*) Alas, I am undone! What shall I do?

FAUST. O, my leg, my leg! Help, Mephistophilis! call the officers. My leg, my leg!

MEPH. Come, villain, to the constable.

HORSE-C. O lord, sir, let me go, and I'll give you forty dollars more.

MEPH. Where be they?

HORSE-C. I have none about me. Come to my ostry and I'll give them you.

MEPH. Begone quickly. [HORSE-COURSER *runs away.*]

FAUST. What, is he gone? Farewell he! Faustus has his leg again, and the horse-courser, I take it, a bottle of hay for his labor. Well, this trick shall cost him forty dollars more.

[*Enter* WAGNER.]

How now, Wagner, what's the news with thee?

WAG. Sir, the Duke of Vanholt doth earnestly entreat your company.

FAUST. The Duke of Vanholt! an honorable gentleman, to whom I must be no niggard of my cunning. Come Mephistophilis, let's away to him. [*Exeunt.*]

SCENE XII.

Court of the DUKE.

[*Enter the* DUKE *and the* DUCHESS, FAUSTUS, *and* MEPHISTOPHILIS.]

DUKE. Believe me, Master Doctor, this merriment hath much pleased me.

FAUST. My gracious lord, I am glad it contents you so well.—But it may be, madam, you take no delight in this. I have heard that great bellied women do long for some dainties or other: what is it, madam? tell me, and you shall have it.

DUCHESS. Thanks, good Master Doctor; and for I see your courteous intent to pleasure me, I will not hide from you the thing my heart desires; and were it now summer, as it is January and the dead time of winter, I would desire no better meat than a dish of ripe grapes.

FAUST. Alas, madam, that's nothing! Mephistophilis, begone. [*Exit* MEPHISTOPHILIS.] Were it a greater thing than this, so it would content you, you should have it.

[*Enter* MEPHISTOPHILIS *with the grapes.*]

Here they be, madam; wilt please you taste on them?

DUKE. Believe me, Master Doctor, this makes me wonder above the rest, that being in the dead time of winter, and in the month of January, how you should come by these grapes.

FAUST. If it like your grace, the year is divided into two circles over the whole world, that, when it is here winter with us, in the contrary circle it is summer with them, as in India, Saba, and farther countries in the East; and by means of a swift spirit that I have I had them brought hither, as you see.—How do you like them, madam; be they good?

DUCHESS. Believe me, Master Doctor, they be the best grapes that e'er I tasted in my life before.

FAUST. I am glad they content you so, madam.

DUKE. Come, madam, let us in, where you must well reward this learned man for the great kindness he hath showed to you.

DUCHESS. And so I will, my lord; and, whilst I live, rest beholding for this courtesy.

FAUST. I humbly thank your grace.

DUKE. Come, Master Doctor, follow us and receive your reward. [*Exeunt.*]

SCENE XIII.

FAUSTUS' *study.*

[*Enter* WAGNER *solus.*]

WAG. I think my master means to die shortly,
For he hath given to me all his goods
And yet, methinks, if that death were [so] near,
He would not banquet, and carouse and swill
Amongst the students, as even now he doth,
Who are at supper with such belly-cheer
As Wagner ne'er beheld in all his life.
See where they come! belike the feast is ended.

[*Enter* FAUSTUS, *with two or three* SCHOLARS *and* MEPHISTOPHILIS.]

1 SCHOL. Master Doctor Faustus, since our conference about fair ladies, which was the beautifullest in all the world, we have determined with ourselves that Helen of Greece was the admirablest lady that ever lived: therefore, Master Doctor, if you will do us that favor, as to let us see that peerless dame of Greece, whom all the world admires for majesty, we should think ourselves much beholding unto you.

FAUST. Gentlemen,
For that I know your friendship is unfeignèd,
And Faustus' custom is not to deny
The just requests of those that wish him well,
You shall behold that peerless dame of Greece,
No otherways for pomp and majesty,
Than when Sir Paris crossed the seas with her,
And brought the spoils to rich Dardania.
Be silent, then, for danger is in words.

[*Music sounds and* HELEN *passeth over the stage.*]

2 SCHOL. Too simple is my wit to tell her praise,
Whom all the world admires for majesty.

3 SCHOL. No marvel though the angry Greeks pursued
With ten years' war the rape of such a queen,
Whose heavenly beauty passeth all compare.

1 SCHOL. Since we have seen the pride of Nature's works,
And only paragon of excellence,

[*Enter an* OLD MAN.]

Let us depart; and for this glorious deed
Happy and blest be Faustus evermore.

FAUST. Gentlemen, farewell—the same I wish to you.

[*Exeunt* SCHOLARS *and* WAGNER.]

OLD MAN. Ah, Doctor Faustus, that I might prevail

To guide thy steps unto the way of life,
By which sweet path thou may'st attain the goal
That shall conduct thee to celestial rest!
Break heart, drop blood, and mingle it with tears,
Tears falling from repentant heaviness
Of thy most vile and loathsome filthiness,
The stench whereof corrupts the inward soul
With such flagitious crimes of heinous sins
As no commiseration may expel,
But mercy, Faustus, of thy Saviour sweet,
Whose blood alone must wash away thy guilt.

FAUST. Where art thou, Faustus? wretch, what hast thou done?
Damned art thou, Faustus, damned; despair and die!
Hell calls for right, and with a roaring voice
Says, "Faustus! come! thine hour is [almost] come!"
And Faustus now will come to do thee right.

[MEPHISTOPHILIS *gives him a dagger.*]

OLD MAN. Ah stay, good Faustus, stay thy desperate steps!
I see an angel hovers o'er thy head,
And, with a vial full of precious grace,
Offers to pour the same into thy soul:
Then call for mercy, and avoid despair.

FAUST. Ah, my sweet friend, I feel
Thy words do comfort my distressèd soul.
Leave me a while to ponder on my sins.

OLD MAN. I go, sweet Faustus, but with heavy cheer,
Fearing the ruin of thy hopeless soul. [*Exit.*]

FAUST. Accursèd Faustus, where is mercy now?
I do repent; and yet I do despair;
Hell strives with grace for conquest in my breast:
What shall I do to shun the snares of death?

MEPH. Thou traitor, Faustus, I arrest thy soul
For disobedience to my sovereign lord;
Revolt, or I'll in piecemeal tear thy flesh.

FAUST. Sweet Mephistophilis, entreat thy lord
To pardon my unjust presumption.
And with my blood again I will confirm
My former vow I made to Lucifer.

MEPH. Do it then quickly, with unfeignèd heart,
Lest greater danger do attend thy drift. [FAUSTUS *stabs his arm and writes on a paper with his blood.*]

FAUST. Torment, sweet friend, that base and crookèd age,
That durst dissuade me from thy Lucifer,
With greatest torments that our hell affords.

MEPH. His faith is great: I cannot touch his soul;
But what I may afflict his body with
I will attempt, which is but little worth.

FAUST. One thing, good servant, let me crave of thee,

To glut the longing of my heart's desire—
That I might have unto my paramour
That heavenly Helen, which I saw of late,
Whose sweet embracings may extinguish clean
These thoughts that do dissuade me from my vow,
And keep mine oath I made to Lucifer.

MEPH. Faustus, this or what else thou shalt desire
Shall be performed in twinkling of an eye.

[*Enter* HELEN.]

FAUST. Was this the face that launched a thousand ships
And burnt the topless towers of Ilium?
Sweet Helen, make me immortal with a kiss. [*Kisses her.*]
Her lips suck forth my soul; see where it flies!
Come, Helen, come, give me my soul again.
Here will I dwell, for heaven be in these lips,
And all is dross that is not Helena.
I will be Paris, and for love of thee,
Instead of Troy, shall Wittenberg be sacked
And I will combat with weak Menelaus,
And wear thy colors on my plumèd crest:
Yea, I will wound Achilles in the heel,
And then return to Helen for a kiss.
O, thou art fairer than the evening air
Clad in the beauty of a thousand stars;
Brighter art thou than flaming Jupiter
When he appeared to hapless Semele:
More lovely than the monarch of the sky
In wanton Arethusa's azured arms:
And none but thou shalt be my paramour! [*Exeunt.*]

[*Enter the* OLD MAN.]

OLD MAN. Accursèd Faustus, miserable man,
That from thy soul exclud'st the grace of heaven,
And fly'st the throne of his tribunal seat!

[*Enter* DEVILS.]

Satan begins to sift me with his pride:
As in this furnace God shall try my faith.
My faith, vile hell, shall triumph over thee.
Ambitious fiends! see how the heavens smile
At your repulse, and laugh your state to scorn!
Hence, hell! for hence I fly unto my God. [*Exeunt.*]

SCENE XIV.

The same.

[*Enter* FAUSTUS *with the* SCHOLARS.]

FAUST. Ah, gentlemen!

1 SCHOL. What ails Faustus?

FAUST. Ah, my sweet chamber-fellow, had I lived with thee, then had I lived still! but now I die eternally. Look, comes he not, comes he not?

2 SCHOL. What means Faustus?

3 SCHOL. Belike he is grown into some sickness by being over solitary.

1 SCHOL. If it be so, we'll have physicians to cure him. 'Tis but a surfeit. Never fear, man.

FAUSTUS. A surfeit of deadly sin that hath damned both body and soul.

2 SCHOL. Yet, Faustus, look up to heaven: remember God's mercies are infinite.

FAUST. But Faustus' offence can ne'er be pardoned: the serpent that tempted Eve may be saved, but not Faustus. Ah, gentlemen, hear me with patience, and tremble not at my speeches! Though my heart pants and quivers to remember that I have been a student here these thirty years, O, would I had never seen Wittenberg, never read book! And what wonders I have done, all Germany can witness, yea, all the world; for which Faustus hath lost both Germany and the world, yea heaven itself, heaven, the seat of God, the throne of the blessed, the kingdom of joy; and must remain in hell for ever, hell, ah, hell, for ever! Sweet friends! what shall become of Faustus being in hell for ever?

3 SCHOL. Yet, Faustus, call on God.

FAUST. On God, whom Faustus hath abjured! on God, whom Faustus hath blasphemed! Ah, my God, I would weep, but the Devil draws in my tears. Gush forth blood instead of tears! Yea, life and soul! O, he stays my tongue! I would lift up my hands, but see, they hold them, they hold them!

ALL. Who, Faustus?

FAUST. Lucifer and Mephistophilis. Ah, gentlemen, I gave them my soul for my cunning!

ALL. God forbid!

FAUST. God forbade it indeed; but Faustus hath done it: for vain pleasure of twenty-four years hath Faustus lost eternal joy and felicity. I writ them a bill with mine own blood: the date is expired; the time will come, and he will fetch me.

1 SCHOL. Why did not Faustus tell us of this before, that divines might have prayed for thee?

FAUST. Oft have I thought to have done so: but the Devil threatened to tear me in pieces if I named God; to fetch both body and soul if

I once gave ear to divinity: and now 'tis too late. Gentlemen, away! lest you perish with me.

2 SCHOL. O, what shall we do to [save] Faustus?

FAUST. Talk not of me, but save yourselves, and depart.

3 SCHOL. God will strengthen me. I will stay with Faustus.

1 SCHOL. Tempt not God, sweet friend; but let us into the next room, and there pray for him.

FAUST. Ay, pray for me, pray for me! and what noise soever ye hear, come not unto me, for nothing can rescue me.

2 SCHOL. Pray thou, and we will pray that God may have mercy upon thee.

FAUST. Gentlemen, farewell: if I live till morning I'll visit you: if not——Faustus is gone to hell.

ALL. Faustus, farewell. [*Exeunt* SCHOLARS.]

[*The clock strikes eleven.*]

FAUST. Ah, Faustus,
Now hast thou but one bare hour to live,
And then thou must be damned perpetually!
Stand still, you ever-moving spheres of heaven,
That time may cease, and midnight never come;
Fair Nature's eye, rise, rise again and make
Perpetual day; or let this hour be but
A year, a month, a week, a natural day,
That Faustus may repent and save his soul!
O lente, lente, currite noctis equi![31]
The stars move still, time runs, the clock will strike,
The Devil will come, and Faustus must be damned.
Oh, I'll leap up to my God! Who pulls me down?
See, see where Christ's blood streams in the firmament!
One drop would save my soul—half a drop: ah, my Christ!
Ah, rend not my heart for naming of my Christ!
Yet will I call on him: O, spare me, Lucifer!—
Where is it now? 'tis gone; and see where God
Stretcheth out his arm, and bends his ireful brows!
Mountain and hills come, come and fall on me,
And hide me from the heavy wrath of God!
No! no!
Then will I headlong run into the earth;
Earth gape! O, no, it will not harbor me!
You stars that reigned at my nativity,
Whose influence hath allotted death and hell,
Now draw up Faustus like a foggy mist
Into the entrails of yon laboring clouds,
That when you vomit forth into the air,
My limbs may issue from their smoky mouths,
So that my soul may but ascend to heaven,

[*The clock strikes the half hour.*]

31 [Run slowly, slowly, horses of the night.]

Ah, half the hour is past! 'twill all be past anon!
O God!
If thou wilt not have mercy on my soul,
Yet for Christ's sake whose blood hath ransomed me,
Impose some end to my incessant pain;
Let Faustus live in hell a thousand years—
A hundred thousand, and—at last—be saved!
O, no end is limited to damnèd souls!
Why wert thou not a creature wanting soul?
Or why is this immortal that thou hast?
Ah, Pythagoras' metempsychosis! were that true,
This soul should fly from me, and I be changed
Unto some brutish beast! all beasts are happy,
For, when they die,
Their souls are soon dissolved in elements;
But mine must live, still to be plagued in hell.
Curst be the parents that engendered me!
No, Faustus: curse thyself; curse Lucifer
That hath deprived thee of the joys of heaven.
[*The clock strikes twelve.*]
O, it strikes, it strikes! Now, body, turn to air,
Or Lucifer will bear thee quick to hell. [*Thunder and lightning.*]
O soul, be changed into little water-drops,
And fall into the ocean—ne'er be found.
My God! my God! look not so fierce on me!

[*Enter* DEVILS.]

Adders and serpents, let me breathe awhile!
Ugly hell, gape not! come not, Lucifer!
I'll burn my books!—Ah Mephistophilis! [*Exeunt with him.*]

[*Enter* CHORUS.]

CHO. Cut is the branch that might have grown full straight,
And burnèd is Apollo's laurel bough,
That sometime grew within this learnèd man.
Faustus is gone; regard his hellish fall,
Whose fiendful fortune may exhort the wise
Only to wonder at unlawful things,
Whose deepness doth entice such forward wits
To practise more than heavenly power permits. [*Exit.*]

Terminat hora diem; terminat auctor opus.[32]

32 [The hour ends the day; the author ends the work.]

III

THE TRAGIC EXPERIENCE
Out of Passion—Perception

INTRODUCTION

I

AWARENESS, as we have seen, leads to aspiration. Just as surely, aspiration sometimes results in disappointment, sorrow, defeat, tragedy. Not all heroes live happily forever after. Achilles dies, shot through the heel by the arrow of ignoble Paris. King Arthur fades away, defeated, into the mists of Avalon. Faustus, sated with knowledge and experience, is snatched into hell. Even the most successful heroes end in dusty death. The poet James Shirley, speaking about the death of heroes in *The Contention of Ajax and Ulysses*, sums it up thus:

> The glories of our blood and state,
> Are shadows, not substantial things.
> There is no armor against fate,
> Death lays his icy hand on kings,
> Sceptor and crown,
> Must tumble down,
> And in the dust be equal made,
> With the poor crooked scythe and spade.

But if defeat of some kind is man's fate, it is not a cause for despair. We may agree with Bacon when he praises the uses of adversity: "Certainly virtue is like precious odors, most fragrant when they are incensed or crushed: for prosperity doth best discover vices; but adversity doth best discover virtue."

His stern doctrine regards adversity both as the unavoidable predicament of man and as a possible blessing. Man does not achieve his proper measure by attempting to escape or avoid the sufferings that are his by reason of his fallible human nature, of his personal limitations, and of the multiplied defects of his society. Rather he achieves it by meeting defeat with intelligence, grace, and fortitude. He can make the most of his defeat by giving utterance to his thoughts, by enlarging his range of human sympathy, by understanding the implications of suffering, by discovering the true meaning of adversity. In short, man measures himself, in good part, by his response to suffering. If all men must suffer, then surely we may put man to the test by asking, "To what end did he suffer? What good was born of that suffering? Did his suffering ennoble him, or did it render him numb and inexpressive, or bitter and resentful?"

In literature these questions do not, indeed should not, elicit short substantive responses. A poem is not an answer to a questionnaire, nor is a story, however long, capable of expressing the whole range of tragic responses. The form of expression supplies a context for, and hence tends to impose restrictions on, the particular tragic response. A sonnet, for example, by convention develops one situation and *its* appropriate response. A short story is limited by the point of view of the characters and by the tragic possibilities of a single situation. A drama is confined to that aspect of tragedy contained within the action; it merely suggests what has happened before and barely hints at what happens later. Hence we may expect that literature will present human suffering—defeat, adversity, disgrace, alienation, death—within the limitations of a particular form of discourse. We may take it for granted, too, that for a comprehensive view of tragedy we must consult a variety of literary forms.

II

LET us see just what this means in terms of three stories that begin this section. The three stories have a common theme: death. Leo Tolstoy's "Three Deaths" is the most universal in that it comprehends the greatest range of human experience. In swift succession we encounter three responses to the fact of death. Mme. Shírkin is a rich, decayed beauty, suffering as much from "impotent malevolence" as from tuberculosis. She feels acutely the isolation of the sick. Her vigorous maid, the station-master's blooming daughter and her friend, and her attentive (but healthy) husband all seem to mock her. Sickness has narrowed her sensibility to an overwhelming fear of death—a death she will not accept. " 'Oh, my God, what is it for?' she said, and her tears flowed faster."

Uncle Theodore, the dying drover, is a peasant. His sufferings, unlike those of Mme. Shírkin, are unattended. He is a dying animal, begrudged a corner to die in. Yet he expects no more. "Don't be cross with me. . . . I shall soon leave your corner empty." Willingly, he surrenders his new boots to Mme. Shírkin's driver, Sergéy, signalizing thereby his acceptance of the inevitable.

In contrast to Uncle Theodore, Mme. Shírkin breaks under pressure. In the face of her mother's hysteria and her husband's solicitude she expresses her resignation. She receives the sacraments from the priest. Yet, a moment later, she begs her husband to send for a tradesman who is alleged to cure the sick with herbs. The lady, Tolstoy clearly implies, does not know the meaning of death; she had not understood the words of the psalm, the expression of her own faith while she was alive. As she lies dead, her stern majestic face seemingly attentive, Tolstoy asks: "But had she even now understood those solemn words?"

In his fourth section Tolstoy completes his story with a third death, that is, with the episode in which Sergéy fells a tree in order to hew a cross for Uncle Theodore's grave. The language takes on a lyrical tone. The tree marked for felling becomes a person and the forest a field of folk. When the tree is cut, the forest grows still. Then "the trees flaunted the beauty of their motionless branches still more joyously in the newly cleared space." Life renews itself, life goes on, the forest survives the tree, life survives the death of the individual. The crux of the story is a refraction of the psalm: "They die and return to their dust. Thou sendest forth thy spirit; they are created; and thou renewest the face of the earth."

Tolstoy is concerned with the ordinary, natural, yet universal, fact of death, and of how some representative human beings respond to it. In "The Blue Hotel," Stephen Crane is concerned with murder. In a broad sense, he is asking Tolstoy's questions: How does a man die? Is there any purpose in his life and death? His particular question, however, is: Who is responsible for the death of the Swede, the main character?

There are two answers, both partly true. The first is—destiny, the second is—the Swede himself. Destiny—the end in a pool of blood on a barroom floor, with his dead eyes staring at the legend on the cash register, "This registers the amount of your purchase"—this destiny stalks the Swede from the beginning of the story. The hotel, with its gay coat of paint, tempts him. Scully, the proprietor, completes the "seduction" with his greeting at the railroad station. Fate provides two companions—the cowboy and Mr. Blanc, the educated Easterner, who join Scully and his son Johnnie to form an unhappy company. Fate decrees the blizzard that forces the men to remain indoors. Fate whispers the premonition of death that provokes what it seems to warn against. Fate thwarts every effort to forestall the Swede's involvement in the game of cards, itself a symbol of destiny. Fate leads the Swede to fight with Johnnie and the gambler.

At the same time, Crane makes us see that the Swede connives with fate. The author describes him at the beginning as being "shaky and quick-eyed," fearful and furtive, hysterically suspicious of "Nebraska," and of his companions at the blue hotel. Abjectly fearful, he is also abjectly humble as he protests that he does not want to fight, he does not want to be killed, he will leave the house. But after he drinks with Scully, he becomes arrogant and boisterous. He "fizzed like a fire-wheel."

> At six-o'clock supper . . . [he] domineered the whole feast . . . he gazed, brutally disdainful, into every face. His voice rang through the room. Once when he jabbed out harpoon-fashion with his fork to pinion a biscuit, the weapon nearly impaled the hand of the Easterner, which had been stretched quietly out for the same biscuit.

He begins to curse and whack the playing board. His rage at Johnnie's cheating is excessive. Excessive too is his berserk fury in the fight with Johnnie, and his jeering pride at his victory. By the time he reaches the saloon, the Swede has come full circle—from the fear of the man who would not fight to the swaggering insolence and the culpable blindness of the drunken bully. His character, as the Greek adage has it, is his fate. "The Swede fell with a cry of supreme astonishment."

Yet neither the Swede, nor Fate, nor the two together are entirely responsible. The gambler need not have used his long knife. Scully need not have persuaded the Swede to remain at the hotel. Johnnie need not have cheated. The Easterner need not have denied that he saw Johnnie cheating. And the cowboy need not have provoked the Swede's blood-lust. In short everyone, each in some proportion, is guilty of the Swede's death. Crane's judgment is explicitly summed up in the Easterner's final words to the cowboy.

> Every sin is the result of a collaboration. We, five of us, have collaborated in the murder of this Swede. . . . you, I, Johnnie, old Scully; and that fool of an unfortunate gambler came merely as a culmination, the apex of a human movement, and gets all the punishment.

While "The Blue Hotel" points to our personal participation in a specific human tragedy, "The Lottery," by Shirley Jackson, compels us, however shrinkingly, to admit to a collective responsibility. The success of this story is due in part to its deceptively plain surface. The style seems to be that of a literate secretary of a women's club reporting the annual village raffle. References to the stones and to the little black box, while faintly ominous, are neutralized by repeated allusions to the antiquity and the ritual character of the lottery. What has often been done, we feel, must be normal, and what is normal must be safe. We are reassured, too, by the matter-of-fact dialogue of the villagers. We never get to know them well, since they are faintly characterized, but we feel we have known people just like them.

Gradually we sense the seriousness of the lottery in the sudden hush that falls on the crowd and in the villagers' nervous and humorless grins. The tension mounts as the slips of paper in the black box dwindle. When Mrs. Hutchinson cries out, "It wasn't fair," we recognize a piercing apprehension. The debate on fairness, decided against the Hutchinsons, leads to the sudden, but prepared for, climax.

The end is shocking. The appalling nature of the ritual sacrifice seems at first an ironic trick. But "The Lottery" is more than a shocker; it is also a parable on collective guilt. Society, the story implies, needs a victim, a scapegoat whose death will propitiate the gods. Significantly, the author refers frequently to the antiquity and formality of the ritual. Once she relates it directly to the half-remembered fertility rites of primitive times. Old Man Warner, irritated by the suggestion that the lottery is out of date, speaks out angrily. His voice is that of prehistoric memory warning his fellow tribesmen that, unless the victim be sacrificed, they will revert to a still more primitive savagery.

> "Pack of crazy fools," he said. "Listening to the young folks, nothing's good enough for *them*. Next thing you know, they'll be wanting to go back to living in caves, nobody work any more, live *that* way for a while. Used to be a saying about 'Lottery in June, corn be heavy soon.' First thing you know, we'd all be eating stewed chickweed and acorns. There's always been a lottery." he added petulantly.

Thus a deadly parallel is set up between prehistoric and modern communities: both have victimized an innocent individual. We cannot help recalling how, in our times, communities have visited their frustrations on the unpopular general, the innocent bystander, the expendable philosopher, the foreign race.

III

WE BEGAN our discussion of the stories of Tolstoy, Crane, and Miss Jackson by saying that each form of literature, whether it be short story, poem, or drama, to some extent imposes limits on the range of tragic experience. One reading of the stories may confirm this view, especially when we ask ourselves the larger questions: How does the suffering described in these stories reveal the measure of man? Are the stories concerned with man in general rather than with the fate of particular men? How do they explain man's nature and purpose?

The stories provide only partial revelations. The reader comes to see that some of the causes of suffering reside in self-concern, in culpable human weakness, in a cowardly consent to the erroneous opinions of the majority. But the positive ideals are, necessarily, briefly alluded to or are present by remote implication. While the chief characters of these three stories are excellent representatives of humanity at a level, they are not representative of humanity at its highest reach. The characters lack both intellectual depth and range and a point of view that permits them to experience suffering at the same time as they recognize and reflect upon the meaning of that suffering.

Unless we are content to measure human response at its average level, we must look for a kind of character who represents humanity at its height. Four such characters appear in Plato's *Apology: On the Death of Socrates,* Sophocles' *Oedipus Rex,* Shelley's "Adonais," and Hopkins' "The Wreck of the Deutschland." Taken together they show us how man at his best—man as philosopher, as king, as poet, as saint—responds to human suffering.

Although the Socrates of Plato's *Apology* is based on an historical figure, the real man, as Werner Jaeger has remarked, "shed most of his personality as he entered history and became for all eternity 'a representative man.'" Socrates' students admired him as much for his moral courage as for his subtle method of philosophical inquiry.

In real life both his moral courage and his dialectical skill got him into trouble. As a member of the Committee of the Senate he refused to agree to the common trial of eight commanders accused of negligence. On another occasion he refused to sanction a judicial murder planned by the oligarchy then in power. It was said that his teaching stimulated youth to question not only the "theology" of the contemporary religious myths but even the political processes of the state. His enemies brought him to trial on two charges:

(1) of not worshipping the gods whom the state worships, but introducing new and unfamiliar religious practice;

(2) and further, of corrupting the young. The prosecutor demands the death penalty.

The first charge was never made clear; the second actually referred to Socrates' teaching. Socrates' defense in court in effect challenged the moral integrity and the intellectual principles of the jury itself. He was condemned to death.

After Socrates' death Plato, his most eminent student, resolved to keep his memory alive by writing an account of his trial. His *Apology* is based upon the historical record, but it is primarily a fictional presentation of a great man and a great thinker. In the *Apology* Socrates is represented as seizing an opportunity to sum up his life's work. He demonstrates his Socratic method of searching for the truth by trial and error, question and answer. Thus he shows that human wisdom consists not in the pretension to knowledge but in the humble awareness that man knows very little. True wisdom consists in the steady pursuit of virtue. "For I do nothing," he says, "but go about persuading you all, old and young alike, not to take thought for your persons or your properties, but first and chiefly to care about the greatest improvement of the soul."

Socrates justifies his philosophy in practice as well as by reason. When the jury condemned him to death he crowned his defense by manifesting how a wise man accepts adversity. Death, he tells them, can be a blessing rather than a curse:

> Wherefore, O judges, be of good cheer about death, and know of a certainty, that no evil can happen to a good man, either in life or after death. . . . I am not angry with my condemners, or with my accusers; they have done me no harm, although they did not mean to do me any good; and for this I may gently blame them.

Just before he died, as Plato narrates it in his *Phaedo*, Socrates concluded his long discourse on the immortality of the soul by prophesying that the pure soul will live on in mansions fairer still: "Wherefore, Simmias, seeing all these things, what ought not we do that we may obtain virtue and wisdom in this life? Fair is the prize, and the hope great!"

Sophocles' Oedipus ("swollen foot"), like Socrates, is another "representative" man. But whereas Socrates represents virtue and wisdom born of thought, Oedipus represents virtue and wisdom born of impassioned suffering. Indeed few will deny what Jaeger said of Oedipus: "He was suffering humanity personified." To understand this let us see who Oedipus was, what he suffered, and why he was at first overwhelmed by suffering and then purified by it.

To say Oedipus is a king is not merely to give his lineage and title: he is a king in more than the legal sense of the word. As his Greek title, *tyrannos,* suggests, Oedipus earns the throne by his extraordinary intelligence, courage, and strength. He is a king in the sense that he is a born ruler. He respects the gods, he is decisive in times of crisis, a vigorous orator and reasoner, a father of his people, a liberator, a guide, a physician, a priestlike figure, and an approachable friend. His habit of command evokes not resentment but trusting obedience. He is, in short, man in the fullest measure of man, superb in his strength of spirit, mind, and body. Other men aspire to his

> Wealth, power, craft of statesmanship!
> Kingly position, everywhere admired!

What happens to Oedipus is so appalling that the final chant of the chorus seems a chilling understatement:

Men of Thebes: look upon Oedipus.
This is the king who solved the famous riddle
And towered up, most powerful of men.
No mortal eyes but looked on him with envy,
Yet in the end ruin swept over him.

"Look upon Oedipus." He is an exile, an unwitting parricide cursed by the gods. He gouges out his own eyes; Iocastê, both his wife and mother, commits suicide; their children are cursed with him. Yet what happens to Oedipus is perhaps less dreadful than the way it happens. Had he had no part in his own miserable fate, had he been altogether virtuous and wise, he might, like Socrates, have lamented the occasion but cast no blame on himself. But he himself had proudly promised to "bring what is dark to light." He had been insolent to Teiresias and to Creon, persistent in his self-righteous hunt for the criminal. Hence, when his fortunes are completely reversed, Oedipus recognizes how, step by step from his rejection of Teiresias' prophecy to his questioning of the shepherd, he himself collaborated in his own ruin.

Recognition that he is the criminal and that he must suffer the penalties set forth in his own decree results in a torrent of grief, shame, despair, self-accusation. But these emotions, overwhelming though they be, tend to bring the mind to a balance, a poise. They correct and purify Oedipus' earlier pride and insolence and they help the audience to see what man's true measure is. Man is godlike, yet not a god; he is a lawgiver, yet subject to a divine order whose applications he cannot foresee. Man is not, in Protagoras' words, the measure of all things. Rather he is measured by

The laws of the pure universe
From highest heaven handed down.

And to understand this, even in and through pain and sorrow, is to be cleansed. The chorus suggests as much in the play's concluding lines:

Let every man in mankind's frailty
Consider his last day; and let none
Presume on his good fortune until he find
Life, at his death, a memory without pain.

Shelley's "Adonais," an elegy on the death of John Keats, proposes a third representative figure, the poet. True, John Keats is also an historical person, but in this poem he is, like Socrates, a symbol rather than an individual. Shelley saw Keats—mistakenly it so happens—as the victim of the arrogant stupidity of his critics. The savage criticism of Keats's "Endymion," which appeared in the *Quarterly Review* in 1818, "produced the most violent effect on his susceptible mind," wrote Shelley, and ultimately resulted in his death. This historical misinterpretation, however, is not essential to the poem, whose main purpose is to praise the poet, to mourn his death, and to offer consolation to the living. Here again, as in the figures of Socrates and Oedipus, we see passion or suffering give birth in Adonais to a special kind of perception.

In the convention of the elegy, Shelley begins with an invocation to Urania, the Muse who inspires poetry. The imagery establishes a tone of lofty requiem, ritually solemn and dignified, yet deeply personal. There follows a long section in which personifications of Keats's dreams, his "passion-wingèd Ministers of thought," together with figures of mythology and fellow poets such as Milton, Byron, Moore, Chatterton and, in Stanzas 31–34, Shelley himself—all pay tribute to the dead poet. Briefly, in two stanzas, 36 and 37, the speaker curses the *Quarterly Review*. The poem resumes its dignified tone in the consoling lines:

> Peace, peace! he is not dead, he doth not sleep—
> He hath awakened from the dream of life—

The stanzas that follow restate, in superb images, the view that Keats, by virtue of his devotion to his poetic ideals, is now part of an eternal Light, Beauty, Benediction, and Love:

> The Soul of Adonais, like a star,
> Beacons from the abode where the Eternal are.

Thus in Shelley's vision death is a passage into the white radiance of eternity. Like other Romantic poets, he found in Plato's eternal forms, if not a formal creed, at least a sustaining fiction or a vehicle for his intuitive belief in immortality.

The main figure in Hopkins' "The Wreck of the Deutschland," the tall nun who drowns in the storm, is, in one accepted sense of the term, a saint. Why she deserves that title, and how in earning it she reveals another way in which man can respond to suffering, is the story of Hopkins' poem.

In Part I the poet addresses a question to God—here the personal triune God of Christianity rather than the indefinite impersonal deity invoked by Plato, Socrates, and Shelley. "And dost thou touch me afresh?" the speaker inquires. "Over again I feel thy finger and find thee." There follows a deeply personal meditation in which the speaker in the poem tells of his first encounter with God. This early terrifying experience leads to the understanding that Christ's suffering, "the dense and the driven Passion," is the truest epiphany of His glory. Man then, the meditation goes, participates in that glory through a sharing of the Passion.

Thus the stage is set for a dramatic rendering of the shipwreck in Part II. The first sixteen stanzas form an intensely compressed descriptive narrative of the wreck. In Stanza 17 the nun appears, "breasting the babble" of wailing women and children. She is a "lioness, a prophetess," and her call "rode over the storm's brawling." She is one with martyrs, with the saints marked by the suffering and the joy of Christ. In the height of the storm she prays: "O Christ, Christ, come quickly." This prayer, according to the poet, indicates that she is accepting her cross and christening "her wild-worst Best." Her own reward, in Stanza 28, is the presence of the Master. She earns mercy for others, for she is "a blown beacon of light," a bell that startles the poor sheep back to the mercy of God. Thus the nun becomes, by participation, another Christ, praying, suffering, redeeming herself and others, and, through her death, rising to her glory.

Socrates, Oedipus, Adonais, and the nun are four heroic figures who show how man can respond to human suffering. The key word here is *respond.* None of them is a dumb oracle. Their lives tell us that death is a fact of life, perhaps the most important fact, and that death is an implied question: For what purpose do you live? Each has an answer, yet each recognizes that human life, in its beginnings as in its end, is shrouded in ennobling mystery.

STORIES

Leo Tolstoy

THREE DEATHS

A TALE

1

IT WAS autumn. Two vehicles were going along the highway at a quick trot. In the first sat two women: a lady, thin and pale, and a maidservant, plump and rosy and shining. The maid's short dry hair escaped from under her faded bonnet and her red hand in its torn glove kept pushing it back by fits and starts; her full bosom, covered by a woollen shawl, breathed health, her quick black eyes now watched the fields as they glided past the window, now glanced timidly at her mistress, and now restlessly scanned the corners of the carriage. In front of her nose dangled her mistress's bonnet, pinned to the luggage carrier, on her lap lay a puppy, her feet were raised on the boxes standing on the floor and just audibly tapped against them to the creaking of the coach-springs and the clatter of the window panes.

Having folded her hands on her knees and closed her eyes, the lady swayed feebly against the pillows placed at her back, and, frowning slightly, coughed inwardly. On her head she had a white nightcap, and a blue kerchief was tied round her delicate white throat. A straight line receding under the cap parted her light brown, extremely flat, pomaded hair, and there was something dry and deathly about the whiteness of the skin of that wide parting. Her features were delicate and handsome, but her skin was flabby and rather sallow, though there was a hectic flush on her cheeks. Her lips were dry and restless, her scanty eyelashes had no curl in them, and her cloth travelling coat fell in straight folds over a sunken breast. Though her eyes were closed her face bore an expression of weariness, irritation, and habitual suffering.

A footman, leaning on the arms of his seat, was dozing on the box. The mail-coach driver, shouting lustily, urged on his four big sweating horses, occasionally turning to the other driver who called to him from the calèche behind. The broad parallel tracks of the tyres spread themselves evenly and fast on the muddy, chalky surface of the road. The

THREE DEATHS: From *Nine Stories*, 1855–63 by Leo Tolstoy, translated by Louise and Aylmer Maude, 1934. Reprinted by permission of the publishers, Oxford University Press, London.

sky was grey and cold and a damp mist was settling on the fields and road. It was stuffy in the coach and there was a smell of Eau-de-Cologne and dust. The invalid drew back her head and slowly opened her beautiful dark eyes, which were large and brilliant.

"Again," she said, nervously pushing away with her beautiful thin hand an end of her maid's cloak which had lightly touched her foot, and her mouth twitched painfully. Matrësha gathered up her cloak with both hands, rose on her strong legs, and seated herself farther away, while her fresh face grew scarlet. The lady, leaning with both hands on the seat, also tried to raise herself so as to sit up higher, but her strength failed her. Her mouth twisted, and her whole face became distorted by a look of impotent malevolence and irony. "You might at least help me! . . . No, don't bother! I can do it myself, only don't put your bags or anything behind me, for goodness' sake! . . . No, better not touch me since you don't know how to!" The lady closed her eyes and then, again quickly raising her eyelids, glared at the maid. Matrësha, looking at her, bit her red nether lip. A deep sigh rose from the invalid's chest and turned into a cough before it was completed. She turned away, puckered her face, and clutched her chest with both hands. When the coughing fit was over she once more closed her eyes and continued to sit motionless. The carriage and calèche entered a village. Matrësha stretched out her thick hand from under her shawl and crossed herself.

"What is it?" asked her mistress.

"A post-station, madam."

"I am asking why you crossed yourself."

"There's a church, madam."

The invalid turned to the window and began slowly to cross herself, looking with large wide-open eyes at the big village church her carriage was passing.

The carriage and calèche both stopped at the post-station and the invalid's husband and doctor stepped out of the calèche and went up to the coach.

"How are you feeling?" asked the doctor, taking her pulse.

"Well, my dear, how are you—not tired?" asked the husband in French. "Wouldn't you like to get out?"

Matrësha, gathering up the bundles, squeezed herself into a corner so as not to interfere with their conversation.

"Nothing much, just the same," replied the invalid. "I won't get out."

Her husband after standing there a while went into the station-house, and Matrësha, too, jumped out of the carriage and ran on tiptoe across the mud and in at the gate.

"If I feel ill, it's no reason for you not to have lunch," said the sick woman with a slight smile to the doctor, who was standing at her window.

"None of them has any thought for me," she added to herself as soon as the doctor, having slowly walked away from her, ran quickly up the steps to the station-house. "They are well, so they don't care. Oh, my God!"

"Well, Edward Ivánovich?" said the husband, rubbing his hands as he met the doctor with a merry smile. "I have ordered the lunch-basket to be brought in. What do you think about it?"

"A capital idea," replied the doctor.

"Well, how is she?" asked the husband with a sigh, lowering his voice and lifting his eyebrows.

"As I told you: it is impossible for her to reach Italy—God grant that she gets even as far as Moscow, especially in this weather."

"But what are we to do? Oh, my God, my God!" and the husband hid his eyes with his hand. "Bring it here!" he said to the man who had brought in the lunch-basket.

"She ought to have stayed at home," said the doctor, shrugging his shoulders.

"But what could I do?" rejoined the husband. "You know I used every possible means to get her to stay. I spoke of the expense, of our children whom we had to leave behind, and of my business affairs, but she would not listen to anything. She is making plans for life abroad as if she were in good health. To tell her of her condition would be to kill her."

"But she is killed already—you must know that, Vasíli Dmítrich. A person can't live without lungs, and new lungs won't grow. It is sad and hard, but what is to be done? My business and yours is to see that her end is made as peaceful as possible. It's a priest who is needed for that."

"O, my God! Think of my condition, having to remind her about her will. Come what may I can't tell her that, you know how good she is . . ."

"Still, try to persuade her to wait till the roads are fit for sledging," said the doctor, shaking his head significantly, "or something bad may happen on the journey."

"Aksyúsha, hello Aksyúsha!" yelled the station-master's daughter, throwing her jacket over her head and stamping her feet on the muddy back porch. "Come and let's have a look at the Shírkin lady: they say she is being taken abroad for a chest trouble, and I've never seen what consumptive people look like!"

She jumped onto the threshold, and seizing one another by the hand the two girls ran out of the gate. Checking their pace, they passed by the coach and looked in at the open window. The invalid turned her head towards them but, noticing their curiosity, frowned and turned away.

"De-arie me!" said the station-master's daughter, quickly turning her head away. "What a wonderful beauty she must have been, and see what she's like now! It's dreadful. Did you see, did you, Aksyúsha?"

"Yes, how thin!" Aksyúsha agreed. "Let's go and look again, as if we were going to the well. See, she has turned away, and I hadn't seen her yet. What a pity, Másha!"

"Yes, and what mud!" said Másha, and they both ran through the gate.

"Evidently I look frightful," thought the invalid. "If only I could get abroad quicker, quicker. I should soon recover there."

"Well, my dear, how are you?" said her husband, approaching her and still chewing.

"Always the same question," thought the invalid, "and he himself is eating."

"So-so," she murmured through her closed teeth.

"You know, my dear, I'm afraid you'll get worse travelling in this weather, and Edward Ivánovich says so too. Don't you think we'd better turn back?"

She remained angrily silent.

"The weather will perhaps improve and the roads be fit for sledging; you will get better meanwhile, and we will all go together."

"Excuse me. If I had not listened to you for so long, I should now at least have reached Berlin, and have been quite well."

"What could be done, my angel? You know it was impossible. But now if you stayed another month you would get nicely better, I should have finished my business, and we could take the children with us."

"The children are well, but I am not."

"But do understand, my dear, that if in this weather you should get worse on the road. . . . At least you would be at home."

"What of being at home? . . . To die at home?" answered the invalid, flaring up. But the word "die" evidently frightened her, and she looked imploringly and questioningly at her husband. He hung his head and was silent. The invalid's mouth suddenly widened like a child's, and tears rolled down her cheeks. Her husband hid his face in his handkerchief and stepped silently away from the carriage.

"No, I will go on," said the invalid, and lifting her eyes to the sky she folded her hands and began whispering incoherent words: "Oh, my God, what is it for?" she said, and her tears flowed faster. She prayed long and fervently, but her chest ached and felt as tight as before; the sky, the fields, and the road were just as grey and gloomy, and the autumnal mist fell, neither thickening nor lifting, and settled on the muddy road, the roofs, the carriage, and the sheepskin coats of the drivers, who talking in their strong merry voices were greasing the wheels and harnessing the horses.

2

THE carriage was ready but the driver still loitered. He had gone into the drivers' room at the station. It was hot, stuffy, and dark there, with an oppressive smell of baking bread, cabbage, sheepskin garments, and humanity. Several drivers were sitting in the room, and a cook was busy at the oven, on the top of which lay a sick man wrapped in sheepskins.

"Uncle Theodore! I say, Uncle Theodore!" said the young driver, entering the room in his sheepskin coat with a whip stuck in his belt, and addressing the sick man.

"What do you want Theodore for, lazybones?" asked one of the drivers. "There's your carriage waiting for you."

"I want to ask for his boots; mine are quite worn out," answered the young fellow, tossing back his hair and straightening the mittens tucked in his belt. "Is he asleep? I say, Uncle Theodore!" he repeated, walking over to the oven.

"What is it?" answered a weak voice, and a lean face with a red beard looked down from the oven, while a broad, emaciated, pale, and hairy hand pulled up the coat over the dirty shirt covering his angular shoulder.

"Give me a drink, lad. . . . What is it you want?"

The lad handed him up a dipper with water.

"Well, you see, Theodore," he said, stepping from foot to foot, "I expect you don't need your new boots now; won't you let me have them? I don't suppose you'll go about any more."

The sick man, lowering his weary head to the shiny dipper and immersing his sparse drooping moustache in the turbid water, drank feebly but eagerly. His matted beard was dirty, and his sunken clouded eyes had difficulty in looking up at the lad's face. Having finished drinking he tried to lift his hand to wipe his wet lips, but he could not do so, and rubbed them on the sleeve of his coat instead. Silently, and breathing heavily through his nose, he looked straight into the lad's eyes, collecting his strength.

"But perhaps you have promised them to someone else?" asked the lad. "If so, it's all right. The worst of it is, it's wet outside and I have to go about my work, so I said to myself: 'suppose I ask Theodore for his boots; I expect he doesn't need them.' If you need them yourself—just say so."

Something began to rumble and gurgle in the sick man's chest; he doubled up and began to choke with an abortive cough in his throat.

"Need them indeed!" the cook snapped out unexpectedly so as to be heard by the whole room. "He hasn't come down from the oven for more than a month! Hear how he's choking—it makes me ache inside just to hear him. What does he want with boots? They won't bury him in new boots. And it was time long ago—God forgive me the sin! See how he chokes. He ought to be taken into the other room or somewhere. They say there are hospitals in the town. Is it right that he should take up the whole corner?—there's no more to be said. I've no room at all, and yet they expect cleanliness!"

"Hullo, Sergéy! Come along and take your place, the gentlefolk are waiting!" shouted the drivers' overseer, looking in at the door.

Sergéy was about to go without waiting for a reply, but the sick man, while coughing, let him understand by a look that he wanted to give him an answer.

"Take my boots, Sergéy," he said when he had mastered the cough and rested a moment. "But listen. . . . Buy a stone for me when I die," he added hoarsely.

"Thank you, uncle. Then I'll take them, and I'll buy a stone for sure."

"There, lads, you heard that?" the sick man managed to utter, and then bent double again and began to choke.

"All right, we heard," said one of the drivers. "Go and take your seat, Sergéy, there's the overseer running back. The Shírkin lady is ill, you know."

Sergéy quickly pulled off his unduly big, dilapidated boots and threw them under a bench. Uncle Theodore's new boots just fitted him, and having put them on he went to the carriage with his eyes fixed on his feet.

"What fine boots! Let me grease them," said a driver, who held some axle-grease in his hand, as Sergéy climbed onto the box and gathered up the reins. "Did he give them to you for nothing?"

"Why, are you envious?" Sergéy replied, rising and wrapping the skirts of his coat under his legs. "Off with you! Gee up, my beauties!" he shouted to the horses, flourishing the whip, and the carriage and calèche with their occupants, portmanteaux, and trunks rolled rapidly along the wet road and disappeared in the grey autumnal mist.

The sick driver was left on the top of the oven in the stuffy room and, unable to relieve himself by coughing, turned with an effort onto his other side and became silent.

Till late in the evening people came in and out of the room and dined there. The sick man made no sound. When night came, the cook climbed up onto the oven and stretched over his legs to get down her sheepskin coat.

"Don't be cross with me, Nastásya," said the sick man. "I shall soon leave your corner empty."

"All right, all right, never mind," muttered Nastásya. "But what is it that hurts you? Tell me, uncle."

"My whole inside has wasted away. God knows what it is!"

"I suppose your throat hurts when you cough?"

"Everything hurts. My death has come—that's how it is. Oh, oh, oh!" moaned the sick man.

"Cover up your feet like this," said Nastásya, drawing his coat over him as she climbed down from the oven.

A night-light burnt dimly in the room. Nastásya and some ten drivers slept on the floor or on the benches, loudly snoring. The sick man groaned feebly, coughed, and turned about on the oven. Towards morning he grew quite quiet.

"I had a queer dream last night," said Nastásya next morning, stretching herself in the dim light. "I dreamt that Uncle Theodore got down from the oven and went out to chop wood. 'Come, Nastásya,' he says, 'I'll help you!' and I say, 'How can you chop wood now?', but he just seizes the axe and begins chopping quickly, quickly, so that the chips fly all about. 'Why,' I say, 'haven't you been ill?' 'No,' he says, 'I am well,' and he swings the axe so that I was quite frightened. I gave a cry and woke up. I wonder whether he is dead! Uncle Theodore! I say, Uncle Theodore!"

Theodore did not answer.

"True enough he may have died. I'll go and see," said one of the drivers, waking up.

The lean hand covered with reddish hair that hung down from the oven was pale and cold.

"I'll go and tell the station-master," said the driver. "I think he is dead."

Theodore had no relatives: he was from some distant place. They buried him next day in the new cemetery beyond the wood, and Nastásya went on for days telling everybody of her dream, and of having been the first to discover that Uncle Theodore was dead.

3

SPRING had come. Rivulets of water hurried down the wet streets of the city, gurgling between lumps of frozen manure; the colours of the people's clothes as they moved along the streets looked vivid and their voices sounded shrill. Behind the garden-fences the buds on the trees were swelling and their branches were just audibly swaying in the fresh breeze. Everywhere transparent drops were forming and falling. . . . The sparrows chirped, and fluttered awkwardly with their little wings. On the sunny side of the street, on the fences, houses, and trees, everything was in motion and sparkling. There was joy and youth everywhere in the sky, on the earth, and in the hearts of men.

In one of the chief streets fresh straw had been strewn on the road before a large, important house, where the invalid who had been in a hurry to go abroad lay dying.

At the closed door of her room stood the invalid's husband and an elderly woman. On the sofa a priest sat with bowed head, holding something wrapped in his stole. In a corner of the room the sick woman's old mother lay on an invalid chair weeping bitterly: beside her stood one maidservant holding a clean handkerchief, waiting for her to ask for it; while another was rubbing her temples with something and blowing under the old lady's cap onto her grey head.

"Well, may Christ aid you, dear friend," the husband said to the elderly woman who stood near him at the door. "She has such confidence in you and you know so well how to talk to her, so persuade her as well as you can, my dear—go to her." He was about to open the door, but her cousin stopped him, pressing her handkerchief several times to her eyes and giving her head a shake.

"Well, I don't think I look as if I had been crying now," said she and, opening the door herself, went in.

The husband was in great agitation and seemed quite distracted. He walked towards the old woman, but while still several steps from her turned back, walked about the room, and went up to the priest. The priest looked at him, raised his eyebrows to heaven, and sighed: his thick, greyish beard also rose as he sighed and then came down again.

"My God, my God!" said the husband.

"What is to be done?" said the priest with a sigh, and again his eyebrows and beard rose and fell.

"And her mother is here!" said the husband almost in despair. "She won't be able to bear it. You see, loving her as she does . . . I don't know! If you would only try to comfort her, Father, and persuade her to go away."

The priest got up and went to the old woman.

"It is true, no one can appreciate a mother's heart," he said—"but God is merciful."

The old woman's face suddenly twitched all over, and she began to hiccup hysterically.

"God is merciful," the priest continued when she grew a little calmer. "Let me tell you of a patient in my parish who was much worse than Mary Dmítrievna, and a simple tradesman cured her in a short time with various herbs. That tradesman is even now in Moscow.

I told Vasíli Dmítrich—we might try him. . . . It would at any rate comfort the invalid. To God all is possible."

"No, she will not live," said the old woman. "God is taking her instead of me," and the hysterical hiccuping grew so violent that she fainted.

The sick woman's husband hid his face in his hands and ran out of the room.

In the passage the first person he met was his six-year-old son, who was running full speed after his younger sister.

"Won't you order the children to be taken to their mamma?" asked the nurse.

"No, she doesn't want to see them—it would upset her."

The boy stopped a moment, looked intently into his father's face, then gave a kick and ran on, shouting merrily.

"She pretends to be the black horse, Papa!" he shouted, pointing to his sister.

Meanwhile in the other room the cousin sat down beside the invalid, and tried by skilful conversation to prepare her for the thought of death. The doctor was mixing a draught at another window.

The patient, in a white dressing gown, sat up in bed supported all round by pillows, and looked at her cousin in silence.

"Ah, my dear friend," she said, unexpectedly interrupting her, "don't prepare me! Don't treat me like a child. I am a Christian. I know it all. I know I have not long to live, and know that if my husband had listened to me sooner I should now have been in Italy and perhaps—no, certainly—should have been well. Everybody told him so. But what is to be done? Evidently this is God's wish. We have all sinned heavily. I know that, but I trust in God's mercy everybody will be forgiven, probably all will be forgiven. I try to understand myself. I have many sins to answer for, dear friend, but then how much I have had to suffer! I try to bear my sufferings patiently . . ."

"Then shall I call the priest, my dear? You will feel still more comfortable after receiving communion," said her cousin.

The sick woman bent her head in assent.

"God forgive me, sinner that I am!" she whispered.

The cousin went out and signalled with her eyes to the priest.

"She is an angel!" she said to the husband, with tears in her eyes. The husband burst into tears; the priest went into the next room; the invalid's mother was still unconscious, and all was silent there. Five minutes later he came out again, and after taking off his stole, straightened out his hair.

"Thank God she is calmer now," he said, "and wishes to see you."

The cousin and the husband went into the sickroom. The invalid was silently weeping, gazing at an icon.

"I congratulate you, my dear,"[1] said her husband.

"Thank you! How well I feel now, what inexpressible sweetness I feel!" said the sick woman, and a soft smile played on her thin lips. "How merciful God is! Is He not? Merciful and all powerful!" and again she looked at the icon with eager entreaty and her eyes full of tears.

Then suddenly, as if she remembered something, she beckoned to her husband to come closer.

"You never want to do what I ask . . . " she said in a feeble and dissatisfied voice.

The husband, craning his neck, listened to her humbly.

"What is it, my dear?"

"How many times have I not said that these doctors don't know anything; there are simple women who can heal, and who do cure. The priest told me . . . there is also a tradesman . . . Send!"

"For whom, my dear?"

"O God, you don't want to understand anything!" . . . And the sick woman's face puckered and she closed her eyes.

The doctor came up and took her hand. Her pulse was beating more and more feebly. He glanced at the husband. The invalid noticed that gesture and looked round in affright. The cousin turned away and began to cry.

"Don't cry, don't torture yourself and me," said the patient. "Don't take from me the last of my tranquillity."

"You are an angel," said the cousin, kissing her hand.

"No, kiss me here! Only dead people are kissed on the hand. My God, my God!"

That same evening the patient was a corpse, and the body lay in a coffin in the music room of the large house. A deacon sat alone in that big room reading the psalms of David through his nose in a monotonous voice. A bright light from the wax candles in their tall silver candlesticks fell on the pale brow of the dead woman, on her heavy wax-like hands, on the stiff folds of the pall which brought out in awesome relief the knees and the toes. The deacon without understanding the words read on monotonously, and in the quiet room the words sounded strangely and died away. Now and then from a distant room came the sounds of children's voices and the patter of their feet.

"Thou hidest thy face, they are troubled," said the psalter. "Thou takest away their breath, they die and return to their dust. Thou sendest forth thy spirit, they are created: and thou renewest the face of the earth. The glory of the Lord shall endure for ever."

The dead woman's face looked stern and majestic. Neither in the clear cold brow nor in the firmly closed lips was there any movement.

1 A Russian greeting after receiving the sacrament of Holy Communion.

She seemed all attention. But had she even now understood those solemn words?

4

A MONTH later a stone chapel was being erected over the grave of the deceased woman. Over the driver's tomb there was still no stone, and only the light green grass sprouted on the mound which served as the only token of the past existence of a man.

"It will be a sin, Sergéy," said the cook at the station-house one day, "if you don't buy a stone for Theodore. You kept saying it's winter, it's winter!' but why don't you keep your word now? You know I witnessed it. He has already come back once to ask you to do it; if you don't buy him one, he'll come again and choke you."

"But why? I'm not backing out of it," replied Sergéy. "I'll buy a stone as I said I would, and give a ruble and a half for it. I haven't forgotten it, but it has to be fetched. When I happen to be in town I'll buy one."

"You might at least put up a cross—you ought to—else it's really wrong," interposed an old driver. "You know you are wearing his boots."

"Where can I get a cross? I can't cut one out of a log."

"What do you mean, can't cut one out of a log? You take an axe and go into the forest early, and you can cut one there. Cut down a young ash or something like that, and you can make a cross of it . . . you may have to treat the forester to vodka; but one can't afford to treat him for every trifle. There now, I broke my splinter-bar and went and cut a new one, and nobody said a word."

Early in the morning, as soon as it was daybreak, Sergéy took an axe and went into the wood.

A cold white cover of dew, which was still falling untouched by the sun, lay on everything. The east was imperceptibly growing brighter, reflecting its pale light on the vault of heaven still veiled by a covering of clouds. Not a blade of grass below, nor a leaf on the topmost branches of the trees, stirred. Only occasionally a sound of wings amid the brushwood, or a rustling on the ground, broke the silence of the forest. Suddenly a strange sound, foreign to Nature, resounded and died away at the outskirts of the forest. Again the sound was heard, and was rhythmically repeated at the foot of the trunk of one of the motionless trees. A tree-top began to tremble in an unwonted manner, its juicy leaves whispered something, and the robin who had been sitting in one of its branches fluttered twice from place to place with a whistle, and jerking its tail sat down on another tree.

The axe at the bottom gave off a more and more muffled sound, sappy white chips were scattered on the dewy grass and a slight creaking was heard above the sound of the blows. The tree, shuddering in its whole body, bent down and quickly rose again, vibrating with fear on its roots. For an instant all was still, but the tree bent again, a crashing sound came from its trunk, and with its branches breaking and its boughs hanging down it fell with its crown on the damp earth.

The sounds of the axe and of the footsteps were silenced. The robin whistled and flitted higher. A twig which it brushed with its wings shook a little and then with all its foliage grew still like the rest. The trees flaunted the beauty of their motionless branches still more joyously in the newly cleared space.

The first sunbeams, piercing the translucent cloud, shone out and spread over earth and sky. The mist began to quiver like waves in the hollows, the dew sparkled and played on the verdure, the transparent cloudlets grew whiter, and hurriedly dispersed over the deepening azure vault of the sky. The birds stirred in the thicket and, as though bewildered, twittered joyfully about something; the sappy leaves whispered gladly and peacefully on the treetops, and the branches of those that were living began to rustle slowly and majestically over the dead and prostrate tree.

Stephen Crane

THE BLUE HOTEL

1

THE Palace Hotel at Fort Romper was painted a light blue, a shade that is on the legs of a kind of heron, causing the bird to declare its position against any background. The Palace Hotel, then, was always screaming and howling in a way that made the dazzling winter landscape of Nebraska seem only a gray swampish hush. It stood alone on the prairie, and when the snow was falling the town two hundred yards away was not visible. But when the traveller alighted at the railway station he was obliged to pass the Palace Hotel before he could come upon the company of low clapboard houses which composed Fort Romper, and it was not to be thought that any traveller could pass the Palace Hotel without looking at it. Pat Scully, the proprietor, had proved himself a master of strategy when he chose his paints. It is true that on clear days, when the great transcontinental expresses, long lines of swaying Pullmans, swept through Fort Romper, passengers were overcome at the sight, and the cult that knows the brown-reds and subdivisions of the dark greens of the East expressed shame, pity, horror, in a laugh. But to the citizens of this prairie town and to the people who would naturally stop there, Pat Scully had performed a feat. With this opulence and splendor, these creeds, classes, egotisms, that streamed through Romper on the rails day after day, they had no color in common.

As if the display delights of such a blue hotel were not sufficiently enticing, it was Scully's habit to go every morning and evening to meet the leisurely trains that stopped at Romper and work his seductions upon any man that he might see wavering, gripsack in hand.

One morning, when a snow-crusted engine dragged its long string of freight cars and its one passenger coach to the station, Scully performed the marvel of catching three men. One was a shaky and quick-eyed Swede, with a great shining cheap valise; one was a tall bronzed cowboy, who was on his way to a ranch near the Dakota line; one was a little silent man from the East, who didn't look it, and didn't announce it. Scully practically made them prisoners. He was so nimble and merry and kindly that each probably felt it would be the height of brutality to try to escape. They trudged off over the creaking board sidewalks in the wake of the eager little Irishman. He wore a heavy fur cap squeezed tightly down on his head. It caused his two red ears to stick out stiffly, as if they were made of tin.

At last, Scully, elaborately, with boisterous hospitality, conducted them through the portals of the blue hotel. The room which they entered was small. It seemed to be merely a proper temple for an enormous stove, which, in the center, was humming with godlike violence. At various points on its surface the iron had become luminous and glowed yellow from the heat. Beside the stove Scully's son Johnnie was playing High-Five with an old farmer who had whiskers both gray and sandy. They were quarrelling. Frequently the old farmer turned his face toward a box of sawdust—colored brown from tobacco juice—that was behind the stove, and spat with an air of great impatience and irritation. With a loud flourish of words Scully destroyed the game of cards, and bustled his son up-stairs with part of the baggage of the new guests. He himself conducted them to three basins of the coldest water in the world. The cowboy and the Easterner burnished themselves fiery red with this water, until it seemed to be some kind of metal polish. The Swede, however, merely dipped his fingers gingerly and with trepidation. It was notable that throughout this series of small ceremonies the three travellers were made to feel that Scully was very benevolent. He was conferring great favors upon them. He handed the towel from one to another with an air of philanthropic impulse.

Afterward they went to the first room, and, sitting about the stove, listened to Scully's officious clamor at his daughters, who were preparing the midday meal. They reflected in the silence of experienced men who tread carefully amid new people. Nevertheless, the old farmer, stationary, invincible in his chair near the warmest part of the stove, turned his face from the sawdust-box frequently and addressed a glowing commonplace to the strangers. Usually he was answered in short but adequate sentences by either the cowboy or the Easterner. The Swede said nothing. He seemed to be occupied in making furtive estimates of each man in the room. One might have thought that he had the sense of silly suspicion which comes to guilt. He resembled a badly frightened man.

Later, at dinner, he spoke a little, addressing his conversation entirely to Scully. He volunteered that he had come from New York, where for ten years he had worked as a tailor. These facts seemed to strike Scully as fascinating, and afterward he volunteered that he had lived at Romper for fourteen years. The Swede asked about the crops and the price of labor. He seemed barely to listen to Scully's extended replies. His eyes continued to rove from man to man.

Finally, with a laugh and a wink, he said that some of these Western communities were very dangerous; and after his statement he straightened his legs under the table, tilted his head, and laughed again, loudly. It was plain that the demonstration had no meaning to the others. They looked at him wondering and in silence.

2

AS THE men trooped heavily back into the front room, the two little windows presented views of a turmoiling sea of snow. The huge arms of the wind were making attempts—mighty, circular, futile—to embrace the flakes as they sped. A gate-post like a still man with a blanched face stood aghast amid this profligate fury. In a hearty voice Scully announced the presence of a blizzard. The guests of the blue hotel, lighting their pipes, assented with grunts of lazy masculine contentment. No island of the sea could be exempt in the degree of this little room with its humming stove. Johnnie, son of Scully, in a tone which defined his opinion of his ability as a card-player, challenged the old farmer of both gray and sandy whiskers to a game of High-Five. The farmer agreed with a contemptuous and bitter scoff. They sat close to the stove, and squared their knees under a wide board. The cowboy and the Easterner watched the game with interest. The Swede remained near the window, aloof, but with a countenance that showed signs of an inexplicable excitement.

The play of Johnnie and the gray-beard was suddenly ended by another quarrel. The old man arose while casting a look of heated scorn at his adversary. He slowly buttoned his coat, and then stalked with fabulous dignity from the room. In the discreet silence of all the other men the Swede laughed. His laughter rang somehow childish. Men by this time had begun to look at him askance, as if they wished to inquire what ailed him.

A new game was formed jocosely. The cowboy volunteered to become the partner of Johnnie, and they all then turned to ask the Swede to throw in his lot with the little Easterner. He asked some questions about the game, and, learning that it wore many names, and that he had played it when it was under an alias, he accepted the invitation. He strode toward the men nervously, as if he expected to be assaulted. Finally, seated, he gazed from face to face and laughed shrilly. This laugh was so strange that the Easterner looked up quickly, the cowboy sat intent and with his mouth open, and Johnnie paused, holding the cards with still fingers.

Afterward there was a short silence. Then Johnnie said, "Well, let's get at it. Come on now!" They pulled their chairs forward until their knees were bunched under the board. They began to play, and their interest in the game caused the others to forget the manner of the Swede.

The cowboy was a board-whacker. Each time that he held superior cards he whanged them, one by one, with exceeding force, down upon the improvised table, and took the tricks with a glowing air of prowess and pride that sent thrills of indignation into the hearts of his opponents. A game with a board-whacker in it is sure to become intense. The countenances of the Easterner and the Swede were miserable whenever the cowboy thundered down his aces and kings, while Johnnie, his eyes gleaming with joy, chuckled and chuckled.

Because of the absorbing play none considered the strange ways of the Swede. They paid strict heed to the game. Finally, during a lull caused by a new deal, the Swede suddenly addressed Johnnie: "I suppose there have been a good many men killed in this room." The jaws of the others dropped and they looked at him.

"What in hell are you talking about?" said Johnnie.

The Swede laughed again his blatant laugh, full of a kind of false courage and defiance. "Oh, you know what I mean all right," he answered.

"I'm a liar if I do!" Johnnie protested. The card was halted, and the men stared at the Swede. Johnnie evidently felt that as the son of the proprietor he should make a direct inquiry. "Now, what might you be drivin' at, mister?" he asked. The Swede winked at him. It was a wink full of cunning. His fingers shook on the edge of the board. "Oh, maybe you think I have been to nowheres. Maybe you think I'm a tenderfoot?"

"I don't know nothin' about you," answered Johnnie, "and I don't give a damn where you've been. All I got to say is that I don't know what you're driving at. There hain't never been nobody killed in this room."

The cowboy, who had been steadily gazing at the Swede, then spoke: "What's wrong with you, mister?"

Apparently it seemed to the Swede that he was formidably menaced. He shivered and turned white near the corners of his mouth. He sent an appealing glance in the direction of the little Easterner. During these moments he did not forget to wear his air of advanced pot-valor. "They say they don't know what I mean," he remarked mockingly to the Easterner.

The latter answered after prolonged and cautious reflection. "I don't understand you," he said, impassively.

The Swede made a movement then which announced that he thought he had encountered treachery from the only quarter where he had expected sympathy, if not help. "Oh, I see you are all against me. I see—"

The cowboy was in a state of deep stupefaction. "Say," he cried, as he tumbled the deck violently down upon the board, "say, what are you gittin' at, hey?"

The Swede sprang up with the celerity of a man escaping from a snake on the floor. "I don't want to fight," he shouted. "I don't want to fight!"

The cowboy stretched his long legs indolently and deliberately. His hands were in his pockets. He spat into the sawdust-box. "Well, who the hell thought you did?" he inquired.

The Swede backed rapidly toward a corner of the room. His hands were out protectingly in front of his chest, but he was making an obvious struggle to control his fright. "Gentlemen," he quavered, "I suppose I am going to be killed before I can leave this house! I suppose I am going to be killed before I can leave this house!" In his eyes was the dying-swan look. Through the windows could be seen the snow turning blue in the shadow of dusk. The wind tore at the house, and some loose thing beat regularly against the clapboards like a spirit tapping.

A door opened, and Scully himself entered. He paused in surprise as he noted the tragic attitude of the Swede. Then he said, "What's the matter here?"

The Swede answered him swiftly and eagerly: "These men are going to kill me."

"Kill you!" ejaculated Scully. "Kill you! What are you talkin'?"

The Swede made the gesture of a martyr.

Scully wheeled sternly upon his son. "What is this, Johnnie?"

The lad had grown sullen. "Damned if I know," he answered. "I can't make no sense to it." He began to shuffle the cards, fluttering them together with an angry snap. "He says a good many men have been killed in this room, or something like that. And he says he's goin' to be killed here too. I don't know what ails him. He's crazy, I shouldn't wonder."

Scully then looked for explanation to the cowboy, but the cowboy simply shrugged his shoulders.

"Kill you?" said Scully again to the Swede. "Kill you? Man, you're off your nut."

"Oh, I know," burst out the Swede. "I know what will happen. Yes, I'm crazy—yes. Yes, of course, I'm crazy—yes. But I know one thing—" There was a sort of sweat of misery and terror upon his face. "I know I won't get out of here alive."

The cowboy drew a deep breath, as if his mind was passing into the last stages of dissolution. "Well, I'm doggoned," he whispered to himself.

Scully wheeled suddenly and faced his son. "You've been troublin' this man!"

Johnnie's voice was loud with its burden of grievance. "Why, good Gawd, I ain't done nothin' to 'im."

The Swede broke in. "Gentlemen, do not disturb yourselves. I will leave this house. I will go away, because"—he accused them dramatically with his glance—"because I do not want to be killed."

Scully was furious with his son. "Will you tell me what is the matter, you young divil? What's the matter, anyhow? Speak out!"

"Blame it!" cried Johnnie in despair, "don't I tell you I don't know? He—he says we want to kill him, and that's all I know. I can't tell what ails him."

The Swede continued to repeat: "Never mind, Mr. Scully; never mind. I will leave this house. I will go away, because I do not wish to be killed. Yes, of course, I am crazy—yes. But I know one thing! I will go away. I will leave this house. Never mind, Mr. Scully, never mind. I will go away."

"You will not go 'way," said Scully. "You will not go 'way until I hear the reason of this business. If anybody has troubled you I will take care of him. This is my house. You are under my roof, and I will not allow any peaceable man to be troubled here." He cast a terrible eye upon Johnnie, the cowboy, and the Easterner.

"Never mind, Mr. Scully; never mind. I will go away. I do not wish to be killed." The Swede moved toward the door which opened upon the stairs. It was evidently his intention to go at once for his baggage.

"No, no," shouted Scully peremptorily; but the white-faced man slid by him and disappeared. "Now," said Scully severely, "what does this mane?"

Johnnie and the cowboy cried together: "Why, we didn't do nothin' to 'im!"

Scully's eyes were cold. "No," he said, "you didn't?"

Johnnie swore a deep oath. "Why, this is the wildest loon I ever see. We didn't do nothin' at all. We were jest sittin' here playin' cards, and he—"

The father suddenly spoke to the Easterner. "Mr. Blanc," he asked, "what has these boys been doin'?"

The Easterner reflected again. "I didn't see anything wrong at all," he said at last, slowly.

Scully began to howl. "But what does it mane?" He stared ferociously at his son. "I have a mind to lather you for this, my boy."

Johnnie was frantic. "Well, what have I done?" he bawled at his father.

3

"I THINK you are tongue-tied," said Scully finally to his son, the cowboy, and the Easterner; and at the end of this scornful sentence he left the room.

Upstairs the Swede was swiftly fastening the straps of his great valise. Once his back happened to be half turned toward the door, and, hearing a noise there, he wheeled and sprang up, uttering a loud cry. Scully's wrinkled visage showed grimly in the light of the small lamp he carried. This yellow effulgence, streaming upward, colored only his prominent features, and left his eyes, for instance, in mysterious shadow. He resembled a murderer.

"Man! man!" he exclaimed, "have you gone daffy?"

"Oh, no! Oh, no!" rejoined the other. "There are people in this world who know pretty nearly as much as you do—understand?"

For a moment they stood gazing at each other. Upon the Swede's deathly pale cheeks were two spots brightly crimson and sharply edged, as if they had been carefully painted. Scully placed the light on the table and sat himself on the edge of the bed. He spoke ruminatively. "By cracky, I never heard of such a thing in my life. It's a complete muddle. I can't, for the soul of me, think how you ever got this idea into your head." Presently he lifted his eyes and asked: "And did you sure think they were going to kill you?"

The Swede scanned the old man as if he wished to see into his mind. "I did," he said at last. He obviously suspected that this answer might precipitate an outbreak. As he pulled on a strap his whole arm shook, the elbow wavering like a bit of paper.

Scully banged his hand impressively on the footboard of the bed. "Why, man, we're goin' to have a line of ilictric street-cars in this town next spring."

"'A line of electric street-cars,'" repeated the Swede, stupidly.

"And," said Scully, "there's a new railroad goin' to be built down from Broken Arm to here. Not to mintion the four churches and the smashin' big brick schoolhouse. Then there's the big factory, too. Why, in two years Romper'll be a met-tro-*pol*-is."

Having finished the preparation of his baggage, the Swede straightened himself. "Mr. Scully," he said, with sudden hardihood, "how much do I owe you?"

"You don't owe me anythin'," said the old man, angrily.

"Yes, I do," retorted the Swede. He took seventy-five cents from his pocket and tendered it to Scully; but the latter snapped his fingers in disdainful refusal. However, it happened that they both stood gazing in a strange fashion at three silver pieces on the Swede's open palm.

"I'll not take your money," said Scully at last. "Not after what's been goin' on here." Then a plan seemed to strike him. "Here," he cried, picking up his lamp and moving toward the door. "Here! Come with me a minute."

"No," said the Swede, in overwhelming alarm.

"Yes," urged the old man. "Come on! I want you to come and see a picter—just across the hall—in my room."

The Swede must have concluded that his hour was come. His jaw dropped and his teeth showed like a dead man's. He ultimately followed Scully across the corridor, but he had the step of one hung in chains.

Scully flashed the light high on the wall of his own chamber. There was revealed a ridiculous photograph of a little girl. She was leaning against a balustrade of gorgeous decoration, and the formidable bang to her hair was prominent. The figure was as graceful as an upright sled-stake, and, withal, it was of the hue of lead. "There," said Scully, tenderly, "that's the picter of my little girl that died. Her name was Carrie. She had the purtiest hair you ever saw! I was that fond of her, she—"

Turning then, he saw that the Swede was not contemplating the picture at all, but, instead, was keeping keen watch on the gloom in the rear.

"Look, man!" cried Scully, heartily. "That's the picter of my little gal that died. Her name was Carrie. And then here's the picter of my oldest boy. Michael. He's a lawyer in Lincoln, an' doin' well. I gave that boy a grand eddication, and I'm glad for it now. He's a fine-boy. Look at 'im now. Ain't he bold as blazes, him there in Lincoln, an honored an' respicted gintleman! An honored and respicted gintleman," concluded Scully with a flourish. And, so saying, he smote the Swede jovially on the back.

The Swede faintly smiled.

"Now," said the old man, "there's only one more thing." He dropped suddenly to the floor and thrust his head beneath the bed. The Swede could hear his muffled voice. "I'd keep it under me piller if it wasn't for that boy Johnnie. Then there's the old woman—Where is it now? I never put it twice in the same place. Ah, now come out with you!"

Presently he backed clumsily from under the bed, dragging with him an old coat rolled into a bundle. "I've fetched him," he muttered. Kneeling on the floor, he unrolled the coat and extracted from its heart a large yellow-brown whiskey-bottle.

His first manœuver was to hold the bottle up to the light. Reassured, apparently, that nobody had been tampering with it, he thrust it with a generous movement toward the Swede.

The weak-kneed Swede was about to eagerly clutch this element of strength, but he suddenly jerked his hand away and cast a look of horror upon Scully.

"Drink," said the old man affectionately. He had risen to his feet, and now stood facing the Swede.

There was a silence. Then again Scully said: "Drink!"

The Swede laughed wildly. He grabbed the bottle, put it to his mouth; and as his lips curled absurdly around the opening and his throat worked, he kept his glance, burning with hatred, upon the old man's face.

4

AFTER the departure of Scully the three men, with the cardboard still upon their knees, preserved for a long time an astounded silence. Then Johnnie said: "That's the doddangedest Swede I ever see."

"He ain't no Swede," said the cowboy, scornfully.

"Well, what is he then?" cried Johnnie. "What is he then?"

"It's my opinion," replied the cowboy deliberately, "he's some kind of a Dutchman." It was a venerable custom of the country to entitle as Swedes all light-haired men who spoke with a heavy tongue. In consequence the idea of the cowboy was not without its daring. "Yes, sir," he repeated. "It's my opinion this feller is some kind of a Dutchman."

"Well, he says he's a Swede, anyhow," muttered Johnnie, sulkily. He turned to the Easterner: "What do you think, Mr. Blanc?"

"Oh, I don't know," replied the Easterner.

"Well, what do you think makes him act that way?" asked the cowboy.

"Why, he's frightened." The Easterner knocked his pipe against a rim of the stove. "He's clear frightened out of his boots."

"What at?" cried Johnnie and the cowboy together.

The Easterner reflected over his answer.

"What at?" cried the others again.

"Oh, I don't know, but it seems to me this man has been reading dime novels, and he thinks he's right out in the middle of it—the shootin' and stabbin' and all."

"But," said the cowboy, deeply scandalized, "this ain't Wyoming, ner none of them places. This is Nebrasker."

"Yes," added Johnnie, "an' why don't he wait till he gits *out West?*"

The travelled Easterner laughed. "It isn't different there even—not in these days. But he thinks he's right in the middle of hell."

Johnnie and the cowboy mused long.

"It's awful funny," remarked Johnnie at last.

"Yes," said the cowboy. "This is a queer game. I hope we don't git snowed in, because then we'd have to stand this here man bein' around with us all the time. That wouldn't be no good."

"I wish pop would throw him out," said Johnnie.

Presently they heard a loud stamping on the stairs, accompanied by ringing jokes in the voice of old Scully, and laughter, evidently from the Swede. The men around the stove stared vacantly at each other. "Gosh!" said the cowboy. The door flew open, and old Scully, flushed and anecdotal, came into the room. He was jabbering at the Swede, who followed him, laughing bravely. It was the entry of two roisterers from a banquet hall.

"Come now," said Scully sharply to the three seated men, "move up and give us a chance at the stove." The cowboy and the Easterner obediently sidled their chairs to make room for the new-comers. Johnnie, however, simply arranged himself in a more indolent attitude, and then remained motionless.

"Come! Git over, there," said Scully.

"Plenty of room on the other side of the stove," said Johnnie.

"Do you think we want to sit in the draught?" roared the father.

But the Swede here interposed with a grandeur of confidence. "No, no. Let the boy sit where he likes," he cried in a bullying voice to the father.

"All right! All right!" said Scully deferentially. The cowboy and the Easterner exchanged glances of wonder.

The five chairs were formed in a crescent about one side of the stove. The Swede began to talk; he talked arrogantly, profanely, angrily. Johnnie, the cowboy, and the Easterner maintained a morose silence, while old Scully appeared to be receptive and eager, breaking in constantly with sympathetic ejaculations.

Finally the Swede announced that he was thirsty. He moved in his chair, and said that he would go for a drink of water.

"I'll git it for you," cried Scully at once.

"No," said the Swede, contemptuously. "I'll get it for myself." He arose and stalked with the air of an owner off into the executive parts of the hotel.

As soon as the Swede was out of hearing Scully sprang to his feet and whispered intensely to the others: "Up-stairs he thought I was tryin' to poison 'im."

"Say," said Johnnie, "this makes me sick. Why don't you throw 'im out in the snow?"

"Why, he's all right now," declared Scully. "It was only that he was from the East, and he thought this was a tough place. That's all. He's all right now."

The cowboy looked with admiration upon the Easterner. "You were straight," he said. "You were on to that there Dutchman."

"Well," said Johnnie to his father, "he may be all right now, but I don't see it. Other time he was scared, but now he's too fresh."

Scully's speech was always a combination of Irish brogue and idiom, Western twang and idiom, and scraps of curiously formal diction taken from the story-books and newspapers. He now hurled a strange mass of language at the head of his son. "What do I keep? What do I keep? What do I keep?" he demanded, in a voice of thunder. He slapped his knee impressively, to indicate that he himself was going to make reply, and that all should heed. "I keep a hotel," he shouted. "A hotel, do you mind? A guest under my roof has sacred privileges. He is to be intimidated by none. Not one word shall he hear that would prijudice him in favor of goin' away. I'll not have it. There's no place in this here town where they can say they iver took in a guest of mine because he was afraid to stay here." He wheeled suddenly upon the cowboy and the Easterner. "Am I right?"

"Yes, Mr. Scully," said the cowboy, "I think you're right."

"Yes, Mr. Scully," said the Easterner, "I think you're right."

5

AT SIX-O'CLOCK supper, the Swede fizzed like a fire-wheel. He sometimes seemed on the point of bursting into riotous song, and in all his madness he was encouraged by old Scully. The Easterner was encased in reserve, the cowboy sat in wide-mouthed amazement, forgetting to eat, while Johnnie wrathily demolished great plates of food. The daughters of the house, when they were obliged to replenish the biscuits, approached as warily as Indians, and, having succeeded in their purpose, fled with ill-concealed trepidation. The Swede domineered the whole feast, and he gave it the appearance of a cruel bacchanal. He seemed to have grown suddenly taller; he gazed, brutally disdainful, into every face. His voice rang through the room. Once when he jabbed out harpoon-fashion with his fork to pinion a biscuit, the weapon nearly impaled the hand of the Easterner, which had been stretched quietly out for the same biscuit.

After supper, as the men filed toward the other room, the Swede smote Scully ruthlessly on the shoulder. "Well, old boy, that was a good, square meal." Johnnie looked hopefully at his father; he knew that shoulder was tender from an old fall; and, indeed, it appeared for a moment as if Scully was going to flame out over the matter, but in the end he smiled a sickly smile and remained silent. The others understood from his manner that he was admitting his responsibility for the Swede's new view-point.

Johnnie, however, addressed his parent in an aside. "Why don't you license somebody to kick you downstairs?" Scully scowled darkly by way of reply.

When they were gathered about the stove, the Swede insisted on another game of High-Five. Scully gently deprecated the plan at first, but the Swede turned a wolfish glare upon him. The old man subsided, and the Swede canvassed the others. In his tone there was always a great threat. The cowboy and the Easterner both remarked indifferently that they would play. Scully said that he would presently have to go to meet the 6.58 train, and so the Swede turned menacingly upon Johnnie. For a moment their glances crossed like blades, and then Johnnie smiled and said, "Yes, I'll play."

They formed a square, with the little board on their knees. The Easterner and the Swede were again partners. As the play went on, it was noticeable that the cowboy was not board-whacking as usual. Meanwhile, Scully, near the lamp, had put on his spectacles and, with an appearance curiously like an old priest, was reading a newspaper. In time he went out to meet the 6.58 train, and, despite his precautions, a gust of polar wind whirled into the room as he opened the door. Besides scattering the cards, it chilled the players to the marrow. The Swede cursed frightfully. When Scully returned, his entrance disturbed a cosy and friendly scene. The Swede again cursed. But presently they were once more intent, their heads bent forward and their hands moving swiftly. The Swede had adopted the fashion of board-whacking.

Scully took up his paper and for a long time remained immersed in matters which were extraordinarily remote from him. The lamp burned badly, and once he stopped to adjust the wick. The newspaper, as he turned from page to page, rustled with a slow and comfortable sound. Then suddenly he heard three terrible words: "You are cheatin'!"

Such scenes often prove that there can be little of dramatic import in environment. Any room can present a tragic front; any room can be comic. This little den was now hideous as a torture-chamber. The new faces of the men themselves had changed it upon the instant. The Swede held a huge fist in front of Johnnie's face, while the latter looked steadily over it into the blazing orbs of his accuser. The Easterner had grown pallid; the cowboy's jaw had dropped in that expression of bovine amazement which was one of his important mannerisms. After the three words, the first sound in the room was made by Scully's paper as it floated forgotten to his feet. His spectacles had also fallen from his nose, but by a clutch he had saved them in air. His hand, grasping the spectacles, now remained poised awkwardly and near his shoulder. He stared at the card-players.

Probably the silence was while a second elapsed. Then, if the floor had been suddenly twitched out from under the men they could not have moved quicker. The five had projected themselves headlong toward a common point. It happened that Johnnie, in rising to hurl himself upon the Swede, had stumbled slightly because of his curiously instinctive care for the cards and the board. The loss of the moment allowed time for the arrival of Scully, and also allowed the cowboy time to give the Swede a great push which sent him staggering back. The men found tongue together, and hoarse shouts of rage, appeal, or fear burst from every throat. The cowboy pushed and jostled feverishly at the Swede, and the Easterner and Scully clung wildly to Johnnie; but through the smoky air, above the swaying bodies of the peace-compellers, the eyes of the two warriors ever sought each other in glances of challenge that were at once hot and steely.

Of course the board had been overturned, and now the whole company of cards was scattered over the floor, where the boots of the men trampled the fat and painted kings and queens as they gazed with their silly eyes at the war that was waging above them.

Scully's voice was dominating the yells. "Stop now! Stop, I say! Stop, now—"

Johnnie, as he struggled to burst through the rank formed by Scully and the Easterner, was crying, "Well, he says I cheated! He says I cheated! I won't allow no man to say I cheated! If he says I cheated, he's a —— ——!"

The cowboy was telling the Swede, "Quit, now! Quit, d'ye hear —

The screams of the Swede never ceased: "He did cheat! I saw him! I saw him—"

As for the Easterner, he was importuning in a voice that was not heeded: "Wait a moment, can't you? Oh, wait a moment. What's the good of a fight over a game of cards? Wait a moment—"

In this tumult no complete sentences were clear. "Cheat"—

"Quit"— "He says"—these fragments pierced the uproar and rang out sharply. It was remarkable that, whereas Scully undoubtedly made the most noise, he was the least heard of any of the riotous band.

Then suddenly there was a great cessation. It was as if each man had paused for breath; and although the room was still lighted with the anger of men, it could be seen that there was no danger of immediate conflict, and at once Johnnie, shouldering his way forward, almost succeeded in confronting the Swede. "What did you say I cheated for? What did you say I cheated for? I don't cheat, and I won't let no man say I do!"

The Swede said, "I saw you! I saw you!"

"Well," cried Johnnie, "I'll fight any man what says I cheat!"

"No, you won't," said the cowboy. "Not here."

"Ah, be still, can't you?" said Scully, coming between them.

The quiet was sufficient to allow the Easterner's voice to be heard. He was repeating, "Oh, wait a moment, can't you? What's the good of a fight over a game of cards? Wait a moment!"

Johnnie, his red face appearing above his father's shoulder, hailed the Swede again. "Did you say I cheated?"

The Swede showed his teeth. "Yes."

"Then,'" said Johnnie, "we must fight."

"Yes, fight," roared the Swede. He was like a demoniac. "Yes, fight! I'll show you what kind of a man I am! I'll show you who you want to fight! Maybe you think I can't fight! Maybe you think I can't! I'll show you, you skin, you card-sharp! Yes, you cheated! You cheated! You cheated!"

"Well, let's go at it, then, mister," said Johnnie, coolly.

The cowboy's brow was beaded with sweat from his efforts in intercepting all sorts of raids. He turned in despair to Scully. "What are you goin' to do now?"

A change had come over the Celtic visage of the old man. He now seemed all eagerness; his eyes glowed.

"We'll let them fight," he answered, stalwartly. "I can't put up with it any longer. I've stood this damned Swede till I'm sick. We'll let them fight."

6

THE men prepared to go out-of-doors. The Easterner was so nervous that he had great difficulty in getting his arms into the sleeves of his new leather coat. As the cowboy drew his fur cap down over his ears his hands trembled. In fact, Johnnie and old Scully were the only ones who displayed no agitation. These preliminaries were conducted without words.

Scully threw open the door. "Well, come on," he said. Instantly a terrific wind caused the flame of the lamp to struggle at its wick, while a puff of black smoke sprang from the chimney-top. The stove was in mid-current of the blast, and its voice swelled to equal the roar of the storm. Some of the scarred and bedabbled cards were caught up from the floor and dashed helplessly against the farther wall. The men lowered their heads and plunged into the tempest as into a sea.

No snow was falling, but great whirls and clouds of flakes, swept up from the ground by the frantic winds, were streaming southward with the speed of bullets. The covered land was blue with the sheen of an unearthly satin, and there was no other hue save where, at the low, black railway station—which seemed incredibly distant—one light gleamed like a tiny jewel. As the men floundered into a thigh-deep drift, it was known that the Swede was bawling out something. Scully went to him, put a hand on his shoulder, and projected an ear. "What's that you say?" he shouted.

"I say," bawled the Swede again, "I won't stand much show against this gang. I know you'll all pitch on me."

Scully smote him reproachfully on the arm. "Tut, man!" he yelled. The wind tore the words from Scully's lips and scattered them far alee.

"You are all a gang of—" boomed the Swede, but the storm also seized the remainder of this sentence.

Immediately turning their backs upon the wind, the men had swung around a corner to the sheltered side of the hotel. It was the function of the little house to preserve here, amid this great devastation of snow, an irregular V-shape of heavily encrusted grass, which crackled beneath the feet. One could imagine the great drifts piled against the windward side. When the party reached the comparative peace of this spot it was found that the Swede was still bellowing.

"Oh, I know what kind of a thing this is! I know you'll all pitch on me. I can't lick you all!"

Scully turned upon him panther-fashion. "You'll not have to whip all of us. You'll have to whip my son Johnnie. An' the man what troubles you durin' that time will have me to dale with."

The arrangements were swiftly made. The two men faced each other, obedient to the harsh commands of Scully, whose face, in the subtly luminous gloom, could be seen set in the austere impersonal lines that are pictured on the countenances of the Roman veterans. The Easterner's teeth were chattering, and he was hopping up and down like a mechanical toy. The cowboy stood rock-like.

The contestants had not stripped off any clothing. Each was in his ordinary attire. Their fists were up, and they eyed each other in a calm that had the elements of leonine cruelty in it.

During this pause, the Easterner's mind, like a film, took lasting impressions of three men—the iron-nerved master of the ceremony; the Swede, pale, motionless, terrible; and Johnnie, serene yet ferocious, brutish yet heroic. The entire prelude had in it a tragedy greater than the tragedy of action, and this aspect was accentuated by the long, mellow cry of the blizzard, as it sped the tumbling and wailing flakes into the black abyss of the south.

"Now!" said Scully.

The two combatants leaped forward and crashed together like bullocks. There was heard the cushioned sound of blows, and of a curse squeezing out from between the tight teeth of one.

As for the spectators, the Easterner's pent-up breath exploded from him with a pop of relief, absolute relief from the tension of the preliminaries. The cowboy bounded into the air with a yowl. Scully was immovable as from supreme amazement and fear at the fury of the fight which he himself had permitted and arranged.

For a time the encounter in the darkness was such a perplexity of flying arms that it presented no more detail than would a swiftly revolving wheel. Occasionally a face, as if illumined by a flash of light, would shine out, ghastly and marked with pink spots. A moment later, the men might have been known as shadows, if it were not for the involuntary utterance of oaths that came from them in whispers.

Suddenly a holocaust of warlike desire caught the cowboy, and he bolted forward with the speed of a broncho. "Go it, Johnnie! go it! Kill him! Kill him!"

Scully confronted him. "Kape back," he said; and by his glance the cowboy could tell that this man was Johnnie's father.

To the Easterner there was a monotony of unchangeable fighting that was an abomination. This confused mingling was eternal to his sense, which was concentrated in a longing for the end, the priceless end. Once the fighters lurched near him, and as he scrambled hastily backward he heard them breathe like men on the rack.

"Kill him, Johnnie! Kill him! Kill him! Kill him!" The cowboy's face was contorted like one of those agony masks in museums.

"Keep still," said Scully, icily.

Then there was a sudden loud grunt, incomplete, cut short, and Johnnie's body swung away from the Swede and fell with sickening heaviness to the grass. The cowboy was barely in time to prevent the mad Swede from flinging himself upon his prone adversary. "No, you don't" said the cowboy, interposing an arm. "Wait a second."

Scully was at his son's side. "Johnnie! Johnnie, me boy!" His voice had a quality of melancholy tenderness. "Johnnie! Can you go on with it?" He looked anxiously down into the bloody, pulpy face of his son.

There was a moment of silence, and then Johnnie answered in his ordinary voice, "Yes, I—it—yes."

Assisted by his father he struggled to his feet. "Wait a bit now till you git your wind," said the old man.

A few paces away the cowboy was lecturing the Swede. "No, you don't! Wait a second!"

The Easterner was plucking at Scully's sleeve. "Oh, this is enough," he pleaded. "This is enough! Let it go as it stands. This is enough!"

"Bill," said Scully, "git out of the road." The cowboy stepped aside. "Now." The combatants were actuated by a new caution as they advanced toward collision. They glared at each other, and then the Swede aimed a lightning blow that carried with it his entire weight. Johnnie was evidently half stupid from weakness, but he miraculously dodged, and his fist sent the overbalanced Swede sprawling.

The cowboy, Scully, and the Easterner burst into a cheer that was like a chorus of triumphant soldiery, but before its conclusion the Swede had scuffled agilely to his feet and come in berserk abandon at his foe. There was another perplexity of flying arms, and Johnnie's body again swung away and fell, even as a bundle might fall from a roof. The Swede instantly staggered to a little wind-waved tree and leaned upon it, breathing like an engine, while his savage and flame-lit eyes roamed from face to face as the men bent over Johnnie. There was a splendor of isolation in his situation at this time which the Easterner felt once when, lifting his eyes from the man on the ground, he beheld that mysterious and lonely figure, waiting.

"Are you any good yet, Johnnie?" asked Scully in a broken voice.

The son gasped and opened his eyes languidly. After a moment he answered, "No—I ain't—any good—any—more." Then, from shame and bodily ill, he began to weep, the tears furrowing down through the blood-stains on his face. "He was too—too—too heavy for me."

Scully straightened and addressed the waiting figure. "Stranger," he said, evenly, "it's all up with our side." Then his voice changed into that vibrant huskiness which is commonly the tone of the most simple and deadly announcements. "Johnnie is whipped."

Without replying, the victor moved off on the route to the front door of the hotel.

The cowboy was formulating new and unspellable blasphemies. The Easterner was startled to find that they were out in a wind that seemed to come direct from the shadowed arctic floes. He heard again the wail of the snow as it was flung to its grave in the south. He knew now that all this time the cold had been sinking into him deeper and deeper, and he wondered that he had not perished. He felt indifferent to the condition of the vanquished man.

"Johnnie, can you walk?" asked Scully.

"Did I hurt—hurt him any?" asked the son.

"Can you walk, boy? Can you walk?"

Johnnie's voice was suddenly strong. There was a robust impatience in it. "I asked you whether I hurt him any!"

"Yes, yes, Johnnie," answered the cowboy, consolingly; "he's hurt a good deal."

They raised him from the ground, and as soon as he was on his feet he went tottering off, rebuffing all attempts at assistance. When the party rounded the corner they were fairly blinded by the pelting of the snow. It burned their faces like fire. The cowboy carried Johnnie through the drift to the door. As they entered, some cards again rose from the floor and beat against the wall.

The Easterner rushed to the stove. He was so profoundly chilled that he almost dared to embrace the glowing iron. The Swede was not in the room. Johnnie sank into a chair and, folding his arms on his knees, buried his face in them. Scully, warming one foot and then the other at a rim of the stove, muttered to himself with Celtic mournfulness. The cowboy had removed his fur cap, and with a dazed and rueful air he was running one hand through his tousled locks. From overhead they could hear the creaking of boards, as the Swede tramped here and there in his room.

The sad quiet was broken by the sudden flinging open of a door that led toward the kitchen. It was instantly followed by an inrush of women. They precipitated themselves upon Johnnie amid a chorus of lamentation. Before they carried their prey off to the kitchen, there to be bathed and harangued with that mixture of sympathy and abuse which is a feat of their sex, the mother straightened herself and fixed old Scully with an eye of stern reproach. "Shame be upon you, Patrick Scully!" she cried. "Your own son, too. Shame be upon you!"

"There, now! Be quiet, now!" said the old man, weakly.

"Shame be upon you, Patrick Scully!" The girls, rallying to this slogan, sniffed disdainfully in the direction of those trembling accomplices, the cowboy and the Easterner. Presently they bore Johnnie away, and left the three men to dismal reflection.

7

I'D LIKE to fight this here Dutchman myself," said the cowboy, breaking a long silence.

Scully wagged his head sadly. "No, that wouldn't do. It wouldn't be right. It wouldn't be right."

"Well, why wouldn't it?" argued the cowboy. "I don't see no harm in it."

"No," answered Scully, with mournful heroism. "It wouldn't be right. It was Johnnie's fight, and now we mustn't whip the man just because he whipped Johnnie."

"Yes, that's true enough," said the cowboy; "but—he better not get fresh with me, because I couldn't stand no more of it."

"You'll not say a word to him," commanded Scully, and even then they heard the tread of the Swede on the stairs. His entrance was made theatric. He swept the door back with a bang and swaggered to the middle of the room. No one looked at him. "Well," he cried, insolently, at Scully, "I s'pose you'll tell me now how much I owe you?"

The old man remained stolid. "You don't owe me nothin'."

"Huh!" said the Swede, "huh! Don't owe 'im nothin'."

The cowboy addressed the Swede. "Stranger, I don't see how you come to be so gay around here."

Old Scully was instantly alert. "Stop!" he shouted, holding his hand forth, fingers upward. "Bill, you shut up!"

The cowboy spat carelessly into the sawdust-box. "I didn't say a word, did I?" he asked.

"Mr. Scully," called the Swede, "how much do I owe you?" It was seen that he was attired for departure, and that he had his valise in his hand.

"You don't owe me nothin'," repeated Scully in the same imperturbable way.

"Huh!" said the Swede. "I guess you're right. I guess if it was any way at all, you'd owe me somethin'. That's what I guess." He turned to the cowboy. " 'Kill him! Kill him! Kill him!' " he mimicked, and then guffawed victoriously. " 'Kill him!' " He was convulsed with ironical humor.

But he might have been jeering the dead. The three men were immovable and silent, staring with glassy eyes at the stove.

The Swede opened the door and passed into the storm, giving one derisive glance backward at the still group.

As soon as the door was closed, Scully and the cowboy leaped to their feet and began to curse. They trampled to and fro, waving their arms and smashing into the air with their fists. "Oh, but that was a hard minute!" wailed Scully. "That was a hard minute! Him there leerin' and scoffin'! One bang at his nose was worth forty dollars to me that minute! How did you stand it, Bill?"

"How did I stand it?" cried the cowboy in a quivering voice. "How did I stand it? Oh!"

The old man burst into sudden brogue. "I'd loike to take that Swade," he wailed, "and hould 'im down on a shtone flure and bate 'im to a jelly wid a shtick!"

The cowboy groaned in sympathy. "I'd like to git him by the neck and ha-ammer him"—he brought his hand down on a chair with a noise like a pistol-shot—"hammer that there Dutchman until he couldn't tell himself from a dead coyote!"

"I'd bate 'im until he—"

"I'd show *him* some things—"

And then together they raised a yearning, fanatic cry—"Oh-o-oh! if we only could—"

"Yes!"

"Yes!"

"And then I'd—"

"O-o-oh!"

8

THE Swede, tightly gripping his valise, tacked across the face of the storm as if he carried sails. He was following a line of little naked, gasping trees which, he knew, must mark the way of the road. His face, fresh from the pounding of Johnnie's fists, felt more pleasure than pain in the wind and the driving snow. A number of square shapes loomed upon him finally, and he knew them as the houses of the main body of the town. He found a street and made travel along it, leaning heavily upon the wind whenever, at a corner, a terrific blast caught him.

He might have been in a deserted village. We picture the world as thick with conquering and elate humanity, but here, with the bugles of the tempest pealing, it was hard to imagine a peopled earth. One viewed the existence of man then as a marvel, and conceded a glamor of wonder to these lice which were caused to cling to a whirling, fire-smitten, ice-locked, disease-stricken, space-lost bulb. The conceit of man was explained by this storm to be the very engine of life. One was a coxcomb not to die in it. However, the Swede found a saloon.

In front of it an indomitable red light was burning, and the snow-flakes were made blood-color as they flew through the circumscribed territory of the lamp's shining. The Swede pushed open the door of the saloon and entered. A sanded expanse was before him, and at the end of it four men sat about a table drinking. Down one side of the room extended a radiant bar, and its guardian was leaning upon his elbows listening to the talk of the men at the table. The Swede dropped his valise upon the floor and, smiling fraternally upon the barkeeper, said, "Gimme some whiskey, will you?" The man placed a bottle, a whiskey-glass, and a glass of ice-thick water upon the bar. The Swede poured himself an abnormal portion of whiskey and drank it in three gulps. "Pretty bad night," remarked the bartender, indifferently. He was making the pretension of blindness which is usually a distinction of his class; but it could have been seen that he was furtively studying the half-erased blood-stains on the face of the Swede. "Bad night," he said again.

"Oh, it's good enough for me," replied the Swede, hardily, as he poured himself some more whiskey. The barkeeper took his coin and manœuvered it through its reception by the highly nickelled cash-machine. A bell rang; a card labelled "20 cts." had appeared.

"No," continued the Swede, "this isn't too bad weather. It's good enough for me."

"So?" murmured the barkeeper, languidly.

The copious drams made the Swede's eyes swim, and he breathed a trifle heavier. "Yes, I like this weather. I like it. It suits me." It was apparently his design to impart a deep significance to these words.

"So?" murmured the bartender again. He turned to gaze dreamily at the scroll-like birds and bird-like scrolls which had been drawn with soap upon the mirrors in back of the bar.

"Well, I guess I'll take another drink," said the Swede, presently. "Have something?"

"No, thanks; I'm not drinkin'," answered the bartender. Afterward he asked, "How did you hurt your face?"

The Swede immediately began to boast loudly. "Why, in a fight. I thumped the soul out of a man down here at Scully's hotel."

The interest of the four men at the table was at last aroused.

"Who was it?" said one.

"Johnnie Scully," blustered the Swede. "Son of the man what runs it. He will be pretty near dead for some weeks, I can tell you. I made a nice thing of him, I did. He couldn't get up. They carried him in the house. Have a drink?"

Instantly the men in some subtle way encased themselves in reserve. "No, thanks," said one. The group was of curious formation. Two were prominent local business men; one was the district attorney; and one was a professional gambler of the kind known as "square." But a scrutiny of the group would not have enabled an observer to pick the gambler from the men of more reputable pursuits. He was, in fact, a man so delicate in manner, when among people of fair class, and so judicious in his choice of victims, that in the strictly masculine part of the town's life he had come to be explicitly trusted and admired. People called him a thoroughbred. The fear and contempt with which his craft was regarded were undoubtedly the reason why his quiet dignity shone conspicuous above the quiet dignity of men who might be merely hatters, billiard-markers, or grocery-clerks. Beyond an occasional unwary traveller who came by rail, this gambler was supposed to prey solely upon reckless and senile farmers, who, when flush with good crops, drove into town in all the pride and confidence of an absolutely invulnerable stupidity. Hearing at times in circuitous fashion of the despoilment of such a farmer, the important men of Romper invariably laughed in contempt of the victim, and if they thought of the wolf at all, it was with a kind of pride at the knowledge that he would never dare think of attacking their wisdom and courage. Besides, it was popular that this gambler had a real wife and two real children in a neat cottage in a suburb, where he led an exemplary home life; and when any one even suggested a discrepancy in his character, the crowd immediately vociferated descriptions of this virtuous family circle. Then men who led exemplary home lives, and men who did not lead exemplary home lives, all subsided in a bunch, remarking that there was nothing more to be said.

However, when a restriction was placed upon him—as, for instance, when a strong clique of members of the new Pollywog Club refused to permit him, even as a spectator, to appear in the rooms of the organization—the candor and gentleness with which he accepted the judgment disarmed many of his foes and made his friends more desperately partisan. He invariably distinguished between himself and a respectable Romper man so quickly and frankly that his manner actually appeared to be a continual broadcast compliment.

And one must not forget to declare the fundamental fact of his entire position in Romper. It is irrefutable that in all affairs outside his business, in all matters that occur eternally and commonly between man and man, this thieving card-player was so generous, so just, so moral, that, in a contest, he could have put to flight the consciences of nine-tenths of the citizens of Romper.

And so it happened that he was seated in this saloon with the two prominent local merchants and the district attorney.

The Swede continued to drink raw whiskey, meanwhile babbling at the barkeeper and trying to induce him to indulge in potations. "Come on. Have a drink. Come on. What—no? Well, have a little one, then. By gawd, I've whipped a man to-night, and I want to celebrate. I whipped him good, too. Gentlemen," the Swede cried to the men at the table, "have a drink?"

"Ssh!" said the barkeeper.

The group at the table, although furtively attentive, had been pretending to be deep in talk, but now a man lifted his eyes toward the Swede and said, shortly, "Thanks. We don't want any more."

At this reply the Swede ruffled out his chest like a rooster. "Well," he exploded, "it seems I can't get anybody to drink with me in this town. Seems so, don't it? Well!"

"Ssh!" said the barkeeper.

"Say," snarled the Swede, "don't you try to shut me up. I won't have it. I'm a gentleman, and I want people to drink with me. And

I want 'em to drink with me now. *Now*—do you understand?" He rapped the bar with his knuckles.

Years of experience had calloused the bartender. He merely grew sulky. "I hear you," he answered.

"Well," cried the Swede, "listen hard then. See those men over there? Well, they're going to drink with me, and don't you forget it. Now you watch."

"Hi!" yelled the barkeeper, "this won't do!"

"Why won't it?" demanded the Swede. He stalked over to the table, and by chance laid his hand upon the shoulder of the gambler. "How about this?" he asked wrathfully. "I asked you to drink with me."

The gambler simply twisted his head and spoke over his shoulder. "My friend, I don't know you."

"Oh, hell!" answered the Swede, "come and have a drink."

"Now, my boy," advised the gambler, kindly, "take your hand off my shoulder and go 'way and mind your own business." He was a little, slim man, and it seemed strange to hear him use this tone of heroic patronage to the burly Swede. The other men at the table said nothing.

"What! You won't drink with me, you little dude? I'll make you, then! I'll make you!" The Swede had grasped the gambler frenziedly at the throat, and was dragging him from his chair. The other men sprang up. The barkeeper dashed around the corner of his bar. There was a great tumult, and then was seen a long blade in the hand of the gambler. It shot forward, and a human body, this citadel of virtue, wisdom, power, was pierced as easily as if it had been a melon. The Swede fell with a cry of supreme astonishment.

The prominent merchants and the district attorney must have at once tumbled out of the place backward. The bartender found himself hanging limply to the arm of a chair and gazing into the eyes of a murderer.

"Henry," said the latter, as he wiped his knife on one of the towels that hung beneath the bar rail, "you tell 'em where to find me. I'll be home, waiting for 'em." Then he vanished. A moment afterward the barkeeper was in the street dinning through the storm for help and, moreover, companionship.

The corpse of the Swede, alone in the saloon, had its eyes fixed upon a dreadful legend that dwelt atop of the cash-machine: "This registers the amount of your purchase."

9

MONTHS later, the cowboy was frying pork over the stove of a little ranch near the Dakota line, when there was a quick thud of hoofs outside, and presently the Easterner entered with the letters and the papers.

"Well," said the Easterner at once, "the chap that killed the Swede has got three years. Wasn't much, was it?"

"He has? Three years?" The cowboy poised his pan of pork, while he ruminated upon the news. "Three years. That ain't much."

"No. It was a light sentence," replied the Easterner as he unbuckled his spurs. "Seems there was a good deal of sympathy for him in Romper."

"If the bartender had been any good," observed the cowboy, thoughtfully, "he would have gone in and cracked that there Dutchman on the head with a bottle in the beginnin' of it and stopped all this here murderin'."

"Yes, a thousand things might have happened," said the Easterner, tartly.

The cowboy returned his pan of pork to the fire, but his philosophy continued. "It's funny, ain't it? If he hadn't said Johnnie was cheatin' he'd be alive this minute. He was an awful fool. Game played for fun, too. Not for money. I believe he was crazy."

"I feel sorry for that gambler," said the Easterner.

"Oh, so do I," said the cowboy. "He don't deserve none of it for killin' who he did."

"The Swede might not have been killed if everything had been square."

"Might not have been killed?" exclaimed the cowboy. "Everythin' square? Why, when he said that Johnnie was cheatin' and acted like such a jackass? And then in the saloon he fairly walked up to git hurt?" With these arguments the cowboy browbeat the Easterner and reduced him to rage.

"You're a fool!" cried the Easterner, viciously. "You're a bigger jackass than the Swede by a million majority. Now let me tell you one thing. Let me tell you something. Listen! Johnnie *was* cheating!"

" 'Johnnie,' " said the cowboy, blankly. There was a minute of silence, and then he said, robustly, "Why, no. The game was only for fun."

"Fun or not," said the Easterner, "Johnnie was cheating. I saw him. I know it. I saw him. And I refused to stand up and be a man. I let the Swede fight it out alone. And you—you were simply puffing around the place and wanting to fight. And then old Scully himself! We are all in it! This poor gambler isn't even a noun. He is kind of an adverb. Every sin is the result of a collaboration. We, five of us, have collaborated in the murder of this Swede. Usually there are from a dozen to forty women really involved in every murder, but in this case it seems to be only five men—you, I, Johnnie, old Scully; and that fool of an unfortunate gambler came merely as a culmination, the apex of a human movement, and gets all the punishment."

The cowboy, injured and rebellious, cried out blindly into this fog of mysterious theory: "Well, I didn't do anythin', did I?"

Shirley Jackson

THE LOTTERY

THE morning of June 27th was clear and sunny, with the fresh warmth of a full-summer day; the flowers were blossoming profusely and the grass was richly green. The people of the village began to gather in the square, between the post office and the bank, around ten o'clock; in some towns there were so many people that the lottery took two days and had to be started on June 26th, but in this village, where there were only about three hundred people, the whole lottery took less than two hours, so it could begin at ten o'clock in the morning and still be through in time to allow the villagers to get home for noon dinner.

The children assembled first, of course. School was recently over for the summer, and the feeling of liberty sat uneasily on most of them; they tended to gather together quietly for a while before they broke into boisterous play, and their talk was still of the classroom and the teacher, of books and reprimands. Bobby Martin had already stuffed his pockets full of stones, and the other boys soon followed his example, selecting the smoothest and roundest stones; Bobby and Harry Jones and Dickie Delacroix—the villagers pronounced this name "Dellacroy"—eventually made a great pile of stones in one corner of the square and guarded it against the raids of the other boys. The girls stood aside, talking among themselves, looking over their shoulders at the boys, and the very small children rolled in the dust or clung to the hands of their older brothers or sisters.

Soon the men began to gather, surveying their own children, speaking of planting and rain, tractors and taxes. They stood together, away from the pile of stones in the corner, and their jokes were quiet and they smiled rather than laughed. The women, wearing faded house dresses and sweaters, came shortly after their menfolk. They greeted one another and exchanged bits of gossip as they went to join their husbands. Soon the women, standing by their husbands, began to call to their children, and the children came reluctantly, having to be

---

called four or five times. Bobby Martin ducked under his mother's grasping hand and ran, laughing, back to the pile of stones. His father spoke up sharply, and Bobby came quickly and took his place between his father and his oldest brother.

The lottery was conducted—as were the square dances, the teen-age club, the Halloween program—by Mr. Summers, who had time and energy to devote to civic activities. He was a round-faced, jovial man and he ran the coal business, and people were sorry for him, because he had no children and his wife was a scold. When he arrived in the square, carrying the black wooden box, there was a murmur of conversation among the villagers, and he waved and called, "Little late today, folks." The postmaster, Mr. Graves, followed him, carrying a three-legged stool, and the stool was put in the center of the square and Mr. Summers set the black box down on it. The villagers kept their distance, leaving a space between themselves and the stool, and when Mr. Summers said, "Some of you fellows want to give me a hand?" there was a hesitation before two men, Mr. Martin and his oldest son, Baxter, came forward to hold the box steady on the stool while Mr. Summers stirred up the papers inside it.

The original paraphernalia for the lottery had been lost long ago, and the black box now resting on the stool had been put into use even before Old Man Warner, the oldest man in town, was born. Mr. Summers spoke frequently to the villagers about making a new box, but no one liked to upset even as much tradition as was represented by the black box. There was a story that the present box had been made with some pieces of the box that had preceded it, the one that had been constructed when the first people settled down to make a village here. Every year, after the lottery, Mr. Summers began talking again about a new box, but every year the subject was allowed to fade off without anything's being done. The black box grew shabbier each year; by now it was no longer completely black but splintered badly along one side to show the original wood color, and in some places faded or stained.

Mr. Martin and his oldest son, Baxter, held the black box securely on the stool until Mr. Summers had stirred the papers thoroughly with his hand. Because so much of the ritual had been forgotten or discarded, Mr. Summers had been successful in having slips of paper substituted for the chips of wood that had been used for generations. Chips of wood, Mr. Summers had argued, had been all very well when the village was tiny, but now that the population was more than three hundred and likely to keep on growing, it was necessary to use something that would fit more easily into the black box. The night before the lottery, Mr. Summers and Mr. Graves made up the slips of paper and put them in the box, and it was then taken to the safe of Mr. Summers' coal company and locked up until Mr. Summers was ready to take it to the square next morning. The rest of the year, the box was put away, sometimes one place, sometimes another; it had spent one year in Mr. Graves's barn and another year underfoot in the post office, and sometimes it was set on a shelf in the Martin grocery and left there.

There was a great deal of fussing to be done before Mr. Summers declared the lottery open. There were the lists to make up—of heads of families, heads of households in each family, members of each household in each family. There was the proper swearing-in of Mr. Summers by the postmaster, as the official of the lottery; at one time, some people remembered, there had been a recital of some sort, performed by the official of the lottery, a perfunctory, tuneless chant that had been rattled off duly each year; some people believed that the official of the lottery used to stand just so when he said or sang it, others believed that he was supposed to walk among the people, but years and years ago this part of the ritual had been allowed to lapse. There had been, also, a ritual salute, which the official of the lottery had had to use in addressing each person who came up to draw from the box, but this also had changed with time, until now it was felt necessary only for the official to speak to each person approaching. Mr. Summers was very good at all this; in his clean white shirt and blue jeans, with one hand resting carelessly on the black box, he seemed very proper and important as he talked interminably to Mr. Graves and the Martins.

Just as Mr. Summers finally left off talking and turned to the assembled villagers, Mrs. Hutchinson came hurriedly along the path to the square, her sweater thrown over her shoulders, and slid into place in the back of the crowd. "Clean forgot what day it was," she said to Mrs. Delacroix, who stood next to her, and they both laughed softly. "Thought my old man was out back stacking wood," Mrs. Hutchinson went on, "and then I looked out the window and the kids was gone, and then I remembered it was the twenty-seventh and came a-running." She dried her hands on her apron, and Mrs. Delacroix said, "You're in time, though. They're still talking away up there."

Mrs. Hutchinson craned her neck to see through the crowd and found her husband and children standing near the front. She tapped Mrs. Delacroix on the arm as a farewell and began to make her way through the crowd. The people separated good-humoredly to let her through; two or three people said, in voices just loud enough to be heard across the crowd, "Here comes your Missus, Hutchinson," and "Bill, she made it after all." Mrs. Hutchinson reached her husband, and Mr. Summers, who had been waiting, said cheerfully, "Thought we were going to have to get on without you, Tessie." Mrs. Hutchinson said, grinning, "Wouldn't have me leave m'dishes in the sink, now, would you, Joe?," and soft laughter ran through the crowd as the people stirred back into position after Mrs. Hutchinson's arrival.

"Well, now," Mr. Summers said soberly, "guess we better get started, get this over with, so's we can go back to work. Anybody ain't here?"

"Dunbar," several people said. "Dunbar, Dunbar."

Mr. Summers consulted his list. "Clyde Dunbar," he said. "That's right. He's broke his leg, hasn't he? Who's drawing for him?"

"Me, I guess," a woman said, and Mr. Summers turned to look at her. "Wife draws for her husband," Mr. Summers said. "Don't you have a grown boy to do it for you, Janey?" Although Mr. Summers and everyone else in the village knew the answer perfectly well, it was the business of the official of the lottery to ask such questions formally. Mr. Summers waited with an expression of polite interest while Mrs. Dunbar answered.

"Horace's not but sixteen yet," Mrs. Dunbar said regretfully. "Guess I gotta fill in for the old man this year."

"Right," Mr. Summers said. He made a note on the list he was holding. Then he asked, "Watson boy drawing this year?"

A tall boy in the crowd raised his hand. "Here," he said. "I'm drawing for m'mother and me." He blinked his eyes nervously and ducked his head as several voices in the crowd said things like "Good fellow, Jack," and "Glad to see your mother's got a man to do it."

"Well," Mr. Summers said, "guess that's everyone. Old Man Warner make it?"

"Here," a voice said, and Mr. Summers nodded.

A sudden hush fell on the crowd as Mr. Summers cleared his throat and looked at the list. "All ready?" he called. "Now, I'll read the names—heads of families first—and the men come up and take a paper out of the box. Keep the paper folded in your hand without looking at it until everyone has had a turn. Everything clear?"

The people had done it so many times that they only half listened to the directions; most of them were quiet, wetting their lips, not looking around. Then Mr. Summers raised one hand high and said, "Adams." A man disengaged himself from the crowd and came forward. "Hi, Steve," Mr. Summers said, and Mr. Adams said, "Hi, Joe." They grinned at one another humorlessly and nervously. Then Mr. Adams reached into the black box and took out a folded paper. He held it firmly by one corner as he turned and went hastily back to his place in the crowd, where he stood a little apart from his family, not looking down at his hand.

"Allen," Mr. Summers said. "Anderson. . . . Bentham."

"Seems like there's no time at all between lotteries any more," Mrs.

Delacroix said to Mrs. Graves in the back row. "Seems like we got through with the last one only last week."

"Time sure goes fast," Mrs. Graves said.

"Clark. . . . Delacroix."

"There goes my old man," Mrs. Delacroix said. She held her breath while her husband went forward.

"Dunbar," Mr. Summers said, and Mrs. Dunbar went steadily to the box while one of the women said, "Go on, Janey," and another said, "There she goes."

"We're next," Mrs. Graves said. She watched while Mr. Graves came around from the side of the box, greeted Mr. Summers gravely, and selected a slip of paper from the box. By now, all through the crowd there were men holding the small folded papers in their large hands, turning them over and over nervously. Mrs. Dunbar and her two sons stood together, Mrs. Dunbar holding the slip of paper.

"Harburt. . . . Hutchinson."

"Get up there, Bill," Mrs. Hutchinson said, and the people near her laughed.

"Jones."

"They do say," Mr. Adams said to Old Man Warner, who stood next to him, "that over in the north village they're talking of giving up the lottery."

Old Man Warner snorted. "Pack of crazy fools," he said. "Listening to the young folks, nothing's good enough for *them*. Next thing you know, they'll be wanting to go back to living in caves, nobody work any more, live *that* way for a while. Used to be a saying about 'Lottery in June, corn be heavy soon.' First thing you know, we'd all be eating stewed chickweed and acorns. There's *always* been a lottery," he added petulantly. "Bad enough to see young Joe Summers up there joking with everybody."

"Some places have already quit lotteries," Mrs. Adams said.

"Nothing but trouble in *that*," Old Man Warner said stoutly. "Pack of young fools."

"Martin." And Bobby Martin watched his father go forward. "Overdyke. . . . Percy."

"I wish they'd hurry," Mrs. Dunbar said to her older son. "I wish they'd hurry."

"They're almost through," her son said.

"You get ready to run tell Dad," Mrs. Dunbar said.

Mr. Summers called his own name and then stepped forward precisely and selected a slip from the box. Then he called, "Warner."

"Seventy-seventh year I been in the lottery," Old Man Warner said as he went through the crowd. "Seventy-seventh time."

"Watson." The tall boy came awkwardly through the crowd. Someone said, "Don't be nervous, Jack," and Mr. Summers said, "Take your time, son."

"Zanini."

After that, there was a long pause, a breathless pause, until Mr. Summers, holding his slip of paper in the air, said, "All right, fellows." For a minute, no one moved, and then all the slips of paper were opened. Suddenly, all the women began to speak at once, saying, "Who is it?," "Who's got it?," "Is it the Dunbars?," "Is it the Watsons?" Then the voices began to say, "It's Hutchinson. It's Bill," "Bill Hutchinson's got it."

"Go tell your father," Mrs. Dunbar said to her older son.

People began to look around to see the Hutchinsons. Bill Hutchinson was standing quiet, staring down at the paper in his hand. Suddenly, Tessie Hutchinson shouted to Mr. Summers, "You didn't give him time enough to take any paper he wanted. I saw you. It wasn't fair!"

"Be a good sport, Tessie," Mrs. Delacroix called, and Mrs. Graves said, "All of us took the same chance."

"Shut up, Tessie," Bill Hutchinson said.

"Well, everyone," Mr. Summers said, "that was done pretty fast, and now we've got to be hurrying a little more to get done in time." He consulted his next list. "Bill," he said, "you draw for the Hutchinson family. You got any other households in the Hutchinsons?"

"There's Don and Eva," Mrs. Hutchinson yelled. "Make *them* take their chance!"

"Daughters draw with their husbands' families, Tessie," Mr. Summers said gently. "You know that as well as anyone else."

"It wasn't *fair*," Tessie said.

"I guess not, Joe," Bill Hutchinson said regretfully. "My daughter draws with her husband's family, that's only fair. And I've got no other family except the kids."

"Then, as far as drawing for families is concerned, it's you," Mr. Summers said in explanation, "and as far as drawing for households is concerned, that's you, too. Right?"

"Right," Bill Hutchinson said.

"How many kids, Bill?" Mr. Summers asked formally.

"Three," Bill Hutchinson said. "There's Bill, Jr., and Nancy, and little Dave. And Tessie and me."

"All right, then," Mr. Summers said. "Harry, you got their tickets back?"

Mr. Graves nodded and held up the slips of paper. "Put them in the box, then," Mr. Summers directed. "Take Bill's and put it in."

"I think we ought to start over," Mrs. Hutchinson said, as quietly as she could. "I tell you it wasn't *fair*. You didn't give him time enough to choose. *Every*body saw that."

Mr. Graves had selected the five slips and put them in the box, and he dropped all the papers but those onto the ground, where the breeze caught them and lifted them off.

"Listen, everybody," Mrs. Hutchinson was saying to the people around her.

"Ready, Bill?" Mr. Summers asked, and Bill Hutchinson, with one quick glance around at his wife and children, nodded.

"Remember," Mr. Summers said, "take the slips and keep them folded until each person has taken one. Harry, you help little Dave." Mr. Graves took the hand of the little boy, who came willingly with him up to the box. "Take a paper out of the box, Davy," Mr. Summers said. Davy put his hand into the box and laughed. "Take just *one* paper," Mr. Summers said. "Harry, you hold it for him." Mr. Graves took the child's hand and removed the folded paper from the tight fist and held it while little Dave stood next to him and looked up at him wonderingly.

"Nancy next," Mr. Summers said. Nancy was twelve, and her school friends breathed heavily as she went forward, switching her skirt, and took a slip daintily from the box. "Bill, Jr.," Mr. Summers said, and Billy, his face red and his feet overlarge, nearly knocked the box over as he got a paper out. "Tessie," Mr. Summers said. She hesitated for a minute, looking around defiantly, and then set her lips and went up to the box. She snatched a paper out and held it behind her.

"Bill," Mr. Summers said, and Bill Hutchinson reached into the box and felt around, bringing his hand out at last with the slip of paper in it.

The crowd was quiet. A girl whispered, "I hope it's not Nancy," and the sound of the whisper reached the edges of the crowd.

"It's not the way it used to be," Old Man Warner said clearly. "People ain't the way they used to be."

"All right," Mr. Summers said. "Open the papers. Harry, you open little Dave's."

Mr. Graves opened the slip of paper and there was a general sigh through the crowd as he held it up and everyone could see that it was blank. Nancy and Bill, Jr., opened theirs at the same time, and both beamed and laughed, turning around to the crowd and holding their slips of paper above their heads.

"Tessie," Mr. Summers said. There was a pause, and then Mr. Summers looked at Bill Hutchinson, and Bill unfolded his paper and showed it. It was blank.

"It's Tessie," Mr. Summers said, and his voice was hushed. "Show us her paper, Bill."

Bill Hutchinson went over to his wife and forced the slip of paper out of her hand. It had a black spot on it, the black spot Mr. Summers had made the night before with the heavy pencil in the coal-company office. Bill Hutchinson held it up, and there was a stir in the crowd.

"All right, folks," Mr. Summers said. "Let's finish quickly."

Although the villagers had forgotten the ritual and lost the original black box, they still remembered to use stones. The pile of stones the boys had made earlier was ready; there were stones on the ground with the blowing scraps of paper that had come out of the box. Mrs. Delacroix selected a stone so large she had to pick it up with both hands and turned to Mrs. Dunbar. "Come on," she said. "Hurry up."

Mrs. Dunbar had small stones in both hands, and she said, gasping for breath, "I can't run at all. You'll have to go ahead and I'll catch up with you."

The children had stones already, and someone gave little Davy Hutchinson a few pebbles.

Tessie Hutchinson was in the center of a cleared space by now, and she held her hands out desperately as the villagers moved in on her. "It isn't fair," she said. A stone hit her on the side of the head.

Old Man Warner was saying, "Come on, come on, everyone." Steve Adams was in the front of the crowd of villagers, with Mrs. Graves beside him.

"It isn't fair, it isn't right." Mrs. Hutchinson screamed, and then they were upon her.

ESSAYS

Sir Francis Bacon

OF ADVERSITY

It was an high speech of Seneca (after the manner of the Stoics): *That the good things which belong to prosperity are to be wished; but the good things that belong to adversity are to be admired. Bona rerum secundarum optabilia, adversarum mirabilia.* Certainly, if miracles be the command over nature, they appear most in adversity. It is yet a higher speech of his than the other (much too high for a heathen): *It is true greatness to have in one the frailty of a man, and the security of a god. Vere magnum, habere fragilitatem hominis, securitatem dei.* This would have done better in poesy, where transcendencies are more allowed. And the poets indeed have been busy with it; for it is in effect the thing which is figured in that strange fiction of the ancient poets, which seemeth not to be without mystery; nay, and to have some approach to the state of a Christian: that *Hercules, when he went to unbind Prometheus* (by whom human nature is represented), *sailed the length of the great ocean in an earthen pot or pitcher:* lively describing Christian resolution, that saileth in the frail bark of the flesh through the waves of the world. But to speak in a mean. The virtue of prosperity is temperance; the virtue of adversity is fortitude; which in morals is the more heroical virtue. Prosperity is the blessing of the Old Testament; adversity is the blessing of the New; which carrieth the greater benediction, and the clearer revelation of God's favour. Yet even in the Old Testament, if you listen to David's harp, you shall hear as many hearse-like airs as carols; and the pencil of the Holy Ghost hath laboured more in describing the afflictions of Job than the felicities of Solomon. Prosperity is not without many fears and distastes; and adversity is not without comforts and hopes. We see in the needleworks and embroideries, it is more pleasing to have a lively work upon a sad and solemn ground, than to have a dark and melancholy work upon a lightsome ground: judge therefor of the pleasure of the heart by the pleasure of the eye. Certainly virtue is like precious odours, most fragrant when they are incensed or crushed: for prosperity doth best discover vice; but adversity doth best discover virtue.

Plato

APOLOGY: ON THE DEATH OF SOCRATES

How you, O Athenians, have been affected by my accusers, I cannot tell; but I know that they almost made me forget who I was—so persuasively did they speak; and yet they have hardly uttered a word of truth. But of the many falsehoods told by them, there was one which quite amazed me;—I mean when they said that you should be upon your guard and not allow yourselves to be deceived by the force of my eloquence. To say this, when they were certain to be detected as soon as I opened my lips and proved myself to be anything but a great speaker, did indeed appear to me most shameless—unless by the force of eloquence they mean the force of truth; for if such is their meaning, I admit that I am eloquent. But in how different a way from theirs! Well, as I was saying, they have scarcely spoken the truth at all; but from me you shall hear the whole truth: not, however, delivered after their manner in a set oration duly ornamented with words and phrases. No, by heaven! but I shall use the words and arguments which occur to me at the moment; for I am confident in the justice of my cause:[1] at my time of life I ought not to be appearing before you, O men of Athens, in the character of a juvenile orator—let no one expect it of me. And I must beg of you to grant me a favour:—if I defend myself in my accustomed manner, and you hear me using the words which I have been in the habit of using in the agora, at the tables of the money-changers, or anywhere else, I would ask you not to be surprised, and not to interrupt me on this account. For I am more than seventy years of age, and appearing now for the first time in a court of law, I am quite a stranger to the language of the place; and therefore I would have you regard me as if I were really a stranger, whom you would excuse if he spoke in his native tongue, and after the fashion of his country:—Am I making an unfair request of you? Never mind the manner, which may or may not be good; but think only of the truth of my words, and give heed to that: let the speaker speak truly and the judge decide justly. . . .

And first, I have to reply to the older charges and to my first accusers, and then I will go on to the later ones. For of old I have had many accusers, who have accused me falsely to you during many years; and I am more afraid of them than of Anytus and his associates,

1 Or, I am certain that I am right in taking this course.

who are dangerous, too, in their own way. But far more dangerous are the others, who began when you were children, and took possession of your minds with their falsehoods, telling of one Socrates, a wise man, who speculated about the heaven above, and searched into the earth beneath, and made the worse appear the better cause. The disseminators of this tale are the accusers whom I dread; for their hearers are apt to fancy that such enquirers do not believe in the existence of the gods. And they are many, and their charges against me are of ancient date, and they were made by them in the days when you were more impressible than you are now—in childhood, or it may have been in youth—and the cause when heard went by default, for there was none to answer. And hardest of all, I do not know and cannot tell the names of my accusers; unless in the chance case of a comic poet. All who from envy and malice have persuaded you—some of them having first convinced themselves—all this class of men are most difficult to deal with; for I cannot have them up here, and cross-examine them, and therefore I must simply fight with shadows in my own defence, and argue when there is no one who answers. I will ask you then to assume with me, as I was saying, that my opponents are of two kinds; one recent, the other ancient: and I hope that you will see the propriety of my answering the latter first, for these accusations you heard long before the others, and much oftener.

Well, then, I must make my defence, and endeavour to clear away in a short time, a slander which has lasted a long time. May I succeed, if to succeed be for my good and yours, or likely to avail me in my cause! The task is not an easy one; I quite understand the nature of it. And so leaving the event with God, in obedience to the law I will now make my defence.

I will begin at the beginning, and ask what is the accusation which has given rise to the slander of me, and in fact has encouraged Meletus to prefer this charge against me. Well, what do the slanderers say? They shall be my prosecutors, and I will sum up their words in an affidavit: "Socrates is an evildoer, and a curious person, who searches into things under the earth and in heaven, and he makes the worse appear the better cause; and he teaches the aforesaid doctrines to others." Such is the nature of the accusation: it is just what you have yourselves seen in the comedy of Aristophanes, who has introduced a man whom he calls Socrates, going about and saying that he walks in air, and talking a deal of nonsense concerning matters of which I do not pretend to know either much or little—not that I mean to speak disparagingly of any one who is a student of natural philosophy. I should be very sorry if Meletus could bring so grave a charge against me. But the simple truth is, O Athenians, that I have nothing to do with physical speculations. Very many of those here present are witnesses to the truth of this, and to them I appeal. Speak then, you who have heard me, and tell your neighbours whether any of you have ever known me hold forth in few words or in many upon such matters. . . . You hear their answer. And from what they say of this part of the charge you will be able to judge of the truth of the rest.

As little foundation is there for the report that I am a teacher, and take money; this accusation has no more truth in it than the other. Although, if a man were really able to instruct mankind, to receive money for giving instruction would, in my opinion, be an honour to him. There is Gorgias of Leontium, and Prodicus of Ceos, and Hippias of Elis, who go the round of the cities, and are able to persuade the young men to leave their own citizens by whom they might be taught for nothing, and come to them whom they not only pay, but are thankful if they may be allowed to pay them. There is at this time a Parian philosopher residing in Athens, of whom I have heard; and I came to hear of him in this way:—I came across a man who has spent a world of money on the Sophists, Callias, the son of Hipponicus, and knowing that he had sons, I asked him: "Callias," I said, "if your two sons were foals or calves, there would be no difficulty in finding some one to put over them; we should hire a trainer of horses, or a farmer, probably, who would improve and perfect them in their own proper virtue and excellence; but as they are human beings, whom are you thinking of placing over them? Is there any one who understands human and political virtue? You must have thought about the matter, for you have sons; is there any one?" "There is," he said. "Who is he?" said I; "and of what country? and what does he charge?" "Evenus the Parian," he replied; "he is the man, and his charge is five minae." Happy is Evenus, I said to myself, if he really has this wisdom, and teaches at such a moderate charge. Had I the same, I should have been very proud and conceited; but the truth is that I have no knowledge of the kind.

I dare say, Athenians, that some one among you will reply, "Yes, Socrates, but what is the origin of these accusations which are brought against you; there must have been something strange which you have been doing? All these rumours and this talk about you would never have arisen if you had been like other men: tell us, then, what is the cause of them, for we should be sorry to judge hastily of you." Now, I regard this as a fair challenge, and I will endeavour to explain to you the reason why I am called wise and have such an evil fame. Please to attend then. And although some of you may think that I am joking, I declare that I will tell you the entire truth. Men of Athens, this reputation of mine has come of a certain sort of wisdom which I possess. If you ask me what kind of wisdom, I reply, wisdom such as may perhaps be attained by man, for to that extent I am inclined to believe that I am wise; whereas the persons of whom I was speaking have a superhuman wisdom, which I may fail to describe, because I have it not myself; and he who says that I have, speaks falsely, and is taking away my character. And here, O men of Athens, I must beg you not to interrupt me, even if I seem to say something extravagant. For the word which I will speak is not mine. I will refer you to a witness who is worthy of credit; that witness shall be the god of Delphi—he will tell you about my wisdom, if I have any, and of what sort it is. You must have known Chaerephon; he was early a friend of mine, and also a friend of yours, for he shared in the recent exile of the people, and returned with you. Well, Chaerephon, as you know, was very impetuous in all his doings, and he went to Delphi and boldly asked the oracle to tell him whether—as I was saying, I must beg you not to interrupt—he asked the oracle to tell him whether any one was wiser than I was, and the Pythian prophetess answered, that there was no man wiser. Chaerephon is dead himself; but his brother, who is in court, will confirm the truth of what I am saying.

Why do I mention this? Because I am going to explain to you why I have such an evil name. When I heard the answer, I said to myself, What can the god mean? and what is the interpretation of his riddle? for I know that I have no wisdom, small or great. What then can he mean when he says that I am the wisest of men? And yet he is a god, and cannot lie; that would be against his nature. After long consideration, I thought of a method of trying the question. I reflected that if I could only find a man wiser than myself, then I might go to the god with a refutation in my hand. I should say to him, "Here is a man who is wiser than I am; but you said that I was the wisest." Accordingly I went to one who had the reputation of wisdom, and observed him—his name I need not mention; he was a politician whom I selected for examination—and the result was as follows: When I began to talk with him, I could not help thinking that he was not really wise, although he was thought wise by many, and still wiser by himself; and thereupon I tried to explain to him that he thought himself wise, but was not really wise; and the consequence was that he hated me, and his enmity was shared by several who were present and heard me. So I left him, saying to myself, as I went away: Well, although I do not suppose that either of us knows anything really beautiful and good, I am better off than he is,—for he knows nothing, and thinks that he knows; I neither know nor think that I know. In this latter particular, then, I seem to have slightly the advantage of him. Then I went to another who had still higher pretensions to wisdom, and my conclusion was exactly the same. Whereupon I made another enemy of him, and of many others besides him.

Then I went to one man after another, being not unconscious of the enmity which I provoked, and I lamented and feared this: but necessity was laid upon me,—the word of God, I thought, ought to be considered first. And I said to myself, Go I must to all who appear to know, and find out the meaning of the oracle. And I swear to you, Athenians, by the dog I swear!—for I must tell you the truth—the result of my mission was just this: I found that the men most in repute were all but the most foolish; and that others less esteemed were really wiser and better. I will tell you the tale of my wanderings and of the "Herculean" labours, as I may call them, which I endured only to find at last the oracle irrefutable. After the politicians, I went to the poets; tragic, dithyrambic, and all sorts. And there, I said to myself, you will be instantly detected; now you will find out that you are more ignorant than they are. Accordingly I took them some of the most elaborate passages in their own writings, and asked what was the meaning of them—thinking that they would teach me something. Will you believe me? I am almost ashamed to confess the truth, but I must say that there is hardly a person present who would not have talked better about their poetry than they did themselves. Then I knew that not by wisdom do poets write poetry, but by a sort of genius and inspiration; they are like diviners or soothsayers who also say many fine things, but do not understand the meaning of them. The poets appeared to me to be much in the same case; and I further observed that upon the strength of their poetry they believed themselves to be the wisest of men in other things in which they were not wise. So I departed, conceiving myself to be superior to them for the same reason that I was superior to the politicians.

At last I went to the artisans. I was conscious that I knew nothing at all, as I may say, and I was sure that they knew many fine things; and here I was not mistaken, for they did know many things of which I was ignorant, and in this they certainly were wiser than I was. But I observed that even the good artisans fell into the same error as the poets;—because they were good workmen they thought that they also knew all sorts of high matters, and this defect in them overshadowed their wisdom; and therefore I asked myself on behalf of the oracle, whether I would like to be as I was, neither having their knowledge nor their ignorance, or like them in both; and I made answer to myself and to the oracle that I was better off as I was.

This inquisition has led to my having many enemies of the worst and most dangerous kind, and has given occasion also to many calumnies. And I am called wise, for my hearers always imagine that I myself possess the wisdom which I find wanting in others: but the truth is, O men of Athens, that God only is wise; and by his answer he intends to show that the wisdom of men is worth little or nothing; he is not speaking of Socrates, he is only using my name by way of illustration, as if he said, He, O men, is the wisest, who, like Socrates, knows that his wisdom is in truth worth nothing. And so I go about the world obedient to the god, and search and make enquiry into the wisdom of any one, whether citizen or stranger, who appears to be wise; and if he is not wise, then in vindication of the oracle I show him that he is not wise; and my occupation quite absorbs me, and I have no time to give either to any public matter of interest or to any concern of my own, but I am in utter poverty by reason of my devotion to the god. . . .

Some one will say: And are you not ashamed, Socrates, of a course of life which is likely to bring you to an untimely end? To him I may fairly answer: There you are mistaken: a man who is good for anything ought not to calculate the chance of living or dying; he ought only to consider whether in doing anything he is doing right or wrong—acting the part of a good man or of a bad. Whereas, upon your view, the heroes who fell at Troy were not good for much, and the son of Thetis above all, who altogether despised danger in comparison with disgrace; and when he was so eager to slay Hector, his goddess mother said to him, that if he avenged his companion Patroclus, and slew Hector, he would die himself—"Fate," she said, in these or the like words, "waits for you next after Hector"; he, receiving this warning, utterly despised danger and death, and instead of fearing them, feared rather to live in dishonour, and not to avenge his friend. "Let me die forthwith," he replies, "and be avenged of my enemy, rather than abide here by the beaked ships, a laughing stock and a burden of the earth." Had Achilles any thought of death and danger? For wherever a man's place is, whether the place which he has chosen or that in which he has been placed by a commander, there he ought to remain in the hour of danger; he should not think of death or of anything but of disgrace. And this, O men of Athens, is a true saying.

Strange, indeed, would be my conduct, O men of Athens, if I, who, when I was ordered by the generals whom you chose to command me at Potidaea and Amphipolis and Delium, remained where they placed me, like any other man, facing death—if now, when, as I conceive and imagine, God orders me to fulfil the philosopher's mission of searching into myself and other men, I were to desert my post through fear of death, or any other fear; that would indeed be strange, and I might justly be arraigned in court for denying the existence of the gods, if I disobeyed the oracle because I was afraid of death, fancying that I was wise when I was not wise. For the fear of death is indeed the pretence of wisdom, and not real wisdom, being a pretence of knowing the unknown; and no one knows whether death, which men in their fear apprehend to be the greatest evil, may not be the greatest good. Is not this ignorance of a disgraceful sort, the ignorance which is the conceit that a man knows what he does not know? And in this respect only I believe myself to differ from men in general, and may perhaps claim to be wiser than they are:—that whereas I know but little of the world below, I do not suppose that I know: but I do know that injustice and disobedience to a better, whether God or man, is evil and dishonourable, and I will never fear or avoid a possible good rather than a certain evil. And therefore if you let me go now, and are not convinced by Anytus, who said that since I had been prosecuted I must be put to death (or if not that I ought never to have been prosecuted at all); and that if I escape now, your sons will all be utterly ruined by listening to my words—if you say to me, Socrates, this time we will not mind Anytus, and you shall be let off, but upon one condition, that you are not to enquire and speculate in this way any more, and that if you are caught doing so again you shall die;—if this was the condition on which you let me go, I should reply: Men of Athens, I honour and love you; but I shall obey God rather than you, and while I have life and strength I shall never cease from the practice and teaching of philosophy, exhorting any one whom I meet and saying to him after my manner: You, my friend,—a citizen of the great and mighty and wise city of Athens,—are you not ashamed of heaping up the greatest amount of money and honour and reputation, and caring so little about wisdom and truth and the greatest improvement of the soul, which you never regard or heed at all? And if the person with whom I am arguing, says: Yes, but I do care; then I do not leave him or let him go at once; but I proceed to interrogate and examine and cross-examine him, and if I think that he has no virtue in him, but only says that he has, I reproach him with undervaluing the greater, and overvaluing the less. And I shall repeat the same words to every one whom I meet, young and old, citizen and alien, but especially to the citizens, inasmuch as they are my brethren. For know that this is the command of God; and I believe that no greater good has ever happened in the State than my service to the God. For I do nothing but go about persuading you all, old and young alike, not to take thought for your persons or your properties, but first and chiefly to care about the greatest improvement of the soul. I tell you that virtue is not given by money, but that from virtue comes money and every other good of man, public as well as private. This is my teaching, and if this is the doctrine which corrupts the youth, I am a mischievous person. But if any one says that this is not my teaching, he is speaking an untruth. Wherefore, O men of Athens, I say to you, do as Anytus bids or not as Anytus bids, and either acquit me or not; but whichever you do, understand that I shall never alter my ways, not even if I have to die many times. . . .

There are many reasons why I am not grieved, O men of Athens, at the vote of condemnation. I expected it, and am only surprised that the votes are so nearly equal; for I had thought that the majority against me would have been far larger; but now, had thirty votes gone over to the other side, I should have been acquitted. And I may say, I think, that I have escaped Meletus. I may say more; for without the assistance of Anytus and Lycon, any one may see that he would not have had a fifth part of the votes, as the law requires, in which case he would have incurred a fine of a thousand drachmae.

And so he proposes death as the penalty. And what shall I propose on my part, O men of Athens? Clearly that which is my due. And what is my due? What returns shall be made to the man who has never had the wit to be idle during his whole life; but has been careless of what the many care for—wealth, and family interests, and military offices, and speaking in the assembly, and magistracies, and plots, and parties. Reflecting that I was really too honest a man to be a politician and live, I did not go where I could do no good to you or to myself; but where I could do the greatest good privately to every one of you, thither I went, and sought to persuade every man among you that he must look to himself, and seek virtue and wisdom before he looks to his private interests, and look to the State before he looks to the interests of the State; and that this should be the order which he observes in all his actions. What shall be done to such an one? Doubtless some good thing, O men of Athens, if he has his reward; and the good should be of a kind suitable to him. What would be a reward suitable to a poor man who is your benefactor, and who desires leisure that he may instruct you? There can be no reward so fitting as maintenance in the Prytaneum, O men of Athens, a reward which he deserves far more than the citizen who has won the prize at Olympia in the horse or chariot race, whether the chariots were drawn by two horses or by many. For I am in want, and he has enough; and he only gives you the appearance of happiness, and I give you the reality. And if I am to estimate the penalty fairly, I should say that maintenance in the Prytaneum is the just return.

Perhaps you think that I am braving you in what I am saying now, as in what I said before about the tears and prayers. But this is not so. I speak rather because I am convinced that I never intentionally wronged any one, although I cannot convince you—the time has been too short; if there were a law at Athens, as there is in other cities, that a capital cause should not be decided in one day, then I believe that I should have convinced you. But I cannot in a moment refute great slanders; and, as I am convinced that I never wronged another, I will assuredly not wrong myself. I will not say of myself that I deserve any evil, or propose any penalty. Why should I? Because I am afraid of the penalty of death which Meletus proposes? When I do not know whether death is a good or an evil, why should I propose a penalty which would certainly be an evil? Shall I say imprisonment? And why should I live in prison, and be the slave of the magistrate of the year—of the Eleven? Or shall the penalty be a fine, and imprisonment until the fine is paid? There is the same objection. I should have to lie in prison, for money I have none, and cannot pay. And if I say exile (and this may possibly be the penalty which you will affix), I must indeed be blinded by the love of life if I am so irrational as to expect that when you, who are my own citizens, cannot endure my discourses and words, and have found them so grievous and odious that you will have no more of them, others are likely to endure me. No, indeed, men of Athens, that is not very likely. And what a life should I lead, at my age, wandering from city to city, ever changing my place of exile, and always being driven out! For I am quite sure that wherever I go, there, as here, the young men will flock to me; and if I drive them away, their elders will drive me out at their request; and if I let them come, their fathers and friends will drive me out for their sakes.

Some one will say: Yes, Socrates, but cannot you hold your tongue, and then you may go into a foreign city, and no one will interfere with you? Now, I have great difficulty in making you understand my answer to this. For if I tell you that to do as you say would be a disobedience to the God, and therefore that I cannot hold my tongue, you will not believe that I am serious; and if I say again that daily to discourse about virtue, and of those other things about which you hear me examining myself and others, is the greatest good of man, and that the unexamined life is not worth living, you are still less likely to believe me. Yet I say what is true, although a thing of which it is hard for me to persuade you. Also, I have never been accustomed to think that I deserve to suffer any harm. Had I money I might have estimated the offence at what I was able to pay, and not have been much the worse. But I have none, and therefore I must ask you to proportion the fine to my means. Well, perhaps I could afford a mina, and therefore I propose that penalty: Plato, Crito, Critobulus, and Apollodorus, my friends here, bid me say thirty minae, and they will be the sureties. Let thirty minae be the penalty; for which sum they will be ample security to you.

[The jury voted the death penalty.]

Not much time will be gained, O Athenians, in return for the evil name which you will get from the detractors of the city, who will say that you killed Socrates, a wise man; for they will call me wise, even although I am not wise, when they want to reproach you. If you had waited a little while, your desire would have been fulfilled in the course of nature. For I am far advanced in years, as you may perceive, and not far from death. I am speaking now not to all of you, but only to those who have condemned me to death. And I have another thing to say to them: You think that I was convicted because I had no words of the sort which would have procured my acquittal—I mean, if I had thought fit to leave nothing undone or unsaid. Not so; the deficiency which led to my conviction was not of words—certainly not. But I had not the boldness or impudence or inclination to address you as you would have liked me to do, weeping and wailing and lamenting, and saying and doing many things which you have been accustomed to hear from others, and which, as I maintain, are unworthy of me. I thought at the time that I ought not to do anything common or mean when in danger: nor do I now repent of the style of my defence; I would rather die having spoken after my manner, than speak in your manner and live. For neither in war nor yet at law ought I or any man to use every way of escaping death. Often in battle there can be no doubt that if a man will throw away his arms, and fall on his knees before his pursuers, he may escape death; and in other dangers there are other ways of escaping death, if a man is willing to say and do anything. The difficulty, my friends, is not to avoid death, but to avoid unrighteousness; for that runs faster than death. I am old and move slowly, and the slower runner has overtaken me, and my accusers are keen and quick, and the faster runner, who is unrighteousness, has overtaken them. And now I depart hence condemned by you to suffer the penalty of death,—they too go their ways condemned by the truth to suffer the penalty of villainy and wrong; and I must abide by my award—let them abide by theirs. I suppose that these things may be regarded as fated,—and I think that they are well.

And now, O men who have condemned me, I would fain prophesy to you; for I am about to die, and in the hour of death men are gifted with prophetic power. And I prophesy to you who are my murderers, that immediately after my departure punishment far heavier than you have inflicted on me will surely await you. Me you have killed because you wanted to escape the accuser, and not to give an account of your lives. But that will not be as you suppose: far otherwise. For I say that there will be more accusers of you than there are now; accusers whom hitherto I have restrained: and as they are younger they will be more inconsiderate with you, and you will be more offended at them. If you think that by killing men you can prevent someone from censuring your evil lives, you are mistaken; that is not a way of escape which is either possible or honourable; the easiest and the noblest way is not to be disabling others, but to be improving yourselves. This is the prophecy which I utter before my departure to the judges who have condemned me.

Friends, who would have acquitted me, I would like also to talk with you about the thing which has come to pass, while the magistrates are busy, and before I go to the place at which I must die. Stay then a little, for we may as well talk with one another while there is time. You are my friends, and I should like to show you the meaning of this event which has happened to me. O my judges—for you I may truly call judges—I should like to tell you of a wonderful circumstance. Hitherto the divine faculty of which the internal oracle is the source has constantly been in the habit of opposing me even about trifles, if I was going to make a slip or error in any matter; and now as you see there has come upon me that which may be thought, and is generally believed to be, the last and worst evil. But the oracle made no sign of opposition, either when I was leaving my house in the morning, or when I was on my way to the court, or while I was speaking, at anything which I was going to say; and yet I have often been stopped in the middle of a speech, but now in nothing I either said or did touching the matter in hand has the oracle opposed me. What do I take to be the explanation of this silence? I will tell you. It is an intimation that what has happened to me is a good, and that those of us who think that death is an evil are in error. For the customary sign would surely have opposed me had I been going to evil and not to good.

Let us reflect in another way, and we shall see that there is great reason to hope that death is a good; for one of two things—either death is a state of nothingness and utter unconsciousness, or, as men say, there is a change and migration of the soul from this world to another. Now if you suppose that there is no consciousness, but a sleep like the sleep of him who is undisturbed even by dreams, death will be an unspeakable gain. For if a person were to select the night in which his sleep was undisturbed even by dreams, and were to compare with this the other days and nights of his life, and then were to tell us how many days and nights he had passed in the course of his life better and more pleasantly than this one, I think that any man, I will not say a private man, but even the great king will not find many such days or nights, when compared with the others. Now if death be of such a nature, I say that to die is gain; for eternity is then only a single night. But if death is the journey to another place, and there, as men say, all the dead abide, what good, O my friends and judges, can be greater than this? If indeed when the pilgrim arrives in the world below, he is delivered from the professors of justice in this world, and finds the true judges who are said to give judgment there, Minos and Rhadamanthus and Aeacus and Triptolemus, and other sons of God who were righteous in their own life, that pilgrimage will be worth making. What would not a man give if he might converse with Orpheus and Musaeus and Hesiod and Homer? Nay, if this be true, let me die again and again. I myself, too, shall have a wonderful interest in there meeting and conversing with Palamedes, and Ajax the son of Telamon, and any other ancient hero who has suffered death through an unjust judgment; and there will be no small pleasure, as I think, in comparing my own sufferings with theirs. Above all, I shall then be able to continue my search into true and false knowledge; as in this world, so also in the next; and I shall find out who is wise, and who pretends to be wise, and is not. What would not a man give, O judges, to be able to examine the leader of the great Trojan expedition; or Odysseus or Sisyphus, or numberless others, men and women too! What infinite delight would there be in conversing with them and asking them questions! In another world they do not put a man to death for asking questions: assuredly not. For besides being happier than we are, they will be immortal, if what is said is true.

Wherefore, O judges, be of good cheer about death, and know of a certainty, that no evil can happen to a good man, either in life or after death. He and his are not neglected by the gods; nor has my own approaching end happened by mere chance. But I see clearly that the time had arrived when it was better for me to die and be released from trouble; wherefore the oracle gave no sign. For which reason, also, I am not angry with my condemners, or with my accusers; they have done me no harm, although they did not mean to do me any good; and for this I may gently blame them.

Still I have a favor to ask of them. When my sons are grown up, I would ask you, O my friends, to punish them; and I would have you trouble them, as I have troubled you, if they seem to care about riches, or anything, more than about virtue; or if they pretend to be something when they are really nothing,—then reprove them, as I have reproved you, for not caring about that for which they ought to care, and thinking they are something when they are really nothing. And if you do this, both I and my sons will have received justice at your hands.

The hour of departure has arrived, and we go our ways—I to die, and you to live. Which is better God only knows.

POETRY

Anonymous

EDWARD

"Why dois your brand[1] sae drap wi bluid,
Edward, Edward,
Why dois your brand sae drap wi bluid,
And why sae sad gang yee O?"
"O I hae killed my hauke sae guid,
Mither, mither,
O I hae killed my hauke sae guid,
And I had nae mair bot hee O."

"Your haukis bluid was nevir sae reid,
Edward, Edward,
Your haukis bluid was nevir sae reid,
My deir son I tell thee O."
"O I hae killed my reid-roan steid,
Mither, mither,
O I hae killed my reid-roan steid,
That erst was sae fair and frie O."

"Your steid was auld, and ye hae gat mair,
Edward, Edward,
"Your steid was auld, and ye hae gat mair,
Sum other dule ye drie[2] O."
"O I hae killed my fadir deir,
Mither, mither,
O I hae killed my fadir deir,
Alas, and wae is mee O!"

"And whatten penance wul ye drie for that,
Edward, Edward?
And whatten penance wul ye drie for that?
My deir son, now tell me O."
"Ile set my feit in yonder boat,
Mither, mither,
Ile set my feit in yonder boat,
And Ile fare ovir the sea O."

1 Sword. 2 Sorrow you suffer.

"And what wul ye doe wi your towirs and your ha,
Edward, Edward?
And what wul ye doe wi your towirs and your ha,
That were sae fair to see O?"
"Ile let thame stand tul they doun fa,
Mither, mither,
Ile let thame stand tul they doun fa,
For here nevir mair maun I bee O."

"And what wul ye leive to your bairns and your wife,
Edward, Edward?
And what wul ye leive to your bairns and your wife,
Whan ye gang ovir the sea O?"
"The warldis room, late them beg thrae life,
Mither, mither,
The warldis room, late them beg thrae life,
For thame nevir mair wul I see O."

"And what wul ye leive to your ain mither deir,
Edward, Edward?
And what wul ye leive to your ain mither deir?
My deir son, now tell me O."
"The curse of hell frae me sall ye beir,
Mither, mither,
The curse of hell frae me sall ye beir,
Sic counseils ye gave to me O."

William Shakespeare

SONNET 66

TIRED with all these, for restful death I cry,
As to behold desert a beggar born,
And needy nothing trimmed in jollity,
And purest faith unhappily forsworn,
And gilded honour shamefully misplaced,
And maiden virtue rudely strumpeted,
And right perfection wrongfully disgraced,
And strength by limping sway disablèd,
And art made tongue-tied by authority,
And folly—doctor-like—controlling skill,
And simple truth miscalled simplicity,
And captive good attending captain ill:
Tired with all these, from these would I be gone,
Save that, to die, I leave my love alone.

William Shakespeare

SONNET 73

That time of year thou mayst in me behold
When yellow leaves, or none, or few, do hang
Upon those boughs which shake against the cold,
Bare ruined choirs, where late the sweet birds sang.
In me thou see'st the twilight of such day
As after sunset fadeth in the west,
Which by and by black night doth take away,
Death's second self that seals up all in rest.
In me thou see'st the glowing of such fire,
That on the ashes of his youth doth lie,
As the death-bed whereon it must expire
Consumed with that which it was nourished by.
 This thou perceiv'st, which makes thy love more strong
 To love that well, which thou must leave ere long.

William Shakespeare

SONNET 146

Poor soul, the centre of my sinful earth,
Thrall to these rebel powers that thee array,
Why dost thou pine within and suffer dearth,
Painting thy outward walls so costly gay?
Why so large cost, having so short a lease,
Dost thou upon thy fading mansion spend?
Shall worms, inheritors of this excess,
Eat up thy charge? Is this thy body's end?
Then, soul, live thou upon thy servant's loss,
And let that pine to aggravate thy store;
Buy terms divine in selling hours of dross;
Within be fed, without be rich no more:
 So shalt thou feed on Death, that feeds on men,
 And Death once dead, there's no more dying then.

William Blake

ON ANOTHER'S SORROW

Can I see another's woe,
And not be in sorrow too?
Can I see another's grief,
And not seek for kind relief?

Can I see a falling star,
And not feel my sorrow's share?
Can a father see his child
Weep, nor be with sorrow filled?

Can a mother sit and hear
An infant groan, an infant fear?
No, no! never can it be!
Never, never can it be!

And can he who smiles on all
Hear the wren with sorrows small,
Hear the small bird's grief and care,
Hear the woes that infants bear,

And not sit beside the nest,
Pouring pity in their breast;
And not sit the cradle near,
Weeping tear on infant's tear;

And not sit both night and day,
Wiping all our tears away?
O! no never can it be!
Never, never can it be!

He doth give his joy to all;
He becomes an infant small;
He becomes a man of woe;
He doth feel the sorrow too.

Think not thou canst sigh a sigh
And thy maker is not by;
Think not thou canst weep a tear
And thy maker is not near.

O! he gives to us his joy
That our grief he may destroy;
Till our grief is fled and gone
He doth sit by us and moan.

Robert Burns

OPEN THE DOOR TO ME, OH!

OH, OPEN the door, some pity to shew,
Oh, open the door to me, oh!
Tho' thou has been false, I'll ever prove true,
Oh, open the door to me, oh!

Cauld is the blast upon my pale cheek,
But caulder thy love for me, oh!
The frost that freezes the life at my heart,
Is nought to my pains fra thee, oh!

The wan moon is setting behind the white wave,
And time is setting with me, oh!
False friends, false love, farewell! for mair
I'll ne'er trouble them, nor thee, oh!

She has open'd the door, she has open'd it wide;
She sees his pale corse on the plain, oh!
My true love! she cried, and sank down by his side,
Never to rise again, oh!

Percy Bysshe Shelley

ADONAIS: AN ELEGY ON THE DEATH OF JOHN KEATS, AUTHOR OF ENDYMION, HYPERION, ETC.

'Αστὴρ πρὶν μὲν ἔλαμπες ἐνὶ ζωοῖσιν Ἑῷος.
νῦν δὲ θανὼν λάμπεις Ἕσπερος ἐν φθιμένοις.[1]
—PLATO

PREFACE

Φάρμακον ἦλθε, Βίων, ποτὶ σὸν στόμα, φάρμκον εἶδες.
πῶς τευ τοῖς χείλεσσι ποτέδραμε, κοὐκ ἐγλυκάνθη;
τις δὲ βροτὸς τοσσοῦτον ἀνάμερος, ἢ κεράσαι τοι,
ἢ δοῦναι λαλέοντι τὸ φάρμακον; ἔκφυγεν ᾠδάν.[2]
—MOSCHUS, EPITAPH. BION

IT IS my intention to subjoin to the London edition of this poem a criticism upon the claims of its lamented object to be classed among the writers of the highest genius who have adorned our age. My known repugnance to the narrow principles of taste on which several of his earlier compositions were modelled prove at least that I am an impartial judge. I consider the fragment of *Hyperion* as second to nothing that was ever produced by a writer of the same years.

John Keats died at Rome of a consumption, in his twenty-fourth

1 Thou wert the morning star among the living,
Ere thy fair light had fled:
Now, having died, thou art as Hesperus, giving
New splendor to the dead.—SHELLEY "To Stella."

2 Poison came, Bion, to thy mouth; poison thou didst know.
To such lips as thine it came, and it came unsweetened.
What mortal could be so cruel to mix poison for thee?
Who that had heard thee sing could give thee venom?
Only he who had no music in his soul.—EDITOR

year, on the —— of —— 1821; and was buried in the romantic and lonely cemetery of the Protestants in that city, under the pyramid which is the tomb of Cestius, and the massy walls and towers, now mouldering and desolate, which formed the circuit of ancient Rome. The cemetery is an open space among the ruins, covered in winter with violets and daisies. It might make one in love with death, to think that one should be buried in so sweet a place.

The genius of the lamented person to whose memory I have dedicated these unworthy verses was not less delicate and fragile than it was beautiful; and where cankerworms abound, what wonder if its young flower was blighted in the bud? The savage criticism on his *Endymion*, which appeared in the *Quarterly Review*, produced the most violent effect on his susceptible mind; the agitation thus originated ended in the rupture of a blood-vessel in the lungs; a rapid consumption ensued, and the succeeding acknowledgements from more candid critics of the true greatness of his powers were ineffectual to heal the wound thus wantonly inflicted.

It may be well said that these wretched men know not what they do. They scatter their insults and their slanders without heed as to whether the poisoned shaft lights on a heart made callous by many blows or one like Keats's composed of more penetrable stuff. One of their associates is, to my knowledge, a most base and unprincipled calumniator. As to *Endymion*, was it a poem, whatever might be its defects, to be treated contemptuously by those who had celebrated, with various degrees of complacency and panegyric, *Paris*, and *Woman*, and a *Syrian Tale*, and Mrs. Lefanu, and Mr. Barrett, and Mr. Howard Payne, and a long list of the illustrious obscure? Are these the men who in their venal good nature presumed to draw a parallel between the Rev. Mr. Milman and Lord Byron? What gnat did they strain at here, after having swallowed all those camels? Against what woman taken in adultery dares the foremost of these literary prostitutes to cast his opprobrious stone? Miserable man! you, one of the meanest, have wantonly defaced one of the noblest specimens of the workmanship of God. Nor shall it be your excuse, that, murderer as you are, you have spoken daggers, but used none.

The circumstances of the closing scene of poor Keats's life were not made known to me until the *Elegy* was ready for the press. I am given to understand that the wound which his sensitive spirit had received from the criticism of *Endymion* was exasperated by the bitter sense of unrequited benefits; the poor fellow seems to have been hooted from the stage of life, no less by those on whom he had wasted the promise of his genius, than those on whom he had lavished his fortune and his care. He was accompanied to Rome, and attended in his last illness by Mr. Severn, a young artist of the highest promise, who, I have been informed, "almost risked his own life, and sacrificed every prospect to unwearied attendance upon his dying friend." Had I known these circumstances before the completion of my poem, I should have been tempted to add my feeble tribute of applause to the more solid recompense which the virtuous man finds in the recollection of his own motives. Mr. Severn can dispense with a reward from "such stuff as dreams are made of." His conduct is a golden augury of the success of his future career—may the unextinguished Spirit of his illustrious friend animate the creations of his pencil, and plead against Oblivion for his name!

1

I weep for Adonais—he is dead!
O, weep for Adonais—though our tears
Thaw not the frost which binds so dear a head!
And thou, sad Hour, selected from all years
To mourn our loss, rouse thy obscure compeers,
And teach them thine own sorrow, say: "With me
Died Adonais; till the Future dares
Forget the Past, his fate and fame shall be
An echo and a light unto eternity!"

2

Where wert thou, mighty Mother, when he lay,
When thy Son lay, pierced by the shaft which flies
In darkness? where was lorn Urania
When Adonais died? With veilèd eyes,
'Mid listening Echoes, in her Paradise
She sate, while one, with soft enamoured breath,
Rekindled all the fading melodies,
With which, like flowers that mock the corse beneath,
He had adorned and hid the coming bulk of Death.

3

Oh, weep for Adonais—he is dead!
Wake, melancholy Mother, wake and weep!
Yet wherefore? Quench within their burning bed
Thy fiery tears, and let thy loud heart keep
Like his, a mute and uncomplaining sleep;
For he is gone, where all things wise and fair
Descend—oh, dream not that the amorous Deep
Will yet restore him to the vital air;
Death feeds on his mute voice, and laughs at our despair.

4

Most musical of mourners, weep again!
Lament anew, Urania!—He died,

Who was the Sire of an immortal strain,
Blind, old, and lonely, when his country's pride,
The priest, the slave, and the liberticide,
Trampled and mocked with many a loathéd rite
Of lust and blood; he went, unterrified,
Into the gulf of death; but his clear Sprite
Yet reigns o'er earth; the third among the sons of light.

5

Most musical of mourners, weep anew!
Not all to that bright station dared to climb;
And happier they their happiness who knew,
Whose tapers yet burn through that night of time
In which suns perished; others more sublime,
Struck by the envious wrath of man or god,
Have sunk, extinct in their refulgent prime;
And some yet live, treading the thorny road,
Which leads, through toil and hate, to Fame's serene abode.

6

But now, thy youngest, dearest one, has perished—
The nursling of thy widowhood, who grew,
Like a pale flower by some sad maiden cherished,
And fed with true-love tears, instead of dew;
Most musical of mourners, weep anew!
Thy extreme hope, the loveliest and the last,
The bloom, whose petals nipped before they blew
Died on the promise of the fruit, is waste;
The broken lily lies—the storm is overpast.

7

To that high Capital, where kingly Death
Keeps his pale court in beauty and decay,
He came; and bought, with price of purest breath,
A grave among the eternal.—Come away!
Haste, while the vault of blue Italian day
Is yet his fitting charnel-roof! while still
He lies, as if in dewy sleep he lay;
Awake him not! surely he takes his fill
Of deep and liquid rest, forgetful of all ill.

8

He will awake no more, oh, never more!—
Within the twilight chamber spreads apace
The shadow of white Death, and at the door
Invisible Corruption waits to trace
His extreme way to her dim dwelling-place;

The eternal Hunger sits, but pity and awe
Soothe her pale rage, nor dares she to deface
So fair a prey, till darkness, and the law
Of change, shall o'er his sleep the mortal curtain draw.

9

Oh, weep for Adonais!—The quick Dreams,
The passion-wingèd Ministers of thought,
Who were his flocks, whom near the living streams
Of his young spirit he fed, and whom he taught
The love which was its music, wander not,—
Wander no more, from kindling brain to brain,
But droop there, whence they sprung; and mourn their lot
Round the cold heart, where, after their sweet pain,
They ne'er will gather strength, or find a home again.

10

And one with trembling hands clasps his cold head,
And fans him with her moonlight wings, and cries;
"Our love, our hope, our sorrow, is not dead;
See, on the silken fringe of his faint eyes,
Like dew upon a sleeping flower, there lies
A tear some Dream has loosened from his brain."
Lost Angel of a ruined Paradise!
She knew not 'twas her own; as with no stain
She faded, like a cloud which had outwept its rain.

11

One from a lucid urn of starry dew
Washed his light limbs as if embalming them;
Another clipped her profuse locks, and threw
The wreath upon him, like an anadem,
Which frozen tears instead of pearls begem;
Another in her wilful grief would break
Her bow and wingèd reeds, as if to stem
A greater loss with one which was more weak;
And dull the barbèd fire against his frozen cheek.

12

Another Splendour on his mouth alit,
That mouth,whence it was wont to draw the breath
Which gave it strength to pierce the guarded wit,
And pass into the panting heart beneath
With lightning and with music: the damp death
Quenched its caress upon his icy lips;
And, as a dying meteor stains a wreath
Of moonlight vapour, which the cold night clips,
It flushed through his pale limbs, and passed to its eclipse.

13

And others came . . . Desires and Adorations,
Wingèd Persuasions and veiled Destinies,
Splendours, and Glooms, and glimmering Incarnations
Of hopes and fears, and twilight Phantasies;
And Sorrow with her family of Sighs,
And Pleasure, blind with tears, led by the gleam
Of her own dying smile instead of eyes,
Came in slow pomp;—the moving pomp might seem
Like pageantry of mist on an autumnal stream.

14

All he had loved, and moulded into thought,
From shape, and hue, and odour, and sweet sound,
Lamented Adonais. Morning sought
Her eastern watch-tower, and her hair unbound,
Wet with the tears which should adorn the ground,
Dimmed the aëreal eyes that kindle day;
Afar the melancholy thunder moaned,
Pale Ocean in unquiet slumber lay,
And the wild Winds flew round, sobbing in their dismay.

15

Lost Echo sits amid the voiceless mountains,
And feeds her grief with his remembered lay,
And will no more reply to winds or fountains,
Or amorous birds perched on the young green spray,
Or herdsman's horn, or bell at closing day;
Since she can mimic not his lips, more dear
Than those for whose disdain she pined away
Into a shadow of all sounds;—a drear
Murmur,between their songs, is all the woodmen hear.

16

Grief made the young Spring wild, and she threw down
Her kindling buds, as if she Autumn were,
Or they dead leaves; since her delight is flown,
For whom should she have waked the sullen year?
To Phoebus was not Hyacinth so dear
Nor to himself Narcissus, as to both
Thou, Adonais: wan they stand and sere
Amid the faint companions of their youth,
With dew all turned to tears; odour, to sighing ruth.

17

Thy spirit's sister, the lorn nightingale
Mourns not her mate with such melodious pain;

Not so the eagle, who like thee could scale
Heaven, and could nourish in the sun's domain
Her mighty youth with mourning, doth complain,
Soaring and screaming round her empty nest,
As Albion wails for thee: the curse of Cain
Light on his head who pierced thy innocent breast,
And scared the angel soul that was its earthly guest!

18

Ah, woe is me! Winter is come and gone,
But grief returns with the revolving year;
The airs and streams renew their joyous tone;
The ants, the bees, the swallows reappear;
Fresh leaves and flowers deck the dead Seasons' bier;
The amorous birds now pair in every brake,
And build their mossy homes in field and brere;
And the green lizard, and the golden snake,
Like unimprisoned flames, out of their trance awake.

19

Through wood and stream and field and hill and Ocean
A quickening life from the Earth's heart has burst
As it has ever done, with change and motion,
From the great morning of the world when first
God dawned on Chaos; in its stream immersed,
The lamps of Heaven flash with a softer light;
All baser things pant with life's sacred thirst;
Diffuse themselves; and spend in love's delight,
The beauty and the joy of their renewèd might.

20

The leprous corpse, touched by this spirit tender,
Exhales itself in flowers of gentle breath;
Like incarnations of the stars, when splendour
Is changed to fragrance, they illumine death
And mock the merry worm that wakes beneath;
Nought we know, dies. Shall that alone which knows
Be as a sword consumed before the sheath
By sightless lightning?—the intense atom glows
A moment, then is quenched in a most cold repose.

21

Alas! that all we loved of him should be,
But for our grief, as if it had not been,
And grief itself be mortal! Woe is me!
Whence are we, and why are we? of what scene
The actors or spectators? Great and mean

Meet massed in death, who lends what life must borrow.
As long as skies are blue, and fields are green,
Evening must usher night, night urge the morrow,
Month follow month with woe, and year wake year to sorrow.

22

He will awake no more, oh, never more!
"Wake thou," cried Misery, "childless Mother, rise
Out of thy sleep, and slake, in thy heart's core,
A wound more fierce than his, with tears and sighs."
And all the Dreams that watched Urania's eyes,
And all the Echoes whom their sister's song
Had held in holy silence, cried: "Arise!"
Swift as a Thought by the snake Memory stung,
From her ambrosial rest the fading Splendour sprung.

23

She rose like an autumnal Night, that springs
Out of the East, and follows wild and drear
The golden Day, which, on eternal wings,
Even as a ghost abandoning a bier,
Had left the Earth a corpse. Sorrow and fear
So struck, so roused, so rapped Urania;
So saddened round her like an atmosphere
Of stormy mist; so swept her on her way
Even to the mournful place where Adonais lay.

24

Out of her secret Paradise she sped,
Through camps and cities rough with stone, and steel,
And human hearts, which to her aery tread
Yielding not, wounded the invisible
Palms of her tender feet where'er they fell:
And barbèd tongues, and thoughts more sharp than they,
Rent the soft Form they never could repel,
Whose sacred blood, like the young tears of May,
Paved with eternal flowers that undeserving way.

25

In the death-chamber for a moment Death,
Shamed by the presence of that living Might,
Blushed to annihilation, and the breath
Revisited those lips, and Life's pale light
Flashed through those limbs, so late her dear delight.
"Leave me not wild and drear and comfortless,
As silent lightning leaves the starless night!
Leave me not!" cried Urania: her distress
Roused Death: Death rose and smiled, and met her vain caress.

26

"Stay yet awhile! speak to me once again;
Kiss me, so long but as a kiss may live;
And in my heartless breast and burning brain
That word, that kiss, shall all thoughts else survive,
With food of saddest memory kept alive,
Now thou art dead, as if it were a part
Of thee, my Adonais! I would give
All that I am to be as thou now art!
But I am chained to Time, and cannot thence depart!

27

"O gentle child, beautiful as thou wert,
Why didst thou leave the trodden paths of men
Too soon, and with weak hands though mighty heart
Dare the unpastured dragon in his den?
Defenceless as thou wert, oh, where was then
Wisdom the mirrored shield, or scorn the spear?
Or hadst thou waited the full cycle, when
Thy spirit should have filled its crescent sphere,
The monsters of life's waste had fled from thee like deer.

28

"The herded wolves, bold only to pursue;
The obscene ravens, clamorous o'er the dead;
The vultures to the conqueror's banner true
Who feed where Desolation first has fed,
And whose wings rain contagion;—how they fled,
When, like Apollo, from his golden bow
The Pythian of the age one arrow sped
And smiled!—The spoilers tempt no second blow,
They fawn on the proud feet that spurn them lying low.

29

"The sun comes forth and many reptiles spawn;
He sets, and each ephemeral insect then
Is gathered into death without a dawn,
And the immortal stars awake again;
So is it in the world of living men:
A godlike mind soars forth, in its delight
Making earth bare and veiling heaven, and when
It sinks, the swarms that dimmed or shared its light
Leave to its kindred lamps the spirit's awful night."

30

Thus ceased she: and the mountain shepherds came,
Their garlands sere, their magic mantles rent;

The Pilgrim of Eternity, whose fame
Over his living head like Heaven is bent,
An early but enduring monument,
Came, veiling all the lightnings of his song
In sorrow; from her wilds Ierne sent
The sweetest lyrist of her saddest wrong,
And Love taught Grief to fall like music from his tongue.

31

Midst others of less note, came one frail Form,
A phantom among men; companionless
As the last cloud of an expiring storm
Whose thunder is its knell; he, as I guess,
Had gazed on Nature's naked loveliness,
Actaeon-like, and now he fled astray
With feeble steps o'er the world's wilderness,
And his own thoughts, along that rugged way,
Pursued, like raging hounds, their father and their prey.

32

A pardlike Spirit beautiful and swift—
A Love in desolation masked;—a Power
Girt round with weakness;—it can scarce uplift
The weight of the superincumbent hour;
It is a dying lamp, a falling shower,
A breaking billow;—even whilst we speak
Is it not broken? On the withering flower
The killing sun smiles brightly: on a cheek
The life can burn in blood, even while the heart may break.

33

His head was bound with pansies overblown,
And faded violets, white, and pied, and blue;
And a light spear topped with a cypress cone,
Round whose rude shaft dark ivy-tresses grew
Yet dripping with the forest's noonday dew,
Vibrated, as the ever-beating heart
Shook the weak hand that grasped it; of that crew
He came the last, neglected and apart;
A herd-abandoned deer struck by the hunter's dart.

34

All stood aloof, and at his partial moan
Smiled through their tears; well knew that gentle band
Who in another's fate now wept his own,
As in the accents of an unknown land
He sung new sorrow; sad Urania scanned

The Stranger's mien, and murmured: "Who art thou?"
He answered not, but with a sudden hand
Made bare his branded and ensanguined brow,
Which was like Cain's or Christ's—oh! that it should be so!

35

What softer voice is hushed over the dead?
Athwart what brow is that dark mantle thrown?
What form leans sadly o'er the white death-bed,
In mockery of monumental stone,
The heavy heart heaving without a moan?
If it be He, who, gentlest of the wise,
Taught, soothed, loved, honoured the departed one,
Let me not vex, with inharmonious sighs,
The silence of that heart's accepted sacrifice.

36

Our Adonais has drunk poison—oh!
What deaf and viperous murderer could crown
Life's early cup with such a draught of woe?
The nameless worm would now itself disown:
It felt, yet could escape, the magic tone
Whose prelude held all envy, hate, and wrong,
But what was howling in one breast alone,
Silent with expectation of the song,
Whose master's hand is cold, whose silver lyre unstrung.

37

Live thou, whose infamy is not thy fame!
Live! fear no heavier chastisement from me,
Thou noteless blot on a remembered name!
But be thyself, and know thyself to be!
And ever at thy season be thou free
To spill the venom when thy fangs o'erflow;
Remorse and Self-contempt shall cling to thee;
Hot Shame shall burn upon thy secret brow,
And like a beaten hound tremble thou shalt—as now.

38

Nor let us weep that our delight is fled
Far from these carrion kites that scream below;
He wakes or sleeps with the enduring dead;
Thou canst not soar where he is sitting now—
Dust to the dust! but the pure spirit shall flow
Back to the burning fountain whence it came,
A portion of the Eternal, which must glow
Through time and change, unquenchably the same,
Whilst thy cold embers choke the sordid hearth of shame.

39

Peace, peace! he is not dead, he doth not sleep—
He hath awakened from the dream of life—
'Tis we, who lost in stormy visions, keep
With phantoms an unprofitable strife,
And in mad trance, strike with our spirit's knife
Invulnerable nothings.—*We* decay
Like corpses in a charnel; fear and grief
Convulse us and consume us day by day,
And cold hopes swarm like worms within our living clay.

40

He has outsoared the shadow of our night;
Envy and calumny and hate and pain,
And that unrest which men miscall delight,
Can touch him not and torture not again;
From the contagion of the world's slow stain
He is secure, and now can never mourn
A heart grown cold, a head grown gray in vain;
Nor, when the spirit's self has ceased to burn,
With sparkless ashes load an unlamented urn.

41

He lives, he wakes—'tis Death is dead, not he;
Mourn not for Adonais.—Thou young Dawn,
Turn all thy dew to splendour, for from thee
The spirit thou lamentest is not gone;
Ye caverns and ye forests, cease to moan!
Cease, ye faint flowers and fountains, and thou Air,
Which like a mourning veil thy scarf hadst thrown
O'er the abandoned Earth, now leave it bare
Even to the joyous stars which smile on its despair!

42

He is made one with Nature: there is heard
His voice in all her music, from the moan
Of thunder, to the song of night's sweet bird;
He is a presence to be felt and known
In darkness and in light, from herb and stone,
Spreading itself where'er that Power may move
Which has withdrawn his being to its own;
Which wields the world with never-wearied love,
Sustains it from beneath, and kindles it above.

43

He is a portion of the loveliness
Which once he made more lovely: he doth bear

His part, while the one Spirit's plastic stress
Sweeps through the dull dense world, compelling there,
All new successions to the forms they wear;
Torturing th' unwilling dross that checks its flight
To its own likeness, as each mass may bear;
And bursting in its beauty and its might
From trees and beasts and men into the Heaven's light.

44

The splendours of the firmament of time
May be eclipsed, but are extinguished not;
Like stars to their appointed height they climb,
And death is a low mist which cannot blot
The brightness it may veil. When lofty thought
Lifts a young heart above its mortal lair,
And love and life contend in it, for what
Shall be its earthly doom, the dead live there
And move like winds of light on dark and stormy air.

45

The inheritors of unfulfilled renown
Rose from their thrones, built beyond mortal thought,
Far in the Unapparent. Chatterton
Rose pale,—his solemn agony had not
Yet faded from him; Sidney, as he fought
And as he fell and as he lived and loved
Sublimely mild, a Spirit without spot,
Arose; and Lucan, by his death approved:
Oblivion as they rose shrank like a thing reproved.

46

And many more, whose names on Earth are dark,
But whose transmitted effluence cannot die
So long as fire outlives the parent spark,
Rose, robed in dazzling immortality.
"Thou art become as one of us," they cry,
"It was for thee yon kingless sphere has long
Swung blind in unascended majesty,
Silent alone amid an Heaven of Song.
Assume thy wingèd throne, thou Vesper of our throng!"

47

Who mourns for Adonais? Oh, come forth,
Fond wretch! and know thyself and him aright.
Clasp with thy panting soul the pendulous Earth;
As from a centre, dart thy spirit's light
Beyond all worlds, until its spacious might

Satiate the void circumference: then shrink
Even to a point within our day and night;
And keep thy heart light lest it make thee sink
When hope has kindled hope, and lured thee to the brink.

48

Or go to Rome, which is the sepulchre,
Oh, not of him, but of our joy: 'tis nought
That ages, empires, and religions there
Lie buried in the ravage they have wrought;
For such as he can lend,—they borrow not
Glory from those who made the world their prey;
And he is gathered to the kings of thought
Who waged contention with their time's decay,
And of the past are all that cannot pass away.

49

Go thou to Rome,—at once the Paradise,
The grave, the city, and the wilderness;
And where its wrecks like shattered mountains rise,
And flowering weeds, and fragrant copses dress
The bones of Desolation's nakedness
Pass, till the spirit of the spot shall lead
Thy footsteps to a slope of green access
Where, like an infant's smile, over the dead
A light of laughing flowers along the grass is spread;

50

And gray walls moulder round, on which dull Time
Feeds, like slow fire upon a hoary brand;
And one keen pyramid with wedge sublime,
Pavilioning the dust of him who planned
This refuge for his memory, doth stand
Like flame transformed to marble; and beneath,
A field is spread, on which a newer band
Have pitched in Heaven's smile their camp of death,
Welcoming him we lose with scarce extinguished breath.

51

Here pause: these graves are all too young as yet
To have outgrown the sorrow which consigned
Its charge to each; and if the seal is set,
Here, on one fountain of a mourning mind,
Break it not thou! too surely shalt thou find
Thine own well full, if thou returnest home,
Of tears and gall. From the world's bitter wind
Seek shelter in the shadow of the tomb.
What Adonais is, why fear we to become?

52

The One remains, the many change and pass;
Heaven's light forever shines, Earth's shadows fly;
Life, like a dome of many-coloured glass,
Stains the white radiance of Eternity,
Until Death tramples it to fragments.—Die,
If thou wouldst be with that which thou dost seek!
Follow where all is fled!—Rome's azure sky,
Flowers, ruins, statues, music, words, are weak
The glory they transfuse with fitting truth to speak.

53

Why linger, why turn back, why shrink, my Heart?
Thy hopes are gone before: from all things here
They have departed; thou shouldst now depart!
A light is passed from the revolving year,
And man, and woman; and what still is dear
Attracts to crush, repels to make thee wither.
The soft sky smiles,—the low wind whispers near:
'Tis Adonais calls! oh, hasten thither,
No more let Life divide what Death can join together.

54

That Light whose smile kindles the Universe,
That Beauty in which all things work and move,
That Benediction which the eclipsing Curse
Of birth can quench not, that sustaining Love
Which through the web of being blindly wove
By man and beast and earth and air and sea,
Burns bright or dim, as each are mirrors of
The fire for which all thirst; now beams on me,
Consuming the last clouds of cold mortality.

55

The breath whose might I have invoked in song
Descends on me; my spirit's bark is driven,
Far from the shore, far from the trembling throng
Whose sails were never to the tempest given;
The massy earth and spherèd skies are riven!
I am borne darkly, fearfully, afar;
Whilst, burning through the inmost veil of Heaven,
The soul of Adonais, like a star,
Beacons from the abode where the Eternal are.

Samuel Taylor Coleridge

DEJECTION: AN ODE

Late, late yestreen I saw the new Moon,
With the old Moon in her arms;
And I fear, I fear, my Master dear!
We shall have a deadly storm.
BALLAD OF SIR PATRICK SPENCE

1

WELL! If the Bard was weather-wise, who made
The grand old ballad of Sir Patrick Spence,
This night, so tranquil now, will not go hence
Unroused by winds, that ply a busier trade
Than those which mould yon cloud in lazy flakes,
Or the dull sobbing draft, that moans and rakes
Upon the strings of this Æolian lute,
Which better far were mute.
For lo! the New-moon winter-bright!
And overspread with phantom light,
(With swimming phantom light o'erspread
But rimmed and circled by a silver thread)
I see the old Moon in her lap, foretelling
The coming-on of rain and squally blast.
And oh! that even now the gust were swelling,
And the slant night-shower driving loud and fast!
Those sounds which oft have raised me, whilst they awed,
And sent my soul abroad,
Might now perhaps their wonted impulse give,
Might startle this dull pain, and make it move and live!

2

A grief without a pang, void, dark, and drear,
A stifled, drowsy, unimpassioned grief,
Which finds no natural outlet, no relief,
In word, or sigh, or tear—
O Lady! in this wan and heartless mood,
To other thoughts by yonder throstle wooed,
All this long eve, so balmy and serene,
Have I been gazing on the western sky,
And its peculiar tint of yellow green:
And still I gaze—and with how blank an eye!
And those thin clouds above, in flakes and bars,
That give away their motion to the stars;
Those stars, that glide behind them or between,
Now sparkling, now bedimmed, but always seen:

Yon crescent Moon, as fixed as if it grew
In its own cloudless, starless lake of blue;
I see them all so excellently fair,
I see, not feel, how beautiful they are!

3

My genial spirits fail;
And what can these avail
To lift the smothering weight from off my breast?
It were a vain endeavor,
Though I should gaze forever
On that green light that lingers in the west:
I may not hope from outward forms to win
The passion and the life, whose fountains are within.

4

O Lady! we receive but what we give,
And in our life alone does Nature live:
Ours is her wedding garment, ours her shroud!
And would we aught behold, of higher worth,
Than that inanimate cold world allowed
To the poor loveless ever-anxious crowd,
Ah! from the soul itself must issue forth
A light, a glory, a fair luminous cloud
Enveloping the Earth—
And from the soul itself must there be sent
A sweet and potent voice, of its own birth,
Of all sweet sounds the life and element!

5

O pure of heart! thou need'st not ask of me
What this strong music in the soul may be!
What, and wherein it doth exist,
This light, this glory, this fair luminous mist,
This beautiful and beauty-making power.
Joy, virtuous Lady! Joy that ne'er was given,
Save to the pure, and in their purest hour,
Life, and Life's effluence, cloud at once and shower,
Joy, Lady! is the spirit and the power,
Which wedding Nature to us gives in dower
A new Earth and new Heaven,
Undreamt of by the sensual and the proud—
Joy is the sweet voice, Joy the luminous cloud—
We in ourselves rejoice!
And thence flows all that charms or ear or sight,
All melodies the echoes of that voice,
All colours a suffusion from that light.

6

There was a time when, though my path was rough,
  This joy within me dallied with distress,
And all misfortunes were but as the stuff
  Whence Fancy made me dreams of happiness:
For hope grew round me, like the twining vine,
And fruits, and foliage, not my own, seemed mine.
But now afflictions bow me down to earth:
Nor care I that they rob me of my mirth;
    But oh! each visitation
Suspends what nature gave me at my birth,
  My shaping spirit of Imagination.
For not to think of what I needs must feel,
  But to be still and patient, all I can;
And haply by abstruse research to steal
  From my own nature all the natural man—
  This was my soul resource, my only plan:
Till that which suits a part infects the whole,
And now is almost grown the habit of my soul.

7

Hence, viper thoughts, that coil around my mind,
    Reality's dark dream!
I turn from you, and listen to the wind,
  Which long has raved unnoticed. What a scream
Of agony by torture lengthened out
That lute sent forth! Thou Wind, that rav'st without,
  Bare crag, or mountain tairn, or blasted tree,
Or pine grove whither woodman never clomb,
Or lonely house, long held the witches' home,
  Methinks were fitter instruments for thee,
Mad lutanist! who in this month of showers,
Of dark-brown gardens, and of peeping flowers,
Mak'st devils' yule, with worse than wintry song,
The blossoms, buds, and timorous leaves among.
  Thou actor, perfect in all tragic sounds!
Thou mighty poet, e'en to frenzy bold!
    What tell'st thou now about?
    'Tis of the rushing of an host in rout,
  With groans, of trampled men, with smarting wounds—
At once they groan with pain, and shudder with the cold!
But hush! there is a pause of deepest silence!
  And all that noise, as of a rushing crowd,
With groans, and tremulous shudderings—all is over—
  It tells another tale, with sounds less deep and loud!

A tale of less affright,
And tempered with delight,
As Otway's self had framed the tender lay—
'Tis of a little child
Upon a lonesome wild,
Not far from home, but she hath lost her way:
And now moans low in bitter grief and fear,
And now screams loud, and hopes to make her mother hear.

8

'Tis midnight, but small thoughts have I of sleep:
Full seldom may my friend such vigils keep!
Visit her, gentle Sleep! with wings of healing,
And may this storm be but a mountain-birth,
May all the stars hang bright above her dwelling,
Silent as though they watched the sleeping Earth!
With light heart may she rise,
Gay fancy, cheerful eyes,
Joy lift her spirit, joy attune her voice;
To her may all things live, from pole to pole,
Their life the eddying of her living soul!
O simple spirit, guided from above,
Dear Lady! friend devoutest of my choice,
Thus mayest thou ever, evermore rejoice.

Gerard Manley Hopkins

THE WRECK OF THE DEUTSCHLAND

To the
happy memory of five Franciscan Nuns
exiles by the Falk Laws[1]
drowned between midnight and morning of
Dec. 7th, 1875

PART THE FIRST

1

THOU mastering me
God! giver of breath and bread;
World's strand, sway of the sea;
Lord of living and dead;

1 Anti-Catholic legislation sponsored by Bismark's party in 1873–74.

Thou hast bound bones and veins in me, fastened me flesh,
And after it almost unmade, what with dread,
Thy doing: and dost thou touch me afresh?
Over again I feel thy finger and find thee.

2

I did say yes
O at lightning and lashed rod;
Thou heardst me truer than tongue confess
Thy terror, O Christ, O God;
Thou knowest the walls, altar and hour and night:
The swoon of a heart that the sweep and the hurl of thee trod
Hard down with a horror of height:
And the midriff astrain with leaning of, laced with fire of stress.

3

The frown of his face
Before me, the hurtle of hell
Behind, where, where was a, where was a place?
I whirled out wings that spell
And fled with a fling of the heart to the heart of the Host.
My heart, but you were dovewinged, I can tell,
Carrier-witted, I am bold to boast,
To flash from the flame to the flame then, tower from the grace
to the grace.

4

I am soft sift
In an hourglass—at the wall
Fast, but mined with a motion, a drift,
And it crowds and it combs to the fall;
I steady as a water in a well, to a poise, to a pane,
But roped with, always, all the way down from the tall
Fells or flanks of the voel, a vein
Of the gospel proffer, a pressure, a principle, Christ's gift.

5

I kiss my hand
To the stars, lovely-asunder
Starlight, wafting him out of it; and
Glow, glory in thunder;
Kiss my hand to the dappled-with-damson west:
Since, tho' he is under the world's splendour and wonder,
His mystery must be instressed, stressed;
For I greet him the days I meet him, and bless when I understand.

6

Not out of his bliss
Springs the stress felt
Nor first from heaven (and few know this)
Swings the stroke dealt—
Stroke and a stress that stars and storms deliver,
That guilt is hushed by, hearts are flushed by and melt—
But it rides time like riding a river
(And here the faithful waver, the faithless fable and miss).

7

It dates from day
Of his going in Galilee;
Warm-laid grave of a womb-life grey;
Manger, maiden's knee;
The dense and the driven Passion, and frightful sweat;
Thence the discharge of it, there its swelling to be,
Though felt before, though in high flood yet—
What none would have known of it, only the heart, being
hard at bay,

8

Is out with it! Oh,
We lash with the best or worst
Word last! How a lush-kept plush-capped sloe
Will, mouthed to flesh-burst,
Gush!—flush the man, the being with it, sour or sweet,
Brim, in a flash, full!—Hither then, last or first,
To hero of Calvary, Christ,'s feet—
Never ask if meaning it, wanting it, warned of it—men go.

9

Be adored among men,
God, three-numberèd form;
Wring thy rebel, dogged in den,
Man's malice, with wrecking and storm.
Beyond saying sweet, past telling of tongue,
Thou art lightning and love, I found it, a winter and warm;
Father and fondler of heart thou hast wrung:
Hast thy dark descending and most art merciful then.

10

With an anvil-ding
And with fire in him forge thy will
Or rather, rather then, stealing as Spring
Through him, melt him but master him still:
Whether at once, as once at a crash Paul,
Or as Austin, a lingering-out swéet skíll,
Make mercy in all of us, out of us all
Mastery, but be adored, but be adored King.

PART THE SECOND

11

'Some find me a sword; some
The flange and the rail; flame,
Fang, or flood' goes Death on drum,
And storms bugle his fame.
But wé dream we are rooted in earth—Dust!
Flesh falls within sight of us, we, though our flower the same,
Wave with the meadow, forget that there must
The sour-scythe cringe, and the blear share come.

12

On Saturday sailed from Bremen,
American-outward-bound,
Take settler and seamen, tell men with women,
Two hundred souls in the round—
O Father, not under thy feathers nor ever as guessing
The goal was a shoal, of a fourth the doom to be drowned;
Yet did the dark side of the bay of thy blessing
Not vault them, the millions of rounds of thy mercy not reeve
even them in?

13

Into the snows she sweeps,
Hurling the haven behind,
The Deutschland, on Sunday; and so the sky keeps,
For the infinite air is unkind,
And the sea flint-flake, black-backed in the regular blow,
Sitting Eastnortheast, in cursed quarter, the wind;
Wiry and white-fiery and whirlwind-swivellèd snow
Spins to the widow-making unchilding unfathering deeps.

14

She drove in the dark to leeward,
She struck—not a reef or a rock
But the combs of a smother of sand: night drew her
Dead to the Kentish Knock;
And she beat the bank down with her bows and the ride of
her keel:
The breakers rolled on her beam with ruinous shock;
And canvas and compass, the whorl and the wheel
Idle for ever to waft her or wind her with, these she endured.

15

Hope had grown grey hairs,
Hope had mourning on,
Trenched with tears, carved with cares,
Hope was twelve hours gone;

And frightful a nightfall folded rueful a day
Nor rescue, only rocket and lightship, shone,
And lives at last were washing away:
To the shrouds they took,—they shook in the hurling and horrible airs.

16

One stirred from the rigging to save
The wild woman-kind below,
With a rope's end round the man, handy and brave—
He was pitched to his death at a blow,
For all his dreadnought breast and braids of thew:
They could tell him for hours, dandled the to and fro
Through the cobbled foam-fleece, what could he do
With the burl of the fountains of air, buck and the flood of the wave?

17

They fought with God's cold—
And they could not and fell to the deck
(Crushed them) or water (and drowned them) or rolled
With the sea-romp over the wreck.
Night roared, with the heart-break hearing a heart-broke rabble,
The woman's wailing, the crying of child without check—
Till a lioness arose breasting the babble,
A prophetess towered in the tumult, a virginal tongue told.

18

Ah, touched in your bower of bone
Are you! turned for an exquisite smart,
Have you! make words break from me here all alone,
Do you!—mother of being in me, heart.
O unteachably after evil, but uttering truth,
Why, tears! is it? tears; such a melting, a madrigal start!
Never-eldering revel and river of youth,
What can it be, this glee? the good you have there of your own?

19

Sister, a sister calling
A master, her master and mine!—
And the inboard seas run swirling and hawling;
The rash smart sloggering brine
Blinds her; but she that weather sees one thing, one;
Has one fetch in her: she rears herself to divine
Ears, and the call of the tall nun
To the men in the tops and the tackle rode over the storm's brawling.

20

She was first of a five and came
Of a coifèd sisterhood.
(O Deutschland, double a desperate name!
O world wide of its good!
But Gertrude, lily, and Luther, are two of a town,
Christ's lily and beast of the waste wood:
From life's dawn it is drawn down,
Abel is Cain's brother and breasts they have sucked the same.)

21

Loathed for a love men knew in them,
Banned by the land of their birth,
Rhine refused them. Thames would ruin them;
Surf, snow, river and earth
Gnashed: but thou art above, thou Orion of light;
Thy unchancelling poising palms were weighing the worth,
Thou martyr-master: in thy sight
Storm flakes were scroll-leaved flowers, lily showers—sweet
heaven was astrew in them.

22

Five! the finding and sake
And cipher of suffering Christ.
Mark, the mark is of man's make
And the word of it Sacrificed.
But he scores it in scarlet himself on his own bespoken,
Before-time-taken, dearest prizèd and priced—
Stigma, signal, cinquefoil token
For lettering of the lamb's fleece, ruddying of the rose-flake.

23

Joy fall to thee, father Francis,
Drawn to the Life that died;
With the gnarls of the nails in thee, niche of the lance, his
Lovescape crucified
And seal of his seraph-arrival! and these thy daughters
And five-livèd and leavèd favour and pride,
Are sisterly sealed in wild waters,
To bathe in his fall-gold mercies, to breathe in his all-fire glances.

24

Away in the loveable west,
On a pastoral forehead of Wales,
I was under a roof here, I was at rest,
And they the prey of the gales;

She to the black-about air, to the breaker, the thickly
Falling flakes, to the throng that catches and quails
Was calling "O Christ, Christ, come quickly":
The cross to her she calls Christ to her, christens her wild-worst
Best.

25

The majesty! what did she mean?
Breathe, arch and original Breath.
Is it love in her of the being as her lover had been?
Breathe, body of lovely Death.
They were else-minded then, altogether, the men
Woke thee with a *we are perishing* in the weather of Gen-
nesareth.
Or is it that she cried for the crown then,
The keener to come at the comfort for feeling the combating
keen?

26

For how to the heart's cheering
The down-dugged ground-hugged grey
Hovers off, the jay-blue heavens appearing
Of pied and peeled May!
Blue-beating and hoary-glow height; or night, still higher,
With belled fire and the moth-soft Milky Way,
What by your measure is the heaven of desire,
The treasure never eyesight got, nor was ever guessed what for
the hearing?

27

No, but it was not these.
The jading and jar of the cart,
Time's tasking, it is fathers that asking for ease
Of the sodden-with-its-sorrowing heart,
Not danger, electrical horror; then further it finds
The appealing of the Passion is tenderer in prayer apart:
Other, I gather, in measure her mind's
Burden, in wind's burly and beat of endragonèd seas.

28

But how shall I . . . make me room there:
Reach me a . . . Fancy, come faster—
Strike you the sight of it? look at it loom there,
Thing that she . . . there then! the Master,
Ipse,[2] the only one, Christ, King, Head:
He was to cure the extremity where he had cast her;
Do, deal, lord it with living and dead;
Let him ride, her pride, in his triumph, despatch and have done
with his doom there.

2 [Himself.]

29

Ah! there was a heart right
There was single eye!
Read the unshapeable shock night
And knew the who and the why;
Wording it how but by him that present and past,
Heaven and earth are word of, worded by?—
The Simon Peter of a soul! to the blast
Tarpeian-fast, but a blown beacon of light.

30

Jesu, heart's light,
Jesu, maid's son,
What was the feast followed the night
Thou hadst glory of this nun?—
Feast of the one woman without stain.
For so conceivèd, so to conceive thee is done;
But here was heart-throe, birth of a brain,
Word, that heard and kept thee and uttered thee outright.

31

Well, she has thee for the pain, for the
Patience; but pity of the rest of them!
Heart, go and bleed at a bitterer vein for the
Comfortless unconfessed of them—
No not uncomforted: lovely-felicitous Providence
Finger of a tender of, O of a feathery delicacy, the breast of the
Maiden could obey so, be a bell to, ring of it, and
Startle the poor sheep back! is the shipwrack then a harvest, does
tempest carry the grain for thee?

32

I admire thee, master of the tides,
Of the Yore-flood, of the year's fall;
The recurb and the recovery of the gulf's sides,
The girth of it and the wharf of it and the wall;
Stanching, quenching ocean of a motionable mind;
Ground of being, and granite of it: past all
Grasp God, throned behind
Death with a sovereignty that heeds but hides, bodes but abides;

33

With a mercy that outrides
The all of water, an ark
For the listener; for the lingerer with a love glides
Lower than death and the dark;

A vein for the visiting of the past-prayer, pent in prison,
The-last-breath penitent spirits—the uttermost mark
Our passion-plungèd giant risen,
The Christ of the Father compassionate, fetched in the storm of his strides.

34

Now burn, new born to the world,
Doubled-naturèd name,
The heaven-flung, heart-fleshed, maiden-furled
Miracle-in-Mary-of-flame,
Mid-numbered He in three of the thunder-throne!
Not a dooms-day dazzle in his coming nor dark as he came;
Kind, but royally reclaiming his own;
A released shower, let flash to the shire, not a lightning of fire hard-hurled.

35

Dame, at our door
Drowned, and among our shoals,
Remember us in the roads, the heaven-haven of the Reward:
Our King back, oh, upon English souls!
Let him easter in us, be a dayspring to the dimness of us, be a crimson-cresseted east,
More brightening her, rare-dear Britain, as his reign rolls,
Pride, rose, prince, hero of us, high-priest,
Our hearts' charity's hearth's fire, our thoughts' chivalry's throng's Lord.

Emily Dickinson

AFTER GREAT PAIN A FORMAL FEELING COMES

After great pain, a formal feeling comes—
The nerves sit ceremonious like tombs;
The stiff heart questions—was it He that bore?
And yesterday—or centuries before?

The feet mechanical go round
A wooden way,
Of ground or air or Ought,
Regardless grown;
A quartz contentment like a stone.

This is the hour of lead—
Remembered, if outlived,
As freezing persons recollect
The snow—
First chill, then stupor, then
The letting go.

Shaemas O'Sheel

THEY WENT FORTH TO BATTLE BUT THEY ALWAYS FELL

THEY went forth to battle but they always fell;
Their eyes were fixed upon the sullen shields;
Nobly they fought and bravely, but not well,
And sank heart-wounded by a subtle spell.
They knew not fear that to the foeman yields,
They were not weak, as one who vainly wields
A futile weapon; yet the sad scrolls tell
How on the hard-fought field they always fell.

It was a secret music that they heard,
A sad sweet plea for pity and for peace;
And that which pierced the heart was but a word,
Though the white breast was red-lipped where the sword
Pressed a fierce cruel kiss, to put surcease
On its hot thirst, but drank a hot increase.
Ah, they by some strange troubling doubt were stirred,
And died for hearing what no foeman heard.

They went forth to battle but they always fell:
Their might was not the might of lifted spears;
Over the battle-clamor came a spell
Of troubling music, and they fought not well.
Their wreaths are willows and their tribute, tears;
Their names are old sad stories in men's ears;
Yet they will scatter the red hordes of Hell,
Who went to battle forth and always fell.

James Agee

SONNET 2

OUR doom is in our being. We began
In hunger eager more than ache of hell:
And in that hunger became each a man
Ravened with hunger death alone may spell:
And in that hunger live, as lived the dead,
Who sought, as now we seek, in the same ways,
Nobly, and hatefully, what angel's-bread
Might ever stand us out these short few days.
So is this race in this wild hour confounded:
And though you rectify the big distress,
And kill all outward wrong where wrong abounded,
Your hunger cannot make this hunger less
Which breeds all wrath and right, and shall not die
In earth, and finds some hope upon the sky.

SONNET 2: From *Permit Me Voyage* by James Agee, 1934. Reprinted by permission of the publisher, Yale University Press.

DRAMA

Sophocles
OEDIPUS REX

PROLOGUE	[Oedipus, Suppliants, Priest, Creon]
PÁRODOS	[Chorus]
SCENE I	[Oedipus, Choragos, Teiresias]
ODE I	[Chorus]
SCENE II	[Creon, Choragos, Oedipus, Iocastê]
ODE II	[Chorus]
SCENE III	[Iocastê, Messenger, Oedipus, Choragos]
ODE III	[Chorus]
SCENE IV	[Oedipus, Choragos, Messenger, Shepherd]
ODE IV	[Chorus]
ÉXODOS	[Second Messenger, Choragos, Oedipus, Creon, Antigonê, Ismenê]

PERSONS REPRESENTED:

OEDIPUS	MESSENGER
A PRIEST	SHEPHERD OF LAÏOS
CREON	SECOND MESSENGER
TEIRESIAS	CHORUS OF THEBAN ELDERS
IOCASTE	

THE SCENE: *Before the palace of Oedipus, King of Thebes. A central door and two lateral doors open onto a platform which runs the length of the façade. On the platform, right and left, are altars; and three steps lead down into the "orchestra," or chorus-ground. At the beginning of the action these steps are crowded by suppliants who have brought branches and chaplets of olive leaves and who lie in various attitudes of despair.* OEDIPUS *enters.*

PROLOGUE

OEDIPUS: My children, generations of the living
In the line of Kadmos, nursed at his ancient hearth:

Why have you strewn yourselves before these altars
In supplication, with your boughs and garlands?
The breath of incense rises from the city
With a sound of prayer and lamentation.
Children,
I would not have you speak through messengers,
And therefore I have come myself to hear you—
I, Oedipus, who bear the famous name. [*To a* PRIEST:]
You, there, since you are eldest in the company,
Speak for them all, tell me what preys upon you,
Whether you come in dread, or crave some blessing:
Tell me, and never doubt that I will help you
In every way I can; I should be heartless
Were I not moved to find you suppliant here.

PRIEST: Great Oedipus, O powerful King of Thebes!
You see how all the ages of our people
Cling to your altar steps: here are boys
Who can barely stand alone, and here are priests
By weight of age, as I am a priest of God,
And young men chosen from those yet unmarried;
As for the others, all that multitude,
They wait with olive chaplets in the squares,
At the two shrines of Pallas, and where Apollo
Speaks in the glowing embers.
Your own eyes
Must tell you: Thebes is in her extremity
And can not lift her head from the surge of death.
A rust consumes the buds and fruits of the earth;
The herds are sick; children die unborn,
And labor is vain. The god of plague and pyre
Raids like detestable lightning through the city,
And all the house of Kadmos is laid waste,
All emptied, and all darkened: Death alone
Battens upon the misery of Thebes.

You are not one of the immortal gods, we know;
Yet we have come to you to make our prayer
As to the man of all men best in adversity
And wisest in the ways of God. You saved us
From the Sphinx, that flinty singer, and the tribute
We paid to her so long; yet you were never
Better informed than we, nor could we teach you:
It was some god breathed in you to set us free.

Therefore, O mighty King, we turn to you:
Find us our safety, find us a remedy,
Whether by counsel of the gods or men.
A king of wisdom tested in the past

Can act in a time of troubles, and act well.
Noblest of men, restore
Life to your city! Think how all men call you
Liberator for your triumph long ago;
Ah, when your years of kingship are remembered,
Let them not say *We rose, but later fell*—
Keep the State from going down in the storm!
Once, years ago, with happy augury,
You brought us fortune; be the same again!
No man questions your power to rule the land:
But rule over men, not over a dead city!
Ships are only hulls, citadels are nothing,
When no life moves in the empty passageways.

OEDIPUS: Poor children! You may be sure I know
All that you longed for in your coming here.
I know that you are deathly sick; and yet,
Sick as you are, not one is as sick as I.
Each of you suffers in himself alone
His anguish, not another's; but my spirit
Groans for the city, for myself, for you.
I was not sleeping, you are not waking me.
No, I have been in tears for a long while
And in my restless thought walked many ways.
In all my search, I found one helpful course,
And that I have taken: I have sent Creon,
Son of Menoikeus, brother of the Queen,
To Delphi, Apollo's place of revelation,
To learn there, if he can,
What act or pledge of mine may save the city.
I have counted the days, and now, this very day,
I am troubled, for he has overstayed his time.
What is he doing? He has been gone too long.
Yet whenever he comes back, I should do ill
To scant whatever hint the god may give.

PRIEST: It is a timely promise. At this instant
They tell me Creon is here.

OEDIPUS: O Lord Apollo!
May his news be fair as his face is radiant!

PRIEST: It could not be otherwise: he is crowned with bay,
The chaplet is thick with berries.

OEDIPUS: We shall soon know;
He is near enough to hear us now.

[*Enter* CREON.]

O Prince:
Brother: son of Menoikeus:
What answer do you bring us from the god?

CREON: It is favorable. I can tell you, great afflictions

Will turn out well, if they are taken well.
OEDIPUS: What was the oracle? These vague words
Leave me still hanging between hope and fear.
CREON: Is it your pleasure to hear me with all these
Gathered around us? I am prepared to speak,
But should we not go in?
OEDIPUS: Let them all hear it.
It is for them I suffer, more than for myself.
CREON: Then I will tell you what I heard at Delphi.

In plain words
The god commands us to expel from the land of Thebes
An old defilement we are sheltering.
It is a deathly thing, beyond cure;
We must not let it feed upon us longer.
OEDIPUS: What defilement? How shall we rid ourselves of it?
CREON: By exile or death, blood for blood. It was
Murder that brought the plague-wind on the city.
OEDIPUS: Murder of whom? Surely the god has named him?
CREON: My lord: long ago Laïos was our king,
Before you came to govern us.
OEDIPUS: I know;
I learned of him from others; I never saw him.
CREON: He was murdered; and Apollo commands us now
To take revenge upon whoever killed him.
OEDIPUS: Upon whom? Where are they? Where shall we find a clue
To solve that crime, after so many years?
CREON: Here in this land, he said.
If we make enquiry,
We may touch things that otherwise escape us.
OEDIPUS: Tell me: Was Laïos murdered in his house,
Or in the fields, or in some foreign country?
CREON: He said he planned to make a pilgrimage.
He did not come home again.
OEDIPUS: And was there no one,
No witness, no companion, to tell what happened?
CREON: They were all killed but one, and he got away
So frightened that he could remember one thing only.
OEDIPUS: What was that one thing? One may be the key
To everything, if we resolve to use it.
CREON: He said that a band of highwaymen attacked them,
Outnumbered them, and overwhelmed the King.
OEDIPUS: Strange, that a highwayman should be so daring—
Unless some faction here bribed him to do it.
CREON: We thought of that. But after Laïos' death
New troubles arose and we had no avenger.
OEDIPUS: What troubles could prevent your hunting down the killers?
CREON: The riddling Sphinx's song

Made us deaf to all mysteries but her own.
OEDIPUS: Then once more I must bring what is dark to light.
It is most fitting that Apollo shows,
As you do, this compunction for the dead.
You shall see how I stand by you, as I should,
To avenge the city and the city's god,
And not as though it were for some distant friend,
But for my own sake, to be rid of evil.
Whoever killed King Laïos might—who knows?—
Decide at any moment to kill me as well.
By avenging the murdered king I protect myself.

Come, then, my children: leave the altar steps,
Lift up your olive boughs!
One of you go
And summon the people of Kadmos to gather here.
I will do all that I can; you may tell them that. [*Exit a* PAGE.]
So, with the help of God,
We shall be saved—or else indeed we are lost.
PRIEST: Let us rise, children. It was for this we came,
And now the King has promised it himself.
Phoibos has sent us an oracle; may he descend
Himself to save us and drive out the plague.
[*Exeunt* OEDIPUS *and* CREON *into the palace by the central door. The* PRIEST *and the* SUPPLIANTS *disperse* R *and* L. *After a short pause the* CHORUS *enters the orchestra.*]

PÁRODOS

STROPHE 1

CHORUS: What is the god singing in his profound
Delphi of gold and shadow?
What oracle for Thebes, the sunwhipped city?

Fear unjoints me, the roots of my heart tremble.

Now I remember, O Healer, your power, and wonder:
Will you send doom like a sudden cloud, or weave it
Like nightfall of the past?

Ah no: be merciful, issue of holy sound:
Dearest to our expectancy: be tender!

ANTISTROPHE 1

Let me pray to Athenê, the immortal daughter of Zeus,
And to Artemis her sister
Who keeps her famous throne in the market ring,
And to Apollo, bowman at the far butts of heaven—

O gods, descend! Like three streams leap against
The fires of our grief, the fires of darkness;
Be swift to bring us rest!

As in the old time from the brilliant house
Of air you stepped to save us, come again!

STROPHE 2

Now our afflictions have no end,
Now all our stricken host lies down
And no man fights off death with his mind;

The noble plowland bears no grain,
And groaning mothers can not bear—

See, how our lives like birds take wing,
Like sparks that fly when a fire soars,
To the shore of the god of evening.

ANTISTROPHE 2

The plague burns on, it is pitiless,
Though pallid children laden with death
Lie unwept in the stony ways,

And old gray women by every path
Flock to the strand about the altars

There to strike their breasts and cry
Worship of Phoibos in wailing prayers:
Be kind, God's golden child!

STROPHE 3

There are no swords in this attack by fire,
No shields, but we are ringed with cries.
Send the besieger plunging from our homes
Into the vast sea-room of the Atlantic
Or into the waves that foam eastward of Thrace—

For the day ravages what the night spares—

Destroy our enemy, lord of the thunder!
Let him be riven by lightning from heaven!

ANTISTROPHE 3

Phoibos Apollo, stretch the sun's bowstring,
That golden cord, until it sing for us,
Flashing arrows in heaven!
Artemis, Huntress,
Race with flaring lights upon our mountains!

O scarlet god, O golden-banded brow,
O Theban Bacchos in a storm of Maenads,

[*Enter* OEDIPUS, *center.*]

Whirl upon Death, that all the Undying hate!
Come with blinding torches, come in joy!

SCENE I

OEDIPUS: Is this your prayer? It may be answered. Come,
Listen to me, act as the crisis demands,
And you shall have relief from all these evils.

Until now I was a stranger to this tale,
As I had been a stranger to the crime.
Could I track down the murderer without a clue?
But now, friends,
As one who became a citizen after the murder,
I make this proclamation to all Thebans:
If any man knows by whose hand Laïos, son of Labdakos,
Met his death, I direct that man to tell me everything,
No matter what he fears for having so long withheld it.
Let it stand as promised that no further trouble
Will come to him, but he may leave the land in safety.

Moreover: If anyone knows the murderer to be foreign,
Let him not keep silent: he shall have his reward from me.
However, if he does conceal it; if any man
Fearing for his friend or for himself disobeys this edict,
Hear what I propose to do:

I solemnly forbid the people of this country,
Where power and throne are mine, ever to receive that man
Or speak to him, no matter who he is, or let him
Join in sacrifice, lustration, or in prayer.
I decree that he be driven from every house,
Being, as he is, corruption itself to us: the Delphic
Voice of Zeus has pronounced this revelation.
Thus I associate myself with the oracle
And take the side of the murdered king.

As for the criminal, I pray to God—
Whether it be a lurking thief, or one of a number—
I pray that that man's life be consumed in evil and wretchedness.
And as for me, this curse applies no less
If it should turn out that the culprit is my guest here,
Sharing my hearth.
You have heard the penalty.

I lay it on you now to attend to this
For my sake, for Apollo's, for the sick
Sterile city that heaven has abandoned.
Suppose the oracle had given you no command:
Should this defilement go uncleansed for ever?
You should have found the murderer: your king,
A noble king, had been destroyed!
Now I,
Having the power that he held before me,
Having his bed, begetting children there
Upon his wife, as he would have, had he lived—
Their son would have been my children's brother,
If Laïos had had luck in fatherhood!
(But surely ill luck rushed upon his reign)—
I say I take the son's part, just as though
I were his son, to press the fight for him
And see it won! I'll find the hand that brought
Death to Labdakos' and Polydoros' child,
Heir of Kadmos' and Agenor's line.
And as for those who fail me,
May the gods deny them the fruit of the earth,
Fruit of the womb, and may they rot utterly!
Let them be wretched as we are wretched, and worse!

For you, for loyal Thebans, and for all
Who find my actions right, I pray the favor
Of justice, and of all the immortal gods.

CHORAGOS: Since I am under oath, my lord, I swear
I did not do the murder, I can not name
The murderer. Might not the oracle
That has ordained the search tell where to find him?
OEDIPUS: An honest question. But no man in the world
Can make the gods do more than the gods will.
CHORAGOS: There is one last expedient—
OEDIPUS: Tell me what it is.
Though it seem slight, you must not hold it back.
CHORAGOS: A lord clairvoyant to the lord Apollo,
As we all know, is the skilled Teiresias.
One might learn much about this from him, Oedipus.
OEDIPUS: I am not wasting time:
Creon spoke of this, and I have sent for him—
Twice, in fact; it is strange that he is not here.
CHORAGOS: The other matter—that old report—seems useless.
OEDIPUS: Tell me. I am interested in all reports.
CHORAGOS: The King was said to have been killed by highwaymen.
OEDIPUS: I know. But we have no witnesses to that.
CHORAGOS: If the killer can feel a particle of dread,
Your curse will bring him out of hiding!

OEDIPUS: No.
The man who dared that act will fear no curse.

[*Enter the blind seer* TEIRESIAS, *led by a* PAGE.]

CHORAGOS: But there is one man who may detect the criminal.
This is Teiresias, this is the holy prophet
In whom, alone of all men, truth was born.

OEDIPUS: Teiresias: seer: student of mysteries,
Of all that's taught and all that no man tells,
Secrets of Heaven and secrets of the earth:
Blind though you are, you know the city lies
Sick with plague; and from this plague, my lord,
We find that you alone can guard or save us.

Possibly you did not hear the messengers?
Apollo, when we sent to him,
Sent us back word that this great pestilence
Would lift, but only if we established clearly
The identity of those who murdered Laïos.

They must be killed or exiled.
Can you use
Birdflight or any art of divination
To purify yourself, and Thebes, and me
From this contagion? We are in your hands.
There is no fairer duty
Than that of helping others in distress.

TEIRESIAS: How dreadful knowledge of the truth can be
When there's no help in truth! I knew this well,
But did not act on it: else I should not have come.

OEDIPUS: What is troubling you? Why are your eyes so cold?

TEIRESIAS: Let me go home. Bear your own fate, and I'll
Bear mine. It is better so: trust what I say.

OEDIPUS: What you say is ungracious and unhelpful
To your native country. Do not refuse to speak.

TEIRESIAS: When it comes to speech, your own is neither temperate
Nor opportune. I wish to be more prudent.

OEDIPUS: In God's name, we all beg you—

TEIRESIAS: You are all ignorant.
No; I will never tell you what I know.
Now it is my misery; then, it would be yours.

OEDIPUS: What! You do know something, and will not tell us?
You would betray us all and wreck the State?

TEIRESIAS: I do not intend to torture myself, or you.
Why persist in asking? You will not persuade me.

OEDIPUS: What a wicked old man you are! You'd try a stone's
Patience! Out with it! Have you no feeling at all?

TEIRESIAS: You call me unfeeling. If you could only see
The nature of your own feelings . . .

OEDIPUS: Why,
Who would not feel as I do? Who could endure
Your arrogance toward the city?
TEIRESIAS: What does it matter!
Whether I speak or not, it is bound to come.
OEDIPUS: Then, if "it" is bound to come, you are bound to tell me.
TEIRESIAS: No, I will not go on. Rage as you please.
OEDIPUS: Rage? Why not!
And I'll tell you what I think:
You planned it, you had it done, you all but
Killed him with your own hands: if you had eyes,
I'd say the crime was yours, and yours alone.
TEIRESIAS: So? I charge you, then,
Abide by the proclamation you have made:
From this day forth
Never speak again to these men or to me;
You yourself are the pollution of this country.
OEDIPUS: You dare say that! Can you possibly think you have
Some way of going free, after such insolence?
TEIRESIAS: I have gone free. It is the truth sustains me.
OEDIPUS: Who taught you shamelessness? It was not your craft.
TEIRESIAS: You did. You made me speak. I did not want to.
OEDIPUS: Speak what? Let me hear it again more clearly.
TEIRESIAS: Was it not clear before? Are you tempting me?
OEDIPUS: I did not understand it. Say it again.
TEIRESIAS: I say that you are the murderer whom you seek.
OEDIPUS: Now twice you have spat out infamy. You'll pay for it!
TEIRESIAS: Would you care for more? Do you wish to be really angry?
OEDIPUS: Say what you will. Whatever you say is worthless.
TEIRESIAS: I say you live in hideous shame with those
Most dear to you. You can not see the evil.
OEDIPUS: It seems you can go on mouthing like this for ever.
TEIRESIAS: I can, if there is power in truth.
OEDIPUS: There is:
But not for you, not for you,
You sightless, witless, senseless, mad old man!
TEIRESIAS: You are the madman. There is no one here
Who will not curse you soon, as you curse me.
OEDIPUS: You child of endless night! You can not hurt me
Or any other man who sees the sun.
TEIRESIAS: True: it is not from me your fate will come.
That lies within Apollo's competence,
As it is his concern.
OEDIPUS: Tell me:
Are you speaking for Creon, or for yourself?
TEIRESIAS: Creon is no threat. You weave your own doom.
OEDIPUS: Wealth, power, craft of statesmanship!

Kingly position, everywhere admired!
What savage envy is stored up against these,
If Creon, whom I trusted, Creon my friend,
For this great office which the city once
Put in my hands unsought—if for this power
Creon desires in secret to destroy me!

He has bought this decrepit fortune-teller, this
Collector of dirty pennies, this prophet fraud—
Why, he is no more clairvoyant than I am!
Tell us:
Has your mystic mummery ever approached the truth?
When that hellcat the Sphinx was performing here,
What help were you to these people?
Her magic was not for the first man who came along:
It demanded a real exorcist. Your birds—
What good were they? or the gods, for the matter of that?
But I came by,
Oedipus, the simple man, who knows nothing—
I thought it out for myself, no birds helped me!
And this is the man you think you can destroy,
That you may be close to Creon when he is king!
Well, you and your friend Creon, it seems to me,
Will suffer most. If you were not an old man,
You would have paid already for your plot.

CHORAGOS: We can not see that his words or yours
Have been spoken except in anger, Oedipus,
And of anger we have no need. How can God's will
Be accomplished best? That is what most concerns us.

TEIRESIAS: You are a king. But where argument's concerned
I am your man, as much a king as you.
I am not your servant, but Apollo's.
I have no need of Creon to speak for me.

Listen to me. You mock my blindness, do you?
But I say that you, with both your eyes, are blind:
You can not see the wretchedness of your life,
Nor in whose house you live, no, nor with whom.
Who are your father and mother? Can you tell me?
You do not even know the blind wrongs
That you have done them, on earth and in the world below.
But the double lash of your parents' curse will whip you
Out of this land some day, with only night
Upon your precious eyes.
Your cries then—where will they not be heard?
What fastness of Kithairon will not echo them?
And that bridal-descant of yours—you'll know it then,

The song they sang when you came here to Thebes
And found your misguided berthing.
All this, and more, that you can not guess at now,
Will bring you to yourself among your children.

Be angry, then. Curse Creon. Curse my words.
I tell you, no man that walks upon the earth
Shall be rooted out more horribly than you.
OEDIPUS: Am I to bear this from him?—Damnation
Take you! Out of this place! Out of my sight!
TEIRESIAS: I would not have come at all if you had not asked me.
OEDIPUS: Could I have told that you'd talk nonsense, that
You'd come here to make a fool of yourself, and of me?
TEIRESIAS: A fool? Your parents thought me sane enough.
OEDIPUS: My parents again!—Wait: who were my parents?
TEIRESIAS: This day will give you a father, and break your heart.
OEDIPUS: Your infantile riddles! Your damned abracadabra!
TEIRESIAS: You were a great man once at solving riddles.
OEDIPUS: Mock me with that if you like; you will find it true.
TEIRESIAS: It was true enough. It brought about your ruin.
OEDIPUS: But if it saved this town?
TEIRESIAS: [*To the* PAGE:] Boy, give me your hand.
OEDIPUS: Yes, boy; lead him away.
—While you are here
We can do nothing. Go, leave us in peace.
TEIRESIAS: I will go when I have said what I have to say.
How can you hurt me? And I tell you again:
The man you have been looking for all this time,
The damned man, the murderer of Laïos,
That man is in Thebes. To your mind he is foreign-born,
But it will soon be shown that he is a Theban,
A revelation that will fail to please.
A blind man,
Who has his eyes now; a penniless man, who is rich now;
And he will go tapping the strange earth with his staff
To the children with whom he lives now he will be
Brother and father—the very same; to her
Who bore him, son and husband—the very same
Who came to his father's bed, wet with his father's blood.

Enough. Go think that over.
If later you find error in what I have said,
You may say that I have no skill in prophecy.
[*Exit* TEIRESIAS, *led by his* PAGE.
OEDIPUS *goes into the palace.*]

ODE I

STROPHE 1

CHORUS: The Delphic stone of prophecies
Remembers ancient regicide
And a still bloody hand.
That killer's hour of flight has come.
He must be stronger than riderless
Coursers of untiring wind,
For the son of Zeus armed with his father's thunder
Leaps in lightning after him;
And the Furies follow him, the sad Furies.

ANTISTROPHE 1

Holy Parnassos' peak of snow
Flashes and blinds that secret man,
That all shall hunt him down:
Though he may roam the forest shade
Like a bull gone wild from pasture
To rage through glooms of stone.
Doom comes down on him; flight will not avail him;
For the world's heart calls him desolate,
And the immortal Furies follow, for ever follow.

STROPHE 2

But now a wilder thing is heard
From the old man skilled at hearing Fate in the wing-beat of a bird.
Bewildered as a blown bird, my soul hovers and can not find
Foothold in this debate, or any reason or rest of mind.
But no man ever brought—none can bring
Proof of strife between Thebes' royal house,
Labdakos' line, and the son of Polybos;
And never until now has any man brought word
Of Laïos' dark death staining Oedipus the King.

ANTISTROPHE 2

Divine Zeus and Apollo hold
Perfect intelligence alone of all tales ever told;
And well though this diviner works, he works in his own night;
No man can judge that rough unknown or trust in second sight
For wisdom changes hands among the wise.
Shall I believe my great lord criminal
At a raging word that a blind old man let fall?
I saw him, when the carrion woman faced him of old,
Prove his heroic mind! These evil words are lies.

SCENE II

CREON: Men of Thebes:
I am told that heavy accusations
Have been brought against me by King Oedipus.

I am not the kind of man to bear this tamely.

If in these present difficulties
He holds me accountable for any harm to him
Through anything I have said or done—why, then,
I do not value life in this dishonor.
It is not as though this rumor touched upon
Some private indiscretion. The matter is grave.
The fact is that I am being called disloyal
To the State, to my fellow citizens, to my friends.
CHORAGOS: He may have spoken in anger, not from his mind.
CREON: But did you not hear him say I was the one
Who seduced the old prophet into lying?
CHORAGOS: The thing was said; I do not know how seriously.
CREON: But you were watching him! Were his eyes steady?
Did he look like a man in his right mind?
CHORAGOS: I do not know.
I can not judge the behavior of great men.
But here is the King himself.

[*Enter* OEDIPUS.]

OEDIPUS: So you dared come back
Why? How brazen of you to come to my house.
You murderer!
Do you think I do not know
That you plotted to kill me, plotted to steal my throne?
Tell me, in God's name: am I coward, a fool,
That you should dream you could accomplish this?
A fool who could not see your slippery game?
A coward, not to fight back when I saw it?
You are the fool, Creon, are you not? hoping
Without support or friends to get a throne?
Thrones may be won or bought: you could do neither.
CREON: Now listen to me. You have talked: let me talk, too.
You can not judge unless you know the facts.
OEDIPUS: You speak well: there is one fact; but I find it hard
To learn from the deadliest enemy I have.
CREON: That above all I must dispute with you.
OEDIPUS: That above all I will not hear you deny.
CREON: If you think there is anything good in being stubborn
Against all reason, then I say you are wrong.
OEDIPUS: If you think a man can sin against his own kind
And not be punished for it, I say you are mad.

CREON: I agree. But tell me: what have I done to you?
OEDIPUS: You advised me to send for that wizard, did you not?
CREON: I did. I should do it again.
OEDIPUS: Very well. Now tell me:
How long has it been since Laïos—
CREON: What of Laïos?
OEDIPUS: Since he vanished in that onset by the road?
CREON: It was long ago, a long time.
OEDIPUS: And this prophet,
Was he practicing here then?
CREON: He was! and with honor, as now.
OEDIPUS: Did he speak of me at that time?
CREON: He never did;
At least, not when I was present.
OEDIPUS: But . . . the enquiry?
I suppose you held one?
CREON: We did, but we learned nothing.
OEDIPUS: Why did the prophet not speak against me then?
CREON: I do not know; and I am the kind of man
Who holds his tongue when he has no facts to go on.
OEDIPUS: There's one fact that you know, and you could tell it.
CREON: What fact is that? If I know it, you shall have it.
OEDIPUS: If he were not involved with you, he could not say
That it was I who murdered Laïos.
CREON: If he says that, you are the one that knows it!—
But now it is my turn to question you.
OEDIPUS: Put your questions. I am no murderer.
CREON: First, then: You married my sister?
OEDIPUS: I married your sister.
CREON: And you rule the kingdom equally with her?
OEDIPUS: Everything that she wants she has from me.
CREON: And I am the third, equal to both of you?
OEDIPUS: That is why I call you a bad friend.
CREON: No. Reason it out, as I have done.
Think of this first: Would any sane man prefer
Power, with all a king's anxieties,
To that same power and the grace of sleep?
Certainly not I.
I have never longed for the king's power—only his rights.
Would any wise man differ from me in this?
As matters stand, I have my way in everything
With your consent, and no responsibilities.
If I were king, I should be a slave to policy.

How could I desire a scepter more
Than what is now mine—untroubled influence?
No, I have not gone mad; I need no honors,
Except those with the perquisites I have now.

I am welcome everywhere; every man salutes me,
And those who want your favor seek my ear,
Since I know how to manage what they ask.
Should I exchange this ease for that anxiety?
Besides, no sober mind is treasonable.
I hate anarchy
And never would deal with any man who likes it.

Test what I have said. Go to the priestess
At Delphi, ask if I quoted her correctly.
And as for this other thing: if I am found
Guilty of treason with Teiresias,
Then sentence me to death! You have my word
It is a sentence I should cast my vote for—
But not without evidence!
You do wrong
When you take good men for bad, bad men for good.
A true friend thrown aside—why, life itself
Is not more precious!
In time you will know this well:
For time, and time alone, will show the just man,
Though scoundrels are discovered in a day.

CHORAGOS: This is well said, and a prudent man would ponder it.
Judgments too quickly formed are dangerous.
OEDIPUS: But is he not quick in his duplicity?
And shall I not be quick to parry him?
Would you have me stand still, hold my peace, and let
This man win everything, through my inaction?
CREON: And you want—what is it, then? To banish me?
OEDIPUS: No, not exile. It is your death I want,
So that all the world may see what treason means.
CREON: You will persist, then? You will not believe me?
OEDIPUS: How can I believe you?
CREON: Then you are a fool.
OEDIPUS: To save myself?
CREON: In justice, think of me.
OEDIPUS: You are evil incarnate.
CREON: But suppose that you are wrong?
OEDIPUS: Still I must rule.
CREON: But not if you rule badly.
OEDIPUS: O city, city!
CREON: It is my city, too!
CHORAGOS: Now, my lords, be still. I see the Queen,
Iocastê, coming from her palace chambers;
And it is time she came, for the sake of you both.
This dreadful quarrel can be resolved through her.

[*Enter* IOCASTE.]

IOCASTE: Poor foolish men, what wicked din is this?
With Thebes sick to death, is it not shameful
That you should rake some private quarrel up? [*To* OEDIPUS:]
Come into the house.
—And you, Creon, go now:
Let us have no more of this tumult over nothing.
CREON: Nothing? No, sister: what your husband plans for me
Is one of two great evils: exile or death.
OEDIPUS: He is right.
Why, woman I have caught him squarely
Plotting against my life.
CREON: No! Let me die
Accurst if ever I have wished you harm!
IOCASTE: Ah, believe it, Oedipus!
In the name of the gods, respect this oath of his
For my sake, for the sake of these people here!

STROPHE 1

CHORAGOS: Open your mind to her, my lord. Be ruled by her, I beg you!
OEDIPUS: What would you have me do?
CHORAGOS: Respect Creon's word. He has never spoken like a fool,
And now he has sworn an oath.
OEDIPUS: You know what you ask?
CHORAGOS: I do.
OEDIPUS: Speak on, then.
CHORAGOS: A friend so sworn should not be baited so,
In blind malice, and without final proof.
OEDIPUS: You are aware, I hope, that what you say
Means death for me, or exile at the least.

STROPHE 2

CHORAGOS: No, I swear by Helios, first in Heaven!
May I die friendless and accurst,
The worst of deaths, if ever I meant that!
It is the withering fields
That hurt my sick heart:
Must we bear all these ills,
And now your bad blood as well?
OEDIPUS: Then let him go. And let me die, if I must,
Or be driven by him in shame from the land of Thebes.
It is your unhappiness, and not his talk,
That touches me.
As for him—
Wherever he is, I will hate him as long as I live.
CREON: Ugly in yielding, as you were ugly in rage!
Natures like yours chiefly torment themselves.
OEDIPUS: Can you not go? Can you not leave me?

CREON: I can.
You do not know me; but the city knows me,
And in its eyes I am just, if not in yours. [*Exit* CREON.]

ANTISTROPHE 1

CHORAGOS: Lady Iocastê, did you not ask the King to go to his chambers?
IOCASTE: First tell me what has happened.
CHORAGOS: There was suspicion without evidence; yet it rankled
As even false charges will.
IOCASTE: On both sides?
CHORAGOS: On both.
IOCASTE: But what was said?
CHORAGOS: Oh let it rest, let it be done with!
Have we not suffered enough?
OEDIPUS: You see to what your decency has brought you:
You have made difficulties where my heart saw none.

ANTISTROPHE 2

CHORAGOS: Oedipus, it is not once only I have told you—
You must know I should count myself unwise
To the point of madness, should I now forsake you—
You, under whose hand,
In the storm of another time,
Our dear land sailed out free.
But now stand fast at the helm!
IOCASTE: In God's name, Oedipus, inform your wife as well:
Why are you so set in this hard anger?
OEDIPUS: I will tell you, for none of these men deserves
My confidence as you do. It is Creon's work,
His treachery, his plotting against me.
IOCASTE: Go on, if you can make this clear to me.
OEDIPUS: He charges me with the murder of Laïos.
IOCASTE: Has he some knowledge? Or does he speak from hearsay?
OEDIPUS: He would not commit himself to such a charge,
But he has brought in that damnable soothsayer
To tell his story.
IOCASTE: Set your mind at rest.
If it is a question of soothsayers, I tell you
That you will find no man whose craft gives knowledge
Of the unknowable.
Here is my proof:

An oracle was reported to Laïos once
(I will not say from Phoibos himself, but from
His appointed ministers, at any rate)
That his doom would be death at the hands of his own son—
His son, born of his flesh and of mine!

Now, you remember the story: Laïos was killed
By marauding strangers where three highways meet;
But his child had not been three days in this world
Before the King had pierced the baby's ankles
And left him to die on a lonely mountainside.

Thus, Apollo never caused that child
To kill his father, and it was not Laïos' fate
To die at the hands of his son, as he had feared.
This is what prophets and prophecies are worth!
Have no dread of them.
It is God himself
Who can show us what he wills, in his own way.

OEDIPUS: How strange a shadowy memory crossed my mind,
Just now while you were speaking; it chilled my heart.
IOCASTE: What do you mean? what memory do you speak of?
OEDIPUS: If I understand you, Laïos was killed
At a place where three roads meet.
IOCASTE: So it was said;
We have no later story.
OEDIPUS: Where did it happen?
IOCASTE: Phokis, it is called: at a place where the Theban Way
Divides into the roads toward Delphi and Daulia.
OEDIPUS: When?
IOCASTE: We had the news not long before you came
And proved the right to your succession here.
OEDIPUS: Ah, what net has God been weaving for me?
IOCASTE: Oedipus! Why does this trouble you?
OEDIPUS: Do not ask me yet.
First, tell me how Laïos looked, and tell me
How old he was.
IOCASTE: He was tall, his hair just touched
With white; his form was not unlike your own.
OEDIPUS: I think that I myself may be accurst
By my own ignorant edict.
IOCASTE: You speak strangely.
It makes me tremble to look at you, my King.
OEDIPUS: I am not sure that the blind man can not see.
But I should know better if you were to tell me—
IOCASTE: Anything—though I dread to hear you ask it.
OEDIPUS: Was the King lightly escorted, or did he ride
With a large company, as a ruler should?
IOCASTE: There were five men with him in all: one was a herald;
And a single chariot, which he was driving.
OEDIPUS: Alas, that makes it plain enough!
But who—
Who told you how it happened?
IOCASTE: A household servant,

The only one to escape.
OEDIPUS: And is he still
A servant of ours?
IOCASTE: No; for when he came back at last
And found you enthroned in the place of the dead king,
He came to me, touched my hand with his, and begged
That I would send him away to the frontier district
Where only the shepherds go—
As far away from the city as I could send him.
I granted his prayer; for although the man was a slave,
He had earned more than this favor at my hands.
OEDIPUS: Can he be called back quickly?
IOCASTE: Easily.
But why?
OEDIPUS: I have taken too much upon myself
Without enquiry; therefore I wish to consult him.
IOCASTE: Then he shall come.
But am I not one also
To whom you might confide these fears of yours?
OEDIPUS: That is your right; it will not be denied you,
Now least of all; for I have reached a pitch
Of wild foreboding. Is there anyone
To whom I should sooner speak?

Polybos of Corinth is my father.
My mother is a Dorian: Meropê.
I grew up chief among the men of Corinth
Until a strange thing happened—
Not worth my passion, it may be, but strange.

At a feast, a drunken man maundering in his cups
Cries out that I am not my father's son!

I contained myself that night, though I felt anger
And a sinking heart. The next day I visited
My father and mother, and questioned them.
They stormed,
Calling it all the slanderous rant of a fool;
And this relieved me. Yet the suspicion
Remained always aching in my mind;
I knew there was talk; I could not rest;
And finally, saying nothing to my parents,
I went to the shrine at Delphi.
The god dismissed my question without reply;
He spoke of other things.
Some were clear,
Full of wretchedness, dreadful, unbearable:

As, that I should lie with my own mother, breed
Children from whom all men would turn their eyes;
And that I should be my father's murderer.

I heard all this, and fled. And from that day
Corinth to me was only in the stars
Descending in that quarter of the sky,
As I wandered farther and farther on my way
To a land where I should never see the evil
Sung by the oracle. And I came to this country
Where, so you say, King Laïos was killed.

I will tell you all that happened there, my lady.

There were three highways
Coming together at a place I passed;
And there a herald came towards me, and a chariot
Drawn by horses, with a man such as you describe
Seated in it. The groom leading the horses
Forced me off the road at his lord's command;
But as this charioteer lurched over towards me
I struck him in my rage. The old man saw me
And brought his double goad down upon my head
As I came abreast.
He was paid back, and more!
Swinging my club in this right hand I knocked him
Out of his car, and he rolled on the ground.
I killed him.

I killed them all.
Now if that stranger and Laïos were—kin,
Where is a man more miserable than I?
More hated by the gods? Citizen and alien alike
Must never shelter me or speak to me—
I must be shunned by all.
And I myself
Pronounced this malediction upon myself!

Think of it: I have touched you with these hands,
These hands that killed your husband. What defilement!

Am I all evil, then? It must be so,
Since I must flee from Thebes, yet never again
See my own countrymen, my own country,
For fear of joining my mother in marriage
And killing Polybos, my father.
Ah,

If I was created so, born to this fate,
Who could deny the savagery of God?

O holy majesty of heavenly powers!
May I never see that day! Never!
Rather let me vanish from the race of men
Than know the abomination destined me!
CHORAGOS: We too, my lord, have felt dismay at this.
But there is hope: you have yet to hear the shepherd.
OEDIPUS: Indeed, I fear no other hope is left me.
IOCASTE: What do you hope from him when he comes?
OEDIPUS: This much:
If his account of the murder tallies with yours,
Then I am cleared.
IOCASTE: What was it that I said
Of such importance?
OEDIPUS: Why, "marauders," you said,
Killed the King, according to this man's story.
If he maintains that still, if there were several,
Clearly the guilt is not mine: I was alone.
But if he says one man, singlehanded, did it,
Then the evidence all points to me.
IOCASTE: You may be sure that he said there were several;
And can he call back that story now? He cán not.
The whole city heard it as plainly as I.
But suppose he alters some detail of it:
He can not ever show that Laïos' death
Fulfilled the oracle: for Apollo said
My child was doomed to kill him; and my child—
Poor baby!—it was my child that died first.

No. From now on, where oracles are concerned,
I would not waste a second thought on any.
OEDIPUS: You may be right.
But come: let someone go
For the shepherd at once. This matter must be settled.
IOCASTE: I will send for him.
I would not wish to cross you in anything,
And surely not in this.—Let us go in. [*Exeunt into the palace.*]

ODE II

STROPHE 1

CHORUS: Let me be reverent in the ways of right,
Lowly the paths I journey on;
Let all my words and actions keep
The laws of the pure universe
From highest Heaven handed down.

For Heaven is their bright nurse,
Those generations of the realms of light;
Ah, never of mortal kind were they begot,
Nor are they slaves of memory, lost in sleep:
Their Father is greater than Time, and ages not.

ANTISTROPHE 1

The tyrant is a child of Pride
Who drinks from his great sickening cup
Recklessness and vanity,
Until from his high crest headlong
He plummets to the dust of hope.
That strong man is not strong.
But let no fair ambition be denied;
May God protect the wrestler for the State
In government, in comely policy,
Who will fear God, and on His ordinance wait.

STROPHE 2

Haughtiness and the high hand of disdain
Tempt and outrage God's holy law;
And any mortal who dares hold
No immortal Power in awe
Will be caught up in a net of pain:
The price for which his levity is sold.
Let each man take due earnings, then,
And keep his hands from holy things,
And from blasphemy stand apart—
Else the crackling blast of heaven
Blows on his head, and on his desperate heart;
Though fools will honor impious men,
In their cities no tragic poet sings.

ANTISTROPHE 2

Shall we lose faith in Delphi's obscurities,
We who have heard the world's core
Discredited, and the sacred wood
Of Zeus at Elis praised no more?
The deeds and the strange prophecies
Must make a pattern yet to be understood.
Zeus, if indeed you are lord of all,
Throned in light over night and day,
Mirror this in your endless mind:
Our masters call the oracle
Words on the wind, and the Delphic vision blind!
Their hearts no longer know Apollo,
And reverence for the gods has died away.

SCENE III

[*Enter* IOCASTE.]

IOCASTE: Princes of Thebes, it has occurred to me
To visit the altars of the gods, bearing
These branches as a suppliant, and this incense.
Our King is not himself: his noble soul
Is overwrought with fantasies of dread,
Else he would consider
The new prophecies in the light of the old.
He will listen to any voice that speaks disaster,
And my advice goes for nothing. [*She approaches the altar, right.*]
To you, then, Apollo,
Lycean lord, since you are nearest, I turn in prayer.
Receive these offerings, and grant us deliverance
From defilement. Our hearts are heavy with fear
When we see our leader distracted, as helpless sailors
Are terrified by the confusion of their helmsman.

[*Enter* MESSENGER.]

MESSENGER: Friends, no doubt you can direct me:
Where shall I find the house of Oedipus,
Or, better still, where is the King himself?
CHORAGOS: It is this very place, stranger; he is inside.
This is his wife and mother of his children.
MESSENGER: I wish her happiness in a happy house,
Blest in all the fulfillment of her marriage.
IOCASTE: I wish as much for you: your courtesy
Deserves a like good fortune. But now, tell me:
Why have you come? What have you to say to us?
MESSENGER: Good news, my lady, for your house and your husband.
IOCASTE: What news? Who sent you here?
MESSENGER: I am from Corinth.
The news I bring ought to mean joy for you,
Though it may be you will find some grief in it.
IOCASTE: What is it? How can it touch us in both ways?
MESSENGER: The word is that the people of the Isthmus
Intend to call Oedipus to be their king.
IOCASTE: But old King Polybos—is he not reigning still?
MESSENGER: No. Death holds him in his sepulchre.
IOCASTE: What are you saying? Polybos is dead?
MESSENGER: If I am not telling the truth, may I die myself.
IOCASTE: [*To a* MAIDSERVANT:] Go in, go quickly; tell this to your master.

O riddlers of God's will, where are you now!
This was the man whom Oedipus, long ago,

Feared so, fled so, in dread of destroying him—
But it was another fate by which he died.

[*Enter* OEDIPUS, *center.*]

OEDIPUS: Dearest Iocastê, why have you sent for me?
IOCASTE: Listen to what this man says, and then tell me
What has become of the solemn prophecies.
OEDIPUS: Who is this man? What is his news for me?
IOCASTE: He has come from Corinth to announce your father's death!
OEDIPUS: Is it true, stranger? Tell me in your own words.
MESSENGER: I can not say it more clearly: the King is dead.
OEDIPUS: Was it by treason? Or by an attack of illness?
MESSENGER: A little thing brings old men to their rest.
OEDIPUS: It was sickness, then?
MESSENGER: Yes, and his many years.
OEDIPUS: Ah!
Why should a man respect the Pythian hearth, or
Give heed to the birds that jangle above his head?
They prophesied that I should kill Polybos,
Kill my own father; but he is dead and buried,
And I am here—I never touched him, never,
Unless he died of grief for my departure,
And thus, in a sense, through me. No. Polybos
Has packed the oracles off with him underground.
They are empty words.
IOCASTE: Had I not told you so?
OEDIPUS: You had; it was my faint heart that betrayed me.
IOCASTE: From now on never think of those things again.
OEDIPUS: And yet—must I not fear my mother's bed?
IOCASTE: Why should anyone in this world be afraid,
Since Fate rules us and nothing can be foreseen?
A man should live only for the present day.

Have no more fear of sleeping with your mother:
How many men, in dreams, have lain with their mothers!
No reasonable man is troubled by such things.
OEDIPUS: That is true; only—
If only my mother were not still alive!
But she is alive. I can not help my dread.
IOCASTE: Yet this news of your father's death is wonderful.
OEDIPUS: Wonderful. But I fear the living woman.
MESSENGER: Tell me, who is this woman that you fear?
OEDIPUS: It is Meropê, man; the wife of King Polybos.
MESSENGER: Meropê? Why should you be afraid of her?
OEDIPUS: An oracle of the gods, a dreadful saying.
MESSENGER: Can you tell me about it or are you sworn to silence?
OEDIPUS: I can tell you, and I will.
Apollo said through his prophet that I was the man

Who should marry his own mother, shed his father's blood
With his own hands. And so, for all these years
I have kept clear of Corinth, and no harm has come—
Though it would have been sweet to see my parents again.

MESSENGER: And is this the fear that drove you out of Corinth?
OEDIPUS: Would you have me kill my father?
MESSENGER: As for that
You must be reassured by the news I gave you.
OEDIPUS: If you could reassure me, I would reward you,
MESSENGER: I had that in mind, I will confess: I thought
I could count on you when you returned to Corinth.
OEDIPUS: No: I will never go near my parents again.
MESSENGER: Ah, son, you still do not know what you are doing—
OEDIPUS: What do you mean? In the name of God tell me!
MESSENGER: —If these are your reasons for not going home.
OEDIPUS: I tell you, I fear the oracle may come true.
MESSENGER: And guilt may come upon you through your parents?
OEDIPUS: That is the dread that is always in my heart.
MESSENGER: Can you not see that all your fears are groundless?
OEDIPUS: How can you say that? They are my parents, surely?
MESSENGER: Polybos was not your father.
OEDIPUS: Not my father?
MESSENGER: No more your father than the man speaking to you.
OEDIPUS: But you are nothing to me!
MESSENGER: Neither was he.
OEDIPUS: Then why did he call me son?
MESSENGER: I will tell you:
Long ago he had you from my hands, as a gift.
OEDIPUS: Then how could he love me so, if I was not his?
MESSENGER: He had no children, and his heart turned to you.
OEDIPUS: What of you? Did you buy me? Did you find me by chance?
MESSENGER: I came upon you in the crooked pass of Kithairon.
OEDIPUS: And what were you doing there?
MESSENGER: Tending my flocks.
OEDIPUS: A wandering shepherd?
MESSENGER: But your savior, son, that day.
OEDIPUS: From what did you save me?
MESSENGER: Your ankles should tell you that.
OEDIPUS: Ah, stranger, why do you speak of that childhood pain?
MESSENGER: I cut the bonds that tied your ankles together.
OEDIPUS: I have had the mark as long as I can remember.
MESSENGER: That was why you were given the name you bear.
OEDIPUS: God! Was it my father or my mother who did it?
Tell me!
MESSENGER: I do not know. The man who gave you to me
Can tell you better than I.
OEDIPUS: It was not you that found me, but another?

MESSENGER: It was another shepherd gave you to me.
OEDIPUS: Who was he? Can you tell me who he was?
MESSENGER: I think he was said to be one of Laïos' people.
OEDIPUS: You mean the Laïos who was king here years ago?
MESSENGER: Yes; King Laïos; and the man was one of his herdsmen.
OEDIPUS: Is he still alive? Can I see him?
MESSENGER: These men here
Know best about such things.
OEDIPUS: Does anyone here
Know this shepherd that he is talking about?
Have you seen him in the fields, or in the town?
If you have, tell me. It is time things were made plain.
CHORAGOS: I think the man he means is that same shepherd
You have already asked to see. Iocastê perhaps
Could tell you something.
OEDIPUS: Do you know anything
About him, Lady? Is he the man we have summoned?
Is that the man this shepherd means?
IOCASTE: Why think of him?
Forget this herdsman. Forget it all.
This talk is a waste of time.
OEDIPUS: How can you say that,
When the clues to my true birth are in my hands?
IOCASTE: For God's love, let us have no more questioning!
Is your life nothing to you?
My own is pain enough for me to bear.
OEDIPUS: You need not worry. Suppose my mother a slave,
And born of slaves: no baseness can touch you.
IOCASTE: Listen to me, I beg you: do not do this thing!
OEDIPUS: I will not listen; the truth must be made known.
IOCASTE: Everything that I say is for your own good!
OEDIPUS: My own good
Snaps my patience, then; I want none of it.
IOCASTE: You are fatally wrong! May you never learn who you are!
OEDIPUS: Go, one of you, and bring the shepherd here.
Let us leave this woman to brag of her royal name.
IOCASTE: Ah, miserable!
That is the only word I have for you now.
That is the only word I can ever have. [*Exit into the palace.*]
CHORAGOS: Why has she left us, Oedipus? Why has she gone
In such a passion of sorrow? I fear this silence:
Something dreadful may come of it.
OEDIPUS: Let it come!
However base my birth, I must know about it.
The Queen, like a woman, is perhaps ashamed
To think of my low origin. But I
Am a child of Luck; I can not be dishonored.

Luck is my mother; the passing months, my brothers,
Have seen me rich and poor.
If this is so,
How could I wish that I were someone else?
How could I not be glad to know my birth?

ODE III

STROPHE

CHORUS: If ever the coming time were known
To my heart's pondering,
Kithairon, now by Heaven I see the torches
At the festival of the next full moon,
And see the dance, and hear the choir sing
A grace to your gentle shade:
Mountain where Oedipus was found,
O mountain guard of a noble race!
May the god who heals us lend his aid,
And let that glory come to pass
For our king's cradling-ground.

ANTISTROPHE

Of the nymphs that flower beyond the years,
Who bore you, royal child,
To Pan of the hills or the timberline Apollo,
Cold in delight where the upland clears,
Or Hermês for whom Kyllenê's heights are piled?
Or flushed as evening cloud,
Great Dionysos, roamer of mountains,
He—was it he who found you there,
And caught you up in his own proud
Arms from the sweet god-ravisher
Who laughed by the Muses' fountains?

SCENE IV

OEDIPUS: Sirs: though I do not know the man,
I think I see him coming, this shepherd we want:
He is old, like our friend here, and the men
Bringing him seem to be servants of my house.
But you can tell, if you have ever seen him.

[*Enter* SHEPHERD *escorted by servants.*]

CHORAGOS: I know him, he was Laïos' man. You can trust him.
OEDIPUS: Tell me first, you from Corinth: is this the shepherd
We were discussing?
MESSENGER: This is the very man.

OEDIPUS: [*To* SHEPHERD:] Come here. No, look at me. You must answer
Everything I ask.—You belonged to Laïos?
SHEPHERD: Yes: born his slave, brought up in his house.
OEDIPUS: Tell me: what kind of work did you do for him?
SHEPHERD: I was a shepherd of his, most of my life.
OEDIPUS: Where mainly did you go for pasturage?
SHEPHERD: Sometimes Kithairon, sometimes the hills near-by.
OEDIPUS: Do you remember ever seeing this man out there?
SHEPHERD: What would he be doing there? This man?
OEDIPUS: This man standing here. Have you ever seen him before?
SHEPHERD: No. At least, not to my recollection.
MESSENGER: And that is not strange, my lord. But I'll refresh
His memory: he must remember when we two
Spent three whole seasons together, March to September,
On Kithairon or thereabouts. He had two flocks;
I had one. Each autumn I'd drive mine home
And he would go back with his to Laïos' sheepfold.—
Is this not true, just as I have described it?
SHEPHERD: True, yes; but it was all so long ago.
MESSENGER: Well, then: do you remember, back in those days,
That you gave me a baby boy to bring up as my own?
SHEPHERD: What if I did? What are you trying to say?
MESSENGER: King Oedipus was once that little child.
SHEPHERD: Damn you, hold your tongue!
OEDIPUS: No more of that!
It is your tongue needs watching, not this man's.
SHEPHERD: My King, my Master, what is it I have done wrong?
OEDIPUS: You have not answered his question about the boy.
SHEPHERD: He does not know . . . He is only making trouble . . .
OEDIPUS: Come, speak plainly, or it will go hard with you.
SHEPHERD: In God's name, do not torture an old man!
OEDIPUS: Come here, one of you; bind his arms behind him.
SHEPHERD: Unhappy king! What more do you wish to learn?
OEDIPUS: Did you give this man the child he speaks of?
SHEPHERD: I did.
And I would to God I had died that very day.
OEDIPUS: You will die now unless you speak the truth.
SHEPHERD: Yet if I speak the truth, I am worse than dead.
OEDIPUS: Very well; since you insist upon delaying—
SHEPHERD: No! I have told you already that I gave him the boy.
OEDIPUS: Where did you get him? From your house? From somewhere else?
SHEPHERD: Not from mine, no. A man gave him to me.
OEDIPUS: Is that man here? Do you know whose slave he was?
SHEPHERD: For God's love, my King, do not ask me any more!
OEDIPUS: You are a dead man if I have to ask you again.
SHEPHERD: Then . . . Then the child was from the palace of Laïos.

OEDIPUS: A slave child? or a child of his own line?
SHEPHERD: Ah, I am on the brink of dreadful speech!
OEDIPUS: And I of dreadful hearing. Yet I must hear.
SHEPHERD: If you must be told, then . . .
They said it was Laïos' child;
But it is your wife who can tell you about that.
OEDIPUS: My wife!—Did she give it to you?
SHEPHERD: My lord, she did.
OEDIPUS: Do you know why?
SHEPHERD: I was told to get rid of it.
OEDIPUS: An unspeakable mother!
SHEPHERD: There had been prophecies . . .
OEDIPUS: Tell me.
SHEPHERD: It was said that the boy would kill his own father.
OEDIPUS: Then why did you give him over to this old man?
SHEPHERD: I pitied the baby, my King,
And I thought that this man would take him far away
To his own country.
He saved him—but for what a fate!
For if you are what this man says you are,
No man living is more wretched than Oedipus.
OEDIPUS: Ah God!
It was true!
All the prophecies!
—Now,
O Light, may I look on you for the last time!
I, Oedipus,
Oedipus, damned in his birth, in his marriage damned,
Damned in the blood he shed with his own hand!
[*He rushes into the palace.*]

ODE IV

STROPHE 1

CHORUS: Alas for the seed of men.
What measure shall I give these generations
That breathe on the void and are void
And exist and do not exist?

Who bears more weight of joy
Than mass of sunlight shifting in images,
Or who shall make his thought stay on
That down time drifts away?

Your splendor is all fallen.

O naked brow of wrath and tears,
O change of Oedipus!

I who saw your days call no man blest—
Your great days like ghósts góne.

ANTISTROPHE 1

That mind was a strong bow.

Deep, how deep you drew it then, hard archer,
At a dim fearful range,
And brought dear glory down!

You overcame the stranger—
The virgin with her hooking lion claws—
And though death sang, stood like a tower
To make pale Thebes take heart.

Fortress against our sorrow!

Divine king, giver of laws,
Majestic Oedipus!
No prince in Thebes had ever such renown,
No prince won such grace of power.

STROPHE 2

And now of all men ever known
Most pitiful is this man's story:
His fortunes are most changed, his state
Fallen to a low slave's
Ground under bitter fate.

O Oedipus, most royal one!
The great door that expelled you to the light
Gave at night—ah, gave night to your glory:
As to the father, to the fathering son.

All understood too late.

How could that queen whom Laïos won,
The garden that he harrowed at his height,
Be silent when that act was done?

ANTISTROPHE 2

But all eyes fail before time's eye,
All actions come to justice there.
Though never willed, though far down the deep past,
Your bed, your dread sirings,
Are brought to book at last.
Child by Laïos doomed to die,
Then doomed to lose that fortunate little death,

Would God you never took breath in this air
That with my wailing lips I take to cry:

For I weep the world's outcast.

I was blind, and now I can tell why:
Asleep, for you had given ease of breath
To Thebes, while the false years went by.

ÉXODOS

[*Enter, from the palace,* SECOND MESSENGER.]

SECOND MESSENGER: Elders of Thebes, most honored in this land,
What horrors are yours to see and hear, what weight
Of sorrow to be endured, if, true to your birth,
You venerate the line of Labdakos!
I think neither Istros nor Phasis, those great rivers,
Could purify this place of the corruption
It shelters now, or soon must bring to light—
Evil not done unconsciously, but willed.

The greatest griefs are those we cause ourselves.
CHORAGOS: Surely, friend, we have grief enough already;
What new sorrow do you mean?
SECOND MESSENGER: The Queen is dead.
CHORAGOS: Iocastê? Dead? But at whose hand?
SECOND MESSENGER: Her own.
The full horror of what happened you can not know,
For you did not see it; but I, who did, will tell you
As clearly as I can how she met her death.

When she had left us,
In passionate silence, passing through the court,
She ran to her apartment in the house,
Her hair clutched by the fingers of both hands.
She closed the doors behind her; then, by that bed
Where long ago the fatal son was conceived—
That son who should bring about his father's death—
We heard her call upon Laïos, dead so many years,
And heard her wail for the double fruit of her marriage,
A husband by her husband, children by her child.
Exactly how she died I do not know:
For Oedipus burst in moaning and would not let us
Keep vigil to the end: it was by him
As he stormed about the room that our eyes were caught.
From one to another of us he went, begging a sword,

Cursing the wife who was not his wife, the mother
Whose womb had carried his own children and himself.
I do not know: it was none of us aided him,
But surely one of the gods was in control!
For with a dreadful cry
He hurled his weight, as though wrenched out of himself,
At the twin doors: the bolts gave, and he rushed in.
And there we saw her hanging, her body swaying
From the cruel cord she had noosed about her neck.
A great sob broke from him, heartbreaking to hear,
As he loosed the rope and lowered her to the ground.

I would blot out from my mind what happened next!
For the King ripped from her gown the golden brooches
That were her ornament, and raised them, and plunged them down
Straight into his own eyeballs, crying, "No more,
No more shall you look on the misery about me,
The horrors of my own doing! Too long you have known
The faces of those whom I should never have seen,
Too long been blind to those for whom I was searching!
From this hour, go in darkness!" And as he spoke,
He struck at his eyes—not once, but many times;
And the blood spattered his beard,
Bursting from his ruined sockets like red hail.

So from the unhappiness of two this evil has sprung,
A curse on the man and woman alike. The old
Happiness of the house of Labdakos
Was happiness enough: where is it today?
It is all wailing and ruin, disgrace, death—all
The misery of mankind that has a name—
And it is wholly and for ever theirs.

CHORAGOS: Is he in agony still? Is there no rest for him?

SECOND MESSENGER: He is calling for someone to lead him to the gates
So that all the children of Kadmos may look upon
His father's murderer, his mother's—no,
I can not say it!
And then he will leave Thebes,
Self-exiled, in order that the curse
Which he himself pronounced may depart from the house.
He is weak, and there is none to lead him,
So terrible is his suffering.
But you will see:
Look, the doors are opening; in a moment
You will see a thing that would crush a heart of stone.

[*The central door is opened;* OEDIPUS, *blinded, is led in.*]

CHORAGOS: Dreadful indeed for men to see.
Never have my own eyes
Looked on a sight so full of fear.

Oedipus!
What madness came upon you, what daemon
Leaped on your life with heavier
Punishment than a mortal man can bear?
No: I can not even
Look at you, poor ruined one.
And I would speak, question, ponder,
If I were able. No.
You make me shudder.
OEDIPUS: God. God.
Is there a sorrow greater?
Where shall I find harbor in this world?
My voice is hurled far on a dark wind.
What has God done to me?
CHORAGOS: Too terrible to think of, or to see.

STROPHE 1

OEDIPUS: O cloud of night,
Never to be turned away: night coming on,
I can not tell how: night like a shroud!
My fair winds brought me here.
O God. Again
The pain of the spikes where I had sight,
The flooding pain
Of memory, never to be gouged out.
CHORAGOS: This is not strange.
You suffer it all twice over, remorse in pain,
Pain in remorse.

ANTISTROPHE 1

OEDIPUS: Ah dear friend
Are you faithful even yet, you alone?
Are you still standing near me, will you stay here,
Patient, to care for the blind?
The blind man!
Yet even blind I know who it is attends me,
By the voice's tone—
Though my new darkness hide the comforter.
CHORAGOS: Oh fearful act!
What god was it drove you to rake black
Night across your eyes?

STROPHE 2

OEDIPUS: Apollo. Apollo. Dear
Children, the god was Apollo.

He brought my sick, sick fate upon me.
But the blinding hand was my own!
How could I bear to see
When all my sight was horror everywhere?

CHORAGOS: Everywhere; that is true.

OEDIPUS: And now what is left?
Images? Love? A greeting even,
Sweet to the senses? Is there anything?
Ah, no, friends: lead me away.
Lead me away from Thebes.
Lead the great wreck
And hell of Oedipus, whom the gods hate.

CHORAGOS: Your fate is clear, you are not blind to that.
Would God you had never found it out!

ANTISTROPHE 2

OEDIPUS: Death take the man who unbound
My feet on that hillside
And delivered me from death to life! What life?
If only I had died,
This weight of monstrous doom
Could not have dragged me and my darlings down.

CHORAGOS: I would have wished the same.

OEDIPUS: Oh never to have come here
With my father's blood upon me! Never
To have been the man they call his mother's husband!
Oh accurst! Oh child of evil,
To have entered that wretched bed—
the selfsame one!
More primal than sin itself, this fell to me.

CHORAGOS: I do not know how I can answer you.
You were better dead than alive and blind.

OEDIPUS: Do not counsel me any more. This punishment
That I have laid upon myself is just.
If I had eyes,
I do not know how I could bear the sight
Of my father, when I came to the house of Death,
Or my mother: for I have sinned against them both
So vilely that I could not make my peace
By strangling my own life.
Or do you think my children,
Born as they were born, would be sweet to my eyes?
Ah never, never! Nor this town with its high walls,
Nor the holy images of the gods.
For I,
Thrice miserable!—Oedipus, noblest of all the line
Of Kadmos, have condemned myself to enjoy
These things no more, by my own malediction

Expelling that man whom the gods declared
To be a defilement in the house of Laïos.
After exposing the rankness of my own guilt,
How could I look men frankly in the eyes?
No, I swear it,
If I could have stifled my hearing at its source,
I would have done it and made all this body
A tight cell of misery, blank to light and sound:
So I should have been safe in a dark agony
Beyond all recollection.
Ah Kithairon!
Why did you shelter me? When I was cast upon you,
Why did I not die? Then I should never
Have shown the world my execrable birth.

Ah Polybos! Corinth, city that I believed
The ancient seat of my ancestors: how fair
I seemed, your child! And all the while this evil
Was cancerous within me!
For I am sick
In my daily life, sick in my origin.

O three roads, dark ravine, woodland and way
Where three roads met: you, drinking my father's blood,
My own blood, spilled by my own hand: can you remember
The unspeakable things I did there, and the things
I went on from there to do?
O marriage, marriage!
The act that engendered me, and again the act
Performed by the son in the same bed—
Ah, the net
Of incest, mingling fathers, brothers, sons,
With brides, wives, mothers: the last evil
That can be known by men: no tongue can say
How evil!
No. For the love of God, conceal me
Somewhere far from Thebes; or kill me; or hurl me
Into the sea, away from men's eyes for ever.

Come, lead me. You need not fear to touch me.
Of all men, I alone can bear this guilt.

[*Enter* CREON.]

CHORAGOS: We are not the ones to decide; but Creon here
May fitly judge of what you ask. He only
Is left to protect the city in your place.
OEDIPUS: Alas, how can I speak to him? What right have I
To beg his courtesy whom I have deeply wronged?

CREON: I have not come to mock you, Oedipus,
Or to reproach you, either.
[*To* ATTENDANTS:]—You, standing there:

If you have lost all respect for man's dignity,
At least respect the flame of Lord Helios:
Do not allow this pollution to show itself
Openly here, an affront to the earth
And Heaven's rain and the light of day. No, take him
Into the house as quickly as you can.
For it is proper
That only the close kindred see his grief.
OEDIPUS: I pray you in God's name, since your courtesy
Ignores my dark expectation, visiting
With mercy this man of all men most execrable:
Give me what I ask—for your good, not for mine.
CREON: And what is it that you would have me do?
OEDIPUS: Drive me out of this country as quickly as may be
To a place where no human voice can ever greet me.
CREON: I should have done that before now—only,
God's will had not been wholly revealed to me.
OEDIPUS: But his command is plain: the parricide
Must be destroyed. I am that evil man.
CREON: That is the sense of it, yes; but as things are,
We had best discover clearly what is to be done.
OEDIPUS: You would learn more about a man like me?
CREON: You are ready now to listen to the god.
OEDIPUS: I will listen. But it is to you
That I must turn for help. I beg you, hear me.

The woman in there—
Give her whatever funeral you think proper:
She is your sister.
—But let me go, Creon!
Let me purge my father's Thebes of the pollution
Of my living here, and go out to the wild hills,
To Kithairon, that has won such fame with me,
The tomb my mother and father appointed for me,
And let me die there, as they willed I should.
And yet I know
Death will not ever come to me through sickness
Or in any natural way: I have been preserved
For some unthinkable fate. But let that be.

As for my sons, you need not care for them.
They are men, they will find some way to live.
But my poor daughters, who have shared my table,
Who never before have been parted from their father—

Take care of them, Creon; do this for me.
And will you let me touch them with my hands
A last time, and let us weep together?
Be kind, my lord,
Great prince, be kind!
Could I but touch them,
They would be mine again, as when I had my eyes.

[*Enter* ANTIGONE *and* ISMENE, *attended*.]

Ah, God!
Is it my dearest children I hear weeping?
Has Creon pitied me and sent my daughters?

CREON: Yes, Oedipus: I knew that they were dear to you
In the old days, and know you must love them still.

OEDIPUS: May God bless you for this—and be a friendlier
Guardian to you than he has been to me!

Children, where are you?
Come quickly to my hands: they are your brother's—
Hands that have brought your father's once clear eyes
To this way of seeing—
Ah dearest ones,
I had neither sight nor knowledge then, your father
By the woman who was the source of his own life!
And I weep for you—having no strength to see you—,
I weep for you when I think of the bitterness
That men will visit upon you all your lives.
What homes, what festivals can you attend
Without being forced to depart again in tears?
And when you come to marriageable age,
Where is the man, my daughters, who would dare
Risk the bane that lies on all my children?
Is there any evil wanting? Your father killed
His father; sowed the womb of her who bore him;
Engendered you at the fount of his own existence!
That is what they will say of you.

Then, whom
Can you ever marry? There are no bridegrooms for you,
And your lives must wither away in sterile dreaming.

O Creon, son of Menoikeus!
You are the only father my daughters have,
Since we, their parents, are both of us gone for ever.
They are your own blood: you will not let them
Fall into beggary and loneliness;
You will keep them from the miseries that are mine!
Take pity on them; see, they are only children,

Friendless except for you. Promise me this,
Great Prince, and give me your hand in token of it.
[CREON *clasps his right hand.*]
Children:
I could say much, if you could understand me,
But as it is, I have only this prayer for you:
Live where you can, be happy as you can—
Happier, please God, than God has made your father!
CREON: Enough. You have wept enough. Now go within.
OEDIPUS: I must; but it is hard.
CREON: Time eases all things.
OEDIPUS: But you must promise—
CREON: Say what you desire.
OEDIPUS: Send me from Thebes!
CREON: God grant that I may!
OEDIPUS: But since God hates me . . .
CREON: No, he will grant your wish.
OEDIPUS: You promise?
CREON: I can not speak beyond my knowledge.
OEDIPUS: Then lead me in.
CREON: Come now, and leave your children.
OEDIPUS: No! Do not take them from me!
CREON: Think no longer
That you are in command here, but rather think
How, when you were, you served your own destruction.
[*Exeunt into the house all but the* CHORUS;
the CHORAGOS *chants directly to the audience:*]
CHORAGOS: Men of Thebes: look upon Oedipus.

This is the king who solved the famous riddle
And towered up, most powerful of men.
No mortal eyes but looked on him with envy,
Yet in the end ruin swept over him.

Let every man in mankind's frailty
Consider his last day; and let none
Presume on his good fortune until he find
Life, at his death, a memory without pain.

Francis Fergusson

OEDIPUS REX: THE TRAGIC RHYTHM OF ACTION

. . . quel secondo regno dove l'umano spirito si purga.[1]
—*Purgatorio*, Canto I

I suppose there can be little doubt that *Oedipus Rex* is a crucial instance of drama, if not *the* play which best exemplifies this art in its essential nature and its completeness. It owes its position partly to the fact that Aristotle founded his definitions upon it. But since the time of Aristotle it has been imitated, rewritten, and discussed by many different generations, not only of dramatists, but also of moralists, psychologists, historians, and other students of human nature and destiny.

Though the play is thus generally recognized as an archetype, there has been little agreement about its meaning or its form. It seems to beget, in every period, a different interpretation and a different dramaturgy. From the seventeenth century until the end of the eighteenth, a Neoclassic and rationalistic interpretation of *Oedipus*, of Greek tragedy, and of Aristotle, was generally accepted; and upon this interpretation was based the dramaturgy of Corneille and Racine. Nietzsche, under the inspiration of Wagner's *Tristan und Isolde*, developed a totally different view of it, and thence a different theory of drama. These two views of Greek tragedy, Racine's and Nietzsche's, still provide indispensable perspectives upon *Oedipus*. They show a great deal about modern principles of dramatic composition; and they show, when compared, how central and how essential Sophocles' drama is. In the two essays following, the attempt is made to develop the analogies, the similarities and differences, between these three conceptions of drama.

In our day a conception of *Oedipus* seems to be developing which is neither that of Racine nor that of Nietzsche. This view is based upon the studies which the Cambridge School, Fraser, Cornford, Harrison, Murray, made of the ritual origins of Greek tragedy. It also owes a great deal to the current interest in myth as a way of ordering human experience. *Oedipus*, we now see, is both myth and ritual. It assumes and employs these two ancient ways of understanding and

1 [(And I will sing) of that second realm where the human spirit is purged.]

---

representing human experience, which are prior to the arts and sciences and philosophies of modern times. To understand it (it now appears) we must endeavor to recapture the habit of significant make-believe, of the direct perception of action, which underlies Sophocles' theater.

If *Oedipus* is to be understood in this way, then we shall have to revise our ideas of Sophocles' dramaturgy. The notion of Aristotle's theory of drama, and hence of Greek dramaturgy, which still prevails (in spite of such studies as Butcher's of the *Poetics*) is largely colored by Neoclassic taste and rationalistic habits of mind. If we are to take it that Sophocles was imitating action before theory, instead of after it, like Racine, then both the elements and the form of his composition appear in a new light.

In the present essay the attempt is made to draw the deductions, for Sophocles' theater and dramaturgy, which the present view of *Oedipus* implies. We shall find that the various traditional views of this play are not so much wrong as partial.

Oedipus: MYTH AND PLAY

WHEN Sophocles came to write his play[2] he had the myth of Oedipus to start with. Laius and Jocasta, King and Queen of Thebes, are told by the oracle that their son will grow up to kill his father and marry his mother. The infant, his feet pierced, is left on Mount Kitharon to die. But a shepherd finds him and takes care of him; at last gives him to another shepherd, who takes him to Corinth, and there the King and Queen bring him up as their own son. But Oedipus—"Club-foot"—is plagued in his turn by the oracle; he hears that he is fated to kill his father and marry his mother; and to escape that fate he leaves Corinth never to return. On his journey he meets an old man with his servants; gets into a dispute with him, and kills him and all his followers. He comes to Thebes at the time when the Sphinx is preying upon that City; solves the riddle which the Sphinx propounds, and saves the City. He marries the widowed Queen, Jocasta; has several children by her; rules prosperously for many years. But, when Thebes is suffering under a plague and a drought, the oracle reports that the gods are angry because Laius' slayer is unpunished. Oedipus, as King, undertakes to find him; discovers that he is himself the culprit and that Jocasta is his own mother. He blinds himself and goes into exile. From this time forth he becomes a sort of sacred relic, like the bones of a saint; perilous, but "good medicine" for the community that possesses him. He dies, at last, at Athens, in a grove sacred to the Eumenides, female spirits of fertility and night.

2 [In this essay the names of some of the characters are spelled differently from the *Oedipus Rex* translation immediately preceding.—Editors of the Princeton edition.]

It is obvious, even from this sketch, that the myth, which covers several generations, has as much narrative material as *Gone with the Wind*. We do not know what versions of the story Sophocles used. It is the way of myths that they generate whole progenies of elaborations and varying versions. They are so suggestive, seem to say so much, yet so mysteriously, that the mind cannot rest content with any single form, but must add, or interpret, or simplify—reduce to terms which the reason can accept. Mr. William Troy suggests that "what is possibly most in order at the moment is a thoroughgoing refurbishment of the medieval fourfold method of interpretation, which was first developed, it will be recalled, for just such a purpose—to make at least partially available to the reason that complex of human problems which are embedded, deep and imponderable, in the Myth."[3] It appears that Sophocles, in his play, succeeded in preserving the suggestive mystery of the Oedipus myth, while presenting it in a wonderfully unified dramatic form; and this drama has all the dimensions which the fourfold method was intended to explore.

Everyone knows that when Sophocles planned the plot of the play itself, he started almost at the end of the story, when the plague descends upon the City of Thebes which Oedipus and Jocasta had been ruling with great success for a number of years. The action of the play takes less than a day, and consists of Oedipus' quest for Laius' slayer—his consulting the Oracle of Apollo, his examination of the Prophet, Tiresias, and of a series of witnesses, ending with the old Shepherd who gave him to the King and Queen of Corinth. The play ends when Oedipus is unmistakenly revealed as himself the culprit.

At this literal level, the play is intelligible as a murder mystery. Oedipus takes the role of District Attorney; and when he at last convicts himself, we have a twist, a *coup de théâtre*, of unparalleled excitement. But no one who sees or reads the play can rest content with its literal coherence. Questions as to its meaning arise at once: Is Oedipus really guilty, or simply a victim of the gods, of his famous complex, of fate, of original sin? How much did he know, all along? How much did Jocasta know? The first, and most deeply instinctive effort of the mind, when confronted with this play, is to endeavor to reduce its meanings to some set of rational categories.

The critics of the Age of Reason tried to understand it as a fable of the enlightened moral will, in accordance with the philosophy of that time. Voltaire's version of the play, following Corneille, and his comments upon it, may be taken as typical. He sees it as essentially a struggle between a strong and righteous Oedipus, and the malicious and very human gods, aided and abetted by the corrupt priest Tiresias; he makes it an antireligious tract, with an unmistakable moral to sat-

3 "Myth, Method and the Future," by William Troy. *Chimera,* spring, 1946.

isfy the needs of the discursive intellect. In order to make Oedipus "sympathetic" to his audience, he elides, as much as possible, the incest motif; and he adds an irrelevant love story. He was aware that his version and interpretation were not those of Sophocles but, with the complacent provinciality of his period, he attributes the difference to the darkness of the age in which Sophocles lived.

Other attempts to rationalize *Oedipus Rex* are subtler than Voltaire's, and take us further toward an understanding of the play. Freud's reduction of the play to the concepts of his psychology reveals a great deal, opens up perspectives which we are still exploring. If one reads *Oedipus* in the light of Fustel de Coulanges' *The Ancient City*, one may see it as the expression of the ancient patriarchal religion of the Greeks. And other interpretations of the play, theological, philosophical, historical, are available, none of them wrong, but all partial, all reductions of Sophocles' masterpiece to an alien set of categories. For the peculiar virtue of Sophocles' presentation of the myth is that it preserves the ultimate mystery by focusing upon the tragic human at a level beneath, or prior to any rationalization whatever. The plot is so arranged that we see the action, as it were, illumined from many sides at once.

By starting the play at the end of the story, and showing on-stage only the last crucial episode in Oedipus' life, the past and present action of the protagonist are revealed together; and, in each other's light, are at last felt as one. Oedipus' quest for the slayer of Laius becomes a quest for the hidden reality of his own past; and as that slowly comes into focus, like repressed material under psychoanalysis—with sensory and emotional immediacy, yet in the light of acceptance and understanding—his immediate quest also reaches its end: he comes to see himself (the Savior of the City) and the guilty one, the plague of Thebes, at once and at one.

This presentation of the myth of Oedipus constitutes, in one sense, an "interpretation" of it. What Sophocles saw as the essence of Oedipus' nature and destiny, is not what Seneca or Dryden or Cocteau saw; and one may grant that even Sophocles did not exhaust the possibilities in the materials of the myth. But Sophocles' version of the myth does not constitute a "reduction" in the same sense as the rest.

I have said that the action which Sophocles shows is a quest, the quest for Laius' slayer; and that as Oedipus' past is unrolled before us his whole life is seen as a kind of quest for his true nature and destiny. But since the object of the quest is not clear until the end, the seeking action takes many forms, as its object appears in different lights. The object, indeed, the final perception, the "truth," looks so different at the end from what it did at the beginning that Oedipus' action itself may seem not a quest, but its opposite, a flight. Thus it would be hard to say, simply, that Oedipus either succeeds or fails. He succeeds; but his success is his undoing. He fails to find what, in one way, he sought; yet from another point of view his search is brilliantly successful. The same ambiguities surround his effort to discover who and what he is. He seems to find that he is nothing; yet thereby finds himself. And what of his relation to the gods? His quest may be regarded as a heroic attempt to escape their decrees, or as an attempt, based upon some deep natural faith, to discover what their wishes are, and what true obedience would be. In one sense Oedipus suffers forces he can neither control nor understand, the puppet of fate; yet at the same time he wills and intelligently intends his every move.

The meaning, or spiritual content of the play, is not to be sought by trying to resolve such ambiguities as these. The spiritual content of the play is the tragic action which Sophocles directly presents; and this action is in its essence *zweideutig*:[4] triumph and destruction, darkness and enlightenment, mourning and rejoicing, at any moment we care to consider it. But this action has also a shape: a beginning, middle, and end, in time. It starts with the reasoned purpose of finding Laius' slayer. But this aim meets unforeseen difficulties, evidences which do not fit, and therefore shake the purpose as it was first understood; and so the characters suffer the piteous and terrible sense of the mystery of the human situation. From this suffering or passion, with its shifting visions, a new perception of the situation emerges; and on that basis the purpose of the action is redefined, and a new movement starts. This movement, or tragic rhythm of action, constitutes the shape of the play as a whole; it is also the shape of each episode, each discussion between principles with the chorus following. Mr. Kenneth Burke has studied the tragic rhythm in his *Philosophy of Literary Form*, and also in *A Grammar of Motives*, where he gives the three moments traditional designations which are very suggestive: *Poiema, Pathema, Mathema*[5] They may also be called, for convenience, Purpose, Passion (or Suffering) and Perception. It is this tragic rhythm of action which is the substance or spiritual content of the play, and the clue to its extraordinarily comprehensive form.

In order to illustrate these points in more detail, it is convenient to examine the scene between Oedipus and Tiresias with the chorus following it. This episode, being early in the play (the first big agon), presents, as it were, a preview of the whole action and constitutes a clear and complete example of action in the tragic rhythm.

4 [Ambiguous.]

5 [Purpose, Passion, Perception.]

HERO AND SCAPEGOAT: THE AGON BETWEEN OEDIPUS AND TIRESIAS

The scene between Oedipus and Tiresias comes after the opening sections of the play. We have seen the citizens of Thebes beseeching their King to find some way to lift the plague which is on the City. We have had Oedipus' entrance (majestic, but for his tell-tale limp) to reassure them, and we have heard the report which Creon brings from the Delphic Oracle; that the cause of the plague is the unpunished murder of Laius, the former king. Oedipus offers rewards to anyone who will reveal the culprit, and he threatens with dire punishment anyone who conceals or protects him. In the meantime, he decides, with the enthusiastic assent of the chorus, to summon Tiresias as the first witness.

Tiresias is that suffering seer whom Sophocles uses in *Antigone* also to reveal a truth which other mortals find it hard and uncomfortable to see. He is physically blind, but Oedipus and chorus alike assume that if anyone can see who the culprit is, it is Tiresias, with his uncanny inner vision of the future. As Tiresias enters, led by a boy, the chorus greets him in these words:[6]

> CHORUS: But the man to convict him is here. Look: they are bringing the one human being in whom the truth is native, the godlike seer.

Oedipus is, at this point in the play, at the opposite pole of experience from Tiresias: he is hero, monarch, helmsman of the state, the solver of the Sphinx's riddle, the triumphant being. He explains his purpose in the following proud clear terms:

> OEDIPUS. O Tiresias, you know all things: what may be told, and the unspeakable: things of earth and things of heaven. You understand the City (though you do not see it) in its present mortal illness—from which to save us and protect us, we find, Lord, none but you. For you must know, in case you haven't heard it from the messengers, that Apollo, when we asked him, told us there was one way only with this plague: to discover Laius' slayers, and put them to death or send them into exile. Therefore you must not jealously withhold your omens, whether of birds or other visionary way, but save yourself and the City —save me, save all of us—from the defilement of the dead. In your hand we are. There is no handsomer work for a man, than to bring, with what he has, what help he can.

This speech is the prologue of the scene, and the basis of the agon or struggle which follows. This struggle in effect analyzes Oedipus'

6 I am responsible for the English of this scene. The reader is referred to *Oedipus Rex*, translated by Dudley Fitts and Robert Fitzgerald (New York: Harcourt, Brace and Co., 1949), a very handsome version of the whole play. [See p. 377.]

purpose; places it in a wider context, reveals it as faulty and dubious. At the end of the scene Oedipus loses his original purpose altogether, and suffers a wave of rage and fear, which will have to be rationalized in its turn before he can "pull himself together" and act again with a clear purpose.

In the first part of the struggle, Oedipus takes the initiative, while Tiresias, on the defensive, tries to avoid replying:

TIRESIAS. Oh, oh. How terrible to know, when nothing can come of knowing! Indeed, I had lost the vision of these things, or I should never have come.

OEDIPUS. What things? . . . In what discouragement have you come to us here!

TIR. Let me go home. I shall endure this most easily, and so will you, if you do as I say.

OED. But what you ask is not right. To refuse your word is disloyalty to the City that has fed you.

TIR. But I see that your demands are exorbitant, and lest I too suffer such a—

OED. For the sake of the gods, if you know, don't turn away! Speak to us, we are your suppliants here.

TIR. None of you understands. But I—I never will tell my misery. Or yours.

OED. What are you saying? You know, but tell us nothing? You intend treachery to us, and death to the City?

TIR. I intend to grieve neither myself nor you. Why then do you try to know? You will never learn from me.

OED. Ah, evil old man! You would anger a stone! You will say *nothing?* Stand futile, speechless before us?

TIR. You curse my temper, but you don't see the one that dwells in you; no, you must blame me.

OED. And who would *not* lose his temper, if he heard you utter your scorn of the City?

TIR. It will come. Silent though I be.

OED. Since it will come, it is your duty to inform me.

TIR. I shall say no more. Now, if you like, rage to your bitter heart's content.

OED. Very well: in my "rage" I shall hold back nothing which I now begin to see. I think you planned that deed, even performed it, though not with your own hands. If you could see, I should say that the work was yours alone.

In the last speech quoted, Oedipus changes his tack, specifying his purpose differently; he accuses Tiresias, and that makes Tiresias attack. In the next part of the fight the opponents trade blow for blow:

TIR. You would? I charge you, abide by the decree you uttered: from this day forth, speak neither to these present, nor to me, unclean as you are, polluter of the earth!

OED. You have the impudence to speak out words like these! And now how do you expect to escape?

TIR. I have escaped. The truth strengthens and sustains me.

OED. Who taught you the truth? Not your prophet's art.

TIR. You did; you force me against my will to speak.

OED. Speak what? Speak again, that I may understand better.

TIR. *Didn't* you understand? Or are you goading me?

OED. I can't say I really grasp it: speak again.

TIR. I say you are the murderer of the man whose murderer you seek.

OED. You won't be glad to have uttered that curse twice.

TIR. Must I say more, so you may rage the more?

OED. As much as you like—all is senseless.

TIR. I say you do not know your own wretchedness, nor see in what shame you live with those you love.

OED. Do you think you can say that forever with impunity?

TIR. If the truth has power.

OED. It has, with all but you: helpless is truth with you: for you are blind, in eye, in ear, in mind.

TIR. You are the impotent one: you utter slanders which every man here will apply to you.

OED. You have your being only in the night; you couldn't hurt me or any man who sees the sun.

TIR. No. Your doom is not to fall by me. Apollo suffices for that, he will bring it about.

OED. Are these inventions yours, or Creon's?

TIR. Your wretchedness is not Creon's, it is yours.

OED. O wealth, and power, and skill—which skill, in emulous life, brings low—what envy eyes you! if for this kingly power which the City gave into my hands, unsought—if for *this* the faithful Creon, my friend from the first, has stalked me in secret, yearning to supplant me! if he has bribed this juggling wizard, this deceitful beggar, who discerns his profit only, blind in his own art!

Tell me now, tell me where you have proved a true diviner? Why, when the song-singing sphinx was near, did you not speak deliverance to the people? Her riddles were not for any comer to solve, but for the mantic art, and you were apparently instructed neither by birds nor by any sign from the gods. Yet when I came, I, Oedipus, all innocent, I stopped her song. No birds taught me, by my own wit I found the answer. And it is I whom you wish to banish, thinking that you will then stand close to Creon's throne.

You and your ally will weep, I think, for this attempt; and in fact, if you didn't seem to be an old man, you would already have learned, in pain, of your presumption.

In this part the beliefs, the visions, and hence the purposes of the antagonists are directly contrasted. Because both identify themselves so completely with their visions and purposes, the fight descends from the level of dialectic to a level below the rational altogether: it becomes cruelly *ad hominem.*[7] We are made to see the absurd incommensurability of the very beings of Oedipus and Tiresias; they shrink from one another as from the uncanny. At the end of the round, it is Oedipus who has received the deeper wound; and his great speech, "O wealth and power," is a far more lyric utterance than the ordered exposition with which he began.

The end of this part of the fight is marked by the intervention of the chorus, which endeavors to recall the antagonists to the most general version of purpose which they supposedly share: the discovery of the truth and the service of the gods:

CHORUS. To us it appears that this man's words were uttered in anger, and yours too, Oedipus. No need for that: consider how best to discharge the mandate of the god.

The last part of the struggle shows Tiresias presenting his whole vision, and Oedipus, on the defensive, shaken to the depths:

TIR. Although you rule, we have equally the right to reply; in that I too have power. Indeed, I live to serve, not you, but Apollo; and I shall not be enrolled under Creon, either. Therefore I say, since you have insulted even my blindness, that though you have eyesight, you do not see what misery you are in, nor where you are living, nor with whom. Do you know whence you came? No, nor that you are the enemy of your own family, the living and the dead. The double prayer of mother and father shall from this land hound you in horror—who now see clearly, but then in darkness.

Where then will your cry be bounded? What part of Kitharon not echo it quickly back, when you shall come to understand that marriage, to which you sailed on so fair a wind, homelessly home? And many other evils which you do not see will bring you to yourself at last, your children's equal.

Scorn Creon, therefore, and my words: you will be struck down more terribly than any mortal.

OED. Can I really hear such things from him? Are you not gone? To death? To punishment? Not fled from this house?

TIR. I should never have come if you hadn't called me.

OED. I didn't know how mad you would sound, or it would have been a long time before I asked you here to my house.

TIR. This is what I am; foolish, as it seems to you; but wise, to the parents who gave you birth.

OED. To whom? Wait: *who* gave me birth?

7 [Directed to the person rather than to the subject.]

TIR. This day shall give you birth, and death.
OED. In what dark riddles you always speak.
TIR. Aren't you the best diviner of riddles?
OED. Very well: mock that gift, which, you will find, is mine.
TIR. That very gift was your undoing.
OED. But if I saved the City, what does it matter?
TIR. So be it. I am going. Come, boy, lead me.
OED. Take him away. Your presence impedes and trips me; once you are gone, you can do no harm.
TIR. I shall go when I have done my errand without fear of your frowns, for they can't hurt me. I tell you, then, that the man whom you have long been seeking, with threats and proclamations, Laius' slayer, is here. He is thought to be an alien, but will appear a native Theban, and this circumstance will not please him. Blind, who once could see; destitute, who once was rich, leaning on a staff, he will make his way through a strange land. He will be revealed as brother and father of his own children; of the woman who bore him, both son and husband; sharer of his father's bed; his father's killer.

Go in and ponder this. If you find it wrong, say then I do not understand the prophetic vision.

Oedipus rushes off-stage, his clear purpose gone, his being shaken with fear and anger. Tiresias departs, led by his boy. The chorus is left to move and chant, suffering the mixed and ambivalent feelings, the suggestive but mysterious images, which the passion in which the agon eventuated produces in them:

CHORUS
Strophe I. Who is it that the god's voice from the Rock of Delphi says
Accomplished the unspeakable with murderous hands?
Time now that windswift
Stronger than horses
His feet take flight.
In panoply of fire and lightning
Now springs upon him the son of Zeus
Whom the dread follow,
The Fates unappeasable.
Antistrophe I. New word, like light, from snowy Parnassus:
Over all the earth trail the unseen one.
For in rough wood,
In cave or rocks,
Like bull bereft—stampeded, futile
He goes, seeking with futile foot to
Flee the ultimate
Doom, which ever
Lives and flies over him.
Strophe II. In awe now, and soul's disorder, I neither accept
The augur's wisdom, nor deny: I know not what to say.

I hover in hope, see neither present nor future.
Between the House of Laius
And Oedipus, I do not hear, have never heard, of any feud:
I cannot confirm the public charge against him, to help
Avenge the dark murder.
Antistrophe II. Zeus and Apollo are wise, and all that is mortal
They know: but whether that human seer knows more than I
There is no way of telling surely, though in wisdom
A man may excel.
Ah, never could I, till I see that word confirmed, consent to blast him!
Before all eyes the winged songstress, once, assailed him;
Wise showed he in that test, and to the City, tender; in my heart
I will call him evil never.

The chorus is considered in more detail below. At this point I merely wish to point out that Oedipus and Tiresias show, in their agon, the "purpose" part of the tragic rhythm; that this turns to "passion," and that the chorus presents the passion and also the new perception which follows. This new perception is that of Oedipus as the possible culprit. But his outlines are vague; perhaps the vision itself is illusory, a bad dream. The chorus has not yet reached the end of its quest; that will come only when Oedipus, in the flesh before them, is unmistakably seen as the guilty one. We have reached merely a provisional resting-place, the end of the first figure in which the tragic rhythm is presented. But this figure is a reduced version of the shape of the play as a whole, and the fleeting and unwelcome image of Oedipus as guilty corresponds to the final perception or epiphany, the full-stop, with which the play ends.

Oedipus: RITUAL AND PLAY

The Cambridge School of Classical Anthropologists has shown in great detail that the form of Greek tragedy follows the form of a very ancient ritual, that of the *Enniautos-Daimon,* or seasonal god.[8] This was one of the most influential discoveries of the last few generations, and it gives us new insights into *Oedipus* which I think are not yet completely explored. The clue to Sophocles' dramatizing of the myth of Oedipus is to be found in this ancient ritual, which had a similar form and meaning—that is, it also moved in the "tragic rhythm."

Experts in classical anthropology, like experts in other fields, dispute innumerable questions of fact and of interpretation which the layman can only pass over in respectful silence. One of the thornier questions seems to be whether myth or ritual came first. Is the ancient ceremony merely an enactment of the Ur-Myth of the year-god—At-

8 See especially Jane Ellen Harrison's *Ancient Art and Ritual,* and her *Themis* which contains an "Excursus on the ritual forms preserved in Greek Tragedy" by Professor Gilbert Murray.

tis, or Adonis, or Osiris, or the "Fisher-King"—in any case that Hero-King-Father-High-Priest who fights with his rival, is slain and dismembered, then rises anew with the spring season? Or did the innumerable myths of this kind arise to "explain" a ritual which was perhaps mimed or danced or sung to celebrate the annual change of season?

For the purpose of understanding the form and meaning of *Oedipus*, it is not necessary to worry about the answer to this question of historic fact. The figure of Oedipus himself fulfills all the requirements of the scapegoat, the dismembered king or god-figure. The situation in which Thebes is presented at the beginning of the play—in peril of its life; its crops, its herds, its women mysteriously infertile, signs of a mortal disease of the City, and the disfavor of the gods—is like the withering which winter brings, and calls, in the same way, for struggle, dismemberment, death, and renewal. And this tragic sequence is the substance of the play. It is enough to know that myth and ritual are close together in their genesis, two direct imitations of the perennial experience of the race.

But when one considers *Oedipus* as a ritual one understands it in ways which one cannot by thinking of it merely as a dramatization of a story, even that story. Harrison has shown that the Festival of Dionysos, based ultimately upon the yearly vegetation ceremonies, included *rites de passage*,[9] like that celebrating the assumption of adulthood—celebrations of the mystery of individual growth and development. At the same time, it was a prayer for the welfare of the whole City; and this welfare was understood not only as material prosperity, but also as the natural order of the family, the ancestors, the present members, and the generations still to come, and, by the same token, obedience to the gods who were jealous, each in his own province, of this natural and divinely sanctioned order and proportion.

We must suppose that Sophocles' audience (the whole population of the City) came early, prepared to spend the day in the bleachers. At their feet was the semicircular dancing-ground for the chorus, and the thrones for the priests, and the altar. Behind that was the raised platform for the principal actors, backed by the all-purpose, emblematic façade, which would presently be taken to represent Oedipus' palace in Thebes. The actors were not professionals in our sense, but citizens selected for a religious office, and Sophocles himself had trained them and the chorus.

This crowd must have had as much appetite for thrills and diversion as the crowds who assemble in our day for football games and musical comedies, and Sophocles certainly holds the attention with an exciting show. At the same time his audience must have been alert

9 [Ceremonies of growth.]

for the fine points of poetry and dramaturgy, for *Oedipus* is being offered in competition with other plays on the same bill. But the element which distinguishes this theater, giving it its unique directness and depth, is the *ritual expectancy* which Sophocles assumed in his audience. The nearest thing we have to this ritual sense of theater is, I suppose, to be found at an Easter performance of the *Mattias Passion.* We also can observe something similar in the dances and ritual mummery of the Pueblo Indians. Sophocles' audience must have been prepared, like the Indians standing around their plaza, to consider the playing, the make-believe it was about to see—the choral invocations, with dancing and chanting; the reasoned discourses and the terrible combats of the protagonists; the mourning, the rejoicing, and the contemplation of the final stage-picture or epiphany—as imitating and celebrating the mystery of human nature and destiny. And this mystery was at once that of individual growth and development, and that of the precarious life of the human City.

I have indicated how Sophocles presents the life of the mythic Oedipus in the tragic rhythm, the mysterious quest of life. Oedipus is shown seeking his own true being; but at the same time and by the same token, the welfare of the City. When one considers the ritual form of the whole play, it becomes evident that it presents the tragic but perennial, even normal, quest of the whole City for its well-being. In this larger action, Oedipus is only the protagonist, the first and most important champion. This tragic quest is realized by all the characters in their various ways; but in the development of the action as a whole it is the chorus alone that plays a part as important as that of Oedipus; its counterpart, in fact. The chorus holds the balance between Oedipus and his antagonists, marks the progress of their struggles, and restates the main theme, and its new variation, after each dialogue or agon. The ancient ritual was probably performed by a chorus alone without individual developments and variations, and the chorus, in *Oedipus,* is still the element that throws most light on the ritual form of the play as a whole.

The chorus consists of twelve or fifteen "Elders of Thebes." This group is not intended to represent literally all of the citizens either of Thebes or of Athens. The play opens with a large delegation of Theban citizens before Oedipus' palace, and the chorus proper does not enter until after the prologue. Nor does the chorus speak directly for the Athenian audience; we are asked throughout to make-believe that the theater is the agora at Thebes; and at the same time Sophocles' audience is witnessing a ritual. It would, I think, be more accurate to say that the chorus represents the point of view and the faith of Thebes as a whole, and, by analogy, of the Athenian audience. Their errand before Oedipus' palace is like that of Sophocles' audience in the theater: they are watching a sacred combat, in the issue of which they have an all-important and official stake. Thus they represent the audience and the citizens in a particular way—not as a mob formed in response to some momentary feeling, but rather as an organ of a highly self-conscious community: something closer to the "conscience of the race" than to the overheated affectivity of a mob.

According to Aristotle, a Sophoclean chorus is a character that takes an important role in the action of the play, instead of merely making incidental music between the scenes, as in the plays of Euripides. The chorus may be described as a group personality, like an old Parliament. It has its own traditions, habits of thought and feeling, and mode of being. It exists, in a sense, as a living entity, but not with the sharp actuality of an individual. It perceives; but its perception is at once wider and vaguer than that of a single man. It shares, in its way, the seeking action of the play as a whole; but it cannot act in all the modes; it depends upon the chief agonists to invent and try out the detail of policy, just as a rather helpless but critical Parliament depends upon the Prime Minister to act but, in its less specific form of life, survives his destruction.

When the chorus enters after the prologue, with its questions, its invocation of the various gods, and its focus upon the hidden and jeopardized welfare of the City—Athens or Thebes—the list of essential *dramatis personæ*,[10] as well as the elements needed to celebrate the ritual, is complete, and the main action can begin. It is the function of the chorus to mark the stages of this action, and to perform the suffering and perceiving part of the tragic rhythm. The protagonist and his antagonists develop the "purpose" with which the tragic sequence begins; the chorus, with its less than individual being, broods over the agons, marks their stages with a word (like that of the chorus leader in the middle of the Tiresias scene), and (expressing its emotions and visions in song and dance) suffers the results, and the new perception at the end of the fight.

The choral odes are lyrics but they are not to be understood as poetry, the art of words, only, for they are intended also to be danced and sung. And though each chorus has its own shape, like that of a discrete lyric—its beginning, middle, and end—it represents also one passion or pathos in the changing action of the whole. This passion, like the other moments in the tragic rhythm, is felt at so general, or, rather, so deep a level that it seems to contain both the mob ferocity that Nietzsche felt in it and, at the other extreme, the patience of prayer. It is informed by faith in the unseen order of nature and the gods, and moves through a sequence of modes of suffering. This may

10 [Cast of characters.]

be illustrated from the chorus I have quoted at the end of the Tiresias scene.

It begins (close to the savage emotion of the end of the fight) with images suggesting that cruel "Bacchic frenzy" which is supposed to be the common root of tragedy and of the "old" comedy: "In panoply of fire and lightning / The son of Zeus now springs upon him." In the first antistrophe these images come together more clearly as we relish the chase; and the fleeing culprit, as we imagine him, begins to resemble Oedipus, who is lame, and always associated with the rough wilderness of Kitharon. But in the second strophe, as though appalled by its ambivalent feelings and the imagined possibilities, the chorus sinks back into a more dark and patient posture of suffering, "in awe," "hovering in hope." In the second antistrophe this is developed into something like the orthodox Christian attitude of prayer, based on faith, and assuming the possiblity of a hitherto unimaginable truth and answer: "Zeus and Apollo are wise," etc. The whole chorus then ends with a new vision of Oedipus, of the culprit, and of the direction in which the welfare of the City is to be sought. This vision is still colored by the chorus's human love of Oedipus as Hero, for the chorus has still its own purgation to complete, cannot as yet accept completely either the suffering in store for it, or Oedipus as scapegoat. But it marks the end of the first complete "purpose-passion-perception" unit, and lays the basis for the new purpose which will begin the next unit.

It is also to be noted that the chorus changes the scene which we, as audience, are to imagine. During the agon between Oedipus and Tiresias, our attention is fixed upon their clash, and the scene is literal, close, and immediate: before Oedipus' palace. When the fighters depart and the choral music starts, the focus suddenly widens, as though we had been removed to a distance. We become aware of the interested City around the bright arena; and beyond that, still more dimly, of Nature, sacred to the hidden gods. Mr. Burke has expounded the fertile notion that human action may be understood in terms of the scene in which it occurs, and vice versa: the scene is defined by the mode of action. The chorus's action is not limited by the sharp, rationalized purposes of the protagonist; its mode of action, more patient, less sharply realized, is cognate with a wider, if less accurate, awareness of the scene of human life. But the chorus's action, as I have remarked, is not that of passion itself (Nietzsche's cosmic void of night) but suffering informed by the faith of the tribe in a human and a divinely sanctioned natural order: "If such deeds as these are honored," the chorus asks after Jocasta's impiety, "why should I dance and sing?" (lines 894, 895). Thus it is one of the most important functions of the chorus to reveal, in its widest and most mysterious extent, the theater of human life which the play, and indeed the whole Festival of Dionysos, assumed, Even when the chorus does not speak, but only watches, it maintains this theme and this perspective—ready to take the whole stage when the fighters depart.

If one thinks of the movement of the play, it appears that the tragic rhythm analyzes human action temporally into successive modes, as a crystal analyzes a white beam of light spatially into the colored bands of the spectrum. The chorus, always present, represents one of these modes, and at the recurrent moments when reasoned purpose is gone, it takes the stage with its faith-informed passion, moving through an ordered succession of modes of suffering, to a new perception of the immediate situation.

SOPHOCLES AND EURIPIDES, THE RATIONALIST

Oedipus Rex is a changing image of human life and action which could have been formed only in the mirror of the tragic theater of the Festival of Dionysos. The perspectives of the myth, of the rituals, and of the traditional *hodos*, the way of life of the City—"habits of thought and feeling" which constitute the traditional wisdom of the race—were all required to make this play possible. That is why we have to try to regain these perspectives if we are to understand the written play which has come down to us: the analysis of the play leads to an analysis of the theater in which it was formed.

But though the theater was there, everyone could not use it to the full: Sophocles was required. This becomes clear if one considers the very different use which Euripides, Sophocles' contemporary, makes of the tragic theater and its ritual forms.

Professor Gilbert Murray has explained in detail how the tragic form is derived from the ritual form; and he has demonstrated the ritual forms which are preserved in each of the extant Greek tragedies. In general, the ritual had its agon, or sacred combat, between the old king, or god or hero, and the new, corresponding to the agons in the tragedies, and the clear "purpose" moment of the tragic rhythm. It had its *Sparagmos*,[11] in which the royal victim was literally or symbolically torn asunder, followed by the lamentation and/or rejoicing of the chorus: elements which correspond to the moments of "passion." The ritual had its messenger, its recognition scene, and its epiphany; various plot devices for representing the moment of "perception" which follows the "pathos." Professor Murray, in a word, studies the art of tragedy in the light of ritual forms, and thus, throws a really new light upon Aristotle's *Poetics*. The parts of the ritual would appear to correspond to parts of the plot, like recognitions and

11 [Immolation.]

scenes of suffering, which Aristotle mentions, but, in the text which has come down to us, fails to expound completely. In this view, both the ritual and the more highly elaborated and individualized art of tragedy would be "imitating" action in the tragic rhythm; the parts of the ritual, and the parts of the plot, would both be devices for showing forth the three movements of this rhythm.

Professor Murray, however, does not make precisely these deductions. Unlike Aristotle, he takes the plays of Euripides, rather than Sophocles' *Oedipus*, as the patterns of the tragic form. That is because his attitude to the ritual forms is like Euripides' own: he responds to their purely theatrical effectiveness, but has no interest or belief in the pre-rational image of human nature and destiny which the ritual conveyed; which Sophocles felt as still alive and significant for his generation, and presented once more in Oedipus. Professor Murray shows that Euripides restored the literal ritual much more accurately than Sophocles—his epiphanies, for example, are usually the bodily showing-forth of a very human god, who cynically expounds his cruel part in the proceedings; while the "epiphany" in *Oedipus*, the final tableau of the blind old man with his incestuous brood, merely conveys the moral truth which underlay the action, and implies the anagoge: human dependence upon a mysterious and divine order of nature. Perhaps these distinctions may be summarized as follows: Professor Murray is interested in the ritual forms in abstraction from all content; Sophocles saw also the spiritual content of the old forms: understood them at a level deeper than the literal, as imitations of an action still "true" to life in his sophisticated age.

Though Euripides and Sophocles wrote at the same time and for the same theater, one cannot understand either the form or the meaning of Euripides' plays on the basis of Sophocles' dramaturgy. The beautiful lyrics sung by Euripides' choruses are, as I have said, incidental music rather than organic parts of the action; they are not based upon the feeling that all have a stake in the common way of life and therefore in the issue of the present action. Euripides' individualistic heroes find no light in their suffering, and bring no renewal to the moral life of the community: they are at war with the very clear, human, and malicious gods, and what they suffer, they suffer unjustly and to no good end. Where Sophocles' celebrated irony seems to envisage the *condition humaine*[12] itself—the plight of the psyche in a world which is ultimately mysterious to it—Euripides' ironies are all aimed at the incredible "gods" and at the superstitions of those who believe in them. In short, if these two writers both used the tragic theater, they did so in very different ways.

Verral's *Euripides the Rationalist* shows very clearly what the

12 [Human plight.]

basis of Euripides' dramaturgy is. His use of myth and ritual is like that which Cocteau or, still more exactly, Sartre makes of them—for parody or satirical exposition, but without any belief in their meaning. If Euripides presents the plight of Electra in realistic detail, it is because he wants us to feel the suffering of the individual without benefit of any objective moral or cosmic order—with an almost sensational immediacy: he does not see the myth, as a whole, as significant as such. If he brings Apollo, in the flesh, before us, it is not because he "believes" in Apollo, but because he disbelieves in him, and wishes to reveal this figment of the Greek imagination as, literally, incredible. He depends as much as Sophocles upon the common heritage of ritual and myth: but he "reduces" its form and images to the uses of parody and metaphorical illustration, in the manner of Ovid and of the French Neoclassic tradition. And the human action he reveals is the extremely modern one of the psyche caught in the categories its reason invents, responding with unmitigated sharpness to the feeling of the moment, but cut off from the deepest level of experience, where the mysterious world is yet felt as real and prior to our inventions, demands, and criticisms.

Though Sophocles was not using the myths and ritual forms of the tragic theater for parody and to satirize their tradition, it does not appear that he had any more naïve belief in their literal validity than Euripides did. He would not, for his purpose, have had to ask himself whether the myth of Oedipus conveyed any historic facts. He would not have had to believe that the performance of *Oedipus*, or even the Festival of Dionysos itself, would assure the Athenians a good crop of children and olives. On the contrary he must have felt that the tragic rhythm of action which he discerned in the myth, which he felt as underlying the forms of the ritual, and which he realized in so many ways in his play, was a deeper version of human life than any particular manifestation of it, or any conceptual understanding of it, whether scientific and rationalistic, or theological; yet potentially including them all. If one takes Mr. Troy's suggestion, one might say, using the Medieval notion of fourfold symbolism, that Sophocles might well have taken myth and ritual as literally "fictions," yet still have accepted their deeper meanings—trope, allegory, and anagoge—as valid.

Oedipus: THE IMITATION OF AN ACTION

The general notion we used to compare the forms and spiritual content of tragedy and of ancient ritual was the "imitation of action." Ritual imitates action in one way, tragedy in another; and Sophocles' use of ritual forms indicates that he sensed the tragic rhythm common to both.

But the language, plot, characters of the play may also be understood in more detail and in relation to each other as imitations, in their various media, of the one action. I have already quoted Coleridge on the unity of action: "not properly a rule," he calls it, "but in itself the great end, not only of the drama, but of the epic, lyric, even to the candle-flame cone of an epigram—not only of poetry, but of poesy in general, as the proper generic term inclusive of all the fine arts, as its species."[13] Probably the influence of Coleridge partly accounts for the revival of this notion of action which underlies the recent studies of poetry which I have mentioned. Mr. Burke's phrase, "language as symbolic action," expresses the idea, and so does his dictum: "The poet spontaneously knows that 'beauty *is* as beauty *does*' (that the 'state' must be embodied in an 'actualization')." (*Four Tropes.*)

This idea of action, and of the play as the imitation of an action, is ultimately derived from the *Poetics*. This derivation is explained in the Appendix. At this point I wish to show how the complex form of *Oedipus*—its plot, characters, and discourse—may be understood as the imitation of a certain action.

The action of the play is the quest for Laius' slayer. That is the over-all aim which informs it—"to find the culprit in order to purify human life," as it may be put. Sophocles must have seen this seeking action as the real life of the Oedipus myth, discerning it through the personages and events as one discerns "life in a plant through the green leaves." Moreover, he must have seen this particular action as a type, or crucial instance, of human life in general; and hence he was able to present it in the form of the ancient ritual which also presents and celebrates the perennial mystery of human life and action. Thus by "action" I do not mean the events of the story but the focus or aim of psychic life from which the events, in that situation, result.

If Sophocles was imitating action in this sense, one may schematically imagine his work of composition in three stages, three mimetic acts: 1. He makes the plot: i.e., arranges the events of the story in such a way as to reveal the seeking action from which they come. 2. He develops the characters of the story as individualized forms of "quest." 3. He expresses or realizes their actions by means of the words they utter in the various situations of the plot. This scheme, of course, has nothing to do with the temporal order which the poet may really have followed in elaborating his composition, nor to the order we follow in becoming acquainted with it; we start with the words, the "green leaves." The scheme refers to the "hierarchy of actualizations" which we may eventually learn to see in the completed work.

13 The essay on *Othello*.

1. The first act of imitation consists in making the plot or arrangement of incidents. Aristotle says that the tragic poet is primarily a maker of plots, for the plot is the "soul of a tragedy," its formal cause. The arrangement which Sophocles made of the events of the story—starting near the end, and rehearsing the past in relation to what is happening now—already to some degree actualizes the tragic quest he wishes to show, even before we sense the characters as individuals or hear them speak and sing.

(The reader must be warned that this conception of the plot is rather unfamiliar to us. Usually we do not distinguish between the plot as the form of the play and the plot as producing a certain effect upon the audience—excitement, "interest," suspense, and the like. Aristotle also uses "plot" in this second sense. The mimicry of art has a further purpose, or final—as distinguished from its formal—cause, i.e., to reach the audience. Thinking of the Athenian theater, he describes the plot as intended to show the "universal," or to rouse and purge the emotions of pity and terror. These two meanings of the word—the form of the action, and the device for reaching the audience—are also further explained in the Appendix. At this point I am using the word *plot* in the first sense: as the form, the first actualization, of the tragic action.)

2. The characters, or agents, are the second actualization of the action. According to Aristotle, "the agents are imitated mainly with a view to the action"—i.e., the soul of the tragedy is there already in the order of events, the tragic rhythm of the life of Oedipus and Thebes; but this action may be more sharply realized and more elaborately shown forth by developing individual variations upon it. It was with this principle in mind that Ibsen wrote to his publisher, after two years of work on *The Wild Duck*, that the play was nearly complete, and he could now proceed to "the more energetic individuation of the characters."

If one considers the Oedipus-Tiresias scene which I have quoted, one can see how the characters serve to realize the action of the whole. They reveal, at any moment, a "spectrum of action" like that which the tragic rhythm spread before us in temporal succession, at the same time offering concrete instances of almost photographic sharpness. Thus Tiresias "suffers" in the darkness of his blindness while Oedipus pursues his reasoned "purpose"; and then Tiresias effectuates his "purpose" of serving his mantic vision of the truth, while Oedipus "suffers" a blinding passion of fear and anger. The agents also serve to move the action ahead, develop it in time, through their conflicts. The chorus meanwhile, in some respects between, in others deeper, than the antagonists, represents the interests of that resolution, that final chord of feeling, in which the end of

very important

the action, seen ironically and sympathetically as one, will be realized.

3. The third actualization is in the words of the play. The seeking action which is the substance of the play is imitated first in the plot, second in the characters, and third in the words, concepts, and forms of discourse wherein the characters "actualize" their psychic life in its shifting forms, in response to the everchanging situations of the play. If one thinks of plotting, characterization, and poetry as successive "acts of imitation" by the author, one may also say that they constitute, in the completed work, a hierarchy of forms; and that the words of the play are its "highest individuation." They are the "green leaves" which we actually perceive; the product and the sign of the one "life of the plant" which, by an imaginative effort, one may divine behind them all.

At this point one encounters again Mr. Burke's theory of "language as symbolic action," and the many contemporary studies of the arts of poetry which have been made from this point of view. It would be appropriate to offer a detailed study of Sophocles' language, using the modern tools of analysis, to substantiate my main point. But this would require the kind of knowledge of Greek which a Jebb spent his life to acquire; and I must be content to try to show, in very general terms, that the varied forms of the poetry of *Oedipus* can only be understood on a histrionic basis: i.e., as coming out of a direct sense of the tragic rhythm of *action.*

In the Oedipus-Tiresias scene, there is a "spectrum of the forms of discourse" corresponding to the "spectrum of action" which I have described. It extends from Oedipus' opening speech—a reasoned exposition not, of course, without feeling but based essentially upon clear ideas and a logical order—to the choral chant, based upon sensuous imagery and the "logic of feeling." Thus it employs, in the beginning, the principle of composition which Mr. Burke calls "syllogistic progression," and, at the other end of the spectrum, Mr. Burke's "progression by association and contrast." When the Neoclassic and rationalistic critics of the seventeenth century read *Oedipus,* they saw only the order of reason; they did not know what to make of the chorus. Hence Racine's drama of "Action as Rational": a drama of static situations, of clear concepts and merely illustrative images. Nietzsche, on the other hand, saw only the passion of the chorus; for his insight was based on *Tristan,* which is composed essentially in sensuous images, and moves by association and contrast according to the logic of feeling: the drama which takes "action as passion." Neither point of view enables one to see how the scene, as a whole, hangs together.

If the speeches of the characters and the songs of the chorus are only the foliage of the plant, this is as much as to say that the life and meaning of the whole is never literally and completely present in any one formulation. It takes *all* of the elements—the shifting situation, the changing and developing characters, and their reasoned or lyric utterances, to indicate, in the round, the action Sophocles wishes to convey. Because this action takes the form of reason as well as passion, and of contemplation by way of symbols; because it is essentially moving (in the tragic rhythm); and because it is shared in different ways by all the characters, the play has neither literal unity nor the rational unity of the truly abstract idea, or "univocal concept." Its parts and its moments are one only "by analogy"; and just as the Saints warn us that we must believe in order to understand, so we must "make believe," by a sympathetic and imitative act of the histrionic sensibility, in order to get what Sophocles intended by his play.

It is the histrionic basis of Sophocles' art which makes it mysterious to us, with our demands for conceptual clarity, or for the luxury of yielding to a stream of feeling and subjective imagery. But it is this also which makes it so crucial an instance of the art of the theater in its completeness, as though the author understood "song, spectacle, thought, and diction" in their primitive and subtle roots. And it is the histrionic basis of drama which "undercuts theology and science."

ANALOGUES OF THE "TRAGIC RHYTHM"

In the present study I propose to use *Oedipus* as a landmark, and to relate subsequent forms of drama to it. For it presents a moving image at the nascent moment of highest valency, of a way of life and action which is still at the root of our culture.

Professor Buchanan remarks, in *Poetry and Mathematics*, that the deepest and most elaborate development of the tragic rhythm is to be found in the *Divine Comedy*. The *Purgatorio* especially, though an epic and not a drama, evidently moves in the tragic rhythm, both as a whole and in detail. The daylight climb up the mountain, by moral effort, and in the light of natural reason, corresponds to the first moment, that of "purpose." The night, under the sign of Faith, Hope and Charity, when the Pilgrim can do nothing by his own unaided efforts, corresponds to the moments of passion and perception. The Pilgrim, as he pauses, mulls over the thoughts and experiences of the day; he sleeps and dreams, seeing ambivalent images from the mythic dreaming of the race, which refer, also, both to his own "suppressed desires" and to his own deepest aspirations. These images gradually solidify and clarify, giving place to a new perception of his situation. This rhythm, repeated in varied forms, carries the Pilgrim from the superficial but whole-hearted motivations of childhood, in the Antipurgatorio, through the divided counsels of the growing soul, to the new innocence, freedom, and integrity of the Terrestrial Paradise—the realm of *The Tempest* or of *Oedipus at Colonos*. The same rhythmic conception governs also the detail of the work, down to the *terza rima* itself—that verse-form which is clear at any moment in its literal fiction yet essentially moving ahead and pointing to deeper meanings.

Because Dante keeps his eye always upon the tragic moving of the psyche itself, his vision, like that of Sophocles, is not limited by any of the forms of thought whereby we seek to fix our experience—in which we are idolatrously expiring, like the coral animal in its shell. But Professor Buchanan shows that the abstract shape, at least, of the tragic rhythm is to be recognized in other and more limited or specialized cultural forms as well. "This pattern," he writes, "is the Greek view of life. It is the method of their and our science, history and philosophy. . . . The Greek employment of it had been humanistic in the main. . . . The late Middle Ages and the Renaissance substituted natural objects for the heroes of vicarious tragedies, the experiments in the laboratory. They put such objects under controlled conditions, introduced artificial complications, and waited for the answering pronouncement of fate. The crucial experiment is the crisis of an attempt to rationalize experience, that is, to force it into our analogies. Purgation and recognition are now called elimination of false hypotheses and verification. The shift is significant, but the essential tragic pattern of tragedy is still there."

The tragic rhythm is, in a sense, the shape of Racinian tragedy, even though Racine was imitating action as essentially rational, and would have called the moments of the rhythm exposition, complication, crisis, and denouement, to satisfy the reason. It is in a way the shape of *Tristan*, though action in that play is reduced to passion, the principles of composition to the logic of feeling. Even the over-all shape of *Hamlet* is similar, though the sense of pathos predominates, and the whole is elaborated in such subtle profusion as can only be explained with reference to Dante and the Middle Ages.

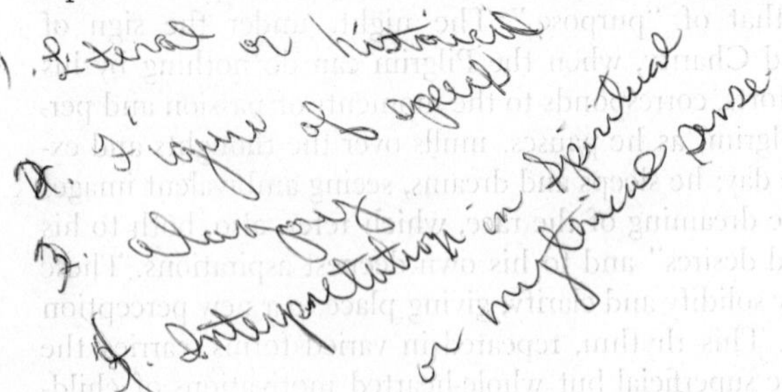

IV

THE COMIC EXPERIENCE

Out of Perception—Laughter

INTRODUCTION

I

"MAN IS the only animal that laughs and weeps; for he is the only animal that is struck with the difference between what things are, and what they ought to be."

This sentence from Hazlitt's essay "On Wit and Humor" goes to the heart of both tragic and comic experience. In tragedy we see or sense what ought to be. Oedipus, by virtue of his character and achievements, ought to be a happy man. Socrates, by virtue of his wisdom, ought to live out his days as a revered philosopher. Adonais, the poet, by virtue of the power and beauty of his thought and language, ought to be admired. The tall nun, by virtue of her holiness and courage, ought not to be drowned.

But Oedipus is condemned to a living hell of remorse; Socrates is sentenced to death; Adonais is scourged by ridicule; the nun perishes. We weep for them, because we perceive the difference between what "ought to be" and their actual predicament. We are involved in their predicament because the tragic writer has dwelt upon their suffering, even though, as we have indicated, he has in each case distilled an elixir of resignation or hope from the tragedy.

In comedy we also see or sense what ought to be. Why do we laugh at the pretensions of Walter Mitty, the hero of James Thurber's small classic of American humor? A man, we say, ought to be himself and ought to know himself for what he is. Hence we perceive at once the incongruity of Walter Mitty's daydreams. He pictures himself as Commander Walter Mitty navigating his SN202 "through the worst storm in twenty years of Navy flying"; as Dr. Walter Mitty coolly fixing the anesthetizer and then taking over the operation; as Walter Mitty, the crack shot; as Captain Mitty, the intrepid but nonchalant military hero. Yet he is actually a henpecked, middle-aged man who drives his car to Waterbury, is scored off by a cop and a parking-lot attendant, forgets what he was sent to purchase, and waits patiently for his wife in a hotel lobby. At the end, he projects his sense of frustration in an image of a condemned man before a firing squad scornfully refusing a handkerchief.

Walter Mitty's daydreams, emphasizing as they do the incongruity between his aspirations and his actual situation, are predominantly comic. They make us laugh, even though we can detect in them a vein of sadness. The same story, we feel, might have verged toward tragedy. Walter Mitty is close to the melancholy Chaplinesque clown, and to his tragic brother, the dulled and leveled man of a collective society who, in futile rebellion against his fate, slakes his thirst for heroism on romantic dreams.

Thus, we see that tragedy and comedy both derive from perception of the incongruity between things as they are and things as they ought to be. What distinguishes comedy from tragedy is the way the incongruity is presented. In tragedy the incongruity is presented as a *fatal* loss—of life, of reputation, of happiness; in comedy it is presented as an absurdity. In tragedy the incongruity "shocks and wounds the mind"; in comedy it relaxes and entertains. In tragedy we participate, by sympathetic identification, in the misfortunes of the hero; in comedy we stand at an emotional distance: we are observers rather than participants. In short, the incongruity of tragedy is painful while that of comedy is painless.

When we say that tragedy and comedy are reverse sides of the same coin we imply that the complete man must exercise his comic sense as well as his tragic sense. Man is both a laughing *and* a weeping animal. To achieve a balance between laughing and weeping, he needs to see life as delightfully amusing, ridiculous, absurd, and nonsensical, as well as seriously meaningful. The perception of comic incongruities not only relaxes his spirit—too often tautened by his anxieties and strivings—but serves also to refine his sense of the truth. While scorn and ridicule are not reliable tests of the truth, educated laughter can help to mark the line where good sense deviates into folly, the golden mean into mediocrity, human aspirations into vain ambition.

The comic sense is a bright spirit, often wayward, always hard to define. Thus, while we may describe tragic experience by the term tragedy without causing too much ambiguity, we need a variety of expressions even to approximate an accurate description of the range of comic experience. Educated laughter, comedy, humor, wit, satire, the perception of man's defects and excesses—all these terms are needed to do justice to the different aspects of comic experience.

To describe its range, we must account for at least three of its principal elements—spontaneity, correction, and reconciliation.

II

SPONTANEITY / Spontaneity designates the free play of the mind delighting in the droll, the absurd, the ridiculous, each for its own sake. Spontaneous comedy has no serious intention to improve our morals or to set our thinking straight. Often it is marked by a delight in verbal high jinks, the use of puns, personifications, absurd parallels, outrageous hyperboles, and madly perverted logic. Thus Rabelais, in *Pantagruel*, makes fun of lawyers by presenting their thoughts in language that sounds learned, logical, and profound, yet makes no sense.

> For the common custom of the Salic Law is such that the first firebrand who flays and dishorns the cow, and blows his nose in a full concert of instruments without sol-faing the cobbler's stitches, should in time of nightmare sublimate the penury of his thingumajig. . . .

In a similar vein, Lewis Carroll tells the fantastic story of the Boojum as if it had the reality of an historical event, and T. S. Eliot amuses us in "Macavity" by using the bated-breath style of a Scotland Yard murder mystery for the whimsical account of a criminal cat.

But, for the most part, verbal humor and wit are closely connected with the perception of some incongruity in a character or a situation or in the interconnection of one with the other. Thus, in Eudora Welty's "Why I Live at the P.O.," the language is humorous chiefly because it reveals "Sister's" half-righteous, half-wrong-headed, but always hare-brained objections to her treatment at the hands of Mama, Papa-Daddy, Uncle Rondo and, most of all, her sibling, Stella-Rondo. "Sister" is very amusing, and by her use of language we perceive how amusing she is.

The language in A. P. Herbert's "The Negotiable Cow" is even more hilarious, but it is linked less with the revelation of character than with a farcical situation. Mr. Albert Haddock chooses to write his check for payment of his income tax on the flank of a cow, which he tenders at the Collector's office. When the check is refused (due to the cow's resentment at being endorsed on its abdomen), Mr. Haddock is forced to lead the cow away. A crowd collects around the cow in Trafalgar Square and Constable Boot arrests Mr. Haddock for obstructing traffic. Now Mr. Haddock is a defendant against two charges, one brought by the Inland Revenue Service for failure to pay taxes, the other by the constable for disorderly conduct.

Mr. Haddock's defense and Sir Basil String's decision are reported in impeccable legal prose. Not once does the tone of judicial logic falter. Yet the whole machinery of justice, replete with citations of legal authorities, serves to prolong an ingenious practical joke—a joke that invokes the law against the law.

III

CORRECTION / The second element in the comic experience is correction. Correction, as we use the term, designates that kind of comedy that criticizes human action with a view toward the purging of error or vice. Louis Kronenberger writes:

> Comedy is criticism. If through laughter at others we purge ourselves of certain spiteful and ungenerous instincts . . . that is not quite the whole of it. Comedy need not be hostile to idealism; it need only show how far human beings fall short of the ideal. . . . Comedy is criticism, then, because it exposes human beings for what they are in contrast to what they profess to be. . . . Always it is the enemy, not of virtue or idealism, but of hypocrisy and pretense. . . .

Corrective comedy does not lack amusement, for all its emphasis on criticism. It could hardly hope to win our attention if it were flatly didactic or intemperately moralistic. On the contrary, it achieves its critical aim chiefly because it delights the reader while it guides him; like sports, it mingles its benefits with its pleasures. In fact, because corrective comedy must sail close to the rocks and shoals of instruction, it has developed many special literary pleasures, which Dostoevsky successfully employs in his novella *The Crocodile*.

By the end of Dostoevsky's acidulously comic tale, only the unperceptive reader fails to realize that it takes aim at the folly of men. The target is avant-garde humanitarianism. Dostoevsky's humanitarians pity the crocodile who swallowed Ivan Matveich rather than poor Ivan himself. In the name of advanced economic theory and progress, the newspaper writers, Ivan's old friend Timofey Semyonich, his wife Elena, even Semyon Semyonich, the sympathetic narrator himself, all come round to thinking that Ivan is better off forgotten than saved.

This unmistakable satire on the reversal of human values in Russia of 1865 emphasizes, in the telling, the amusing or absurd aspects of human nature. We laugh at the caricature of the German proprietors, at Elena's coquetries, at Timofey Semyonich's bureaucratic concern with legal procedures and, above all, at their involvement with the future success of the crocodile business. Moreover, Ivan's fatuous delusion that in the bowels of the crocodile he can make a name for himself as a scientific observer and an economic theorist, and the newspaper commentators' totally mistaken reading of the situation reduce to absurdity the whole complex of rationalizations. Dostoevsky does not argue; he simply lets his characters act out their folly in ridiculous speeches and gestures.

Hence we come to accept his corrective aim because we have seen for ourselves that those who profess to be enlightened are in fact the slaves of their personal desires and of the pressure of collective attitudes. Dostoevsky, like most good comic writers, is careful to focus attention on painless incongruity and to pass over the painful possibilities that lurk beneath the surface of his fantastic situation. He deals less with a completely realized individual with whom we might be tempted to identify than he does with the typical characteristics of that individual.

Most corrective comedy concerns a typical human folly. Thus Horace, in his Epode 2, popularly known as "The Happy Man," puts into the mouth of Alfius, a Roman usurer, a romantic eulogy of the good life on a family farm. But the kind of life Alfius admires, and he does so with elegance and perspicuity, he does not pursue. Not for him, any more than for a contemporary tycoon, the bucolic joys of sowing and reaping, early rising and early sleeping. Thus while we may not share in Alfius' hypocrisy, we recognize it as a typical failing of human nature and we ruminate on the discrepancy between human ideals and human practice.

Alexander Pope's poem—"Epistle II. To a Lady"—for all its special concern with aristocratic London society of the eighteenth century, also underlines common human defects. Rufa is beautiful in public view, but at home she wears a dirty smock and greases her face; Silia is all meekness, but becomes enraged when someone observes a pimple on her nose; Narcissa oscillates between piety and libertinage; Flavia dies "of nothing but a rage to live." In this composite picture, "Woman's at best a contradiction still." It is this contradiction, no less true of men, though they display it differently, that is at the heart of Pope's satire on the follies of women. And again, while we enjoy the wit with which these follies are expressed, we see in Pope's polished mirror some likenesses to our own flawed and foolish characters.

In Pope the corrective element is clearly marked. One cannot ignore his unified purpose, his consistently ironic tone, his devastating contrasts, his accumulation of incongruities. Nor can one mistake Robert Burns's moral in "To a Louse," or G. K. Chesterton's contempt for compromise in "The World State," or Robert Graves's denunciation of service mentality in "1805." But just as often the comic experience presents the corrective element as by-play, a sidelong thrust, or digression. Thus Andrew Marvell's "To His Coy Mistress" (see p. 535), though not a comedy, is at times sportive. In these two lines,

> The grave's a fine and private place,
> But none, I think, do there embrace.

he aims to correct his lady's shyness. In *Don Juan*, Byron digresses from the romance of Don Juan and Haidee to write a generalized satire on a certain type of poet. His poet, who pretends to sincerity, is a pliable fellow who will give his audience what it wants to hear.

> He lied with such a fervor of intention
> There was no doubt he earned his laureate pension

In pursuing the digression, Byron improvises a scene in which his chameleonic poet performs. The digression at an end, Byron resumes his interrupted story of Don Juan's love affair.

IV

RECONCILIATION / The third element in the comic experience is reconciliation. We use this term to describe comedies that may be serious, but are certainly not tragedies; comedies that may be spontaneous, but are not in the main humorous; or comedies that may be corrective, but are not predominantly satirical or didactic. Comedies of this sort not only describe events that begin in misfortune and end in prosperity, they also reconcile the discords and paradoxes of human experience. The hero, originally involved in a tangle of debts, wins his fortune in Australia. The heroine, suspected of infidelity, is proved virtuous and constant. The true heir, supplanted by his evil brother, is identified by a birthmark and claims his title. Or, on a more sophisticated level, the young poet, at first emotionally tormented, ultimately finds his way to inner peace; or the old philosopher, starting with the conviction that the world is a senseless muddle, comes to see it as a meaningful mystery.

But reconciliation does not mean merely that the loose ends of a plot are neatly tied up before the last curtain. Resolution of this sort may be an outward or technical sign that the inner difficulties of the story are reconciled. On the other hand, it may mean that the author has come to an end without reaching a conclusion. A true reconciliation is not the packaging of events, but rather the artistic explanation of how the opposites of good and evil, youth and age, the real and the ideal may be harmonized.

One of man's most persistent intuitions is that the harmony of opposites underlies the order of the universe; that chaos, or disorder, is an affront to his intelligence and a threat to his happiness. John Dryden summed up a long tradition in "A Song for St. Cecilia's Day":

> From harmony, from heav'nly harmony
> This universal frame began;
> When Nature underneath a heap
> Of jarring atoms lay,
> And could not heave her head,

The tuneful Voice was heard from high,
"Arise, ye more than dead."
Then cold and hot and moist and dry
In order to their stations leap
And Music's pow'r obey.
From harmony, from heav'nly harmony
This universal frame began:
From harmony to harmony
Through all the compass of the notes it ran,
The diapason closing full in Man.

Man has always felt, too, that harmony was possible even in the turbulent human sphere, provided of course man could discover the key to a reconciliation of opposites. Hence every important philosopher has devoted much of his thought to the problem of how, in a world where evil certainly exists, good can triumph and happiness can be achieved. The same conundrum haunts the poet and the artist. They have tried to solve it, not only by appropriating the thoughts of the philosophers but, more importantly, by creating imaginary worlds where reconciliations cannot be frustrated either by the outrages of fortune or the perversities of logic. The golden age of the mythologists, the Arcadia of the pastoral poets, the magical forests of medieval romancers—all are symbols of attempted reconciliations. Perhaps the most successful of all these attempts is Shakespeare's *The Tempest*.

In the last act Prospero, by virtue of his magic, triumphs in all his endeavors. The innocent, after being tried, receive their reward. Prospero is restored to his dukedom; Ferdinand and Miranda are safely engaged to marry; Ariel is freed. Conversely, the guilty—Antonio, Prospero's evil brother; Sebastian, the conniving Prince of Naples; and even Alonso, the King of Naples—are conscience-stricken. Since detection of their crimes diminishes their power to do evil, they are punished, forgiven, and restored to society. Caliban, Stephano, and Trinculo are, each according to measure, chastised and reconciled to their masters. The play ends in a luminous halo of understanding. Miranda exclaims:

Oh, wonder!
How many godly creatures are there here!
How beauteous mankind is! Oh, brave new world,
That has such people in't!

Gonzalo rejoices over the rediscovery of Ferdinand, and sees in the Prince's marriage to Miranda the reconciliation of Milan and Naples. The gods have wrought good from evil.

Was Milan thrust from Milan, that his issue
Should become King of Naples? Oh, rejoice
Beyond a common joy! And set it down
With gold on lasting pillars. In one voyage
Did Claribel her husband find at Tunis
And Ferdinand, her brother, find a wife
Where he himself was lost, Prospero his dukedom
In a poor isle, and all of us ourselves
When no man was his own.

The last line in Gonzalo's speech suggests that each man was also reconciled to himself. Under Prospero's spells each had come to know himself for what he was. Even Prospero knows himself better. Prospero, the supreme enchanter, had earlier identified his own fault as neglect of his duties.

I, thus neglecting worldly ends, all dedicated
To closeness and the bettering of my mind
With that which, but by being so retired,
O'erprized all popular rate, in my false brother
Awaked an evil nature.

Now, at the end of the play, he willingly foregoes his magic powers and prepares to resume his duties in the world of Milan where, however, "Every third thought shall be [his] grave." Thus Prospero's final action brings into harmony the imagined world of the enchanted isle and the real world, now touched with magic.

Reconciliation on the poetic scale attained in *The Tempest* cannot be reduced to rough-hewn ethical norms. The play is not a mere allegory of good and evil in which Prospero stands for providence, Ariel for the spirit, Caliban for sensuality, Miranda for original innocence, Antonio for human evil, and so on. Too much of it is sheer imagination. Like music, and *The Tempest* is full of song, the play sweeps along in obedience to its own inner rhythm, with alternations of storm and tranquillity, of murderous plots and lyric interludes, of spectacle and song, of high comedy and raucous burlesque, of delicate fantasy and brutal realism. It is held together as much by mood as by tightly woven incident, as much by the symbolism of beneficent magic as by an appeal to our common sense.

Yet we realize that, while the play appeals directly to our sense of beauty, it does not, for that reason, ignore our desire for truth. As W. H. Auden has remarked, Ariel, the free spirit, symbolic of beauty, is a rival but not an antagonist of Prospero, the benign philosopher, symbolic of wisdom. And who will say that Shakespeare's great comedy of reconciliation does not also reconcile the offices of Ariel and Prospero?

STORIES

James Thurber

THE SECRET LIFE OF WALTER MITTY

"WE'RE going through!" The Commander's voice was like thin ice breaking. He wore his full-dress uniform, with the heavily braided white cap pulled down rakishly over one cold gray eye. "We can't make it, sir. It's spoiling for a hurricane, if you ask me." "I'm not asking you, Lieutenant Berg," said the Commander. "Throw on the power lights! Rev her up to 8500! We're going through!" The pounding of the cylinders increased: ta-pocketa-pocketa-pocketa-*pocketa-pocketa*. The Commander stared at the ice forming on the pilot window. He walked over and twisted a row of complicated dials. "Switch on No. 8 auxiliary!" he shouted. "Switch on No. 8 auxiliary!" repeated Lieutenant Berg. "Full strength in No. 3 turret!" shouted the Commander. "Full strength in No. 3 turret!" The crew, bending to their various tasks in the huge, hurtling eight-engined Navy hydroplane, looked at each other and grinned. "The Old Man'll get us through," they said to one another. "The Old Man ain't afraid of hell!"

"Not so fast! You're driving too fast!" said Mrs. Mitty. "What are you driving so fast for?"

"Hmm?" said Walter Mitty. He looked at his wife, in the seat beside him, with shocked astonishment. She seemed grossly unfamiliar, like a strange woman who had yelled at him in a crowd. "You were up to fifty-five," she said. "You know I don't like to go more than forty. You were up to fifty-five." Walter Mitty drove on toward Waterbury in silence, the roaring of the SN202 through the worst storm in twenty years of Navy flying fading in the remote, intimate airways of his mind. "You're tensed up again," said Mrs. Mitty. "It's one of your days. I wish you'd let Dr. Renshaw look you over."

Walter Mitty stopped the car in front of the building where his wife went to have her hair done. "Remember to get those overshoes while I'm having my hair done," she said. "I don't need overshoes," said Mitty. She put her mirror back into her bag. "We've been all through that," she said, getting out of the car. "You're not a young man any longer." He raced the engine a little. "Why don't you wear your gloves? Have you lost your gloves?" Walter Mitty reached in a pocket and brought out the gloves. He put them on, but after she had turned and gone into the building and he had driven on to a red light, he took them off again. "Pick it up, brother!" snapped a cop as the light changed, and Mitty hastily pulled on his gloves and lurched ahead. He drove around the streets aimlessly for a time, and then he drove past the hospital on his way to the parking lot.

. . . "It's the millionaire banker, Wellington McMillan," said the pretty nurse. "Yes?" said Walter Mitty, removing his gloves slowly. "Who has the case?" "Dr. Renshaw and Dr. Benbow, but there are two specialists here, Dr. Remington from New York and Dr. Pritchard-Mitford from London. He flew over." A door opened down a long, cool corridor and Dr. Renshaw came out. He looked distraught and haggard. "Hello, Mitty," he said. "We're having the devil's own time with McMillan, the millionaire banker and close personal friend of Roosevelt. Obstreosis of the ductal tract. Tertiary. Wish you'd take a look at him." "Glad to," said Mitty.

In the operating room there were whispered introductions: "Dr. Remington, Dr. Mitty. Dr. Pritchard-Mitford, Dr. Mitty." "I've read your book on streptothricosis," said Pritchard-Mitford, shaking hands. "A brilliant performance, sir." "Thank you," said Walter Mitty. "Didn't know you were in the States, Mitty," grumbled Remington. "Coals to Newcastle, bringing Mitford and me up here for a tertiary." "You are very kind," said Mitty. A huge, complicated machine, connected to the operating table, with many tubes and wires, began at this moment to go pocketa-pocketa-pocketa. "The new anesthetizer is giving away!" shouted an intern. "There is no one in the East who knows how to fix it." "Quiet, man!" said Mitty, in a low, cool voice. He sprang to the machine, which was now going pocketa-pocketa-queep-pocketa-queep. He began fingering delicately a row of glistening dials. "Give me a fountain pen!" he snapped. Someone handed him a fountain pen. He pulled a faulty piston out of the machine and inserted the pen in its place. "That will hold for ten minutes," he said. "Get on with the operation." A nurse hurried over and whispered to Renshaw, and Mitty saw the man turn pale. "Coreopsis has set in," said Renshaw nervously. "If you would take over, Mitty?" Mitty looked at him and at the craven figure of Benbow, who drank, and at the grave, uncertain faces of the two great specialists. "If you wish," he said. They slipped a white gown on him; he adjusted a mask and drew on thin gloves; nurses handed him shining . . .

"Back it up, Mac! Look out for that Buick!" Walter Mitty jammed on the brakes. "Wrong lane, Mac," said the parking-lot attendant, looking at Mitty closely. "Gee. Yeh," muttered Mitty. He began cautiously to back out of the lane marked "Exit Only." "Leave her set there," said the attendant. "I'll put her away." Mitty got out of the car. "Hey, better leave the key." "Oh," said Mitty, handing the man the ignition key. The attendant vaulted into the car, backed it up with insolent skill, and put it where it belonged.

They're so damn cocky, thought Walter Mitty, walking along Main Street; they think they know everything. Once he had tried to take his chains off, outside New Milford, and he had got them wound around the axles. A man had had to come out in a wrecking car and unwind them, a young, grinning garage-man. Since then Mrs. Mitty always made him drive to a garage to have the chains taken off. The next time, he thought, I'll wear my right arm in a sling; they won't grin at me then. I'll have my right arm in a sling and they'll see I couldn't possibly take the chains off myself. He kicked at the slush on the sidewalk. "Overshoes," he said to himself, and he began looking for a shoe store.

When he came out into the street again, with the overshoes in a box under his arm, Walter Mitty began to wonder what the other thing was his wife had told him to get. She had told him, twice before they set out from their house for Waterbury. In a way he hated these weekly trips to town—he was always getting something wrong. Kleenex, he thought, Squibb's, razor blades? No. Tooth paste, toothbrush, bicarbonate, carborundum, initiative and referendum? He gave it up. But she would remember it. "Where's the what's-its-name?" she would ask. "Don't tell me you forgot the what's-its-name." A newsboy went by shouting something about the Waterbury trial.

. . . "Perhaps this will refresh your memory." The District Attorney suddenly thrust a heavy automatic at the quiet figure on the witness stand. "Have you ever seen this before?" Walter Mitty took the gun and examined it expertly. "This is my Webley-Vickers 50.80," he said calmly. An excited buzz ran around the courtroom. The Judge rapped for order. "You are a crack shot with any sort of firearms, I believe?" said the District Attorney, insinuatingly. "Objection!" shouted Mitty's attorney. "We have shown that the defendant could not have fired the shot. We have shown that he wore his right arm in a sling on the night of the fourteenth of July." Walter Mitty raised his hand briefly and the bickering attorneys were stilled. "With any known make of gun," he said evenly. "I could have killed Gregory Fitzhurst at three hundred feet *with my left hand.*" Pandemonium broke loose in the courtroom. A woman's scream rose above the bedlam and suddenly a lovely, dark-haired girl was in Walter Mitty's arms. The District Attorney struck at her savagely. Without rising from his chair, Mitty let the man have it on the point of the chin. "You miserable cur!"

"Puppy biscuit," said Walter Mitty. He stopped walking and the buildings of Waterbury rose up out of the misty courtroom and surrounded him again. A woman who was passing laughed. "He said 'Puppy biscuit,' " she said to her companion. "That man said 'Puppy biscuit' to himself." Walter Mitty hurried on. He went into an A. & P., not the first one he came to but a smaller one farther up the street. "I want some biscuit for small, young dogs," he said to the clerk. "Any special brand, sir?" The greatest pistol shot in the world thought a moment. "It says 'Puppies Bark for It' on the box," said Walter Mitty.

His wife would be through at the hairdresser's in fifteen minutes, Mitty saw in looking at his watch, unless they had trouble drying it; sometimes they had trouble drying it. She didn't like to get to the hotel first; she would want him to be there waiting for her as usual. He found a big leather chair in the lobby, facing a window, and he put the overshoes and the puppy biscuit on the floor beside it. He picked up an old copy of *Liberty* and sank down into the chair. "Can Germany Conquer the World Through the Air?" Walter Mitty looked at the pictures of bombing planes and of ruined streets.

. . . "The cannonading has got the wind up in young Raleigh, sir," said the sergeant. Captain Mitty looked up at him through tousled hair. "Get him to bed," he said wearily, "with the others. I'll fly alone." "But you can't, sir," said the sergeant anxiously. "It takes two men to handle that bomber and the Archies are pounding hell out of the air. Von Richtman's circus is between here and Saulier." "Somebody's got to get that ammunition dump," said Mitty. "I'm going over. Spot of brandy?" He poured a drink for the sergeant and one for himself. War thundered and whined around the dug-out and battered at the door. There was a rending of wood, and splinters flew through the room. "A bit of a near thing," said Captain Mitty carelessly. "The box barrage is closing in," said the sergeant. "We only live once, Sergeant," said Mitty, with his faint, fleeting smile. "Or do we?" He poured another brandy and tossed it off. "I never see a man could hold his brandy like you, sir," said the sergeant. "Begging your pardon, sir." Captain Mitty stood up and strapped on his huge Webley-Vickers automatic. "It's forty kilometers through hell, sir," said the sergeant. Mitty finished one last brandy. "After all," he said softly, "what isn't?" The pounding of the cannon increased; there was the rat-tat-tatting of machine guns, and from somewhere came the menacing pocketa-pocketa-pocketa of the new flame-throwers. Walter Mitty walked to the door of the dugout humming "Auprès de Ma Blonde." He turned and waved to the sergeant. "Cheerio!" he said. . . .

Something struck his shoulder. "I've been looking all over this hotel for you," said Mrs. Mitty. "Why do you have to hide in this old chair? How did you expect me to find you?" "Things close in," said Walter Mitty vaguely. "What?" Mrs. Mitty said. "Did you get the what's-its-name? The puppy biscuit? What's in that box?" "Overshoes," said Mitty. "Couldn't you have put them on in the store?" "I was thinking," said Walter Mitty. "Does it ever occur to you that I am sometimes thinking?" She looked at him. "I'm going to take your temperature when I get you home," she said.

They went out through the revolving doors that made a faintly derisive whistling sound when you pushed them. It was two blocks to the parking lot. At the drugstore on the corner she said, "Wait here for me. I forgot something. I won't be a minute." She was more than a minute. Walter Mitty lighted a cigarette. It began to rain, rain with sleet in it. He stood up against the wall of the drugstore, smoking. . . . He put his shoulders back and his heels together. "To hell with the handkerchief," said Walter Mitty scornfully.

Eudora Welty
WHY I LIVE AT THE P.O.

I WAS getting along fine with Mama, Papa-Daddy and Uncle Rondo until my sister Stella-Rondo just separated from her husband and came back home again. Mr. Whitaker! Of course I went with Mr. Whitaker first, when he first appeared here in China Grove, taking "Pose Yourself" photos, and Stella-Rondo broke us up. Told him I was one-sided. Bigger on one side than the other, which is a deliberate, calculated falsehood: I'm the same. Stella-Rondo is exactly twelve months to the day younger than I am and for that reason she's spoiled.

She's always had anything in the world she wanted and then she'd throw it away. Papa-Daddy gave her this gorgeous Add-a-Pearl necklace when she was eight years old and she threw it away playing baseball when she was nine, with only two pearls.

So as soon as she got married and moved away from home the first thing she did was separate! From Mr. Whitaker! This photographer with the popeyes she said she trusted. Came home from one of those towns up in Illinois and to our complete surprise brought this child of two.

Mamma said she like to made her drop dead for a second. "Here you had this marvelous blonde child and never so much as wrote your mother a word about it," says Mama. "I'm thoroughly ashamed of you." But of course she wasn't.

Stella-Rondo just calmly takes off this *hat*, I wish you could see it. She says, "Why, Mama, Shirley-T.'s adopted, I can prove it."

"How?" says Mama, but all I says was, "H'm!" There I was over the hot stove, trying to stretch two chickens over five people and a completely unexpected child into the bargain, without one moment's notice.

"What do you mean—'H'm'?" says Stella-Rondo, and Mama says, "I heard that, Sister."

I said that oh, I didn't mean a thing, only that whoever Shirley-T. was, she was the spit-image of Papa-Daddy if he'd cut off his beard, which of course he'd never do in the world. Papa-Daddy's Mama's papa and sulks.

Stella-Rondo got furious! She said, "Sister, I don't need to tell you you got a lot of nerve and always did have and I'll thank you to make no future reference to my adopted child whatsoever."

"Very well," I said. "Very well, very well. Of course I noticed at once she looks like Mr. Whitaker's side too. That frown. She looks like a cross between Mr. Whitaker and Papa-Daddy."

"Well, all I can say is she isn't."

"She looks exactly like Shirley Temple to me," says Mama, but Shirley-T. just ran away from her.

So the first thing Stella-Rondo did at the table was turn Papa-Daddy against me.

"Papa-Daddy," she said. He was trying to cut up his meat. "Papa-Daddy!" I was taken completely by surprise. Papa-Daddy is about a million years old and's got this long-long beard. "Papa-Daddy, Sister says she fails to understand why you don't cut off your beard."

So Papa-Daddy l-a-y-s down his knife and fork! He's real rich. Mama says he is, he says he isn't. So he says, "Have I heard correctly? You don't understand why I don't cut off my beard?"

"Why," I says, "Papa-Daddy, of course I understand, I did not say any such of a thing, the idea!"

He says, "Hussy!"

I says, "Papa-Daddy, you know I wouldn't any more want you to cut off your beard than the man in the moon. It was the farthest thing from my mind! Stella-Rondo sat there and made that up while she was eating breast of chicken."

But he says, "So the postmistress fails to understand why I don't cut off my beard. Which job I got you through my influence with the government. 'Bird's nest'—is that what you call it?"

Not that it isn't the next to smallest P.O. in the entire state of Mississippi.

I says, "Oh, Papa-Daddy," I says, "I didn't say any such of a thing, I never dreamed it was a bird's nest, I have always been grateful though this is the next to smallest P.O. in the state of Mississippi, and I do not enjoy being referred to as a hussy by my own grandfather."

But Stella-Rondo says, "Yes, you did say it too. Anybody in the world could of heard you, that had ears."

"Stop right there," says Mama, looking at *me*.

So I pulled my napkin straight back through the napkin ring and left the table.

As soon as I was out of the room Mama says, "Call her back, or she'll starve to death," but Papa-Daddy says, "This is the beard I started growing on the Coast when I was fifteen years old." He would of gone on till nightfall if Shirley-T. hadn't lost the Milky Way she ate in Cairo.

So Papa-Daddy says, "I am going out and lie in the hammock, and you can all sit here and remember my words: I'll never cut off my beard as long as I live, even one inch, and I don't appreciate it in you at all." Passed right by me in the hall and went straight out and got in the hammock.

It would be a holiday. It wasn't five minutes before Uncle Rondo suddenly appeared in the hall in one of Stella-Rondo's flesh-colored kimonos, all cut on the bias, like something Mr. Whitaker probably thought was gorgeous.

"Uncle Rondo!" I says. "I didn't know who that was! Where are you going?"

"Sister," he says, "get out of my way, I'm poisoned."

"If you're poisoned stay away from Papa-Daddy," I says. "Keep out of the hammock. Papa-Daddy will certainly beat you on the head if you come within forty miles of him. He thinks I deliberately said he ought to cut off his beard after he got me the P.O., and I've told him and told him and told him, and he acts like he just don't hear me. Papa-Daddy must of gone stone deaf."

"He picked a fine day to do it then," says Uncle Rondo, and before you could say "Jack Robinson" flew out in the yard.

What he'd really done, he'd drunk another bottle of that prescription. He does it every single Fourth of July as sure as shooting, and it's horribly expensive. Then he falls over in the hammock and snores. So he insisted on zigzagging right on out to the hammock, looking like a half-wit.

Papa-Daddy woke up with this horrible yell and right there without moving an inch he tried to turn Uncle Rondo against me. I heard every word he said. Oh, he told Uncle Rondo I didn't learn to read till I was eight years old and he didn't see how in the world I ever got the mail put up at the P.O., much less read it all, and he said if Uncle Rondo could only fathom the lengths he had gone to to get me that job! And he said on the other hand he thought Stella-Rondo had a brilliant mind and deserved credit for getting out of town. All the time he was just lying there swinging as pretty as you please and looping out his beard, and poor Uncle Rondo was *pleading* with him to slow down the hammock, it was making him as dizzy as a witch to watch it. But that's what Papa-Daddy likes about a hammock. So Uncle Rondo was too dizzy to get turned against me for the time being. He's Mama's only brother and is a good case of a one-track mind. Ask anybody. A certified pharmacist.

Just then I heard Stella-Rondo raising the upstairs window. While she was married she got this peculiar idea that it's cooler with the windows shut and locked. So she has to raise the window before she can make a soul hear her outdoors.

So she raises the window and says, "*Oh!*" You would have thought she was mortally wounded.

Uncle Rondo and Papa-Daddy didn't even look up, but kept right on with what they were doing. I had to laugh.

I flew up the stairs and threw the door open! I says, "What in the wide world's the matter, Stella-Rondo? You mortally wounded?"

"No," she says, "I am not mortally wounded but I wish you would do me the favor of looking out that window there and telling me what you see."

So I shade my eyes and look out the window.

"I see the front yard," I says.

"Don't you see any human beings?" she says.

"I see Uncle Rondo trying to run Papa-Daddy out of the hammock," I says. "Nothing more. Naturally, it's so suffocating-hot in the house, with all the windows shut and locked, everybody who cares to stay in their right mind will have to go out and get in the hammock before the Fourth of July is over."

"Don't you notice anything different about Uncle Rondo?" asks Stella-Rondo.

"Why, no, except he's got on some terrible-looking flesh-colored contraption I wouldn't be found dead in, is all I can see," I says.

"Never mind, you won't be found dead in it, because it happens to be part of my trousseau, and Mr. Whitaker took several dozen photographs of me in it," says Stella-Rondo. "What on earth could Uncle Rondo *mean* by wearing part of my trousseau out in the broad open daylight without saying so much as 'Kiss my foot,' *knowing* I only got home this morning after my separation and hung my negligee up on the bathroom door, just as nervous as I could be?"

"I'm sure I don't know, and what do you expect me to do about it?" I says. "Jump out the window?"

"No, I expect nothing of the kind. I simply declare that Uncle Rondo looks like a fool in it, that's all," she says. "It makes me sick to my stomach."

"Well, he looks as good as he can," I says. "As good as anybody in reason could." I stood up for Uncle Rondo, please remember. And I said to Stella-Rondo, "I think I would do well not to criticize so freely if I were you and came home with a two-year-old child I had never said a word about, and no explanation whatever about my separation."

"I asked you the instant I entered this house not to refer one more time to my adopted child, and you gave me your word of honor you would not," was all Stella-Rondo would say, and started pulling out every one of her eyebrows with some cheap Kress tweezers.

So I merely slammed the door behind me and went down and made some green-tomato pickle. Somebody had to do it. Of course Mama had turned both the niggers loose; she always said no earthly power could hold one anyway on the Fourth of July, so she wouldn't even try. It turned out that Jaypan fell in the lake and came within a very narrow limit of drowning.

So Mama trots in. Lifts up the lid and says, "H'm! Not very good for your Uncle Rondo in his precarious condition, I must say. Or poor little adopted Shirley-T. Shame on you!"

That made me tired. I says, "Well, Stella-Rondo had better thank her lucky stars it was her instead of me came trotting in with that very peculiar-looking child. Now if it had been me that trotted in from Illinois and brought a peculiar-looking child of two, I shudder to think of the reception I'd of got, much less controlled the diet of an entire family."

"But you must remember, Sister, that you were never married to Mr. Whitaker in the first place and didn't go up to Illinois to live," says Mama, shaking a spoon in my face. "If you had I would of been just as overjoyed to see you and your little adopted girl as I was to see Stella-Rondo, when you wound up with your separation and came on back home."

"You would not," I says.

"Don't contradict me, I would," says Mama.

But I said she couldn't convince me though she talked till she was blue in the face. Then I said, "Besides, you know as well as I do that that child is not adopted."

"She most certainly is adopted," says Mama, stiff as a poker.

I says, "Why, Mama, Stella-Rondo had her just as sure as anything in this world, and just too stuck up to admit it."

"Why, Sister," said Mama. "Here I thought we were going to have a pleasant Fourth of July, and you start right out not believing a word your own baby sister tells you!"

"Just like Cousin Annie Flo. Went to her grave denying the facts of life," I reminded Mama.

"I told you if you ever mentioned Annie Flo's name I'd slap your face," says Mama, and slaps my face.

"All right, you wait and see," I says.

"I," says Mama, "*I* prefer to take my children's word for anything when it's humanly possible." You ought to see Mama, she weighs two hundred pounds and has real tiny feet.

Just then something perfectly horrible occurred to me.

"Mama," I says, "can that child talk?" I simply had to whisper! "Mama, I wonder if that child can be—you know—in any way? Do you realize," I says, "that she hasn't spoken one single, solitary word to a human being up to the minute? This is the way she looks," I says, and I looked like this.

Well, Mama and I just stood there and stared at each other. It was horrible!

"I remember well that Joe Whitaker frequently drank like a fish," says Mama. "I believed to my soul he drank *chemicals*." And without another word she marches to the foot of the stairs and calls Stella-Rondo.

"Stella-Rondo? O-o-o-o-o! Stella-Rondo!"

"What?" says Stella-Rondo from upstairs. Not even the grace to get up off the bed.

"Can that child of yours talk?" asks Mama.

Stella-Rondo says, "Can she what?"

"Talk! Talk!" says Mama. "Burdyburdyburdyburdy!"

So Stella-Rondo yells back, "Who says she can't talk?"

"Sister says so," says Mama.

"You didn't have to tell me, I know whose word of honor don't mean a thing in this house," says Stella-Rondo.

And in a minute the loudest Yankee voice I ever heard in my life yells out, "OE'm Pop-OE the Sailor-r-r-r Ma-a-an!" and then somebody jumps up and down in the upstairs hall. In another second the house would of fallen down.

"Not only talks, she can tap-dance!" calls Stella-Rondo. "Which is more than some people I won't name can do."

"Why, the little precious darling thing!" Mama says, so surprised. "Just as smart as she can be!" Starts talking baby talk right there. Then she turns on me. "Sister, you ought to be thoroughly ashamed!

Run upstairs this instant and apologize to Stella-Rondo and Shirley-T."

"Apologize for what?" I says. "I merely wondered if the child was normal, that's all. Now that she's proved she is, why, I have nothing further to say."

But Mama just turned on her heel and flew out, furious. She ran right upstairs and hugged the baby. She believed it was adopted. Stella-Rondo hadn't done a thing but turn her against me from upstairs while I stood there helpless over the hot stove. So that made Mama, Papa-Daddy and the baby all on Stella-Rondo's side.

Next, Uncle Rondo.

I must say that Uncle Rondo has been marvelous to me at various times in the past and I was completely unprepared to be made to jump out of my skin, the way it turned out. Once Stella-Rondo did something perfectly horrible to him—broke a chain letter from Flanders Field—and he took the radio back he had given her and gave it to me. Stella-Rondo was furious! For six months we all had to call her Stella instead of Stella-Rondo, or she wouldn't answer. I always thought Uncle Rondo had all the brains of the entire family. Another time he sent me to Mammoth Cave, with all expenses paid.

But this would be the day he was drinking that prescription, the Fourth of July.

So at supper Stella-Rondo speaks up and says she thinks Uncle Rondo ought to try to eat a little something. So finally Uncle Rondo said he would try a little cold biscuits and ketchup, but that was all. So *she* brought it to him.

"Do you think it wise to disport with ketchup in Stella-Rondo's flesh-colored kimono?" I says. Trying to be considerate! If Stella-Rondo couldn't watch out for her trousseau, somebody had to.

"Any objections?" asks Uncle Rondo, just about to pour out all the ketchup.

"Don't mind what she says, Uncle Rondo," says Stella-Rondo. "Sister has been devoting this solid afternoon to sneering out my bedroom window at the way you look."

"What's that?" says Uncle Rondo. Uncle Rondo has got the most terrible temper in the world. Anything is liable to make him tear the house down if it comes at the wrong time.

So Stella-Rondo says, "Sister says, 'Uncle Rondo certainly does look like a fool in that pink kimono!' "

Do you remember who it was really said that?

Uncle Rondo spills out all the ketchup and jumps out of his chair and tears off the kimono and throws it down on the dirty floor and puts his foot on it. It had to be sent all the way to Jackson to the cleaners and re-pleated.

"So that's your opinion of your Uncle Rondo, is it?" he says. "I look like a fool, do I? Well, that's the last straw. A whole day in this house with nothing to do, and then to hear you come out with a remark like that behind my back!"

"I didn't say any such of a thing, Uncle Rondo," I says, "and I'm not saying who did, either. Why, I think you look all right. Just try to take care of yourself and not talk and eat at the same time," I says. "I think you better go lie down."

"Lie down my foot," says Uncle Rondo. I ought to of known by that he was fixing to do something perfectly horrible.

So he didn't do anything that night in the precarious state he was in—just played Casino with Mama and Stella-Rondo and Shirley-T. and gave Shirley-T. a nickel with a head on both sides. It tickled her nearly to death, and she called him "Papa." But at 6:30 A.M. the next morning, he threw a whole five-cent package of some unsold one-inch firecrackers from the store as hard as he could into my bedroom and they every one went off. Not one bad one in the string. Anybody else, there'd be one that wouldn't go off.

Well, I'm just terribly susceptible to noise of any kind, the doctor has always told me I was the most sensitive person he had ever seen in his whole life, and I was simply prostrated. I couldn't eat! People tell me they heard it as far as the cemetery, and old Aunt Jep Patterson, that had been holding her own so good, thought it was Judgment Day and she was going to meet her whole family. It's usually so quiet here.

And I'll tell you it didn't take me any longer than a minute to make up my mind what to do. There I was with the whole entire house on Stella-Rondo's side and turned against me. If I have anything at all I have pride.

So I just decided I'd go straight down to the P.O. There's plenty of room there in the back, I says to myself.

Well! I made no bones about letting the family catch on to what I was up to. I didn't try to conceal it.

The first thing they knew, I marched in where they were all playing Old Maid and pulled the electric oscillating fan out by the plug, and everything got real hot. Next I snatched the pillow I'd done the needlepoint on right off the davenport from behind Papa-Daddy. He went "Ugh!" I beat Stella-Rondo up the stairs and finally found my charm bracelet in her bureau drawer under a picture of Nelson Eddy.

"So that's the way the land lies," says Uncle Rondo. There he was, piecing on the ham. "Well, Sister, I'll be glad to donate my army cot if you got any place to set it up, providing you'll leave right this minute and let me get some peace." Uncle Rondo was in France.

"Thank you kindly for the cot and 'peace' is hardly the word I would select if I had to resort to firecrackers at 6:30 A.M. in a young girl's bedroom," I says back to him. "And as to where I intend to go, you seem to forget my position as postmistress of China Grove, Mississippi," I says. "I've always got the P.O."

Well, that made them all sit up and take notice.

I went out front and started digging up some four-o'clocks to plant around the P.O.

"Ah-ah-ah!" says Mama, raising the window. "Those happen to be my four-o'clocks. Everything planted in that star is mine. I've never known you to make anything grow in your life."

"Very well," I says. "But I take the fern. Even you, Mama, can't stand there and deny that I'm the one watered that fern. And I happen to know where I can send in a box top and get a packet of one thousand mixed seeds, no two the same kind, free."

"Oh, where?" Mama wants to know.

But I says, "Too late. You 'tend to your house, and I'll 'tend to mine. You hear things like that all the time if you know how to listen to the radio. Perfectly marvelous offers. Get anything you want free."

So I hope to tell you I marched in and got that radio, and they could of all bit a nail in two, especially Stella-Rondo, that it used to belong to, and she well knew she couldn't get it back, I'd sue for it like a shot. And I very politely took the sewing-machine motor I helped pay the most on to give Mama for Christmas back in 1929, and a good big calendar, with the first-aid remedies on it. The thermometer and the Hawaiian ukulele certainly were rightfully mine, and I stood on the step-ladder and got all my watermelon-rind preserves and every fruit and vegetable I'd put up, every jar. Then I began to pull the tacks out of the bluebird wall vases on the archway to the dining room.

"Who told you you could have those, Miss Priss?" says Mama, fanning as hard as she could.

"I bought 'em and I'll keep track of 'em," I says. "I'll tack 'em up one on each side of the post-office window, and you can see 'em when you come to ask me for your mail, if you're so dead to see 'em."

"Not I! I'll never darken the door to that post office again if I live to be a hundred," Mama says. "Ungrateful child! After all the money we spent on you at the Normal."

"Me either," says Stella-Rondo. "You can just let my mail lie there and *rot*, for all I care. I'll never come and relieve you of a single, solitary piece."

"I should worry," I says. "And who you think's going to sit down and write you all those big fat letters and postcards, by the way? Mr. Whitaker? Just because he was the only man ever dropped down in China Grove and you got him—unfairly—is he going to sit down and write you a lengthy correspondence after you come home giving no rhyme nor reason whatsoever for your separation and no explanation for the presence of that child? I may not have your brilliant mind, but I fail to see it."

So Mama says, "Sister, I've told you a thousand times that Stella-Rondo simply got homesick, and this child is far too big to be hers," and she says, "Now, why don't you all just sit down and play Casino?"

Then Shirley-T. sticks out her tongue at me in this perfectly horrible way. She has no more manners than the man in the moon. I told her she was going to cross her eyes like that some day and they'd stick.

"It's too late to stop me now," I says. "You should have tried that yesterday. I'm going to the P.O. and the only way you can possibly see me is to visit me there."

So Papa-Daddy says, "You'll never catch me setting foot in that post office, even if I should take a notion into my head to write a letter some place." He says, "I won't have you reachin' out of that little old window with a pair of shears and cuttin' off any beard of mine. I'm too smart for you!"

"We all are," says Stella-Rondo.

But I said, "If you're so smart, where's Mr. Whitaker?"

So then Uncle Rondo says, "I'll thank you from now on to stop reading all the orders I get on postcards and telling everybody in China Grove what you think is the matter with them," but I says, "I draw my own conclusions and will continue in the future to draw them." I says, "If people want to write their inmost secrets on penny postcards, there's nothing in the wide world you can do about it, Uncle Rondo."

"And if you think we'll ever *write* another postcard you're sadly mistaken," says Mama.

"Cutting off your nose to spite your face then," I says. "But if you're all determined to have no more to do with the U.S. mail, think of this: What will Stella-Rondo do now, if she wants to tell Mr. Whitaker to come after her?"

"Wah!" says Stella-Rondo. I knew she'd cry. She had a conniption fit right there in the kitchen.

"It will be interesting to see how long she holds out," I says. "And now—I am leaving."

"Good-bye," says Uncle Rondo.

"Oh, I declare," says Mama, "to think that a family of mine should quarrel on the Fourth of July, or the day after, over Stella-Rondo leaving old Mr. Whitaker and having the sweetest little adopted child! It looks like we'd all be glad!"

"Wah!" says Stella-Rondo, and has a fresh conniption fit.

"*He* left *her*—you mark my words," I says. "That's Mr. Whitaker.

I know Mr. Whitaker. After all, I knew him first. I said from the beginning he'd up and leave her. I foretold every single thing that's happened."

"Where did he go?" asks Mama.

"Probably to the North Pole, if he knows what's good for him," I says.

But Stella-Rondo just bawled and wouldn't say another word. She flew to her room and slammed the door.

"Now look what you've gone and done, Sister," says Mama. "You go apologize."

"I haven't got time, I'm leaving," I says.

"Well, what are you waiting around for?" asks Uncle Rondo.

So I just picked up the kitchen clock and marched off, without saying "Kiss my foot" or anything, and never did tell Stella-Rondo good-bye.

There was a nigger girl going along on a little wagon right in front.

"Nigger girl," I says, "come help me haul these things down the hill, I'm going to live in the post office."

Took her nine trips in her express wagon. Uncle Rondo came out on the porch and threw her a nickel.

And that's the last I've laid eyes on any of my family or my family laid eyes on me for five solid days and nights. Stella-Rondo may be telling the most horrible tales in the world about Mr. Whitaker, but I haven't heard them. As I tell everybody, I draw my own conclusions.

But oh, I like it here. It's ideal, as I've been saying. You see, I've got everything cater-cornered, the way I like it. Hear the radio? All the war news. Radio, sewing machine, book ends, ironing board and that great big piano lamp—peace, that's what I like. Butter-bean vines planted all along the front where the strings are.

Of course, there's not much mail. My family are naturally the main people in China Grove, and if they prefer to vanish from the face of the earth, for all the mail they get or the mail they write, why, I'm not going to open my mouth. Some of the folks here in town are taking up for me and some turned against me. I know which is which. There are always people who will quit buying stamps just to get on the right side of Papa-Daddy.

But here I am, and here I'll stay. I want the world to know I'm happy.

And if Stella-Rondo should come to me this minute, on bended knees, and *attempt* to explain the incidents of her life with Mr. Whitaker, I'd simply put my fingers in both my ears and refuse to listen.

Fyodor Dostoevsky

THE CROCODILE

A TRUE STORY OF HOW A GENTLEMAN OF A CERTAIN AGE AND OF RESPECTABLE APPEARANCE WAS SWALLOWED ALIVE BY THE CROCODILE IN THE ARCADE, AND OF THE CONSEQUENCES THAT FOLLOWED.

Ohè Lambert! Où est Lambert?
As tu vu Lambert?[1]

1

ON THE thirteenth of January of this present year, 1865, at half-past twelve in the day, Elena Ivanovna, the wife of my cultured friend Ivan Matveich, who is a colleague in the same department, and may be said to be a distant relation of mine, too, expressed the desire to see the crocodile now on view at a fixed charge in the Arcade. As Ivan Matveich had already in his pocket his ticket for a tour abroad (not so much for the sake of his health as for the improvement of his mind), and was consequently free from his official duties and had nothing whatever to do that morning, he offered no objection to his wife's irresistible fancy, but was positively aflame with curiosity himself.

"A capital idea!" he said, with the utmost satisfaction. "We'll have a look at the crocodile! On the eve of visiting Europe it is well to acquaint ourselves on the spot with its indigenous inhabitants." And with these words, taking his wife's arm, he set off with her at once for the Arcade. I joined them, as I usually do, being an intimate friend of the family. I have never seen Ivan Matveich in a more agreeable frame of mind than he was on that memorable morning—how true it is that we know not beforehand the fate that awaits us! On entering the Arcade he was at once full of admiration for the splendors of the building, and when we reached the shop in which the monster lately arrived in Petersburg was being exhibited, he volunteered to pay the quarter-ruble for me to the crocodile owner—a thing which had never happened before. Walking into a little room, we observed that besides the crocodile there were in it parrots of the species known as cockatoo, and also a group of monkeys in a special case in a recess. Near the en-

1 [Oh, Lambert! Where is Lambert? Have you seen Lambert?]

THE CROCODILE: Reprinted with permission of The Macmillan Company from *An Honest Thief and Other Stories* by Fyodor Dostoevsky, tr. by Constance Garnett.

trance, along the left wall stood a big tin tank that looked like a bath covered with a thin iron grating, filled with water to the depth of two inches. In this shallow pool was kept a huge crocodile, which lay like a log absolutely motionless and apparently deprived of all its faculties by our damp climate, so inhospitable to foreign visitors. This monster at first aroused no special interest in any one of us.

"So this is the crocodile!" said Elena Ivanovna, with a pathetic cadence of regret. "Why, I thought it was . . . something different."

Most probably she thought it was made of diamonds. The owner of the crocodile, a German, came out and looked at us with an air of extraordinary pride.

"He has a right to be," Ivan Matveich whispered to me, "he knows he is the only man in Russia exhibiting a crocodile."

This quiet nonsensical observation I ascribe also to the extremely good-humored mood which had overtaken Ivan Matveich, who was on other occasions of rather envious disposition.

"I fancy your crocodile is not alive," said Elena Ivanovna, piqued by the irresponsive stolidity of the proprietor, and addressing him with a charming smile in order to soften his churlishness—a maneuver so typically feminine.

"Oh, no, madam," the latter replied in broken Russian; and instantly moving the grating half off the tank, he poked the monster's head with a stick.

Then the treacherous monster, to show that it was alive, faintly stirred its paws and tail, raised its snout and emitted something like a prolonged snuffle.

"Come, don't be cross, Karlchen," said the German caressingly, gratified in his vanity.

"How horrid that crocodile is! I am really frightened," Elena Ivanovna twittered, still more coquettishly. "I know I shall dream of him now."

"But he won't bite you if you do dream of him," the German retorted gallantly, and was the first to laugh at his own jest, but none of us responded.

"Come, Semyon Semyonich," said Elena Ivanovna, addressing me exclusively, "let us go and look at the monkeys. I am awfully fond of monkeys; they are such darlings . . . and the crocodile is horrid."

"Oh, don't be afraid, my dear!" Ivan Matveich called after us, gallantly displaying his manly courage to his wife. "This drowsy denison of the realms of the Pharaohs will do us no harm." And he remained by the tank. What is more, he took his glove and began tickling the crocodile's nose with it, wishing, as he said afterwards, to induce him to snort. The proprietor showed his politeness to a lady by following Elena Ivanovna to the case of monkeys.

So everything was going well, and nothing could have been fore seen. Elena Ivanovna was quite skittish in her raptures over the monkeys, and seemed completely taken up with them. With shrieks of delight she was continually turning to me, as though determined not to notice the proprietor, and kept gushing with laughter at the resemblance she detected between these monkeys and her intimate friends and acquaintances. I, too, was amused, for the resemblance was unmistakable. The German did not know whether to laugh or not, and so at last was reduced to frowning. And it was at that moment that a terrible, I may say unnatural, scream set the room vibrating. Not knowing what to think, for the first moment I stood still, numb with horror, but noticing that Elena Ivanovna was screaming too, I quickly turned around—and what did I behold! I saw—oh heavens!—I saw the luckless Ivan Matveich in the terrible jaws of the crocodile, held by them round the waist, lifted horizontally in the air and desperately kicking. Then—one moment, and no trace remained of him. But I must describe it in detail, for I stood all the while motionless, and had time to watch the whole process taking place before me with an attention and interest such as I never remember to have felt before. "What," I thought at that critical moment, "what if all that had happened to me instead of Ivan Matveich—how unpleasant it would have been for me!"

But to return to my story. The crocodile began by turning the unhappy Ivan Matveich in his terrible jaws so that he could swallow his legs first; then bringing up Ivan Matveich, who kept trying to jump out and clutching at the sides of the tank, sucked him down again as far as his waist. Then bringing him up again, gulped him down, and so again and again. In this way Ivan Matveich was visibly disappearing before our eyes. At last, with a final gulp, the crocodile swallowed my cultured friend entirely, this time leaving no trace of him. From the outside of the crocodile we could see the protuberances of Ivan Matveich's figure as he passed down the inside of the monster. I was on the point of screaming again when destiny played another treacherous trick upon us. The crocodile made a tremendous effort, probably oppressed by the magnitude of the object he had swallowed, once more opened his terrible jaws, and with a final hiccup he suddenly let the head of Ivan Matveich pop out for a second, with an expression of despair on his face. In that brief instant the spectacles dropped off his nose to the bottom of the tank. It seemed as though that despairing countenance had only popped out to cast one last look on the objects around it, to take its last farewell of all earthly pleasures. But it had not time to carry out its intention; the crocodile made another effort, gave a gulp and instantly it vanished again—this time for ever. This appearance and disappearance of a still living human head was so horrible, but at the same [time]—either from its rapidity and unexpectedness or from the dropping of the spectacles—there was something so comic about it that I suddenly quite unexpectedly exploded with laughter. But pulling myself together and realising that to laugh at such a moment was not the thing for an old family friend, I turned at once to Elena Ivanovna and said with a sympathetic air:

"Now it's all over with our friend Ivan Matveich!"

I cannot even attempt to describe how violent was the agitation of Elena Ivanovna during the whole process. After the first scream she seemed rooted to the spot, and stared at the catastrophe with apparent indifference, though her eyes looked as though they were starting out of her head; then she suddenly went off into a heart-rending wail, but I seized her hands. At this instant the proprietor, too, who had at first been also petrified by horror, suddenly clasped his hands and cried, gazing upwards:

"Oh my crocodile! *Oh mein allerliebster Karlchen! Mutter, Mutter, Mutter!*"[2]

A door at the rear of the room opened at this cry, and the *Mutter*, a rosy-cheeked, elderly but dishevelled woman in a cap made her appearance, and rushed with a shriek to her German.

A perfect Bedlam followed. Elena Ivanovna kept shrieking out the same phrase, as though in a frenzy, "Flay him! flay him!" apparently entreating them—probably in a moment of oblivion—to flay somebody for something. The proprietor and *Mutter* took no notice whatever of either of us; they were both bellowing like calves over the crocodile.

"He did for himself! He will burst himself at once, for he did swallow a *ganz* official!" cried the proprietor.

"*Unser Karlchen, unser allerliebster Karlchen wird sterben,*"[3] howled his wife.

"We are bereaved and without bread!" chimed in the proprietor.

"Flay him! flay him! flay him!" clamored Elena Ivanovna, clutching at the German's coat.

"He did tease the crocodile. For what did your man tease the crocodile?" cried the German, pulling away from her. "You will if *Karlchen wird* burst, therefore pay, *das war mein Sohn, das war mein einziger Sohn.*"[4]

I must own I was intently indignant at the sight of such egoism in the German and the cold-heartedness of his dishevelled *Mutter*; at the same time Elena Ivanovna's reiterated shriek of "Flay him! flay him!" troubled me even more and absorbed at last my whole atten-

2 [Oh, my most beloved Karl! Mother, Mother, Mother!]
3 [Our Karl, our most beloved Karl, will die.]
4 [This was my son, this was my only son.]

tion, positively alarming me. I may as well say straight off that I entirely misunderstood this strange exclamation: it seemed to me that Elena Ivanovna had for the moment taken leave of her senses, but nevertheless wishing to avenge the loss of her beloved Ivan Matveich, was demanding by way of compensation that the crocodile should be severely thrashed, while she was meaning something quite different. Looking round at the door, not without embarrassment, I began to entreat Elena Ivanovna to calm herself, and above all not to use the shocking word "flay." For such a reactionary desire here, in the midst of the Arcade and of the most cultured society, not two paces from the hall where at this very minute Mr. Lavrov was perhaps delivering a public lecture, was not only impossible but unthinkable, and might at any moment bring upon us the hisses of culture and the caricatures of Mr. Stepanov. To my horror I was immediately proved to be correct in my alarmed suspicions: the curtain that divided the crocodile room from the little entry where the quarter-rubles were taken suddenly parted, and in the opening there appeared a figure with moustaches and beard, carrying a cap, with the upper part of its body bent a long way forward, though the feet were scrupulously held beyond the threshold of the crocodile room in order to avoid the necessity of paying the entrance money.

"Such a reactionary desire, madam," said the stranger, trying to avoid falling over in our direction and to remain standing outside the room, "does no credit to your development, and is conditioned by lack of phosphorus in your brain. You will be promptly held up to shame in the *Chronicle of Progress* and in our satirical prints . . ."

But he could not complete his remarks; the proprietor coming to himself, and seeing with horror that a man was talking in the crocodile room without having paid entrance money, rushed furiously at the progressive stranger and turned him out with a punch from each fist. For a moment both vanished from our sight behind a curtain, and only then I grasped that the whole uproar was about nothing. Elena Ivanovna turned out quite innocent; she had, as I have mentioned already, no idea whatever of subjecting the crocodile to a degrading corporal punishment, and had simply expressed the desire that he should be opened and her husband released from his interior.

"What! You wish that my crocodile be perished!" the proprietor yelled, running in again. "No! let your husband be perished first, before my crocodile! . . . *Mein Vater*[5] showed crocodile, *mein Grossvater*[5] showed crocodile, *mein Sohn*[5] will show crocodile, and I will show crocodile! All will show crocodile! I am known to *ganz Europa*,[6] and you are not known to *ganz Europa*, and you must pay me a *strafe!*"[7]

5 [My father; my grandfather; my son.] 6 [All of Europe.] 7 [Fine.]

"*Ja, ja,*" put in the vindictive German woman, "we shall not let you go. *Strafe*, since Karlchen is burst!"

"And, indeed, it's useless to flay the creature," I added calmly, anxious to get Elena Ivanovna away home as quickly as possible, "as our dear Ivan Matveich is by now probably soaring somewhere in the empyrean."

"My dear"—we suddenly heard, to our intense amazement, the voice of Ivan Matveich—"my dear, my advice is to apply direct to the superintendent's office, as without the assistance of the police the German will never be made to see reason."

These words, uttered with firmness and aplomb, and expressing an exceptional presence of mind, for the first minute so astounded us that we could not believe our ears. But, of course, we ran at once to the crocodile's tank, and with equal reverence and incredulity listened to the unhappy captive. His voice was muffled, thin and even squeaky, as though it came from a considerable distance. It reminded one of a jocose person who, covering his mouth with a pillow, shouts from an adjoining room, trying to mimic the sound of two peasants calling to one another in a deserted plain or across a wide ravine—a performance to which I once had the pleasure of listening in a friend's house at Christmas.

"Ivan Matveich, my dear, and so you are alive!" faltered Elena Ivanovna.

"Alive and well," answered Ivan Matveich, "and, thanks to the Almighty, swallowed without any damage whatever. I am only uneasy as to the view my superiors may take of the incident; for after getting a permit to go abroad I've got into a crocodile, which seems anything but clever."

"But, my dear, don't trouble your head about being clever; first of all we must somehow excavate you from where you are," Elena Ivanovna interrupted.

"Excavate!" cried the proprietor. "I will not let my crocodile be excavated. Now the *publicum* will come many more, and I will *fünfzig*[8] kopeks ask and Karlchen will cease to burst."

"*Gott sei dank!*"[9] put in his wife.

"They are right," Ivan Matveich observed tranquilly; "the principles of economics before everything."

"My dear! I will fly at once to the authorities and lodge a complaint, for I feel that we cannot settle this mess by ourselves."

"I think so too," observed Ivan Matveich; "but in our age of industrial crisis it is not easy to rip open the belly of a crocodile without economic compensation, and meanwhile the inevitable question presents itself: What will the German take for his crocodile? And with it

8 [Fifty.]

9 [Thank God!]

another: How will it be paid? For, as you know, I have no means . . ."

"Perhaps out of your salary . . ." I observed timidly, but the proprietor interrupted me at once.

"I will not the crocodile sell; I will for three thousand the crocodile sell! I will for four thousand the crocodile sell! Now the *publicum* will come very many. I will for five thousand the crocodile sell!"

In fact he gave himself insufferable airs. Covetousness and a revolting greed gleamed joyfully in his eyes.

"I am going!" I cried indignantly.

"And I! I too! I shall go to Andrey Osipich himself. I will soften him with my tears," whined Elena Ivanovna.

"Don't do that, my dear," Ivan Matveich hastened to interpose. He had long been jealous of Andrey Osipich on his wife's account, and he knew she would enjoy going to weep before a gentleman of refinement, for tears suited her.

"And I don't advise you to do so either, my friend," he added, addressing me. "It's no good plunging headlong in that slap-dash way; there's no knowing what it may lead to. You had much better go today to Timofey Semyonich, as though to pay an ordinary visit; he is an old-fashioned and by no means brilliant man, but he is trustworthy, and what matters most of all, he is straightforward. Give him my greetings and describe the circumstances of the case. And since I owe him seven rubles over our last game of cards, take the opportunity to pay him the money; that will soften the stern old man. In any case his advice may serve as a guide for us. And meanwhile take Elena Ivanovna home. . . . Calm yourself my dear," he continued, addressing her. "I am weary of these outcries and feminine squabblings, and should like a nap. It's soft and warm in here, though I have hardly had time to look round in this unexpected haven."

"Look round! Why, is it light in there?" cried Elena Ivanovna in a tone of relief.

"I am surrounded by impenetrable night," answered the poor captive; "but I can feel and, so to speak, have a look round with my hands. . . . Good-by; set your mind at rest and don't deny yourself recreation and diversion. Till tomorrow! And you, Semyon Semyonich, come to me in the evening, and as you are absent-minded and may forget it, tie a knot in your handkerchief."

I confess I was glad to get away, for I was overtired and somewhat bored. Hastening to offer my arm to the disconsolate Elena Ivanovna, whose charms were only enhanced by her agitation, I hurriedly led her out of the crocodile room.

"The charge will be another quarter-ruble in the evening," the proprietor called after us.

"Oh, dear, how greedy they are!" said Elena Ivanovna, looking at herself in every mirror on the walls of the Arcade, and evidently aware that she was looking prettier than usual.

"The principles of economics," I answered with some emotion, proud that passers-by should see the lady on my arm.

"The principles of economics," she drawled in a touching little voice. "I did not in the least understand what Ivan Matveich said about those horrid economics just now."

"I will explain to you," I answered, and began at once telling her of the beneficial effects of the introduction of foreign capital into our country, upon which I had read an article in the *Petersburg News* and the *Voice* that morning.

"How strange it is," she interrupted, after listening for some time. "But do leave off, you horrid man. What nonsense you are talking. . . . Tell me, do I look purple?"

"You look perfect, and not purple!" I observed, seizing the opportunity to pay her a compliment.

"Naughty man!" she said complacently. "Poor Ivan Matveich," she added a minute later, putting her little head on one side coquettishly. "I am really sorry for him. Oh, dear!" she cried suddenly, "how is he going to have his dinner . . . and . . . and . . . what will he do . . . if he wants anything?"

"An unforeseen question," I answered, perplexed in my turn. To tell the truth, it had not entered my head, so much more practical are women than we men in the solution of the problems of daily life!

"Poor dear! how could he have got into such a mess . . . nothing to amuse him, and in the dark. . . . How vexing it is that I have no photograph of him. . . . And so now I am a sort of widow," she added, with a seductive smile, evidently interested in her new position. "Hm! . . . I am sorry for him, though."

It was, in short, the expression of the very natural and intelligible grief of a young and interesting wife for the loss of her husband. I took her home at last, soothed her, and after dining with her and drinking a cup of aromatic coffee, set off at six o'clock to Timofey Semyonich, calculating that at that hour all married people of settled habits would be sitting or lying down at home.

Having written this first chapter in a style appropriate to the incident recorded, I intend to proceed in a language more natural though less elevated, and I beg to forewarn the reader of the fact.

2

THE venerable Timofey Semyonich met me rather nervously, as though somewhat embarrassed. He led me to his tiny study and shut the door carefully, "that the children may not hinder us," he added with evident uneasiness. There he made me sit down on a chair by the writing table, sat down himself in an easy chair, wrapped round him the skirts of his old wadded dressing gown, and assumed an official and even severe air, in readiness for anything, though he was not my chief nor Ivan Matveich's, and had hitherto been reckoned as a colleague and even a friend.

"First of all," he said, "take note that I am not a person in authority, but just such a subordinate official as you and Ivan Matveich. . . . I have nothing to do with it, and do not intend to mix myself up in the affair."

I was surprised to find that he apparently knew all about it already. In spite of that I told him the whole story over in detail. I spoke with positive excitement, for I was at that moment fulfilling the obligations of a true friend. He listened without special surprise, but with evident signs of suspicion.

"Only fancy," he said, "I always believed that this would be sure to happen to him."

"Why, Timofey Semyonich? It is a very unusual incident in itself . . ."

"I admit it. But Ivan Matveich's whole career in the service was leading up to this end. He was flighty—conceited indeed. It was always 'progress' and ideas of all sorts, and this is what progress brings people to!"

"But this is a most unusual incident and cannot possibly serve as a general rule for all progressives."

"Yes, indeed it can. You see, it's the effect of overeducation, I assure you. For overeducation leads people to poke their noses into all sorts of places, especially where they are not invited. Though perhaps you know best," he added, as though offended. "I am an old man and not of much education. I began as a soldier's son, and this year has been the jubilee of my service."

"Oh, no, Timofey Semyonich, not at all. On the contrary, Ivan Matveich is eager for your advice; he is eager for your guidance. He implores it, so to say, with tears."

"So to say, with tears! Hm! Those are crocodile's tears and one cannot quite believe in them. Tell me, what possessed him to want to go abroad? And how could he afford to go? Why, he has no private means!"

"He had saved the money from his last bonus," I answered plaintively. "He only wanted to go for three months—to Switzerland . . . to the land of William Tell."

"William Tell? Hm!"

"He wanted to meet the spring at Naples, to see the museums, the customs, the animals . . ."

"Hm! The animals! I think it was simply from pride. What animals? Animals, indeed! Haven't we animals enough? We have museums, menageries, camels. There are bears quite close to Petersburg! And here he's got inside a crocodile himself . . ."

"Oh, come, Timofey Semyonich! The man is in trouble, the man appeals to you as to a friend, as to an older relation, craves for advice—and you reproach him. Have pity at least on the unfortunate Elena Ivanovna!"

"You are speaking of his wife? A charming little lady," said Timofey Semyonich, visibly softening and taking a pinch of snuff with relish. "Particularly prepossessing. And so plump, and always putting her pretty little head on one side. . . . Very agreeable. Andrey Osipich was speaking of her only the other day."

"Speaking of her?"

"Yes, and in very flattering terms. Such a bust, he said, such eyes, such hair. . . . A sugarplum, he said, not a lady—and then he laughed. He is still a young man, of course." Timofey Semyonich blew his nose with a loud noise. "And yet, young though he is, what a career he is making for himself."

"That's quite a different thing, Timofey Semyonich."

"Of course, of course."

"Well, what do you say then, Timofey Semyonich?"

"Why, what can I do?"

"Give advice, guidance, as a man of experience, a relative! What are we to do? What steps are we to take? Go to the authorities and . . ."

"To the authorities? Certainly not," Timofey Semyonich replied hurriedly. "If you ask my advice, you had better, above all, hush the matter up and act, so to speak, as a private person. It is a suspicious incident, quite unheard of. Unheard of, above all; there is no precedent for it, and it is far from creditable. . . . And so discretion above all. . . . Let him lie there a bit. We must wait and see . . ."

"But how can we wait and see, Timofey Semyonich? What if he is stifled there?"

"Why should he be? I think you told me that he made himself fairly comfortable there?"

I told him the whole story over again. Timofey Semyonich pondered.

"Hm!" he said, twisting his snuffbox in his hands. "To my mind it's really a good thing he should lie there a bit, instead of going abroad. Let him reflect at his leisure. Of course he mustn't be stifled, and so he must take measures to preserve his health, avoiding a cough, for instance, and so on. . . . And as for the German, it's my personal opinion he is within his rights, and even more so than the other side, because it was the other party who got into *his* crocodile without asking permission, and not *he* who got into Ivan Matveich's crocodile without asking permission, though, so far as I recollect, the latter has no crocodile. And a crocodile is private property, and so it is impossible to slit him open without compensation."

"For the saving of human life, Timofey Semyonich."

"Oh, well, that's a matter for the police. You must go to them."

"But Ivan Matveich may be needed in the department. He may be asked for."

"Ivan Matveich needed? Ha-ha! Besides, he is on leave, so that we may ignore him—let him inspect the countries of Europe! It will be a different matter if he doesn't turn up when his leave is over. Then we shall ask for him and make inquiries."

"Three months! Timofey Semyonich, for pity's sake!"

"It's his own fault. Nobody thrust him there. At this rate we should have to get a nurse to look after him at government expense, and that is not allowed for in the regulations. But the chief point is that the crocodile is private property, so that the principles of economics apply in this question. And the principles of economics are paramount. Only the other evening, at Luka Andreich's, Ignati Prokofyich was saying so. Do you know Ignati Prokofyich? A capitalist, in a big way of business, and he speaks so fluently. 'We need industrial development,' he said; 'there is very little development among us. We must create it. We must create capital, so we must create a middle class, the so-called bourgeoisie. And as we haven't capital we must attract it from abroad. We must, in the first place, give facilities to foreign companies to buy up lands in Russia as is done now abroad. The communal holding of land is poison, is ruin.' And, you know, he spoke with such heat; well, that's all right for him—a wealthy man, and not in the service. 'With the communal system,' he said, 'there will be no improvement in industrial development or agriculture. Foreign companies,' he said, 'must as far as possible buy up the whole of our land in big lots, and then split it up, split it up, split it up, in the smallest parts possible'—and do you know he pronounced the words 'split it up' with such determination—'and then sell it as private property. Or rather, not sell it, but simply let it. When,' he said, 'all the land is in the hands of foreign companies they can fix any rent they like. And so the peasant will work three times as much for his daily bread and he can be turned out at pleasure. So that he will feel it, will be submissive and industrious, and will work three times as much for the same wages. But as it is, with the commune, what does he care? He knows he won't die of hunger, so he is lazy and drunken. And meanwhile money will be attracted into Russia, capital will be created and the bourgeoisie will spring up. The English political and literary paper, *The Times*, in an article the other day on our finances stated that the reason our financial position was so unsatisfactory was that we had no middle class, no big fortunes, no accommodating proletariat.' Ignati Prokofyich speaks well. He is an orator. He wants to lay a report on the subject before the authorities, and then to get it published in the *News*. That's something very different from verses like Ivan Matveich's . . ."

"But how about Ivan Matveich?" I put in, after letting the old man babble on.

Timofey Semyonich was sometimes fond of talking and showing that he was not behind the times, but knew all about things.

"How about Ivan Matveich? Why, I am coming to that. Here we are, anxious to bring foreign capital into the country—and only consider: as soon as the capital of a foreigner, who has been attracted to Petersburg, has been doubled through Ivan Matveich, instead of protecting the foreign capitalist, we are proposing to rip open the belly of his original capital—the crocodile. Is it consistent? To my mind, Ivan Matveich, as the true son of his fatherland, ought to rejoice and to be proud that through him the value of a foreign crocodile has been doubled and possibly even trebled. That's just what is wanted to attract capital. If one man succeeds, mind you, another will come with a crocodile, and a third will bring two or three of them at once, and capital will grow up about them—there you have a bourgeoisie. It must be encouraged."

"Upon my word, Timofey Semyonich!" I cried, "you are demanding almost supernatural self-sacrifice from poor Ivan Matveich."

"I demand nothing, and I beg you, before everything—as I have said already—to remember that I am not a person in authority and so cannot demand anything of any one. I am speaking as a son of the fatherland, that is, not as the *Son of the Fatherland*, but as a son of the fatherland. Again, what possessed him to get into the crocodile? A respectable man, a man of good grade in the service, lawfully married—and then to behave like that! Is it consistent?"

"But it was an accident."

"Who knows? And where is the money to compensate the owner to come from?"

"Perhaps out of his salary, Timofey Semyonich?"

"Would that be enough?"

"No, it wouldn't, Timofey Semyonich," I answered sadly. "The proprietor was at first alarmed that the crocodile would burst, but as soon as he was sure that it was all right, he began to bluster and was delighted to think that he could double the charge for entry."

"Treble and quadruple perhaps! The public will simply stampede the place now, and crocodile owners are smart people. Besides, it's not Lent yet, and people are keen on diversions, and so I say again, the great thing is that Ivan Matveich should preserve his incognito, don't let him be in a hurry. Let everybody know, perhaps, that he is in the crocodile, but don't let them be officially informed of it. Ivan Matveich is in particularly favorable circumstances for that, for he is reckoned to be abroad. It will be said he is in the crocodile, and we will refuse to believe it. That is how it can be managed. The great thing is that he should wait; and why should he be in a hurry?"

"Well, but if . . ."

"Don't worry, he has a good constitution . . ."

"Well, and afterwards, when he has waited?"

"Well, I won't conceal from you that the case is exceptional in the highest degree. One doesn't know what to think of it, and the worst of it is there is no precedent. If we had a precedent we might have something to go by. But as it is, what is one to say? It will certainly take time to settle it."

A happy thought flashed upon my mind.

"Cannot we arrange," I said, "that if he is destined to remain in the entrails of the monster and it is the will of Providence that he should remain alive, that he should send in a petition to be reckoned as still serving?"

"Hm! . . . Possibly as on leave and without salary . . ."

"But couldn't it be with salary?"

"On what grounds?"

"As sent on a special commission."

"What commission and where?"

"Why, into the entrails, the entrails of the crocodile. . . . So to speak, for exploration, for investigation of the facts on the spot. It would, of course, be a novelty, but that is progressive and would at the same time show zeal for enlightenment."

Timofey Semyonich thought a little.

"To send a special official," he said at last, "to the inside of a crocodile to conduct a special inquiry is, in my personal opinion, an absurdity. It is not in the regulations. And what sort of special inquiry could there be there?"

"The scientific study of nature on the spot, in the living subject. The natural sciences are all the fashion nowadays, botany. . . . He could live there and report his observations. . . . For instance, concerning digestion or simply habits. For the sake of accumulating facts."

"You mean as statistics. Well, I am no great authority on that subject, indeed I am no philosopher at all. You say 'facts'—we are overwhelmed with facts as it is, and don't know what to do with them. Besides, statistics are a danger."

"In what way?"

"They are a danger. Moreover, you will admit he will report facts, so to speak, lying like a log. And, can one do one's official duties lying like a log? That would be another novelty and a dangerous one; and again, there is no precedent for it. If we had any sort of precedent for it, then, to my thinking, he might have been given the job."

"But no live crocodiles have been brought over hitherto, Timofey Semyonich."

"Hm . . . yes," he reflected again. "Your objection is a just one, if you like, and might indeed serve as a ground for carrying the matter further; but consider again, that if with the arrival of living crocodiles government clerks begin to disappear, and then on the ground that they are warm and comfortable there, expect to receive the official sanction for their position, and then take their ease there . . . you must admit it would be a bad example. We should have every one trying to go the same way to get a salary for nothing."

"Do your best for him, Timofey Semyonich. By the way, Ivan Matveich asked me to give you seven rubles he had lost to you at cards."

"Ah, he lost that the other day at Nikifor Nikiforich's. I remember. And how gay and amusing he was—and now!"

The old man was genuinely touched.

"Intercede for him, Timofey Semyonich!"

"I will do my best. I will speak in my own name, as a private person, as though I were asking for information. And meanwhile, you find out indirectly, unofficially, how much would the proprietor consent to take for his crocodile?"

Timofey Semyonich was visibly more friendly.

"Certainly," I answered. "And I will come back to you at once to report."

"And his wife . . . is she alone now? Is she depressed?"

"You should call on her, Timofey Semyonich."

"I will. I thought of doing so before; it's a good opportunity. . . . And what on earth possessed him to go and look at the crocodile. Though, indeed, I should like to see it myself."

"Go and see the poor fellow, Timofey Semyonich."

"I will. Of course, I don't want to raise his hopes by doing so. I shall go as a private person. . . . Well, goodbye, I am going to Nikifor Nikiforich's again; shall you be there?"

"No, I am going to see the poor prisoner."

"Yes, now he is a prisoner! . . . Ah, that's what comes of thoughtlessness!"

I said good-by to the old man. Ideas of all kinds were straying through my mind. A good-natured and most honest man, Timofey Semyonich, yet, as I left him, I felt pleased at the thought that he had celebrated his fiftieth year of service, and that Timofey Semyonichs are now a rarity among us. I flew at once, of course, to the Arcade to tell poor Ivan Matveich all the news. And, indeed, I was moved by curiosity to know how he was getting on in the crocodile and how it was possible to live in a crocodile. And, indeed, was it possible to live in a crocodile at all? At times it really seemed to me as though it were all an outlandish, monstrous dream, especially as an outlandish monster was the chief figure in it.

3

AND yet it was not a dream, but actual, indubitable fact. Should I be telling the story if it were not? But to continue.

It was late, about nine o'clock, before I reached the Arcade, and I had to go into the crocodile room by the back entrance, for the German had closed the shop earlier than usual that evening. Now in the seclusion of domesticity he was walking about in a greasy old frock coat, but he seemed three times as pleased as he had been in the morning. It was evidently that he had no apprehensions now, and that the public had been coming "many more." The *Mutter* came out later, evidently to keep an eye on me. The German and the *Mutter* frequently whispered together. Although the shop was closed he charged me a quarter-ruble. What unnecessary exactitude!

"You will every time pay; the public will one ruble, and you one quarter pay; for you are the good friend of your good friend; and I a friend respect . . ."

"Are you alive, are you alive, my cultured friend?" I cried, as I approached the crocodile, expecting my words to reach Ivan Matveich from a distance and to flatter his vanity.

"Alive and well," he answered, as though from a long way off or from under the bed, though I was standing close beside him. "Alive and well; but of that later. . . . How are things going?"

As though purposely not hearing the question, I was just beginning with sympathetic haste to question him how he was, what it was like in the crocodile, and what, in fact, there was inside a crocodile. Both friendship and common civility demanded this. But with capricious annoyance he interrupted me.

"How are things going?" he shouted, in a shrill and on this occasion particularly revolting voice, addressing me peremptorily as usual.

I described to him my whole conversation with Timofey Semyonich down to the smallest detail. As I told my story I tried to show my resentment in my voice.

"The old man is right," Ivan Matveich pronounced as abruptly as usual in his conversation with me. "I like practical people, and can't endure sentimental milksops. I am ready to admit, however, that your idea about a special commission is not altogether absurd. I certainly have a great deal to report, both from a scientific and from an ethical point of view. But now all this has taken a new and unexpected aspect, and it is not worth while to trouble about mere salary. Listen attentively. Are you sitting down?"

"No, I am standing up."

"Sit down on the floor if there is nothing else, and listen attentively."

Resentfully I took a chair and put it down on the floor with a bang, in my anger.

"Listen," he began dictatorially. "The public came today in masses. There was no room left in the evening, and the police came in to keep order. At eight o'clock, that is, earlier than usual, the proprietor thought it necessary to close the shop and end the exhibition to count the money he had taken and prepare for tomorrow more conveniently. So I know there will be a regular fair tomorrow. And we may assume that all the most cultivated people in the capital, the ladies and the best society, the foreign ambassadors, the leading lawyers and so on, will all be present. What's more, people will be flowing here from the remotest provinces of our vast and interesting empire. The upshot of it is that I am the cynosure of all eyes, and though hidden to sight, I am eminent. I shall teach the idle crowd. Taught by experience, I shall be an example of greatness and resignation to fate! I shall be, so to say, a pulpit from which to instruct mankind. The mere biological details I can furnish about the monster I am inhabiting are of priceless value. And so, far from repining at what has happened, I confidently hope for the most brilliant of careers."

"You won't find it wearisome?" I asked sarcastically.

What irritated me more than anything was the extreme pomposity of his language. Nevertheless, it all rather disconcerted me. "What on earth, what, can this frivolous blockhead find to be so cocky about?" I muttered to myself. "He ought to be crying instead of being cocky."

"No!" he answered my observation sharply, "for I am full of great ideas, only now can I at leisure ponder over the amelioration of the lot of humanity. Truth and light will come forth now from the crocodile. I shall certainly develop a new economic theory of my own and I shall be proud of it—which I have hitherto been prevented from doing by my official duties and by trivial distractions. I shall refute everything and be a new Fourier. By the way, did you give Timofey Semyonich the seven rubles?"

"Yes, out of my own pocket," I answered, trying to emphasise that fact in my voice.

"We will settle it," he answered superciliously. "I confidently expect my salary to be raised, for who should get a raise if not I? I am of the utmost service now. But to business. My wife?"

"You are, I suppose, inquiring after Elena Ivanovna?"

"My wife?" he shouted, this time in a positive squeal.

There was no help for it! Meekly, though gnashing my teeth, I told him how I had left Elena Ivanovna. He did not even hear me out.

"I have special plans in regard to her," he began impatiently. "If I am celebrated *here*, I wish her to be celebrated *there*. Savants, poets, philosophers, foreign mineralogists, statesmen, after conversing in the morning with me, will visit her *salon* in the evening. From next week onwards she must have an 'At Home' every evening. With my salary doubled, we shall have the means for entertaining, and as the entertainment must not go beyond tea and hired footmen—that's settled. Both here and there they will talk of me. I have long thirsted for an opportunity for being talked about, but could not attain it, fettered by my humble position and low grade in the service. And now all this has been attained by a simple gulp on the part of the crocodile. Every word of mine will be listened to, every utterance will be thought over, repeated, printed. And I'll teach them what I am worth! They shall understand at last what abilities they have allowed to vanish in the entrails of a monster. 'This man might have been Foreign Minister or might have ruled a kingdom,' some will say. 'And that man did not rule a kingdom,' others will say. In what way am I inferior to a Garnier-Pagesishki or whatever they are called? My wife must be a worthy second—I have brains, she has beauty and charm. 'She is beautiful, and that is why she is his wife,' some will say. 'She is beautiful *because* she is his wife,' others will amend. To be ready for anything let Elena Ivanovna buy tomorrow the Encyclopedia edited by Andrey Krayevski, that she may be able to converse on any topic. Above all, let her be sure to read the political leader in the *Petersburg News*, comparing it every day with the *Voice*. I imagine that the proprietor will consent to take me sometimes with the crocodile to my wife's brilliant *salon*. I will be in a tank in the middle of the magnificent drawing room, and I will scintillate with witticisms which I will prepare in the morning. To the statesmen I will impart my projects; to the poet I will speak in rhyme; with the ladies I can be amusing and charming without impropriety, since I shall be no danger to their husbands' peace of mind. To all the rest I shall serve as a pattern of resignation to fate and the will of Providence. I shall make my wife a brilliant literary lady; I shall bring her forward and explain her to the public; as my wife she must be full of the most striking virtues; and if they are right in calling Andrey Alexandrovich our Russian Alfred de Musset, they will be still more right in calling her our Russian Yevgenia Tour."

I must confess that although this wild nonsense was rather in Ivan Matveich's habitual style, it did occur to me that he was in a fever and delirious. It was the same, everyday Ivan Matveich, but magnified twenty times.

"My friend," I asked him, "are you hoping for a long life? Tell me, in fact, are you well? How do you eat, how do you sleep, how do you breathe? I am your friend, and you must admit that the incident is most unnatural, and consequently my curiosity is most natural."

"Idle curiosity and nothing else," he pronounced sententiously, "but you shall be satisfied. You ask how I am managing in the entrails of the monster? To begin with, the crocodile, to my amusement, turns out to be perfectly empty. His inside consists of a sort of huge empty sack made of gutta-percha, like the elastic goods sold in the Gorokhovi Street, in the Morskaya, and, if I am not mistaken, in the Voznesenski Prospect. Otherwise, if you think of it, how could I find room?"

"Is it possible?" I cried, in a surprise that may well be understood. "Can the crocodile be perfectly empty?"

"Perfectly," Ivan Matveich maintained sternly and impressively. "And in all probability, it is so constructed by the laws of Nature. The crocodile possesses nothing but jaws furnished with sharp teeth, and besides the jaws, a tail of considerable length—that is all, properly speaking. The middle part between these two extremities is an empty space enclosed by something of the nature of gutta-percha, probably really gutta-percha."

"But the ribs, the stomach, the intestines, the liver, the heart?" I interrupted quite angrily.

"There is nothing, absolutely nothing of all that, and probably there never has been. All that is the idle fancy of frivolous travellers. As one inflates an air cushion, I am now with my person inflating the crocodile. He is incredibly elastic. Indeed, you might, as the friend of the family, get in with me if you were generous and self-sacrificing enough—and even with you here there would be room to spare. I even think that in the last resort I might send for Elena Ivanovna. However, this void, hollow formation of the crocodile is quite in keeping with the teachings of natural science. If, for instance, one had to construct a new crocodile, the question would naturally present itself. What is the fundamental characteristic of the crocodile? The answer is clear: to swallow human beings. How is one, in constructing the crocodile, to secure that he should swallow people? The answer is clearer still: construct him hollow. It was settled by physics long ago that Nature abhors a vacuum. Hence the inside of the crocodile must be hollow so that it may abhor the vacuum, and consequently swallow and so fill itself with anything it can come across. And that is the sole rational cause why every crocodile swallows men. It is not the same in the constitution of man: the emptier a man's head is, for instance, the less he feels the thirst to fill it, and that is the one exception to the general rule. It is all as clear as day to me now. I have deduced it by my own observation and experience, being, so to say, in the very bowels of Nature, in its retort, listening to the throbbing of its pulse. Even etymology supports me, for the very word crocodile means voracity. Crocodile—*crocodillo*—is evidently an Italian word, dating perhaps from the Egyptian Pharaohs, and evidently derived from the French verb *croquer*, which means to eat, to devour, in general to absorb nourishment. All these remarks I intend to deliver as my first lecture in Elena Ivanovna's *salon* when they take me there in the tank."

"My friend, oughtn't you at least to take some purgative?" I cried involuntarily.

"He is in a fever, a fever, he is feverish!" I repeated to myself in alarm.

"Nonsense!" he answered contemptuously. "Besides, in my present position it would be most inconvenient. I knew, though, you would be sure to talk of taking medicine."

"But, my friend, how . . . how do you take food now? Have you dined today?"

"No, but I am not hungry, and most likely I shall never take food again. And that, too, is quite natural; filling the whole interior of the crocodile I make him feel always full. Now he need not be fed for some years. On the other hand, nourished by me, he will naturally impart to me all the vital juices of his body; it is the same as with some accomplished coquettes who embed themselves and their whole persons for the night in raw steak, and then, after their morning bath, are fresh, supple, buxom and fascinating. In that way nourishing the crocodile, I myself obtain nourishment from him, consequently we mutually nourish one another. But as it is difficult even for a crocodile to digest a man like me, he must, no doubt, be conscious of a certain weight in his stomach—an organ which he does not, however, possess—and that is why, to avoid causing the creature suffering, I do not often turn over, and although I could turn over I do not do so from humanitarian motives. This is the one drawback of my present position, and in an allegorical sense Timofey Semyonich was right in saying I was lying like a log. But I will prove that even lying like a log—nay, that only lying like a log—one can revolutionize the lot of mankind. All the great ideas and movements of our newspapers and magazines have evidently been the work of men who were lying like logs; that is why they call them divorced from the realities of life—but what does it matter, their saying that! I am constructing now a complete system of my own, and you wouldn't believe how easy it is! You have only to creep into a secluded corner or into a crocodile, to shut your eyes, and you immediately devise a perfect millennium for mankind. When you went away this afternoon I set to work at once and have already invented three systems, now I am preparing the fourth. It is true that at first one must refute everything that has gone before, but from the crocodile it is so easy to refute it; besides, it all becomes clearer, seen from the inside of the crocodile. . . . There are some drawbacks, though small ones, in my position, however; it is somewhat damp here and covered with a sort of slime; moreover, there is a smell of india rubber like the smell of my old goloshes. That is all, there are no other drawbacks."

"Ivan Matveich," I interrupted, "all this is a miracle in which I can scarcely believe. And can you, can you intend never to dine again?"

"What trivial nonsense you are troubling about, you thoughtless, frivolous creature! I talk to you about great ideas, and you . . . Understand that I am sufficiently nourished by the great ideas which light up the darkness in which I am enveloped. The good-natured proprietor has, however, after consulting the kindly *Mutter*, decided with her that they will every morning insert into the monster's jaws a bent metal tube, something like a whistle pipe, by means of which I can absorb coffee or broth with bread soaked in it. The pipe has already been requested in the neighborhood, but I think this is superfluous luxury. I hope to live at least a thousand years, if it is true that crocodiles live so long, which, by the way—good thing I thought of it—you had better look up in some natural history tomorrow and tell me, for I may have been mistaken and have mixed it up with some excavated monster. There is only one reflection rather troubles me: as I am dressed in cloth and have boots on, the crocodile can obviously not digest me. Besides, I am alive, and so am opposing the process of digestion with my whole will power; for you can understand that I do not wish to be turned into what all nourishment turns into, for that would be too humiliating for me. But there is one thing I am afraid of: in a thousand years the cloth of my coat, unfortunately of Russian make, may decay, and then, left without clothing, I might perhaps, in spite of my indignation, begin to be digested; and though by day nothing would induce me to allow it, at night, in my sleep, when a man's will deserts him, I may be overtaken by the humiliating destiny of a potato, a pancake, or veal. Such an idea reduces me to fury. This alone is an argument for the revision of the tariff and the encouragement of the importation of English cloth, which is stronger and so will withstand Nature longer when one is swallowed by a crocodile. At the first opportunity I will impart this idea to some statesman and at the same time to the political writers on our Petersburg dailies. Let them publish it abroad. I trust this will not be the only idea they will borrow from me. I foresee that every morning a regular crowd of them, provided with quarter-rubles from the editorial office, will be flocking round me to seize my ideas on the telegrams of the previous day. In brief, the future presents itself to me in the rosiest light."

"Fever, fever!" I whispered to myself.

"My friend, and freedom?" I asked, wishing to learn his views thoroughly. "You are, so to speak, in prison, while every man has a right to the enjoyment of freedom."

"You are a fool," he answered. "Savages love independence, wise men love order; and if there is no order . . ."

"Ivan Matveich, spare me, please!"

"Hold your tongue and listen!" he squealed, vexed at my interrupting him. "Never has my spirit soared as now. In my narrow refuge there is only one thing that I dread—the literary criticisms of the monthlies and the hiss of our satirical papers. I am afraid that thoughtless visitors, stupid and envious people and nihilists in general, may turn me into ridicule. But I will take measures. I am impatiently awaiting the response of the public tomorrow, and especially the opinion of the newspapers. You must tell me about the papers tomorrow."

"Very good; to-morrow I will bring a perfect pile of papers with me."

"Tomorrow it is too soon to expect reports in the newspapers, for it will take four days for it to be advertised. But from today come to me every evening by the back way through the yard. I am intending to employ you as my secretary. You shall read the newspapers and magazines to me, and I will dictate to you my ideas and give you commissions. Be particularly careful not to forget the foreign dispatches. Let all the European dispatches be here every day. But enough; most likely you are sleepy by now. Go home, and do not think of what I said just now about criticisms: I am not afraid of it, for the critics themselves are in critical position. One has only to be wise and virtuous and one will certainly get on to a pedestal. If not Socrates, then Diogenes, or perhaps both of them together—that is my future rôle among mankind."

So frivolously and boastfully did Ivan Matveich hasten to express himself before me, like feverish weak-willed women who, as we are told by the proverb, cannot keep a secret. All that he told me about the crocodile struck me as most suspicious. How was it possible that the crocodile was absolutely hollow? I don't mind betting that he was bragging from vanity and partly to humiliate me. It is true that he was an invalid and one must make allowances for invalids; but I must frankly confess, I never could endure Ivan Matveich. I have been trying all my life, from a child up, to escape from his tutelage and have not been able to. A thousand times over I have been tempted to break with him altogether, and every time I have been drawn to him again, as though I were still hoping to prove something to him or to revenge myself on him. A strange thing, this friendship! I can positively assert that nine-tenths of my friendship for him was made up of malice. On this occasion, however, we parted with genuine feeling.

"Your friend a very clever man!" the German said to me in an undertone as he moved to see me out; he had been listening all the time attentively to our conversation.

"*À propos*," I said, "while I think of it: how much would you ask for your crocodile in case any one wanted to buy it?"

Ivan Matveich, who heard the question, was waiting with curiosity for the answer; it was evident that he did not want the German to ask too little; anyway, he cleared his throat in a peculiar way on hearing my question.

At first the German would not listen—was positively angry.

"No one will dare my own crocodile to buy!" he cried furiously, and turned as red as a boiled lobster. "Me not want to sell the crocodile! I would not for the crocodile a million thalers take. I took a hundred and thirty thalers from the public today, and I shall tomorrow ten thousand take, and then a hundred thousand every day I shall take. I will not him sell."

Ivan Matveich positively chuckled with satisfaction. Controlling myself—for I felt it was a duty to my friend—I hinted coolly and reasonably to the crazy German that his calculations were not quite correct, that if he makes a hundred thousand every day, all Petersburg will have visited him in four days, and then there will be no one left to bring him rubles, that life and death are in God's hands, that the crocodile may burst or Ivan Matveich may fall ill and die, and so on and so on.

The German grew pensive.

"I will him drops from the chemist's get," he said, after pondering, "and will save your friend that he die not."

"Drops are all very well," I answered, "but consider, too, that the thing may get into the law courts. Ivan Matveich's wife may demand the restitution of her lawful spouse. You are intending to get rich, but do you intend to give Elena Ivanovna a pension?"

"No, me not intend," said the German in stern decision.

"No, we not intend," said the *Mutter*, with positive malignancy.

"And so would it not be better for you to accept something now, at once, a secure and solid though moderate sum, than to leave things to chance? I ought to tell you that I am inquiring simply from curiosity."

The German drew the *Mutter* aside to consult with her in a corner where there stood a case with the largest and ugliest monkey of his collection.

"Well, you will see!" said Ivan Matveich.

As for me, I was at that moment burning with the desire, first, to give the German a thrashing, next, to give the *Mutter* an even sounder one, and, thirdly, to give Ivan Matveich the soundest thrashing of all for his boundless vanity. But all this paled beside the answer of the rapacious German.

After consultation with the *Mutter* he demanded for his crocodile fifty thousand rubles in bonds of the last Russian loan with lottery voucher attached, a brick house in Gorohovy Street with a chemist's shop attached, and in addition the rank of Russian colonel.

"You see!" Ivan Matveich cried triumphantly. "I told you so! Apart from this last senseless desire for the rank of a colonel, he is perfectly right, for he fully understands the present value of the monster he is exhibiting. The economic principle before everything!"

"Upon my word!" I cried furiously to the German. "But what should you be made a colonel for? What exploit have you performed? What service have you done? In what way have you gained military glory? You are really crazy!"

"Crazy!" cried the German, offended. "No, a person very sensible, but you very stupid! I have a colonel deserved for that I have a crocodile shown and in him a live *hofrath*[10] sitting! And a Russian can a crocodile not show and a live *hofrath* in him sitting! Me extremely clever man and much wish colonel to be!"

"Well, good-by, then, Ivan Matveich!" I cried, shaking with fury, and I went out of the crocodile room almost at a run.

I felt that in another minute I could not have answered for myself. The unnatural expectations of these two blockheads were insupportable. The cold air refreshed me and somewhat moderated my indignation. At last, after spitting vigorously fifteen times on each side, I took a cab, got home, undressed and flung myself into bed. What vexed me more than anything was my having become his secretary. Now I was to die of boredom there every evening, doing the duty of a true friend! I was ready to beat myself for it, and I did, in fact, after putting out the candle and pulling up the bedclothes, punch myself several times on the head and various parts of my body. That somewhat relieved me, and at last I fell asleep fairly soundly, in fact, for I was very tired. All night long I could dream of nothing but monkeys, but towards morning I dreamt of Elena Ivanovna.

10 [Councillor.]

4

THE monkeys I dreamed about, I surmise, because they were shut up in the case at the German's; but Elena Ivanovna was a different story.

I may as well say at once, I loved the lady, but I make haste—post-haste—to make a qualification. I loved her as a father, neither more nor less. I judge that because I often felt an irresistible desire to kiss her little head or her rosy cheek. And although I never carried out this inclination, I would not have refused even to kiss her lips. And not merely her lips, but her teeth, which always gleamed so charmingly like two rows of pretty, well-matched pearls when she laughed. She laughed extraordinarily often. Ivan Matveich in demonstrative moments used to call her his "darling absurdity"—a name extremely happy and appropriate. She was a perfect sugarplum, and that was all one could say of her. Therefore, I am utterly at a loss to understand what possessed Ivan Matveich to imagine his wife as a Russian Yevgenia Tour? Anyway, my dream, with the exception of the monkeys, left a most pleasant impression upon me, and going over all the incidents of the previous day as I drank my morning cup of tea, I resolved to go and see Elena Ivanovna at once on my way to the office—which, indeed, I was bound to do as the friend of the family.

In a tiny little room out of the bedroom—the so-called little drawing room, though their big drawing room was little too—Elena Ivanovna was sitting, in some half-transparent morning wrapper, on a smart little sofa before a little tea table, drinking coffee out of a little cup in which she was dipping a minute biscuit. She was ravishingly pretty, but struck me as being at the same time rather pensive.

"Ah, that's you, naughty man!" she said, greeting me with an absent-minded smile. "Sit down, featherhead, have some coffee. Well, what were you doing yesterday? Were you at the masquerade?"

"Why, were you? I don't go, you know. Besides, yesterday I was visiting our captive. . . ." I sighed and assumed a pious expression as I took the coffee.

"Whom? . . . What captive? . . . Oh, yes! Poor fellow! Well, how is he—bored? Do you know . . . I wanted to ask you . . . I suppose I can ask for a divorce now?"

"A divorce!" I cried in indignation and almost spilled the coffee. "It's that swarthy fellow," I thought to myself bitterly.

There was a certain swarthy gentleman with little moustaches who was something in the architectural line, and who came far too often to see them, and was extremely skillful in amusing Elena Ivanovna. I must confess I hated him and there was no doubt that he had succeeded in seeing Elena Ivanovna yesterday either at the masquerade or even here, and putting all sorts of nonsense into her head.

"Why," Elena Ivanovna rattled off hurriedly, as though it were a lesson she had learnt, "if he is going to stay on in the crocodile, perhaps not come back all his life, while I sit waiting for him here. A husband ought to live at home, and not in a crocodile. . . ."

"But that was an unforeseen occurrence," I was beginning, in very comprehensible agitation.

"Oh, no, don't talk to me, I won't listen, I won't listen," she cried, suddenly getting quite cross. "You are always against me, you wretch! There's no doing anything with you, you will never give me any advice! Other people tell me that I can get a divorce because Ivan Matveich will not get his salary now."

"Elena Ivanovna! is it you I hear!" I exclaimed pathetically. "What villain could have put such an idea into your head? And divorce on such a trivial ground as a salary is quite impossible. And poor Ivan Matveich, poor Ivan Matveich is, so to speak, burning with love for you even in the bowels of the monster. What's more, he is melting away with love like a lump of sugar. Yesterday while you were enjoying yourself at the masquerade, he was saying that he might in the last resort send for you as his lawful spouse to join him in the entrails of the monster, especially as it appears the crocodile is exceedingly roomy, not only able to accommodate two but even three persons. . . .

And then I told her all that interesting part of my conversation the night before with Ivan Matveich.

"What, what!" she cried, in surprise. "You want me to get into the monster too, to be with Ivan Matveich? What an idea! And how am I to get in there, in my hat and crinoline? Heavens, what foolishness! And what should I look like while I was getting into it, and very likely there would be some one there to see me! It's absurd! And what should I have to eat there? And . . . and . . . and what should I do there when . . . Oh, my goodness, what will they think of next? . . . And what should I have to amuse me there? . . . You say there's a smell of gutta-percha? And what should I do if we quarrelled—should we have to go on staying there side by side? Foo, how horrid!"

"I agree, I agree with all those arguments, my sweet Elena Ivanovna," I interrupted, striving to express myself with that natural enthusiasm which always overtakes a man when he feels the truth is on his side. "But one thing you have not appreciated in all this, you have not realized that he cannot live without you if he is inviting you there; that is a proof of love, passionate, faithful, ardent love. . . . You have thought too little of his love, dear Elena Ivanovna!"

"I won't, I won't, I won't hear anything about it!" waving me off with her pretty little hand with glistening pink nails that had just been washed and polished. "Horrid man! You will reduce me to tears! Get into it yourself, if you like the prospect. You are his friend, get in and keep him company, and spend your life discussing some tedious science. . . ."

"You are wrong to laugh at this suggestion"—I checked the frivolous woman with dignity—"Ivan Matveich has invited me as it is. You, of course, are summoned there by duty; for me, it would be an act of generosity. But when Ivan Matveich described to me last night the elasticity of the crocodile, he hinted very plainly that there would be room not only for you two, but for me also as a friend of the family, especially if I wished to join you, and therefore . . ."

"How so, the three of us?" cried Elena Ivanovna, looking at me in surprise. "Why, how should we . . . are we going to be all three there together? Ha-ha-ha! How silly you both are! Ha-ha-ha! I shall certainly pinch you all the time, you wretch! Ha-ha-ha! Ha-ha-ha!"

And falling back on the sofa, she laughed till she cried. All this—the tears and the laughter—were so fascinating that I could not resist rushing eagerly to kiss her hand, which she did not oppose, though she did pinch my ears lightly as a sign of reconciliation.

Then we both grew very cheerful, and I described to her in detail all Ivan Matveich's plans. The thought of her evening receptions and her *salon* pleased her very much.

"Only I should need a great many new dresses," she observed, "and so Ivan Matveich must send me as much of his salary as possible and as soon as possible. Only . . . only I don't know about that," she added thoughtfully. "How can he be brought here in the tank? That's very absurd. I don't want my husband to be carried about in a tank. I should feel quite ashamed for my visitors to see it. . . . I don't want that, no, I don't."

"By the way, while I think of it, was Timofey Semyonich here yesterday?"

"Oh, yes, he was; he came to comfort me, and do you know, we played cards all the time. He played for sweetmeats, and if I lost he was to kiss my hands. What a wretch he is! And only fancy, he almost came to the masquerade with me, really!"

"He was carried away by his feelings!" I observed. "And who would not be with you, you charmer?"

"Oh, get along with your compliments! Stay, I'll give you a pinch as a parting present. I've learnt to pinch awfully well lately. Well, what do you say to that? By the way, you say Ivan Matveich spoke several times of me yesterday?"

"N-no, not exactly. . . . I must say he was thinking more now of the fate of humanity, and wants . . ."

"Oh, let him! You needn't go on! I am sure it's fearfully boring. I'll go and see him some time. I shall certainly go tomorrow. Only not today; I've got a headache, and besides, there will be such a lot of people there today. . . . They'll say, 'That's his wife,' and I shall feel ashamed. . . . Good-by. You will be . . . there this evening, won't you?"

"To see him, yes. He asked me to go and take him the papers."

"That's capital. Go and read to him. But don't come and see me today. I am not well, and perhaps I may go and see some one. Good-by, you naughty man."

"It's that swarthy fellow is going to see her this evening," I thought.

At the office, of course, I gave no sign of being consumed by these cares and anxieties. But soon I noticed some of the most progressive papers seemed to be passing particularly rapidly from hand to hand among my colleagues, and were being read with an extremely serious expression of face. The first one that reached me was the *News-sheet*, a paper of no particular party but humanitarian in general, for which it was regarded with contempt among us, though it was read. Not without surprise I read in it the following paragraph:

"Yesterday strange rumors were circulating among the spacious ways and sumptuous buildings of our vast metropolis. A certain well-known *bon-vivant* of the highest society, probably weary of the *cuisine* at Borel's and at the X. Club, went into the Arcade, into the place where an immense crocodile recently brought to the metropolis is being exhibited, and insisted on its being prepared for his dinner. After bargaining with the proprietor he at once set to work to devour him (that is, not the proprietor, a very meek and punctilious German, but his crocodile), cutting juicy morsels with his penknife from the living animal, and swallowing them with extraordinary rapidity. By degrees the whole crocodile disappeared into the vast recesses of his stomach, so that he was even on the point of attacking an ichneumon, a constant companion of the crocodile, probably imagining that the latter would be as savoury. We are by no means opposed to that new article of diet with which foreign *gourmands* have long been familiar. We have, indeed, predicted that it would come. English lords and travellers make up regular parties for catching crocodiles in Egypt, and consume the back of the monster cooked like beefsteak, with mustard, onions and potatoes. The French who followed in the train of Lesseps prefer the paws baked in hot ashes, which they do, however, in opposition to the English, who laugh at them. Probably both ways would be appreciated among us. For our part, we are delighted at a new branch of industry, of which our great and varied fatherland stands pre-eminently in need. Probably before the year is out crocodiles will be brought in hundreds to replace this first one, lost in the stomach of a Petersburg *gourmand*. And why should not the crocodile be acclimatized among us in Russia? If the water of the Neva is too cold for these interesting strangers, there are ponds in the capital and rivers and lakes outside it. Why not breed crocodiles at Pargolovo, for instance, or at Pavlovsk, in the Presensky Ponds and in Samoteka in Moscow? While providing agreeable, wholesome nourishment for our fastidious *gourmands,* they might at the same time entertain the ladies who walk about these ponds and instruct the children in natural history. The crocodile skin might be used for making jewel cases, boxes, cigar cases, pocketbooks, and possibly more than one thousand saved up in the greasy notes that are peculiarly beloved of merchants might be laid by in crocodile skin. We hope to return more than once to this interesting topic."

Though I had foreseen something of the sort, yet the reckless inaccuracy of the paragraph overwhelmed me. Finding no one with whom to share my impression, I turned to Prokhor Savitch who was sitting opposite to me, and noticed that the latter had been watching me for some time, while in his hand he held the *Voice* as though he were on the point of passing it to me. Without a word he took the *News-sheet* from me, and as he handed me the *Voice* he drew a line with his nail against an article to which he probably wished to call my attention. This Prokhor Savitch was a very queer man; a taciturn old bachelor, he was not on intimate terms with any of us, scarcely spoke to any one in the office, always had an opinion of his own about everything, but could not bear to impart it to any one. He lived alone. Hardly any one among us had ever been in his lodging.

This was what I read in the *Voice.*

"Every one knows that we are progressive and humanitarian and want to be on a level with Europe in this respect. But in spite of all our exertions and the efforts of our paper we are still far from maturity, as may be judged from the shocking incident which took place yesterday in the Arcade and which we predicted long ago. A foreigner arrives in the capital bringing with him a crocodile which he begins exhibiting in the Arcade. We immediately hasten to welcome a new branch of useful industry such as our powerful and varied fatherland stands in great need of. Suddenly yesterday at four o'clock in the afternoon a gentleman of exceptional stoutness enters the foreigner's shop in an intoxicated condition, pays his entrance money, and immediately without any warning leaps into the jaws of the crocodile, who was forced, of course, to swallow him, if only from an instinct of self-preservation, to avoid being crushed. Tumbling into the inside of the crocodile, the stranger at once dropped asleep. Neither the shouts of the foreign proprietor, nor the lamentations of his terrified family, nor threats to send for the police made the slightest impression. Within the crocodile was heard nothing but laughter and a promise to flay him (sic), though the poor mammal, compelled to swallow such a mass, was vainly shedding tears. An uninvited guest is worse than a Tartar. But in spite of the proverb the insolent visitor would not leave. We do not know how to explain such barbarous incidents which prove our lack of culture and disgrace us in the eyes of foreigners. The recklessness of the Russian temperament has found a fresh outlet. It may be asked what was the object of the uninvited visitor? A warm and comfortable abode? But there are many excellent houses in the capital with very cheap and comfortable lodgings, with the Neva water laid on, and a staircase lighted by gas, frequently with a hall porter maintained by the proprietor. We would call our readers' attention to the barbarous treatment of domestic animals: it is difficult, of course, for the crocodile to digest such a mass all at once, and now he lies swollen out to the size of a mountain, awaiting death in insufferable agonies. In Europe persons guilty of inhumanity towards domestic animals have long been punished by law. But in spite of our European enlightenment, in spite of our European pavements, in spite of the European architecture of our houses, we are still far from shaking off our time-honored traditions.

'Though the houses are new, the conventions are old.'

"And, indeed, the houses are not new, at least the staircases in them are not. We have more than once in our paper alluded to the fact that in the Petersburg Side in the house of the merchant Lukyanov the steps of the wooden staircase have decayed, fallen away, and have long been a danger for Afimya Skapidarov, a soldier's wife who works in the house, and is often obliged to go up the stairs with water or armfuls of wood. At last our predictions have come true: yesterday evening at half-past eight Afimya Skapidarov fell down with a basin of soup and broke her leg. We do not know whether Lukyanov will mend his staircase now, Russians are often wise after the event, but the victim of Russian carelessness has by now been taken to the hospital. In the same way we shall never cease to maintain that the house-porters who clear away the mud from the wooden pavement in the Viborgsky Side ought not to spatter the legs of passersby, but should throw the mud up into heaps as is done in Europe," and so, and so on.

"What's this?" I asked in some perplexity, looking at Prokhor Savitch. "What's the meaning of it?"

"How do you mean?"

"Why, upon my word! Instead of pitying Ivan Matveich, they pity the crocodile!"

"What of it? They have pity even for a beast, a *mammal*. We must be up to Europe, mustn't we? They have a very warm feeling for crocodiles there too. He-he-he!"

Saying this, queer old Prokhor dived into his papers and would not utter another word.

I stuffed the *Voice* and the *News-sheet* into my pocket and collected as many old copies of the newspaper as I could find for Ivan Matveich's diversion in the evening, and though the evening was far off, yet on this occasion I slipped away from the office early to go to the Arcade and look, if only from a distance, at what was going on there, and listen to the various remarks and currents of opinion. I foresaw that there would be a regular crush there, and turned up the collar of my coat to meet it. I somehow felt rather shy—so unaccustomed are we to publicity. But I feel that I have no right to report my own prosaic feelings when faced with this remarkable and original incident.

Sir Alan P. Herbert

THE NEGOTIABLE COW

BOARD OF INLAND REVENUE v. HADDOCK; REX v. HADDOCK

"WAS THE cow crossed?"

"No, your worship, it was an open cow."

These and similar passages provoked laughter at Bow Street to-day when the Negotiable Cow case was concluded.

Sir Joshua Hoot, K.C. (appearing for the Public Prosecutor): Sir Basil, these summonses, by leave of the Court, are being heard together, an unusual but convenient arrangement.

The defendant, Mr. Albert Haddock, has for many months, in spite of earnest endeavors on both sides, been unable to establish harmonious relations between himself and the Collector of Taxes. The Collector maintains that Mr. Haddock should make over a large part of his earnings to the Government. Mr. Haddock replies that the proportion demanded is excessive, in view of the inadequate services or consideration which he himself has received from that Government. After an exchange of endearing letters, telephone calls, and even cheques, the sum demanded was reduced to fifty-seven pounds; and about this sum the exchange of opinions continued.

On the 31st of May the Collector was diverted from his respectable labours by the apparition of a noisy crowd outside his windows. The crowd, Sir Basil, has been attracted by Mr. Haddock, who was leading a large white cow of malevolent aspect. On the back and sides of the cow were clearly stencilled in red ink the following words:

To the London and Literary Bank, Ltd.
Pay the Collector of Taxes, who is no gentleman, on Order, the sum of fifty-seven pounds (and may he rot!).
£57/0/0 ALBERT HADDOCK

Mr. Haddock conducted the cow into the Collector's office, tendered it to the Collector in payment of income-tax and demanded a receipt.

Sir Basil String: Did the cow bear the statutory stamp?

Sir Joshua: Yes, a twopenny stamp was affixed to the dexter horn. The Collector declined to accept the cow, objecting that it would be difficult or even impossible to pay the cow into the bank. Mr. Haddock, throughout the interview, maintained the friendliest demeanour;[1] and he now remarked that the Collector could endorse the cow to any third party to whom he owed money, adding that there must be many persons in that position. The Collector then endeavoured to endorse the cheque——

Sir Basil String: Where?

Sir Joshua: On the back of the cheque, Sir Basil, that is to say, on the abdomen of the cow. The cow, however, appeared to resent endorsement and adopted a menacing posture. The Collector, abandoning the attempt, declined finally to take the cheque. Mr. Haddock led the cow away and was arrested in Trafalgar Square for causing an obstruction. He has also been summoned by the Board of Inland Revenue for nonpayment of income-tax.

Mr. Haddock, in the witness-box, said that he had tendered a cheque in payment of income-tax, and if the Commissioners did not like his cheque they could do the other thing. A cheque was only an order to a bank to pay money to the person in possession of the cheque or a person named on the cheque. There was nothing in statute or customary law to say that that order must be written on a piece of paper of specified dimensions. A cheque, it was well known, could be written on a piece of notepaper. He himself had drawn cheques on the backs of menus, on napkins, on handkerchiefs, on the labels of wine-bottles; all these cheques had been duly honoured by his bank and passed through the Bankers' Clearing House. He could see no distinction in law between a cheque written on a napkin and a cheque written on a cow. The essence of each document was a written order to pay money, made in the customary form and in accordance with statutory requirements as to stamps, etc. A cheque was admittedly not legal tender in the sense that it could not lawfully be refused; but it was accepted by custom as a legitimate form of payment. There were funds in his bank sufficient to meet the cow; the

1 *"Mars est celare martem."* (Selden, *Mare Clausum,* lib. I c. 21). [War conceals war. A play on the adage: Art conceals art.]

Commissioners might not like the cow, but, the cow having been tendered, they were estopped from charging him with failure to pay. (Mr. Haddock here cited *Spowers* v. *The Strand Magazine*, *Lucas* v. *Finck*, and *Wadsworth* v. *The Metropolitan Water Board*.)

As to the action of the police, Mr. Haddock said it was a nice thing if in the heart of the commercial capital of the world a man could not convey a negotiable instrument down the street without being arrested. He had instituted proceedings against Constable Boot for false imprisonment.

Cross-examined as to motive, witness said that he had no cheque-forms available and, being anxious to meet his obligations promptly, had made use of the only material to hand. Later he admitted that there might have been present in his mind a desire to make the Collector of Taxes ridiculous. But why not? There was no law against deriding the income-tax.[2]

Sir Basil String (*after the hearing of further evidence*): This case has at least brought to the notice of the Court a citizen who is unusual both in his clarity of mind and integrity of behaviour. No thinking man can regard those parts of the Finance Acts which govern the income-tax with anything but contempt. There may be something to be said—not much—for taking from those who have inherited wealth a certain proportion of that wealth for the service of the State and the benefit of the poor and needy; and those who by their own ability, brains, industry, and exertion have earned money may reasonably be invited to surrender a small portion of it towards the maintenance of those public services by which they benefit, to wit, the Police, the Navy, the Army, the public sewers, and so forth. But to compel such individuals to bestow a large part of their earnings upon other individuals, whether by way of pensions, unemployment grants, or education allowances, is manifestly barbarous and indefensible. Yet this is the law. The original and only official basis of taxation was that individual citizens, in return for their money, received collectively some services from the State, the defence of their property and persons, the care of their health or the education of their children. All that has now gone. Citizen A, who has earned money, is commanded simply to give it to Citizens B, C, and D, who have not, and by force of habit this has come to be regarded as a normal and proper proceeding, whatever the comparative industry or merits of Citizens A, B, C, and D. To be alive has become a virtue, and the mere capacity to inflate the lungs entitles Citizen B to a substantial share in the laborious earnings of Citizen A. The defendant, Mr. Haddock, repels and resents this doctrine, but, since it has received

2 Cf. Magna Carta: "*Jus ridendi nulli negabimus.*" [No one is denied the right to laughter.]

the sanction of Parliament, he dutifully complies with it. Hampered by practical difficulties, he took the first step he could to discharge his legal obligations to the State. Paper was not available, so he employed instead a favourite cow. Now, there can be nothing obscene, offensive, or derogatory in the presentation of a cow by one man to another. Indeed, in certain parts of our Empire the cow is venerated as a sacred animal. Payment in kind is the oldest form of payment, and payment in kind more often than not meant payment in cattle. Indeed, during the Saxon period, Mr. Haddock tells us, cattle were described as *viva pecunia,* or "living money," from their being received as payment on most occasions, at certain regulated prices.[3] So that, whether the cheque was valid or not, it was impossible to doubt the validity of the cow; and whatever the Collector's distrust of the former it was at least his duty to accept the latter and credit Mr. Haddock's account with its value. But, as Mr. Haddock protested in his able argument, an order to pay is an order to pay, whether it is made on the back of an envelope or on the back of a cow. The evidence of the bank is that Mr. Haddock's account was in funds. From every point of view, therefore, the Collector of Taxes did wrong, by custom if not by law, in refusing to take the proffered animal, and the summons issued at his instance will be discharged.

As for the second charge, I hold again that Constable Boot did wrong. It cannot be unlawful to conduct a cow through the London streets. The horse, at the present time a much less useful animal, constantly appears in those streets without protest, and the motor-car, more unnatural and unattractive still, is more numerous than either animal. Much less can the cow be regarded as an improper or unlawful companion when it is invested (as I have shown) with all the dignity of a bill of exchange.

If people choose to congregate in one place upon the apparition of Mr. Haddock with a promissory cow, then Constable Boot should arrest the people, not Mr. Haddock. Possibly, if Mr. Haddock had paraded Cockspur Street with a paper cheque for one million pounds made payable to bearer, the crowd would have been as great, but that is not to say that Mr. Haddock would have broken the law. In my judgment Mr. Haddock has behaved throughout in the manner of a perfect knight, citizen, and taxpayer. The charge brought by the Crown is dismissed; and I hope with all my heart that in his action against Constable Boot Mr. Haddock will be successful. What is the next case, please?

3 Mandeville uses *Catele* for "price" (Wharton's Law Lexicon).

ESSAYS

Dylan Thomas

A VISIT TO AMERICA

ACROSS the United States of America, from New York to California and back, glazed, again, for many months of the year there streams and sings for its heady supper a dazed and prejudiced procession of European lecturers, scholars, sociologists, economists, writers, authorities on this and that and even, in theory, on the United States of America. And, breathlessly between addresses and receptions, in planes and trains and boiling hotel bedroom ovens, many of these attempt to keep journals and diaries. At first, confused and shocked by shameless profusion and almost shamed by generosity, unaccustomed to such importance as they are assumed, by their hosts, to possess, and up against the barrier of a common language, they write in their note-books like demons, generalizing away, on character and culture and the American political scene. But, towards the middle of their middle-aged whisk through middle-western clubs and universities, the fury of the writing flags; their spirits are lowered by the spirit with which they are everywhere strongly greeted and which, in over-increasing doses, they themselves lower; and they begin to mistrust themselves, and their reputations—for they have found, too often, that an audience will receive a lantern-lecture on, say, ceramics, with the same uninhibited enthusiasm that it accorded the very week before to a paper on the Modern Turkish Novel. And, in their diaries, more and more do such entries appear as, "No way of escape!" or "Buffalo!" or "I am beaten," until at last they cannot write a word. And, twittering all over, old before their time, with eyes like rissoles in the sand, they are helped up the gangway of the home-bound liner by kind bosom friends (of all kinds and bosoms) who boister them on the back, pick them up again, thrust bottles, sonnets, cigars, addresses into their pockets, have a farewell party in their cabin, pick them up again, and, snickering and yelping, are gone: to wait at the dockside for another boat from Europe and another batch of fresh, green lecturers.

There they go, every spring, from New York to Los Angeles: ex-

---

hibitionists, polemicists, histrionic publicists, theological rhetoricians, historical hoddy-doddies, balletomanes, ulterior decorators, windbags, and bigwigs and humbugs, men in love with stamps, men in love with steaks, men after millionaires' widows, men with elephantiasis of the reputation (huge trunks and teeny minds), authorities on gas, bishops, best sellers, editors looking for writers, writers looking for publishers, publishers looking for dollars, existentialists, serious physicists with nuclear missions, men from the B.B.C. who speak as though they had the Elgin Marbles in their mouths, potboiling philosophers, professional Irishmen (very lepri-corny), and I am afraid, fat poets with slim volumes. And see, too, in that linguaceous stream, the tall monocled men, smelling of saddle soap and club arm-chairs, their breath a nice blending of whiskey and fox's blood, with big protruding upper-class tusks and county moustaches, presumably invented in England and sent abroad to advertise *Punch,* who lecture to women's clubs on such unlikely subjects as "The History of Etching in the Shetland Islands." And the brassy-bossy men-women, with corrugated-iron perms, and hippo hides, who come, self-announced, as "ordinary British housewives," to talk with rich minked chunks of American matronhood about the iniquity of the Health Services, the criminal sloth of the miners, the visible tail and horns of Mr. Aneurin Bevan, and the fear of everyone in England to go out alone at night because of the organized legions of cosh boys against whom the police are powerless owing to the refusal of those in power to equip them with revolvers and to flog to ribbons every adolescent offender on any charge at all. And there shiver and teeter also, meek and driven, those British authors unfortunate enough to have written, after years of unadventurous forgotten work, one bad novel which became enormously popular on both sides of the Atlantic. At home, when success first hit them, they were mildly delighted; a couple of literary luncheons went sugar-tipsy to their heads, like the washing sherry served before those luncheons; and perhaps, as the lovely money rolled lushly in, they began to dream in their moony writers' way, of being able to retire to the country, keep wasps (or was it bees?), and never write another lousy word. But in come the literary agent's triggermen and the publisher's armed narks: "You must go to the States and make a Personal Appearance. Your novel is *killing* them over there, and we're not surprised either. You must go round the States lecturing to women." And the inoffensive writers, who've never dared lecture anyone, let alone women—they are frightened of women, they do not understand women, they write about women as creatures that never existed, and the women lap it up—these sensitive plants cry out: "But what shall be lecture about?"

"The English Novel."

"I don't read novels."

"Great Women in Fiction."

"I don't like fiction *or* women."

But off they're wafted, first class, in the plush bowels of the *Queen Victoria* with a list of engagements long as a New York menu or a half-hour with a book by Charles Morgan, and soon they are losing their little cold-as-goldfish paw in the great general glutinous handshake of a clutch of enveloping hostesses. I think, by the way, that it was Ernest Raymond, the author of *Tell England*, who once made a journey round the American women's clubs, being housed and entertained at each small town he stopped at by the richest and largest and furriest lady available. On one occasion he stopped at some little station, and was met, as usual, by an enormous motor-car full of a large hornrimmed business man, looking *exactly* like a large hornrimmed business man on the films—and his roly-poly pearly wife. Mr. Raymond sat with her in the back of the car, and off they went, the husband driving. At once, she began to say how utterly delighted she and her husband and the committee were to have him at their Women's Literary and Social Guild, and to compliment him on his books. "I don't think I've ever, in all my life, enjoyed a book so much as *Sorrel and Son*," she said. "What you don't know about human nature! I think Sorrel is one of the most beautiful characters ever portrayed."

Ernest Raymond let her talk on, while he stared, embarrassed, in front of him. All he could see were the three double chins that her husband wore at the back of his neck. On and on she gushed in praise of *Sorrel and Son* until he could stand it no longer. "I quite agree with you," he said. "A beautiful book indeed. But I'm afraid I didn't write *Sorrel and Son*. It was written by an old friend of mine, Mr. Warwick Deeping."

And the large hornrimmed double-chinned husband at the wheel said without turning: "Caught again, Emily."

See the garrulous others, also, gabbing and garlanded from one nest of culture-vultures to another: people selling the English way of life and condemning the American way as they swig and guzzle through it; people resurrecting the theories of surrealism for the benefit of remote parochial female audiences who did not know it was dead, not having ever known it had been alive; people talking about Etruscan pots and pans to a bunch of dead pans and wealthy pots in Boston. And there, too, in the sticky thick of lecturers moving across the continent black with clubs, go the foreign poets, catarrhal troubadours, lyrical one-night-standers, dollar-mad nightingales, remittance-bards from at home, myself among them booming with the worst.

Did we pass one another, *en route*, all unknowing, I wonder, one of us, spry-eyed, with clean, white lectures and a soul he could call his own, going buoyantly west to his remunerative doom in the great State University factories, another returning dog-eared as his clutch of poems and his carefully typed impromptu asides? I ache for us both. There one goes, unsullied as yet, in his Pullman pride, toying, oh boy, with a blunderbuss bourbon, being smoked by a large cigar, riding out to the wide open spaces of the faces of his waiting audience. He carries, besides his literary baggage, a new, dynamic razor, just on the market, bought in New York, which operates at the flick of a thumb, but cuts the thumb to the bone; a tin of new shaving-lather which is worked with the other, unbleeding, thumb and covers not only the face but the whole bath-room and, instantly freezing, makes an arctic, icicled cave from which it takes two sneering bell-boys to extract him; and, of course, a nylon shirt. This, he dearly believed from the advertisements, he could himself wash in his hotel, hang to dry overnight, and put on, without ironing, in the morning. (In my case, no ironing was needed, for as someone cruelly pointed out in print, I looked, anyway, like an unmade bed.)

He is vigorously welcomed at the station by an earnest crew-cut platoon of giant collegiates, all chasing the butterfly culture with net, note-book, poison-bottle, pin, and label, each with at least thirty-six terribly white teeth, and is nursed away, as heavily gently as though he were an imbecile rich aunt with a short prospect of life, into a motor-car in which, for a mere fifty miles or so travelled at poet-breaking speed, he assures them of the correctness of their assumption that he is half-witted by stammering inconsequential answers in an over-British accent to the genial questions about what international conference Stephen Spender might be attending at the moment or the reactions of British poets to the work of a famous American whose name he did not know or catch. He is then taken to a small party of only a few hundred people all of whom hold the belief that what a visiting lecturer needs before he trips on to the platform is just enough martinis so that he can trip *off* the platform as well. And, clutching his explosive glass, he is soon contemptuously dismissing, in a flush of ignorance and fluency, the poetry of those androgynous literary ladies with three names who produce a kind of verbal ecto-plasm to order as a waiter dishes up spaghetti—only to find that the fiercest of these, a wealthy huntress of small, seedy lions (such as himself), who stalks the middle-western bush with ears and rifle cocked, is his hostess for the evening. Of the lecture he remembers little but the applause and maybe two questions: "Is it true that the young English intellectuals are *really* psychological?" or, "I always carry Kierkegaard in my pocket. What do you carry?"

Late at night, in his room, he fills a page of his journal with a confused, but scathing, account of his first engagement; summarizes American advanced education in a paragraph that will be meaningless to-morrow, and falls to sleep where he is immediately chased through long, dark thickets by a Mrs. Mabel Frankincense Mehaffey, with a tray of martinis and lyrics.

And there goes the other happy poet bedraggedly back to New York which struck him all of a sheepish never-sleeping heap at first but which seems to him now, after the ulcerous rigours of a lecturer's spring, a haven cosy as toast, cool as an icebox, and safe as skyscrapers.

Max Beerbohm

LAUGHTER

M. BERGSON, in his well-known essay on this theme, says . . . [sic] well, he says many things; but none of these, though I have just read them, do I clearly remember, nor am I sure that in the act of reading I understood any of them. That is the worst of these fashionable philosophers—or rather, the worst of me. Somehow I never manage to read them till they are just going out of fashion, and even then I don't seem able to cope with them. About twelve years ago, when every one suddenly talked to me about Pragmatism and William James, I found myself moved by a dull but irresistible impulse to try Schopenhauer, of whom, years before that, I had heard that he was the easiest reading in the world, and the most exciting and amusing. I wrestled with Schopenhauer for a day or so, in vain. Time passed; M. Bergson appeared "and for his hour was lord of the ascendant"; I tardily tackled William James. I bore in mind, as I approached him, the testimonials that had been lavished on him by all my friends. Alas, I was insensible to his thrillingness. His gaiety did not make me gay. His crystal clarity confused me dreadfully. I could make nothing of William James. And now, in the fullness of time, I have been floored by M. Bergson.

It distresses me, this failure to keep pace with the leaders of thought as they pass into oblivion. It makes me wonder whether I am, after all, an absolute fool. Yet surely I am not that. Tell me of a man or a woman, a place or an event, real or fictitious: surely you will find me a fairly intelligent listener. Any such narrative will present to me some image, and will stir me to not altogether fatuous thoughts. Come to me in some grievous difficulty: I will talk to you like a father, even like

---

a lawyer. I'll be hanged if I haven't a certain mellow wisdom. But if you are by way of weaving theories as to the nature of things in general, and if you want to try those theories on some one who will luminously confirm them or powerfully rend them, I must, with a hang-dog air, warn you that I am not your man. I suffer from a strong suspicion that things in general cannot be accounted for through any formula or set of formulae, and that any one philosophy, howsoever new, is no better than another. That is in itself a sort of philosophy, and I suspect it accordingly; but it has for me the merit of being the only one I can make head or tail of. If you try to expound any other philosophic system to me, you will find not merely that I can detect no flaw in it (except the one great flaw just suggested), but also that I haven't, after a minute or two, the vaguest notion of what you are driving at. "Very well," you say, "instead of trying to explain all things at once, I will explain some little, simple, single thing." It was for sake of such shorn lambs as myself, doubtless, that M. Bergson sat down and wrote about—Laughter. But I have profited by his kindness no more than if he had been treating of the Cosmos. I cannot tread even a limited space of air. I have a gross satisfaction in the crude fact of being on hard ground again, and I utter a coarse peal of—Laughter.

At least, I say I do so. In point of fact, I have merely smiled. Twenty years ago, ten years ago, I should have laughed, and have professed to you that I had merely smiled. A very young man is not content to be very young, nor even a young man to be young: he wants to share the dignity of his elders. There is no dignity in laughter, there is much of it in smiles. Laughter is but a joyous surrender, smiles give token of mature criticism. It may be that in the early ages of this world there was far more laughter than is to be heard now, and that aeons hence laughter will be obsolete, and smiles universal—every one, always, mildly, slightly, smiling. But it is less useful to speculate as to mankind's past and future than to observe men. And you will have observed with me in the club-room that young men at most times look solemn, whereas old men or men of middle age mostly smile; and also that those young men do often laugh out loud and long among themselves, while we others—the gayest and best of us in the most favourable circumstances—seldom achieve more than our habitual act of smiling. Does the sound of that laughter jar on us? Do we liken it to the crackling of thorns under a pot? Let us do so. There is no cheerier sound. But let us not assume it to be laughter of fools because we sit quiet. It is absurd to disapprove of what one envies, or to wish a good thing were no more because it has passed out of our possession.

But (it seems that I must begin every paragraph by questioning the sincerity of what I have just said) *has* the gift of laughter been withdrawn from me? I protest that I do still, at the age of forty-seven, laugh often and loud and long. But not, I believe, so long and loud and often as in my less smiling youth. And I am proud, nowadays, of laughing, and grateful to any one who makes me laugh. That is a bad sign. I no longer take laughter as a matter of course. I realise, even after reading M. Bergson on it, how good a thing it is. I am qualified to praise it.

As to what is most precious among the accessories to the world we live in, different men hold different opinions. There are people whom the sea depresses, whom mountains exhilarate. Personally, I want the sea always—some not populous edge of it for choice; and with it sunshine, and wine, and a little music. My friend on the mountain yonder is of tougher fibre and sterner outlook, disapproves of the sea's laxity and instability, has no ear for music and no palate for the grape, and regards the sun as a rather enervating institution, like central heating in a house. What he likes is a grey day and the wind in his face; crags at a great altitude; and a flask of whisky. Yet I think that even he, if we were trying to determine from what inner sources mankind derives the greatest pleasure in life, would agree with me that only the emotion of love takes higher rank than the emotion of laughter. Both these emotions are partly mental, partly physical. It is said that the mental symptoms of love are wholly physical in origin. They are not the less ethereal for that. The physical sensations of laughter, on the other hand, are reached by a process whose starting-point is in the mind. They are not the less "gloriously of our clay." There is laughter that goes so far as to lose all touch with its motive, and to exist only, grossly, in itself. This is laughter at its best. A man to whom such laughter has often been granted may happen to die in a work-house. No matter. I will not admit that he has failed in life. Another man, who has never laughed thus, may be buried in Westminster Abbey, leaving more than a million pounds overhead. What then? I regard him as a failure.

Nor does it seem to me to matter one jot how such laughter is achieved. Humour may rollick on high planes of fantasy or in depths of silliness. To many people it appeals only from those depths. If it appeal to them irresistibly, they are more enviable than those who are sensitive only to the finer kind of joke and not so sensitive as to be mastered and dissolved by it. Laughter is a thing to be rated according to its own intensity.

Many years ago I wrote an essay in which I poured scorn on the fun purveyed by the music halls, and on the great public for which that fun was quite good enough. I take that callow scorn back. I fancy that the fun itself was better than it seemed to me, and might not have displeased me if it had been wafted to me in private, in presence of a few friends. A public crowd, because of a lack of broad impersonal humanity in me, rather insulates than absorbs me. Amidst the guffaws of a thousand strangers I become unnaturally grave. If these people were the entertainment, and I the audience, I should be sympathetic enough. But to be one of them is a position that drives me spiritually aloof. Also, there is to me something rather dreary in the notion of going anywhere for the specific purpose of being amused. I prefer that laughter shall take me unawares. Only so can it master and dissolve me. And in this respect, at any rate, I am not peculiar. In music halls and such places, you may hear loud laughter, but—not see silent laughter, not see strong men weak, helpless, suffering, gradually convalescent, dangerously relapsing. Laughter at its greatest and best is not there.

To such laughter nothing is more propitious than an occasion that demands gravity. To have good reason for not laughing is one of the surest aids. Laughter rejoices in bonds. If music halls were schoolrooms for us, and the comedians were our schoolmasters, how much less talent would be needed for giving us how much more joy! Even in private and accidental intercourse, few are the men whose humour can reduce us, be we never so susceptible, to paroxysms of mirth. I will wager that nine tenths of the world's best laughter is laughter *at*, not *with*. And it is the people set in authority over us that touch most surely our sense of the ridiculous. Freedom is a good thing, but we lose through it golden moments. The schoolmaster to his pupils, the monarch to his courtiers, the editor to his staff—how priceless they are! Reverence is a good thing, and part of its value is that the more we revere a man, the more sharply are we struck by anything in him (and there is always much) that is incongruous with his greatness. And herein lies one of the reasons why as we grow older we laugh less. The men we esteemed so great are gathered to their fathers. Some of our coevals may, for aught we know, be very great, but good heavens! we can't esteem *them so*. . . .

William Hazlitt

ON WIT AND HUMOUR

MAN is the only animal that laughs and weeps; for he is the only animal that is struck with the difference between what things are, and what they ought to be. We weep at what thwarts or exceeds our desires in serious matters: we laugh at what only disappoints our expectations in trifles. We shed tears from sympathy with real and necessary distress; as we burst into laughter from want of sympathy with that which is unreasonable and unnecessary, the absurdity of which provokes our spleen or mirth, rather than any serious reflections on it.

To explain the nature of laughter and tears, is to account for the condition of human life; for it is in a manner compounded of these two! It is a tragedy or a comedy—sad or merry, as it happens. The crimes and misfortunes that are inseparable from it, shock and wound the mind when they once seize upon it, and when the pressure can no longer be borne, seek relief in tears: the follies and absurdities that men commit, or the odd accidents that befall them, afford us amusement from the very rejection of these false claims upon our sympathy and end in laughter. If everything that went wrong, if every vanity or weakness in another gave us a sensible pang, it would be hard indeed: but as long as the disagreeableness of the consequences of a sudden disaster is kept out of sight by the immediate oddity of the circumstances, and the absurdity or unaccountableness of a foolish action is the most striking thing in it, the ludicrous prevails over the pathetic, and we receive pleasure instead of pain from the farce of life which is played before us, and which discomposes our gravity as often as it fails to move our anger or our pity!

Tears may be considered as the natural and involuntary resource of the mind overcome by some sudden and violent emotion, before it has had time to reconcile its feelings to the change of circumstances: while laughter may be defined to be the same sort of convulsive and involuntary movement, occasioned by mere surprise or contrast (in the absence of any more serious emotion), before it has time to reconcile its belief to contradictory appearances. If we hold a mask before our face, and approach a child with this disguise on, it will at first, from the oddity and incongruity of the appearance, be inclined to laugh; if we go nearer to it, steadily, and without saying a word, it will begin to be alarmed, and be half inclined to cry: if we suddenly take off the mask, it will recover from its fears, and burst out a-laughing; but if, instead of presenting the old well-known countenance, we have concealed a satyr's head or some frightful caricature behind the first mask, the suddenness of the change will not in this case be a source of merriment to it, but will convert its surprise into an agony of consternation, and will make it scream out for help, even though it may be convinced that the whole is a trick at bottom. . . .

To understand or define the ludicrous, we must first know what the serious is. Now the serious is the habitual stress which the mind lays upon the expectation of a given order of events, following one another with a certain regularity and weight of interest attached to them. When this stress is increased beyond its usual pitch of intensity, so as to overstrain the feelings by the violent opposition of good to bad, or of objects to our desires, it becomes the pathetic or tragical. The ludicrous, or comic, is the unexpected loosening or relaxing this stress below its usual pitch of intensity, by such an abrupt transposition of the order of our ideas, as taking the mind unawares, throws it off its guard, startles it into a lively sense of pleasure, and leaves no time nor inclination for painful reflections.

The essence of the laughable then is the incongruous, the disconnecting one idea from another, or the jostling of one feeling against another. The first and most obvious cause of laughter is to be found in the simple succession of events, as in the sudden shifting of a disguise, or some unlooked-for accident, without any absurdity of character or situation. The accidental contradiction between our expectations and the event can hardly be said, however, to amount to the ludicrous: it is merely laughable. The ludicrous is where there is the same contradiction between the object and our expectations, heightened by some deformity or inconvenience, that is, by its being contrary to what is customary or desirable; as the ridiculous, which is the highest degree of the laughable, is that which is contrary not only to custom but to sense and reason, or is a voluntary departure from what we have a right to expect from those who are conscious of absurdity and propriety in words, looks, and actions.

Of these different kinds or degrees of the laughable, the first is the most shallow and short-lived; for the instant the immediate surprise of a thing's merely happening one way or another is over, there is nothing to throw us back upon our former expectation, and renew our wonder at the event a second time. The second sort, that is, the ludicrous arising out of the improbable or distressing, is more deep and lasting, either because the painful catastrophe excites a greater curiosity, or because the old impression, from its habitual hold on the imagination, still recurs mechanically, so that it is longer before we can seriously make up our minds to the unaccountable deviation from it. The third sort, or the ridiculous arising out of absurdity as well as improbability, that is, where the defect or weakness is of a man's own seeking, is the most refined of all, but not always so pleasant as the last, because the same contempt and disapprobation which sharpens and subtilises our sense of the impropriety, adds a severity to it inconsistent with perfect ease and enjoyment. This last species is properly the province of satire. The principle of contrast is, however, the same in all the stages, in the simply laughable, the ludicrous, the ridiculous; and the effect is only the more complete, the more durably and pointedly this principle operates. . . .

You cannot force people to laugh: you cannot give a reason why they should laugh: they must laugh of themselves, or not at all. As we laugh from a spontaneous impulse, we laugh the more at any restraint upon this impulse. We laugh at a thing merely because we ought not. If we think we must not laugh, this perverse impediment makes our temptation to laugh the greater; for by endeavouring to keep the obnoxious image out of sight, it comes upon us more irresistibly and repeatedly; and the inclination to indulge our mirth, the longer it is held back, collects its force, and breaks out the more violently in peals of laughter. In like manner, any thing we must not think of makes us laugh, by its coming upon us by stealth and unawares, and from the very efforts we make to exclude it. A secret, a loose word, a wanton jest, make people laugh. Aretine laughed himself to death at hearing a lascivious story. Wickedness is often made a substitute for wit; and in most of our good old comedies, the intrigue of the plot and the double meaning of the dialogue go hand-in-hand, and keep up the ball with wonderful spirit between them. The consciousness, however it may arise, that there is something that we ought to look grave at, is almost always a signal for laughing outright: we can hardly keep our countenance at a sermon, a funeral, or a wedding. What an excellent old custom was that of throwing the stocking! What a deal of innocent mirth has been spoiled by the disuse of it!—It is not an easy matter to preserve decorum in courts of justice. The smallest circumstance that interferes with the solemnity of the proceedings throws the whole place into an uproar of laughter. People at the point of death often say smart things. Sir Thomas More jested with his executioner. Rabelais and Wycherley both died with a *bon-mot* in their mouths.

Misunderstandings, (*malentendus*) where one person means one thing, and another is aiming at something else, are another great source of comic humour, on the same principle of ambiguity and contrast. There is a high-wrought instance of this in the dialogue between Aimwell and Gibbet, in the Beaux' Stratagem, where Aimwell mistakes his companion for an officer in a marching regiment, and Gibbet takes it for granted that the gentleman is a highwayman. The alarm and consternation occasioned by some one saying to him, in the course of common conversation, "I apprehend you," is the most ludicrous thing in that admirably natural and powerful performance, Mr. Emery's Robert Tyke. Again, unconsciousness in the person himself of what he is about, or of what others think of him, is also a great heightener of the sense of absurdity. It makes it come the fuller home upon us from his insensibility to it. His simplicity sets off the satire, and gives it a finer edge. It is a more extreme case still where the person is aware of being the object of ridicule, and yet seems perfectly reconciled to it as a matter of course. So wit is often the more forcible and pointed for being dry and serious, for it then seems as if the speaker himself had no intention in it, and we were the first to find it out. Irony, as a species of wit, owes its force to the same principle. In such cases it is the contrast between the appearance and the reality, the suspense of belief, and the seeming incongruity, that gives point to the ridicule, and makes it enter the deeper when the first impression is overcome. Excessive impudence, as in the Liar; or excessive modesty, as in the hero of She Stoops to Conquer; or a mixture of the two, as in the Busy Body, are equally amusing. Lying is a species of wit and humour. To lay any thing to a person's charge from which he is perfectly free, shews spirit and invention; and the more incredible the effrontery, the greater is the joke.

There is nothing more powerfully humorous than what is called *keeping* in comic character, as we see it very finely exemplified in Sancho Panza and Don Quixote. The proverbial phlegm and the romantic gravity of these two celebrated persons may be regarded as the height of this kind of excellence. The deep feeling of character strengthens the sense of the ludicrous. Keeping in comic character is consistency in absurdity; a determined and laudable attachment to the incongruous and singular. The regularity completes the contradiction; for the number of instances of deviation from the right line, branching out in all directions, shews the inveteracy of the original bias to any extravagance or folly, the natural improbability, as it were, increasing every time with the multiplication of chances for a return to common sense, and in the end mounting up to an incredible and unaccountably ridiculous height, when we find our expectations as invariably baffled. The most curious problem of all is this truth of absurdity to itself. That reason and good sense should be consistent, is not wonderful: but that caprice, and whim, and fantastical prejudice, should be uniform and infallible in their results, is the surprising thing. But while this characteristic clue to absurdity helps on the ridicule, it also softens and harmonises its excesses; and the ludicrous is here blended with a certain beauty and decorum, from this very truth of habit and sentiment, or from the principle of similitude in dissimilitude. The devotion to nonsense, and enthusiasm about trifles, is highly affecting as a moral lesson: it is one of the striking weaknesses and greatest happinesses of our nature. That which excites so lively and lasting an interest in itself, even though it should not be wisdom, is not despicable in the sight of reason and humanity. We cannot suppress the smile on the lip; but the tear should also stand ready to start from the eye. . . .

Humour is the describing the ludicrous as it is in itself; wit is the exposing it, by comparing or contrasting it with something else. Humour is, as it were, the growth of nature and accident; wit is the product of art and fancy. Humour, as it is shewn in books, is an imitation of the natural or acquired absurdities of mankind, or of the ludicrous in accident, situation, and character: wit is the illustrating and heightening the sense of that absurdity by some sudden and unexpected likeness or opposition of one thing to another, which sets off the quality we laugh at or despise in a still more contemptible or striking point of view. Wit, as distinguished from poetry, is the imagination or fancy inverted, and so applied to given objects, as to make the little look less, the mean more light and worthless; or to divert our admiration or wean our affections from that which is lofty and impressive, instead of producing a more intense admiration and exalted passion, as poetry does. Wit may sometimes, indeed, be shewn in compliments as well as satire; as in the common epigram—

> Accept a miracle, instead of wit:
> See two dull lines with Stanhope's pencil writ.

But then the mode of paying it is playful and ironical, and contradicts itself in the very act of making its own performance an humble foil to another's. Wit hovers round the borders of the light and trifling, whether in matters of pleasure or pain; for as soon as it describes the serious seriously, it ceases to be wit, and passes into a different form. Wit is, in fact, the eloquence of indifference, or an ingenious and striking exposition of those evanescent and glancing impressions of objects which affect us more from surprise or contrast to the train of our ordinary and literal preconceptions, than from anything in the objects themselves exciting our necessary sympathy or lasting hatred. The favourite employment of wit is to add littleness to littleness, and heap contempt on insignificance by all the arts of petty and incessant warfare; or if it ever affects to aggrandise, and use the language of hyperbole, it is only to betray into derision by a fatal comparison, as in the mock-heroic; or if it treats of serious passion, it must do it so as to lower the tone of intense and high-wrought sentiment, by the introduction of burlesque and familiar circumstances. . . . Wit and humour (comparatively speaking, or taking the extremes to judge of the gradations by) appeal to our indolence, our vanity, our weakness, and insensibility; serious and impassioned poetry appeals to our strength, our magnanimity, our virtue, and humanity. Any thing is sufficient to heap contempt upon an object; even the bare suggestion of a mischievous allusion to what is improper, dissolves the whole charm, and puts an end to our admiration of the sublime or beautiful. Reading the finest passage in Milton's Paradise Lost in a false tone, will make it seem insipid and absurd. The cavilling at, or invidiously pointing out, a few slips of the pen, will embitter the pleasure, or alter our opinion of a whole work, and make us throw it down in disgust. The critics are aware of this vice and infirmity in our nature, and play upon it with periodical success. The meanest weapons are strong enough for this kind of warfare, and the meanest hands can wield them. Spleen can subsist on any kind of food. The shadow of a doubt, the hint of an inconsistency, a word, a look, a syllable, will destroy our best-formed convictions. What puts this argument in as striking a point of view as any thing, is the nature of parody or burlesque, the secret of which lies merely in transposing or applying at a venture to any thing, or to the lowest objects, that which is applicable only to certain given things, or to the highest matters. "From the sublime to the ridiculous, there is but one step." The slightest want of unity of impression destroys the sublime; the detection of the smallest incongruity is an infallible ground to rest the ludicrous upon. But in serious poetry, which aims at rivetting our affections, every blow must tell home. The missing a single time is fatal, and undoes the spell. . . .

Lastly, there is a wit of sense and observation, which consists in the acute illustration of good sense and practical wisdom, by means of some far-fetched conceit or quaint imagery. The matter is sense, but the form is wit. Thus the lines in Pope—

> Tis with our judgments as our watches, none
> Go just alike; yet each believes his own——

are witty, rather than poetical; because the truth they convey is a mere dry observation on human life, without elevation or enthusiasm, and the illustration of it is of that quaint and familiar kind that is merely curious and fanciful. Cowley is an instance of the same kind in almost all his writings. Many of the jests and witticisms in the best comedies are moral aphorisms and rules for the conduct of life, sparkling with wit and fancy in the mode of expression. The ancient philosophers also abounded in the same kind of wit, in telling home truths in the most unexpected manner.—In this sense Æsop was the greatest wit and moralist that ever lived. Ape and slave, he looked askance at human nature, and beheld its weaknesses and errors transferred to another species. Vice and virtue were to him as plain as any objects of sense. He saw in man a talking, absurd, obstinate, proud, angry animal; and clothed these abstractions with wings, or a beak, or tail, or claws, or long ears, as they appeared embodied in these hieroglyphics in the brute creation. His moral philosophy is natural history. He makes an ass bray wisdom, and a frog croak humanity. The store of moral truth, and the fund of invention in exhibiting it in eternal forms, palpable and intelligible, and delightful to children and grown persons, and to all ages and nations, are almost miraculous. The invention of a fable is to me the most enviable exertion of human genius: it is the discovering a truth to which there is no clue, and which, when once found out, can never be forgotten. . . .

E. B. White

SOME REMARKS ON HUMOR

ANALYSTS have had their go at humor, and I have read some of this interpretative literature, but without being greatly instructed. Humor can be dissected, as a frog can, but the thing dies in the process and the innards are discouraging to any but the pure scientific mind.

In a newsreel theatre the other day I saw a picture of a man who had developed the soap bubble to a higher point than it had ever before reached. He had become the ace soap bubble blower of America, had perfected the business of blowing bubbles, refined it, doubled it, squared it, and had even worked himself up into a convenient lather. The effect was not pretty. Some of the bubbles were too big to be beautiful, and the blower was always jumping into them or out of them, or playing some sort of unattractive trick with them. It was, if anything, a rather repulsive sight. Humor is a little like that: it won't stand much blowing up, and it won't stand much poking. It has a certain fragility, an evasiveness, which one had best respect. Essentially, it is a complete mystery. A human frame convulsed with laughter, and the laughter becoming hysterical and uncontrollable, is as far out of balance as one shaken with the hiccoughs or in the throes of a sneezing fit.

One of the things commonly said about humorists is that they are really very sad people—clowns with a breaking heart. There is some truth in it, but it is badly stated. It would be more accurate, I think, to say that there is a deep vein of melancholy running through everyone's life and that the humorist, perhaps more sensible of it than some others, compensates for it actively and positively. Humorists fatten on trouble. They have always made trouble pay. They struggle along with a good will and endure pain cheerfully, knowing how well it will serve them in the sweet by and by. You find them wrestling with foreign languages, fighting folding ironing boards and swollen drainpipes, suffering the terrible discomfort of tight boots (or as Josh Billings wittily called them, "tite" boots). They pour out

SOME REMARKS ON HUMOR: From *The Second Tree From the Corner* by E. B. White. Reprinted with the permission of Harper & Row, Publishers, Incorporated. This is an adaptation of the Preface to *A Subtreasury of American Humor* edited by Katharine S. White and E. B. White (Coward-McCann).

their sorrows profitably, in a form that is not quite fiction nor quite fact either. Beneath the sparkling surface of these dilemmas flows the strong tide of human woe.

Practically everyone is a manic depressive of sorts, with his up moments and his down moments, and you certainly don't have to be a humorist to taste the sadness of situation and mood. But there is often a rather fine line between laughing and crying, and if a humorous piece of writing brings a person to the point where his emotional responses are untrustworthy and seem likely to break over into the opposite realm, it is because humor, like poetry, has an extra content. It plays close to the big hot fire which is Truth, and sometimes the reader feels the heat.

The world likes humor, but it treats it patronizingly. It decorates its serious artists with laurel, and its wags with Brussels sprouts. It feels that if a thing is funny it can be presumed to be something less than great, because if it were truly great it would be wholly serious. Writers know this, and those who take their literary selves with great seriousness are at considerable pains never to associate their name with anything funny or flippant or nonsensical or "light." They suspect it would hurt their reputation, and they are right. Many a poet writing today signs his real name to his serious verse and a pseudonym to his comical verse, being unwilling to have the public discover him in any but a pensive and heavy moment. It is a wise precaution. (It is often a bad poet, too.)

When I was reading over some of the parody diaries of Franklin P. Adams, I came across this entry for April 28, 1926:

> Read H. Canby's book, *Better Writing*, very excellent. But when he says, "A sense of humour is worth gold to any writer," I disagree with him vehemently. For the writers who amass the greatest gold have, it seems to me, no sense of humour; and I think also that if they had, it would be a terrible thing for them, for it would paralyze them so that they would not write at all. For in writing, emotion is more to be treasured than a sense of humour, and the two are often in conflict.

That is a sound observation. The conflict is fundamental. There constantly exists, for a certain sort of person of high emotional content, at work creatively, the danger of coming to a point where something cracks within himself or within the paragraph under construction—cracks and turns into a snicker. Here, then, is the very nub of the conflict: the careful form of art, and the careless shape of life itself. What a man does with this uninvited snicker (which may closely resemble a sob, at that) decides his destiny. If he resists it, conceals it, destroys it, he may keep his architectural scheme intact and save his building, and the world will never know. If he gives in to it, he becomes a humorist, and the sharp brim of the fool's cap leaves a mark forever on his brow.

I think the stature of humor must vary some with the times. The court fool in Shakespeare's day had no social standing and was no better than a lackey, but he did have some artistic standing and was listened to with considerable attention, there being a well-founded belief that he had the truth hidden somewhere about his person. Artistically he stood probably higher than the humorist of today, who has gained social position but not the ear of the mighty. (Think of the trouble the world would save itself if it would pay some attention to nonsense!) A narrative poet at court, singing of great deeds, enjoyed a higher standing than the fool and was allowed to wear fine clothes; yet I suspect that the ballad singer was more often than not a second-rate stooge, flattering his monarch lyrically, while the fool must often have been a first-rate character, giving his monarch good advice in bad puns.

In the British Empire of our time, satirical humor of the Gilbert and Sullivan sort enjoys a solid position in the realm, and *Punch*, which is as British as vegetable marrow, is socially acceptable everywhere an Englishman is to be found. The *Punch* editors not only write the jokes but they help make the laws of England. Here in America we have an immensely humorous people in a land of milk and honey and wit, who cherish the ideal of the "sense" of humor and at the same time are highly suspicious of anything that is nonserious. Whatever else an American believes or disbelieves about himself, he is absolutely sure he has a sense of humor.

Frank Moore Colby, one of the most intelligent humorists operating in this country in the early years of the century, in an essay called "The Pursuit of Humor" described how the American loves and guards his most precious treasure:

> . . . Now it is the commonest thing in the world to hear people call the absence of a sense of humor the one fatal defect. No matter how owlish a man is, he will tell you that. It is a miserable falsehood, and it does incalculable harm. A life without humor is like a life without legs. You are haunted by a sense of incompleteness, and you cannot go where your friends go. You are somewhat of a burden. But the only really fatal thing is the shamming of humor when you have it not. There are people whom nature meant to be solemn from their cradle to their grave. They are under bonds to remain so. In so far as they are true to themselves they are safe company for any one; but outside their proper field they are terrible. Solemnity is relatively a blessing, and the man who was born with it should never be encouraged to wrench himself away.
>
> We have praised humor so much that we have started an insincere cult, and there are many who think they must glorify it when they

> hate it from the bottom of their hearts. False humor-worship is the deadliest of social sins, and one of the commonest. People without a grain of humor in their composition will eulogize it by the hour. Men will confess to treason, murder, arson, false teeth, or a wig. How many of them will own up to a lack of humor? The courage that could draw this confession from a man would atone for everything.

Relatively few American humorists have become really famous, so that their name is known to everyone in the land in the way that many novelists and other solemn literary characters have become famous. Mark Twain made it. He had, of course, an auspicious start, since he was essentially a story teller and his humor was an added attraction. (It was also very, very good.) In the 1920's and 30's, Ring Lardner was the idol of professional humorists and of plenty of other people, too; but I think I am correct in saying that at the height of his career he was not one of the most widely known literary figures in this country, and the name Lardner was not known to the millions but only to the thousands. He never reached Mr. and Mrs. America and all the ships at sea, to the extent that Mark Twain reached them, and I doubt if he ever will. On the whole, humorists who give pleasure to a wide audience are the ones who create characters and tell tales, the ones who are story tellers at heart. Lardner told stories and gave birth to some characters, but I think he was a realist and a parodist and a satirist first of all, not essentially a writer of fiction. The general public needs something to get a grip on—a Penrod, a Huck Finn, a Br'er Rabbit, or a Father Day. The subtleties of satire and burlesque and nonsense and parody and criticism are not to the general taste; they are for the top (or, if you want, for the bottom) layer of intellect. Clarence Day, for example, was relatively inconspicuous when he was oozing his incomparable "Thoughts without Words," which are his best creations; he became generally known and generally loved only after he had brought Father to life. (Advice to young writers who want to get ahead without any annoying delays: don't write about Man, write about *a* man.)

I was interested, in reading De Voto's "Mark Twain in Eruption," to come across some caustic remarks of Mr. Clemens's about an anthology of humor which his copyright lawyer had sent him and which Mark described as "a great fat, coarse, offensive volume." He was not amused. "This book is a cemetery," he wrote.

> In this mortuary volume [he went on] I find Nasby, Artemus Ward, Yawcob Strauss, Derby, Burdette, Eli Perkins, the Danbury News Man, Orpheus C. Kerr, Smith O'Brien, Josh Billings, and a score of others, maybe two score, whose writings and sayings were once in everybody's mouth but are now heard of no more and are no longer mentioned. Seventy-eight seems an incredible crop of well-known humorists for one

forty-year period to have produced, and yet this book has not harvested the entire crop—far from it. It has no mention of Ike Partington, once so welcome and so well known; it has no mention of Doesticks, nor of the Pfaff crowd, nor of Artemus Ward's numerous and perishable imitators, nor of three very popular Southern humorists whose names I am not able to recall, nor of a dozen other sparkling transients whose light shone for a time but has now, years ago, gone out.

Why have they perished? Because they were merely humorists. Humorists of the "mere" sort cannot survive. Humor is only a fragrance, a decoration. Often it is merely an odd trick of speech and of spelling, as in the case of Ward and Billings and Nasby and the "Disbanded Volunteer," and presently the fashion passes and the fame along with it.

Not long ago I plunged back fifty to a hundred years into this school of dialect humor that Mark Twain found perishable. Then was the heyday of the crackerbarrel philosopher, sometimes wise, always wise-seeming, and when read today rather dreary. It seemed to me, in reading the dialect boys, that a certain basic confusion often exists in the use of tricky or quaint or illiterate spelling to achieve a humorous effect. I mean, it is not always clear whether the author intends his character to be writing or speaking—and I, for one, feel that unless I know at least this much about what I am reading, I am off to a bad start. For instance, here are some spellings from the works of Petroleum V. Nasby: he spells "would" *wood,* "of" *uv,* "you" *yoo,* "hence" *hentz,* "office" *offis.*

Now, it happens that I pronounce "office" *offis.* And I pronounce "hence" *hentz,* and I even pronounce "of" *uv.* Therefore, I infer that Nasby's character is supposed not to be speaking but to be writing. Yet in either event, justification for this perversion of the language is lacking; for if the character is speaking, the queer spelling is unnecessary, since the pronunciation is almost indistinguishable from the natural or ordinary pronunciation, and if the character is writing, the spelling is most unlikely. Who ever wrote "uv" for "of"? Nobody. Anyone who knows how to write at all knows how to spell a simple world like "of." If you can't spell "of" you wouldn't be able to spell anything and wouldn't be attempting to set words to paper—much less words like "solissitood." A person who can't spell "of" is an illiterate, and the only time such a person attempts to write anything down is in a great crisis. He doesn't write political essays or diaries or letters or satirical paragraphs.

In the case of Dooley, the Irish dialect is difficult but worth the effort, and it smooths out after the first hundred miles. Finley Peter Dunne was a sharp and gifted humorist, who wrote no second-rate stuff, and he had the sympathetic feeling for his character which is indispensable. This same sympathy is discernible in contemporary Jewish humor—in the work of Milt Gross, Arthur Kober, Leonard Q. Ross. It is sympathy, not contempt or derision, that makes their characters live. Lardner's ballplayer was born because the author had a warm feeling for ballplayers, however boyish or goofy. The spelling in all these cases is not a device for gaining a humorous effect but a necessary tool for working the material, which is inherently humorous.

I suspect that the popularity of all dialect stuff derives in part from flattery of the reader—giving him a pleasant sensation of superiority which he gets from working out the intricacies of misspelling, and the satisfaction of detecting boorishness or illiteracy in someone else. This is not the whole story but it has some bearing in the matter. Incidentally, I am told by an authority on juvenile literature that dialect is tops with children. They like to puzzle out the words. When they catch on to the thing, they must feel that first fine glow of maturity—the ability to exercise higher intellectual powers than those of the character they are looking at.

But to get back to Mark Twain and the "great fat, coarse volume" that offended him so:

> There are those [he continued], who say that a novel should be a work of art solely, and you must not preach in it, you must not teach in it. That may be true as regards novels but it is not true as regards humor. Humor must not professedly teach, and it must not professedly preach, but it must do both if it would live forever. By forever I mean thirty years. With all its preaching it is not likely to outlive so long a term as that. The very things it preaches about, and which are novelties when it preaches about them, can cease to be novelties and become commonplaces in thirty years. Then that sermon can thenceforth interest no one.
>
> I have always preached. That is the reason that I have lasted thirty years. If the humor came of its own accord and uninvited, I have allowed it a place in my sermon, but I was not writing the sermon for the sake of humor. I should have written the sermon just the same, whether any humor applied for admission or not. I am saying these vain things in this frank way because I am a dead person speaking from the grave. Even I would be too modest to say them in life. I think we never become really and genuinely our entire and honest selves until we are dead—and not then until we have been dead years and years. People ought to start dead, and then they would be honest so much earlier.

I don't think I agree that humor must preach in order to live; it need only speak the truth—and I notice it usually does. But there is no question at all that people ought to start dead.

POETRY

Horace
EPODE 2

"A MAN is happy when, far from the business world,
like the earliest tribe of men
he cultivates the family farm with his team,
and is free from usury's ties
(not as a soldier, stirred by the trumpet's wild cry,
nor quaking in an angry sea),
when he keeps away from the Forum and the proud
doorways of influential men.
This is his life: when the shoots of his vines mature,
he marries them to tall poplars,
or, in a secluded valley, he looks over
his lowing cattle as they graze,
and pruning away useless branches with his hook,
grafts more fruitful ones to the trees,
or he puts up pressed honey in his well-scrubbed jars
or shears the struggling, helpless sheep;
above all, when through his lands Autumn lifts his head
with a crown of ripening fruit,
how delighted he is, plucking the grafted pears
and the purple cluster of grapes
as your offering, Priapus, and Silvanus,
protector of boundary lines.
How pleasant to rest, sometimes beneath an old oak,
sometimes on a carpet of grass;
all the while the brook glides by between its high banks,
the birds are trilling in the trees,
and the splashing waters of springs play counterpoint,
a summons to easy slumber.
But when the time of winter and thunderous Jove
comes on with its rain and its snow,
with his pack of hounds from here, from there, he forces
the fierce boars towards the ready nets,
or stretches a wide-meshed net on its polished pole,
a snare for the greedy thrushes,
and the trembling rabbit and the far-flying crane
he traps in his noose, a good catch.

Who would not forget, in such a life, the sorrows
and cares that accompany love?
But if a chaste wife would do her part in caring
for the home and the dear children,
like a Sabine woman or the sunburned wife of
a strong Apulian farmer,
would pile seasoned firewood beside the sacred hearth
for her weary husband's return,
and shutting the frisky flock in their wattled pen,
would milk their swollen udders dry,
and bringing out this year's wine, still sweet in its cask,
would prepare a home-cooked supper,
I could not be more pleased by Lake Lucrine oysters,
or by turbot or by scarfish,
should winter as it roars over Eastern waters
drive some of them near our seacoast;
no African hen or Ionian pheasant
would make its way to my belly
more enjoyably than olives chosen from the
ripest branches in the orchard,
or leaves of meadow-loving sorrel and mallows
that are good for a sick body,
or a lamb slaughtered on the Feast of Boundaries,
or a kid retrieved from a wolf.
How delightful, at such a feast, to see the flock
hurrying home from the pasture,
to see the worn-out oxen as with weary necks
they drag along the upturned plow,
and the homebred slaves, that crowd a rich house, in place
about the gleaming household gods."

When Alfius the usurer had said all this,
on the brink of a country life,
he collected all of his money on the Ides,
invested it on the Calends.

Alexander Pope

EPISTLE II. TO A LADY[1]

Of the Characters of Women

NOTHING so true as what you once let fall,
"Most Women have no Characters at all."
Matter too soft a lasting mark to bear,
And best distinguished by black, brown, or fair.

1 [Presumed to be Martha Blount, one of Pope's closest friends.]

How many pictures on one Nymph we view,
All how unlike each other, all how true!
Arcadia's Countess, here, in ermined pride,
Is, there, Pastora by a fountain side.
Here Fannia, leering on her own good man,
And there, a naked Leda with a Swan.
Let then the Fair one beautifully cry,
In Magdalen's loose hair and lifted eye,
Or dressed in smiles of sweet Cecilia shine,
With simpering Angels, Palms, and Harps divine;
Whether the Charmer sinner it, or saint it,
If Folly grow romantic, I must paint it.
Come then, the colours and the ground prepare!
Dip in the Rainbow, trick her off in Air;
Choose a firm Cloud, before it fall, and in it
Catch, ere she change, the Cynthia of this minute.
Rufa, whose eye quick-glancing o'er the Park,
Attracts each light gay meteor of a spark,
Agrees as ill with Rufa studying Locke,
As Sappho's diamonds with her dirty smock;
Or Sappho at her toilet's greasy task,[2]
With Sappho fragrant at an evening Masque:
So morning Insects that in muck begun,
Shine, buzz, and flyblow in the setting sun.
How soft is Silia! fearful to offend;
The Frail one's advocate, the Weak one's friend:
To her, Calista proved her conduct nice;
And good Simplicius asks of her advice.
Sudden, she storms! she raves! You tip the wink,
But spare your censure; Silia does not drink.
All eyes may see from what the change arose,
All eyes may see—a Pimple on her nose.
Papillia, wedded to her amorous spark,
Sighs for the shades—"How charming is a Park!"
A Park is purchased, but the Fair he sees
All bathed in tears—"Oh, odious, odious Trees!"
Ladies, like variegated Tulips, show;
'Tis to their Changes half their charms we owe;
Fine by defect, and delicately weak,
Their happy Spots the nice admirer take,
'Twas thus Calypso once each heart alarmed,
Awed without Virtue, without Beauty charmed;
Her tongue bewitched as oddly as her Eyes,
Less Wit than Mimic, more a Wit than wise;
Strange graces still, and stranger flights she had,
Was just not ugly, and was just not mad;

2 [Presumed to be Lady Mary Wortley Montagu, who had incurred Pope's displeasure.]

Yet ne'er so sure our passion to create,
As when she touched the brink of all we hate.
Narcissa's nature, tolerably mild,
To make a wash, would hardly stew a child;
Has even been proved to grant a Lover's prayer,
And paid a Tradesman once to make him stare;
Gave alms at Easter, in a Christian trim,
And made a Widow happy, for a whim.
Why then declare Good nature is her scorn,
When 'tis by that alone she can be borne?
Why pique all mortals, yet affect a name?
A fool to Pleasure, yet a slave to Fame:
Now deep in Taylor and the Book of Martyrs,
Now drinking citron with his Grace and Chartres:
Now Conscience chills her, and now Passion burns;
And Atheism and Religion take their turns;
A very Heathen in the carnal part,
Yet still a sad, good Christian at her heart.
See Sin in State, majestically drunk;
Proud as a Peeress, prouder as a Punk;
Chaste to her husband, frank to all beside,
A teeming Mistress, but a barren Bride.
What then? let Blood and Body bear the fault,
Her Head's untouched, that noble Seat of Thought:
Such this day's doctrine—in another fit
She sins with Poets through pure Love of Wit.
What has not fired her bosom or her brain?
Cæsar and Tallboy, Charles and Charlemagne.
As Helluo, late Dictator of the Feast,
The Nose of Hautgout, and the Tip of Taste,
Critiqued your wine, and analysed your meat,
Yet on plain Pudding deigned at home to eat;
So Philomedé, lecturing all mankind
On the soft Passion, and the Taste refined,
Th' Address, the Delicacy—stoops at once,
And makes her hearty meal upon a Dunce.
Flavia's a Wit, has too much sense to Pray;
To Toast our wants and wishes, is her way;
Nor asks of God, but of her Stars, to give
The mighty blessing, "while we live, to live."
Then all for Death, that Opiate of the soul!
Lucretia's dagger, Rosamonda's bowl.
Say, what can cause such impotence of mind?
A spark too fickle, or a Spouse too kind.
Wise Wretch! with Pleasures too refined to please;
With too much Spirit to be e'er at ease;
With too much Quickness ever to be taught;
With too much Thinking to have common Thought:

You purchase Pain with all that Joy can give,
And die of nothing but a Rage to live.
  Turn then from Wits; and look on Simo's Mate,
No Ass so meek, no Ass so obstinate.
Or her, that owns her Faults, but never mends,
Because she's honest, and the best of Friends.
Or her, whose life the Church and Scandal share,
For ever in a Passion, or a Prayer.
Or her, who laughs at Hell, but (like her Grace)
Cries, "Ah! how charming, if there's no such place!"
Or who in sweet vicissitude appears
Of Mirth and Opium, Ratafie and Tears,
The daily Anodyne, and nightly Draught,
To kill those foes to Fair ones, Time and Thought.
Woman and Fool are two hard things to hit;
For true No-meaning puzzles more than Wit.
  But what are these to great Atossa's mind?[3]
Scarce once herself, by turns all Womankind!
Who, with herself, or others, from her birth
Finds all her life one warfare upon earth:
Shines, in exposing Knaves, and painting Fools,
Yet is, whate'er she hates and ridicules.
No Thought advances, but her Eddy Brain
Whisks it about, and down it goes again.
Full sixty years the World has been her Trade,
The wisest Fool much Time has ever made.
From loveless youth to unrespected age,
No passion gratified except her Rage.
So much the Fury still outran the Wit,
The Pleasure missed her, and the Scandal hit.
Who breaks with her, provokes Revenge from Hell,
But he's a bolder man who dares be well.
Her every turn with Violence pursued,
Nor more a storm her Hate than Gratitude:
To that each Passion turns, or soon or late;
Love, if it makes her yield, must make her hate:
Superiors? death! and Equals? what a curse!
But an Inferior not dependant? worse.
Offend her, and she knows not to forgive;
Oblige her, and she'll hate you while you live:
But die, and she'll adore you—Then the Bust
And Temple rise—then fall again to dust.
Last night, her Lord was all that's good and great;
A Knave this morning and his Will a Cheat.
Strange! by the Means defeated of the Ends,
By Spirit robbed of Power, by Warmth of Friends,

3 [Atossa was the daughter of Cyrus, King of Persia, 550–529 B.C., presumed here to represent Sarah, Duchess of Marlborough.]

By Wealth of Followers! without one distress
Sick of herself through very selfishness!
Atossa, cursed with every granted prayer,
Childless with all her Children, wants an Heir.
To Heirs unknown descends th' unguarded store,
Or wanders, Heaven-directed, to the Poor.
Pictures like these, dear Madam, to design,
Asks no firm hand, and no unerring line;
Some wandering touches, some reflected light,
Some flying stroke alone can hit 'em right:
For how should equal Colours do the knack?
Chameleons who can paint in white and black?
"Yet Chloe sure was formed without a spot"—
Nature in her then erred not, but forgot.
"With every pleasing, every prudent part,
Say, what can Chloe want?"—She wants a Heart.
She speaks, behaves, and acts just as she ought;
But never, never, reached one generous Thought.
Virtue she finds too painful an endeavour,
Content to dwell in Decencies for ever.
So very reasonable, so unmoved,
As never yet to love, or to be loved.
She, while her Lover pants upon her breast,
Can mark the figures on an Indian chest;
And when she sees her Friend in deep despair,
Observes how much a Chintz exceeds Mohair.
Forbid it Heaven, a Favour or a Debt
She e'er chould cancel—but she may forget.
Safe is your Secret still in Chloe's ear;
But none of Chloe's shall you ever hear.
Of all her Dears she never slandered one,
But cares not if a thousand are undone.
Would Chloe know if you're alive or dead?
She bids her Footman put it in her head.
Chloe is prudent—Would you too be wise?
Then never break your heart when Chloe dies.
One certain Portrait may (I grant) be seen,
Which Heaven has varnished out, and made a *Queen*:
THE SAME FOR EVER! and described by all
With Truth and Goodness, as with Crown and Ball.
Poets heap Virtues, Painters Gems at will,
And show their zeal, and hide their want of skill.
'Tis well—but, Artists! who can paint or write,
To draw the Naked is your true delight.
That robe of Quality so struts and swells,
None see what Parts of Nature it conceals:
Th' exactest traits of Body or of Mind,
We owe to models of an humble kind.

If QUEENSBURY to strip there's no compelling,
'Tis from a Handmaid we must take a Helen.
From Peer or Bishop 'tis no easy thing
To draw the man who loves his God, or King:
Alas! I copy (or my draught would fail)
From honest Máhomet, or plain Parson Hale.
But grant, in Public Men sometimes are shown,
A Woman's seen in Private life alone:
Our bolder Talents in full light displayed;
Your Virtues open fairest in the shade.
Bred to disguise, in Public 'tis you hide;
There, none distinguish twixt your Shame or Pride,
Weakness or Delicacy; all so nice,
That each may seem a Virtue, or a Vice.
In Men, we various Ruling Passions find;
In Women, two almost divide the kind;
Those, only fixed, they first or last obey,
The Love of Pleasure, and the Love of Sway.
That, Nature gives; and where the lesson taught
Is but to peace, can Pleasure seem a fault?
Experience, this; by Man's oppression curst,
They seek the second not to lose the first.
Men, some to Business, some to Pleasure take;
But every Woman is at heart a Rake:
Men, some to Quiet, some to public Strife;
But every Lady would be Queen for life.
Yet mark the fate of a whole Sex of Queens!
Power all their end, but Beauty all the means:
In Youth they conquer, with so wild a rage,
As leaves them scarce a subject in their Age:
For foreign glory, foreign joy, they roam;
No thought of peace or happiness at home.
But Wisdom's triumph is well-timed Retreat,
As hard a science to the Fair as Great!
Beauties, like Tyrants, old and friendless grown,
Yet hate repose, and dread to be alone,
Worn out in public, weary every eye,
Nor leave one sigh behind them when they die.
Pleasures the sex, as children Birds, pursue,
Still out of reach, yet never out of view;
Sure, if they catch, to spoil the Toy at most,
To covet flying, and regret when lost:
At last, to follies Youth could scarce defend,
It grows their Age's prudence to pretend;
Ashamed to own they gave delight before,
Reduced to feign it, when they give no more:
As Hags hold Sabbaths, less for joy than spite,
So these their merry, miserable Night;

Still round and round the Ghosts of Beauty glide,
And haunt the places where their Honour died.
See how the World its Veterans rewards!
A Youth of Frolics, an old Age of Cards;
Fair to no purpose, artful to no end,
Young without Lovers, old without a Friend;
A Fop their Passion, but their Prize a Sot;
Alive, ridiculous, and dead, forgot!
Ah! Friend! to dazzle let the Vain design;
To raise the Thought, and touch the Heart be thine!
That Charm shall grow, while what fatigues the Ring,
Flaunts and goes down, an unregarded thing:
So when the Sun's broad beam has tired the sight,
All mild ascends the Moon's more sober light,
Serene in Virgin Modesty she shines,
And unobserved the glaring Orb declines.
Oh, blest with Temper, whose unclouded ray
Can make tomorrow cheerful as today;
She, who can love a Sister's charms, or hear
Sighs for a Daughter with unwounded ear;
She, who ne'er answers till a Husband cools,
Or, if she rules him, never shows she rules;
Charms by accepting, by submitting sways,
Yet has her humour most, when she obeys;
Let Fops or Fortune fly which way they will;
Disdains all loss of Tickets, or Codille;
Spleen, Vapours, or Smallpox, above them all,
And Mistress of herself, though China fall.
And yet, believe me, good as well as ill,
Woman's at best a Contradiction still.
Heaven, when it strives to polish all it can
Its last best work, but forms a softer Man;
Picks from each sex, to make the Favorite blest,
Your love of Pleasure, our desire of Rest:
Blends, in exception to all general rules,
Your Taste of Follies, with our Scorn of Fools:
Reserve with Frankness, Art with Truth allied,
Courage with Softness, Modesty with Pride;
Fixed Principles, with Fancy ever new;
Shakes all together, and produces—You.
Be this a Woman's Fame: with this unblest,
Toasts live a scorn, and Queens may die a jest.
This Phœbus promised (I forget the year)
When those blue eyes first opened on the sphere;
Ascendant Phœbus watched that hour with care,
Averted half your Parents' simple Prayer;
And gave you Beauty, but denied the Pelf
That buys your sex a Tyrant o'er itself.

The generous God, who Wit and Gold refines,
And ripens Spirits as he ripens Mines,
Kept Dross for Duchesses, the world shall know it,
To you gave Sense, Good Humour, and a Poet.

George Gordon, Lord Byron

FROM CANTO III, DON JUAN

LXXVIII

AND NOW they were diverted by their suite,
Dwarfs, dancing-girls, black eunuchs, and a poet,
Which made their new establishment complete;
The last was of great fame, and liked to show it;
His verses rarely wanted their due feet—
And for his theme—he seldom sung below it,
He being paid to satirise or flatter,
As the psalm says, "inditing a good matter."

LXXIX

He praised the present, and abused the past,
Reversing the good custom of old days,
An Eastern anti-jacobin at last
He turn'd, preferring pudding to *no* praise—
For some few years his lot had been o'ercast
By his seeming independent in his lays,
But now he sung the Sultan and the Pacha
With truth like Southey, and with verse like Crashaw.

LXXX

He was a man who had seen many changes,
And always changed as true as any needle;
His polar star being one which rather ranges,
And not the fix'd—he knew the way to wheedle:
So vile he 'scaped the doom which oft avenges;
And being fluent (save indeed when fee'd ill),
He lied with such a fervour of intention—
There was no doubt he earn'd his laureate pension.

LXXXI

But he had genius,—when a turncoat has it,
The "Vates irritabilis" takes care
That without notice few full moons shall pass it;
Even good men like to make the public stare:—
But to my subject—let me see—what was it?—
Oh!—the third canto—and the pretty pair—
Their loves, and feasts, and house, and dress, and mode
Of living in their insular abode.

LXXXII

Their poet, a sad trimmer, but no less
  In company a very pleasant fellow,
Had been the favourite of full many a mess
  Of men, and made them speeches when half mellow;
And though his meaning they could rarely guess,
  Yet still they deign'd to hiccup or to bellow
The glorious meed of popular applause,
Of which the first ne'er knows the second cause.

LXXXIII

But now being lifted into high society,
  And having pick'd up several odds and ends
Of free thoughts in his travels, for variety,
  He deem'd being in a lone isle, among friends,
That without any danger of a riot, he
  Might for long lying make himself amends;
And singing as he sung in his warm youth,
Agree to a short armistice with truth.

LXXXIV

He had travell'd 'mongst the Arabs, Turks, and Franks,
  And knew the self-loves of the different nations;
And having lived with people of all ranks,
  Had something ready upon most occasions—
Which got him a few presents and some thanks.
  He varied with some skill his adulations;
To "do at Rome as Romans do," a piece
Of conduct was which he observed in Greece.

LXXXV

Thus, usually, when he was asked to sing,
  He gave the different nations something national;
'Twas all the same to him—"God save the king,"
  Or "Ça ira,"[1] according to the fashion all:
His muse made increment of anything,
  From the high lyric down to the low rational:
If Pindar sang horse-races, what should hinder
Himself from being as pliable as Pindar?

LXXXVI

In France, for instance, he could write a chanson;
  In England a six-canto quarto tale;
In Spain he'd make a ballad or romance on
  The last war—much the same in Portugal;

1 [That will be.]

In Germany, the Pegasus he'd prance on
  Would be old Goethe's—(see what says DeStaël);
In Italy he'd ape the "Trecentisti";
In Greece, he'd sing some sort of hymn like this t' ye:

1

The isles of Greece, the isles of Greece!
  Where burning Sappho loved and sung,
Where grew the arts of war and peace,
  Where Delos rose, and Phoebus sprung!
Eternal summer gilds them yet,
But all, except their sun, is set.

2

The Scian and the Teian muse,
  The hero's harp, the lover's lute,
Have found the fame your shores refuse:
  Their place of birth alone is mute
To sounds which echo further west
Than your sires' "Islands of the Blest."

3

The mountains look on Marathon—
  And Marathon looks on the sea;
And musing there an hour alone,
  I dream'd that Greece might still be free;
For standing on the Persians' grave,
I could not deem myself a slave.

4

A king sate on the rocky brow
  Which looks o'er sea-born Salamis;
And ships, by thousands, lay below,
  And men in nations;—all were his!
He counted them at break of day—
And when the sun set where were they?

5

And where are they? and where art thou,
  My country? On thy voiceless shore
The heroic lay is tuneless now—
  The heroic bosom beats no more!
And must thy lyre, so long divine,
  Degenerate into hands like mine?

6

'Tis something, in the dearth of fame,
  Though link'd among a fetter'd race,

To feel at least a patriot's shame,
  Even as I sing, suffuse my face;
For what is left the poet here?
For Greeks a blush—for Greece a tear.

7

Must *we* but weep o'er days more blest?
  Must *we* but blush?—Our fathers bled.
Earth! render back from out thy breast
  A remnant of our Spartan dead!
Of the three hundred grant but three,
To make a new Thermopylæ!

8

What, silent still? and silent all?
  Ah! no;—the voices of the dead
Sound like a distant torrent's fall,
  And answer, "Let one living head,
But one arise,—we come, we come!"
'Tis but the living who are dumb.

9

In vain—in vain: strike other chords;
  Fill high the cup with Samian wine!
Leave battles to the Turkish hordes,
  And shed the blood of Scio's vine!
Hark! rising to the ignoble call—
How answers each bold Bacchanal!

10

You have the Pyrrhic dance as yet;
  Where is the Pyrrhic phalanx gone?
Of two such lessons, why forget
  The nobler and the manlier one?
You have the letters Cadmus gave—
Think ye he meant them for a slave?

11

Fill high the bowl with Samian wine!
  We will not think of themes like these!
It made Anacreon's song divine:
  He served—but served Polycrates—
A tyrant; but our masters then
Were still, at least, our countrymen.

12

The tyrant of the Chersonese
  Was freedom's best and bravest friend;

That tyrant was Miltiades!
Oh! that the present hour would lend
Another despot of the kind!
Such chains as his were sure to bind.

13

Fill high the bowl with Samian wine!
On Suli's rock, and Parga's shore,
Exists the remnant of a line
Such as the Doric mothers bore;
And there, perhaps, some seed is sown,
The Heracleidan blood might own.

14

Trust not for freedom to the Franks—
They have a king who buys and sells;
In native swords, and native ranks,
The only hope of courage dwells:
But Turkish force, and Latin fraud,
Would break your shield, however broad.

15

Fill high the bowl with Samian wine!
Our virgins dance beneath the shade—
I see their glorious black eyes shine;
But gazing on each glowing maid,
My own the burning tear-drop laves,
To think such breasts must suckle slaves.

16

Place me on Sunium's marbled steep,
Where nothing, save the waves and I,
May hear our mutual murmurs sweep;
There, swan-like, let me sing and die:
A land of slaves shall ne'er be mine—
Dash down yon cup of Samian wine!

LXXXVII

Thus sung, or would, or could, or should have sung,
The modern Greek, in tolerable verse;
If not like Orpheus quite, when Greece was young,
Yet in these times he might have done much worse:
His strain display'd some feeling—right or wrong;
And feeling, in a poet, is the source
Of others' feeling; but they are such liars,
And take all colours—like the hands of dyers.

LXXXVIII

But words are things, and a small drop of ink,
Falling like dew, upon a thought, produces
That which makes thousands, perhaps millions, think;
'Tis strange, the shortest letter which man uses
Instead of speech, may form a lasting link
Of ages; to what straits old Time reduces
Frail man, when paper—even a rag like this,
Survives himself, his tomb, and all that's his!

LXXXIX

And when his bones are dust, his grave a blank,
His station, generation, even his nation,
Become a thing, or nothing, save to rank
In chronological commemoration,
Some dull MS. oblivion long has sank,
Or graven stone found in a barrack's station
In digging the foundation of a closet,
May turn his name up, as a rare deposit.

XC

And glory long has made the sages smile;
'Tis something, nothing, words, illusion, wind—
Depending more upon the historian's style
Than on the name a person leaves behind:
Troy owes to Homer what whist owes to Hoyle:
The present century was growing blind
To the great Marlborough's skill in giving knocks,
Until his late Life by Archdeacon Coxe.

XCI

Milton's the prince of poets—so we say;
A little heavy, but no less divine:
An independent being in his day—
Learn'd, pious, temperate in love and wine;
But his life falling into Johnson's way,
We're told this great high priest of all the Nine
Was whipt at college—a harsh sire—odd spouse,
For the first Mrs. Milton left his house.

XCII

All these are, *certes*,[2] entertaining facts,
Like Shakespeare's stealing deer. Lord Bacon's bribes;
Like Titus' youth, and Cæsar's earliest acts;
Like Burns (whom Doctor Currie well describes);
Like Cromwell's pranks;—but although truth exacts
These amiable descriptions from the scribes,

2 [Certainly.]

As most essential to their hero's story,
They do not much contribute to his glory.

XCIII

All are not moralists, like Southey, when
He prated to the world of "Pantisocracy";
Or Wordsworth unexcised, unhired, who then
Season'd his pedlar poems with democracy;
Or Coleridge, long before his flighty pen
Let to the Morning Post its aristocracy;
When he and Southey, following the same path,
Espoused two partners (milliners of Bath).

XCIV

Such names at present cut a convict figure,
The very Botany Bay in moral geography;
Their loyal treason, renegado rigour,
Are good manure for their more bare biography,
Wordsworth's last quarto, by the way, is bigger
Than any since the birthday of typography;
A drowsy frowzy poem, call'd the "Excursion,"
Writ in a manner which is my aversion.

XCV

He there builds up a formidable dyke
Between his own and others' intellect:
But Wordsworth's poem, and his followers, like
Joanna Southcote's Shiloh, and her sect,
Are things which, in this century don't strike
The public mind,—so few are the elect;
And the new births of both their stale virginities
Have proved but dropsies, taken for divinities.

XCVI

But let me to my story: I must own,
If I have any fault, it is digression,
Leaving my people to proceed alone,
While I soliloquize beyond expression:
But these are my addresses from the throne,
Which put off business to the ensuing session:
Forgetting each omission is a loss to
The world, not quite so great as Ariosto.

Robert Burns

TO A LOUSE, ON SEEING ONE ON A LADY'S BONNET AT CHURCH

HA! WHERE ye gaun, ye crowlan ferlie![1]
Your impudence protects you sairly:
I canna say but ye strunt rarely,
Owre gawze and lace;
Tho' faith! I fear ye dine but sparely
On sic a place.

Ye ugly, creepan, blastet wonner,
Detested, shunn'd, by saunt an' sinner,
How daur ye set your fit upon her,
Sae fine a Lady?
Gae somewhere else and seek your dinner
On some poor body.

Swith, in some beggar's haffet[2] squattle,
There ye may creep, and sprawl, and sprattle,
Wi' ither kindred, jumping cattle,
In shoals and nations;
Whare horn nor bane ne'er daur unsettle,
Your thick plantations.

Now haud you there, ye're out o' sight,
Below the fatt'rels, snug and tight,
Na, faith ye yet! ye'll no be right,
Till ye've got on it,
The vera tapmost, towrin height
O' Miss's bonnet.

My sooth! right bauld ye set your nose out,
As plump an' gray as onie grozet.[3]
O for some rank mercurial rozet,[4]
Or fell[5], red smeddum![6]
I'd gie you sic a hearty dose o't,
Wad dress your droddum![7]

I wad na been surpriz'd to spy
You on an auld wife's flannen toy;[8]
Or aiblins[9] some bit duddie[10] boy,
On's wyliecoat;[11]

1 Wonder. 2 Sideburns. 3 Gooseberry. 4 Ointment. 5 Deadly. 6 Ointment. 7 Breech. 8 Flannel cap. 9 Perhaps. 10 Ragged. 11 Undershirt.

But Miss's fine Lunardi, fye!
How daur ye do't?

O Jenny dinna toss your head,
An' set your beauties a' abread!
Ye little ken what cursèd speed
The blastie's makin!
Thae winks and finger-ends, I dread,
Are notice takin!

O wad some Pow'r the giftie gie us
To see oursels as others see us!
It wad frae monie a blunder free us
An' foolish notion:
What airs in dress an' gait wad lea'e us,
And ev'n Devotion!

Lewis Carroll

THE BAKER'S TALE

THEY roused him with muffins—they roused him with ice—
They roused him with mustard and cress—
They roused him with jam and judicious advice—
They set him conundrums to guess.

When at length he sat up and was able to speak,
His sad story he offered to tell;
And the Bellman cried "Silence! Not even a shriek!"
And excitedly tingled his bell.

There was silence supreme! Not a shriek, not a scream,
Scarcely even a howl or a groan,
As the man they called "Ho!" told his story of woe
In an antediluvian tone.

"My father and mother were honest, though poor—"
"Skip all that !" cried the Bellman in haste.
"If it once becomes dark, there's no chance of a Snark—
We have hardly a minute to waste!"

"I skip forty years," said the Baker, in tears,
"And proceed without further remark
To the day when you took me aboard of your ship
To help you in hunting the Snark.

THE BAKER'S TALE: From "The Hunting of the Snark" by Lewis Carroll.

"A dear uncle of mine (after whom I was named)
Remarked when I bade him farewell—"
"Oh, skip your dear uncle!" the Bellman exclaimed,
As he angrily tingled his bell.

"He remarked to me then," said that mildest of men,
" 'If your Snark be a Snark, that is right:
Fetch it home by all means—you may serve it with greens,
And it's handy for striking a light.

" 'You may seek it with thimbles—and seek it with care,
You may hunt it with forks and hope;
You may threaten its life with a railway-share;
You may charm it with smiles and soap—' "

("That's exactly the method," the Bellman bold
In a hasty parenthesis cried,
"That's exactly the way I have always been told
That the capture of Snarks should be tried!")

" 'But oh, beamish nephew, beware of the day,
If your Snark be a Boojum! For then
You will softly and suddenly vanish away
And never be met with again!'

"It is this, it is this that oppresses my soul,
When I think of my uncle's last words:
And my heart is like nothing so much as a bowl
Brimming over with quivering curds!

"It is this, it is this—" "We have had that before!"
The Bellman indignantly said.
And the Baker replied "Let me say it once more.
It is this, it is this that I dread!

"I engage with the Snark—every night after dark—
In a dreamy delirious fight:
I serve it with greens in those shadowy scenes,
And I use it for striking a light:

"But if ever I meet with a Boojum, that day,
In a moment (of this I am sure),
I shall softly and suddenly vanish away—
And the notion I cannot endure!"

John Godfrey Saxe

THE BLIND MEN AND THE ELEPHANT

It was six men of Indostan
   To learning much inclined,
Who went to see the Elephant
   (Though all of them were blind),
That each by observation
   Might satisfy his mind.

The *First* approached the Elephant,
   And happening to fall
Against his broad and sturdy side,
   At once began to bawl:
"God bless me! but the Elephant
   Is very like a wall!"

The *Second*, feeling of the tusk,
   Cried, "Ho! what have we here
So very round and smooth and sharp?
   To me 'tis mighty clear
This wonder of an Elephant
   Is very like a spear!"

The *Third* approached the animal,
   And happening to take
The squirming trunk within his hands,
   Thus boldly up and spake:
"I see," quoth he, "the Elephant
   Is very like a snake!"

The *Fourth* reached out an eager hand,
   And felt about the knee.
"What most this wondrous beast is like
   Is mighty plain," quoth he;
" 'Tis clear enough, the Elephant
   Is very like a tree!"

The *Fifth* who chanced to touch the ear,
   Said: "E'en the blindest man
Can tell what this resembles most;
   Deny the fact who can
This marvel of an Elephant
   Is very like a fan!"

The *Sixth* no sooner had begun
About the beast to grope,
Than, seizing on the swinging tail
That fell within his scope,
"I see," quoth he, "the Elephant
Is very like a rope!"

And so these men of Indostan
Disputed loud and long,
Each in his own opinion
Exceeding stiff and strong,
Though each was partly in the right,
And all were in the wrong!

Robert Graves

1805

At Viscount Nelson's lavish funeral,
While the mob milled and yelled about St. Paul's,
A General chatted with an Admiral:

"One of your Colleagues, Sir, remarked today
That Nelson's *exit*, though to be lamented,
Falls not inopportunely, in its way."

"He was a thorn in our flesh," came the reply—
"The most bird-witted, unaccountable,
Odd little runt that ever I did spy.

"One arm, one peeper, vain as Pretty Poll,
A meddler, too, in foreign politics
And gave his heart in pawn to a plain moll.

"He would dare lecture us Sea Lords, and then
Would treat his ratings as though men of honour
And play at leap-frog with his midshipmen!

"We tried to box him down, but up he popped,
And when he banged Napoleon at the Nile
Became too much the hero to be dropped.

"You've heard that Copenhagen 'blind eye' story?
We'd tied him to Nurse Parker's apron-strings—
By G–d, he snipped them through and snatched the glory!"

1805: From *Collected Poems,* published by Doubleday & Co., Inc., and Cassell & Co., Inc.

"Yet," cried the General, "six-and-twenty sail
  Captured or sunk by him off Tráfalgár—
That writes a handsome *finis* to the tale."

"Handsome enough. The seas are England's now.
  That fellow's foibles need no longer plague us.
He died most creditably, I'll allow."

"And, Sir, the secret of his victories?"
  "By his unServicelike, familiar ways, Sir,
He made the whole Fleet love him, damn his eyes!"

G. K. Chesterton

THE WORLD STATE

OH, HOW I love Humanity,
  With love so pure and pringlish,
And how I hate the horrid French,
  Who never will be English!

The International Idea,
  The largest and the clearest,
Is welding all the nations now,
  Except the one that's nearest.

This compromise has long been known,
  This scheme of partial pardons,
In ethical societies
  And small suburban gardens—

The villas and the chapels where
  I learned with little labour
The way to love my fellow-man
  And hate my next-door neighbour.

Andrew Marvell

TO HIS COY MISTRESS

HAD WE but world enough and time,
  This coyness, Lady, were no crime.
We would sit down and think which way
To walk and pass our long love's day.

Thou by the Indian Ganges' side
Shouldst rubies find: I by the tide
Of Humber would complain. I would
Love you ten years before the Flood,
And you should, if you please, refuse
Till the conversion of the Jews.
My vegetable love should grow
Vaster than empires, and more slow;
An hundred years should go to praise
Thine eyes and on thy forehead gaze;
Two hundred to adore each breast,
But thirty thousand to the rest:
An age at least to every part,
And the last age should show your heart.
For, Lady, you deserve this state;
Nor would I love at lower rate.

But at my back I always hear
Time's wingèd chariot hurrying near;
And yonder all before us lie
Deserts of vast eternity.
Thy beauty shall no more be found,
Nor, in thy marble vault, shall sound
My echoing song; then worms shall try
That long preserv'd virginity,
And your quaint honour turn to dust,
And into ashes all my lust.
The grave's a fine and private place,
But none, I think, do there embrace.
Now therefore, while the youthful hue
Sits on thy skin like morning dew,
And while thy willing soul transpires
At every pore with instant fires,
Now let us sport us while we may,
And now, like amorous birds of prey,
Rather at once our time devour
Than languish in his slow-chapt power.
Let us roll all our strength and all
Our sweetness up into one ball,
And tear our pleasures with rough strife
Thorough the iron gates of life.
Thus, though we cannot make our sun
Stand still, yet we will make him run.

John Gay

THE RAT-CATCHER AND THE CATS

THE RATS by night such mischief did,
Betty was every morning chid:
They undermined whole sides of bacon,
Her cheese was sapped, her tarts were taken,
Her pasties, fenced with thickest paste,
Were all demolished and laid waste.
She cursed the cat for want of duty,
Who left her foes a constant booty.
An engineer, of noted skill,
Engaged to stop the growing ill,
From room to room he now surveys
Their haunts, their works, their secret ways,
Finds where they 'scape an ambuscade,
And whence the nightly sally's made.
An envious cat, from place to place,
Unseen, attends his silent pace.
She saw that, if his trade went on,
The purring race must be undone,
So, secretly removes his baits,
And every stratagem defeats.
Again he sets the poisoned toils,
And puss again the labour foils.
"What foe (to frustrate my designs)
My schemes thus nightly countermines?"
Incensed, he cries: "This very hour
The wretch shall bleed beneath my power."
So said, a ponderous trap he brought,
And in the fact poor puss was caught.
"Smuggler," says he, "thou shalt be made
A victim to our loss of trade."
The captive cat with piteous mews
For pardon, life and freedom sues.
"A sister of the science spare,
One int'rest is our common care."
"What insolence!" the man replied,
"Shall cats with us the game divide?
Were all your interloping band
Extinguished, or expelled the land,
We rat-catchers might raise our fees,
Sole guardians of a nation's cheese!"
A cat, who saw the lifted knife,
Thus spoke, and saved her sister's life:

"In every age and clime we see,
Two of a trade can ne'er agree:
Each hates his neighbour for encroaching;
Squire stigmatizes squire for poaching;
Beauties with beauties are in arms,
And scandal pelts each other's charms;
Kings too their neighbour kings dethrone,
In hope to make the world their own.
But let us limit our desires,
Not war like beauties, kings and squires,
For though we both one prey pursue,
There's game enough for us and you."

T. S. Eliot

MACAVITY: THE MYSTERY CAT

MACAVITY's a Mystery Cat; he's called the Hidden Paw—
For he's the master criminal who can defy the Law.
He's the bafflement of Scotland Yard, the Flying Squad's despair:
For when they reach the scene of crime—*Macavity's not there!*

Macavity, Macavity, there's no one like Macavity,
He's broken every human law, he breaks the law of gravity.
His powers of levitation would make a fakir stare,
And when you reach the scene of crime—*Macavity's not there!*
You may seek him in the basement, you may look up in the air—
But I tell you once and once again, *Macavity's not there!*
Macavity's a ginger cat, he's very tall and thin;
You would know him if you saw him, for his eyes are sunken in.
His brow is deeply lined with thought, his head is highly domed;
His coat is dusty from neglect, his whiskers are uncombed.
He sways his head from side to side, with movements like a snake;
And when you think he's half asleep, he's always wide awake.

Macavity, Macavity, there's no one like Macavity,
For he's a fiend in feline shape, a monster of depravity.
You may meet him in a by-street, you may see him in the square
But when a crime's discovered, then *Macavity's not there!*

He's outwardly respectable. (They say he cheats at cards.)
And his footprints are not found in any file of Scotland Yard's.
And when the larder's looted, or the jewel-case is rifled,
Or when the milk is missing, or another Peke's been stifled,

Or the greenhouse glass is broken, and the trellis past repair—
Ay, there's the wonder of the thing! *Macavity's not there!*

And when the Foreign Office find a Treaty's gone astray,
Or the Admiralty lose some plans and drawings by the way,
There may be a scrap of paper in the hall or on the stair—
But it's useless to investigate—*Macavity's not there!*
And when the loss has been disclosed, the Secret Service say:
"It *must* have been Macavity!"—but he's a mile away.
You'll be sure to find him resting, or a-licking of his thumbs,
Or engaged in doing complicated long division sums.
Macavity, Macavity, there's no one like Macavity,
There never was a Cat of such deceitfulness and suavity.
He always has an alibi, and one or two to spare:
At whatever time the deed took place—MACAVITY WASN'T THERE!
And they say that all the Cats whose wicked deeds are widely known
(I might mention Mungojerrie, I might mention Griddlebone)
Are nothing more than agents for the cat who all the time
Just controls their operations: the Napoleon of Crime.

Phyllis McGinley

VILLAGE SPA

BY SCRIBBLED names on walls, by telephone number,
  Cleft heart, bold slogan, carved in every booth,
This sanctum shall be known. This holy lumber
  Proclaims a temple dedicate to Youth.
Daily in garments lawful to their tribe,
  In moccasins and sweaters, come the Exalted
To lean on spotty counters and imbibe
  Their ritual Cokes or drink a chocolate malted.

This refuge is their own. Here the cracked voice,
  Giving the secret passwords, does not falter.
And here the monstrous deity of their choice
  Sits bellowing from his fantastic altar,
A juke-box god, enshrined and well at home,
  Dreadful with neon, shuddering with chrome.

Walter Learned

TO CRITICS

WHEN I was seventeen I heard
    From each censorious tongue,
"I'd not do that if I were you;
    You see you're rather young."

Now that I number forty years,
    I'm quite as often told
Of this or that I shouldn't do
    Because I'm quite too old.

O carping world! If there's an age
    Where youth and manhood keep
An equal poise, alas! I must
    Have passed it in my sleep.

DRAMA

William Shakespeare

THE TEMPEST

INTRODUCTION

by G. B. Harrison

SO FAR as is known *The Tempest* was Shakespeare's last comedy, and it contains some of his finest and maturest blank verse. It is a fairy tale, but Shakespeare has used it to illustrate the theme of reconciliation; wrongs committed in one generation are set right in the happiness of the next.

Shakespeare also achieved a remarkable feat of plot construction: he not only brings the two generations together, but actually preserves the unity of time: the action on the stage occurs within the time of real events, and almost in one place.

The play opens with a stirring, noisy scene, a ship at sea in great peril. The ship runs aground. Then in the quiet that follows, there enter an elderly man and his daughter, and at this point we are given the glimpse of past history which is necessary before the story can be understood. Miranda falls asleep, whereupon Ariel—a spirit of the air—appears. Except to Prospero and to the audience, Ariel, unless assuming a disguise, is always invisible.

We are next introduced to Caliban, who in contrast with Ariel is a creature all earth. He is Shakespeare's portrait of the horrid savage, whose mother was a witch and father a devil. With such heredity one hardly expects refinement. Yet Shakespeare is always fair to Caliban. He has his case and is allowed to state it. It is not surprising that he should be fascinated by Stephano and Trinculo, with their divine liquor.

The plot is now on the move, and hereafter Prospero makes his victims dance to his music. Ferdinand comes in, and at first glance, he and Miranda "change eyes." But Prospero, so that things may not be too easy for Ferdinand, pretends to be rough and terrifying, and from that moment Ferdinand becomes Miranda's slave.

After this idyllic scene, a very different and less ideal set of people are introduced. They are Prospero's wrongers, Alonso, the father of Ferdinand, and the wicked pair Sebastian and Antonio. Also in this party is Gonzalo, the old councilor, who is a sort of refined version of Polonius. The bold, bad men Sebastian and Antonio plot Alonso's murder so nicely and so grimly. Their conversation is admirably invented—neither of them quite likes to give plain words to a plain, dirty action. But this is a fairy tale, and no blood is to be shed; besides, Prospero and Ariel always have the situation well in hand. So Alonso is saved and the party wander to their predestined meeting with Prospero.

Next, to clean the palate of the unpleasant taste of this scene, follows a passage of first-class low comedy. Trinculo, the jester, encounters the cowering Caliban. There is a kind of parody here of Miranda's first sight of a human being. Then comes Stephano, the drunken butler, and finds Trinculo covered by Caliban's cloak, and all three go off inspired by liquor.

Shakespeare then repeats the pattern. Ferdinand and Miranda pass from love to courtship and a pledging of troth. To high romance the natural contrast is low comedy when Stephano, Trinculo, and Caliban re-enter, with Caliban the only man among them with a plan. He will murder Prospero.

Now Prospero has everything ready for the conversion of Alonso, and to crown Alsonso's sorrow there comes the sudden, unexpected, overwhelming denunciation of Ariel. Thereafter Prospero, knowing that all is as he would have it, relents toward Ferdinand and accepts him, and in honor of the lovers presents a little wedding masque, which is suddenly broken off as he remembers the plot.

The play is now working toward an end. The three plotters, Caliban, Stephano, and Trinculo, are punished; they were poor plotters after all. A few gay cloths on a line easily turned them aside. Finally, all Prospero's enemies are brought before him and forgiven. To Alonso, his son is restored, and both old men are reconciled in the happiness of their children. *The Tempest* is a very simple story.

Of his comedies, certainly *The Tempest* is Shakespeare's greatest dramatic poem. Unlike most of his other plays, it is better in the reading than on the stage.

DATE AND SOURCE OF THE PLAY: *The Tempest* was performed at Court on November 1, 1611, and was then probably a new play. It was again acted as one of fourteen plays performed for the wedding festivities of the Princess Elizabeth with the Elector Palatine on February 14, 1613. It was first printed in the first folio in 1623, and the text is good. There is no known source for the story, but the idea of the shipwreck was suggested by a disaster to Sir Thomas Gates' expedition to Virginia; Gates' flagship was wrecked in the Bermudas. Accounts describing the wreck were being printed in the autumn of 1610.

DRAMATIS PERSONAE

ALONSO, *King of Naples*
SEBASTIAN, *his brother*
PROSPERO, *the right Duke of Milan*
ANTONIO, *his brother, the usurping Duke of Milan*
FERDINAND, *son to the King of Naples*
GONZALO, *an honest old councilor*
ADRIAN, FRANCISCO } *lords*
CALIBAN, *a savage and deformed slave*
TRINCULO, *a jester*
STEPHANO, *a drunken butler*
MASTER *of a ship*
BOATSWAIN
MARINERS
MIRANDA, *daughter to Prospero*
ARIEL, *an airy spirit*
IRIS, CERES, JUNO, NYMPHS, REAPERS } *presented by spirits*
OTHER SPIRITS, *attending on Prospero*

SCENE: *A ship at sea; an unihabited island.*

ACT I

SCENE I.

On a ship at sea. A tempestuous noise of thunder and lightning heard.°

[*Enter a* SHIPMASTER *and a* BOATSWAIN.]

MAST. Boatswain!
BOATS. Here, master. What cheer?
MAST. Good,° speak to the mariners. Fall to't yarely,° or we run ourselves aground. Bestir, bestir. [*Exit.*]

[*Enter* MARINERS.]

BOATS. Heigh, my hearts! Cheerly, cheerly, my hearts! Yare, yare! Take in the topsail.° Tend° to the master's whistle. Blow till thou burst thy wind, if room° enough!

[*Enter* ALONSO, SEBASTIAN, ANTONIO, FERDINAND, GONZALO, *and others.*]

ALON. Good boatswain, have care. Where's the master? Play the men.°

ACT I, SC. i: s.d., *On . . . heard:* When the scene opens the ship is in great danger. The wind is blowing hard from the sea; on the landward side lies the rocky island, and between there is too little sea room for her to sail past without being driven ashore by the drift. 3. *Good:* my good man. 4. *yarely:* quickly, smartly. 7. *Take . . . topsail:* i.e., to lessen the drift. *Tend:* attend. 9. *room:* sea room. 11. *Play . . . men:* act like men.

BOATS. I pray now, keep below.

ANT. Where is the master, boatswain?

BOATS. Do you not hear him? You mar our labor. Keep your cabins. You do assist the storm.

GON. Nay, good, be patient.

BOATS. When the sea is. Hence! What cares these roarers for the name of King! To cabin. Silence! Trouble us not.

GON. Good, yet remember whom thou has aboard.

BOATS. None that I more love than myself. You are a councilor. If you can command these elements to silence, and work the peace of the present,° we will not hand a rope more. Use your authority. If you cannot, give thanks you have lived so long, and make yourself ready in your cabin for the mischance of the hour, if it so hap. Cheerly, good hearts! Out of our way, I say. [*Exit.*]

GON. I have great comfort from this fellow. Methinks he hath no drowning mark upon him, his complexion is perfect gallows.° Stand fast, good Fate, to his hanging. Make the rope of his destiny our cable, for our own doth little advantage. If he be not born to be hanged, our case is miserable. [*Exeunt.*]

[*Re-enter* BOATSWAIN.]

BOATS. Down with the topmast! Yare! Lower, lower! Bring her to try with main course.° [*A cry within.*] A plague upon this howling! They are louder than the weather or our office.°

[*Re-enter* SEBASTIAN, ANTONIO, *and* GONZALO.]

Yet again! What do you here? Shall we give o'er, and drown? Have you a mind to sink?

SEB. A pox o' your throat, you bawling, blasphemous, incharitable dog!

BOATS. Work you, then.

ANT. Hang, cur! Hang, you whoreson,° insolent noisemaker. We are less afraid to be drowned than thou art.

GON. I'll warrant him for drowning,° though the ship were no stronger than a nutshell and as leaky as an unstanched wench.

BOATS. Lay her ahold,° ahold! Set her two courses.° Off to sea again, lay her off.

[*Enter* MARINERS *wet.*]

MAR. All lost! To prayers, to prayers! All lost!

BOATS. What, must our mouths be cold?°

24. *work . . . present*: bring us peace at once. 32–33. *hath . . . gallows*: Genzalo remembers the proverb "He that is born to be hanged will never be drowned," and the boatswain looks like a gallows bird. 38. *try . . . course*: i.e., use only the mainsail to heave her to. *course*: sail. 40. *office*: business. 46. *whoreson*: bastard. 49. *warrant . . . drowning*: guarantee him against drowning. 52. *ahold*: close to the wind. 52–53. *two courses*: two sails; i.e., set the foresail as well. The maneuver of heaving-to has failed; the boatswain now hopes to get the ship moving into the wind enough to pass the island. 56. *mouths be cold*: Here the boatswain abandons hope and falls to drinking.

GON. The King and Prince at prayers! Let's assist them,
For our case is as theirs.

SEB. I'm out of patience.

ANT. We are merely cheated of our lives by drunkards.
This wide-chapped° rascal—would thou mightst lie drowning
The washing of ten tides!°

GON. He'll be hanged yet,
Though every drop of water swear against it
And gape at widest to glut° him.

[*A confused noise within:* "Mercy on us!"—"We split, we split!"—"Farewell my wife and children!"—"Farewell, brother!"—"We split, we split, we split!"]

ANT. Let's all sink with the King.

SEB. Let's take leave of him. [*Exeunt* ANTONIO *and* SEBASTIAN.]

GON. Now would I give a thousand furlongs of sea for an acre of barren ground, long heath,° brown furze,° anything. The wills above be done! But I would fain die a dry death. [*Exeunt.*]

SCENE II.

The island. Before PROSPERO'S *cell.*

[*Enter* PROSPERO *and* MIRANDA.]

MIRA. If by your art, my dearest father, you have
Put the wild waters in this roar, allay° them.
The sky, it seems, would pour down stinking pitch
But that the sea, mounting to the welkin's° cheek,
Dashes the fire out. Oh, I have suffered
With those that I saw suffer! A brave vessel,
Who had no doubt some noble creature in her,
Dashed all to pieces. Oh, the cry did knock
Against my very heart! Poor souls, they perished!
Had I been any god of power, I would
Have sunk the sea within the earth or ere
It should the good ship so have swallowed and
The fraughting° souls within her.

PRO. Be collected.°
No more amazement. Tell your piteous heart
There's no harm done.

MIRA. Oh, woe the day!

PRO. No harm.
I have done nothing but in care of thee,
Of thee, my dear one, thee, my daughter, who

60. *wide-chapped*: large-cheeked, because full of liquor. 61. *washing . . . tides*: Pirates were hanged on the seashore and left until three high tides had passed over them. 63. *glut*: swallow. 71. *long heath*: rough grass. 72. *furze*: a prickly bushy shrub.

Sc. ii: 2. *allay*: abate. 4. *welkin*: sky. 13. *fraughting*: lit., who were her freight. *collected*: calm.

Art ignorant of what thou art, naught knowing
Of whence I am, nor that I am more better
Than Prospero, master of a full° poor cell,
And thy no greater father.

MIRA. More to know
Did never meddle° with my thoughts.

PRO. 'Tis time
I should inform thee farther. Lend thy hand,
And pluck my magic garment from me.—So.
[*Lays down his mantle.*]
Lie there, my art. Wipe thou thine eyes, have comfort.
The direful spectacle of the wreck, which touched
The very virtue of compassion in thee,
I have with such provision° in mine art
So safely ordered that there is no soul,
No, not so much perdition° as a hair,
Betid° to any creature in the vessel
Which thou heard'st cry, which thou saw'st sink. Sit down,
For thou must now know farther.

MIRA. You have often
Begun to tell me what I am, but stopped,
And left me to a bootless inquisition,°
Concluding "Stay, not yet."

PRO. The hour's now come,
The very minute bids thee ope thine ear.
Obey, and be attentive. Canst thou remember
A time before we came unto this cell?
I do not think thou canst, for then thou wast not
Out° three years old.

MIRA. Certainly, sir, I can.

PRO. By what? By any other house or person?
Of anything the image tell me that
Hath kept with thy remembrance.

MIRA. 'Tis far off,
And rather like a dream than an assurance
That my remembrance warrants. Had I not
Four or five women once that tended me?

PRO. Thou hadst, and more, Miranda. But how is it
That this lives in thy mind? What seest thou else
In the dark backward and abysm of time?°
If thou remember'st aught ere thou camest here,
How thou camest here thou mayst.

MIRA. But that I do not.

20. *full*: exceedingly. 22. *meddle*: interfere; i.e., cause to be curious. 28. *provision*: foresight. 30. *perdition*: loss. 31. *Betid*: befallen. 35. *bootless inquisition*: vain inquiry. 41. *Out*: more than. 50. *abysm of time*: i.e., the past, which is like a dark abyss.

PRO. Twelve year since, Miranda, twelve year since,
Thy father was the Duke of Milan, and
A prince of power.
MIRA. Sir, are not you my father?
PRO. Thy mother was a piece of virtue, and
She said thou wast my daughter, and thy father
Was Duke of Milan, and his only heir
A Princess, no worse issued.
MIRA. Oh, the Heavens!
What foul play had we that we came from thence?
Or blessèd was't we did?
PRO. Both, both, my girl.
By foul play, as thou say'st, were we heaved thence,
But blessedly holp° hither.
MIRA. Oh, my heart bleeds
To think o' the teen° that I have turned you to,
Which is from my remembrance! Please you, farther.
PRO. My brother, and thy uncle, called Antonio—
I pray thee mark me—that a brother should
Be so perfidious!—he whom, next thyself,
Of all the world I loved, and to him put
The manage° of my state—as at that time
Through all the signories° it was the first,
And Prospero the prime° Duke, being so reputed
In dignity, and for the liberal arts°
Without a parallel, those being all my study—
The government I cast upon my brother,
And to my state grew stranger, being transported
And rapt in secret studies. Thy false uncle—
Dost thou attend me?
MIRA. Sir, most heedfully.
PRO. Being once perfected° how to grant suits,
How to deny them, who to advance, and who
To trash for overtopping,° new-created°
The creatures that were mine, I say, or changed 'em,
Or else new-formed 'em—having both the key°
Of officer and office, set all hearts i' the state
To what tune pleased his ear, that now he was
The ivy which had hid my princely trunk,
And sucked my verdure out on't. Thou attend'st not.
MIRA. Oh, good sir, I do.
PRO. I pray thee, mark me.

63. *holp*: helped. 64. *teen*: sorrow. 70. *manage*: management. 71. *signories*: lordships. 72. *prime*: leading. 73. *liberal arts*: academic learning. 79. *perfected*: become perfect by practice. 81. *trash . . . overtopping*: check for running ahead, a metaphor from training a pack of hounds. *new-created*: made them new creatures—by tampering with their loyalty. 83. *key*: tool used for tuning a stringed instrument.

I, thus neglecting worldly ends, all dedicated
To closeness° and the bettering of my mind
With that which, but by being so retired,°
O'erprized all popular rate,° in my false brother
Awaked an evil nature. And my trust,
Like a good parent, did beget of him
A falsehood in its contrary as great
As my trust was, which had indeed no limit,
A confidence sans° bound. He being thus lorded,
Not only with what my revenue yielded,
But what my power might else exact, like one
Who having into truth, by telling of it,
Made such a sinner of his memory,
To credit his own lie, he did believe
He was indeed the Duke°—out o' the substitution,
And executing the outward face of royalty,
With all prerogative°—Hence his ambition growing——
Dost thou hear?

MIRA. Your tale, sir, would cure deafness.

PRO. To have no screen between this part he played
And him he played it for, he needs will be
Absolute Milan.° Me, poor man, my library
Was dukedom large enough. Of temporary royalties°
He thinks me now incapable; confederates,°
So dry° he was for sway, wi' the King of Naples
To give him annual tribute, do him homage,
Subject his coronet to his crown,° and bend
The dukedom, yet unbowed—alas, poor Milan!—
To most ignoble stooping.

MIRA. Oh, the Heavens!

PRO. Mark his condition, and the event,° then tell me
If this might be a brother.

MIRA. I should sin
To think but nobly of my grandmother.
Good wombs have borne bad sons.

PRO. Now the condition.
This King of Naples, being an enemy
To me inveterate, hearkens my brother's suit.
Which was that he, in lieu o' the premises,°
Of homage, and I know not how much tribute,

90. *closeness*: privacy. 91. *but . . . retired*: except that it kept me away from state affairs. 92. *O'erprized . . . rate*: was worth more than it is commonly regarded. 97. *sans*: without. 97–103. *He . . . Duke*: he, getting such greatness not only from my wealth but also by abusing my power, began to believe as he had hitherto pretended, that he was in truth the Duke. 103–05. *out . . . prerogative*: from being my substitute and acting outwardly as Duke with all the rights of a ruler. 109. *Absolute Milan*: Duke of Milan in fact. 110. *temporal royalties*: worldly power. 111. *confederates*: conspires. 112. *dry*: thirsty. 114. *Subject . . . crown*: i.e., pay homage as to his overlord. The coronet was worn as a symbol by rulers of lower rank than that of King. 127. *event*: sequel. 123. *in . . . premises*: in return for these conditions.

Should presently° extirpate° me and mine
Out of the dukedom, and confer fair Milan,
With all the honors, on my brother. Whereon,
A treacherous army levied, one midnight
Fated to the purpose did Antonio open
The gates of Milan, and, i' the dead of darkness
The ministers for the purpose hurried thence
Me and thy crying self.

MIRA. Alack, for pity!
I, not remembering how I cried out then,
Will cry it o'er again. It is a hint°
That wrings mine eyes to't.

PRO. Hear a little further,
And then I'll bring thee to the present business
Which now's upon 's, without the which this story
Were most impertinent.

MIRA. Wherefore did they not
That hour destroy us?

PRO. Well demanded, wench.
My tale provokes that question. Dear, they durst not,
So dear the love my people bore me, nor set
A mark so bloody on the business, but
With colors fairer painted their foul ends.
In few,° they hurried us aboard a bark,
Bore us some leagues to sea, where they prepared
A rotten carcass of a butt,° not rigged,
Nor tackle, sail, nor mast. The very rats
Instinctively have quit it. There they hoist us,
To cry to the sea that roared to us, to sigh
To the winds, whose pity, sighing back again,
Did us but loving wrong.

MIRA. Alack, what trouble
Was I then to you!

PRO. Oh, a cherubin
Thou wast that did preserve me. Thou didst smile,
Infusèd with a fortitude from Heaven,
When I have decked the sea with drops full salt.
Under my burden groaned, which raised in me
An undergoing stomach° to bear up
Against what should ensue.

MIRA. How came we ashore?

PRO. By Providence divine.
Some food we had, and some fresh water, that
A noble Neapolitan, Gonzalo,
Out of his charity, who being then appointed
Master of this design, did give us, with

125. *presently*: immediately. *extirpate*: root out. 134. *hint*: occasion. 144. *In few*: in a few words. 146. *butt*: tub. 157. *undergoing stomach*: courage to endure, the stomach being regarded as the seat of valor.

Rich garments, linens, stuffs, and necessaries,
Which since have steaded much.° So, of his gentleness,
Knowing I loved my books, he furnished me
From mine own library with volumes that
I prize above my dukedom.

MIRA. Would I might
But ever see that man!

PRO. Now I arise. [*Resumes his mantle.*]
Sit still, and hear the last of our sea sorrow.
Here in this island we arrived, and here
Have I, thy schoolmaster, made thee more profit
Than other princes can that have more time
For vainer hours, and tutors not so careful.

MIRA. Heavens thank you for't! And now I pray you, sir,
For still 'tis beating° in my mind, your reason
For raising this sea storm?

PRO. Know thus far forth.°
By accident most strange, bountiful Fortune,
Now my dear lady,° hath mine enemies
Brought to this shore. And by my prescience°
I find my zenith° doth depend upon
A most auspicious star, whose influence
If now I court not,° but omit, my fortunes
Will ever after droop. Here cease more questions.
Thou art inclined to sleep, 'tis a good dullness,
And give it way. I know thou canst not choose. [MIRANDA *sleeps.*]
Come away, servant, come. I am ready now.
Approach, my Ariel, come.

[*Enter* ARIEL.]

ARI. All hail, great master! Grave sir, hail! I come
To answer thy best pleasure, be 't to fly,
To swim, to dive into the fire, to ride
On the curled clouds, to thy strong bidding task°
Ariel and all his quality.°

PRO. Hast thou, spirit,
Performed to point° the tempest that I bade thee?

ARI. To every article.
I boarded the King's ship. Now on the beak,
Now in the waist,° the deck, in every cabin,
I flamed amazement.° Sometime I'd divide,

165. *have . . . much*: have been of great benefit. 176. *beating*: throbbing. 177. *Know . . . forth*: i.e., I will now tell you more. 179. *Now . . . lady*: Fortune (once my foe) is now kind to me. 180. *prescience*: foreknowledge. 181. *zenith*: the highest point of my fortunes. 183. *court not*: do not seek to win. 192. *task*: impose a task on. 193. *quality*: ability. 194. *to point*: in all points, exactly. 197. *waist*: that part of the ship which lies between forecastle and poop. 198. *flamed amazement*: appeared in the form of fire which caused amazement. This phenomenon, known as Saint Elmo's fire or a corposant, is sometimes seen on ships during a storm.

And burn in many places; on the topmast,
The yards and bowsprit, would I flame distinctly,
Then meet and join. Jove's lightnings, the precursors°
O' the dreadful thunderclaps, more momentary
And sight-outrunning were not. The fire and cracks
Of sulphurous roaring the most mighty Neptune
Seem to besiege, and make his bold waves tremble—
Yea, his dread trident shake.

PRO. My brave spirit!
Who was so firm, so constant, that this coil°
Would not infect his reason?

ARI. Not a soul
But felt a fever of the mad° and played
Some tricks of desperation.° All but mariners
Plunged in the foaming brine, and quit the vessel,
Then all afire with me. The King's son, Ferdinand,
With hair upstaring—then like reeds, not hair—
Was the first man that leaped, cried, "Hell is empty,
And all the devils are here."

PRO. Why, that's my spirit!
But was not this nigh shore?

ARI. Close by, my master.

PRO. But are they, Ariel, safe?

ARI. Not a hair perished,
On their sustaining° garments not a blemish,
But fresher than before. And, as thou badest me,
In troops I have dispersed them 'bout the isle.
The King's son have I landed by himself,
Whom I left cooling of the air with sighs
In an odd angle° of this isle, and sitting
His arms in this sad knot.°

PRO. Of the King's ship,
The mariners, say how thou hast disposed,
And all the rest o' the fleet.

ARI. Safely in harbor
Is the King's ship—in the deep nook where once
Thou call'dst me up at midnight to fetch dew
From the still-vexed Bermoothes,° there she's hid.
The mariners all under hatches stowed,
Who, with a charm joined to their suffered labor,°
I have left asleep. And for the rest o' the fleet,
Which I dispersed, they all have met again,
And are upon the Mediterranean flote,°
Bound sadly home for Naples,

201. *precursors*: forerunners. 207. *coil*: confusion. 209. *fever . . . mad*: fever of madness. 210. *tricks of desperation*: desperate tricks. 218. *sustaining*: which bore them up. 223. *angle*: corner. 224. *in . . . knot*: sadly folded. Ariel imitates the posture. 229. *still-vexed Bermoothes*: ever stormy Bermudas. 231. *joined . . . labor*: as well as the labor they had endured. 234. *flote*: sea.

Supposing that they saw the King's ship wrecked
And his great person perish.
PRO. Ariel, thy charge
Exactly is performed. But there's more work.
What is the time o' the day?
ARI. Past the midseason.
PRO. At least two glasses.° The time 'twixt six and now
Must by us both be spent most preciously.
ARI. Is there more toil? Since thou dost give me pains,°
Let me remember° thee what thou hast promisèd,
Which is not yet performed me.
PRO. How now? Moody?
What is't thou canst demand?
ARI. My liberty.
PRO. Before the time be out? No more!
ARI. I prithee
Remember I have done thee worthy service,
Told thee no lies, made thee no mistakings, served
Without or grudge or grumblings. Thou didst promise
To bate° me a full year.
PRO. Dost thou forget
From what a torment I did free thee?
ARI. No.
PRO. Thou dost, and think'st it much to tread the ooze
Of the salt deep,
To run upon the sharp wind of the North,
To do me business in the veins o' the earth
When it is baked with frost.
ARI. I do not, sir.
PRO. Thou liest, malignant thing! Hast thou forgot
The foul witch Sycorax, who with age and envy
Was grown into a hoop?° Hast thou forgot her?
ARI. No, sir.
PRO. Thou hast. Where was she born?
Speak, tell me.
ARI. Sir, in Argier.°
PRO. Oh, was she so? I must
Once in a month recount what thou hast been,
Which thou forget'st. This damned witch Sycorax,
For mischiefs manifold and sorceries terrible
To enter human hearing,° from Argier,
Thou know'st, was banished. For one thing she did°
They would not take her life. Is not this true?
ARI. Aye, sir.

240. *glasses*: i.e., hours; turns of the hourglass. 242. *pains*: toil. 243. *remember*: remind. 250. *bate*: abate, lessen. 259. *grown . . . hoop*: bent double. 261. *Argier*: Algiers. 265. *To . . . hearing*: for a human being to hear. 266. *one . . . did*: This good action is not recalled.

PRO. This blue-eyed° hag was hither brought with child,
And here was left by the sailors. Thou, my slave,
As thou report'st thyself, wast then her servant.
And, for thou wast a spirit too delicate
To act her earthy and abhorred commands,
Refusing her grand hests,° she did confine thee,
By help of her more potent ministers
And in her most unmitigable° rage,
Into a cloven pine. Within which rift
Imprisoned thou didst painfully remain
A dozen years. Within which space she died,
And left thee there, where thou didst vent thy groans
As fast as mill wheels strike.° Then was this island—
Save for the son that she did litter here,
A freckled whelp hag-born°—not honored with
A human shape.
ARI. Yes, Caliban her son.
PRO. Dull thing, I say so, he, that Caliban
Whom now I keep in service. Thou best know'st
What torment I did find thee in. Thy groans
Did make wolves howl and penetrate the breasts
Of ever-angry bears. It was a torment
To lay upon the damned, which Sycorax
Could not again undo. It was mine art,
When I arrived and heard thee, that made gape
The pine and let thee out.
ARI. I thank thee, master.
PRO. If thou more murmur'st, I will rend an oak°
And peg thee in his knotty entrails till
Thou hast howled away twelve winters.
ARI. Pardon, master.
I will be correspondent° to command,
And do my spiriting° gently.
PRO. Do so, and after two days
I will discharge thee.
ARI. That's my noble master!
What shall I do? Say what. What shall I do?
PRO. Go make thyself like a nymph o' the sea.
Be subject to no sight but thine and mine, invisible
To every eyeball else. Go take this shape,
And hither come in't. Go, hence with diligence!
[*Exit* ARIEL.]
Awake, dear heart, awake! Thou hast slept well.
Awake!

269. *blue-eyed*: with dark rings under the eyes. 274. *hests*: commands. 276. *unmitigable*: absolute. 281. *mill . . . strike*: i.e., the continuous clack of a water mill. 283. *hag-born*: child of a hag. 294. *rend an oak*: i.e., a far worse torment than imprisonment in a pine. 297. *correspondent*: agreeable, submissive. 298. *spiriting*: my work as a spirit.

MIRA. The strangeness of your story put
Heaviness in me.
PRO. Shake it off. Come on,
We'll visit Caliban my slave, who never
Yields us kind answer.
MIRA. 'Tis a villain, sir,
I do not love to look on.
PRO. But, as 'tis,
We cannot miss° him. He does make our fire,
Fetch in our wood, and serves in offices
That profit us. What ho! Slave! Caliban!
Thou earth,° thou! Speak
CAL. [*Within*] There's wood enough within.
PRO. Come forth, I say! There's other business for thee.
Come, thou tortoise! When?

[*Re-enter* ARIEL *like a water nymph.*]

Fine apparition! My quaint° Ariel,
Hark in thine ear.
ARI. My lord, it shall be done. [*Exit.*]
PRO. Thou poisonous slave, got° by the Devil himself
Upon thy wicked dam,° come forth!

[*Enter* CALIBAN.]

CAL. As wicked dew as e'er my mother brushed
With raven's feather from unwholesome fen
Drop on you both! A southwest° blow on ye
And blister you all o'er!
PRO. For this, be sure, tonight thou shalt have cramps,
Side stitches that shall pen thy breath up. Urchins°
Shall, for that vast° of night that they may work,
All exercise on thee. Thou shalt be pinched
As thick as honeycomb, each pinch more stinging
Than bees that made 'em.
CAL. I must eat my dinner.
This island's mine, by Sycorax my mother,
Which thou takest from me. When thou camest first,
Thou strokedst me, and madest much of me, wouldst give me
Water with berries in't.° And teach me how
To name the bigger light, and how the less,
That burn by day and night. And then I loved thee,
And showed thee all the qualities° o' th' isle,
The fresh springs, brine pits, barren place and fertile.
Cursèd be I that did so! All the charms

311. *miss*: do without. 314. *earth*: lump of dirt. 317. *quaint*: elegant. 319. *got*: begotten. 320. *dam*: mother. 323. *southwest*: regarded as an unhealthy wind. 326. *Urchins*: goblins, or hedgehogs. 327. *vast*: desolate period. 334. *Water . . . in't*: Shakespeare apparently took this from William Strachey's account of the Bermuda shipwreck, which records that the castaways made a pleasant drink from cedar berries. 337. *qualities*: good spots.

Of Sycorax, toads, beetles, bats, light on you!
For I am all the subjects that you have,
Which first was mine own king. And here you sty° me
In this hard rock whiles you do keep from me
The rest o' th' island.

PRO. Thou most lying slave,
Whom stripes° may move, not kindness! I have used thee,
Filth as thou art, with human care, and lodged thee
In mine own cell till thou didst seek to violate
The honor of my child.

CAL. Oh ho, oh ho! Would 't had been done!
Thou didst prevent me. I had peopled else
This isle with Calibans.

PRO. Abhorrèd slave,
Which any print° of goodness wilt not take,
Being capable of all ill! I pitied thee,
Took pains to make thee speak, taught thee each hour
One thing or other. When thou didst not, savage,
Know thine own meaning, but wouldst gabble like
A thing most brutish, I endowed thy purposes
With words that made them known. But thy vile race,
Though thou didst learn, had that in't which good natures
Could not abide to be with. Therefore wast thou
Deservedly confined into this rock,
Who hadst deserved more than a prison.

CAL. You taught me language, and my profit on't
Is I know how to curse. The red plague° rid° you
For learning° me your language!

PRO. Hagseed,° hence!
Fetch us in fuel, and be quick, thou'rt best,
To answer other business. Shrug'st thou, malice?
If thou neglect'st, or dost unwillingly
What I command, I'll rack thee with old° cramps,
Fill all thy bones with achés,° make thee roar
That beasts shall tremble at thy din.

CAL. No, pray thee.
[*Aside*] I must obey. His art is of such power
It would control my dam's god, Setebos,
And make a vassal° of him.

PRO. So, slave. Hence! [*Exit* CALIBAN.]

[*Re-enter* ARIEL, *invisible, playing and singing;* FERDINAND *following.*]

ARI. [*Sings.*]

"Come unto these yellow sands,
And then take hands.

342. *sty*: pen. 345. *stripes*: blows. 352. *print*: impression. 364. *red plague*: bubonic plague. *rid*: destroy. 365. *learning*: teaching. *Hagseed*: son of a hag. 369. *old*: abundant. 370. *aches*: a two-syllable word, pronounced like "h's." 374. *vassal*: slave.

Curtsied when you have and kissed
The wild waves whist,°
Foot it featly° here and there,
And, sweet sprites, the burden° bear."

BURDEN. [*Dispersedly*]° "Hark, hark"
"Bowwow."

ARI. "The watchdogs bark."

BURDEN. [*Dispersedly*] "Bowwow."

ARI. "Hark, hark! I hear
The strain of strutting chanticleer
Cry Cock-a-diddle-dow."

FER. Where should this music be? I' th' air or th' earth?
It sounds no more, and, sure, it waits upon
Some god o' th' island. Sitting on a bank,
Weeping again the King my father's wreck,
This music crept by me upon the waters,
Allaying both their fury and my passion°
With its sweet air. Thence I have followed it,
Or it hath drawn me rather. But 'tis gone.
No, it begins again.

ARI. [*Sings.*]

"Full fathom five thy father lies,
Of his bones are coral made,
Those are pearls that were his eyes.
Nothing of him that doth fade
But doth suffer a sea change
Into something rich and strange.
Sea nymphs hourly ring his knell."

BURDEN. "Dingdong."

ARI. "Hark! Now I hear them.—Dingdong, bell."

FER. The ditty does remember my drowned father.
This is no mortal business, nor no sound
That the earth owes.°—I hear it now above me.

PRO. The fringèd curtains of thine eye advance,°
And say what thou seest yond.

MIRA. What is't? A spirit?
Lord, how it looks about! Believe me, sir,
It carries a brave form.° But 'tis a spirit.

PRO. No, wench, it eats and sleeps and hath such senses
As we have, such. This gallant which thou seest
Was in the wreck, and but he's something stained
With grief, that's beauty's canker,° thou mightst call him
A goodly person. He hath lost his fellows,
And strays about to find 'em.

379. *whist*: silent. 380. *featly*: smartly. 381. *burden*: refrain. 382. [s.d.] *Dispersedly*: from different sides. 392. *passion*: emotion, sorrow. 407. *owes*: owns, possesses. 408. *advance*: raise. 411. *brave form*: fine shape. 415. *canker*: maggot.

MIRA. I might call him
A thing divine, for nothing natural
I ever saw so noble.
PRO. [*Aside*] It goes on,° I see,
As my soul prompts it. Spirit, fine spirit! I'll free thee
Within two days for this.
FER. Most sure, the goddess
On whom these airs attend!° Vouchsafe my prayer
May know if you remain upon this island,°
And that you will some good instruction give
How I may bear me° here. My prime request,
Which I do last pronounce, is, O you wonder!
If you be maid or no?°
MIRA. No wonder, sir,
But certainly a maid.
FER. My language! Heavens!
I am the best of them° that speak this speech,
Were I but where 'tis spoken.
PRO. How? The best?
What wert thou if the King of Naples heard thee?
FER. A Single° thing, as I am now, that wonders
To hear thee speak of Naples. He does hear me,
And that he does I weep. Myself am Naples,
Who with mine eyes, never since at ebb,° beheld
The King my father wrecked.
MIRA. Alack, for mercy!
FER. Yes, faith, and all his lords, the Duke of Milan
And his brave son being twain.°
PRO. [*Aside*] The Duke of Milan
And his more braver daughter could control thee,
If now 'twere fit to do't. At the first sight
They have changed eyes.° Delicate Ariel,
I'll set thee free for this. [*To* FERDINAND] A word, good sir.
I fear you have done yourself some wrong. A word.
MIRA. Why speaks my father so ungently? This
Is the third man that e'er I saw, the first
That e'er I sighed for. Pity move my father
To be inclined my way!
FER. Oh, if a virgin,
And your affection not gone forth,° I'll make you
The Queen of Naples.
PRO. Soft, sir! One word more.

419. *It . . . on*: i.e., Prospero's plan that Miranda and Ferdinand shall fall in love. 422. *attend*: wait on. 422–23. *Vouchsafe . . . island*: grant my prayer, which is to know whether you inhabit this island. 425. *bear me*: behave myself. 427. *maid or no*: i.e., a mortal or a goddess. 429. *best of them*: i.e., I am now King of Naples since my father's death. 432. *single*: lonely. 435. *never . . . ebb*: i.e., have not ceased to flow. 438. *twain*: i.e., two of those drowned. 441. *changed eyes*: fallen in love. 448. *gone forth*: i.e., been bestowed on someone else.

[*Aside*] They are both in either's powers. But this swift business
I must uneasy make, lest too light winning
Make the prize light. [*To* FERDINAND] One word more. I charge
thee
That thou attend me. Thou dost here usurp
The name thou owest not, and hast put thyself
Upon this island as a spy, to win it
From me, the lord on 't.
FER. No, as I am a man.
MIRA. There's nothing ill can dwell in such a temple.°
If the ill spirit have so fair a house,
Good things will strive to dwell with 't.
PRO. Follow me.
Speak not you for him, he's a traitor. Come,
I'll manacle thy neck and feet together.
Sea water shalt thou drink, thy food shall be
The fresh-brook mussels, withered roots, and husks
Wherein the acorn cradled. Follow.
FER. No.
I will resist such entertainment till
Mine enemy has more power. [*Draws, and is charmed from moving.*]
MIRA. O dear Father,
Make not too rash a trial of him, for
He's gentle, and not fearful.°
PRO. What! I say,
My foot my tutor?° Put thy sword up, traitor,
Who makest a show but darest not strike, thy conscience
Is so possessed with guilt. Come from thy ward,°
For I can here disarm thee with this stick
And make thy weapon drop.
MIRA. Beseech you, Father.
PRO. Hence! Hang not on my garments.
MIRA. Sir, have pity.
I'll be his surety.
PRO. Silence! One word more
Shall make me chide thee, if not hate thee. What!
An advocate for an impostor! Hush!
Thou think'st there is no more such shapes as he,
Having seen but him and Caliban. Foolish wench!
To the most of men this is a Caliban,
And they to him are angels.
MIRA. My affections
Are, then, most humble. I have no ambition
To see a goodlier man.

457. *temple*: i.e., beautiful body. 468. *fearful*: to be feared. 469. *my . . . tutor*: The head is the tutor to the body, but Miranda (who is by nature subordinate and so the foot) is trying to tell her father what he should do. 471. *ward*: position of defense.

PRO. Come on, obey.
Thy nerves° are in their infancy again,
And have no vigor in them.
FER. So they are.
My spirits, as in a dream, are all bound up.
My father's loss, the weakness which I feel,
The wreck of all my friends, nor this man's threats,
To whom I am subdued, are but light to me
Might I but through my prison once a day
Behold this maid. All corners else o' th' earth
Let liberty make use of, space enough
Have I in such a prison.
PRO. [*Aside*] It works.
[*To* FERDINAND] Come on.
Thou hast done well, fine Ariel!
[*To* FERDINAND] Follow me.
[*To* ARIEL] Hark what thou else shalt do me.
MIRA. Be of comfort.
My father's of a better nature, sir,
Than he appears by speech. This is unwonted°
Which now came from him.
PRO. Thou shalt be as free
As mountain winds. But then exactly do
All points of my command.
ARI. To the syllable.
PRO. Come, follow. Speak not for him. [*Exeunt.*]

ACT II

SCENE I.

Another part of the island.

[*Enter* ALONSO, SEBASTIAN, ANTONIO, GONZALO, ADRIAN, FRANCISCO, *and others.*]

GON. Beseech you, sir, be merry. You have cause,
So have we all, of joy, for our escape
Is much beyond our loss. Our hint° of woe
Is common. Every day some sailor's wife,
The masters of some merchant,° and the merchant,°
Have just our theme of woe. But for the miracle—
I mean our preservation—few in millions
Can speak like us. Then wisely, good sir, weigh
Our sorrow with our comfort.

484. *nerves*: sinews. 497. *unwonted*: unusual.
ACT II, Sc. i: 3. *hint*: occasion. See I.ii.134. 5. *masters . . . merchant*: captains of merchant ships. *the merchant*: i.e., the owner.

ALON. Prithee, peace.
SEB. He receives comfort like cold porridge.
ANT. The visitor° will not give him o'er so.
SEB. Look, he's winding up the watch of his wit.
By and by it will strike.
GON. Sir——
SEB. One. Tell.°
GON. When every grief is entertained° that's offered,
Comes to the entertainer——
SEB. A dollar.
GON. Dolor comes to him, indeed. You have spoken truer than you purposed.
SEB. You have taken it wiselier than I meant you should.
GON. Therefore, my lord——
ANT. Fie, what a spendthrift is he of his tongue!
ALON. I prithee, spare.
GON. Well, I have done. But yet——
SEB. He will be talking.
ANT. Which, of he or Adrian, for a good wager, first begins to crow?
SEB. The old cock.
ANT. The cockerel.
SEB. Done. The wager?
ANT. A laughter.°
SEB. A match!
ADR. Though this island seem to be desert——
SEB. Ha, ha, ha!—So, you're paid.°
ADR. Uninhabitable, and almost inaccessible——
SEB. Yet——
ADR. Yet——
ANT. He could not miss 't.°
ADR. It must needs be of subtle, tender, and delicate temperance.
ANT. Temperance was a delicate wench.
SEB. Aye, and a subtle, as he most learnedly delivered.°
ADR. The air breathes upon us here most sweetly.
SEB. As if it had lungs, and rotten ones.
ANT. Or as 'twere perfumed by a fen.
GON. Here is everything advantageous to life.
ANT. True—save means to live.
SEB. Of that there's none, or little.
GON. How lush and lusty the grass looks! How green!
ANT. The ground indeed is tawny.

11. *visitor*: visiting minister. *See T Night,* IV.ii.25–26. Sebastian means that Gonzalo will insist on having his say whether Alonso wishes to hear it or not. 15. *Tell*: count. 16. *entertained*: received. 33. *A laughter*: the winner is to have the laugh on the loser, on the principle of the proverb "He laughs that wins." Cf. *Oth,* IV.i.126. (Kittredge). 36. *Ha . . . paid*: F1 divides the speech: "*Sebastian:* Ha, ha, ha. *Antonio:* So, you're paid"; i.e., you've had your laugh as winner. 40. *He . . . miss't*: i.e., if he begins the first clause with "though," he is sure to follow it up with a "yet." 45. *delivered*: declared.

SEB. With an eye° of green in't.
ANT. He misses not much.
SEB. No, he doth but mistake the truth totally.
GON. But the rarity° of it is—which is indeed almost beyond credit°——
SEB. As many vouched° rarities are.
GON. That our garments, being, as they were, drenched in the sea, hold notwithstanding their freshness and glosses, being rather new-dyed than stained with salt water.
ANT. If but one of his pockets could speak,° would it not say he lies?
SEB. Aye, or very falsely pocket up his report.
GON. Methinks our garments are now as fresh as when we put them on first in Afric, at the marriage of the King's fair daughter Claribel to the King of Tunis.
SEB. 'Twas a sweet marriage, and we prosper well in our return.
ADR. Tunis was never graced° before with such a paragon to° their Queen.
GON. Not since Widow Dido's° time.
ANT. Widow! A pox° o' that! How came that widow in?° Widow Dido!
SEB. What if he had said "Widower Aeneas" too? Good Lord, how you take it!
ADR. "Widow Dido," said you? You make me study of that. She was of Carthage, not of Tunis.
GON. This Tunis, sir, was Carthage.
ADR. Carthage?
GON. I assure you, Carthage.
ANT. His word is more than the miraculous harp.°
SEB. He hath raised the wall, and houses too.
ANT. What impossible matter will he make easy next?
SEB. I think he will carry this island home in his pocket, and give it his son for an apple.
ANT. And, sowing the kernels of it in the sea, bring forth more islands.
GON. Aye.
ANT. Why, in good time.
GON. Sir, we were talking that our garments seem now as fresh as when we were at Tunis at the marriage of your daughter, who is now Queen.
ANT. And the rarest that e'er came there.
SEB. Bate,° I beseech you, Widow Dido.

55. *eye*: tinge. 58. *rarity*: strange thing. 59. *credit*: belief. 60. *vouched*: guaranteed. 65. *pockets . . . speak*: i.e., his pockets are still wet. 74. *graced*: honored. 75. *to*: for. 76. *Widow Dido*: Dido was the Queen of Carthage (near the modern Tunis) who entertained Aeneas on his way from Troy to Italy. She was a widow and had vowed eternal fidelity to the memory of her husband, but she fell in love with Aeneas. When he deserted her, she committed suicide. 77. *pox*: plague; lit., venereal disease. 77–78. *How . . . in*: why do you call her a widow? 86. *His . . . harp*: According to the legends told by Ovid, the walls of Thebes came together at the music of Amphion's harp. By a like miracle Gonzalo has erected a Carthage at Tunis. 100. *Bate*: except.

ANT. Oh, Widow Dido! Aye, Widow Dido.
GON. Is not, sir, my doublet° as fresh as the first day I wore it? I mean, in a sort.°
ANT. That sort was well fished for.°
GON. When I wore it at your daughter's marriage?
ALON. You cram these words into mine ears against
The stomach of my sense. Would I had never
Married my daughter there! For, coming thence,
My son is lost and, in my rate,° she too
Who is so far from Italy removed
I ne'er again shall see her. O thou mine heir
Of Naples and of Milan, what strange fish
Hath made his meal on thee?
FRAN. Sir, he may live.
I saw him beat the surges° under him,
And ride upon their backs. He trod the water,
Whose enmity he flung aside, and breasted
The surge most swoln° that met him. His bold head
'Bove the contentious waves he kept, and oared
Himself with his good arms in lusty stroke
To the shore, that o'er his wave-worn basis bowed,°
As stooping to relieve him. I not doubt
He came alive to land.
ALON. No, no, he's gone.
SEB. Sir, you may thank yourself for this great loss,
That would not bless our Europe with your daughter,
But rather lose her to an African,
Where she, at least, is banished from your eye
Who hath cause to wet° the grief on 't.
ALON. Prithee, peace.
SEB. You were kneeled to, and importuned otherwise,
By all of us, and the fair soul herself
Weighed° between loathness° and obedience, at
Which end o' the beam° should bow. We have lost your son,
I fear, forever. Milan and Naples have
Mo° widows in them of this business' making
Than we bring men to comfort them.
The fault's your own.
ALON. So is the dear'st° o' the loss.
GON. My lord Sebastian,
The truth you speak doth lack some gentleness,
And time to speak it in. You rub the sore
When you should bring the plaster.

102. *doublet*: short, close-fitting jacket. 103. *in a sort*: after a fashion. 104. *That . . . for*: i.e., he had to add "after a fashion." 109. *rate*: estimation. 114. *surges*: waves. 117. *swoln*: swollen. 120. *his . . . bowed*: hung over its base, which had been worn away by the sea. 127. *wet*: weep for. 130. *Weighed*: balanced. *loathness*: reluctance. 131. *end . . . beam*: which scale should sink. 133. *Mo*: more. 135. *dear'st*: most grievous.

SEB. Very well.
ANT. And most chirurgeonly.°
GON. It is foul weather in us all, good sir,
When you are cloudy.
SEB. Foul weather?
ANT. Very foul.
GON. Had I plantation° of this isle, my lord——
ANT. He'd sow 't with nettle seed.
SEB. Or docks, or mallows.°
GON. And were the King on 't, what would I do?
SEB. 'Scape being drunk for want of wine.
GON. I' the commonwealth° I would by contraries°
Execute all things, for no kind of traffic°
Would I admit, no name of magistrate.
Letters° should not be known; riches, poverty,
And use of service,° none; contract,° succession,°
Bourn,° bound° of land, tilth,° vineyard, none;
No use of metal,° corn, or wine, or oil;
No occupation°—all men idle, all;
And women too, but innocent and pure;
No sovereignty——
SEB. Yet he would be King on't.
ANT. The latter end of his commonwealth forgets the beginning.
GON. All things in common nature should produce
Without sweat or endeavor. Treason, felony,
Sword, pike, knife, gun, or need of any engine°
Would I not have. But Nature should bring forth,
Of it° own kind, all foison,° all abundance,
To feed my innocent people.
SEB. No marrying 'mong his subjects?
ANT. None, man—all idle, whores and knaves.
GON. I would with such perfection govern, sir,
To excel the Golden Age.°
SEB. 'Save° His Majesty!
ANT. Long live Gonzalo!
GON. And—do you mark me, sir?
ALON. Prithee, no more. Thou dost talk nothing to me.
GON. I do well believe your Highness, and did it to minister occasion° to these gentlemen, who are of such sensible° and nimble lungs that they always use to laugh at nothing.

140. *chirurgeonly*: like a good surgeon. 143. *plantation*: colonization, but Antonio pretends to take it literally as "planting." 144. *docks or mallows*: common English weeds. 147. *I' . . . commonwealth*: This passage was taken from one of Montaigne's *Essays*. *by contraries*: contrary to the usual plan. 148. *traffic*: trade. 150. *Letters*: learning. 151. *use of service*: no one should have servants. *contract*: legal agreements. *succession*: right of inheritance. 152. *Bourn*: boundary. *bound*: limit; i.e., private property rights. *tilth*: tillage. 153. *use of metal*: i.e., exchange of money. 154. *occupation*: manual labor. 161. *engine*: instrument of warfare. 163. *it*: its. *foison*: plenty. 168. *Golden Age*: the days of perfect innocence at the beginning of the world. *'Save*: God save. 173. *minister occasion*: provide opportunity 174. *sensible*: sensitive.

ANT. 'Twas you we laughed at.
GON. Who in this kind of merry fooling am nothing to you. So you may continue and laugh at nothing still.
ANT. What a blow was there given!
SEB. An° it had not fallen flat-long.°
GON. You are gentlemen of brave mettle,° you would lift the moon out of her sphere° if she would continue in it five weeks without changing.

[*Enter* ARIEL (*invisible*) *playing solemn music.*]

SEB. We would so, and then go a-batfowling.°
ANT. Nay, good my lord, be not angry.
GON. No, I warrant you, I will not adventure my discretion so weakly.°
Will you laugh me asleep, for I am very heavy?
ANT. Go sleep, and hear us.

[*All sleep except* ALONSO, SEBASTIAN, *and* ANTONIO.]

ALON. What, all so soon asleep! I wish mine eyes
Would, with themselves, shut up my thoughts. I find
They are inclined to do so.
SEB. Please you, sir,
Do not omit the heavy offer° of it.
It seldom visits sorrow. When it doth,
It is a comforter.
ANT. We, two, my lord,
Will guard your person while you take your rest,
And watch your safety.
ALON. Thank you.—Wondrous heavy.
[ALONSO *sleeps. Exit* ARIEL.]
SEB. What a strange drowsiness possesses them!
ANT. It is the quality° o' the climate.
SEB. Why
Doth it not then our eyelids sink? I find not
Myself disposed to sleep.
ANT. Nor I. My spirits are nimble.
They fell together all, as by consent,
They dropped as by a thunderstroke. What might,
Worthy Sebastian?—Oh, what might?—No more.—
And yet methinks I see it in thy face,
What thou shouldst be. The occasion speaks thee,° and
My strong imagination sees a crown
Dropping upon thy head.
SEB. What, art thou waking?°

181. *An*: if. *flat-long*: on the flat side of the sword. 182. *mettle*: material, stuff. 183. *sphere*: course. 185. *batfowling*: hunting for birds at night with the aid of torches and sticks or bats. 187–88. *adventure . . . weakly*: risk my reputation as a discreet man so easily, by showing anger at such as you. 194. *omit . . . offer*: do not lose this chance of sleeping. 200. *quality*: nature. 207. *occasion . . . thee*: opportunity calls you. 209. *waking*: awake.

ANT. Do you not hear me speak?
SEB. I do, and surely
It is a sleepy language, and thou speak'st
Out of thy sleep. What is it thou didst say?
This is a strange repose, to be asleep
With eyes wide-open—standing, speaking, moving,
And yet so fast asleep.
ANT. Noble Sebastian,
Thou let'st thy fortune sleep—die, rather—wink'st
Whiles thou art waking.
SEB. Thou dost snore distinctly.
There's meaning in thy snores.
ANT. I am more serious than my custom. You
Must be so too, if heed me,° which to do
Trebles thee o'er.°
SEB. Well, I am standing water.°
ANT. I'll teach you how to flow.°
SEB. Do so. To ebb
Hereditary sloth instructs me.
ANT. Oh,
If you but knew how you the purpose cherish
Whiles thus you mock it! How, in stripping it,
You more invest it! Ebbing men, indeed,
Most often do so near the bottom run
By their own fear or sloth.°
SEB. Prithee, say on.
The setting° of thine eye and cheek proclaim
A matter° from thee, and a birth, indeed,
Which throes thee much to yield.°
ANT. Thus, sir.
Although this lord of weak remembrance, this,°
Who shall be of as little memory
When he is earthed, hath here almost persuaded—
For he's a spirit of persuasion, only
Professes to persuade—the King his son's alive,
'Tis as impossible that he's undrowned
As he that sleeps here swims.
SEB. I have no hope
That he's undrowned.
ANT. Oh, out of that "no hope"

220. *if . . . me*: if you will listen to me. 221. *Trebles . . . o'er*: makes you three times the man you are. *standing water*: i.e., at the turning of the tide, which for a while neither ebbs nor flows. 222. *flow*: advance (like the rising tide). 224–28. *If . . . sloth*: if you would only realize how much you are moved by the prospect of becoming King, even while you mock it; how in stripping it of its glamour you make it more attractive. *Ebbing men* (i.e., the lazy and unambitious) often run aground through fear or sloth. 229. *setting*: expression. 230. *matter*: something serious. 231. *throes . . . yield*: is very painful to bring forth. 232. *this . . . this*: i.e., Francisco. See ll 113–122.

What great hope have you! No hope that way is
Another way so high a hope that even
Ambition cannot pierce a wink beyond,
But doubt discovery there.° Will you grant with me
That Ferdinand is drowned?

SEB. He's gone.

ANT. Then tell me,
Who's the next heir of Naples?

SEB. Claribel.

ANT. She that is Queen of Tunis, she that dwells
Ten leagues beyond man's life,° she that from Naples
Can have no note, unless the sun were post°—
The man i' the moon's too slow—till newborn chins
Be rough and razorable.° She that from whom
We all were sea-swallowed, though some cast° again,
And by that destiny, to perform an act
Whereof what's past is prologue, what to come,
In yours and my discharge.°

SEB. What stuff is this! How say you?
'Tis true, my brother's daughter's Queen of Tunis,
So is she heir of Naples, 'twixt which regions
There is some space.

ANT. A space whose every cubit
Seems to cry out, "How shall that Claribel
Measure us° back to Naples? Keep° in Tunis,
And let Sebastian wake." Say this were death
That now hath seized them—why, they were no worse
Than now they are. There be that can rule Naples
As well as he that sleeps, lords that can prate
As amply and unnecessarily
As this Gonzalo. I myself could make
A chough of as deep chat.° Oh, that you bore
The mind that I do! What a sleep were this
For your advancement! Do you understand me?

SEB. Methinks I do.

ANT. And how does your content
Tender your own good fortune?

SEB. I remember
You did supplant your brother Prospero.

ANT. True.
And look how well my garments sit upon me,

240–43. *No . . . there*: i.e., your certainty that the true heir is drowned gives you a greater hope in another direction (i.e., of being King yourself), where even your ambition cannot look higher. 247. *Ten . . . life*: ten leagues farther than a man could travel in his lifetime. 248. *post*: messenger. 249–50. *newborn . . . razorable*: i.e., newborn children are grown men. 251. *cast*: vomited up. 254. *discharge*: task to be performed. 259. *Measure us*: retrace her journey after us. *Keep*: let her remain. 266. *chough . . . chat*: I could make a jackdaw (*chough*, rhyming with rough) talk as profoundly as he does.

Much feater° than before. My brother's servants
Were then my fellows,° now they are my men.°

SEB. But—for your conscience.

ANT. Aye, sir, where lies that? It 'twere a kibe,
'Twould put me to my slipper.° But I feel not
This deity in my bosom. Twenty consciences,
That stand 'twixt me and Milan, candied be they,
And melt ere they molest!° Here lies your brother,
No better than the earth he lies upon
If he were that which now he's like, that's dead.
Whom I, with this obedient steel, three inches of it,
Can lay to bed forever whiles you, doing thus,
To the perpetual wink° for aye might put
This ancient morsel, this Sir Prudence who
Should not upbraid our course. For all the rest
They'll take suggestion as a cat laps milk,
They'll tell the clock to° any business that
We say befits the hour.

SEB. Thy case, dear friend,
Shall be my precedent. As thou got'st Milan,
I'll come by Naples. Draw thy sword. One stroke
Shall free thee from the tribute which thou payest,
And I the King shall love thee.

ANT. Draw together,
And when I rear my hand, do you the like,
To fall° it on Gonzalo.

SEB. Oh, but one word.

[*They talk apart.*]

[*Re-enter* ARIEL, *invisible.*]

ARI. My master through his art foresees the danger
That you, his friend, are in, and sends me forth—
For else his project dies—to keep them living.

[*Sings in* GONZALO'S *ear.*]

"While you here do snoring lie,
Open-eyed conspiracy
His time° doth take.
If of life you keep a care,
Shake off slumber, and beware.
Awake, awake!"

ANT. Then let us both be sudden.

GON. Now, good angels

273. *feater*: more trimly. 274. *fellows*: equals. *men*: servants. 276–77. *kibe . . . slipper*: a chilblain which would make me wear a slipper. 278–80. *Twenty . . . molest*: i.e., if twenty consciences had stood between me and the dukedom of Milan, I should have let them melt like candy before they would have disturbed me. Other editors take "candied" to mean "frozen." 285. *perpetual wink*: everlasting sleep. 289. *tell . . . to*: say it is time for. 296. *fall*: let fall. 302. *time*: opportunity.

Preserve the King! [*They wake.*]
ALON. Why, how now? Ho, awake!—Why are you drawn?
Wherefore this ghastly looking?
GON. What's the matter?
SEB. Whiles we stood here securing° your repose,
Even now, we heard a hollow burst of bellowing
Like bulls, or rather lions. Did 't not wake you?
It struck mine ear most terribly.
ALON. I heard nothing.
ANT. Oh, 'twas a din to fright a monster's ear,
To make an earthquake! Sure, it was the roar
Of a whole herd of lions.
ALON. Heard you this, Gonzalo?
GON. Upon mine honor, sir, I heard a humming,
And that a strange one too, which did awake me.
I shaked you, sir, and cried. As mine eyes opened
I saw their weapons drawn.—There was a noise,
That's verily.° 'Tis best we stand upon our guard,
Or that we quit this place. Let's draw our weapons.
ALON. Lead off this ground, and let's make further search
For my poor son.
GON. Heavens keep him from these beasts!
For he is sure i' th' island.
ALON. Lead away.
ARI. Prospero my lord shall know what I have done.
So, King, go safely on to seek thy son. [*Exeunt.*]

SCENE II.

Another part of the island.

[*Enter* CALIBAN *with a burden of wood. A noise of thunder heard.*]

CAL. All the infections that the sun sucks up
From bogs, fens, flats, on Prosper fall, and make him
By inchmeal° a disease! His spirits hear me,
And yet I needs must curse. But they'll nor pinch,
Fright me with urchin shows,° pitch me i' the mire,
Nor lead me, like a firebrand,° in the dark
Out of my way, unless he bid 'em. But
For every trifle are they set upon me—
Sometime like apes, that mow° and chatter at me,
And after bite me; then like hedgehogs, which
Lie tumbling in my barefoot way and mount°
Their pricks at my footfall. Sometime am I

310. *securing*: keeping safe. 321. *verily*: truth.
Sc. ii: 3. *inchmeal*: by inches. 5. *urchin shows*: the appearance of goblins. See I.ii.326. 6. *firebrand*: will-o'-the-wisp. 9. *mow*: make faces. 11. *mount*: raise.

All wound with adders, who with cloven tongues
Do hiss me into madness.

[*Enter* TRINCULO.]

Lo, now, lo!
Here comes a spirit of his, and to torment me
For bringing wood in slowly. I'll fall flat.
Perchance he will not mind me.

TRIN. Here's neither bush nor shrub to bear off any weather at all, and another storm brewing, I hear it sing i' the wind. Yond same black cloud, yond huge one, looks like a foul bombard° that would shed his liquor. If it should thunder as it did before, I know not where to hide my head. Yond same cloud cannot choose but fall by pailfuls. What have we here? A man or a fish? Dead or alive? A fish—he smells like a fish, a very ancient and fishlike smell, a kind of not of the newest Poor John.° A strange fish! Were I in England now, as once I was, and had but this fish painted,° not a holiday fool there but would give a piece of silver. There would this monster make a man°—any strange beast there makes a man. When they will not give a doit° to relieve a lame beggar, they will lay out ten to see a dead Indian. Legged like a man! And his fins like arms! Warm, o' my troth! I do now let loose my opinion, hold it no longer—this is no fish, but an islander that hath lately suffered by a thunderbolt. [*Thunder.*] Alas, the storm is come again! Best way is to creep under his gaberdine,° there is no other shelter hereabout. Misery acquaints a man with strange bedfellows. I will here shroud° till the dregs of the storm be past.

[*Enter* STEPHANO, *singing, a bottle in his hand.*]

STE. "I shall no more to sea, to sea,
Here shall I die ashore——"
This is a very scurvy° tune to sing at a man's funeral.
Well, here's my comfort. [*Drinks. Sings.*]
"The master, the swabber, the boatswain, and I,
The gunner, and his mate,
Loved Mall, Meg, and Marian, and Margery,
But none of us cared for Kate.
For she had a tongue with a tang,°
Would cry to a sailor, Go hang!
She loved not the savor° of tar nor of pitch,
Yet a tailor might scratch her where'er she did itch.
Then, to sea, boys, and let her go hang!"
This is a scurvy tune too, but here's my comfort. [*Drinks.*]

CAL. Do not torment me.—Oh!

21. *bombard*: large black leathern jug for carrying liquor. 27. *Poor John*: dried salt hake. 29. *had . . . painted*: had a poster of this fish painted. 31. *make a man*: i.e., his fortune. 32. *doit*: a small Dutch coin, a cent. 39. *gaberdine*: cloak. 41. *shroud*: cover myself. 46. *scurvy*: "lousy." 52. *tang*: a sharp sound. 54. *savor*: taste.

STE. What's the matter? Have we devils here? Do you put tricks
upon 's with salvages° and men of Ind,° ha? I have not 'scaped
drowning to be afeard now of your four legs, for it hath been said,
As proper° a man as ever went on four legs cannot make him 62
give ground. And it shall be said so again while Stephano breathes
at nostrils.

CAL. The spirit torments me.—Oh! 66

STE. This is some monster of the isle with four legs, who hath got, as
I take it, an ague.° Where the devil should he learn our language?
I will give him some relief, if it be but for that. If I can recover°
him, and keep him tame, and get to Naples with him, he's a present for any emperor that ever trod on neat's leather.° 73

CAL. Do not torment me, prithee, I'll bring my wood home faster.

STE. He's in his fit now, and does not talk after the wisest. He shall
taste of my bottle. If he have never drunk wine afore, it will go near
to remove his fit. If I can recover him, and keep him tame, I will
not take too much for him.° He shall pay for him that hath him,
and that soundly. 81

CAL. Thou dost me yet but little hurt, thou wilt anon, I know it by
thy trembling.° Now Prosper works upon thee. 84

STE. Come on your ways. Open your mouth, here is that which will
give language to you, cat. Open your mouth, this will shake your
shaking, I can tell you, and that soundly. You cannot tell who's
your friend. Open your chaps° again. 89

TRIN. I should know that voice. It should be—but he is drowned,
and these are devils.—Oh, defend me! 92

STE. Four legs and two voices—a most delicate monster! His forward voice, now, is to speak well of his friend, his backward voice
is to utter foul speeches and to detract. If all the wine in my bottle
will recover him, I will help his ague. Come.—Amen! I will pour
some in thy other mouth. 99

TRIN. Stephano!

STE. Doth thy other mouth call me? Mercy, mercy! This is a devil
and no monster. I will leave him, I have no long spoon.° 103

TRIN. Stephano! If thou beest Stephano, touch me, and speak to me,
for I am Trinculo—be not afeard—thy good friend Trinculo.

STE. If thou beest Trinculo, come forth. I'll pull thee by the lesser
legs. If any be Trinculo's legs, these are they. Thou art very
Trinculo indeed! How camest thou to be the siege° of this mooncalf?° Can he vent Trinculos? 111

TRIN. I look him to be killed with a thunderstroke. But art thou not

60. *salvages*: savages. 60–61. *men of Ind*: natives of India. 63. *proper*: fine. 68. *ague*: fever, which makes him shiver. 71. *recover*: cure. 73. *neat's leather*: i.e., shoes. 79–80. *I . . . him*: I'll not take even an excessive price. 83. *trembling*: Trinculo is the trembler, for he believes that the voice of Stephano comes from a ghost. Trinculo is a natural coward. 89. *chaps*: chops, jaws. 103. *I . . . spoon*: "He that sups with the Devil needs a long spoon"—a proverb from the time when men dipped into a common dish. A long spoon was needed, as the Devil's claws were long and sharp, and his table manners nasty. 110. *siege*: excrement. *mooncalf*: misshapen monster, freak.

drowned, Stephano? I hope, now, thou art not drowned. Is the storm overblown? I hid me under the dead mooncalf's gaberdine for fear of the storm. And art thou living, Stephano? O Stephano, two Neapolitans 'scaped!

STE. Prithee do not turn me about, my stomach is not constant.°

CAL. [*Aside*] These be fine things, an if they be not sprites.
That's a brave god, and bears celestial liquor.
I will kneel to him.

STE. How didst thou 'scape? How camest thou hither? Swear, by this bottle, how thou camest hither. I escaped upon a butt of sack,° which the sailors heaved o'erboard, by this bottle, which I made of the bark of a tree with mine own hands, since I was cast ashore.

CAL. I'll swear upon that bottle to be thy true subject, for the liquor is not earthly.

STE. Here, swear, then, how thou escapedst.

TRIN. Swam ashore, man, like a duck. I can swim like a duck, I'll be sworn.

STE. Here, kiss the book. Though thou canst swim like a duck, thou art made like a goose.

TRIN. O Stephano, hast any more of this?

STE. The whole butt, man. My cellar is in a rock by the seaside, where my wine is hid. How now, mooncalf! How does thine ague?

CAL. Hast thou not dropped from Heaven?

STE. Out o' the moon, I do assure thee. I was the man 'i the moon when time was.°

CAL. I have seen thee in her, and I do adore thee. My mistress showed me thee, and thy dog, and thy bush.°

STE. Come, swear to that, kiss the book. I will furnish it anon with new contents. Swear.

TRIN. By this good light, this is a very shallow monster! I afeard of him! A very weak monster! The man i' the moon! A most poor credulous monster! Well drawn,° monster, in good sooth!°

CAL. I'll show thee every fertile inch o' th' island,
And I will kiss thy foot. I prithee be my god.

TRIN. By this light, a most perfidious and drunken monster!
When's god's asleep, he'll rob his bottle.

CAL. I'll kiss thy foot, I'll swear myself thy subject.

STE. Come on, then, down, and swear.

TRIN. I shall laugh myself to death at this puppy-headed monster. A most scurvy monster! I could find in my heart to beat him——

STE. Come, kiss.

TRIN. But that the poor monster's in drink. An abominable monster!

CAL. I'll show thee the best springs, I'll pluck thee berries,

119. *constant*: steady. Trinculo is pawing him all over, and turning him round in his excitement. 125. *sack*: a dry wine from Spain. For Falstaff on the merits of sack, see *II Hen IV,* IV.iii.102–35. 142. *when . . . was*: once upon a time. 144–45. *thee . . . bush*: the man in the moon had his dog and bush of thorns, as Quince knew. See *MND,* III.i.60. 151. *drawn*: sucked. *sooth*: truth.

I'll fish for thee, and get thee wood enough.
A plague upon the tyrant that I serve!
I'll bear him no more sticks, but follow thee,
Thou wondrous man.

TRIN. A most ridiculous monster, to make a wonder of a poor drunkard!

CAL. I prithee let me bring thee where crabs° grow.
And I with my long nails will dig thee pignuts,°
Show thee a jay's nest, and instruct thee how
To snare the nimble marmoset.° I'll bring thee
To clustering filberts, and sometimes I'll get thee
Young scamels° from the rock. Wilt thou go with me?

STE. I prithee now, lead the way, without any more talking. Trinculo, the King and all our company else being drowned, we will inherit here. Here, bear my bottle, fellow Trinculo, we'll fill him by and by again.

CAL. [*Sings drunkenly.*]

"Farewell, master, farewell, farewell!"

TRIN. A howling monster, a drunken monster!

CAL. "No more dams I'll make for fish.
Nor fetch in firing
At requiring,
Nor scrape trencher,° nor wash dish.
'Ban, 'Ban, Cacaliban
Has a new master.—Get a new man."

Freedom, heyday! Heyday, freedom! Freedom, heyday, freedom!

STE. O brave monster! Lead the way. [*Exeunt.*]

ACT III

SCENE I.

Before PROSPERO'S *cell.*

[*Enter* FERDINAND, *bearing a log.*]

FER. There be some sports are painful, and their labor
Delight in them sets off.° Some kinds of baseness
Are nobly undergone, and most poor matters
Point° to rich ends. This my mean task
Would be as heavy to me as odious, but

171. *crabs*: crab apples. 172. *pignut*: called also earthnut, a plant producing edible tubers. 174. *marmoset*: kind of small monkey. 176. *scamels*: a much-discussed word which does not occur elsewhere and so has been variously interpreted or emended, the likeliest guess being *seamel:* sea gull. 187. *trencher*: wooden plate.

ACT III, SC. i: 1–2. *their . . . off*: the delight which they bring outweighs the fatigue. 4. *Point*: lead.

The mistress which I serve quickens° what's dead
And makes my labors pleasures. Oh, she is
Ten times more gentle than her father's crabbèd,
And he's composed of harshness. I must remove
Some thousands of these logs, and pile them up,
Upon a sore injunction.° My sweet mistress
Weeps when she sees me work, and says such baseness
Had never like executor.° I forget.
But these sweet thoughts do even refresh my labors,
Most busy lest when I do it.°

[*Enter* MIRANDA, *and* PROSPERO *at a distance,° unseen.*]

MIRA. Alas, now, pray you
Work not so hard. I would the lightning had
Burned up those logs that you are enjoined to pile!
Pray set it down and rest you. When this burns,
'Twill weep° for having wearied you. My father
Is hard at study, pray now, rest yourself.
He's safe for these three hours.
FER. O most dear mistress,
The sun will set before I shall discharge
What I must strive to do.
MIRA. If you'll sit down,
I'll bear your logs the while. Pray give me that,
I'll carry it to the pile.
FER. No, precious creature,
I had rather crack my sinews, break my back,
Than you should such dishonor undergo
While I sit lazy by.
MIRA. It would become me
As well as it does you. And I should do it
With much more ease, for my goodwill is to it,
And yours it is against.
PRO. Poor worm, thou art infected!
This visitation° shows it.
MIRA. You look wearily.
FER. No, noble mistress, 'tis fresh morning with me
When you are by at night. I do beseech you—
Chiefly that I might set it in my prayers—
What is your name?
MIRA. Miranda.—O my father,

6. *quickens*: brings to life. 11. *injunction*: a command enforced with penalties against disobedience. 13. *executor*: performer. 15. *Most . . . it*: This line has been much discussed and may be corrupt. It means apparently "I am most busy when I am idle, for then I think so many sweet thoughts." *lest*: least. [s.d.] *and . . . distance*: F1 simply reads "Enter Miranda and Prospero." They obviously do not enter together, and on the Elizabethan stage probably Prospero entered on the balcony above, as later (III.iii.19). The balcony was a most convenient place for eavesdroppers. 19. *weep*: i.e., drip with sap when burning. 32. *visitation*: visit.

I have broke your hest° to say so!
FER. Admired Miranda!°
Indeed the top° of admiration! Worth
What's dearest to the world! Full many a lady
I have eyed with best regard, and many a time
The harmony of their tongues hath into bondage
Brought my too diligent ear. For several° virtues
Have I liked several women, never any
With so full soul but some defect in her
Did quarrel with the noblest grace she owed,
And put it to the foil.° But you, oh, you,
So perfect and so peerless, are created
Of every creature's best!
MIRA. I do not know
One of my sex, no woman's face remember
Save, from my glass, mine own. Nor have I seen
More that I may call men than you, good friend,
And my dear father. How features are abroad,
I am skill-less of.° But, by my modesty,
The jewel in my dower, I would not wish
Any companion in the world but you,
Nor can imagination form a shape
Besides yourself to like of. But I prattle
Something too wildly, and my father's precepts
I therein do forget.
FER. I am, in my condition,
A prince, Miranda, I do think, a king—
I would not so!—and would no more endure
This wooden slavery° than to suffer
The flesh fly blow° my mouth. Hear my soul speak.
The very instant that I saw you did
My heart fly to your service, there resides,
To make me slave to it, and for your sake
Am I this patient logman.
MIRA. Do you love me?
FER. O Heaven, O earth, bear witness to this sound,
And crown what I profess with kind event°
If I speak true! If hollowly, invert
What best is boded° me to mischief! I,
Beyond all limit of what else i' the world,
Do love, prize, honor you.
MIRA. I am a fool
To weep at what I am glad of.

37. *hest*: command. *Admired Miranda*: a play on her name, for *miranda* in Latin means "she who ought to be wondered at." "Admired" at this time had a stronger meaning than today. 38. *top*: summit. 42. *several*: separate, individual. 46. *put . . . foil*: bring it to disgrace. 52–53. *features . . . of*: I have no experience of how people look elsewhere. 62. *wooden slavery*: i.e., task of having to carry wood. 63. *blow*: lay its eggs on, foul. 69. *event*: result. 71. *What . . . boded*: the best fate that is prophesied.

PRO. Fair encounter
Of two most rare affections! Heavens rain grace
On that which breeds between 'em!

FER. Wherefore weep you?

MIRA. At mine unworthiness, that dare not offer
What I desire to give, and much less take
What I shall die to want.° But this is trifling,
And all the more it seeks to hide itself,
The bigger bulk it shows. Hence, bashful cunning!
And prompt me, plain and holy innocence!
I am your wife, if you will marry me.
If not, I'll die your maid. To be your fellow°
You may deny me, but I'll be your servant,
Whether you will or no.

FER. My mistress, dearest,
And I thus humble ever.

MIRA. My husband, then?

FER. Aye, with a heart as willing°
As bondage e'er of freedom. Here's my hand.

MIRA. And mine, with my heart in 't. And now farewell
Till half an hour hence.

FER. A thousand thousand!°

[*Exeunt* FERDINAND *and* MIRANDA *severally.*°]

PRO. So glad of this as they I cannot be,
Who° are surprised withal,° but my rejoicing
At nothing can be more. I'll to my book,
For yet ere suppertime must I perform
Much business appertaining. [*Exit.*]

SCENE II.

Another part of the island.

[*Enter* CALIBAN, STEPHANO, *and* TRINCULO.]

STE. Tell not me.—When the butt is out, we will drink water, not a drop before. Therefore bear up,° and board 'em. Servant-monster, drink to me.

TRIN. Servant-monster! The folly of this island!° They say there's but five upon this isle. We are three of them. If th' other two be brained like us, the state totters.

STE. Drink, servant-monster, when I bid thee. Thy eyes are almost set° in thy head.

TRIN. Where should they be set else? He were a brave monster indeed if they were set in his tail.

79. *want*: be without. 84. *fellow*: equal. See II.i.274. 88. *willing*: eager. 91. *thousand thousand*: i.e., farewells. [s.d.] *severally*: by different exists. 93. *Who*: i.e., Ferdinand and Miranda. *withal*: therewith.

Sc. ii: 2. *bear up*: crowd on more sail. 5. *The . . . island*: what a silly place this island is. 10. *set*: closed, dazed with drink.

STE. My man-monster hath drowned his tongue in sack. For my part, the sea cannot drown me. I swam, ere I could recover the shore, five-and-thirty leagues° off and on. By this light, thou shalt be my lieutenant, monster, or my standard.°

TRIN. Your lieutenant, if you list. He's no standard.

STE. We'll not run, Monsieur Monster.

TRIN. Nor go neither, but you'll lie, like dogs, and yet say nothing neither.

STE. Mooncalf, speak once in thy life, if thou beest a good mooncalf.

CAL. How does thy Honor? Let me lick thy shoe. I'll not serve him, he is not valiant.

TRIN. Thou liest, most ignorant monster. I am in case° to jostle a constable. Why, thou deboshed° fish thou, was there ever man a coward that hath drunk so much sack as I today? Wilt thou tell a monstrous lie, being but half a fish and half a monster?

CAL. Lo, how he mocks me! Wilt thou let him, my lord?

TRIN. "Lord," quoth he! That a monster should be such a natural!°

CAL. Lo, lo, again! Bite him to death, I prithee.

STE. Trinculo, keep a good tongue in your head. If you prove a mutineer—the next tree! The poor monster's my subject, and he shall not suffer indignity.

CAL. I thank my noble lord. Wilt thou be pleased to hearken once again to the suit I made to thee?

STE. Marry,° will I. Kneel and repeat it. I will stand, and so shall Trinculo.

[*Enter* ARIEL, *invisible.*]

CAL. As I told thee before, I am subject to a tyrant, a sorcerer, that by his cunning hath cheated me of the island.

ARI. Thou liest.

CAL. Thou liest,° thou jesting monkey thou.
I would my valiant master would destroy thee!
I do not lie.

STE. Trinculo, if you trouble him any more in 's tale, by this hand, I will supplant° some of your teeth.

TRIN. Why, I said nothing.

STE. Mum, then, and no more. Proceed.

CAL. I say, by sorcery he got this isle.
From me he got it. If thy greatness will
Revenge it on him—for I know thou darest,
But this thing dare not—

STE. That's most certain.

CAL. Thou shalt be lord of it, and I'll serve thee.

STE. How now shall this be compassed?°

15. *league*: three miles. 17. *standard*: standard-bearer (or ensign), the junior officer in the company, the others being the captain and the lieutenant. Caliban is now too unsteady to be a satisfactory *standard*. 29. *in case*: in a condition. *deboshed*: debauched. 38. *natural*: born fool. 46. *Marry*: Mary, by the Virgin. 52. *Thou liest*: Caliban supposes the voice to be Trinculo's. 56. *supplant*: displace. 66. *compassed*: brought about.

Canst thou bring me to the party?

CAL. Yea, yea, my lord. I'll yield him thee asleep, Where thou mayst knock a nail into his head.

ARI. Thou liest, thou canst not.

CAL. What a pied ninny's° this! Thou scurvy patch!°
I do beseech thy greatness, give him blows,
And take his bottle from him. When that's gone,
He shall drink naught but brine, for I'll not show him
Where the quick freshes° are.

STE. Trinculo, run into no further danger. Interrupt the monster one word further and, by this hand, I'll turn my mercy out o' doors and make a stockfish° of thee.

TRIN. Why, what did I? I did nothing. I'll go farther off.

STE. Didst thou not say he lied?

ARI. Thou liest.

STE. Do I so? Take thou that. [*Beats him.*] As you like this, give me the lie° another time.

TRIN. I did not give the lie. Out o' your wits, and hearing too? A pox o' your bottle! This can sack and drinking do. A murrain° on your monster, and the devil take your fingers!

CAL. Ha, ha, ha!

STE. Now, forward with your tale.—Prithee, stand farther off.

CAL. Beat him enough. After a little time
I'll beat him too.

STE. Stand farther.—Come, proceed.

CAL. Why, as I told thee, 'tis a custom with him
I' th' afternoon to sleep. There thou mayst brain him,
Having first seized his books, or with a log
Batter his skull, or paunch° him with a stake,
Or cut his weasand° with thy knife. Remember
First to possess his books, for without them
He's but a sot, as I am, nor hath not
One spirit to command. They all do hate him
As rootedly° as I. Burn but his books.
He has brave utensils°—for so he calls them—
Which, when he has a house, he'll deck withal.
And that most deeply to consider is
The beauty of his daughter. He himself
Calls her a nonpareil.° I never saw a woman
But only Sycorax my dam and she,
But she as far surpasseth Sycorax
As great'st does least.

STE. Is it so brave a lass?

71. *pied ninny*: patched fool, because Trinculo as a jester wears motley, the "patched" or particolored dress of his profession. *patch*: fool. 75. *quick freshes*: running springs of fresh water. 79. *stockfish*: dried, salted cod, beaten to make it tender. 85. *give . . . lie*: call me a liar. 88. *murrain*: plague. 98. *paunch*: stab him in the belly. 99. *weasand*: windpipe. 103. *rootedly*: fixedly. 104. *utensils*: furnishings. 108. *nonpareil*: without an equal.

CAL. Aye, lord, she will become thy bed, I warrant, And bring thee forth brave brood.

STE. Monster, I will kill this man. His daughter and I will be King and Queen—save our Graces!—and Trinculo and thyself shall be Viceroys. Dost thou like the plot, Trinculo?

TRIN. Excellent.

STE. Give me thy hand. I am sorry I beat thee, but while thou livest keep a good tongue in thy head.

CAL. Within this half-hour will he be asleep.
Wilt thou destroy him then?

STE. Aye, on mine honor.

ARI. This will I tell my master.

CAL. Thou makest me merry, I am full of pleasure.
Let us be jocund. Will you troll° the catch°
You taught me but whilere?°

STE. At thy request, monster, I will do reason,° any reason.—
Come on, Trinculo, let us sing.
[*Sings*.] "Flout° 'em and scout° 'em,
And scout 'em and flout 'em.
Thought is free."

CAL. That's not the tune.

[ARIEL *plays the tune on a tabor° and pipe*.]

STE. What is this same?

TRIN. This is the tune of our catch, played by the picture of Nobody.°

STE. If thou beest a man, show thyself in thy likeness. If thou beest a devil, take 't as thou list.

TRIN. Oh, forgive me my sins!

STE. He that dies pays all debts. I defy thee. Mercy upon us!

CAL. Art thou afeard?

STE. No, monster, not I.

CAL. Be not afeard. The isle is full of noises,°
Sounds and sweet airs that give delight and hurt not.
Sometimes a thousand twangling instruments
Will hum about mine ears, and sometime voices
That, if I then had waked after long sleep,
Will make me sleep again. And then, in dreaming,
The clouds methought would open and show riches
Ready to drop upon me, that when I waked,
I cried to dream again.

STE. This will prove a brave kingdom to me, where I shall have my music for nothing.

CAL. When Prospero is destroyed.

STE. That shall be by and by.° I remember the story.

126. *troll*: sing. *catch*: See *T Night*, II.iii.60,n. 127. *whilere*: just now. 128. *reason*: anything within reason. 130. *Flout*: mock. *scout*: deride. 133. [s.d.] *tabor*: small drum. 136. *picture of Nobody*: i.e., by an invisible player. There is a picture of Nobody in a play called *Nobody and Some-body*, printed 1606. It is all head and no body, like Humpty Dumpty. 144. *noises*: music. 156. *by . . . by*: in the near future.

TRIN. The sound is going away. Let's follow it, and after do our work.
STE. Lead, monster, we'll follow. I would I could see this taborer, he lays it on.
TRIN. Wilt come? I'll follow, Stephano. [*Exeunt.*]

SCENE III.

Another part of the island.

[*Enter* ALONSO, SEBASTIAN, ANTONIO, GONZALO, ADRIAN, FRANCISCO, *and others.*]

GON. By'r Lakin,° I can go no further, sir.
My old bones ache. Here's a maze trod, indeed,
Through forthrights and meanders!° By your patience,
I needs must rest me.
ALON. Old lord, I cannot blame thee,
Who am myself attached with° weariness,
To the dulling of my spirits. Sit down and rest.
Even here I will put off my hope, and keep it
No longer for my flatterer. He is drowned
Whom thus we stray to find, and the sea mocks
Our frustrate° search on land. Well, let him go.
ANT. [*Aside to* SEBASTIAN] I am right glad that he's so out of hope.
Do not, for one repulse, forgo the purpose
That you resolved to effect.
SEB. [*Aside to* ANTONIO] The next advantage
Will we take throughly.°
ANT. [*Aside to* SEBASTIAN] Let it be tonight,
For now they are oppressed with travel, they
Will not, nor cannot, use such vigilance
As when they are fresh.
SEB. [*Aside to* ANTONIO] I say tonight. No more.

[*Solemn and strange music.*]

ALON. What harmony is this?—My good friends, hark!
GON. Marvelous sweet music!

[*Enter* PROSPERO *above, invisible. Enter several strange Shapes, bringing in a banquet.*° *They dance about it with gentle actions of salutation, and, inviting the King, etc., to eat, they depart.*]

ALON. Give us kind keepers, Heavens!—What were these?
SEB. A living drollery.° Now° I will believe
That there are unicorns, that in Arabia

Sc. iii: 1. *By'r Lakin*: by Our Lady. 2–3. *Here's . . . meanders*: we have wandered as in a maze by straight paths (*forthrights*) and winding paths (*meanders*). 5. *attached with*: overcome by; lit., arrested. 10. *frustrate*: vain. 14. *throughly*: thoroughly. 19. [s.d.] *banquet*: light refreshments, such as fruit and jellies. 21. *drollery*: puppet show. 21–27. *Now . . . 'em*: i.e., after this we can believe any fantastic traveler's yarn.

There is one tree, the phoenix'° throne, one phoenix
At this hour reigning there.

ANT. I'll believe both,
And what does else want credit,° come to me
And I'll be sworn 'tis true. Travelers ne'er did lie,
Though fools at home condemn 'em.

GON. If in Naples
I should report this now, would they believe me?
If I should say I saw such islanders—
For, certes,° these are people of the island—
Who, though they are of monstrous shape, yet note,
Their manners are more gentle-kind than of
Our human generation° you shall find
Many—nay, almost any.

PRO. [*Aside*] Honest lord,
Thou hast said well, for some of you there present
Are worse than devils.

ALON. I cannot too much muse°
Such shapes, such gesture, and such sound, expressing—
Although they want the use of tongue—a kind
Of excellent dumb discourse.

PRO. [*Aside*] Praise in departing.°

FRAN. They vanished strangely.

SEB. No matter, since
They have left their viands behind, for we have stomachs.—
Will 't please you taste of what is here?

ALON. Not I.

GON. Faith, sir, you need not fear. When we were boys,
Who would believe that there were mountaineers
Dewlapped° like bulls, whose throats had hanging at 'em
Wallets of flesh? Or that there were such men
Whose heads stood in their breasts?° Which now we find
Each putter-out of five for one° will bring us
Good warrant of.

23. *phoenix*: a mythical bird. According to the legend only one phoenix was alive at a time. It lived for five hundred years. Then it built itself a nest of spices, which were set alight by the rapid beating of its wings. From the ashes a new phoenix was born. 25. *want credit*: is not believed. 30. *certes*: certainly. 33. *generation*: breed. 36. *muse*: wonder at. 39. *Praise in departing*: a proverb meaning "Don't give thanks for your entertainment until you see how it will end." 45. *Dewlapped*: having folds of loose skin hanging from the throat. 46–47. *men . . . breasts*: Sir Walter Raleigh in his account of Guiana (1595) noted "a nation of people whose heads appear not above their shoulders; which though it may be thought a mere fable, yet for mine own part I am resolved it is true, because every child in the provinces of Arromaia and Canuri affirms the same. They are called Ewaipanoma. They are reported to have their eyes in their shoulders, and their mouths in the middle of their breasts, and that a long train of hair groweth backward between their shoulders." 48. *putter-out . . . one*: In Shakespeare's time voyages to distant and strange ports were so risky that the traveler sometimes left a sum of money with a merchant at home on condition that he should receive five times the amount if he returned; if he did not, the premium was forfeited.

ALON. I will stand to and feed,
Although my last. No matter, since I feel
The best is past. Brother, my lord the Duke,
Stand to, and do as we.

[*Thunder and lightning. Enter* ARIEL, *like a harpy,*° *claps his wings upon the table, and, with a quaint device,*° *the banquet vanishes.*]

ARI. You are three men of sin, whom Destiny—
That hath to instrument this lower world
And what is in 't°—the never-surfeited° sea
Hath caused to belch up you. And on this island,
Where man doth not inhabit—you 'mongst men
Being most unfit to live. I have made you mad,
And even with suchlike valor men hang and drown
Their proper° selves

[ALONZO, SEBASTIAN, *etc., draw their swords.*]

You fools! I and my fellows
Are ministers of Fate. The elements
Of whom your swords are tempered may as well
Wound the loud winds, or with bemocked-at stabs
Kill the still-closing° waters, as diminish
One dowle° that's in my plume.° My fellow ministers
Are like invulnerable. If you could hurt,
Your swords are now too massy° for your strengths,
And will not be uplifted. But remember—
For that's my business to you—that you three
From Milan did supplant good Prospero,
Exposed unto the sea, which hath requit° it,
Him and his innocent child. For which foul deed
The powers, delaying not forgetting, have
Incensed the seas and shores—yea, all the creatures—
Against your peace. Thee of thy son, Alonso,
They have bereft, and do pronounce by me
Lingering perdition°—worse than any death
Can be at once—shall step by step attend
You and your ways. Whose wraths to guard you from—
Which here, in this most desolate isle, else falls
Upon your heads—is nothing but° heart sorrow
And a clear° life ensuing.

52. [s.d.] *harpy*: a foul creature, half bird of prey, half woman. This episode was suggested by an event in Virgil's *Aeneid* when the harpies seize and foul the food of Aeneas and his followers. *quaint device*: piece of ingenious stage machinery. 53–55. *Destiny . . . in 't*: Destiny (Providence), which uses this world below and its powers as its instrument. 55. *never-surfeited*: never overfull. A surfeit is an excess of food. Even the sea, which can retain most things, cannot stomach Alonso and his fellow sinners. 60. *proper*: own. 64. *still-closing*: always closing up; i.e., which cannot be wounded. 65. *dowle*: downy feather. *plume*: wing. 67. *massy*: heavy. 71. *requit*: paid back. 77. *perdition*: destruction. 81. *is . . . but*: i.e., only repentance will guard you from destruction. 82. *clear*: innocent.

[*He vanishes in thunder; then, to soft music, enter the Shapes again, and dance, with mocks° and mows,° and carrying out the table.*]

PRO. Bravely the figure of this harpy hast thou
Performed, my Ariel, a grace it had, devouring.°
Of my instruction hast thou nothing bated°
In what thou hadst to say. So, with good life°
And observation° strange,° my meaner ministers°
Their several kinds° have done. My high charms work,
And these mine enemies are all knit up°
In their distractions.° They now are in my power,
And in these fits I leave them while I visit
Young Ferdinand—whom they suppose is drowned—
And his and mine loved darling. [*Exit above.*]

GON. I' the name of something holy, sir, why stand you
In this strange stare?

ALON. Oh, it is monstrous, monstrous!
Methought the billows spoke, and told me of it,
The winds did sing it to me, and the thunder,
That deep and dreadful organ pipe, pronounced
The name of Prosper. It did bass my trespass.°
Therefore my son i' th' ooze is bedded, and
I'll seek him deeper than e'er plummet° sounded,
And with him there lie mudded. [*Exit.*]

SEB. But one fiend at a time,
I'll fight their legions o'er.

ANT. I'll be thy second.
[*Exeunt* SEBASTIAN *and* ANTONIO.]

GON. All three of them are desperate. Their great guilt,
Like poison given to work a great time after,
Now 'gins to bite the spirits. I do beseech you
That are of suppler joints, follow them swiftly,
And hinder them from what this ecstasy°
May now provoke them to.

ADR. Follow, I pray you. [*Exeunt.*]

[s.d.] *mocks*: mocking gestures. *mows*: grimaces. 84. *grace . . . devouring*: the action of devouring was splendidly (*bravely*) performed. 85. *bated*: abated, left out. 86. *with . . . life*: realistically. 87. *observation*: obedience. *strange*: unusual. *meaner ministers*: lesser servants. 88. *several kinds*: particular tasks. 89. *knit up*: entangled. 90. *distractions*: fits of madness. 99. *bass my trespass*: proclaim my sin in a deep note. 101. *plummet*: the lead weight at the end of a cord used by sailors to discover the depth of the water. 108. *ecstasy*: mad fit. See *Haml*, III.iv.137–44.

ACT IV

SCENE I.

Before PROSPERO'S *cell.*

[*Enter* PROSPERO, FERDINAND, *and* MIRANDA.]

PRO. If I have too austerely punished you,
Your compensation makes amends. For I
Have given you here a third° of mine own life,
Or that for which I live, who once again
I tender° to thy hand. All thy vexations
Were but my trials of thy love, and thou
Hast strangely° stood the test. Here, afore Heaven,
I ratify this my rich gift. O Ferdinand,
Do not smile at me that I boast her off,°
For thou shalt find she will outstrip all praise
And make it halt° behind her.
FER. I do believe it
Against an oracle.°
PRO. Then, as my gift, and thine own acquistion
Worthily purchased, take my daughter. But
If thou dost break her virgin knot before
All sanctimonious° ceremonies may
With full and holy rite be ministered,
No sweet aspersion° shall the Heavens let fall
To make this contract grow;° but barren hate,
Sour-eyed disdain, and discord shall bestrew
The union of your bed with weeds so loathly
That you shall hate it both. Therefore take heed,
As Hymens° lamps shall light you.
FER. As I hope
For quiet days, fair issue,° and long life,
With such love as 'tis now, the murkiest den,
The most opportune place, the strong'st suggestion°
Our worser genius° can, shall never melt
Mine honor into lust, to take away
The edge of that day's celebration
When I shall think or Phoebus' steeds are foundered,
Or Night kept chained below.°

ACT IV, SC. i: 3. *third*: i.e., a great part of. 5. *tender*: hand over. 7. *strangely*: exceptionally. 9. *boast . . . off*: boast about her. 11. *halt*: come limping; i.e., she will excel all praise. 12. *Against an oracle*: i.e., even if a god had said the contrary. 16. *sanctimonious*: religious. 18. *aspersion*: blessing; lit., sprinkling. 19. *grow*: prosper. 23. *Hymen*: the god of marriage. 24. *issue*: children. 26. *suggestion*: temptation. 27. *worser genius*: evil angel. 30–31. *or . . . below*: either the horses of the Sun have fallen or Night has been imprisoned; i.e., my wedding day, when night seems never to come.

PRO. Fairly spoke.
Sit, then, and talk with her, she is thine own.
What, Ariel! My industrious servant, Ariel!

[*Enter* ARIEL.]

ARI. What would my potent master? Here I am.
PRO. Thou and thy meaner fellows your last service
Did worthily perform, and I must use you
In such another trick. Go bring the rabble,
O'er whom I give thee power, here to this place.
Incite them to quick motion, for I must
Bestow upon the eyes of this young couple
Some vanity° of mine art. It is my promise,
And they expect it from me.
ARI. Presently?°
PRO. Aye, with a twink.°
ARI. Before you can say, "come," and "go,"
And breathe twice and cry, "so, so,"
Each one, tripping on his toe,
Will be here with mop° and mow.
Do you love me, master? No?
PRO. Dearly, my delicate Ariel. Do not approach
Till thou dost hear me call.
ARI. Well, I conceive.° [*Exit.*]
PRO. Look thou be true. Do not give dalliance°
Too much the rein. The strongest oaths are straw
To the fire i' the blood. Be more abstemious,
Or else, good night your vow!
FER. I warrant you, sir,
The white cold virgin snow upon my heart
Abates the ardor of my liver.°
PRO. Well.
Now come, my Ariel! Bring a corollary°
Rather than want° a spirit. Appear, and pertly!°
No tongue! All eyes! Be silent. [*Soft music.*]

[*Enter* IRIS.°]

IRIS. Ceres,° most bounteous lady, thy rich leas°
Of wheat, rye, barley, vetches, oats, and pease;
Thy turfy mountains, where live nibbling sheep,

41. *vanity*: display. 42. *Presently*: at once. 43. *twink*: the twinkling of an eye. 47. *mop*: grimace. 50. *conceive*: understand. 51. *dalliance*: fondling. 56. *liver*: passion. The liver was regarded as the seat of passion. 57. *corollary*: excess; i.e., too many rather than too few. 58. *want*: be without. *pertly*: briskly. 59. [s.d.] *Enter Iris*: Prospero now produces a little wedding masque in honor not only of the lovers, Ferdinand and Miranda, but as a compliment to the Princess Elizabeth and her bridegroom before whom *The Tempest* was acted in 1613. *Iris*: the female messenger of the gods, also the personification of the rainbow. 60. *Ceres*: goddess of corn and plenty. *leas*: arable lands.

And flat meads° thatched with stover,° them to keep;
Thy banks with pioned and twilled brims,°
Which spongy April at thy hest° betrims°
To make cold nymphs chaste crowns; and thy broom° groves,
Whose shadow the dismissed° bachelor loves,
Being lasslorn;° thy pole-clipped° vineyard;
And thy sea marge,° sterile and rocky-hard,
Where thou thyself dost air—the Queen o' the Sky,°
Whose watery arch° and messenger am I,
Bids thee leave these, and with her sovereign grace,
Here on this grassplot, in this very place,
To come and sport.—Her peacocks° fly amain.°
Approach, rich Ceres, her to entertain.

[*Enter* CERES.]

CER. Hail, many-colored messenger, that ne'er
Dost disobey the wife of Jupiter;
Who, with thy saffron° wings, upon my flowers
Diffusest honey drops, refreshing showers,
And with each end of thy blue bow dost crown
My bosky° acres and my unshrubbed down,°
Rich scarf° to my proud earth.—Why hath thy Queen
Summoned me hither, to this short-grassed green?
IRIS. A contract of true love to celebrate,
And some donation° freely to estate°
On the blest lovers.
CER. Tell me, heavenly bow,
If Venus or her son, as thou dost know,
Do now attend the Queen? Since they did plot
The means that dusky Dis° my daughter got,
Her and her blind boy's° scandaled° company
I have forsworn.
IRIS. Of her society
Be not afraid. I met Her Deity
Cutting the clouds towards Paphos,° and her son
Dove-drawn° with her. Here thought they to have done
Some wanton charm upon this man and maid,

63. *meads*: meadows. *thatched . . . stover*: covered over with grass for fodder. 64. *pioned . . . brims*: a difficult phrase, much disputed and emended. The likeliest explanation is that *pioned* means dug, and *twilled,* heaped up; i.e., with high banks. 65. *hest*: command. *betrims*: trims with wild flowers, especially kingcups, a kind of buttercup that grows by streams. 66. *broom*: a shrub with yellow flowers. 67. *dismissed*: rejected. 68. *lasslorn*: without his girl. *pole-clipped*: poles embraced by vines. 69. *sea marge*: seashore. 70. *Queen . . . Sky*: the goddess Juno, wife of Jupiter. 71. *watery arch*: i.e., the rainbow. 74. *peacocks*: birds sacred to Juno. *amain*: swiftly. 78. *saffron*: yellow. 81. *bosky*: wooded. *unshrubbed down*: rolling open country, without shrubs. 82. *scarf*: adornment. 85. *donation*: present. *estate*: donate. 89. *dusky Dis*: Pluto, god of the underworld, and so dark. He seized Ceres' daughter Persephone and carried her down to his kingdom. 90. *blind boy*: Cupid. *scandaled*: scandalous. 93. *Paphos*: in Sicily, a town sacred to Venus. 94. *Dove-drawn*: in a chariot drawn by doves.

Whose vows are, that no bedright shall be paid
Till Hymen's torch° be lighted. But in vain,
Mars's hot minion° is returned again.
Her waspish-headed° son has broke his arrows,
Swears he will shoot no more, but play with sparrows,
And be a boy right out.

CER. High'st Queen of state,
Great Juno, comes. I know her by her gait.

[*Enter* JUNO.]

JUNO. How does my bounteous sister? Go with me
To bless this twain, that they may prosperous be,
And honored in their issue.

[*They sing.*]

JUNO. "Honor, riches, marriage blessing,
Long continuance, and increasing,
Hourly joys be still° upon you!
Juno sings her blessings on you."

CER. "Earth's increase, foison° plenty,
Barns and garners never empty,
Vines with clustering bunches growing,
Plants with goodly burden bowing,
Spring come to you at the farthest
In the very end of harvest!°
Scarcity and want shall shun you,
Ceres' blessing so is on you."

FER. This is a most majestic vision, and
Harmonious charmingly. May I be bold
To think these spirits?

PRO. Spirits which by mine art
I have from their confines° called to enact
My present fancies.°

FER. Let me live here ever.
So rare a wondered° father and a wise
Makes this place Paradise.

[JUNO *and* CERES *whisper, and send* IRIS *on employment.*]

PRO. Sweet, now silence!
Juno and Ceres whisper seriously,
There's something else to do. Hush, and be mute,
Or else our spell is marred.

IRIS. You nymphs, called Naiads,° of the windring° brooks,

97. *Hymen's torch*: The torches of the wedding god were lit to escort bride and bridegroom to bed. 98. *Mars's . . . minion*: Mars' lusty darling; i.e., Venus. 99. *waspish-headed*: quick-tempered. 108. *still*: always. 110. *foison*: bounteous harvest. 114–115. *Spring . . . harvest*: may spring follow autumn; i.e., may there be no bitterness of winter in your lives. Cf. *Ant & Cleo*, V.ii.86–88 for a similar image. 121. *confines*: places of confinement. 122. *fancies*: devices of my imagination. 123. *wondered*: wonderful. 128. *Naiads*: water nymphs. *windring*: wandering, winding.

With your sedged° crowns and ever-harmless looks,
Leave your crisp° channels, and on this green land
Answer your summons. Juno does command.
Come, temperate° nymphs, and help to celebrate
A contract of true love. Be not too late.

[*Enter certain* NYMPHS.]

You sunburned sicklemen,° of August weary,
Come hither from the furrow, and be merry.
Make holiday, your rye-straw hats put on,
And these fresh nymphs encounter every one
In country footing.°

[*Enter certain* REAPERS, *properly habited. They join with the* NYMPHS *in a graceful dance, towards the end whereof* PROSPERO *starts suddenly, and speaks. After which, to a strange, hollow, and confused noise, they heavily° vanish.*]

PRO. [*Aside*] I had forgot that foul conspiracy
Of the beast Caliban and his confederates
Against my life. The minute of their plot
Is almost come. [*To the* SPIRITS] Well done! Avoid,° no more!
FER. This is strange. Your father's in some passion
That works him strongly.
MIRA. Never till this day
Saw I him touched with anger so distempered.°
PRO. You do look, my son, in a movèd sort,°
As if you were dismayed. Be cheerful, sir.
Our revels now are ended. These our actors,
As I foretold you, were all spirits, and
Are melted into air, into thin air.
And, like the baseless fabric° of this vision,
The cloud-capped towers, the gorgeous palaces,
The solemn temples, the great globe itself—
Yea, all which it inherit—shall dissolve
And, like this insubstantial pageant faded,
Leave not a rack° behind. We are such stuff
As dreams are made on, and our little life
Is rounded° with a sleep. Sir, I am vexed.
Bear with my weakness, my old brain is troubled.
Be not disturbed with my infirmity.
If you be pleased, retire into my cell,
And there repose. A turn or two I'll walk,

129. *sedged*: covered with sedge, a kind of water grass. 130. *crisp*: curled, rippling. 132. *temperate*: chaste. 134. *sicklemen*: reapers, who cut the wheat with sickles. 138. *footing*: dancing. s.d., *heavily*: sorrowfully. 142. *Avoid*: be gone. 145. *distempered*: disturbed. 146. *moved sort*: as if you were distressed. 151. *baseless fabric*: unreal stuff. 156. *rack*: cloud. 158. *rounded*: completed; i.e., life is but a moment of consciousness in an everlasting sleep.

To still my beating° mind.
FER. & MIRA. We wish your peace. [*Exeunt.*]
PRO. Come with a thought. I thank thee, Ariel.
Come.

[*Enter* ARIEL.]

ARI. Thy thoughts I cleave to. What's thy pleasure?
PRO. Spirit,
We must prepare to meet with Caliban.
ARI. Aye, my commander. When I presented° Ceres,
I thought to have told thee of it, but I feared
Lest I might anger thee.
PRO. Say again, where didst thou leave these varlets?°
ARI. I told you, sir, they were red-hot with drinking,
So full of valor that they smote the air
For breathing in their faces, beat the ground
For kissing of their feet, yet always bending°
Toward their project. Then I beat my tabor.
At which, like unbacked° colts, they pricked their ears,
Advanced their eyelids, lifted up their noses
As° they smelt music. So I charmed their ears,
That, calflike, they my lowing followed through
Toothed briers, sharp furzes,° pricking goss,° and thorns
Which entered their frail shins. At last I left them
I' the filthy-mantled° pool beyond your cell,
There dancing up to the chins, that the foul lake
O'erstunk their feet.
PRO. This was well done, my bird.
Thy shape invisible retain thou still.
The trumpery° in my house, go bring it hither,
For stale° to catch these thieves.
ARI. I go, I go. [*Exit.*]
PRO. A devil, a born devil, on whose nature
Nurture° can never stick, on whom my pains,
Humanely taken, all, all lost, quite lost.
And as with age his body uglier grows,
So his mind cankers.° I will plague them all,
Even to roaring.

[*Re-enter* ARIEL, *loaden with glistering° apparel, etc.*]

Come, hang them on this line.°

163. *beating*: throbbing. Cf. I.ii.176. 167. *presented*: either introduced the masques or acted the part of Ceres. There is, however, very little time for a change of costume between Ariel's exit at l. 50 and Ceres' entry at l. 75. 170. *varlets*: knaves. 174. *bending*: inclining. 176. *unbacked*: never saddled. 178. *As*: as if. 180. *furzes*: See I.i.72,n. *goss*: gorse. 182. *filthy-mantled*: covered with scum. 186. *trumpery*: cheap finery. 187. *stale*: bait. 189. *Nurture*: education. 192. *cankers*: grows malignant. 193. [s.d.] *glistering*: glittering. *line*: lime tree.

[PROSPERO *and* ARIEL *remain, invisible. Enter* CALIBAN, STEPHANO, *and* TRINCULO, *all wet.*]

CAL. Pray you, tread softly, that the blind mole may not
Hear a footfall. We now are near his cell.

STE. Monster, your fairy, which you say is a harmless fairy, has done little better than played the jack° with us.

TRIN. Monster, I do smell all horse piss, at which my nose is in great indignation.

STE. So is mine. Do you hear, monster? If I should take a displeasure against you, look you—

TRIN. Thou wert but a lost monster.

CAL. Good my lord, give me thy favor still.
Be patient, for the prize I'll bring thee to
Shall hoodwink this mischance.° Therefore speak softly.
All's hushed as midnight yet.

TRIN. Aye, but to lose our bottles in the pool—

STE. There is not only disgrace and dishonor in that, monster, but an infinite loss.

TRIN. That's more to me than my wetting. Yet this is your harmless fairy, monster.

STE. I will fetch off° my bottle, though I be o'er ears° for my labor.

CAL. Prithee, my King, be quiet. See'st thou here,
This is the mouth o' the cell. No noise, and enter.
Do that good mischief which may make this island
Thine own forever, and I, thy Caliban,
For aye thy footlicker.

STE. Give me thy hand. I do begin to have bloody thoughts.

TRIN. O King Stephano!° O peer! O worthy Stephano! Look what a wardrobe here is for thee!

CAL. Let it alone, thou fool, it is but trash.

TRIN. Oh ho, monster! We know what belongs to a frippery.° O King Stephano!

STE. Put off that gown, Trinculo. By this hand, I'll have that gown.

TRIN. Thy Grace shall have it.

CAL. The dropsy drown this fool! What do you mean
To dote thus on such luggage?° Let's alone,
And do the murder first. If he awake
From toe to crown he'll fill our skins with pinches,
Make us strange stuff.

STE. Be you quiet, monster. Mistress° line, is not this my jerkin? Now is the jerkin under the line. Now, jerkin, you are like to lose your hair and prove a bald jerkin.

TRIN. Do, do. We steal by line and level, an 't like your Grace.

197. *jack*: knave. 206. *hoodwink . . . mischance*: blindfold this misfortune; i.e., make us forget it. 213. *fetch off*: rescue. 214. *o'er ears*: up to my ears in the pond. 222. *O . . . Stephano*: The sight of all the clothes reminds Trinculo of the old ballad "King Stephen was a worthy peer." See *Oth*, II.iii.92–99. 226. *frippery*: secondhand-clothes shop. 231. *luggage*: baggage, which will hinder them. 235–40. *Mistress . . .*

STE. I thank thee for that jest—here's a garment for 't. Wit shall not go unrewarded while I am King of this country. "Steal by line and level" is an excellent pass of pate°—there's another garment for 't.

TRIN. Monster, come, put some lime° upon your fingers, and away with the rest.

CAL. I will have none on 't. We shall lose our time,
And all be turned to barnacles,° or to apes
With foreheads villainous low.

STE. Monster, lay to your fingers. Help to bear this away where my hogshead of wine is, or I'll turn you out of my kingdom. Go to, carry this.

TRIN. And this.

STE. Aye, and this.

[*A noise of hunters heard. Enter divers* SPIRITS, *in shape of dogs and hounds, hunting them about,* PROSPERO *and* ARIEL *setting them on.*]

PRO. Hey, Mountain, hey!

ARI. Silver! There it goes, Silver!

PRO. Fury, Fury! There, Tyrant,° there! Hark, hark!

[CALIBAN, STEPHANO, *and* TRINCULO *are driven out.*]

Go charge my goblins that they grind their joints
With dry convulsions. Shorten up their sinews
With agèd cramps,° and more pinch-spotted make them
Than pard° or cat-o'-mountain.°

ARI. Hark, they roar!

PRO. Let them be hunted soundly. At this hour
Lie at my mercy all mine enemies.
Shortly shall all my labors end, and thou
Shalt have the air at freedom. For a little
Follow, and do me service. [*Exeunt.*]

Grace: These lines have mystified editors, and indeed elaborate Elizabethan jokes, especially when made by a half-drunk butler, are not always easy to follow. Stephano begins by addressing the lime tree as "Mistress Line" as if he were talking to the dealer in an old-clothes shop. He appeals to her to decide whether the jerkin is his or Trinculo's. Having taken the jerkin for himself, he then puns on "under the line" (i.e., south of the Equator), where the various skin diseases common to long voyages in the tropics caused hair to fall out. Trinculo caps the remark by a further pun on "line and level"; i.e., "on the square," lit., by the bricklayer's instruments for ensuring perpendicular and horizontal exactness. 245. *pass of pate*: sally of wit. 246. *lime*: birdlime, to make them sticky, because Caliban disgustedly drops the garments. 249. *barnacles*: tree geese. It was believed, even by serious botanists, that from the barnacles, which grow on rotten wood immersed in sea water, emerged creatures which grew into birds like geese. 256-58. *Mountain . . . Silver . . . Fury . . . Tyrant*: the names of the hounds. 261 *aged cramps*: the cramps which come with old age. 262. *pard*: leopard. *cat-o'-mountain*: mountain cat.

ACT V

SCENE I.

Before the cell of PROSPERO.

[*Enter* PROSPERO *in his magic robes, and* ARIEL.]

PRO. Now does my project gather to a head.
My charms crack not,° my spirits obey, and Time
Goes upright with his carriage.° How's the day?
ARI. On the sixth hour, at which time, my lord,
You said our work should cease.
PRO. I did say so
When first I raised the tempest. Say, my spirit,
How fares the King and 's followers?
ARI. Confined together
In the same fashion as you gave in charge,
Just as you left them—all prisoners, sir,
In the line grove° which weather-fends° your cell.
They cannot budge till your release. The King,
His brother, and yours abide all three distracted,
And the remainder mourning over them,
Brimful of sorrow and dismay. But chiefly
Him that you termed, sir, "The good old lord, Gonzalo."
His tears run down his beard like winter's drops
From eaves of reeds.° Your charm so strongly works 'em
That if you now beheld them, your affections
Would become tender.
PRO. Dost thou think so, spirit?
ARI. Mine would, sir, were I human.
PRO. And mine shall.
Hast thou, which art but air, a touch, a feeling
Of their afflictions, and shall not myself,
One of their kind, that relish° all as sharply,
Passion° as they, be kindlier moved than thou art?
Though with their high wrongs I am struck to the quick,
Yet with my nobler reason 'gainst my fury
Do I take part. The rarer action is
In virtue than in vengeance.° They being penitent,
The sole drift° of my purpose doth extend
Not a frown further. Go release them, Ariel.
My charms I'll break, their senses I'll restore,
And they shall be themselves.

ACT V, SC. i: 2. *crack not*: do not break down. 2–3. *Time . . . carriage*: Time bears his burden without stooping, because it has now grown so light. 10. *line grove*: grove of lime trees. *weather-fends*: protects from the weather. 17. *eaves of reeds*: a thatched roof. 23. *relish*: feel. 24. *Passion*: suffer emotion. 27–28. *rarer . . . vengeance*: it is a finer action to be self-controlled than to take vengeance. 29. *drift*: intention.

ARI. I'll fetch them, sir. [*Exit.*]
PRO. Ye elves of hills, brooks, standing lakes, and groves,
And ye that on the sands with printless foot°
Do chase the ebbing Neptune° and do fly him
When he comes back; you demipuppets° that
By moonshine do the green sour° ringlets° make,
Whereof the ewe not bites; and you whose pastime
Is to make midnight mushrooms° that rejoice
To hear the solemn curfew,° by whose aid—
Weak masters though ye be—I have bedimmed
The noontide sun, called forth the mutinous winds,
And 'twixt the green sea and the azured vault°
Set roaring war. To the dread rattling thunder
Have I given fire, and rifted° Jove's stout oak
With his own bolt. The strong-based promontory
Have I made shake, and by the spurs° plucked up
The pine and cedar. Graves at my command
Have waked their sleepers, oped, and let 'em forth
By my so potent art. But this rough magic
I here abjure, and when I have required
Some heavenly music—which even now I do—
To work mine end upon their senses, that
This airy charm is for, I'll break my staff,
Bury it certain fathoms in the earth,
And deeper than did ever plummet° sound
I'll drown my book.° [*Solemn music.*]

[*Re-enter* ARIEL *before; then* ALONSO, *with a frantic gesture, attended by* GONZALO; SEBASTIAN *and* ANTONIO *in like manner, attended by* ADRIAN *and* FRANCISCO. *They all enter the circle which* PROSPERO *had made, and there stand charmed, which* PROSPERO *observing, speaks:*]

A solemn air,° and the best comforter
To an unsettled fancy, cure thy brains,
Now useless, boiled° within thy skull! There stand,
For you are spell-stopped.
Holy Gonzalo, honorable man,
Mine eyes, even sociable° to the show of thine,
Fall° fellowly° drops. The charm dissolves apace,°
And as the morning steals upon the night,

34. *printless foot*: without leaving a footprint. 35. *ebbing Neptune*: i.e., the outgoing tide. 36. *demipuppets*: tiny creatures, half the size of a puppet. 37. *sour*: i.e., unacceptable to the cattle. *ringlets*: fairy rings, circles of grass of a darker green often seen in English meadows, supposed to be caused by the fairies dancing in a ring. 39. *midnight mushrooms*: As mushrooms grow in a single night, they were thought to be the work of fairies. 40. *curfew*: rung at 9 P.M. to warn people to go indoors. Thereafter the fairies can work without interruption. 43. *azured vault*: blue sky. 45. *rifted*: split. 47. *spurs*: roots. 56. *plummet*: See III.iii.101,n. 57. *book*: i.e., of magic spells. 58. *air*: musical air. 60. *boiled*: boiling. Cf. *MND*, V.i.4, "Lovers and madmen have such seething brains." 63. *sociable*: of fellow feeling. 64. *Fall*: let fall. *fellowly*: in sympathy. *apace*: quickly.

Melting the darkness, so their rising senses
Begin to chase the ignorant fumes° that mantle°
Their clearer reason. O good Gonzalo,
My true preserver, and a loyal sir
To him thou follow'st! I will pay thy graces
Home° both in word and deed. Most cruelly
Didst thou, Alonso, use me and my daughter.
Thy brother was a furtherer in the act.
Thou art pinched for 't now, Sebastian. Flesh and blood,
You, brother mine, that entertained ambition,
Expelled remorse° and nature, who with Sebastian—
Whose inward pinches therefore are most strong—
Would here have killed your King, I do forgive thee,
Unnatural though thou art. Their understanding
Begins to swell, and the approaching tide
Will shortly fill the reasonable shore°
That now lies foul and muddy. Not one of them
That yet looks on me, or would know me. Ariel,
Fetch me the hat and rapier in my cell.
I will discase° me, and myself present
As I was sometime Milan.° Quickly, spirit.
Thou shalt ere long be free.

ARI. [*Sings and helps to attire him.*]

"Where the bee sucks, there suck I.
In a cowslip's bell I lie,
There I couch° when owls do cry.
On the bat's back I do fly
After summer merrily.
Merrily, merrily shall I live now
Under the blossom that hangs on the bough."

PRO. Why, that's my dainty Ariel! I shall miss thee,
But yet thou shalt have freedom. So, so, so.°
To the King's ship, invisible as thou art.
There shalt thou find the mariners asleep
Under the hatches. The master and the boatswain
Being awake, enforce them to this place,
And presently, I prithee.

ARI. I drink the air before me, and return
Or ere your pulse twice beat. [*Exit.*]

GON. All torment, trouble, wonder, and amazement
Inhabits here. Some heavenly power guide us
Out of this fearful country!

67. *ignorant fumes*: mists of ignorance. *mantle*: cloak. 70–71. *pay . . . Home*: reward your kind deeds fully. 76. *remorse*: pity. 81. *reasonable shore*: shore of reason; i.e., sanity is beginning to flow back like the incoming tide. 85. *discase*: remove my outer garment. Prospero is still in his magic robe and so not recognized by his former associates. 86. *As . . . Milan*: as I was when I was Duke of Milan. 90. *couch*: lie. 96. *So, so, so*: "so," used thus, often indicates movement. Cf. *Lear,* III.vi.90.

PRO. Behold, Sir King,
The wrongèd Duke of Milan, Prospero.
For more assurance that a living prince
Does now speak to thee, I embrace thy body,
And to thee and thy company I bid
A hearty welcome.

ALON. Whether thou be'st he or no,
Or some enchanted trifle° to abuse° me,
As late I have been, I not know. Thy pulse
Beats, as of° flesh and blood, and since I saw thee,
The affliction of my mind amends, with which,
I fear, a madness held me. This must crave—
An if this be at all°—a most strange story.
Thy dukedom I resign, and do entreat
Thou pardon me my wrongs.°—But how should Prospero
Be living and be here?

PRO. First, noble friend,
Let me embrace thine age, whose honor cannot
Be measured or confined.

GON. Whether this be
Or be not, I'll not swear.

PRO. You do yet taste
Some subtilties° o' the isle, that will not let you
Believe things certain. Welcome, my friends all!
[*Aside to* SEBASTIAN *and* ANTONIO] But you, my brace of lords, were I so minded,
I here could pluck His Highness' frown upon you,
And justify you traitors. At this time
I will tell no tales.

SEB. [*Aside*] The Devil speaks in him.

PRO. No.
For you, most wicked sir, whom to call brother
Would even infect my mouth, I do forgive
Thy rankest fault—all of them—and require
My dukedom of thee, which perforce I know
Thou must restore.

ALON. If thou be'st Prospero,
Give us particulars of thy preservation—
How thou hast met us here, who three hours since
Were wrecked upon this shore, where I have lost—
How sharp the point of this remembrance is!—
My dear son Ferdinand.

PRO. I am woe for't,° sir.

ALON. Irreparable is the loss, and Patience
Says it is past her cure.

112. *enchanted trifle*: hallucination caused by enchantment. *abuse*: deceive. 114. *as of*: as if composed of. 117. *An . . . all*: if this is really true. 119. *my wrongs*: the wrongs which I have committed. 123–24. *You . . . subtilties*: you still have the taste of the magic nature. 139. *woe for't*: sorry for it.

PRO. I rather think
You have not sought her help of whose soft grace
For the like loss I have her sovereign° aid,
And rest myself content.
ALON. You the like loss!
PRO. As great to me as late, and, supportable
To make the dear loss, have I means much weaker
Than you may call to comfort you, for I
Have lost my daughter.
ALON. A daughter?
O Heavens, that they were living both in Naples,
The King and Queen there! That they were, I wish
Myself were mudded in that oozy bed
Where my son lies. When did you lose your daughter?
PRO. In this last tempest. I perceive these lords
At this encounter do so much admire°
That they devour their reason, and scarce think
Their eyes do offices of truth,° their words
Are natural breath. But howsoe'er you have
Been jostled from your senses, know for certain
That I am Prospero, and that very Duke
Which was thrust forth of Milan, who most strangely
Upon this shore where you were wrecked was landed,
To be the lord on 't. No more yet of this,
For 'tis a chronicle of day by day,
Not a relation for a breakfast, nor
Befitting this first meeting. Welcome, sir.
This cell's my Court. Here have I few attendants,
And subjects none abroad. Pray you look in.
My dukedom since you have given me again,
I will requite° you with as good a thing,
At least bring forth a wonder to content ye
As much as me my dukedom.

[*Here* PROSPERO *discovers*° FERDINAND *and* MIRANDA *playing at chess.*]

MIRA. Sweet lord, you play me false.
FER. No, my dear'st love,
I would not for the world.
MIRA. Yes, for a score of kingdoms you should wrangle,
And I would call it fair play.
ALON. If this prove
A vision of the island, one dear son
Shall I twice lose.

143. *sovereign*: all-powerful. 154. *admire*: wonder. 156. *offices of truth*: true service. 169. *requite*: pay back. 171. [s.d.] *discovers*: reveals by drawing back the curtain.

SEB. A most high miracle!
FER. Though the seas threaten, they are merciful.
I have cursed them without cause. [*Kneels.*]
ALON. Now all the blessings
Of a glad father compass thee about!
Arise, and say how thou camest here.
MIRA. Oh, wonder!
How many goodly creatures are there here!
How beauteous mankind is! Oh, brave new world,
That has such people in 't!
PRO. 'Tis new to thee.
ALON. What is this maid with whom thou wast at play?
Your eld'st° acquaintance cannot be three hours.
Is she the goddess that hath severed us,
And brought us thus together?
FER. Sir, she is mortal,
But by immortal Providence she's mine.
I chose her when I could not ask my father
For his advice, nor thought I had one. She
Is daughter to this famous Duke of Milan,
Of whom so often I have heard renown
But never saw before, of whom I have
Received a second life, and second father
This lady makes him to me.
ALON. I am hers.
But oh, how oddly will it sound that I
Must ask my child° forgiveness!
PRO. There, sir, stop.
Let us not burden our remembrances with
A heaviness that's gone.
GON. I have inly wept,
Or should have spoke ere this. Look down, you gods,
And on this couple drop a blessèd crown!
For it is you that have chalked forth° the way
Which brought us hither.
ALON. I say Amen, Gonzalo!
GON. Was Milan thrust from Milan, that his issue
Should become Kings of Naples? Oh, rejoice
Beyond a common joy! And set it down
With gold on lasting pillars. In one voyage
Did Claribel her husband find at Tunis
And Ferdinand, her brother, found a wife
Where he himself was lost, Prospero his dukedom
In a poor isle, and all of us ourselves
When no man was his own.
ALON. [*To* FERDINAND *and* MIRANDA] Give me your hands.

186. *eld'st*: longest. 198. *my child*: i.e., Miranda, who is about to become his daughter-in-law. 203. *chalked forth*: marked out (as with a chalk line).

Let grief and sorrow still embrace° his heart
That doth not wish you joy!

GON. Be it so! Amen!

[*Re-enter* ARIEL, *with the* MASTER *and* BOATSWAIN *amazedly° following.*]

Oh, look, sir, look, sir! Here is more of us.
I prophesied if a gallows were on land,
This fellow could not drown.° Now, blasphemy,°
That swear'st grave o'erboard,° not an oath on shore?
Hast thou no mouth by land? What is the news?

BOATS. The best news is that we have safely found
Our King and company. The next, our ship—
Which, but three glasses since, we gave out split—
Is tight and yare and bravely rigged as when
We first put out to sea.

ARI. [*Aside to* PROSPERO] Sir, all this service
Have I done since I went.

PRO. [*Aside to* ARIEL] My tricksy° spirit!

ALON. These are not natural events, they strengthen
From strange to stranger. Say, how came you hither?

BOATS. If I did think, sir, I were well awake,
I'd strive to tell you. We were dead of sleep,
And—how we know not—all clapped° under hatches,
Where, but even now, with strange and several noises
Of roaring, shrieking, howling, jingling chains,
And mo diversity of sounds, all horrible,
We were awaked, straightway at liberty.
Where we, in all her trim, freshly beheld
Our royal, good, and gallant ship, our master
Capering° to eye her.—On a trice, so please you,
Even in a dream, were we divided from them,
And were brought moping hither.

ARI. [*Aside to* PROSPERO] Was 't well done?

PRO. [*Aside to* ARIEL] Bravely, my diligence. Thou shalt be free.

ALON. This is as strange a maze as e'er men trod,
And there is in this business more than nature
Was ever conduct of. Some oracle
Must rectify° our knowledge.

PRO. Sir, my liege,
Do not infest your mind with beating on
The strangeness of this business. At picked leisure
Which shall be shortly, single° I'll resolve° you,
Which to you shall seem probable, of every

214. *still embrace*: always cling to. 215. [s.d.] *amazedly*: in amazement. 217–18. *gallows . . . drown*: see I.i.32–33. 218. *blasphemy*: you blasphemer. 219. *That . . . o'erboard*: that by your swearing drives the grace of God away. 226. *tricksy*: clever. 231. *clapped*: shut in. 238. *Capering*: dancing for joy. 245. *rectify*: prove true. 248. *single*: alone. *resolve*: inform.

These happened accidents. Till when, be cheerful,
And think of each thing well. [*Aside to* ARIEL] Come hither, spirit.
Set Caliban and his companions free,
Untie the spell. [*Exit* ARIEL.] How fares my gracious sir?
There are yet missing of your company
Some few odd lads that you remember not.

[*Re-enter* ARIEL, *driving in* CALIBAN, STEPHANO, *and* TRINCULO, *in their stolen apparel.*]

STE. Every man shift for all the rest, and let no man take care for himself, for all is but fortune.—
Coragio,° bully-monster, coragio!
TRIN. If these be true spies° which I wear in my head, here's a goodly sight.
CAL. Oh, Setebos, these be brave spirits indeed!
How fine my master is! I am afraid
He will chastise me.
SEB. Ha, ha!
What things are these, my lord Antonio?
Will money buy 'em?
ANT. Very like. One of them
Is a plain fish, and no doubt marketable.
PRO. Mark but the badges° of these men, my lords.
Then say if they be true. This misshapen knave,
His mother was a witch, and one so strong
That could control the moon, make flows and ebbs,
And deal in her command,° without her power.°
These three have robbed me, and this demidevil—
For he's a bastard one—had plotted with them
To take my life. Two of these fellows you
Must know and own, this thing of darkness I
Acknowledge mine.
CAL. I shall be pinched to death.
ALON. Is not this Stephano, my drunken butler?
SEB. He is drunk now. Where had he wine?
ALON. And Trinculo is reeling ripe. Where should they
Find this grand liquor that hath gilded 'em?°—
How camest thou in this pickle?
TRIN. I have been in such a pickle since I saw you last that I fear me will never out of my bones. I shall not fear flyblowing.°
SEB. Why, how now, Stephano!
STE. Oh, touch me not.—I am not Stephano, but a cramp.
PRO. You'd be King o' the isle, sirrah?
STE. I should have been a sore one, then.

258. *Coragio*: courage. 259. *spies*: eyes. 267. *badges*: A nobleman's servant wore a badge displaying his master's coat of arms. 271. *deal . . . command*: i.e., take over the moon's power of controlling the tides. *without . . . power*: without the aid of the moon. 280. *gilded 'em*: made them glow. 284. *fear flyblowing*: i.e., shall never go bad, for I have been so well pickled.

ALON. This is a strange thing as e'er I looked on.
[*Pointing to* CALIBAN.]
PRO. He is as disproportioned in his manners°
As in his shape. Go, sirrah, to my cell.
Take with you your companions. As you look
To have my pardon, trim° it handsomely.
CAL. Aye, that I will, and I'll be wise hereafter,
And seek for grace.° What a thrice-double ass
Was I to take this drunkard for a god
And worship this dull fool!
PRO. Go to, away!
ALON. Hence, and bestow your luggage where you found it.
SEB. Or stole it, rather.
[*Exeunt* CALIBAN, STEPHANO, *and* TRINCULO.]
PRO. Sir, I invite your Highness and your train
To my poor cell, where you shall take your rest
For this one night. Which, part of it, I'll waste
With such discourse as I not doubt shall make it
Go quick away—the story of my life,
And the particular accidents° gone by
Since I came to this isle. And in the morn
I'll bring you to your ship, and sc to Naples,
Where I have hope to see the nuptial
Of these our dear-belovèd solemnized,
And thence retire me to my Milan, where
Every third thought shall be my grave.
ALON. I long
To hear the story of your life, which must
Take the ear strangely.
PRO. I'll deliver all,
And promise you calm seas, auspicious° gales,
And sail so expeditious that shall catch
Your royal fleet far off. [*Aside to* ARIEL] My Ariel, chick,
That is thy charge. Then tc the elements
Be free, and fare thou well! Please you, draw near. [*Exeunt.*]

EPILOGUE°

SPOKEN BY PROSPERO

Now my charms are all o'erthrown,
And what strength I have's mine own,
Which is most faint. Now, 'tis true,
I must be here confined by you,

290. *manners*: behavior. 293. *trim*: make tidy. 295. *grace*: favor. 305. *accidents*: events. 314. *auspicious*: favorable.

Epilogue: A concluding epilogue is fairly common in Elizabethan plays, especially those performed before a Courtly audience. It is usually a conventional apology for

Or sent to Naples. Let me not,
Since I have my dukedom got,
And pardoned the deceiver, dwell
In this bare island by your spell,
But release me from my bands°
With the help of your good hands.°
Gentle breath° of yours my sails
Must fill, or else my project fails,
Which was to please. Now I want°
Spirits to enforce, art to enchant,
And my ending is despair
Unless I be relieved by prayer
Which pierces so that it assaults
Mercy itself, and frees all faults.
As you from crimes would pardoned be,
Let your indulgence set me free.

the inadequacies of the performance, and an appeal for applause. Cf. the epilogues in *MND, AYLI,* and *II Hen IV*. 9. *bands*: bonds. 10. *good hands*: i.e., by clapping. 11. *Gentle breath*: kindly criticism. 13. *want*: lack.

THOUGHT AND LANGUAGE

The Modes of Science and the Modes of Art

INTRODUCTION

I

FROM time immemorial the classic definition of man has been expressed in the sentence: Man is a rational animal. In this definition man is differentiated from other animals by his ability to reason, that is, by his ability to think and to speak. The two faculties are, for all practical purposes, regarded as identical. Thought is the internal word; speech is the external word, first sounded and eventually written. To express oneself is to say or write what one thinks; to speak or write is a thinking out into language. To ask—What do you think?—is to demand an answer in speech or writing. Hence in the twelfth century an early humanist, John of Salisbury, took it for granted that:

> To inquire into the effective force of speech and to investigate the truth and meaning of what is said are precisely or practically the same. A word's force consists in its meaning. Without the latter it is empty, useless, dead. Just as the soul animates the body, so, in a way, meaning breathes life into a word.

Nor are we in modern times less certain that the power of thought and language is the distinctive mark of man. Susanne Langer writes:

> The process of envisaging facts, values, hopes and fears underlies our whole behavior pattern; and this process is reflected in an extraordinary phenomenon found always, and only, in human societies—the phenomenon of language. Language is the highest and most amazing achievement of the symbolistic human mind. The power it bestows is almost inestimable, for without it anything properly called "thought" is impossible.

If thought and language are marks of man's distinctive rational power, then literature, which we may describe as man's best thoughts in man's best language, is clearly a most important measure of his achievement. In previous chapters we saw how man expresses his awareness, his aspirations, and his responses to the experiences of tragedy and comedy in and through literature. Since literature is a thinking out into language we may say that we have already touched upon the theme of this chapter. So we have.

But here we need to explore in greater detail the relationship between two modes of thought and two modes of language for reasons that become apparent as soon as we read the first three selections—Liam O'Flaherty's short story, Conrad Arensberg's essay, and G. M. Brady's poem. Common to all three is the subject, the Irish farmer. Not inconceivably, an historian might cite each work as a description of the role of the farmer seen in terms of his environment. He might notice other similarities among them, such as the poverty of the people, the interconnectedness of man and the soil, the independence of the family units.

On the other hand, a literary critic might find the three works markedly different in character. "Two Lovely Beasts" is fundamentally a story of men, specifically of Colm Derrane and his family. It leaps with feeling. Its language goes directly through ear and eye to the reader's heart. From the opening scene when Kate Higgins comes running into the Derrane kitchen, squats on the floor, and laments her dead cow, to the final scene when Derrane defies his wife and the villagers in his ruthless ambition to make money, Liam O'Flaherty speaks in the vivid rhythms and tones of country folk who are really thinking *and* feeling and acting. So, too, does G. M. Brady in his poem "The Settled Men." Here again is the story of men—not of individual men, but of successive generations of men who toil in loneliness. Its language—the compressed and suggestive language befitting a poem—reaches the heart too, though more solemnly and more reflectively.

But "Countrymen at Work" by Conrad Arensberg, for all its professed intention to clothe its subjects "in flesh and blood," is fundamentally an economic and anthropological study rather than an intimate story of men. Indeed, a literary critic who looks in this essay for evidence of *human* action might be tempted to say that Arensberg considers men as things rather than as persons, as economic or social facts rather than as the living, independent worlds of thought and feeling represented in the story of O'Flaherty and the poem of Brady.

This judgment could be made on the basis of language alone. Note how Arensberg, O'Flaherty, and Brady treat one aspect of the farmer's life.

ARENSBURG:

That the small farmer is a family man even at work is important for the study of human behaviour. Eight out of ten people working in agriculture in Ireland work not for wages and salaries but by virtue of their family relationship. The work a man does and the directions he gives and receives take form within a social group. That fact yields an opportunity for the anthropologist.

O'FLAHERTY:

The whole Derrane family received this news in open-mouthed silence. It was a calamity that affected every household in the village. Each family had but a single cow. By traditional law, those who had milk were bound to share it with those who had none. So that the death of one cow, no matter to whom she belonged, was a calamity that affected all.

"Bloody woe!" Colm said at length. "Bloody mortal woe! That's a terrible blow and you after losing your husband only the other day. There you are now with a houseful of weak children and no cow. Ah! Bloody woe!"

BRADY: Gravely, as gravely they live as the stones
That wall about their season-worried fields.
When death's encroaching wind unsettles hold
One falls, one stone, one man whose loss
Opens a door of prayer on every hearth.
Then without hesitancy or fear
Another thrusts into the vacant place.

Arensberg's language is colored by a scientific attitude. His people are classified by their "family relationship"; their actions are "facts" that yield "an opportunity for the anthropologist." While he is not unsympathetic to his subjects, neither does he respond to their sufferings. O'Flaherty and Brady also depict human behavior within a "social group." But in both cases their language focuses on the human reaction to the fact. Colm speaks for the whole human family when he cries "Bloody woe!" Brady suggests the human response to calamity when he writes of "one man whose loss / Opens a door of prayer on every hearth."

Yet it would be misleading to say that O'Flaherty and Brady demonstrate that good writing reveals the human heart and that Arensberg's prose reveals a mind deadened to human feeling. In "Countrymen at Work" Arensberg employs scientific language the better to emphasize the general condition of the class he has defined as "small farmers." In short, he speaks a language appropriate to a scientific way of thinking, just as O'Flaherty and Brady speak a language appropriate to a more intensely personal or poetic way of thinking.

Just as Arensberg's style may be inappropriate in most fiction and poetry, so the style of O'Flaherty and Brady may well be inappropriate in essays that express the thoughts of science. We say "may be" rather than "is" because, as we shall see, while scientific knowledge and poetic knowledge differ, they are not always opposed. Indeed, at the highest level—that is, in the mind of a great thinker—they are often combined in a marvelous equilibrium.

II

SCIENTIFIC knowledge, in its broadest sense, is the application of the laws of reason to the data of human experience. As T. H. Huxley points out in "The Method of Scientific Investigation," scientific knowledge is simply the mode by which we reason about phenomena precisely or exactly. That mode is then defined as the way of induction and deduction. What these two words mean is clearly indicated in the examples Huxley develops throughout his essay. The chief characteristics of scientific knowledge are care and completeness in observation and inference. By the same token the chief characteristics of a scientific style are a logical precision in the choice of words, a spelling out of details, an explicit statement of the reasons that lead up to an inference. In highly specialized scientific articles, the language is often as abstract and arid as the symbols used in mathematics. In more popular scientific expositions—and Huxley's own essay is a case in point—the language is more familiar, at times even dramatic. Nevertheless scientific language serves one main purpose—to render exactly and precisely reasonings about phenomena.

Poetic knowledge, on the other hand, is usually described as the intuitive perception of human experience—a perception in which the logical element, if it be present at all, is suffused with feeling, imagination, sensation. This kind of knowledge is less concerned with facts or, as Keats puts it, with "the consecutive reasoning of the philosopher," than it is with imagination. "O for a Life of Sensations rather than of Thoughts!" Keats writes in his letter to Benjamin Bailey. Then he speaks of the suddenness of imaginative experience, its quality of surprise, its unanalyzable delights. Thoughts of this kind cannot be as logically precise as thoughts about the way a clock works. Nor can one scrutinize the following sentence, taken from the same letter, in the same manner that one would examine the statements embodying one of Huxley's carefully developed inductions:

> If a Sparrow come before my Window I take part in its existence and pick about the Gravel.

To some, Keats's imaginative identification, or empathy, with the sparrow may seem nonsensical. Yet it expresses precisely a truth of the imagination of the kind that underlies, and inspires, his own great "Ode on a Grecian Urn." In that poem the word *urn,* for instance, is not just a word designating an object; it is a symbol, an image that stands for the permanence and tranquillity of beauty. *Urn,* used symbolically, is as precise in its way as the word *deduction* is in Huxley's essay.

At first glance then we note a significant difference between scientific knowledge and poetic knowledge. A closer scrutiny of the style of Huxley's essay and of Keats's poem points to other differences. The diction differs in tone and color. The sentences differ in rhythm and sound. The whole pattern of each composition has a different strain. The difference between scientific knowledge and poetic knowledge is further emphasized when we read Wallace Stevens' "An Ordinary Evening in New Haven," which appears to ignore the laws of consecutive reasoning as well as the precisions of logical discourse.

Yet, once we recognize these important differences, once we do not expect Huxley or Dubos to discuss the field of scientific knowledge in the manner of Keats or Stevens or, vice versa, once we do not expect Stevens to write poetry in the manner of Huxley or Dubos, we may then observe that scientific thought and poetic thought are not wholly and forever isolated from each other. Science, for example, does not disdain the imagination. Indeed it depends upon intuition no less than it does upon careful analysis and verification.

Significantly, René Dubos entitles his historical study of the rise of science "Dreams of Reason." And those dreams are intuitions that science, biology in particular, aspires to be free of mechanical restrictions. Thus Dubos writes:

> Science does not progress only by inductive, analytical knowledge. The imaginative speculations of the mind come first, the verification and the analytic breakdown come only later. And imagination depends upon a state of emotional and intellectual freedom which makes the mind receptive to the impressions that it receives from the world in its confusing, overpowering, but enriching totality. . . . I believe that in most cases the creative scientific act comes before the operations which lead to the establishment of truth; together they make science.

If scientists may, indeed must, employ creative imagination (normally regarded as the hallmark of poetry), is the reverse also true?

Can poets avail themselves of scientific modes of thought and expression and still remain poets? In "Logic and Lyric," J. V. Cunningham argues cogently that they can, and do. The point of his essay (incidentally an outstanding example of the academic or "research" paper) is that, contrary to prevailing critical assumptions, poetry, even lyric poetry, is not antithetical to reason, logic, and science. On the contrary, it may not only be "subject to logical analysis," it may also be logical in form. He argues specifically that Andrew Marvell's "To His Coy Mistress," William Dunbar's "Lament for the Makaris," and Thomas Nashe's "Adieu, farewell, earth's bliss," are all founded on that form of logical reason called syllogism. In each of the three poems, Cunningham concludes, "the experience of the poem is the experience of syllogistic thinking with its consequences for feeling, attitude, and action. . . . It is a poetical experience and a logical, and it is both at once."

Persuasive though this view is, we need not carry it beyond its proper limits. Possibly every poem may be reduced to a syllogism. But some poems and most stories and dramas follow the pattern of history rather than of logic. They attempt to answer the questions: What happened? What happened after that? Does what happened after all have a meaning? Sometimes, as we observed in our discussion of the comedy of reconciliation (p. 444), some answers are given. Sometimes, as we have seen in our discussion of the comedy of nonsense (p. 441), there is no "logical" explanation in any usual sense of the word logical. In his "A Defence of Nonsense," G. K. Chesterton reminds us that reality often has a most illogical shape. The world, he assures us, is not explainable in terms of a beneficent rationalism. It sometimes offers, rather, "a picture of huge and undecipherable unreason." One must believe and wonder at this mystery.

> Nonsense and faith (strange as the conjunction may seem) are the two supreme symbolic assertions of the truth that to draw out the soul of things with a syllogism is as impossible to draw out Leviathan with a hook.

Hence, while imaginative writers often think and write in a scientific manner, they also dream dreams and see visions and set them forth in language which, in making us understand that we do not understand, does not conform to the precisions of science.

Thus far we have been exploring the internal relationship between two modes of thought and language. We have recognized that a precise, unemotional, objective style is consonant with the scientific mode of thought, and that a more personal, vivid, emotional style is consonant with the poetic mode. We have recognized, too, that, despite their differences, the two modes of thought and language are sometimes united in a work of literature. Now we address ourselves to another aspect of the relationship between thought and language—an aspect which we will call *external* because it is concerned with the effect of traditions, conventions, or history on the development of good style.

III

In his book *English Prose Style,* Sir Herbert Read begins by stressing the importance of unity. By unity he means the identification of the mind in all its processes with language in all its processes. He finds the source of that unity in the force of the writer's predominant passion:

> The sense of the quality of words; the use of appropriate epithets and images; the organization of the period, the paragraph and the plot; the arts of exposition and of narrative; all the gifts of thought and sensibility—these are only dry perfections unless they are moved by a spirit which is neither intelligence nor emotion, but the sustained power of reason. And by reason in this context I do not mean ratiocination or rationality, but . . . "the widest evidence of the senses, and of all processes and instincts developed in the history of man. It is the sum total of awareness, ordained and ordered to some specific end or object of attention." Such a quality . . . is no innate instinct, but a conscious achievement.

Unity, then, is the result of an impassioned idea or ideal, and all great writers achieve their style not by following rules in a pedantic way but, as in the case of Swift, by the force of "a particular insight into the world, a particular view of life, a predominating passion." Thus it is, too, in the cases of Newman, James and Pater, Dryden and Addison, Johnson and Gibbon, Reynolds and Frazer. Yet, for all this emphasis on the internal relation between personal intuition and style, Read recognizes that the quality of a great writer depends not only on self-development, but also upon his assimilation of ideas outside himself. The writer molds himself, but he is in turn molded by his age, his traditions and, in the literary sense, by the state of the language. What gives his style its unity or "strain of address" is the blending of "the common tradition, the technical tradition of written English," with his personal intuition.

Edmund Wilson's essay "Is Verse a Dying Technique?" is also concerned with the question of what constitutes a good style. His special purpose is to demonstrate, by tracing the development of literary theory and practice, that "the technique of prose today seems . . . to be absorbing the technique of verse; but it is showing itself quite equal to that work of the imagination which caused men to call

Homer 'divine': that re-creation, in the harmony and logic of words, of the cruel confusion of life." Whether he succeeds in establishing his main point is disputable. But in the course of his argument he does succeed in illuminating the equally important point that the forms of literature depend in part upon shifting anthropological and sociological points of view. When, as in Greece, music and literature were learned together, literature tended to approximate the condition of music. Hence verse was a normal mode of expression. The same was true in the Elizabethan Age when poets accepted the centrality of music in poetry.

But when men cease to sing their lyrics and ballads and narratives, when, in short, they write more for the eye than for the ear, as in Augustan Rome and Augustan England, verse loses its central impulse. More recently, when the invention of the printing press coincided with the rise of vast urban populations, the novel became popular. Some novels inherited the classical features of poetry. Others, however, wore the sprawling face of popular journalism: "Their authors, no longer schooled in the literary tradition of the Renaissance, speak the practical everyday language of the dominant middle class, which has destroyed the Renaissance world." But these authors are not, for that reason, less important than the aristocratic Renaissance artists they have supplanted. They are simply different. So goes Mr. Wilson's argument.

A good style, then, is not one that is good once and for all, the same in every language and every age. It is not passed on like an heirloom, never to be altered or adjusted to the pressures of social change. Rather it is ever adapted to new uses, to a newly conceived purpose of an author, to a newly felt need of a reader or hearer, to a newly developed form of communication.

To recognize this principle of change is to protect ourselves against false assumptions about literature and the consequent false judgments of literary values. As we remarked above, we should not judge Arensberg's essay by the standards that apply to O'Flaherty's short story or to Brady's poem. Neither should we apply the same standards to a Greek tragedy and to a Dostoevsky novel. Sophocles did indeed write a perfect tragedy. In *The Brothers Karamazov* Dostoevsky did not write like Sophocles. But Dostoevsky wrote something very great in a different way for a different time.

We must be on guard, then, against supposing that literature must always appeal to us through its old forms. In his "Sight, Sound, and Fury" Marshall MacLuhan shows how the new media, newspapers, radio, films, and television, have already revolutionized our literary technique. "Have four centuries of book-culture," he asks, "hypnotized us into such concentration on the content of books and the new media that we cannot see that the very form of any medium of communication is as important as anything that it conveys?" We fail to understand Joyce, Pound, or Eliot, he implies, because we apply standards derived from the techniques of printed books and from the more ancient oral tradition. But these new writers have absorbed the techniques of the new media. Hence the reader should approach Joyce, Pound, or Eliot as they would an "historical newsreel of persons, myths, ideas, and events with [a] thematic musical score built in."

Cinematic form, as MacLuhan sees it, is a way of knowing that resembles the process of human cognition itself. Hence it reflects substantial human values. For, if we understand the process of human cognition in its full range—of sensation, memory, imagination, reason, and intuition—and if we understand the way thoughts are formed and expressed, we come close to understanding man's nature. Moreover, we encounter that nature not in the abstract but in its actual operation.

The study of thought and language is the study of thought in language, the study of man in his most characteristic human activity. Small wonder then that, of all the criteria we apply to man, the criteria derived from language and literature give us a most accurate gauge of what man can be and what he can become, of his powers and of his limitations.

Liam O'Flaherty

TWO LOVELY BEASTS

THE DERRANES were having breakfast when a neighbour called Kate Higgins came running into their kitchen. She squatted on the floor by the wall to the right of the door, threw her apron over her face, and began to wail at the top of her voice in most heart-rending fashion.

"God between us and harm!" said Mrs. Derrane, as she came over from the table. "What happened to you?"

She put an arm about the shoulders of the wailing neighbour and added tenderly, "Tell us what happened, so that we can share your sorrow."

Colm Derrane came over with his mouth full of food. He had a mug of tea in his hand. The six children followed him. They all stood in a half circle about Kate Higgins, who continued to wail incontinently.

"Speak up in God's name," Colm said, after swallowing what he had been munching. "Speak to us so that we can help you, woman."

It was some time before Kate desisted from her lamentation. Then she suddenly removed her apron from before her face and looked fiercely at Colm through wild blue eyes that showed no sign of tears. She was a skinny little woman, with a pale face that was deeply lined with worry. Her husband had died a few months previously, leaving her with a large family that she was struggling to rear on next to nothing.

"Will you buy a calf?" she said to Colm in an angry tone.

"A calf?" said Colm in surprise. "I didn't know your cow had . . ."

"She dropped it a little while ago," the woman interrupted. "Then she died herself. Lord save us, she lay down and stretched herself out flat on the grass and shook her legs and that was all there was to it. She's as dead as a doornail. There isn't a spark left in her. It must have been poison that she dragged up out of the ground with her teeth, while she was mad with the calf sickness."

The whole Derrane family received this news in open-mouthed silence. It was a calamity that affected every household in the village. Each family had but a single cow. By traditional law, those who had

---

milk were bound to share it with those who had none. So that the death of one cow, no matter to whom she belonged, was a calamity that affected all.

"Bloody woe!" Colm said at length. "Bloody mortal woe! That's a terrible blow and you after losing your husband only the other day. There you are now with a houseful of weak children and no cow. Ah! Bloody woe!"

"No use talking, Colm," Kate Higgins said fiercely. "Buy the calf from me. I'm asking you to do it for the love of God. He must get suck quickly or else he'll die of hunger. He'll stretch out there on the grass beside his mother and die, unless he gets suck. Buy him from me."

Colm and his wife looked at one another in perplexity. Their faces were racked with pity for their neighbour.

"Bloody woe!" Colm kept muttering under his breath.

There was no sign of pity in the faces of the children. They moved back to the table slowly after a few moments of open-mouthed consternation. They kept glancing over their shoulders at Kate Higgins with aversion. They hated her, now that they understood her calamity threatened to diminish their milk supply.

"I'm asking you for the love of God," Kate Higgins continued in a tone that had become quite savage. "The price will help me buy a new cow. I must have a cow for the children. The doctor said they must have plenty of milk, the two youngest of them especially. They are ailing, the poor creatures. Your cow has a fine udder, God bless her. She calved only a few days ago. She won't feel my fellow at her teats in addition to her own. She'll be well able for the two of them, God bless her. She will, faith, and she'll leave plenty of milk for yourselves into the bargain. Praise be to God, I never saw such a fine big udder as she has."

Colm was on the point of speaking when his wife interrupted him.

"You know how it is with us," Mrs. Derrane said. "We are giving milk to three houses already. Their cows aren't due to calve for more than three weeks yet. We'll have to help you as well, now that your cow is gone. So how could we feed a second calf? It would be against the law of God and of the people. We couldn't leave neighbours without milk in order to fill a calf's belly."

Kate Higgins jumped to her feet and put her clenched fits against her lean hips.

"The calf will die unless you buy him," she cried ferociously. "There is nobody else to take him but you people. Nobody else has a cow after calving. The price would help me buy another cow. I must have a cow for the children. The doctor said . . ."

"That's enough, woman," Colm interrupted. "I'll put him on our cow for a couple of days. In the meantime, maybe you could get someone in another village to buy him."

Kate Higgins grew calm at once on hearing this offer. Tears came into her wild blue eyes.

"God spare your health, Colm," she said gently. "I was afraid he'd die of hunger before he could get suck. That would be the end of me altogether. I'd have nothing at all left if he died on me, stretched out on the grass beside his mother. When you have a few pounds, it's easier to borrow more than if you have none at all. God spare the two of you."

Colm went with her to the field, where they were already skinning the dead cow. He took the red bull calf in his arms to the paddock where his own cow was grazing. She consented to give the stranger suck after some persuasion.

"He's lovely, sure enough," Colm said as he looked with admiration at the wine-dark hide of the sucking calf. "I thought my own calf this year looked like a champion, but he's only in the half-penny place compared to this one."

"He'll be a champion all right," Kate Higgins said. "He has the breed in him. Why wouldn't he? Nothing would do my husband, Lord have mercy on him, but to spend ten royal shillings for the use of the Government bull. Nothing less would satisfy him, 'faith. He wasn't much to look at, poor man, but he always liked to have the best of everything."

She suddenly rushed over to Colm and put her lips close to his ear. Now her wild blue eyes were full of cunning.

"You should buy him, Colm," she whispered. "Buy him and put him with your own calf. Then you'll have the makings of the two finest yearlings that were ever raised in this townland. You'll be the richest man in the village. You'll be talked about and envied from one end of the parish to the other."

Colm turned his back to her and took off his cap. He was quite young and yet his skull had already began to go bald along the crown. He was a big awkward fellow with pigeon toes and arms that were exceptionally long, like those of an ape. He was noted in the district for his strength, his immense energy and his eagerness for work.

"Arrah! How could I buy him from you?" he said in a low voice. "How could I feed him and so many people depending on the milk?"

Then he turned towards her suddenly and raised his voice to a shout, as if he were arguing with some wild thought in his own mind.

"I have only twenty acres of land," he cried angrily. "The whole of it is practically barren. You wouldn't find more than a few inches of soil in the deepest part of it. You wouldn't find a foot of ground in all

I possess where you could bury a spade to the haft. Bloody woe! Woman, I tell you that I haven't one good single half-acre. There is hardly enough grass for my cow, not to mention my unfortunate horse. You could count the bones right through my poor horse's hide. I'm hard put every year to find grass for my yearling. Woman alive, sure there isn't a man in this village that could feed two yearlings. It would be madness for me to try it."

"The English have started fighting the Germans a second time," Kate Higgins whispered. "They won't stop until they have dragged the whole world again into the war with them. The fight will last for years and years, same as it did before. There will be a big price for everything fit to eat. A man that would have two lovely beasts for sale . . ."

"Stop tempting me with your foolish talk, woman," Colm interrupted.

"Your cow could easily feed the two calves," Kate continued. "She could do it without any bother at all. She'd have plenty, beside, for yourselves and the neighbours. You needn't worry about grass, either. There's always plenty of grass for rent in the village of Pusach. You'll have plenty of money to spare for buying any extra grass you'll need, because there is going to be a great price for potatoes and fish. Man alive, there will be lashings of money, same as before. During the other big war, you remember, they were even buying rotten dogfish. I declare to my God they were. They paid famine prices for the rotten dogfish that the storms threw up on the beach beyond there."

Colm turned away from her again and lowered his voice to a whisper.

"It would be madness for me to try it," he said. "Nobody ever tried to raise two yearlings in this village. We all have the same amount of rocky land, twenty acres a head."

"You're different from everybody else, Colm," Kate said, raising her voice and speaking very rapidly. "The others only do what they have to do. They do barely enough to keep themselves and their families alive. You go out of your way looking for work. You never turn aside from an opportunity to earn an extra shilling. You are at it night and day. The spunk is in you. There is no end to your strength. Oh! Indeed, it's well known that there is no holding you, where there is a job of work to be done. You spit on your hands and away you go like a wild stallion. God bless you, there is the strength of ten men in your body and you're not afraid to use it. You deserve to prosper on account of your willingness. You deserve to be rich and famous. All you need is courage."

"Nobody ever tried it," Colm whispered hoarsely. "Nobody ever did. It would be madness to try it."

Kate Higgins stepped back from him and threw out her arms in a dramatic gesture.

"Let you be the first, then," she shouted. "There's nothing stopping you but a want of courage. Let you be the first. Let you show them how to do it, Colm."

Colm also raised his voice to a shout as he answered her fiercely.

"Stop your foolish talk, woman," he said. "He can suck on my cow for a couple of days, but I promise you no more."

Kate walked away from him hurriedly, gesticulating with both arms.

"Two lovely beasts!" she shouted back at him, when she was at a distance. "Think of that now. There's nothing standing in your way but a want of courage."

"Not another word out of you now," Colm shouted after her at the top of his voice. "What you're saying is against the law of God."

Even so, he could hardly sleep a wink that night through thinking of what the woman had said. In the morning he broached the idea of buying the calf during conversation with his wife.

"That's a lovely calf Kate Higgins has," he said. "It's a pity we can't buy it."

"Buy it?" said his wife. "Yerrah! How could we do that?"

"There is going to be a great price for beasts on account of the war," Colm continued. "With the English and the Germans at it again . . ."

"Have sense, man," his wife said. "Unless you've taken leave of your gumption, you know well it's impossible for us to buy that calf. Not even if we had grass for it, which we haven't."

"All the same," Colm said, "that young fellow makes my mouth water. I never saw such a young champion."

"Yerrah! How could we leave the neighbours without milk?" his wife said.

"I'm only talking, that's all," Colm said. "There is no harm in talk."

"Well! Say no more about it," his wife said. "People might hear you and be scandalized."

"You never saw such a colour as that calf has," Colm said as he went out of the house. "He's so red that he's almost black."

Kate Higgins came to him again that day, while he was smashing rocks with a sledge-hammer in the corner of a little field that he was trying to make arable. She began to pester him once more with the idea of having "two lovely beasts." He threw down the sledge-hammer and ran over to the fence against which she leant.

"Why don't you leave me alone?" he shouted at her. "Go to some other village and find a buyer for him."

"I've enquired everywhere," Kate Higgins said. "It's no use, Colm. Unless you buy him, I'll have to give him to the butcher at Kilmacalla. The few shillings that I'll get for his flesh and his hide won't be much. However, they'll be better than nothing."

"I promised to let him suck for a couple of days," Colm shouted. "I can promise you no more. I can't let the neighbours go without the milk that is due to them."

"It will be a mortal sin to slaughter such a lovely young fellow," Kate said as she walked away hurriedly. "What else can I do, though? I must get a pound or two, by hook or by crook. Then I can borrow more. I have to make up the price of a new cow one way or another. The doctor said that the young ones must have plenty of milk. Otherwise they'll die. So he said. He did, 'faith."

After the woman had gone, Colm went to the paddock for another look at the young bull calf that had a wine-dark hide.

"It would be a mortal sin surely to slaughter such a lovely creature," he said aloud. "He'll be every inch a champion if he lives."

Then his heart began to beat wildly as he watched the two calves cavort together with their tails in the air. He became intoxicated by the idea of possessing them both.

"Two lovely beasts!" he whispered.

He went for a walk to the cliff tops instead of returning to his sledge-hammer. He stood on the brink of the highest cliff and looked down into the sea.

"Two lovely beasts!" he whispered again.

Then a frenzied look came into his pale blue eyes. He took off his cap and threw it on the ground behind him.

"Sure I have the courage," he muttered fiercely.

He spread his legs, leaned forward slightly and held out his hands in front of his hips, with the palms upturned and the fingers slightly crooked. He began to tremble.

"I have plenty of courage," he muttered.

The skin on the upper part of his forehead and on top of his baldish skull looked very pale above the brick-red colour of his bony cheeks. He had a long narrow face, thick lips, and buck teeth. His short nose had a very pointed ridge. His mouse-coloured hair stuck out in ugly little bunches above his ears and at the nape of his neck. His shoes were in tatters. His frieze trousers were covered with patches of varying colours. His grey shirt was visible through the numerous holes in his blue woollen sweater.

Yet he looked splendid and even awe-inspiring, in spite of his physical ugliness and his uncouth dress, as he stood poised that way on the brink of the tall cliff above the thundering sea, leaning forward on widespread legs, with his long arms stretched out and his fingers turned slightly inward on his open palms, trembling with a frenzy of desire.

After a while he turned away from the sea and picked up his cap. He felt very tired as he walked homeward with downcast head. His arms swung limply by his sides. He kept glancing furtively from side to side, as if he were conscious of having committed a crime up there on the cliff top and feared pursuit as a consequence. There was a hard look in his pale blue eyes.

Again that night he could not sleep. He lay on his back thinking of the two lovely beasts and how he wanted to possess them. The thought gave him both pleasure and pain. The pleasure was like that derived from the anticipation of venery. The pain came from his conscience.

During the morning of the following day, Kate Higgins came to him again. She was wearing her best clothes.

"I'm on my way to the butcher at Kilmacalla," she said to him.

"All right," Colm said to her. "How much do you want for the calf?"

He was so excited by the decision at which he had arrived that he consented to the price she asked without bargaining.

"Come to the house with me," he said. "I'll hand over the money to you."

"God spare your health," Kate Higgins said. "With that money I can begin at once to look for another cow. When you have a few pounds you can always borrow more."

Mrs. Derrane got very angry when her husband came into the kitchen with Kate Higgins and asked her for the family purse.

"Is it to buy that calf?" she said.

"Hand me the purse," Colm repeated.

"Devil a bit of me," his wife said. "It would be against the law of God to put the people's milk into a calf's heathen belly. I won't give it to you."

Colm gripped the front of her bodice with his left hand and shook her.

"Hand it over, woman," he said in a low voice.

Her anger passed at once. She was a big, muscular woman, almost as strong as her husband and possessed of a stern will. Indeed, she had dominated Colm's simple nature ever since their marriage until now. Whenever he tried to rebel against her decisions, he had always been easily defeated. He had shouted, broken articles of furniture and even struck her cruel blows from time to time. She had always merely waited with folded arms and set jaws until his foolish anger had spent itself. Now it was different. He did not shout and she saw something in his pale blue eyes that frightened her.

So that she went quickly to the great chest and brought him the long cloth purse.

"What's come over you?" she said to him while he was undoing the string. "What are the neighbours going to say about this?"

Colm unrolled the purse and thrust his hand deep down into the long inner pocket. He again looked his wife straight in the eyes.

"Shut up, woman," he said quietly. "From now on don't meddle with things that don't concern you. I'm master in this house. Do you hear?"

Again she became frightened by what she saw in his eyes. She turned away from him. "May God forgive you," she said. "I hope you have thought well about this before doing it."

"I've never in my life thought more about anything," Colm said.

Kate Higgins never uttered one word of thanks when she was given the money. She stuffed the notes into the front pocket of her skirt and rushed from the house. "I'll go now," she cried as she hurried down the yard, "to try and get company for these few pounds. Those that have give only to those that have. To those that have not only crumbs are given, same as to a dog."

When Colm went that evening to the meeting place, on the brow of the little hill that faced the village, silence fell among the men who were assembled there. He threw himself on the ground, put his back to a rock and lit his pipe. The others began to discuss the weather in subdued tones after a little while. Then again there was silence.

At length a man named Andy Gorum turned to Colm and said, "We heard you bought the calf from Kate Higgins."

"I did," said Colm.

"Is it to slaughter him you bought him?" Gorum said.

"No," said Colm.

"Do you intend to rear him?" Gorum said.

"I do," said Colm.

Gorum got to his feet slowly and clasped his hands behind the small of his back. He came over and stood in front of Colm. He was an elderly man, very small and thin, with a wrinkled face that was the colour of old parchment. His eyes were weak and they had hardly any lashes, like those of a man blind from birth. He was the village leader because of his wisdom.

"I'm sorry you are doing this, Colm," he said. "You are a good man and everybody belonging to you was good, away back through the generations. This is a bad thing you intend to do, though."

"How could it be bad to help a widow?" Colm said.

"You know well it won't help a widow if you rear that calf on the people's milk," Gorum said.

"She begged me and begged me," Colm said, raising his voice. "She kept at me the whole time. How could I refuse her? She said that she had to have the money for another cow. She said her children would die unless . . ."

"You know you are breaking the law," Gorum interrupted. "It's no use trying to talk yourself out of it."

"How could it be against the law to help a widow?" Colm shouted.

"Indeed, it isn't," Gorum said. "We'll all help her, please God, as much as we can. That's how we live here in our village, by helping one another. Our land is poor and the sea is wild. It's hard to live. We only manage to live by sticking together. Otherwise we'd all die. It's too wild and barren here for any one man to stand alone. Whoever tries to stand alone and work only for his own profit becomes an enemy of all."

Colm jumped to his feet. He towered over Gorum.

"Are you calling me an enemy for helping a widow?" he shouted.

"If you put into a calf's belly," Gorum said, "the milk that you owe your neighbours, everybody will be against you."

"I'll do what I please," Colm shouted.

Thereupon he rushed from the meeting place.

"Come back, neighbour," Gorum called after him in a tone of entreaty.

"I have the courage to do what I think is right," Colm shouted.

"We are all fond of you," Gorum said. "We don't want to turn against you. Come back to us and be obedient to the law."

"I'll do what I think is right," Colm shouted as he crossed the stile into his yard. "I'll raise those two beasts if it's the last thing I'll do in this world. Let any man that dares try to stop me."

The Derranes became outcasts in the village from that day forward. Nobody spoke to them. Nobody gave them any help. Nobody entered their house. All other doors were closed against them.

Even Kate Higgins turned against her benefactors in most shameful fashion. Contrary to her expectations, the hapless woman was unable to borrow any more money, except for a solitary pound that she got from an aunt after lengthy importunities. Neither was she able to find any cow for sale, although she tramped the parish from end to end, over and over again. Her house went to rack and ruin during her continued absence. The ungoverned children burned the furniture to keep themselves warm. They grew so savage and filthy that the neighbour women removed their own children from all contact with them.

Unbalanced by her misfortunes, Kate forsook her peasant frugality and brought tidbits home to her starving brood after each fruitless day of wandering. The poor woman lacked courage to face them empty-handed. In that way she soon spent every penny of the money that she got from Colm and her aunt. There was none of it left after two months. When she had nothing more to give the little ones on her return, as they clutched at her apron with their filthy hands and whined pitifully for food, her mind began to get crazed.

She took to reviling Colm at the top of her voice in the roadway outside her house as she shuffled homeward with the fall of night.

"Colm Derrane is sold to the devil," she cried. "He put bad luck on me. I was grateful to him when he bought my calf, thinking he was doing me a favour and that I could borrow more, to put with what he gave me and make up the price of a new cow. Devil a bit of it. There was a curse on his money. People told me it was on account of the war they were unwilling to part with any of their share. They said they were bound to clutch all they had, for fear of disaster. The truth is that they would not lend to a woman that sold a calf to an enemy of the people. Here I am now without a red copper in my skirt, without a cow or a husband and my children ailing. They'll die on me, the poor little creatures, without the milk that the doctor ordered for them. I have no strength to care for them. I'm so tired every evening after my walking that I can't even pick the lice out of their hair. Ah! the poor little creatures! May God have pity on my orphans!"

Colm paid no more heed to this abuse than he did to the hostility of the people. After his outburst of anger on being told he was to be treated as an outcast, he maintained strict control over his temper. He became dour and silent and indifferent, except when he was in the presence of the two young beasts that he loved. It was only then that he smiled and uttered words of tenderness.

"Oh! You lovely creatures!" he said to them, as he watched them suck at the cow's teats. "Drink up now and be strong. Don't leave a drop of that milk in the udder. I want the two of you to be champions."

He was as ruthless toward his family as he was tender toward the calves. He only brought into the house enough milk to colour the tea. He let the calves swallow all the rest. Lest there might be any cheating, he forbade his wife and children to go near the cow under threat of dire punishment.

His wife came to him shortly after the calves were weaned. "I can go without butter," she protested, "although the children tear the heart in me with their whining. They keep asking when there is going to be some. It is too much, though, when I can't get enough buttermilk to make our bread rise. All I ask is enough milk for one churning."

"You can't have it," Colm said coldly. "I can't let the calves go in want, just for the sake of making our bread rise. We can eat it flat just as well. Calves must get a good foundation during the first few months, by having every hole and corner of their bellies well stuffed the whole time. That's how they get bone and muscle and balance and plenty of room. Then it's easy, when the time comes, to pile on the good hard meat. The foundation will be there to carry the load."

His wife kept looking at him in amazement while he spoke. She could not understand how a man, who had formerly been so kind and considerate of his family's needs, could suddenly become so ruthless. She burst into tears after he had finished. "God will punish you for being cruel," she said.

"Silence," said Colm. "Don't take liberties, woman."

Midsummer came. That was the season of abundance for the poor people of that village. The new potatoes were being dug. The young onions were succulent in the house gardens. There was plenty of milk and butter. Great baskets of pollock and rock fish and bream and mackerel were brought each day from the sea. The hens were laying and the spare cockerels from the spring hatchings made broth for the delicate. At suppertime the people gorged themselves on their favorite dish of mashed new potatoes, with butter and scallions and boiled fish and fresh buttermilk. The scallions were chopped fine and mixed with the potatoes. Then a great lump of yellow butter was pressed down into the center of the steaming dish. The table was laid before the open door, so that the people could hear the birds singing in the drowsy twilight and see the red glory of the sunset on the sea while they ate. The men waddled out afterward to the village meeting place, sending clouds of tobacco smoke into the air from their pipes. They lay down on their backs against the rocks and listened to the bird music in raptured content. Now and again one of them joined his voice to those of the birds and gave thanks to God for His gracious bounty.

It was then that Mrs. Derrane rose up in rebellion against her husband. She took the tongs from the hearth one evening and stood in front of him. "I'll stand no more of this, Colm," she said fiercely. "Here we are, living on potatoes and salt while the neighbours are feasting. Everything is put aside for the calves. My curse on the pair of them. You won't even let us eat a bit of fresh fish. By your leave, you made me salt every single fish that you brought into the house this spring, to be sold later on, so that you can have money to buy grass for your beasts. We have to scavenge along the shore, the children and myself, looking for limpets and periwinkles, same as people did during the famine. Lord save us, the lining of our stomachs is torn into shreds from the purging that the limpets give us. We are put to shame, rummaging like seagulls for stinking food, while the people of our village are feasting. There has to be an end to this, or else I'll take the children and follow my face out of the house. You'll have to get rid of that calf you bought. Then we can live as we did before. We'll be outcasts no longer."

Colm got to his feet and looked at her coldly.

"I'm going to raise those two calves," he said solemnly, "even if you and the children and myself have to eat dung while I'm doing it. Let other people fill their bellies in midsummer and remain poor. I want to rise in the world. A man can do that only by saving."

His wife raised the tongs and threatened him with them.

"I'll have none of it," she cried. "I'm telling you straight to your face. You have to give in to me or I'll split your skull with these tongs."

"Put down those tongs," Colm said quietly.

"Are you going to get rid of that calf?" said his wife.

"Put them down," said Colm.

"I'll kill you with them," shouted his wife, becoming hysterical.

She struck at him with all her force, but he jumped aside nimbly and evaded the blow. Then he closed with her and quickly locked her arms behind her back.

"I'm going to give you a lesson now," he said quietly. "I'm going to chastise you in a way that you'll remember."

He dragged her down to the hearth.

"Call the neighbours," his wife cried to the children. "Run out into the yard and call the people to come and save me from this murderer."

The children ran out into the yard and began to call for help as Colm took down a dried sally rod that lay stretched on wooden pegs along the chimney place.

"You'll be obedient in future, my good woman," he said. "On my solemn oath you will."

He began to flog her. She tried to bite his legs. Then he put her flat on the ground and laid his foot to her back.

"I'll kill you when I get a chance," she cried. "I'll have your life while you are asleep."

Then she folded her arms beneath her face, gritted her teeth and received his blows in silence. He had to go on beating her for a long time before the sturdy creature surrendered and begged for mercy.

"All right, then," Colm said calmly when she had done so. "Do you promise to be obedient from now on and to make no more trouble about the calf?"

"I promise," his wife said.

"Get up, then, in God's name," Colm said gently, "and call in the children."

His wife looked up at him sideways in amazement. She did not rise. It puzzled her that he was so calm and spoke to her with tenderness, after having beaten her without mercy.

"Get up, woman," he continued. "Don't let us behave like this any more. It gives scandal to the children."

Then he took her tenderly in his arms and raised her to her feet. She ran out into the yard without looking at him.

"Get into the house," she said sternly to the children. "In with you."

She turned to some neighbours, who had come in answer to the children's cries for help. They were standing out in the lane, in doubt as to whether they should enter the yard of a household that were outcast.

"What brought you here?" Mrs. Derrane shouted at them. "It's not for our good that you came. Be off now and mind your own business."

That night in bed, she clasped Colm in her arms and put her cheek against his breast. "I thought it was the devil got into you," she whispered, as tears rolled down her cheeks. "Now I know different. You are trying to raise your family up in the world, while I'm only a hindrance to you and a dead weight around your neck. From now on, though, I'm going to help you. I will, faith!"

Colm took her head between his big rough hands and kissed her on the crown. "God spare your health, darling," he said. "With your help there will be no stopping us."

Seeing their parents happily united again, the children also became imbued with enthusiasm. They willingly consented to make sacrifices for the common effort. Even the youngest boy, barely five years old, had a little job to do every day. The whole family worked like bees in a hive.

The village people soon became so impressed by this turn of events that they began to question the justice of their conduct towards the Derrane family.

"If what he is doing is bad, why does he prosper?" they said to one another. "Isn't it more likely that God is blessing his effort to rise in the world? Maybe it's us that are wicked on account of our laziness?"

At the village meeting place, Andy Gorum strove with all his skill to hold the men steadfast against Colm.

"You'll soon see him come back to us on his knees," Gorum said, "and he begging for mercy. He may seem to prosper now. His two calves are growing powerfully. His wife and children and himself are working night and day. He has a nimble hand in everything worth money. Wait till winter comes, though. Then he won't be able to find grass for his beasts. The butcher of Kilmacalla has bought a herd of black cattle, to fatten them for the fighting English. He has rented all the spare grass in the village of Pusach. Many more big people in the district have bought herds on account of the war. There won't be a single blade of grass left anywhere for a poor man to rent. The big people will have it all clutched. Colm will have to slaughter that dark-skinned calf. I declare to my God we'll be eating that dark fellow's meat when the Christmas candles are lit."

Gorum's prophecy proved false and Colm was able to find grass owing to the tragedy that again struck the Higgins family. As summer passed, the village people were no longer able to give more than the barest help to the widow and her orphans. Neither did the distraught woman put to the best use what little there was given. Indeed, she now turned on the whole village as she had formerly turned on Colm, denouncing the community at the top of her voice.

"Ah! Woe!" she cried as she marched back and forth before the houses in her bare feet. "Almighty God was cruel when he left me a widow among people that are worse than the heathen Turks. There I am, with my clutch of delicate creatures, without bite or sup from morning to night. You wouldn't see a good rush of smoke out of my chimney top from Monday to Saturday. All I have to burn on my hearth is cow dung and a few miserable briers. There isn't a hot drop for the children's bellies. Ah! Woe! My curse on the hard hearts of my neighbours!"

There was a spell of cold weather toward the end of September and the two youngest children fell victims to it. They both died in the same week of pneumonia. The second death unhinged the mother's reason. Leaving the child unburied in the house, she wandered away at dead of night, with hardly a stitch of clothes on her starved body. They found her marching along the cliff tops on the evening of the following day and took her to the lunatic asylum. The remaining five children, finding no relatives willing to shelter them, were also lodged in a public institution. It then became apparent that the widow owed money right and left. Her creditors, who were chiefly shopkeepers of Kilmacalla, began to quarrel about disposal of the house and land. The case was brought into the district court.

"Here is my chance," Colm said to his wife. "Here is where I might be able to get grass this winter for my beasts."

On the day the case was to be tried, he put on his best clothes, took the family purse and went to the courthouse at Kilmacalla. After listening to the arguments of the rival lawyers for some time, he got leave to address the magistrate.

"Your honour," he said, "it would be an injustice to the children, if that farm is auctioned now, or divided up among these shopkeepers.

It would be taking the bread out of the children's mouths. They have a right to do what they please later on with that land. When they grow up and come out into the world, it's for them to say if the land is to be sold, or given to one of themselves in order to raise a family on it. In the meantime, let me rent it from them, your honour. Year after year I'll pay good rent for it on the nail. Everybody knows me, sir. I'm a man of my word. I never went back on a pennyworth of promises in my natural life. Any man will tell you that, from the parish priest on down. The mother's debts can be paid out of the rent in no time at all. What more would these shopkeepers want, unless they are land-grabbers? In God's name, your honour, you'll be behaving like a Christian if you let me rent it, instead of letting these people slice it out among themselves. God bless you, sir!"

The magistrate finally agreed to Colm's suggestion for settling the dispute.

"Praised be God!" Colm cried on his return home. "I am secure now against the winter. Nothing can stop me from now on. In God's name, the two beasts are as good as raised."

Gorum was furious at this turn of events. He attacked Colm savagely that evening at the meeting place.

"There is a bloody heathen for you!" he cried. "The two little ones are barely dead in their graves when the bloodsucker that robbed them of their milk puts his two calves grazing on their mother's share. Ay! His two calves are lovely, sure enough. Why wouldn't they? Didn't they grow fat and strong on the milk that the little dead children should have drunk? Ah! The poor little dead creatures! It's a fine state of affairs truly, with two children dead and two beasts rolling in fat on their share of food. Mother of God! That's a cursed state of affairs for you! Beasts given rich food and children let die of hunger! Damnation has surely fallen on our village when such things are let happen here."

The men jeered at these remarks,. They had lost faith in the old man.

"You are envious of Colm," they said to Gorum. "You are jealous of his success and his wisdom. You are no longer a wise man. Hatred has made a windbag of you."

One by one, they entered Colm's house, sat by his hearth and shared their pipes with him. Their wives brought presents to Mrs. Derrane and knitted with her on Sunday after Mass, at the women's hillock. The men came to Colm for advice, just as they had hitherto gone to Gorum. They put Colm in the place of honour at the meeting place. There was silence when he spoke.

"God is good to us," Colm said to his wife.

"He is, faith," Mrs. Derrane said. "Praised be His name."

Even so, it became more and more difficult for the family to make ends meet. The rent for the widow's farm put a heavy strain on their purse. The children's enthusiasm vanished during the winter in face of continual hunger. It became almost impossible to make them do a hand's turn.

Mrs. Derrane also forgot her solemn promise of co-operation and began to grumble out loud, when Colm would not allow even an egg for the Christmas dinner.

"Great God!" she said. "There is a limit to everything. We haven't seen fish or meat since spring. You wouldn't let us buy a piece of holly or a coloured candle. We are a disgrace to the whole village, with nothing on our table but potatoes and salt for the feast of Our Lord."

"Silence," Colm said. "This is no time of the year to become impudent."

To cap it all, he ordered that the cloth made from that year's wool be sold, instead of turning it into garments for the household.

"Our rags will do us well enough for another year," he said. "In any case, patched clothes are just as warm as new ones."

Everybody in the house got terribly thin and weak. Yet Colm's iron will buoyed them up to such an extent that there was no illness.

"We have only to hold on a little while," he kept saying, "and have courage. Then we'll rise in the world. We'll be rich and famous, from one end of the parish to the other."

He himself looked like a skeleton, for he practically went without food in order that the children might have as much as possible.

"You'll kill yourself," his wife said, when he began to prepare the ground for the spring sowing. "You look like a sick man. For God's sake, let me take money out of the purse and buy a pig's cheek for you."

"Silence, woman," Colm said. "Not a penny must be touched. I have a plan. We'll need all we have and more, to make my new plan work. It's not easy to become rich, I tell you."

The cow relieved the desperate plight of the family by having her calf a month earlier than usual, during the first week of March.

The children became gay once more, for they were given plenty of the new milk to drink. There was buttermilk to make the bread rise. There was even beautiful salty yellow butter, fresh from the churn and with pale drops of water glistening on its surface, to spread thickly on the long slices of crusty griddle cake.

The happy children began to whisper excitedly to one another in the evenings about the coming spring fair, when great riches were to come into the house from the sale of the pigs and the yearlings.

Over and over again, they discussed the toys and trinkets that their mother would buy them in the town on fair day, as a reward for their help in raising the two beasts.

They were continually running to the field where the yearlings were gorging themselves on the luscious young grass.

"They are champions," they cried boastfully as they stared at the animals over the top of the stone fence. "Nobody ever before saw such lovely beasts."

Colm put an end to the children's dreams a few days before the fair.

"Listen to me, all of you," he told the family one evening after supper. "You have worked hard helping me with the two beasts. They are now fine yearlings, God bless them. We'll all have to work a little harder, though, so as to make them the two best bullocks that were ever seen."

Mrs. Derrane was dumbfounded on hearing this news. She dropped on to a stool and fanned her face with her apron.

"Are you out of your mind, Colm?" she said at length. "How could we keep those two beasts another year? How could we keep two bullocks? Won't we have this year's calf, too, growing up and eating on us?"

"I have a plan," Colm said. "We are going to open a shop."

His wife made the sign of the Cross on her forehead and looked at him in horror.

"Why not?" said Colm. "It's only shopkeepers that rise in the world."

"Are you crazy?" his wife said. "Where would we get the money to open a shop?"

"All we need is courage," Colm said. "The few pounds we have saved, together with the price of the pigs, will be enough to open it. I'm telling you, woman, that all we need is courage and willingness. If we all work hard together, night and day . . ."

"God Almighty!" his wife interrupted. "You've gone mad. Those two beasts have gone to your head."

"Now, then," said Colm. "That's not true at all. I was never wiser in my life. The war will last for years yet. It's only now the real fury is coming on the fighting nations. Very well, then. While the mad people are fighting and killing each other, let us make money out of them and rise in the world. There is going to be a demand for everything that can be eaten. There will be a price for everything fit to make your mouth water. Food is going to be more precious than gold. So will clothes. In God's name, then, let us open a shop and stock it with goods. Let us go around the parish with our horse and cart, buying up everything the people have to sell, eggs and butter and carrigeen moss and fish and wool and hides and potatoes. We'll buy everything that can be carted away. We can pay them for what we buy with shop goods. Do you see? Then we'll sell what we buy from the people over in the town at a profit. Later on, we can buy sheep as well and . . ."

"Arrah! You're stark crazy," his wife interrupted angrily. "Stop talking like that, man alive, in front of the children."

At this moment all the children burst into tears, no longer able to contain their disappointment.

"Stop whinging," Colm shouted, as he leaped to his feet. "Is it crying you are because there will be nothing for you from the fair? Is it for sweets and crackers you are crying and dai-dais? All right, then. I'm telling you now there will be plenty of sweets and dai-dais for you when we have a shop. There will be sweets every day and dai-dais, too. Do you hear me? Every day in the year will be like a fair day for you."

His uncouth face, worn to the bone by privation and worry, now glowed with the light of ecstasy, as he struggled to wheedle his family into co-operation with his ambition to rise in the world. Such was the power of the idea that possessed him, that the children stopped crying almost at once. They listened with eagerness to his fantastic promises. Their little faces became as radiant as his own.

His wife also became affected, as she saw her dour husband trying to win over the children by means of smiles and gaiety and honeyed words.

"I wouldn't believe it," she said, "only for I see it with my own two eyes."

Tears rolled down her cheeks and her upper lip trembled. "In fifteen years," she muttered, as she rubbed her eyes with a corner of her apron, "I never once saw him dance one of the children on his knee. No, faith, I never once saw him shake a rattle in front of a whinging baby. Yet there he is now, all of a sudden, trying to make a showman of himself. God Almighty! Only for I see it with my own two eyes . . ."

"He must have touched the magic stone," said the astonished people of the village. "Everything he handles turns into lashings of money."

Andy Gorum alone continued to prophesy that misfortune would fall on Colm for attempting to "stand alone and rise above the people."

"You just wait," Gorum kept shouting on the hill before the village. "God will strike him down when he least expects it. Those two beasts, that are now so lovely, will never reach the fair green alive on their four legs."

This prophecy proved to be just as false as the previous one that Gorum had made. All through the winter and the following spring, Colm and his family lavished the greatest care on the two beasts that had brought them prosperity. So that they were really champions on fair day. The bullock with the wine-dark hide was acknowledged by all to be the finest animal of his age ever seen in the district. He fetched top price.

Tears poured down Colm's cheeks as he walked back from the railway station with his wife, after parting with his beasts.

"Those two lovely beasts brought me luck," he said. "I feel lonely for them now that they are gone. Only for them, I'd never think of rising in the world. Praised be God! He works in strange ways. He strikes one down and raises up another."

"True for you," his wife said. "Praised be His holy name! Who are we, miserable sinners that we are, to question His mysterious ways?"

"Only for that cow dying on Kate Higgins," Colm continued, "we'd always be land slaves, wrestling with starvation to the end of our days and never getting the better of any bout. Look at us now, woman. We're on our way towards riches. God alone knows where we'll stop."

"Enough of that talk now," his wife said. "Don't let arrogance get hold of us. Don't let us be boastful. The people are already becoming envious of us. I can see a begrudging look in the eyes of the neighbours."

"That's true," Colm said. "That's why I'm thinking of opening a shop in the town. It might be better to take ourselves out of the sight of people that knew us poor."

"A shop in the town?" his wife said. "Don't get too big for your boots, Colm."

"No fear," Colm said. "I know what I'm doing. I'm going to hire a few men and begin buying in earnest. There's money to be picked up by the bushel all over the place. All we need is courage, woman."

"In God's name!" his wife said.

When they were hitching the mare to their new jaunting car for the journey home, Andy Gorum came along with a group of intoxicated men.

"The mills of God grind slow," Gorum shouted, "but they grind sure. The bloodsuckers are taking the food out of our country. They are giving it to the fighting foreigners, while our children die of hunger. We are barefooted and in rags, but they give our wool and our hides to the war people. They are taking all our lovely beasts across the seas to fill the bellies of pagans. The time will soon come, though, when the bloodsuckers that are robbing us will be struck down by the hand of Almighty God. They will roast in Hell for the everlasting ages."

As Colm drove away in his new green jaunting car, quite a number of people whistled after him in hostility and derision. Now that he had risen so far, he had again become an enemy.

His gaunt face looked completely unaware of their jeers. His pale blue eyes stared fixedly straight ahead, cold and resolute and ruthless.

"There will be no end to the riches we'll have when we are shopkeepers," Colm continued. "We can have bacon for breakfast. Yes, indeed, we can eat great big rashers of it every morning in the year, except Fridays. The people of the village will be coming to smell the lovely food that's frying on our pan. Oh! I'm telling you that we can have bellies on us like tourists. We'll hardly be able to carry ourselves, as we walk the road, on account of our fat. We'll have ribbons as well and velvet and a mirror in every room."

His wife and children were won over completely to his side once more. So they all went to work with enthusiasm and the shop was speedily installed. It was an immediate success. People came from a long distance in order to trade with the courageous man, who was trying to raise two bullocks on twenty acres of barren rocks.

"Blood in ounce!" the people said. "He'll never be able to do it, but you have to admire his courage all the same. He'll very likely end up in the asylum with Kate Higgins, but more power to him for trying. He's a credit to the parish."

When Colm went round with his horse and cart, accompanied by one or other of the children, everybody was eager to do business with him. The people sold him whatever they had available and they forbore to drive a hard bargain. He soon had to take the house and barn that belonged to Kate Higgins, in order to store the great mass of his goods. Within a few months he was making trips to the town twice a week and getting high prices for all he had to sell.

Money kept coming into the house so quickly and in such large quantities that his wife became frightened.

"May God keep pride and arrogance out of our hearts," she used to say, as she stuffed the notes into the long cloth purse. "It's dangerous to get rich so quickly."

"Have no fear, woman," Colm said to her. "We denied ourselves and we didn't lose heart when times were bad. So now God is giving us a big hansel as a reward. Be grateful, woman, and have no fear."

The promises that he had made to the children were fulfilled. There was full and plenty in the house. The little girls had ribbons to their hair and dai-dais to amuse their leisure. His wife got a velvet dress and a hat with feathers. There was bacon for breakfast.

Conrad M. Arensberg

COUNTRYMEN AT WORK

To bring you closer to the way of life we glimpsed through the window of old custom, I must try to clothe it in flesh and blood. It will not do to make the mistake of etherealizing it. Men everywhere face the same first necessities; they must live; they must feed, clothe and shelter themselves.

My subject, then, is the countryman at work. How does he make his livelihood in the Irish countryside? What is the work he does, and what are his incentives and rewards? Economic interpretations of history, sociology, anthropology are the fashion. What understanding can an economic inquiry yield us?

The first task in such an inquiry is to clear away the ground one is to examine. To look at the work of the countryman of rural Ireland demands dipping into the economics of the whole Free State. The countryman occupies an important place which must be recognized. It should not be discouraging that the task involves recourse to cold statistics. After all, the greatest array of numbers is a mere count of some sort of human activity; one can remember the living beings behind them. In the search for the countryman, one can break through census records and production figures to find him pursuing his daily and annual round.

The task is simplified immensely by the fact that in 1926 the Free State Government undertook a complete census of the country. In the tables prepared there, the countrymen distinguish themselves in a variety of ways. They are the most numerous group in the country. Out of nearly three million inhabitants, one million eight hundred thousand, or 63 per cent, live in rural areas, outside cities and towns. Not all these country-dwellers are farmers, of course, but the vast majority are. Fifty-one per cent of all occupied persons, male and female, in southern Ireland work at agriculture.

But these agriculturists are not all alike, of course. Distinctions appear among them which are important to an understanding of the countryman. For example, the farms on which they work differ widely in size. Relative proportions of small and large farms vary with different parts of the country, but nevertheless small farms predominate in all Ireland. A farm over 200 acres is a rarity, comparatively

---

COUNTRYMEN AT WORK: Reprinted with permission of the publisher from *The Irish Countryman* by Conrad M. Arensberg. First published by The Macmillan Company in 1937.

speaking; most of them do not reach 100 acres. Thirty or fifty acres is the average size.

When one looks at the numbers of people these farms support, however, the small holdings come forward much more strongly. There are many more persons supported upon farms under thirty acres than there are on farms over fifty. In fact, one could almost say "the smaller the farm the greater number of persons it supports." The plurality of Irish farmers support themselves upon farms averaging from fifteen to thirty acres in area. Almost eight of every ten persons working in agriculture live by small-farm production.

By our standards, a farm under thirty acres or even under fifty acres is very small. So it is regarded in Ireland. When I call the Irish countryman a small farmer, I am following standards the Irish use themselves. Yet, to deal with the life of the small farmers is to deal with that of the single largest group on the land.

Furthermore, that group is concentrated in the west and south of Ireland. Historical and economic currents have massed the population in the more rugged "mountainy" regions of south and west. A county of the rich central plain, such as Meath, where large farms are most numerous, has a density of about fifty persons per square mile. But a poorer, mountainous county such as Mayo, where small farms are very numerous indeed, supports seventy-five persons per square mile or an almost 50 per cent greater density.

But do those who support themselves by small farms form a true category? Are they a group unto themselves, or are they a numeration meaningless for the student of human behaviour? Statistics have a way of revealing real categories in life, but they also send one upon many false scents. One must use them with proper care. In such a case as this, care consists in discovering correlations and fitting them into wholes. For example, one learns little or nothing of various kinds of human beings if one counts only single characteristics. On the other hand, if one counts a wide variety of numerable features and finds one human group distinguishing itself again and again within this wide variety, one is justified in thinking one is dealing with a class of which the individuals are instances.

So it is with the economic data in the Irish records. The small farmers do appear as a true category. They reveal themselves in the cold figures as a class with habits of life of its own, different in kind and in quantitative expression from all others.

Rather than delay over the reasoning which leads to this conclusion, I should prefer to recite the distinguishing marks in the economic sphere.

First, it is clear that the small farmers practise a type of agriculture all their own. Their products differ widely from those of the large farmers, sometimes in kind, sometimes in proportion. The large farmer is a cattleman, a stockman. The small farmer is typically what we have come to call in this country "a subsistence farmer." Both depend primarily upon livestock, for Ireland is a country of grass and pasturage, depending less upon tillage than any other European land. But their economies are quite distinct. The small farmer cultivates a "garden" of oats, rye, potatoes, cabbage and turnips, and devotes his pasture and the hay of his fields to milch cattle. He sells his cows' increase each year. He keeps large numbers of hens and a few pigs. But the milch cow is the centre round which this economy revolves. Nearly all he raises he consumes at home; his family and his farm animals take the greater part of his produce. It is only his surplus and his annual crop of calves which break out of the circle of subsistence and in so doing bring him the only monetary income he receives.

In all this he differs considerably from the big farmer, particularly the so-called "rancher" of Irish agriculture. The big farmer is primarily a producer of beef. He concentrates upon the production of fattened stock. Upon this market he relies for the supplies which feed himself and his labourers. If he is wealthier and much more of a man of business, he is also nearly entirely dependent upon the whims of price and demand.

Naturally, then, the small farmer and big farmer play quite distinct roles in the economics of exchange, distribution and commerce. The small farmer disposes of his cattle, usually calves of his own breeding, quite differently. He sells this surplus to the dealer, the middleman, the big farmer. As calves grow up they move from the small farm to the large. It is the large farmer who grazes them until they are ready for the English table. Consequently, the local cattle fair is still the small farmer's mart, as it was in the middle ages. The big farmer, on the other hand, sells direct to shippers and exporters. In this system, which represents an immense cattle trade within Ireland, moving cattle endlessly from west to east, from small farms to ranches, and on to their final market in England, the big farmer acts, partly at least, as a commercial middleman or "processer." In many ways the "economic war" with England, which the de Valera government is waging today in an effort to wean Ireland from its dependence upon an English market, is necessarily an attack upon the big farmer. . . .

With all this, it is natural that the small farmers should be different consumers from the rest. They live upon a different diet. They eat very little meat, confining themselves to bacon and occasional poultry. Eggs are a great staple and the potato has only slowly retreated from its place of honour, though the countryman makes sure he shall not allow it to betray him as it did in the time of the Famine.

Milk, especially in the form of butter, is consumed more than in any European country. All this the small farmer raises at home. Bread and tea, English invaders of the last century, are now the commonest diet of all, and represent the one staple which he must buy off the farm. This last he shares with the big farmer and the townsman, but otherwise he buys little of the meats and the shop products which fall to the lot of townsman and big farmer.

Neither type of farmer has much use for mechanized agriculture as we know it; for both are cattlemen. Nevertheless, the small farmer differs again in the tools he uses. He is the one who clings to hand tools; in poorer districts he must rely upon spade, flail, and scythe. The size of his farm and the poor quality of his land confine him to the manual tools.

Lastly, big farmers and small farmers work their lands quite differently. On the big farm, the farmer-owner uses hired labour. On the small farm, the owner relies upon the united efforts of his family. The countryman's subsistence farming is a family economy in which all members of the family take part—sons, daughters and other relatives. He differs completely in this regard from the large farmer, who is an employer and whose hands are wage earners.

This recitation of the distinguishing marks of peasant economics serves a purpose. It reveals in a roundabout manner what sort of livelihood it is that the countryman wrests from his land. He works a small farm with the help of his family. He raises a small garden of potatoes and a few other foodstuffs which feed both himself and his beasts, which beasts feed him in their return. He need go to town only for clothing and sundries, for flour and tea, and to sell at the fairs the calves and yearlings which bring in his principal monetary income and provide thus for whatever he cannot produce at home. These cattle go to big farmers, ranchers and shippers; and with the sale his participation in trade and commerce, in "business," is finished except for his account with the shopkeeper (and in later years, the creamery). As you can well imagine, it is a livelihood little connected with the outside world, and now that agrarian reform has made him full owner of his holding, it is little open to disturbance from the outside.

This is the external view of the small farm. It is the view that usually satisfies the economist. But if one probes deeper and looks at the small farmer's livelihood from within, a fuller picture appears.

That the small farmer is a family man even at work is important for the study of human behaviour. Eight out of ten people working in agriculture in Ireland work not for wages and salaries but by virtue of their family relationship. The work a man does and the directions he gives and receives take form within a social group. That fact yields an opportunity for the anthropologist. Here, in a modern country, is an economy in which there are other controls on labour than those we know—money, contracts, individual profit. To understand these controls is to reach at least one nucleus of the countryman's way of life.

In County Clare, as in all rural Ireland, the small farmer's family lives upon the holding it works. As a rule, the farmhouse is an isolated building standing upon its own ground and forming an integral part of the holding. This is the familiar type of farm we know; Meizen calls it the *Einzelhof*.[1] There are many other types of settlement in Ireland: villages whose fields lie round about in somewhat the fashion of the Russian *mir*[2]; striping fields; and the crazy-quilt pattern of "rundale"; but the *Einzelhof* has won out historically. Anyway, whatever the type of holding, the farm family spends its entire life upon it: sleeping, eating, giving birth and dying there, and sallying forth every day for work. Whether or not there is a topographic identity between house and land, there is a social one. The countryside knows the farm as a unit. The farm shares the name of the family working it. It is inalienably associated with them.

Since cattle play so large a part in rural economy, it is natural that this unit should be known and judged as "the place of so many cows." For in Clare the land is valued for its pasture. It is divided into "field" for grazing, and "meadow" where the grass is cut for hay, and "garden," the small tillage plot. In mountain areas, it may also include rough mountain grazing, called "mountain," and wherever possible, it includes a "bit of bog" for "turf" for the year's fuel. When a small farmer tells you he "has the place of four cows" he sums up this sort of farm, judging it for its ability to support himself and his family in the country manner and to give pasture to four milch cows. In the phrase he epitomizes rural economy.

Ordinarily the house opens directly into the "haggard," as the farmyard is called. There in the haggard are the cabins in which cattle are housed and the various sheds and stalls, often built into the masonry of the house itself. In them, farm machines, tools and carts are kept and crops and seed are stored. Hens and other poultry roam at will through the haggard and are housed there, and in one of the sheds pig or pigs find their quarters. The winter's supply of fodder stands there in the form of the great hayrick. The straw-covered pit of turnips and mangels, not far away, will serve for men and cattle; and the turf-rick is near at hand.

B- The family with which this unit is associated centres its activity round house and haggard. Even for the men, whose work lies primarily in field, garden and meadow, work centres round the house for a

1 [A type of farm.] 2 [Farm.]

good part of the year. If I give you a sketch of this activity as my co-workers and I saw it day after day in several rural communities in Clare, I hope to throw its general features into relief. Following the countryman at his work, we can learn what his role is, what determines it, and what keeps him to it; we can see its controls and the organization of labour it entails.

The first duty of the farm family's day falls to "the woman of the house." Before the others are up, she rakes together such live ashes as remain in the slaked turf fire, puts down new sods, and rekindles the blaze. Then she hangs the kettle on the hook over the hearth, making ready for the first tea of the day. All day long the kettle will hang there, for at any moment she must be ready to serve a cup of tea to husband, children and visitors. With the first tea comes breakfast: bread, eggs and milk.

By the time breakfast is over, the household is ready for its workaday life. Then men are up and dressed for the day's tasks, and the farm wife and mother who serves them and stands by unwilling to sit down till they have had their fill, has begun her daily round. She takes her place later with her daughters and young children who help her throughout the day.

But familiar housework is not the whole of the woman's duty. Her work takes her beyond the house door. After breakfast she takes the milk buckets and goes to milk the cows in the sheds. This is merely one of many trips she makes out into the haggard, for fuel, for water, and to feed the animals and poultry. Milking over, she must not rest, for the whole process of converting milk to butter is her charge. She is an expert at the churn.

Her human charges fed, she must feed the animals in their turn. The full-grown cattle and the horse are not her charge, but she must tend calves and pigs and fowl. Milk and potatoes must be prepared for them all.

Before noon, she hangs a second kettle from the hook. This time she fills it with potatoes for the family. In season, she will add white cabbage, and a portion or two of bacon or salt pork. By the time this is ready the men will be in from the fields impatient for their dinner.

For the men have not been idle. The farmer-father and husband wakes his sons, inspects the cattle and horse, if there is one, and gives them hay and water. If the day is fine, he sallies forth to the fields; if not, and the weather confines him to house and haggard, he has still plenty to do, in building walls, repairing and making machine parts, harness and tools.

Dinner unites the family for the first time since breakfast. Only children of school age are absent and their share of the meal is saved till later. As before, the women and children do not eat till the men have finished. But as the women serve, they all talk about the experiences of the day. It is the chief time of general family conversation. Only the children are silent, for in rural Ireland a well-behaved child is a silent one.

After dinner, work begins anew. For the women chores are much the same as in the morning. Should routine duties come to a pause, there is still plenty to do. Washing, mending, knitting must be done; and their hands are never idle.

The great staple, bread, is baked daily, upon the "griddle" at the hearth. The women may bake at any time, and even late in the evening when the family is gathered round the fire, their last task may be to bake for supper of bread and tea.

At four in the "evening," as the countryman divides the day, children arrive from school, to be fed and questioned. For they are important purveyors of news. Later, the men are home from the fields, driving the cattle home, bedding them for the night. The woman must serve supper and milk the cows, bringing the milk in to separate. But though her day is over with the separating, she may not sit idly with the men for long beside the evening's fire. Children, knitting, and baking can still be attended to; tradition and proverb demand that "one woman in the house be always working."

Work round house and haggard is continuous; it varies little from season to season. It involves a continuous activity by which the household group orders its life and fulfils its first needs in the midst of a carefully patterned regularity of habit. What variation there is, is itself confined to a narrow range. Certain chores are divided among days of the week, but they show nothing of the swift change of a Solomon Grundy. A farmer's wife of Clare divided her week more rigidly in describing it than she did in practice. "On Monday," she said, "I do the washing, on Tuesday the ironing, on Thursday I make butter, on Friday to market, on Saturday I get ready for Sunday, and on Sunday I go to mass and do as little as I can." Really it is only on Sunday that any change seriously alters the daily round; for the country-people are strict Sabbatarians, at least regarding work.

Work on "land" beyond the haggard and the house is less restricted. It has a greater range over the farm and offers a wider variety of tasks round the year. There is a wider freedom of choice among tasks as well. Soil and climate are just as insistent as is the household, but they do not force such narrow regularities.

Yet each season brings a task the farmer must perform. Custom and rivalry in the community restrict him as well. He is in fact less free to choose the date of sowing than his wife the hour of dinner. Long-established tradition and ancestral experience imprint upon his mind the best dates for planting, for reaping, for harrowing, for breeding cattle, and so forth. The farmer is caught, willingly of course, in a mesh of rivalries, competitions, condemnations, which binds him the more strongly to the community's patterning of his yearly round.

The seasonal rhythm of farm work reaches its low in winter. On bitter wet days little can be done beyond the haggard wall, as we have noted. All the many tasks of patching and repair are men's work, they fall to the farmer-father and his sons. The annual round is theirs, as the daily one belongs to the women.

For the countryman, the Christmas season, from the beginning of Advent to the Epiphany or "Little Christmas," is the dead of winter. All farm work is at a standstill. The farmer is free to devote the season to holiday. Outside the weather is unsettled, a cold rain falling on the sodden fields. For him the year has stopped and is waiting to renew its forces.

With the Epiphany, the succession of bitter wet days does not end, but holiday does. One's mind turns to the earnest work of the year to come. The farmer plans his spring planting. On drier days he can clean ditches and drains; he can lay in seed and repair machines. In the evenings, conversation on visits and at home revolves round the coming planting and calving, and traditional experience goes from mouth to mouth. In fact, it is the time for all new plans, for it is Shrovetide, the season of match-making and marriage.

St. Bridget's Day, February 1, marks the beginning of spring. For St. Bridget promised every second day thereafter would be "hard." The return of the "hard" days of wind and clear weather herald the land's drying-off. Through February and March, gardens must be prepared, potatoes planted, fields made ready for the return of the cattle to them. Each "hard" day is more than welcome, for then work in the fields can go on. By St. Patrick's Day, they say in Clare, the potatoes should all be "down"; after that there still remains much to do, though the worst is over. St. Patrick promised that after his day *every* day would "come hard."

Through the rest of the spring, work is at its most intense. Potatoes must be "stirred" and "landed"; other root crops "put down." March and April see the birth of calves and the beginning of the season of greater milk yields and intensified butter-making. Before that in February and March the "great spring fairs" take place, and the year's buying and selling of cattle must be done.

Then, gradually, with the return of warm weather and the drying-off of the land, Irish summer begins. May is often the first summer month. Soon the bogs are dry enough for cutting the year's supply of turf and for stacking it to dry under the summer warmth at the bog's edge.

Once the turf is cut and stacked, the first fruits of the farmer's labour begin to appear. The first crop is cabbage, which was planted at odd times very early. It is practically the only green of the diet and old people remember June or July *an chabáiste*, "the hungry month," when a delayed potato crop might condemn them to a month or more of semi-starvation upon cabbage. Today new varieties of potatoes mature as early as June. But the mature potatoes mark no harvest; they are turned out of the ridges with spade and plough as they are needed.

The first true harvest, and the most important one of the year, is the haymaking. Mowing begins in late July or early August. The haymaking is a race against time and rainy weather. Every effort must be bent to mow, rake, dry and stack the grasses, first in small haycocks, then in the great hayrick in the haggard, before rain brings rot to the lush crop. The farmers speak of it aptly when they call it "saving the hay."

Corn crops, oats and rye, come in next, and then through September, October and November the other roots, mangels and turnips, must be "pulled." Turf must be brought down to the haggard from the bogricks; and everything made ready for man and cattle for the coming winter. Autumn fairs bring a new high in buying and selling cattle; and with the last of them, winter sets in again and Advent has returned. In late November the farmer may turn over his gardens with the plough, to prepare them for the spring. As he follows the furrow, he can look back upon a year ended and forward upon a new one to begin.

Yet, unvarying as this yearly round is, and much as the recurrent patterns of work in garden, meadow and field follow the farmer year after year, from boyhood to death, this work—man's round—is freer and more various, even perhaps more arduous, than woman's. We must remember this difference. It reflects an important dichotomy between the sexes in the organization of labour.

We can see this dichotomy even when the group works as a unit. At various crucial points in the annual round we have just followed, the whole family bends to the tasks at hand together. At potato planting, turf-cutting and haymaking, one can see them working in unison. Even the young children contribute their share to the common rhythm of the task. Yet the woman's role is separate. It is auxiliary; the simpler, less arduous tasks fall to her. The heavier work and command of the enterprise rests with the men. The plough, the harrow, the mower, the scythe, the spade and the turf-cutting *slán* are regarded as masculine implements. The attitudes of the countryside forbid a woman's using them. In the same way, they heap ridicule upon the thought of a man's interesting himself in the feminine sphere, in poultry, or in the churning.

Immemorial folklore bolsters this division. The woman is unlucky to masculine enterprises, for instance: it is dangerous to see a woman on the road to the fair. Likewise, man is dangerous to the woman's work. If he so much as takes his lighted pipe out of the house while she is churning, he may "take the butter," through fairy magic.

In this dichotomy, of course, the male sphere bears higher value. But dichotomy implies no derogation. Man's role and woman's role are complementary; both are indispensable patterns of skill without which the farm family cannot live. And for that reason each is reciprocal to the other. Each feels a right to expect good work from the other, in his or her proper sphere. A good husband is a skilful farmer; a good wife is a skilful, willing household worker and auxiliary field hand. The family makes its way through a nice adjustment of these reciprocal roles. A small farmer of mid-Clare describes the situation in his own words:

"Here is something I want to tell you and you can put it in your head and take it back with you. The small farmer (in Ireland) has to have an intelligent wife or he won't last long. He may do for a few years, but after that he can't manage. You take children's clothes . . . if she knows how to buy material and make the clothes she saves a lot of money, and there are a thousand ways an intelligent woman makes money." Here his wife interrupted him and asked, "What about the tillage?" "That's all right," he went on. "But if it wasn't for the woman the farmer wouldn't last, and when he is getting a wife for one of his sons, he should look to a house where there has been an industrious and intelligent woman, because she has taught her daughters how to work and that is what is needed."

Here, then, we have one important control in work. The division of labour between the sexes arises within a larger field of interests and mutual obligations. It is a function of the relationship of husband and wife within the family.

But it is more, too. The attitudes of the countryside toward men's work and women's work show that their respective skills are regarded also as integral parts of the personalities of all men and women of the countryman's own kind. Here we can see how strongly social dispositions influence both mind and vocabulary. "Natural" is a word very frequently on the countryman's lips. Thus, it is "natural" for a woman to be a better milker, her smaller hands are proof. And it is laughably "unnatural" that a man should bother about the sale of eggs. This division is embedded in tradition, too. Luogh still tells a humorous old tale of the spades, men's tools, that used to work of themselves in the olden days, till a woman forgot to say "God bless the work" to them. This division is bolstered in magic, too, for the "coulter of a plough," that masculine implement, can bring back the butter the fairies have taken.

The division of labour between the sexes is not the only important division within the countryman's pattern of farm work. Work is divided just as much upon the basis of age. Within the masculine sphere, male family members divide the practice of masculine techniques. Within the feminine sphere, there are similar divisions.

Let us look at the men at their work. The father and husband is normally owner and director of the enterprise. The farm and its income are vested in him. The farm bears his name in the community and sons are spoken of as his "boys." In the draining of a field or the sale of cattle at a fair, the sons, even though fully adult, work under their father's eye, and refer necessary decisions to him.

But this relationship is much more than economic. Perhaps the best way of describing it is to trace its development. The child forms part of the productive unit which is his own family. His growing up is also an apprenticeship. He learns the techniques which will make him a full-fledged member of his class; but there is no divorce between technical and non-technical training. All he learns fits him for one end—to become a farmer-father-husband in a family of his own.

The child see his father as owner, director and principal worker of the farm. From his example, he learns which are men's tasks and he learns to value the skills they demand. In family deliberations he learns, too, the nice balance between the needs of household and land. It is true he learns these techniques in a narrow school; his father makes sure that he does not deviate from the right and traditional pattern, which folklore, adage and the censure of the village support. But he learns well, by example, competition and practice.

This process is the daily experience of many years; it is very gradual and is embedded in traditional social life. The boy's first duties, as soon as he can speak and walk, are to run on petty errands to neighbours and near-by friends. Until he is seven and passes through first communion, his place is in the house with the women, and he shares the same bed with his sisters. After that year, he leaves his mother's apron strings, and is slowly drawn into men's ways; he is thrown more and more with elder brothers and sleeps with them henceforward. In remote regions he takes off girl's clothing for the first time; for girl's clothing has protected him from the fairies, they say. Both socially and economically he is becoming a male, but his male status is still very little. By the time he is ten or eleven, he is brought home from school when needed to take part in the important agricultural work of the year. But not until he passes confirmation and leaves school, usually at the same time, does he take on full men's work and assume men's clothing. Even then, as he reaches maturity, and takes on more and more the heavy tasks of the farm, he never escapes his father's direction. Only when his father makes over the farm to him, at death or at his own marriage, can he assume command, and with it full adult status.

Economic apprenticeship is thus a process of conditioning within the family. But there is no separation of economic and non-economic spheres. The father's direction of the enterprise coincides with his dominant, controlling role as parent and adult; the boy learns work as he learns manhood.

Also, the child grows up within the full complex of life within the farm family. His first petty errands are a mere incident in the relationship he builds up with his parents and brothers. He learns not only his work but the whole code of conduct which constitutes the folkways of his class, at their hands. This conduct is itself part of his relation to them. It ranges all the way from the errands he runs for his superiors in the family to the learning of his prayers and the development of the sentiments which make sexual behaviour of any kind an offence, and of that within the family, incest.

Consequently, in so well-knit a group, the command which his father (and his mother) exercises over the son in farm work is only one aspect of that control. His subordination continues as long as his father lives. Even though the major work of the farm devolves upon the son and his brothers, they have no control of the direction of farm work nor the disposal of the farm's income. I say the son and his brothers, for all the sons are equal in this subordination; rural Ireland knows neither primogeniture nor junior right. As long as they remain at home upon the farm they share this status equally.

The behaviour that reflects this state of affairs can be readily observed. Sons go to market and fair from the time they are ten or twelve, but they buy or sell little if anything. Father and sons can be seen together at the local markets, but it is the father who does the bargaining. Their attitudes are in agreement with this arrangement. Once I asked a countryman about it at a potato market in Clare. He explained he could not leave his post for long because his full-grown son wasn't well enough known yet and was not yet a good hand at selling. If a son in Luogh and other Clare communities wants a half-crown to go to a hurley match, he must get it from his father. The son may earn money in employment off the farm, on the roads, or as a labourer, but even then he is expected to contribute everything he receives to the household, as long as he remains on the farm. Very often, as the author saw in Luogh, in work on land division, the old fellows will walk to the pay-off to collect for themselves the wages their sons earned.

You will say, perhaps, that all this has a very familiar ring; it is characteristic of closely knit farm families everywhere. So it is, but we are prone to disregard the familiar; we forget that the familiar stuff of life has often more important implications than the exotic. In the Irish countryside we must not undervalue the familiar. For the implications of these factors of family life are the signposts along the road.

In the countryside this subordination of the sons does not gradually come to an end. It is a constant. Even at forty-five and fifty, if the old couple have not yet made over the farm, the countryman remains a "boy," both in farm work and in the rural vocabulary. In 1933, a deputy to the Dail raised considerable laughter in the sophisticated Dublin papers when he inadvertently used the country idiom in expressing country realities. He pleaded for special treatment in land division for "boys of forty-five and older"—boys who have nothing in prospect but to wait for their father's farm. For "boyhood" in this instance is a social status rather than a physiological state. A countryman complained to me in words which tell the whole story. "You can be a boy forever," he said, "as long as the old fellow is alive."

Had we more time we might devote a long inquiry to this relationship, to its affective content, to the mutual respect and pride of father and son. The Irish countryside values the stern father perhaps more highly than the indulgent one; the peasant father takes great pride in a sturdy successor and competent fellow-worker. Camaraderie and intimacy may not flourish between them; but deeper felt affections underlie formal respect and gruff command. The Irish mother, compassionate, indulgent, is of course a counterpoise to this stern paternality. She has an emotional role in the balance of reciprocal sentiments as indispensable to the family's existence as the economic role she plays. Freud might illuminate us about the sort of conflicts such a human structure engenders, but he has little to say of the far more important, and more apparent, balance of emotional forces which it entails.

For this balance is the health of a complete social organism. The countryman who occupies boyhood status so long ordinarily does not revolt. His economic dependence galls him perhaps at times, but he cannot regard it as an injustice. That dependence is itself a product of healthy balance. He has expectancies and prospects; father and mother owe him obligations for which he can and does wait; emotional bonds are fiercely strong, for there is little opportunity to diffuse them. The solidarity of his own family is strengthened through competition with other socio-economic units. The endless petty disputes of the countryside over rights of way, boundaries, cattle trespasses, drainages, are much more than defences of property. "The two grandfathers" of the contestants "began it" is the usual defence in court. That solidarity is a mountain of strength against the outside world. "Defending Tim Flanagan's title" is the jocular way of describing armed resistance to eviction in the country districts in Clare. For Tim Flanagan worked a farm with ten strong adult sons; evicting ten armed stalwarts is no small matter for the best of police. Sons and brothers are a better title than the clearest deed.

The controls in farm work, then, are those of a social group—the family. The countryman at work is little concerned with the usual economic categories. He is a family man. He may be the shrewdest of traders and the best of farmers, but what gives him his occupational status, determines his pattern of work, provides his incentive, is a set of dispositions arising in the balanced interests and reciprocal obligations of the social group to which he belongs.

Concl.

G. M. Brady

THE SETTLED MEN

NO SLY USURPING dream defeats the will
Of these whose kingdoms are their careful crops.
Only the unwatched weeds breed loss,
Only the thoughtless sky contests
Against the slow resourcefulness of these
Who move between bare weathering headlands,
Moving until the stubborn heart is stayed.

Gravely, as gravely they live as the stones
That wall about their season-worried fields.
When death's encroaching wind unsettles hold
One falls, one stone, one man whose loss
Opens a door of prayer on every hearth.
Then without hesitancy or fear
Another thrusts into the vacant place.

Across their skies the sun leans sometimes or
The tall rain swings. The white day like a blade
Slips into night's sheath gradually, night

THE SETTLED MEN: From the poetry collection *New Irish Poets* edited by Devin A. Garrity. Published 1948 by The Devin-Adair Co., New York.

That nurses no sprouting fantasies of wealth,
But stretches a shadow on the marriage bed,
And in its darkness breeds the hands,
The hands of future toil and later ghosts.

Within their boundaries of clutching field
They are the uncommuning men. Absent
Is History, busy with war and loss.
Above them loneliness circles like a bird.
Beneath their silences the hard land yields.
Tall on Time's hill, they breathe the plucking air,
These men who through the centuries grew gaunt.

Thomas Henry Huxley

THE METHOD OF SCIENTIFIC INVESTIGATION

THE METHOD of scientific investigation is nothing but the expression of the necessary mode of working of the human mind. It is simply the mode at which all phenomena are reasoned about, rendered precise and exact. There is no more difference, but there is just the same kind of difference, between the mental operations of a man of science and those of an ordinary person as there is between the operations and methods of a baker or of a butcher weighing out his goods in common scales and the operations of a chemist in performing a difficult and complex analysis by means of his balance and finely graduated weights. It is not that the action of the scales in the one case and the balance in the other differ in the principles of their construction or manner of working; but the beam of one is set on an infinitely finer axis than the other and of course turns by the addition of a much smaller weight.

You will understand this better, perhaps, if I give you some familiar example. You have all heard it repeated, I dare say, that men of science work by means of induction and deduction, and that by the help of these operations they, in a sort of sense, wring from nature certain other things which are called natural laws and causes, and that out of these, by some cunning skill of their own, they build up hypotheses and theories. And it is imagined by many that the operations of the common mind can be by no means compared with these processes, and that they have to be acquired by a sort of special apprenticeship to the craft. To hear all these large words you would think that the mind of a man of science must be constituted differ-

THE METHOD OF SCIENTIFIC INVESTIGATION: From *Darwiniana* by Thomas Henry Huxley. Reprinted by permission of the publishers, Appleton-Century-Crofts, Inc.

ently from that of his fellow men; but if you will not be frightened by terms, you will discover that you are quite wrong and that all these terrible apparatus are being used by yourselves every day and every hour of your lives.

There is a well-known incident in one of Molière's plays where the author makes the hero express unbounded delight on being told that he had been talking prose during the whole of his life. In the same way I trust that you will take comfort and be delighted with yourselves on the discovery that you have been acting on the principles of inductive and deductive philosophy during the same period. Probably there is not one here who has not in the course of the day had occasion to set in motion a complex train of reasoning of the very same kind, though differing of course in degree, as that which a scientific man goes through in tracing the causes of natural phenomena.

A very trivial circumstance will serve to exemplify this. Suppose you go into a fruiterer's shop, wanting an apple. You take up one, and on biting it you find it is sour; you look at it and see that it is hard and green. You take up another one, and that too is hard, green, and sour. The shopman offers you a third; but before biting it you examine it and find that it is hard and green, and you immediately say that you will not have it, as it must be sour like those that you have already tried.

Nothing can be more simple than that, you think; but if you will take the trouble to analyze and trace out into its logical elements what has been done by the mind, you will be greatly surprised. In the first place you have performed the operation of induction. You found that in two experiences hardness and greenness in apples go together with sourness. It was so in the first case, and it was confirmed by the second. True, it is a very small basis, but still it is enough to make an induction from; you generalize the facts, and you expect to find sourness in apples where you get hardness and greenness. You found upon that a general law that all hard and green apples are sour; and that, so far as it goes, is a perfect induction. Well, having got your natural law in this way, when you are offered another apple which you find is hard and green, you say, "All hard and green apples are sour; this apple is hard and green; therefore this apple is sour." That train of reasoning is what logicians call a syllogism and has all its various parts and terms—its major premise, its minor premise, and its conclusion. And by the help of further reasoning, which if drawn out would have to be exhibited in two or three other syllogisms, you arrive at your final determination, "I will not have that apple." So that, you see, you have, in the first place, established a law by induction, and upon that you have founded a deduction and reasoned out the special conclusion of the particular case. Well now, suppose, having not your law, that at some time afterwards you are discussing the qualities of apples with a friend. You will say to him, "It is a very curious thing, but I find that all hard and green apples are sour!" Your friend says to you, "But how do you know that?" You at once reply, "Oh, because I have tried them over and over again and have always found them to be so." Well, if we were talking science instead of common sense, we should call that an experimental verification. And if still opposed you go further and say, "I have heard from the people in Somersetshire and Devonshire, where a large number of apples are grown, that they have observed the same thing. It is also found to be the case in Normandy and in North America. In short, I find it to be the universal experience of mankind wherever attention has been directed to the subject." Whereupon, your friend, unless he is a very unreasonable man, agrees with you and is convinced that you are quite right in the conclusion you have drawn. He believes, although perhaps he does not know he believes it, that the more extensive verifications are, that the more frequently experiments have been made and results of the same kind arrived at, that the more varied the conditions under which the same results have been attained the more certain is the ultimate conclusion, and he disputes the question no further. He sees that the experiment has been tried under all sorts of conditions as to time, place, and people with the same result; and he says with you, therefore, that the law you have laid down must be a good one and he must believe it.

In science we do the same thing; the philosopher exercises precisely the same faculties, though in a much more delicate manner. In scientific inquiry it becomes a matter of duty to expose a supposed law to every possible kind of verification, and to take care, moreover, that this is done intentionally and not left to mere accident as in the case of the apples. And in science, as in common life, our confidence in a law is in exact proportion to the absence of variation in the result of our experimental verifications. For instance, if you let go your grasp of an article you may have in your hand, it will immediately fall to the ground. That is a very common verification of one of the best established laws of nature, that of gravitation. The method by which men of science established the existence of that law is exactly the same as that by which we have established the trivial proposition about the sourness of hard and green apples. But we believe it in such an extensive, thorough, and unhesitating manner because the universal experience of mankind verifies it, and we can verify it ourselves at any time; and that is the strongest possible foundation on which any natural law can rest.

So much by way of proof that the method of establishing laws in science is exactly the same as that pursued in common life. Let us now turn to another matter (though really it is but another phase of the same question), and that is the method by which from the relations of certain phenomena we prove that some stand in the position of causes towards the others.

I want to put the case clearly before you, and I will therefore show you what I mean by another familiar example. I will suppose that one of you, on coming down in the morning to the parlor of your house, finds that a teapot and some spoons which had been left in the room on the previous evening are gone; the window is open, and you observe the mark of a dirty hand on the window-frame; and perhaps, in addition to that, you notice the impress of a hobnailed shoe on the gravel outside. All these phenomena have struck your attention instantly, and before two seconds have passed you say, "Oh, somebody has broken open the window, entered the room, and run off with the spoons and the teapot!" That speech is out of your mouth in a moment. And you will probably add, "I know there has; I am quite sure of it." You mean to say exactly what you know; but in reality what you have said has been the expression of what is, in all essential particulars, an hypothesis. You do not *know* it at all; it is nothing but an hypothesis rapidly framed in your own mind! And it is an hypothesis founded on a long train of inductions and deductions.

What are those inductions and deductions, and how have you got at this hypothesis? You have observed, in the first place, that the window is open; but by a train of reasoning involving many inductions and deductions, you have probably arrived long before at the general law—and a very good one it is—that windows do not open of themselves; and you therefore conclude that something has opened the window. A second general law that you have arrived at in the same way is that teapots and spoons do not go out of a window spontaneously, and you are satisfied that, as they are not now where you left them, they have been removed. In the third place, you look at the marks on the window and the shoe marks outside, and you say that in all previous experience the former kind of mark has never been produced by anything else but the hand of a human being; and the same experience shows that no other animal but man at present wears shoes with hobnails on them such as would produce the marks in the gravel. I do not know, even if we could discover any of those "missing links" that are talked about, that they would help us to any other conclusion! At any rate the law which states our present experience is strong enough for my present purpose. You next reach the conclusion that as these kinds of marks have not been left by any other animal than man, or are liable to be formed in any other way than by a mans' hand and shoe, the marks in question have been formed by

a man in that way. You have, further, a general law founded on observation and experience, and that too is, I am sorry to say, a very universal and unimpeachable one—that some men are thieves; and you assume at once from all these premises—and that is what constitutes your hypothesis—that the man who made the marks outside and on the window sill opened the window, got into the room, and stole your teapot and spoons. You have now arrived at a *vera causa;* you have assumed a cause which it is plain is competent to produce all the phenomena you have observed. You can explain all these phenomena only by the hypothesis of a thief. But that is an hypothetical conclusion, of the justice of which you have no absolute proof at all; it is only rendered highly probable by a series of inductive and deductive reasonings.

I suppose your first action, assuming that you are a man of ordinary common sense and that you have established this hypothesis to your own satisfaction, will very likely be to go off for the police and set them on the track of the burglar with the view to the recovery of your property. But just as you are starting with this object, some person comes in and on learning what you are about says, "My good friend, you are going on a great deal too fast. How do you know that the man who really made the marks took the spoons? It might have been a monkey that took them, and the man may have merely looked in afterwards." You would probably reply, "Well, that is all very well, but you see it is contrary to all experience of the way teapots and spoons are abstracted; so that, at any rate, your hypothesis is less probable than mine." While you are talking the thing over in this way, another friend arrives, one of that good kind of people that I was talking of a little while ago.

And he might say, "Oh, my dear sir, you are certainly going on a great deal too fast. You are most presumptuous. You admit that all these occurrences took place when you were fast asleep, at a time when you could not possibly have known anything about what was taking place. How do you know that the laws of nature are not suspended during the night? It may be that there has been some kind of supernatural interference in this case." In point of fact, he declares that your hypothesis is one of which you cannot at all demonstrate the truth and that you are by no means sure that the laws of nature are the same when you are asleep as when you are awake.

Well, now, you cannot at the moment answer that kind of reasoning. You feel that your worthy friend has you somewhat at a disadvantage. You will feel perfectly convinced in your own mind, however, that you are quite right, and you will say to him, "My good friend, I can only be guided by the natural probabilities of the case, and if you will be kind enough to stand aside and permit me to pass,

I will go and fetch the police." Well, we will suppose that your journey is successful and that by good luck you meet with a policeman; that eventually the burglar is found with your property on his person and the marks correspond to his hand and to his boots. Probably any jury would consider those facts a very good experimental verification of your hypothesis touching the cause of the abnormal phenomena observed in your parlor, and would act accordingly.

Now, in this supposititious case I have taken phenomena of a very common kind in order that you might see what are the different steps in an ordinary process of reasoning, if you will only take the trouble to analyze it carefully. All the operations I have described, you will see, are involved in the mind of any man of sense in leading him to a conclusion as to the course he should take in order to make good a robbery and punish the offender. I say that you are led, in that case, to your conclusion by exactly the same train of reasoning as that which a man of science pursues when he is endeavoring to discover the origin and laws of the most occult phenomena. The process is, and always must be, the same; and precisely the same mode of reasoning was employed by Newton and Laplace in their endeavors to discover and define the causes of the movements of the heavenly bodies as you, with your own common sense, would employ to detect a burglar. The only difference is that, the nature of the inquiry being more abstruse, every step has to be most carefully watched so that there may not be a single crack or flaw in your hypothesis. A flaw or crack in many of the hypotheses of daily life may be of little or no moment as affecting the general correctness of the conclusions at which we may arrive; but in a scientific inquiry a fallacy, great or small, is always of importance and is sure to be in the long run constantly productive of mischievous if not fatal results.

Do not allow yourselves to be misled by the common notion that an hypothesis is untrustworthy simply because it is an hypothesis. It is often urged in respect to some scientific conclusion that, after all, it is only an hypothesis. But what more have we to guide us in nine-tenths of the most important affairs of daily life than hypotheses, and often very ill-based ones? So that in science, where the evidence of an hypothesis is subjected to the most rigid examination, we may rightly pursue the same course. You may have hypotheses and hypotheses. A man may say, if he likes, that the moon is made of green cheese; that is an hypothesis. But another man, who has devoted a great deal of time and attention to the subject and availed himself of the most powerful telescopes and the results of the observations of others, declares that in his opinion it is probably composed of materials very similar to those of which our own earth is made up; and that is also only an hypothesis. But I need not tell you that there is an enormous difference in the value of the two hypotheses. That one which is based on sound scientific knowledge is sure to have a corresponding value; and that which is a mere hasty random guess is likely to have but little value. Every great step in our progress in discovering causes has been made in exactly the same way as that which I have detailed to you. A person observing the occurrence of certain facts and phenomena asks, naturally enough, what kind of operation known to occur in nature applied to the particular case, will unravel and explain the mystery. Hence you have the scientific hypothesis; and its value will be proportionate to the care and completeness with which its basis has been tested and verified. It is in these matters as in the commonest affairs of practical life: the guess of the fool will be folly, while the guess of the wise man will contain wisdom. In all cases you see that the value of the result depends on the patience and faithfulness with which the investigator applies to his hypothesis every possible kind of verification.

René Dubos

DREAMS OF REASON

THE REVOLUTIONARY advances of the past two centuries suggest that almost any problem of human welfare can be solved if it is properly formulated and if its solution is diligently pursued. As a student of experimental medicine, I take it for granted that progress can be made in the control of any disease to which we address ourselves with enough energy. I feel confident, also, that physicists, chemists, and engineers can provide us with almost any kind of earthly good. I even believe that sociologists and politicians will find ways of improving relations among men, even though the result may be peace without love. From penicillin to supersonic flight, from the control of personality to space exploration, from elimination of child labor to universal suffrage, the twentieth century has been marked by many scientific and social achievements which are so startling as to dwarf the miracles of the legendary ages.

Despite all these modern miracles, there are many among us who speak regretfully of the old times and tend to place the golden age in the past rather than in the future. And, in fact, the many beautiful things that have come to us from the past are eloquent witnesses to a kind of happiness that we may well envy our an-

---

cestors: the lyrical outbursts of poets, the smiling angels in Gothic cathedrals, the glamourous feasts of the Renaissance, the gay celebrations of primitive country folk. How often we long for the profound and genuine happiness of yesteryear!

The disenchanted mood of today, of course, has its origin in the fact that happiness does not depend only upon comfort and contentment. Illiterates may well be contented and morons even more so—still more, perhaps, the proverbially contented cow or the well-fed household cat. But the further man evolves from his animal origin, the less happiness he can find in the mere removal of discomfort and in the satisfactions of the body. Every fulfillment, whatever its nature, is likely to create a new need and thus become a source of new dissatisfaction. The endless urge for some new experience, the tendency to look for goals beyond the attainable, are traits which differentiate man from other forms of life. These aspirations have led him to establish his dominance over the natural world, but certainly they are endlessly creating for him new problems which make of health and of happiness mirages that are ever receding into the future.

Until the end of the eighteenth century most of material civilization had been built out of practices evolved either empirically from the very experience of day-to-day life or from discoveries made by accident without prior scientific knowledge. In fact, much of science itself arose from these empirical achievements. Then, systematic scientific knowledge derived from laboratory experimentation rapidly overtook practical life, and scientists increasingly became the innovators and indeed the governors of human existence. It can be said that the scientific age began when, from toiling obscurely in the rear of the empirical procedures, science stepped forward and held up the torch in front. By the middle of the nineteenth century, scientific investigations undertaken in a search for pure knowledge began to suggest practical applications and inventions. Faraday's electro-magnetic experiments led to the dynamo and other electromagnetic machines; Maxwell's studies of waves led to wireless telegraphy; Pasteur's work revolutionized fermentation industries and the practice of medicine, etc., etc.

As a result of this change, the business of everyday life is now carried out with the tools provided by science, and, more importantly, the very character of human existence is now molded by the products of scientific technology. While these facts are obvious and acknowledged by all—by those who deprecate them as well as by those who delight in them—it is not so well recognized that the direction of scientific effort during the past three centuries, and therefore the whole trend of modern life, has been markedly conditioned by an attitude fostered by the creators of utopias. They fostered the view that nature must be studied not so much to be understood as to be mastered and exploited by man.

The urge to control nature is probably the most characteristic aspect of Western civilization. It has not yet been proven, however, that this ideal is the best for human life. After all, great civilizations have been created in the past, and much profound happiness has been experienced, based on the philosophy that man must strive for harmony with the rest of nature instead of behaving toward it as a dominating lord and an exploiting master. It is much too early to be sure that Galileo, Watt, and Edison have contributed more lastingly to human advancement and happiness than have Socrates, Lao-tse, and Francis of Assisi.

The ethical problems posed by the utilization of knowledge are, of course, as old as mankind. But it is only during modern times that the question has become practically important as a result of the increasing effectiveness of scientific methods, and of the fact that science is now valued more for its social uses than as natural philosophy. In a recent address Ritchie Calder stated that "scientists leave their discoveries like foundlings on the doorstep of society. The step-parents do not know how to bring them up." Clearly, this attitude is no longer permissible now that scientific discoveries can have such far-reaching and lasting effects on human existence—indeed, on the fate of the human race. It is for society, of course, to decide what goals it wishes to reach and what risks it is willing to take. But it is the task of the scientific community to formulate as clearly as possible and to make public the probable consequences of any step that it takes and of any action that it advocates. In other words, the responsibility of the scientist does not stop when he has developed the knowledge and techniques that lead to a process or a product. Beyond that, he must secure and make public the kind of information on which the social body as a whole can base the value judgments that alone will decide long-range policies.

The relation of science to society has changed and become more complex during modern times. Three hundred years ago Bacon and his followers were justified in claiming that the important problem was to learn *how* to do things. There was then so little that could be done! Soon it became apparent that the most effective method of progress was to try to understand natural phenomena, their *whys* as much as their *hows*. Now it can be said that it is possible to achieve almost anything we want—so great is the effectiveness of technology based on the experimental method. Thus, the main issue for scientists and for society as a whole is now to decide *what* to do among all the things that could be done and should be done.

Unless scientists are willing to give hard thought—indeed, their hearts—to this latter aspect of their social responsibilities, they may find themselves someday in the position of the Sorcerer's Apprentice, unable to control the forces they have unleashed. And they may have to confess, like Captain Ahab in *Moby Dick*, that all their methods are sane, their goal mad.

The perennial fascination of Greek philosophy lies in its concern with the kind of knowledge that led man out of his brutish existence. Science would be just an instrument for comfort and power, not a cultural force, if it did not help man to transcend his animal origin. Whatever their selfish interests and their commitments to practical ends, most scientists cling to the faith—respected in the spirit even though often betrayed in action—that to work for knowledge and truth is the highest form of scientific duty. Ideally, and to a large extent actually, science is part of the collective effort for the humanization of mankind.

Modern science has been immensely successful in discovering facts and inventing techniques. But only a few minds in each generation have been able to percieve the laws of the cosmos and to communicate them in a meaningful form to their less gifted fellow men. As to understanding the nature of the universe and of the human condition, it is questionable whether we have progressed much during the past two thousand years.

Let us look at the field of biology. It seems to me that the scientific attitude of modern biologists is conditioned to a very large extent by assumptions about the mind-matter problem which were made a few centuries ago and which are accepted as a basis of operation without concern for their validity, even by those who do not really believe in them.

During the early seventeenth century, as is well known, René Descartes asserted that the human body and the human soul are two separate entities and that the body is a machine which, therefore, can be studied as such. This was a convenient assumption and one which has proved extremely useful for certain kinds of scientific pursuits. Immediately following Descartes, scientists applied what they knew of mechanics to the body machine and found that its structure and functions were compatible with the knowledge derived from lifeless systems. Then the chemists and the physicists engaged in similar studies and found that the phenomena associated with life obey at each step the same physicochemical laws that operate in the inanimate world. At the present time this approach to the study of the structure and functions of living things is culminating in the marvelous achievements of molecular biology.

The fact that Descartes's assumptions have led to such great scientific advances does not prove, however, that these assumptions are correct. There is no evidence whatever that the body and the mind are two separate entities, and despite the triumphs of molecular biology, it has not yet been proven that the living body is only a machine and that life is merely a complex integration of known physicochemical forces. I realize that in raising this question I may seem to be reviving the vitalistic doctrine with all its false intellectual mysticism. But, in my opinion, I am doing nothing of the sort. I am only emphasizing that the machine view of living things is buried so deep in the modern subconscious that few scientists ever try to bring it to the surface to examine its significance in the bright light of critical knowledge. And I believe that the acceptance of an oversimplified mechanistic theory of life has narrowed considerably the front of progress in biological sciences.

Increasingly during recent decades the study of biological problems has been influenced by two large assumptions which at first sight appear to be based on hard-boiled scientific common sense, but in reality are still *sub judice*.[1] One is that life can be understood only by analyzing the mechanisms linking the molecular and the animate worlds; the other is that the arrow of influence between these two worlds points in only one direction, from the molecular lifeless components to the more complex patterns of organization found in living things. These two assumptions have been immensely fruitful because they have encouraged investigators to break down phenomena and structures into smaller and simpler components, ultimately to be described in terms of identifiable chemical forces and substances. Moreover, they provide the easiest and safest approach to biology. They free the scientist from the need to engage in soul searching about the philosophical meaning of life, since in the final analysis they equate living processes with the reactions of inanimate matter. Finally, they permit an endless series of laboratory operations, because to disintegrate and analyze is far easier than to build up complex functioning organisms or even to investigate them as a whole. In the words of Professor Homer W. Smith:

> I would define mechanism, as we use the word today, as designating the belief that all the activities of the living organism are ultimately to be explained in terms of its component molecular parts. This was Descartes's greatest contribution to philosophy. . . . Abandon Cartesian mechanism and you will close up every scientific biological laboratory in the world at once, you will turn back the clock by three full centuries.

1 [Literally, under the judge, i.e., being investigated.]

It is likely, however, that if the analytical breakdown of living things into simpler and ever simpler components is not supplemented by a more synthetic approach, it will lead the biologist into areas of knowledge concerned not with the essential characteristics of life but with a few selected phenomena which happen to be associated with living processes. To accept this limitation is an attitude of intellectual security and may be the better part of wisdom, but it denies scientists the chance to gain deeper insight into larger biological realities. As a contrast to the unphilosophical endless accretion of "scientific" facts concerning living *matter*, it is stimulating to rediscover in Aristotle's writing the entrancing throb of life. Darwin had this experience on reading William Ogle's translation of *The Parts of Animals*. "I had not the most remote notion what a wonderful man he was," wrote Darwin. "Linnaeus and Cuvier have been my two gods, though in very different ways, but they were mere schoolboys to old Aristotle."

It seems to me that a return to the Aristotelian philosophy, far from being a retreat, would enlarge the scope of the biological sciences. Biology will run dry unless it becomes more receptive than it is presently to unsuspected phenomena, unpredictable on the basis of what is already known. Science does not progress only by inductive, analytical knowledge. The imaginative speculations of the mind come first, the verification and the analytic breakdown come only later. And imagination depends upon a state of emotional and intellectual freedom which makes the mind receptive to the impressions that it receives from the world in its confusing, overpowering, but enriching totality. We must try to experience again the receptivity of the young ages of science when it was socially acceptable to marvel. What Baudelaire said of art applies equally well to science: "Genius is youth recaptured." More prosaically, I believe that in most cases the creative scientific act comes before the operations which lead to the establishment of truth; together they make science.

Nothing could illustrate better the change that occurred in the focus of the scientific community during the Industrial Revolution than the sudden and complete disappearance of the term "natural philosophy." The schism between science and philosophy was the result of two forces which operated almost simultaneously. One was the recognition that knowledge could be used for creating wealth and power; the other was the rapid accumulation of new and unexpected facts which engendered a sense of humility before the complexity of nature and rendered scientists shy of extrapolating from factual knowledge into speculative thoughts. Then humility evolved into scorn for speculation, and today the statement "This is not science, this is philosophy" rules out of scientific discussion any statement that goes a step beyond established fact.

Yet it is apparent that today, as in the past, many scientists—among them some of the most brilliant and most effective—are eager to escape from the austere discipline of factual knowledge and to experience again the intoxication of philosophical thought. They may distrust Plato, but, like him, they seem to regard philosophy as the "dear delight." Witness the flurry of speculative books published by scientists as soon as some discovery enlarges the scope of their knowledge. The theory of evolution has been used by biologists as a platform to erect or justify religious, political, and economic philosophies. Familiarity with modern theoretical physics seems to warrant opinions not only on the structure of matter and its relation to energy but also on the nature of life, the existence of free will, or the symbolism of language.

This return to scientific philosophy negates, it seems to me, the fears so commonly expressed that scientists are becoming a class apart from the rest of society by developing a culture without contact with the rest of human life. It is true, of course, that within the area of his particular work each scientist becomes so specialized that he finds it difficult to communicate on scientific subjects except with other workers in the same specialized field. But this situation is not peculiar to science. It exists just as much in other forms of learning—in philology or Moslem culture as much as in mathematics or genetics. Moreover, science should not be regarded as one single discipline concerning which sweeping statements can be made, any more than this can be done for the so-called humanities. With regard to the knowledge and operations defined by their techniques, the biologist and the mathematician are as far apart as they are from the student of Sanskrit or from the art critic, and as these are from each other. We must accept as a fact that the modern world is made up of an immense number of specialized groups, intellectually separated by experience, words, and the meaning of symbols. In my opinion, there are not "two cultures," even though C. P. Snow has made the expression famous. There are a multiplicity of intellectual occupations, each of which fortunately has several points of contact with human life. Whatever his field of specialization, the scholar can be understood beyond the confines of his guild—but only if he is willing to raise his language above the jargon of his trade. The scholar must learn to speak to man.

As we have seen, the transformations of human life which have taken place during the past hundred years are the realizations of the utopias formulated by the seventeenth- and eighteenth-century philosophers. Not so long ago the role of the scientist in this enterprise appeared straightforward and all to the good; each advance in scientific knowledge eventually resulted in some contributions to human health and happiness. Confident of the ultimate beneficence of his work, the scientist had good reasons to keep aloof from social problems. It is obvious, however, that the situation is now changing rapidly, and one can anticipate that the scientist will face more and more problems of conscience as the social power of science continues to increase.

The issues that immediately come to mind are certain obvious threats to mankind such as those associated with atomic power or with population pressures. In fact, however, the scientist's responsibility is involved in many other issues which appear less dramatic, perhaps, but are probably as important in the long run and more difficult to solve because less clearly defined. Until very recent times so little could be done to deal with the obvious shortages and sufferings in the world that the most urgent need was to develop techniques for the production of material wealth and for the control of disease. Now the power of science is so great that almost any desired method, gadget, or product can be developed if we are willing to devote enough resources to the task. And it is precisely the confidence that utopias can now be converted into realities which creates urgent ethical problems for the scientist.

The question of how to do things was a purely technical one that could be decided on scientific criteria; but the choice of *what* to do, among all the things that can be done, clearly implies some concern with ultimate social consequences. There is no longer any thoughful person who believes that the conversion of science into more power, more wealth, or more drugs necessarily adds to health and happiness or improves the human condition. Indeed, haphazard scientific technology pursued without regard for its relevance to the meaning of human life could spell the end of civilization. Unless he becomes concerned with social philosophy, the scientist will increasingly hear the words of Oscar Wilde applied to him: that he knows the price of everything, but the value of nothing.

J. V. Cunningham

LOGIC AND LYRIC

IN THIS ESSAY I shall propose the question: May the principal structure of a poem be of a logical rather than of an alogical sort? For example, to confine ourselves to the Old Logic: May a lyric be solely or predominantly the exposition of a syllogism? and may the propositions of the lyric, one by one, be of the sort to be found in a logical syllogism?

The incautious romantic will deny the possibility, and with a repugnance of feeling that would preclude any further discussion. For logic and lyric are generally regarded as opposites, if not as contradictory terms. "It is a commonplace," says a recent writer on logic, "that poetry and logic have nothing to do with each other, that they are even opposed to one another."[1] You will find this explicitly stated, sometimes with the substitution of "science" for "logic," in most of the school handbooks on the study of literature, in most of the introductions to poetry. "The peculiar quality of poetry," we read in one of these, "can be distinguished from that of prose if one thinks of the creative mind as normally expressing itself in a variety of literary forms ranged along a graduated scale between the two contrasted extremes of scientific exposition and lyrical verse." And, a little later, "[Poetry] strives for a conviction begotten of the emotions rather than of the reason." Consequently, we are told, "The approach of poetry is indirect. It proceeds by means of suggestion, implication, reflection. Its method is largely symbolical. It is more interested in connotations than in denotations."[2] This is common doctrine. Poetry is in some way concerned with emotion rather than with reason, and its method is imaginative, indirect, implicit rather than explicit, symbolical rather than discursive, concerned with what its terms suggest rather than with what they state. The kind of poetry which most fully possesses and exhibits these concerns, methods, and qualities is generally thought to be the lyric, and hence the lyric, of all poetry, is regarded as the most antithetical to reason, logic, and science.

This was not always the case. In the eighth century, for example,

1 Richard von Mises, *Positivism* (Cambridge, Mass., 1951), p. 289.

2 Harold R. Walley and J. Harold Wilson, *The Anatomy of Literature* (New York, 1934), pp. 143, 144.

LOGIC AND LYRIC: Reprinted from *Modern Philology*, LI, August 1953, by permission of The University of Chicago Press.

a scholiast of the school of Alcuin regarded not only grammar and rhetoric but dialectic or logic also as the disciplines that nourish and form a poet. In the medieval and Renaissance traditions of commentary on Aristotle's logic, poetic is sometimes regarded as a part, a subdivision, of logic—as, indeed, I consider it myself. So late as the eighteenth century, David Hume writes in an essay *Of the Standard of Taste:* "Besides, every kind of composition, even the most poetical, is nothing but a chain of propositions and reasonings; not always indeed the justest and most exact, but still plausible and specious, however disguished by the coloring of the imagination." And even today the writer on logic whom I quoted earlier asserts, in denial of the commonplace: "Every poem, except in rare extreme cases, contains judgements and implicit propositions, and thus becomes subject to logical analysis."[3]

But may the chain of propositions and reasonings be not merely plausible and specious but even sufficiently just and exact? May the poem be not merely subject to logical analysis but logic in form? May, to return to our point, the subject and structure of a poem be conceived and expressed syllogistically? Anyone at all acquainted with modern criticism and the poems that are currently in fashion will think in this connection of Marvell's "To His Coy Mistress." The apparent structure of that poem is an argumentative syllogism, explicitly stated. "Had we but world enough and time," the poet says,

> This coyness, Lady, were no crime . . .
>
> But at my back I always hear
> Time's winged chariot hurrying near . . .
>
> Now, therefore . . .
> . . . let us sport us while we may.

If we had all the space and time in the world, we could delay consummation. But we do not. Therefore. The structure is formal. The poet offers to the lady a practical syllogism, and if she assents to it, the appropriate consequence, he hopes, will follow:

> Had we but world enough, and time,
> This coyness, Lady, were no crime;
> We would sit down and think which way
> To walk and pass our long love's day.

3 Scholiast cited in Otto Bird, "The Seven Liberal Arts," in Joseph T. Shipley, ed., *Dictionary of World Literature* (New York, 1943), p. 55; J. E. Spingarn, *A History of Literary Criticism in the Renaissance,* 2d ed. (New York, 1908), pp. 24–27; David Hume, *Philosophical Works* (Boston and Edinburgh, 1854), III, 264; von Mises, *loc. cit.*

Thou by the Indian Ganges side
Shouldst rubies find; I by the tide
Of Humber would complain. I would
Love you ten years before the Flood,
And you should, if you please, refuse
Till the conversion of the Jews.

My vegetable love should grow
Vaster than empires, and more slow.
A hundred years should go to praise
Thine eyes and on thy forehead gaze;
Two hundred to adore each breast;
But thirty thousand to the rest;
An age at least to every part,
And the last age should show your heart;
For, Lady, you deserve this state,
Nor would I love at lower rate.

But at my back I always hear
Time's winged chariot hurrying near;
And yonder all before us lie
Deserts of vast eternity.
Thy beauty shall no more be found,
Nor in thy marble vault shall sound
My echoing song; then worms shall try
That long preserved virginity,
And your quaint honor turn to dust,
And into ashes all my lust:
The grave's a fine and private place,
But none, I think, do there embrace.

Now, therefore, while the youthful hue
Sits on thy skin like morning dew,
And while thy willing soul transpires
At every pore with instant fires,
Now let us sport us while we may,
And now, like amorous birds of prey,
Rather at once our time devour
Than languish in his slow-chapt power.
Let us roll all our strength and all
Our sweetness up into one ball,
And tear our pleasures with rough strife
Thorough the iron gates of life:
Thus, though we cannot make our sun
Stand still, yet we will make him run.[4]

4 Modernized from H. M. Margouliouth, ed., *The Poems and Letters* (Oxford, 1927), Vol. II.

The logical nature of the argument here has been generally recognized, though often with a certain timidity. Mr. Eliot hazards: "the three strophes of Marvell's poem have something like a syllogistic relation to each other." And in a recent scholarly work we read: "The dialectic of the poem lies not only or chiefly in the formal demonstration explicit in its three stanzas, but in all the contrasts evoked by its images and in the play between the immediately sensed and the intellectually apprehended."[5] That is, the logic is recognized, but minimized, and our attention is quickly distracted to something more reputable in a poem, the images of the characteristic tension of metaphysical poetry. For Mr. Eliot the more important element in this case is a principle of order common in modern poetry and often employed in his own poems. He points out that the theme of Marvell's poem is "one of the great traditional commonplaces of European literature . . . the theme of . . . *Gather ye rosebuds,* of *Go, lovely rose*." "Where the wit of Marvell," he continues, "renews the theme is in the variety and order of the images." The dominant principle of order in the poem, then, is an implicit one rather than the explicit principle of the syllogism, and implicit in the succession of images.

Mr. Eliot explains the implicit principle of order in this fashion:

> In the first of the three paragraphs Marvell plays with a fancy that begins by pleasing and leads to astonishment. . . . We noticed the high speed, the succession of concentrated images, each magnifying the original fancy. When this process has been carried to the end and summed up, the poem turns suddenly with that surprise which has been one of the most important means of poetic effect since Homer:
>
> But at my back I always hear
> Time's winged chariot hurrying near,
> And yonder all before us lie
> Deserts of vast eternity.
>
> A whole civilization resides in these lines:
>
> Pallida Mors aequo pulsat pede pauperum
> tabernas
> Regumque turres . . .[6]
>
> A modern poet, had he reached the height, would very likely have closed on this moral reflection.

5 T. S. Eliot, *Selected Essays,* new ed. (New York, 1950), p. 254; Helen C. White, Ruth C. Wallerstein, and Ricardo Quintana, eds., *Seventeenth Century Verse and Prose* (New York, 1951), I, 454.

6 [Pale Death with impartial foot knocks at the door of poor men's hovels and of kings' palaces. Horace, *Odes,* IV. 13.]

What is meant by this last observation becomes clear a little later, where it is said that the wit of the poem "forms the crescendo and diminuendo of a scale of great imaginative power."[7] The structure of the poem, then, is this: It consists of a succession of images increasing in imaginative power to the sudden turn and surprise of the image of time, and then decreasing to the conclusion. But is there any sudden turn and surprise in the image of time? and does the poem consist of a succession of images?

This talk of images is a little odd, since there seem to be relatively few in the poem if one means by "image" what people usually do—a descriptive phrase that invites the reader to project a sensory construction. The looming imminence of Time's winged chariot is, no doubt, an image, though not a full-blown one, since there is nothing in the phrasing that properly invites any elaboration of sensory detail. But when Mr. Eliot refers to "successive images" and cites "my *vegetable* love," with *vegetable* italicized, and "Till the conversion of the Jews," one suspects that he is provoking images where they do not textually exist. There is about as much of an image in "Till the conversion of the Jews" as there would be in "till the cows come home," and it would be a pyschiatrically sensitive reader who would immediately visualize the lowing herd winding slowly o'er the lea. But "my *vegetable* love" will make the point. I have no doubt that Mr. Eliot and subsequent readers do find an image here. They envisage some monstrous and expanding cabbage, but they do so in ignorance. *Vegetable* is no vegetable but an abstract and philosophical term, known as such to the educated man of Marvell's day. Its context is the doctrine of the three souls: the rational, which in man subsumes the other two; the sensitive, which men and animals have in common and which is the principle of motion and perception; and, finally, the lowest of the three, the vegetable soul, which is the only one that plants possess and which is the principle of generation and corruption, of augmentation and decay. Marvell says, then, my love, denied the exercise of sense but possessing the power of augmentation, will increase "Vaster than empires." It is an intellectual image, and hence no image at all but a conceit. For if one calls any sort of particularity or detail in a poem an "image," the use of the wrong word will invite the reader to misconstrue his experience in terms of images, to invent sensory constructions and to project them on the poem. . . .

But if the poem is not a succession of images, does it exhibit that other principle which Mr. Eliot ascribes to it—the turn and surprise which he finds in the abrupt introduction of Time's chariot and which forms a sort of fulcrum on which the poem turns?

7 Eliot, pp. 253–55.

Subsequent critics have certainly felt that it has. In a current textbook we read:

> The poem begins as a conventional love poem in which the lover tries to persuade his mistress to give in to his entreaties. But with the introduction of the image of the chariot in l. 21, the poem becomes obsessed by the terrible onrush of time, and the love theme becomes scarcely more than an illustration of the effect which time has upon human life.

And the leading scholar in the field, a man who is generally quite unhappy with Mr. Eliot's criticism, nevertheless says:

> the poet sees the whole world of space and time as the setting for two lovers. But wit cannot sustain the pretence that youth and beauty and love are immortal, and with a quick change of tone—like Catullus' *nobis cum semel occidit brevis lux*[8] or Horace's *sed Timor et Minae*[9]—the theme of time and death is developed with serious and soaring directness.[10]

These, I believe, are not so much accounts of the poem as accounts of Mr. Eliot's reading of the poem. Let us question the fact. Does the idea of time and death come as any surprise in this context? The poem began, "Had we but world enough and Time." That is, it began with an explicit condition contrary to fact, which, by all grammatical rules, amounts to the assertion that we do not have world enough and time. There is no surprise whatever when the proposition is explicitly made in line 21. It would rather have been surprising if it had not been made. Indeed, the only question we have in this respect, after we have read the first line, is: How many couplets will the poem expend on the ornamental reiteration of the initial proposition before he comes to the expected *but?* The only turn in the poem is the turn which the structure of the syllogism has led us to await. . . .

In brief, the general structure of Marvell's poem is syllogistic, and it is located in the Renaissance tradition of formal logic and of rhetoric. The structure exists in its own right and as a kind of expandable filing system. It is a way of disposing of, of making a place for, elements of a different order: in this case, Clevelandizing conceits and erotic propositions in the tradition of Jonson and Herrick. These reiterate the propositions of the syllogism. They do

8 [When our brief day once and for all takes flight. Catullus, *Carmina,* V. 5.]
9 [But fear and threats. . . . Horace, *Odes,* III. 1.]
10 Wright Thomas and Stuart Gerry Brown, eds., *Reading Poems* (New York, 1941), p. 702; Douglas Bush, *English Literature in the Earlier Seventeenth Century* (Oxford, 1945), p. 163.

not develop the syllogism and they are not required by the syllogism; they are free and extra. There could be more or less of them, since there is nothing in the structure that determines the number of interpolated couplets. It is a matter of tact and a matter of the appetite of the writer and the reader.

The use of a structure as a kind of expandable filing system is common enough in the Renaissance. The narrative structure of a Shakespearean play can be regarded as a structure of this order. It exists in its own right, of course, but it is also a method for disposing various kinds of material of other orders—a set speech or passion here, an interpolated comic routine in another place. The structure offers a series of hooks upon which different things can be hung. Whether the totality will then form a whole, a unity, is a question of interpretation and a question of value. It is a question, for example, of what sort of unity is demanded and whether there are various sorts.

In Marvell's poem, only the general structure is syllogistic; the detail and development are of another order, and critics have been diligent in assigning the poetic quality of the whole to the non-syllogistic elements. Is it possible, then, to write a lyric that will be wholly or almost wholly syllogistic? It is. There is such a lyric in the *Oxford Book of English Verse*, a lyric of somewhat lesser repute than Marvell's but still universally conceded to possess the true lyrical power. It is Dunbar's "Lament for the Makaris."

The structure of Dunbar's poem is the structure of the traditional syllogism with which everyone is acquainted: *All men are mortal, I am a man;* together with a concluding practical syllogism, *What must be, must be accepted, but I must die.* The syllogism is developed in two ways, both characteristic methods in the logical tradition of the later Middle Ages. It begins with the immediate induction from experience of the leading principle, the major premise:

> I that in heill wes and gladness,
> Am trublit now with gret seiknes,
> An feblit with infermite;
> *Timor mortis conturbat me.*[11]

The experience, then, is the sudden alteration from health to illness, and this yields the generalization:

> Our plesance heir is all vane glory,
> This fals warld is bot transitory,
> The flesche is brukle, the Fend is sle;
> *Timor mortis conturbat me.*

11 [The fear of death throws me into panic.]

The premise, then, is: This false world is but transitory; and it is presently expressed in more restricted terms:

The stait of man dois change and vary,
Now sound, now seik, now blith, now sary,
Now dansand mery, now like to dee;
Timor mortis conturbat me.

The syllogism is now developed by another form of induction, and this development accounts for the remainder of the poem, except for the last stanza. It is developed through induction by simple enumeration in support and explication of the major premise, but with this special feature, that the induction proceeds by a hierarchical method. Nothing could be more characteristic of medieval logic. The argument is: If everything sublunary changes and varies, is mortal, then every estate of man is mortal; and the poet enumerates the estates:

On to the ded gois all Estatis,
Princis, Prelotis, and Potestatis,
Baith riche and pur of al degre;
Timor mortis conturbat me. . . .

He takis the campion in the stour,
The capitane closit in the tour,
The lady in bour full of bewte;
Timor mortis conturbat me.

He sparis no lord for his piscence,
Na clerk for his intelligence;
His awful strak may no man fle;
Timor mortis conturbat me.

Art, magicianis, and astrologgis,
Rhetoris, logicianis, and theologgis,
Thame helpis no conclusionis sle;
Timor mortis conturbat me.

If all estates must die, then poets, too, must die. And now Dunbar proceeds by a simple enumeration, a roll call, of poets:

He has done petuously devour
The noble Chaucer, of makaris flour,
The Monk of Bery, and Gower, all thre;
Timor mortis conturbat me.

The gud Syr Hew of Eglintoun,
And eik Heryot, and Wyntoun,
He has tane out of this cuntre;
Timor mortis conturbat me.

He continues to enumerate poet after poet whom death has taken, until he comes finally to his friendly enemy, the poet, Kennedy, and to himself.

Gud Maister Walter Kennedy
In point of dede lyis veraly,
Gret reuth it were that so suld be;
Timor mortis conturbat me.

Sen he has all my brether tane,
He wil nocht lat me lif alane,
Of forse I man his nyxt pray be;
Timor mortis conturbat me.

Therefore, I must die, concludes the syllogism. And now follows the practical syllogism, the act of resignation:

Sen for the deid remeid is none,
Best is that we dede dispone,
Eftir our deid that lif may we;
Timor mortis conturbat me.[12]

Almost every proposition in the poem is strictly controlled by the syllogistic structure. The exceptions are the refrain and a certain number of affective sentences: "He has done petuously devour / The noble Chaucer" and "Gret reuth it wer that so suld be." These direct the feeling of the poem. Yet, though the poem is so completely determined by logical method and logical structure, it has seemed, and justly, to generations of readers to be a moving poem and properly poetical.

I shall conclude with another poem of the same sort, a lyric of even greater renown in modern criticism. This is the song from *Summer's Last Will and Testament* by Thomas Nashe, "Adieu, farewell, earth's bliss." It, too, has a refrain, though in English, a response from the Litany of Saints which was customarily recited through the streets of London in time of plague. The poem, like Dunbar's, consists of a series of discrete, self-inclosed stanzas, in which each line is end-stopped. The structure of the poem is, like Dunbar's and Marvell's, a practical syllogism explicitly propounded, though not quite so formally as in the preceding poem. It opens

12. W. Mackay Mackenzie, ed., *The Poems* (Edinburgh, 1932), pp. 20–23.

with the rejection of earthly happiness. The argument is, to begin with the suppressed premise: True happiness is certain, but the world is uncertain; therefore worldly happiness is not true happiness. The world is uncertain since it is subject to the certainty of death and change. Nor can the goods of this world buy continued life, or the art of medicine procure it: the plague increases. What is best in this life—and here we have the structure of the next three stanzas—beauty, prowess, and wit, all fade:

> Haste therefore each degree
> To welcome destiny.

For the world after death is certain, and its happiness true happiness:

> Adieu, farewell, earth's bliss!
> This world uncertain is:
> Fond are life's lustful joys,
> Death proves them all but toys.
> None from his darts can fly;
> I am sick, I must die—
>   Lord, have mercy on us.
>
> Rich men, trust not in wealth,
> Gold cannot buy you health;
> Physic himself must fade;
> All things to end are made;
> The plague full swift goes by;
> I am sick, I must die—
>   Lord, have mercy on us.
>
> Strength stoops unto the grave,
> Worms feed on Hector brave;
> Swords may not fight with fate;
> Earth still holds ope her gate;
> Come, come! the bells do cry—
> I am sick, I must die—
>   Lord, have mercy on us.
>
> Wit with his wantonness
> Tasteth death's bitterness;
> Hell's executioner
> Hath no ears for to hear
> What vain art can reply;
> I am sick, I must die—
>   Lord, have mercy on us.

Haste therefore each degree
To welcome destiny;
Heaven is our heritage;
Earth but a player's stage;
Mount we unto the sky;
I am sick, I must die—
    Lord, have mercy on us.[13]

The poem is a series of fairly literal propositions, some exactly in logical form: *This world uncertain is, All things to end are made, Queens have died young and fair, Haste therefore each degree.* They are such propositions as might have been translated from the *Summa contra Gentiles* of Thomas Aquinas, and they are located in that general tradition. Thomas, for instance, discusses the following questions: That human happiness does not consist in carnal pleasures; that man's happiness does not consist in glory; that man's happiness does not consist in wealth; that happiness does not consist in worldly power; that happiness does not consist in the practice of art; that man's ultimate happiness is not in this life, "for if there is ultimate happiness in this life, it will certainly be lost, at least by death."[14] But these are the propositions of Nashe's lyric, some literally, some more figuratively put.

Of the propositions in the poem, perhaps the most figurative is *Strength stoops unto the grave,* which yet is fairly literal as we see the suggestion of an aged figure bent over more and more until he is almost prone. And there are, of course, affective elements in the poem, as in *death's bitterness* and *Hell's executioner.* But the special distinction of the poem and the source of an unusual quality of feeling perhaps lies in the meter as much as in anything else. The six-syllable line glides from a regular iambic pattern into a triple movement—accented, unaccented, accented—and back again as if both were its mode of being and neither had precedence over the other:

Beauty is but a flower
Which wrinkles will devour;
Brightness falls from the air;
Queens have died young and fair.

The poem in this respect belongs to a curious episode in the history of English meter; for this phenomenon appears only, to my knowl-

13 Modernized from Ronald B. McKerrow, ed., *Works* (London, 1904–10), III, 283.

14 *Contra Gentiles* iii, 27, 29–31, 36, 48, in *Opera omnia* (Rome, 1882–1948), Vol. XIV; Anton C. Pegis, ed., *Basic Writings of Saint Thomas Aquinas* (New York, 1945), Vol. II.

edge, in the songs written within a fairly short period, of perhaps ten or twenty years, in the 1590's and early 1600's. Of a similar sort is Shakespeare's:

> Come away, come away, death
> And in sad cypress let me be laid;
> Fly away, fly away, breath;
> I am slain by a fair cruel maid.

But the special distinction of the poem has usually been found in the line, *Brightness falls from the air.* This is certainly a proposition of a different order from those we have discussed, and one that has excited the sensibilities of innumerable modern readers. It is a line in the symbolist tradition. One remembers how Stephen Dedalus in the *Portrait of the Artist as a Young Man* recalls the line, though at first in an altered form:

> She had passed through the dusk. And therefore the air was silent save for one soft hiss that fell. And therefore the tongues about him had ceased their babble. Darkness was falling.
>
> *Darkness falls from the air.*
>
> A trembling joy, lambent as a faint light, played like a fairy host around him. But why? Her passage through the darkening air or the verse with its black vowels and its opening sound, rich and lutelike?
>
> He walked away slowly towards the deeper shadows at the end of the colonnade, beating the stone softly with his stick to hide his revery from the students whom he had left: and allowed his mind to summon back to itself the age of Dowland and Byrd and Nash.
>
> Eyes, opening from the darkness of desire, eyes that dimmed the breaking east. What was their languid grace but the softness of chambering? And what was their shimmer but the shimmer of the scum that mantled the cesspool of the court of a slobbering Stuart. And he tasted in the language of memory ambered vines, dying fallings of sweet airs, and proud pavan. . . .
>
> The images he had summoned gave him no pleasure. They were secret and enflaming but her image was not entangled by them. . . .
>
> Yes; and it was not darkness that fell from the air. It was brightness.
>
> *Brightness falls from the air.*
>
> He had not even remembered rightly Nash's line. All the images it had awakened were false.[15]

15 James Joyce, *A Portrait of the Artist as a Young Man* ("Modern Library" ed.; New York, 1928), pp. 273–75.

But all the images it had awakened were false for still another reason. The line as Joyce quotes it is certainly an evocative line, a line in the symbolist tradition, and hence apt and fitted to entangle itself in reverie. But it seems out of place in the poem. It is so much a line in the symbolist tradition that the historical scholar grows wary and suspicious. He turns to the text. He looks in the great modern edition of Nashe, the edition of McKerrow, and he finds that the editor records with a sigh: "It is to be hoped that Nashe meant 'ayre,' but I cannot help strongly suspecting that the true reading is 'hayre,' which gives a more obvious, but far inferior, sense."[16] So we have the alternatives: *Brightness falls from the air* or *Brightness falls from the hair*. But the latter is a literal account of the effect of age and death. The proposition so read is of the same order as all the other propositions in the poem, of the same order as *Queens have died young and fair*. There is no doubt, then, as to the correct reading. In fact, the symbolistic line, however good, is a bad line in context, since it is out of keeping. And so the poem loses its last claim to modernity. It becomes a Renaissance poem. It returns to the park of logic from the forest of reverie. The experience of the poem is the experience of syllogistic thinking with its consequences for feeling, attitude, and action. It is a mode of experience that the Renaissance practiced and cherished, and expressed with power, dignity, and precision. It is a poetical experience and a logical, and it is both at once.

G. K. Chesterton

A DEFENCE OF NONSENSE

THERE ARE two equal and eternal ways of looking at this twilight world of ours: we may see it as the twilight of evening or the twilight of morning; we may think of anything, down to a fallen acorn, as a descendant or as an ancestor. There are times when we are almost crushed, not so much with the load of the evil as with the load of the goodness of humanity, when we feel that we are nothing but the inheritors of a humiliating splendour. But there are other times when everything seems primitive, when the ancient stars are only sparks blown from a boy's bonfire, when the whole earth seems so young and experimental that even the white hair of the aged, in

16 McKerrow, IV, 440.

A DEFENCE OF NONSENSE: From *The Defendant* by G. K. Chesterton. Reprinted by permission of Miss D. E. Collins.

the fine biblical phrase, is like almond trees that blossom, like the white hawthorn grown in May. That it is good for a man to realise that he is "the heir of all the ages" is pretty commonly admitted; it is a less popular but equally important point that it is good for him sometimes to realise that he is not only an ancestor, but an ancestor of primal antiquity; it is good for him to wonder whether he is not a hero, and to experience ennobling doubts as to whether he is not a solar myth.

The matters which most thoroughly evoke this sense of the abiding childhood of the world are those which are really fresh, abrupt, and inventive in any age; and if we were asked what was the best proof of this adventurous youth in the nineteenth century we should say, with all respect to its portentous sciences and philosophies, that it was to be found in the rhymes of Mr. Edward Lear and in the literature of nonsense. *The Dong with the Luminous Nose,* at least, is original, as the first ship and the first plough were original.

It is true in a certain sense that some of the greatest writers the world has seen—Aristophanes, Rabelais, and Sterne—have written nonsense; but unless we are mistaken, it is in a widely different sense. The nonsense of these men was satiric—that is to say, symbolic; it was a kind of exuberant capering round a discovered truth. There is all the difference in the world between the instinct of satire, which, seeing in the Kaiser's moustaches something typical of him, draws them continually larger and larger; and the instinct of nonsense which, for no reason whatever, imagines what those moustaches would look like on the present Archbishop of Canterbury if he grew them in a fit of absence of mind. We incline to think that no age except our own could have understood that the Quangle-Wangle meant absolutely nothing, and the Lands of the Jumblies were absolutely nowhere. We fancy that if the account of the knave's trial in *Alice in Wonderland* had been published in the seventeenth century it would have been bracketed with Bunyan's *Trial of Faithful* as a parody on the state prosecutions of the time. We fancy that if *The Dong with the Luminous Nose* had appeared in the same period every one would have called it a dull satire on Oliver Cromwell.

It is altogether advisedly that we quote chiefly from Mr. Lear's *Nonsense Rhymes.* To our mind he is both chronologically and essentially the father of nonsense; we think him superior to Lewis Carroll. In one sense, indeed, Lewis Carroll has a great advantage. We know what Lewis Carroll was in daily life: he was a singularly serious and conventional don, universally respected, but very much of a pedant and something of a Philistine. Thus his strange double life in earth and in dreamland emphasises the idea that lies at the back of nonsense—the idea of *escape,* of escape into a world where things are not fixed horribly in an eternal appropriateness, where apples grow on pear trees, and any odd man you meet may have three legs. Lewis Carroll, living one life in which he would have thundered morally against any one who walked on the wrong plot of grass, and another life in which he would cheerfully call the sun green and the moon blue, was, by his very divided nature, his one foot on both worlds, a perfect type of the position of modern nonsense. His Wonderland is a country populated by insane mathematicians. We feel the whole is an escape into a world of masquerade; we feel that if we could pierce their disguises, we might discover that Humpty Dumpty and the March Hare were Professors and Doctors of Divinity enjoying a mental holiday. This sense of escape is certainly less emphatic in Edward Lear, because of the completeness of his citizenship in the world of unreason. We do not know his prosaic biography as we know Lewis Carroll's. We accept him as a purely fabulous figure, on his own description of himself:

> His body is perfectly spherical,
> He weareth a runcible hat.

While Lewis Carroll's Wonderland is purely intellectual, Lear introduces quite another element—the element of the poetical and even emotional. Carroll works by the pure reason, but this is not so strong a contrast; for, after all, mankind in the main has always regarded reason as a bit of a joke. Lear introduces his unmeaning words and his amorphous creatures not with the pomp of reason, but with the romantic prelude of rich hues and haunting rhythms,

> Far and few, far and few,
> Are the lands where the Jumblies live,

is an entirely different type of poetry to that exhibited in *Jabberwocky*. Carroll, with a sense of mathematical neatness, makes his whole poem a mosaic of new and mysterious words. But Edward Lear, with more subtle and placid effrontery, is always introducing scraps of his own elvish dialect into the middle of simple and rational statements, until we are almost stunned into admitting that we know what they mean. There is a genial ring of common sense about such lines as,

> For his aunt Jobiska said "Every one knows
> That a Pobble is better without his toes,"

which is beyond the reach of Carroll. The poet seems so easy on the matter that we are almost driven to pretend that we see his meaning, that we know the peculiar difficulties of a Pobble, that we are as old travellers in the "Gromboolian Plain" as he is.

Our claim that nonsense is a new literature (we might almost say a new sense) would be quite indefensible if nonsense were nothing more than a mere aesthetic fancy. Nothing sublimely artistic has ever arisen out of mere art, any more than anything essentially reasonable has ever arisen out of the pure reason. There must always be a rich moral soil for any great aesthetic growth. The principle of *art for art's sake* is a very good principle if it means that there is a vital distinction between the earth and the tree that has its roots in the earth; but it is a very bad principle if it means that the tree could grow just as well with its roots in the air. Every great literature has always been allegorical—allegorical of some view of the whole universe. The *Iliad* is only great because all life is a battle, the *Odyssey* because all life is a journey, the Book of Job because all life is a riddle. There is one attitude in which we think that all existence is summed up in the word "ghosts"; another, and somewhat better one, in which we think it is summed up in the words A *Midsummer Night's Dream.* Even the vulgarest melodrama or detective story can be good if it expresses something of the delight in sinister possibilities—the healthy lust for darkness and terror which may come on us any night in walking down a dark lane. If, therefore, nonsense is really to be the literature of the future, it must have its own version of the Cosmos to offer; the world must not only be tragic, romantic, and religious, it must be nonsensical also. And here we fancy that nonsense will, in a very unexpected way, come to the aid of the spiritual view of things. Religion has for centuries been trying to make men exult in the "wonders" of creation, but it has forgotten that a thing cannot be completely wonderful so long as it remains sensible. So long as we regard a tree as an obvious thing, naturally and reasonably created for a giraffe to eat, we cannot properly wonder at it. It is when we consider it as a prodigious wave of the living soil sprawling up to the skies for no reason in particular that we take off our hats, to the astonishment of the park-keeper. Everything has in fact another side to it, like the moon, the patroness of nonsense. Viewed from that other side, a bird is a blossom broken loose from its chain of stalk, a man a quadruped begging on its hind legs, a house a gigantesque hat to cover a man from the sun, a chair an apparatus of four wooden legs for a cripple with only two.

This is the side of things which tends most truly to spiritual wonder. It is significant that in the greatest religious poem existent, the Book of Job, the argument which convinces the infidel is not (as has been represented by the merely rational religionism of the eighteenth century) a picture of the ordered beneficence of the Creation; but, on the contrary, a picture of the huge and undecipherable unreason of it. "Hast Thou sent the rain upon the desert where no man is?" This simple sense of wonder at the shapes of things, and at their exuberant independence of our intellectual standards and our trivial definitions, is the basis of spirituality as it is the basis of nonsense. Nonsense and faith (strange as the conjunction may seem) are the two supreme symbolic assertions of the truth that to draw out the soul of things with a syllogism is as impossible as to draw out Leviathan with a hook. The well-meaning person who, by merely studying the logical side of things, has decided that "faith is nonsense," does not know how truly he speaks; later it may come back to him in the form that nonsense is faith.

John Keats
LETTER TO BENJAMIN BAILEY

November 22, 1817.

ADDRESS: Mr. B. Bailey /Magdalen Hall/ Oxford—
POSTMARKS: Leatherhead and 22 No 1817.

MY DEAR BAILEY,

I will get over the first part of this (*un*said) Letter as soon as possible for it relates to the affair of poor Crips—To a Man of your nature such a Letter as Haydon's must have been extremely cutting—What occasions the greater part of the World's Quarrels? simply this, two Minds meet and do not understand each other time enough to prevent any shock or surprise at the conduct of either party—As soon as I had known Haydon three days I had got enough of his character not to have been surprised at such a Letter as he has hurt you with. Nor when I knew it was it a principle with me to drop his acquaintance although with you it would have been an imperious feeling. I wish you knew all that I think about Genius and the Heart—and yet I think you are thoroughly acquainted with my innermost breast in that respect, or you could not have known me even thus long and still hold me worthy to be your dear friend. In passing however I must say of one thing that has pressed upon me lately and encreased my Humility and capability of submission and that is this truth—Men of Genius are great as certain ethereal Chemicals operating on the Mass of neutral intellect—by [*for* but] they have not any individuality, any determined Character—I would call the top and head of those who have a proper self Men of Power—

But I am running my head into a Subject which I am certain I could not do justice to under five years S[t]udy and 3 vols octavo—and moreover long to be talking about the Imagination—so my dear

Bailey do not think of this unpleasant affair if possible—do not—I defy any harm to come of it—I defy. I'll . . . write to Crips this Week and request him to tell me all his goings on from time to time by Letter wherever I may be—it will all go on well so don't because you have suddenly discover'd a Coldness in Haydon suffer yourself to be teased. Do not my dear fellow. O I wish I was as certain of the end of all your troubles as that of your momentary start about the authenticity of the Imagination. I am certain of nothing but of the holiness of the Heart's affections and the truth of Imagination—What the imagination seizes as Beauty must be truth—whether it existed before or not—for I have the same Idea of all our Passions as of Love they are all in their sublime, creative of essential Beauty. In a Word, you may know my favorite Speculation by my first Book and the little song I sent in my last—which is a representation from the fancy of the probable mode of operating in these Matters. The Imagination may be compared to Adam's dream—he awoke and found it truth. I am the more zealous in this affair, because I have never yet been able to perceive how any thing can be known for truth by consequitive reasoning—and yet it must be. Can it be that even the greatest Philosopher ever arrived at his goal without putting aside numerous objections. However it may be, O for a Life of Sensations rather than of Thoughts! It is "a Vision in the form of Youth" a Shadow of reality to come—and this consideration has further convinced me for it has come as auxiliary to another favorite Speculation of mine, that we shall enjoy ourselves here after by having what we called happiness on Earth repeated in a finer tone and so repeated. And yet such a fate can only befall those who delight in Sensation rather than hunger as you do after Truth. Adam's dream will do here and seems to be a conviction that Imagination and its empyreal reflection is the same as human Life and its Spiritual repetition. But as I was saying—the simple imaginative Mind may have its rewards in the repeti[ti]on of its own silent Working coming continually on the Spirit with a fine Suddenness—to compare great things with small—have you never by being Surprised with an old Melody—in a delicious place—by a delicious voice, fe[l]t over again your very Speculations and Surmises at the time it first operated on your Soul—do you not remember forming to yourself the singer's face more beautiful that [*for* than] it was possible and yet with the elevation of the Moment you did not think so—even then you were mounted on the Wings of Imagination so high—that the Prototype must be here after—that delicious face you will see. What a time! I am continually running away from the subject—sure this cannot be exactly the case with a complex Mind—one that is imaginative and at the same time careful of its fruits—who would exist partly on Sensation partly on thought—to whom it is necessary that years should bring the philosophic Mind—such an one I consider your's and therefore it is necessary to your eternal Happiness that you not only drink this old Wine of Heaven, which I shall call the redigestion of our most ethereal Musings on Earth; but also increase in knowledge and know all things. I am glad to hear you are in a fair way for Easter—you will soon get through your unpleasant reading and then!—but the world is full of troubles and I have not much reason to think myself pestered with many—I think Jane or Marianne has a better opinion of me than I deserve—for really and truly I do not think my Brothers illness connected with mine—you know more of the real Cause than they do nor have I any chance of being rack'd as you have been—You perhaps at one time thought there was such a thing as Worldly Happiness to be arrived at, at certain periods of time marked out—you have of necessity from your disposition been thus led away—I scarcely remember counting upon any happiness—I look not for it if it be not in the present hour—nothing startles me beyond the Moment. The setting Sun will always set me to rights—or if a Sparrow come before my Window I take part in its existence and pick about the Gravel. The first thing that strikes me on hearing a Misfortune having befalled another is this. "Well it cannot be helped—he will have the pleasure of trying the resources of his spirit"—and I beg now my dear Bailey that hereafter should you observe anything cold in me not to but [*for* put] it to the account of heartlessness but abstraction—for I assure you I sometimes feel not the influence of a Passion or affection during a whole week—and so long this sometimes continues I begin to suspect myself and the genui[ne]ness of my feelings at other times—thinking them a few barren Tragedy-tears—My Brother Tom is much improved—he is going to Devonshire—whither I shall follow him—at present I am just arrived at Dorking to change the Scene—change the Air and give me a spur to wind up my Poem, of which there are wanting 500 Lines. I should have been here a day sooner but the Reynoldses persuaded me to stop in Town to meet your friend Christie. There were Rice and Martin—we talked about Ghosts. I will have some talk with Taylor and let you know—when please God I come down at Christmas. I will find that Examiner if possible. My best regards to Gleig. My Brothers [*sic*] to you and Mrs Bentley's

Your affectionate friend

John Keats—

I want to say much more to you—a few hints will set me going. Direct Burford Bridge near dorking

John Keats

ODE ON A GRECIAN URN

1

THOU STILL unravished bride of quietness,
Thou foster-child of Silence and slow Time,
Slyvan historian, who canst thus express
A flowery tale more sweetly than our rhyme:
What leaf-fringed legend haunts about thy shape
Of dieties or mortals, or of both,
In Tempe or the dales of Arcady?
What men or gods are these? What maidens loth?
What mad pursuit? What struggle to escape?
What pipes and timbrels? What wild ecstasy?

2

Heard melodies are sweet, but those unheard
Are sweeter; therefore, ye soft pipes, play on;
Not to the sensual ear, but, more endeared,
Pipe to the spirit ditties of no tone:
Fair youth, beneath the trees, thou canst not leave
Thy song, nor ever can those trees be bare;
Bold Lover, never, never canst thou kiss,
Though winning near the goal—yet, do not grieve;
She cannot fade, though thou hast not thy bliss,
For ever wilt thou love, and she be fair!

3

Ah, happy, happy boughs! that cannot shed
Your leaves, nor ever bid the Spring adieu;
And, happy melodist, unwearied,
For ever piping songs for ever new.
More happy love! more happy, happy love!
For ever warm and still to be enjoyed,
For ever panting, and for ever young;
All breathing human passion far above,
That leaves a heart high-sorrowful and cloyed,
A burning forehead, and a parching tongue.

4

Who are these coming to the sacrifice?
To what green altar, O mysterious priest,
Lead'st thou that heifer lowing at the skies,
And all her silken flanks with garlands drest?

What little town by river or sea shore,
  Or mountain-built with peaceful citadel,
    Is emptied of this fold, this pious morn?
And, little town, thy streets for evermore
  Will silent be; and not a soul to tell
    Why thou art desolate, can e'er return.

5

O Attic shape! Fair attitude! with brede
  Of marble men and maidens overwrought,
With forest branches and the trodden weed;
  Thou, silent form! dost tease us out of thought
As doth eternity: Cold Pastoral!
  When old age shall this generation waste,
    Thou shalt remain, in midst of other woe
  Than ours, a friend to man, to whom thou say'st,
"Beauty is truth, truth beauty,"—that is all
    Ye know on earth, and all ye need to know.

Wallace Stevens

AN ORDINARY EVENING IN NEW HAVEN

I

THE EYE'S plain version is a thing apart,
The vulgate of experience. Of this,
A few words, an and yet, and yet, and yet—

As part of the never-ending meditation,
Part of the question that is a giant himself:
Of what is this house composed if not of the sun,

These houses, these difficult objects, dilapidate
Appearances of what appearances,
Words, lines, not meanings, not communications,

Dark things without a double, after all,
Unless a second giant kills the first—
A recent imagining of reality,

Much like a new resemblance of the sun,
Down-pouring, up-springing and inevitable,
A larger poem for a larger audience,

AN ORDINARY EVENING IN NEW HAVEN: Reprinted in part from *The Collected Poems of Wallace Stevens* by permission of Alfred A. Knopf, Inc.

As if the crude collops came together as one,
A mythological form, a festival sphere,
A great bosom, beard and being, alive with age.

II

Reality is the beginning not the end,
Naked Alpha, not the hierophant Omega,
Of dense investiture, with luminous vassals.

It is the infant A standing on infant legs,
Not twisted, stooping, polymathic Z,
He that kneels always on the edge of space

In the pallid perceptions of its distances.
Alpha fears men or else Omega's men
Or else his prolongations of the human.

These characters are around us in the scene.
For one it is enough; for one it is not;
For neither is it profound absentia,

Since both alike appoint themselves the choice
Custodians of the glory of the scene,
The immaculate interpreters of life.

But that's the difference: in the end and the way
To the end. Alpha continues to begin.
Omega is refreshed at every end.

III

We keep coming back and coming back
To the real: to the hotel instead of the hymns
That fall upon it out of the wind. We seek

The poem of pure reality, untouched
By trope or deviation, straight to the word,
Straight to the transfixing object, to the object

At the exactest point at which it is itself,
Transfixing by being purely what it is,
A view of New Haven, say, through the certain eye,

The eye made clear of uncertainty, with the sight
Of simple seeing, without reflection. We seek
Nothing beyond reality. Within it,

Everything, the spirit's alchemicana
Included, the spirit that goes roundabout
And through included, not merely the visible,

The solid, but the movable, the moment,
The coming on of feasts and the habits of saints,
The pattern of the heavens and high, night air.

IV

In the metaphysical streets of the physical town
We remember the lion of Juda and we save
The phrase . . . Say of each lion of the spirit

It is a cat of a sleek transparency
That shines with a nocturnal shine alone.
The great cat must stand potent in the sun.

The phrase grows weak. The fact takes up the strength
Of the phrase. It contrives the self-same evocations
And Juda becomes New Haven or else must.

In the metaphysical streets, the profoundest forms
Go with the walker subtly walking there.
These he destroys with wafts of wakening,

Free from their majesty and yet in need
Of majesty, of an invincible clou,
A minimum of making in the mind,

A verity of the most veracious men,
The propounding of four seasons and twelve months.
The brilliancy at the central of the earth.

V

The poem is the cry of its occasion,
Part of the res itself and not about it.
The poet speaks the poem as it is,

Not as it was: part of the reverberation
Of a windy night as it is,when the marble statues
Are like newspapers blown by the wind. He speaks

By sight and insight as they are. There is no
Tomorrow for him. The wind will have passed by,
The statues will have gone back to be things about.

The mobile and the immobile flickering
In the area between is and was are leaves,
Leaves burnished in autumnal burnished trees

And leaves in whirlings in the gutters, whirlings
Around and away, resembling the presence of thought,
Resembling the presences of thoughts, as if,

In the end, in the whole psychology, the self,
The town, the weather, in a casual litter,
Together, said words of the world are the life of the world.

VI

Among time's images, there is not one
Of this present, the venerable mask above
The dilapidation of dilapidations.

The oldest-newest day is the newest alone.
The oldest-newest night does not creak by,
With lanterns, like a celestial ancientness.

Silently it heaves its youthful sleep from the sea—
The Oklahoman—the Italian blue
Beyond the horizon with its masculine,

Their eyes closed, in a young palaver of lips.
And yet the wind whimpers oldly of old age
In the western night. The venerable mask,

In this perfection, occasionally speaks
And something of death's poverty is heard.
This should be tragedy's most moving face.

It is a bough in the electric light
And exhalations in the eaves, so little
To indicate the total leaflessness.

VII

Professor Eucalyptus said, "The search
For reality is as momentous as
The search for god." It is the philosopher's search

For an interior made exterior
And the poet's search for the same exterior made
Interior: breathless things broodingly abreath

With the inhalations of original cold
And of original earliness. Yet the sense
Of cold and earliness is a daily sense,

Not the predicate of bright origin.
Creation is not renewed by images
Of lone wanderers. To re-create, to use

The cold and earliness and bright origin
Is to search. Likewise to say of the evening star,
The most ancient light in the most ancient sky,

That it is wholly an inner light, that it shines
From the sleepy bosom of the real, re-creates,
Searches a possible for its possibleness.

VIII

If it should be true that reality exists
In the mind: the tin plate, the loaf of bread on it,
The long-bladed knife, the little to drink and her

Misericordia, it follows that
Real and unreal are two in one: New Haven
Before and after one arrives or, say,

Bergamo on a postcard, Rome after dark,
Sweden described, Salzburg with shaded eyes
Or Paris in conversation at a café.

This endlessly elaborating poem
Displays the theory of poetry,
As the life of poetry. A more severe,

More harassing master would extemporize
Subtler, more urgent proof that the theory
Of poetry is the theory of life,

As it is, in the intricate evasions of as,
In things seen and unseen, created from nothingness,
The heavens, the hells, the worlds, the longed-for lands.

IX

The last leaf that is going to fall has fallen.
The robins are là-bas, the squirrels, in tree-caves,
Huddle together in the knowledge of squirrels.

The wind has blown the silence of summer away.
It buzzes beyond the horizon or in the ground:
In mud under ponds, where the sky used to be reflected.

The barrenness that appears is an exposing.
It is not part of what is absent, a halt
For farewells, a sad hanging on for remembrances.

It is a coming on and a coming forth.
The pines that were fans and fragrances emerge,
Staked solidly in a gusty grappling with rocks.

The glass of the air becomes an element—
It was something imagined that has been washed away.
A clearness has returned. It stands restored.

It is not an empty clearness, a bottomless sight.
It is a visibility of thought,
In which hundreds of eyes, in one mind, see at once.

X

The less legible meanings of sounds, the little reds
Not often realized, the lighter words
In the heavy drum of speech, the inner men

Behind the outer shields, the sheets of music
In the strokes of thunder, dead candles at the window
When day comes, fire-foams in the motions of the sea,

Flickings from finikin to fine finikin
And the general fidget from busts of Constantine
To photographs of the late president, Mr. Blank,

These are the edgings and inchings of final form,
The swarming activities of the formulae
Of statement, directly and indirectly getting at,

Like an evening evoking the spectrum of violet,
A philosopher practicing scales on his piano,
A woman writing a note and tearing it up.

It is not in the premise that reality
Is a solid. It may be a shade that traverses
A dust, a force that traverses a shade.

XI

In the land of the lemon trees, yellow and yellow were
Yellow-blue, yellow-green, pungent with citron-sap,
Dangling and spangling, the mic-mac of mocking birds.

In the land of the elm trees, wandering mariners
Looked on big women, whose ruddy-ripe images
Wreathed round and round the round wreath of autumn.

They rolled their r's, there, in the land of the citrons.
In the land of big mariners, the words they spoke
Were mere brown clods, mere catching weeds of talk.

When the mariners came to the land of the lemon trees,
At last, in that blond atmosphere, bronzed hard,
They said, "We are back once more in the land of the elm trees,

But folded over, turned round." It was the same,
Except for the adjectives, an alteration
Of words that was a change of nature, more

Than the difference that clouds make over a town.
The countrymen were changed and each constant thing.
Their dark-colored words had redescribed the citrons.

. . . .

Joseph N. Riddel

WALLACE STEVENS' "VISIBILITY OF THOUGHT"

. . . .

"An ordinary Evening in New Haven" (*CP*, p. 465) is the last of Stevens' long poems, and appropriately it brings together the predilections of an illustrious career. There is hardly an instance in the poem when one is not aware of that sigh with which he begins one of his last poems: "It makes so little difference, at so much more/Than seventy, where one looks, one has been there before" (*CP*, p. 522). Coming as it did so closely following his seventieth year, it is without doubt an attempt at some kind of summary

WALLACE STEVENS' "VISIBILITY OF THOUGHT": Extracts from an article which appeared in *PMLA,* Vol. LXXVII, No. 4, Part 1 (September 1962). Used by permission of The Modern Language Association of America. *CP* throughout refers to *Collected Poems.*

—not a farewell nor even a confession that the springs of imagination are giving out, but rather one of those concentrations of sensibility that makes the long poem a characteristic of his every volume. One feels almost certain that the long poem was never a problem for Stevens, that indeed it is but an extended series of shorter poems which, because of innate qualities, fall almost casually into an ordered whole.

The history of the poem is indicative of its design. It was written expressly for the one-thousandth meeting of the Connecticut Academy of Arts and Sciences, the original version, which first appeared in the Academy's *Transactions* (December 1949), consisting of only eleven of the final thirty-one poems to appear later in *The Auroras of Autumn.* The original pieces are scattered through the final version as follows: i, vi, ix, xi, xii, xvi, xxii, xxviii, xxx, xxxi, xxix.[1] The inversion, in the final draft, of the concluding poems is revealing. The conclusion to the shorter sequence is an apostrophe to the reality of language, to "words" that effect a "change of nature," while the concluding poem of the final version expresses the broader perspective of a rounded contemplative experience. Words, in the final version, become only one manifestation of the poet's imagined reality, which is more appropriately the felt thought of meditation; theory gives way to feeling.

"An Ordinary Evening" is significant mainly for the affirmative way it re-emphasizes all that Stevens has believed in over the years. It makes no new contributions to his aesthetic, but all of the standard ideas and arguments for poetry are revived and reconstituted: reality is a synthesis of subjective self and objective world; the poem is a manifestation of this synthesis, and thus a kind of reality itself; this imagined reality is not a forced but a natural creation; the experiences which lead to the creation of poetry are analogous to spiritual experiences; poetry as reality is integral to life, and for the poet the "theory of poetry" will be the "theory of life." These among others are the explicit arguments, calculated heresies which have become the poet's assured responses in defense of his medium. It is revealing that a number of the poem's most succinct metaphors are aphorisms which he had published years before as "Materia Poetica" (most appear in the "Adagia" of *Opus Posthumous*), aphorisms which regularly punctuate the meditation and give it the semblance of an intellectual argument. As a poem of meditation, it moves fluidly between the level of statement and the emotional clothing that makes thought visible.

There is, then, an integral relation between the ideas and the de-

1 See S. F. Morse, *Wallace Stevens, A Preliminary Checklist of His Published Writings, 1898-1954* (New Haven, Conn.: Yale Univ. Library, 1954), p. 54.

sign, if there is a design at all. Samuel French Morse insists that the poem is as predictably outlined as "Notes Toward a Supreme Fiction," with its tripartite divisions and coda. According to Morse, "An Ordinary Evening" can be divided roughly into: (1) ten poems which treat aspects and definitions of reality; (2) ten which present man's search for satisfactions (and thus forms) in this reality; and (3) ten which deal with the interpenetrations of internal and external reality.[2] But even this, which is generally accurate, hardly gives the poem as tight a design as "Notes." I should like to suggest rather that the poem develops by associative "blocks" of idea, by discontinuity and divertissement, and is ultimately tied together only by the order of the mind itself and its natural habits of reflection, though the overall design and poetic treatment are deliberate and not at all impulsive recording. There is an apparent progression in the poem, as Morse says, from the abstract to a more emotional or personal questioning and resolution. But the dialectic is not progressive; poems of an almost purely theoretical nature occur intermittently.

The poet's continuous struggle, of course, is to balance internal and external worlds, to find some meaningful synthesis between the self and the matrix of its residence, both actual and memorable. Meditation grows out of the images which arise from contact with a scene he has known before, and therefore one compounded of past and present. There are always flickerings of New Haven in the poet's ideas, both the actual scene and the ideas accumulating about it; and his response to this world, as in the second poem, is meant both to absorb "these houses" into the "transparent dwellings of the self" and to obtain from this act spiritual sanctions. The poem's development, then, can be outlined in terms of related themes, however arbitrary such an outline and however unimportant the argument itself:[3]

Poems i–ii: provide the basis of meditation by providing a problem, here most obviously the relation of a self to the environment in which it dwells.

iii–viii: develop out of the initial problem: whether reality is the thing itself, the idea of the thing, or some balance of the two; the problem, stated simply, is the relationship of sense perception to forms of reality.

ix–x: conclude the questioning of reality by indicating that neither pure mind nor pure thing is conceivable, and that to embrace either is to distort one's world.

2 "An Examination of the Practice and Theory of Wallace Stevens" (unpubl. diss., Boston Univ., 1952), pp. 279–280. See also, "The Motive for Metaphor," *Origin V*, II (Spring 1952), 54.

3 [The following outline considers the entire poem and thus supplies the context of the eleven sections of it reprinted above, pp. 678–84.]

xi–xvi: elevate the I-thou drama into the more abstract relation of man's physical to his metaphysical worlds, and indicate the spiritual need for the latter as well as the undeniable truth that the metaphysical is no more than the imaginative extension of the physical.

xvii–xviii: consider the same question in terms of man's life in the commonplace world, which he both loves and desires to transcend.

xix–xx: present the opposite problem, the life lived in the uncommon, the imaginative world which was once a religious world; but now the religious imagination distorts its reality in search of a purer realm.

xxi–xxiii: answer the previous problems much in the manner of poems ix and x, but suggest that the union of pure reality and pure imagination gives us the only reality we can know.

xxiv–xxvi: explore the nature of this new reality in relation to forms of belief; and find it closely associated with old mythological forms, forms of spiritual experience conceived in spatially concrete images as opposed to the vague moral forms of modern religions.

xxvii–xxviii: suggest that poetry as an analogue of this new reality is therefore interrelated with life, and thus that a "theory of poetry" is a "theory of life."

xxix: celebrates language as a mediate reality, and thereby extends the argument for poetry.

xxx–xxxi: resolve the problem by returning to the experience of the aging man and the life of meditation as resistance to the rock; the meditation therefore circles back to the beginning which prompted it, the experience of a commonplace world which sets off the "never-ending meditation," indicating that life is just this tension between self and the rock.

There is hardly an argument here—only the blandly repeated insistence on one truth. The mind moves at will among the familiar things and ideas which have long since become a habit for it. It may well be, as Frank Doggett says, that to pursue the apparent meanings of the individual poems is to destroy their existence as poetry, "like telling dreams or describing music." But that would be no less true of any of the long poems and would identify Stevens with practitioners of the "pure" which he repudiates. I think rather that one can follow the argument and its repetitions at one remove from the poem, as the matter on which he orders his verbal excursions. Stevens very often uses conceptual order where another poet might appropriate a mythical analogue. There is, in short, a rational content here, however platitudinous and obvious.

The first two stanzas of Poem 1 establish the theme and direction:

The eye's plain version is a thing apart,
The vulgate of experience. Of this,
A few words, an and yet, and yet, and yet—

As part of the never-ending meditation,
Part of the question that is the giant himself.

The "eye's plain version" is similar to the "vital, arrogant, fatal, dominant X" of "The Motive for Metaphor" (*CP*, p. 288): i.e., the barest perceptual abstraction. The opening tropes present the motive, the need for man to personalize his reality, to grasp its fleeting and evasive nature, to pursue it with endless metaphorical "and yet(s)." Experience, then, resolves into a "never-ending meditation," a creation, as the last stanza indicates, of a "mythological form," of imaginative cosmos out of experiential chaos: the form of the "giant" or poem. And poem two picks up the motif in terms of the immediate situation, the physical New Haven and that which he transmutes in his subjective embrace into the "transparent dwellings of the self," the "Impalpable habitations." The balance of internal and external world, then, is attained in meditation:

In the perpetual reference, object
Of the perpetual meditation, point
Of the enduring, visionary love,

Obscure, in colors whether of the sun
Or mind, uncertain in the clearest bells,
The spirit's speeches, the indefinite,

Confused illuminations and sonorities,
So much ourselves, we cannot tell apart
The idea and the bearer-being of the idea.

The concluding statement echoes the paradox of Yeats's "Among School Children"; the "idea" and its "bearer-being" are metaphorical equivalents of dance and dancer. Stevens' figure, however, is not a paradox at all, but the synthesis of perceptual experience, elementary poetry as it were. Yeats's haunting paradox of the inseparable conjunction of act and actor, and by extension of thing and idea, is interpreted by Stevens as the enduring opposition at the bottom of all experience. The remaining twenty-nine poems are concerned primarily with the variable and possible relations of the two opposites, the variety of balances in the imaginative life which conjoins the "idea" and its "bearer-being."

Sir Herbert Read

UNITY

"ALL THE laws of good writing," wrote Pater in his "Essay on Style," "aim at a unity or identity of the mind in all the processes by which the word is associated to its import. . . . To give the phrase, the sentence, the structural member, the entire composition, song, or essay, a similar unity with its subject and its self:—style is in the right way when it tends towards that."

Such is the final aim of rhetoric—the balance and reconciliation as Coleridge put it, "of a more than usual state of emotion with more than usual order; judgment ever awake and steady self-possession with enthusiasm and feeling profound or vehement." But it was Gerard Manley Hopkins, in a letter to Coventry Patmore, who came closest to defining the quality in a prose style essential for such unity. He called it "the strain of address":

> . . . When I read your prose and when I read Newman's and some other modern writers' the same impression is borne in on me: no matter how beautiful the thought, nor, taken singly, with what happiness expressed, you do not know what *writing prose* is. At bottom what you do and what Cardinal Newman does is to think aloud, to think with pen to paper. In this process there are certain advantages; they may outweigh those of a perfect technic, but at any rate they exclude that; they exclude the belonging technic; the belonging rhetoric, the own proper eloquence of written prose. Each thought is told off singly and there follows a pause and this breaks the continuity, the *contentio*,[1] the strain of address, which writing should usually have.
>
> The beauty, the eloquence, of good prose cannot come wholly from the thought. With Burke it does and varies with the thought; when therefore the thought is sublime so does the style appear to be. But in fact Burke had no style properly so called: his style was colourlessly to transmit his thought. Still he was an orator in form and followed the common oratorical tradition, so that his writing has the strain of address I speak of above.
>
> But Newman does not follow the common tradition—of writing. His tradition is that of cultured, the most highly educated, conversation; it is the flower of the best Oxford life. Perhaps this gives it a charm of unaffected and personal sincerity that nothing else could. Still he shirks the technic of written prose and shuns the tradition of

1 [The full exercise of power.]

> written English. He seems to be thinking "Gibbon is the last great master of traditional English prose; he is its perfection: I do not propose to emulate him; I begin all over again from the language of conversation, of common life."
>
> You too seem to me to be saying to yourself "I am writing prose, not poetry; it is bad taste and a confusion of kinds to employ the style of poetry in prose: the style of prose is to shun the style of poetry and to express one's thoughts with point." But the style of prose is a positive thing and not the absence of verse-forms and pointedly expressed thoughts are single hits and give no continuity of style.
>
> *Further Letters of Gerard Manley Hopkins.*[2]

There is a famous passage in the *Biographia Literaria* where Coleridge, speaking of the poet's "images," remarks that these do not of themselves characterize the poet—"They become proofs of original genius only so far as they are modified by a predominant passion, or by associated thoughts or images awakened by that passion." Coleridge had in mind the unity of a poetic composition, and he contends that such unity is imposed on the poet's expression only by virtue of a sustained mood or passion. What Coleridge had in mind *on an intense scale* for the composition of poetry, Hopkins wished to extend to the writing of prose. Adopting Coleridge's phrase, we might say that all the modes of rhetoric which we have been considering become proofs of original genius only so far as they are modified by a predominant passion in the writer. The sense of the quality of words; the use of appropriate epithets and images; the organization of the period, the paragraph and the plot; the arts of exposition and of narrative; all the gifts of thought and sensibility—these are only dry perfections unless they are moved by a spirit which is neither intelligence nor emotion, but the sustained power of reason. And by reason in this context I do not mean ratiocination or rationality, but, as I have said in another connection, "the widest evidence of the senses, and of all processes and instincts developed in the history of man. It is the sum total of awareness, ordained and ordered to some specific end or object of attention."[3] Such a quality in a writer is no innate instinct, but a conscious achievement. It is more than character, because it necessarily implies intelligence; and it is more than personality, because it necessarily implies a realm of absolute ideals. A life of reason is more than a life of self-development, because it is also a life of self-devotion, of service to outer and autocratic abstractions.

This is merely to say that a good style is not the making of a great writer; and the corollary is, that a great writer is always a good

2 Oxford Univ. Press, 1938, p. 231.
3 *Reason and Romanticism* (London, Faber and Gwyer, 1926), p. 27.

stylist. The greatest English prose writers Swift, Milton, Taylor, Hooker, Berkeley, Shelley, are great not only by virtue of their prose style, but also by virtue of the profundity of their outlook on the world. And these are not separable and distinct virtues, but two aspects of one reality. The thought seems to mould and accentuate the style, and the style reacts to mould and accentuate the thought. It is one process of creation, one art, one aim.

In the last chapter I have defined true eloquence as determined by the dominance of some idea in the mind of the writer, ordering the rhetoric to the single purpose of that idea. If for "idea" we substitute the word "ideal" we have a definition of the quality which I am concerned with now. Not merely ideal, but a life of ideals, is perhaps a more accurate conception. But even this is a dangerous phrase, for it must be further desiderated that the ideals are intelligent—not sentimental, or unreal. Sentimental ideals will, it is true, give rise to a predominating passion of a sort. But there is a hierarchy in everything, and the higher the concept the more difficult it is to differentiate the subtle graduations of value. A certain degree of passion is to be found in a writer like Walter Pater; his style is everywhere definitely his own; it has character and it has beauty, and we feel that such an outer unity must spring from an inner unity. But how describe this inner unity, in Pater's case? It is a subtle matter, and some critics have doubted if anything more considerable than just a self-consuming passion for style, an educated taste, an abnormal sensibility for the tonal value of words, could be deduced. These qualities are not to be despised, but contrast them with the qualities of another writer whose style is equally integral and equally eloquent—I mean John Henry Newman. Newman's aim in writing was almost directly contrary to Pater's; he tells us (*Letters*, II. 477, quoted by Canon Beeching in Craik's *English Prose*, v. 444) that he has never written for writing's sake, but that his one and single desire and aim had been "to do what is so difficult, viz. to explain clearly and exactly my meaning; this has been the whole principle of all my corrections and re-writings." The eloquence that is undeniably his, one of the most persuasive in English literature, in the first instance owes little to conscious rhetoric or composition. It is a spirit, in his case definitely recognizable as the religious spirit, which finds the modes of its eloquence inherent in its moods. "Newman's style being in its lowest terms an effort after a clear and exact representation of his thought, it follows that not a little of the fascination it exercises is the influence of the writer's beautiful and subtle mind, which it clothes in light and transparent vesture."[4] In kind, it is the eloquence of Vanzetti; but unlike Vanzetti's eloquence it is not

4 Canon Beeching, *op. cit.* p. 444.

created by a stress of emotion, but is a sustained state, a predominating passion—passion always, in this context, implying control.

Newman is perhaps not a good example to take, except as a contrast to Pater. Newman's passion is too subtle, and too little understood. Swift is easier of comprehension, and admirable for "predominance." I do not for a moment pretend that his sardonic humour is a simple matter, or one for vulgar explication. But whatever the diagnosis, its symptoms are plain to be seen; and they are not to be explained in the terms of rhetoric and composition. They depend on a particular insight into the world, a particular view of life, a predominating passion. We may not altogether like this passion, since it strikes at the roots of all complacency and satisfaction, but we cannot explain the style without it.

Henry James provides a still more illuminating example. He developed a very complex and a very personal style, a style which has encountered a good deal of shallow depreciation. But, once his mind was made up, the aim of Henry James was essentially the same as Newman's—to explain clearly and exactly his meaning, and not to bother about writing for writing's sake. Now the "meaning" which Henry James was concerned to express was generally very complicated. It was concerned with life at its finest creative point—the point where moral judgments are formed. The deeper this penetrating mind delved into the psychological complexity of human motives the more involved his world became. But it was obviously the real world, the only world worth describing, once your course is set that way. Henry James went ahead, fearlessly, irretrievably, into regions where few are found who care to follow him. He was driven by a force far more powerful than "writing for writing's sake," by what he himself would have called a sacred rage, by what Coleridge called a predominating passion.

The question to consider, in this final chapter, is to what extent this predominating passion that gives a style its unity, its strain of address, is a personal intuition ("judgment ever awake and steady self-possession"), to what extent a common tradition, the technical tradition of written English.

The ordinary use of the word "tradition" implies a "handing down" of something vital—a torch, lit in the remote past, whose light is the only light capable of guiding us in the particular darkness surrounding us at the moment of present existence. There is a good deal to be said for this conception: it implies continuity; it also implies activity. It is not, however, completely satisfactory, if only for the fact that it makes no provision for the athletes of the metaphor, who race from point to point with the burning brand. It assumes, so to speak, that a runner is miraculously there at the relay point, to seize the torch from the exhausted fore-runner. But such an assumption is a begging of the whole question:

> ... if the only form of tradition, of handing down, consisted in following the ways of the immediate generation before us in a blind or timid adherence to its successes, "tradition" should positively be discouraged. We have seen many such simple currents soon lost in the sand; and novelty is better than repetition. Tradition is a matter of much wider significance. It cannot be inherited, and if you want it you must obtain it by great labour. It involves, in the first place, the historical sense ... and the historical sense involves a perception, not only of the pastness of the past, but of its presence; the historical sense compels a man to write not merely with his own generation in his bones, but with a feeling that the whole of the literature of Europe from Homer and within it the whole of the literature of his own country has a simultaneous existence and composes a simultaneous order.[5]

In this passage, and more generally in the essay from which it is taken, Mr. Eliot has succeeded in showing how little tradition is a mere question of blind "following," but is rather the presence in the writer of a particular kind of sensibility. It is a sensibility, not only to historical continuity, but also to historical wholeness, or integrity. To realize this age-long integrity is necessarily to feel the irrelevance of those idiosyncrasies upon which, as we saw in Chapter XII, the personal writer depends. It is only possible to come to this realization by a process of education. Through the interplay of sensibility and experience there arises this particular style which we describe as traditional; in a more general sense such interplay gives rise to the phenomenon of *Taste.*

A tradition in prose (as in poetic) style first takes shape when a body of critical opinion crystallizes around the idiomatic structure of a language. For some time influences—personal, imitative, even social and religious—have been moulding a language; a point occurs when suddenly it is realized that these influences have resulted in an appropriateness: in a fit relation of sound, sense and conversational ease. Such a moment came in English literature in the second half of the seventeenth century, and particularly in the person of Dryden, who has been commonly recognized as the starting point of the main traditional style in English. This is not to say that there were not writers before his time who were contributory to this tradition—for besides Tillotson, whom Dryden acknowledged, too generously, as his master, there is what I am tempted to call the whole firmament of fixed stars—Bunyan, Milton, Taylor, Browne, Donne, Bacon, Hooker, the Bible translators, and Malory. Among these authors

5 T. S. Eliot, *The Sacred Wood* (1920), Methuen, pp. 44–45.

there are, indeed, visible relationships and even (as, for example, in the case of Bunyan and the English Bible) direct descents. But there is no corporate literary sense; most of our early writers are solitary writers; sometimes therefore idiosyncratic, like Sir Thomas Browne; but more often instructed by some conscious discipline. But by Dryden's time the corporate sense had been born; literature had become a profession, and something like professional pride was engendered. Dryden himself was the first writer to be wholly conscious of this sense, and it is a tribute to his real greatness that he himself became its first exemplar.

Let us now examine a series of fairly short but typical passages from those writers whom we may regard as constituting the English tradition, beginning with Dryden:

> But to return from this digression to a farther account of my poem; I must crave leave to tell you, that as I have endeavoured to adorn it with noble thoughts, so much more to express those thoughts with elocution. The composition of all poems is, or ought to be, of wit; and wit in the poet, or *Wit writing* (if you will give me leave to use a school-distinction), is no other than the faculty of imagination in the writer, which, like a nimble spaniel, beats over and ranges through the field of memory, till it springs the quarry it hunted after; or, without metaphor, which searches over all the memory for the species or ideas of those things which it designs to represent. *Wit written* is that which is well defined, the happy result of thought, or product of imagination. But to proceed from wit, in the general notion of it, to the proper wit of an Heroic or Historical Poem, I judge it chiefly to consist in the delightful imagining of persons, actions, passions, or things. 'Tis not the jerk or sting of an epigram, nor the seeming contradiction of a poor antithesis (the delight of an ill-judging audience in a play of rhyme), nor the jingle of a more poor paronomasia; neither is it so much the morality of a grave sentence, affected by Lucan, but more sparingly used by Virgil; but it is some lively and apt description, dressed in such colours of speech, that it sets before your eyes the absent object, as perfectly, and more delightfully than nature. So then the first happiness of the poet's imagination is properly invention, or finding of the thought; the second is fancy, or the variation, deriving, or moulding, of that thought, as the judgment represents it proper to the subject; the third is elocution, or the art of clothing and adorning that thought, so found and varied, in apt, significant, and sounding words: the quickness of the imagination is seen in the invention, the fertility in the fancy, and the accuracy in the expression. For the two first of these, Ovid is famous amongst the poets; for the latter, Virgil. Ovid images more often the movements and affections of the mind, either combating between two contrary passions, or extremely discomposed by one. His words therefore are the least part of his care; for he pictures nature in disorder, with which the study and

choice of words is inconsistent. This is the proper wit of dialogue or discourse, and consequently of the Drama, where all that is said is supposed to be the effect of sudden thought; which, though it excludes not the quickness of wit in repartees, yet admits not a too curious election of words, too frequent allusions, or use of tropes, or, in fine, anything that shows remoteness of thought, or labour in the writer. On the other side, Virgil speaks not so often to us in the person of another, like Ovid, but in his own: he relates almost all things as from himself, and thereby gains more liberty than the other, to express his thoughts with all the graces of elocution, to write more figuratively, and to confess as well the labour as the force of his imagination.

JOHN DRYDEN, *Preface to Annus Mirabilis.*

Nothing is more pleasant to the fancy, than to enlarge it-self by degrees in its contemplation of the various proportions which its several objects bear to each other, when it compares the body of man to the bulk of the whole earth, the earth to the circle it describes round the sun, that circle to the sphere of the fixt stars, the sphere of the fixt stars to the circuit of the whole creation, the whole creation it self to the infinite space that is every where diffused about it; or when the imagination works downward, and considers the bulk of a human body in respect of an animal, a hundred times less than a mite, the particular limbs of such an animal, the different springs which actuate the limbs, the spirits which set these springs a going, and the proportionable minuteness of these several parts, before they have arrived at their full growth and perfection. But if, after all this, we take the least particle of these animal spirits, and consider its capacity of being wrought into a world, that shall contain within those narrow dimensions a heaven and earth, stars and planets, and every different species of living creatures, in the same analogy and proportion they bear to each other in our own universe; such a speculation, by reason of its nicety, appears ridiculous to those who have not turned their thoughts that way, though at the same time it is founded on no less than the evidence of a demonstration. Nay, we may yet carry it farther, and discover in the smallest particle of this little world a new and inexhausted fund of matter, capable of being spun out into another universe.

JOSEPH ADDISON, *Spectator, No.* 420

Rasselas went often to an assembly of learned men, who met at stated times to unbend their minds, and compare their opinions. Their manners were somewhat coarse, but their conversation was instructive, and their disputations acute, though sometimes too violent, and often continued till neither controvertist remembered upon what question they began. Some faults were almost general among them: everyone was desirous to dictate to the rest, and every one was pleased to hear the genius or knowledge of another depreciated.

In this assembly Rasselas was relating his interview with the hermit, and the wonder with which he heard him censure a course of life which he had so deliberately chosen, and so laudably followed. The sentiments of the hearers were various. Some were of opinion, that the folly of his choice had been justly punished by condemnation to perpetual perseverance. One of the youngest among them, with great vehemence, pronounced him a hypocrite. Some talked of the right of society to the labour of individuals, and considered retirement as a desertion of duty. Others readily allowed, that there was a time when the claims of the people were satisfied, and when a man might properly sequester himself to review his life, and purify his heart.

One who appeared more affected with the narrative than the rest, thought it likely, that the hermit would in a few years, go back to his retreat, and perhaps, if shame did not restrain, or death intercept him, return once more from his retreat into the world: "For the hope of happiness," said he, "is so strongly impressed, that the longest experience is not able to efface it. Of the present state, whatever it be, we feel, and are forced to confess, the misery; yet, when the same state is again at a distance, imagination paints it as desirable. But the time will surely come, when desire will be no longer our torment, and no man shall be wretched but by his own fault."

"This," said a philosopher, who had heard him with tokens of great impatience, "is the present condition of a wise man. The time is already come, when none are wretched but by their own fault. Nothing is more idle, than to inquire after happiness, which nature has kindly placed within our reach. The way to be happy is to live according to nature, in obedience to that universal and unalterable law with which every heart is originally impressed; which is not written on it by precept, but engraven by destiny; not instilled by education, but infused at our nativity. He that lives according to nature will suffer nothing from the delusions of hope, or importunities of desire: he will receive and reject with equability of temper; and act or suffer as the reason of things shall alternately prescribe. Other men may amuse themselves with subtle definitions, or intricate ratiocination. Let them learn to be wise by easier means: let them observe the hind of the forest, and the linnet of the grove: let them consider the life of animals, whose motions are regulated by instinct; they obey their guide and are happy. Let us therefore, at length, cease to dispute, and learn to live; throw away the encumbrance of precepts, which they who utter them with so much pride and pomp do not understand, and carry with us this simple and intelligible maxim, That deviation from nature is deviation from happiness."

When he had spoken, he looked round him with a placid air, and enjoyed the consciousness of his own beneficence. "Sir," said the prince, with great modesty, "as I, like all the rest of mankind, am desirous of felicity, my closest attention has been fixed upon your discourse: I doubt not the truth of a position which a man so learned has so confidently advanced. Let me only know what it is to live according to nature."

"When I find young men so humble and so docile," said the philosopher, "I can deny them no information which my studies have enabled me to afford. To live according to nature, is to act always with due regard to the fitness arising from the relations and qualities of causes and effects; to concur with the great and unchangeable scheme of universal felicity; to co-operate with the general disposition and tendency of the present system of things."

The prince soon found that this was one of the sages whom he should understand less as he heard him longer. He therefore bowed and was silent, and the philosopher, supposing him satisfied, and the rest vanquished, rose up and departed with the air of a man that had co-operated with the present system.

Samuel Johnson, *Rasselas*.

The renewal, or perhaps the improvement, of my English life was embittered by the alteration of my own feelings. At the age of twenty-one I was, in my proper station of a youth, delivered from the yoke of education, and delighted with the comparative state of liberty and affluence. My filial obedience was natural and easy; and in the gay prospect of futurity, my ambition did not extend beyond the enjoyment of my books, my leisure, and my patrimonial estate, undisturbed by the cares of a family and the duties of a profession. But in the militia I was armed with power; in my travels, I was exempt from control; and as I approached, as I gradually passed my thirtieth year, I began to feel the desire of being master in my own house. The most gentle authority will sometimes frown without reason, the most cheerful submission will sometimes murmur without cause; and such is the law of our imperfect nature, that we must either command or obey; that our personal liberty is supported by the obsequiousness of our own dependants. While so many of my acquaintance were married or in parliament, or advancing with a rapid step in the various roads of honour and fortune, I stood alone, immovable and insignificant; for after the monthly meeting of 1770, I had even withdrawn myself from the militia, by the resignation of an empty and barren commission. My temper is not susceptible of envy, and the view of successful merit has always excited my warmest applause. The miseries of a vacant life were never known to a man whose hours were insufficient for the inexhaustible pleasures of study. But I lamented that at the proper age I had not embraced the lucrative pursuits of the law or of trade, the chances of civil office or India adventure, or even the fat slumbers of the church; and my repentance became more lively as the loss of time was more irretrievable. Experience showed me the use of grafting my private consequence on the importance of a great professional body; the benefits of those firm connexions which are cemented by hope and interest, by gratitude and emulation, by the mutual exchange of services and favours. From the emoluments of a profession I might have derived an ample fortune, or a competent income, instead of being stinted to the same narrow allowance, to be increased only by an event which I sincerely deprecated. The progress and the knowledge of our domestic disorders aggravated my anxiety, and I began to apprehend that I might be left in my old age without the fruits either of industry or inheritance.

EDWARD GIBBON, *Memoirs of my Life and Writings.*

If any man had a right to look down upon the lower accomplishments as beneath his attention, it was certainly Michel Angelo: nor can it be thought strange, that such a mind should have slighted or have been withheld from paying due attention to all those graces and embellishments of art, which have diffused such lustre over the works of other painters.

It must be acknowledged, however, that together with these, which we wish he had more attended to, he has rejected all the false, though specious ornaments, which disgrace the works of even the most esteemed artists; and, I will venture to say, that when those higher excellencies are more known and cultivated by the artists and patrons of arts, his fame and credit will increase with our increasing knowledge. His name will then be held in the same veneration as it was in the enlightened age of Leo the Tenth; and it is remarkable that the reputation of this truly great man has been continually declining as the art itself has declined. For I must remark to you, that it has long been much on the decline, and that our only hope of its revival will consist in your being thoroughly sensible of its deprivation and decay. It is to Michel Angelo that we owe even the existence of Raffaelle; it is to him Raffaelle owes the grandeur of his style. He was taught by him to elevate his thoughts, and to conceive his subjects with dignity. His genius, however, formed to blaze and to shine, might, like fire in combustible matter, for ever have lain dormant, if it had not caught a spark by its contact with Michel Angelo; and though it never burst out with *his* extraordinary heat and vehemence, yet it must be acknowledged to be a more pure, regular, and chaste flame. Though our judgment must, upon the whole, decide in favour of Raffaelle, yet he never takes such a firm hold and entire possession of the mind as to make us desire nothing else, and to feel nothing wanting. The effect of the capital works of Michel Angelo perfectly corresponds to what Bouchardon said he felt from reading Homer; his whole frame appeared to himself to be enlarged, and all nature which surrounded him, diminished to atoms.

SIR JOSHUA REYNOLDS, *The Fifth Discourse.*

If an Age of Religion has thus everywhere, as I venture to surmise, been preceded by an Age of Magic, it is natural that we should enquire what causes have led mankind, or rather a portion of them, to abandon magic as a principle of faith and practice and to betake themselves to religion instead. When we reflect upon the multitude, the variety, and the complexity of facts to be explained, and the scantiness of our information regarding them, we shall be ready to acknowledge that a full and satisfactory solution of so profound a problem is hardly to be hoped for, and that the most we can do in the present state of our knowledge is to hazard a more or less plausible conjecture. With all due diffidence, then, I would suggest that a tardy recognition of the inherent falsehood and barrenness of magic set the more thoughtful part of mankind to cast about for a truer theory of nature and a more fruitful method of turning her resources to account. The shrewder intelligences must in time have come to perceive that magical ceremonies and incantations did not really effect the results which they were designed to produce, and which the majority of their simpler fellows still believed that they did actually produce. This great discovery of the inefficacy of magic must have wrought a radical though probably slow revolution in the minds of those who had the sagacity to make it. The discovery amounted to this, that men for the first time recognised their inability to manipulate at pleasure certain natural forces which hitherto they had believed to be completely within their control. It was a confession of human ignorance and weakness. Man saw that he had taken for causes what were no causes, and that all his efforts to work by means of these imaginary causes had been vain. His painful toil had been wasted, his curious ingenuity had been squandered to no purpose. He had been pulling at strings to which nothing was attached; he had been marching, as he thought, straight to the goal, while in reality he had only been treading in a narrow circle. Not that the effects which he had striven so hard to produce did not continue to manifest themselves. They were still produced, but not by him. The rain still fell on the thirsty ground: the sun still pursued his daily, and the moon her nightly journey across the sky: the silent procession of the seasons still moved in light and shadow, in cloud and sunshine across the earth: men were still born to labour and sorrow, and still, after a brief sojourn here, were gathered to their fathers in the long home hereafter. All things indeed went on as before, yet all seemed different to him from whose eyes the old scales had fallen. For he could no longer cherish the pleasing illusion that it was he who guided the earth and the heaven in their courses, and that they would cease to perform their great evolutions were he to take his feeble hand from the wheel. In the death of his enemies and his friends he no longer saw a proof of the resistless potency of his own or of hostile enchantments; he now knew that friends and foes alike had succumbed to a force stronger than any that he could wield, and in obedience to a destiny which he was powerless to control.

Sir James G. Frazer, *The Golden Bough*.[6]

It is impossible, in the course of these short extracts, to feel the full flow of a traditional style. As we read an author, say Dryden or Addison or Gibbon, a distinct knowledge of the *pattern* of his style is formed in our mind. Between such authors as I have quoted one can easily perceive a similarity of pattern. It is not only a similarity,

6 Macmillan, pp. 56–57, Abridged Edition.

but also a development. At each change of author the pattern, though formed of the same elements, is given a slight turn, which we may ascribe to the author's personality. But the author is conscious all the time of a certain objective mould into which he is content to fit as much of his expression as the mould will take. Here and there a phrase slips over, such as "yet admits not a too curious election of words,"—which is purely Dryden's, or "to unbend their minds, and compare their opinions," "the consciousness of his own beneficence," "the air of a man that had co-operated with the present system," which are purely Johnson's. But these, and other phrases which could be quoted from these authors, are phrases only. Tradition is concerned more with the tone and temper of expression, and so with the period rather than the phrase, with the paragraph rather than the period, and with the general *manner* of the whole rather than the conduct of the parts. It is embodied in a sense of personal decency rather than in a code of rhetoric; it is an ideal of character rather than a system of rules. But it is character which expresses itself consciously, as is implied in the word "ideal." It is not the "humour" of Jonson, nor the "charm" and "personality" of the writers we have discussed in Chapter XII. It is, that is to say, a positive style, and when Francis Jeffrey criticized Swift it was from the point of view of this positiveness:

> Of his style, it has been usual to speak with great, and, we think, exaggerated praise. It is less mellow than Dryden's, less elegant than Pope's or Addison's, less noble than Lord Bolingbroke's, and utterly without the glow and loftiness which belonged to our earlier masters. It is radically a low and homely style, without grace and without affectation, and chiefly remarkable for a great choice and profusion of common words and expressions.

That it is not altogether just to regard Swift's style from this point of view I have remarked in my Introduction, in relation to the hypothesis of Pure Prose (see p. xii). But Jeffrey, himself a follower of the tradition he is praising, is justified if we allow the force of that tradition. And its force is the force that comes of all disciplines, all dogma and all co-ordinate aims. Nothing, in the end, is so wearisome as idiosyncrasy and waywardness; the universal alone is stable, and a universal style is an impersonal style. Certain writers, like Swift, may get away with a technique of "thinking aloud," but the quality of their mind assures the dignity of their style. Less talented writers will, like Gibbon or like Stevenson, set themselves a standard and sedulously ape it. Such dependence has serious defects. It leads to a mechanical structure, to timidity of phrasing (a timidity not inconsistent with an occasional kick over the traces) and rigidity of rhythm. It is apt to sacrifice fluidity to formality. It is obvious that a tradition which can control personality in the interests of uniformity can also mark the absence of personality by wearing the outer garments of such an uniformity. Given an easy command of words, it is not difficult to build them into a shoddy structure which in appearance at least is indistinguishable from real architecture. Nothing, in any art, is so easy to fake as the grand manner. Coleridge perceived this:

> After the Revolution, the spirit of the nation became much more commercial than it had been before; a learned body, or clerisy, as such, gradually disappeared, and literature in general began to be addressed to the common miscellaneous public. That public had become accustumed to, and required, a strong stimulus; and to meet the requisitions of the public taste, a style was produced which by combining triteness of thought with singularity and excess of manner of expression, was calculated at once to soothe ignorance and to flatter vanity. The thought was carefully kept down to the immediate apprehension of the commonest understanding, and the dress was as anxiously arranged for the purpose of making the thought appear something very profound. The essence of this style consisted in a mock antithesis, that is, an opposition of mere sounds, in a rage for personification, the abstract made animate, far-fetched metaphors, strange phrases, metrical scraps, in everything, in short, but genuine prose.
>
> *Lecture XIV.*

The tradition we have described, that beginning with Dryden and still prevalent to-day, is only one tradition. Other traditions are possible, though perhaps only by evolution. Here again the analogy of manners in society would seem to hold good. There is, after all, a difference of tone between Dryden and Sir Joshua Reynolds, but it is difficult to know how much of this difference should be ascribed to a difference in personality. Not everything, for merely a change in the face value (or "purchasing power") of words is enough to effect a difference in tone, and therefore in tradition. But discounting these temporal changes we must still hazard this axiom: that in matters of style tradition is a good instrument but a bad machine. It is a discipline that needs to be informed by the originating forces of mental energy, clear vision, and fine sensibility.

Edmund Wilson

IS VERSE A DYING TECHNIQUE?

THE MORE one reads the current criticism of poetry by poets and their reviewers, the more one becomes convinced that the discussion is proceeding on false assumptions. The writers may belong to different schools, but they all seem to share a basic confusion.

This confusion is the result of a failure to think clearly about what is meant by the words "prose," "verse," and "poetry"—a question which is sometimes debated but which never gets straightened out. Yet are not the obvious facts as follows?

What we mean by the words "prose" and "verse" are simply two different techniques of literary expression. Verse is written in lines with a certain number of metrical feet each; prose is written in paragraphs and has what we call rhythm. But what is "poetry," then? What I want to suggest is that "poetry" formerly meant one kind of thing but that it now means something different, and that one ought not to generalize about "poetry" by taking all the writers of verse, ancient, medieval and modern, away from their various periods and throwing them together in one's mind, but to consider both verse and prose in relation to their functions at different times.

The important thing to recognize, it seems to me, is that the literary technique of verse was once made to serve many purposes for which we now, as a rule, use prose. Solon, the Athenian statesman, expounded his political ideas in verse; the *Works and Days* of Hesiod are a shepherd's calendar in verse; his *Theogony* is versified mythology; and almost everything that in contemporary writing would be put into prose plays and novels was versified by the Greeks in epics or plays.

It is true that Aristotle tried to discriminate. "We have no common name," he wrote, "for a mime of Sophron or Xenarchus and a Socratic conversation; and we should still be without one even if the imitation in the two instances were in trimeters or elegiacs or some other kind of verse—though it is the way with people to tack on 'poet' to the name of a meter, and talk of elegiac-poets and epic-poets, thinking that they call them poets not by reason of the imitative nature of their work, but indiscriminately by reason of the meter they write in. Even if a theory of medicine or physical philosophy be put forth in a metrical form, it is usual to describe the writer in

IS VERSE A DYING TECHNIQUE?: From *The Triple Thinkers* by Edmund Wilson, Oxford University Press, 1948. Reprinted by permission of the author.

this way; Homer and Empedocles, however, have really nothing in common apart from their meter; so that, if the one is to be called a poet, the other should be termed a physicist rather than a poet."

But he admitted that there was no accepted name for the creative —what he calls the "imitative"—art which had for its mediums both prose and verse; and his posterity followed the custom of which he had pointed out the impropriety by calling anything in a meter a "poem." The Romans wrote treatises in verse on philosophy and astronomy and farming. The "poetic" of Horace's *Ars Poetica* applies to the whole range of ancient verse—though Horace did think it just as well to mingle the "agreeable" with the "useful"—and this essay in literary criticism is itself written in meter. "Poetry" remained identified with verse; and since for centuries both dramas and narratives continued largely to be written in verse, the term of which Aristotle had noticed the need—a term for imaginative literature itself, irrespective of literary techniques—never came into common use.

But when we arrive at the nineteenth century, a new conception of "poetry" appears. The change is seen very clearly in the doubts which began to be felt as to whether Pope were really a poet. Now, it is true that a critic like Johnson would hardly have assigned to Pope the position of pre-eminence he does at any other period than Johnson's own; but it is *not* true that only a critic of the latter part of the eighteenth century, a critic of an "age of prose," would have considered Pope a poet. Would not Pope have been considered a poet in any age before the age of Coleridge?

But the romantics were to redefine "poetry." Coleridge, in the *Biographia Literaria,* denies that any excellent work in meter may be properly called a "poem." "The final definition . . ." he says, "may be thus worded. A poem is that species of composition which is opposed to works of science by proposing for its *immediate* object pleasure, not truth; and from all other species—(having *this* object in common with it)—it is discriminated by proposing to itself such delight from the *whole* as is compatible with a distinct gratification from each component part." This would evidently exclude the *Ars Poetica* and the *De Rerum Natura,* whose immediate objects are as much truth as pleasure. What is really happening here is that for Coleridge the function of "poetry" is becoming more specialized. Why? Coleridge answers this question in formulating an objection which may be brought against the first part of his definition: "But the communication of pleasure may be the immediate object of a work not metrically composed; and that object may have been in a high degree attained, as in novels and romances." Precisely; and the novels and romances were formerly written in verse, whereas they are now usually written in prose. In Coleridge's time, tales in verse were more and more giving place to prose novels. Before long, novels in verse such as *Aurora Leigh* and *The Ring and the Book* were to seem more or less literary oddities. "Poetry," then, for Coleridge, has become something which, unless he amends his definition, may equally well be written in prose: Isaiah and Plato and Jeremy Taylor will, as he admits, be describable as "poetry." Thereafter, he seems to become somewhat muddled; but he finally arrives at the conclusion that the "peculiar property of poetry" is "the property of exciting a more continuous and equal attention than the language of prose aims at, whether colloquial or written."

The truth is that Coleridge is having difficulties in attempting to derive his new conception of poetry from the literature of the past, which has been based on the old conception. Poe, writing thirty years later, was able to get a good deal further. Coleridge had said—and it seems to have been really what he was principally trying to say—that "a poem of any length neither can be, nor ought to be, all poetry." (Yet are not the *Divine Comedy* and Shakespeare's tragedies "all poetry"? Or rather, in the case of these masterpieces, is not the work as a whole really a "poem" maintained, as it is, at a consistently high level of intensity and style and with the effects of the different parts dependent on one another?) Poe predicted that "no very long poem would ever be popular again," and made "poetry" mean something even more special by insisting that it should approach the indefiniteness of music. The reason why no very long poem was ever to be popular again was simply that verse as a technique was then passing out of fashion in every department of literature except those of lyric poetry and the short idyl. The long poems of the past—Shakespeare's plays, the *Divine Comedy*, the Greek dramatists and Homer—were going to continue to be popular; but writers of that caliber in the immediate future were not going to write in verse.

Matthew Arnold was to keep on in Coleridge's direction, though by a route somewhat different from Poe's. He said, as we have heard so repeatedly, that poetry was at bottom a criticism of life; but, though one of the characteristics which true poetry might possess was "moral profundity," another was "natural magic," and "eminent manifestations of this magical power of poetry" were "very rare and very precious." "Poetry" is thus, it will be seen, steadily becoming rarer. Arnold loved quoting passages of natural magic and he suggested that the lover of literature should carry around in his mind as touchstones a handful of such topnotch passages to test any new verse he encountered. His method of presenting the poets makes poetry seem fleeting and quintessential. Arnold was not happy till he had edited Byron and Wordsworth in such a way as to make it appear that their "poetry" was a kind of elixir which had to be distilled from the mass of their work—rather difficult in Byron's case: a production like *Don Juan* does not really give up its essence in the sequences excerpted by Arnold.

There was, to be sure, some point in what Arnold was trying to do for these writers: Wordsworth and Byron both often wrote badly and flatly. But they would not have lent themselves at all to this high-handed kind of anthologizing if it had not been that, by this time, it had finally become almost impossible to handle large subjects successfully in verse. Matthew Arnold could have done nothing for Dante by reducing him to a little book of extracts—nor, with all Shakespeare's carelessness, for Shakespeare. The new specialized idea of poetry appears very plainly and oddly when Arnold writes about Homer: the *Iliad* and the *Odyssey*, which had been for the Greeks fiction and scripture, have come to appear to this critic long stretches of ancient legend from which we may pick out little crystals of moral profundity and natural magic.

And in the meantime the ideas of Poe, developed by the Symbolists in France, had given rise to the *Art poétique* of Verlaine, so different from that of Horace: "Music first of all . . . no Color only the *nuance!* . . . Shun Point, the murderer, cruel Wit and Laughter the impure . . . Take eloquence and wring its neck! . . . Let your verse be the luck of adventure flung to the crisp morning wind that brings us a fragrance of thyme and mint—and all the rest is literature."

Eliot and Valéry followed. Paul Valéry, still in the tradition of Poe, regarded a poem as a specialized machine for producing a certain kind of "state." Eliot called poetry a "superior amusement," and he anthologized, in both his poems and his essays, even more fastidiously than Arnold. He, too, has his favorite collection of magical and quintessential passages; and he possesses an uncanny gift for transmitting to them a personal accent and imbuing them with a personal significance. And as even those passages of Eliot's poems which have not been imitated or quoted often seemed to have been pieced together out of separate lines and fragments, so his imitators came to work in broken mosaics and "pinches of glory"—to use E. M. Forster's phrase about Eliot—rather than with conventional stanzas.

The result has been an optical illusion. The critic, when he read the classic, epic, eclogue, tale or play, may have grasped it and enjoyed it as a whole; yet when the reader reads the comment of the critic, he gets the impression, looking back on the poem, that the *Divine Comedy*, say, so extraordinarily sustained and so beautifully integrated, is remarkable mainly for Eliot-like fragments. Once we know Matthew Arnold's essay, we find that the ἀνήριθμον γέλασμα [many-twinkling smile of Ocean] of Aeschylus and the "daffodils that come before the swallow dares" of Shakespeare tend to stick out from their contexts in a way that they hardly deserve to. Matthew Arnold, unintentionally and unconsciously, has had the effect of making the poet's "poetry" seem to be concentrated in the phrase or the line.

Finally, Mr. A. E. Housman, in his lecture on *The Name and Nature of Poetry*, has declared that he cannot define poetry. He can only become aware of its presence by the symptoms he finds it producing: "Experience has taught me, when I am shaving of a morning, to keep watch over my thought, because if a line of poetry strays into my memory, my skin bristles so that the razor ceases to act. This particular symptom is accompanied by a shiver down the spine; there is another which consists in a constriction of the throat and a precipitation of water to the eyes; and there is a third which I can only describe by borrowing a phrase from one of Keats's last letters, where he says, speaking of Fanny Brawne, 'everything that reminds me of her goes through me like a spear.' The seat of this sensation is the pit of the stomach."

One recognizes these symptoms; but there are other things, too, which produce these peculiar sensations: scenes from prose plays, for example (the final curtain of *The Playboy of the Western World* could make one's hair stand on end when it was first done by the Abbey Theater), passages from prose novels (Stephen Daedalus' broodings over his mother's death in the opening episode of *Ulysses* and the end of Mrs. Bloom's soliloquy), even scenes from certain historians, such as Mirabeau's arrival in Aix at the end of Michelet's *Louis XVI*, even passages in a philosophical dialogue: the conclusion of Plato's Symposium. Though Housman does praise a few long poems, he has the effect, like these other critics, of creating the impression that "poetry" means primarily lyric verse, and this only at its most poignant or most musical moments.

Now all that has been said here is, of course, not intended to belittle the value of what such people as Coleridge and Poe, Arnold and Eliot have written on the subject of poetry. These men are all themselves first-class poets; and their criticism is very important because it constitutes an attempt to explain what they have aimed at in their own verse, of what they have conceived, in their age, to be possible or impossible for their medium.

Yet one feels that in the minds of all of them a certain confusion persists between the new idea of poetry and the old—between Coleridge's conception, on the one hand, and Horace's, on the other;

that the technique of prose is inevitably tending more and more to take over the material which had formerly provided the subjects for compositions in verse, and that, as the two techniques of writing are beginning to appear, side by side or combined, in a single work, it is becoming more and more impossible to conduct any comparative discussion of literature on a basis of this misleading division of it into the department of "poetry" and of "prose."

One result of discussion on this basis, especially if carried on by verse-writers, is the creation of an illusion that contemporary "poets" of relatively small stature (though of however authentic gifts) are the true inheritors of the genius and carriers-on of the tradition of Aeschylus, Sophocles and Virgil, Dante, Shakespeare and Milton. Is it not time to discard the word "poetry" or to define it in such a way as to take account of the fact that the most intense, the most profound, the most beautifully composed and the most comprehensive of the great works of literary art (which for these reasons are also the most thrilling and give us most prickly sensations while shaving) have been written sometimes in verse technique, sometimes in prose technique, depending partly on the taste of the author, partly on the mere current fashion? It is only when we argue these matters that we become involved in absurdities. When we are reading, we appraise correctly. Matthew Arnold cites examples of that "natural magic" which he regards as one of the properties of "poetry" from Chateaubriand and Maurice de Guérin, who did not write verse but prose, as well as from Shakespeare and Keats; and he rashly includes Molière among the "larger and more splendid luminaries in the poetical heaven," though Molière was scarcely more "poetic" in any sense except perhaps that of "moral profundity" when he wrote verse than when he wrote prose and would certainly not have versified at all if the conventions of his time had not demanded it. One who has first come to Flaubert at a sensitive age when he is also reading Dante may have the experience of finding that the paragraphs of the former remain in his mind and continue to sing just as the lines of the latter do. He has got the prose by heart unconsciously just as he has done with favorite passages of verse; he repeats them, admiring the form, studying the choice of words, seeing more and more significance in them. He realizes that, though Dante may be greater than Flaubert, Flaubert belongs in Dante's class. It is simply that by Flaubert's time the Dantes present their visions in terms of prose drama or fiction rather than of epics in verse. At any other period, certainly, *La Tentation de Saint Antoine* would have been written in verse instead of prose.

And if one happens to read Virgil's *Georgics* not long after having read Flaubert, the shift from verse to prose technique gets the plainest demonstration possible. If you think of Virgil with Tennyson, you have the illusion that the Virgilian poets are shrinking; but if you think of Virgil with Flaubert, you can see how a great modern prose-writer has grown out of the great classical poets. Flaubert somewhere —I think, in the Goncourt journal—expresses his admiration for Virgil; and, in method as well as in mood, the two writers are often akin. Flaubert is no less accomplished in his use of words and rhythms than Virgil; and the poet is as successful as the novelist in conveying emotion through objective statement. The *Georgics* were seven years in the writing, as *Madame Bovary* was six. And the fact that—in *Madame Bovary* especially—Flaubert's elegiac feeling as well as his rural settings run so close to the characteristic vein of Virgil makes the comparison particularly interesting. Put the bees of the *Georgics*, for example, whose swarming Virgil thus describes:

aethere in alto
Fit sonitus, magnum mixtae glomerantur in orbem
Praecipitesque cadunt

[High in air the din arises, they gather confusedly into a great ball, and drop headlong down]

beside the bees seen and heard by Emma Bovary on an April afternoon: "quelquefois les abeilles, tournoyant dans la lumière, frappaient contre les carreaux commes des balles d'or rebondissantes [sometimes the bees, turning in the light, struck against the glass panes like rebounding golden balls]." Put

Et iam summa procul villarum culmina fumant,
Maioresque cadunt altis de montibus umbrae

[and now the tall roofs of the farms smoke in the distance, and larger shadows fall from the high mountains]

beside: "La tendresse des anciens jours leur revenait au coeur, abondante et silencieuse comme la rivière qui coulait, avec autant de mollesse qu'en apportait le parfum des seringas, et projetait dans leurs souvenirs des ombres plus démesurées et plus mélancoliques que celles des saules immobiles qui s'allongeaient sur l'herbe [The tenderness of the old days reawoke in their hearts, full and silent as the flowing river, soft as the aroma of the syringas, and cast on their memories shadows longer and more melancholy than those of the motionless willows which lengthened on the grass]." And compare Virgil's sadness and wistfulness with the sadness and nostalgia of Flaubert: the melancholy of the mountainous pastures laid waste by the cattle plague:

> *desertaque regna*
> *Pastorum, et longe saltus lateque vacantes*
> [the realms of the shepherds deserted, and the lawns left desolate far and wide]

with the modern desolations of Paris in *L'Éducation sentimentale*: "Les rues étaient désertes. Quelquefois une charrette lourde passait, en ébranlant les pavés [The streets were deserted. Sometimes a heavy cart passed, shaking the paving stones]," etc.; or Palinurus, fallen into the sea, swimming with effort to the coast of Italy, but only to be murdered and left there "naked on the unknown sand," while his soul, since his corpse lies unburied, must forever be excluded from Hades, or Orpheus still calling Eurydice when his head has been torn from his body, till his tongue has grown cold and the echo of his love has been lost among the river banks—compare these with Charles Bovary, a schoolboy, looking out on fine summer evenings at the sordid streets of Rouen and sniffing for the good country odors, "qui ne vanaient pas jusqu'à lui [which never came to him]"—("tendebantque manus ripae ulterioris amore") [and were stretching forth their hands in longing for the opposite bank]—or with the scene in which Emma Bovary receives her father's letter and remembers the summers of her girlhood, with the galloping colts and the bees, and knows that she has spent all her illusions in maidenhood, in marriage, in adultery, as a traveler leaves something of his money at each of the inns of the road.

We find, in this connection, in Flaubert's letters the most explicit statements. "To desire to give verse-rhythm to prose, yet to leave it prose and very much prose," he wrote to Louise Colet (March 27, 1853), "and to write about ordinary life as histories and epics are written, yet without falsifying the subject, is perhaps an absurd idea. Sometimes I almost think it is. But it may also be a great experiment and very original." The truth is that Flaubert is a crucial figure. He is the first great writer in prose deliberately to try to take over for the treatment of ambitious subjects the delicacy, the precision and the intensity that have hitherto been identified with verse. Henrik Ibsen, for the poetic drama, played a role hardly less important. Ibsen began as a writer of verse and composed many short and non-dramatic poems as well as *Peer Gynt* and *Brand* and his other plays in verse, but eventually changed over to prose for the concentrated Sophoclean tragedies that affected the whole dramatic tradition. Thereafter the dramatic "poets"—the Chekhovs, the Synges and the Shaws (Hauptmann had occasional relapses)—wrote almost invariably in prose. It was by such that the soul of the time was given its dramatic expression: there was nothing left for Rostand's alexandrines but fireworks and declamation.

In the later generation, James Joyce, who had studied Flaubert and Ibsen as well as the great classical verse-masters, set out to merge the two techniques. Dickens and Herman Melville had occasionally resorted to blank verse for passages which they meant to be elevated, but these flights had not matched their context, and the effect had not been happy. Joyce, however, now, in *Ulysses*, has worked out a new medium of his own which enables him to exploit verse metrics in a texture which is basically prose; and he has created in *Finnegans Wake* a work of which we cannot say whether it ought, in the old-fashioned phraseology, to be described as prose or verse. A good deal of *Finnegans Wake* is written in regular meter and might perfectly well be printed as verse, but, except for the intepolated songs, the whole thing is printed as prose. As one reads it, one wonders, in any case, how anything could be demanded of "poetry" by Coleridge with his "sense of novelty and freshness with old and familiar objects," by Poe with his indefiniteness of music, by Arnold with his natural magic, by Verlaine with his nuance, by Eliot with his unearthliness, or by Housman with his bristling of the beard, which the *Anna Livia Plurabelle* chapter (or canto) does not fully supply.

If, then, we take literature as a whole for our field, we put an end to many futile controversies—the controversies, for example, as to whether or not Pope is a poet, as to whether or not Whitman is a poet. If you are prepared to admit that Pope is one of the great English writers, it is less interesting to compare him with Shakespeare—which will tell you something about the development of English verse but not bring out Pope's peculiar excellence—than to compare him with Thackeray, say, with whom he has his principal theme—the vanity of the world—in common and who throws into relief the more passionate pulse and the solider art of Pope. And so the effort to apply to Whitman the ordinary standards of verse has hindered the appreciation of his careful and exquisite art.

If, in writing about "poetry," one limits oneself to "poets" who compose in verse, one excludes too much of modern literature, and with it too much of life. The best modern work in verse has been mostly in the shorter forms, and it may be that our lyric poets are comparable to any who have ever lived, but we have had no imaginations of the stature of Shakespeare or Dante, who have done their major work in verse. The horizon and even the ambition of the contemporary writer of verse has narrowed with the specialization of the function of verse itself. (Though the novelists Proust and Joyce are both masters of what used to be called "numbers," the verses of the first are negligible and those of the second minor.)

Would not D. H. Lawrence, for example, if he had lived a century earlier, probably have told his tales, as Byron and Crabbe did: in verse? Is it not just as correct to consider him the last of the great English romantic poets as one of the most original of modern English novelists? Must we not, to appreciate Virginia Woolf, be aware that she is trying to do what Jane Austen or George Eliot were doing?

Recently the techniques of prose and verse have been getting mixed up at a bewildering rate—with the prose technique steadily gaining. You have had the verse technique of Ezra Pound gradually changing into prose technique. You have had William Faulkner, who began by writing verse, doing his major work in prose fiction without ever quite mastering prose, so that he may at any moment upset us by interpolating a patch of verse. You have had Robinson Jeffers, in narrative "poems" which are as much novels as some of Lawrence's, reeling out yards of what are really prose dithyrambs with a loose hexametric base: and you have had Carl Sandburg, of *The People, Yes*, producing a queer kind of literature which oscillates between something like verse and something like the paragraphs of a newspaper "column."

Sandburg and Pound have, of course, come out of the old *vers libre*, which, though prose-like, was either epigrammatic or had the rhythms of the Whitmanesque chant. But since the Sandburg-Pound generation, a new development in verse has taken place. The sharpness and the energy disappear; the beat gives way to demoralized weariness. Here the "sprung-rhythm" of Gerard Manley Hopkins has sometimes set the example. But the difference is that Hopkins' rhythms convey agitation and tension, whereas the rhythms of MacNeice and Auden let down the taut traditions of lyric verse with an effect that is often comic and probably intended to be so—these poets are not far at moments from the humorous rhymed prose of Ogden Nash. And finally—what is very strange to see—Miss Edna St. Vincent Millay in *Conversation at Midnight*, slackening her old urgent pace, dimming the ring of her numbers, has given us a curious example of metrics in full dissolution, with the stress almost entirely neglected, the lines running on for paragraphs and even the rhymes sometimes fading out. In some specimens of this recent work, the beat of verse has been so slurred and muted that it might almost as well have been abandoned. We have at last lived to see the day when the ballads of Gilbert and Hood, written without meter for comic effect in long lines that look and sound like paragraphs, have actually become the type of a certain amount of serious poetry.

You have also the paradox of Eliot attempting to revive the verse-drama with rhythms which, adapting themselves to the rhythms of colloquial speech, run sometimes closer to prose. And you have Mr. Maxwell Anderson trying to renovate the modern theater by bringing back blank verse again—with the result that, once a writer of prose dialogue distinguished by some color and wit, he has become, as a dramatic poet, banal and insipid beyond belief. The trouble is that no verse technique is more obsolete today than blank verse. The old iambic pentameters have no longer any relation whatever to the tempo and language of our lives. Yeats was the last who could write them, and he only because he inhabited, in Ireland and in imagination, a grandiose anachronistic world. You cannot deal with contemporary events in an idiom which was already growing trite in Tennyson's and Arnold's day; and if you try to combine the rhythm of blank verse with the idiom of ordinary talk, you get something—as in Anderson's *Winterset*—which lacks the merits of either. Nor can you try to exploit the worked-out rhythm without also finding yourself let in for the antiquated point of view. The comments on the action in *Winterset* are never the expression of sentiments which we ourselves could conceivably feel in connection with the events depicted: they are the echoes of Greek choruses and Elizabethan soliloquies reflecting upon happenings of a different kind.

Thus if the poets of the Auden-MacNeice school find verse turning to prose in their hands, like the neck of the flamingo in Lewis Carroll with which Alice tried to play croquet, Mr. Anderson, returning to blank verse, finds himself in the more awkward predicament of the girl in the fairy tale who could never open her mouth without having a toad jump out.

But what has happened? What, then, is the cause of this disuse into which verse technique has been falling for at least the last two hundred years? And what are we to expect in the future? Is verse to be limited now to increasingly specialized functions and finally to go out altogether? Or will it recover the domains it has lost?

To find out, if it is possible to do so, we should be forced to approach this change from the anthropological and sociological points of view. Is verse a more primitive technique than prose? Are its fixed rules like the syntax of languages, which are found to have been stiffer and more complicated the further back one goes? Aside from the question of the requirements of taste and the self-imposed difficulties of form which have always, in any period, been involved in the production of great works of art, does the easy flexibility, say, of modern English prose bear to the versification of Horace the same relation that English syntax bears to Horace's syntax, or that Horace's bears to that of the Eskimos?

It seems obvious that one of the important factors in the history of the development of verse must have been its relations with music. Greek verse grew up in fusion with music: verse and music were learned together. It was not till after Alexander the Great that prosody was detached from harmony. The Greek name for "prose" was "bare words"—that is, words divorced from music. But what the Romans took over and developed was a prosody that was purely literary. This, I believe, accounts for the fact that we seem to find in Greek poetry, if we compare it with Latin poetry, so little exact visual observation. Greek poetry is mainly for the ear. Compare a landscape in one of the choruses of Sophocles or Aristophanes with a landscape of Virgil or Horace: the Greeks are *singing* about the landscape, the Romans are fixing it for the eye of the mind; and it is Virgil and Horace who lead the way to all the later picture poetry down to our own Imagists. Again, in the Elizabethan age, the English were extremely musical: the lyrics of Campion could hardly have been composed apart from their musical settings; and Shakespeare is permeated with music. When Shakespeare wants to make us see something, he is always compelling and brilliant; but the effect has been liquefied by music so that it sometimes gives a little the impression of objects seen under water. The main stream of English poetry continues to keep fairly close to music through Milton, the musician's son, and even through the less organ-voiced Dryden. What has really happened with Pope is that the musical background is no longer there and that the ocular sense has grown sharp again. After this, the real music of verse is largely confined to lyrics—songs—and it becomes more and more of a trick to write them so that they seem authentic—that is, so that they sound like something sung. It was the aim of the late-nineteenth-century Symbolists, who derived their theory from Poe, to bring verse closer to music again, in opposition to the school of the Parnassians, who cultivated an opaque objectivity. And the excellence of Miss Millay's lyrics is obviously connected with her musical training, as the metrical parts of Joyce—such as the Sirens episode in *Ulysses,* which attempts to render music, the response to a song of its hearer—are obviously associated with his vocal gifts. (There is of course a kind of poetry which produces plastic effects not merely by picture-making through explicit descriptions or images, but by giving the language itself—as Allen Tate is able to do—a plastic quality rather than a musical one.)

We might perhaps see a revival of verse in a period and in a society in which music played a leading role. It has long played a great role in Russia; and in the Soviet Union at the present time you find people declaiming poetry at drinking parties or while traveling on boats and trains almost as readily as they burst into song to the accordion or the balalaika, and flocking to poetry-readings just as they do to concerts. It is possible that the Russians at the present time show more of an appetite for "poetry," if not always for the best grade of literature, than any of the Western peoples. Their language, half-chanted and strongly stressed, in many ways extremely primitive, provides by itself, as Italian does, a constant stimulus to the writing of verse.

Here in the United States, we have produced some of our truest poetry in the folk-songs that are inseparable from their tunes. One is surprised, in going through the collections of American popular songs (of Abbé Niles and W. C. Handy, of Carl Sandburg, of the various students trained by Professor Kittredge), which have appeared during the last ten or fifteen years, to discover that the peopling of the continent has had as a by-product a body of folk-verse not unworthy of comparison with the similar material that went to make Percy's *Reliques*. The air of the popular song will no doubt be carrying the words that go with it into the "poetry" anthologies of the future when many of the set-pieces of "poetry," which strain to catch a music gone with Shakespeare, will have come to seem words on the page, incapable of reverberation or of flight from between the covers.

Another pressure that has helped to discourage verse has undoubtedly been the increased demand for reading matter which has been stimulated by the invention of the printing press and which, because ordinary prose is easier to write than verse, has been largely supplied by prose. Modern journalism has brought forth new art-forms; and you have had not only the masterpieces of fiction of such novelists as Flaubert and Joyce, who are also consummate artists in the sense that the great classical poets were, but also the work of men like Balzac and Dickens which lacks the tight organization and the careful attention to detail of the classical epic or drama, and which has to be read rapidly in bulk. The novels of such writers are the epics of societies: they have neither the concision of the folk-song nor the elegance of the forms of the court; they sprawl and swarm over enormous areas like the city populations they deal with. Their authors, no longer schooled in the literary tradition of the Renaissance, speak the practical everyday language of the dominant middle class, which has destroyed the Renaissance world. Even a writer like Dostoevsky rises out of this weltering literature. You cannot say that his insight is less deep, that his vision is less noble or narrower, or that his mastery of his art is less complete than that of the great poets of the past. You can say only that what he achieves he achieves by somewhat different methods.

The technique of prose today seems thus to be absorbing the technique of verse; but it is showing itself quite equal to that work of the imagination which caused men to call Homer "divine": that re-creation, in the harmony and logic of words, of the cruel confusion of life. Not, of course, that we shall have Dante and Shakespeare redone in some prose form any more than we shall have Homer in prose. In art, the same things are not done again or not done again except as copies. The point is that literary techniques are tools, which the masters of the craft have to alter in adapting them to fresh uses. To be too much attached to the traditional tools may be sometimes to ignore the new masters.

Susanne K. Langer
LANGUAGE AND CREATIVE THOUGHT

OF ALL born creatures, man is the only one that cannot live by bread alone. He lives as much by symbols as by sense report, in a realm compounded of tangible things and virtual images, of actual events and omnious portents, always between fact and fiction. For he sees not only actualities but meanings. He has, indeed, all the impulses and interests of animal nature; he eats, sleeps, mates, seeks comfort and safety, flees pain, falls sick and dies, just as cats and bears and fishes and butterflies do. But he has something more in his repertoire, too—he has laws and religions, theories and dogmas, because he lives not only through sense but through symbols. That is the special asset of his mind, which makes him the master of earth and all its progeny.

By the agency of symbols—marks, words, mental images, and icons of all sorts—he can hold his ideas for contemplation long after their original causes have passed away. Therefore, he can think of things that are not presented or even suggested by his actual environment. By associating symbols in his mind, he combines things and events that were never together in the real world. This gives him the power we call imagination. Further, he can symbolize only part of an idea and let the rest go out of consciousness; this gives him the faculty that has been his pride throughout the ages—the power of abstraction. The combined effect of these two powers is inestimable. They are the roots of his supreme talent, the gift of reason. . . .

A symbol is not the same thing as a sign; that is a fact that psychologists and philosophers often overlook. All intelligent animals use signs; so do we. To them as well as to us sounds and smells and motions are signs of food, danger, the presence of other beings, or of rain or storm. Furthermore, some animals not only attend to signs but produce them for the benefit of others. Dogs bark at the door to be let in; rabbits thump to call each other; the cooing of doves

LANGUAGE AND CREATIVE THOUGHT: Reprinted from the January 1944 issue of *Fortune* magazine by special permission.

and the growl of a wolf defending his kill are unequivocal signs of feelings and intentions to be reckoned with by other creatures.

We use signs just as animals do, though with considerable more elaboration. We stop at red lights and go on green; we answer calls and bells, watch the sky for coming storms, read trouble or promise or anger in each other's eyes. That is animal intelligence raised to the human level. Those of us who are dog lovers can probably all tell wonderful stories of how high our dogs have sometimes risen in the scale of clever sign interpretation and sign using.

A sign is anything that announces the existence or the imminence of some event, the presence of a thing or a person, or a change in a state of affairs. There are signs of the weather, signs of danger, signs of future good or evil, signs of what the past has been. In every case a sign is closely bound up with something to be noted or expected in experience. It is always a part of the situation to which it refers, though the reference may be remote in space and time. In so far as we are led to note or expect the signified event we are making correct use of a sign. This is the essence of rational behavior, which animals show in varying degrees. It is entirely realistic, being closely bound up with the actual objective course of history—learned by experience, and cashed in or voided by further experience.

If man had kept to the straight and narrow path of sign using, he would be like the other animals, though perhaps a little brighter. He would not talk, but grunt and gesticulate and point. He would make his wishes known, give warnings, perhaps develop a social system like that of bees and ants, with such a wonderful efficiency of communal enterprise that all men would have plenty to eat, warm apartments—all exactly alike and perfectly convenient—to live in, and everybody could and would sit in the sun or by the fire, as the climate demanded, not talking but just basking, with every want satisfied, most of his life. The young would romp and make love, the old would sleep, the middle-aged would do the routine work almost unconsciously and eat a great deal. But that would be the life of a social, superintelligent, purely sign-using animal.

To us who are human, it does not sound very glorious. We want to go places and do things, own all sorts of gadgets that we do not absolutely need, and when we sit down to take it easy we want to talk. Rights and property, social position, special talents and virtues, and above all our ideas, are what we live for. We have gone off on a tangent that takes us far away from the mere biological cycle that animal generations accomplish; and that is because we can use not only signs but symbols.

A symbol differs from a sign in that it does not announce the presence of the object, the being, condition, or what not, which is its meaning, but merely *brings this thing to mind.* It is not a mere "substitute sign" to which we react as though it were the object itself. The fact is that our reaction to hearing a person's name is quite different from our reaction to the person himself. There are certain rare cases where a symbol stands directly for its meaning: in religious experience, for instance, the Host is not only a symbol but a Presence. But symbols in the ordinary sense are not mystic. They are the same sort of thing that ordinary signs are; only they do not call our attention to something necessarily present or to be physically dealt with—they call up merely a conception of the thing they "mean."

The difference between a sign and a symbol is, in brief, that a sign causes us to think or act *in face of* the thing signified, whereas a symbol causes us to think *about* the thing symbolized. Therein lies the great importance of symbolism for human life, its power to make this life so different from any other animal biography that generations of men have found it incredible to suppose that they were of purely zoological origin. A sign is always embedded in reality, in a present that emerges from the actual past and stretches to the future; but a symbol may be divorced from reality altogether. It may refer to what is *not* the case, to a mere idea, a figment, a dream. It serves, therefore, to liberate thought from the immediate stimuli of a physically present world; and that liberation marks the essential difference between human and nonhuman mentality. Animals think, but they think *of* and *at* things; men think primarily *about* things. Words, pictures, and memory images are symbols that may be combined and varied in a thousand ways. The result is a symbolic structure whose meaning is a complex of all their respective meanings, and this kaleidoscope of *ideas* is the typical product of the human brain that we call the "stream of thought."

The process of transforming all direct experience into imagery or into that supreme mode of symbolic expression, language, has so completely taken possession of the human mind that it is not only a special talent but a dominant, organic need. All our sense impressions leave their traces in our memory not only as signs disposing our practical reactions in the future but also as symbols, images representing our *ideas* of things; and the tendency to manipulate ideas, to combine and abstract, mix and extend them by playing with symbols, is man's outstanding characteristic. It seems to be what his brain most naturally and spontaneously does. Therefore his primitive mental function is not judging reality, but *dreaming his desires.*

Dreaming is apparently a basic function of human brains, for it is free and unexhausting like our metabolism, heartbeat, and breath. It is easier to breathe than to refrain from breathing. The symbolic character of dreams is fairly well established. Symbol mongering, on this ineffectual, uncritical level, seems to be instinctive, the fulfillment of an elementary need rather than the purposeful exercise of a high and difficult talent.

The special power of man's mind rests on the evolution of this special activity, not on any transcendently high development of animal intelligence. We are not immeasurably higher than other animals; we are different. We have a biological need and with it a biological gift that they do not share.

Because man has not only the ability but the constant need of *conceiving* what has happened to him, what surrounds him, what is demanded of him—in short, of symbolizing nature, himself, and his hopes and fears—he has a constant and crying need of *expression.* What he cannot express, he cannot *conceive;* what he cannot conceive is chaos, and fills him with terror.

If we bear in mind this all-important craving for expression we get a new picture of man's behaviour; for from this trait spring his powers and his weaknesses. The process of symbolic transformation that all our experiences undergo is nothing more nor less than the process of *conception,* which underlies the human faculties of abstraction and imagination.

When we are faced with a strange or difficult situation, we cannot react directly, as other creatures do, with flight, aggression, or any such simple instinctive pattern. Our whole reaction depends on how we manage to conceive the situation—whether we cast it in a definite dramatic form, whether we see it as a disaster, a challenge, a fulfillment of doom, or a fiat of the Divine Will. In words or dreamlike images, in artistic or religious or even in cynical form, we must *construe* the events of life. There is great virtue in the figure of speech, "I can *make* nothing of it," to express a failure to understand something. Thought and memory are processes of *making* the thought content and the memory image; the pattern of our ideas is given by the symbols through which we express them. And in the course of manipulating those symbols we inevitably distort the original experience, as we abstract certain features of it, embroider and reinforce those features with other ideas, until the conception we project on the screen of memory is quite different from anything in our real history.

Conception is a necessary and elementary process; what we do with our conception is another story. That is the entire history of human culture—of intelligence and morality, folly and superstition, ritual, language, and the arts—all the phenomena that set man apart from, and above, the rest of the animal kingdom. As the religious mind has to make all human history a drama of sin and salvation in order to define its own moral attitudes, so a scientist wrestles with the mere presentation of "the facts" before he can reason about them. The process of *envisaging* facts, values, hopes, and fears underlies our whole behavior pattern; and this process is reflected in the evolution of an extraordinary phenomenon found always, and only, in human societies—the phenomenon of language.

Language is the highest and most amazing achievement of the symbolistic human mind. The power it bestows is almost inestimable, for without it anything properly called "thought" is impossible. The birth of language is the dawn of humanity. The line between man and beast—between the highest ape and the lowest savage—is the language line. Whether the primitive Neanderthal man was anthropoid or human depends less on his cranial capacity, his upright posture, or even his use of tools and fire, than on one issue we shall probably never be able to settle—whether or not he spoke.

In all physical traits and practical responses, such as skills and visual judgments, we can find a certain continuity between animal and human mentality. Sign using is an ever evolving, ever improving function throughout the whole animal kingdom, from the lowly worm that shrinks into his hole at the sound of an approaching foot, to the dog obeying his master's command, and even to the learned scientist who watches the movements of an index needle.

This continuity of the sign-using talent has led psychologists to the belief that language is evolved from the vocal expressions, grunts and coos and cries, whereby animals vent their feelings or signal their fellows; that man has elaborated this sort of communion to the point where it makes a perfect exchange of ideas possible.

I do not believe that this doctrine of the origin of language is correct. The essence of language is symbolic, not signific; we use it first and most vitally to formulate and hold ideas in our own minds. Conception, not social control, is its first and foremost benefit.

Watch a young child that is just learning to speak play with a toy; he says the name of the object, e.g.: "Horsey! horsey! horsey!" over and over again, looks at the object, moves it, always saying the name to himself or to the world at large. It is quite a time before he talks to anyone in particular; he talks first of all to himself. This is his way of forming and fixing the *conception* of the object in his mind, and around this conception all his knowledge of it grows. Names are the essence of language; for the *name* is what abstracts the conception of the horse from the horse itself, and lets the mere idea recur at the speaking of the name. This permits the conception gathered from one horse experience to be exemplified again by another instance of a horse, so that the notion embodied in the name is a general notion.

To this end, the baby uses a word long before he asks for the object; when he wants his horsey he is likely to cry and fret, because he is reacting to an actual environment, not forming ideas. He uses the animal language of *signs* for his wants; talking is still a purely symbolic process—its practical value has not really impressed him yet.

Language need not be vocal; it may be purely visual, like written language, or even tactual, like the deaf-mute system of speech; but it *must be denotative*. The sounds, intended or unintended, whereby animals communicate do not constitute a language, because they are signs, not names. They never fall into an organic pattern, a meaningful syntax of even the most rudimentary sort, as all language seems to do with a sort of driving necessity. That is because signs refer to actual situations, in which things have obvious relations to each other that require only to be noted; but symbols refer to ideas, which are not physically there for inspection, so their connections and features have to be represented. This gives all true language a natural tendency toward growth and development, which seems almost like a life of its own. Languages are not invented; they grow with our need for expression.

In contrast, animal "speech" never has a structure. It is merely an emotional response. Apes may greet their ration of yams with a shout of "Nga!" But they do not say "Nga" between meals. If they could *talk* about their yams instead of just saluting them, they would be the most primitive men instead of the most anthropoid of beasts. They would have ideas, and tell each other things true or false, rational or irrational; they would make plans and invent laws and sing their own praises, as men do.

The history of speech is the history of our human descent. Yet the habit of transforming morality into symbols, of contemplating and combining and distorting symbols, goes beyond the confines of language. All *images* are symbols, which make us think about the things they mean.

This is the source of man's great interest in "graven images," and in *mere appearances* like the face of the moon or the human profiles he sees in rocks and trees. There is no limit to the meanings he can read into natural phenomena. As long as this power is undisciplined, the sheer enjoyment of finding meanings in everything, the elaboration of concepts without any regard to truth and usefulness seems to run riot; superstition and ritual in their pristine strength go through what some anthropologists have called a "vegetative" stage, where the dream-like symbols, gods and ghouls and rites, multiply like the overgrown masses of life in a jungle. From this welter of symbolic forms emerge the images that finally govern a civilization; the great symbols of religion, society, and selfhood.

What does an image "mean"? Anything it is thought to resemble.

It is only because we can abstract quite unobvious forms from the actual appearance of things that we see line drawings in two dimensions as images of colored, three-dimensional objects, find the likeness of a dipper in a constellation of seven stars, or see a face on a pansy. Any circle may represent the sun or moon; an upright monolith may be a man.

Whenever we can fancy a similarity we tend to see something represented. The first thing we do, upon seeing a new shape, is to assimilate it to our own idea of something that it resembles, something that is known and important to us. Our most elementary concepts are of our own actions, and the limbs or organs that perform them; other things are named by comparison with them. The opening of a cave is its mouth, the divisions of a river its arms. Language, and with it all articulate thought, grows by this process of unconscious metaphor. Every new idea urgently demands a word; if we lack a name for it, we call it after the first namable thing seen to bear even a remote analogy to it. Thus all the subtle and variegated vocabulary of a living language grows up from a few roots of very general application; words as various in meaning as "gentle" and "ingenious" and "general" spring from the one root "ge" meaning "to give life."

Yet there are conceptions that language is constitutionally unfit to express. The reason for this limitation of our verbal powers is a subject for logicians and need not concern us here. The point of interest to us is that, just as rational, discursive thought is bound up with language, so the life of feeling, of direct personal and social consciousness, the emotional stability of man and his sense of orientation in the world are bound up with images directly given to his senses. Fire and water, noise and silence, high mountains and deep caverns, the brief beauty of flowers, the persistent grin of a skull. There seem to be irresistible parallels to the expressive forms we find in nature and the forms of our inner life; thus the use of light to represent all things good, joyful, comforting, and of darkness to express all sorts of sorrow, despair, or horror, is so primitive as to be well-nigh unconscious.

A flame is a soul; a star is a hope; the silence of winter is death. All such images, which serve the purpose of metaphorical thinking, are *natural symbols*. They have not conventionally assigned meanings, like words, but recommend themselves even to a perfectly untutored mind, a child's or a savage's, because they are definitely articulated *forms*, and to see something expressed in such forms is a universal human talent. We do not have to learn to use natural symbols; it is one of our primitive activities.

The fact that sensuous forms of natural processes have a significance beyond themselves makes the range of our symbolism, and with it the horizon of our consciousness, much wider and deeper than language. This is the source of ritual, mythology, and art. Ritual is a symbolic rendering of certain emotional *attitudes*, which have become articulate and fixed by being constantly expressed. Mythology is man's image of his world, and of himself in the world. Art is the exposition of his own subjective history, the life of feeling, the human spirit in all its adventures. . . .

Marshall McLuhan

SIGHT, SOUND, AND THE FURY

On his recent visit to America, Roy Campbell mentioned that when Dylan Thomas had discovered he could read poetry on the radio, this discovery transformed his later poetry for the better. Thomas discovered a new dimension in his language when he established a new relation with the public.

Until Gutenberg, poetic publication meant the reading or singing of one's poems to a small audience. When poetry began to exist primarily on the printed page, in the seventeenth century, there occurred that strange mixture of sight and sound later known as "metaphysical poetry" which has so much in common with modern poetry.

American colonization began when the only culture available to most men was that of the printed book. European culture was then, as now, as much an affair of music, painting, sculpture, and communication as it was of literature. So that to this day North Americans associate culture mainly with books. But, paradoxically, it is in North America that the new media of sight and sound have had the greatest popular sway. Is it precisely because we make the widest separation between culture and our new media that we are unable to see the new media as serious culture? Have four centuries of book-culture hypnotized us into such concentration on the content of books and the new media that we cannot see that the very form of any medium of communication is as important as anything that it conveys?

Ireland is perhaps the only part of the English-speaking world where the oral tradition of culture has strongly persisted in spite of the printed page. And Ireland has given us Wilde, Shaw, Yeats, Synge, and Joyce in recent years—all of them masters of the magic of the spoken word. A Ballynooley farmer who returned to Ireland from

SIGHT, SOUND, AND THE FURY: From *The Commonweal*, April 9, 1954. Reprinted by permission of the editor of *The Commonweal*.

America said to his neighbor: "In three years I didn't meet a man who could sing a ballad, let alone compose one on his feet."

The printed page was itself a highly specialized (and spatialized) form of communication. In 1500 A.D. it was revolutionary. And Erasmus was perhaps the first to grasp the fact that the revolution was going to occur above all in the classroom. He devoted himself to the production of textbooks and to the setting up of grammar schools. The printed book soon liquidated two thousand years of manuscript culture. It created the solitary student. It set up the rule of private interpretation against public disputation. It established the divorce between "literature and life." It created a new and highly abstract culture because it was itself a mechanized form of culture. Today, when the textbook has yielded to the classroom project and the classroom as social workshop and discussion group, it is easier for us to notice what was going on in 1500. Today we know that the turn to the visual on one hand, that is, to photography, and to the auditory media of radio and public address systems on the other hand, has created a totally new environment for the educational process.

André Malraux has recently popularized the notion of the art revolution of our time in his *Museum Without Walls*. His theme is that the picture book today can embrace a greater range of art than any museum. By bringing such a range of art within portable compass, however, it has changed even the painter's approach to painting. Again, it is not just a question of message, image, or content. The picture book as a museum without walls has for the artist a new technical meaning, just as for the spectator pictorial communication means a large but unconscious shift in his ways of thought and feeling.

We have long been accustomed to the notion that a person's beliefs shape and color his existence. They provide the windows which frame, and through which he views, all events. We are less accustomed to the notion that the shapes of a technological environment are also idea-windows. Every shape (gimmick or metropolis), every situation planned and realized by man's factive intelligence, is a window which reveals or distorts reality. Today when power technology has taken over the entire global environment to be manipulated as the material of art, nature has disappeared with nature-poetry. And the effectiveness of the classroom has diminished with the decline of the monopoly of book-culture. If Erasmus saw the classroom as the new stage for the drama of the printing-press, we can see today that the new situation for young and old alike is classrooms without walls. The entire urban environment has become aggressively pedagogic. Everybody and everything has a message to declare, a line to plug.

This is the time of transition from the commercial age, when it was the production and distribution of commodities which occupied the ingenuity of men. Today we have moved from the production of packaged goods to the packaging of information. Formerly we invaded foreign markets with goods. Today we invade whole cultures with packaged information, entertainment, and ideas. In view of the instantaneous global scope of the new media of sight and sound, even the newspaper is slow. But the press ousted the book in the nineteenth century because the book arrived too late. The newspaper page was not a mere enlargement of the book page. It was, like the movie, a new collective art form.

To retrace some of this ground, it will help to recall that in the *Phaedrus*, Plato argued that the new arrival of writing would revolutionize culture for the worse. He suggested that it would substitute reminiscence for thought and mechanical learning for the true dialectic of the living quest for truth by discourse and conversation. It was as if he foresaw the library of Alexandria and the unending exegesis upon previous exegesis of the scholiasts and grammarians.

It would seem that the great virtue of writing is its power to arrest the swift process of thought for steady contemplation and analysis. Writing is the translation of the audible into the visual. In large measure it is the spatialization of thought. Yet writing on papyrus and parchment fostered a very different set of mental habits from those we associate with print and books. In the first place silent reading was unknown until the macadamized, streamlined surfaces of the printed page arrived to permit swift traverse of the eye alone. In the second place, difficulty of access to manuscripts impelled students to memorize so far as possible everything they read. This led to encyclopedism, but also to having on tap in oral discourse one's entire erudition.

The child at school in the Middle Ages had first to make his own copies of texts from dictation. He had next to compile his own grammar and lexicon and commonplace book. The arrival of plenty of cheap, uniform, printed texts changed all this. The mechanization of writing by means of the assembly line of movable type speedily expanded the range of available reading and just as quickly reduced the habit of oral discourse as a way of learning. During the sixteenth century, however, a degree of equilibrium persisted between oral and written learning which we associate with the special excellence of Elizabethan drama, sermon, and poetry.

In the reverse direction, much of the vivid energy of American speech and writing in the twentieth century is the result of the movement away from book-culture towards oral communication. This non-literary direction of speech has been felt to a much smaller degree in England and in Europe during the same period. Radio in particular has encouraged the return to the panel discussion and the round-table. But the spontaneous move towards the seminar and class discussion as learning process has been helped by press and photography too, in so far as these have challenged the monopoly of the book.

Above all, the habits of the business community in demanding conference and discussion as the swift way of establishing insight into method and procedure in various specialized branches of business—these have prompted the new reliance on speech as a means of discovery. It is significant, for example, that the atomic physicists found that only by daily, face-to-face association could they get on with their tasks during the past war.

It has long been a truism that changes in material culture cause shifts in the patterns of the entire culture. The ancient road made possible armies and empires and destroyed the isolated city states of Greece. But the road depended in the first place on writing. Behind the imperial command of great land areas stood the written word in easily transportable form. In the nineteenth century the newspapers, especially after the telegraph, paid for new roads and faster transport by land and sea. The press altered the forms of government, and the telegraph brought secret diplomacy to an end. When events in Egypt or Russia, London, Paris, or New York were known everywhere at once, the time for secret negotiation was reduced to hours and minutes. And the great national populations of the world, alerted and emotionalized by the press, could confront one another immediately for a show-down.

Printing had from the first fostered nationalism because the vernaculars with their large reading publics were more profitable to commercial publishers than Latin. The press has pushed this nationalism to its ultimate point. There it remains. But photography and movies, like music and painting, are international in their power of appeal. The power of pictures to leap over national frontiers and prejudices is well-known, for good and ill.

One aspect of the press deserves special comment in this same respect. The contents of newspapers, their messages and information, have steadily promoted nationalism. But the form of the newspaper page is powerfully inter-cultural and international. The unformulated message of an assembly of news items from every quarter of the globe is that the world today is one city. All war is civil war. All suffering is our own. So that regardless of the political line, or the time or the place, the mere format of the press exerts a single pressure. Basic acceptance of this fact is recorded in the steady weakening of interest in political parties everywhere.

From the point of view of its format, the press as a daily cross-section of the globe is a mirror of the technological instruments of communication. It is the popular daily book, the great collective poem, the universal entertainment of our age. As such it has modified poetic techniques and in turn has already been modified by the newer media of movie, radio, and television. These represent revolutions in communication as radical as printing itself. In fact, they are "magic casements opening on the foam of perilous seas," on which few of us have yet ventured in thought, art or living. If Erasmus was the first to size up and exploit the printing-press as a new force in art and education, James Joyce was the first to seize upon newspaper, radio, movie, and television to set up his "verbivocovisual" drama in *Finnegans Wake*. Pound and Eliot are, in comparison with Joyce, timid devotees of the book as art form. But most of the difficulties which the ordinary person encounters with the poetry of Pound and Eliot disappear if it is viewed as a historical newsreel of persons, myths, ideas, and events with thematic musical score built in. Joyce had a much greater trust of language and reality than Pound or Eliot. By contrast they give their language and reality the Hollywood glamor treatment. Joyce is closer to a De Sica film with its awareness of the intimate riches of the most ordinary scenes and situations.

But the reader who approaches Pound, Eliot, and Joyce alike as exploiters of the cinematic aspects of language will arrive at appreciation more quickly than the one who unconsciously tries to make sense of them by reducing their use of the new media of communication to the abstract linear forms of the book page.

The basic fact to keep in mind about the movie camera and projector is their resemblance to the process of human cognition. That is the real source of their magical, transforming power. The camera rolls up the external world on a spool. It does this by rapid still shots. The projector unwinds this spool as a kind of magic carpet which conveys the enchanted spectator anywhere in the world in an instant. The camera records and analyzes the daylight world with more than human intensity because of the forty-five degree angle of the camera eye. The projector reveals this daylight world on a dark screen where it becomes a dream world.

The wonderful resemblance in all this to human cognition extends at least this far: in cognition we have to interiorize the exterior world. We have to recreate in the medium of our senses and inner faculties the drama of existence. This is the work of the *logos poietikos*, the agent intellect. In speech we utter that drama which we have analogously recreated within us. In speech we make or *poet* the world even as we may say that the movie parrots the world. Languages themselves are thus the greatest af all works of art. They are the collective hymns to existence. For in cognition itself is the whole of the poetic process. But the artist differs from most men in his power to arrest and then reverse the stages of human apprehension. He learns how to embody the stages of cognition (Aristotle's "plot") in an exterior work which can be held up for contemplation.

Even in this respect the movie resembles the cognitive process since the daylight world which the camera rolls up on the spool is reversed and projected to become the magical dream world of the audience. But all media of communication share something of this cognitive character which only a Thomist vision of existence and cognition dare do justice to.

Television, for example, differs from the movie in the immediacy with which it picks up and renders back the visible. The TV camera is like the microphone in relation to the voice. The movie has no such immediacy of pick-up and feedback. As we begin to look into the inevitably cognitive character of the various media we soon get over the jitters that come from exclusive concern with any one form of communication.

In his *Theory of the Film,* Bela Balazs notes how "the discovery of printing gradually rendered illegible the faces of men. So much could be read from paper that the method of conveying meaning by facial expression fell into desuetude. Victor Hugo wrote once that the printed book took over the part played by the cathedral in the Middle Ages and became the carrier of the spirit of the people. But the thousands of books tore the one spirit. . . . into thousands of opinions . . . tore the church into a thousand books. The visible spirit was thus turned into a legible spirit and visual culture into a culture of concepts."

Before printing, a reader was one who discerned and probed riddles. After printing, it meant one who scanned, who skipped along the macadamized surfaces of print. Today at the end of that process we have come to equate reading skill with speed and distraction rather than wisdom. But print, the mechanization of writing, was succeeded in the nineteenth century by photography and then by the mechanization of human gesture in the movie. This was followed by the mechanization of speech in telephone, phonograph and radio. In the talkies, and finally with TV, came the mechanization of the totality of human expression, of voice, gesture, and human figure in action.

Each of these steps in the mechanization of human expression was comparable in its scope to the revolution brought about by the mechanization of writing itself. The changes in the ways of human association, social and political, were telescoped in time and so hidden from casual observers.

If there is a truism in the history of human communication it is that any innovation in the external means of communication brings in its train shock on shock of social change. One effect of writing was to make possible cities, roads, armies, and empires. The letters of the alphabet were indeed the dragon's teeth. The printed book not only fostered nationalism but made it possible to bring the world of the past into every study. The newspaper is a daily book which brings a slice of all the cultures of the world under our eyes every day. To this extent it reverses the tendency of the printing press to accentuate merely national culture. Pictorial journalism and reportage tend strongly in the same international direction. But is this true of radio? Radio has strengthened the oral habit of communication and extended it, via the panel and round-table, to serious learning. Yet radio seems to be a form which also strengthens the national culture. Merely oral societies, for example, are the ultimate in national exclusiveness.

A group of us recently performed an experiment with a large group of students. We divided them into four sections and assigned each section to a separate communication channel. Each section got the identical lecture simultaneously, but one read it, one heard it as a regular lecture in a studio, one heard it on radio and one heard and saw it as a TV broadcast. Immediately afterwards we administered a quiz to determine apprehension and understanding of this new and difficult material. The TV section came out on top, then the radio section, then the studio, and reading sections at the bottom. This was a totally unexpected result and it is too soon to generalize; but it is quite certain that the so-called mass media are not necessarily ordained to be channels of popular entertainment only.

It is "desirable" in thinking about the new media that we should recall that buildings are mass communications and that the first mechanical medium was print from movable type. In fact, the discovery of movable type was the ancestor of all assembly lines, and it would be foolish to overlook the impact of the technological form involved in print on the psychological life of readers. To overlook this would be as unrealistic as to ignore rhythm and tempo in music. Likewise it is only common sense to recognize that the general situation created by a communicative channel and its audience is a large part of that in which and by which the individuals commune. The encoded message cannot be regarded as a mere capsule or pellet produced at one point and consumed at another. Communication is communication all along the line.

One might illustrate from sports. The best brand of football played before fifty people would lack something of the power to communicate. The large enthusiastic crowd is necessary to represent the community at large, just as the players enact a drama which externalizes certain motivations and tensions in the communal life which would not otherwise be visible or available for audience participation. In India huge crowds assemble to experience "*darshan,*" which they consider to occur when they are massed in the presence of a visible manifestation of their collective life.

The new media do something similar for us in the West. Movies, radio, and TV establish certain personalities on a new plane of existence. They exist not so much in themselves but as types of collective life felt and perceived through a mass medium. L'il Abner, Bob Hope, Donald Duck, and Marilyn Monroe become points of collective awareness and communication for an entire society. And as technology increasingly undertakes to submit the entire planet as well as the contents of consciousness to the purposes of man's factive intelligence, it behooves us to consider the whole process of magical transformation involved in the media acutely and extensively.

From this point of view it should be obvious, for example, that the framers of the Hollywood morality code were operating with a very inadequate set of perceptions and concepts about the nature of the movie medium. Modern discussions of censorship, in the same way, are helplessly tied to conceptions borrowed from book culture alone. And the defenders of book culture have seldom given any thought to any of the media as art forms, the book least of all. The result is that their "defense" might as well be staged on an abandoned movie lot for all the effect it has on the actual situation.

When I wrote *The Mechanical Bride* some years ago I did not realize that I was attempting a defense of book culture against the new media. I can now see that I was trying to bring some of the critical awareness fostered by literary training to bear on the new media of sight and sound. My strategy was wrong, because my obsession with literary values blinded me to much that was actually happening for good and ill. What we have to defend today is not the values developed in any particular culture or by any one mode of communication. Modern technology presumes to attempt a total transformation of man and his environment. This calls in turn for an inspection and defense of all human values. And so far as merely human aid goes, the citadel of this defense must be located in analytical awareness of the nature of the creative process involved in human cognition. For it is in this citadel that science and technology have already established themselves in their manipulation of the new media.

PART TWO

What Is Man's Measure?

VI

THE MEASURE OF EXCELLENCE

The Habitual Vision of Greatness

INTRODUCTION

I

MEASURE—the word means a standard, a gauge, a criterion, or a test. Thus we measure weight in ounces and pounds, volume in pints and quarts, length in inches and feet, time in minutes and hours, electrical current in volts and amperes. We live by measure. Scales, clocks, calendars, maps, tables, charts, averages, compasses, barometers, and thermometers are but a few of the measures that man uses in the ordinary conduct of his life and in the ordinary pursuit of scientific knowledge. We trust in the measures we have and seek to make them more exact; we keep trying to measure the quantity, magnitude, and energy of newly discovered elements the better to understand ourselves and our universe.

We know, however, that scientists can measure and test man only up to a point. Anatomists, biologists, chemists, physicists, even with instruments of unerring accuracy, cannot penetrate man's inner being. The physical organ called the heart may in time be completely understood. The metaphorical heart, the center of man's personality, will never yield its secrets to X rays, stethoscopes, or instruments of bodily measurement. When that heart is disclosed it is through artistic expression, chiefly through literature. As Cardinal Newman has noted in *The Idea of a University*:

> Literature stands related to man as science stands to nature; it is his history. Man is composed of body and soul; he thinks and he acts; he has appetites, passions, affections, motives, designs; he has within him the lifelong struggle of duty with inclination; he has an intellect fertile and capacious; he is formed for society, and society multiplies and diversifies in endless combinations his personal characteristics,

> moral and intellectual. All this constitutes his life; of all this Literature is the expression; so that Literature is to man in some sort what autobiography is to the individual; it is his Life and Remains.

If literature is a faithful history of what man has been and what he has done, it is also in good part a description of what he is. Literature takes man's measure; it provides norms for comparing and judging his experiences and for gauging his future possibilities. At the same time, literature warns us not to predict the future solely on the basis of the past. Man can grow and develop in a way that defies the expectations aroused by his previous history. He can and does move up and down the material and spiritual scales, just as his civilizations rise and fall.

Man's achievement is not only the expression of his inner or personal powers; it is a movement toward a goal, an objective, an ideal. Hence man seeks to fulfill his measure both by expressing his own personality and by reaching toward ideals that, from time to time, attract him with compelling force. A new ideal, or an old one freshly realized, can put man to a new test and stimulate him to new achievement.

II

IN OUR day, the most talked about ideal is that of intellectual excellence. True, men in other ages, especially the Greeks and Romans and the medieval and Renaissance Europeans, strove for excellence. (See Section II). But the motives for the pursuit of excellence in the past were chiefly personal perfection or professional advancement. Today we are aware of a more urgent motive. The failures to achieve excellence may result, we have been warned, in the collapse of democratic society and eventually in the loss of personal freedom. As John Gardner writes:

> Those who are most deeply devoted to a democratic society must be precisely the ones who insist upon excellence, who insist that free men are capable of the highest standards of performance, who insist that a free society can be a great society in the richest sense of that phrase. The idea for which this nation stands will not survive if the highest goal free men can set themselves is an amiable mediocrity.

Gardner's essay states the problem in the widest terms. He is concerned with excellence in all fields of knowledge: liberal, professional, and technological. In our times, he argues, we face difficult decisions which require both "the wisest possible leadership" and "competence on the part of individuals at every level of our society." Wise leadership and competent service are impossible without a willing acceptance of standards, and standards often go against the national tolerance of laziness and complacency, "the desire for a fast buck, the American fondness for short cuts, and the reluctance to criticize slackness. . . ."

This general assessment of the present state of American culture is no mere reflection of the author's professional interest in improving American education. Rather it is a summary of innumerable formal reports and informal personal histories, most of which deplore the tendency to "level down" standards to the abilities of the average student. Two of these reports on American education are Claude M. Fuess's "The Retreat from Excellence" and Herbert Gold's "A Dog in Brooklyn, A Girl in Detroit," subtitled "A Life Among the Humanities."

Fuess's essay is an undisguised argument addressed to the mature American citizen. Its central thesis—"that statecraft should . . . counteract the blight which mediocrity has been casting over our boasted culture"—is supported by incisive examples of that blight. "We live in an age of the average, and even the average is not as high as it should or could be," he writes. All classes of society tend to resist criticism of their mediocrity and to depend upon the orthodox optimism of the American mood for a public decision against the charges of the reformers. Many Americans, he goes on to say, not only actively favor the low standards that protect mediocrity, but they also actively oppose the development of the superior student. "We have neglected that small group of potential leaders through whom human happiness has in the past been attainable and attained."

At the end of his spirited discussion of the cult of mediocrity Fuess suggests that "we should put up a sign 'Wanted: A Satirist' and hope for his energizing appearance." In the few years since this essay was written numerous satires have appeared. Even more effective perhaps than these exposures of our educational follies are the personal histories of highly intelligent young men and women who have themselves experienced the ironies, tragic as well as comic, of higher education. None of these is more moving than Herbert Gold's account of his brief career as a teacher of the humanities in an American university.

Written in the intensely vivid, witty, and personal style that has earned its author a very high place among young American novelists, "A Dog in Brooklyn" reports "a succession of classroom events which, retrospectively, seems to have determined [the author's] abandonment of formal dealing with [the Humanities]." The main incidents of the narrative, the students' reaction to the anecdotes of the dog in Brooklyn, their attitude toward automobiles, their response to the traffic accident and its tragic-comic consequences, their attitude toward reading and examinations, all lead up to a huge frustration. Clotilda Adams, like most of her classmates, is not able "to respond adequately to the facts," either the facts of ordinary life or the facts of literature or the facts of the classroom. Clotilda Adams does not pass the course, "but she [is] nevertheless admitted on probation to the student teacher programme because of the teacher shortage and the great need to educate our children in these perilous times. Of today."

Gold abandoned teaching, partly because he recognized his own superior talents for writing, partly because he was baffled by the great confusion of an educational program that not only tolerates mediocrity but, by a "peculiar combination of ignorance and jadedness," actively obscures the reality of the world we live in. "Words fade; our experience does not touch; we make do with babble and time-serving. We need to learn the meaning of words, the meaning of the reality those words refer to; we must clasp reality close."

III

THE VIEWS of John Gardner, Claude Fuess, and Herbert Gold present a challenge to American society as a whole and to the present generation of college students in particular. While they are not wholly negative in their criticism—Gold points to the positive principle "Particular life is still the best map to truth"—they do stress the failure of our society to achieve intellectual excellence. To find out just what excellence is we need to identify the standards of excellence and to study them in their concrete manifestations.

The traditional custodians of excellence are those scholars and writers whose views, having passed repeated scrutiny by a large body of critics, are widely accepted as representative. Three such spokesmen are presented in Section IV: Sir Richard Livingstone, T. S. Eliot, and Alfred North Whitehead.

In "The Essentials of Education" Livingstone begins by observing that the common feature of all colleges is the professed aim to teach what is first-rate in whatever courses the student studies. But there are many courses of study, in humanities, science, and technology. "The difficulty with education, as with life, is that it has so many fields. . . . Which, then, are the most important fields?" One such field is vocational. We ought to know what is first-rate in the profession or business we hope to enter. But, since in this field "the modern world does well," and since it is rarely ignored, he proceeds to emphasize the need to know what is first-rate in the humanities—in literature and the fine arts, philosophy, theology, and so on.

The two humanities that show man "full face" are history and literature; of these two literature is regarded as the more excellent.

> There we hear him talking aloud to the world, but really talking to himself, putting on paper the feelings that come to him, so that in literature is recorded every thought, every vision, every fancy, every emotion that has ever passed through the human mind. What a record! Is there any better way of learning what men are . . . ?

If literature is *the* truly excellent subject because it brings us closer to the human heart, we still need to know what is excellent in literature. We can readily identify excellence of subject matter. Stories of great men lift up the mind; as Disraeli observed, "to believe in the heroic makes heroes." But literature does not always portray heroes. Sometimes its excellence consists in its power to reveal the unheroic. And here we may be deceived by the counterfeit coin of pseudo-literature. Livingstone supplies a test. We can recognize what is truly excellent by asking the question: Does the literary work make us aware both of the immediate and the timeless?

If Sir Richard Livingstone furnishes us with a general test of the excellence of literature, T. S. Eliot in "What Is a Classic?" provides a special test of excellence of one kind of literature. In Eliot's view a classic work of literature is not merely the book of a "standard" author who is read in the schools or of an author who represents a "classical" period of a given language, but the work of one who possesses maturity.

A classic is mature in three different ways. First, "a classic can only occur when a civilisation is mature." Thus, while Sir Thomas Malory's *Morte D'Arthur* is a medieval classic, it is not a classic in Eliot's sense because medieval society in England was unsophisticated, at least in comparison to that of Greece and Rome, or to that of Italy and France at a later date. Second, a classic can only occur "when a language and literature are mature." Hence those who write in a primitive tongue and who have no literary models may possess individual genius but they are not classic. Although the author of *Beowulf* may impress us more than Virgil does, he is not classic. Third, a classic can only occur when the mind of the poet is mature. An immature poet, however mature his society and its language and literature, is not a classic poet.

> A mature literature, therefore, has a history behind it: a history, that is not merely a chronicle, an accumulation of manuscripts and writings of this kind and that, but an ordered though unconscious progress of a language to realise its own potentialities within its own limitations.

A classic is marked by "maturity of mind, maturity of manners, maturity of language and perfection of the common style." For Eliot, Virgil is the classic writer par excellence. Dante is his closest competitor among writers in modern European languages. Shakespeare, Milton, and Molière only approximate Virgil's classic quality.

The value of the classic, according to Eliot, is not that it gives us a model to imitate. He points out that, on the contrary:

> every great work of poetry tends to make impossible the production of equally great works of the same kind. . . . No first-rate poet would attempt to do again, what has already been done as well as it can be done in his language. . . . The classic poet . . . exhausts, not a form only, but the language of his time.

A great classic writer, in a sense, mines all the gold for himself. What the classic does provide, however, is a criterion of excellence. "We need it in order to judge our individual poets, though we refuse to judge our literature as a whole in comparison with one which has produced a classic." The classic is our clue to the first-rate: "without the constant application of the classical measure . . . we tend to become provincial."

Many will agree that Eliot's extended definition of this one measure of literary excellence is as explicit as one can become without slipping into pedantic details. In describing the classic standard, too, he has suggested that other kinds of literature have their appropriate standards and that excellence may be judged by reference to those standards.

If an individual art such as literature has its standards of excellence may we say that the college or university, where all arts and sciences are offered, also has a standard? To put it otherwise, is there a common trait that will describe excellence in all teaching and learning? Does the first-rate teacher or student of economics share a quality with the first-rate teacher or student of the fine arts?

In Sir Richard Livingstone's essay, these questions are not fully explored. In Alfred North Whitehead's "Universities and Their Function" they are directly confronted. Whitehead's springboard is the presence of the business school in a modern university. At first glance such a school, particularly on a large scale, threatens to distract many from the pursuit of excellence in the humanities and science. Business, as a university subject, is highly experimental. It has as yet few standards, and it seems to aim less at the cultivation of the intellect for its own sake than it does at immediate public service and private profit. All the more reason then, Whitehead implies, for going to the heart of the matter. Does business belong in a university whose hallmark is intellectual excellence? Conversely, what is the excellence proper to the university and can it be conveyed in a school of business?

The purpose of a university is not primarily the education of the student or the research by the faculty but "the imaginative consideration of learning." Throughout his essay *imagination,* understood as imaginative thought, is the key word. Imagination works as an illuminating force, an energizer, a source of vision, an adventuring spirit that brings zest to life. Imagination is not divorced from knowledge, nor is knowledge very useful without imagination. "Fools act on imagination without knowledge; pedants act on knowledge without imagination."

Whether business studies will develop imaginative scholarship, the touchstone, and indeed the ultimate measure of the success of a university, is still to be determined. But if business schools are to achieve excellence, and if the society they serve is to achieve it also, then both the school and the society must be inspired by imagination.

> Imagination is a gift which has often been associated with great commercial peoples—with Greece, with Florence, with Venice, with the learning of Holland, and with the poetry of England. Commerce and imagination thrive together. It is a gift which all must pray for their country who desire for it that abiding greatness achieved by Athens:—
>
> Her citizens, imperial spirits,
> Rule the present from the past.
>
> For American education no smaller ideal can suffice.

IV

POETRY and imagination are normally and rightly associated with the expression of intense human emotions, not of philosophical arguments about intellectual excellence. We look to poets less for reasons than for insights, less for explanations than for implications. Yet the poets together with all their fellow artists have defined excellence for us perhaps more effectively than have philosophers, educators, and critics. They do so, first, by their persuasive praise and blame of the characters of men and women and of their ways of life and thought; second, by their portrayal of perfection and of its opposite; and third, by their representation, in imaginative terms, of the complexities, indeed the paradoxes, involved in the pursuit of excellence.

Praise and blame—the words remind us that early poets sang the praises of famous men in epics, elegies, odes, and hymns, that religious poets composed psalms of thanksgiving and adoration, that lyric poets paid homage to their light and dark ladies, that ballad-writers have cried up the heroes of the hour. Poetry is largely made up of praise: of Homer for Achilles, of Virgil for Aeneas, of Dante for Beatrice, of Milton for Lycidas, of Shelley for Keats, of Tennyson for Arthur Hallam, of Walt Whitman for the common man. By the same token poets have condemned tyrants, demagogues, usurers, adulterers, the seven deadly sins, and a plethora of lesser follies in invectives, satires, parodies, epigrams, and ironic comedies.

Often praise or blame is the expression of personal feeling born of ignorance or blind affection or disguised malice. But when praise or blame are both sincere and discriminating, they often reveal the writer's norm of excellence. Ben Jonson's eulogy of Shakespeare applies the writer's standards to his subject. To say that Shakespeare is the soul of his age and a delight and a wonder is to reflect the classical canon that literature first gives pleasure or delight. The extended comparison of Shakespeare with Greek, Latin, and other "classic" authors reflects Eliot's view that the classics provide our norms of literary excellence. Nature (reality) and art (representation) are united in Shakespeare:

> For though the poet's matter nature be,
> His art doth give the fashion. . . .

Shakespeare, Jonson continues, is a supreme artist because he has re-created nature and fathered a living race "in his well-turnèd and true-filèd lines."

Thus, in the course of his eulogy Jonson not only expresses his personal admiration and affection for Shakespeare but he states, in a condensed and oblique form, the classical standards of excellence that were held in the Renaissance.

So, too, in "Under Which Lyre" W. H. Auden's humorous attack upon the followers of Apollo and his praise of Hermes, implies, again obliquely, a theory of literature that emphasizes imaginative freedom. In her "In Praise of Diversity" Phyllis McGinley in blaming conformity for the world's woes and in extolling individual differences clarifies her standard of excellence.

Writers also establish standards of excellence by their portrayal of perfection or of its opposite. In art, the perfect moment when a truth stands revealed, when a scene gives the direction to an action, or when an image discloses the secret of a heart—is the concrete embodiment of a standard of excellence. When we hear a Bach concerto or see Michelangelo's David or stand before the Parthenon we know we are in the presence of the norm of excellence itself. Bach *is* harmony, Michelangelo *is* symmetry, the Parthenon *is* classical poise. By being what they are they establish that norm. In the same manner a poem or story or drama that catches some aspect of reality at its perfect moment defines both the excellence that inheres in that reality and the excellence of the artistic operation.

"The Windhover" has often been cited as just such an excellent portrayal of an excellent thing. In the octet of the sonnet, the speaker describes a falcon at early morning. He observes intently the bird's movements, his hovering, his upward dart, his spiraling, his wide smooth swing, his command of himself and his element. The falcon is "caught" in the sense that he is seen in an action that perfectly expresses just what he is. The standard of excellence for the falcon is his expression, his power of flight. The speaker is stirred by "the achieve of, the mastery of the thing."

In the sestet, the speaker turns the thought upon himself, as if to inquire whether he too can achieve excellence through action. He can do so, according to many interpreters of the poem, by day-to-day endurance ("shéer plód") in the service of Christ. He, the speaker, can achieve his selfhood, his mastery, in self-sacrifice. "And the fire that breaks from thee" then—that is, from himself in union with Christ—is "a billion/ Times told lovelier" than the "brute beauty and valour and act" of the plummeting bird. Man's most expressive act, his cooperation with God's will, is infinitely more beautiful than the falcon's.

"The Windhover" catches the action in a larger sense than our paraphrase might suggest. The poem is more than a statement. Its rhythm, imagery, and sound are all closely interrelated to form a coherent literary whole. Hence we respond to its highly charged and intricately ordered language as well as to its accurate observations and poignant emotions and thoughts. The poem, in short, catches the perfect moment of the bird—and, by analogy, man's perfect moment. Moreover, it catches bird and man in a perfect pattern of language. This in itself is an "achieve of, [a] mastery of" the verbal "thing."

Robert Browning's "Andrea del Sarto" is a longer, more detailed, and more complex study of the theme of excellence. Just as Hopkins catches the essential character of the windhover in its self-expressive flight, so Browning catches the character of the great Italian Renaissance painter in a moment of significant choice, a choice that reveals Andrea exactly as he is.

In this poem Andrea is speaking to his wife Lucrezia. As twilight settles on Florence the exhausted painter tells Lucrezia that he will do what she asks—paint a picture for a friend of a friend and give her the money. In turn he asks her to sit with him by the window, "Both of one mind, as married people use,/ Quietly, quietly, the evening through." He reviews his paintings, which are scattered about his studio. As it is an autumn evening in Florence, so it is the autumn evening of his life. The artist, contemplating his career, says:

> . . . the whole seems to fall into a shape
> As if I saw alike my work and self
> And all that I was born to be and do,
> A twilight-piece. . . .

Andrea knows that he had great genius and many opportunities. In craftsmanship he excelled all his Renaissance competitors. Noble patrons had encouraged him, the greatest critics had praised him. Yet, compared with Michelangelo and Raphael, he lacked true excellence.

> I am judged.
> There burns a truer light of God in them. . . .

Andrea's art is placid and perfect, theirs less perfect but inspired. While he grasped at the immediately perfectible, they aspired to ultimate perfection. He recognizes their superiority, saying:

> Ah, but a man's reach should exceed his grasp,
> Or what's a heaven for?

Thus far, Andrea's monologue has revealed a series of significant choices. He had chosen to marry Lucrezia; he had consented to paint for money; he had absconded with the King of France's gold and dared not leave his house "For fear of chancing on the Paris lords." In short, while he might have achieved Raphael's glory and Michelangelo's magnificence of soul, he chose Lucrezia, he chose to be satisfied with the second-rate.

These choices, however revealing, merely foreshadow the crucial moment of the poem when Andrea, having failed to persuade Lucrezia to remain with him, consents to her assignation with a "cousin," and then makes his final revealing decision. He imagines that he will have a second chance—in heaven—to compete with Leonardo, Raphael, and Michelangelo. But once again he chooses as he did before:

> So—still they overcome
> Because there's still Lucrezia,—as I choose.

Andrea, in that final moment of decision where he confirms the earlier decisions that have led up to it, stands before us completely revealed. In delineating his character as a man and an artist Browning has measured Andrea against his rivals. He invokes the standards of true excellence to show why Andrea says rightly: "I am judged."

But we must note, too, that Browning's language, like that of Hopkins, displays its own kind of excellence. If a man reveals his personal character by a series of significant choices, so too does a literary artist reveal his artistic character by a series of choices in the making of his poem. By this standard, Browning's success in "Andrea del Sarto" can only be questioned by those who cannot tolerate the kind of poem he chose to write. But granted his subject and theme, Browning's decisions are exactly right.

The frame is right because the dramatic monologue, a form that Browning himself brought to perfection, permits the speaker to describe, to narrate, and to explain exterior events and, more importantly, to reveal his interior feelings. Further, it permits him to analyze his conscious and deliberate actions and, again more importantly, to express his spontaneous and unanalyzed drives. Thus Andrea may plausibly shift from a description of his studio and the Florentine setting to an account of his past, returning to the present to caress his wife and, unconsciously, to give himself away by his uxorious complaints and his weak excuses for his failure.

The tone is right. Andrea's voice is that of a tired, disappointed man, too defeated to shout in rage against his unhappy lot. Yet, though the key is low, the verse hums with a vigor that conveys to us, through its energetic irony, how the great artists might have responded to life.

The imagery is right. "A common greyness silvers everything," everything, that is, that pertains to Andrea, whereas, in contrast, the colors associated with true excellence are golden: "Too live the life grew, golden and not grey."

The pace is right: slow and crepuscular when Andrea meditates on his life within the four walls "that make his home," rapid and excited when he recalls his days of glory in France. "A good time, was it not, my kingly days?"

V

THE essays, stories, and poems that we have been discussing in this section all point up the theme of excellence: what it is and what it is not; what the standards of excellence are in life, in education, in literature; how individual works of literature manifest the excellent and the excellent way of expressing the excellent. Now we turn to two long stories, one by Henry James and one by Willa Cather, and a famous play by Molière. All three dramatize the complexities, and the paradoxes, that are involved in the pursuit of excellence.

That true excellence sometimes meets with misunderstanding goes without saying. Excellence is the result of a gift of nature, the exercise of discriminating choice, and the commitment to a severe and, in the eyes of ordinary men, an alienating discipline. The excellent artist, for example, possesses superlative gifts of intelligence and taste that set him apart from the average person and often provoke envy or contempt. The excellent artist rejects the mediocre and thus may seem arrogant when he is merely being discriminating. Finally, compelled by his passion to make things right, he "scorns delights and lives laborious days" and, thus detached from common tasks and ordinary society, is often misunderstood. Yet these misunderstandings, however tragic they be, may result in the clarification of true excellence.

In "The Next Time" Henry James tells the story of Ralph Limbert, a gifted author faced with the necessity of making a living. He cannot, however, accommodate himself to the taste of an age "of trash triumphant." Unlike his wife's relative, the best-selling Mrs. Highmore, he cannot make the public bite and wag "their great collective tail artlessly for more." His gift, according to his friend, the narrator of the tale, is his distinctive way of recording life. Limbert feels that:

> The only success worth one's powder was success in the line of one's idiosyncrasy. Consistency was in itself distinction, and what was talent but the art of being completely whatever it was that one happened to be? One's things were characteristic or they were nothing.

Hence his efforts to succeed as journalist, writer, and editor fail. He stoops as low as he can. But try as he might, Limbert cannot write "tremendous trash" or achieve "the mediocrity that attaches, that endears." Each next time, he resolves to do the popular thing. But each next time he fails:

> The thing was charming with all his charm and powerful with all his power: it was an unscrupulous, an unsparing, a shameless merciless masterpiece. . . . The perversity of the effort . . . had been frustrated by the purity of the gift.

Limbert, in short, is so obsessed with the exquisite, so habituated to the excellent, that he cannot make a sow's ear out of a silk purse. He finally abandons the attempt to be popular and, in his last work, floats away "into a reckless consciousness of [his] art." True excellence, in this dramatic tale, is the acceptance of the law of one's talent, and that talent achieves its measure "when of a beautiful subject his expression was complete."

Willa Cather's "A Sculptor's Funeral" deals with another misunderstanding between the artist in pursuit of his goal of excellence and a social group that measures him by its own very different standards. The story opens at a Kansas railroad siding, where a group of townspeople await the arrival of a train bearing the body of the distinguished local sculptor, Harvey Merrick. They convey the body to the Merrick home, where Henry Steavens, the young Bostonian disciple of the sculptor, witnesses, "with a shudder of unutterable repulsion," the self-indulgent hysteria of Annie Merrick, the sculptor's mother. As he listens to the mourners, Steavens reconstructs the "whole miserable boyhood" of his master:

> All this raw, biting ugliness had been the portion of the man whose mind was to become an exhaustless gallery of beautiful impressions—so sensitive that the mere shadow of a poplar leaf flickering against a

> sunny wall would be etched and held there forever. . . . Whatever he touched, he revealed its holiest secret; liberated it from enchantment and restored it to its pristine loveliness. Upon whatever he had come in contact with, he had left a beautiful record of the experience—a sort of ethereal signature; a scent, a sound, a color that was his own.

Steavens then discovers the real tragedy of Harvey Merrick's life. He had always suspected that Merrick had been struck a blow that had cut deep into his soul and stained his life forever with a terrified sadness. Steavens confirms the suspicion during the wake. The townspeople analyze Harvey Merrick with an arrogant stupidity. One, in much sorrow, says "It's too bad the old man's sons didn't turn out better"; another says "Harve never could have handled stock none"; another adds "Harve never was much account for anything practical"; and a fourth advises that "What Harve needed, of all people, was a course in some first-class Kansas City business college." In short, what Harve should have been, in the eyes of his Kansas neighbors, was what they had made of their own sons: boys yoked to the making of money and to knavery. "You wanted them to be successful rascals . . ." roars Jim Laird in a fit of revulsion.

> There was only one boy ever raised in this borderland between ruffianism and civilization who didn't come to grief, and you hated Harvey Merrick more for winning out than you hated all the other boys who got under the wheels.

In "The Next Time" and "The Sculptor's Funeral," Henry James and Willa Cather both clarify the meaning of artistic excellence by a dramatic contrast between the goals of Ralph Limbert and Harvey Merrick and those of a vulgar, obsessively commercial society. These stories, and countless others, enter an indirect plea for excellence. Although it seems inconceivable that anyone would plead against excellence, there is a sense in which the pursuit of excellence can become obsessive. One's admiration for the best can lead to an unjust contempt for the simply good; love of fineness can deviate into mere fastidiousness; honesty can crumble into scrupulosity. When this happens the pursuit of excellence may lead to an excess of idealism that resembles Don Quixote's mad pursuit of honor.

In *The Misanthrope* Molière presents in the character of Alceste a man whose standards of excellence, in life and in literature, are so uncompromising that he is tempted to resign from the society of his day, if not from the whole human race. The play begins with an argument between Alceste and his friend, Philinte. Philinte has just parted from another friend whom he had greeted with effusive politeness. Alceste regards Philinte's cordiality as extravagant and insincere:

Esteem is founded on comparison:
To honor all men is to honor none.
Since you embrace this indiscriminate vice,
Your friendship comes at far too cheap a price. . . .

Philinte is astonished that Alceste will not agree that social custom permits one to be outwardly more cordial than he might inwardly feel:

In certain cases it would be uncouth
And most absurd to speak the naked truth. . . .
Wouldn't the social fabric come undone
If we were wholly frank with everyone?

Not at all thinks Alceste. There is too much condonation, indeed flattery, of vice and folly: "Mankind has grown so base,/ I mean to break with the whole human race."

To Philinte, the basis of Alceste's misanthropy is a perfectionist view of human nature. "I take men as they are, or let them be,/ And teach my soul to bear their frailty." Alceste on the other hand is perpetually indignant because he finds men knavish, unjust, and insincere.

In the scenes that follow Alceste acts according to his rigorous code. Because of his unsparing criticism of Oronte's sonnet he almost comes to blows with his rival in love. He bullies the worldly widow, Célimène, with whom he is, inconsistently, in love and whom he wishes to marry. He refuses to make the "normal" political maneuvers to defend himself in court and loses his law suit. Although in the end he finds in Eliante a woman of virtuous beauty whose sincerity matches his own, she rejects him in favor of Philinte and Alceste resolves to flee

this bitter world where vice is king
And seek some spot unpeopled and apart
Where I'll be free to have an honest heart.

Philinte's last words echo the argument of the opening lines: "Let's do everything we can,/ To change the mind of this unhappy man."

Clearly Molière offers no easy solution to the problem, implied throughout *The Misanthrope,* of whether an honest man, who is also logical, can find a place in society without compromising his own standards of excellence. On the one hand the answer seems to be that he cannot. The glittering world of seventeenth-century French high society seems utterly corrupt. Hypocrisy, like an evil scent, oozes through a false skin of elegance and wit. Given Alceste's combination of honesty and logic, he can find no acceptable place for himself. To Philinte's argument that man's conniving provides the honest man with a chance to philosophize, "And that is virtue's noblest exercise," Alceste responds, "My reason bids me go, for my own good." Alceste's response seems unanswerable. Yet it is also an unreasonable response for all its logic because Alceste allows himself to be trapped in contradictions of his own making. He loves Célimène who is unworthy of his love, but he feels unworthy of loving Eliante, who, he knows, is truly worthy of his love. His sincerity, while heroic, is less intellectual than it is emotional. He fails to see that love is not based on feelings of devotion; it is based, in Eliante's words, "on sweet accords of temper and of taste." In short, Alceste might have maintained his standards while he remained within society had he, like Eliante, kept clear the line between his intellectual ideals and his emotional attitudes.

The Misanthrope ends then without a clear answer to its main questions. As Martin Turnell remarks in *The Classical Moment:*

> The catharsis lies in the clarifying of our feelings, in the perception that social adjustment is a personal matter where in the last resort no facile slogan or philosophical system can help us; and the "message," if we must have one, is that we must have courage to create our own "order," whatever the cost, instead of yielding to the temptation of an easy escape.

The pursuit of excellence, we may conclude from the selections from James, Willa Cather, and Molière, is not without its ambiguities. One of them is the paradox that excellence, like the ideal woman of Wordsworth's poem, should not always be "too bright or good/ For human nature's daily food."

ESSAYS

John Gardner
THE PURSUIT OF EXCELLENCE

WILLIAM JAMES said, "Democracy is on trial, and no one knows how it will stand the ordeal. . . . What its critics now affirm is that its preferences are inveterately for the inferior. So it was in the beginning, they say, and so it will be world without end. Vulgarity enthroned and institutionalized, elbowing everything superior from the highway, this, they tell us, is our irremediable destiny. . . ."

William James himself did not believe that this was our destiny. Nor do I. But the danger is real and not imagined. Democracy as we know it has proved its vitality and its durability. We may be proud of its accomplishments. But let us not deceive ourselves. The specter that William James raised still haunts us.

I once asked a highly regarded music teacher what was the secret of his extraordinary success with students. He said, "First I teach them that it is better to do it well than to do it badly. Many have never been taught the pleasure and pride in setting standards and then living up to them."

Standards! That is a word for every American to write on his bulletin board. We must face the fact that there are a good many things in our character and in our national life which are inimical to standards—laziness, complacency, the desire for a fast buck, the American fondness for short cuts, reluctance to criticize slackness, to name only a few. Every thinking American knows in his heart that we must sooner or later come to terms with these failings. . . .

Anyone concerned with excellence in our society must understand and take into account the social complexities that surround the subject. Only the fainthearted and the easily confused will be daunted by these complexities. Tougher-minded Americans will see that a clear view of the complexities opens the way to constructive action.

And constructive action is desperately needed. The transformations of technology and the intricacies of modern social organization have given us a society more complex and baffling than ever before. And before us is the prospect of having to guide it through changes more ominous than any we have known. This will require the wisest possible leadership. But it will also require competence on the part of individuals at every level of our society.

The importance of competence as a condition of freedom has been widely ignored (as some newly independent nations are finding to their sorrow). An amiable fondness for the graces of a free society is not enough. Keeping a free society free—and vital and strong—is no job for the half-educated and the slovenly. Free men must be competent men. In a society of free men, competence is an elementary duty. Men and women doing competently whatever job is theirs to do tone up the whole society. And the man who does a slovenly job—whether he is a janitor or a judge, a surgeon or a technician—lowers the tone of the society. So do the chiselers of high and low degree, the sleight-of-hand artists who always know how to gain an advantage without honest work. They are the regrettable burdens of a free society.

But excellence implies more than competence. It implies a striving for the highest standards in every phase of life. We need individual excellence in all its forms—in every kind of creative endeavor, in political life, in education, in industry—in short, universally.

Those who are most deeply devoted to a democratic society must be precisely the ones who insist upon excellence, who insist that free men are capable of the highest standards of performance, who insist that a free society can be a great society in the richest sense of that phrase. The idea for which this nation stands will not survive if the highest goal free men can set themselves is an amiable mediocrity.

We are just beginning to understand that free men must set their own difficult goals and be their own hard taskmasters. Since the beginning of time, most humans have had to work hard either because physical survival demanded it or because their taskmasters required it. Now, thanks to our prosperity, we don't have to put out great effort for physical survival; and a free people has no taskmasters.

With such an unprecedented release from outward pressures, free men fall easily into the error of thinking that no effort is required of them. It is easy for them to believe that freedom and justice are inexpensive commodities, always there, like the air they breathe, and not things they have to earn, be worthy of, fight for and cherish.

Nothing could be more dangerous to the future of our society.

Free men must set their own goals. There is no one to tell them what to do; they must do it for themselves. They must be quick to apprehend the kinds of effort and performance their society needs, and they must demand that kind of effort and performance of themselves and of their fellows. They must cherish what Whitehead called "the habitual vision of greatness." If they have the wisdom and courage to demand much of themselves—as individuals and as a society—they may look forward to long-continued vitality. But a free society that is passive, inert and preoccupied with its own diversions and comforts will not last long. And freedom won't save it.

Today any reference to the weaknesses of our society is seen in the context of our international rivalries of the moment. But long, long before such rivalries were formed we were committed, as free men, to the arduous task of building a great society—not just a strong one, not just a rich one, but a great society. This is a pact we made with ourselves.

De Tocqueville was not speaking rhetorically when he said, ". . . there is nothing more arduous than the apprenticeship of liberty." And he might have added that the apprenticeship is unending—the unchanging requirement of a free society's survival is that each generation rediscover this truth. As Chesterton put it, "The world will never be safe for democracy—it is a dangerous trade."

But who ever supposed that it would be easy?

Claude M. Fuess

THE RETREAT FROM EXCELLENCE

A WORRIED mother recently called me by telephone to ask me to intervene for her son, who had failed to win a scholarship at a well-known private school.

"How did he do on his tests?" I asked.

"I don't know," she confessed plaintively. "But what difference does that make? He's a lot better than most boys who get scholarships!"

I tried to explain to her that this lad, in our democracy, could in due season marry and vote and run for office and qualify for social security, but that when he applied for financial aid at a school, he entered into a contest in which he had to match his brain power against that of others. But the mother just didn't understand that the mere fact of her son's existence doesn't make him the equal of anybody in competition.

Her attitude is a significant illustration of a pattern which is recognizable throughout our society. The pattern is simply that we

THE RETREAT FROM EXCELLENCE: From *Saturday Review,* March 26, 1960. Reprinted by permission of *Saturday Review* and the author.

are increasingly ignoring the important differences among people. In New England a school custodian (a modern euphemism for "janitor") often receives a higher salary than the teacher whose room he cleans. This has always seemed to me somewhat absurd, and once when I said so at a meeting a man rose and asked indignantly, "Why not? He works just as hard, doesn't he?" The prolonged and intensive training of a mathematics instructor seemed to this critic entirely irrelevant. After all, one citizen is as valuable as another!

We live in an age of the average, and even the average is not as high as it should or could be. I have spent some time in hospitals and know how reassuring it is to be attended by a physician who knows his business, who thinks and speaks and acts with the confidence acquired by thorough training. After you have been examined by a nurse who barely differentiates the patella from the esophagus, how cheering it is to come under the tender care of a professional who doesn't wield a hypodermic needle as if it were an ice pick. The current incompetence is due, I am told, largely to lack of competition. Nurses are needed so badly that hospitals take what they can get—and the "take" is often astonishing.

That one citizen is as good as another is a favorite American axiom, supposed to express the very essence of our Constitution and way of life. But just what do we mean when we utter that platitude? One surgeon is not as good as another. One plumber is not as good as another. We soon become aware of this when we require the attention of either. Yet in political and economic matters we appear to have reached a point where knowledge and specialized training count for very little. A newspaper reporter is sent out on the street to collect the views of various passers-by on such a question as "Should the United States defend Formosa?" The answer of the bar-fly who doesn't even know where the island is located, or that it is an island, is quoted in the next edition just as solemnly as that of the college teacher of history. With the basic tenets of democracy —that all men are born free and equal and are entitled to life, liberty, and the pursuit of happiness—no decent American can possibly take issue. But that the opinion of one citizen on a technical subject is just as authoritative as that of another is manifestly absurd. And to accept the opinions of all comers as having the same value is surely to encourage a cult of mediocrity.

Recent prognostications for the 1960s over radio and television, and even in legislative halls, have been preponderantly optimistic. The orthodox American mood today is confident and complacent. Very little mention has been made of significant changes which, whether we approve of them or not, have taken place since the close of World War I, and which have had and are having far-reaching

consequences. The current tendency to reduce everybody to the same level is illustrated not only in the broad results of our taxation policies but also in such matters as the adjustment of the school curriculum to the abilities of the average or below-average pupils. Having moved almost unconsciously toward achieving the greatest good for the greatest number, we have neglected that small group of potential leaders through whom human happiness has in the past been attainable and attained.

The prevalence of a cult of mediocrity is evident in many phases of our national economy. Out of many trends a few samples will prove this point. One of the more obvious is the system under which all workmen, regardless of skill or attitude, receive the same pay for the same job. Under the existing policy nobody has any incentive for toiling harder or longer or more effectively than his less aggressive neighbors. Everybody is familiar with union regulations forbidding a member to lay more than a specified number of bricks in an eight-hour day. Those who are able to lay more, and would like to lay more for more money, find themselves frustrated. I have argued this matter with labor leaders, who insist that it is more important to protect the normal, or below-normal, workman than to encourage the exceptionally eager one. It should be possible to do both. The present tendency, however, is to eliminate competition among employees and thus to restrain the ambitious laborer. Clearly this policy does not, indeed cannot, stimulate increased production. The principle of "leveling down" is here perfectly illustrated in one of its worst aspects.

The widespread acceptance in our country of the doctrine of promotion by seniority alone has had much the same consequences. Let me illustrate what often happens in education. A teacher of average ability, once appointed to a school or college staff, can be sure of moving up automatically as retirement or death removes his older colleagues; and because of this guarantee, ambition frequently ebbs away. The amount of dead wood among faculty members of forty-five or older is considerable, as any honest dean will testify. Yet to advance a younger but much abler associate ahead of one of these comfortably situated elder professors is virtually an impossibility unless the old-timer strays from the marital fold or becomes a Communist suspect—which he is unlikely to do. Again I am aware that the existing system has its staunch defenders, and it unquestionably does favor some entirely respectable men and women. But of its contribution to the lowering of quality there can be little doubt.

The forces promoting mediocrity in our schools are too well known to require extensive documentation. The Carnegie Foundation for the Advancement of Teaching, summarizing some of the problems created by these forces, says:

> Very large numbers of superior students are still not working up to their capacity, not being challenged to their best performance, not pursuing the hard intellectual programs which will develop their talents.

George F. Kennan, writing as a historian observing current events, refers scathingly to an educational system in which "quality has been extensively sacrificed to quantity." In a majority of secondary schools, the emphasis is not primarily on scholastic attainment; the vacations are too long, the standards are too low, and too much emphasis is placed on games. Parenthetically, it may be observed that athletics are *not* mediocre—at least not in the United States.

Nor is this deadening effect confined to educational areas. *Look* magazine, in an article entitled "Our Military Manpower Scandal," quotes the Cordiner Committee as saying that the army has "no adequate incentive system." It adds, "There is no extra pay for doing your job well." One officer, who left the Air Force to enter business, said, "Those people were ahead of me and were going to stay ahead of me. This kills aggressiveness in a young officer." It has been suggested as a basic reform that the armed forces should break with the traditional promotion system, so that the best men could advance more rapidly.

Perhaps recognition of the philosophy underlying such practices has already damaged the competitive spirit of young Americans. College graduates entering business are reported to be more interested in security than in competition. The inclination to "take a chance" or indulge in a "calculated risk" is said to be not so prevalent as it was in our pioneer days. Recently I spent an afternoon with the chairman of one of the most enterprising manufacturing companies in America. He was lamenting that on his team, as he called it, he could discover few with the originality and resourcefulness required for dynamic leadership. We have, he said, dozens of fine-looking, well-groomed fellows for routine assignments. What he wanted was a few restless men with imagination, ready to break loose from conventional procedure and move into untried fields. Desire for security and mediocrity belong together.

Even in politics specialized knowledge is far from obligatory. Where I live, aspirants for office stress the fact that they are good family men, with a covey of children, as if demonstrated fecundity made them better law-makers. In certain instances candidates are actually hampered by an acquaintance with history or economics. And if the results of elections seem to offer an advantage to mediocrity, whose fault is it? A considerable proportion of voters is prepared to accept garrulity, back-slapping, vague enthusiasm, and expressed good intentions as substitutes for talent.

As a practical asset, demonstrated skill is unimportant when community appointments are concerned. Recently in Cambridge, Massachusetts, the issue of veterans' preference for public school teachers was vigorously debated. The heads of local veterans' organizations argued that any former serviceman, no matter what grades he had received on his qualification tests, should be given an appointment ahead of non-servicemen who had passed with higher marks. The commander of the local American Legion post was quoted as asking, "What difference do a few points on an examination make anyhow?" The assumption was that virtually anybody could teach school. Perhaps this feeling is responsible for some of our present difficulties in education.

Much the same criticism may be made of the policy of giving "home town" applicants preference for salaried jobs, no matter what their ability. In this case, as in many others, some attribute other than professional excellence is used for the decision.

The American distrust of cleverness or quickness of mind, or indeed of conspicuous intellectual ability, has been noted by foreign observers. A young Korean, a graduate student at Harvard, wrote recently in the *Christian Science Monitor* some candid comments on the United States, in which he said:

> The American people want their President to be one of them. They would like to elect to the Presidency a man like themselves. They do not want the President to be the "great leader," "hero," or "superman," whose vision, outlook, and philosophy are remote from theirs. Instead they want their President's tastes, outlook, and philosophy to be similar to theirs.

It is significant that the number of first-rate statesmen in the United States of the post-Revolutionary period, when the country had a population of not much over three million, was greater than it is today when we have 180,000,000. One of the reasons, perhaps, is that our generation has reversed the pattern and established a cult, not of genius but of mediocrity, by its approval of conformity and orthodoxy and the kindred colorless virtues which keep a social organism static. Various observers deplore the growing tendency to distrust those who are different, those who deviate in their thinking or writing or behavior from what we have been taught to consider normal. Uniformity of ideas seems to be regarded as a protection against the dangers of so-called radical thought. Although we concede that, in theory, heterogeneity is essential to progress, we give it little encouragement in our own vicinity.

Let me call new witnesses. Arthur E. Fetridge, predicting the course television will take during the coming year, says, "I may be wrong, but certainly all the signs point to mediocrity and more mediocrity. The more commonplace a presentation the more people watch it. . . . The masses say they want mediocrity, and until the sponsor says he won't give it to them any more but instead forces them to accept something far better, mediocrity is what we are going to get."

In his latest book, "The American Conscience," Roger Burlingame has summed all this up in one succinct paragraph:

> We are prosperous. We are complacent. Religion has become, for the most part, a social convention. . . . Skill is anonymous, thought is under pressure to conform, security has replaced venture as a dominant aim, intellect is in the discard, and politics are dictated by . . . mediocrity.

Fortunately, despite Mr. Burlingame's well-justified pessimism, some signs of a revolt are evident, especially in education. Thomas Jefferson, whose democracy cannot well be questioned, deliberately advocated an educational policy in Virginia which would gradually eliminate the unfit and open the way to brilliant students. Public inertia kept his program from being put into operation, but today even hard-boiled, thrifty taxpayers are advocating the early identification of talented boys and girls, and their proper training on their way through school, college, and university. We have at last become fearful that the Soviets are producing more competent experts, particularly in the fields of science and modern languages, and fear may do for us what prosperity has been unable to accomplish. To meet this sudden challenge from a "barbaric" country we have already in some degree begun to sort out the young, using native aptitude as one of the criteria, and we are offering these gifted boys and girls the opportunity of going as far and as fast as they can. Everybody should have a fair chance, and the ablest should win.

Against this program for developing excellence are allied several evil forces: the sinister operations of politicians who thrive on public ignorance; the corrupting power of the press through its appeals to mass psychology; the decline of the pioneer spirit; the general relaxation of people seeking a fast and often a criminal buck; and the enervating influence of widespread luxury. These are no new phenomena in a democracy, but they have been spreading farther and reaching deeper in our times than in any American period with which I am familiar. And their combined effect is to promote the commonplace, the average, and the mediocre.

It can be argued that the United States and the Soviet Union, without either intent or realization, have been exchanging national philosophies. In our insistence that all men and women engaged in the same jobs should be compensated in the same amount, regardless of activity or quantity and quality of production, we have been moving toward the fundamental principles of Marxism. The Russians, on the other hand, convinced that exceptional energy and ability are national assets and should therefore be well rewarded, have adopted some of the stimulating practices associated with the capitalistic system. If they find a brilliant scientist, they apparently offer him unusual opportunities and privileges; and they now pay gifted writers, musicians, and even teachers, salaries which make their positions worth competing for. Richard L. Strout has reported that in the Soviet Union a university professor may receive from $35,000 to $50,000 at the current rate of exchange. He adds significantly, "Anybody who sees the sputnik as an isolated phenomenon is shortsighted. It is not a race between sputniks but a race between schools."

One truth is almost self-evident. Widespread mediocrity in key places, in business or education and even in the armed forces, can be deadening, even destructive, to any country. For Americans it is at the moment vital to provide a cultural climate in which exceptionally high intelligence is detected and subsidized accordingly. So much that is good is going on in these United States, and a small number of dedicated people are doing so much on so many levels, that our mass degeneration seems pitiful. Possibly we have been anesthetized by material prosperity and lack the vigor to move into action. Perhaps we should put up a sign "Wanted: A Satirist" and hope for his energizing appearance. But somehow our national leadership in religion, in education, and in statecraft should rise to the occasion and counteract the blight which mediocrity has been casting over our boasted culture.

Herbert Gold

A DOG IN BROOKLYN, A GIRL IN DETROIT: A LIFE AMONG THE HUMANITIES

WHAT better career for a boy who seeks to unravel the meaning of our brief span on earth than that of philosopher? We all wonder darkly, in the forbidden hours of the night, punishing our parents and building a better world, with undefined terms. Soon, however, most of us learn to sleep soundly; or we take to pills or love-making; or we call ourselves insomniacs, not philosophers. A few attempt to define the terms.

There is no code number for the career of philosophy in school, the Army, or out beyond in real life. The man with a peculiar combination of melancholic, nostalgic, and reforming instincts stands at three possibilities early in his youth. He can choose to be a hero, an artist, or a philosopher. In olden times, war, say, or the need to clean out the old west, might make up his mind for him. The old west had been pretty well cleaned up by the time I reached a man's estate, and Gary Cooper could finish the job. Heroism was an untimely option. With much bureaucratic confusion I tried a bit of heroic war, got stuck in the machine, and returned to the hectic, Quonset campus of the G.I. Bill, burning to Know, Understand, and Convert. After a season of ferocious burrowing in books, I was ready to be a Teacher, which seemed a stern neighbour thing to Artist and Philosopher. I took on degrees, a Fulbright fellowship, a wife, a child, a head crammed with foolish questions and dogmatic answers despite the English school of linguistic analysis. I learned to smile, pardner, when I asked questions of philosophers trained at Oxford or Cambridge, but I asked them nonetheless. I signed petitions against McCarthy, wrote a novel, went on a treasure hunt, returned to my roots in the Middle West and stood rooted there, discussed the menace of the mass media, and had another child.

By stages not important here, I found myself teaching the Humanities at Wayne University in Detroit. I am now going to report a succession of classroom events which, retrospectively, seems to have determined my abandonment of formal dealing with this subject. The evidence does not, however, render any conclusion about education in the "Humanities" logically impregnable. It stands for a state of mind and is no substitute for formal argument. However, states of mind are important in this area of experience and meta-experience. However and however: it happens that most of the misty exaltation of the blessed vocation of the teacher issues from the offices of deans, editors, and college presidents. The encounter with classroom reality has caused many teachers, like Abelard meeting the relatives of Eloïse, to lose their bearings. Nevertheless this is a memoir, not a campaign, about a specific life in and out of the Humanities. Though I am not a great loss to the History of Everything in Culture, my own eagerness to teach is a loss to me.

News item of a few years ago. A young girl and her date are walking along a street in Brooklyn, New York. The girl notices that they are being followed by an enormous Great Dane. The dog is behaving peculiarly, showing its teeth and making restless movements. A moment later, sure enough, the dog, apparently maddened, leaps slavering upon the girl, who is borne to earth beneath its weight. With only an instant's hesitation, the boy jumps on the dog. Its fangs sunk in one, then in the other, the dog causes the three of them to roll like beasts across the sidewalk.

A crowd gathers at a safe distance to watch. No one interferes. They display the becalmed curiosity of teevee viewers.

A few moments later a truckdriver, attracted by the crowd, pulls his vehicle over to the kerb. This brave man is the only human being stirred personally enough to leave the role of passive spectator. Instantaneously analysing the situation, he leaps into the struggle—*attacking and beating the boy.* He has naturally assumed that the dog must be protecting an innocent young lady from the unseemly actions of a juvenile delinquent.

I recounted this anecdote in the classroom in order to introduce a course which attempted a summary experience of Humanities 610 for a monumental nine credits. There were a number of points to be made about the passivity of the crowd ("don't get involved," "not my business") and the stereotypical reaction of the truck driver who had been raised to think of man's best friend as not another human being but a dog. In both cases, addicted to entertainment and clichés, the crowd and the trucker could not recognise what was actually happening before their eyes; they responded irrelevantly to the suffering of strangers; they were not a part of the main. This led us to a discussion of the notion of "community." In a closely-knit society, the people on the street would have known the couple involved and felt a responsibility towards them. In a large city, everyone is a stranger. (Great art can give a sense of the brotherhood of men. Religion used to do this, too.) "Any questions?" I asked, expecting the authority of religion to be defended.

An eager hand shot up. Another. Another. Meditative bodies sprawled in their chairs. "Are all New Yorkers like that?" "Well, what can you do if there's a mad dog and you're not expecting it?" "Where does it say in what great book how you got to act in Brooklyn?"

I took note of humour in order to project humorousness. I found myself composing my face in the look of thought which teevee panellists use in order to project thinking. I discovered a serious point to elaborate—several. I mentioned consciousness and relevance and the undefined moral suggestion implied by the labour which produces any work of art or mind. A girl named Clotilda Adams asked me: "Why don't people try to get along better in this world?"

Somewhat digressively, we then discussed the nature of heroism, comparing the behaviour of the boy and the truck driver. Both took extraordinary risks; why? We broke for cigarettes in the autumn air outside. Then, for fifty minutes more, we raised these interesting questions, referring forward to Plato, Aristotle, St. Thomas, Dostoevsky, Tolstoy, William James, and De Gaulle; and then boy, dog, girl, truck driver and crowd were left with me and the crowned ghosts of history in the deserted room while my students went on to Phys Ed, Music Appreciation, Sosh, and their other concerns. Having been the chief speaker, both dramatist and analyst, I was exalted by the lofty ideas floated up into the air around me. I was a little let down to return to our real life in which dog-eat-dog is man's closest pal. Fact. Neither glory nor pleasure nor power, and certainly not wisdom, provided the goal of my students. Not even wealth was the aim of most of them. They sought to make out, to do all right, more prideful than amorous in love, more security-hungry than covetous in status. I saw my duty as a teacher: Through the Humanities, to awaken them to the dream of mastery over the facts of our lives. I saw my duty plain: Through the Humanities, to lead them toward the exaltation of knowledge and the calm of control. I had a whole year in which to fulfil this obligation. It was a two-semester course.

Before she left the room, Clotilda Adams said, "You didn't answer my question." Fact.

Outside the university enclave of glass and grass, brick and trees, Detroit was agonising in its last big year with the big cars. Automation, dispersion of factories, and imported automobiles were eroding a precarious confidence. Fear was spreading; soon the landlords would offer to decorate apartments and suffer the pain. Detroit remembered the war years with nostalgia. Brave days, endless hours, a three-shift clock, insufficient housing, men sleeping in the all-night, triple-feature movies on Woodward and Grand River. Though the area around the Greyhound and Trailways stations was still clotted with the hopeful out of the hill country of the mid-south and the driven from the deep south—they strolled diagonally across the boulevards, entire families holding hands—some people suspected what was already on its way down the road: twenty per cent unemployment in Detroit.

The semester continued. We churned through the great books. One could classify my students in three general groups, intelligent, mediocre, and stupid, allowing for the confusions of three general factors—background, capacity, and interest. This was how we classified the Humanities, too: ancient, medieval, and modern. It made a lot of sense, and it made me itch, scratch, and tickle. Series of three form nice distinctions. According to Jung and other authorities, they have certain mythic significances. The course was for nine credits. All the arts were touched upon. We obeyed Protagoras; man, just man, was our study. When I cited him—"the proper study of man is Man"—Clotilda Adams stirred uneasily in her seat. "By which Protagoras no doubt meant woman, too," I assured her. She rested.

Now imagine the winter coming and enduring, with explosions of storm and exfoliations of gray slush, an engorged industrial sky overhead and sinus trouble all around. The air was full of acid and a purplish, spleeny winter mist. Most of Detroit, in Indian times before the first French trappers arrived, had been a swamp and below sea level. The swamp was still present, but invisible; city stretched out in all directions, crawling along the highways. Though Detroit was choked by a dense undergrowth of streets and buildings, irrigated only by super-highways, its work was done with frantic speed. The Rouge plant roared, deafened. The assembly lines clanked to the limit allowed by the UAW. The old Hudson factory lay empty, denuded, waiting to become a parking lot. Then the new models were being introduced! Buick! Pontiac! Dodge! Ford and Chevrolet! Ford impudently purchased a huge billboard faced towards the General Motors Building on Grand Boulevard. General Motors retaliated by offering free ginger ale to all comers, and a whole bottle of Vernor's to take home if you would only consent to test-drive the new Oldsmobile, the car with the . . . I've forgotten what it had that year. All over town the automobile companies were holding revival meetings; hieratic salesmen preached to the converted and the hangers-back alike; lines at the loan companies stretched through the revolving doors and out on to the winter pavements. But many in those lines were trying to get additional financing on their last year's cars. The new models were an indifferent success despite all the uproar of display and Detroit's patriotic attention to it. Searchlights sliced up the heavens while the city lay under flu.

Teachers at Wayne University soon learn not to tease the American Automobile. *Lése*[1] Chrysler was a moral offence, an attack on the livelihood and the sanctity of the American garage. Detroit was a town in which men looked at hub caps as men elsewhere have sometimes looked at ankles. The small foreign car found itself treated with a violent Halloween kidding-on-the-square, scratched, battered, and smeared (another Jungian series of three!). A passionate and sullen town, Detroit had no doubts about its proper business. All it doubted was everything else.

I often failed at inspiring my students to do the assigned reading. Many of them had part time jobs in the automobile industry or its

1 [Crime against . . .]

annexes. Even a Philosopher found it difficult to top the argument, "I couldn't read the book this week, I have to *work*," with its implied reproach for a scholar's leisure. But alas, many of these stricken proletarians drove freshly-minted automobiles. They worked in order to keep up the payments, racing like laboratory mice around the cage of depreciation. Certain faculty deep thinkers, addicted to broad understanding of the problems of others, argued that these students were so poor they *had* to buy new cars in order to restore their confidence. The finance companies seemed to hear their most creative expressions, not me. Deep in that long Detroit winter, I had the task of going from the pre-Socratic mystics all the way to Sartre, for nine credits. Like an audio-visual monkey, I leapt from movie projector to records to slides, with concurrent deep labour in book and tablet. We read *The Brothers Karamazov*, but knowing the movie did not give credit. We studied *The Waste Land*, and reading the footnotes did not suffice. We listened to Wanda Landowska play the harpsichord on records. We sat in the dark before a slide of Seurat's "La Grande Jatte" while I explained the importance of the measles of *pointillisme* to students who only wanted to see life clear and true, see it comfortably. Clotilda Adams said that this kind of painting hurt her eyes. She said that there was too much reading for one course—"piling it on. This isn't the only course we take." She said that she liked music, though. Moses only had to bring the Law down the mountain to the children of Israel; I had to bring it pleasingly.

We made exegeses. I flatly turned down the request of a dean that I take attendance. As a statesmanlike compromise, I tested regularly for content and understanding.

Then, on a certain morning, I handed back some quiz papers at the beginning of class. Out on the street, a main thoroughfare through town, it was snowing; this was one of those magical days of late winter snowfall—pale, cold, clean, and the entire city momentarily muffled by the silence of snow. The room hissed with steam heat; a smell of galoshes and mackinaws arose from the class. "Let us not discuss the test—let us rise above grades. Let us try to consider nihilism as a byproduct of the Romantic revival——" I had just begun my lecture when an odd clashing, lumping noise occurred on Cass Avenue. "Eliot's later work, including *The Four Quartets*, which we will not discuss here. . ."

But I was interrupted by a deep sigh from the class. A product of nihilism and the romantic revival? No. It was that strange tragic sigh of horror and satisfaction. Out in the street, beyond the window against which I stood, a skidding truck had sideswiped a taxi. The truckdriver had parked and gone into a drugstore. The cab was smashed like a cruller. From the door, the driver had emerged, stumbling drunkenly on the icy road, holding his head. There was blood on his head. There was blood on his hands. He clutched his temples. The lines of two-way traffic, moving very slowly in the snow and ice, carefully avoided hitting him. There were streaks of perforated and patterned snow, frothed up by tyres. He was like an island around which the sea of traffic undulated in slow waves; but he was an island that moved in the sea and held hands to head. He slid and stumbled back and forth, around and about his cab in the middle of the wide street. He was in confusion, in shock. Even at this distance I could see blood on the new-fallen snow. Drivers turned their heads upon him like angry Halloween masks, but did not get involved. Snow spit at his feet.

No one in the class moved. The large window through which we gazed was like a screen, with the volume turned down by habit, by snow, by a faulty tube. As the teacher, my authority took precedence. I ran out to lead the cab driver into the building. An elderly couple sat huddled in the car, staring at the smashed door, afraid to come out the other. They said they were unhurt.

I laid the man down on the floor. He was bleeding from the head and his face was a peculiar purplish colour, with a stubble of beard like that of a dead man. There was a neat prick in his forehead where the union button in his cap had been driven into the skin. I sent a student to call for an ambulance. The cab driver's colour was like that of the bruised industrial sky. "You be okay till the ambulance——?"

Foolish question. No alternative. No answer.

We waited. The class was restless. When they weren't listening to me, or talking to themselves, or smudging blue books in an exam, they did not know what to do in this room devoted to the specialised absorption of ideas. Silence. Scraping of feet, crisping of paper. We watched the slow-motion traffic on the street outside.

The cab driver moved once in a rush, turning over face down against the floor, with such force that I thought he might break his nose. Then slowly, painfully, as if in a dream, he turned back and lay staring at the ceiling. His woollen lumberjack soaked up the blood trickling from one ear; the blood travelled up separated cilia of wool which drew it in with a will of their own. There was a swaying, osmotic movement like love-making in the eager little wisps of wool. An astounded ring of Humanities 610 students watched, some still holding their returned quiz papers. One girl in particular, Clotilda Adams, watched him and me with her eyes brilliant, wet, and bulging, and her fist crumpling the paper. I tried by imagining it to force the ambulance through the chilled and snowfallen city. I saw it weaving around the injured who strutted with shock over ice and drift, its single red Cyclop's eye turning, the orderlies hunched over on benches, chewing gum and cursing the driver. The ambulance did not arrive. Clotilda Adams' eye had a thick, impenetrable sheen over it. She watched from the cab driver to me as if we were in some way linked. When would the authorities get there? When the medics? There must have been many accidents in town, and heart attacks, and fires with cases of smoke inhalation.

Before the ambulance arrived, the police were there. They came strolling into the classroom with their legs apart, as if they remembered ancestors who rode the plains. Their mouths were heavy in thought. They had noses like salamis, red and mottled with fat. They were angry at the weather, at the school, at the crowd, at me, and especially at the prostrate man at our feet. He gave them a means to the creative expression of pique. (Everyone needs an outlet.)

Now Clotilda Adams took a step backward, and I recall thinking this odd. She had been treading hard near the pool of blood about the cab-driver, but when the cops strolled up, she drifted toward the outer edge of the group of students, with a sly look of caution in her downcast, sideways-cast eyes. Her hand still crisped at the returned exam paper. This sly, lid-fallen look did not do her justice. She was a hard little girl of the sort often thought to be passionate—skinny but well-breasted, a high hard rump with a narrow curve, a nervous mouth.

The two policemen stood over the body of the cab driver. They stared at him in the classic pose—one cop with a hand resting lightly on the butt of his gun and the other on his butt, the younger cop with lips so pouted that his breath made a snuffling sound in his nose. They both had head colds. Their Ford was pulled up on the snow-covered lawn outside, with raw muddled marks of tread in the soft dirt. When the snow melted, there would be wounded streaks in the grass. The cab driver closed his eyes under the finicking, distasteful examination. At last one spoke: "See your driver's licence."

The cab driver made a clumsy gesture towards his pocket. The cop bent and went into the pocket. He flipped open the wallet, glanced briefly at the photographs and cash, glanced at me, and then began lip-reading the licence.

The cab-driver was in a state of shock. There was a mixture of thin and thick blood on his clothes and messing the floor. "This man is badly hurt," I said. "Can't we get him to the hospital first?"

"This is only your *driver* licence," the cop said slowly, having carefully read through Colour of Hair: *Brn,* Colour of Eyes: *Brn,* and checked each item with a stare at the man on the floor. "Let me see your chauffeur licence."

"He's badly hurt," I said. "Get an ambulance."

"Teach'," said the older cop, "you know your business? We know ours."

"It's on the way," said the other. "Didn't you call it yourself?"

"No, one of the students. . . ." I said.

He grinned with his great victory. "So—don't you trust your pupils neither?"

Shame. I felt shame at this ridicule of my authority in the classroom. A professor is not a judge, a priest, or a sea captain; he does not have the right to perform marriages on the high seas of audio-visual aids and close reasoning. But he is more than an intercom between student and fact; he can be a stranger to love for his students, but not to a passion for his subject; he is a student himself; his pride is lively. The role partakes of a certain heft and control. There is power to make decisions, power to abstain, power to bewilder, promote, hold back, adjust, and give mercy; power, an investment of pride, a risk of shame.

Clotilda Adams, still clutching her exam, stared at me with loathing. She watched me bested by the police. She barely glanced, and only contemptuously, at the man bleeding from the head on the floor. She moved slightly forward again in order to participate fully in an action which apparently had some important meaning for her. She had lost her fear of the police when she saw how we all stood with them. The limits were established.

The police were going through the cab-driver's pockets. They took out a folding pocket-knife and cast significant looks at it and at each other. It had a marbled plastic hilt, like a resort souvenir. It was attached to a key ring.

"Hey!" one said to the half-conscious man. "What's this knife for?"

"Where'd you get them keys?" the other demanded, prodding the cabbie with his toe.

"A *skeleton* key. These cab companies," one of the cops decided to explain to Clotilda Adams, who was standing nearby, "they get the dregs. Hillbillies, you know?"

I said nothing, found nothing to say. I now think of Lord Acton's famous law, which is accepted as true the way it was uttered. The opposite is also true—the commoner's way: Having no power corrupts; having absolutely no power corrupts absolutely.

The bleeding seemed to have stopped. The cab-driver sat up, looking no better, with his bluish, greenish, drained head hanging between his knees. His legs were crumpled stiffly. He propped himself on his hands. The police shot questions at him. He mumbled, mumbled, explained, explained.

"How long you been in Detroit? How come you come out of the mountains?"

"Why you pick up this fare?"

"What makes you think Cass is a one-way street?"

Mumbling and mumbling, explaining and explaining, the cab driver tried to satisfy them. He also said: "Hurt. Maybe you get me to the hospital, huh? Hurt real bad."

"Maybe," said one of the cops, "maybe we take you to the station house first. That boy you hit says reckless driving. I think personally you'd flunk the drunk test—what you think, Teach'?"

I sent one of the students to call for an ambulance again. In the infinitesimal pause between my suggestion and his action, an attentive reluctant expectant caesura, I put a dime in his hand for the call. One of the cops gave me that long look described by silent movie critics as the slow burn. "They drive careful," he finally said. "It's snowing. They got all that expensive equipment."

The snow had started again outside the window. The skid-marks on the lawn were covered. Though the sky was low and gray, the white sifting down gave a peaceful village glow to this industrial Detroit. Little gusts barely rattled the windows. With the class, the cops, and the driver, we were living deep within a snowy paperweight. I felt myself moving very slowly, swimming within thick glass, like the loosened plastic figure in a paperweight. The snow came down in large torn flakes, all over the buildings of Wayne University, grass, trees, and the pale radiance of a network of slow-motion super-highways beyond. Across the street a modern building —glass and aluminium strips—lay unfinished in this weather. Six months ago there had been a student boarding house on that spot, filled with the artists and the beat, the guitar-wielders and the modern dancers, with a tradition going all the way back to the Korean war. Now there were wheelbarrows full of frozen cement; there were intentions to build a Japanese garden, with Japanese proportions and imported goldfish.

My student returned from the telephone. He had reached a hospital.

The cab driver was fading away. Rootlets of shock hooded his eyes: the lid was closing shut. A cop asked him another question—what the button on his cap stood for—it was a union button—and then the man just went reclining on his elbow, he slipped slowly down, he lay in the little swamp of crusted blood on the floor. You know what happens when milk is boiled? The crust broke like the crust of boiled milk when a spoon goes into coffee. The cop stood with a delicate, disgusted grimace on his face. What a business to be in, he seemed to be thinking. In approximately ten years, at age forty-two, he could retire and sit comfortable in an undershirt, with a non-returnable can of beer, before the colour teevee. He could relax, He could *start* to relax. But in the meantime—nag, nag, nag. Drunk cabbies, goddam hillbillies. The reckless driver on the floor seemed to sleep. His lips moved. He was alive.

Then a puffing intern rushed into the room. I had not heard the ambulance. The policeman gave room and the intern kneeled. He undid his bag. The orderlies glanced at the floor and went back out for their stretcher.

I stood on one side of the body, the kneeling intern with his necklace of stethoscope, and the two meditative cops. On the other side was the group of students, and at their head, like a leader filled with wrath, risen in time of crisis, stood Clotilda Adams, still clutching her exam paper. There were tears in her eyes. She was in a fury. She had been thinking all this time, and now her thinking had issue: *rage*. Over the body she handed me a paper, crying out, "I don't think I deserved a *D* on that quiz. I answered all the questions. I can't get my credit for Philo of Ed without I get a *B* off you."

I must have looked at her with pure stupidity on my face. There is a Haitian proverb: Stupidity won't kill you, but it'll make you sweat a lot. She took the opportunity to make me sweat, took my silence for guilt, took my open-mouthed gaze for weakness. She said: "If I was a white girl, you'd grade me easier."

Guilt, a hundred years, a thousand years of it; pity for the disaster of ignorance and fear, pity for ambition rising out of ignorance; adoration of desire; trancelike response to passion—passion which justifies itself because passionate. . . . I looked at her with mixed feelings. I could not simply put her down. In order to *put down,* your own mind must be made up, put down. She had beauty and dignity, stretched tall and wrathful, with teeth for biting and eyes for striking dead.

"But I know my rights," she said, "*mister*. My mother told me about your kind—lent my father money on his car and then hounded him out of town. He's been gone since fifty-three. But you can't keep us down forever, no sir, you can't always keep us down—"

She was talking and I was yelling. She was talking and yelling about injustice and I, under clamps, under ice, was yelling in a whisper about the sick man. She was blaming me for all her troubles, all the troubles she had seen, and I was blaming her for not seeing what lay before her, and we were making an appointment to meet in my office and discuss this thing more calmly, Miss Adams. Okay. All right. Later.

The police, the doctor, the orderlies, and the injured cab driver were gone. The police car out front was gone and the snow was covering its traces. The janitor came in and swept up the bloodstains with green disinfectant powder. The frightened couple in the cab were released. They all disappeared silently into the great city, into the routine of disaster and recovery of a great city. I dismissed the class until tomorrow.

The next day I tried to explain to Miss Adams what I meant about her failing to respond adequately to the facts of our life together. Her mouth quivered. Yesterday rage; today a threat of tears. What did I mean she wasn't *adequate?* What did I know about adequate anyhow? Nothing. Just a word. Agreed, Miss Adams. I was trying to say that there were two questions at issue between us—her exam grade and her choice of occasion to dispute it. I would like to discuss each matter separately. I tried to explain why putting the two events together had disturbed me. I tried to explain the notions of empirical evidence and metaphor. Finally I urged her to have her exam looked at by the head of the department, but she refused because she knew in advance that he would support me. "White is Right," she said.

"Do you want to drop out of the class?"

"No. I'll stay," she said with a sudden patient, weary acceptance of her fate. "I'll do what I can."

"I'll do what I can too," I said.

She smiled hopefully at me. She was tuckered out by the continual alert for combat everywhere. She was willing to forgive and go easy. When she left my office, this smile, shy, pretty, and conventional, tried to tell me that she could be generous—a friend.

We had come to Thomas Hobbes and John Locke in our tour through time and the river of humanities. I pointed out that the English philosophers were noted for clarity and eloquence of style. I answered this question: The French? Isn't French noted for clarity? Yes, they too, but they were more abstract. On the whole. In general.

The class took notes on the truths we unfolded together. Spring came and the snow melted. There was that brief Detroit flowering of the new season—jasmine and hollyhocks—which, something like it, must have captivated the Frenchman Antoine de la Mothe Cadillac when he paused on the straits of Detroit in 1701. University gardeners planted grass seed where the patrol car had parked on the lawn. The new models, all except the Cadillac, were going at mean discounts.

"The 'Humanities,' " wrote Clotilda Adams in her final essay, "are a necessary additive to any teacher's development worth her 'salt' in the perilous times of today. The West and the 'Free World' must stand up to the war of ideas against the 'Iron' Curtain." This was in answer to a question about Beethoven, Goethe, and German romanticism. She did not pass the course, but she was nevertheless admitted on probation to the student teacher programme because of the teacher shortage and the great need to educate our children in these perilous times. Of today.

Humanities 610 provided ballast for the ship of culture as it pitched and reeled in the heavy seas of real life; I lashed myself to the mast, but after hearing the siren song of grand course outlines, I cut myself free and leaned over the rail with the inside of my lip showing.

It would be oversimplifying to say that I left off teaching Humanities merely because of an experience. Such an argument is fit to be published under the title "I was a Teen-Age Humanities Professor." I also left for fitter jobs, more money, a different life. Still, what I remember of the formal study of Truth and Beauty, for advanced credit in education, is a great confusion of generalities, committees, conferences, audio-visual importunities, and poor contact. "Contact!" cried the desperate deans and chairmen, like radio operators in ancient war movies. And much, much discussion of how to get through to the students. How to get through? Miss Adams and Mr. Gold, cab driver and Thomas Hobbes, policemen and the faceless student who paused an instant for a dime for the telephone—we all have to discover how relevant we are to each other. Or do we *have* to? No, we can merely perish, shot down like mad dogs or diminished into time with no more than a glimpse of the light.

Words fade; our experience does not touch; we make do with babble and time-serving. We need to learn the meaning of words, the meaning of the reality those words refer to; we must clasp reality close. We cannot flirt forever, brown-nosing or brow-beating. We must act and build out of our own spirits. How? How? We continually need new politics, new cities, new marriages and families, new ways of work and leisure. We also need the fine old ways. For me, the primitive appeal to pleasure and pain of writing stories is a possible action, is the way in and out again, as teaching was not. As a teacher, I caught my students too late and only at the top of their heads, at the raw point of pride and ambition, and I had not enough love and pressure as a teacher to open the way through their intentions to the common humanity which remains locked within. As a writer, I could hope to hit them in their bodies and needs, where lusts and ideals are murkily nurtured together, calling to the prime fears and joys directly, rising with them from the truths of innocence into the truths of experience.

The peculiar combination of ignorance and jadedness built into most institutions is a desperate parody of personal innocence, personal experience. Nevertheless, education, which means a drawing out—even formal education, a formal drawing out—is a variety of experience, and experience is the only evidence we have. After evidence comes our thinking upon it. Do the scientists, secreting their honey in distant hives, hear the barking of the black dog which follows them? Will the politicians accept the lead of life, or will they insist on a grade of *B* in Power and Dominion over a doomed race? We need to give proper answers to the proper questions.

Particular life is still the best map to truth. When we search our hearts and strip our pretences, we all know this. Particular life—we know only what we *know*. Therefore the policemen stay with me: I have learned to despise most authority. The cab driver remains in his sick bleeding: pity for the fallen and helpless. And I think of Clotilda Adams in her power and weakness; like the cops, she has an authority of stupidity; like the victim of an accident, she is fallen and helpless. But some place, since we persist in our cold joke against the ideal of democracy, the cops still have the right to push people around, Clotilda is leading children in the Pledge of Allegiance. We must find a way to teach better and to learn.

Sir Richard Livingstone

THE ESSENTIALS OF EDUCATION

A TRAVELER who studies the menu on a transatlantic liner or, indeed, in some American hotels has a paralyzing sensation. There is so much to eat—far more than he can possibly digest. One sometimes has the same feeling about education, which also offers an enormous bill of fare. Almost any dish can be found in it, from Greek to stenography, from music to economics. How are we to choose from this bewildering profusion? What dishes ought we to order if we wish not merely to fill ourselves up, but to get the

THE ESSENTIALS OF EDUCATION: From *The Atlantic Monthly*, January 1952. Reprinted by permission of the author's executors.

nourishment necessary to a healthy life, to become really educated people?

That question cannot be answered without asking and answering another—what is education for? If that problem were suddenly put to pupils in school, or to students in college, or even to their parents, I doubt if all of them could, on the spur of the moment, give a clear and convincing reply. Most of us are educated because our parents wish it, or because attendance at school is a habit of our society, or because it is compulsory, or because it is apparently necessary to success in the world. But these, though at the moment they may be conclusive reasons for desiring education or at any rate submitting to it, will not by themselves secure our getting from it what it has to give; and if we go to school or college with no more definite reasons at the back of our minds, we are likely to rise from our meal there replete perhaps but ill-nourished. Let me, therefore, start by asking what we should seek in education. In answering this question, I shall ignore important but lesser objects of it, in order to concentrate on the most important of all.

Get hold of the catalogues of the colleges in the United States. You will find courses in innumerable subjects. Is there any common feature in these courses? Is there any aim which all of them have? I think that there is a common feature and that every course given has a similar aim. They all aim at the first-rate; the purpose of every course is to help the student to learn what is first-rate in the particular subject which he studies. If it is a course in English, the aim is that he should know what is good English; if it is a course in agriculture, that he should know the best methods in farming; if it is a course in cookery or in dressmaking it is to show the pupil how to cook or to make dresses really well. The same is true of a course in any other subject—its aim is to show what is first-rate in that subject. This is the common thread that runs through all education. Whether we are teachers or students we ought to get firmly in our minds the idea that whatever else may come by the way, education will be incomplete and unsatisfactory if it fails to give a clear view of what is first-rate in the subject studied. Otherwise we may have got some knowledge, but we shall not have got education.

Here then is a first answer to the question, what is the aim of education? Its aim is to know the first-rate in any subject that we study, with a view to achieving it as nearly as our powers allow. If we could fix this firmly in our minds, we should not stumble through a variety of lessons, lectures, and books like a drunk man, only partially aware where we are or what we are doing. We should cease to think that we go to school or college to pass examinations or to secure degrees or diplomas or to satisfy our teachers, though these may be and are incidental and limited objectives. We should have brought order into our education by realizing its true aim and we should have deepened in our minds through practice the sense that a worthy purpose in life is the desire for excellence, the pursuit of the first-rate.

So far, so good. But a very important question remains unanswered. We should desire excellence, pursue the first-rate. But in what fields? The difficulty with education, as with life, is that it has so many fields. One would like to know the first-rate in all of them, but that is impossible for the limited mind and energy of man. Which, then, are the most important fields—or, narrowing the problem further, which are those in which every human being ought to know the first-rate? These should enter into the education of all.

The most obvious field is our job in life, our vocation in the usual sense of the word. Clearly, whatever it is, we ought to know the first-rate, the best methods to employ. In this field of vocational education, the modern world does well: we have a conscience about it or, at any rate, a sense of its importance; our provision of vocational education is good, and in engineering or medicine, commerce or technology, nursing or hotelkeeping, or any other of these activities which make up material civilization, we believe in quality, in the first-rate; we have a clear idea of what it means and we often achieve it. I shall, therefore, say nothing more about vocational studies. It is perhaps the only branch of education in which we are entirely successful, and there is no risk of its being ignored.

An educated man should know what is first-rate in those activities which spring from the creative and intellectual faculties of human nature, such as literature, art, architecture, and music. I should like to add science and philosophy, but in these two subjects it is difficult for any but the expert to estimate quality, and many educated people have not the close knowledge necessary to judge work in them. On the other hand everyone has close and daily contact with the other four. Architecture surrounds him in every city, literature meets him on every bookstall, music assails his ears on his radio set and from every juke box; and art in its protean aspects of form and color is a part of daily life. The architecture may often be bad, the literature and music often puerile, the art often undeserving of the name; but that is all the more reason why we should be able, in all of them, to distinguish good from bad.

To judge by the literature offered us in hotel bookstands and by most of the music played on the radio and by juke boxes, we might be more discriminating in these fields than we are. If it be said that music and art and literature are not essentials of life but its frills, I would reply that, if so, it is curious that they are among the few immortal things in the world, and that, should a man wish to be remembered two thousand years hence, the only certain way is to write a great poem or book, compose a great symphony, paint a great picture, carve a great sculpture, or build a great building. If you have any doubts about this, consider why long-dead people like Plato and Shakespeare, Michelangelo and Raphael, Ictinus and Bramante, are remembered today.

I have argued that no one has a right to feel himself educated if he does not know what is first-rate in his daily occupation and (so far as this is possible) in those fields where the creative and intellectual powers of man are revealed. But there is another job much more difficult than teaching or nursing or business or medicine, in which we are all concerned—the job of living; and there surely, as much as in any other pursuit, we need to know what is first-rate. Is not our education very incomplete if we do not know what is excellent in human nature and in life; if in that field we are taken in by second-rate, shoddy stuff? Here our age is far less successful than in medicine, or engineering, or the sciences.

We need clearer standards; or, to put it more simply, we need to have a clearer idea about the distinction between first-rate and second-rate, between good and bad, in conduct and in life. Ignorance on this vital subject is written all over modern civilization. Our age contains a great deal of good—as much perhaps as any age. But I doubt if there has ever been an age in which good and bad were so mixed together and the public as a whole so lacking in standards by which to distinguish them. The tares grow with the wheat and the difference between wheat and tares escapes notice. If anyone thinks that I am exaggerating, let him look at our films and, even more, at our advertisements, our radio, and at many of our newspapers. Those responsible for some of these do far more harm than any murderer: for the films, the radio, the press are among the chief influences which form the public view, impressing on it the view of life which they embody.

2

BUT where does one learn what is first-rate? The only way to learn it is to meet it. A medical student will learn something from seeing a great surgeon in the operating theater, or a great doctor in the hospital wards, which all the textbooks in the world cannot tell him. If anyone wishes to know how to teach, let him go and see a great teacher in the classroom; if he wishes to know what good painting or good banking is, let him search out the best examples he can find in them. In any field the only way to learn what is first-rate is to see it. And the same surely is true in life itself. If we wish to know what the good life is we must make the acquaintance and, if possible, keep the company of those who have known its meaning and, better still, of those who have lived it. But who are they? And where shall we meet them?

It is in order that we may meet them, that what we call the humanities come into the curriculum. They are the subjects which deal with man. But there are humanities and humanities; the word is vague, embracing many subjects: theology, philosophy, literature, history, anthropology, psychology, languages, politics, and social studies; even economics and geography. Clearly they differ widely and are only united in virtue of one element common to all of them—they are concerned with man. But it is a formidable list—enough to burst any curriculum and to overwork any brain.

We must choose among them and decide which of all this multitude is the most important for our purposes. All have their value for one purpose or another. If, for instance, we are going to deal with primitive people, we must have some familiarity with anthropology; if we are going into politics or business, we must have some knowledge of economics. All these subjects in one way or another throw a light on man and his goings on. The least human of the humanities at least glances at man. But we are looking, not for the subjects which glance at man or throw side lights on him, but for those which show him full face, and, moreover, show him at his best, so that we can know what he is, at his best. And here such subjects as psychology or economics or anthropology, important as they are in other ways, give no real help. In them we see only a fragment of ourselves, a part of human nature and not the best or the most characteristic part. If we wish to see man full face, it is to religion, literature, and history that we must turn.

Of religion I will not speak; admittedly in its highest forms it contains the purest and finest archetypes of human excellences, though it can be "taught" (as it was to me at school) with almost no reference to these aspects of it. Its surprising neglect in much of education shows how little we are concerned to hold up to our pupils the noblest examples of living.

Of the other two, history and literature, the former is perhaps the less illuminating. It is not so personal as literature. Mainly, it is the record of man as a social being, making societies which grow ever more complicated; it is the record of the fortunes of these societies, their successes and failures, the storms which shattered them or which they rode out, the wisdom and folly, the virtues and vices, of the officers and the crews of many ships of the state. But it becomes more personal in its biographical aspects, and there we may find light on human nature and its excellence.

If we are to find it, mere passive reading of a biography is not enough. We must go to it with questions, taking some famous man and asking what he owes to his heredity, to his environment and to the circumstances of his time, and to his education in the narrow sense of the word. (To the last I am afraid it will be found that in most cases the debt is small.) Note what are the decisive moments in his life, what opportunities he seized or missed; his difficulties and how far he overcame or was baffled by them; his successes; his mistakes and failures; what he did and what he failed to do; his contribution to his age and its importance at the time—and afterwards; his qualities and defects; whether he had the long sight to view problems *sub specie aeternitatis,*[1] in the light of all time and all existence, or only the short sight which suffices to deal with the immediate needs of the hour; whether he is significant for all ages or merely for his own. Then, in order that greatness may not be confused with goodness, ask whether or not, in Plato's words, "he arrayed his soul in the jewels proper to its nature, justice and temperance and courage and truth."

If, however, we wish to see man, as I put it, full face, it is to literature that we must turn. There we hear him talking aloud to the world, but really talking to himself, putting on paper the feelings that come to him, so that in literature is recorded every thought, every vision, every fancy, every emotion that has ever passed through the human mind. What a record! Is there any better way of learning what men are, so far as it can be learned from books and not from meeting human beings; and, however good our opportunities of meeting them, a lifetime of human contacts could not give us as wide an experience of human nature as literature can give.

Of course all literature does not give us a portrait of human excellence; it shows us human nature but not necessarily, or always, human nature at its best. And just as in history one must distinguish between greatness and goodness, and not be dazzled by the genius of a Napoleon or a Bismarck, a Hitler or a Lenin, into ignoring the evil which they did and which lives after them, so in literature and art one must avoid a similar mistake and not allow the genius of a writer to blind us to what is unworthy or inadequate in his vision of life. For our purpose, which is to know the best in human nature, we must turn to the writers that show it. Fortunately—and it can hardly be accident—the greatest writers have also the noblest vision.

3

MERELY from an academic point of view, merely as a matter of curiosity, it is natural to wish to know what is first-rate. But also it has

1 [Under the aspect of eternity.]

its practical uses for the conduct of our own lives. I do not say that to know the first-rate is the same thing as to achieve it. Unfortunately it is not. Everyone knows what the Roman poet meant when he said, "*Video meliora proboque; deteriora sequor*—I see what is best and I approve it. I follow what is worse." And Saint Paul says much the same thing when he says, "When I would do good, evil is present with me." Yet the people we live with in literature and history, in the world of thought, do affect our outlook and even our conduct, just as the people with whom we live in our homes or our daily work affect it. Evil communications corrupt good mores, but good communications improve them. There is an element of truth in Disraeli's words: "Nurture your mind with great thoughts; to believe in the heroic makes heroes."

Further, without these studies, we shall never know what the world is really like. Our education tends to be superficial. I am not using the word in a bad sense. I only mean that much of it is concerned with the surface of life and tells us nothing of its depths. The surface is very important; we need the skills and knowledge required to cope with the immediate problems of our day. We need economics and social studies and anthropology and the rest. But important as they are, they do not take us down to the ultimate issues and realities of life; they are superficial.

Literature itself can be superficial and much of it is so. Noel Coward or Hemingway is superficial compared with Shaw. Shaw is superficial as compared with Dante or Shakespeare, who show us greater depths in human nature than we shall find in these lesser men. I am not suggesting that we should not read Shaw or Coward. I only say that unless we are content with a superficial view of life, we should also read writers who have deeper and longer views, who will open our eyes and keep them open to realities to which they are apt to grow dim.

The tenseness and strain of our daily occupations favor short sight. We have to focus our eyes on the business of the moment, and the power of long vision is easily lost. But man needs a long vision in life and should view it through bifocal spectacles. Through one lens he sees the immediate business of the moment; otherwise he will not do that business well. Through the other he sees life and our occupations and himself in the light of what Plato calls all time and all existence.

If anyone asks what these words mean, he has only to visit the Lincoln Memorial at Washington and read the inscriptions on its walls: the Gettysburg speech and—even more—the magnificent close of the Second Inaugural; or, more simply, he can read them in any good library. Let him then ask himself if these words do not take us below the surface of political life down to permanent issues. Politicians in all countries are continually making speeches; few of them are of this kind; it would be better for the world if they were. Lincoln was a man with bifocal vision, a practical statesman, dealing all the time with the day-to-day problems of politics and war. Yet he was a man who at the same time saw them in the light of eternal issues. The feeling which these words of Lincoln give is given in one way or another by all great literature—by the Bible, by Plato and the great Greeks, by Dante, by Shakespeare. They enlarge our vision. Read them, make them your companions through life; otherwise you may live on its surface and forget its depths.

Surely it is a tenable philosophy that when we meet goodness and greatness we are in the presence of something fundamental in the universe—solid ground that remains firm whatever convulsions shake the world. Surely it is in them that one meets the real human being. Another side of man is real too—the dark, petty, sensual side, where his quarrels and jealousies and hates and greeds and passions take their rise. But if I had to find the essential characteristic thing in man I should not find it, like Marx, in the economic animal—or, like Freud and many modern novelists, in a sex-ridden phantom; I should find it in man straining his eyes to catch sight of the vision of a better world, and to incorporate what he can see in the life of himself and his society. Is not that the real human being? And when you consider history, is it not through men and women of this type that the progress most worth making has come about? Are not these the lines on which the world has advanced and will continue to advance towards something better?

We need, said Burke, in his stately language, to auspicate all our proceedings with the old warning of the Church, "*Sursum corda*—Lift up your hearts." But how, from the levels of our ordinary lives, our average minds, can we raise ourselves, if only for a space, to heights beyond our own capacity, even beyond our normal vision? The answer is that we can raise ourselves on the shoulders of those who have walked on higher levels. What unaided we could not do we can do by their help.

Religion is the greatest instrument for so raising us. It is amazing that a person not intellectually bright, perhaps not even educated, is capable of grasping, and living by, something so advanced as the principles of Christianity. Yet that is a common phenomenon. It is not, however, in my province to talk about religion, but rather to stress the power which great literature and the great personalities whom we meet in it and in history have to open and enlarge our minds, and to show us what is first-rate in human personality and human character by showing us goodness and greatness. Any education which neglects that is incomplete and a very inadequate preparation for life.

T. S. Eliot

WHAT IS A CLASSIC?

IN THE whole of European literature there is no poet who can furnish the texts for a more significant variety of discourse than Virgil. The fact that he symbolises so much in the history of Europe, and represents such central European values, is the justification for our founding a society to preserve his memory: the fact that he is so central and so comprehensive is my justification for this address. For if Virgil's poetry were a subject upon which only scholars should presume to speak, you would not have put me in this position, or have cared to listen to what I have to say. I am emboldened by the reflection, that no specialised knowledge or proficiency can confer the exclusive title to talk about Virgil. Speakers of the most diverse capacities, can bring his poetry to bear upon matters within their competence; can hope to contribute, from those studies to which they have given their minds, to the elucidation of his value; can try to offer, for the general use, the benefit of whatever wisdom Virgil may have helped them to acquire, in relation to their own experience of life. Each can give his testimony of Virgil in relation to those subjects which he knows best, or upon which he has most deeply reflected: that is what I meant by variety. In the end, we may all be saying the same thing in different ways: and that is what I meant by significant variety.

The subject which I have taken is simply the question: "What is a classic?" It is not a new question. There is, for instance, a famous essay by Ste. Beuve with this title: whether it is a misfortune or not, that—not having read it for some thirty-odd years—accidents of the present time have prevented me from re-reading it before preparing this address, I hope to find out as soon as libraries are more accessible and books more plentiful. The pertinence of asking this question, with Virgil particularly in mind, is obvious: whatever the definition we arrive at, it cannot be one which excludes Virgil—we may say confidently that it must be one which will expressly reckon with him. But before I go farther, I should like to dispose of certain prejudices and anticipate certain misunderstandings. I do not aim to supersede, or to outlaw, any use of the word "classic" which precedent has made permissible. The word has, and will continue to have, several meanings in several contexts: I am concerned with one meaning in one context. In defining the term in this way, I do not bind myself, for the future, not to use the term in any of the other ways in which it has been used. If, for instance, you find me on some future occasion, in writing, in public speech, or in conversation, using the word "classic" merely to mean a "standard author" in any language—using it merely as an indication of the greatness, or of the permanence and importance of a writer in his own field, as when we speak of *The Fifth Form at St. Dominic's* as a classic of schoolboy fiction, or *Handley Cross* as a classic of the hunting field —you are not to expect an apology. And there is a very interesting book called *A Guide to the Classics,* which tells you how to pick the Derby winner. On other occasions, I permit myself to mean by "the classics," either Latin and Greek literature *in toto,* or the greatest authors of those languages, as the context indicates. And, finally, I think that the account of the classic which I propose to give here should remove it from the area of the antithesis between "classic" and "romantic"—a pair of terms belonging to literary politics, and therefore arousing passions which I should wish, on this occasion, Aeolus to contain in the bag.

This leads me to my next point. According to the terms of the classic-romantic controversy, the rules of that game, to call any work of art "classical," implies either the highest praise or the most contemptuous abuse, according to the party to which one belongs. It implies certain particular merits or faults: either the perfection of form, or the absolute of frigidity. But I want to define one kind of art, and am not concerned that it is absolutely and in every respect *better* or *worse* than another kind. I shall enumerate certain qualities which I should expect the classic to display. But I do not say that, if a literature is to be a great literature, it must have any one author, or any one period, in which all these qualities are manifested. If, as I think, they are all to be found in Virgil, that is not to assert that he is the greatest poet who ever wrote—such an assertion about any poet seems to me meaningless—and it is certainly not to assert that Latin literature is greater than any other literature. We need not consider it as a defect of any literature, if no one author, or no one period, is completely classical; or if, as is true of English literature, the period which most nearly fills the classical definition is not the greatest. I think that those literatures, of which English is one of the most eminent, in which the classical qualities are scattered between various authors and several periods, may well be the richer. Every language has its own resources, and its own limitations. The conditions of a language, and the conditions of the history of the people who speak it, may put out of question the expectation of a classical period, or a classical author. That is not in itself any more a matter for regret than it is for gratulation. It did happen that the history of Rome was such, the character of the Latin language was such, that at a certain moment a uniquely classical poet was possible: though we must remember that it needed that particular poet, and a lifetime of labour on the part of that poet, to make the classic out of his material. And, of course, Virgil couldn't know that *that* was what he was doing. He was, if any poet ever was, acutely aware of what he was trying to do: the one thing he couldn't aim at, or know that he was doing, was to compose a classic: for it is only by hindsight, and in historical perspective, that a classic can be known as such.

If there is one word on which we can fix, which will suggest the maximum of what I mean by the term "a classic," it is the word *maturity*. I shall distinguish between the universal classic, like Virgil, and the classic which is only such in relation to the other literature in its own language, or according to the view of life of a particular period. A classic can only occur when a civilisation is mature; when a language and a literature are mature; and it must be the work of a mature mind. It is the importance of that civilisation and of that language, as well as the comprehensiveness of the mind of the individual poet, which gives the universality. To define *maturity* without assuming that the hearer already knows what it means, is almost impossible: let us say then, that if we are properly mature, as well as educated persons, we can recognise maturity in a civilisation and in a literature, as we do in the other human beings whom we encounter. To make the meaning of maturity really apprehensible—indeed, even to make it acceptable—to the immature, is perhaps impossible. But if we are mature we either recognise maturity immediately, or come to know it on more intimate acquaintance. No reader of Shakespeare, for instance, can fail to recognise, increasingly as he himself grows up, the gradual ripening of Shakespeare's mind: even a less developed reader can perceive the rapid development of Elizabethan literature and drama as a whole, from early Tudor crudity to the plays of Shakespeare, and perceive a decline in the work of Shakespeare's successors. We can also observe, upon a little conversance, that the plays of Christopher Marlowe exhibit a greater maturity of mind and of style, than the plays which Shakespeare wrote at the same age: it is interesting to speculate whether, if Marlowe had lived as long as Shakespeare, his development would have continued at the same pace. I doubt it: for we observe some minds maturing earlier than others, and we observe that those which mature very early do not always develop very far. I raise this point as a reminder, first that the value of maturity depends upon the value of that which matures, and second, that we should know when we are concerned with the maturity of individual writers, and when with the relative maturity of literary periods. A writer who individually has a more mature mind, may belong to a less mature period than another, so that in that respect his work will be less mature. The maturity of a literature is the reflection of that of the society in which it is produced: an individual author—notably Shakespeare and Virgil—can do much to develop his language: but he cannot bring that language to maturity unless the work of his predecessors has prepared it for his final touch. A mature literature, therefore, has a history behind it: a history, that is not merely a chronicle, an accumulation of manuscripts and writings of this kind and that, but an ordered though unconscious progress of a language to realise its own potentialities within its own limitations.

It is to be observed, that a society, and a literature, like an individual human being, do not necessarily mature equally and concurrently in every respect. The precocious child is often, in some obvious ways, childish for his age in comparison with ordinary children. Is there any one period of English literature to which we can point as being fully mature, comprehensively and in equilibrium? I do not think so: and, as I shall repeat later, I hope it is not so. We cannot say that any individual poet in English has in the course of his life become a more mature man than Shakespeare: we cannot even say that any poet has done so much, to make the English language capable of expressing the most subtle thought or the most refined shades of feeling. Yet we cannot but feel that a play like Congreve's *Way of the World* is in some way more mature than any play of Shakespeare's: but only in this respect, that it reflects a more mature society—that is, it reflects a greater maturity of *manners*. The society for which Congreve wrote was, from our point of view, coarse and brutal enough: yet it is nearer to ours than the society of the Tudors: perhaps for that reason we judge it the more severely. Nevertheless, it was a society more polished and less provincial: its mind was shallower, its sensibility more restricted; it has lost some promise of maturity but realised another. So to maturity of *mind* we must add maturity of *manners*.

The progress towards maturity of language is, I think, more easily recognized and more readily acknowledged in the development of prose, than in that of poetry. In considering prose we are less distracted by individual differences in greatness, and more inclined to demand approximation towards a common standard, a common vocabulary and a common sentence structure: it is often, in fact, the prose which departs the farthest from these common standards, which is individual to the extreme, that we are apt to denominate "poetic prose." At a time when England had already accomplished miracles in poetry, her prose was relatively immature, developed sufficiently for certain purposes but not for others: at that same time, when the French language had given little promise of poetry as great as that in English, French prose was much more mature than English prose. You have only to compare any Tudor writer with Montaigne—and Montaigne himself, as a stylist, is only a precursor, his style not ripe enough to fulfil the French requirements for the classic. Our prose was ready for some tasks before it could cope with others: a Malory could come along before a Hooker, a Hooker before a Hobbes, and a Hobbes before an Addison. Whatever difficulties we have in applying this standard to poetry, it is possible to see the development of a classic prose is the development towards a *common style*. By this I do not mean that the best writers are indistinguishable from each other. The essential and characteristic differences remain: it is not that the differences are less, but that they are more subtle and refined. To a sensitive palate the difference between the prose of Addison and that of Swift will be as marked as the difference between two vintage wines to a connoisseur. What we find, in a period of classic prose, is not a mere common convention of writing, like the common style of newspaper leader writers, but a community of taste. The age which precedes a classic age, may exhibit both eccentricity and monotony: monotony, because the resources of the language have not yet been explored, and eccentricity because there is yet no generally accepted standard—if, indeed, that can be called eccentric where there is no centre. Its writing may be at the same time pedantic and licentious. The age following a classic age, may also exhibit eccentricity and monotony: monotony because the resources of the language have, for the time at least, been exhausted, and eccentricity because originality comes to be more valued than correctness. But the age in which we find a common style, will be an age when society has achieved a moment of order and stability, of equilibrium and harmony; as the age which manifests the greatest extremes of individual style will be an age of development or an age of decay.

Maturity of language may naturally be expected to accompany maturity of mind and manners. We may expect the language to approach maturity at the moment when it has a critical sense of the past, a confidence in the present, and no conscious doubt of the future. In literature, this means that the poet is aware of his predecessors, and that we are aware of the predecessors behind his work, as we may be aware of ancestral traits in a person who is at the same time individual and unique. The predecessors should be themselves great and honoured: but their accomplishment must be such as to suggest still undeveloped resources of the language, and not such as to oppress the younger writers with the fear that everything that can be done has been done, in their language. The poet, certainly, in a mature age, may still obtain stimulus from the hope of doing something that his predecessors have not done; he may even be in revolt against them, as a promising adolescent may revolt against the beliefs, the habits and the manners of his parents; but, in retrospect, we can see that he is also the continuer of their traditions, that he preserves essential family characteristics, and that his difference of behaviour is a difference in the circumstances of another age. And, on the other hand, just as we sometimes observe men whose lives are overshadowed by the fame of a father or grandfather, men of whom any achievement of which they are capable appears comparatively insignificant, so a late age of poetry may be consciously impotent to compete with its distinguished paternity. We meet poets of this kind at the end of any age, poets with a sense of the past only, or alternatively, poets whose hope of the future is founded upon the attempt to renounce the past. The persistence of literary creativeness in any people, accordingly, consists in the maintenance of an unconscious balance between tradition in the larger sense—the collective personality, so to speak, realised in the literature of the past—and the originality of the living generation.

We cannot call the literature of the Elizabethan period, great as it is, wholly mature: we cannot call it classical. No close parallel can be drawn between the development of Greek and Latin literature, for Latin had Greek behind it; still less can we draw a parallel between these and any modern literature, for modern literatures had both Latin and Greek behind them. In the Renaissance there is an early semblance of maturity, which is borrowed from antiquity. We are aware of approaching nearer to maturity with Milton. Milton was in a better position to have a critical sense of the past—of a past in English literature—than his great predecessors. To read Milton is to be confirmed in respect for the genius of Spenser, and in gratitude to Spenser for having contributed towards making the verse of Milton possible. Yet the style of Milton is not a classic style: it is a style of language still in formation, the style of a writer whose *masters* were not English, but Latin and to a less degree Greek. This, I think, is only saying what Johnson and in turn Landor said, when they complained of Milton's style not being quite English. Let us qualify this judgement by saying immediately that Milton did much to develop the language. One of the signs of approach towards a classic style is a development towards greater complexity of sentence and period structure. Such development is apparent in the single work of

Shakespeare, when we trace his style from the early to the late plays: we can even say that in his late plays he goes as far in the direction of complexity as is possible within the limits of dramatic verse, which are narrower than those of other kinds. But complexity for its own sake is not a proper goal: its purpose must be, first, the precise expression of finer shades of feeling and thought; second, the introduction of greater refinement and variety of music. When an author appears, in his love of the elaborate structure, to have lost the ability to say anything simply; when his addiction to pattern becomes such that he says things elaborately which should properly be said simply, and thus limits his range of expression, the process of complexity ceases to be quite healthy, and the writer is losing touch with the spoken language. Nevertheless, as verse develops, in the hands of one poet after another, it tends from monotony to variety, from simplicity to complexity; as it declines, it tends towards monotony again, though it may perpetuate the formal structure to which genius gave life and meaning. You will judge for yourselves how far this generalisation is applicable to the predecessors and followers of Virgil: we can all see this secondary monotony in the eighteenth century imitators of Milton—who himself is never monotonous. There comes a time when a new simplicity, even a relative crudity, may be the only alternative.

You will have anticipated the conclusion towards which I have been approaching: that those qualities of the classic which I have so far mentioned—maturity of mind, maturity of manners, maturity of language and perfection of the common style—are most nearly to be illustrated, in English literature, in the eighteenth century; and, in poetry, most in the poetry of Pope. If that were all I had to say on the matter, it would certainly not be new, and it would not be worth saying. That would be merely proposing a choice between two errors at which men have arrived before: one, that the eighteenth century is (as it thought itself) the finest period of English literature; and the other, that the classical idea should be wholly discredited. My own opinion is, that we have no classic age, and no classic poet, in English; that when we see why this is so, we have not the slightest reason for regret; but that, nevertheless, we must maintain the classic ideal before our eyes. Because we must maintain it, and because the English genius of language has had other things to do than to realise it, we cannot afford either to reject or to overrate the age of Pope; we cannot see English literature as a whole, or aim rightly in the future, without a critical appreciation of the degree to which the classical qualities are exemplified in the work of Pope: which means that unless we are able to enjoy the work of Pope, we cannot arrive at a full understanding of English poetry.

It is fairly obvious that the realisation of classical qualities by Pope was obtained at a high price—to the exclusion of some greater potentialities of English verse. Now, to some extent, the sacrifice of some potentialities in order to realise others, is a condition of artistic creation, as it is a condition of life in general. In life the man who refuses to sacrifice anything, to gain anything else, ends in mediocrity or failure; though, on the other hand, there is the specialist who has sacrificed too much for too little, or who has been born too completely the specialist to have had anything to sacrifice. But in the English eighteenth century, we have reason for feeling that too much was excluded. There was the mature mind: but it was a narrow one. English society and English letters were not provincial, in the sense that they were not isolated from, and not lingering behind, the best European society and letters. Yet the age itself was, in a manner of speaking, a provincial age. When one thinks of a Shakespeare, a Jeremy Taylor, a Milton, in England—of a Racine, a Molière, a Pascal, in France—in the seventeenth century, one is inclined to say that the eighteenth century had perfected its formal garden, only by restricting the area under cultivation. We feel that if the classic is really a worthy ideal, it must be capable of exhibiting an amplitude, a catholicity, to which the eighteenth century cannot lay claim; qualities which are present in some great authors, like Chaucer, who cannot be regarded in my sense as classics of English literature; and which are fully present in the mediaeval mind of Dante. For in the Divine Comedy, if anywhere, we find the classic in a modern European language. In the eighteenth century, we are oppressed by the limited range of sensibility, and especially in the scale of religious feeling. It is not that, in England at least, the poetry is not Christian. It is not even that the poets were not devout Christians: for a pattern of orthodoxy of principle, and sincere piety of feeling, you may look long before you find a poet more genuine than Samuel Johnson. Yet there are evidences of a deeper religious sensibility in the poetry of Shakespeare, whose belief and practice can be only a matter of conjecture. And this restriction of religious sensibility itself produces a kind of provinciality (though we must add that in this sense the nineteenth century was more provincial still): the provinciality which indicates the disintegration of Christendom, the decay of a common belief and a common culture. It would seem then, that the eighteenth century, in spite of its classical achievement—an achievement, I believe, which still has great importance as an example for the future—was lacking some condition which makes the creation of a true classic possible. What this condition is, we must return to Virgil to discover.

I should like first to rehearse the characteristics which I have already attributed to the classic, with special application to Virgil, to his language, his civilisation, and the particular moment in the history of that language and civilisation at which he arrived. Maturity of mind: this needs history, and the consciousness of history. Consciousness of history cannot be fully awake, except where there is other history than the history of the poet's own people: we need this in order to see our own place in history. There must be the knowledge of the history of at least one other highly civilised people, and of a people whose civilisation is sufficiently cognate to have influenced and entered into our own. This is a consciousness which the Romans had, and which the Greeks, however much more highly we may estimate their achievement—and indeed, we may respect it all the more on this account—could not possess. It was a consciousness, certainly, which Virgil himself did much to develop. From the beginning, Virgil, like his contemporaries and immediate predecessors, was constantly adapting and using the discoveries, traditions and inventions of Greek poetry: to make use of a foreign literature in this way marks a further stage of civilisation beyond making use only of the earlier stages of one's own—though I think we can say that no poet has ever shown a finer sense of proportion than Virgil, in the uses he made of Greek and of earlier Latin poetry. It is this development of one literature, or one civilisation, in relation to another, which gives a peculiar significance to the subject of Virgil's epic. In Homer, the conflict between the Greeks and the Trojans is hardly larger in scope than a feud between one Greek city-state and a coalition of other city-states: behind the story of Aeneas is the consciousness of a more radical distinction, a distinction, which is at the same time a statement of *relatedness*, between two great cultures, and, finally, of their reconciliation under an all-embracing destiny.

Virgil's maturity of mind, and the maturity of his age, are exhibited in this awareness of history. With maturity of mind I have associated maturity of manners and absence of provinciality. I suppose that, to a modern European suddenly precipitated into the past, the social behaviour of the Romans and the Athenians would seem indifferently coarse, barbarous and offensive. But if the poet can portray something superior to contemporary practice, it is not in the way of anticipating some later, and quite different code of behaviour, but by an insight into what the conduct of his own people at his own time might be, at its best. House parties of the wealthy, in Edwardian England, were not exactly what we read of in the pages of Henry James: but Mr. James's society was an idealisation, of a kind, of *that* society, and not an anticipation of any other. I think that we are conscious, in Virgil more than any other Latin poet—for Catullus and Propertius seem ruffians, and Horace somewhat plebian, by comparison—of a refinement of manners springing from a delicate sensibility, and particularly in that test of manners, private and public conduct between the sexes. It is not for me, in a gathering of people, all of whom may be better scholars than I, to review the story of Aeneas and Dido. But I have always thought the meeting of Aeneas with the shade of Dido, in Book VI, not only one of the most poignant, but one of the most civilised passages in poetry. It is complex in meaning and economical in expression, for it not only tells us about the attitude of Dido—what is still more important is what it tells us about the attitude of Aeneas. Dido's behaviour appears almost as a projection of Aeneas' own conscience: this, we feel, is the way in which Aeneas' conscience would *expect* Dido to behave to him. The point, it seems to me, is not that Dido is unforgiving—though it is important that, instead of railing at him, she merely snubs him—perhaps the most telling snub in all poetry: what matters most is, that Aeneas does not forgive himself—and this, significantly, in spite of the fact of which he is well aware, that all that he has done has been in compliance with destiny, or in consequence of the machinations of gods who are themselves, we feel, only instruments of a greater inscrutable power. Here, what I chose as an instance of civilised manners, proceeds to testify to civilised consciousness and conscience: but all of the levels at which we may consider a particular episode, belong to one whole. It will be observed, finally, that the behaviour of Virgil's characters (I might except Turnus, the man without a destiny) never appears to be according to some purely local or tribal code of manners: it is, in its time, both Roman and European. Virgil certainly, on the plane of manners, is not provincial.

To attempt to demonstrate the maturity of language and style of Virgil is, for the present occasion, a superfluous task: many of you could perform it better than I, and I think that we should all be in accord. But it is worth repeating that Virgil's syle would not have been possible without a literature behind him, and without his having a very intimate knowledge of this literature: so that he was, in a sense, re-writing Latin poetry—as when he borrows a phrase or a device from a predecessor and improves upon it. He was a learned author, all of whose learning was relevant to his task; and he had, for his use, just enough literature behind him and not too much. As for maturity of style, I do not think that any poet has ever developed a greater command of the complex structure, both of sense and sound, without losing the resource of direct, brief and startling simplicity when the occasion required it. On this I need not dilate: but I think it is worth while to say a word more about the *common style*, because this is something which we cannot perfectly illustrate from English poetry, and we are therefore apt to pay not enough deference to it. In modern European literature, the closet approximation to the ideal of a common style, is probably to be found in Dante and in

Racine; the nearest we have to it in English poetry is Pope, and Pope's is a common style which, in comparison, is of a very narrow range. A common style is one which makes us exclaim, not "this is a man of genius using the language" but "this realises the genius of the language." We do not say this when we read Pope, because we are too conscious of all the resources of the English speech upon which Pope does not draw; we can at most say "this realises the genius of the English language of a particular epoch." We do not say this when we read Shakespeare or Milton, because we are always conscious of the greatness of the man, and of the miracles that *he* is performing with the language; we come nearer perhaps with Chaucer—but that Chaucer is using a different, from our point of view a cruder speech. And Shakespeare and Milton, as later history shows, left open many possibilities of other uses of English in poetry: whereas, after Virgil, it is truer to say that no great development was possible, until the Latin language became something different.

At this point I should like to return to a question which I have already suggested: the question whether the achievement of a classic, in the sense in which I have been using the term throughout, is, for the people and the language of its origin, altogether an unmixed blessing—even though it is unquestionably a ground for pride. To have this question raised in one's mind, it is almost enough simply to have contemplated Latin poetry after Virgil, to have considered the extent to which later poets lived and worked under the shadow of his greatness: so that we praise or dispraise them, according to standards which he set—admiring them, sometimes, for discovering some variation which was new, or even for merely rearranging patterns of words so as to give a pleasing faint reminder of the remote original. We may raise a rather different question, when we view Italian poetry after Dante: for the later Italian poets did not imitate Dante, and had this advantage, that they lived in a world which was more rapidly changing, so that there was obviously something different for them to do; they provoke no direct disastrous comparison. But English poetry, and French poetry also, may be considered fortunate in this: that the greatest poets have exhausted only particular areas. We cannot say that, since the age of Shakespeare, and respectively since the time of Racine, there has been any really first-rate poetic drama in England or in France; since Milton, we have had no great epic poem, though there have been great long poems. It is true that every supreme poet, classic or not, tends to exhaust the ground he cultivates, so that it must, after yielding a diminishing crop, finally be left in fallow for some generations.

Here you may object that the effect on a literature which I am imputing to the classic, results not from the classic character of that work, but simply from its greatness: for I have denied to Shakespeare and to Milton the title of classics, in the sense in which I am employing the term throughout, and yet have admitted that no supremely great poetry of the same kind has been written since. You may or may not be disposed to accept the distinction which I shall make. That every great work of poetry tends to make impossible the production of equally great works of the same kind is indisputable. The reason may be stated partly in terms of conscious purpose: no first-rate poet would attempt to do again, what has already been done as well as it can be done in his language. It is only after the language—its cadence, still more than vocabulary and syntax—has, with time and social change, sufficiently altered, that another dramatic poet as great as Shakespeare, or another epic poet as great as Milton, can become possible. Not only every great poet, but every genuine, though lesser poet, fulfils once for all some possibility of the language, and so leaves one possibility less for his successors. The vein that he has exhausted may be a very small one; or may represent some major form of poetry, the epic or dramatic. But what the great poet has exhausted is merely one form, and not the whole language. The classic poet, on the other hand, exhausts, not a form only, but the language of his time; and when he is a wholly classic poet, the language of his time will be the language in its perfection. So that it is not the poet alone of whom we have to take account, but the language in which he writes: it is not merely that a classic poet exhausts the language, but that an exhaustible language is the kind which may produce a classic poet.

We may be inclined to ask, then, whether we are not fortunate in possessing a language which, instead of having produced a classic, can boast a rich variety in the past, and the possibility of further novelty in the future? Now while we are *inside* a literature, while we speak the same language, and have fundamentally the same culture as that which produced the literature of the past, we want to maintain two things: a pride in what our literature has already accomplished, and a belief in what it may still accomplish in the future. If we cease to believe in the future, the past would cease to be fully *our* past: it would become the past of a dead civilisation. And this consideration must operate with particular cogency upon the minds of those who are engaged in the attempt to add to the store of English literature. There is no classic in English: therefore, any living poet can say, there is still hope that I—and those after me, for no one can face with equanimity, once he understands what is implied, the thought of being the *last* poet—may be able to write something which will be worth preserving. But from the aspect of eternity, such interest in the future has no meaning: when two languages are both dead languages, we cannot say that one is greater, because of the number and variety of its poets, or the other because its genius is more completely expressed in the work of one poet. What I wish to affirm, at one and the same time, is this: that, because English is a living language and the language in which we live, we may be glad that it has never completely realised itself in the work of one classic poet; but that, on the other hand, the classic criterion is of vital importance to us. We need it in order to judge our individual poets, though we refuse to judge our literature as a whole in comparision with one which has produced a classic. Whether a literature does culminate in a classic, is a matter of fortune. It is largely, I suspect, a question of the degree of fusion of the elements within that language; so that the Latin languages can approximate more closely to the classic, not simply because they are Latin, but because they are more homogeneous than English, and therefore tend more naturally towards the *common style:* whereas English, being the most various of great languages in its constituents, tends to variety rather than perfection, needs the longest time to realise its potency, and still contains, perhaps, more unexplored possibilities. It has, perhaps, the greatest capacity for changing, and yet remaining itself.

I am now approaching the distinction between the relative and the absolute classic, the distinction between the literature which can be called classic in relation to its own language, and that which is classic in relation to a number of other languages. But first I wish to record one more characteristic of the classic, beyond those I have enumerated, which will help to establish this dictinction, and to mark the difference between such a classic as Pope and such a classic as Virgil. It is convenient to recapitulate certain assertions which I made earlier.

I suggested, at the beginning, that a frequent, if not universal feature of the maturing of individuals may be a process of selection (not altogether conscious), of the development of some potentialities to the exclusion of others; and that a similarity may be found in the development of language and literature. If this is so, we should expect to find that in a minor classic literature, such as our own of the late seventeenth and the eighteenth century, the elements excluded, to arrive at maturity, will be more numerous or more serious; and that satisfaction in the result, will always be qualified by our awareness of the possibilities of the language, revealed in the work of earlier authors, which have been ignored. The classic age of English literature is not representative of the total genius of the race: as I have intimated, we cannot say that that genius is wholly realised in any one period—with the result that we can still, by referring to one or another period of the past, envisage possibilities for the future. The English language is one which offers wide scope for legitimate divergencies of style; it seems to be such that no one age, and certainly no one writer, can establish a norm. The French language has seemed to be much more closely tethered to a normal style; yet, even in French, though the language appeared to have established itself, once for all, in the seventeenth century, there is an *esprit gaulois*,[1] an element of richness present in Rabelais and in Villon, the awareness of which may qualify our judgement of the *wholeness* of Racine or Molière, for we may feel that it is not only unrepresented but unreconciled. We may come to the conclusion, then, that the perfect classic must be one in which the whole genius of a people will be latent, if not all revealed; and that it can only appear in a language such that its whole genius can be present at once. We must accordingly add, to our list of characteristics of the classic, that of *comprehensiveness*. The classic must, within its formal limitations, express the maximum possible of the whole range of feeling which represents the character of the people who speak that language. It will represent this at its best, and it will also have the widest appeal: among the people to which it belongs, it will find its response among all classes and conditions of men.

When a work of literature has, beyond this comprehensiveness in relation to its own language, an equal significance in relation to a number of foreign literatures, we may say that it has also *universality*. We may for instance speak justly enough of the poetry of Goethe as constituting a classic, because of the place which it occupies in its own language and literature. Yet, because of its partiality, of the impermanence of some of its content, and the germanism of the sensibility; because Goethe appears, to a foreign eye, limited by his age, by his language, and by his culture, so that he is unrepresentative of the whole European tradition, and, like our own nineteenth century authors, a little provincial, we cannot call him a *universal* classic. He is a universal author, in the sense that he is an author with whose works every European ought to be acquainted: but that is a different thing. Nor, on one count or another, can we expect to find the proximate approach to the classic in *any* modern language. It is necessary to go to the two dead languages: it is important that they are dead, because through their death we have come into our inheritance—the fact that they are dead would in itself give them no value, apart from the fact that all the peoples of Europe are their beneficiaries. And of all the great poets of Greece and Rome, I think that it is to Virgil that we owe the most for our standard of the classic: which, I will repeat, is not the same thing as pretending that he is the greatest, or the one to whom we are in every

1 [Gallic spirit.]

way the most indebted—it is of a particular debt that I speak. His comprehensiveness, his peculiar kind of comprehensiveness, is due to the unique position in our history of the Roman Empire and the Latin language: a position which may be said to conform to its *destiny*. This sense of destiny comes to consciousness in the Aeneid. Aeneas is himself, from first to last, a "man in fate," a man who is neither an adventurer nor a schemer, neither a vagabond nor a careerist, a man fulfilling his destiny, not under compulsion or arbitrary decree, and certainly from no stimulus to glory, but by surrendering his will to a higher power behind the gods who would thwart or direct him. He would have preferred to stop in Troy, but he becomes an exile, and something greater and more significant than any exile; he is exiled for a purpose greater than he can know, but which he recognises; and he is not, in a human sense, a happy or successful man. But he is the symbol of Rome; and, as Aeneas is to Rome, so is ancient Rome to Europe. Thus Virgil acquires the centrality of the unique classic; he is at the centre of European civilisation, in a position which no other poet can share or usurp. The Roman Empire and the Latin language were not any empire and any language, but an empire and a language with a unique destiny in relation to ourselves; and the poet in whom that Empire and that language came to consciousness and expression is a poet of unique destiny.

If Virgil is thus the consciousness of Rome and the supreme voice of her language, he must have a significance for us which cannot be expressed wholly in terms of literary appreciation and criticism. Yet, adhering to the problems of literature, or to the terms of literature in dealing with life, we may be allowed to imply more than we state. The value of Virgil to us, in literary terms, is in providing us with a critical criterion. We may, as I have said, have reasons to rejoice that this criterion is provided by a poet writing in a different language from our own: but that is not a reason for rejecting the criterion. To preserve the classical standard, and to measure every individual work of literature by it, is to see that, while our literature as a whole may contain everything, every single work in it may be defective in something. This may be a necessary defect, a defect without which some quality present would be lacking: but we must see it as a defect, at the same time that we see it as a necessity. In the absence of this standard of which I speak, a standard we cannot keep clearly before us if we rely on our own literature alone, we tend, first to admire works of genius for the wrong reasons—as we extol Blake for his *philosophy*, and Hopkins for his *style*: and from this we proceed to greater error, to giving the second-rate equal rank with the first-rate.

In short, without the constant application of the classical measure, which we owe to Virgil more than to any other one poet, we tend to become provincial.

By "provincial" I mean here something more than I find in the dictionary definitions. I mean more, for instance, than "wanting the culture of polish of the capital," though, certainly, Virgil was of the Capital, to a degree which makes any later poet of equal stature look a little provincial; and I mean more than "narrow in thought, in culture, in creed"—a slippery definition this, for, from a modern liberal point of view, Dante was "narrow in thought, in culture, in creed," yet it may be the Broad Churchman, rather than the Narrow Churchman, who is the more provincial. I mean also a distortion of values, the exclusion of some, the exaggeration of others, which springs, not from lack of wide geographical perambulation, but from applying standards acquired within a limited area, to the whole of human experience; which confounds the contingent with the essential, the ephemeral with the permanent. In our age, when men seem more than ever prone to confuse wisdom with knowledge, and knowledge with information, and to try to solve problems of life, in terms of engineering, there is coming into existence a new kind of provincialism which perhaps deserves a new name. It is a provincialism, not of space, but of time; one for which history is merely the chronicle of human devices which have served their turn and been scrapped, one for which the world is the property solely of the living, a property in which the dead hold no shares. The menace of this kind of provincialism is, that we can all, all the peoples on the globe, be provincials together; and those who are not content to be provincials, can only become hermits. If this kind of provincialism led to greater tolerance, in the sense of forbearance, there might be more to be said for it; but it seems more likely to lead to our becoming indifferent, in matters where we ought to maintain a distinctive dogma or standard, and to our becoming intolerant, in matters which might be left to local or personal preference. We may have as many varieties of religion as we like, provided we all send our children to the same schools. But my concern here is only with the corrective to provincialism in literature. We need to remind ourselves that, as Europe is a whole (and still, in its progressive mutilation and disfigurement, the organism out of which any greater world harmony must develop), so European literature is a whole, the several members of which cannot flourish, if the same blood-stream does not circulate throughout the whole body. The blood-stream of European literature is Latin and Greek—not as two systems of circulation, but one, for it is through Rome that our parentage in Greece must be traced. What common measure of excellence have we in literature, among our several languages, which is not the classical measure? What mutual intelligibility can we hope to preserve, except in our common heritage of thought and feeling in those two languages, for the understanding of which, no European people is in any position of advantage over any other? No modern language could aspire to the universality of Latin, even though it came to be spoken by millions more than ever spoke Latin, and even though it came to be the universal means of communication between peoples of all tongues and cultures. No modern language can hope to produce a classic, in the sense in which I have called Virgil a classic. Our classic, the classic of all Europe, is Virgil.

In our several literatures, we have much wealth of which to boast, to which Latin has nothing to compare; but each literature has its greatness, not in isolation, but because of its place in a larger pattern set in Rome. I have spoken of the new seriousness—*gravity* I might say—the new insight into history, illustrated by the dedication of Aeneas to Rome, to a future far beyond his living achievement. *His* reward was hardly more than a narrow beachhead and a political marriage in a weary middle age: his youth interred, its shadow moving with the shades the other side of Cumae. And so, I said, one envisages the destiny of ancient Rome. So we may think of Roman literature: at first sight, a literature of limited scope, with a poor muster of great names, yet universal as no other literature can be; a literature unconsciously sacrificing, in compliance to its destiny in Europe, the opulence and variety of later tongues, to produce, for us, the classic. It is sufficient that this standard should have been established once for all: the task does not have to be done again. But the maintenance of the standard is the price of our freedom, the defence of freedom against chaos. We may remind ourselves of this obligation, by our annual observance of piety towards the great ghost who guided Dante's pilgrimage: who, as it was his function to lead Dante towards a vision he could never himself enjoy, led Europe towards the Christian culture which he could never know; and who, speaking for the last time in the new Italian speech, said in farewell

il temporal foco e l'eterno
veduto hai, figlio, e sei venuto in parte
dov' io per me più oltre non discerno.

Son, the temporal fire and the eternal, hast
thou seen, and art come to a place where I,
of myself, discern no further.

Alfred North Whitehead

UNIVERSITIES AND THEIR FUNCTION

1

THE expansion of universities is one marked feature of the social life in the present age. All countries have shared in this movement, but more especially America, which thereby occupies a position of honor. It is, however, possible to be overwhelmed even by the gifts of good fortune; and this growth of universities, in number of institutions, in size, and in internal complexity of organisation, discloses some danger of destroying the very sources of their usefulness, in the absence of a widespread understanding of the primary functions which universities should perform in the service of a nation. These remarks, as to the necessity for reconsideration of the function of universities, apply to all the more developed countries. They are only more especially applicable to America, because this country has taken the lead in a development which, under wise guidance, may prove to be one of the most fortunate forward steps which civilisation has yet taken.

This article will only deal with the most general principles, though the special problems of the various departments in any university are, of course, innumerable. But generalities require illustration, and for this purpose I choose the business school of a university. This choice is dictated by the fact that business schools represent one of the newer developments of university activity. They are also more particularly relevant to the dominant social activities of modern nations, and for that reason are good examples of the way in which the national life should be affected by the activities of its universities. Also at Harvard, where I have the honour to hold office, the new foundation of a business school on a scale amounting to magnificence has just reached its completion.

There is a certain novelty in the provision of such a school of training, on this scale of magnitude, in one of the few leading universities of the world. It marks the culmination of a movement which for many years past has introduced analogous departments throughout American universities. This is a new fact in the university world; and it alone would justify some general reflections upon the purpose of a university education, and upon the proved importance of that purpose for the welfare of the social organism.

The novelty of business schools must not be exaggerated. At no time have universities been restricted to pure abstract learning. The University of Salerno in Italy, the earliest of European universities, was devoted to medicine. In England, at Cambridge, in the year 1316, a college was founded for the special purpose of providing "clerks for the King's service." Universities have trained clergy, medical men, lawyers, engineers. Business is now a highly intellectualised vocation, so it well fits into the series. There is, however, this novelty: the curriculum suitable for a business school, and the various modes of activity of such a school, are still in the experimental stage. Hence the peculiar importance of recurrence to general principles in connection with the moulding of these schools. It would, however, be an act of presumption on my part if I were to enter upon any consideration of details, or even upon types of policy affecting the balance of the whole training. Upon such questions I have no special knowledge, and therefore have no word of advice.

2

THE universities are schools of education, and schools of research. But the primary reason for their existence is not to be found either in the mere knowledge conveyed to the students or in the mere opportunities for research afforded to the members of the faculty.

Both these functions could be performed at a cheaper rate, apart from these very expensive institutions. Books are cheap, and the system of apprenticeship is well understood. So far as the mere imparting of information is concerned, no university has had any justification for existence since the popularisation of printing in the fifteenth century. Yet the chief impetus to the foundation of universities came after that date, and in more recent times has even increased.

The justification for a university is that it preserves the connection between knowledge and the zest of life, by uniting the young and the old in the imaginative consideration of learning. The university imparts information, but it imparts it imaginatively. At least, this is the function which it should perform for society. A university which fails in this respect has no reason for existence. This atmosphere of excitement, arising from imaginative consideration, transforms knowledge. A fact is no longer a bare fact: it is invested with all its possibilities. It is no longer a burden on the memory: it is energising as the poet of our dreams, and the architect of our purposes.

Imagination is not to be divorced from the facts: it is a way of illuminating the facts. It works by eliciting the general principles which apply to the facts, as they exist, and then by an intellectual survey of alternative possibilities which are consistent with those principles. It enables men to construct an intellectual vision of a new world, and it preserves the zest of life by the suggestion of satisfying purposes.

Youth is imaginative, and if the imagination be strengthened by discipline this energy of imagination can in great measure be preserved through life. The tragedy of the world is that those who are imaginative have but slight experience, and those who are experienced have feeble imaginations. Fools act on imagination without knowledge; pedants act on knowledge without imagination. The task of a university is to weld together imagination and experience.

The initial discipline of imagination in its period of youthful vigor requires that there be no responsibility for immediate action. The habit of unbiased thought, whereby the ideal variety of exemplifications is discerned in its derivation from general principles, cannot be acquired when there is the daily task of preserving a concrete organisation. You must be free to think rightly and wrongly, and free to appreciate the variousness of the universe undisturbed by its perils.

These reflections upon the general functions of a university can be at once translated in terms of the particular functions of a business school. We need not flinch from the assertion that the main function of such a school is to produce men with a greater zest for business. It is a libel upon human nature to conceive that zest for life is the product of pedestrian purposes directed toward the narrow routine of material comforts. Mankind by its pioneering instinct, and in a hundred other ways, proclaims falsehood of that lie.

In the modern complex social organism, the adventure of life cannot be disjoined from intellectual adventure. Amid simpler circumstances, the pioneer can follow the urge of his instinct, directed toward the scene of his vision from the mountain top. But in the complex organisations of modern business the intellectual adventure of analysis, and of imaginative reconstruction, must precede any successful reorganisation. In a simpler world, business relations were simpler, being based on the immediate contact of man with man and on immediate confrontation with all relevant material circumstances. To-day business organisation requires an imaginative grasp of the psychologies of populations engaged in differing modes of occupation; of populations scattered through cities, through mountains, through plains; of populations on the ocean, and of populations in mines, and of populations in forests. It requires an imaginative grasp of conditions in the tropics, and of conditions in temperate zones. It requires an imaginative grasp of the interlocking interests of great organisations, and of the reactions of the whole complex to any change in one of its elements. It requires an imaginative understanding of laws of political economy, not merely in the abstract, but also with the power to construe them in terms of the particular circumstances of a concrete business. It requires some knowledge of the habits of government, and of the variations of those habits under diverse conditions. It requires an imaginative vision of the binding forces of any human organisation, a sympathetic vision of the limits of human nature and of the conditions which evoke loyalty of service. It requires some knowledge of the laws of health, and of the laws of fatigue, and of the conditions for sustained reliability. It requires an imaginative understanding of the social effects of the conditions of factories. It requires a sufficient conception of the rôle of applied science in modern society. It requires that discipline of character which can say "yes" and "no" to other men, not by reason of blind obstinacy, but with firmness derived from a conscious evaluation of relevant alternatives.

The universities have trained the intellectual pioneers of our civilisation—the priests, the lawyers, the statesmen, the doctors, the men of science, and the men of letters. They have been the home of those ideals which lead men to confront the confusion of their present times. The Pilgrim Fathers left England to found a state of society according to the ideals of their religious faith; and one of their earlier acts was the foundation of Harvard University in Cambridge, named after that ancient mother of ideals in England, to which so many of them owed their training. The conduct of business now requires intellectual imagination of the same type as that which in former times has mainly passed into those other occupations; and the universities are the organisations which have supplied this type of mentality for the service of the progress of the European races.

In early mediæval history the origin of universities was obscure and almost unnoticed. They were a gradual and natural growth. But their existence is the reason for the sustained, rapid progressiveness of European life in so many fields of activity. By their agency the adventure of action met the adventure of thought. It would not have been possible antecedently to have divined that such organisations would have been successful. Even now, amid the imperfections of all things human, it is sometimes difficult to understand how they succeed in their work. Of course there is much failure in the work of universities. But, if we take a broad view of history, their success has been remarkable and almost uniform. The cultural histories of Italy, of France, of Germany, of Holland, of Scotland, of England, of the United States, bear witness to the influence of universities. By "cultural history" I am not chiefly thinking of the lives of scholars;

I mean the energising of the lives of those men who gave to France, to Germany, and to other countries that impress of types of human achievement which, by their addition to the zest of life, form the foundation of our patriotism. We love to be members of society which can do those things.

There is one great difficulty which hampers all the higher types of human endeavour. In modern times this difficulty has even increased in its possibilities for evil. In any large organisation the younger men, who are novices, must be set to jobs which consist in carrying out fixed duties in obedience to orders. No president of a large corporation meets his youngest employee at his office door with the offer of the most responsible job which the work of that corporation includes. The young men are set to work at a fixed routine, and only occasionally even see the president as he passes in and out of the building. Such work is a great discipline. It imparts knowledge, and it produces reliability of character; also it is the only work for which the young men, in that novice stage, are fit, and it is the work for which they are hired. There can be no criticism of the custom, but there may be an unfortunate effect—prolonged routine work dulls the imagination.

The result is that qualities essential at a later stage of a career are apt to be stamped out in an earlier stage. This is only an instance of the more general fact, that necessary technical excellence can only be acquired by a training which is apt to damage those energies of mind which should direct the technical skill. This is the key fact in education, and the reason for most of its difficulties.

The way in which a university should function in the preparation for an intellectual career, such as modern business or one of the older professions, is by promoting the imaginative consideration of the various general principles underlying that career. Its students thus pass into their period of technical apprenticeship with their imaginations already practised in connecting details with general principles. The routine then receives its meaning, and also illuminates the principles which give it that meaning. Hence, instead of a drudgery issuing in a blind rule of thumb, the properly trained man has some hope of obtaining an imagination disciplined by detailed facts and by necessary habits.

Thus the proper function of a university is the imaginative acquisition of knowledge. Apart from this importance of the imagination, there is no reason why business men, and other professional men, should not pick up their facts bit by bit as they want them for particular occasions. A university is imaginative or it is nothing—at least nothing useful.

3

IMAGINATION is a contagious disease. It cannot be measured by the yard, or weighed by the pound, and then delivered to the students by members of the faculty. It can only be communicated by a faculty whose members themselves wear their learning with imagination. In saying this, I am only repeating one of the oldest of observations. More than two thousand years ago the ancients symbolised learning by a torch passing from hand to hand down the generations. That lighted torch is the imagination of which I speak. The whole art in the organisation of a university is the provision of a faculty whose learning is lighted up with imagination. This is the problem of problems in university education; and unless we are careful the recent vast extension of universities in number of students and in variety of activities—of which we are so justly proud—will fail in producing its proper results, by the mishandling of this problem.

The combination of imagination and learning normally requires some leisure, freedom from restraint, freedom from harassing worry, some variety of experiences, and the stimulation of other minds diverse in opinion and diverse in equipment. Also there is required the excitement of curiosity, and the self-confidence derived from pride in the achievements of the surrounding society in procuring the advance of knowledge. Imagination cannot be acquired once and for all, and then kept indefinitely in an ice box to be produced periodically in stated quantities. The learned and imaginative life is a way of living, and is not an article of commerce.

It is in respect to the provision and utilisation of these conditions for an efficient faculty that the two functions of education and research meet together in a university. Do you want your teachers to be imaginative? Then encourage them to research. Do you want your researchers to be imaginative? Then bring them into intellectual sympathy with the young at the most eager, imaginative period of life, when intellects are just entering upon their mature discipline. Make your researchers explain themselves to active minds, plastic and with the world before them; make your young students crown their period of intellectual acquisition by some contact with minds gifted with experience of intellectual adventure. Education is discipline for the adventure of life; research is intellectual adventure; and the universities should be homes of adventure shared in common by young and old. For successful education there must always be a certain freshness in the knowledge dealt with. It must either be new in itself or it must be invested with some novelty of application to the new world of new times. Knowledge does not keep any better than fish. You may be dealing with knowledge of the old species, with some old truth; but somehow or other it must come to the students, as it were, just drawn out of the sea and with the freshness of its immediate importance.

It is the function of the scholar to evoke into life wisdom and beauty which, apart from his magic, would remain lost in the past. A progressive society depends upon its inclusion of three groups—scholars, discoverers, inventors. Its progress also depends upon the fact that its educated masses are composed of members each with a tinge of scholarship, a tinge of discovery, and a tinge of invention. I am here using the term "discovery" to mean the progress of knowledge in respect to truths of some high generality, and the term "invention" to mean the progress of knowledge in respect to the application of general truths in particular ways subservient to present needs. It is evident that these three groups merge into each other, and also that men engaged in practical affairs are properly to be called inventors so far as they contribute to the progress of society. But any one individual has his own limitation of function, and his own peculiar needs. What is important for a nation is that there shall be a very close relation between all types of its progressive elements, so that the study may influence the market place, and the market place the study. Universities are the chief agencies for this fusion of progressive activities into an effective instrument of progress. Of course they are not the only agencies, but it is a fact that to-day the progressive nations are those in which universities flourish.

It must not be supposed that the output of a university in the form of original ideas is solely to be measured by printed papers and books labeled with the names of their authors. Mankind is as individual in its mode of output as in the substance of its thoughts. For some of the most fertile minds composition in writing, or in a form reducible to writing, seems to be an impossibility. In every faculty you will find that some of the more brilliant teachers are not among those who publish. Their originality requires for its expression direct intercourse with their pupils in the form of lectures, or of personal discussion. Such men exercise an immense influence; and yet, after the generation of their pupils has passed away, they sleep among the innumerable unthanked benefactors of humanity. Fortunately, one of them is immortal—Socrates.

Thus it would be the greatest mistake to estimate the value of each member of a faculty by the printed work signed with his name. There is at the present day some tendency to fall into this error; and an emphatic protest is necessary against an attitude on the part of authorities which is damaging to efficiency and unjust to unselfish zeal.

But, when all such allowances have been made, one good test for the general efficiency of a faculty is that as a whole it shall be producing in published form its quota of contributions of thought. Such a quota is to be estimated in weight of thought, and not in number of words.

This survey shows that the management of a university faculty has no analogy to that of a business organisation. The public opinion of the faculty, and a common zeal for the purposes of the university, form the only effective safeguards for the high level of university work. The faculty should be a band of scholars, stimulating each other, and freely determining their various activities. You can secure certain formal requirements, that lectures are given at stated times and that instructors and students are in attendance. But the heart of the matter lies beyond all regulation.

The question of justice to the teachers has very little to do with the case. It is perfectly just to hire a man to perform any legal services under any legal conditions as to times and salary. No one need accept the post unless he so desires.

The sole question is, What sort of conditions will produce the type of faculty which will run a successful university? The danger is that it is quite easy to produce a faculty entirely unfit—a faculty of very efficient pedants and dullards. The general public will only detect the difference after the university has stunted the promise of youth for scores of years.

The modern university system in the great democratic countries will only be successful if the ultimate authorities exercise singular restraint, so as to remember that universities cannot be dealt with according to the rules and policies which apply to the familiar business corporations. Business schools are no exception to this law of university life. There is really nothing to add to what the presidents of many American universities have recently said in public on this topic. But whether the effective portion of the general public, in America or other countries, will follow their advice appears to be doubtful. The whole point of a university, on its educational side, is to bring the young under the intellectual influence of a band of imaginative scholars. There can be no escape from proper attention to the conditions which—as experience has shown—will produce such a band.

4

THE two premier universities of Europe, in age and in dignity, are the University of Paris and the University of Oxford. I will speak of my own country because I know it best. The University of Oxford may have sinned in many ways. But, for all her deficiencies, she has throughout the ages preserved one supreme merit, beside which all failures in detail are as dust in the balance: for century after century, throughout the long course of her existence, she has produced bands of scholars who treated learning imaginatively. For that service alone, no one who loves culture can think of her without emotion.

But it is quite unnecessary for me to cross the ocean for my examples. The author of the Declaration of Independence, Mr. Jefferson, has some claim to be the greatest American. The perfection of his various achievements certainly places him among the few great men of all ages. He founded a university, and devoted one side of his complex genius to placing that university amid every circumstance which could stimulate the imagination—beauty of buildings, of situation, and every other stimulation of equipment and organisation.

There are many other universities in America which can point my moral, but my final example shall be Harvard—the representative university of the Puritan movement. The New England Puritans of the seventeenth and eighteenth centuries were the most intensely imaginative people, restrained in their outward expression, and fearful of symbolism by physical beauty, but, as it were, racked with the intensity of spiritual truths intellectually imagined. The Puritan faculties of those centuries must have been imaginative indeed, and they produced great men whose names have gone round the world. In later times Puritanism softened, and, in the golden age of literary New England, Emerson, Lowell, and Longfellow set their mark upon Harvard. The modern scientific age then gradually supervenes, and again in William James we find the typical imaginative scholar.

To-day business comes to Harvard; and the gift which the University has to offer is the old one of imagination, the lighted torch which passes from hand to hand. It is a dangerous gift, which has started many a conflagration. It we are timid as to that danger, the proper course is to shut down our universities. Imagination is a gift which has often been associated with great commercial peoples—with Greece, with Florence, with Venice, with the learning of Holland, and with the poetry of England. Commerce and imagination thrive together. It is a gift which all must pray for their country who desire for it that abiding greatness achieved by Athens:—

> Her citizens, imperial spirits,
> Rule the present from the past.

For American education no smaller ideal can suffice.

POETRY

John Norris of Bemerton

THE ASPIRATION

How long great God, how long must I
Immured in this dark prison lie!
Where at the gate and avenues of sense
My Soul must watch to have intelligence:
Where but faint gleams of thee salute my sight,
Like doubtful moonshine in a cloudy night.
When shall I leave this magic Sphere
And be all mind, all eye, all ear.

How cold this clime! and yet my sense
Perceives even here thy influence.
Even here thy strong, magnetic charms I feel
And pant and tremble like the amorous steel.
To lower good, and beauties less divine,
Sometimes my erroneous needle does decline
But yet so strong the sympathy
It turns, and points again to thee.

I long to see this excellence
Which at such distance strikes my sense.
My impatient Soul struggles to disengage
Her wings from the confinement of her cage.
Would'st thou great Love this prisoner once set free
How would she hasten to be link'd with thee!
She'd for no angel's conduct stay
But fly and love on all the way.

Ben Jonson

TO THE MEMORY OF MY BELOVED THE AUTHOR, MASTER WILLIAM SHAKESPEARE, AND WHAT HE HATH LEFT US

To draw no envy, Shakespeare, on thy name,
Am I thus ample to thy book and fame,
While I confess thy writings to be such
As neither man nor Muse can praise too much.

'Tis true, and all men's suffrage. But these ways
Were not the paths I meant unto thy praise:
For seeliest ignorance on these may light,
Which, when it sounds at best, but echoes right;
Or blind affection, which doth ne'er advance
The truth, but gropes, and urgeth all by chance;
Or crafty malice might pretend this praise,
And think to ruin where it seemed to raise.
These are as some infamous bawd or whore
Should praise a matron—What could hurt her more?
But thou art proof against them, and, indeed,
Above the ill fortune of them, or the need.
I therefore will begin. Soul of the age!
The applause, delight, the wonder of our stage,
My Shakespeare, rise! I will not lodge thee by
Chaucer or Spenser, or bid Beaumont lie
A little further to make thee a room:
Thou art a monument without a tomb,
And art alive still while thy book doth live,
And we have wits to read and praise to give.
That I not mix thee so, my brain excuses,
I mean with great, but disproportioned Muses;
For, if I thought my judgment were of years,
I should commit thee surely with thy peers,
And tell how far thou didst our Lyly outshine,
Or sporting Kyd, or Marlowe's mighty line.
And though thou hadst small Latin and less Greek,
From thence to honor thee I would not seek
For names, but call forth thundering Aeschylus,
Euripides, and Sophocles to us,
Pacuvius, Accius, him of Cordova dead,
To life again, to hear thy buskin tread
And shake a stage; or when thy socks were on,
Leave thee alone for the comparison
Of all that insolent Greece or haughty Rome
Sent forth, or since did from their ashes come.
Triumph, my Britain; thou hast one to show
To whom all scenes of Europe homage owe.
He was not of an age, but for all time!
And all the Muses still were in their prime
When like Apollo he came forth to warm
Our ears, or like a Mercury to charm.
Nature herself was proud of his designs,
And joyed to wear the dressing of his lines,
Which were so richly spun, and woven so fit,
As, since, she will vouchsafe no other wit:
The merry Greek, tart Aristophanes,
Neat Terence, witty Plautus, now not please,

But antiquated and deserted lie,
As they were not of nature's family.
Yet must I not give nature all; thy Art,
My gentle Shakespeare, must enjoy a part:
For though the poet's matter nature be,
His Art doth give the fashion; and that he
Who casts to write a living line must sweat
(Such as thine are) and strike the second heat
Upon the Muses' anvil, turn the same,
And himself with it, that he thinks to frame,
Or for the laurel he may gain a scorn;
For a good poet's made as well as born.
And such wert thou! Look how the father's face
Lives in his issue; even so the race
Of Shakespeare's mind and manners brightly shines
In his well-turnèd and true-filèd lines,
In each of which he seems to shake a lance,
As brandished at the eyes of ignorance.
Sweet swan of Avon, what a sight it were
To see thee in our waters yet appear,
And make those flights upon the banks of Thames
That so did take Eliza and our James!
But stay; I see thee in the hemisphere
Advanced and made a constellation there!
Shine forth, thou star of poets, and with rage
Or influence chide or cheer the drooping stage,
Which, since thy flight from hence, hath mourned like night,
And despairs day, but for thy volume's light.

Gerard Manley Hopkins

THE WINDHOVER: TO CHRIST OUR LORD

I CAUGHT this morning's minion, king-
dom of daylight's dauphin, dapple-dawn-drawn Falcon, in his riding
Of the rolling level underneath him steady air, and striding
High there, how he rung upon the rein of a wimpling wing
In his ecstasy! then off, off forth on swing,
As a skate's heel sweeps smooth on a bow-bend: the hurl and gliding
Rebuffed the big wind. My heart in hiding
Stirred for a bird,—the achieve of, the mastery of the thing!

Brute beauty and valour and act, oh, air, pride, plume, here
  Buckle! AND the fire that breaks from thee then, a billion
Times told lovelier, more dangerous, O my chevalier!

  No wonder of it: shéer plód makes plough down sillion
Shine, and blue-bleak embers, ah my dear,
  Fall, gall themselves, and gash gold-vermillion.

Robert Browning

ANDREA DEL SARTO

Called "the Faultless Painter"

BUT DO not let us quarrel any more,
No, my Lucrezia; bear with me for once:
Sit down and all shall happen as you wish.
You turn your face, but does it bring your heart?
I'll work then for your friend's friend, never fear,
Treat his own subject after his own way,
Fix his own time, accept too his own price,
And shut the money into this small hand
When next it takes mine. Will it? tenderly?
Oh, I'll content him,—but tomorrow, Love!
I often am much wearier than you think,
This evening more than usual, and it seems
As if—forgive now—should you let me sit
Here by the window with your hand in mine
And look a half-hour forth on Fiesole,
Both of one mind, as married people use,
Quietly, quietly, the evening through,
I might get up tomorrow to my work
Cheerful and fresh as ever. Let us try.
Tomorrow how you shall be glad for this!
Your soft hand is a woman of itself,
And mine the man's bared breast she curls inside.
Don't count the time lost, either; you must serve
For each of the five pictures we require—
It saves a model. So! keep looking so—
My serpentining beauty, rounds on rounds!
—How could you ever prick those perfect ears,
Even to put the pearl there! oh, so sweet—
My face, my moon, my everybody's moon,
Which everybody looks on and calls his,
And, I suppose, is looked on by in turn,
While she looks—no one's: very dear, no less!
You smile? why, there's my picture ready made.

There's what we painters call our harmony!
A common greyness silvers everything,—
All in a twilight, you and I alike
—You, at the point of your first pride in me
(That's gone, you know),—but I, at every point;
My youth, my hope, my art, being all toned down
To yonder sober pleasant Fiesole.
There's the bell clinking from the chapel-top;
That length of convent-wall across the way
Holds the trees safer, huddled more inside;
The last monk leaves the garden; days decrease
And autumn grows, autumn is everything.
Eh? the whole seems to fall into a shape
As if I saw alike my work and self
And all that I was born to be and do,
A twilight-piece. Love, we are in God's hand.
How strange now, looks the life he makes us lead;
So free we seem, so fettered fast we are!
I feel he laid the fetter: let it lie!
This chamber for example—turn your head—
All that's behind us! you don't understand
Nor care to understand about my art,
But you can hear at least when people speak;
And that cartoon, the second from the door
—It is the thing, Love! So such things should be—
Behold Madonna! I am bold to say.
I can do with my pencil what I know,
What I see, what at bottom of my heart
I wish for, if I ever wish so deep—
Do easily, too—when I say perfectly
I do not boast, perhaps: yourself are judge
Who listened to the Legate's talk last week.
And just as much they used to say in France.
At any rate 'tis easy, all of it,
No sketches first, no studies, that's long past—
I do what many dream of all their lives
—Dream? strive to do, and agonize to do,
And fail in doing. I could count twenty such
On twice your fingers, and not leave this town,
Who strive—you don't know how the others strive
To paint a little thing like that you smeared
Carelessly passing with your robes afloat,—
Yet do much less, so much less, Someone says,
(I know his name, no matter) so much less!
Well, less is more, Lucrezia: I am judged.
There burns a truer light of God in them,
In their vexed, beating, stuffed, and stopped-up brain,
Heart, or whate'er else, than goes on to prompt
This low-pulsed forthright craftsman's hand of mine.

Their works drop groundward, but themselves, I know,
Reach many a time a heaven that's shut to me,
Enter and take their place there sure enough,
Though they come back and cannot tell the world.
My works are nearer heaven, but I sit here.
The sudden blood of these men! at a word—
Praise them, it boils, or blame them, it boils too.
I, painting from myself and to myself,
Know what I do, am unmoved by men's blame
Or their praise either. Somebody remarks
Morello's outline there is wrongly traced,
His hue mistaken; what of that? or else,
Rightly traced and well ordered; what of that?
Speak as they please, what does the mountain care?
Ah, but a man's reach should exceed his grasp,
Or what's a heaven for? All is silver-grey
Placid and perfect with my art: the worse!
I know both what I want and what might gain,
And yet how profitless to know, to sigh
"Had I been two, another and myself,
Our head would have o'erlooked the world!" No doubt.
Yonder's a work now, of that famous youth
The Urbinate who died five years ago.
('Tis copied, George Vasari sent it me.)
Well, I can fancy how he did it all,
Pouring his soul, with kings and popes to see,
Reaching, that heaven might so replenish him,
Above and through his art—for it gives way;
That arm is wrongly put—and there again—
A fault to pardon in the drawing's lines,
Its body, so to speak: its soul is right,
He means right—that, a child may understand.
Still, what an arm! and I could alter it:
But all the play, the insight and the stretch—
Out of me, out of me! And wherefore out?
Had you enjoined them on me, given me soul,
We might have risen to Rafael, I and you!
Nay, Love, you did give all I asked, I think—
More than I merit, yes, by many times.
But had you—oh, with the same perfect brow,
And perfect eyes, and more than perfect mouth,
And the low voice my soul hears, as a bird
The fowler's pipe, and follows to the snare—
Had you, with these the same, but brought a mind!
Some women do so. Had the mouth there urged
"God and the glory! never care for gain.
The present by the future, what is that?
Live for fame, side by side with Agnolo!

Rafael is waiting; up to God, all three!"
I might have done it for you. So it seems:
Perhaps not. All is as God over-rules.
Besides, incentives come from the soul's self;
The rest avail not. Why do I need you?
What wife had Rafael, or has Agnolo?
In this world, who can do a thing, will not;
And who would do it, cannot, I perceive:
Yet the will's somewhat—somewhat, too, the power—
And thus we half-men struggle. At the end,
God, I conclude, compensates, punishes,
'Tis safer for me, if the award be strict,
That I am something underrated here,
Poor this long while, despised, to speak the truth.
I dared not, do you know, leave home all day,
For fear of chancing on the Paris lords.
The best is when they pass and look aside;
But they speak sometimes; I must bear it all.
Well may they speak! That Francis, that first time,
And that long festal year at Fontainebleau!
I surely then could sometimes leave the ground,
Put on the glory, Rafael's daily wear,
In that humane great monarch's golden look,—
One finger in his beard or twisted curl
Over his mouth's good mark that made the smile,
One arm about my shoulder, round my neck,
The jingle of his gold chain in my ear,
I painting proudly with his breath on me,
All his court round him, seeing with his eyes,
Such frank French eyes, and such a fire of souls
Profuse, my hand kept plying by those hearts,—
And, best of all, this, this, this face beyond,
This in the background, waiting on my work,
To crown the issue with a last reward!
A good time, was it not, my kingly days?
And had you not grown restless . . . but I know—
'Tis done and past; 'twas right, my instinct said;
Too live the life grew, golden and not grey,
And I'm the weak-eyed bat no sun should tempt
Out of the grange whose four walls make his world.
How could it end in any other way?
You called me, and I came home to your heart.
The triumph was—to reach and stay there; since
I reached it ere the triumph, what is lost?
Let my hands frame your face in your hair's gold,
You beautiful Lucrezia that are mine!
"Rafael did this, Andrea painted that;
The Roman's is the better when you pray,

But still the other's Virgin was his wife—"
Men will excuse me. I am glad to judge
Both pictures in your presence; clearer grows
My better fortune, I resolve to think.
For, do you know, Lucrezia, as God lives,
Said one day Agnolo, his very self,
To Rafael . . . I have known it all these years . . .
(When the young man was flaming out his thoughts
Upon a palace-wall for Rome to see,
Too lifted up in heart because of it)
"Friend, there's certain sorry little scrub
Goes up and down our Florence, none cares how,
Who, were he set to plan and execute
As you are, pricked on by your popes and kings,
Would bring the sweat into that brow of yours!"
To Rafael's!—And indeed the arm is wrong.
I hardly dare . . . yet, only you to see,
Give the chalk here—quick, thus the line should go!
Ay, but the soul! he's Rafael! rub it out!
Still, all I care for, if he spoke the truth,
(What he? why, who but Michel Agnolo?
Do you forget already words like those?)
If really there was such a chance, so lost,—
Is, whether you're—not grateful—but more pleased.
Well, let me think so. And you smile indeed!
This hour has been an hour! Another smile?
If you would sit thus by me every night
I should work better, do you comprehend?
I mean that I should earn more, give you more.
See, it is settled dusk now; there's a star;
Morello's gone, the watch-lights show the wall,
The cue-owls speak the name we call them by.
Come from the window, Love,—come in, at last,
Inside the melancholy little house
We built to be so gay with. God is just.
King Francis may forgive me; oft at nights
When I look up from painting, eyes tired out,
The walls become illumined, brick from brick
Distinct, instead of mortar, fierce bright gold,
That gold of his I did cement them with!
Let us but love each other. Must you go?
That Cousin here again? he waits outside?
Must see you—you, and not with me? Those loans?
More gaming debts to pay? you smiled for that?
Well, let smiles buy me! have you more to spend?
While hand and eye and something of a heart
Are left me, work's my ware, and what's it worth?
I'll pay my fancy. Only let me sit

The grey remainder of the evening out,
Idle, you call it, and muse perfectly
How I could paint, were I but back in France,
One picture, just one more—the Virgin's face,
Not yours this time! I want you at my side
To hear them—that is, Michel Agnolo—
Judge all I do and tell you of its worth.
Will you? To-morrow, satisfy your friend.
I take the subjects for his corridor,
Finish the portrait out of hand—there, there,
And throw him in another thing or two
If he demurs; the whole should prove enough
To pay for this same Cousin's freak. Beside,
What's better and what's all I care about,
Get you the thirteen scudi for the ruff!
Love, does that please you? Ah, but what does he,
The Cousin! what does he to please you more?

I am grown peaceful as old age to-night.
I regret little, I would change still less.
Since there my past life lies, why alter it?
The very wrong to Francis!—it is true
I took his coin, was tempted and complied,
And built this house and sinned, and all is said.
My father and my mother died of want.
Well, had I riches of my own? you see
How one gets rich! Let each one bear his lot.
They were born poor, lived poor, and poor they died:
And I have laboured somewhat in my time
And not been paid profusely. Some good son
Paint my two hundred pictures—let him try!
No doubt, there's something strikes a balance. Yes,
You loved me quite enough, it seems to-night.
This must suffice me here. What would one have?
In Heaven, perhaps, new chances, one more chance—
Four great walls in the New Jerusalem,
Meted on each side by the angel's reed,
For Leonard, Rafael, Agnolo and me
To cover—the three first without a wife,
While I have mine! So—still they overcome
Because there's still Lucrezia,—as I choose.

Again the Cousin's whistle! Go, my Love.

W. H. Auden

UNDER WHICH LYRE

A Reactionary Tract for the Times

Ares at last has quit the field,
The bloodstains on the bushes yield
To seeping showers.
And in their convalescent state
The fractured towns associate
With summer flowers.

Encamped upon the college plain
Raw veterans already train
As freshman forces;
Instructors with sarcastic tongue
Shepherd the battle-weary young
Through basic courses.

Among bewildering appliances
For mastering the arts and sciences
They stroll or run,
And nerves that never flinched at slaughter
Are shot to pieces by the shorter
Poems of Donne.

Professors back from secret missions
Resume their proper eruditions,
Though some regret it;
They liked their dictaphones a lot,
They met some big wheels and do not
Let you forget it.

But Zeus' inscrutable decree
Permits the will to disagree
To be pandemic,
Ordains that vaudeville shall preach,
And every commencement speech
Be a polemic.

Let Ares doze, that other war
Is instantly declared once more
'Twixt those who follow
Precocious Hermes all the way
And those who without qualms obey
Pompous Apollo.

Brutal like all Olympic games,
Though fought with smiles and Christian names
    And less dramatic,
This dialectic strife between
The civil gods is just as mean,
    And more fanatic.

What high immortals do in mirth
Is life and death on Middle Earth;
    Their a-historic
Antipathy forever gripes
All ages and somatic types:
    The sophomoric

Who face the future's darkest hints
With giggles or with prairie squints
    As stout as Cortez,
And those who like myself turn pale
As we approach with ragged sail
    The fattening forties.

The sons of Hermes love to play,
And only do their best when they
    Are told they oughtn't;
Apollo's children never shrink
From boring jobs but have to think
    Their work important.

Related by antithesis,
A compromise between them is
    Impossible;
Respect perhaps, but friendship never:
Falstaff the fool confronts forever
    The prig Prince Hal.

So, standing here, surrounded by
The eyes of Miltons and the high
    Foreheads of Shaws,
A Hermes man, I call on you,
Phi-Beta-Kappa brethren, to
    Defend his cause.

If he would leave the self alone,
Apollo's welcome to the throne,
    Fasces and falcons;
He loves to rule, has always done it;
The earth would soon, did Hermes run it,
    Be like the Balkans.

But, jealous of our god of dreams,
His common sense in secret schemes
To rule the heart;
Unable to invent the lyre,
Creates with simulated fire
Official art.

And when he occupies a college,
Truth is replaced by Useful Knowledge;
He pays particular
Attention to Commercial Thought,
Public Relations, Hygiene, Sport,
In his curricula.

Athletic, extrovert and crude,
For him, to work in solitude
Is the offense,
The goal a populous Nirvana:
His shield bears this device: *Mens sana*
Qui mal y pense.[1]

Today his arms, we must confess,
From Right to Left have met success,
His banners wave
From Yale to Princeton, and the news
From Broadway to the Book Reviews
Is very grave.

His radio Homers all day long
In over-Whitmanated song
That does not scan,
With adjectives laid end to end,
Extol the doughnut and commend
The Common Man.

His too each homely lyric thing
On sport or spousal love or spring
Or dogs or dusters,
Invented by some courthouse bard
For recitation by the yard
In filibusters.

To him ascend the prize orations
And sets of fugal variations
On some folk ballad,
While dietitians sacrifice
A glass of prune juice or a nice
Marshmallow salad.

1 [The mind is sane which thinks evil.]

Charged with his compound of sensational
Sex plus some undenominational
        Religious matter,
Enormous novels by co-eds
Rain down on our defenseless heads
        Till our teeth chatter.

In fake Hermetic uniforms
Behind our battle-line, in swarms
        That keep alighting,
His existentialists declare
That they are in complete despair,
        Yet go on writing.

No matter. He shall be defied.
We have the ladies on our side.
        What though his threat
To organize us grow more critical?
Zeus willing, we, the unpolitical
        Shall best him yet.

Lone scholars, sniping from the walls
Of learned periodicals,
        Our facts defend,
Our intellectual marines,
Landing in Little Magazines,
        Capture a trend.

By night our student Underground
At cocktail parties whisper round
        From ear to ear;
Fat figures in the public eye
Collapse next morning, ambushed by
        Some witty sneer.

In our morale must lie our strength:
So, that we may behold at length
        Routed Apollo's
Battalions melt away like fog,
Keep well the Hermetic Decalogue,
        Which runs as follows:

Thou shalt not do as the dean pleases,
Thou shalt not write thy doctor's thesis
        On education,
Thou shalt not worship projects nor
Shalt thou or thine bow down before
        Administration.

Thou shalt not answer questionnaires
Or quizzes upon World Affairs,
Nor with compliance
Take any test. Thou shalt not sit
With statisticians nor commit
A social science.

Thou shalt not be on friendly terms
With guys in advertising firms,
Nor speak with such
As read the Bible for its prose,
Nor, above all, make love to those
Who wash too much.

Thou shalt not live within thy means
Nor on plain water and raw greens.
If thou must choose
Between the chances, choose the odd;
Read the *New Yorker*; trust in God;
And take short views.

Phyllis McGinley

IN PRAISE OF DIVERSITY

Since this ingenious earth began
To shape itself from fire and rubble;
Since God invented man, and man
At once fell to, inventing trouble,
One virtue, one subversive grace
Has chiefly vexed the human race.

One whimsical beatitude,
Concocted for his gain and glory,
Has man most stoutly misconstrued
Of all the primal category—
Counting no blessing, but a flaw,
That Difference is the mortal law.

Adam, perhaps, while toiling late,
With life a book still strange to read in,
Saw his new world, now variegate,
And mourned, "It was not so in Eden,"
Confusing thus from the beginning
Unlikeness with original sinning.

And still the sons of Adam's clay
  Labor in person or by proxy
At altering to a common way
  The planet's holy heterodoxy.
Till now, so dogged is the breed,
Almost it seems that they succeed.

One shrill, monotonous, level note
  The human orchestra's reduced to.
Man casts his ballot, turns his coat,
  Gets born, gets buried as he used to,
Makes war, makes love—but with a kind
Of masked and universal mind.

His good has no nuances. He
  Doubts or believes with total passion.
Heretics choose for heresy
  Whatever's the prevailing fashion.
Those wearing Tolerance for a label
Call other views intolerable.

"For or Against" 's the only rule,
  Damned are the unconvinced, the floaters.
Now all must go to public school,
  March with the League of Women Voters,
Or else for safety get allied
With a unanimous Other Side.

There's white, there's black; no tint between.
  Truth is a plane that was a prism.
All's Blanshard that's not Bishop Sheen.
  All's treason that's not patriotism.
Faith, charity, hope—now all must fit
One pattern or its opposite.

Or so it seems. Yet who would dare
  Deny that nature planned it other,
When every freckled thrush can wear
  A dapple various from his brother,
When each pale snowflake in the storm
Is false to some imagined norm?

Recalling then what surely was
  The earliest bounty of Creation:
That not a blade among the grass
  But flaunts its difference with elation,
Let us devoutly take no blame
If similar does not mean the same.

And grateful for the wit to see
  Prospects through doors we cannot enter,
Ah! let us praise Diversity
  Which holds the world upon its center.
Praise *con amor'* or *furioso*
The large, the little, and the soso.

Rejoice that under cloud and star
  The planet's more than Maine or Texas.
Bless the delightful fact there are
  Twelve months, nine muses, and two sexes;
And infinite in earth's dominions
Arts, climates, wonders, and opinions.

Praise ice and ember, sand and rock,
  Tiger and dove and ends and sources;
Space travelers, and who only walk
  Like mailmen round familiar courses;
Praise vintage grapes and tavern Grappas,
And bankers and Phi Beta Kappas;

Each in its moment justified,
  Praise knowledge, theory, second guesses;
That which must wither or abide;
  Prim men, and men like wildernesses;
And men of peace and men of mayhem
And pipers and the ones who pay 'em.

Praise the disheveled, praise the sleek;
  Austerity and hearts-and-flowers;
People who turn the other cheek
  And extroverts who take cold showers;
Saints we can name a holy day for
And infidels the saints can pray for.

Praise youth for pulling things apart,
  Toppling the idols, breaking leases;
Then from the upset apple-cart
  Praise oldsters picking up the pieces.
Praise wisdom, hard to be a friend to,
And folly one can condescend to.

Praise what conforms and what is odd,
  Remembering, if the weather worsens
Along the way, that even God
  Is said to be three separate Persons.
Then upright or upon the knee,
Praise Him that by His courtesy,

For all our prejudice and pains,
Diverse His creature still remains.

Kevin Sullivan

WHAT WAS PROMISE IN THE BUD

WHAT was promise in the bud
fails of fulness in the fruit;
only half of what is good
is completely understood:
half is hidden in the root.

For all things that beauty are
open only partly—part
undiscovered in the eye,
ear or mind or memory,
escapes the heart.

WHAT WAS PROMISE IN THE BUD: By Kevin Sullivan from the poetry collection *From One Word* edited by John Gilland Brunini. Published 1950 by The Devin-Adair Co., New York.

STORIES

Henry James

THE NEXT TIME

MRS. HIGHMORE's errand this morning was odd enough to deserve commemoration: she came to ask me to write a notice of her great forthcoming work. Her great works have come forth so frequently without my assistance that I was sufficiently entitled on this occasion to open my eyes; but what really made me stare was the ground on which her request reposed, and what prompts a note of the matter is the train of memory lighted by that explanation. Poor Ray Limbert, while we talked, seemed to sit there between us: she reminded me that my acquaintance with him had begun, eighteen years ago, with her having come in, precisely as she came to-day before luncheon, to bespeak my charity for him. If she didn't know then how little my charity was worth she's at least enlightened now, and this is just what makes the drollery of her visit. As I hold up the torch to the dusky years—by which I mean as I cipher up with a pen that stumbles and stops the figured column of my reminiscences—I see that Limbert's public hour, or at least my small apprehension of it, is rounded by those two occasions. It was *finis,* with a little moralising flourish, that Mrs. Highmore seemed to trace to-day at the bottom of the page. "One of the most voluminous writers of the time," she has often repeated this sign; but never, I daresay, in spite of her professional command of appropriate emotion, with an equal sense of that mystery and that sadness of things which to people of imagination generally hover over the close of human histories. This romance at any rate is bracketed by her early and her late appeal; and when its melancholy protrusions had caught the declining light again from my half-hour's talk with her I took a private vow to recover while that light still lingers something of the delicate flush, to pick out with a brief patience the perplexing lesson.

It was wonderful to see how for herself Mrs. Highmore had already done so: she wouldn't have hesitated to announce to me what was the matter with Ralph Limbert, or at all events to give me a glimpse of the high admonition she had read in his career. There

---

could have been no better proof of the vividness of this parable, which we were really in our pleasant sympathy quite at one about, than that Mrs. Highmore of all hardened sinners, should have been converted. It wasn't indeed news to me: she impressed on me that for the last ten years she had wanted to do something artistic, something as to which she was prepared not to care a rap whether or no it should sell. She brought home to me further that it had been mainly seeing what her brother-in-law did and how he did it that had wedded her to this perversity. As *he* didn't sell, dear soul, and as several persons, of whom I was one, thought highly of that, the fancy had taken her—taken her even quite early in her prolific course—of reaching, if only once, the same heroic eminence. She yearned to be, like Limbert, but of course only once, an exquisite failure. There was something a failure was, a failure in the market, that a success somehow wasn't. A success was as prosaic as a good dinner: there was nothing more to be said about it than that you had had it. Who but vulgar people, in such a case, made gloating remarks about the courses? It was often by such vulgar people that a success was attested. It made, if you came to look at it, nothing but money; that is, it made so much that any other result showed small in comparison. A failure now could make—oh with the aid of immense talent of course, for there were failures and failures—such a reputation! She did me the honour—she had often done it—to intimate that what she meant by reputation was seeing *me* toss a flower. If it took a failure to catch a failure I was by my own admission well qualified to place the laurel. It was because she had made so much money and Mr. Highmore had taken such care of it that she could treat herself to an hour of pure glory. She perfectly remembered that as often as I had heard her heave that sigh I had been prompt with my declaration that a book sold might easily be as glorious as a book unsold. Of course she knew this, but she knew also that it was the age of trash triumphant and that she had never heard me speak of anything that had "done well" exactly as she had sometimes heard me speak of something that hadn't—with just two or three words of respect which, when I used them, seemed to convey more than they commonly stood for, seemed to hush the discussion up a little, as for the very beauty of the secret.

I may declare in regard to these allusions that, whatever I then thought of myself as a holder of the scales, I had never scrupled to laugh out at the humour of Mrs. Highmore's pursuit of quality at any price. It had never rescued her even for a day from the hard doom of popularity, and though I never gave her my word for it there was no reason at all why it should. The public *would* have her, as her husband used roguishly to remark; not indeed that, making her bargains, standing up to her publishers, and even in his higher flights to her reviewers, he ever had a glimpse of her attempted conspiracy against her genius, or rather, as I may say, against mine. It wasn't that when she tried to be what she called subtle (for wasn't Limbert subtle, and wasn't I?) her fond consumers, bless them, didn't suspect the trick nor show what they thought of it: they straightway rose on the contrary to the morsel she had hoped to hold too high, and, making but a big cheerful bite of it, wagged their great collective tail artlessly for more. It was not given to her not to please, not granted even to her best refinements to affright. I had always respected the mystery of those humiliations, but I was fully aware this morning that they were practically the reason why she had come to me. Therefore when she said with the flush of a bold joke in her kind coarse face, "What I feel is, you know, that *you* could settle me if you only would," I knew quite well what she meant. She meant that of old it had always appeared to be the fine blade (as some one had hyperbolically called it) of my particular opinion that snapped the silken thread by which Limbert's chance in the market was wont to hang. She meant that my favour was compromising, that my praise indeed was fatal. I had cultivated the queer habit of seeing nothing in certain celebrities, of seeing overmuch in an occasional nobody, and of judging from a point of view that, say what I would for it (and I had a monstrous deal to say), mostly remained perverse and obscure. Mine was in short the love that killed, for my subtlety, unlike Mrs. Highmore's, produced no tremor of the public tail. She hadn't forgotten how, toward the end, when his case was worst, Limbert would absolutely come to me with an odd shy pathos in his eyes and say: "My dear fellow, I think I've done it this time, if you'll only keep quiet." If my keeping quiet in those days was to help him to appear to have hit the usual taste, for the want of which he was starving, so now my breaking-out was to help Mrs. Highmore to appear to have hit the unusual.

The moral of all this was that I had frightened the public too much for our late friend, but that as she was not starving this was exactly what her grosser reputation required. And then, she good-naturedly and delicately intimated, there would always be, if further reasons were wanting, the price of my clever little article. I think she gave that hint with a flattering impression—spoiled child of the booksellers as she is—that the offered fee for my clever little articles is heavy. Whatever it is, at any rate, she had evidently reflected that poor Limbert's anxiety for his own profit used to involve my sacrificing mine. Any inconvenience that my obliging her might entail would not in fine be pecuniary. Her appeal, her motive, her fantastic thirst for quality and her ingenious theory of my influence struck me all as excellent comedy, and when I consented at hazard to oblige her she left me the sheets of her new novel. I could plead no inconvenience and have been looking them over; but I'm frankly appalled at what she expects of me. What's she thinking of, poor dear, and what has put it into her head that the muse of "quality" has ever sat with her for so much as three minutes? Why does she suppose that she has been "artistic"? She hasn't been anything whatever, I surmise, that she hasn't inveterately been. What does she imagine she has left out? What does she conceive she has put in? She has neither left out nor put in anything. I shall have to write her an embarrassed note. The book doesn't exist and there's nothing in life to say about it. How can there be anything but the same old faithful rush for it?

1

THIS rush had already begun when, early in the seventies, in the interest of her prospective brother-in-law, she approached me on the singular ground of the unencouraged sentiment I had entertained for her sister. Pretty pink Maud had cast me out, but I appear to have passed in the flurried little circle for a magnanimous youth. Pretty pink Maud, so lovely then, before her troubles, that dusky Jane was gratefully conscious of all she made up for, Maud Stannace, very literary too, very languishing and extremely bullied by her mother, had yielded, invidiously as it might have struck me, to Ray Limbert's suit, which Mrs. Stannace wasn't the woman to stomach. Mrs. Stannace was seldom the woman to do anything: she had been shocked at the way her children, with the grubby taint of their father's blood —he had published pale Remains or flat Conversations of *his* father —breathed the alien air of authorship. If not the daughter, nor even the niece, she was, if I'm not mistaken, the second cousin of a hundred earls and a great stickler for relationship, so that she had other views for her brilliant child, especially after her quiet one— such had been her original discreet forecast of the producer of eighty volumes—became the second wife of an ex-army-surgeon, already the father of four children. Mrs. Stannace had too manifestly dreamed it would be given to pretty pink Maud to detach some one of the noble hundred, who wouldn't be missed, from the cluster. It was because she cared only for cousins that I unlearnt the way to her house, which she had once reminded me was one of the few paths of gentility I could hope to tread. Ralph Limbert, who belonged to nobody and had done nothing—nothing even at Cambridge—had only the uncanny spell he had cast on her younger daughter to recommend him; but if her younger daughter had a spark of filial feeling she wouldn't commit the indecency of deserting for his sake a deeply dependent and intensely aggravated mother.

These things I learned from Jane Highmore, who, as if her books had been babies—they remained her only ones—had waited till after marriage to show what she could do, and now bade fair to surround her satisfied spouse (he took, for some mysterious reason, a part of the credit) with a little family, in sets of triplets, which properly handled would be the support of his declining years. The young couple, neither of whom had a penny, were now virtually engaged: the thing was subject to Ralph's putting his hand on some regular employment. People more enamoured couldn't be conceived, and Mrs. Highmore, honest woman, who had moreover a professional sense for a love-story, was eager to take them under her wing. What was wanted was a decent opening for Limbert, which it had occurred to her I might assist her to find, though indeed I had not yet found any such matter for myself. But it was well known that I was too particular, whereas poor Ralph, with the easy manners of genius, was ready to accept almost anything to which a salary, even a small one, was attached. If he could only for instance get a place on a newspaper the rest of his maintenance would come freely enough. It was true that his two novels, one of which she had brought to leave with me, had passed unperceived, and that to her, Mrs. Highmore personally, they didn't irresistibly appeal; but she could all the same assure me that I should have only to spend ten minutes with him—and our encounter must speedily take place—to receive an impression of latent power.

Our encounter took place soon after I had read the volumes Mrs. Highmore had left with me, in which I recognised an intention of a sort that I had then pretty well given up the hope of meeting. I daresay that without knowing it I had been looking out rather hungrily for an altar of sacrifice: however that may be, I submitted when I came across Ralph Limbert to one of the rarest emotions of my literary life, the sense of an activity in which I could critically rest. The rest was deep and salutary, and has not been disturbed to this hour. It has been a long large surrender, the luxury of dropped discriminations. He couldn't trouble me, whatever he did, for I practically enjoyed him as much when he was worse as when he was better. It was a case, I suppose, of natural prearrangement, in which, I hasten to add, I keep excellent company. We're a numerous band, partakers of the same repose, who sit together in the shade of the tree, by the plash of the fountain, with the glare of the desert round us and no great vice that I know of but the habit perhaps of estimating people a little too much by what they think of a certain style. If it had been laid upon these few pages, none the less, to be the history of an enthusiasm, I shouldn't have undertaken them: they're concerned with Ralph Limbert in relations to which I was a stranger or in which I participated but by sympathy. I used to talk about his work, but I seldom talk now: the brotherhood of the faith have become, like the Trappists, a silent order. If to the day of his death, after mortal disenchantments, the impression he first produced always evoked the word "ingenuous," those to whom his face was familiar can easily imagine what it must have been when it still had the light of youth. I had never seen a man of genius show so for passive, a man of experience so off his guard. At the time I made his acquaintance this freshness was all unbrushed. His foot had begun to stumble, but he was full of big intentions and of sweet Maud Stannace. Black-haired and pale, deceptively languid, he had the eyes of a clever child and the voice of a bronze bell. He saw more even than I had done in the girl he was engaged to; as time went on I became conscious that we had both, properly enough, seen rather more than there was. Our odd situation, that of the three of us, became perfectly possible from the moment I recognised how much more patience he had with her than I should have had. I was happy at not having to supply this quantity, and she, on her side, found pleasure in being able to be impertinent to me without incurring the reproach of the bad wife.

Limbert's novels appeared to have brought him no money: they had only brought him, so far as I could then make out, tributes that took up his time. These indeed brought him from several quarters some other things, and on my part at the end of three months *The Blackport Beacon*. I don't to-day remember how I obtained for him the London correspondence of the great northern organ, unless it was through somebody's having obtained it for myself. I seem to recall that I got rid of it in Limbert's interest, urging on the editor that he was much the better man. The better man was naturally the man who had pledged himself at the altar to provide for a charming woman. We were neither of us good, as the event proved, but he had the braver badness. *The Blackport Beacon* rejoiced in two London correspondents—one a supposed haunter of political circles, the other a votary of questions sketchily classified as literary. They were both expected to be lively, and what was held out to each was that it was honourably open to him to be livelier than the other. I recollect the political correspondent of that period and how the problem offered to Ray Limbert was to try to be livelier than Pat Moyle. He had not yet seemed to me so candid as when he undertook this exploit, which brought matters to a head with Mrs. Stannace, inasmuch as her opposition to the marriage now logically fell to the ground. It's all tears and laughter as I look back upon that admirable time, in which nothing was so romantic as our intense vision of the real. No fool's paradise ever rustled such a cradle-song.

It was anything but Bohemia—it was the very temple of Mrs. Grundy. We knew we were too critical, and that made us sublimely indulgent; we believed we did our duty or wanted to, and that made us free to dream. But we dreamed over the multiplication-table; we were nothing if not practical. Oh the long smokes and sudden happy thoughts, the knowing hints and banished scruples! The great thing was for Limbert to bring out his next book, which was just what his delightful engagement with the *Beacon* would give him leisure and liberty to do. The kind of work, all human and elastic and suggestive, was capital experience: in picking up things for his bi-weekly letter he would pick up life as well, he would pick up literature. The new publications, the new pictures, the new people—there would be nothing too novel for us and nobody too sacred. We introduced everything and everybody into Mrs. Stannace's drawing-room, of which I again became a familiar.

Mrs. Stannace, it was true, thought herself in strange company; she didn't particularly mind the new books, though some of them seemed queer enough, but to the new people she had decided objections. It was notorious, however, that poor Lady Robeck secretly wrote for one of the papers, and the thing had certainly, in its glance at the doings of the great world, a side that might be made attractive. But we were going to make every side attractive and we had everything to say about the sort of thing a paper like the *Beacon* would want. To give it what it would want and to give it nothing else was not doubtless an inspiring but was a perfectly respectable task, especially for a man with an appealing bride and a contentious mother-in-law. I thought Limbert's first letters as charming as the type allowed, though I won't deny that in spite of my sense of the importance of concessions I was just a trifle disconcerted at the way he had caught the tone. The tone was of course to be caught, but need it have been caught so in the act? The creature was even cleverer, as Maud Stannace said, than she had ventured to hope. Verily it was a good thing to have a dose of the wisdom of the serpent. If it had to be journalism—well, it *was* journalism. If he had to be "chatty" —well, he *was* chatty. Now and then he made a hit that—it was stupid of me—brought the blood to my face. I hated him to be so personal; but still, if it would make his fortune——! It wouldn't of course directly, but the book would, practically and in the sense to which our pure ideas of fortune were confined; and these things were all for the book. The daily balm meanwhile was in what one knew of the book—there were exquisite things to know; in the quiet monthly cheques from Blackport and in the deeper rose of Maud's little preparations, which were as dainty, on their tiny scale, as if she had been a humming-bird building a nest. When at the end of three months her betrothed had fairly settled down to his correspondence —in which Mrs. Highmore was the only person, so far as we could discover, disappointed, even she moreover being in this particular tortuous and possibly jealous; when the situation had assumed such a comfortable shape it was quite time to prepare. I published at that moment my first volume, mere faded ink to-day, a little collection of literary impressions, odds and ends of criticism contributed to a journal less remunerative but also less chatty than the *Beacon*, small ironies and ecstasies, great phrases and mistakes; and the very week it came out poor Limbert devoted half of one of his letters to it, with the happy sense this time of gratifying both himself and me as well as the Blackport breakfast-tables. I remember his saying it wasn't literature, the stuff, superficial stuff, he had to write about me; but what did that matter if it came back, as we knew, to the making for literature in the roundabout way? I had sold the thing, I recall, for ten pounds, and with the money I bought in Vigo Street a quaint piece of old silver for Maud Stannace, which I carried her with my own hand as a wedding-gift. In her mother's small drawing-room, a faded bower of photography fenced in and bedimmed by folding screens out of which sallow persons of fashion with dashing signatures looked at you from retouched eyes and little windows of plush, I was left to wait long enough to feel in the air of the house a hushed vibration of disaster. When our young lady came in she was very pale and *her* eyes too had been retouched.

"Something horrid has happened," I at once said; and having really all along but half-believed in her mother's meagre permission, I risked with an unguarded groan the introduction of Mrs. Stannace's name.

"Yes, she has made a dreadful scene; she insists on our putting it off again. We're very unhappy: poor Ray has been turned off." Her tears recommenced to flow.

I had such a good conscience that I stared. "Turned off what?"

"Why, his paper of course. The *Beacon* has given him what he calls the sack. They don't like his letters—they're not the style of thing they want."

My blankness could only deepen. "Then what style of thing, in God's name, *do* they want?"

"Something more chatty."

"More?" I cried, aghast.

"More gossipy, more personal. They want 'journalism.' They want tremendous trash."

"Why, that's just what his letters have *been*!" I broke out.

This was strong, and I caught myself up, but the girl offered me the pardon of a beautiful wan smile. "So Ray himself declares. He says he has stooped so low."

"Very well—he must stoop lower. He *must* keep the place."

"He can't!" poor Maud wailed. "He says he has tried all he knows, has been abject, has gone on all-fours, has crawled like a worm; and that if they don't like that——"

"He accepts his dismissal?" I interposed in dismay.

She gave a tragic shrug. "What other course is open to him? He wrote to them that such work as he has done is the very worst he can do for the money."

"Therefore," I pressed with a flash of hope, "they'll offer him more for worse?"

"No indeed," she answered, "they haven't even offered him to go on at a reduction. He isn't funny enough."

I reflected a moment. "But surely such a thing as his notice of my book——!"

"It was your wretched book that was the last straw! He should have treated it superficially."

"Well, if he didn't——!" I began. Then I checked myself. "*Je vous porte malheur.*"[1]

She didn't deny this; she only went on: "What on earth is he to do?"

"He's to do better than the monkeys! He's to write!"

"But what on earth are we to marry on?"

I considered once more. "You're to marry on 'The Major Key.' "

2

"THE MAJOR KEY" was the new novel, and the great thing accordingly was to finish it; a consummation for which three months of the *Beacon* had in some degree prepared the way. The action of that journal was indeed a shock, but I didn't know then the worst, didn't know that in addition to being a shock it was also a symptom. It was the first hint of the difficulty to which poor Limbert was eventually to succumb. His state was the happier, of a truth, for his not immediately seeing all it meant. Difficulty was the law of life, but one could thank heaven it was quite abnormally present in that awful connexion. There was the difficulty that inspired, the difficulty of "The Major Key" to wit, which it was after all base to sacrifice to the turning of somersaults for pennies. These convictions my friend beguiled his fresh wait by blandly entertaining: not indeed, I think, that the failure of his attempt to be chatty didn't leave him slightly humiliated. If it was bad enough to have grinned

1 [I bring you bad luck.]

through a horse-collar it was very bad indeed to have grinned in vain. Well, he would try no more grinning or at least no more horse-collars. The only success worth one's powder was success in the line of one's idiosyncrasy. Consistency was in itself distinction, and what was talent but the art of being completely whatever it was that one happened to be? One's things were characteristic or they were nothing. I look back rather fondly on our having exchanged in those days these admirable remarks and many others; on our having been very happy too, in spite of postponements and obscurities, in spite also of such occasional hauntings as could spring from our lurid glimpse of the fact that even twaddle cunningly calculated was far above people's heads. It was easy to wave away spectres by the reflexion that all one had to do was not to write for people; it was certainly not for people that Limbert wrote while he hammered at "The Major Key." The taint of literature was fatal only in a certain kind of air, which was precisely the kind against which we had now closed our window. Mrs. Stannace rose from her crumpled cushions as soon as she had obtained an adjournment, and Maud looked pale and proud, quite victorious and superior, at her having obtained nothing more. Maud behaved well, I thought, to her mother, and well indeed, for a girl who had mainly been taught to be flowerlike, to every one. What she gave Ray Limbert for her fine abundant needs made him then and ever pay for; but the gift was liberal, almost wonderful—an assertion I make even while remembering to how many clever women, early and late, his work has been dear. It was not only that the woman he was to marry was in love with him, but that—this was the strangeness—she had really seen almost better than any one what he could do. The greatest strangeness was that she didn't want him to do something different. This boundless belief was indeed the main way of her devotion; and as an act of faith it naturally asked for miracles. She was a rare wife for a poet, if she was not perhaps the best to have been picked out for a poor man.

Well, we were to have the miracles of all events and we were in a perfect state of mind to receive them. There were more of us every day, and we thought highly even of our friend's odd jobs and pot-boilers. The *Beacon* had had no successor, but he found some quiet corners and stray chances. Perpetually poking the fire and looking out of the window, he was certainly not a monster of facility, but he was, thanks perhaps to a certain method in that madness, a monster of certainty. It wasn't every one, however, who knew him for this: many editors printed him but once. He was getting a small reputation as a man it was well to have the first time; he created obscure apprehensions as to what might happen the second. He was good for making an impression, but no one seemed exactly to know what the impression was good for when made. The reason was simply that they had not seen yet "The Major Key," that fiery-hearted rose as to which we watched in private the formation of petal after petal and flame after flame. Nothing mattered but this, for it had already elicited a splendid bid, much talked about in Mrs. Highmore's drawing-room, where at this point my reminiscences grow particularly thick. *Her* roses bloomed all the year and her sociability increased with her row of prizes. We had an idea that we "met every one" there—so we naturally thought when we met each other. Between our hostess and Ray Limbert flourished the happiest relation, the only cloud on which was that her husband eyed him rather askance. When he was called clever this personage wanted to know what he had to "show"; and it was certain that he showed nothing that could compare with Jane Highmore. Mr. Highmore took his stand on accomplished work and, turning up his coat-tails, warmed his rear with a good conscience at the neat bookcase in which the generations of triplets were chronologically arranged. The harmony between his companions rested on the fact that, as I have already hinted, each would have liked so much to be the other. Limbert couldn't but have a feeling about a woman who in addition to being the best creature and her sister's backer would have made, could she have condescended, such a success with the *Beacon*. On the other hand Mrs. Highmore used freely to say: "Do you know, he'll do exactly the thing that *I* want to do? I shall never do it myself, but he'll do it instead. Yes, he'll do *my* thing, and I shall hate him for it—the wretch." Hating him was her pleasant humour, for the wretch was personally to her taste.

She prevailed on her own publisher to promise to take "The Major Key" and to engage to pay a considerable sum down, as the phrase is, on the presumption of its attracting attention. This was good news for the evening's end at Mrs. Highmore's when there were only four or five left and cigarettes ran low; but there was better to come, and I have never forgotten how, as it was I who had the good fortune to bring it, I kept it back on one of those occasions, for the sake of my effect, till only the right people remained. The right people were now more and more numerous, but this was a revelation addressed only to a choice residuum—a residuum including of course Limbert himself, with whom I haggled for another cigarette before I announced that as a consequence of an interview I had had with him that afternoon, and of a subtle argument I had brought to bear, Mrs. Highmore's pearl of publishers had agreed to put forth the new book as a serial. He was to "run" it in his magazine and he was to pay ever so much more for the privilege. I produced a fine gasp which presently found a more articulate relief, but poor Limbert's voice failed him once for all—he knew he was to walk away with me—and it was some one else who asked me what my subtle argument had been. I forget what florid description I then gave of it: to-day I've no reason not to confess that it had resided in the simple plea that the book was exquisite. I had said: "Come, my dear friend, be original; just risk it for that!" My dear friend seemed to rise to the chance, and I followed up my advantage, permitting him honestly no illusion as to the nature of the thing. He clutched interrogatively at two or three attenuations, but I dashed them aside, leaving him face to face with the formidable truth. It was just a pure gem: was he the man not to flinch? His danger appeared to have acted on him as the anaconda acts on the rabbit; fascinated and paralysed, he had been engulfed in the long pink throat. When a week before, at my request, Limbert had left with me for a day the complete manuscript, beautifully copied out by Maud Stannace, I had flushed with indignation at its having to be said of the author of such pages that he hadn't the common means to marry. I had taken the field in a great glow to repair this scandal, and it was therefore quite directly my fault if three months later, when "The Major Key" began to run, Mrs. Stannace was driven to the wall. She had made a condition of a fixed income, and at last a fixed income was achieved.

She had to recognise it, and after much prostration among the photographs she recognised it to the extent of accepting some of the convenience of it in the form of a project for a common household, to the expenses of which each party should proportionately contribute. Jane Highmore made a great point of her not being left alone, but Mrs. Stannace herself determined the proportion, which on Limbert's side at least and in spite of many other fluctuations was never altered. His income had been "fixed" with a vengeance: having painfully stooped to the comprehension of it Mrs. Stannace rested on this effort to the end and asked no further question on the subject. "The Major Key" in other words ran ever so long, and before it was half out Limbert and Maud had been married and the common household set up. These first months were probably the happiest in the family annals, with wedding-bells and budding laurels, the quiet assured course of the book and the friendly familiar note, round the corner, of Mrs. Highmore's big guns. They gave Ralph time to block in another picture as well as to let me know after a while that he had the happy prospect of becoming a father. We had at times some dispute as to whether "The Major Key" was making an impression, but our difference could only be futile so long as we were not agreed as to what an impression consisted of. Several persons wrote to the author and several others asked to be introduced to him: wasn't that an impression? One of the lively "weeklies," snapping at the deadly "monthlies," said the whole thing was "grossly inartistic"—wasn't *that*? It was somewhere else proclaimed "a wonderfully subtle character-study"—wasn't that too? The strongest effect doubtless was produced on the publisher when, in its lemon-coloured volumes, like a little dish of three custards, the book was at last served cold: he never got his money back and so far as I know has never got it back to this day. "The Major Key" was rather a great performance than a great success. It converted readers into friends and friends into lovers; it placed the author, as the phrase is—placed him all too definitely; but it shrank to obscurity in the account of sales eventually rendered. It was in short an exquisite thing, but it was scarcely a thing to have published and certainly not a thing to have married on. I heard all about the matter, for my intervention had much exposed me. Mrs. Highmore was emphatic as to the second volume's having given her ideas, and the ideas are probably to be found in some of her works, to the circulation of which they have even perhaps contributed. This was not absolutely yet the very thing she wanted to do—though on the way to it. So much, she informed me, she particularly perceived in the light of a critical study that I put forth in a little magazine; a thing the publisher in his advertisements quoted from profusely, and as to which there sprang up some absurd story that Limbert himself had written it. I remember that on my asking some one why such an idiotic thing had been said my interlocutor replied: "Oh because, you know, it's just the way he *would* have written!" My spirit sank a little perhaps as I reflected that with such analogies in our manner there might prove to be some in our fate.

It was during the next four or five years that our eyes were open to what, unless something could be done, that fate, at least on Limbert's part, might be. The thing to be done was of course to write the book, the book that would make the difference, really justify the burden he had accepted and consummately express his power. For the works that followed upon "The Major Key" he had inevitably to accept conditions the reverse of brilliant, at a time too when the strain upon his resources had begun to show sharpness. With three babies in due course, an ailing wife and a complication still greater than these, it became highly important that a man should do only his best. Whatever Limbert did was his best; so at least each time I thought and so I unfailingly said somewhere, though it was not my saying it, heaven knows, that made the desired difference. Every one else indeed said it, and there was among multiplied worries always the comfort that his position was quite assured. The two books that followed "The Major Key" did more than anything else to assure it, and Jane Highmore was always crying out: "You stand alone, dear Ray; you stand absolutely alone!" Dear Ray used to leave me in no doubt of how he felt the truth of this in feebly-attempted discussions with his bookseller. His sister-in-law gave him good advice into the bargain; she was a repository of knowing hints, of esoteric learning. These things were doubtless not the less valuable to him for bearing wholly on the question of how a reputation might be with a little gumption, as Mrs. Highmore said, "worked." Save when she occasionally bore testimony to her desire to do, as Limbert did, something some day for her own very self, I never heard her speak of the literary motive as if it were distinguishable from the pecuniary. She cocked up his hat, she pricked up his prudence for him, reminding him that as one seemed to take one's self so the silly world was ready to take one. It was a fatal mistake to be too candid even with those who were all right—not to look and to talk prosperous, not at least to pretend one had beautiful sales. To listen to her you would have thought the profession of letters a wonderful game of bluff. Wherever one's idea began it ended somehow in inspired paragraphs in the newspapers. "*I* pretend, I assure you, that you're going off like wildfire—I can at least do that for you!" she often declared, prevented as she was from doing much else by Mr. Highmore's insurmountable objection to *their* taking Mrs. Stannace.

I couldn't help regarding the presence of this latter lady in Limbert's life as the major complication: whatever he attempted it appeared given to him to achieve as best he could in the mere margin of the space in which she swung her petticoats. I may err in the belief that she practically lived on him, for though it was not in him to follow adequately Mrs. Highmore's counsel there were exasperated confessions he never made, scant domestic curtains he rattled on their rings. I may exaggerate in the retrospect his apparent anxieties, for these after all were the years when his talent was freshest and when as a writer he most laid down his line. It wasn't of Mrs. Stannace nor even as time went on of Mrs. Limbert that we mainly talked when I got at longer intervals a smokier hour in the little grey den from which we could step out, as we used to say, to the lawn. The lawn was the back-garden, and Limbert's study was behind the dining-room, with folding doors not impervious to the clatter of the children's tea. We sometimes took refuge from it in the depths—a bush and a half deep—of the shrubbery, where was a bench that gave us while we gossiped a view of Mrs. Stannace's tiara-like headdress nodding at an upper window. Within doors and without Limbert's life was overhung by an awful region that figured in his conversation, comprehensively and with unpremeditated art, as Upstairs. It was Upstairs that the thunder gathered, that Mrs. Stannace kept her accounts and her state, that Mrs. Limbert had her babies and her headaches, that the bells for ever jangled at the maids, that everything imperative in short took place—everything that he had somehow, pen in hand, to meet, to deal with and dispose of, in the little room on the garden-level. I don't think he liked to go Upstairs, but no special burst of confidence was needed to make me feel that a terrible deal of service went. It was the habit of the ladies of the Stannace family to be extremely waited on, and I've never been in a house where three maids and a nursery-governess gave such an impression of a retinue. "Oh they're so deucedly, so hereditarily fine!"—I remember how that dropped from him in some worried hour. Well, it was because Maud was so universally fine that we had both been in love with her. It was not an air, moreover, for the plaintive note: no private inconvenience could long outweigh for him the great happiness of these years—the happiness that sat with us when we talked and that made it always amusing to talk, the sense of his being on the heels of success, coming closer and closer, touching it at last, knowing that he should touch it again and hold it fast and hold it high. Of curse when we said success we didn't mean exactly what Mrs. Highmore for instance meant. He used to quote at me as a definition something from a nameless page of my own, some stray dictum to the effect that the man of his craft had achieved it when of a beautiful subject his expression was complete. Well, wasn't Limbert's in all conscience complete?

3

IT WAS bang upon this completeness all the same that the turn arrived, the turn I can't say of his fortune—for what was that?—but of his confidence, of his spirits and, what was more to the point, of his system. The whole occasion on which the first symptom flared out is before me as I write. I had met them both at dinner: they were diners who had reached the penultimate stage—the stage which in theory is a rigid selection and in practice a wan submission. It was late in the season and stronger spirits than theirs were broken; the night was close and the air of the banquet such as to restrict conversation to the refusal of dishes and consumption to the sniffing of a flower. It struck me all the more that Mrs. Limbert was flying her flag. As vivid as a page of her husband's prose, she had one of those flickers of freshness that are the miracle of her sex and one of those expensive dresses that are the miracle of ours. She had also a neat brougham in which she had offered to rescue an old lady from the possibilities of a queer cab-horse; so that when she had rolled away with her charge I proposed a walk home with her husband, whom I had overtaken on the doorstep. Before I had gone far with him he told me he had news for me—he had accepted, of all people and of all things, an "editorial position." It had come to pass that very day, from one hour to another, without time for appeals or ponderations: Mr. Bousefield, the proprietor of a "high-class monthly," making, as they said, a sudden change, had dropped on him heavily out of the blue. It was all right—there was a salary and an idea, and both of them, as such things went, rather high. We took our way slowly through the vacant streets, and in the explanations and revelations that as we lingered under lamp-posts I drew from him I found with an apprehension that I tried to gulp down a foretaste of the bitter end. He told me more than he had ever told me yet. He couldn't balance accounts—that was the trouble: his expenses were too rising a tide. It was imperative he should at last make money, and now he must work only for that. The need this last year had gathered the force of a crusher: it had rolled over him and laid him on his back. He had his scheme; this time he knew what he was about; on some good occasion, with leisure to talk it over, he would tell me the blest whole. His editorship would help him, and for the rest he must help himself. If he couldn't they would have to do something fundamental—change their life altogether, give up London, move into the country, take a house at thirty pounds a year, send their children to the Boardschool. I saw he was excited, and he admitted he was: he had waked out of a trance. He had been on the wrong tack; he had piled mistake on mistake. It was the vision of his remedy that now excited him: ineffably, grotesquely simple, it had yet come to him only within a day or two. No, he wouldn't tell me what it was; he would give me the night to guess, and if I shouldn't guess it would be because I was as big an ass as himself. However, a lone man might be an ass: he had room in his life for his ears. Ray had a burden that demanded a back: the back must therefore now be properly instituted. As to the editorship, it was simply heaven-sent, being not at all another case of *The Blackport Beacon* but a case of the very opposite. The proprietor, the great Mr. Bousefield, had approached him precisely because his name, which was to be on the cover, *didn't* represent the chatty. The whole thing was to be—oh on fiddling little lines of course—a protest against the chatty. Bousefield wanted him to be himself; it was for himself Bousefield had picked him out. Wasn't it beautiful and brave of Bousefield? He wanted literature, he saw the great reaction coming, the way the cat was going to jump. "Where will you get literature?" I woefully asked; to which he replied with a laugh that what he had to get was not literature but only what Bousefield would take for it.

In that single phrase I without more ado discovered his famous remedy. What was before him for the future was not to do his work but to do what somebody else would take for it. I had the question out with him on the next opportunity, and of all the lively discussions into which we had been destined to drift it lingers in my mind as the liveliest. This was not, I hasten to add, because I disputed his conclusions: it was an effect of the very force with which, when I had fathomed his wretched premises, I took them to my soul. It was very well to talk with Jane Highmore about his standing alone: the eminent relief of this position had brought him to the verge of ruin. Several persons admired his books—nothing was less contestable; but they appeared to have a mortal objection to acquiring them by subscription or by purchase; they begged or borrowed or stole, they delegated one of the party perhaps to commit the volumes to memory and repeat them, like the bards of old, to listening multitudes. Some ingenious theory was required at any rate to account for the inexorable limits of his circulation. It wasn't a thing for five people to live on; therefore either the objects circulated must change their nature or the organisms to be nourished must. The former change was perhaps the easier to consider first. Limbert considered it with sovereign ingenuity from that time on, and the ingenuity, greater even than any I had yet had occasion to admire in him, made the whole next stage of his career rich in curiosity and suspense.

"I've been butting my skull against a wall," he had said in those hours of confidence; "and, to be as sublime a blockhead, if you'll allow me the word, you, my dear fellow, have kept sounding the charge. We've sat prating here of 'success,' heaven help us, like chanting monks in a cloister, hugging the sweet delusion that it lies somewhere in the work itself, in the expression, as you said, of one's subject or the intensification, as somebody else somewhere says, of one's note. One has been going on in short as if the only thing to do were to accept the law of one's talent, and thinking that if certain consequences didn't follow it was only because one wasn't logical enough. My disaster has served me right—I mean for using that ignoble word at all. It's a mere distributor's, a mere hawker's word. What *is* 'success' anyhow? When a book's right it's right—shame to it surely if it isn't. When it sells it sells—it brings money like potatoes or beer. If there's dishonour one way and inconvenience the other, it certainly is comfortable, but it as certainly isn't glorious, to have escaped them. People of delicacy don't brag either about their probity or about their luck. Success be hanged!—I want to sell. It's a question of life and death. I must study the way. I've studied too much the other way—I know the other way now, every inch of it. I must cultivate the market—it's a science like another. I must go in for an infernal cunning. It will be very amusing, I foresee that; I shall lead a dashing life and drive a roaring trade. I haven't been obvious—I must *be* obvious. I haven't been popular—I must *be* popular. It's another art—or perhaps it isn't an art at all. It's something else; one must find out *what* it is. Is it something awfully queer?—you blush!—something barely decent? All the greater incentive to curiosity! Curiosity's an immense motive, we shall have tremendous sport. 'They all do it'—doesn't somebody sing at a music hall?—it's only a question of how. Of course I've everything to unlearn; but what's life, as Jane Highmore says, but a lesson? I must get all I can, all she can give me, from Jane. She can't explain herself much; she's all intuition; her processes are obscure; it's the spirit that swoops down and catches her up. But I must study her reverently in her works. Yes, you've defied me before, but now my loins are girded: I declare I'll *read* one of them—I really will; I'll put it through if I perish!"

I won't pretend he made all these remarks at once; but there wasn't one that he didn't make at one time or another, for suggestion and occasion were plentiful enough, his life being now given up altogether to his new necessity. It wasn't a question of his having or not having, as they say, my intellectual sympathy: the brute force of the pressure left no room for judgement; it made all emotion a mere recourse to the spyglass. I watched him as I should have watched a long race or a long chase, irresistibly siding with him, yet much occupied with the calculation of odds. I confess indeed that my heart, for the endless stretch he covered so fast, was often in my throat. I saw him peg away over the sun-dappled plain, I saw him double and wind and gain and lose; and all the while I secretly entertained a conviction. I wanted him to feed his many mouths, but at the bottom of all things was my sense that if he should succeed in doing so in this particular way I should think less well of him. Now I had an absolute terror of that. Meanwhile so far as I could I backed him up, I helped him: all the more that I had warned him immensely at first, smiled with a compassion it was very good of him not to have found exasperating over the complacency of his assumption that a man could escape from himself. Ray Limbert at all events would certainly never escape; but one could make believe for him, make believe very hard—an undertaking in which at first Mr. Bousefield was visibly a blessing. Ralph was delightful on the business of this being at last my chance too—my chance, so miraculously vouchsafed, to appear with a certain luxuriance. He didn't care how often he printed me, for wasn't it exactly in my direction Mr. Bousefield held the cat was going to jump? This was the least he could do for me. I might write on anything I liked—on anything at least but Mr. Limbert's second manner. He didn't wish attention strikingly called to his second manner; it was to operate insidiously;

people were to be left to believe they had discovered it long ago. "Ralph Limbert? Why, when did we ever live without him?"—that's what he wanted them to say. Besides, they hated manners—let sleeping dogs lie. His understanding with Mr. Bousefield—on which he had had not at all to insist; it was the excellent man who insisted—was that he should run one of his beautiful stories in the magazine. As to the beauty of his story, however, Limbert was going to be less admirably straight than as to the beauty of everything else. That was another reason why I mustn't write about his new line: Mr. Bousefield was not to be too definitely warned that such a periodical was exposed to prostitution. By the time he should find it out for himself the public—*le gros public*—would have bitten, and then perhaps he would be conciliated and forgive. Everything else would be literary in short, and above all *I* would be; only Ralph Limbert wouldn't—he'd chuck up the whole thing sooner. He'd be vulgar, he'd be vile, he'd be abject: he'd be elaborately what he hadn't been before.

I duly noticed that he had more trouble in making "everything else" literary than he had at first allowed for; but this was largely counteracted by the ease with which he was able to obtain that his mark shouldn't be overshot. He had taken well to heart the old lesson of the *Beacon;* he remembered that he was after all there to keep his contributors down much rather than to keep them up. I thought at times that he kept them down a trifle too far, but he assured me that I needn't be nervous: he had his limit—his limit was inexorable. He would reserve pure vulgarity for his serial, over which he was sweating blood and water; elsewhere it should be qualified by the prime qualifications, the mediocrity that attaches, that endears. Bousefield, he allowed, was proud, was difficult, nothing was really good enough for him but the middling good: he himself, however, was prepared for adverse comment, resolute for his noble course. Hadn't Limbert, moreover, in the event of a charge of laxity from headquarters the great strength of being able to point to my contributions? Therefore I must let myself go, I must abound in my peculiar sense, I must be a resource in case of accidents. Limbert's vision of accidents hovered mainly over the sudden awakening of Mr. Bousefield to the stuff that in the department of fiction his editor was palming off. He would then have to confess in all humility that this was not what the old boy wanted, but I should be all the more there as a salutary specimen. I would cross the scent with something showily impossible, splendidly unpopular—I must be sure to have something on hand. I always had plenty on hand—poor Limbert needn't have worried: the magazine was forearmed each month by my care with a retort to any possible accusation of trifling with

Mr. Bousefield's standard. He had admitted to Limbert, after much consideration indeed, that he was prepared to be perfectly human; but he had added that he was not prepared for an abuse of this admission. The thing in the world I think I least felt myself was an abuse, even though—as I had never mentioned to my friendly editor—I too had my project for a bigger reverberation. I daresay I trusted mine more than I trusted Limbert's; at all events the golden mean in which, for the special case, he saw his salvation as an editor was something I should be most sure of were I to exhibit it myself. I exhibited it month after month in the form of a monstrous levity, only praying heaven that my editor might now not tell me, as he had so often told me, that my result was awfully good. I knew what that would signify—it would signify, sketchily speaking, disaster. What he did tell me heartily was that it was just what his game required; his new line had brought with it an earnest assumption—earnest save when we privately laughed about it—of the locutions proper to real bold enterprise. If I tried to keep him in the dark even as he kept Mr. Bousefield there was nothing to show that I wasn't tolerably successful: each case therefore presented a promising analogy for the other. He never noticed my descent, and it was accordingly possible Mr. Bousefield would never notice his. But would nobody notice it at all?—that was a question that added a prospective zest to one's possession of a critical sense. So much depended upon it that I was rather relieved than otherwise not to know the answer too soon. I waited in fact a year—the trial-year for which Limbert had cannily engaged with Mr. Bousefield; the year as to which, through the same sharpened shrewdness, it had been conveyed in the agreement between them that Mr. Bousefield wasn't to intermeddle. It had been Limbert's general prayer that we would during this period let him quite alone. His terror of my direct rays was a droll dreadful force that always operated: he explained it by the fact that I understood him too well, expressed too much of his intention, saved him too little from himself. The less he was saved the more he didn't sell: I positively interpreted, and that was simply fatal.

I held my breath accordingly; I did more—I closed my eyes, I guarded my treacherous ears. He induced several of us to do that—of such devotions we were capable—so that, not even glancing at the thing from month to month and having nothing but his shamed anxious silence to go by, I participated only vaguely in the little hum that surrounded his act of sacrifice. It was blown about the town that the public would be surprised; it was hinted, it was printed, that he was making a desperate bid. His new work was spoken of as "more calculated for general acceptance." These tidings produced in some quarters much reprobation, and nowhere more, I think, than on the part of certain persons who had never read a word of him, or assuredly had never spent a shilling on him, and who hung for hours over the other attractions of the newspaper that announced his abasement. So much asperity cheered me a little—seemed to signify that he might really be doing something. On the other hand, I had a distinct alarm; some one sent me for some alien reason an American journal—containing frankly more than that source of affliction—in which was quoted a passage from our friend's last instalment. The passage—I couldn't for my life help reading it—was simply superb. Ah he *would* have to move to the country if that was the worst he could do! It gave me a pang to see how little after all he had improved since the days of his competition with Pat Moyle. There was nothing in the passage quoted in the American paper that Pat would for a moment have owned.

During the last weeks, as the opportunity of reading the complete thing drew near, one's suspense was barely endurable, and I shall never forget the July evening on which I put it to rout. Coming home to dinner I found the two volumes on my table, and I sat up with them half the night, dazed, bewildered, rubbing my eyes, wondering at the monstrous joke. *Was* it a monstrous joke, his second manner—was *this* the new line, the desperate bid, the scheme for more general acceptance and the remedy for material failure? Had he made a fool of all his following, or had he most injuriously made a still bigger fool of himself? Obvious?—where the deuce was it obvious? Popular?—how on earth could it be popular? The thing was charming with all his charm and powerful with all his power: it was an unscrupulous, an unsparing, a shameless merciless masterpiece. It was, no doubt, like the old letters to the *Beacon*, the worst he could do; but the perversity of the effort, even though heroic, had been frustrated by the purity of the gift. Under what illusion had he laboured, with what wavering treacherous compass had he steered? His honour was inviolable, his measurements were all wrong. I was thrilled with the whole impression and with all that came crowding in its train. It was too grand a collapse—it was too hideous a triumph; I exulted almost with tears—I lamented with a strange delight. Indeed as the short night waned and, threshing about in my emotion, I fidgeted to my high-perched window for a glimpse of the summer dawn, I became at last aware that I was staring at it out of eyes that had compassionately and admiringly filled. The eastern sky, over the London house tops, had a wonderful tragic crimson. That was the colour of his magnificent mistake.

4

IF SOMETHING less had depended on my impression I daresay I should have communicated it as soon as I had swallowed my breakfast; but the case was so embarrassing that I spent the first half of the day in reconsidering it, dipping into the book again, almost feverishly turning its leaves and trying to extract from them, for my friend's benefit, some symptom of reassurance, some ground for felicitation. This rash challenge had consequences merely dreadful; the wretched volumes, imperturbable and impeccable, with their shyer secrets and their second line of defence, were like a beautiful woman more denuded or a great symphony on a new hearing. There was something quite sinister in the way they stood up to me. I couldn't, however, be dumb—that was to give the wrong tinge to my disappointment; so that later in the afternoon, taking my courage in both hands, I approached with a vain tortuosity poor Limbert's door. A smart victoria waited before it, in which, from the bottom of the street, I saw that a lady who had apparently just issued from the house was settling herself. I recognised Jane Highmore and instantly paused till she should drive down to me. She soon met me halfway and directly she saw me stopped her carriage in agitation. This was a relief—it postponed a moment the sight of that pale fine face of our friend's fronting me for the right verdict. I gathered from the flushed eagerness with which Mrs. Highmore asked me if I had heard the news that a verdict of some sort had already been rendered.

"What news?—about the book?"

"About that horrid magazine. They're shockingly upset. He has lost his position—he has had a fearful flare-up with Mr. Bousefield."

I stood there blank, but not unaware in my blankness of how history repeats itself. There came to me across the years Maud's announcement of their ejection from the *Beacon,* and dimly, confusedly, the same explanation was in the air. This time, however, I had been on my guard; I had had my suspicion. "He has made it too flippant?" I found breath after an instant to inquire.

Mrs. Highmore's vacuity exceeded my own. "Too 'flippant'? He had made it too oracular; Mr. Bousefield says he has killed it." Then perceiving my stupefaction: "Don't you know what has happened?" she pursued; "isn't it because in his trouble, poor love, he has sent for you that you've come? You've heard nothing at all? Then you had better know before you see them. Get in here with me—I'll take you a turn and tell you." We were close to the Park, the Regent's, and when with extreme alacrity I had placed myself beside her and the carriage had begun to enter it she went on: "It was what

I feared, you know. It reeked with culture. He keyed it up too high."

I felt myself sinking in the general collapse. "What are you talking about?"

"Why, about that beastly magazine. They're all on the streets. I shall have to take mamma."

I pulled myself together. "What on earth, then, did Bousefield want? He said he wanted intellectual power."

"Yes, but Ray overdid it."

"Why, Bousefield said it was a thing he *couldn't* overdo."

"Well, Ray managed: he took Mr. Bousefield too literally. It appears the thing has been doing dreadfully, but the proprietor couldn't say anything, because he had covenanted to leave the editor quite free. He describes himself as having stood there in a fever and seen his ship go down. A day or two ago the year was up, so he could at last break out. Maud says he did break out quite fearfully—he came to the house and let poor Ray have it. Ray gave it him back—he reminded him of his own idea of the way the cat was going to jump."

I gasped with dismay. "Has Bousefield abandoned that idea? *Isn't* the cat going to jump?"

Mrs. Highmore hesitated. "It appears she doesn't seem in a hurry. Ray at any rate has jumped too far ahead of her. He should have temporised a little, Mr. Bousefield says; but I'm beginning to think, you know," said my companion, "that Ray *can't* temporise." Fresh from my emotion of the previous twenty-four hours I was scarcely in a position to disagree with her. "He published too much pure thought."

"Pure thought?" I cried. "Why, it struck me so often—certainly in a due proportion of cases—as pure drivel!"

"Oh you're more keyed up than he! Mr. Bousefield says that of course he wanted things that were suggestive and clever, things that he could point to with pride. But he contends that Ray didn't allow for human weakness. He gave everything in too stiff doses."

Sensibly, I fear, to my neighbour, I winced at her words—I felt a prick that made me meditate. Then I said: "Is that, by chance, the way he gave *me*?" Mrs. Highmore remained silent so long that I had somehow the sense of a fresh pang; and after a minute, turning in my seat, I laid my hand on her arm, fixed my eyes on her face, and pursued pressingly: "Do you suppose it to be to my 'Occasional Remarks' that Mr. Bousefield refers?"

At last she met my look. "Can you bear to hear it?"

"I think I can bear anything now."

"Well then, it was really what I wanted to give you an inkling of. It's largely over you that they've quarrelled. Mr. Bousefield wants him to chuck you."

I grabbed her arm again. "And our friend *won't?*"

"He seems to cling to you. Mr. Bousefield says no magazine can afford you."

I gave a laugh that agitated the very coachman. "Why, my dear lady, has he any idea of my price?"

"It isn't your price—he says you're dear at any price: you do so much to sink the ship. Your 'Remarks' are called 'Occasional,' but nothing could be more deadly regular; you're there month after month and you're never anywhere else. And you supply no public want."

"I supply the most delicious irony."

"So Ray appears to have declared. Mr. Bousefield says that's not in the least a public want. No one can make out what you're talking about and no one would care if he could. I'm only quoting *him*, mind."

"Quote, quote—if Ray holds out. I think I must leave you now, please: I must rush back to express to him what I feel."

"I'll drive you to his door. That isn't all," said Mrs. Highmore. And on the way, when the carriage had turned, she communicated the rest. "Mr. Bousefield really arrived with an ultimatum: it had the form of something or other by Minnie Meadows."

"Minnie Meadows?" I was stupefied.

"The new lady-humourist every one seems talking about. It's the first of a series of screaming sketches for which poor Ray was to find a place."

"Is *that* Mr. Bousefield's idea of literature?"

"No, but he says it's the public's, and you've got to take *some* account of the public. *Aux grands maux les grands remèdes.*[2] They had a tremendous lot of ground to make up, and no one would make it up like Minnie. She would be the best concession they could make to human weakness; she would strike at least this note of showing that it wasn't going to be quite all—well, all *you*. Now Ray draws the line at Minnie; he won't stoop to Minnie; he declines to touch, to look at Minnie. When Mr. Bousefield—rather imperiously, I believe—made Minnie a *sine qua non*[3] of his retention of his post he said something rather violent, told him to go to some unmentionable place and take Minnie with him. That of course put the fat on the fire. They had really a considerable scene."

"So had he with the *Beacon* man," I musingly replied. "Poor dear, he seems born for considerable scenes; It's on Minnie, then, they've really split?" Mrs. Highmore exhaled her despair in a sound which I took for an assent, and when we had rolled a little further I rather inconsequently and to her visible surprise broke out of my

2 [For great faults, great remedies.]

3 [Necessity.]

reverie. "It will never do in the world—he *must* stoop to Minnie!"

"It's too late—and what I've told you still isn't all. Mr. Bousefield raises another objection."

"What other, pray?"

"Can't you guess?"

I wondered. "No more of Ray's fiction?"

"Not a line. That's something else no magazine can stand. Now that his novel has run its course Mr. Bousefield's distinctly disappointed."

I fairly bounded in my place. "Then it may do?"

Mrs. Highmore looked bewildered. "Why so, if he finds it too dull?"

"Dull? Ralph Limbert? He's as fine as the spray of a lawn-irrigator."

"It comes to the same thing, when your lawn's as coarse as a turnip field. Mr. Bousefield had counted on something that *would* do, something that would have a wider acceptance. Ray says he wants gutter-pipes and slop-buckets." I collapsed again; my flicker of elation dropped to a throb of quieter comfort; and after a moment's silence I asked my neighbour if she had herself read the work our friend had just put forth. "No," she returned, "I gave him my word at the beginning, on his urgent request, that I wouldn't."

"Not even as a book?"

"He begged me never to look at it at all. He said he was trying a low experiment. Of course I knew what he meant and I entreated him to let me just for curiosity take a peep. But he was firm, he declared he couldn't bear the thought that a woman like me should see him in the depths."

"He's only, thank God, in the depths of distress," I answered. "His experiment's nothing worse than a failure."

"Then Bousefield *is* right—his circulation won't budge?"

"It won't move one, as they say in Fleet Street. The book has extraordinary beauty."

"Poor duck—after trying so hard!" Jane Highmore sighed with real tenderness. "What *will*, then, become of them?"

I was silent an instant. "You must take your mother."

She was silent too. "I must speak of it to Cecil!" she presently said. Cecil is Mr. Highmore, who then entertained, I knew, strong views on the inadjustability of circumstances in general to the idiosyncrasies of Mrs. Stannace. He held it supremely happy that in an important relation she should have met her match. Her match was Ray Limbert—not much of a writer but a practical man. "The dear things still think, you know," my companion continued, "that the book will be the beginning of their fortune. Their illusion, if you're right, will be rudely dispelled."

"That's what makes me dread to face them. I've just spent with his volumes an unforgettable night. His illusion has lasted because so many of us have been pledged till this moment to turn our faces the other way. We haven't known the truth and have therefore had nothing to say. Now that we do know it indeed we have practically quite as little. I hang back from the threshold. How can I follow up with a burst of enthusiasm such a catastrophe as Mr. Bousefield's visit?"

As I turned uneasily about my neighbour more comfortably snuggled. "Well, I'm glad, then, I haven't read him and have nothing unpleasant to say!" We had come back to Limbert's door, and I made the coachman stop short of it. "But he'll try again, with that determination of his: he'll build his hopes on the next time."

"On what else has he built them from the very first? It's never the present for him that bears the fruit; that's always postponed and for somebody else: there has always to be another try. I admit that his idea of a 'new line' has made him try harder than ever. It makes no difference," I brooded, still timorously lingering; "his achievement of his necessity, his hope of a market, will continue to attach itself to the future. But the next time will disappoint him as each last time has done—and then the next and the next and the next!"

I found myself seeing it all with a clearness almost inspired: it evidently cast a chill on Mrs. Highmore. "Then what on earth will become of him?" she plaintively repeated.

"I don't think I particularly care what may become of *him*," I returned with a conscious reckless increase of my exaltation; "I feel it almost enough to be concerned with what may become of one's enjoyment of him. I don't know in short what will become of his circulation; I'm only quite at my ease as to what will become of his work. It will simply keep all its quality. He'll try again for the common with what he'll believe to be a still more infernal cunning, and again the common will fatally elude him, for his infernal cunning will have been only his genius in an ineffectual disguise." We sat drawn up by the pavement, facing poor Limbert's future as I saw it. It relieved me in a manner to know the worst, and I prophesied with an assurance which as I look back upon it strikes me as rather remarkable. "*Que voulez-vous?*"[4] I went on; "you can't make a sow's ear of a silk purse! It's grievous indeed if you like—there are people who can't be vulgar for trying. *He* can't—it wouldn't come off, I promise you, even once. It takes more than trying—it comes by

4 [What do you want?]

grace. It happens not to be given to Limbert to fall. He belongs to the heights—he breathes there, he lives there, and it's accordingly to the heights I must ascend," I said as I took leave of my conductress, "to carry him this wretched news from where *we* move!"

5

A FEW months were sufficient to show how right I had been about his circulation. It didn't move one, as I had said; it stopped short in the same place, fell off in a sheer descent, like some precipice gaped up at by tourists. The public, in other words, drew the line for him as sharply as he had drawn it for Minnie Meadows. Minnie has skipped with a flouncing caper over his line, however; whereas the mark traced by a lustier cudgel has been a barrier insurmountable to Limbert. Those next times I had spoken of to Jane Highmore, I see them simplified by retrocession. Again and again he made his desperate bid—again and again he tried to. His rupture with Mr. Bousefield caused him in professional circles, I fear, to be thought impracticable, and I'm perfectly aware, to speak candidly, that no sordid advantage ever accrued to him from such public patronage of my performances as he had occasionally been in a position to offer. I reflect for my comfort that any injury I may have done him by untimely application of a faculty of analysis which could point to no converts gained by honourable exercise was at least equalled by the injury he did himself. More than once, as I have hinted, I held my tongue at his request, but my frequent plea that such favours weren't politic never found him, when in other connexions there was an opportunity to give me a lift, anything but indifferent to the danger of the association. He let them have me, in a word, whenever he could; sometimes in periodicals in which he had credit, sometimes only at dinner. He talked about me when he couldn't get me in, but it was always part of the bargain that I shouldn't make him a topic. "How can I successfully serve you if you do?" he used to ask: he was more afraid than I thought he ought to have been of the charge of tit for tat. I didn't care, for I never could distinguish tat from tit; but, as I've intimated, I dropped into silence really more than anything else because there was a certain fascinated observation of his course which was quite testimony enough and to which in this huddled conclusion of it he practically reduced me.

I see it all foreshortened, his wonderful remainder—see it from the end backward, with the direction widening toward me as if on a level with the eye. The migration to the country promised him at first great things—smaller expenses, larger leisure, conditions eminently conducive on each occasion to the possible triumph of the next time. Mrs. Stannace, who altogether disapproved of it, gave as one of her reasons that her son-in-law, living mainly in a village on the edge of a goose-green, would be deprived of that contact with the great world which was indispensable to the painter of manners. She had the showiest arguments for keeping him in touch, as she called it, with good society; wishing to know with some force where, from the moment he ceased to represent it from observation, the novelist could be said to be. In London fortunately a clever man was just a clever man; there were charming houses in which a person of Ray's undoubted ability, even though without the knack of making the best use of it, could always be sure of a quiet corner for watching decorously the social kaleidoscope. But the kaleidoscope of the goose-green, what in the world was that, and what such delusive thrift as drives about the land (with a fearful account for flys from the inn) to leave cards on the country magnates? This solicitude for Limbert's subject-matter was the specious colour with which, deeply determined not to affront mere tolerance in a cottage, Mrs. Stannace overlaid her indisposition to place herself under the heel of Cecil Highmore. She knew that he ruled Upstairs as well as down, and she clung to the fable of the association of interests in the north of London. The Highmores had a better address, they lived now in Stanhope Gardens; but Cecil was fearfully artful—he wouldn't hear of an association of interests nor treat with his mother-in-law save as a visitor. She didn't like false positions; but on the other hand she didn't like the sacrifice of everything she was accustomed to. Her universe at all events was a universe of card-leavings and charming houses, and it was fortunate that she couldn't, Upstairs, catch the sound of the doom to which, in his little grey den, describing to me his diplomacy, Limbert consigned alike the country magnates and the opportunities of London. Despoiled of every guarantee she went to Stanhope Gardens like a mere maidservant, with restrictions on her very luggage, while during the year that followed this upheaval Limbert, strolling with me on the goose-green, to which I often ran down, played extravagantly over the theme that with what he was now going in for it was a positive comfort not to have the social kaleidoscope. With a cold-blooded trick in view, what had life or manners or the best society or flys from the inn to say to the question? It was as good a place as another to play his new game. He had found a quieter corner than any corner of the great world, and a damp old house at tenpence a year, which, beside leaving him all his margin to educate his children, would allow of the supreme luxury of his frankly presenting himself as a poor man. This was a convenience that *ces dames*,[5] as he called them, had never yet fully permitted him.

5 [These ladies.]

It rankled in me at first to see his reward so meagre, his conquest so mean; but the simplification effected had a charm that I finally felt: it was a forcing-house for the three or four other fine miscarriages to which his scheme was evidently condemned. I limited him to three or four, having had my sharp impression, in spite of the perpetual broad joke of the thing, that a spring had really broken in him on the occasion of that deeply disconcerting sequel to the episode of his editorship. He never lost his sense of the grotesque want, in the difference made, of adequate relation to the effort that had been the intensest of his life. He had carried from that moment a charge of shot, and it slowly worked its way to a vital part. As he met his embarrassments each year with his punctual false remedy I wondered periodically where he found the energy to return to the attack. He did it every time with a rage more blanched, but it was clear to me that the tension must finally snap the cord. We got again and again the irrepressible work of art, but what did *he* get, poor man, who wanted something so different? There were likewise odder questions than this in the matter, phenomena more curious and mysteries more puzzling, which often for sympathy, if not for illumination, I intimately discussed with Mrs. Limbert. She had her burdens, dear lady: after the removal from London and a considerable interval she twice again became a mother. Mrs. Stannace too, in a more restricted sense, exhibited afresh, in relation to the home she had abandoned, the same exemplary character. In her poverty of guarantees at Stanhope Gardens there had been least of all, it appeared, a proviso that she shouldn't resentfully revert again from Goneril to Regan. She came down to the goose-green like Lear himself, with fewer knights, or at least baronets, and the joint household was at last patched up. It fell to pieces and was put together on various occasions before Ray Limbert died. He was ridden to the end by the superstition that he had broken up Mrs. Stannace's original home on pretences that had proved hollow, and that if he hadn't given Maud what she might have had he could at least give her back her mother. I was always sure that a sense of the compensations he owed was half the motive of the dogged pride with which he tried to wake up the libraries. I believed Mrs. Stannace still had money, though she pretended that, called upon at every turn to retrieve deficits, she had long since poured it into the general fund. This conviction haunted me; I suspected her of secret hoards, and I said to myself that she couldn't be so infamous as not some day on her death-bed to leave everything to her less opulent daughter. My compassion for the Limberts led me to hover perhaps indiscreetly round that closing scene, to dream of some happy time when such an accession of means would make up a little for their present penury.

This, however, was crude comfort, as in the first place I had nothing definite to go by and in the second I held it for more and more indicated that Ray wouldn't outlive her. I never ventured to sound him as to what in this particular he hoped or feared, for after the crisis marked by his leaving London I had new scruples about suffering him to be reminded of where he fell short. The poor man was in truth humiliated, and there were things as to which that kept us both silent. In proportion as he tried more fiercely for the market the old plaintive arithmetic, fertile in jokes, dropped from our conversation. We joked immensely still about the process, but our treatment of the results became sparing and superficial. He talked as much as ever, with monstrous arts and borrowed hints, of the traps he kept setting, but we all agreed to take merely for granted that the animal was caught. This propriety had really dawned upon me the day that, after Mr. Bousefield's visit, Mrs. Highmore put me down at his door. Mr. Bousefield at that juncture had been served up to me anew, but after we had disposed of him we came to the book, which I was obliged to confess I had already rushed through. It was from this moment—the moment at which my terrible impression of it had blinked out at his anxious query—that the image of his scared face was to abide with me. I couldn't attentuate then—the cat was out of the bag; but later, each of the next times, I did, I acknowledge, attentuate. We all did religiously, so far as was possible; we cast ingenious ambiguities over the strong places, the beauties that betrayed him most, and found ourselves in the queer position of admirers banded to mislead a confiding artist. If we stifled our cheers however, if we dissimulated our joy, our fond hypocrisy accomplished little, for Limbert's finger was on a pulse that told a plainer story. It was a satisfaction to have secured a greater freedom with his wife, who at last, much to her honour, entered into the conspiracy and whose sense of responsibility was flattered by the frequency of our united appeal to her for some answer to the marvellous riddle. We had all turned it over till we were tired of it, threshing out the question of why the note he strained every chord to pitch for common ears should invariably insist on addressing itself to the angels. Being, as it were, ourselves the angels, we had only a limited quarrel in each case with the event; but its inconsequent character, given the forces set in motion, was peculiarly baffling. It was like an interminable sum that wouldn't come straight; nobody had the time to handle so many figures. Limbert gathered, to make his pudding, dry bones and dead husks; how, then, was one to formulate the law that made the dish prove a feast? What was the cerebral treachery that defied his own vigilance? There was some obscure interference of taste, some obsession of the exquisite. All one could say was that genius was a fatal disturber or that the unhappy man had no effectual *flair*. When he went abroad to gather garlic he came home with heliotrope.

I hasten to add that if Mrs. Limbert was not directly illuminating she was yet rich in anecdote and example, having found a refuge from mystification exactly where the rest of us had found it, in a more devoted embrace and the sense of a finer glory. Her disappointments and eventually her privations had been many, her discipline severe; but she had ended by accepting the long grind of life and was now quite willing to take her turn at the mill. She was essentially one of us—she always understood. Touching and admirable at the last, when through the unmistakable change in Limbert's health her troubles were thickest, was the spectacle of the particular pride that she wouldn't have exchanged for prosperity. She had said to me once—only once, in a gloomy hour of London days when things were not going at all—that one really had to think him a very great man, since if one didn't one would be rather ashamed of him. She had distinctly felt it at first—and in a very tender place—that almost every one passed him on the road; but I believe that in these final years she would almost have been ashamed of him if he had suddenly gone into editions. It's certain indeed that her complacency was not subjected to that shock. She would have liked the money immensely, but she would have missed something she had taught herself to regard as rather rare. There's another remark I remember her making, a remark to the effect that of course if she could have chosen she would have liked him to be Shakespeare or Scott, but that failing this she was very glad he wasn't—well, she named the two gentlemen, but I won't. I daresay she sometimes laughed out to escape an alternative. She contributed passionately to the capture of the second manner, foraging for him further afield than he could conveniently go, gleaning in the barest stubble, picking up shreds to build the nest and in particular, in the study of the great secret of how, as we always said, they all did it, laying waste of the circulating libraries. If Limbert had a weakness he rather broke down in his reading. It was fortunately not till after the appearance of "The Hidden Heart" that he broke down in everything else. He had had rheumatic fever in the spring, when the book was but half-finished, and this ordeal had in addition to interrupting his work enfeebled his powers of resistance and greatly reduced his vitality. He recovered from the fever and was able to take up the book again, but the organ of life was pronounced ominously weak and it was enjoined upon him with some sharpness that he should lend himself to no worries. It might have struck me as on the cards that his worries would now be surmountable, for when he began to mend he expressed to me a conviction almost contagious that he had never yet made so adroit a bid as in the idea of "The Hidden Heart." It is grimly droll to reflect that this superb little composition, the shortest of his novels but perhaps the loveliest, was planned from the first as an "adventure-story" on approved lines. It was the way they all did the adventure-story that he had tried dauntlessly to emulate. I wonder how many readers ever divined to which of their book-shelves "The Hidden Heart" was so exclusively addressed. High medical advice early in the summer had been quite viciously clear as to the inconvenience that might ensue to him should he neglect to spend the winter in Egypt. He was not a man to neglect anything; but Egypt seemed to us all then as unattainable as a second edition. He finished "The Hidden Heart" with the energy of apprehension and desire, for if the book should happen to do what "books of that class," as the publisher said, sometimes did, he might well have a fund to draw on. As soon as I read the fine deep thing I knew, as I had known in each case before, exactly how well it would do. Poor Limbert in this long business always figured to me an undiscourageable parent to whom only girls kept being born. A bouncing boy, a son and heir, was devoutly prayed for and almanacks and old wives consulted; but the spell was inveterate, incurable, and "The Hidden Heart" proved, so to speak, but another female child. When the winter arrived accordingly Egypt was out of the question. Jane Highmore, to my knowledge, wanted to lend him money, and there were even greater devotees who did their best to induce him to lean on them. There was so marked a "movement" among his friends that a very considerable sum would have been at his disposal; but his stiffness was invincible: it had its root, I think, in his sense, on his own side, of sacrifices already made. He had sacrificed honour and pride, and he had sacrificed them precisely to the question of money. He would evidently, should he be able to go on, have to continue to sacrifice them, but it must be all in the way to which he had now, as he considered, hardened himself. He had spent years in plotting for favour, and since on favour he must live it could only be as a bargain and a price.

He got through the early part of the season better than we feared, and I went down in great elation to spend Christmas on the goose-green. He told me late on Christmas Eve, after our simple domestic revels had sunk to rest and we sat together by the fire, how he had been visited the night before in wakeful hours by the finest fancy for a really good thing that he had ever felt descend in the darkness. "It's just the vision of a situation that contains, upon my honour, everything," he said, "and I wonder I've never thought of it before." He didn't describe it further, contrary to his common practice, and

I only knew later, by Mrs. Limbert, that he had begun "Derogation" and was completely full of his subject. It was, however, a subject he wasn't to live to treat. The work went on for a couple of months in quiet mystery, without revelations even to his wife. He hadn't invited her to help him to get up his case—she hadn't taken the field with him as on his previous campaigns. We only knew he was at it again, but that less even than ever had been said about the impression to be made on the market. I saw him in February and thought him sufficiently at ease. The great thing was that he was immensely interested and was pleased with the omens. I got a strange stirring sense that he had not consulted the usual ones and indeed that he had floated away into a grand indifference, into a reckless consciousness of art. The voice of the market had suddenly grown faint and far: he had come back at the last, as people so often do, to one of the moods, the sincerities of his prime. Was he really, with a blurred sense of the urgent, doing something now only for himself? We wondered and waited—we felt he was a little confused. What had happened, I was afterwards satisfied, was that he had quite forgotten whether he generally sold or not. He had merely waked up one morning again in the country of the blue and had stayed there with a good conscience and a great idea. He stayed till death knocked at the gate, for the pen dropped from his hand only at the moment when, from sudden failure of the heart, his eyes, as he sank back in his chair, closed for ever. "Derogation" is a splendid fragment; it evidently would have been one of his high successes. I am not prepared to say it would have waked up the libraries.

Willa Cather

THE SCULPTOR'S FUNERAL

A GROUP of the townspeople stood on the station siding of a little Kansas town, awaiting the coming of the night train, which was already twenty minutes overdue. The snow had fallen thick over everything; in the pale starlight the line of bluffs across the wide, white meadows south of the town made soft, smoke-coloured curves against the clear sky. The men on the siding stood first on one foot and then on the other, their hands thrust deep into their trousers pockets, their overcoats open, their shoulders screwed up with the cold; and they glanced from time to time toward the southeast,

---

where the railroad track wound along the river shore. They conversed in low tones and moved about restlessly, seeming uncertain as to what was expected of them. There was but one of the company who looked as if he knew exactly why he was there, and he kept conspicuously apart; walking to the far end of the platform, returning to the station door, then pacing up the track again, his chin sunk in the high collar of his overcoat, his burly shoulders drooping forward, his gait heavy and dogged. Presently he was approached by a tall, spare, grizzled man clad in a faded Grand Army suit, who shuffled out from the group and advanced with a certain deference, craning his neck forward until his back made the angle of a jackknife three-quarters open.

"I reckon she's a-goin' to be pretty late agin tonight, Jim," he remarked in a squeaky falsetto. "S'pose it's the snow?"

"I don't know," responded the other man with a shade of annoyance, speaking from out an astonishing cataract of red beard that grew fiercely and thickly in all directions.

The spare man shifted the quill toothpick he was chewing to the other side of his mouth. "It ain't likely that anybody from the East will come with the corpse, I s'pose," he went on reflectively.

"I don't know," responded the other, more curtly than before.

"It's too bad he didn't belong to some lodge or other. I like an order funeral myself. They seem more appropriate for people of some repytation," the spare man continued, with an ingratiating concession in his shrill voice, as he carefully placed his toothpick in his vest pocket. He always carried the flag at the G.A.R. funerals in the town.

The heavy man turned on his heel, without replying, and walked up the siding. The spare man rejoined the uneasy group. "Jim's ez full ez a tick, ez ushel," he commented commiseratingly.

Just then a distant whistle sounded, and there was a shuffling of feet on the platform. A number of lanky boys, of all ages, appeared as suddenly and slimily as eels wakened by the crack of thunder; some came from the waiting-room, where they had been warming themselves by the red stove, or half asleep on the slat benches; others uncoiled themselves from baggage trucks or slid out of express wagons. Two clambered down from the driver's seat of a hearse that stood backed up against the siding. They straightened their stooping shoulders and lifted their heads, and a flash of momentary animation kindled their dull eyes at that cold, vibrant scream, the worldwide call for men. It stirred them like the note of a trumpet, just as it had often stirred the man who was coming home tonight, in his boyhood.

The night express shot, red as a rocket, from out the eastward marsh lands and wound along the river shore under the long lines of shivering poplars that sentinelled the meadows, the escaping steam hanging in grey masses against the pale sky and blotting out the Milky Way. In a moment the red glare from the headlight streamed up the snow-covered track before the siding and glittered on the wet, black rails. The burly man with the dishevelled red beard walked swiftly up the platform toward the approaching train, uncovering his head as he went. The group of men behind him hesitated, glanced questioningly at one another, and awkwardly followed his example. The train stopped, and the crowd shuffled up to the express car just as the door was thrown open, the man in the G.A.R. suit thrusting his head forward with curiosity. The express messenger appeared in the doorway, accompanied by a young man in a long ulster and travelling cap.

"Are Mr. Merrick's friends here?" inquired the young man.

The group on the platform swayed uneasily. Philip Phelps, the banker, responded with dignity: "We have come to take charge of the body. Mr. Merrick's father is very feeble and can't be about."

"Send the agent out here," growled the express messenger, "and tell the operator to lend a hand."

The coffin was got out of its rough-box and down on the snowy platform. The townspeople drew back enough to make room for it and then formed a close semicircle about it, looking curiously at the palm leaf which lay across the black cover. No one said anything. The baggage man stood by his truck, waiting to get at the trunks. The engine panted heavily, and the fireman dodged in and out among the wheels with his yellow torch and long oil-can, snapping the spindle boxes. The young Bostonian, one of the dead sculptor's pupils who had come with the body, looked about him helplessly. He turned to the banker, the only one of that black, uneasy, stoop-shouldered group who seemed enough of an individual to be addressed.

"None of Mr. Merrick's brothers are here?" he asked uncertainly.

The man with the red beard for the first time stepped up and joined the others. "No, they have not come yet; the family is scattered. The body will be taken directly to the house." He stooped and took hold of one of the handles of the coffin.

"Take the long hill road up, Thompson; it will be easier on the horses," called the livery-man as the undertaker snapped the door of the hearse and prepared to mount to the driver's seat.

Laird, the red-bearded lawyer, turned again to the stranger: "We didn't know whether there would be any one with him or not," he explained. "It's a long walk, so you'd better go up in the hack." He pointed to a single battered conveyance, but the young man replied stiffly: "Thank you, but I think I will go up with the hearse. If you don't object," turning to the undertaker, "I'll ride with you."

They clambered up over the wheels and drove off in the starlight up the long, white hill toward the town. The lamps in the still village were shining from under the low, snow-burdened roofs; and beyond, on every side, the plains reached out into emptiness, peaceful and wide as the soft sky itself, and wrapped in a tangible, white silence.

When the hearse backed up to a wooden sidewalk before a naked, weather-beaten frame house, the same composite, ill-defined group that had stood upon the station siding was huddled about the gate. The front yard was an icy swamp, and a couple of warped planks, extending from the sidewalk to the door, made a sort of rickety footbridge. The gate hung on one hinge, and was opened wide with difficulty. Steavens, the young stranger, noticed that something black was tied to the knob of the front door.

The grating sound made by the casket, as it was drawn from the hearse, was answered by a scream from the house; the front door was wrenched open, and a tall, corpulent woman rushed out bareheaded into the snow and flung herself upon the coffin, shrieking: "My boy, my boy! And this is how you've come home to me!"

As Steavens turned away and closed his eyes with a shudder of unutterable repulsion, another woman, also tall, but flat and angular, dressed entirely in black, darted out of the house and caught Mrs. Merrick by the shoulders, crying sharply: "Come, come, mother; you musn't go on like this!" Her tone changed to one of obsequious solemnity as she turned to the banker: "The parlour is ready, Mr. Phelps."

The bearers carried the coffin along the narrow boards, while the undertaker ran ahead with the coffin-rests. They bore it into a large, unheated room that smelled of dampness and disuse and furniture polish, and set it down under a hanging lamp ornamented with jingling glass prisms and before a "Rogers group" of John Alden and Priscilla, wreathed with smilax. Henry Steavens stared about him with the sickening conviction that there had been a mistake, and that he had somehow arrived at the wrong destination. He looked at the clover-green Brussels, the fat plush upholstery, among the hand-painted china placques and panels and vases, for some mark of identification,—for something that might once conceivably have belonged to Harvey Merrick. It was not until he recognized his friend in the crayon portrait of a little boy in kilts and curls, hanging above the piano, that he felt willing to let any of these people approach the coffin.

"Take the lid off, Mr. Thompson; let me see my boy's face," wailed the elderly woman between her sobs. This time Steavens looked fearfully, almost beseechingly into her face, red and swollen under its masses of strong, black, shiny hair. He flushed, dropped his eyes, and then, almost incredulously, looked again. There was a kind of power about her face—a kind of brutal handsomeness, even; but it was scarred and furrowed by violence, and so coloured and coarsened by fiercer passions that grief seemed never to have laid a gentle finger there. The long nose was distended and knobbed at the end, and there were deep lines on either side of it; her heavy, black brows almost met across her forehead, her teeth were large and square, and set far apart—teeth that could tear. She filled the room; the men were obliterated, seemed tossed about like twigs in an angry water, and even Steavens felt himself being drawn into the whirlpool.

The daughter—the tall, raw-boned woman in crepe, with a mourning comb in her hair which curiously lengthened her long face—sat stiffly upon the sofa, her hands, conspicuous for their large knuckles, folded in her lap, her mouth and eyes drawn down, solemnly awaiting the opening of the coffin. Near the door stood a mulatto woman, evidently a servant in the house, with a timid bearing and an emaciated face pitifully sad and gentle. She was weeping silently, the corner of her calico apron lifted to her eyes, occasionally suppressing a long, quivering sob. Steavens walked over and stood beside her.

Feeble steps were heard on the stairs, and an old man, tall and frail, odorous of pipe smoke, with shaggy, unkempt grey hair and a dingy beard, tobacco stained about the mouth, entered uncertainly. He went slowly up to the coffin and stood rolling a blue cotton handkerchief between his hands, seeming so pained and embarrassed by his wife's orgy of grief that he had no consciousness of anything else.

"There, there, Annie, dear, don't take on so," he quavered timidly, putting out a shaking hand and awkwardly patting her elbow. She turned and sank upon his shoulder with such violence that he tottered a little. He did not even glance toward the coffin, but continued to look at her with a dull, frightened, appealing expression, as a spaniel looks at the whip. His sunken cheeks slowly reddened and burned with miserable shame. When his wife rushed from the room, her daughter strode after her with set lips. The servant stole up to the coffin, bent over it for a moment, and then slipped away to the kitchen, leaving Steavens, the lawyer, and the father to themselves. The old man stood looking down at his dead son's face. The sculptor's splendid head seemed even more noble in its rigid stillness than in life. The dark hair had crept down upon the wide forehead; the face seemed strangely long, but in it there was not that repose we expect to find in the faces of the dead. The brows were so drawn that there were two deep lines above the beaked nose, and the chin was thrust forward defiantly. It was as though the strain of life had been so sharp and bitter that death could not at once relax the tension and smooth the countenance into perfect peace—as though he were still guarding something precious, which might even yet be wrested from him.

The old man's lips were working under his stained beard. He turned to the lawyer with timid deference: "Phelps and the rest are comin' back to set up with Harve, ain't they?" he asked. "Thank 'ee Jim, thank 'ee." He brushed the hair back gently from his son's forehead. "He was a good boy, Jim; always a good boy. He was ez gentle ez a child and the kindest of 'em all—only we didn't none of us ever understand him." The tears trickled slowly down his beard and dropped upon the sculptor's coat.

"Martin, Martin! Oh, Martin! come here," his wife wailed from the top of the stairs. The old man started timorously: "Yes, Annie, I'm coming." He turned away, hesitated, stood for a moment in miserable indecision; then reached back and patted the dead man's hair softly, and stumbled from the room.

"Poor old man, I didn't think he had any tears left. Seems as if his eyes would have gone dry long ago. At his age nothing cuts very deep," remarked the lawyer.

Something in his tone made Steavens glance up. While the mother had been in the room, the young man had scarcely seen any one else; but now, from the moment he first glanced into Jim Laird's florid face and blood-shot eyes, he knew that he had found what he had been heartsick at not finding before—the feeling, the understanding, that must exist in some one, even here.

The man was red as his beard, with features swollen and blurred by dissipation, and a hot, blazing blue eye. His face was strained—that of a man who is controlling himself with difficulty—and he kept plucking at his beard with a sort of fierce resentment. Steavens, sitting by the window, watched him turn down the glaring lamp, still its jangling pendants with an angry gesture, and then stand with his hands locked behind him, staring down into the master's face. He could not help wondering what link there had been between the porcelain vessel and so sooty a lump of potter's clay.

From the kitchen an uproar was sounding; when the dining-room opened, the import of it was clear. The mother was abusing the maid for having forgotten to make the dressing for the chicken salad which had been prepared for the watchers. Steavens had never heard anything in the least like it; it was injured, emotional, dramatic abuse, unique and masterly in its excruciating cruelty, as violent and unrestrained as had been her grief of twenty minutes before. With a shudder of disgust the lawyer went into the dining-room and closed the door into the kitchen.

"Poor Roxy's getting it now," he remarked when he came back. "The Merricks took her out of the poor-house years ago; and if her loyalty would let her, I guess the poor old thing could tell tales that would curdle your blood. She's the mulatto woman who was standing in here a while ago, with her apron to her eyes. The old woman is a fury; there never was anybody like her. She made Harvey's life a hell for him when he lived at home; he was so sick ashamed of it. I never could see how he kept himself sweet."

"He was wonderful," said Steavens slowly, "wonderful; but until tonight I have never known how wonderful."

"That is the eternal wonder of it, anyway; that it can come even from such a dung heap as this," the lawyer cried, with a sweeping gesture which seemed to indicate much more than the four walls within which they stood.

"I think I'll see whether I can get a little air. The room is so close I am beginning to feel rather faint," murmured Steavens, struggling with one of the windows. The sash was stuck, however, and would not yield, so he sat down dejectedly and began pulling at his collar. The lawyer came over, loosened the sash with one blow of his big red fist and sent the window up a few inches. Steavens thanked him, but the nausea which had been gradually climbing into his throat for the last half hour left him with but one desire—a desperate feeling that he must get away from this place with what was left of Harvey Merrick. Oh, he comprehended well enough now the quiet bitterness of the smile that he had seen so often on his master's lips!

Once when Merrick returned from a visit home, he brought with him a singularly feeling and suggestive bas-relief of a thin, faded old woman, sitting and sewing something pinned to her knee; while a full-lipped, full-blooded little urchin, his trousers, held up by a single gallows, stood beside her, impatiently twitching her gown to call her attention to a butterfly he had caught. Steavens, impressed by the tender and delicate modelling of the thin, tired face, had asked him if it were his mother. He remembered the dull flush that had burned up in the sculptor's face.

The lawyer was sitting in a rocking-chair beside the coffin, his head thrown back and his eyes closed. Steavens looked at him earnestly, puzzled at the line of the chin, and wondering why a man should conceal a feature of such distinction under that disfiguring shock of beard. Suddenly, as though he felt the young sculptor's keen glance, Jim Laird opened his eyes.

"Was he always a good deal of an oyster?" he asked abruptly. "He was terribly shy as a boy."

"Yes, he was an oyster, since you put it so," rejoined Steavens. "Although he could be very fond of people, he always gave one the impression of being detached. He disliked violent emotion; he was reflective, and rather distrustful of himself—except, of course, as regarded his work. He was sure enough there. He distrusted men pretty thoroughly and women even more, yet somehow without believing ill of them. He was determined, indeed, to believe the best; but he seemed afraid to investigate."

"A burnt dog dreads the fire," said the lawyer grimly, and closed his eyes.

Steavens went on and on, reconstructing that whole miserable boyhood. All this raw, biting ugliness had been the portion of the man whose mind was to become an exhaustless gallery of beautiful impressions—so sensitive that the mere shadow of a poplar leaf flickering against a sunny wall would be etched and held there for ever. Surely, if ever a man had the magic word in his finger tips, it was Merrick. Whatever he touched, he revealed its holiest secret; liberated it from enchantment and restored it to its pristine loveliness. Upon whatever he had come in contact with, he had left a beautiful record of the experience—a sort of ethereal signature; a scent, a sound, a colour that was his own.

Steavens understood now the real tragedy of his master's life; neither love nor wine, as many had conjectured; but a blow which had fallen earlier had cut deeper than anything else could have done—a shame not his, and yet so unescapably his, to hide in his heart from his very boyhood. And without—the frontier warfare; the yearning of a boy, cast ashore upon a desert of newness and ugliness and sordidness, for all that is chastened and old, and noble with traditions.

At eleven o'clock the tall, flat woman in black announced that the watchers were arriving, and asked them to "step into the dining-room." As Steavens rose, the lawyer said dryly: "You go on—it'll be a good experience for you. I'm not equal to that crowd tonight; I've had twenty years of them."

As Steavens closed the door after him he glanced back at the lawyer, sitting by the coffin in the dim light, with his chin resting on his hand.

The same misty group that had stood before the door of the express car shuffled into the dining-room. In the light of the kerosene lamp they separated and became individuals. The minister, a pale, feeble-looking man with white hair and blond chin-whiskers, took his seat beside a small side table and placed his Bible upon it. The Grand Army man sat down behind the stove and tilted his chair back comfortably against the wall, fishing his quill toothpick from his waistcoat pocket. The two bankers, Phelps and Elder, sat off in a corner behind the dinner-table, where they could finish their discussion of the new usury law and its effect on chattel security loans. The real estate agent, an old man with a smiling, hypocritical face, soon joined them. The coal and lumber dealer and the cattle shipper sat on opposite sides of the hard-coal burner, their feet on the nickel-work. Steavens took a book from his pocket and began to read. The talk around him ranged through various topics of local interest while the house was quieting down. When it was clear that the members of the family were in bed, the Grand Army man hitched his shoulders and, untangling his long legs, caught his heels on the rounds of his chair.

"S'pose there'll be a will, Phelps?" he queried in his weak falsetto.

The banker laughed disagreeably, and began trimming his nails with a pearl-handled pocket-knife.

"There'll scarcely be any need for one, will there?" he queried in his turn.

The restless Grand Army man shifted his position again, getting his knees still nearer his chin. "Why, the ole man says Harve's done right well lately," he chirped.

The other banker spoke up. "I reckon he means by that Harve ain't asked him to mortgage any more farms lately, so as he could go on with his education."

"Seems like my mind don't reach back to a time when Harve wasn't bein' edycated," tittered the Grand Army man.

There was a general chuckle. The minister took out his handkerchief and blew his nose sonorously. Banker Phelps closed his knife with a snap. "It's too bad the old man's sons didn't turn out better," he remarked with reflective authority. "They never hung together. He spent money enough on Harve to stock a dozen cattle-farms, and he might as well have poured it into Sand Creek. If Harve had stayed at home and helped nurse what little they had, and gone into stock on the old man's bottom farm, they might all have been well fixed. But the old man had to trust everything to tenants and was cheated right and left."

"Harve never could have handled stock none," interposed the cattleman. "He hadn't it in him to be sharp. Do you remember when he bought Sander's mules for eight-year olds, when everybody in town knew that Sander's father-in-law give 'em to his wife for a wedding present eighteen years before, an' they was full-grown mules then?"

The company laughed discreetly, and the Grand Army man rubbed his knees with a spasm of childish delight.

"Harve never was much account for anything practical, and he shore was never fond of work," began the coal and lumber dealer. "I mind the last time he was home; the day he left, when the old man was out to the barn helpin' his hand hitch up to take Harve to the train, and Cal Moots was patchin' up the fence; Harve, he come out on the step and sings out, in his lady-like voice: 'Cal Moots, Cal Moots! please come cord my trunk.' "

"That's Harve for you," approved the Grand Army man. "I kin hear him howlin' yet, when he was a big feller in long pants and his mother used to whale him with a rawhide in the barn for lettin' the cows git foundered in the cornfield when he was drivin' 'em home from pasture. He killed a cow of mine that-a-way onct—a pure Jersey and the best milker I had, an' the ole man had to put up for her. Harve, he was watchin' the sun set acrost the marshes when the anamile got away."

"Where the old man made his mistake was in sending the boy East to school," said Phelps, stroking his goatee and speaking in a deliberate, judicial tone. "There was where he got his head full of nonsense. What Harve needed, of all people, was a course in some first-class Kansas City business college."

The letters were swimming before Steavens' eyes. Was it possible that these men did not understand, that the palm on the coffin meant nothing to them? The very name of their town would have remained forever buried in the postal guide had it not been now and again mentioned in the world in connection with Harvey Merrick's. He remembered what his master had said to him on the day of his death, after the congestion of both lungs had shut off any probability of recovery, and the sculptor had asked his pupil to send his body home. "It's not a pleasant place to be lying while the world is moving and doing and bettering," he had said with a feeble smile, "but it rather seems as though we ought to go back to the place we came from, in the end. The townspeople will come in for a look at me; and after they have had their say, I shan't have much to fear from the judgment of God!"

The cattleman took up the comment. "Forty's young for a Merrick to cash in; they usually hang on pretty well. Probably he helped it along with whiskey."

"His mother's people were not long lived, and Harvey never had a robust constitution," said the minister mildly. He would have liked to say more. He had been the boy's Sunday-school teacher, and had been fond of him; but he felt that he was not in a position to speak. His own sons had turned out badly, and it was not a year since one of them had made his last trip home in the express car, shot in a gambling-house in the Black Hills.

"Nevertheless, there is no disputin' that Harve frequently looked upon the wine when it was red, also variegated, and it shore made an oncommon fool of him," moralized the cattleman.

Just then the door leading into the parlour rattled loudly and everyone started involuntarily, looking relieved when only Jim Laird came out. The Grand Army man ducked his head when he saw the spark in his blue, bloodshot eye. They were all afraid of Jim; he was a drunkard, but he could twist the law to suit his client's needs as no other man in all western Kansas could do, and there were many who tried. The lawyer closed the door behind him, leaned back against it and folded his arms, cocking his head a little to one side. When he assumed this attitude in the courtroom, ears were always pricked up, as it usually foretold a flood of withering sarcasm.

"I've been with you gentlemen before," he began in a dry, even tone, "when you've sat by the coffins of boys born and raised in this town; and, if I remember rightly, you were never any too well satisfied when you checked them up. What's the matter, anyhow? Why is it that reputable young men are as scarce as millionaires in Sand City? It might almost seem to a stranger that there was some way something the matter with your progressive town. Why did Ruben Sayer, the brightest young lawyer you ever turned out, after he had come home from the university as straight as a die, take to drinking and forge a check and shoot himself? Why did Bill Merrit's son die of the shakes in a saloon in Omaha? Why was Mr. Thomas's son, here, shot in a gambling-house? Why did young Adams burn his mill to beat the insurance companies and go to the pen?"

The lawyer paused and unfolded his arms, laying one clenched fist quietly on the table. "I'll tell you why. Because you drummed nothing but money and knavery into their ears from the time they wore knickerbockers; because you carped away at them as you've been carping here tonight, holding our friends Phelps and Elder up to them for their models, as our grandfathers held up George Washington and John Adams. But the boys were young, and raw at the business you put them to, and how could they match coppers with such artists as Phelps and Elder? You wanted them to be successful rascals; they were only unsuccessful ones—that's all the difference. There was only one boy ever raised in this borderland between ruffianism and civilization who didn't come to grief, and you hated Harvey Merrick more for winning out than you hated all the other boys who got under the wheels. Lord, Lord, how you did hate him! Phelps, here, is fond of saying that he could buy and sell us all out any time he's a mind to; but he knew Harve wouldn't have given a tinker's damn for his bank and all his cattle farms put together; and a lack of appreciation, that way, goes hard with Phelps.

"Old Nimrod thinks Harve drank too much; and this from such as Nimrod and me!

"Brother Elder says Harve was too free with the old man's money—fell short in filial consideration, maybe. Well, we can all remember the very tone in which brother Elder swore his own father was a liar, in the county court; and we all know that the old man came out of that partnership with his son as bare as a sheared lamb. But maybe I'm getting personal, and I'd better be driving ahead at what I want to say."

The lawyer paused a moment, squared his heavy shoulders, and went on: "Harvey Merrick and I went to school together, back East. We were dead in earnest, and we wanted you all to be proud of us some day. We meant to be great men. Even I, and I haven't lost my sense of humour, gentlemen, I meant to be a great man. I came back here to practise, and I found you didn't in the least want me to be a great man. You wanted me to be a shrewd lawyer—oh, yes! Our veteran here wanted me to get him an increase of pension, because he had dyspepsia; Phelps wanted a new county survey that would put the widow Wilson's little bottom farm inside his south line; Elder wanted to lend money at 5 per cent a month, and get it collected; and Stark here wanted to wheedle old women up in Vermont into investing their annuities in real-estate mortgages that are not worth the paper they are written on. Oh, you needed me hard enough, and you'll go on needing me!

"Well, I came back here and became the damned shyster you wanted me to be. You pretend to have some sort of respect for me; and yet you'll stand up and throw mud at Harvey Merrick, whose soul you couldn't dirty and whose hands you couldn't tie. Oh, you're a discriminating lot of Christians! There have been times when the sight of Harvey's name in some Eastern paper has made me hang my head like a whipped dog; and, again, times when I like to think of him off there in the world, away from all this hog-wallow, climbing the big, clean up-grade he'd set for himself.

"And we? Now that we've fought and lied and sweated and stolen, and hated as only the disappointed strugglers in a bitter, dead little Western town know how to do, what have we got to show for it? Harvey Merrick wouldn't have given one sunset over your marshes for all you've got put together, and you know it. It's not for me to say why, in the inscrutable wisdom of God, a genius should ever have been called from this place of hatred and bitter waters; but I want this Boston man to know that the drivel he's been hearing here tonight is the only tribute any truly great man could have from such a lot of sick, side-tracked, burnt-dog, land-poor sharks as the here-present financiers of Sand City—upon which town may God have mercy!"

The lawyer thrust out his hand to Steavens as he passed him, caught up his overcoat in the hall, and had left the house before the Grand Army man had had time to lift his ducked head and crane his long neck about at his fellows.

Next day Jim Laird was drunk and unable to attend the funeral services. Steavens called twice at his office, but was compelled to start East without seeing him. He had a presentiment that he would hear from him again, and left his address on the lawyer's table; but if Laird found it, he never acknowledged it. The thing in him that Harvey Merrick had loved must have gone underground with Harvey Merrick's coffin; for it never spoke again, and Jim got the cold he died of driving across the Colorado mountains to defend one of Phelps's sons who had got into trouble out there by cutting government timber.

DRAMA

Molière

THE MISANTHROPE

TRANSLATOR'S PREFACE

THE IDEA that comedy is a ritual in which society's laughter corrects individual extravagance is particularly inapplicable to *The Misanthrope*. In this play, society itself is indicted, and though Alceste's criticisms are indiscriminate, they are not unjustified. It is true that falseness and intrigue are everywhere on view; the conventions enforce a routine dishonesty, justice is subverted by influence, love is overwhelmed by calculation, and these things are accepted, even by the best, as "natural." The cold vanity of Oronte, Acaste, and Clitandre, the malignant hypocrisy of Arsinoé, the insincerity of Célimène, are to be taken as exemplary of the age, and Philinte's philosophic tolerance will not quite do in response to such a condition of things. The honest Éliante is the one we are most to trust, and this is partly because she sees that Alceste's intransigence *A quelque chose en soy de noble & d'héroïque.*

But *The Misanthrope* is not only a critique of society; it is also a study of impurity of motive in a critic of society. If Alceste has a rage for the genuine, and he truly has, it is unfortunately compromised and exploited by his vast, unconscious egotism. He is a jealous friend (*Je veux qu'on me distingue*), and it is Philinte's polite effusiveness toward another which prompts his attack on promiscuous civility. He is a jealous lover, and his "frankness" about Oronte's sonnet owes something to the fact that Oronte is his rival, and that the sonnet is addressed to Célimène. Like many humorless and indignant people, he is hard on everybody but himself, and does not perceive it when he fails his own ideal. In one aspect, Alceste seems a moral giant misplaced in a trivial society, having (in George Eliot's phrase) "a certain spiritual grandeur ill-matched with the meanness of opportunity"; in another aspect, he seems an unconscious fraud who magnifies the petty faults of others in order to dramatize himself in his own eyes.

He is, of course, both at once: but the two impressions predominate by turns. A victim, like all around him, of the moral enervation of the times, he cannot consistently be the Man of Honor—simple, magnanimous, passionate, decisive, true. It is his distinction that he is aware of that ideal, and that he can fitfully embody it; his comic flaw consists in a Quixotic confusion of himself with the ideal, a willingness to distort the world for his own self-deceptive and histrionic purposes. Paradoxically, then, the advocate of true feeling and honest intercourse is the one character most artificial, most out-of-touch, most in danger of that nonentity and solitude which all, in the chattery, hollow world of this play, are fleeing. He must play-act continually in order to believe in his own existence, and he welcomes the fact or show of injustice as a dramatic cue. At the close of the play, when Alceste has refused to appeal his lawsuit and has spurned the hand of Célimène, one cannot escape the suspicion that his indignation is in great part instrumental, a desperate means of counterfeiting an identity.

Martin Turnell (whose book *The Classical Moment* contains a fine analysis of *The Misanthrope*) observes that those speeches of Alceste which ring most false are, as it were, parodies of "Cornelian *tirade*." To duplicate this parody-tragic effect in English it was clearly necessary to keep the play in verse, where it would be possible to control the tone more sharply, and to recall our own tragic tradition. There were other reasons, too, for approximating Molière's form. The constant of rhythm and rhyme was needed, in the translation as in the original, for bridging great gaps between high comedy and farce, lofty diction and ordinary talk, deep character and shallow. Again, while prose might preserve the thematic structure of the play, other "musical" elements would be lost, in particular the frequently intricate arrangements of balancing half-lines, lines, couplets, quatrains, and sestets. There is no question that words, when dancing within such patterns, are not their prosaic selves, but have a wholly different mood and meaning.

Consider, finally, two peculiarities of the dialogue of the play: redundancy and logic. When Molière has a character repeat essentially the same thing in three successive couplets, it will sometimes have a very clear dramatic point; but it will always have the intention of stabilizing the idea against the movement of the verse, and of giving a specifically rhetorical pleasure. In a prose rendering, these latter effects are lost, and the passage tends to seem merely prolix. As for logic, it is a convention of *The Misanthrope* that its main characters can express themselves logically, and in the most complex grammar; Molière's dramatic verse, which is almost wholly free of metaphor, derives much of its richness from argumentative virtuosity. Here is a bit of logic from Arsinoé:

> *Madame, l'Amitié doit sur tout éclater*
> *Aux choses qui le plus nous peuvent importer:*
> *Et comme il n'en est point de plus grande importance*
> *Que celles de l'Honneur et de la Bienséance,*
> *Je viens par un avis qui touche vostre honneur*
> *Témoigner l'amitié que pour vous a mon Coeur.*

In prose it might come out like this: "Madam, friendship should most display itself when truly vital matters are in question: and since there are no things more vital than decency and honor, I have come to prove my heartfelt friendship by giving you some advice which concerns your reputation." Even if that were better rendered, it would still be plain that Molière's logic loses all its baroque exuberance in prose; it sounds lawyerish; without rhyme and verse to phrase and emphasize the steps of its progression, the logic becomes obscure like Congreve's, not crystalline and followable as it was meant to be.

For all these reasons, rhymed verse seemed to me obligatory. The choice did not preclude accuracy, and what follows is, I believe, a line-for-line verse translation quite as faithful as any which have been done in prose. I hasten to say that I am boasting only of patience; a translation may, alas, be faithful on all counts, and still lack quality.

One word about diction. This is a play in which French aristocrats of 1666 converse about their special concerns, and employ the moral and philosophical terms peculiar to their thought. Not all my words, therefore, are strictly modern; I had for example to use "spleen" and "phlegm"; but I think that I have avoided the zounds sort of thing, and that at best the diction mediates between then and now, suggesting no one period. There are occasional vulgarities, but for these there is precedent in the original, Molière's people being aristocrats and therefore not genteel.

If this English version is played or read aloud, the names should be pronounced in a fashion *roughly* French, without nasal and uvular agonies. Damon should be *dah-MOAN,* and for rhythmic convenience Arsinoé should be *ar-SIN-oh-eh. . . .*

RICHARD WILBUR

Wellesley, Massachusetts

CHARACTERS

ALCESTE, in love with Célimène
PHILINTE, Alceste's friend
ORONTE, in love with Célimène
CÉLIMÈNE, Alceste's beloved
ÉLIANTE, Célimène's cousin
ARSINOÉ, a friend of Célimène's
ACASTE, CLITANDRE } marquesses
BASQUE, Célimène's servant
A GUARD of the Marshalsea
DUBOIS, Alceste's valet

The scene throughout is in Célimène's house at Paris.

ACT I

SCENE 1

PHILINTE, ALCESTE.

PHILINTE. Now, what's got into you?
ALCESTE. [*Seated.*] Kindly leave me alone.
PHILINTE. Come, come, what is it? This lugubrious tone . . .
ALCESTE. Leave me, I said; you spoil my solitude.
PHILINTE. Oh, listen to me, now, and don't be rude.
ALCESTE. I choose to be rude, Sir, and to be hard of hearing.
PHILINTE. These ugly moods of yours are not endearing;
Friends though we are, I really must insist . . .
ALCESTE. [*Abruptly rising.*] Friends? Friends, you say? Well, cross me off your list.
I've been your friend till now, as you well know;
But after what I saw a moment ago
I tell you flatly that our ways must part.
I wish no place in a dishonest heart.
PHILINTE. Why, what have I done, Alceste? Is this quite just?
ALCESTE. My God, you ought to die of self-disgust.
I call your conduct inexcusable, Sir,
And every man of honor will concur.
I see you almost hug a man to death,
Exclaim for joy until you're out of breath,
And supplement these loving demonstrations
With endless offers, vows, and protestations;
Then when I ask you "Who was that?" I find
That you can barely bring his name to mind!
Once the man's back is turned, you cease to love him,
And speak with absolute indifference of him!
By God, I say it's base and scandalous
To falsify the heart's affections thus;
If I caught myself behaving in such a way,
I'd hang myself for shame, without delay.
PHILINTE. It hardly seems a hanging matter to me;
I hope that you will take it graciously

If I extend myself a slight reprieve,
And live a little longer, by your leave.
ALCESTE. How dare you joke about a crime so grave?
PHILINTE. What crime? How else are people to behave?
ALCESTE. I'd have them be sincere, and never part
With any word that isn't from the heart.
PHILINTE. When someone greets us with a show of pleasure,
It's but polite to give him equal measure,
Return his love the best that we know how,
And trade him offer for offer, vow for vow.
ALCESTE. No, no, this formula you'd have me follow,
However fashionable, is false and hollow,
And I despise the frenzied operations
Of all these barterers of protestations,
These lavishers of meaningless embraces,
These utterers of obliging commonplaces,
Who court and flatter everyone on earth
And praise the fool no less than the man of worth.
Should you rejoice that someone fondles you,
Offers his love and service, swears to be true,
And fills your ears with praises of your name,
When to the first damned fop he'll say the same?
No, no: no self-respecting heart would dream
Of prizing so promiscuous an esteem;
However high the praise, there's nothing worse
Than sharing honors with the universe.
Esteem is founded on comparison:
To honor all men is to honor none.
Since you embrace this indiscriminate vice,
Your friendship comes at far too cheap a price;
I spurn the easy tribute of a heart
Which will not set the worthy man apart:
I choose, Sir, to be chosen; and in fine,
The friend of mankind is no friend of mine.
PHILINTE. But in polite society, custom decrees
That we show certain outward courtesies. . . .
ALCESTE. Ah, no! we should condemn with all our force
Such false and artificial intercourse.
Let men behave like men; let them display
Their inmost hearts in everything they say;
Let the heart speak, and let our sentiments
Not mask themselves in silly compliments.
PHILINTE. In certain cases it would be uncouth
And most absurd to speak the naked truth;
With all respect for your exalted notions,
It's often best to veil one's true emotions.
Wouldn't the social fabric come undone
If we were wholly frank with everyone?

Suppose you met with someone you couldn't bear;
Would you inform him of it then and there?
ALCESTE. Yes.
PHILINTE. Then you'd tell old Emilie it's pathetic
The way she daubs her features with cosmetic
And plays the gay coquette at sixty-four?
ALCESTE. I would.
PHILINTE. And you'd call Dorilas a bore,
And tell him every ear at court is lame
From hearing him brag about his noble name?
ALCESTE. Precisely.
PHILINTE. Ah, you're joking.
ALCESTE. *Au contraire*:
In this regard there's none I'd choose to spare.
All are corrupt; there's nothing to be seen
In court or town but aggravates my spleen.
I fall into deep gloom and melancholy
When I survey the scene of human folly,
Finding on every hand base flattery,
Injustice, fraud, self-interest, treachery. . . .
Ah, it's too much; mankind has grown so base,
I mean to break with the whole human race.
PHILINTE. This philosophic rage is a bit extreme;
You've no idea how comical you seem;
Indeed, we're like those brothers in the play
Called *School for Husbands,* one of whom was prey . . .
ALCESTE. Enough, now! None of your stupid similes.
PHILINTE. Then let's have no more tirades, if you please.
The world won't change, whatever you say or do;
And since plain speaking means so much to you,
I'll tell you plainly that by being frank
You've earned the reputation of a crank,
And that you're thought ridiculous when you rage
And rant against the manners of the age.
ALCESTE. So much the better; just what I wish to hear.
No news could be more grateful to my ear.
All men are so detestable in my eyes,
I should be sorry if they thought me wise.
PHILINTE. Your hatred's very sweeping, is it not?
ALCESTE. Quite right: I hate the whole degraded lot.
PHILINTE. Must all poor human creatures be embraced,
Without distinction, by your vast distaste?
Even in these bad times, there are surely a few . . .
ALCESTE. No, I include all men in one dim view:
Some men I hate for being rogues; the others
I hate because they treat the rogues like brothers,
And, lacking a virtuous scorn for what is vile,
Receive the villain with a complaisant smile.

Notice how tolerant people choose to be
Toward that bold rascal who's at law with me.
His social polish can't conceal his nature;
One sees at once that he's a treacherous creature;
No one could possibly be taken in
By those soft speeches and that sugary grin.
The whole world knows the shady means by which
The low-brow's grown so powerful and rich,
And risen to a rank so bright and high
That virtue can but blush, and merit sigh.
Whenever his name comes up in conversation,
None will defend his wretched reputation;
Call him knave, liar, scoundrel, and all the rest,
Each head will nod, and no one will protest.
And yet his smirk is seen in every house,
He's greeted everywhere with smiles and bows,
And when there's any honor that can be got
By pulling strings, he'll get it, like as not.
My God! It chills my heart to see the ways
Men come to terms with evil nowadays;
Sometimes, I swear, I'm moved to flee and find
Some desert land unfouled by humankind.

PHILINTE. Come, let's forget the follies of the times
And pardon mankind for its petty crimes;
Let's have an end of rantings and of railings,
And show some leniency toward human failings.
This world requires a pliant rectitude;
Too stern a virtue makes one stiff and rude;
Good sense views all extremes with detestation,
And bids us to be noble in moderation.
The rigid virtues of the ancient days
Are not for us; they jar with all our ways
And ask of us too lofty a perfection.
Wise men accept their times without objection,
And there's no greater folly, if you ask me,
Than trying to reform society.
Like you, I see each day a hundred and one
Unhandsome deeds that might be better done,
But still, for all the faults that meet my view,
I'm never known to storm and rave like you.
I take men as they are, or let them be,
And teach my soul to bear their frailty;
And whether in court or town, whatever the scene,
My phlegm's as philosophic as your spleen.

ALCESTE. This phlegm which you so eloquently commend,
Does nothing ever rile it up, my friend?
Suppose some man you trust should treacherously
Conspire to rob you of your property,

And do his best to wreck your reputation?
Wouldn't you feel a certain indignation?
PHILINTE. Why, no. These faults of which you so complain
Are part of human nature, I maintain,
And it's no more a matter for disgust
That men are knavish, selfish and unjust,
Than that the vulture dines upon the dead,
And wolves are furious, and apes ill-bred.
ALCESTE. Shall I see myself betrayed, robbed, torn to bits,
And not . . . Oh, let's be still and rest our wits.
Enough of reasoning, now. I've had my fill.
PHILINTE. Indeed, you would do well, Sir, to be still.
Rage less at your opponent, and give some thought
To how you'll win this lawsuit that he's brought.
ALCESTE. I assure you I'll do nothing of the sort.
PHILINTE. Then who will plead your case before the court?
ALCESTE. Reason and right and justice will plead for me.
PHILINTE. Oh, Lord. What judges do you plan to see?
ALCESTE. Why, none. The justice of my cause is clear.
PHILINTE. Of course, man; but there's politics to fear. . . .
ALCESTE. No, I refuse to lift a hand. That's flat.
I'm either right, or wrong.
PHILINTE. Don't count on that.
ALCESTE. No, I'll do nothing.
PHILINTE. Your enemy's influence
Is great, you know . . .
ALCESTE. That makes no difference.
PHILINTE. It will; you'll see.
ALCESTE. Must honor bow to guile?
If so, I shall be proud to lose the trial.
PHILINTE. Oh, really . . .
ALCESTE. I'll discover by this case
Whether or not men are sufficiently base
And impudent and villainous and perverse
To do me wrong before the universe.
PHILINTE. What a man!
ALCESTE. Oh, I could wish, whatever the cost,
Just for the beauty of it, that my trial were lost.
PHILINTE. If people heard you talking so, Alceste,
They'd split their sides. Your name would be a jest.
ALCESTE. So much the worse for jesters.
PHILINTE. May I enquire
Whether this rectitude you so admire,
And these hard virtues you're enamored of
Are qualities of the lady whom you love?
It much surprises me that you, who seem
To view mankind with furious disesteem,

Have yet found something to enchant your eyes
Amidst a species which you so despise.
And what is more amazing, I'm afraid,
Is the most curious choice your heart has made.
The honest Éliante is fond of you,
Arsinoé, the prude, admires you too;
And yet your spirit's been perversely led
To choose the flighty Célimène instead
Whose brittle malice and coquettish ways
So typify the manners of our days.
How is it that the traits you most abhor
Are bearable in this lady you adore?
Are you so blind with love that you can't find them?
Or do you contrive, in her case, not to mind them?

ALCESTE. My love for that young widow's not the kind
That can't perceive defects; no, I'm not blind.
I see her faults, despite my ardent love,
And all I see I fervently reprove.
And yet I'm weak; for all her falsity,
That woman knows the art of pleasing me,
And though I never cease complaining of her,
I swear I cannot manage not to love her.
Her charm outweighs her faults; I can but aim
To cleanse her spirit in my love's pure flame.

PHILINTE. That's no small task; I wish you all success.
You think then that she loves you?

ALCESTE. Heavens, yes!
I wouldn't love her did she not love me.

PHILINTE. Well, if her taste for you is plain to see,
Why do these rivals cause you such despair?

ALCESTE. True love, Sir, is possessive, and cannot bear
To share with all the world. I'm here today
To tell her she must send that mob away.

PHILINTE. If I were you, and had your choice to make,
Éliante, her cousin, would be the one I'd take;
That honest heart, which cares for you alone,
Would harmonize far better with your own.

ALCESTE. True, true: each day my reason tells me so;
But reason doesn't rule in love, you know.

PHILINTE. I fear some bitter sorrow is in store;
This love . . .

SCENE 2

ORONTE, ALCESTE, PHILINTE.

ORONTE. [*To* ALCESTE.] The servants told me at the door
That Éliante and Célimène were out,
But when I heard, dear Sir, that you were about,

I came to say, without exaggeration,
That I hold you in the vastest admiration,
And that it's always been my dearest desire
To be the friend of one I so admire.
I hope to see my love of merit requited,
And you and I in friendship's bond united.
I'm sure you won't refuse—if I may be frank—
A friend of my devotedness—and rank.

[During this speech of ORONTE'S, ALCESTE *is abstracted, and seems unaware that he is being spoken to. He only breaks off his reverie when* ORONTE *says:]*

It was for you, if you please, that my words were intended.
ALCESTE. For me, Sir?
ORONTE. Yes, for you. You're not offended?
ALCESTE. By no means. But this much surprises me. . . .
The honor comes most unexpectedly. . . .
ORONTE. My high regard should not astonish you;
The whole world feels the same. It is your due.
ALCESTE. Sir . . .
ORONTE. Why, in all the State there isn't one
Can match your merits; they shine, Sir, like the sun.
ALCESTE. Sir . . .
ORONTE. You are higher in my estimation
Than all that's most illustrious in the nation.
ALCESTE. Sir . . .
ORONTE. If I lie, may heaven strike me dead!
To show you that I mean what I have said,
Permit me, Sir, to embrace you most sincerely,
And swear that I will prize our friendship dearly.
Give me your hand. And now, Sir, if you choose,
We'll make our vows.
ALCESTE. Sir . . .
ORONTE. What! You refuse?
ALCESTE. Sir, it's a very great honor you extend:
But friendship is a sacred thing, my friend;
It would be profanation to bestow
The name of friend on one you hardly know.
All parts are better played when well-rehearsed;
Let's put off friendship, and get acquainted first.
We may discover it would be unwise
To try to make our natures harmonize.
ORONTE. By heaven! You're sagacious to the core;
This speech has made me admire you even more.
Let time, then, bring us closer day by day;
Meanwhile, I shall be yours in every way.
If, for example, there should be anything
You wish at court, I'll mention it to the King.

I have his ear, of course; it's quite well known
That I am much in favor with the throne.
In short, I am your servant. And now, dear friend,
Since you have such fine judgment, I intend
To please you, if I can, with a small sonnet
I wrote not long ago. Please comment on it,
And tell me whether I ought to publish it.

ALCESTE. You must excuse me, Sir; I'm hardly fit
To judge such matters.

ORONTE. Why not?

ALCESTE. I am, I fear,
Inclined to be unfashionably sincere.

ORONTE. Just what I ask; I'd take no satisfaction
In anything but your sincere reaction.
I beg you not to dream of being kind.

ALCESTE. Since you desire it, Sir, I'll speak my mind.

ORONTE. *Sonnet.* It's a sonnet. . . . *Hope* . . . The poem's addressed
To a lady who wakened hopes within my breast.
Hope . . . this is not the pompous sort of thing,
Just modest little verses, with a tender ring.

ALCESTE. Well, we shall see.

ORONTE. *Hope* . . . I'm anxious to hear
Whether the style seems properly smooth and clear,
And whether the choice of words is good or bad.

ALCESTE. We'll see, we'll see.

ORONTE. Perhaps I ought to add
That it took me only a quarter-hour to write it.

ALCESTE. The time's irrelevant, Sir: Kindly recite it.

ORONTE. [*Reading.*]

Hope comforts us awhile, 'tis true,
Lulling our cares with careless laughter,
And yet such joy is full of rue,
My Phyllis, if nothing follows after.

PHILINTE. I'm charmed by this already; the style's delightful.

ALCESTE. [*Sotto voce, to* PHILINTE.] How can you say that? Why the thing is frightful.

ORONTE. *Your fair face smiled on me awhile,*
But was it kindness so to enchant me?
'Twould have been fairer not to smile,
If hope was all you meant to grant me.

PHILINTE. What a clever thought! How handsomely you phrase it!

ALCESTE. [*Sotto voce, to* PHILINTE.] You know the thing is trash. How dare you praise it?

ORONTE. *If it's to be my passion's fate*
Thus everlastingly to wait,

Then death will come to set me free:
For death is fairer than the fair;
Phyllis, to hope is to despair
When one must hope eternally.

PHILINTE. The close is exquisite—full of feeling and grace.
ALCESTE. [*Sotto voce, aside.*] Oh, blast the close; you'd better close your face
Before you send your lying soul to hell.
PHILINTE. I can't remember a poem I've liked so well.
ALCESTE. [*Sotto voce, aside.*] Good Lord!
ORONTE. [*To* PHILINTE.] I fear you're flattering me a bit.
PHILINTE. Oh, no!
ALCESTE. [*Sotto voce, aside.*] What else d'you call it, you hypocrite?
ORONTE, [*to* ALCESTE.] But you, Sir, keep your promise now: don't shrink
From telling me sincerely what you think.
ALCESTE. Sir, these are delicate matters; we all desire
To be told that we've the true poetic fire.
But once, to one whose name I shall not mention,
I said, regarding some verse of his invention.
That gentlemen should rigorously control
That itch to write which often afflicts the soul;
That one should curb the heady inclination
To publicize one's little avocation;
And that in showing off one's work of art
One often plays a very clownish part.
ORONTE. Are you suggesting in a devious way
That I ought not . . .
ALCESTE. Oh, that I do not say.
Further, I told him that no fault is worse
Than that of writing frigid, lifeless verse,
And that the merest whisper of such a shame
Suffices to destroy a man's good name.
ORONTE. D'you mean to say my sonnet's dull and trite?
ALCESTE. I don't say that. But I went on to cite
Numerous cases of once-respected men
Who came to grief by taking up the pen.
ORONTE. And am I like them? Do I write so poorly?
ALCESTE. I don't say that. But I told this person, "Surely
You're under no necessity to compose;
Why you should wish to publish, heaven knows.
There's no excuse for printing tedious rot
Unless one writes for bread, as you do not.
Resist temptation, then, I beg of you;
Conceal your pastimes from the public view;
And don't give up, on any provocation,
Your present high and courtly reputation,

To purchase at a greedy printer's shop
The name of silly author and scribbling fop."
These were the points I tried to make him see.
ORONTE. I sense that they are also aimed at me;
But now—about my sonnet—I'd like to be told . . .
ALCESTE. Frankly, that sonnet should be pigeonholed.
You've chosen the worst models to imitate.
The style's unnatural. Let me illustrate:

For example, *Your fair face smiled on me awhile,*
Followed by, *'Twould have been fairer not to smile!*
Or this: *such joy is full of rue;*
Or this: *For death is fairer than the fair;*
Or, *Phyllis, to hope is to despair*
When one must hope eternally!

This artificial style, that's all the fashion,
Has neither taste, nor honesty, nor passion;
It's nothing but a sort of wordy play,
And nature never spoke in such a way.
What, in this shallow age, is not debased?
Our fathers, though less refined, had better taste;
I'd barter all that men admire today
For one old love song I shall try to say:

If the King had given me for my own
Paris, his citadel,
And I for that must leave alone
Her whom I love so well,
I'd say then to the Crown,
Take back your glittering town;
My darling is more fair, I swear,
My darling is more fair.

The rhyme's not rich, the style is rough and old,
But don't you see that it's the purest gold
Beside the tinsel nonsense now preferred,
And that there's passion in its every word?

If the King had given me for my own
Paris, his citadel,
And I for that must leave alone
Her whom I love so well,
I'd say then to the Crown,
Take back your glittering town;
My darling is more fair, I swear,
My darling is more fair.

There speaks a loving heart. [To PHILINTE.] You're laughing, eh?
Laugh on, my precious wit. Whatever you say,

I hold that song's worth all the bibelots
That people hail today with ah's and oh's.
ORONTE. And I maintain my sonnet's very good.
ALCESTE. It's not at all surprising that you should.
You have your reasons; permit me to have mine
For thinking that you cannot write a line.
ORONTE. Others have praised my sonnet to the skies.
ALCESTE. I lack their art of telling pleasant lies.
ORONTE. You seem to think you've got no end of wit.
ALCESTE. To praise your verse, I'd need still more of it.
ORONTE. I'm not in need of your approval, Sir.
ALCESTE. That's good; you couldn't have it if you were.
ORONTE. Come now, I'll lend you the subject of my sonnet;
I'd like to see you try to improve upon it.
ALCESTE. I might, by chance, write something just as shoddy;
But then I wouldn't show it to everybody.
ORONTE. You're most opinionated and conceited.
ALCESTE. Go find your flatterers, and be better treated.
ORONTE. Look here, my little fellow, pray watch your tone.
ALCESTE. My great big fellow, you'd better watch your own.
PHILINTE. [*Stepping between them.*] Oh, please, please, gentlemen!
This will never do.
ORONTE. The fault is mine, and I leave the field to you.
I am your servant, Sir, in every way.
ALCESTE. And I, Sir, am your most abject valet.

SCENE 3

PHILINTE, ALCESTE.

PHILINTE. Well, as you see, sincerity in excess
Can get you into a very pretty mess;
Oronte was hungry for appreciation. . . .
ALCESTE. Don't speak to me.
PHILINTE. What?
ALCESTE. No more conversation.
PHILINTE. Really, now . . .
ALCESTE. Leave me alone.
PHILINTE. If I . . .
ALCESTE. Out of my sight!
PHILINTE. But what . . .
ALCESTE. I won't listen.
PHILINTE. But . . .
ALCESTE. Silence!
PHILINTE. Now, is it polite . . .
ALCESTE. By heaven, I've had enough. Don't follow me.
PHILINTE. Ah, you're just joking. I'll keep you company.

ACT II

SCENE 1

ALCESTE, CÉLIMÈNE.

ALCESTE. Shall I speak plainly, Madam? I confess
Your conduct gives me infinite distress,
And my resentment's grown too hot to smother.
Soon, I foresee, we'll break with one another.
If I said otherwise, I should deceive you;
Sooner or later, I shall be forced to leave you,
And if I swore that we shall never part,
I should misread the omens of my heart.
CÉLIMÈNE. You kindly saw me home, it would appear,
So as to pour invectives in my ear.
ALCESTE. I've no desire to quarrel. But I deplore
Your inability to shut the door
On all these suitors who beset you so.
There's what annoys me, if you care to know.
CÉLIMÈNE. Is it my fault that all these men pursue me?
Am I to blame if they're attracted to me?
And when they gently beg an audience,
Ought I to take a stick and drive them hence?
ALCESTE. Madam, there's no necessity for a stick;
A less responsive heart would do the trick.
Of your attractiveness I don't complain;
But those your charms attract, you then detain
By a most melting and receptive manner,
And so enlist their hearts beneath your banner.
It's the agreeable hopes which you excite
That keep these lovers round you day and night;
Were they less liberally smiled upon,
That sighing troop would very soon be gone.
But tell me, Madam, why it is that lately
This man Clitandre interests you so greatly?
Because of what high merits do you deem
Him worthy of the honor of your esteem?
Is it that your admiring glances linger
On the splendidly long nail of his little finger?
Or do you share the general deep respect
For the blond wig he chooses to affect?
Are you in love with his embroidered hose?
Do you adore his ribbons and his bows?
Or is it that this paragon bewitches
Your tasteful eye with his vast German breeches?
Perhaps his giggle, or his falsetto voice,
Makes him the latest gallant of your choice?

CÉLIMÈNE. You're much mistaken to resent him so.
Why I put up with him you surely know:
My lawsuit's very shortly to be tried,
And I must have his influence on my side.
ALCESTE. Then lose your lawsuit, Madam, or let it drop;
Don't torture me by humoring such a fop.
CÉLIMÈNE. You're jealous of the whole world, Sir.
ALCESTE. That's true,
Since the whole world is well-received by you.
CÉLIMÈNE. That my good nature is so unconfined
Should serve to pacify your jealous mind;
Were I to smile on one, and scorn the rest,
Then you might have some cause to be distressed.
ALCESTE. Well, if I mustn't be jealous, tell me, then,
Just how I'm better treated than other men.
CÉLIMÈNE. You know you have my love. Will that not do?
ALCESTE. What proof have I that what you say is true?
CÉLIMÈNE. I would expect, Sir, that my having said it
Might give the statement a sufficient credit.
ALCESTE. But how can I be sure that you don't tell
The selfsame thing to other men as well?
CÉLIMÈNE. What a gallant speech! How flattering to me!
What a sweet creature you make me out to be!
Well then, to save you from the pangs of doubt,
All that I've said I hereby cancel out;
Now, none but yourself shall make a monkey of you:
Are you content?
ALCESTE. Why, why am I doomed to love you?
I swear that I shall bless the blissful hour
When this poor heart's no longer in your power!
I make no secret of it: I've done my best
To exorcise this passion from my breast;
But thus far all in vain; it will not go;
It's for my sins that I must love you so.
CÉLIMÈNE. Your love for me is matchless, Sir; that's clear.
ALCESTE. Indeed, in all the world it has no peer;
Words can't describe the nature of my passion,
And no man ever loved in such a fashion.
CÉLIMÈNE. Yes, it's a brand-new fashion, I agree:
You show your love by castigating me,
And all your speeches are enraged and rude.
I've never been so furiously wooed.
ALCESTE. Yet you could calm that fury, if you chose.
Come, shall we bring our quarrels to a close?
Let's speak with open hearts, then, and begin . . .

SCENE 2

CÉLIMÈNE, ALCESTE, BASQUE.

CÉLIMÈNE. What is it?
BASQUE. Acaste is here.
CÉLIMÈNE. Well, send him in.

SCENE 3

CÉLIMÈNE, ALCESTE.

ALCESTE. What! Shall we never be alone at all?
You're always ready to receive a call,
And you can't bear, for ten ticks of the clock,
Not to keep open house for all who knock.
CÉLIMÈNE. I couldn't refuse him: he'd be most put out.
ALCESTE. Surely that's not worth worrying about.
CÉLIMÈNE. Acaste would never forgive me if he guessed
That I consider him a dreadful pest.
ALCESTE. If he's a pest, why bother with him then?
CÉLIMÈNE. Heavens! One can't antagonize such men;
Why, they're the chartered gossips of the court,
And have a say in things of every sort.
One must receive them, and be full of charm;
They're no great help, but they can do you harm,
And though your influence be ever so great,
They're hardly the best people to alienate.
ALCESTE. I see, dear lady, that you could make a case
For putting up with the whole human race;
These friendships that you calculate so nicely . . .

SCENE 4

ALCESTE, CÉLIMÈNE, BASQUE.

BASQUE. Madam, Clitandre is here as well.
ALCESTE. Precisely.
CÉLIMÈNE. Where are you going?
ALCESTE. Elsewhere.
CÉLIMÈNE. Stay.
ALCESTE. No, no.
CÉLIMÈNE. Stay, Sir.
ALCESTE. I can't.
CÉLIMÈNE. I wish it.
ALCESTE. No, I must go.
I beg you, Madam, not to press the matter;
You know I have no taste for idle chatter.

CÉLIMÈNE. Stay: I command you.
ALCESTE. No, I cannot stay.
CÉLIMÈNE. Very well; you have my leave to go away.

SCENE 5

ÉLIANTE, PHILINTE, ACASTE, CLITANDRE, ALCESTE, BASQUE.

ÉLIANTE. [*To* CÉLIMÈNE.] The Marquesses have kindly come to call.
Were they announced?
CÉLIMÈNE. Yes. Basque, bring chairs for all.
[BASQUE *provides the chairs, and exits.*]
[*To* ALCESTE.] You haven't gone?
ALCESTE. No; and I shan't depart
Till you decide who's foremost in your heart.
CÉLIMÈNE. Oh, hush.
ALCESTE. It's time to choose; take them, or me.
CÉLIMÈNE. You're mad.
ALCESTE. I'm not, as you shall shortly see.
CÉLIMÈNE. Oh?
ALCESTE. You'll decide.
CÉLIMÈNE. You're joking now, dear friend.
ALCESTE. No, no; you'll choose; my patience is at an end.
CLITANDRE. Madam, I come from court, where poor Cléonte
Behaved like a perfect fool, as is his wont.
Has he no friend to counsel him, I wonder,
And teach him less unerringly to blunder?
CÉLIMÈNE. It's true, the man's a most accomplished dunce;
His gauche behavior charms the eye at once;
And every time one sees him, on my word,
His manner's grown a trifle more absurd.
ACASTE. Speaking of dunces, I've just now conversed
With old Damon, who's one of the very worst;
I stood a lifetime in the broiling sun
Before his dreary monologue was done.
CÉLIMÈNE. Oh, he's a wondrous talker, and has the power
To tell you nothing hour after hour:
If, by mistake, he ever came to the point,
The shock would put his jawbone out of joint.
ÉLIANTE. [*To* PHILINTE.] The conversation takes its usual turn,
And all our dear friends' ears will shortly burn.
CLITANDRE. Timante's a character, Madam.
CÉLIMÈNE. Isn't he, though?
A man of mystery from top to toe,
Who moves about in a romantic mist
On secret missions which do not exist.
His talk is full of eyebrows and grimaces;
How tired one gets of his momentous faces;

He's always whispering something confidential
Which turns out to be quite inconsequential;
Nothing's too slight for him to mystify;
He even whispers when he says "good-by."

ACASTE. Tell us about Géralde.

CÉLIMÈNE. That tiresome ass.
He mixes only with the titled class,
And fawns on dukes and princes, and is bored
With anyone who's not at least a lord.
The man's obsessed with rank, and his discourses
Are all of hounds and carriages and horses;
He uses Christian names with all the great,
And the word Milord, with him, is out of date.

CLITANDRE. He's very taken with Bélise, I hear.

CÉLIMÈNE. She is the dreariest company, poor dear.
Whenever she comes to call, I grope about
To find some topic which will draw her out,
But, owing to her dry and faint replies,
The conversation wilts, and droops, and dies.
In vain one hopes to animate her face
By mentioning the ultimate commonplace;
But sun or shower, even hail or frost
Are matters she can instantly exhaust.
Meanwhile her visit, painful though it is,
Drags on and on through mute eternities,
And though you ask the time, and yawn, and yawn,
She sits there like a stone and won't be gone.

ACASTE. Now for Adraste.

CÉLIMÈNE. Oh, that conceited elf
Has a gigantic passion for himself;
He rails against the court, and cannot bear it
That none will recognize his hidden merit;
All honors given to others give offense
To his imaginary excellence.

CLITANDRE. What about young Cléon? His house, they say,
Is full of the best society, night and day.

CÉLIMÈNE. His cook has made him popular, not he:
It's Cléon's table that people come to see.

ÉLIANTE. He gives a splendid dinner, you must admit.

CÉLIMÈNE. But must he serve himself along with it?
For my taste, he's a most insipid dish
Whose presence sours the wine and spoils the fish.

PHILINTE. Damis, his uncle, is admired no end.
What's your opinion, Madam?

CÉLIMÈNE. Why, he's my friend.

PHILINTE. He seems a decent fellow, and rather clever.

CÉLIMÈNE. He works too hard at cleverness, however.

I hate to see him sweat and struggle so
To fill his conversation with bons mots.
Since he's decided to become a wit
His taste's so pure that nothing pleases it;
He scolds at all the latest books and plays,
Thinking that wit must never stoop to praise,
That finding fault's a sign of intellect,
That all appreciation is abject,
And that by damning everything in sight
One shows oneself in a distinguished light.
He's scornful even of our conversations:
Their trivial nature sorely tries his patience;
He folds his arms, and stands above the battle,
And listens sadly to our childish prattle.

ACASTE. Wonderful, Madam! You hit him off precisely.

CLITANDRE. No one can sketch a character so nicely.

ALCESTE. How bravely, Sirs, you cut and thrust at all
These absent fools, till one by one they fall:
But let one come in sight, and you'll at once
Embrace the man you lately called a dunce,
Telling him in a tone sincere and fervent
How proud you are to be his humble servant.

CLITANDRE. Why pick on us? *Madame's* been speaking, Sir,
And you should quarrel, if you must, with her.

ALCESTE. No, no, by God, the fault is yours, because
You lead her on with laughter and applause,
And make her think that she's the more delightful
The more her talk is scandalous and spiteful.
Oh, she would stoop to malice far, far less
If no such claque approved her cleverness.
It's flatterers like you whose foolish praise
Nourishes all the vices of these days.

PHILINTE. But why protest when someone ridicules
Those you'd condemn, yourself, as knaves or fools?

CÉLIMÈNE. Why, Sir? Because he loves to make a fuss.
You don't expect him to agree with us,
When there's an opportunity to express
His heaven-sent spirit of contrariness?
What other people think, he can't abide;
Whatever they say, he's on the other side;
He lives in deadly terror of agreeing;
'Twould make him seem an ordinary being.
Indeed, he's so in love with contradiction,
He'll turn against his most profound conviction
And with a furious eloquence deplore it,
If only someone else is speaking for it.

ALCESTE. Go on, dear lady, mock me as you please;
You have your audience in ectasies.

PHILINTE. But what she says is true: you have a way
Of bridling at whatever people say;
Whether they praise or blame, your angry spirit
Is equally unsatisfied to hear it.

ALCESTE. Men, Sir, are always wrong, and that's the reason
That righteous anger's never out of season;
All that I hear in all their conversation
Is flattering praise or reckless condemnation.

CÉLIMÈNE. But . . .

ALCESTE. No, no, Madam, I am forced to state
That you have pleasures which I deprecate,
And that these others, here, are much to blame
For nourishing the faults which are your shame.

CLITANDRE. I shan't defend myself, Sir; but I vow
I'd thought this lady faultless until now.

ACASTE. I see her charms and graces, which are many;
But as for faults, I've never noticed any.

ALCESTE. I see them, Sir; and rather than ignore them,
I strenuously criticize her for them.
The more one loves, the more one should object
To every blemish, every least defect.
Were I this lady, I would soon get rid
Of lovers who approved of all I did,
And by their slack indulgence and applause
Endorsed my follies and excused my flaws.

CÉLIMÈNE. If all hearts beat according to your measure,
The dawn of love would be the end of pleasure;
And love would find its perfect consummation
In ecstasies of rage and reprobation.

ÉLIANTE. Love, as a rule, affects men otherwise,
And lovers rarely love to criticize.
They see their lady as a charming blur,
And find all things commendable in her.
If she has any blemish, fault, or shame,
They will redeem it by a pleasing name.
The pale-faced lady's lily-white, perforce;
The swarthy one's a sweet brunette, of course;
The spindly lady has a slender grace;
The fat one has a most majestic pace;
The plain one, with her dress in disarray,
They classify as *beauté négligée;*
The hulking one's a goddess in their eyes,
The dwarf, a concentrate of Paradise;
The haughty lady has a noble mind;
The mean one's witty, and the dull one's kind;
The chatterbox has liveliness and verve,
The mute one has a virtuous reserve.

So lovers manage, in their passion's cause,
To love their ladies even for their flaws.

ALCESTE. But I still say . . .

CÉLIMÈNE. I think it would be nice
To stroll around the gallery once or twice.
What! You're not going, Sirs?

CLITANDRE AND ACASTE. No, Madam, no.

ALCESTE. You seem to be in terror lest they go.
Do what you will, Sirs; leave, or linger on,
But I shan't go till after you are gone.

ACASTE. I'm free to linger, unless I should perceive
Madame is tired, and wishes me to leave.

CLITANDRE. And as for me, I needn't go today
Until the hour of the King's *coucher*.

CÉLIMÈNE. [*To* ALCESTE.] You're joking, surely?

ALCESTE. Not in the least; we'll see
Whether you'd rather part with them, or me.

SCENE 6

ALCESTE, CÉLIMÈNE, ÉLIANTE, ACASTE, PHILINTE, CLITANDRE, BASQUE.

BASQUE [*To* ALCESTE.] Sir, there's a fellow here who bids me state
That he must see you, and that it can't wait.

ALCESTE. Tell him that I have no such pressing affairs.

BASQUE. It's a long tailcoat that this fellow wears,
With gold all over.

CÉLIMÈNE. [*To* ALCESTE.] You'd best go down and see.
Or—have him enter.

SCENE 7

ALCESTE, CÉLIMÈNE, ÉLIANTE, ACASTE, PHILINTE, CLITANDRE, GUARD.

ALCESTE. [*Confronting the* GUARD.] Well, what do you want with me?
Come in, Sir.

GUARD. I've a word, Sir, for your ear.

ALCESTE. Speak it aloud, Sir; I shall strive to hear.

GUARD. The Marshals have instructed me to say
You must report to them without delay.

ALCESTE. Who? Me, Sir?

GUARD. Yes, Sir; you.

ALCESTE. But what do they want?

PHILINTE. [*To* ALCESTE.] To scotch your silly quarrel with Oronte.

CÉLIMÈNE. [*To* PHILINTE.] What quarrel?
PHILINTE. Oronte and he have fallen out
Over some verse he spoke his mind about;
The Marshals wish to arbitrate the matter.
ALCESTE. Never shall I equivocate or flatter!
PHILINTE. You'd best obey their summons; come, let's go.
ALCESTE. How can they mend our quarrel, I'd like to know?
Am I to make a cowardly retraction,
And praise those jingles to his satisfaction?
I'll not recant; I've judged that sonnet rightly.
It's bad.
PHILINTE. But you might say so more politely. . . .
ALCESTE. I'll not back down; his verses make me sick.
PHILINTE. If only you could be more politic!
But come, let's go.
ALCESTE. I'll go, but I won't unsay
A single word.
PHILINTE. Well, let's be on our way.
ALCESTE. Till I am ordered by my lord the King
To praise that poem, I shall say the thing
Is scandalous, by God, and that the poet
Ought to be hanged for having the nerve to show it.
[*To* CLITANDRE *and* ACASTE, *who are laughing.*]
By heaven, Sirs, I really didn't know
That I was being humorous.
CÉLIMÈNE. Go, Sir, go;
Settle your business.
ALCESTE. I shall, and when I'm through,
I shall return to settle things with you.

ACT III

SCENE 1

CLITANDRE, ACASTE.

CLITANDRE. Dear Marquess, how contented you appear;
All things delight you, nothing mars your cheer.
Can you, in perfect honesty, declare
That you've a right to be so debonair?
ACASTE. By Jove, when I survey myself, I find
No cause whatever for distress of mind.
I'm young and rich; I can in modesty
Lay claim to an exalted pedigree;
And owing to my name and my condition
I shall not want for honors and position.
Then as to courage, that most precious trait,
I seem to have it, as was proved of late

Upon the field of honor, where my bearing,
They say, was very cool and rather daring.
I've wit, of course; and taste in such perfection
That I can judge without the least reflection,
And at the theater, which is my delight,
Can make or break a play on opening night,
And lead the crowd in hisses or bravos,
And generally be known as one who knows.
I'm clever, handsome, gracefully polite;
My waist is small, my teeth are strong and white;
As for my dress, the world's astonished eyes
Assure me that I bear away the prize.
I find myself in favor everywhere,
Honored by men, and worshipped by the fair;
And since these things are so, it seems to me
I'm justified in my complacency.

CLITANDRE. Well, if so many ladies hold you dear,
Why do you press a hopeless courtship here?

ACASTE. Hopeless, you say? I'm not the sort of fool
That likes his ladies difficult and cool.
Men who are awkward, shy, and peasantish
May pine for heartless beauties, if they wish,
Grovel before them, bear their cruelties,
Woo them with tears and sighs and bended knees,
And hope by dogged faithfulness to gain
What their poor merits never could obtain.
For men like me, however, it makes no sense
To love on trust, and foot the whole expense.
Whatever any lady's merits be,
I think, thank God, that I'm as choice as she;
That if my heart is kind enough to burn
For her, she owes me something in return;
And that in any proper love affair
The partners must invest an equal share.

CLITANDRE. You think, then, that our hostess favors you?

ACASTE. I've reason to believe that that is true.

CLITANDRE. How did you come to such a mad conclusion?
You're blind, dear fellow. This is sheer delusion.

ACASTE. All right, then: I'm deluded and I'm blind.

CLITANDRE. Whatever put the notion in your mind?

ACASTE. Delusion.

CLITANDRE. What persuades you that you're right?

ACASTE. I'm blind.

CLITANDRE. But have you any proofs to cite?

ACASTE. I tell you I'm deluded.

CLITANDRE. Have you, then,
Received some secret pledge from Célimène?

ACASTE. Oh, no: she scorns me.

CLITANDRE. Tell me the truth, I beg.
ACASTE. She just can't bear me.
CLITANDRE. Ah, don't pull my leg.
Tell me what hope she's given you, I pray.
ACASTE. I'm hopeless, and it's you who win the day.
She hates me thoroughly, and I'm so vexed
I mean to hang myself on Tuesday next.
CLITANDRE. Dear Marquess, let us have an armistice
And make a treaty. What do you say to this?
If ever one of us can plainly prove
That Célimène encourages his love,
The other must abandon hope, and yield,
And leave him in possession of the field.
ACASTE. Now, there's a bargain that appeals to me;
With all my heart, dear Marquess, I agree.
But hush.

SCENE 2

CÉLIMÈNE, ACASTE, CLITANDRE.

CÉLIMÈNE. Still here?
CLITANDRE. 'Twas love that stayed our feet.
CÉLIMÈNE. I think I heard a carriage in the street.
Whose is it? D'you know?

SCENE 3

CÉLIMÈNE, ACASTE, CLITANDRE, BASQUE.

BASQUE. Arsinoé is here,
Madame.
CÉLIMÈNE. Arsinoé, you say? Oh, dear.
BASQUE. Éliante is entertaining her below.
CÉLIMÈNE. What brings the creature here, I'd like to know?
ACASTE. They say she's dreadfully prudish, but in fact
I think her piety . . .
CÉLIMÈNE. It's all an act.
At heart she's worldly, and her poor success
In snaring men explains her prudishness.
It breaks her heart to see the beaux and gallants
Engrossed by other women's charms and talents,
And so she's always in a jealous rage
Against the faulty standards of the age.
She lets the world believe that she's a prude
To justify her loveless solitude,
And strives to put a brand of moral shame
On all the graces that she cannot claim.

But still she'd love a lover; and Alceste
Appears to be the one she'd love the best.
His visits here are poison to her pride;
She seems to think I've lured him from her side;
And everywhere, at court or in the town,
The spiteful, envious woman runs me down.
In short, she's just as stupid as can be,
Vicious and arrogant in the last degree,
And . . .

SCENE 4

ARSINOÉ, CÉLIMÈNE, CLITANDRE, ACASTE.

CÉLIMÈNE. Ah! What happy chance has brought you here?
I've thought about you ever so much, my dear.
ARSINOÉ. I've come to tell you something you should know.
CÉLIMÈNE. How good of you to think of doing so!
[CLITANDRE *and* ACASTE *go out, laughing.*]

SCENE 5

ARSINOÉ, CÉLIMÈNE.

ARSINOÉ. It's just as well those gentlemen didn't tarry.
CÉLIMÈNE. Shall we sit down?
ARSINOÉ. That won't be necessary.
Madam, the flame of friendship ought to burn
Brightest in matters of the most concern,
And as there's nothing which concerns us more
Than honor, I have hastened to your door
To bring you, as your friend, some information
About the status of your reputation.
I visited, last night, some virtuous folk,
And, quite by chance, it was of you they spoke;
There was, I fear, no tendency to praise
Your light behavior and your dashing ways.
The quantity of gentlemen you see
And your by now notorious coquetry
Were both so vehemently criticized
By everyone, that I was much surprised.
Of course, I needn't tell you where I stood;
I came to your defense as best I could,
Assured them you were harmless, and declared
Your soul was absolutely unimpaired.
But there are some things, you must realize,
One can't excuse, however hard one tries,

And I was forced at last into conceding
That your behavior, Madam, is misleading,
That it makes a bad impression, giving rise
To ugly gossip and obscene surmise,
And that if you were more *overtly* good,
You wouldn't be so much misunderstood.
Not that I think you've been unchaste—no! no!
The saints preserve me from a thought so low!
But mere good conscience never did suffice:
One must avoid the outward show of vice.
Madam, you're too intelligent, I'm sure,
To think my motives anything but pure
In offering you this counsel—which I do
Out of a zealous interest in you.

CÉLIMÈNE. Madam, I haven't taken you amiss;
I'm very much obliged to you for this;
And I'll at once discharge the obligation
By telling you about *your* reputation.
You've been so friendly as to let me know
What certain people say of me, and so
I mean to follow your benign example
By offering you a somewhat similar sample.
The other day, I went to an affair
And found some most distinguished people there
Discussing piety, both false and true.
The conversation soon came round to you.
Alas! Your prudery and bustling zeal
Appeared to have a very slight appeal.
Your affectation of a grave demeanor,
Your endless talk of virtue and of honor,
The aptitude of your suspicious mind
For finding sin where there is none to find,
Your towering self-esteem, that pitying face
With which you contemplate the human race,
Your sermonizings and your sharp aspersions
On people's pure and innocent diversions—
All these were mentioned, Madam, and, in fact,
Were roundly and concertedly attacked.
"What good," they said, "are all these outward shows,
When everything belies her pious pose?
She prays incessantly; but then, they say,
She beats her maids and cheats them of their pay;
She shows her zeal in every holy place,
But still she's vain enough to paint her face;
She holds that naked statues are immoral,
But with a naked *man* she'd have no quarrel."
Of course, I said to everybody there
That they were being viciously unfair;

But still they were disposed to criticize you,
And all agreed that someone should advise you
To leave the morals of the world alone,
And worry rather more about your own.
They felt that one's self-knowledge should be great
Before one thinks of setting others straight;
That one should learn the art of living well
Before one threatens other men with hell,
And that the Church is best equipped, no doubt,
To guide our souls and root our vices out.
Madam, you're too intelligent, I'm sure,
To think my motives anything but pure
In offering you this counsel—which I do
Out of a zealous interest in you.

ARSINOÉ. I dared not hope for gratitude, but I
Did not expect so acid a reply;
I judge, since you've been so extremely tart,
That my good counsel pierced you to the heart.

CÉLIMÈNE. Far from it, Madam. Indeed, it seems to me
We ought to trade advice more frequently.
One's vision of oneself is so defective
That it would be an excellent corrective.
If you are willing, Madam, let's arrange
Shortly to have another frank exchange
In which we'll tell each other, *entre nous,*
What you've heard tell of me, and I of you.

ARSINOÉ. Oh, people never censure you, my dear;
It's me they criticize. Or so I hear.

CÉLIMÈNE. Madam, I think we either blame or praise
According to our taste and length of days.
There is a time of life for coquetry,
And there's a season, too, for prudery.
When all one's charms are gone, it is, I'm sure,
Good strategy to be devout and pure:
It makes one seem a little less forsaken.
Some day, perhaps, I'll take the road you've taken:
Time brings all things. But I have time aplenty,
And see no cause to be a prude at twenty.

ARSINOÉ. You give your age in such a gloating tone
That one would think I was an ancient crone;
We're not so far apart, in sober truth,
That you can mock me with a boast of youth!
Madam, you baffle me. I wish I knew
What moves you to provoke me as you do.

CÉLIMÈNE. For my part, Madam, I should like to know
Why you abuse me everywhere you go.
Is it my fault, dear lady, that your hand
Is not, alas, in very great demand?

If men admire me, if they pay me court
And daily make me offers of the sort
You'd dearly love to have them make to you,
How can I help it? What would you have me do?
If what you want is lovers, please feel free
To take as many as you can from me.

ARSINOÉ. Oh, come. D'you think the world is losing sleep
Over that flock of lovers which you keep,
Or that we find it difficult to guess
What price you pay for their devotedness?
Surely you don't expect us to suppose
Mere merit could attract so many beaux?
It's not your virtue that they're dazzled by;
Nor is it virtuous love for which they sigh.
You're fooling no one, Madam; the world's not blind;
There's many a lady heaven has designed
To call men's noblest, tenderest feelings out,
Who has no lovers dogging her about;
From which it's plain that lovers nowadays
Must be acquired in bold and shameless ways,
And only pay one court for such reward
As modesty and virtue can't afford.
Then don't be quite so puffed up, if you please,
About your tawdry little victories;
Try, if you can, to be a shade less vain,
And treat the world with somewhat less disdain.
If one were envious of your amours,
One soon could have a following like yours;
Lovers are no great trouble to collect
If one prefers them to one's self-respect.

CÉLIMÈNE. Collect them then, my dear; I'd love to see
You demonstrate that charming theory;
Who knows, you might . . .

ARSINOÉ. Now, Madam, that will do;
It's time to end this trying interview.
My coach is late in coming to your door,
Or I'd have taken leave of you before.

CÉLIMÈNE. Oh, please don't feel that you must rush away;
I'd be delighted, Madam, if you'd stay.
However, lest my conversation bore you,
Let me provide some better company for you;
This gentleman, who comes most apropos,
Will please you more than I could do, I know.

SCENE 6

ALCESTE, CÉLIMÈNE, ARSINOÉ.

CÉLIMÈNE. Alceste, I have a little note to write
Which simply must go out before tonight;
Please entertain *Madame;* I'm sure that she
Will overlook my incivility.

SCENE 7

ALCESTE, ARSINOÉ.

ARSINOÉ. Well, Sir, our hostess graciously contrives
For us to chat until my coach arrives;
And I shall be forever in her debt
For granting me this little tête-à-tête.
We women very rightly give our hearts
To men of noble character and parts,
And your especial merits, dear Alceste,
Have roused the deepest sympathy in my breast.
Oh, how I wish they had sufficient sense
At court, to recognize your excellence!
They wrong you greatly, Sir. How it must hurt you
Never to be rewarded for your virtue!
ALCESTE. Why, Madam, what cause have I to feel aggrieved?
What great and brilliant thing have I achieved?
What service have I rendered to the King
That I should look to him for anything?
ARSINOÉ. Not everyone who's honored by the State
Has done great services. A man must wait
Till time and fortune offer him the chance.
Your merit, Sir, is obvious at a glance,
And . . .
ALCESTE. Ah, forget my merit; I'm not neglected.
The court, I think, can hardly be expected
To mine men's souls for merit, and unearth
Our hidden virtues and our secret worth.
ARSINOÉ. *Some* virtues, though, are far too bright to hide;
Yours are acknowledged, Sir, on every side.
Indeed, I've heard you warmly praised of late
By persons of considerable weight.
ALCESTE. This fawning age has praise for everyone,
And all distinctions, Madam, are undone.
All things have equal honor nowadays,
And no one should be gratified by praise.

To be admired, one only need exist,
And every lackey's on the honors list.

ARSINOÉ. I only wish, Sir, that you had your eye
On some position at court, however high;
You'd only have to hint at such a notion
For me to set the proper wheels in motion;
I've certain friendships I'd be glad to use
To get you any office you might choose.

ALCESTE. Madam, I fear that any such ambition
Is wholly foreign to my disposition.
The soul God gave me isn't of the sort
That prospers in the weather of a court.
It's all too obvious that I don't possess
The virtues necessary for success.
My one great talent is for speaking plain;
I've never learned to flatter or to feign;
And anyone so stupidly sincere
Had best not seek a courtier's career.
Outside the court, I know, one must dispense
With honors, privilege, and influence;
But still one gains the right, foregoing these,
Not to be tortured by the wish to please.
One needn't live in dread of snubs and slights,
Nor praise the verse that every idiot writes,
Nor humor silly Marquesses, nor bestow
Politic sighs on Madam So-and-So.

ARSINOÉ. Forget the court, then; let the matter rest.
But I've another cause to be distressed
About your present situation, Sir.
It's to your love affair that I refer.
She whom you love, and who pretends to love you,
Is, I regret to say, unworthy of you.

ALCESTE. Why, Madam! Can you seriously intend
To make so grave a charge against your friend?

ARSINOÉ. Alas, I must. I've stood aside too long
And let that lady do you grievous wrong;
But now my debt to conscience shall be paid:
I tell you that your love has been betrayed.

ALCESTE. I thank you, Madam; you're extremely kind.
Such words are soothing to a lover's mind.

ARSINOÉ. Yes, though she *is* my friend, I say again
You're very much too good for Célimène.
She's wantonly misled you from the start.

ALCESTE. You may be right; who knows another's heart?
But ask yourself if it's the part of charity
To shake my soul with doubts of her sincerity.

ARSINOÉ. Well, if you'd rather be a dupe than doubt her,
That's your affair. I'll say no more about her.

ALCESTE. Madam, you know that doubt and vague suspicion
Are painful to a man in my position;
It's most unkind to worry me this way
Unless you've some real proof of what you say.

ARSINOÉ. Sir, say no more: all doubt shall be removed,
And all that I've been saying shall be proved.
You've only to escort me home, and there
We'll look into the heart of this affair.
I've ocular evidence which will persuade you
Beyond a doubt, that Célimène's betrayed you.
Then, if you're saddened by that revelation,
Perhaps I can provide some consolation.

ACT IV

SCENE 1

ÉLIANTE, PHILINTE.

PHILINTE. Madam, he acted like a stubborn child;
I thought they never would be reconciled;
In vain we reasoned, threatened, and appealed;
He stood his ground and simply would not yield.
The Marshals, I feel sure, have never heard
An argument so splendidly absurd.
"No, gentlemen," said he, "I'll not retract.
His verse is bad: extremely bad, in fact.
Surely it does the man no harm to know it.
Does it disgrace him, not to be a poet?
A gentleman may be respected still,
Whether he writes a sonnet well or ill.
That I dislike his verse should not offend him;
In all that touches honor, I commend him;
He's noble, brave, and virtuous—but I fear
He can't in truth be called a sonneteer.
I'll gladly praise his wardrobe; I'll endorse
His dancing, or the way he sits a horse;
But, gentlemen, I cannot praise his rhyme.
In fact, it ought to be a capital crime
For anyone so sadly unendowed
To write a sonnet, and read the thing aloud."
At length he fell into a gentler mood
And, striking a concessive attitude,
He paid Oronte the following courtesies:
"Sir, I regret that I'm so hard to please,
And I'm profoundly sorry that your lyric
Failed to provoke me to a panegyric."
After these curious words, the two embraced,
And then the hearing was adjourned—in haste.

ÉLIANTE. His conduct has been very singular lately;
Still, I confess that I respect him greatly.
The honesty in which he takes such pride
Has—to my mind—its noble, heroic side.
In this false age, such candor seems outrageous;
But I could wish that it were more contagious.
PHILINTE. What most intrigues me in our friend Alceste
Is the grand passion that rages in his breast.
The sullen humors he's compounded of
Should not, I think, dispose his heart to love;
But since they do, it puzzles me still more
That he should choose your cousin to adore.
ÉLIANTE. It does, indeed, belie the theory
That love is born of gentle sympathy,
And that the tender passion must be based
On sweet accords of temper and of taste.
PHILINTE. Does she return his love, do you suppose?
ÉLIANTE. Ah, that's a difficult question, Sir. Who knows?
How can we judge the truth of her devotion?
Her heart's a stranger to its own emotion.
Sometimes it thinks it loves, when no love's there;
At other times it loves quite unaware.
PHILINTE. I rather think Alceste is in for more
Distress and sorrow than he's bargained for;
Were he of my mind, Madam, his affection
Would turn in quite a different direction,
And we would see him more responsive to
The kind regard which he receives from you.
ÉLIANTE. Sir, I believe in frankness, and I'm inclined,
In matters of the heart, to speak my mind.
I don't oppose his love for her; indeed,
I hope with all my heart that he'll succeed,
And were it in my power, I'd rejoice
In giving him the lady of his choice.
But if, as happens frequently enough
In love affairs, he meets with a rebuff—
If Célimène should grant some rival's suit—
I'd gladly play the role of substitute;
Nor would his tender speeches please me less
Because they'd once been made without success.
PHILINTE. Well, Madam, as for me, I don't oppose
Your hopes in this affair; and heaven knows
That in my conversations with the man
I plead your cause as often as I can.
But if those two should marry, and so remove
All chance that he will offer you his love,
Then I'll declare my own, and hope to see
Your gracious favor pass from him to me.

In short, should you be cheated of Alceste,
I'd be most happy to be second best.
ÉLIANTE. Philinte, you're teasing.
PHILINTE. Ah, Madam, never fear;
No words of mine were ever so sincere,
And I shall live in fretful expectation
Till I can make a fuller declaration.

SCENE 2

ALCESTE, ÉLIANTE, PHILINTE.

ALCESTE. Avenge me, Madam! I must have satisfaction,
Or this great wrong will drive me to distraction!
ÉLIANTE. Why, what's the matter? What's upset you so?
ALCESTE. Madam, I've had a mortal, mortal blow.
If Chaos repossessed the universe,
I swear I'd not be shaken any worse.
I'm ruined. . . . I can say no more. . . . My soul . . .
ÉLIANTE. Do try, Sir, to regain your self-control.
ALCESTE. Just heaven! Why were so much beauty and grace
Bestowed on one so vicious and so base?
ÉLIANTE. Once more, Sir, tell us. . . .
ALCESTE. My world has gone to wrack;
I'm—I'm betrayed; she's stabbed me in the back:
Yes, Célimène (who would have thought it of her?)
Is false to me, and has another lover.
ÉLIANTE. Are you quite certain? Can you prove these things?
PHILINTE. Lovers are prey to wild imaginings
And jealous fancies. No doubt there's some mistake. . . .
ALCESTE. Mind your own business, Sir, for heaven's sake.
[*To* ÉLIANTE.]
Madam, I have the proof that you demand
Here in my pocket, penned by her own hand.
Yes, all the shameful evidence one could want
Lies in this letter written to Oronte—
Oronte! whom I felt sure she couldn't love,
And hardly bothered to be jealous of.
PHILINTE. Still, in a letter, appearances may deceive;
This may not be so bad as you believe.
ALCESTE. Once more I beg you, Sir, to let me be;
Tend to your own affairs; leave mine to me.
ÉLIANTE. Compose yourself; this anguish that you feel . . .
ALCESTE. Is something, Madam, you alone can heal.
My outraged heart, beside itself with grief,
Appeals to you for comfort and relief.
Avenge me on your cousin, whose unjust
And faithless nature has deceived my trust;

Avenge a crime your pure soul must detest.
ÉLIANTE. But how, Sir?
ALCESTE. Madam, this heart within my breast
Is yours; pray take it; redeem my heart from her,
And so avenge me on my torturer.
Let her be punished by the fond emotion,
The ardent love, the bottomless devotion,
The faithful worship which this heart of mine
Will offer up to yours as to a shrine.
ÉLIANTE. You have my sympathy, Sir, in all you suffer;
Nor do I scorn the noble heart you offer;
But I suspect you'll soon be mollified,
And this desire for vengeance will subside.
When some belovèd hand has done us wrong
We thirst for retribution—but not for long;
However dark the deed that she's committed,
A lovely culprit's very soon acquitted.
Nothing's so stormy as an injured lover,
And yet no storm so quickly passes over.
ALCESTE. No, Madam, no—this is no lovers' spat;
I'll not forgive her; it's gone too far for that;
My mind's made up; I'll kill myself before
I waste my hopes upon her any more.
Ah, here she is. My wrath intensifies.
I shall confront her with her tricks and lies,
And crush her utterly, and bring you then
A heart no longer slave to Célimène.

SCENE 3

CÉLIMÈNE, ALCESTE.

ALCESTE [*Aside.*] Sweet heaven, help me to control my passion.
CÉLIMÈNE [*Aside.*] Oh, Lord.
[*To* ALCESTE.] Why stand there staring in that fashion?
And what d'you mean by those dramatic sighs,
And that malignant glitter in your eyes?
ALCESTE. I mean that sins which cause the blood to freeze
Look innocent beside your treacheries;
That nothing Hell's or Heaven's wrath could do
Ever produced so bad a thing as you.
CÉLIMÈNE. Your compliments were always sweet and pretty.
ALCESTE. Madam, it's not the moment to be witty.
No, blush and hang your head; you've ample reason,
Since I've the fullest evidence of your treason.
Ah, this is what my sad heart prophesied;
Now all my anxious fears are verified;

My dark suspicion and my gloomy doubt
Divined the truth, and now the truth is out.
For all your trickery, I was not deceived;
It was my bitter stars that I believed.
But don't imagine that you'll go scot-free;
You shan't misuse me with impunity.
I know that love's irrational and blind;
I know the heart's not subject to the mind,
And can't be reasoned into beating faster;
I know each soul is free to choose its master;
Therefore had you but spoken from the heart,
Rejecting my attentions from the start,
I'd have no grievance, or at any rate
I could complain of nothing but my fate.
Ah, but so falsely to encourage me—
That was a treason and a treachery
For which you cannot suffer too severely,
And you shall pay for that behavior dearly.
Yes, now I have no pity, not a shred;
My temper's out of hand; I've lost my head;
Shocked by the knowledge of your double-dealings,
My reason can't restrain my savage feelings;
A righteous wrath deprives me of my senses,
And I won't answer for the consequences.

CÉLIMÈNE. What does this outburst mean? Will you please explain?
Have you, by any chance, gone quite insane?

ALCESTE. Yes, yes, I went insane the day I fell
A victim to your black and fatal spell,
Thinking to meet with some sincerity
Among the treacherous charms that beckoned me.

CÉLIMÈNE. Pooh. Of what treachery can you complain?

ALCESTE. How sly you are, how cleverly you feign!
But you'll not victimize me any more.
Look: here's a document you've seen before.
This evidence, which I acquired today,
Leaves you, I think, without a thing to say.

CÉLIMÈNE. Is this what sent you into such a fit?

ALCESTE. You should be blushing at the sight of it.

CÉLIMÈNE. Ought I to blush? I truly don't see why.

ALCESTE. Ah, now you're being bold as well as sly;
Since there's no signature, perhaps you'll claim . . .

CÉLIMÈNE. I wrote it, whether or not it bears my name.

ALCESTE. And you can view with equanimity
This proof of your disloyalty to me!

CÉLIMÈNE. Oh, don't be so outrageous and extreme.

ALCESTE. You take this matter lightly, it would seem.
Was it no wrong to me, no shame to you,
That you should send Oronte this billet-doux?

CÉLIMÈNE. Oronte! Who said it was for him?
ALCESTE. Why, those
Who brought me this example of your prose.
But what's the difference? If you wrote the letter
To someone else, it pleases me no better.
My grievance and your guilt remain the same.
CÉLIMÈNE. But need you rage, and need I blush for shame,
If this was written to a *woman* friend?
ALCESTE. Ah! Most ingenious. I'm impressed no end;
And after that incredible evasion
Your guilt is clear. I need no more persuasion.
How dare you try so clumsy a deception?
D'you think I'm wholly wanting in perception?
Come, come, let's see how brazenly you'll try
To bolster up so palpable a lie:
Kindly construe this ardent closing section
As nothing more than sisterly affection!
Here, let me read it. Tell me, if you dare to,
That this is for a woman . . .
CÉLIMÈNE. I don't care to.
What right have you to badger and berate me,
And so highhandedly interrogate me?
ALCESTE. Now, don't be angry; all I ask of you
Is that you justify a phrase or two . . .
CÉLIMÈNE. No, I shall not. I utterly refuse,
And you may take those phrases as you choose.
ALCESTE. Just show me how this letter could be meant
For a woman's eyes, and I shall be content.
CÉLIMÈNE. No, no, it's for Oronte; you're perfectly right.
I welcome his attentions with delight,
I prize his character and his intellect,
And everything is just as you suspect.
Come, do your worst now; give your rage free rein;
But kindly cease to bicker and complain.
ALCESTE. [*Aside.*] Good God! Could anything be more inhuman?
Was ever a heart so mangled by a woman?
When I complain of how she has betrayed me,
She bridles, and commences to upbraid me!
She tries my tortured patience to the limit;
She won't deny her guilt; she glories in it!
And yet my heart's too faint and cowardly
To break these chains of passion, and be free,
To scorn her as it should, and rise above
This unrewarded, mad, and bitter love.
[*To* CÉLIMÈNE.] Ah, traitress, in how confident a fashion
You take advantage of my helpless passion,
And use my weakness for your faithless charms
To make me once again throw down my arms!

But do at least deny this black transgression;
Take back that mocking and perverse confession;
Defend this letter and your innocence,
And I, poor fool, will aid in your defense.
Pretend, pretend, that you are just and true,
And I shall make myself believe in you.

CÉLIMÈNE. Oh, stop it. Don't be such a jealous dunce,
Or I shall leave off loving you at once.
Just why should I *pretend*? What could impel me
To stoop so low as that? And kindly tell me
Why, if I loved another, I shouldn't merely
Inform you of it, simply and sincerely!
I've told you where you stand, and that admission
Should altogether clear me of suspicion;
After so generous a guarantee,
What right have you to harbor doubts of me?
Since women are (from natural reticence)
Reluctant to declare their sentiments,
And since the honor of our sex requires
That we conceal our amorous desires,
Ought any man for whom such laws are broken
To question what the oracle has spoken?
Should he not rather feel an obligation
To trust that most obliging declaration?
Enough, now. Your suspicions quite disgust me;
Why should I love a man who doesn't trust me?
I cannot understand why I continue,
Fool that I am, to take an interest in you.
I ought to choose a man less prone to doubt,
And give you something to be vexed about.

ALCESTE. Ah, what a poor enchanted fool I am;
These gentle words, no doubt, were all a sham;
But destiny requires me to entrust
My happiness to you, and so I must.
I'll love you to the bitter end, and see
How false and treacherous you dare to be.

CÉLIMÈNE. No, you don't really love me as you ought.

ALCESTE. I love you more than can be said or thought;
Indeed, I wish you were in such distress
That I might show my deep devotedness.
Yes, I could wish that you were wretchedly poor,
Unloved, uncherished, utterly obscure;
That fate had set you down upon the earth
Without possessions, rank, or gentle birth;
Then, by the offer of my heart, I might
Repair the great injustice of your plight;
I'd raise you from the dust, and proudly prove
The purity and vastness of my love.

CÉLIMÈNE. This is a strange benevolence indeed!
God grant that I may never be in need. . .
Ah, here's Monsieur Dubois, in quaint disguise.

SCENE 4

CÉLIMÈNE, ALCESTE, DUBOIS.

ALCESTE. Well, why this costume? Why those frightened eyes?
What ails you?
DUBOIS. Well, Sir, things are most mysterious.
ALCESTE. What do you mean?
DUBOIS. I fear they're very serious.
ALCESTE. What?
DUBOIS. Shall I speak more loudly?
ALCESTE. Yes; speak out.
DUBOIS. Isn't there someone here, Sir?
ALCESTE. Speak, you lout!
Stop wasting time.
DUBOIS. Sir, we must slip away.
ALCESTE. How's that?
DUBOIS. We must decamp without delay.
ALCESTE. Explain yourself.
DUBOIS. I tell you we must fly.
ALCESTE. What for?
DUBOIS. We mustn't pause to say good-by.
ALCESTE. Now what d'you mean by all of this, you clown?
DUBOIS. I mean, Sir, that we've got to leave this town.
ALCESTE. I'll tear you limb from limb and joint from joint
If you don't come more quickly to the point.
DUBOIS. Well, Sir, today a man in a black suit,
Who wore a black and ugly scowl to boot,
Left us a document scrawled in such a hand
As even Satan couldn't understand.
It bears upon your lawsuit, I don't doubt;
But all hell's devils couldn't make it out.
ALCESTE. Well, well, go on. What then? I fail to see
How this event obliges us to flee.
DUBOIS. Well, Sir: an hour later, hardly more,
A gentleman who's often called before
Came looking for you in an anxious way.
Not finding you, he asked me to convey
(Knowing I could be trusted with the same)
The following message. . . . Now, what *was* his name?
ALCESTE. Forget his name, you idiot. What did he say?
DUBOIS. Well, it was one of your friends, Sir, anyway.
He warned you to begone, and he suggested
That if you stay, you may well be arrested.

ALCESTE. What? Nothing more specific? Think, man, think!
DUBOIS. No, Sir. He had me bring him pen and ink,
And dashed you off a letter which, I'm sure,
Will render things distinctly less obscure.
ALCESTE. Well—let me have it!
CÉLIMÈNE. What *is* this all about?
ALCESTE. God knows; but I have hopes of finding out.
How long am I to wait, you blitherer?
DUBOIS. [*After a protracted search for the letter.*] I must have left it on your table, Sir.
ALCESTE. I ought to . . .
CÉLIMÈNE. No, no, keep your self-control;
Go find out what's behind his rigmarole.
ALCESTE. It seems that fate, no matter what I do,
Has sworn that I may not converse with you;
But, Madam, pray permit your faithful lover
To try once more before the day is over.

ACT V

SCENE 1

ALCESTE, PHILINTE.

ALCESTE. No, it's too much. My mind's made up, I tell you.
PHILINTE. Why should this blow, however hard, compel you . . .
ALCESTE. No, no, don't waste your breath in argument;
Nothing you say will alter my intent;
This age is vile, and I've made up my mind
To have no further commerce with mankind.
Did not truth, honor, decency, and the laws
Oppose my enemy and approve my cause?
My claims were justified in all men's sight;
I put my trust in equity and right;
Yet, to my horror and the world's disgrace,
Justice is mocked, and I have lost my case!
A scoundrel whose dishonesty is notorious
Emerges from another lie victorious!
Honor and right condone his brazen fraud,
While rectitude and decency applaud!
Before his smirking face, the truth stands charmed,
And virtue conquered, and the law disarmed!
His crime is sanctioned by a court decree!
And not content with what he's done to me,
The dog now seeks to ruin me by stating
That I composed a book now circulating,
A book so wholly criminal and vicious
That even to speak its title is seditious!

Meanwhile Oronte, my rival, lends his credit
To the same libelous tale, and helps to spread it!
Oronte! a man of honor and of rank,
With whom I've been entirely fair and frank;
Who sought me out and forced me, willy-nilly,
To judge some verse I found extremely silly;
And who, because I properly refused
To flatter him, or see the truth abused,
Abets my enemy in a rotten slander!
There's the reward of honesty and candor!
The man will hate me to the end of time
For failing to commend his wretched rhyme!
And not this man alone, but all humanity
Do what they do from interest and vanity;
They prate of honor, truth, and righteousness,
But lie, betray, and swindle nonetheless.
Come then: man's vallainy is too much to bear;
Let's leave this jungle and this jackal's lair.
Yes! treacherous and savage race of men,
You shall not look upon my face again.

PHILINTE. Oh, don't rush into exile prematurely;
Things aren't as dreadful as you make them, surely.
It's rather obvious, since you're still at large,
That people don't believe your enemy's charge.
Indeed, his tale's so patently untrue
That it may do more harm to him than you.

ALCESTE. Nothing could do that scoundrel any harm:
His frank corruption is his greatest charm,
And, far from hurting him, a further shame
Would only serve to magnify his name.

PHILINTE. In any case, his bald prevarication
Has done no injury to your reputation,
And you may feel secure in that regard.
As for your lawsuit, it should not be hard
To have the case reopened, and contest
This judgment . . .

ALCESTE. No, no, let the verdict rest.
Whatever cruel penalty it may bring,
I wouldn't have it changed for anything.
It shows the times' injustice with such clarity
That I shall pass it down to our posterity
As a great proof and signal demonstration
Of the black wickedness of this generation.
It may cost twenty thousand francs; but I
Shall pay their twenty thousand, and gain thereby
The right to storm and rage at human evil,
And send the race of mankind to the devil.

PHILINTE. Listen to me. . . .
ALCESTE. Why? What can you possibly say?
Don't argue, Sir; your labor's thrown away.
Do you propose to offer lame excuses
For men's behavior and the times' abuses?
PHILINTE. No, all you say I'll readily concede:
This is a low, conniving age indeed;
Nothing but trickery prospers nowadays,
And people ought to mend their shabby ways.
Yes, man's a beastly creature; but must we then
Abandon the society of men?
Here in the world, each human frailty
Provides occasion for philosophy,
And that is virtue's noblest exercise;
If honesty shone forth from all men's eyes,
If every heart were frank and kind and just,
What could our virtues do but gather dust
(Since their employment is to help us bear
The villainies of men without despair)?
A heart well-armed with virtue can endure. . . .
ALCESTE. Sir, you're a matchless reasoner, to be sure;
Your words are fine and full of cogency;
But don't waste time and eloquence on me.
My reason bids me go, for my own good.
My tongue won't lie and flatter as it should;
God knows what frankness it might next commit,
And what I'd suffer on account of it.
Pray let me wait for Célimène's return
In peace and quiet. I shall shortly learn,
By her response to what I have in view,
Whether her love for me is feigned or true.
PHILINTE. Till then, let's visit Éliante upstairs.
ALCESTE. No, I am too weighed down with somber cares.
Go to her, do; and leave me with my gloom
Here in the darkened corner of this room.
PHILINTE. Why, that's no sort of company, my friend;
I'll see if Éliante will not descend.

SCENE 2

CÉLIMÈNE, ORONTE, ALCESTE.

ORONTE. Yes, Madam, if you wish me to remain
Your true and ardent lover, you must deign
To give me some more positive assurance.
All this suspense is quite beyond endurance.
If your heart shares the sweet desires of mine,
Show me as much by some convincing sign;

And here's the sign I urgently suggest:
That you no longer tolerate Alceste,
But sacrifice him to my love, and sever
All your relations with the man forever.
CÉLIMÈNE. Why do you suddenly dislike him so?
You praised him to the skies not long ago.
ORONTE. Madam, that's not the point. I'm here to find
Which way your tender feelings are inclined.
Choose, if you please, between Alceste and me,
And I shall stay or go accordingly.
ALCESTE. [*Emerging from the corner.*] Yes, Madam, choose; this gentleman's demand
Is wholly just, and I support his stand.
I too am true and ardent; I too am here
To ask you that you make your feelings clear.
No more delays, now; no equivocation;
The time has come to make your declaration.
ORONTE. Sir, I've no wish in any way to be
An obstacle to your felicity.
ALCESTE. Sir, I've no wish to share her heart with you;
That may sound jealous, but at least it's true.
ORONTE. If, weighing us, she leans in your direction . . .
ALCESTE. If she regards you with the least affection . . .
ORONTE. I swear I'll yield her to you there and then.
ALCESTE. I swear I'll never see her face again.
ORONTE. Now, Madam, tell us what we've come to hear.
ALCESTE. Madam, speak openly and have no fear.
ORONTE. Just say which one is to remain your lover.
ALCESTE. Just name one name, and it will all be over.
ORONTE. What! Is it possible that you're undecided?
ALCESTE. What? Can your feelings possibly be divided?
CÉLIMÈNE. Enough: this inquisition's gone too far:
How utterly unreasonable you are!
Not that I couldn't make the choice with ease;
My heart has no conflicting sympathies;
I know full well which one of you I favor,
And you'd not see me hesitate or waver.
But how can you expect me to reveal
So cruelly and bluntly what I feel?
I think it altogether too unpleasant
To choose between two men when both are present;
One's heart has means more subtle and more kind
Of letting its affections be divined,
Nor need one be uncharitably plain
To let a lover know he loves in vain.
ORONTE. No, no, speak plainly; I for one can stand it.
I beg you to be frank.
ALCESTE. And I demand it.

The simple truth is what I wish to know,
And there's no need for softening the blow.
You've made an art of pleasing everyone,
But now your days of coquetry are done:
You have no choice now, Madam, but to choose,
For I'll know what to think if you refuse;
I'll take your silence for a clear admission
That I'm entitled to my worst suspicion.

ORONTE. I thank you for this ultimatum, Sir,
And I may say I heartily concur.

CÉLIMÈNE. Really, this foolishness is very wearing:
Must you be so unjust and overbearing?
Haven't I told you why I must demur?
Ah, here's Éliante; I'll put the case to her.

SCENE 3

ÉLIANTE, PHILINTE, CÉLIMÈNE, ORONTE, ALCESTE.

CÉLIMÈNE. Cousin, I'm being persecuted here
By these two persons, who, it would appear,
Will not be satisfied till I confess
Which one I love the more, and which the less,
And tell the latter to his face that he
Is henceforth banished from my company.
Tell me, has ever such a thing been done?

ÉLIANTE. You'd best not turn to me; I'm not the one
To back you in a matter of this kind:
I'm all for those who frankly speak their mind.

ORONTE. Madam, you'll search in vain for a defender.

ALCESTE. You're beaten, Madam, and may as well surrender.

ORONTE. Speak, speak, you must; and end this awful strain.

ALCESTE. Or don't, and your position will be plain.

ORONTE. A single word will close this painful scene.

ALCESTE. But if you're silent, I'll know what you mean.

SCENE 4

ARSINOÉ, CÉLIMÈNE, ÉLIANTE, ALCESTE, PHILINTE,
ACASTE, CLITANDRE, ORONTE.

ACASTE. [*To* CÉLIMÈNE.] Madam, with all due deference, we two
Have come to pick a little bone with you.

CLITANDRE. [*To* ORONTE *and* ALCESTE.] I'm glad you're present, Sirs; as you'll soon learn,
Our business here is also your concern.

ARSINOÉ. [*To* CÉLIMÈNE.] Madam, I visit you so soon again
Only because of these two gentlemen,

Who came to me indignant and aggrieved
About a crime too base to be believed.
Knowing your virtue, having such confidence in it,
I couldn't think you guilty for a minute,
In spite of all their telling evidence;
And, rising above our little difference,
I've hastened here in friendship's name to see
You clear yourself of this great calumny.

ALCESTE. Yes, Madam, let us see with what composure
You'll manage to respond to this disclosure.
You lately sent Clitandre this tender note.

CLITANDRE. And this one, for Acaste, you also wrote.

ACASTE. [*To* ORONTE *and* ALCESTE.] You'll recognize this writing, Sirs, I think;
The lady is so free with pen and ink
That you must know it all too well, I fear.
But listen: this is something you should hear.

How absurd you are to condemn my lightheartedness in society, and to accuse me of being happiest in the company of others. Nothing could be more unjust; and if you do not come to me instantly and beg pardon for saying such a thing, I shall never forgive you as long as I live. Our big bumbling friend the Viscount . . .

What a shame that he's not here.

Our big bumbling friend the Viscount, whose name stands first in your complaint, is hardly a man to my taste; and ever since the day I watched him spend three-quarters of an hour spitting into a well, so as to make circles in the water, I have been unable to think highly of him. As for the little Marquess . . .

In all modesty gentlemen, that is I.

As for the little Marquess, who sat squeezing my hand for such a long while yesterday, I find him in all respects the most trifling creature alive; and the only things of value about him are his cape and his sword. As for the man with the green ribbons . . .

[*To* ALCESTE.] It's your turn now, Sir.

As for the man with the green ribbons, he amuses me now and then with his bluntness and his bearish ill-humor; but there are many times indeed when I think him the greatest bore in the world. And as for the sonneteer . . .

[*To* ORONTE.] Here's your helping.

And as for the sonneteer, who has taken it into his head to be witty, and insists on being an author in the teeth of opinion, I simply cannot be bothered to listen to him, and his prose wearies me quite as much as his poetry. Be assured that I am not always so well-entertained as you suppose; that I long for your company, more than I dare to say, at all these entertainments to which people drag me; and that the presence of those one loves is the true and perfect seasoning to all one's pleasures.

CLITANDRE. And now for me.

Clitandre, whom you mention, and who so pesters me with his saccharine speeches, is the last man on earth for whom I could feel any affection. He is quite mad to suppose that I love him, and so are you, to doubt that you are loved. Do come to your senses; exchange your suppositions for his; and visit me as often as possible, to help me bear the annoyance of his unwelcome attentions.

It's a sweet character that these letters show,
And what to call it, Madam, you well know.
Enough. We're off to make the world acquainted
With this sublime self-portrait that you've painted.

ACASTE. Madam, I'll make you no farewell oration;
No, you're not worthy of my indignation.
Far choicer hearts than yours, as you'll discover,
Would like this little Marquess for a lover.

SCENE 5

CÉLIMÈNE, ÉLIANTE, ARSINOÉ, ALCESTE, ORONTE, PHILINTE.

ORONTE. So! After all those loving letters you wrote,
You turn on me like this, and cut my throat!
And your dissembling, faithless heart, I find,
Has pledged itself by turns to all mankind!
How blind I've been! But now I clearly see;
I thank you, Madam, for enlightening me.
My heart is mine once more, and I'm content;
The loss of it shall be your punishment.
[*To* ALCESTE.] Sir, she is yours; I'll seek no more to stand
Between your wishes and this lady's hand.

SCENE 6

CÉLIMÈNE, ÉLIANTE, ARSINOÉ, ALCESTE, PHILINTE.

ARSINOÉ. [*To* CÉLIMÈNE.] Madam, I'm forced to speak. I'm far too stirred
To keep my counsel, after what I've heard.
I'm shocked and staggered by your want of morals.
It's not my way to mix in others' quarrels;
But really, when this fine and noble spirit,
This man of honor and surpassing merit,

Laid down the offering of his heart before you,
How *could* you . . .

ALCESTE. Madam, permit me, I implore you,
To represent myself in this debate.
Don't bother, please, to be my advocate.
My heart, in any case, could not afford
To give your services their due reward;
And if I chose, for consolation's sake,
Some other lady, 'twould not be you I'd take.

ARSINOÉ. What makes you think you could, Sir? And how dare you
Imply that I've been trying to ensnare you?
If you can for a moment entertain
Such flattering fancies, you're extremely vain.
I'm not so interested as you suppose
In Célimène's discarded gigolos.
Get rid of that absurd illusion, do.
Women like me are not for such as you.
Stay with this creature, to whom you're so attached;
I've never seen two people better matched.

SCENE 7

CÉLIMÈNE, ÉLIANTE, ALCESTE, PHILINTE.

ALCESTE. [*To* CÉLIMÈNE.] Well, I've been still throughout this exposé,
Till everyone but me has said his say.
Come, have I shown sufficient self-restraint?
And may I now . . .

CÉLIMÈNE. Yes, make your just complaint.
Reproach me freely, call me what you will;
You've every right to say I've used you ill.
I've wronged you, I confess it; and in my shame
I'll make no effort to escape the blame.
The anger of those others I could despise;
My guilt toward you I sadly recognize.
Your wrath is wholly justified, I fear;
I know how culpable I must appear,
I know all things bespeak my treachery,
And that, in short, you've grounds for hating me.
Do so; I give you leave.

ALCESTE. Ah, traitress—how,
How should I cease to love you, even now?
Though mind and will were passionately bent
On hating you, my heart would not consent.
[*To* ÉLIANTE *and* PHILINTE.] Be witness to my madness, both of you;
See what infatuation drives one to;

But wait; my folly's only just begun,
And I shall prove to you before I'm done
How strange the human heart is, and how far
From rational we sorry creatures are.
[*To* CÉLIMÈNE.] Woman, I'm willing to forget your shame,
And clothe your treacheries in a sweeter name;
I'll call them youthful errors, instead of crimes,
And lay the blame on these corrupting times.
My one condition is that you agree
To share my chosen fate, and fly with me
To that wild, trackless, solitary place
In which I shall forget the human race.
Only by such a course can you atone
For those atrocious letters; by that alone
Can you remove my present horror of you,
And make it possible for me to love you.
CÉLIMÈNE. What! *I* renounce the world at my young age,
And die of boredom in some hermitage?
ALCESTE. Ah, if you really loved me as you ought,
You wouldn't give the world a moment's thought;
Must you have me, and all the world beside?
CÉLIMÈNE. Alas, at twenty one is terrified
Of solitude. I fear I lack the force
And depth of soul to take so stern a course.
But if my hand in marriage will content you,
Why, there's a plan which I might well consent to,
And . . .
ALCESTE. No, I detest you now. I could excuse
Everything else, but since you thus refuse
To love me wholly, as a wife should do,
And see the world in me, as I in you,
Go! I reject your hand, and disenthrall
My heart from your enchantments, once for all.

SCENE 8

ÉLIANTE, ALCESTE, PHILINTE.

ALCESTE. [*To* ÉLIANTE.] Madam, your virtuous beauty has no peer;
Of all this world, you only are sincere;
I've long esteemed you highly, as you know;
Permit me ever to esteem you so,
And if I do not now request your hand,
Forgive me, Madam, and try to understand.
I feel unworthy of it; I sense that fate
Does not intend me for the married state,
That I should do you wrong by offering you
My shattered heart's unhappy residue,

And that in short . . .
ÉLIANTE. Your argument's well taken:
Nor need you fear that I shall feel forsaken.
Were I to offer him this hand of mine,
Your friend Philinte, I think, would not decline.
PHILINTE. Ah, Madam, that's my heart's most cherished goal,
For which I'd gladly give my life and soul.
ALCESTE. [*To* ÉLIANTE *and* PHILINTE.] May you be true to all you now profess,
And so deserve unending happiness.
Meanwhile, betrayed and wronged in everything,
I'll flee this bitter world where vice is king,
And seek some spot unpeopled and apart
Where I'll be free to have an honest heart.
PHILINTE. Come, Madam, let's do everything we can
To change the mind of this unhappy man.

VII

THE MEASURE OF LOVE

What Makes the Heroes Valiant and the Poets Sing

INTRODUCTION

I

TO SPEAK of measure in connection with love is to defy a prevailing sentiment to the effect that if love can be measured, it cannot be true love. No popular song writer would tolerate "measured" love because love is held to be measureless. Robert Burns spoke for the lyricists when he wrote:

And I will luve thee still, my dear
Til a' the seas gang dry

Til a' the seas gang dry, my dear,
And the rocks melt wi' the sun;
And I will luve thee still, my dear,
While the sands o' life shall run.

"Give all to love," Ralph Waldo Emerson exhorts us. "All for Love" sums up the stories of Antony and Cleopatra, Paolo and Francesca, Heloise and Abelard, Tristan and Isolde, Romeo and Juliet, Don Quixote and Dulcinea del Toboso, to mention only a few famous lovers. "Love conquers all" is the motto of a half-million subliterary romances that trivialize the airwaves. Love is free; it strikes like lightning; it cannot be denied; it is a law unto itself; "There's beggary in the love that can be reckoned." These and other expressions seem to assert that the true measure of man is his capacity for measureless love, rather than for love according to measure.

Yet, if we study the literary record closely, we find that love does have its measures. In itself love is a force, an energy, that impels man to seek, to possess, and to enjoy a good. But since man is composed of a body and its needs and a soul and its needs, he seeks many different goods. Because he seeks the good of his body, he "loves" food, physical comforts, and the amenities of his home and his society. Because he seeks the good of his mind and soul, he "loves" and enjoys his friends and, in a special way, the intimate companionship and union found in marriage. Because his intellect is powerfully attracted to truth, he also "loves" virtue, goodness, perfection, and wisdom.

Now these three loves—love of things, love of persons, and love of truth—are not always in harmony. Indeed one good is often at war with another. Aeneas must choose between his love for Dido and his love for what he feels to be a higher good, the will of the Gods. Antony faces a choice between Cleopatra and an empire. Alceste in *The Misanthrope* must choose between his friends and his beloved and his love of truth. Love in short can divide and destroy unless a principle of order, some scale or measure, gives direction to its energy.

Is there such a scale? The poets have always assumed that there is. In his study of medieval love poetry called *In Praise of Love*, Maurice Valency points out that the Provençal poets, the most ardent disciples of love, were also the most ardent teachers of order. The special virtue of the true lover, he writes, is "the quality called *mezura*, measure, that inner restraint which governs the appetites and keeps them subject to the intellect." Measure, for the Provençal poets, was both an aesthetic norm and an ethical precept; it was "an equilibrating principle of the soul," equal to valor as the mark of knighthood, a necessary balance wheel to love, and the special virtue equivalent to the classic norm of the golden mean. "Nothing in the world is more highly prized than measure," writes Valency, citing Guillem de Montanhagol, a twelfth-century troubadour poet. "Measure is simply that which amends the defect in what is too much and too little. Reason forms it [measure] midway between these two and makes a virtue out of the two vices by taking from each what it contains of evil."

Measure, of course, was not sought by the Provençal poets for its own sake. Its three qualities—"self-restraint, self-control, self-mastery"—were only means of acquiring that right state of heart which permits the true lover to develop his full human perfection. The true lover, therefore, must put first things first. His self-esteem could give way to, but could not be canceled by, his love for his lady. So too his love for his lady could give way to, but could not be canceled by, his love for honor and truth. Centuries later, Sir Richard Lovelace echoed and reasserted this sense of measure in his poem "To Lucasta: Going to the Wars"—

Tell me not, sweet, I am unkind,
That from the nunnery
Of thy chaste breast and quiet mind
To war and arms I fly.

True, a new mistress now I chase,
The first foe in the field;
And with a stronger faith embrace
A sword, a horse, a shield.

Yet this inconsistency is such
As you too shall adore;
I could not love thee, dear, so much,
Loved I not honor more.

In this poem, to love honor more is not to esteem love less. It is simply to observe a scale or proportion in which love, measured not so much by the intensiy of the lover as it is by the nobility of the object that is loved, yields one of its rights to a higher obligation.

Here, then, in the nobility of the object we discover a measure of love. Our love is rightly ordered when we appreciate the worth of the good we seek to possess and enjoy. We do not give more affection to things than to human beings; we do not place our personal friendships above our respect for truth, our own profit above the common good, or expedience above right. But this measure is not just an ethical norm; it is an aesthetic one as well, as we shall see in a moment.

If an ethical norm is a statement that describes the right way of doing something, an aesthetic norm is a statement that describes the right way of making something. The former is a code of conduct; it measures the right or wrong of human action. The latter is a code of composition; it measures the success or failure of a literary or artistic work. The former praises by approving the action; the latter by approving the manner in which an action is represented.

In one sense, the aesthetic necessity of measure is immediately evident. A work of art cannot be successful if the artist does not observe the golden mean. To put in too much, or to leave out too much —to err by excess or by defect—is to violate the law of measure. To write in a style that is not proportioned to the theme and subject is to violate measure. Indeed, technique, considered in its widest sense as choice of incident, arrangement of details, and style, is both the *means* of achieving an artistic end and the *means* of measuring that achievement. Hence, whenever we say that a writer has chosen the right literary means for expressing a point of view, we are saying in effect that he has, consciously or unconsciously, achieved the mean or the measure of his art. When performance measures up to intention, the aesthetic norm is fulfilled.

But this does not mean that technique alone can explain the total achievement of an artist. Technique is a means toward an end. A writer who has no end—no clear vision of reality or, in the language of our discussion, nothing to measure—has no basis for choosing the appropriate means of measurement. In his destitution, he makes his technique an end in itself. He concentrates on "the best way of writing" rather than on "the best way of writing on a particular theme or subject." Such a writer may express himself, perhaps, but not his subject. The successful writer, on the other hand, has the object to be measured clearly in mind, and he chooses the best available measuring instrument to express it. When he is completely successful his ends and means, the object to be measured and the measurement, blend perfectly. W. B. Yeats gave this thought its most accurate and poetic expression when he wrote:

> O body swayed to music, O brightening glance,
> How can we know the dancer from the dance?

II

THE story writers represented in this section are all concerned with love. They all have something important to say about love, and they all say it differently. They tell us a great deal about the values men and women in love discover for themselves or what values we, the readers, discover by judging their action and reactions.

Jessamyn West's "Mr. Cornelius, I Love You" is the story of Cress Delahanty's discovery of what love truly means. We learn that she has an adolescent crush on Mr. Cornelius, a married man of the same age as her parents. Mr. Cornelius is stricken with tuberculosis. In her daydreams Cress creates a tender idyll in which she nurses him back to health and, in some vague way, enjoys his companionship forever. Her feelings are genuine and intense, her motives are pure. She is in love with Mr. Cornelius and she decides that she must tell him so.

What happens when Cress goes to the one-room tent-house where Mr. Cornelius lies ill leads step-by-step to the replacement of her illusions by reality. Mr. Cornelius's retching partly dispels her romantic anticipations. Mrs. Cornelius, a figure conveniently suppressed in Cress's daydreams, laughs them away.

> Mrs. Cornelius paused in her washing. "What did you come *for*?" she asked.

When Cress says that she has come to tell Mr. Cornelius she loves him, and then does so directly, Mrs. Cornelius laughs:

> not jeering, not angry, not unbelieving, but in the soft delighted way of a person who has received an unexpected gift, a pleasure never dreamed of but one come in the nick of time and most acceptable.

Cress makes the "astounding discovery" that Mr. and Mrs. Cornelius are one person; not "two separated people." "She felt as if her mind, by an infusion of light and warmth, was being forced to expand to accommodate this new idea." As a result Cress's adolescent "crush" develops into a mature friendship. She passes out of the world of daydreams and creates for herself "a single undivided world in which to live," a more substantial world and a more exciting one. She says to her friends Bernadine and Jo, "I think it's the most significant night of my life."

Like "Mr. Cornelius, I Love You," Frank O'Connor's "My Oedipus Complex" is a story of a child discovering the mysterious ways of love. Young Larry has had his mother all to himself during his father's absence in the war. He resents his father's return because it means a bewildering succession of painful changes. He loses his place in the big bed to the "stranger," his right to make noise at any moment in the day, and finally his sense of dignity. When he demands his own cup of tea and is fobbed off with "You can drink from Mummy's saucer," he declares war: "That settle[s] it," he says to himself. "Either Father or I [will] have to leave the house."

The prolonged skirmish that ensues between father and son for the affections of Mummy is one of the most humorous sequences in modern literature. It is also a purposeful comedy in which O'Connor explores with superb irony the interconnected loves of husband and wife, of mother and son, and finally, with the arrival of that poisonous pup, the new baby, of father and son. Love, Larry's experience reveals to us, is neither self-regarding nor exclusive; to survive, it must grow.

Both Jessamyn West and Frank O'Connor present love from the point of view of youth. Their visions of love are, in a sense, measured by the experiences and sensibilities of Cress and Larry. But there are other ways of experiencing different aspects of love. If in youth the norm of love is the distinction between illusion and reality, in maturity the norm is the distinction between fidelity and infidelity. In "Bliss" for instance, Katherine Mansfield takes us into the sophisticated adult world of London literary society where Bertha Young experiences in one evening exaltation and despair.

At the midpoint of the story Bertha sees the lovely pear tree in her garden as a symbol of her own life. "Really—really—she had everything. She was young. Harry and she were as much in love as ever. . . . She had an adorable baby. They didn't have to worry about money." Yet by the end of the evening, during which the corrosive cynicism of her guests has poisoned the atmosphere, Bertha has witnessed her husband's infidelity and the collapse of her hopes. "Oh, what is going to happen now?" she cries. Love, Miss Mansfield seems to warn us, is the prey of all the feline instincts of the world, of the Eddie Warrens who reduce it to "tomato soup," and of the Pearl Fultons who steal by instinct what they do not love.

J. F. Powers' "The Old Bird, A Love Story," resembles "Bliss" in that it describes an adult world and deals with the love between husband and wife. But Powers' point of view (the term here refers to his view of life rather than to his technique in telling a story), is markedly different from Miss Mansfield's. Old Charley Newman experiences no exalted lyric feelings about life or love. While Bertha Young has everything, Newman has nothing—not even a job—and his wife, unlike Bertha's Harry, is neither brilliant nor attractive. But she understands him, completely and relentlessly.

> She was the audience . . . and he was always on stage, the actor who was never taken quite seriously by his audience, no matter how heroic the role. The bad actor and his faithful but not foolish audience. Always! As now! It was not a hopeless situation, but only because she loved him.
>
> She *did* love him.

And because she did, Charlie stumbles on, incompetently but hopefully, pretending that things will turn out well and that he will be able to keep his job after the Christmas layoff, knowing that, although she doesn't believe a word, she will pretend to believe him. "He was the bad actor again. His only audience smiled and loved him."

Not all love stories concern realistic, identifiable human lovers. Some of the best are comic or even satiric tales whose characters are two-dimensional figures or types rather than individuals. Thus in Max Beerbohm's "The Happy Hypocrite" and Evelyn Waugh's "Love Among the Ruins" the figures of Lord George Hell and Miles Plastic are idealized demonstrations, the one of the healing power of love, the other of the dehumanizing effects of lovelessness.

"The Happy Hypocrite" is a subtle and often hilarious blend of circumstantial realism and fantasy. Realism comes first. The setting of regency England is sketched with all the appearance of sober history. The speaker's tone parodies that of an impartial observer who has looked up his facts and can cite contemporary documents to prove them. Shortly, however, Cupid, in the guise of a merry dwarf, lodges an arrow in the wicked heart of Lord George Hell, who proceeds to fall totally in love with the dancer Jenny Mere.

The comic romance burgeons. Lord George's proposal to the beautiful and innocent Jenny, her refusal to marry a man whose face is not saintly, his purchase of a saintlike mask, her acceptance of the masked George, their idyllic marriage, all lead up to the inevitable unmasking. La Gambogi, George's old flame, hunts him down in his cottage retreat in Kensington:

> "False saint," she shrieked, "then *I* will unmask you." . . . There was a loud pop, as though some great cork had been withdrawn, and La Gambogi recoiled. She had torn away the mask. . . . George stood motionless. La Gambogi stared up into his face, and her dark flush died swiftly away. For there, staring back at her, was the man she had unmasked, but, lo! his face was even as his mask had been. Line for line, feature for feature, it was the same. 'Twas a saint's face.

If virtuous love changes Lord George Hell into something of a saint, then the absence of it drives Miles Plastic in "Love Among the Ruins" to pyromania. Evelyn Waugh's satire on the materialistic totalitarian state bears a resemblance to Aldous Huxley's *Brave New World*, George Orwell's *1984*, and W. H. Auden's "To an Unknown Citizen." Like the characters in these terrifying prophecies Waugh's Miles Plastic is "conditioned" or "adjusted."

> No clean-living, God-fearing, Victorian gentleman, he; no complete man of the renaissance; no gentil knight nor dutiful pagan nor, even, noble savage. All that succession of past worthies had gone its way, content to play a prelude to Miles. He was the Modern Man.

How Miles is brought up by the state, how he falls from "grace" and is rehabilitated, how he serves in the Department of Euthanasia in Satellite City, and how he falls in love with the bearded Clara and is promoted to the Ministry of Welfare is a tale imbedded in prolonged ironic description of psychological engineering. Although Waugh satirizes virtually every phase of his imaginary modern state, he is chiefly concerned with its dehumanizing effect upon the individual. And the essence of dehumanization, he makes clear, is its hatred of human love. Human love, which should be the free choice of one's friends, one's wife, one's way of life, is directed, managed, engineered by the state with a false prudence in the interests of political power. Small wonder that tyranny almost necessarily attacks love, for love is the center of the human person, the source of man's independence. If one would subjugate man, one must prevent him from loving.

III

IN ORDINARY usage the word *love* implies sex, for the most typical expression of human love is that of man for woman. And the most typical expression of the love of man for woman (save when the word is cheapened or falsified) is the familiar drama that begins in mutual attraction, advances to courtship, expresses itself in nuptial love, and grows in mutual understanding, consolation, and support.

Yet love, even that between man and woman, is not always synonymous with conjugal affection. As Matthew Arnold points out in his "Dante and Beatrice" Dante loved an earthly Beatrice, but he did not desire to possess her as his wife. Rather he loved her as "his visible symbol of spiritual perfection. . . . Beatrice leads him to this [perfection]; herself symbolizes for him the ineffable beauty and purity for which he longs."

Love has other important meanings. Love includes fraternal love, such as that which King David utters for Jonathan: "Jonathan my brother, so beautiful, so well beloved, beyond all love of women." (II Kings 1, Ronald A. Knox, tr.)

The love of brother for brother or of friend for friend is not that of desire, but of benevolence or good will. A friend seeks not his own good, but the good of his friend and he finds satisfaction in giving and receiving confidence and good will. In his "Of Friendship" Sir Francis Bacon brings to mind what was once celebrated in the tales of Damon and Pythias and Roland and Oliver. Friendship, he writes, "maketh indeed a fair day in the affections . . . but it maketh daylight in the understanding. . . ."

Finally, we need to remind ourselves that love also means charity, that best gift of heaven according to St. Paul, without which everything else goes for nothing:

> Charity is patient, is kind; charity feels no envy; charity is never perverse or proud, never insolent; has no selfish aims, cannot be provoked, does not brood over an injury; takes no pleasure in wrong doing, but rejoices at the victory of truth; sustains, believes, hopes, endures, to the last. (I Corinthians 13, Ronald A. Knox, tr.)

Charity, so described, is a kind of perfection that man can never fully attain but in which he can participate. C. S. Lewis, writing on charity, remarks that "the total and secure transformation of a natural love into a mode of charity is so difficult that perhaps no fallen man has ever come within sight of doing it perfectly."

To recognize that love contains a variety of meanings is a necessary beginning to reading poetry. For poets, far more than most men, are aware of love's multiple dimensions. Poets do not pluck on one string. Shakespeare may write:

Love is not love
Which alters when it alteration finds . . . .
O, no! it is an ever-fixèd mark
That looks on tempests and is never shaken . . . .

But he is equally aware, as Juliet phrases it, that:

At lovers' perjuries
They say Jove laughs . . .
And that Love is at the mercy of Fortune.

A man loves a woman for her nobility or because, like Silvia, she is "holy, fair, and wise" or because, like Wordsworth's ideal woman, she is "a Being breathing thoughtful breath." But he loves her too because in Keats's words "her eyes [are] wild" or as Thomas Moore says "My only books/[are] woman's looks."

Love may be ecstatic, as in Elizabeth Barrett Browning's "How Do I Love Thee," or placid as in Robert Burns's "John Anderson, My Jo"; it may be despairing, as in Matthew Arnold's "Isolation," or confident, as in Ralph Waldo Emerson's "Give All to Love"; it may be a unitive force as in Robert Frost's "The Tuft of Flowers," or a divisive one as in Alice Meynell's "Renouncement."

Yet, whatever aspect of love they sing about, the poets are still concerned with measure. Do the lovers suffer? In "Two in the Campagna" Browning suggests they do because of the difference between "Infinite passion" and the "finite hearts that yearn." A law, too mysterious to be made explicit, punishes excess and defect. Hence Tennyson's Tithonus, to whom the dawn goddess Eos granted immortality but not perpetual youth, cries out that it is a mockery to live forever and forever as an old man:

Let me go; take back thy gift.
Why should a man desire in any way
To vary from the kindly race of men,
Or pass beyond the goal of ordinance,
Where all should pause, as is most meet for all?

Measure plays its part, too, in T. S. Eliot's "The Love Song of J. Alfred Prufrock." Obliquely, with the blurred emphasis of fog, Eliot presents his neurasthenic hero in juxtaposition to positive characters in the work of Dante, Shakespeare, and other writers.

No! I am not Prince Hamlet, nor was meant to be;
Am an attendant lord . . .
Almost, at times, the Fool.

But if law or measure punishes Tithonus for exceeding the human norm and ridicules Prufrock for failing to achieve it, it can also reward and preserve. Edwin Muir puts it well in his "In Love for Long":

This love a moment known
For what I do not know
And in a moment gone
Is like the happy doe
That keeps its perfect laws
Between the tiger's paws
And vindicates its cause.

STORIES

Jessamyn West

MR. CORNELIUS, I LOVE YOU

Mr. and Mrs. Delahanty, Cress, and Cress's friends, Jo Grogan and Bernadine Deevers, sat down to the Delahanty dinner table on Wednesday evening. The table was round with a white cloth that dipped at its four corners to the floor, so that in the dusk of the dining room the cloth seemed actually to be supporting the table. Mrs. Delahanty, who hadn't even expected Cress home for dinner, let alone Jo and Bernadine, felt apologetic about the food which, besides being rather uninviting, was skimpy in amount: a small salmon loaf, Harvard beets, mashed potatoes, and for dessert a cabinet pudding which did nothing to redeem the meal that had gone before. But the girls didn't seem to know or care what they put in their mouths and she decided that strawberries and fresh asparagus would have been wasted on them.

A mockingbird was singing in the orange grove outside the opened windows and the girls listened, a spoonful of cabinet pudding lifted to their opened lips—then, as the song ceased, put the spoons down without having tasted a bite. Mr. and Mrs. Delahanty had given up trying to carry on a conversation with them and treated them as so many portraits ranged round their dining room—"Girls at Dusk," or "Reveries of Youth." They talked their own talk and let the girls dream their dreams, wrap their feet around the rungs of their chairs, and listen (mouths open, eyes closed) to the bird song.

"I saw Doc Mendenhall in town today," Mr. Delahanty said.

Mrs. Delahanty said "Yes?" waiting for whatever it was that made this fact worth reporting, but Bernadine interrupted his train of thought, if he had one, by extending her long arms toward the darkening windows and singing very softly, "Oh night of love, oh beauteous night." Bernadine was barefooted (it was the spring's great fad at high school) though she was eighteen, and wore an elaborate blue voile dress which drifted about her like a sky-stained cloud. Bernadine was to be married the day after school was out and sometimes, Mrs. Delahanty felt, overplayed her role of bride-to-be.

It was already, unbelievably, the last week of school which, in Southern California, is the second week in June, a time climatically as well as scholastically neither one thing nor another, neither spring nor summer, neither truly school nor truly vacation. Class routines had been relaxed but not abandoned. Gradewise, the feeling among the students was that the year was already water over the dam; still they couldn't be positive; some of the teachers were still going through the motions of setting down grades in their record books. Climatically the days started spring-like, damp and gray with threat even of one more unseasonal rain; at 1 P.M. exactly the day did an about-face, took on September inclinations. At that hour the overcast burned away and the tawny grasses, sun-bleached foothills, and smoldering flowers of full summer emerged. It was very confusing after getting up into a dripping cold which made sweaters and open fires necessary, to finish the day barefooted, hot-cheeked, and as naked as possible.

Cress and Jo both wore shorts and halters. Cress had shasta daisies tucked in the V of her halter and Jo Grogan, with those three flame-colored hibiscus in her short dark hair, might have been August itself on any calendar of girls. As the day darkened the white tablecloth grew silvery, the mockingbird retreated deeper into the orchard, and Mrs. Delahanty felt that the whole scene might be unreal, a mirage cast up into the present out of either the past or the future—that girls *had* sat in many a darkening room in years gone by and would so sit in the future; but that "now," the present minute, was unreal, only the past whisking by on its way to the future, or the future casting a long prophetic shadow to rearwards.

"Jo," she said briskly, "if you'll put some more custard on your pudding you might be able to eat it."

"I beg your pardon," said Jo. "Were you speaking to me?"

"Never mind," Mrs. Delahanty told her. "I was only urging you to eat."

"Oh food!" said Cress. "Food. Who cares about food?"

"I do," said Bernadine. "Howie adores puddings. Will you copy down this recipe for me, Mrs. Delahanty? I plan to serve Howie a different pudding every single night for thirty nights. I already have twenty-two recipes."

"Tapioca, jello, and bread," said Jo, sing-songing. "If puddings be the food of love, cook on."

The mockingbird had ceased to sing. The leaves of the bougainvillaea vine which clambered over the dining-room wall rustled faintly. Mrs. Delahanty began taking the spoons from the serving dishes.

Mr. Delahanty remarked in the voice of a man who has had the words in mind for some time, "Doc Mendenhall says that Frank Cornelius had a bad hemorrhage this morning."

Mrs. Delahanty laid the spoons down, clattering. "Oh John!" she said. "I understood he was getting better."

There was a note in her voice of condemnation, as if Mr. Cornelius had not tried hard enough, as if he were a turncoat, a traitor to his generation—and hers. When old people sickened and died, men and women in their seventies and eighties, that was to be expected. But thirty-eight! That was a direct threat to her and John.

"I don't think he's taken very good care of himself," Mr. Delahanty explained. "You can't throw off t.b. just by wishing. You've got to co-operate, rest, stay put. I've seen Cornelius about town off and on all spring. Baseball, things like that. Staggering around half-alive. I saw him yesterday, sitting along the road out by his place. Today, a hemorrhage. He was asking for . . ."

Cress sprang to her feet, interrupting her father. "You mustn't say that. You have no right to say that." She pulled the daisies from the neck of her halter and passed them from hand to hand distractedly. "You don't have any idea what it's like to be dying. Do you?" she insisted.

Mr. Delahanty agreed instantly. "No, I don't, Crescent. The worst I ever had was a touch of shingles."

"Don't be funny," Cress said, her chin quivering. "Don't be funny about death. How can you understand how terrible it is for Mr. Cornelius to think he may die, no matter how much he takes care of himself? And that if he doesn't go out and see the sunshine and people and trees today he may never see them again. Never, never. And you were never a great athlete like Mr. Cornelius, so it's a thousand times worse for him than it would be for you to stay in bed. And you blame him. You blame him for not giving in. You blame him—" She paused, trying to steady her voice. "I hate—I hate *people* who say cruel things like that." She looked at her father and Mr. Delahanty looked back. Then she dropped her daisies onto her plate amidst the uneaten salmon and beets and ran from the room.

Mrs. Delahanty, after the sound of the slammed door had stopped echoing, leaned over and began to gather up the daisies. The two girls excused themselves and left the room.

"What did I say?" Mr. Delahanty asked. "To cause all that?"

Mrs. Delahanty continued without speaking to shake bits of food from the flowers. "Gertrude, did what I said sound cruel and hateful to you?"

"No, John, not to me," she answered. "But then I'm not in love with Mr. Cornelius."

In her bedroom, Cress sat on the floor, her head on the window sill. When she felt an arm about her shoulders, Jo's by the weight and pressure, she said, "Go away, please go away and leave me alone." The arm remained where it was. Jo knew, and so did Bernadine. Not much, because there wasn't much to know, except that she had seen Mr. Cornelius three times to look at him and had spoken to him twice and that she loved him and would willingly die for him.

There was "not much to know" in what was called the outside world; but inside herself, in her dreams and imaginings there was nothing *but* Mr. Cornelius. She had decided out of her experience of loving Mr. Cornelius that the knowledge people had of one another, parents of children, anyway, was almost nothing. She could sit at the dinner table with her father and mother, answering their questions about school, but being in reality thousands of miles away in some hot dry land nursing Mr. Cornelius back to health; and her father and mother never noticed her absence in the least.

In her dreams she and Mr. Cornelius sometimes went away together, Mr. Cornelius saying, "Cress, without knowing it I have been searching for you all of my life. My sickness is no more than the sum of my disappointment, and without you I can never get well."

Sometimes in her dreams Mrs. Cornelius came to her and the gist of what she said was, "My life with Mr. Cornelius has been a failure. He has not many months to live. I do not want to stand between him and his happiness in the little time that is left. Go, with my blessing."

But for the most part Mrs. Cornelius and the Cornelius boys did not exist in her dreams; even the world, as she knew it in what was called "real life," was greatly altered; or, perhaps, simplified. Changed, anyway, so that it consisted of nothing but sunshine, a background of sand or water, and a grassy or sandy bank against which Mr. Cornelius reclined, getting well. And as he got well she waited on him, and talked to him. As a matter of fact, every thought in her mind had become part of an unending monologue directed toward the omnipresent mental image of Mr. Cornelius. Everything she saw immediately became words in a report to Mr. Cornelius; and if, by chance, some experience was so absorbing as to momentarily obscure his image, she made up for it by living the whole scene through once again just for him. Sometimes she imagined that Mr. Cornelius kissed her. She had to be careful about these imaginings however. She had never been kissed, family didn't count, of course, and since she supposed that when you were kissed by the man you loved, the sensations were near to swooning, swooning was what she nearly did whenever she had imaginings of this kind.

Most often she simply helped Mr. Cornelius as he reclined in the midst of the sunny simplified landscape, his thin beautiful face becoming tanned and fuller as his health improved; but not more beautiful. That was impossible. She doted on his hawk-nose and dark crest; she dismissed every other face she saw as pudgy and ill-shaped by comparison. In her dream she picked flowers for Mr. Cornelius, went to the library for him, read to him, smoothed his brow, sometimes kissed him and always, always gazed at him with enraptured eyes. But all the time she was imagining this life with Mr. Cornelius she suffered, because Mr. Cornelius was dying and there was nothing she could do about it; she suffered because she had feelings which she did not know how to express, suffered because she had put the core of her life outside its circumference.

She sat up, and Jo took her arm away. It was still light enough to see Bernadine on the floor leaning against the bed, and Jo by her side. The pitcher of white stock on her desk reflected what light there was, like a moon. The room was quiet and warm and full of misery.

"There is nothing you can do, Cress," Jo said. "You love him and he is dying. You can't do anything about either one. All you can do is to endure it."

"I can do something," Cress said.

"What?" Jo asked.

"I can go to Mr. Cornelius and tell him I love him."

"Oh no," Bernadine said, very shocked. "You can't do that."

"Why not?" Cress asked.

"You don't know whether he loves you or not."

"What does that have to do with it? I'm not going to him to ask him if he loves me. I'm going to tell him that I love him."

"Is that what you really want to do, Cress?" Jo asked.

"No—if you mean by want to, do I feel good about going. I feel awful about going. It makes me feel sick to my stomach to even think about it. It gives me the shakes."

Jo once again put an arm around Cress's shoulders. "It's a fact," she reported to Bernadine. "She's shaking like a leaf."

"Look, Cress," Bernadine said. "I'm almost married myself. It's just a matter of days. For all practical purposes I *am* married. You must think of Mr. Cornelius, Cress, and what he'd feel. I know if Howie was sick and maybe dying he wouldn't want some other woman coming to his sick bed and saying, 'I love you.' The first thing he'd do, I know, is say to me, 'Bernadine, throw this madwoman out.' And that's exactly what Mr. Cornelius is liable to say to you."

"I know it," Cress said bleakly.

"Well, then?" Bernadine asked, pride of reasoning in her voice. "Are you still going?"

Cress huddled silent, unanswering.

"It's probably not a very kind thing to do," Jo suggested in her deep, thoughtful voice. "Go to see him now when he's so sick."

"Oh I *know* that. If I just asked myself what was kind I would never do it. But what has kindness got to do with love? I'm not doing it to be kind to Mr. Cornelius. I'm doing it because I have to."

"Have to?" Jo reminded her, steadily. "You don't have to. Sit right here. Sit still. By morning everything will be different."

"By morning Mr. Cornelius may be dead."

"Well then," Bernadine said, "all your problems will be over. Mr. Cornelius will be dead and you'll be sad. But you won't have bothered him or made a fool of yourself."

"I don't care about making a fool of myself."

"You do care. You're still shaking. And think about Mrs. Cornelius. How's she going to feel about someone barging in on her sick husband, making passionate declarations of love?"

"It wouldn't be passionate. I would just say, very quietly, the minute I got there, 'I love you, Mr. Cornelius.' Then leave."

"Cress," Bernadine said, "what actually do you see yourself doing? You get there, the whole family is around the bed, and doctors and priests too, maybe. What are your plans? To say 'I beg your pardon but I've a little message for Mr. Cornelius'? Then push your way through them all to the bedside, drop on your knee, kiss his wasted hand and say, 'Mr. Cornelius, I love you.' Is that it?"

"Oh, don't heckle her, Bernadine," Jo said.

"What I see myself doing," said Cress, "is telling Mr. Cornelius something I have to tell him."

"How," asked Bernadine, "do you see yourself getting there?" Bernadine had Howie's car while he was in the army and she had driven the girls home from school. "Do you see yourself walking eight miles?"

"If I have to," Cress said.

"O.K.," Bernadine told her. "I'll drive you. And let's go right away and get it over with."

Mr. Cornelius was still living in the small one-room tent-house at the edge of the walnut grove in which his home stood. Here he was away from the noises of his family and was able to get the fresh air he needed. It was nine o'clock when Bernadine stopped the car in front of the Cornelius ranch. A dim light was burning inside the tent-house, but there was nothing to indicate the presence of the crowd of people she had prophesied. "Here we are," she said, turning off the engine.

Cress wished for any catastrophe, however great, which would prevent her from having to leave the car. She felt real hatred for Bernadine and Jo. Why, if they were convinced that she shouldn't come, hadn't they remained steadfast? What kind of friends were they, to give way to their better judgment so weakly? And what were her parents thinking about? Why had they permitted her to go riding off into the night? To tell a strange man she loved him? True, she hadn't told them where she was going nor that she loved a strange man. But what were parents for if not to understand without being told? She blamed them for her fright and unhappiness.

Still anything that *happened* would be better than continuing to live in a make-believe world in which she only dreamed that she told Mr. Cornelius she loved him. And she knew that if Bernadine were to start the car now she would jump out and run toward the tent-house and the declaration which would start her to living inside her dream. She opened the car door and stepped out into the night air which, after the warmth of the car, was damp and cold against her bare legs and arms.

"Cheerio," said Bernadine quite calmly as she was walking away from the car under the dark canopy of the big trees toward the dimly lighted room. Why was it so hard to do what she had set her heart on doing?

She stood at the screened door looking into the room as into a picture. Why did it seem like a picture? The small number of furnishings? Their neat arrangement, dresser balanced by table, chair by bed? The light falling from a bulb, shaded by blue paper, so that part of the room was in deep shadow? But most of all, was it picture-like because she had imagined the room and Mr. Cornelius for so long, that a frame had grown up about them in her mind? Now, would it be possible to break that frame? She opened the screen door, stepped into the room and became a part of the picture by that easy act.

Mr. Cornelius lay on a high narrow bed. He lay very straight, his head supported by three or four pillows and his hands folded across an ice pack which he held to his chest. His eyes were closed and his face, in spite of his illness, was warm with color. At the sight of him all of Cress's doubts left her. Oh Mr. Cornelius, she thought, I do truly love you and I have come at last to tell you.

Without opening his eyes Mr. Cornelius said, "Joyce, I think I'm going to be sick."

Joyce. Cress was surprised at the name. It seemed too gentle for the bus driver. "It's not Joyce, Mr. Cornelius," Cress said. "It's me."

Then Mr. Cornelius opened his eyes and Cress was enchanted all over again by the enormous blaze of being alive and searching and understanding which she saw there.

"It's Cress," he said, in a very low careful voice, "the track-meet girl." Then he closed his eyes. "I'm going to be sick," he said. "Hand me the basin."

The basin, Cress saw, was an enamel wash bowl on the night stand by the bed. She got it, put it on the bed beside Mr. Cornelius.

"Help me," Mr. Cornelius said and Cress helped him the way her mother had helped her when she was sick after her tonsils were out, by putting an arm around his shoulders and supporting him.

"Don't be scared," Mr. Cornelius whispered. "It's not a hemorrhage. I'm just going to lose my supper."

He did and afterwards he lay back against his pillows for a minute or two, then he reached up his hand and rang the bell which was suspended from the headboard of his bed.

"A glass of water," he told Cress, and Cress was holding it for him to rinse his mouth when Mrs. Cornelius arrived. Mrs. Cornelius paid no more attention to her than if she'd been some kind of device to help Mr. Cornelius—like the ice pack or the bell. She took the glass from Cress's hand, slipped her arm around her husband's shoulders and said, "Frank, Frank. Oh thank God, Frank, no more blood. Just your supper and that doesn't matter. I made you eat too much. This was to be expected. If you can swallow a bite or two later I'll fix you another. How do you feel now, honey?"

Cress had backed away from the bed. Mrs. Cornelius was wearing a housecoat or dressing gown of deep red, lightened by wreaths of tiny yellow and white flowers. What she looked like now was not a General in the Russian army but Robert Louis Stevenson's wife, "trusty, dusky, vivid and true with eyes of gold and bramble dew." Her bosom, which had spoiled the lines of her chauffeur's coat, was exactly right for pillowing an invalid's head, and her chestnut hair, curled corkscrew crisp, said "Never give up," as plain as any words, said "Fight on," said "Defy the universe." And all the time she was cradling Mr. Cornelius in her arms, and helping him rinse his mouth she was pressing her cheek to his hair and speaking comforting words through which there ran a mixture of laughing and joking.

"Take this to the bathroom and empty it," she said to Cress when Mr. Cornelius had finished rinsing his mouth. She handed the basin to Cress and nodded toward a door at the back of the room. Cress, ordinarily too squeamish to pull off her own Band-Aids, marched away with it without a word.

When she returned Mr. Cornelius was once more against his pillows and Mrs. Cornelius was wiping his face with a damp cloth.

"Where'd you come from?" she asked Cress as she took the basin from her.

"From out there," Cress said, nodding toward the road. "The girls are waiting for me. In the car," she explained.

Mrs. Cornelius paused in her washing. "What did you come *for?*" she asked.

Cress welcomed the question. It was a wonderful help, like the upward spring of the diving board against her feet when she was reluctant to take off into deep water. Though she no longer had so great a need to say what she had come to say, some change had taken place in her since she had come into the room; what had been locked inside her and had been painful, because unsaid, had somehow, without a word being spoken, gotten itself partially expressed. She was not sure how. Nevertheless she had come to speak certain words. They were the answer to Mrs. Cornelius' question. They were *why* she had come.

So, louder than was necessary, and in a voice cracking with strain she said, "I came to tell Mr. Cornelius I loved him." Then she turned, resolutely, and said the words directly to Mr. Cornelius. "Mr. Cornelius, I love you."

At that Mrs. Cornelius laughed, not jeering, not angry, not unbelieving, but in the soft delighted way of a person who has received an unexpected gift, a pleasure never dreamed of but one come in the nick of time and most acceptable.

"Oh, Frankie," she said, running her hand through Mr. Cornelius' thick black hair, "look at what we've got here."

"What *we've* got," was what she'd said as if, Cress thought, I'd said I loved them both. And then, watching Mr. Cornelius reach for his wife's hand, she saw that there was nothing she could give to Mr. Cornelius without giving it also to Mrs. Cornelius. Because they were not two separated people. They were really one, the way the Bible said. It was an astounding discovery. It was almost too much for her. It held her motionless and speculating. She felt as if her mind, by an infusion of light and warmth, was being forced to expand to accommodate this new idea. And it was an idea which, contrary to all her expectations, she liked. It was exactly what she wanted. Not Mr. Cornelius alone on a stretch of desert sand and she kissing his wasted hand—in spite of her six months' dreaming. What she wanted was Mr. and Mrs. Cornelius. She was so happy for

Mrs. Cornelius' presence she almost took and kissed *her* plump brown unwasted hand.

Mrs. Cornelius, however, was continuing her laughing murmur to her husband. "Frankie," she said, "oh Frankie, you old jackanapes. You old irresistible. What's all this talk about being on your last legs? Done for? Caved in? With school girls coming with professions of love? Pretty school girls. Boy, we're not cashing in our checks just yet. Not us. What's your name, dear?" she asked Cress.

Mr. Cornelius answered in his low half-whispering voice. "She's John Delahanty's daughter, Crescent. They call her Cress at school."

"Well," said Mrs. Cornelius. "I've heard the boys mention you. Where'd you see Frank?"

"At a track meet."

"I stared at her some," Mr. Cornelius said. "Reminded me of you at her age. So alive."

"Was I ever like that?" Mrs. Cornelius asked her husband.

"That's what *I* thought about Mr. Cornelius," Cress said.

"Alive?" asked Mrs. Cornelius.

"Oh yes. More than anyone there. More than the boys. I thought his eyes fed on the sights," she said, daring the poetry of her thoughts.

"Fed?" Mrs. Cornelius studied the word then accepted it. "I see what you mean. Now, Frank," she said, "will you lie still and take care of yourself? Unknown school girls loving you and wanting you to get well. You do, don't you?" she asked Cress.

"Oh yes," Cress said. "I was willing to die for him."

Her voice evidently convinced Mrs. Cornelius. "Oh, Frank," she said, "school girls willing to die for you and you not half trying."

"Mrs. Cornelius," Cress said, wanting, since even partial confession made her feel so much better, to tell everything, "I ought to tell you something else." She stumbled for words. "I ought to tell you what else I planned."

"I bet you planned to run away with Frank and nurse him back to health."

Cress was amazed. "Yes," she said, her face burning with guilt and foolishness, "yes I did. How did you know?"

"Oh Frank, don't it bring it all back to you? No wonder you were reminded of me. *I* was going to run away with the minister," she said, turning to Cress. "Save him from his wife and family. And he *was* the most beautiful man in the world, Frank. You can't hold a candle to your father—never could."

Cress wanted to say something, but she couldn't settle on what. She had too many emotions to express. Exhilaration at being released from the isolation of her dreaming; relief to find that other girls had loved secretly too, but most of all joy to have acted, to have made for herself a single undivided world in which to live.

"Oh Mrs. Cornelius," she said, "oh Mrs. Cornelius . . . ."

"Cress," asked Mrs. Cornelius, "can you play cards? Or checkers?"

"Yes," Cress said, "I can. I like to."

"And read out loud? Of course you can do that, can't you? Why don't you come read to Frank? And play cards with him? It gets so darn lonesome for him. I work. The boys work, and besides they haven't enough patience to sit still. And the good people come in and tell Frank how their uncles or mothers passed away with consumption and for him to be resigned. He needs somebody interested in living, not dying. Would you come?"

"Oh yes. If you want me—if he wants me. I could come every day all summer."

"O.K.," Mrs. Cornelius said, "we'll plan on it. Now you'd better run on. Frank's had a bad day. He's worn out."

Cress looked at Mr. Cornelius. His eyes were closed but he opened them at Mrs. Cornelius' words and made a good-by flicker with the lids.

"Good night," Cress said.

Mrs. Cornelius went to the door with her. "We'll count on you," she said once again and put a hand on Cress's shoulder and gave her a kind of humorous loving shake before she turned away.

Cress flew to the car propelled, it seemed, by the beat of her heart as a bird is propelled by the beat of its wings. The walnut leaves were alive and fluttering in the warm air and all about her mockingbirds were singing like nightingales. As she emerged from the grove she saw the June stars big and heavy-looking like June roses. This is the happiest hour of my life, she thought, and she yearned to do something lovely for the girls, something beautiful and memorable; but all she could think of was to ask them to go to town for milk shakes.

"I could stand some food," Bernadine said, "after all that waiting."

"He was sick," Cress explained, "and Mrs. Cornelius and I had to take care of him."

"Mrs. Cornelius? Did she come out?"

"Of course," Cress answered. "Wouldn't you, if Howie was sick?"

Bernadine had no answer to this. She started the car and after they had gone a mile or so Jo asked, "Did you tell him?"

"Of course."

"Does he love you?" Bernadine asked.

Cress felt sorry for Bernadine. "You're a fine one to be getting married," she said. "Of course he doesn't. He loves Joyce."

"Joyce? Who's Joyce?"

"Mrs. Cornelius. I remind him some of her. I adore Mrs. Cornelius. She is like Mrs. Robert Louis Stevenson and *they* are one person. Mr. and Mrs. Cornelius, I mean. They are truly married. I don't suppose you understand," she said, arrogant with new knowledge, "but what is for the one is for the other. I am going to help her take care of him this summer. Isn't that wonderful? Maybe I can really help him get well. Isn't this the most gloriously beautiful night? Oh, I think it's the most significant night of my life." The two girls were silent, but Cress was too full of her own emotions to notice.

When they went into the soda fountain, she looked at their reflection in the mirror and liked what she saw. The three of them had always been proud of one another. Bernadine had glamour, Jo character, and Cress personality; that was the division they made of themselves. "Look at Bernadine, listen to Cress, and let Jo act," someone had said. Oh, but I've broken through that, Cress thought, I can act, too. She searched for some understanding of the part Mrs. Cornelius had played in that breakthrough. If she had said, "You wicked girl," or made her feel that loving was a terrible thing, would she have been pushed back, fearful, into the narrowness of dreaming, and into dreaming's untruths? She didn't know. She couldn't hold her mind to such abstractions.

"What we want," she said to Lester Riggins, the boy at the fountain, "is simply the most stupendous, colossal, overpowering concoction you ever served."

"This a special night?" Lester asked.

"Super-special."

"How come?"

"Bernadine's going to be married."

"Known that for six months."

"Jo's been accepted for Stanford. With special praise."

"Old stuff."

"Then there's me."

"What about you?"

"I'm alive."

"That's different," Lester said. "Why didn't you tell me in the first place? How do you like it?"

"Being alive? Fine," said Cress. "Better than shooting stars."

"O.K., O.K.," Lester said. "This obviously merits the Riggins' special. Expense any issue?"

"No issue," Cress said.

He brought them something shaped, roughly, like the Eiffel Tower, but more dramatically colored.

"Here it is, girls. Here's to being alive!"

They sank their spoons in it and ate it down, their appetites equal to the whole of it, color, size, sweetness and multiplicity of ingredients.

Frank O'Connor

MY OEDIPUS COMPLEX

FATHER was in the army all through the war—the first war, I mean—so, up to the age of five, I never saw much of him, and what I saw did not worry me. Sometimes I woke and there was a big figure in khaki peering down at me in the candlelight. Sometimes in the early morning I heard the slamming of the front door and the clatter of nailed boots down the cobbles of the lane. These were Father's entrances and exits. Like Santa Claus he came and went mysteriously.

In fact, I rather liked his visits, though it was an uncomfortable squeeze between Mother and him when I got into the big bed in the early morning. He smoked, which gave him a pleasant musty smell, and shaved, an operation of astounding interest. Each time he left a trail of souvenirs—model tanks and Gurkha knives with handles made of bullet cases, and German helmets and cap badges and button-sticks, and all sorts of military equipment—carefully stowed away in a long box on top of the wardrobe, in case they ever came in handy. There was a bit of the magpie about Father; he expected everything to come in handy. When his back was turned, Mother let me get a chair and rummage through his treasures. She didn't seem to think so highly of them as he did.

The war was the most peaceful period of my life. The window of my attic faced southeast. My mother had curtained it, but that had small effect. I always woke with the first light and, with all the responsibilities of the previous day melted, feeling myself rather like the sun, ready to illumine and rejoice. Life never seemed so simple and clear and full of responsibilities as then. I put my feet out from under the clothes—I called them Mrs. Left and Mrs. Right—and invented dramatic situations for them in which they discussed the problems of the day. At least Mrs. Right did; she was very demonstrative, but I hadn't the same control of Mrs. Left, so she mostly contented herself with nodding agreement.

They discussed what Mother and I should do during the day,

---

what Santa Claus should give a fellow for Christmas, and what steps should be taken to brighten the home. There was that little matter of the baby, for instance. Mother and I could never agree about that. Ours was the only house in the terrace without a new baby, and Mother said we couldn't afford one till Father came back from the war because they cost seventeen and six. That showed how simple she was. The Geneys up the road had a baby, and everyone knew they couldn't afford seventeen and six. It was probably a cheap baby, and Mother wanted something really good, but I felt she was too exclusive. The Geneys' baby would have done us fine.

Having settled my plans for the day, I got up, put a chair under the attic window, and lifted the frame high enough to stick out my head. The window overlooked the front gardens of the terrace behind ours, and beyond these it looked over a deep valley to the tall, red-brick houses terraced up the opposite hillside, which were all still in shadow, while those at our side of the valley were all lit up, though with long strange shadows that made them seem unfamiliar; rigid and painted.

After that I went into Mother's room and climbed into the big bed. She woke and I began to tell her of my schemes. By this time, though I never seem to have noticed it, I was petrified in my nightshirt, and I thawed as I talked until, the last frost melted, I fell asleep beside her and woke again only when I heard her below in the kitchen, making the breakfast.

After breakfast we went into town; heard Mass at St. Augustine's and said a prayer for Father, and did the shopping. If the afternoon was fine we either went for a walk in the country or a visit to Mother's great friend in the convent, Mother St. Dominic. Mother had them all praying for Father, and every night, going to bed, I asked God to send him back safe from the war to us. Little, indeed, did I know what I was praying for!

One morning, I got into the big bed, and there, sure enough, was Father in his usual Santa Claus manner, but later, instead of uniform, he put on his best blue suit, and Mother was as pleased as anything. I saw nothing to be pleased about, because, out of uniform, Father was altogether less interesting, but she only beamed, and explained that our prayers had been answered, and off we went to Mass to thank God for having brought Father safely home.

The irony of it! That very day when he came in to dinner he took off his boots and put on his slippers, donned the dirty old cap he wore about the house to save him from colds, crossed his legs, and began to talk gravely to Mother, who looked anxious. Naturally, I disliked her looking anxious, because it destroyed her good looks, so I interrupted him.

"Just a moment, Larry!" she said gently.

This was only what she said when we had boring visitors, so I attached no importance to it and went on talking.

"Do be quiet, Larry!" she said impatiently. "Don't you hear me talking to Daddy?"

This was the first time I had heard those ominous words, "talking to Daddy," and I couldn't help feeling that if this was how God answered prayers, he couldn't listen to them very attentively.

"Why are you talking to Daddy?" I asked with as great a show of indifference as I could muster.

"Because Daddy and I have business to discuss. Now, don't interrupt again!"

In the afternoon, at Mother's request, Father took me for a walk. This time we went into town instead of out to the country, and I thought at first, in my usual optimistic way, that it might be an improvement. It was nothing of the sort. Father and I had quite different notions of a walk in town. He had no proper interest in trams, ships, and horses, and the only thing that seemed to divert him was talking to fellows as old as himself. When I wanted to stop he simply went on, dragging me behind him by the hand; when he wanted to stop I had no alternative but to do the same. I noticed that it seemed to be a sign that he wanted to stop for a long time whenever he leaned against a wall. The second time I saw him do it I got wild. He seemed to be settling himself forever. I pulled him by the coat and trousers, but, unlike Mother who, if you were too persistent, got into a wax and said: "Larry, if you don't behave yourself, I'll give you a good slap," Father had an extraordinary capacity for amiable inattention. I sized him up and wondered would I cry, but he seemed to be too remote to be annoyed even by that. Really, it was like going for a walk with a mountain! He either ignored the wrenching and pummeling entirely, or else glanced down with a grin of amusement from his peak. I had never met anyone so absorbed in himself as he seemed.

At teatime, "talking to Daddy" began again, complicated this time by the fact that he had an evening paper, and every few minutes he put it down and told Mother something new out of it. I felt this was foul play. Man for man, I was prepared to compete with him any time for Mother's attention, but when he had it all made up for him by other people it left me no chance. Several times I tried to change the subject without success.

"You must be quiet while Daddy is reading, Larry," Mother said impatiently.

It was clear that she either genuinely liked talking to Father better than talking to me, or else that he had some terrible hold on her which made her afraid to admit the truth.

"Mummy," I said that night when she was tucking me up, "do you think if I prayed hard God would send Daddy back to the war?"

She seemed to think about that for a moment.

"No, dear," she said with a smile. "I don't think he would."

"Why wouldn't he, Mummy?"

"Because there isn't a war any longer, dear."

"But, Mummy, couldn't God make another war, if he liked?"

"He wouldn't like to, dear. It's not God who makes wars, but bad people."

"Oh!" I said.

I was disappointed about that. I began to think that God wasn't quite what he was cracked up to be.

Next morning I woke at my usual hour, feeling like a bottle of champagne. I put out my feet and invented a long conversation in which Mrs. Right talked of the trouble she had with her own father till she put him in the Home. I didn't quite know what the Home was but it sounded the right place for Father. Then I got my chair and stuck my head out of the attic window. Dawn was just breaking, with a guilty air that made me feel I had caught it in the act. My head bursting with stories and schemes, I stumbled in next door, and in the half-darkness scrambled into the big bed. There was no room at Mother's side so I had to get between her and Father. For the time being I had forgotten about him, and for several minutes I sat bolt upright, racking my brains to know what I could do with him. He was taking up more than his fair share of the bed, and I couldn't get comfortable, so I gave him several kicks that made him grunt and stretch. He made room all right, though. Mother waked and felt for me. I settled back comfortably in the warmth of the bed with my thumb in my mouth.

"Mummy!" I hummed, loudly and contentedly.

"Sssh! dear," she whispered. "Don't wake Daddy!"

This was a new development, which threatened to be even more serious than "talking to Daddy." Life without my early-morning conferences was unthinkable.

"Why?" I asked severely.

"Because poor Daddy is tired."

This seemed to me a quite inadequate reason, and I was sickened by the sentimentality of her "poor Daddy." I never liked that sort of gush; it always struck me as insincere.

"Oh!" I said lightly. Then in my most winning tone: "Do you know where I want to go with you today, Mummy?"

"No, dear," she sighed.

"I want to go down the Glen and fish for thornybacks with my new net, and then I want to go out to the Fox and Hounds, and—"

"Don't-wake-Daddy!" she hissed angrily, clapping her hand across my mouth.

But it was too late. He was awake, or nearly so. He grunted and reached for the matches. Then he stared incredulously at his watch.

"Like a cup of tea, dear?" asked Mother in a meek, hushed voice I had never heard her use before. It sounded almost as though she were afraid.

"Tea?" he exclaimed indignantly. "Do you know what the time is?"

"And after that I want to go up the Rathcooney Road," I said loudly, afraid I'd forget something in all those interruptions.

"Go to sleep at once, Larry!" she said sharply.

I began to snivel. I couldn't concentrate, the way that pair went on, and smothering my early-morning schemes was like burying a family from the cradle.

Father said nothing, but lit his pipe and sucked it, looking out into the shadows without minding Mother or me. I knew he was mad. Every time I made a remark Mother hushed me irritably. I was mortified. I felt it wasn't fair; there was even something sinister in it. Every time I had pointed out to her the waste of making two beds when we could both sleep in one, she had told me it was healthier like that, and now here was this man, this stranger, sleeping with her without the least regard for her health!

He got up early and made tea, but though he brought Mother a cup he brought none for me.

"Mummy," I shouted, "I want a cup of tea, too."

"Yes, dear," she said patiently. "You can drink from Mummy's saucer."

That settled it. Either Father or I would have to leave the house. I didn't want to drink from Mother's saucer; I wanted to be treated as an equal in my own home, so, just to spite her, I drank it all and left none for her. She took that quietly, too.

But that night when she was putting me to bed she said gently:

"Larry, I want you to promise me something."

"What is it?" I asked.

"Not to come in and disturb poor Daddy in the morning. Promise?"

"Poor Daddy" again! I was becoming suspicious of everything involving that quite impossible man.

"Why?" I asked.

"Because poor Daddy is worried and tired and he doesn't sleep well."

"Why doesn't he, Mummy?"

"Well, you know, don't you, that while he was at the war Mummy got the pennies from the Post Office?"

"From Miss MacCarthy?"

"That's right. But now, you see, Miss MacCarthy hasn't any more pennies, so Daddy must go out and find us some. You know what would happen if he couldn't?"

"No," I said, "tell us."

"Well, I think we might have to go out and beg for them like the poor old woman on Fridays. We wouldn't like that, would we?"

"No," I agreed. "We wouldn't."

"So you'll promise not to come in and wake him?"

"Promise."

Mind you, I meant that. I knew pennies were a serious matter, and I was all against having to go out and beg like the old woman on Fridays. Mother laid out all my toys in a complete ring round the bed so that, whatever way I got out, I was bound to fall over one of them.

When I woke I remembered my promise all right. I got up and sat on the floor and played—for hours, it seemed to me. Then I got my chair and looked out the attic window for more hours. I wished it was time for Father to wake; I wished someone would make me a cup of tea. I didn't feel in the least like the sun; instead, I was bored and so very, very cold! I simply longed for the warmth and depth of the big featherbed.

At last I could stand it no longer. I went into the next room. As there was still no room at Mother's side I climbed over her and she woke with a start.

"Larry," she whispered, gripping my arm very tightly, "what did you promise?"

"But I did, Mummy," I wailed, caught in the very act. "I was quiet for ever so long."

"Oh, dear, and you're perished!" she said sadly, feeling me all over. "Now, if I let you stay will you promise not to talk?"

"But I want to talk, Mummy," I wailed.

"That has nothing to do with it," she said with a firmness that was new to me. "Daddy wants to sleep. Now, do you understand that?"

I understood it only too well. I wanted to talk, he wanted to sleep—whose house was it, anyway?

"Mummy," I said with equal firmness, "I think it would be healthier for Daddy to sleep in his own bed."

That seemed to stagger her, because she said nothing for a while.

"Now, once for all," she went on, "you're to be perfectly quiet or go back to your own bed. Which is it to be?"

The injustice of it got me down. I had convicted her out of her own mouth of inconsistency and unreasonableness, and she hadn't even attempted to reply. Full of spite, I gave Father a kick, which she didn't notice but which made him grunt and open his eyes in alarm.

"What time is it?" he asked in a panic-stricken voice, not looking at Mother but the door, as if he saw someone there.

"It's early yet," she replied soothingly. "It's only the child. Go to sleep again. . . . Now, Larry," she added, getting out of bed, "you've wakened Daddy and you must go back."

This time, for all her quiet air, I knew she meant it, and knew that my principal rights and privileges were as good as lost unless I asserted them at once. As she lifted me, I gave a screech, enough to wake the dead, not to mind Father. He groaned.

"That damn child! Doesn't he ever sleep?"

"It's only a habit, dear," she said quietly, though I could see she was vexed.

"Well, it's time he got out of it," shouted Father, beginning to heave in the bed. He suddenly gathered all the bedclothes about him, turned to the wall, and then looked back over his shoulder with nothing showing only two small, spiteful, dark eyes. The man looked very wicked.

To open the bedroom door, Mother had to let me down, and I broke free and dashed for the farthest corner, screeching. Father sat bolt upright in bed.

"Shut up, you little puppy!" he said in a choking voice.

I was so astonished that I stopped screeching. Never, never had anyone spoken to me in that tone before. I looked at him incredulously and saw his face convulsed with rage. It was only then that I fully realized how God had codded me, listening to my prayers for the safe return of this monster.

"Shut up, you!" I bawled, beside myself.

"What's that you said?" shouted Father, making a wild leap out of bed.

"Mick, Mick!" cried Mother. "Don't you see the child isn't used to you?"

"I see he's better fed than taught," snarled Father, waving his arms wildly. "He wants his bottom smacked."

All his previous shouting was as nothing to these obscene words referring to my person. They really made my blood boil.

"Smack your own!" I screamed hysterically. "Smack your own! Shut up! Shut up!"

At this he lost his patience and let fly at me. He did it with the lack of conviction you'd expect of a man under Mother's horrified eyes, and it ended up as a mere tap, but the sheer indignity of being struck at all by a stranger, a total stranger who had cajoled his way back from the war into our big bed as a result of my innocent intercession, made me completely dotty. I shrieked and shrieked, and danced in my bare feet, and Father, looking awkward and hairy in nothing but a short grey army shirt, glared down at me like a mountain out for murder. I think it must have been then that I realized he was jealous too. And there stood Mother in her nightdress, looking as if her heart was broken between us. I hoped she felt as she looked. It seemed to me that she deserved it all.

From that morning out my life was a hell. Father and I were enemies, open and avowed. We conducted a series of skirmishes against one another, he trying to steal my time with Mother and I his. When she was sitting on my bed, telling me a story, he took to looking for some pair of old boots which he alleged he had left behind him at the beginning of the war. While he talked to Mother I played loudly with my toys to show my total lack of concern. He created a terrible scene one evening when he came in from work and found me at his box, playing with his regimental badges, Gurkha knives and button-sticks. Mother got up and took the box from me.

"You mustn't play with Daddy's toys unless he lets you, Larry," she said severely. "Daddy doesn't play with yours."

For some reason Father looked at her as if she had struck him and then turned away with a scowl.

"Those are not toys," he growled, taking down the box again to see had I lifted anything. "Some of those curios are very rare and valuable."

But as time went on I saw more and more how he managed to alienate Mother and me. What made it worse was that I couldn't grasp his method or see what attraction he had for Mother. In every possible way he was less winning than I. He had a common accent and made noises at his tea. I thought for a while that it might be the newspapers she was interested in, so I made up bits of news of my own to read to her. Then I thought it might be the smoking, which I personally thought attractive, and took his pipes and went round the house dribbling into them till he caught me. I even made noises at my tea, but Mother only told me I was disgusting. It all seemed to hinge round that unhealthy habit of sleeping together, so I made a point of dropping into their bedroom and nosing round, talking to myself, so that they wouldn't know I was watching them, but they were never up to anything that I could see. In the end it beat me. It seemed to depend on being grown-up and giving people rings, and I realized I'd have to wait.

But at the same time I wanted him to see that I was only waiting, not giving up the fight. One evening when he was being particularly obnoxious, chattering away well above my head, I let him have it.

"Mummy," I said, "do you know what I'm going to do when I grow up?"

"No, dear," she replied. "What?"

"I'm going to marry you," I said quietly.

Father gave a great guffaw out of him, but he didn't take me in. I knew it must only be pretense. And Mother, in spite of everything, was pleased. I felt she was probably relieved to know that one day Father's hold on her would be broken.

"Won't that be nice?" she said with a smile.

"It'll be very nice," I said confidently. "Because we're going to have lots and lots of babies."

"That's right, dear," she said placidly. "I think we'll have one soon, and then you'll have plenty of company."

I was no end pleased about that because it showed that in spite of the way she gave in to Father she still considered my wishes. Besides, it would put the Geneys in their place.

It didn't turn out like that, though. To begin with, she was very preoccupied—I supposed about where she would get the seventeen and six—and though Father took to staying out late in the evenings it did me no particular good. She stopped taking me for walks, became as touchy as blazes, and smacked me for nothing at all. Sometimes I wished I'd never mentioned the confounded baby—I seemed to have a genius for bringing calamity on myself.

And calamity it was! Sonny arrived in the most appalling hullabaloo—even that much he couldn't do without a fuss—and from the first moment I disliked him. He was a difficult child—so far as I was concerned he was always difficult—and demanded far too much attention. Mother was simply silly about him, and couldn't see when he was only showing off. As company he was worse than useless. He slept all day, and I had to go round the house on tiptoe to avoid waking him. It wasn't any longer a question of not waking Father. The slogan now was "Don't-wake-Sonny!" I couldn't understand why the child wouldn't sleep at the proper time, so whenever Mother's back was turned I woke him. Sometimes to keep him awake I pinched him as well. Mother caught me at it one day and gave me a most unmerciful flaking.

One evening, when Father was coming in from work, I was playing trains in the front garden. I let on not to notice him; instead, I pretended to be talking to myself, and said in a loud voice: "If another bloody baby comes into this house, I'm going out."

Father stopped dead and looked at me over his shoulder.

"What's that you said?" he asked sternly.

"I was only talking to myself," I replied, trying to conceal my panic. "It's private."

He turned and went in without a word. Mind you, I intended it as a solemn warning, but its effect was quite different. Father started being quite nice to me. I could understand that, of course. Mother was quite sickening about Sonny. Even at mealtimes she'd get up and gawk at him in the cradle with an idiotic smile, and tell Father to do the same. He was always polite about it, but he looked so puzzled you could see he didn't know what she was talking about. He complained of the way Sonny cried at night, but she only got cross and said that Sonny never cried except when there was something up with him—which was a flaming lie, because Sonny never had anything up with him, and only cried for attention. It was really painful to see how simple-minded she was. Father wasn't attractive, but he had a fine intelligence. He saw through Sonny, and now he knew that I saw through him as well.

One night I woke with a start. There was someone beside me in the bed. For one wild moment I felt sure it must be Mother, having come to her senses and left Father for good, but then I heard Sonny in convulsions in the next room, and Mother saying: "There! There! There!" and I knew it wasn't she. It was Father. He was lying beside me, wide awake, breathing hard and apparently as mad as hell.

After a while it came to me what he was mad about. It was his turn now. After turning me out of the big bed, he had been turned out himself. Mother had no consideration now for anyone but that poisonous pup, Sonny. I couldn't help feeling sorry for Father. I had been through it all myself, and even at that age I was magnanimous. I began to stroke him down and say: "There! There!" He wasn't exactly responsive.

"Aren't you asleep either?" he snarled.

"Ah, come on and put your arm around us, can't you?" I said, and he did, in a sort of way. Gingerly, I suppose, is how you'd describe it. He was very bony but better than nothing.

At Christmas he went out of his way to buy me a really nice model railway.

Katherine Mansfield

BLISS

ALTHOUGH Bertha Young was thirty she still had moments like this when she wanted to run instead of walk, to take dancing steps on and off the pavement, to bowl a hoop, to throw something up in the air and catch it again, or to stand still and laugh at—nothing—at nothing, simply.

What can you do if you are thirty and, turning the corner of your own street, you are overcome, suddenly, by a feeling of bliss—absolute bliss!—as though you'd suddenly swallowed a bright piece of that late afternoon sun and it burned in your bosom, sending out a little shower of sparks into every particle, into every finger and toe? . . .

Oh, is there no way you can express it without being "drunk and disorderly"? How idiotic civilization is! Why be given a body if you have to keep it shut up in a case like a rare, rare fiddle?

"No, that about the fiddle is not quite what I mean," she thought, running up the steps and feeling in her bag for the key—she'd forgotten it, as usual—and rattling the letter-box. "It's not what I mean, because—Thank you, Mary"—she went into the hall. "Is nurse back?"

"Yes, M'm."

"And has the fruit come?"

"Yes, M'm. Everything's come."

"Bring the fruit up to the dining-room, will you? I'll arrange it before I go upstairs."

It was dusky in the dining-room and quite chilly. But all the same Bertha threw off her coat; she could not bear the tight clasp of it another moment, and the cold air fell on her arms.

But in her bosom there was still that bright glowing place—that shower of little sparks coming from it. It was almost unbearable. She hardly dared to breathe for fear of fanning it higher, and yet she breathed deeply, deeply. She hardly dared to look into the cold mirror—but she did look, and it gave her back a woman, radiant, with smiling, trembling lips, with big, dark eyes and an air of listening, waiting for something . . . divine to happen . . . that she knew must happen . . . infallibly.

Mary brought in the fruit on a tray and with it a glass bowl, and

---

a blue dish, very lovely, with a strange sheen on it as though it had been dipped in milk.

"Shall I turn on the light, M'm?"

"No, thank you. I can see quite well."

There were tangerines and apples stained with strawberry pink. Some yellow pears, smooth as silk, some white grapes covered with a silver bloom and a big cluster of purple ones. These last she had bought to tone in with the new dining-room carpet. Yes, that did sound rather far-fetched and absurd, but it was really why she had bought them. She had thought in the shop: "I must have some purple ones to bring the carpet up to the table." And it had seemed quite sense at the time.

When she had finished with them and had made two pyramids of these bright round shapes, she stood away from the table to get the effect—and it really was most curious. For the dark table seemed to melt into the dusky light and the glass dish and the blue bowl to float in the air. This, of course in her present mood, was so incredibly beautiful. . . . She began to laugh.

"No, no. I'm getting hysterical." And she seized her bag and coat and ran upstairs to the nursery.

Nurse sat at a low table giving Little B her supper after her bath. The baby had on a white flannel gown and a blue woollen jacket, and her dark, fine hair was brushed up into a funny little peak. She looked up when she saw her mother and began to jump.

"Now, my lovey, eat it up like a good girl," said Nurse, setting her lips in a way that Bertha knew, and that meant she had come into the nursery at another wrong moment.

"Has she been good, Nanny?"

"She's been a little sweet all the afternoon," whispered Nanny. "We went to the park and I sat down on a chair and took her out of the pram and a big dog came along and put its head on my knee and she clutched its ear, tugged it. Oh, you should have seen her."

Bertha wanted to ask if it wasn't rather dangerous to let her clutch at a strange dog's ear. But she did not dare to. She stood watching them, her hands by her side, like the poor little girl in front of the rich little girl with the doll.

The baby looked up at her again, stared, and then smiled so charmingly that Bertha couldn't help crying:

"Oh, Nanny, do let me finish giving her her supper while you put the bath things away."

"Well, M'm, she oughtn't to be changed hands while she's eating," said Nanny, still whispering. "It unsettles her; it's very likely to upset her."

How absurd it was. Why have a baby if it has to be kept—not in a case like a rare, rare fiddle—but in another woman's arms?

"Oh, I must!" said she.

Very offended, Nanny handed her over.

"Now, don't excite her after her supper. You know you do, M'm. And I have such a time with her after!"

Thank heaven! Nanny went out of the room with the bath towels.

"Now I've got you to myself, my little precious," said Bertha, as the baby leaned against her.

She ate delightfully, holding up her lips for the spoon and then waving her hands. Sometimes she wouldn't let the spoon go; and sometimes, just as Bertha had filled it, she waved it away to the four winds.

When the soup was finished Bertha turned round to the fire.

"You're nice—you're very nice!" said she, kissing her warm baby. "I'm fond of you. I like you."

And, indeed, she loved Little B so much—her neck as she bent forward, her exquisite toes as they shone transparent in the firelight—that all her feeling of bliss came back again, and again she didn't know how to express it—what to do with it.

"You're wanted on the telephone," said Nanny, coming back in triumph and seizing *her* Little B.

Down she flew. It was Harry.

"Oh, is that you, Ber? Look here. I'll be late. I'll take a taxi and come along as quickly as I can, but get dinner put back ten minutes—will you? All right?"

"Yes, perfectly. Oh, Harry!"

"Yes?"

What had she to say? She'd nothing to say. She only wanted to get in touch with him for a moment. She couldn't absurdly cry: "Hasn't it been a divine day!"

"What is it?" rapped out the little voice.

"Nothing. *Entendu,*"[1] said Bertha, and hung up the receiver, thinking how more than idiotic civilization was.

They had people coming to dinner. The Norman Knights—a very sound couple—he was about to start a theatre, and she was awfully keen on interior decoration, a young man, Eddie Warren, who had just published a little book of poems and whom everybody was asking to dine, and a "find" of Bertha's called Pearl Fulton. What Miss Fulton did, Bertha didn't know. They had met at the club and

1 [Understood, heard, agreed.]

Bertha had fallen in love with her, as she always did fall in love with beautiful women who had something strange about them.

The provoking thing was that, though they had been about together and met a number of times and really talked, Bertha couldn't yet make her out. Up to a certain point Miss Fulton was rarely, wonderfully frank, but the certain point was there, and beyond that she would not go.

Was there anything beyond it? Harry said "No." Voted her dullish, and "cold like all blond women, with a touch, perhaps, of anæmia of the brain." But Bertha wouldn't agree with him: not yet, at any rate.

"No, the way she has of sitting with her head a little on one side, and smiling, has something behind it, Harry, and I must find out what that something is."

"Most likely it's a good stomach," answered Harry.

He made a point of catching Bertha's heels with replies of that kind . . . "liver frozen, my dear girl," or "pure flatulence," or "kidney disease," . . . and so on. For some strange reason Bertha liked this, and almost admired it in him very much.

She went into the drawing-room and lighted the fire; then, picking up the cushions, one by one, that Mary had disposed so carefully, she threw them back on to the chairs and the couches. That made all the difference; the room came alive at once. As she was about to throw the last one she surprised herself by suddenly hugging it to her, passionately, passionately. But it did not put out the fire in her bosom. Oh, on the contrary!

The windows of the drawing-room opened on to a balcony overlooking the garden. At the far end, against the wall, there was a tall, slender pear tree in fullest, richest bloom; it stood perfect, as though becalmed against the jade-green sky. Bertha couldn't help feeling, even from this distance, that it had not a single bud or a faded petal. Down below, in the garden beds, the red and yellow tulips, heavy with flowers, seemed to lean upon the dusk. A grey cat, dragging its belly, crept across the lawn, and a black one, its shadow, trailed after. The sight of them, so intent and so quick, gave Bertha a curious shiver.

"What creepy things cats are!" she stammered, and she turned away from the window and began walking up and down. . . .

How strong the jonquils smelled in the warm room. Too strong? Oh, no. And yet, as though overcome, she flung down on a couch and pressed her hands to her eyes.

"I'm too happy—too happy!" she murmured.

And she seemed to see on her eyelids the lovely pear tree with its wide open blossoms as a symbol of her own life.

Really—really—she had everything. She was young. Harry and she were as much in love as ever, and they got on together splendidly and were really good pals. She had an adorable baby. They didn't have to worry about money. They had this absolutely satisfactory house and garden. And friends—modern, thrilling friends, writers and painters and poets or people keen on social questions—just the kind of friends they wanted. And then there were books, and there was music, and she had found a wonderful little dressmaker, and they were going abroad in the summer, and their new cook made the most superb omelettes. . . .

"I'm absurd. Absurd!" She sat up; but she felt quite dizzy, quite drunk. It must have been the spring.

Yes, it was the spring. Now she was so tired she could not drag herself upstairs to dress.

A white dress, a string of jade beads, green shoes and stockings. It wasn't intentional. She had thought of this scheme hours before she stood at the drawing-room window.

Her petals rustled softly into the hall, and she kissed Mrs. Norman Knight, who was taking off the most amusing orange coat with a procession of black monkeys round the hem and up the fronts.

". . . Why! Why! Why is the middle-class so stodgy—so utterly without a sense of humour! My dear, it's only by a fluke that I am here at all—Norman being the protective fluke. For my darling monkeys so upset the train that it rose to a man and simply ate me with its eyes. Didn't laugh—wasn't amused—that I should have loved. No, just stared—and bored me through and through."

"But the cream of it was," said Norman, pressing a large tortoise-shell-rimmed monocle into his eye, "you don't mind me telling this, Face, do you?" (In their home and among their friends they called each other Face and Mug.) "The cream of it was when she, being full fed, turned to the woman beside her and said: 'Haven't you ever seen a monkey before?' "

"Oh, yes!" Mrs. Norman Knight joined in the laughter. "Wasn't that too absolutely creamy?"

And a funnier thing still was that now her coat was off she did look like a very intelligent monkey—who had even made that yellow silk dress out of scraped banana skins. And her amber earrings; they were like little dangling nuts.

"This is a sad, sad fall!" said Mug, pausing in front of Little B's perambulator. "When the perambulator comes into the hall—" and he waved the rest of the quotation away.

The bell rang. It was lean, pale Eddie Warren (as usual) in a state of acute distress.

"It *is* the right house, *isn't* it?" he pleaded.

"Oh, I think so—I hope so," said Bertha brightly.

"I have had such a *dreadful* experience with a taxi-man; he was *most* sinister. I couldn't get him to *stop*. The *more* I knocked and called the *faster* he went. And *in* the moonlight this *bizarre* figure with the *flattened* head *crouching* over the *lit-tle* wheel. . . ."

He shuddered, taking off an immense white silk scarf. Bertha noticed that his socks were white, too—most charming.

"But how dreadful!" she cried.

"Yes, it really was," said Eddie, following her into the drawing-room. "I saw myself *driving* through Eternity in a *timeless* taxi."

He knew the Norman Knights. In fact, he was going to write a play for N. K. when the theatre scheme came off.

"Well, Warren, how's the play?" said Norman Knight, dropping his monocle and giving his eye a moment in which to rise to the surface before it was screwed down again.

And Mrs. Norman Knight: "Oh, Mr. Warren, what happy socks!"

"I *am* so glad you like them," said he, staring at his feet. "They seem to have got so *much* whiter since the moon rose." And he turned his lean sorrowful young face to Bertha. "There *is* a moon, you know."

She wanted to cry: "I am sure there is—often—often!"

He really was a most attractive person. But so was Face, crouched before the fire in her banana skins, and so was Mug, smoking a cigarette and saying as he flicked the ash: "Why doth the bride-groom tarry?"

"There he is, now."

Bang went the front door open and shut. Harry shouted: "Hullo, you people. Down in five minutes." And they heard him swarm up the stairs. Bertha couldn't help smiling; she knew how he loved doing things at high pressure. What, after all, did an extra five minutes matter? But he would pretend to himself that they mattered beyond measure. And then he would make a great point of coming into the drawing-room, extravagantly cool and collected.

Harry had such a zest for life. Oh, how she appreciated it in him. And his passion for fighting—for seeking in everything that came up against him another test of his power and of his courage—that, too, she understood. Even when it made him just occasionally, to other people, who didn't know him well, a little ridiculous perhaps. . . . For there were moments when he rushed into battle where no battle was. . . . She talked and laughed and positively forgot until he had come in (just as she had imagined) that Pearl Fulton had not turned up.

"I wonder if Miss Fulton has forgotten?"

"I expect so," said Harry. "Is she on the 'phone?"

"Ah! There's a taxi, now." And Bertha smiled with that little air of proprietorship that she always assumed while her women finds were new and mysterious. "She lives in taxis."

"She'll run to fat if she does," said Harry coolly, ringing the bell for dinner. "Frightful danger for blond women."

"Harry—don't," warned Bertha, laughing up at him.

Came another tiny moment, while they waited, laughing and talking, just a trifle too much at their ease, a trifle too unaware. And then Miss Fulton, all in silver, with a silver fillet binding her pale blond hair, came in smiling, her head a little on one side.

"Am I late?"

"No, not at all," said Bertha. "Come along." And she took her arm and they moved into the dining-room.

What was there in the touch of that cool arm that could fan—fan—start blazing—blazing—the fire of bliss that Bertha did not know what to do with?

Miss Fulton did not look at her; but then she seldom did look at people directly. Her heavy eyelids lay upon her eyes and the strange half smile came and went upon her lips as though she lived by listening rather than seeing. But Bertha knew, suddenly, as if the longest, most intimate look had passed between them—as if they had said to each other: "You, too?"—that Pearl Fulton, stirring the beautiful red soup in the grey plate, was feeling just what she was feeling.

And the others? Face and Mug, Eddie and Harry, their spoons rising and falling—dabbing their lips with their napkins, crumbling bread, fiddling with the forks and glasses and talking.

"I met her at the Alpha show—the weirdest little person. She'd not only cut off her hair, but she seemed to have taken a dreadfully good snip off her legs and arms and her neck and her poor little nose as well."

"Isn't she very *liée* with Michael Oat?"

"The man who wrote *Love in False Teeth?*"

"He wants to write a play for me. One act. One man. Decides to commit suicide. Gives all the reasons why he should and why he shouldn't. And just as he has made up his mind either to do it or not to do it—curtain. Not half a bad idea."

"What's he going to call it—'Stomach Trouble'?"

"I *think* I've come across the *same* idea in a lit-tle French review, *quite* unknown in England."

No, they didn't share it. They were dears—dears—and she loved having them there, at her table, and giving them delicious food and wine. In fact, she longed to tell them how delightful they were, and what a decorative group they made, how they seemed to set one another off and how they reminded her of a play by Tchekof!

Harry was enjoying his dinner. It was part of his—well, not his nature, exactly, and certainly not his pose—his—something or other—to talk about food and to glory in his "shameless passion for the white flesh of the lobster" and "the green of pistachio ices—green and cold like the eyelids of Egyptian dancers."

When he looked up at her and said: "Bertha, this is a very admirable *soufflée*!" she almost could have wept with child-like pleasure.

Oh, why did she feel so tender towards the whole world tonight? Everything was good—was right. All that happened seemed to fill again her brimming cup of bliss.

And still, in the back of her mind, there was the pear tree. It would be silver now, in the light of poor dear Eddie's moon, silver as Miss Fulton, who sat there turning a tangerine in her slender fingers that were so pale a light seemed to come from them.

What she simply couldn't make out—what was miraculous—was how she should have guessed Miss Fulton's mood so exactly and so instantly. For she never doubted for a moment that she was right, and yet what had she to go on? Less than nothing.

"I believe this does happen very, very rarely between women. Never between men," thought Bertha. "But while I am making the coffee in the drawing-room perhaps she will 'give a sign.' "

What she meant by that she did not know, and what would happen after that she could not imagine.

While she thought like this she saw herself talking and laughing. She had to talk because of her desire to laugh.

"I must laugh or die."

But when she noticed Face's funny little habit of tucking something down the front of her bodice—as if she kept a tiny, secret hoard of nuts there, too—Bertha had to dig her nails into her hands—so as not to laugh too much.

It was over at last. And: "Come and see my new coffee machine," said Bertha.

"We only have a new coffee machine once a fortnight," said Harry. Face took her arm this time; Miss Fulton bent her head and followed after.

The fire had died down in the drawing-room to a red, flickering "nest of baby phœnixes," said Face.

"Don't turn up the light for a moment. It is so lovely." And down she crouched by the fire again. She was always cold . . . "without her little red flannel jacket, of course," thought Bertha.

At that moment Miss Fulton "gave the sign."

"Have you a garden?" said the cool, sleepy voice.

This was so exquisite on her part that all Bertha could do was to obey. She crossed the room, pulled the curtains apart, and opened those long windows.

"There!" she breathed.

And the two women stood side by side looking at the slender, flowering tree. Although it was so still it seemed, like the flame of a candle, to stretch up, to point, to quiver in the bright air, to grow taller and taller as they gazed—almost to touch the rim of the round, silver moon.

How long did they stand there? Both, as it were, caught in that circle of unearthly light, understanding each other perfectly, creatures of another world, and wondering what they were to do in this one with all this blissful treasure that burned in their bosoms and dropped, in silver flowers, from their hair and hands?

For ever—for a moment? And did Miss Fulton murmur: "Yes. Just *that*." Or did Bertha dream it?

Then the light was snapped on and Face made the coffee and Harry said: "My dear Mrs. Knight, don't ask me about my baby. I never see her. I shan't feel the slightest interest in her until she has a lover," and Mug took his eye out of the conservatory for a moment and then put it under glass again and Eddie Warren drank his coffee and set down the cup with a face of anguish as though he had drunk and seen the spider.

"What I want to do is to give the young men a show. I believe London is simply teeming with first-chop, unwritten plays. What I want to say to 'em is: 'Here's the theatre. Fire ahead.' "

"You know, my dear, I am going to decorate a room for the Jacob Nathans. Oh, I am so tempted to do a fried-fish scheme, with the backs of the chairs shaped like frying pans and lovely chip potatoes embroidered all over the curtains."

"The trouble with our young writing men is that they are still too romantic. You can't put out to sea without being seasick and wanting a basin. Well, why won't they have the courage of those basins?"

"A *dreadful* poem about a *girl* who was *violated* by a beggar *without* a nose in a lit-tle wood. . . ."

Miss Fulton sank into the lowest, deepest chair and Harry handed round the cigarettes.

From the way he stood in front of her shaking the silver box and saying abruptly: "Egyptian? Turkish? Virginian? They're all mixed up," Bertha realized that she not only bored him; he really disliked her. And she decided from the way Miss Fulton said: "No, thank you, I won't smoke," that she felt it, too, and was hurt.

"Oh, Harry, don't dislike her. You are quite wrong about her. She's wonderful, wonderful. And, besides, how can you feel so differently about someone who means so much to me. I shall try to tell you when we are in bed tonight what has been happening. What she and I have shared."

At those last words something strange and almost terrifying darted into Bertha's mind. And this something blind and smiling whispered to her: "Soon these people will go. The house will be quiet—quiet. The lights will be out. And you and he will be alone together in the dark room—the warm bed. . . ."

She jumped up from her chair and ran over to the piano.

"What a pity someone does not play!" she cried. "What a pity somebody does not play."

For the first time in her life Bertha Young desired her husband.

Oh, she'd loved him—she'd been in love with him, of course, in every other way, but just not in that way. And, equally, of course, she'd understood that he was different. They'd discussed it so often. It had worried her dreadfully at first to find that she was so cold, but after a time it had not seemed to matter. They were so frank with each other—such good pals. That was the best of being modern.

But now—ardently! ardently! The word ached in her ardent body! Was this what that feeling of bliss had been leading up to? But then —then—

"My dear," said Mrs. Norman Knight, "you know our shame. We are the victims of time and train. We live in Hampstead. It's been so nice."

"I'll come with you into the hall," said Bertha. "I loved having you. But you must not miss the last train. That's so awful, isn't it?"

"Have a whisky, Knight, before you go?" called Harry.

"No, thanks, old chap."

Bertha squeezed his hand for that as she shook it.

"Good night, good-bye," she cried from the top step, feeling that this self of hers was taking leave of them for ever.

When she got back into the drawing-room the others were on the move.

". . . Then you can come part of the way in my taxi."

"I shall be *so* thankful *not* to have to face *another* drive *alone* after my *dreadful* experience."

"You can get a taxi at the rank just at the end of the street. You won't have to walk more than a few yards."

"That's a comfort. I'll go and put on my coat."

Miss Fulton moved towards the hall and Bertha was following when Harry almost pushed past.

"Let me help you."

Bertha knew that he was repenting his rudeness—she let him go. What a boy he was in some ways—so impulsive—so—simple.

And Eddie and she were left by the fire.

"I *wonder* if you have seen Bilks' *new* poem called *Table d'Hôte*," said Eddie softly. "It's *so* wonderful. In the last Anthology. Have you got a copy? I'd *so* like to *show* it to you. It begins with an *incredibly* beautiful line: 'Why Must it Always be Tomato Soup?' "

"Yes," said Bertha. And she moved noiselessly to a table opposite the drawing-room door and Eddie glided noiselessly after her. She picked up the little book and gave it to him; they had not made a sound.

While he looked it up she turned her head towards the hall. And she saw . . . Harry with Miss Fulton's coat in his arms and Miss Fulton with her back turned to him and her head bent. He tossed the coat away, put his hands on her shoulders and turned her violently to him. His lips said: "I adore you," and Miss Fulton laid her moonbeam fingers on his cheeks and smiled her sleepy smile. Harry's nostrils quivered; his lips curled back in a hideous grin while he whispered: "Tomorrow," and with her eyelids Miss Fulton said: "Yes."

"Here it is," said Eddie. " 'Why Must it Always be Tomato Soup?' It's so *deeply* true, don't you feel? Tomato soup is so *dreadfully* eternal."

"If you prefer," said Harry's voice, very loud, from the hall, "I can phone you a cab to come to the door."

"Oh, no. It's not necessary," said Miss Fulton, and she came up to Bertha and gave her the slender fingers to hold.

"Good-bye. Thank you so much."

"Good-bye," said Bertha.

Miss Fulton held her hand a moment longer.

"Your lovely pear tree!" she murmured.

And then she was gone, with Eddie following, like the black cat following the grey cat.

"I'll shut up shop," said Harry, extravagantly cool and collected.

"Your lovely pear tree—pear tree—pear tree!"

Bertha simply ran over to the long windows.

"Oh, what is going to happen now?" she cried.

But the pear tree was as lovely as ever and as full of flower and as still.

J. F. Powers
THE OLD BIRD, A LOVE STORY

UNEMPLOYED and elderly Mr. Newman sensed there were others, some of them, just as anxious as he was to be put on. But he was the oldest person in the room. He approached the information girl, and for all his show of business, almost brusqueness, he radiated timidity. The man in front of him asked the girl a question, which was also Mr. Newman's.

"Are they doing any hiring today?"

The girl gave the man an application, a dead smile, and told him to take a seat after he had filled it out.

An answer, in any event, ready on her lips, she regarded Mr. Newman. Mr. Newman thought of reaching for an application and saying, "Yes, I'll take a seat," making a kind of joke out of the coincidence—the fellow before him looking for a job, too—only he could see from the others who had already taken seats it was no coincidence. They all had that superior look of people out of work.

"Got an application there for a retired millionaire?" Mr. Newman said, attempting jauntiness. That way it would be easier for her to refuse him. Perhaps it was part of her job to weed out applicants clearly too old to be of any use to the company. Mr. Newman had a real horror of butting in where he wasn't wanted.

The girl laughed, making Mr. Newman feel like a regular devil, and handed him an application. The smile she gave him was alive and it hinted that things were already on a personal basis between him and her and the company.

"You'll find a pen at the desk," she said.

Mr. Newman's bony old hand clawed at his coat pocket and unsnapped a large ancient fountain pen. "I carry my own! See?" In shy triumph he held up the fountain pen, which was orange. He unscrewed it, put it together, and fingered it as though he were actually writing.

But the girl was doing her dead smile at the next one.

Mr. Newman went over to the desk. The application questioned him: Single? Married? Children of your own? Parents living? Living with parents? Salary (expect)? Salary (would take)? Mr. Newman made ready with his fountain pen and in the ensuing minutes he did not lie about his age, his abilities, or past earnings. The salary he expected was modest. He was especially careful about making blots with his pen, which sometimes flowed too freely. He had noted before he started that the application was one of those which calls for the information to be printed. This he had done. Under "DO NOT WRITE BELOW THIS LINE" he had not written.

Mr. Newman read the application over and rose to take it to the information girl. She pointed to a bench. Hesitating for a moment, Mr. Newman seemed bent on giving it to her. He sat down. He got up. His face distraught, he walked unsteadily over to the girl.

Before she could possibly hear him, he started to stammer, "I wonder . . . maybe it will make a difference," his voice both appealing for her mercy and saying it was out of the question—indeed he did not desire it—that she should take a personal interest in him. Then he got control, except for his eyes, which, without really knowing it, were searching the girl's face for the live smile, like the first time.

"I used green ink," he said limply.

"Let's see." The girl took the application, gave both sides a darting scrutiny, looking for mistakes.

"Will it make any difference? If it does and I could have another application, I could——" Mr. Newman had his orange fountain pen out again, as though to match the green on its tip with the ink on the application and thus fully account for what had come about.

"Oh no, I think that'll be all right," the girl said, finally getting the idea. "We're not that fussy." Mr. Newman, however, still appeared worried. "No, that's fine—and neat, too," the girl said. "Mr. *Newman*." She had spoken his name and there was her live smile. Mr. Newman blushed, then smiled a little himself. With perspiring fingers he put the fountain pen together and snapped it in his pocket.

The girl returned the application. Mr. Newman, lingering on, longed to confide in her, to tell her something of himself—why, for instance, he always used green ink; how famous and familiar a few years ago the initials "C. N." in green had been at the old place. Like his friend Jack P. Ferguson (died a few years back, it was in the papers) and the telegram. "Telegram" Ferguson, he was called, because he was always too busy to write. Green ink and telegrams, the heraldry of business. He wanted to tell her of the old days—the time he met Elbert Hubbard and Charley Schwab at a banquet.

Then on this side of the old days he saw a busy girl, busy being busy, who could never understand, and he forced himself to give up hope.

"I thank you," he said, going quickly back to his place on the bench to wait. He sat there rereading his application. Under "DO NOT WRITE BELOW THIS LINE" were some curious symbols. He guessed at their significance: CLN (Clean?); DSPN (Disposition?);

PRSNLTY (Personality, no doubt about that one); PSE (Poise?); FCW (?); LYL (Loyal?); PSBLE LDR (Possible Leader); NTC (?). His fingers were damp with perspiration, and for fear he would present an untidy application, he laid it on his lap and held his hands open at his sides, letting them get cool and dry in case he had to shake hands with the interviewer.

When they were ready to see him, Mr. Newman hustled into a small glass office and stood before a young man. A sign with wooden letters indicated that he was Mr. Shanahan. Mr. Shanahan was reading a letter. Mr. Newman did not look directly at Mr. Shanahan: it was none of Mr. Newman's business—Mr. Shanahan's letter—and he did not want to seem curious or expectant of immediate attention. This was their busy season.

Mr. Shanahan, his eyes still reading the letter, noiselessly extended a hand toward Mr. Newman. A moment later he moved his head and it was then that Mr. Newman saw the hand. Mr. Newman paled. Caught napping! A bad beginning. He hastened to shake Mr. Shanahan's hand, recoiled in time. Mr. Shanahan had only been reaching for the application. Mr. Newman handed it to Mr. Shanahan and said, "Thank you," for some reason.

"Ah, yes. Have a seat." Mr. Shanahan rattled the application in one hand. "What kind of work did you want to do?" Evidently he expected no answer, for he went on to say, "I don't have to tell you, Mr. Newman, there's a labor shortage, expecially in non-defense industries. That, and that alone, accounts for the few jobs we have to offer. We're an old-line house."

"Yes," Mr. Newman said.

"And there aren't any office jobs," Mr. Shanahan continued. "That's the kind of work you've always done?"

"Yes, it is," Mr. Newman said. Mr. Shanahan sucked a tooth sadly.

Mr. Newman was ready now for the part about the company letting him know later.

"How'd you like a temporary job in our shipping room?" Mr. Shanahan said, his eyes suddenly watchful.

For an instant Mr. Newman succeeded in making it plain that he, like any man of his business experience, was meant for better things. A moment later, in an interesting ceremony which took place in his heart, Mr. Newman surrendered his well-loved white collar. He knew that Mr. Shanahan, with that dark vision peculiar to personnel men, had witnessed the whole thing.

"Well . . ." he said.

Mr. Shanahan, the game bagged and bumping from his belt, got cordial now. "How are you, pretty handy with rope?"

He said it in such a flattering way that Mr. Newman trembled under the desire to be worthy. "Yes, I am," he said.

"But can you begin right away?" It was the final test.

"Yes, I can!" Mr. Newman said, echoing some of Mr. Shanahan's spirit. "You bet I can!"

"Well then, follow me!"

Mr. Shanahan guided Mr. Newman through a maze of departments. On an elevator, going down, he revealed what the job paid to start. Mr. Newman nodded vigorously that one could not expect too much to start. Mr. Shanahan told him that he didn't have to tell him that they were a firm known far and wide for fair dealing and that if (for any reason) Mr. Newman ever left them, it should be easy to get another position, and . . . Out of the elevator and in the lower depths, Mr. Shanahan said he would like to make sure Mr. Newman understood the job was only temporary. After the Christmas holidays things were pretty slow in their line. Otherwise, they would be glad to avail themselves of his services the year round. However, the experience Mr. Newman would get here might very well prove invaluable to him in later life. Mr. Newman nodded less vigorously now.

They came to a long table, flat against a wall, extending around a rafterish room fitted out for packing: tough twine and hairy manila rope on giant spools, brown paper on rollers, sticking tape bearing the company's name, crest, and slogan: "A modern house over 100 years *young.*"

Several men were packing things. Mr. Shanahan introduced Mr. Newman to one of them.

"This is your boss, Mr. Hurley. This is Mr. Newman. Mr. Newman's pretty handy with rope. Ought to make an A-1 packer."

"Well . . ." Mr. Newman said, embarrassed before the regular packers.

He shook Mr. Hurley's hard hand.

"I sure hope so," Mr. Hurley said grimly. "This is our busy season."

When Mr. Shanahan had gone Mr. Hurley showed Mr. Newman where he could hang his coat. He told him what he would have to do and what he would be held responsible for. He cited the sad case of the shipment sent out last week to Fargo, North Dakota. The company had lost exactly double the amount of the whole sale, to say nothing of good will. Why? Faulty packing! He urged Mr. Newman to figure it out for himself. He told Mr. Newman that haste made waste, but that they were expected to get incoming orders out of the house on the same day. Not tomorrow. Not the next day. The same day. Finally Mr. Hurley again brought up the case of the shipment sent to Fargo, and seemed pleased with the reaction it got. For Mr. Newman frowned his forehead all out of shape and rolled his head back and forth like a sad old bell, as if to say, "Can such things be?"

"All right, Newman, let's see what you can do!" Mr. Hurley slapped him on the shoulder like a football coach sending in a substitute. Mr. Newman, gritting his false teeth, tackled his first assignment for the company: a half-dozen sets of poker chips, a box of rag dolls, 5,000 small American flags, and a boy's sled going to Waupaca, Wisconsin.

Mr. Newman perspired . . . lost his breath, caught it, tried to break a piece of twine with his bare hands, failed, cut his nose on a piece of wrapping paper, bled, barked his shin on an ice skate, tripped, said a few cuss words to himself . . . perspired.

"We go to lunch at twelve in this section," Mr. Hurley told him in a whisper a few minutes before that time. "If you want to wash up, go ahead now."

But Mr. Newman waited until the whistle blew before he knocked off. He had a shipment he wanted to get off. It was ten after twelve when he punched out.

There was no crowd at the time clock and he had a chance to look the thing over. He tried to summon up a little interest, but all he felt with any intensity was the lone fact that he'd never had to punch a clock before. It had always been enough before that he live by one.

On his lunch hour he did not know where to go. The company had a place where you could eat your lunch, but Mr. Newman had neglected to bring one. Quite reasonably he had not anticipated getting a job and starting on it the same day. After the usual morning of looking around, he had expected to go home and eat a bite with Mrs. Newman.

He walked past a lunch stand twice before he could make certain, without actually staring in the window at the menu painted on the wall, that hamburgers were ten cents and coffee five. He entered the place, then, and ordered with assurance that he would not be letting himself in for more than he could afford. He did not have any money to spare. Would it be better, he wondered, to have payday come soon and get paid for a few days' work, or could he hold out for a week or so and really have something when he did get paid? Leaving the lunch stand, he walked in the direction of the company, but roundabout so he would not get back too soon. Say about fifteen minutes to one. That would give him time to go to the washroom.

"Where did you eat your lunch?" Mr. Hurley asked him the first thing. "I didn't see you in the lunchroom."

"Oh, I ate out," Mr. Newman said, gratified that he'd been missed until he saw that he had offended Mr. Hurley by eating out. "I didn't bring my lunch today," he explained. "Didn't think I'd be working so soon."

"Oh." But Mr. Hurley was still hurt.

"I heard they let you eat your lunch in the building," Mr. Newman said, giving Mr. Hurley his chance.

Mr. Hurley broke down and told Mr. Newman precisely where the employees' lunchroom was, where it wasn't, how to get there from the shipping room, how not to. There were two ways to get there, he said, and he guessed, as for him, he never went the same way twice in a row.

"You know how it is," Mr. Hurley laughed, tying it in with life.

In the end Mr. Newman was laughing with Mr. Hurley, "Well, I guess so." Talking with Mr. Hurley gave Mr. Newman a feeling of rare warmth. It was man-to-man or nothing with Hurley. He hoped there would be other lunch hours like this one. He went back to work at four minutes to one.

During the afternoon Mr. Newman worked up a dislike for the fat fellow next to him, but when they teamed up on a big shipment of toys the fat fellow made some cynical remarks about the company and Mr. Newman relaxed. His kind were harmless as rivals. Mr. Newman thought the company would be better off with employees like himself. And then he was ashamed, for at bottom he admired the fat fellow for his independence. Mr. Newman regretted that he was too old to be independent.

Toward the end of the day he was coming from getting a drink of water when he overheard Mr. Hurley talking with Mr. Shanahan. "Yeah," Mr. Hurley said, "when you said the old bird was handy with rope I thought, boy, he's old enough to think about using some on himself. My God, Shanahan, if this keeps up we'll have to draft them from the old people's home."

Mr. Newman, feeling indecently aged, unable to face them, went for another drink of water. He had to keep moving. When he returned to the shipping room they were all working and Mr. Shanahan was not there.

Just before quitting time, Mr. Hurley came over and congratulated him on his first day's work. He said he thought Mr. Newman would make out all right, and showed him an easier way to cut string. When he suggested that Mr. Newman wash up before the whistle blew, Mr. Newman did not have the faith to refuse. He could not look Mr. Hurley in the eye now and say something about wanting to finish up a shipment. Any extraordinary industry on his part, he knew now, was useless. He was too old. All they could see when they looked at him was an old man. That was the only fact about him. He was an old bird.

"All right, Charley, see you in the morning," Mr. Hurley said.

Mr. Newman slowly brought himself to realize he was "Charley" to Mr. Hurley. He had never before been "Charley" to anyone on such short acquaintance. Probably he would be "Old Charley" before long, which reminded him that Christmas was coming. There was no meaning beyond Christmas in all this sweat and humiliation, but that was enough. He would stick it out.

Mr. Newman was impressed again with the vault-like solemnity of the washroom. The strange dignity of the toilet booths, the resounding marble chips in the floor, the same as statehouses, the plenitude of paper, the rude music of water coursing, the fat washbowls, all resplendent and perfect of their kind, and towels, white as winding sheets, circulating without end . . .

Mr. Newman, young here, luxuriated. Still he was sensible about it. The company was a big company and could no doubt stand a lot of wasting of towels and toilet paper, but Mr. Newman, wanting to be fair, took only what he needed of everything. He would not knowingly abuse a privilege. He read a notice concerning a hospitalization service the company offered the employees. The sensibleness of such a plan appealed strongly to Mr. Newman. He thought he would have to look into that, completely forgetting that he was only on temporary.

At the sound of the five-o'clock whistle Mr. Newman hurried out and took his place in the line of employees at the time clock. When his turn came to punch out, clutching his time card, he was shaking all over. The clock would jam, or stamp the time in the wrong place, or at the last moment, losing confidence in the way he was holding the card, after all his planning, he would somehow stick it in the wrong way. Then there would be shouts from the end of the line, and everybody would know it was all on account of an old bird trying to punch out.

Mr. Newman's heart stopped beating, his body followed a preconceived plan from memory in the lapse, and then his heart started up again. Mr. Newman, a new friend to the machine, had punched out smoothly. One of the mass of company employees heading for home, Mr. Newman, his old body at once tired and tingling, walked so briskly he passed any number of younger people in the corridors. His mood was unfamiliar to him, one of achievement and crazy gaiety. He recognized the information girl ahead of him, passed her, and said over his shoulder:

"Well, good night!"

She smiled in immediate reflex, but it was sobering to Mr. Newman, though she did say good night, that she did not seem to remember him very well, for it had not been the live smile.

At the outside door it was snowing. Mr. Newman bought a newspaper and let the man keep the two cents change. He meant to revive an old tradition with him by reading the paper on the streetcar. There was enough snow on the sidewalk to ease his swollen feet.

It was too crowded on the streetcar to open his paper and he had to stand all the way. His eyes on a placard, he considered the case of a man from Minneapolis who had got welcome relief. Hanging there on a strap, rocking with the elemental heave of the streetcar, he felt utterly weary, a gray old thing. What mattered above all else, though—getting a job—he had accomplished. This he told himself over and over until it became as real as his fatigue and mingled itself with the tortured noise of the streetcar.

His wife met him at the door. One glimpse of his face, he thought, was all she needed and she would know how to treat him tonight. Already she knew something was up and had seen the scratch on his nose. She only said:

"You stayed downtown all day, Charley."

"Yes, I did," he said.

She went to hang up his coat, hat, and scarf. He stepped across the familiar rug to the radiator. He stood there warming his hands and listening to her moving things in the kitchen. He could not bring himself to go there, as he did on any other night before supper, to talk of nothing important or particular, to let the water run till it got cold, to fill their glasses. He had too much to tell her tonight. He had forgotten to remove his rubbers.

"Come on now, Charley."

He took a few steps, hesitated a second, and went straight into the kitchen. He was immediately, as he knew he would be, uneasy. He could think of nothing insignificant to say. His eyes were not meeting hers. The glasses were filled with water. Suddenly he had to look at her. She smiled. It was hard to bear. He *did* have news. But now, he felt, she expected too much.

He bit his lips in irritation and snapped, "Why didn't you let me get the water?" That was beside the point, of course, but it gave him leeway to sit down at the table. He made a project of it. Trying to extend the note of normalcy, he passed things to her. He involved her subtly in passing them back. He wanted her to know there was a time and place for everything and now it was for passing. He invented an unprecedented interest in their silverware. His knife, fork, and spoon absorbed him.

"Where did we get this spoon?" he asked crossly.

It was all wasted. She had revamped her strategy. She appeared amused, and there was about her a determination deeper than his to wait forever. Her being so amused was what struck him as insupportable. He had a dismaying conviction that this was the truest condition of their married life. It ran, more or less, but always present, right through everything they did. She was the audience—that was something like it—and he was always on stage, the actor who was never taken quite seriously by his audience, no matter how heroic the role. The bad actor and his faithful but not foolish audience. Always! As now! It was not a hopeless situation, but only because she loved him.

She *did* love him. Overcome by the idea, he abandoned his silence. He heard himself telling her everything. Not exactly as it was, naturally, but still everything. Not at first about his being handy with rope, nothing about being "Charley" and an old bird, but quite frankly that he was working in the shipping room instead of the office. About Mr. Shanahan, the interviewer—how nice he was, in a way. About the information girl who seemed to take quite an interest in him and who, to his surprise, had said good night to him. Mr. Hurley, his department head, and how to get to the employees' lunchroom. The washroom, plenty of soap and towels, a clean place—clean as her kitchen; she should see it. Where he had lunch, not much of a place. The fat fellow next to him at the table, not exactly loyal to the company, but a very likeable chap . . . and here—he dug into his shirt pocket—was a piece of their sticking tape, as she could see, with their name and trademark.

" 'A modern house,' " she read, " 'over 100 years young'—*young*—well, that's pretty clever."

"Oh, they're an old-line firm," Mr. Newman said.

"I'll have to pack you a lunch then, Charley," she said. She had finally got into the adventure with him.

"I bought a paper tonight," he said. "It's in the other room."

With a little excited movement she parted the organdy curtain at the window. "My, Charley, just look at that!" Snowflakes tumbled in feather confusion past the yellow light burning in the court, wonderfully white against the night, smothering the whole dirty, roaring, guilty city in innocence and silence and beauty.

Mr. Newman squirmed warm inside the thought of everything he could think of—the snow falling, the glow in the kitchen, landing the job, Christmas coming, her . . .

Their supper got cold.

She let the curtain fall together, breathing, "My!"

Reluctantly Mr. Newman assumed the duty he had as husband and only provider—not to be swept away by dreams and snowflakes. He said with the stern wisdom of his generation:

"Keeps up much longer it'll tie up transportation."

"But do you like that kind of work, Charley?"

He assured her most earnestly that he did, knowing she knew he'd do anything to get into an office again. He caught himself on the verge of telling her that working in the shipping room was just the way the company, since it was so old and reliable, groomed its new employees for service in the office. But that sounded too steep and ultimately disastrous. He had to confess it was only temporary work. This pained her, he could see, and he tried to get her mind on something else.

"I'll bet you had no idea your husband was so handy with rope."

He told her how it came on big spools, like telegraph wire. But she did not think this important.

"The people," he said, "the ones I've met at least—well, they all seem very nice."

"Then maybe they'll keep you after Christmas, Charley!"

He looked sharply at her and could tell she was sorry she said that. She understood what must follow. He opened his mouth to speak, said nothing, and then, closing his eyes to the truth he said: "Yes. You know, I think they will. I'm sure of it."

He coughed. That was not the way it was at all. It had happened again. He was the bad actor again. His only audience smiled and loved him.

Max Beerbohm

THE HAPPY HYPOCRITE

NONE, it is said, of all who revelled with the Regent, was half so wicked as Lord George Hell. I will not trouble my little readers with a long recital of his great naughtiness. But it were well they should know that he was greedy, destructive, and disobedient. I am afraid there is no doubt that he often sat up at Carlton House until long after bed-time, playing at games, and that he generally ate and drank more than was good for him. His fondness for fine clothes was such that he used to dress on weekdays quite as gorgeously as good people dress on Sundays. He was thirty-five years old and a great grief to his parents.

And the worst of it was that he set such a bad example to others. Never, never did he try to conceal his wrong-doing; so that, in time,

THE HAPPY HYPOCRITE: Reprinted by permission of Dodd, Mead & Company from *The Happy Hypocrite.*

every one knew how horrid he was. In fact, I think he was proud of being horrid. Captain Tarleton, in his account of *Contemporary Bucks*, suggested that his lordship's great candour was a virtue and should incline us to forgive some of his abominable faults. But, painful as it is to me to dissent from any opinion expressed by one who is now dead, I hold that candour is good only when it reveals good actions or good sentiments, and that, when it reveals evil, itself is evil, even also.

Lord George Hell did, at last, atone for all his faults, in a way that was never revealed to the world during his life-time. The reason of his strange and sudden disappearance from that social sphere, in which he had so long moved and never moved again, I will unfold. My little readers will then, I think, acknowledge that any angry judgment they may have passed upon him must be reconsidered and, it may be, withdrawn. I will leave his lordship in their hands. But my plea for him will not be based upon that candour of his, which some of his friends so much admired. There were, yes! some so weak and so wayward as to think it a fine thing to have an historic title and no scruples. "Here comes George Hell," they would say, "How wicked my lord is looking!" *Noblesse oblige*, you see, and so an aristocrat should be very careful of his good name. Anonymous naughtiness does little harm.

It is pleasant to record that many persons were inobnoxious to the magic of his title and disapproved of him so strongly that, whenever he entered a room where they happened to be, they would make straight for the door and watch him very severely through the keyhole. Every morning when he strolled up Piccadilly they crossed over to the other side in a compact body, leaving him to the companionship of his bad companions on that which is still called the "shady" side. Lord George—σχετλιος[1]—was quite indifferent to this demonstration. Indeed, he seemed wholly hardened, and when ladies gathered up their skirts as they passed him he would lightly appraise their ankles.

I am glad I never saw his lordship. They say he was rather like Caligula, with a dash of Sir John Falstaff, and that sometimes on wintry mornings in St. James's Street young children would hush their prattle and cling in disconsolate terror to their nurses' skirts as they saw him come (that vast and fearful gentleman!) with the east wind ruffling the rotund surface of his beaver, ruffling the fur about his neck and wrists, and striking the purple complexion of his cheeks to a still deeper purple. "King Bogey" they called him in the nurseries. In the hours when they too were naughty, their nurses would predict his advent down the chimney or from the linen-press, and

1 [Merciless.]

then they always "behaved." So that, you see, even the unrighteous are a power for good, in the hands of nurses.

It is true that his lordship was a non-smoker—a negative virtue, certainly, and due, even that, I fear, to the fashion of the day—but there the list of his good qualities comes to an abrupt conclusion. He loved with an insatiable love the town and the pleasures of the town, whilst the ennobling influences of our English lakes were quite unknown to him. He used to boast that he had not seen a buttercup for twenty years, and once he called the country "a Fool's Paradise." London was the only place marked on the map of his mind. London gave him all he wished for. Is it not extraordinary to think that he had never spent a happy day nor a day of any kind in Follard Chase, that desirable mansion in Herts, which he had won from Sir Follard Follard, by a chuck of the dice, at Boodle's, on his seventeenth birthday? Always cynical and unkind, he had refused to give the broken baronet his "revenge." Always unkind and insolent, he had offered to instal him in the lodge—an offer which was, after a little hesitation, accepted. "On my soul, the man's place is a sinecure," Lord George would say; "he never has to open the gate for me."[2] So rust had covered the great iron gates of Follard Chase, and moss had covered its paths. The deer browsed upon its terraces. There were only wild flowers anywhere. Deep down among the weeds and water-lilies of the little stone-rimmed pond he had looked down upon, lay the marble faun, as he had fallen.

Of all the sins of his lordship's life surely not one was more wanton than his neglect of Follard Chase. Some whispered (nor did he ever trouble to deny) that he had won it by foul means, by loaded dice. Indeed no card-player in St. James's cheated more persistently than he. As he was rich and had no wife and family to support, and as his luck was always capital, I can offer no excuse for his conduct. At Carlton House, in the presence of many bishops and cabinet ministers, he once dunned the Regent most arrogantly for 5000 guineas out of which he had cheated him some months before, and went so far as to declare that he would not leave the house till he got it; whereupon His Royal Highness, with that unfailing tact for which he was ever famous, invited him to stay there as a guest, which, in fact, Lord George did, for several months. After this, we can hardly be surprised when we read that he "seldom sat down to the fashionable game of Limbo with less than four, and sometimes with *as many as seven aces* up his sleeve."[3] We can only wonder that he was tolerated at all.

At Garble's, that nightly resort of titled rips and roysterers, he

2 *Lord Coleraine's Correspondence*, p. 101.
3 *Contemporary Bucks*, vol. 1, p. 73.

usually spent the early part of his evenings. Round the illuminated garden, with La Gambogi, the dancer, on his arm and a Bacchic retinue at his heels, he would amble leisurely, clad in Georgian costume, which was not then, of course, fancy dress, as it is now.[4] Now and again, in the midst of his noisy talk, he would crack a joke of the period, or break into a sentimental ballad, dance a little or pick a quarrel. When he tired of such fooling, he would proceed to his box in the tiny *al fresco* theatre and patronize the jugglers, pugilists, play-actors and whatever eccentric persons happened to be performing there.

The stars were splendid and the moon as beautiful as a great camellia one night in May, as his lordship laid his arms upon the cushioned ledge of his box and watched the antics of the Merry Dwarf, a little, curly-headed creature, whose *début* it was. Certainly Garble had found a novelty. Lord George led the applause, and the Dwarf finished his frisking with a pretty song about lovers. Nor was this all. Feats of archery were to follow. In a moment the Dwarf reappeared with a small, gilded bow in his hand and a quiverful of arrows slung at his shoulder. Hither and thither he shot these vibrant arrows, very precisely, several into the bark of the acacias that grew about the overt stage, several into the fluted columns of the boxes, two or three to the stars. The audience was delighted. "*Bravo! Bravo Saggitario!*" murmured Lord George, in the language of La Gambogi, who was at his side. Finally, the waxen figure of a man was carried on by an assistant and propped against the trunk of a tree. A scarf was tied across the eyes of the Merry Dwarf, who stood in a remote corner of the stage. *Bravo* indeed! For the shaft had pierced the waxen figure through the heart or just where the heart would have been, if the figure had been human and not waxen.

Lord George called for port and champagne, and beckoned the bowing homuncle to his box, that he might compliment him on his skill and pledge him in a bumper of the grape.

"On my soul, you have a genius for the bow," his lordship cried with florid condescension. "Come and sit by me, but first let me present you to my divine companion the Signora Gambogi—Virgo and Sagittarius, egad! You may have met on the Zodiac."

"Indeed, I met the Signora many years ago," the Dwarf replied, with a low bow. "But not on the Zodiac, and the Signora perhaps forgets me."

At this speech the Signora flushed angrily, for she was indeed no

4 It would seem, however, that, on special occasions, his lordship indulged in odd costumes. "I have seen him," says Captain Tarleton (vol. 1, p. 69), "attired as a French clown, as a sailor, or in the crimson hose of a Sicilian grandee—*peu beau spectacle* [quite a good spectacle]. He never disguised his face, whatever his costume, however."

longer young, and the Dwarf had a childish face. She thought he mocked her; her eyes flashed. Lord George's twinkled rather maliciously.

"Great is the experience of youth," he laughed. "Pray, are you stricken with more than twenty summers?" "With more than I can count," said the Dwarf. "To the health of your lordship!" and he drained his long glass of wine. Lord George replenished it, and asked by what means or miracle he had acquired his mastery of the bow.

"By long practice," the little thing rejoined; "long practice on human creatures." And he nodded his curls mysteriously.

"On my heart, you are a dangerous box-mate."

"Your lordship were certainly a good target."

Little liking this joke at his bulk, which really rivalled the Regent's, Lord George turned brusquely in his chair and fixed his eyes upon the stage. This time it was the Gambogi who laughed.

A new operette, *The Fair Captive of Samarcand,* was being enacted, and the frequenters of Garble's were all curious to behold the new *débutante,* Jenny Mere, who was said to be both pretty and talented. These predictions were surely fulfilled, when the captive peeped from the window of her wooden turret. She looked so pale under her blue turban. Her eyes were dark with fear; her parted lips did not seem capable of speech. "Is it that she is frightened of us?" the audience wondered. "Or of the flashing scimitar of Aphoschaz, the cruel father who holds her captive?" So they gave her loud applause, and when at length she jumped down, to be caught in the arms of her gallant lover, Nissarah, and, throwing aside her Eastern draperies, did a simple dance, in the convention of Columbine, their delight was quite unbounded. She was very young and did not dance very well, it is true, but they forgave her that. And when she turned in the dance and saw her father with his scimitar, their hearts beat swiftly for her. Nor were all eyes tearless when she pleaded with him for her life.

Strangely absorbed, quite callous of his two companions, Lord George gazed over the footlights. He seemed as one who was in a trance. Of a sudden, something shot sharp into his heart. In pain he sprang to his feet and, as he turned, he seemed to see a winged and laughing child, in whose hand was a bow, fly swiftly away into the darkness. At his side was the Dwarf's chair. It was empty. Only La Gambogi was with him, and her dark face was like the face of a fury.

Presently he sank back into his chair, holding one hand to his heart, that still throbbed from the strange transfixion. He breathed very painfully and seemed scarce conscious of his surroundings. But

La Gambogi knew he would pay no more homage to her now, for that the love of Jenny Mere had come into his heart.

When the operette was over, his love-sick lordship snatched up his cloak and went away without one word to the lady at his side. Rudely he brushed aside Count Karoloff and Mr. FitzClarence, with whom he had arranged to play hazard. Of his comrades, his cynicism, his reckless scorn—of all the material of his existence—he was oblivious now. He had no time for penitence or diffident delay. He only knew that he must kneel at the feet of Jenny Mere and ask her to be his wife.

"Miss Mere," said Garble, "is in her room, resuming her ordinary attire. If your lordship deign to await the conclusion of her humble toilet, it shall be my privilege to present her to your lordship. Even now, indeed, I hear her footfall on the stair."

Lord George uncovered his head and with one hand nervously smoothed his rebellious wig.

"Miss Mere, come hither," said Garble. "This is my Lord George Hell, that you have pleased who by your poor efforts this night will ever be the prime gratification of you. passage through the roseate realms of art."

Little Miss Mere who had never seen a lord, except in fancy or in dreams, curtseyed shyly and hung her head. With a loud crash Lord George fell on his knees. The manager was greatly surprised, the girl greatly embarrassed. Yet neither of them laughed, for sincerity dignified his posture and sent eloquence from its lips.

"Miss Mere," he cried, "give ear, I pray you, to my poor words, nor spurn me in misprision from the pedestal of your beauty, genius, and virtue. All too conscious, alas! of my presumption in the same, I yet abase myself before you as a suitor for your adorable hand. I grope under the shadow of your raven locks. I am dazzled in the light of those translucent orbs, your eyes. In the intolerable whirlwind of your fame I faint and am afraid."

"Sir——" the girl began, simply.

"Say 'My Lord,' " said Garble, solemnly.

"My lord, I thank you for your words. They are beautiful. But indeed, indeed, I can never be your bride."

Lord George hid his face in his hands.

"Child," said Mr. Garble, "let not the sun rise e'er you have retracted those wicked words."

"My wealth, my rank, my irremediable love for you, I throw them at your feet," Lord George cried, piteously. "I would wait an hour, a week, a lustre, even a decade, did you but bid me hope!"

"I can never be your wife," she said, slowly. "I can never be the wife of any man whose face is not saintly. Your face, my lord, mirrors, it may be, true love for me, but it is even as a mirror long tarnished by the reflection of this world's vanity. It is even as a tarnished mirror. Do not kneel to me, for I am poor and humble. I was not made for such impetuous wooing. Kneel, if you please, to some greater, gayer lady. As for my love, it is my own, nor can it ever be torn from me, but given, as true love needs be given, freely. Ah, rise from your knees. That man, whose face is wonderful as the faces of the saints, to him I will give my true love."

Miss Mere, though visibly affected, had spoken this speech with a gesture and elocution so superb, that Mr. Garble could not help applauding, deeply though he regretted her attitude towards his honoured patron. As for Lord George, he was immobile, a stricken oak. With a sweet look of pity, Miss Mere went her way, and Mr. Garble, with some solicitude, helped his lordship to rise from his knees. Out into the night, without a word, his lordship went. Above him the stars were still splendid. They seemed to mock the festoons of little lamps, dim now and guttering in the garden of Garble's. What should he do? No thoughts came; only his heart burnt hotly. He stood on the brim of Garble's lake, shallow and artificial as his past life had been. Two swans slept on its surface. The moon shone strangely upon their white, twisted necks. Should he drown himself? There was no one in the garden to prevent him, and in the morning they would find him floating there, one of the noblest of love's victims. The garden would be closed in the evening. There would be no performance in the little theatre. It might be that Jenny Mere would mourn him. "Life is a prison, without bars," he murmured, as he walked away.

All night long he strode, knowing not whither, through the mysterious streets and squares of London. The watchmen, to whom his figure was most familiar, gripped their staves at his approach, for they had old reason to fear his wild and riotous habits. He did not heed them. Through that dim conflict between darkness and day, which is ever waged silently over our sleep, Lord George strode on in the deep absorption of his love and of his despair. At dawn he found himself on the outskirts of a little wood in Kensington. A rabbit rushed past him through the dew. Birds were fluttering in the branches. The leaves were tremulous with the presage of day, and the air was full of the sweet scent of hyacinths.

How cool the country was! It seemed to cure the feverish maladies of his soul and consecrate his love. In the fair light of the dawn he began to shape the means of winning Jenny Mere, that he had conceived in the desperate hours of the night. Soon an old woodman passed by, and, with rough courtesy, showed him the path that would lead him quickest to the town. He was loth to leave the wood. With Jenny, he thought, he would live always in the country. And he picked a posy of wild flowers for her.

His *rentrée*[5] into the still silent town strengthened his Aracadian resolves. He, who had seen the town so often in its hours of sleep, had never noticed how sinister its whole aspect was. In its narrow streets the white houses rose on either side of him like cliffs of chalk. He hurried swiftly along the unswept pavement. How had he loved this city of evil secrets?

At last he came to St. James's Square, to the hateful door of his own house. Shadows lay like memories in every corner of the dim hall. Through the window of his room a sunbeam slanted across his smooth, white bed, and fell ghastly on the ashen grate.

It was a bright morning in Old Bond Street, and fat little Mr. Aeneas, the fashionable mask-maker, was sunning himself at the door of his shop. His window was lined as usual with all kinds of masks—beautiful masks with pink cheeks, and absurd masks with protuberant chins; curious προσωπα[6] copied from old tragic models; masks of paper for children, of fine silk for ladies, and of leather for working men; bearded or beardless, gilded or waxen (most of them, indeed were waxen), big or little masks. And in the middle of this vain galaxy hung the presentment of a Cyclop's face, carved cunningly of gold, with a great sapphire in its brow.

The sun gleamed brightly on the window and on the bald head and varnished shoes of fat little Mr. Aeneas. It was too early for any customers to come and Mr. Aeneas seemed to be greatly enjoying his leisure in the fresh air. He smiled complacently as he stood there, and well he might, for he was a great artist, and was patronized by several crowned heads and not a few of the nobility. Only the evening before, Mr. Brummell had come into his shop and ordered a light summer mask, wishing to evade for a time the jealous vigilance of Lady Otterton. It pleased Mr. Aeneas to think that his art made him the recipient of so many high secrets. He smiled as he thought of the titled spendthrifts, who, at this moment, *perdus*[7] behind his masterpieces, passed unscathed among their creditors. He was the secular confessor of his day, always able to give absolution. An unique position!

The street was as quiet as a village street. At an open window over the way, a handsome lady, wrapped in a muslin *peignoir*, sat sipping her cup of chocolate. It was La Signora Gambogi, and Mr. Aeneas made her many elaborate bows. This morning, however, her thoughts

5 [Return.] 6 [Masks.] 7 [Lost.]

seemed far away, and she did not notice the little man's polite efforts. Nettled at her negligence, Mr. Aeneas was on the point of retiring into his shop, when he saw Lord George Hell hastening up the street, with a posy of wild flowers in his hand.

"His lordship is up betimes!" he said to himself. "An early visit to La Signora, I suppose."

Not so, however. His lordship came straight towards the mask-shop. Once he glanced up at the Signora's window and looked deeply annoyed when he saw her sitting there. He came quickly into the shop.

"I want the mask of a saint," he said.

"Mask of a saint, my lord? Certainly!" said Mr. Aeneas, briskly. "With or without halo? His Grace the Bishop of St. Aldreds always wears his with a halo. Your lordship does not wish for a halo? Certainly! If your lordship will allow me to take the measurement——"

"I must have the mask to-day," Lord George said. "Have you none ready-made?"

"Ah, I see. Required for immediate wear," murmured Mr. Aeneas, dubiously. "You see, your lordship takes a rather large size." And he looked at the floor.

"Julius!" he cried suddenly to his assistant, who was putting finishing touches to a mask of Barbarossa which the young king of Zürremburg was to wear at his coronation the following week. "Julius! Do you remember the saint's mask we made for Mr. Ripsby, a couple of years ago?"

"Yes, sir," said the boy. "It's stored upstairs."

"I thought so," replied Mr. Aeneas. "Mr. Ripsby only had it on hire. Step upstairs, Julius, and bring it down. I fancy it is just what your lordship would wish. Spiritual, yet handsome."

"Is it a mask that is even as a mirror of true love?" Lord George asked gravely.

"It was made precisely as such," the mask-maker answered. "In fact it was made for Mr. Ripsby to wear at his silver wedding, and was very highly praised by the relatives of Mrs. Ripsby. Will your lordship step into my little room?"

So Mr. Aeneas led the way to his parlour behind the shop. He was elated by the distinguished acquisition to his *clientèle*, for hitherto Lord George had never patronized his business. He bustled round his parlour and insisted that his lordship should take a chair and a pinch from his snuff-box, while the saint's mask was being found.

Lord George's eye travelled along the rows of framed letters from great personages, which lined the walls. He did not see them though, for he was calculating the chances that La Gambogi had not observed him, as he entered the mask-shop. He had come down so early that he thought she would be still abed. That sinister old proverb, *La jalouse se lève de bonne heure*,[8] rose in his memory. His eye fell unconsciously on a large, round mask made of dull silver, with the features of a human face traced over its surface in faint filigree.

"Your lordship wonders what mask that is!" chirped Mr. Aeneas, tapping the thing with one of his little finger nails.

"What is that mask?" Lord George murmured, absently.

"I ought not to divulge, my lord," said the mask-maker. "But I know your lordship would respect a professional secret, a secret of which I am pardonably proud. This," he said, "is a mask for the sun-god, Apollo, whom heaven bless!"

"You astound me," said Lord George.

"Of no less a person, I do assure you. When Jupiter, his father, made him lord of the day, Apollo craved that he might sometimes see the doings of mankind in the hours of night time. Jupiter granted so reasonable a request, and when next Apollo had passed over the sky and hidden in the sea, and darkness had fallen on all the world, he raised his head above the waters that he might watch the doings of mankind in the hours of night time. But," Mr. Aeneas added, with a smile, "his bright countenance made light all the darkness. Men rose from their couches or from their revels, wondering that day was so soon come, and went to their work. And Apollo sank weeping into the sea. 'Surely,' he cried, 'it is a bitter thing that I alone, of all the gods, may not watch the world in the hours of night time. For in those hours, as I am told, men are even as gods are. They spill the wine and are wreathed with roses. Their daughters dance in the light of torches. They laugh to the sound of flutes. On their long couches they lie down at last and sleep comes to kiss their eyelids. None of these things may I see. Wherefore the brightness of my beauty is even as a curse to me and I would put it from me.' And as he wept, Vulcan said to him, 'I am not the least cunning of the gods, nor the least pitiful. Do not weep, for I will give you that which shall end your sorrow. Nor need you put from you the brightness of your beauty.' And Vulcan made a mask of dull silver and fastened it across his brother's face. And that night, thus masked, the sun-god rose from the sea and watched the doings of mankind in the night time. Nor any longer were men abashed by his bright beauty, for it was hidden by the mask of silver. Those whom he had so often seen haggard over their daily tasks, he saw feasting now and wreathed with red roses. He heard them laugh to the sound of flutes, as their daughters danced in the red light of torches. And when at length they lay down upon their soft couches and sleep kissed their

8 [Jealousy rises early.]

eyelids, he sank back into the sea and hid his mask under a little rock in the bed of the sea. Nor have men ever known that Apollo watches them often in the night time, but fancied it to be some pale goddess."

"I myself have always thought it was Diana," said Lord George Hell.

"An error, my lord!" said Mr. Aeneas, with a smile. "*Ecce signum!*"[9] And he tapped the mask of dull silver.

"Strange!" said his lordship. "And pray how comes it that Apollo has ordered of *you* this new mask?"

"He has always worn twelve new masks every year, inasmuch as no mask can endure for many nights the near brightness of his face, before which even a mask of the best and purest silver soon tarnishes, and wears away. Centuries ago, Vulcan tired of making so very many masks. And so Apollo sent Mercury down to Athens, to the shop of Phoron, a Phoenician mask-maker of great skill. Phoron made Apollo's masks for many years, and every month Mercury came to his shop for a new one. When Phoron died, another artist was chosen, and, when he died, another, and so on through all the ages of the world. Conceive, my lord, my pride and pleasure when Mercury flew into my shop, one night last year, and made me Apollo's warrant-holder. It is the highest privilege that any mask-maker can desire. And when I die," said Mr. Aeneas, with some emotion, "Mercury will confer my post upon another."

"And do they pay you for your labour?" Lord George asked.

Mr. Aeneas drew himself up to his full height, such as it was. "In Olympus, my lord," he said, "they have no currency. For any mask-maker, so high a privilege is its own reward. Yet the sun-god is generous. He shines more brightly into my shop than into any other. Nor does he suffer his rays to melt any waxen mask made by me, until its wearer doff it and it be done with." At this moment Julius came in with the Ripsby mask. "I must ask your lordship's pardon, for having kept you so long," pleaded Mr. Aeneas. "But I have a large store of old masks and they are imperfectly catalogued."

It certainly was a beautiful mask, with its smooth, pink cheeks and devotional brows. It was made of the finest wax. Lord George took it gingerly in his hands and tried it on his face. It fitted *à merveille*.[10]

"Is the expression exactly as your lordship would wish?" asked Mr. Aeneas.

Lord George laid it on the table and studied it intently. "I wish it were more as a perfect mirror of true love," he said at length. "It is too calm, too contemplative."

9 [Behold the image.]

10 [Beautifully.]

"Easily remedied!" said Mr. Aeneas. Selecting a fine pencil, he deftly drew the eyebrows closer to each other. With a brush steeped in some scarlet pigment, he put a fuller curve upon the lips. And, behold! it was the mask of a saint who loves dearly. Lord George's heart throbbed with pleasure.

"And for how long does your lordship wish to wear it?" asked Mr. Aeneas.

"I must wear it until I die," replied Lord George.

"Kindly be seated then, I pray," rejoined the little man. "For I must apply the mask with great care. Julius, you will assist me!"

So, while Julius heated the inner side of the waxen mask over a little lamp, Mr. Aeneas stood over Lord George gently smearing his features with some sweet-scented pomade. Then he took the mask and powdered its inner side, quite soft and warm now, with a fluffy puff. "Keep quite still, for one instant," he said, and clapped the mask firmly on his lordship's upturned face. So soon as he was sure of its perfect adhesion, he took from his assistant's hand a silver file and a little wooden spatula, with which he proceeded to pare down the edge of the mask, where it joined the neck and ears. At length, all traces of the "join" were obliterated. It remained only to arrange the curls of the lordly wig over the waxen brow.

The disguise was done. When Lord George looked through the eyelets of his mask into the mirror that was placed in his hand, he saw a face that was saintly, itself a mirror of true love. How wonderful it was! He felt his past was a dream. He felt he was a new man indeed. His voice went strangely through the mask's parted lips, as he thanked Mr. Aeneas.

"Proud to have served your lordship," said that little worthy, pocketing his fee of fifty guineas, while he bowed his customer out.

When he reached the street, Lord George nearly uttered a curse through those sainted lips of his. For there, right in his way, stood La Gambogi, with a small, pink parasol. She laid her hand upon his sleeve and called him softly by his name. He passed her by without a word. Again she confronted him.

"I cannot let go so handsome a lover," she laughed, "even though he spurn me! Do not spurn me, George. Give me your posy of wild flowers. Why, you never looked so lovingly at me in all your life!"

"Madam," said Lord George, sternly, "I have not the honour to know you." And he passed on.

The lady gazed after her lost lover with the blackest hatred in her eyes. Presently she beckoned across the road to a certain spy.

And the spy followed him.

Lord George, greatly agitated, had turned into Piccadilly. It was horrible to have met this garish embodiment of his past on the very threshold of his fair future. The mask-maker's elevating talk about the gods, followed by the initiative ceremony of his saintly mask, had driven all discordant memories from his love-thoughts of Jenny Mere. And then to be met by La Gambogi! It might be that, after his stern words, she would not seek to cross his path again. Surely she would not seek to mar his sacred love. Yet, he knew her dark, Italian nature, her passion for revenge. What was the line in Virgil? *Spretaeque*[11]—something. Who knew but that somehow, sooner or later, she might come between him and his love?

He was about to pass Lord Barrymore's mansion. Count Karoloff and Mr. FitzClarence were lounging in one of the lower windows. Would they know him under his mask? Thank God! they did not. They merely laughed as he went by, and Mr. FitzClarence cried in a mocking voice, "Sing us a hymn, Mr. What-ever-your-saint's-name-is!" The mask, then, at least, was perfect. Jenny Mere would not know him. He need fear no one but La Gambogi. But would not she betray his secret? He sighed.

That night he was going to visit Garble's and to declare his love to the little actress. He never doubted that she would love him for his saintly face. Had she not said, "That man whose face is wonderful as are the faces of the saints, to him I will give my true love?" She could not say now that his face was as a tarnished mirror of love. She would smile on him. She would be his bride. But would La Gambogi be at Garble's?

The operette would not be over before ten that night. The clock in Hyde Park Gate told him it was not yet ten—ten of the morning. Twelve whole hours to wait, before he could fall at Jenny's feet! "I cannot spend that time in this place of memories," he thought. So he hailed a yellow cabriolet and bade the jarvey drive him out to the village of Kensington.

When they came to the little wood where he had been but a few hours ago, Lord George dismissed the jarvey. The sun, that had risen as he stood there thinking of Jenny, shone down on his altered face, but, though it shone very fiercely, it did not melt his waxen features. The old woodman, who had shown him his way, passed by under a load of faggots and did not know him. He wandered among the trees. It was a lovely wood.

Presently he came to the bank of that tiny stream, the Ken, which still flowed there in those days. On the moss of its bank he lay down and let its water ripple over his hand. Some bright pebble glistened under the surface, and, as he peered down at it, he saw in the stream

11 [Spurned. Refers to Juno's anger at Paris's spurning of her beauty. From *The Aeneid,* Book II, line 25.]

the reflection of his mask. A great shame filled him that he should so cheat the girl he loved. Behind that fair mask there would still be the evil face that had repelled her. Could he be so base as to decoy her into love of that most ingenious deception? He was filled with a great pity for her, with a hatred of himself. And yet, he argued, was the mask indeed a mean trick? Surely it was a secret symbol of his true repentance and of his true love. His face was evil, because his life had been evil. He had seen a gracious girl, and of a sudden his very soul had changed. His face alone was the same as it had been. It was not just that his face should be evil still.

There was the faint sound of some one sighing. Lord George looked up, and there, on the further bank, stood Jenny Mere, watching him. As their eyes met, she blushed and hung her head. She looked like nothing but a tall child, as she stood there, with her straight, limp frock of lilac cotton and her sunburnt straw bonnet. He dared not speak; he could only gaze at her. Suddenly there perched astride the bough of a tree, at her side, that winged and laughing child, in whose hand was a bow. Before Lord George could warn her, an arrow had flashed down and vanished in her heart, and Cupid had flown away.

No cry of pain did she utter, but stretched out her arms to her lover, with a glad smile. He leapt quite lightly over the little stream and knelt at her feet. It seemed more fitting that he should kneel before the gracious thing he was unworthy of. But she, knowing only that his face was as the face of a great saint, bent over him and touched him with her hand.

"Surely," she said, "you are that good man for whom I have waited. Therefore do not kneel to me, but rise and suffer me to kiss your hand. For my love of you is lowly, and my heart is all yours."

But he answered, looking up into her fond eyes, "Nay, you are a queen, and I must needs kneel in your presence."

And she shook her head wistfully, and she knelt down, also, in her tremulous ecstasy, before him. And as they knelt, the one to the other, the tears came into her eyes, and he kissed her. Though the lips that he pressed to her lips were only waxen, he thrilled with happiness, in that mimic kiss. He held her close to him in his arms, and they were silent in the sacredness of their love.

From his breast he took the posy of wild flowers that he had gathered.

"They are for you," he whispered, "I gathered them for you, hours ago, in this wood. See! They are not withered."

But she was perplexed by his words and said to him, blushing, "How was it for me that you gathered them, though you had never seen me?"

"I gathered them for you," he answered, "knowing I should soon see you. How was it that you, who had never seen me, yet waited for me?"

"I waited, knowing I should see you at last." And she kissed the posy and put it at her breast.

And they rose from their knees and went into the wood, walking hand in hand. As they went, he asked the names of the flowers that grew under their feet. "These are primroses," she would say. "Did you not know? And these are ladies' feet, and these forget-me-nots. And that white flower, climbing up the trunks of the trees and trailing down so prettily from the branches, is called Astyanax. These little yellow things are buttercups. Did you not know?" And she laughed.

"I know the names of none of the flowers," he said.

She looked up into his face and said timidly, "Is it worldly and wrong of me to have loved the flowers? Ought I to have thought more of those higher things that are unseen?"

His heart smote him. He could not answer her simplicity.

"Surely the flowers are good, and did not you gather this posy for me?" she pleaded. "But if you do not love them, I must not. And I will try to forget their names. For I must try to be like you in all things."

"Love the flowers always," he said. "And teach me to love them."

So she told him all about the flowers, how some grew very slowly and others bloomed in a night; how clever the convolvulus was at climbing, and how shy violets were, and why honeycups had folded petals. She told him of the birds, too, that sang in the wood, how she knew them all by their voices. "That is a chaffinch singing. Listen!" she said. And she tried to imitate its note, that her lover might remember. All the birds, according to her, were good, except the cuckoo, and whenever she heard him sing she would stop her ears, lest she should forgive him for robbing the nests. "Every day," she said, "I have come to the wood, because I was lonely, and it seemed to pity me. But now I have you. And it is glad."

She clung closer to his arm, and he kissed her. She pushed back her straw bonnet, so that it dangled from her neck by its ribands, and laid her little head against his shoulder. For a while he forgot his treachery to her, thinking only of his love and her love. Suddenly she said to him, "Will you try not to be angry with me, if I tell you something? It is something that will seem dreadful to you."

"*Pauvrette,*"[12] he answered, "you cannot have anything very dreadful to tell."

"I am very poor," she said, "and every night I dance in a theatre.

12 [Poor little one.]

It is the only thing I can do to earn my bread. Do you despise me because I dance?" She looked up shyly at him and saw that his face was full of love for her and not angry.

"Do you like dancing?" he asked.

"I hate it," she answered, quickly. "I hate it indeed. Yet—to-night, alas! I must dance again in the theatre."

"You need never dance again," said her lover. "I am rich and I will pay them to release you. You shall dance only for me. Sweetheart, it cannot be much more than noon. Let us go into the town, while there is time, and you shall be made my bride, and I your bride-groom, this very day. Why should you and I be lonely?"

"I do not know," she said.

So they walked back through the wood, taking a narrow path which Jenny said would lead them quickest to the village. And, as they went, they came to a tiny cottage, with a garden that was full of flowers. The old woodman was leaning over its paling, and he nodded to them as they passed.

"I often used to envy the woodman," said Jenny, "living in that dear little cottage."

"Let us live there, then," said Lord George. And he went back and asked the old man if he were not unhappy, living there alone.

" 'Tis a poor life here for me," the old man answered. "No folk come to the wood, except little children, now and again, to play, or lovers like you. But they seldom notice me. And in winter I am alone with Jack Frost. Old men love merrier company than that. Oh! I shall die in the snow with my faggots on my back. A poor life here!"

"I will give you gold for your cottage and whatever is in it, and then you can go and live happily in the town," Lord George said. And he took from his coat a note for two hundred guineas, and held it across the palings.

"Lovers are poor, foolish derry-docks," the old man muttered. "But I thank you kindly, sir. This little sum will keep me cosy, as long as I last. Come into the cottage as soon as can be. It's a lonely place and does my heart good to depart from it."

"We are going to be married this afternoon, in the town," said Lord George. "We will come straight back to our home."

"May you be happy!" replied the woodman. "You'll find me gone when you come."

And the lovers thanked him and went their way.

"Are you very rich?" Jenny asked. "Ought you to have bought the cottage for that great price?"

"Would you love me as much if I were quite poor, little Jenny?" he asked her after a pause.

"I did not know you were rich when I saw you across the stream," she said.

And in his heart Lord George made a good resolve. He would put away from him all his worldly possessions. All the money that he had won at the clubs, fairly or foully, all that hideous accretion of gold guineas, he would distribute among the comrades he had impoverished. As he walked, with the sweet and trustful girl at his side, the vague record of his infamy assailed him, and a look of pain shot behind his smooth mask. He would atone. He would shun no sacrifice that might cleanse his soul. All his fortune he would put from him. Follard Chase he would give back to Sir Follard. He would sell his house in St. James's Square. He would keep some little part of his patrimony, enough for him in the wood, with Jenny, but no more.

"I shall be quite poor, Jenny," he said.

And they talked of the things that lovers love to talk of, how happy they would be together and how economical. As they were passing Herbert's pastry shop, which as my little readers know, still stands in Kensington, Jenny looked up rather wistfully into her lover's ascetic face.

"Should you think me greedy," she asked him, "if I wanted a bun? They have beautiful buns here!"

Buns! The simple word started latent memories of his childhood. Jenny was only a child, after all. Buns! He had forgotten what they were like. And as they looked at the piles of variegated cakes in the window, he said to her, "Which are buns, Jenny? I should like to have one, too."

"I am almost afraid of you," she said. "You must despise me so. Are you so good that you deny yourself all the vanity and pleasure that most people love? It is wonderful not to know what buns are! The round, brown, shiny cakes, with little raisins in them, are buns."

So he bought two beautiful buns, and they sat together in the shop, eating them. Jenny bit hers rather diffidently, but was reassured when he said that they must have buns very often in the cottage. Yes! he, the famous toper and *gourmet* of St. James's, relished this homely fare, as it passed through the insensible lips of his mask to his palate. He seemed to rise, from the consumption of his bun, a better man.

But there was no time to lose now. It was already past two o'clock. So he got a chaise from the inn opposite the pastry-shop, and they were swiftly driven to Doctors' Commons. There he purchased a special license. When the clerk asked him to write his name upon it, he hesitated. What name should he assume? Under a mask he had wooed this girl, under an unreal name he must make her his bride. He loathed himself for a trickster. He had vilely stolen from her the love she would not give him. Even now, should he not confess himself the man whose face had frightened her, and go his way? And yet, surely, it was not just that he, whose soul was transfigured, should bear his old name. Surely George Hell was dead, and his name had died with him. So he dipped a pen in the ink and wrote "George Heaven," for want of a better name. And Jenny wrote "Jenny Mere" beneath it.

An hour later they were married according to the simple rites of a dear little registry office in Covent Garden.

And in the cool evening they went home.

In the cottage that had been the woodman's they had a wonderful honeymoon. No king and queen in any palace of gold were happier than they. For them their tiny cottage was a palace, and the flowers that filled the garden were their couriers. Long and careless and full of kisses were the days of their reign.

Sometimes, indeed, strange dreams troubled Lord George's sleep. Once he dreamt that he stood knocking and knocking at the great door of a castle. It was a bitter night. The frost enveloped him. No one came. Presently he heard a footstep in the hall beyond, and a pair of frightened eyes peered at him through the grill. Jenny was scanning his face. She would not open to him. With tears and wild words he beseeched her, but she would not open to him. Then, very stealthily, he crept round the castle and found a small casement in the wall. It was open. He climbed swiftly, quietly through it. In the darkness of the room some one ran to him and kissed him gladly. It was Jenny. With a cry of joy and shame he awoke. By his side lay Jenny, sleeping like a little child.

After all, what was a dream to him? It could not mar the reality of his daily happiness. He cherished his true penitence for the evil he had done in the past. The past! That was indeed the only unreal thing that lingered in his life. Every day its substance dwindled, grew fainter yet, as he lived his rustic honeymoon. Had he not utterly put it from him? Had he not, a few hours after his marriage, written to his lawyer, declaring solemnly that he, Lord George Hell, had forsworn the world, that he was where no man would find him, that he desired all his worldly goods to be distributed, thus and thus, among these and those of his companions? By this testament he had verily atoned for the wrong he had done, had made himself dead indeed to the world.

No address had he written upon this document. Though its injunctions were final and binding, it could betray no clue of his hiding-place. For the rest, no one would care to seek him out. He, who had done no good to human creature, would pass unmourned out of memory. The clubs, doubtless, would laugh and puzzle over his strange recantations, envious of whomever he enriched. They would say 'twas a good riddance of a rogue and soon forget him.[13] But she, whose prime patron he had been, who had loved him in her vile fashion, La Gambogi, would she forget him easily, like the rest? As the sweet days went by, her spectre, also, grew fainter and less formidable. She knew his mask indeed, but how should she find him in the cottage near Kensington? *Devia dulcedo latebrarum!*[14] He was safe hidden with his bride. As for the Italian, she might search and search—or had forgotten him, in the arms of another lover.

Yes! Few and faint became the blemishes of his honeymoon. At first, he had felt that his waxen mask, though it had been the means of his happiness, was rather a barrier 'twixt him and his bride. Though it was sweet to kiss her through it, to look at her through it with loving eyes, yet there were times when it incommoded him with its mockery. Could he but put it from him! yet, that, of course, could not be. He must wear it all his life. And so, as days went by he grew reconciled to his mask. No longer did he feel it jarring on his face. It seemed to become an integral part of him, and, for all its rigid material, it did forsooth express the one emotion that filled him, true love. The face, for whose sake Jenny gave him her heart, could not but be dear to this George Heaven, also.

Every day chastened him with its joy. They lived a very simple life, he and Jenny. They rose betimes, like the birds, for whose goodness they both had so sincere a love. Bread and honey and little strawberries were their morning fare, and in the evening they had seed cake and dewberry wine. Jenny herself made the wine and her husband drank it, in strict moderation, never more than two glasses.

13 I would refer my little readers once more to the pages of *Contemporary Bucks,* where Captain Tarleton speculates upon the sudden disappearance of Lord George Hell and describes its effect on the town. "Not even the shrewdest," says he, "even gave a guess that would throw a ray of revealing light on the *disparition* of this profligate man. It was supposed that he carried off with him a little dancer from Garble's, at which *haunt of pleasantry* he was certainly on the night he vanished, and whither the young lady never returned again. Garble declared he had been compensated for her perfidy, but that he was sure she had not succumbed to his lordship, having in fact rejected him soundly. Did his lordship, say the cronies, take his life—and hers? *Il n'y a pas d'épreuve.* [There is no need to prove it.]

"The most astonishing matter is that the runaway should have written out a complete will, restoring all money he had won at cards, etc., etc. This certainly corroborates the opinion that he was seized with a sudden repentance and fled over the seas to a foreign monastery, where he died at last in *religious silence.* That's as it may, but many a spendthrift found his pocket clinking with guineas, a not unpleasant sound, I declare. The Regent himself was benefited by the odd will, and old Sir Follard Follard found himself once more in the ancestral home he had forfeited. As for Lord George's mansion in St. James's Square, that was sold with all its appurtenances, and the money fetched by the sale, no bagatelle, was given to various good objects, according to my lord's stated wishes. Well, many of us blessed his name—we had cursed it often enough. Peace to his ashes, in whatever urn they may be resting, on the billows of whatever ocean they float!"

14 [The secret sweetness of seclusion.]

He thought it tasted far better than the Regent's cherry brandy, or the Tokay at Brooks's. Of these treasured topes he had, indeed, nearly forgotten the taste. The wine made from wild berries by his little bride was august enough for his palate. Sometimes, after they had dined thus, he would play the flute to her upon the moonlit lawn, or tell her of the great daisy-chain he was going to make for her on the morrow, or sit silently by her side, listening to the nightingale, till bedtime. So admirably simple were their days.

One morning, as he was helping Jenny to water the flowers, he said to her suddenly, "Sweetheart, we had forgotten!"

"What was there we should forget?" asked Jenny, looking up from her task.

"'Tis the mensiversary of our wedding," her husband answered gravely. "We must not let it pass without some celebration."

"No, indeed," she said, "we must not. What shall we do?"

Between them they decided upon an unusual feast. They would go into the village and buy a bag of beautiful buns and eat them in the afternoon. So soon, then, as all the flowers were watered, they set forth to Herbert's shop, bought the buns and returned home in very high spirits, George bearing a paper bag that held no less than twelve of the wholesome delicacies. Under the plane tree on the lawn Jenny sat her down, and George stretched himself at her feet. They were loth to enjoy their feast too soon. They dallied in childish anticipation. On the little rustic table Jenny built up the buns, one above the other, till they looked like a tall pagoda. When, very gingerly, she had crowned the structure with the twelfth bun, her husband looking on with admiration, she clapped her hands and danced about it. She laughed so loudly (for, though she was only sixteen years old, she had a great sense of humour), that the table shook, and alas! the pagoda tottered and fell to the lawn. Swift as a kitten, Jenny chased the buns, as they rolled, hither and thither, over the grass, catching them deftly with her hand. Then she came back, flushed and merry under her tumbled hair, with her arm full of buns. She began to put them back in the paper bag.

"Dear husband," she said, looking down to him, "why do not you smile too at my folly? Your grave face rebukes me. Smile, or I shall think I vex you. Please smile a little."

But the mask could not smile, of course. It was made for a mirror of true love, and it was grave and immobile. "I am very much amused, dear," he said, "at the fall of the buns, but my lips will not curve to a smile. Love of you has bound them in spell."

"But I can laugh, though I love you. I do not understand." And she wondered. He took her hand in his and stroked it gently, wishing it were possible to smile. Some day, perhaps, she would tire of this monotonous gravity, this rigid sweetness. It was not strange that she should long for a little facile expression. They sat silently.

"Jenny, what is it?" he whispered suddenly. For Jenny, with wide-open eyes, was gazing over his head, across the lawn. "Why do you look frightened?"

"There is a strange woman smiling at me across the palings," she said. "I do not know her."

Her husband's heart sank. Somehow, he dared not turn his head to the intruder. He dreaded who she might be.

"She is nodding to me," said Jenny. "I think she is foreign, for she has an evil face."

"Do not notice her," he whispered. "Does she look evil?"

"Very evil and very dark. She has a pink parasol. Her teeth are like ivory."

"Do not notice her. Think! It is the mensiversary of our wedding, dear!"

"I wish she would not smile at me. Her eyes are like bright blots of ink."

"Let us eat our beautiful buns!"

"Oh, she is coming in!" George heard the latch of the gate jar. "Forbid her to come in!" whispered Jenny, "I am afraid!" He heard the jar of heels on the gravel path. Yet he dared not turn. Only he clasped Jenny's hand more tightly, as he waited for the voice. It was La Gambogi's.

"Pray, pray, pardon me! I could not mistake the back of so old a friend."

With the courage of despair, George turned and faced the woman.

"Even," she smiled, "though his face has changed marvellously."

"Madam," he said, rising to his full height and stepping between her and his bride, "begone, I command you, from the garden. I do not see what good is to be served by the renewal of our acquaintance."

"Acquaintance!" murmured La Gambogi, with an arch of her beetlebrows. "Surely we were friends, rather, nor is my esteem for you so dead that I would crave estrangement."

"Madam," rejoined Lord George, with a tremor in his voice, "you see me happy, living very peacefully with my bride——"

"To whom, I beseech you, old friend, present me."

"I would not," he said hotly, "desecrate her sweet name by speaking it with so infamous a name as yours."

"Your choler hurts me, old friend," said La Gambogi, sinking composedly upon the garden-seat and smoothing the silk of her skirts.

"Jenny," said George, "then do you retire, pending this lady's departure, to the cottage." But Jenny clung to his arm. "I were less frightened at your side," she whispered. "Do not send me away!"

"Suffer her pretty presence," said La Gambogi. "Indeed I am come this long way from the heart of the town, that I may see her, no less than you, George. My wish is only to befriend her. Why should she not set you a mannerly example, giving me welcome? Come and sit by me, little bride, for I have things to tell you. Though you reject my friendship, give me, at least, the slight courtesy of audience. I will not detain you overlong, will be gone very soon. Are you expecting guests, George? *On dirait une masque champêtre!*"[16] She eyed the couple critically. "Your wife's mask," she said, "is even better than yours."

"What does she mean?" whispered Jenny. "Oh, send her away!"

"Serpent," was all George could say, "crawl from our Eden, ere you poison with your venom its fairest denizen."

La Gambogi rose. "Even *my* pride," she cried passionately, "knows certain bounds. I have been forbearing, but even in *my* zeal for friendship I will not be called 'serpent.' I will indeed begone from this rude place. Yet, ere I go, there is a boon I will deign to beg. Show me, oh show me but once again, the dear face I have so often caressed, the lips that were dear to me!"

George started back.

"What does she mean?" whispered Jenny.

"In memory of our old friendship," continued La Gambogi, "grant me this piteous favour. Show me your own face but for one instant, and I vow I will never again remind you that I live. Intercede for me, little bride. Bid him unmask for me. You have more authority over him than I. Doff his mask with your own uxorious fingers."

"What does she mean?" was the refrain of poor Jenny.

"If," said George, gazing sternly at his traitress, "you do not go now, of your own will, I must drive you, man though I am, violently from the garden."

"Doff your mask and I am gone."

George made a step of menace towards her.

"False saint!" she shrieked, "then *I* will unmask you."

Like a panther she sprang upon him and clawed at his waxen cheeks. Jenny fell back, mute with terror. Vainly did George try to free himself from the hideous assailant, who writhed round and round him, clawing, clawing at what Jenny fancied to be his face. With a wild cry, Jenny fell upon the furious creature and tried, with all her childish strength, to release her dear one. The combatives swayed to and fro, a revulsive trinity. There was a loud pop, as

16 [A naughty country lass, perhaps?]

though some great cork had been withdrawn, and La Gambogi recoiled. She had torn away the mask. It lay before her upon the lawn, upturned to the sky.

George stood motionless. La Gambogi stared up into his face, and her dark flush died swiftly away. For there, staring back at her, was the man she had unmasked, but, lo! his face was even as his mask had been. Line for line, feature for feature, it was the same. 'Twas a saint's face.

"Madam," he said, in the calm voice of despair, "your cheek may well blanch, when you regard the ruin you have brought upon me. Nevertheless do I pardon you. The gods have avenged, through you, the imposture I wrought upon one who was dear to me. For that unpardonable sin I am punished. As for my poor bride, whose love I stole by the means of that waxen semblance, of her I cannot ask pardon. Ah, Jenny, Jenny, do not look at me. Turn your eyes from the foul reality that I dissembled." He shuddered and hid his face in his hands. "Do not look at me. I will go from the garden. Nor will I ever curse you with the odious spectacle of my face. Forget me, forget me."

But, as he turned to go, Jenny laid her hands upon his wrists and besought him that he would look at her. "For indeed," she said, "I am bewildered by your strange words. Why did you woo me under a mask? And why do you imagine I could love you less dearly, seeing your own face?"

He looked into her eyes. On their violet surface he saw the tiny reflection of his own face. He was filled with joy and wonder.

"Surely," said Jenny, "your face is even dearer to me, even fairer, than the semblance that hid it and deceived me. I am not angry. 'Twas well that you veiled from me the full glory of your face, for indeed I was not worthy to behold it too soon. But I am your wife now. Let me look always at your own face. Let the time of my probation be over. Kiss me with your own lips."

So he took her in his arms, as though she had been a little child, and kissed her with his own lips. She put her arms round his neck, and he was happier than he had ever been. They were alone in the garden now. Nor lay the mask any longer upon the lawn, for the sun had melted it.

Evelyn Waugh

LOVE AMONG THE RUINS

1

DESPITE their promises at the last Election, the politicians had not yet changed the climate. The State Meteorological Institute had so far produced only an unseasonable fall of snow and two little thunderbolts no larger than apricots. The weather varied from day to day and from county to county as it had done of old, most anomalously.

This was a rich, old-fashioned Tennysonian night.

Strains of a string quartet floated out from the drawing-room windows and were lost amid the splash and murmur of the gardens. In the basin the folded lilies had left a brooding sweetness over the water. No gold fin winked in the porphyry font and any peacock which seemed to be milkily drooping in the moon-shadows was indeed a ghost, for the whole flock of them had been found mysteriously and rudely slaughtered a day or two ago in the first disturbing flush of this sudden summer.

Miles, sauntering among the sleeping flowers, was suffused with melancholy. He did not much care for music and this was his last evening at Mountjoy. Never again, perhaps, would he be free to roam these walks.

Mountjoy had been planned and planted in the years of which he knew nothing; generations of skilled and patient husbandmen had weeded and dunged and pruned; generations of dilettanti had watered it with cascades and jets; generations of collectors had lugged statuary here; all, it seemed, for his enjoyment this very night under this huge moon. Miles knew nothing of such periods and processes, but he felt an incomprehensible tidal pull towards the circumjacent splendors.

Eleven struck from the stables. The music ceased. Miles turned back and, as he reached the terrace, the shutters began to close and the great chandeliers were one by one extinguished. By the light of the sconces which still shone on their panels of faded satin and clouded gold, he joined the company dispersing to bed through the islands of old furniture.

His room was not one of the grand succession which lay along the garden front. Those were reserved for murderers. Nor was it on the floor above, tenanted mostly by sexual offenders. His was a humbler

---

LOVE AMONG THE RUINS: From *Tactical Exercise* by Evelyn Waugh, published by Little, Brown and Company. Reprinted by permission of the author.

wing. Indeed he overlooked the luggage porch and the coal bunker. Only professional men visiting Mountjoy on professional business and very poor relations had been put here in the old days. But Miles was attached to this room, which was the first he had ever called his own in all his twenty years of Progress.

His next-door neighbor, a Mr. Sweat, paused at his door to say good-night. It was only now after twenty months' proximity, when Miles's time was up, that this veteran had begun to unbend. He and a man named Soapy, survivals of another age, had kept themselves to themselves, talking wistfully of cribs they had cracked, of sparklers, of snug bar-parlors where they had met their favorite fences, of strenuous penal days at the Scrubs and on the Moor. They had small use for the younger generation; crime, calvinism and classical music were their interests. But at last Mr. Sweat had taken to nodding, to grunting, and finally, too late for friendship, to speaking to Miles.

"What price the old strings tonight, chum?" he asked.

"I wasn't there, Mr. Sweat."

"You missed a treat. Of course nothing's ever good enough for old Soapy. Made me fair sick to hear Soapy going on all the time. The viola was scratchy, Soapy says. They played the Mozart just like it was Haydn. No feeling in the Debussy pizzicato, says Soapy."

"Soapy knows too much."

"Soapy knows a lot more than some I could mention, schooling or no schooling. Next time they're going to do the Grosse Fugue as the last movement of the B flat. That's something to look forward to, that is, though Soapy says no late Beethoven comes off. We'll see. Leastways, me and Soapy will; *you* won't. You're off tomorrow. Pleased?"

"Not particularly."

"No, no more wouldn't I be. It's a funny thing but I've settled down here wonderful. Never thought I should. It all seemed a bit too posh at first. Not like the old Scrubs. But it's a real pretty place once you're used to it. Wouldn't mind settling here for a lifer if they'd let me. The trouble is there's no security in crime these days. Time was, you knew just what a job was worth, six months, three years; whatever it was, you knew where you were. Now what with prison commissioners and Preventative Custody and Corrective Treatment they can keep you in or push you out just as it suits them. It's not right.

"I'll tell you what it is, chum," continued Mr. Sweat. "There's no understanding of crime these days like what there was. I remember when I was a nipper, the first time I came up before the beak, he spoke up straight: 'My lad,' he says, 'you are embarking upon a course of life that can only lead to disaster and degradation in this world and everlasting damnation in the next.' Now that's talking. It's plain sense and it shows a personal interest. But last time I was up, when they sent me here, they called me an 'anti-social phenomenon;' said I was 'maladjusted.' That's no way to speak of a man what was doing time before they was in long trousers, now is it?"

"They said something of the same kind to me."

"Yes and now they're giving you the push, just like you hadn't no Rights. I tell you it's made a lot of the boys uncomfortable your going out all of a sudden like this. Who'll it be next time, that's what we're wondering?

"I tell you where you went wrong, chum. You didn't give enough trouble. You made it too easy for them to say you was cured. Soapy and me got wise to that. You remember them birds as got done in? That was Soapy and me. They took a lot of killing too; powerful great bastards. But we got the evidence all hid away tidy and if there's ever any talk of me and Soapy being 'rehabilitated' we'll lay it out conspicuous.

"Well, so long, chum. Tomorrow's my morning for Remedial Repose so I daresay you'll be off before I get down. Come back soon."

"I hope so," said Miles and turned alone into his own room.

He stood briefly at the window and gazed his last on the cobbled yard. He made a good figure of a man, for he came of handsome parents and all his life had been carefully fed and doctored and exercised; well clothed too. He wore the drab serge dress that was the normal garb of the period—only certified homosexuals wore colors—but there were differences of fit and condition among these uniforms. Miles displayed the handiwork of tailor and valet. He belonged to a privileged class.

The State had made him.

No clean-living, God-fearing, Victorian gentleman, he; no complete man of the renaissance; no gentil knight nor dutiful pagan nor, even, noble savage. All that succession of past worthies had gone its way, content to play a prelude to Miles. He was the Modern Man.

His history, as it appeared in multuplet in the filing cabinets of numberless State departments, was typical of a thousand others. Before his birth the politicians had succeeded in bringing down his father and mother to penury; they, destitute, had thrown themselves into the simple diversions of the very poor and thus, between one war and the next, set in motion a chain-reaction of divorces which scattered them and their various associates in forlorn couples all over the Free World. The aunt on whom the infant Miles had been quartered was conscribed for work in a factory and shortly afterwards died of boredom at the conveyer-belt. The child was put to safety in an orphanage.

Huge sums were thence forward spent upon him; sums which, fifty years earlier, would have sent whole quiversful of boys to Winchester and New College and established them in the learned professions. In halls adorned with Picassos and Legers he yawned through long periods of Constructive Play. He never lacked the requisite cubic feet of air. His diet was balanced and on the first Friday of every month he was psychoanalyzed. Every detail of his adolescence was recorded and microfilmed and filed, until at the appropriate age he was transferred to the Air Force.

There were no airplanes at the station to which he was posted. It was an institution to train instructors to train instructors to train instructors in Personal Recreation.

There for some weeks he tended a dish-washing machine and tended it, as his adjutant testified at his trial, in an exemplary fashion. The work in itself lacked glory, but it was the normal novitiate. Men from the orphanages provided the hard core of the Forces, a caste apart which united the formidable qualities of Janissary and Junker. Miles had been picked early for high command. Dish-washing was only the beginning. The adjutant, an Orphan too, had himself washed both dishes and officers' underclothes, he testified, before rising to his present position.

Courts Martial had been abolished some years before this. The Forces handed their defaulters over to the civil arm for treatment. Miles came up at quarter sessions. It was plain from the start, when Arson, Wilful Damage, Manslaughter, Prejudicial Conduct and Treason were struck out of the Indictment and the whole reduced to a simple charge of Antisocial Activity, that the sympathies of the Court were with the prisoner.

The Station Psychologist gave his opinion that an element of incendiarism was inseparable from adolescence. Indeed, if checked, it might produce morbid neuroses. For his part he thought the prisoner had performed a perfectly normal act and, moreover, had shown more than normal intelligence in its execution.

At this point some widows, mothers and orphans of the incinerated airmen set up an outcry from the public gallery and were sharply reminded from the Bench that this was a Court of Welfare and not a meeting of the Housewives' Union.

The case developed into a concerted eulogy of the accused. An attempt by the prosecution to emphasize the extent of the damage was rebuked from the Bench.

"The jury," he said, "will expunge from their memories these sentimental details which have been most improperly introduced."

"May be a detail to you," said a voice from the gallery. "He was a good husband to me."

"Arrest that woman," said the Judge.

Order was restored and the panegyrics continued.

At last the Bench summed up. He reminded the jury that it was a first principle of the New Law that no man could be held responsible for the consequences of his own acts. The jury must dismiss from their minds the consideration that much valuable property and many valuable lives had been lost and the cause of Personal Recreation gravely retarded. They had merely to decide whether in fact the prisoner had arranged inflammable material at various judiciously selected points in the Institution and had ignited them. If he had done so, and the evidence plainly indicated that he had, he contravened the Standing Orders of the Institution and was thereby liable to the appropriate penalties.

Thus directed the jury brought in a verdict of guilty coupled with a recommendation of mercy towards the various bereaved persons who from time to time in the course of the hearing had been committed for contempt. The Bench reprimanded the jury for presumption and impertinence in the matter of the prisoners held in contempt, and sentenced Miles to residence during the State's pleasure at Mountjoy Castle (the ancestral seat of a maimed V.C. of the Second World War, who had been sent to a Home for the Handicapped when the place was converted into a jail).

The State was capricious in her pleasures. For nearly two years Miles enjoyed her particular favors. Every agreeable remedial device was applied to him and applied, it was now proclaimed, successfully. Then without warning a few days back, while he lay dozing under a mulberry tree, the unexpected blow had fallen; they had come to him, the Deputy Chief-Guide and the sub-Deputy, and told him bluntly and brutally that he was rehabilitated.

Now on this last night he knew he was to wake tomorrow on a harsh world. Nevertheless he slept and was gently awoken for the last time to the familiar scent of china tea on his bed table, the thin bread and butter, the curtains drawn above the luggage porch, the sunlit kitchen-yard and the stable clock just visible behind the cut-leaf copper beech.

He breakfasted late and alone. The rest of the household were already engaged in the first community-songs of the day. Presently he was called to the Guidance Office.

Since his first day at Mountjoy, when with other entrants Miles had been addressed at length by the Chief Guide on the Aims and Achievements of the New Penology, they had seldom met. The Chief Guide was almost always away addressing penological conferences.

The Guidance Office was the former housekeeper's room stripped now of its plush and patriotic pictures; sadly tricked out instead with standard civil-service equipment, class A.

It was full of people.

"This is Miles Plastic," said the Chief Guide. "Sit down, Miles. You can see from the presence of our visitors this morning what an important occasion this is."

Miles took a chair and looked and saw seated beside the Chief Guide two elderly men whose faces were familiar from the television screen as prominent colleagues in the Coalition Government. They wore open flannel shirts, blazers with numerous pens and pencils protruding from the breast pocket, and baggy trousers. This was the dress of very high politicians.

"The Minister of Welfare and the Minister of Rest and Culture," continued the Chief Guide. "The stars to which we have hitched our wagon. Have the press got the hand-out?"

"Yes, Chief."

"And the photographers are all ready?"

"Yes, Chief."

"Then I can proceed."

He proceeded as he had done at countless congresses, at countless spas and university cities. He concluded, as he always did: "In the New Britain which we are building, there are no criminals. There are only the victims of inadequate social services."

The Minister of Welfare, who had not reached his present eminence without the help of a certain sharpness in debate, remarked: "But I understood that Plastic is from one of our own Orphanages. . . ."

"Plastic is recognized as a Special Case," said the Chief Guide.

The Minister of Rest and Culture, who in the old days had more than once done time himself, said: "Well, Plastic, lad, from all they do say I reckon you've been uncommon smart."

"Exactly," said the Chief Guide. "Miles is our first success, the vindication of the Method."

"Of all the new prisons established in the first glorious wave of Reform, Mountjoy alone has produced a complete case of rehabilitation," the Minister of Welfare said. "You may or may not be aware that the Method has come in for a good deal of criticism both in Parliament and outside. There are a lot of young hot-heads who take their inspiration from our Great Neighbor in the East. You can quote the authorities to them till you're black in the face but they are always pressing for the all latest gadgets of capital and corporal punishment, for chain gangs and solitary confinement, bread and water, the cat-o'-nine-tails, the rope and the block, and all manner of newfangled nonsense. They think we're a lot of old fogeys. Thank goodness we've still got the solid sense of the people behind us, but we're on the defensive now. We have to show results. That's why we're here this morning. To show them results. *You* are our Result!"

These were solemn words and Miles in some measure responded to the occasion. He gazed before him blankly with an expression that might seem to be awe.

"You'd best watch your step now, lad," said the Minister of Rest and Culture.

"Photographs," said the Minister of Welfare, "Yes, shake my hand. Turn towards the cameras. Try to smile."

Bulbs flashed all over the dreary little room.

"Give us a paw, lad," said the Minister of Rest and Culture, taking Miles's hand in his turn. "And no funny business, mind."

Then the politicians departed.

"The Deputy-Chief will attend to all the practical matters," said the Chief wearily. "Go and see him now."

Miles went.

"Well, Miles, from now on I must call you Mr. Plastic," said the Deputy-Chief. "In less than a minute you become a Citizen. This little pile of papers is *You*. When I stamp them, Miles the Problem ceases to exist and Mr. Plastic the Citizen is born. We are sending you to Satellite City, the nearest Population Center, where you will be attached to the Ministry of Welfare as a sub-official. In view of your special training you are not being classified as a Worker. The immediate material rewards, of course, are not as great. But you are definitely in the Service. We have set your foot on the bottom rung of the noncompetitive ladder."

The Deputy Chief Guide picked up the rubber stamp and proceeded to his work of creation. Flip-thump, flip-thump the papers were turned and stained.

"There you are, Mr. Plastic," said the Deputy-Chief handing Miles, as it were, the baby.

At last Miles spoke: "What must I do to get back here?" he asked.

"Come, come, you're rehabilitated now, remember. It is your turn to give back to the State some of the service the State has given you. You will report this morning to the Area Progressive. Transport has been laid on. State be with you, Mr. Plastic. Be careful, that's your Certificate of Human Personality you've dropped—a *vital* document."

2

SATELLITE City, one of a hundred such grand conceptions, was not yet in its teens but already the Dome of Security showed signs of wear. This was the name of the great municipal edifice about which the city was planned. The eponymous dome had looked well enough in the architect's model, shallow certainly but amply making up in girth what it lacked in height, the daring exercise of some new trick of construction. But to the surprise of all, when the building arose and was seen from the ground, the dome blandly vanished. It was hidden forever among the roofs and butting shoulders of the ancillary wings and was never seen again from the outside except by airmen and steeplejacks. Only the name remained. On the day of its dedication, among massed politicians and People's Choirs the great lump of building materials had shone fine as a factory in all its brilliance of glass and new concrete. Since then, during one of the rather frequent week-ends of international panic, it had been camouflaged and its windows blackened. Cleaners were few and usually on strike. So the Dome of Security remained blotched and dingy, the sole permanent building of Satellite City. There were no workers' flats, no officials' garden suburbs, no parks, no playgrounds yet. These were all on the drawing-boards in the surveyor's office, tattered at the edges, ringed by tea cups; their designer long cremated and his ashes scattered among the docks and nettles. Thus the Dome of Security comprised, even more than had been intended, all the aspirations and amenities of the city.

The officials subsisted in perpetual twilight. Great sheets of glass planned to "trap" the sun, admitted few gleams from scratches in their coat of tar. At evening when the electric light came on, there was faint glow, here and there. When, as often, the power-station was "shedding its load" the officials stopped work early and groped their way back to their darkened huts where in the useless refrigerators their tiny rations were quietly putrefying. On working days the officials, male and female, trudged through cigarette ends round and round, up and down what had once been lift-shafts, in a silent, shabby, shadowy procession.

Among these pilgrims of the dusk, in the weeks that followed his discharge from Mountjoy, moved the exiled Miles Plastic.

He was in a key department.

Euthanasia had not been part of the original 1945 Health Service; it was a Tory measure designed to attract votes from the aged and the mortally sick. Under the Bevan-Eden Coalition the Service came into general use and won instant popularity. The Union of Teachers was pressing for its application to difficult children. Foreigners came in such numbers to take advantage of the service that immigration authorities now turned back the bearers of single tickets.

Miles recognised the importance of his appointment even before he began work. On his first evening in the hostel his fellow sub-officials gathered round to question him.

"Euthanasia? I say, you're in luck. They work you jolly hard, of course, but it's the one department that's expanding."

"You'll get promoted before you know your way about."

"Great State! You *must* have pull. Only the very bright boys get posted to Euthanasia."

"I've been in Contraception for five years. It's a blind alley."

"They say that in a year or two Euthanasia will have taken over Pensions."

"You must be an Orphan."

"Yes, I am."

"That accounts for it. Orphans get all the plums. I had a Full Family Life, State help me."

It was gratifying, of course, this respect and envy. It was well to have fine prospects; but for the time being Miles's duties were humble enough.

He was junior sub-official in a staff of half a dozen. The Director was an elderly man called Dr. Beamish, a man whose character had been formed in the nervous '30s, now much embittered, like many of his contemporaries, by the fulfilment of his early hopes. He had signed manifestos in his hot youth, had raised his fist in Barcelona and had painted abstractedly for *Horizon;* he had stood beside Spender at great concourses of Youth, and written "publicity" for the Last Viceroy. Now his reward had come to him. He held the most envied post in Satellite City and, sardonically, he was making the worst of it. Dr. Beamish rejoiced in every attenuation of official difficulties.

Satellite City was said to be the worst served Euthanasia Center in the State. Dr. Beamish's patients were kept waiting so long that often they died natural deaths before he found it convenient to poison them.

His small staff respected Dr. Beamish. They were all of the official class, for it was part of the grim little game which Dr. Beamish played with the higher authorities to economize extravagantly. His department, he maintained, could not, on its present allotment, afford workers. Even the furnace-man and the girl who dispatched unwanted false teeth to the Dental Redistribution Center were sub-officials.

Sub-officials were cheap and plentiful. The Universities turned them out in thousands every year. Indeed, ever since the Incitement to Industry Act of 1955, which exempted workers from taxation—that great and popular measure of reform which had consolidated the now permanent Coalition Government—there had been a nefarious one-way traffic of expensively State-educated officials "passing," as it was called, into the ranks of the workers.

Miles's duties required no special skill. Daily at ten the Service opened its doors to welfare-weary citizens. Miles was the man who opened them, stemmed the too eager rush and admitted the first half-dozen; then he closed the doors on the waiting multitude until a Higher Official gave the signal for the admission of another batch.

Once inside they came briefly under his charge; he set them in order, saw that they did not press ahead of their turn, and adjusted the television set for their amusement. A Higher Official interviewed them, checked their papers and arranged for the confiscation of their property. Miles never passed the door through which they were finally one by one conducted. A faint whiff of cyanide sometimes gave a hint of the mysteries beyond. Meanwhile he swept the waiting room, emptied the wastepaper basket and brewed tea—a worker's job, for which the refinements of Mountjoy proved a too rich apprenticeship.

In his hostel the same reproductions of Leger and Picasso as had haunted his childhood still stared down on him. At the cinema, to which he could afford, at the best, a weekly visit, the same films as he had seen free at Orphanage, Air Force station and prison, flickered and drawled before him. He was a child of Welfare, strictly schooled to a life of boredom, but he had known better than this. He had known the tranquil melancholy of the gardens at Mountjoy. He had known ecstasy when the Air Force Training School had whirled to the stars in a typhoon of flame. And as he moved sluggishly between Dome and hostel there rang in his ears the words of the old lag: "You didn't give enough trouble."

Then one day, in the least expected quarter, in his own drab department, hope appeared.

Miles later remembered every detail of that morning. It had started in the normal way; rather below normal indeed, for they were reopening after a week's enforced idleness. There had been a strike among the coal miners and Euthanasia had been at a standstill. Now the necessary capitulations had been signed, the ovens glowed again, and the queue at the patients' entrance stretched halfway round the dome. Dr. Beamish squinted at the waiting crowd through the periscope and said with some satisfaction: "It will take months to catch up on the waiting list now. We shall have to start making a charge for the service. It's the only way to keep down the demand."

"The Ministry will never agree to that, surely, sir?"

"Damned sentimentalists. My father and mother hanged themselves in their own backyard with their own clothes-line. Now no one will lift a finger to help himself. There's something wrong in the system, Plastic. There are still rivers to drown in, trains—every now and then—to put your head under; gas-fires in some of the huts. The country is full of the natural resources of death, but everyone has to come to us."

It was not often he spoke so frankly before his subordinates. He had overspent during the week's holiday, drunk too much at his hostel with other unemployed colleagues. Always after a strike the senior officials returned to work in low spirits.

"Shall I let the first batch in, sir?"

"Not for the moment," said Dr. Beamish. "There's a priority case to see first, sent over with a pink chit from Drama. She's in the private waiting-room now. Fetch her in."

Miles went to the room reserved for patients of importance. All one wall was of glass. Pressed to it a girl was standing, turned away from him, looking out at the glum queue below. Miles stood, the light in his eyes, conscious only of a shadow which stirred at the sound of the latch and turned, still a shadow merely but of exquisite grace, to meet him. He stood at the door, momentarily struck silent at this blind glance of beauty. Then he said: "We're quite ready for you now, miss."

The girl came nearer. Miles' eyes adjusted themselves to the light. The shadow took form. The full vision was all that the first glance had hinted; more than all, for every slight movement revealed perfection. One feature only broke the canon of pure beauty; a long, silken, corn-gold beard.

She said, with a deep, sweet tone, all unlike the flat conventional accent of the age: "Let it be quite understood that I don't want anything done to me. I consented to come here. The Director of Drama and the Director of Health were so pathetic about it all that I thought it was the least I could do. I said I was quite willing to hear about your service, but I do *not* want anything *done*."

"Better tell him inside," said Miles.

He led her to Dr. Beamish's room.

"Great State!" said Dr. Beamish, with eyes for the beard alone.

"Yes," she said. "It is a shock, isn't it? I've got used to it by now but I can understand how people feel seeing it for the first time."

"Is it real?"

"Pull."

"It *is* strong. Can't they do anything about it?"

"Oh they've tried everything."

Dr. Beamish was so deeply interested that he forgot Miles's presence. "Klugmann's Operation, I suppose?"

"Yes."

"It does go wrong like that every now and then. They had two or three cases at Cambridge."

"I never wanted it done. I never want anything done. It was the Head of the Ballet. He insists on all the girls being sterilized. Apparently you can never dance really well again after you've had a baby. And I did want to dance really well. Now this is what's happened."

"Yes," said Dr. Beamish. "Yes. They're far too slap-dash. They had to put down those girls at Cambridge, too. There was no cure. Well, we'll attend to you, young lady. Have you any arrangements to make or shall I take you straight away?"

"But I don't want to be put down. I told your assistant here, I've simply consented to come at all, because the Director of Drama cried so, and he's rather a darling. I've not the smallest intention of letting you kill me."

While she spoke, Dr. Beamish's geniality froze. He looked at her with hatred, not speaking. Then he picked up the pink form. "Then this no longer applies?"

"No."

"Then for State's sake," said Dr. Beamish, very angry, "What are you wasting my time for? I've got more than a hundred urgent cases waiting outside and you come in here to tell me that the Director of Drama is a darling. I know the Director of Drama. We live side by side in the same ghastly hostel. He's a pest. And I'm going to write a report to the Ministry about this tomfoolery which will make him and the lunatic who thinks he can perform a Klugmann, come round to me begging for extermination. And then I'll put them at the bottom of the queue. Get her out of here, Plastic, and let some sane people in."

Miles led her into the public waiting-room. "What an old beast," she said. "What a perfect beast. I've never been spoken to like that before even in the ballet-school. He seemed so nice at first."

"It's his professional feeling," said Miles. "He was naturally put out at losing such an attractive patient."

She smiled. Her beard was not so thick as quite to obscure her delicate ovoid of cheek and chin. She might have been peeping at him over ripe heads of barley.

Her smiles started in her wide grey eyes. Her lips under her golden moustachios were unpainted, tactile. A line of pale down sprang below them and ran through the center of the chin, spreading and thickening and growing richer in color till it met the full flow of the whiskers, but leaving on either side, clear and tender, two symmetrical zones, naked and provocative. So might have smiled some carefree deacon in the colonnaded school of fifth-century Alexandria and struck dumb the heresiarchs.

"I think your beard is beautiful."

"Do you really? I can't help liking it too. I can't help liking anything about myself, can you?"

"Yes. Oh, yes."

"That's not natural."

Clamor at the outer door interrupted the talk. Like gulls around a lighthouse the impatient victims kept up an irregular flap and slap on the panels.

"We're all ready, Plastic," said a senior official. "What's going on this morning?"

What was going on? Miles could not answer. Turbulent sea birds seemed to be dashing themselves against the light in his own heart.

"Don't go," he said to the girl. "Please, I shan't be a minute."

"Oh, I've nothing to take me away. My department all think I'm half dead by now."

Miles opened the door and admitted an indignant half-dozen. He directed them to their chairs, to the registry. Then he went back to the girl who had turned away slightly from the crowd and drawn a scarf peasantwise round her head, hiding her beard.

"I still don't quite like people staring," she said.

"Our patients are far too busy with their own affairs to notice anyone else," said Miles. "Besides you'd have been stared at all right if you'd stayed on in ballet."

Miles adjusted the television but few eyes in the waiting-room glanced towards it; all were fixed on the registrar's table and the doors beyond.

"Think of them all coming here," said the bearded girl.

"We give them the best service we can," said Miles.

"Yes, of course, I know you do. Please don't think I was finding fault. I only meant, fancy wanting to die."

"One or two have good reasons."

"I suppose you would say that I had. Everyone has been trying to persuade me, since my operation. The medical officials were the worst. They're afraid they may get into trouble for doing it wrong. And then the ballet people were almost as bad. They are so keen on Art that they say: 'You were the best of your class. You can never dance again. How can life be worth living?' What I try to explain is that it's just because I could dance that I *know* life is worth living. That's what Art means to me. Does that sound silly?"

"It sounds unorthodox."

"Ah, but you're not an artist."

"Oh, I've danced all right. Twice a week all through my time at the Orphanage."

"Therapeutic dancing?"

"That's what they called it."

"But, you see, that's quite different from Art."

"Why?"

"Oh," she said with a sudden full intimacy, with fondness, "Oh what a lot you don't know."

The dancer's name was Clara.

3

COURTSHIP was free and easy in this epoch but Miles was Clara's first lover. The strenuous exercises of her training, the austere standards of the corps-de-ballet and her devotion to her art had kept her body and soul unencumbered.

For Miles, child of the State, Sex had been part of the curriculum at every stage of his education; first in diagrams, then in demonstrations, then in application, he had mastered all the antics of procreation. Love was a word seldom used except by politicians and by them only in moments of pure fatuity. Nothing that he had been taught prepared him for Clara.

Once in drama, always in drama. Clara now spent her days mending ballet shoes and helping neophytes on the wall bars. She had a cubicle in a Nissen hut and it was there that she and Miles spent most of their evenings. It was unlike anyone else's quarters in Satellite City.

Two little paintings hung on the walls, unlike any paintings Miles had seen before, unlike anything approved by the Ministry of Art. One represented a goddess of antiquity, naked and rosy, fondling a peacock on a bank of flowers; the other a vast, tree-fringed lake and a party in spreading silken clothes embarking in a pleasure boat under a broken arch. The gilt frames were much chipped but what remained of them was elaborately foliated.

"They're French," said Clara. "More than two hundred years old. My mother left them to me."

All her possessions had come from her mother, nearly enough of them to furnish the little room—a looking glass framed in porcelain flowers, a gilt, irregular clock. She and Miles drank their sad, officially compounded coffee out of brilliant, riveted cups.

"It reminds me of prison," said Miles when he was first admitted there.

It was the highest praise he knew.

On the first evening among this delicate bric-a-brac his lips found the bare twin spaces of her chin.

"I knew it would be a mistake to let the beastly doctor poison me," said Clara complacently.

Full summer came. Another moon waxed over these rare lovers. Once they sought coolness and secrecy among the high cow-parsley and willow-herb of the waste building sites. Clara's beard was all silvered like a patriarch's in the midnight radiance.

"On such a night as this," said Miles, supine, gazing into the face of the moon, "on such a night as this I burned an Air Force Station and half its occupants."

Clara sat up and began lazily smoothing her whiskers, then more vigorously tugged the comb through the thicker, tangled growth of her head, dragging it from her forehead; reordered the clothing which their embraces had loosed. She was full of womanly content and ready to go home. But Miles, all male, *post coitum tristis,* was struck by a chill sense of loss. No demonstration or exercise had prepared him for this strange new experience of the sudden loneliness that follows requited love.

Walking home they talked casually and rather crossly.

"You never go to the ballet now."

"No."

"Won't they give you seats?"

"I suppose they would."

"Then why don't you go?"

"I don't think I should like it. I see them often rehearsing. I don't like it."

"But you lived for it."

"Other interests now."

"Me?"

"Of course."

"You love me more than the ballet?"

"I am very happy."

"Happier than if you were dancing?"

"I can't tell, can I? You're all I've got now."

"But if you could change?"

"I can't."

"If?"

"There's no 'if.' "

"Damn."

"Don't fret, darling. It's only the moon."

And they parted in silence.

November came, a season of strikes; leisure for Miles, unsought and unvalued; lonely periods when the ballet school worked on and the death house stood cold and empty.

Clara began to complain of ill health. She was growing stout.

"Just contentment," she said at first, but the change worried her. "Can it be that beastly operation?" she asked. "I heard the reason they put down one of the Cambridge girls was that she kept growing fatter and fatter."

"She weighed nineteen stone," said Miles. "I know because Dr. Beamish mentioned it. He has strong professional objections to the Klugmann operation."

"I'm going to see the Director of Medicine. There's a new one now."

When she returned from her appointment, Miles, still left idle by the strikers, was waiting for her among her pictures and china. She sat beside him on the bed.

"Let's have a drink," she said.

They had taken to drinking wine together, very rarely because of the expense. The State chose and named the vintage. This month the issue was "Progress Port." Clara kept it in a crimson, white-cut, Bohemian flagon. The glasses were modern, unbreakable and unsightly.

"What did the doctor say?"

"He's very sweet."

"Well?"

"Much cleverer than the one before."

"Did he say it was anything to do with your operation?"

"Oh, yes. Everything to do with it."

"Can he put you right?"

"Yes, he thinks so."

"Good."

They drank their wine.

"That first doctor did make a mess of the operation, didn't he?"

"Such a mess. The new doctor says I'm a unique case. You see, I'm pregnant."

"*Clara.*"

"Yes, it is a surprise, isn't it?"

"This needs thinking about," said Miles.

He thought.

He refilled their glasses.

He said: "It's hard luck on the poor little beast not being an Orphan. Not much opportunity for it. If he's a boy we must try and get him registered as a worker. Of course it might be a girl. Then," brightly, "we could make her a dancer."

"Oh, don't mention dancing," cried Clara, and suddenly began weeping. "Don't speak to me of dancing."

Her tears fell fast. No tantrum this, but deep uncontrolled inconsolable sorrow.

And next day she disappeared.

4

SANTA-CLAUS-TIDE was near. Shops were full of shoddy little dolls. Children in the schools sang old ditties about peace and goodwill. Strikers went back to work in order to qualify for their seasonal bonus. Electric bulbs were hung in the conifers and the furnaces in the Dome of Security roared again. Miles had been promoted. He now sat beside the assistant registrar and helped stamp and file the documents of the dead. It was harder work than he was used to and Miles was hungry for Clara's company. The lights were going out in the Dome and on the Goodwill Tree in the car park. He walked the half-mile of hutments to Clara's quarters. Other girls were waiting for their consorts or setting out to find them in the Recreatorium, but Clara's door was locked. A note, pinned to it read: *Miles, Going away for a bit*. C. Angry and puzzled he returned to his hostel.

Clara, unlike himself, had uncles and cousins scattered about the country. Since her operation she had been shy of visiting them. Now, Miles supposed, she was taking cover among them. It was the manner of her flight, so unlike her gentle ways, that tortured him. For a busy week he thought of nothing else. His reproaches sang in his head as the undertone to all the activities of the day and at night he lay sleepless repeating in his mind every word spoken between them and every act of intimacy.

After a week the thought of her became spasmodic and regular. The subject bored him unendurably. He strove to keep it out of his mind as a man might strive to control an attack of hiccups, and as impotently. Spasmodically, mechanically, the thought of Clara returned. He timed it and found that it came every seven and one-half minutes. He went to sleep thinking of her, he woke up thinking of her. But between times he slept. He consulted the departmental psychiatrist who told him that he was burdened by the responsibility of parentage. But it was not Clara the mother who haunted him, but Clara the betrayer.

Next week he thought of her every twenty minutes. The week after that he thought of her irregularly, though often; only when something outside himself reminded him of her. He began to look at other girls and considered himself cured.

He looked hard at other girls as he passed them in the dim corridors of the Dome and they looked boldly back at him. Then one of them stopped him and said: "I've seen you before with Clara" and at the mention of her name all interest in the other girl ceased in pain. "I went to visit her yesterday."

"Where?"

"In hospital, of course. Didn't you know?"

"What's the matter with her?"

"She won't say. Nor will anyone else at the hospital. She's top secret. If you ask me she's been in an accident and there's some politician involved. I can't think of any other reason for all the fuss. She's covered in bandages and gay as a lark."

Next day, December 25th, was Santa Claus Day; no holiday in the department of Euthanasia, which was an essential service. At dusk Miles walked to the hospital, one of the unfinished edifices, all concrete and steel and glass in front and a jumble of huts behind. The hall porter was engrossed in the television, which was performing an old obscure folk play which past generations had performed on Santa Claus Day, and was now revived and revised as a matter of historical interest.

It was of professional interest to the porter for it dealt with maternity services before the days of Welfare. He gave the number of Clara's room without glancing up from the strange spectacle of an ox and an ass, an old man with a lantern, and a young mother. "People here are always complaining," he said. "They ought to realize what things were like before Progress."

The corridors were loud with relayed music. Miles found the hut he sought. It was marked "Experimental Surgery. Health Officers Only." He found the cubicle. He found Clara sleeping, the sheet pulled up to her eyes, her hair loose on the pillow. She had brought some of her property with her. An old shawl lay across the bed-table. A painted fan stood against the television set. She awoke, her eyes full of frank welcome and pulled the sheet higher, speaking through it.

"Darling, you shouldn't have come. I was keeping it for a surprise."

Miles sat by the bed and thought of nothing to say except: "How are you?"

"Wonderful. They've taken the bandages off today. They won't let me have a looking glass yet but they say everything has been a tremendous success. I'm something very special, Miles—a new chapter in surgical progress."

"But what has happened to you. Is it something to do with the baby?"

"Oh no. At least, it was. That was the first operation. But that's all over now."

"You mean our child?"

"Yes, that had to go. I should never have been able to dance afterwards. I told you all about it. That was why I had the Klugmann operation, don't you remember?"

"But you gave up dancing."

"That's where they've been so clever. Didn't I tell you about the sweet, clever new medical director? He's cured all that."

"Your dear beard."

"Quite gone. An operation the new director invented himself. It's going to be named after him or even perhaps after me. He's so unselfish he wants to call it the Clara Operation. He's taken off all the skin and put on a wonderful new substance, a sort of synthetic rubber that takes grease-paint perfectly. He says the color isn't perfect but that it will never show on the stage. Look, feel it."

She sat up in bed, joyful and proud.

Her eyes and brow were all that was left of the loved face. Below it something quite inhuman, a tight, slippery mask, salmon pink.

Miles stared. In the television screen by the bed further characters had appeared—Food Production Workers. They seemed to declare a sudden strike, left their sheep and ran off at the bidding of some kind of shop-steward in fantastic dress. The machine by the bedside broke into song, an old, forgotten ditty: "O tidings of comfort and joy."

Miles retched unobtrusively. The ghastly face regarded him with fondness and pride. At length the right words came to him; the trite, the traditional sentence uttered by countless lips of generations of baffled and impassioned Englishmen: "I think I shall go for a short walk."

But first he walked only as far as his hostel. There he lay down until the moon moved to his window and fell across his sleepless face. Then he set out, walking far into the fields, out of sight of the Dome of Security, for two hours until the moon was near setting.

He had traveled at random but now the white rays fell on a signpost and he read: "Mountjoy ¾." He strode on with only the stars to light his way till he came to the Castle gates.

They stood open as always, gracious symbol of the new penology. He followed the drive. The whole lightless face of the old house stared at him silently, without rebuke. He knew now what was needed. He carried in his pocket a cigarette lighter which often worked. It worked for him now.

No need for oil here. The dry old silk of the drawing-room curtains lit like paper. Paint and paneling, plaster and tapestry and gilding bowed to the embrace of the leaping flames. He stepped outside. Soon it was too hot on the terrace and he retreated further, to the marble temple at the end of the long walk. The murderers were leaping from the first story windows but the sexual offenders, trapped above, set up a wail of terror. He heard the chandeliers fall and saw the boiling lead cascading from the roof. This was something altogether finer than the strangulation of a few peacocks. He watched exultant as minute by minute the scene disclosed fresh wonders. Great timbers crashed within; outside the lily-pond hissed with falling brands; a vast ceiling of smoke shut out the stars and under it tongues of flame floated away into the tree tops.

Two hours later when the first engine arrived, the force of the fiery storm was already spent. Miles rose from his marble throne and began the long walk home. But he was no longer at all fatigued. He strode out cheerfully with his shadow, cast by the dying blaze, stretching before him along the lane.

On the main road a motorist stopped him and asked: "What's that over there? A house on fire?"

"It was," said Miles. "It's almost out now."

"Looks like a big place. Only Government property, I suppose?"

"That's all," said Miles.

"Well hop in if you want a lift."

"Thanks," said Miles, "I'm walking for pleasure."

5

MILES rose after two hours in bed. The hostel was alive with all the normal activity of morning. The wireless was playing; the sub-officials were coughing over their wash-basins; the reek of State sausages frying in State grease filled the asbestos cubicle. He was slightly stiff after his long walk and slightly footsore, but his mind was as calm and empty as the sleep from which he had awoken. The scorched-earth policy had succeeded. He had made a desert in his imagination which he might call peace. Once before he had burned his childhood. Now his brief adult life lay in ashes; the enchantments that surrounded Clara were one with the splendors of Mountjoy; her great golden beard, one with the tongues of flame that had leaped and expired among the stars; her fans and pictures and scraps of old embroidery, one with the gilded cornices and silk hangings, black, cold and sodden. He ate his sausage with keen appetite and went to work.

All was quiet too at the Department of Euthanasia.

The first announcement of the Mountjoy disaster had been on the early news. Its proximity to Satellite City gave it a special poignancy there.

"It is a significant phenomenon," said Dr. Beamish, "that any bad news has an immediate effect on our service. You see it whenever there is an international crisis. Sometimes I think people only come to us when they have nothing to talk about. Have you looked at our queue today?"

Miles turned to the periscope. Only one man waited outside, old

Parsnip, a poet of the '30s who came daily but was usually jostled to the back of the crowd. He was a comic character in the department, this veteran poet. Twice in Miles's short term he had succeeded in gaining admission but on both occasions had suddenly taken fright and bolted.

"It's a lucky day for Parsnip," said Miles.

"Yes. He deserves some luck. I knew him well once, him and his friend Pimpernell. *New Writing*, the Left Book Club, they were all the rage. Pimpernell was one of my first patients. Hand Parsnip in and we'll finish him off."

So old Parsnip was summoned and that day his nerve stood firm. He passed fairly calmly through the gas chamber on his way to rejoin Pimpernell.

"We might as well knock off for the day," said Dr. Beamish. "We shall be busy again soon when the excitement dies down."

But the politicians seemed determined to keep the excitement up. All the normal features of television were interrupted and curtailed to give place to Mountjoy. Survivors appeared on the screen, among them Soapy, who described how long practice as a cat burglar had enabled him to escape. Mr. Sweat, he remarked with respect, had got clear away. The ruins were surveyed by the apparatus. A sexual maniac with broken legs gave audience from his hospital bed. The Minister of Welfare, it was announced, would make a special appearance that evening to comment on the disaster.

Miles dozed intermittently beside the hostel set and at dusk rose, still calm and free; so purged of emotion that he made his way once more to the hospital and called on Clara.

She had spent the afternoon with looking-glass and make-up box. The new substance of her face fulfilled all the surgeon's promises. It took paint to perfection. Clara had given herself a full mask as though for the lights of the stage; an even creamy white with sudden high spots of crimson on the cheek bones, huge hard crimson lips, eyebrows extended and turned up catwise, the eyes shaded all around with ultramarine and dotted at the corners with crimson.

"You're the first to see me," she said. "I was half-afraid you wouldn't come. You seemed cross yesterday."

"I wanted to see the television," said Miles. "It's so crowded in the hostel."

"So dull today. Nothing except this prison that has been burned down."

"I was there myself. Don't you remember? I often talked of it."

"Did you, Miles? Perhaps so. I've such a bad memory for things that don't concern me. Do you really want to hear the Minister? It would be much cozier to talk."

"It's him I've come for."

And presently the Minister appeared, open-necked as always but without his usual smile; grave to the verge of tears. He spoke for twenty minutes. ". . . The great experiment must go on . . . the martyrs of maladjustment shall not have died in vain. . . . A greater, new Mountjoy shall rise from the ashes of the old. . . ." Eventually tears came—real tears for he held an invisible onion—and trickled down his cheeks. So the speech ended.

"That's all I came for," said Miles, and left Clara to her cocoa-butter and face-towel.

Next day all the organs of public information were still piping the theme of Mountjoy. Two or three patients, already bored with the entertainment, presented themselves for extermination and were happily dispatched. Then a message came from the Regional Director, official-in-chief of Satellite City. He required the immediate presence of Miles in his office.

"I have a move order for you, Mr. Plastic. You are to report to the Ministers of Welfare and Rest and Culture. You will be issued with a Grade A hat, umbrella and brief case for the journey. My congratulations."

Equipped with these insignia of sudden, dizzy promotion, Miles traveled to the capital leaving behind a domeful of sub-officials chattering with envy.

At the terminus an official met him. Together in an official car they drove to Whitehall.

"Let me carry your brief case, Mr. Plastic."

"There's nothing in it."

Miles's escort laughed obsequiously at this risqué joke.

At the Ministry the lifts were in working order. It was a new and alarming experience to enter the little cage and rise to the top of the great building.

"Do they always work here?"

"Not *always*, but very very often."

Miles realized that he was indeed at the heart of things.

"Wait here. I will call you when the Ministers are ready."

Miles looked from the waiting room window at the slow streams of traffic. Just below him stood a strange, purposeless obstruction of stone. A very old man, walking by, removed his hat to it as though saluting an acquaintance. Why? Miles wondered. Then he was summoned to the politicians.

They were alone in their office save for a gruesome young woman. The Minister of Rest and Culture said: "Ease your feet, lad," and indicated a large leatherette armchair.

"Not such a happy occasion, alas, as our last meeting," said the Minister of Welfare.

"Oh, I don't know," said Miles. He was enjoying the outing.

"The tragedy at Mountjoy Castle was a grievous loss to the cause of penology."

"But the great work of Rehabilitation will continue," said the gruesome young woman.

"A greater Mountjoy will arise from the ashes," said the Minister.

"Those noble criminal lives have not been lost in vain."

"Their memory will inspire us."

"Yes," said Miles. "I heard the broadcast."

"Exactly," said the Minister. "Precisely. Then you appreciate, perhaps, what a change the occurrence makes in your own position. From being, as we hoped, the first of a continuous series of successes, you are our only one. It would not be too much to say that the whole future of penology is in your hands. The destruction of Mountjoy Castle by itself was merely a set-back. A sad one, of course, but something which might be described as the growing pains of a great movement. But there is a darker side. I told you, I think, that our great experiment had been made only against considerable opposition. Now—I speak confidentially—that opposition has become vocal and unscrupulous. There is, in fact, a whispering campaign that the fire was no accident but the act of one of the very men whom we were seeking to serve. That campaign must be scotched."

"They can't do us down as easy as they think," said the Minister of Rest and Culture. "Us old dogs know a trick or two."

"Exactly. Counter-propaganda. You are our Exhibit A. The irrefutable evidence of the triumph of our system. We are going to send you up and down the country to lecture. My colleagues have already written your speech. You will be accompanied by Miss Flower here, who will show and explain the model of the new Mountjoy. Perhaps you will care to see it yourself. Miss Flower, the model please."

All the time they were speaking Miles had been aware of a bulky, sheeted object on a table in the window. Miss Flower now unveiled it. Miles gazed in awe.

The object displayed was a familiar, standard packing-case, set on end.

"A rush job," said the Minister of Welfare. "You will be provided with something more elaborate for your tour."

Miles gazed at the box.

It fitted. It fell into place precisely in the void of his mind, satisfying all the needs for which his education had prepared him. The conditioned personality recognized its proper pre-ordained environment. All else was insubstantial; the gardens of Mountjoy, Clara's cracked Crown Derby and her enveloping beard were trophies of a fading dream.

The Modern Man was home.

"There is one further point," continued the Minister of Welfare. "A domestic one but not as irrelevant as it may seem. Have you by any chance formed an attachment in Satellite City? Your dossier suggests that you have."

"Any woman trouble?" explained the Minister of Rest and Culture.

"Oh, yes," said Miles. "Great trouble. But that is over."

"You see, perfect rehabilitation, complete citizenship should include marriage."

"It has not," said Miles.

"That should be rectified."

"Folks like a bloke to be spliced," said the Minister of Rest and Culture. "With a couple of kids."

"There is hardly time for *them*," said the Minister of Welfare. "But we think that psychologically you will have more appeal if you have a wife by your side. Miss Flower here has every qualification."

"Looks are only skin deep, lad," said the Minister of Rest and Culture.

"So if you have no preferable alternative to offer . . . ?"

"None," said Miles.

"Spoken like an Orphan. I see a splendid career ahead of the pair of you."

"When can we get divorced?"

"Come, come Plastic. You mustn't look too far ahead. First things first. You have already obtained the necessary leave from your Director, Miss Flower?"

"Yes, Minister."

"Then off you both go. And State be with you."

In perfect peace of heart Miles followed Miss Flower to the Registrar's office.

Then the mood veered.

Miles felt ill at ease during the ceremony and fidgeted with something small and hard which he found in his pocket. It proved to be his cigarette-lighter, a most uncertain apparatus. He pressed the catch and instantly, surprisingly there burst out a tiny flame—gem-like, hymeneal, auspicious.

ESSAYS

Sir Francis Bacon

OF FRIENDSHIP

IT HAD been hard for him that spake it to have put more truth and untruth together in a few words, than in that speech, *Whosoever is delighted in solitude is either a wild beast or a god.* For it is most true that a natural and secret hatred and aversation towards society, in any man, hath somewhat of the savage beast; but it is most untrue that it should have any character at all of the divine nature; except it proceed, not out of a pleasure in solitude, but out of a love and desire to sequester a man's self for a higher conversation: such as is found to have been falsely and feignedly in some of the heathen; as Epimenides the Candian, Numa the Roman, Empedocles the Sicilian, and Apollonius of Tyana; and truly and really in divers of the ancient hermits and holy fathers of the church. But little do men perceive what solitude is, and how far it extendeth. For a crowd is not company, and faces are but a gallery of pictures, and talk but a tinkling cymbal, where there is no love. The Latin adage meeteth with it a little, *Magna civitas, magna solitudo,*[1] because in a great town friends are scattered; so that there is not that fellowship, for the most part, which is in less neighbourhoods. But we may go further and affirm most truly, that it is a mere and miserable solitude to want true friends, without which the world is but a wilderness; and even in this sense also of solitude, whosoever in the frame of his nature and affections is unfit for friendship, he taketh it of the beast, and not from humanity.

A principal fruit of friendship is the ease and discharge of the fulness and swellings of the heart, which passions of all kinds do cause and induce. We know diseases of stoppings and suffocations are the most dangerous in the body; and it is not much otherwise in the mind: you may take sarza to open the liver, steel to open the spleen, flowers of sulphur for the lungs, castoreum for the brain; but no receipt openeth the heart, but a true friend, to whom you may impart griefs, joys, fears, hopes, suspicions, counsels, and whatsoever lieth upon the heart to oppress it, in a kind of civil shrift or confession.

It is a strange thing to observe how high a rate great kings and

1 [There is great loneliness in great cities.]

monarchs do set upon this fruit of friendship whereof we speak: so great, as they purchase it many times at the hazard of their own safety and greatness. For princes, in regard of the distance of their fortune from that of their subjects and servants, cannot gather this fruit, except (to make themselves capable thereof) they raise some persons to be as it were companions and almost equals to themselves, which many times sorteth to inconvenience. The modern languages give unto such persons the name of *favourites*, or *privadoes;* as if it were matter of grace, or conversation. But the Roman name attaineth the true use and cause thereof, naming them *participes curarum;*[2] for it is that which tieth the knot. And we see plainly that this hath been done, not by weak and passionate princes only, but by the wisest and most politic that ever reigned; who have oftentimes joined to themselves some of their servants, whom both themselves have called *friends*, and allowed others likewise to call them in the same manner, using the word which is received between private men.

L. Sylla, when he commanded Rome, raised Pompey (after surnamed the Great) to that height, that Pompey vaunted himself for Sylla's overmatch. For when he had carried the consulship for a friend of his, against the pursuit of Sylla, and that Sylla did a little resent thereat, and began to speak great, Pompey turned upon him again, and in effect bade him be quiet; *for that more men adored the sun rising than the sun setting.* With Julius Cæsar, Decimus Brutus had obtained that interest, as he set him down in his testament for heir in remainder after his nephew. And this was the man that had power with him to draw him forth to his death. For when Cæsar would have discharged the senate, in regard of some ill presages, and specially a dream of Calpurnia, this man lifted him gently by the arm out of his chair, telling him he hoped he would not dismiss the senate till his wife had dreamt a better dream. And it seemeth his favour was so great, as Antonius, in a letter which is recited *verbatim* in one of Cicero's *Philippics*, calleth him *venefica*, "witch"; as if he had enchanted Cæsar. Augustus raised Agrippa (though of mean birth) to that height, as, when he consulted with Mæcenas about the marriage of his daughter Julia, Mæcenas took the liberty to tell him, *that he must either marry his daughter to Agrippa, or take away his life; there was no third way, he had made him so great.* With Tiberius Cæsar, Sejanus had ascended to that height, as they two were termed and reckoned as a pair of friends. Tiberius in a letter to him saith, *Hæc pro amicitiâ nostrâ non occultavi;*[3] and the whole senate dedicated an altar to Friendship, as

2 [Sharers of our concerns.]
3 [I have not hidden these facts in conformity with our friendship.]

to a goddess, in respect of the great dearness of friendship between them two. The like or more was between Septimius Severus and Plautianus. For he forced his eldest son to marry the daughter of Plautianus; and would often maintain Plautianus in doing affronts to his son; and did write also in a letter to the senate by these words: *I love the man so well, as I wish he may over-live me*. Now if these princes had been as a Trajan, or a Marcus Aurelius, a man might have thought that this had proceeded of an abundant goodness of nature; but being men so wise, for such strength and severity of mind, and so extreme lovers of themselves, as all these were, it proveth most plainly that they found their own felicity (though as great as ever happened to mortal men) but as an half piece, except they mought have a friend to make it entire: and yet, which is more, they were princes that had wives, sons, nephews; and yet all these could not supply the comfort of friendship.

It is not to be forgotten, what Commineus observeth of his first master, Duke Charles the Hardy; namely, that he would communicate his secrets with none; and least of all, those secrets which troubled him most. Whereupon he goeth on and saith, that towards his latter time *that closeness did impair and a little perish his understanding*. Surely Commineus mought have made the same judgement also, if it had pleased him, of his second master, Lewis the Eleventh, whose closeness was indeed his tormentor. The parable of Pythagoras is dark, but true, *Cor ne edito*, "Eat not the heart." Certainly, if a man would give it a hard phrase, those that want friends to open themselves unto are cannibals of their own hearts. But one thing is most admirable (wherewith I will conclude this first fruit of friendship), which is, that this communicating of a man's self to his friend works two contrary effects; for it redoubleth joys, and cutteth griefs in halfs. For there is no man that imparteth his joys to his friends, but he joyeth the more; and no man that imparteth his griefs to his friend, but he grieveth the less. So that it is in truth of operation upon a man's mind, of like virtue as the alchymists use to attribute to their stone for man's body; that it worketh all contrary effects, but still to the good and benefit of nature. But yet, without praying in aid of alchymists, there is a manifest image of this in the ordinary course of nature. For in bodies, union strengtheneth and cherisheth any natural action; and, on the other side, weakeneth and dulleth any violent impression: and even so is it of minds.

The second fruit of friendship is healthful and sovereign for the understanding, as the first is for the affections. For friendship maketh indeed a fair day in the affections, from storm and tempests; but it maketh daylight in the understanding, out of darkness and confusion of thoughts. Neither is this to be understood only of faithful counsel, which a man receiveth from his friend; but before you come to that, certain it is that whosoever hath his mind fraught with many thoughts, his wits and understanding do clarify and break up, in the communicating and discoursing with another: he tosseth his thoughts more easily; he marshalleth them more orderly; he seeth how they look when they are turned into words; finally, he waxeth wiser than himself; and that more by an hour's discourse than by a day's meditation. It was well said by Themistocles to the king of Persia, that *speech was like cloth of Arras, opened and put abroad; whereby the imagery doth appear in figure; whereas in thoughts they lie but as in packs.* Neither is this second fruit of friendship, in opening the understanding, restrained only to such friends as are able to give a man counsel: (they indeed are best); but even without that, a man learneth of himself, and bringeth his own thoughts to light, and whetteth his wits as against a stone, which itself cuts not. In a word, a man were better relate himself to a statua or picture, than to suffer his thoughts to pass in smother.

Add now, to make this second fruit of friendship complete, that other point, which lieth more open, and falleth within vulgar observation; which is faithful counsel from a friend. Heraclitus saith well in one of his enigmas, *Dry light is ever the best.* And certain it is that the light that a man receiveth by counsel from another is drier and purer than that which cometh from his own understanding and judgement; which is ever infused and drenched in his affections and customs. So as there is as much difference between the counsel that a friend giveth, and that a man giveth himself, as there is between the counsel of a friend and of a flatterer. For there is no such flatterer as is a man's self; and there is no such remedy against flattery of a man's self as the liberty of a friend. Counsel is of two sorts; the one concerning manners, the other concerning business. For the first; the best preservative to keep the mind in health is the faithful admonition of a friend. The calling of a man's self to a strict account is a medicine, sometime, too piercing and corrosive. Reading good books of morality is a little flat and dead. Observing our faults in others is sometimes unproper for our case. But the best receipt (best, I say, to work, and best to take) is the admonition of a friend. It is a strange thing to behold what gross errors and extreme absurdities many (especially of the greater sort) do commit, for want of a friend to tell them of them, to the great damage both of their fame and fortune. For, as St. James saith, they are as men, *that look sometimes into a glass, and presently forget their own shape and favour.* As for business, a man may think, if he will, that two eyes see no more than one; or that a gamester seeth always more than a looker-on; or that a man in anger is as wise as he that hath said over the four and twenty letters; or that a musket may be shot off as well upon the arm as upon a rest; and such other fond and high imaginations, to think himself all in all. But when all is done, the help of good counsel is that which setteth business straight. And if any man think that he will take counsel, but it shall be by pieces; asking counsel in one business of one man, and in another business of another man; it is well (that is to say, better perhaps than if he asked none at all); but he runneth two dangers. One, that he shall not be faithfully counselled; for it is a rare thing, except it be from a perfect and entire friend, to have counsel given, but such as shall be bowed and crooked to some ends which he hath that giveth it. The other, that he shall have counsel given, hurtful and unsafe (though with good meaning), and mixed partly of mischief and partly of remedy: even as if you would call a physician, that is thought good for the cure of the disease you complain of, but is unacquainted with your body; and therefore may put you in way for a present cure, but over-throweth your health in some other kind; and so cure the disease and kill the patient. But a friend that is wholly acquainted with a man's estate will beware, by furthering any present business, how he dasheth upon other inconvenience. And therefore rest not upon scattered counsels; they will rather distract and mislead than settle and direct.

After these two noble fruits of friendship (peace in the affections, and support of the judgement) followeth the last fruit, which is like the pomegranate, full of many kernels; I mean aid and bearing a part in all actions and occasions. Here the best way to represent to life the manifold use of friendship is to cast and see how many things there are which man cannot do himself; and then it will appear that it was a sparing speech of the ancients, to say, *that a friend is another himself*: for that a friend is far more than himself. Men have their time, and die many times in desire of some things which they principally take to heart; the bestowing of a child, the finishing of a work, or the like. If a man have a true friend, he may rest almost secure that the care of those things will continue after him. So that a man hath as it were two lives in his desires. A man hath a body, and that body is confined to a place; but where friendship is, all offices of life are as it were granted to him and his deputy. For he may exercise them by his friend. How many things are there which a man cannot, with any face or comeliness say or do himself! A man can scarce allege his own merits with modesty, much less extol them; a man cannot sometimes brook to supplicate or beg; and a number of the like. But all these things are graceful in a friend's mouth, which are blushing in a man's own. So again, a man's person hath many proper relations which he cannot put off. A man cannot speak to his son but as a father; to his wife but as a husband; to his enemy but upon terms: whereas a friend may speak as the case requires, and not as it sorteth with the person. But to enumerate these things were endless: I have given the rule, where a man cannot fitly play his own part: if he have not a friend, he may quit the stage.

Matthew Arnold

DANTE AND BEATRICE

THOSE critics who allegorize the *Divine Comedy*, who exaggerate, or, rather, who mistake the supersensual element in Dante's work, who reduce to nothing the sensible and human element, are hardly worth refuting. They know nothing of the necessary laws under which poetic genius works, of the inevitable conditions under which the creations of poetry are produced. But, in their turn, those other critics err hardly less widely, who exaggerate, or, rather, who mistake the human and real element in Dante's poem; who see, in such a passion as that of Dante for Beatrice, an affection belonging to the sphere of actual domestic life, fitted to sustain the wear and tear of our ordinary daily existence. Into the error of these second critics an accomplished recent translator of Dante, Mr. Theodore Martin, seems to me to have fallen. He has ever present to his mind, when he speaks of the Beatrice whom Dante adored, Wordsworth's picture of

> The perfect woman, nobly planned
> To warn, to comfort, and command;
> And yet a spirit still, and bright
> With something of an angel light.

He is ever quoting these lines in connexion with Dante's Beatrice; ever assimilating to this picture Beatrice as Dante conceived her; ever attributing to Dante's passion a character identical with that of the affection which Wordsworth, in the poem from which these lines are taken, meant to portray. The affection here portrayed by Wordsworth is, I grant, a substantial human affection, inhabiting the domain of real life, at the same time that it is poetical and beautiful. But in order to give this flesh-and-blood character to Dante's passion for Beatrice, what a task has Mr. Martin to perform! how much to shut his eyes to, or to disbelieve! Not perceiving that the vital impulse of Dante's soul is towards reverie and spiritual vision; that the task Dante sets himself is not the task of reconciling poetry and reality, of giving to each its due part, of supplementing the one by the other; but the task of sacrificing the world to the spirit, of making the spirit all in all, of effacing the world in the presence of the spirit—Mr. Martin seeks to find a Dante admirable and complete in the life of the world as well as in the life of the spirit; and when he cannot find him, he invents him. Dante saw the world, and used in his poetry what he had seen; for he was a born artist. But he was essentially aloof from the world, and not complete in the life of the world; for he was a born spiritualist and solitary. Keeping in our minds this, his double character, we may seize the exact truth as to his relations with Beatrice, and steer a right course between the error of those who deliteralize them too much, on the one hand, and that of those who literalize them too much, on the other.

The *Divine Comedy*, I have already said, is no allegory, and Beatrice no mere personification of theology. Mr. Martin is quite right in saying that Beatrice is the Beatrice whom men turned round to gaze at in the streets of Florence; that she is no "allegorical phantom," no "fiction purely ideal." He is quite right in saying that Dante "worships no phantoms," that his passion for Beatrice was a real passion, and that his love-poetry does not deal "in the attributes of celestial charms." He was an artist—one of the greatest artists; and art abhors what is vague, hollow, and impalpable.

Enough to make this fully manifest we have in the *Vita Nuova*. Dante there records how, a boy of ten, he first saw Beatrice, a girl of nine, dressed in crimson; how, a second time, he saw her, nine years later, passing along the street, dressed in white, between two ladies older than herself, and how she saluted him. He records how afterwards she once denied him her salutation; he records the profound impression which, at her father's death, the grief and beauty of Beatrice made on all those who visited her; he records his meeting with her at a party after her marriage, his emotion, and how some ladies present, observing his emotion, "made a mock of him to that most gentle being"; he records her death, and how, a year afterwards, some gentlemen found him, on the anniversary of her death, "sketching an angel on his tablets." He tells us how, a little later, he had a vision of the dead Beatrice "arrayed in the same crimson robe in which she had originally appeared in my eyes and she seemed as youthful as on the day I saw her first." He mentions how, one day, the sight of some pilgrims passing along a particular street in Florence brought to his mind the thought that perhaps these pilgrims, coming from a far country, had never even heard the name of her who filled his thoughts so entirely.

And even in the *Divine Comedy*, composed many years afterwards, and treating of the glorified Beatrice only, one distinct trait of the earthly Beatrice is still preserved—her smile; the *santo riso*[1] of the *Purgatory*, the *dolce riso*[2] of the *Paradise*.

Yes, undoubtedly there was a real Beatrice, whom Dante had seen living and moving before him, and for whom he had felt a passion. This basis of fact and reality he took from the life of the outward world: this basis was indispensable to him, for he was an artist.

But this basis was enough for him as an artist: to have seen Beatrice two or three times, to have felt her beauty, her charm; to have had the emotion of her marriage, her death—this was enough. Art requires a basis of fact, but it also desires to treat this basis of fact with the utmost freedom; and this desire for the first handling of its object is even thwarted when its object is too near, and too real. To have had his relations with Beatrice more positive, intimate, and prolonged, to have had an affection for her into which there entered more of the life of this world, would have even somewhat impeded, one may say, Dante's free use of these relations for the purpose of art. And the artist nature in him was in little danger of being thus impeded; for he was a born solitary.

Thus the conditions of art do not make it necessary that Dante's relations with Beatrice should have been more close and real than the *Vita Nuova* represents them; and the conditions of Dante's own nature do not make it probable. Not the less do such admirers of the poet as Mr. Martin—misconceiving the essential characteristic of chivalrous passion in general, and of Dante's divinization of Beatrice in particular, misled by imagining this "worship for woman," as they call it, to be something which it was not, something involving modern relations in social life between the two sexes—insist upon making out of Dante's adoration of Beatrice a substantial modern love-story, and of arranging Dante's real life so as to turn it into the proper sort of real life for a "worshipper of woman" to lead. The few real incidents of Dante's passion, enumerated in the *Vita Nuova*, sufficient to give to his great poem the basis which it required, are far too scanty to give to such a love-story as this the basis which it requires; therefore they must be developed and amplified. Beatrice was a living woman, and Dante had seen her; but she must become

> The creature not too bright and good
> For human nature's daily food,

of Wordsworth's poem: she must become "pure flesh and blood—beautiful, yet substantial," and "moulded of that noble humanity wherewith Heaven blesses not unfrequently our common earth." Dante had saluted Beatrice, had spoken to her; but this is not enough: he has surely omitted to "record particulars": it is "scarcely

1 [Holy smile.] 2 [Sweet smile.]

credible that he should not have found an opportunity of directly declaring his attachment"; for "in position, education, and appearance he was a man worth any woman," and his face "at that time of his life must have been eminently engaging." Therefore "it seems strange that his love should not have found its issue in marriage"; for "he loved Beatrice as a man loves, and with the passion that naturally perseveres to the possession of its mistress."

However, his love did *not* find its issue in marriage. Beatrice married Messer Simone dei Bardi, to whom, says Mr. Martin, "her hand had been, perhaps lightly or to please her parents, pledged in ignorance of the deep and noble passion which she had inspired in the young poet's heart." But she certainly could not "have been insensible to his profound tenderness and passion"; although whether "she knew of it before her marriage," and whether "she, either then or afterwards, gave it her countenance and approval, and returned it in any way, and in what degree"—questions which, Mr. Martin says, "naturally suggest themselves"—are, he confesses, questions for solving which "the materials are most scanty and unsatisfactory." "Unquestionably," he adds, "it startles and grieves us to find Beatrice taking part with her friends 'in laughing at Dante when he was overcome at first meeting her after her marriage.' But there may," he thinks, "have been causes for this—causes for which, in justice to her, allowance must be made, even as we see that Dante made it." Then, again, as to Messer Simone dei Bardi's feelings about this attachment of Dante to his wife. "It is true," says Mr. Martin, "that we have no direct information on this point;" but "the love of Dante was of an order too pure and noble to occasion distrust, even if the purity of Beatrice had not placed her above suspicion"; but Dante "did what only a great and manly nature could have done—he triumphed over his pain; he uttered no complaint, his regrets were buried within his own heart." "At the same time," Mr. Martin thinks, "it is contrary to human nature that a love unfed by any tokens of favour should retain all its original force; and without wrong either to Beatrice or Dante, we may conclude that an understanding was come to between them, which in some measure soothed his heart, if it did not satisfy it." And "sooner or later, before Beatrice died, we cannot doubt that there came a day when words passed between them which helped to reconcile Dante to the doom that severed her from his side during her all too brief sojourn on earth, when the pent-up heart of the poet swept down the barriers within which it had so long struggled, and he

> Caught up the whole of love, and utter'd it,
> Then bade adieu for ever,

if not to her, yet to all those words which it was no longer meet should be spoken to another's wife."

But Dante married, as well as Beatrice; and so Dante's married life has to be *arranged* also. "It is," says Mr. Martin, "only those who have observed little of human nature, or of their own hearts, who will think that Dante's marriage with Gemma Donati argues against the depth of sincerity of his first love. Why should he not have sought the solace and the support of a generous woman's nature, who, knowing all the truth, was yet content with such affection as he was able to bring to a second love? Nor was that necessarily small. Ardent and affectionate as his nature was, the sympathies of such a woman must have elicited from him a satisfactory response; while, at the same time, without prejudice to the wife's claim on his regard, he might entertain his heavenward dream of the departed Beatrice." The tradition is, however, that Dante did not live happily with his wife; and some have thought that he means to cast a disparaging reflection on his marriage in a passage of the *Purgatory*. I need not say that this sort of thing would never do for Mr. Martin's hero—that hero who can do nothing "inconsistent with the purest respect to her who had been the wedded wife of another, on the one hand, or with his regard for the mother of his children, on the other." Accordingly, "are we to assume," Mr. Martin cries, "that the woman who gave herself to him in the full knowledge that she was not the bride of his imagination, was not regarded by him with the esteem which her devotion was calculated to inspire?" It is quite impossible. "Dante was a true-hearted gentleman, and could never have spoken slightingly of her on whose breast he had found comfort amid many a sorrow, and who had borne to him a numerous progeny—the last a Beatrice." Donna Gemma was a "generous and devoted woman, and she and Dante thoroughly understood each other."

All this has, as applied to real personages, the grave defect of being entirely of Mr. Martin's own imagining. But it has a still graver defect, I think, as applied to Dante, in being so singularly inappropriate to his object. The grand, impracticable Solitary, with keen senses and ardent passions—for nature had made him an artist, and art must be, as Milton says, "sensuous and impassioned"—but with an irresistible bent to the inward life of imagination, vision, and ecstasy; with an inherent impatience of the outward life; the life of distraction, jostling, mutual concession, this man "of a humour which made him hard to get on with," says Petrarch; "melancholy and pensive," says Boccaccio; "by nature abstracted and taciturn, seldom speaking unless he was questioned, and often so absorbed in his own reflections that he did not hear the questions which were put to him"; who could not live with the Florentines, who could not live with Gemma Donati, who could not live with Can Grande della Scala; this lover of Beatrice, but of Beatrice a vision of his youth, hardly at all in contact with him in actual life, vanished from him soon, with whom his imagination could deal freely, whom he could divinize into a fit object for the spiritual longing which filled him—this Dante is transformed, in Mr. Martin's hands, into the hero of a sentimental, but strictly virtuous, novel! To make out Dante to have been eminent for a wise, complete conduct of his outward life, seems to me as unimportant as it is impossible. I can quite believe the tradition, which represents him as not having lived happily with his wife, and attributes her not having joined him in his exile to this cause. I can even believe, without difficulty, an assertion of Boccaccio which excites Mr. Martin's indignation, that Dante's conduct, even in mature life, was at times exceedingly irregular. We know how the followers of the spiritual life tend to be antinomian in what belongs to the outward life: they do not attach much importance to such irregularity themselves; it is their fault, as complete men, that they do not; it is the fault of the spiritual life, as a complete life, that it allows this tendency: by dint of despising the outward life, it loses the control of this life, and of itself when in contact with it. My present business, however, is not to praise or blame Dante's practical conduct of his life, but to make clear his peculiar mental and spiritual constitution. This, I say, disposed him to absorb himself in the inner life, wholly to humble and efface before this the outward life. We may see this in the passage of the *Purgatory* where he makes Beatrice reprove him for his backslidings after she, his visible symbol of spiritual perfection, had vanished from his eyes.

> "For a while"—she says of him to the "pious substances," the angels—"for a while with my countenance I upheld him; showing to him my youthful eyes, with me I led him turned towards the right way.
>
> "Soon as I came on the threshold of my second age, and changed my life, this man took himself from me and gave himself to others.
>
> "When that I had mounted from flesh to spirit, and beauty and spirit were increased unto me, I was to him less dear and less acceptable.
>
> "He turned his steps to go in a way not true, pursuing after false images of good, which fulfil nothing of the promises which they give.
>
> "Neither availed it me that I obtained inspirations to be granted me, whereby, both in dream and otherwise, I called him back; so little heed paid he to them.
>
> "So deep he fell, that, for his salvation all means came short, except to show him the people of perdition.
>
> "The high decree of God would be broken, could Lethe be passed,

and that so fair aliment tasted, without some scot paid of repentance, which pours forth tears."

Here, indeed, and in a somewhat similar passage of the next canto, Mr. Martin thinks that the "obvious allusion" is to certain moral shortcomings, occasional slips, of which (though he treats Boccaccio's imputation as monstrous and incredible) "Dante, with his strong and ardent passions, having, like meaner men, to fight the perennial conflict between flesh and spirit," had sometimes, he supposes, been guilty. An Italian commentator gives at least as true an interpretation of these passages when he says that "in them Dante makes Beatrice, as the representative of theology, lament that he should have left the study of divinity—in which by the grace of Heaven, he might have attained admirable proficiency—to immerse himself in civil affairs with the parties of Florence." But the real truth is, that all the life of the world, its pleasures, its business, its parties, its politics, all is alike hollow and miserable to Dante in comparison with the inward life, the ecstasy of the divine vision; every way which does not lead straight towards this is for him a *via non vera;* every good thing but this is for him a false image of good, fulfilling none of the promises which it gives; for the excellency of the knowledge of this he counts all things but loss. Beatrice leads him to this; herself symbolizes for him the ineffable beauty and purity for which he longs. Even to Dante at twenty-one, when he yet sees the living Beatrice with his eyes, she already symbolizes this for him, she is already not the "creature not too bright and good" of Wordsworth, but a spirit far more than a woman; to Dante at twenty-five composing the *Vita Nuova* she is still more a spirit; to Dante at fifty, when his character has taken its bent, when his genius is come to its perfection, when he is composing his immortal poem, she is a spirit altogether.

C. S. Lewis
CHARITY

. . . .

WE MUST try to relate the human activities called "loves" to that Love which is God. . . . The humblest of us, in a state of Grace, can have some "knowledge-by-acquaintance" (*connaître*), some "tasting," of Love Himself; but man even at his highest sanc-

CHARITY: From *The Four Loves* by C. S. Lewis. © 1960 by Helen Joy Lewis. Reprinted by permission of Harcourt, Brace & World, Inc.

tity and intelligence has no direct "knowledge about" (*savoir*) the ultimate Being—only analogies. We cannot see light, though by light we can see things. Statements about God are extrapolations from the knowledge of other things which the divine illumination enables us to know. I labour these deprecations because, in what follows, my efforts to be clear (and not intolerably lengthy) may suggest a confidence which I by no means feel. I should be mad if I did. Take it as one man's reverie, almost one man's myth. If anything in it is useful to you, use it; if anything is not, never give it a second thought.

God is love. Again, "Herein is love, not that we loved God but that He loved us" (I John 4:10). We must not begin with mysticism, with the creature's love for God, or with the wonderful foretastes of the fruition of God vouchsafed to some in their earthly life. We begin at the real beginning, with love as the Divine energy. This primal love is Gift-love. In God there is no hunger that needs to be filled, only plenteousness that desires to give. The doctrine that God was under no necessity to create is not a piece of dry scholastic speculation. It is essential. Without it we can hardly avoid the conception of what I can only call a "managerial" God; a Being whose function or nature is to "run" the universe, who stands to it as a head-master to a school or a hotelier to a hotel. But to be sovereign of the universe is no great matter to God. In Himself, at home in "the land of the Trinity," he is Sovereign of a far greater realm. We must keep always before our eyes that vision of Lady Julian's in which God carried in His hand a little object like a nut, and that nut was "all that is made." God, who needs nothing, loves into existence wholly superfluous creatures in order that He may love and perfect them. He creates the universe, already foreseeing—or should we say "seeing"? there are no tenses in God—the buzzing cloud of flies about the cross, the flayed back pressed against the uneven stake, the nails driven through the mesial nerves, the repeated incipient suffocation as the body droops, the repeated torture of back and arms as it is time after time, for breath's sake, hitched up. If I may dare the biological image, God is a "host" who deliberately creates His own parasites; causes us to be that we may exploit and "take advantage of" Him. Herein is love. This is the diagram of Love Himself, the inventor of all loves.

God, as Creator of nature, implants in us both Gift-loves and Need-loves. The Gift-loves are natural images of Himself; proximities to Him by resemblance which are not necessarily and in all men proximities of approach. A devoted mother, a beneficent ruler or teacher, may give and give, continually exhibiting the likeness, without making the approach. The Need-loves, so far as I have been able to see, have no resemblance to the Love which God is. They are rather correlatives, opposites; not as evil is the opposite of good, of course, but as the form of the blanc-mange is an opposite to the form of the mould.

But in addition to these natural loves God can bestow a far better gift; or rather, since our minds must divide and pigeon-hole, two gifts.

He communicates to men a share of His own Gift-love. This is different from the Gift-loves He has built into their nature. These never quite seek simply the good of the loved object for the object's own sake. They are biased in favour of those goods they can themselves bestow, or those which they would like best themselves, or those which fit in with a pre-conceived picture of the life they want the object to lead. But Divine Gift-love—Love Himself working in a man—is wholly disinterested and desires what is simply best for the beloved. Again, natural Gift-love is always directed to objects which the lover finds in some way intrinsically lovable—objects to which Affection or Eros or a shared point of view attracts him, or, failing that, to the grateful and the deserving, or perhaps to those whose helplessness is of a winning and appealing kind. But Divine Gift-love in the man enables him to love what is not naturally lovable; lepers, criminals, enemies, morons, the sulky, the superior and the sneering. Finally, by a high paradox, God enables men to have a Gift-love towards Himself. There is of course a sense in which no one can give to God anything which is not already His; and if it is already His what have you given? But since it is only too obvious that we can withhold ourselves, our wills and hearts, from God, we can, in that sense, also give them. What is His by right and would not exist for a moment if it ceased to be His (as the song is the singer's), He has nevertheless made ours in such a way that we can freely offer it back to Him. "Our wills are ours to make them Thine." And as all Christians know there is another way of giving to God; every stranger whom we feed or clothe is Christ. And this apparently is Gift-love to God whether we know it or not. Love Himself can work in those who know nothing of Him. The "sheep" in the parable had no idea either of the God hidden in the prisoner whom they visited or of the God hidden in themselves when they made the visit. (I take the whole parable to be about the judgment of the heathen. For it begins by saying, in the Greek, that the Lord will summon all "the nations" before Him—presumably, the Gentiles, the *Goyim.*)

That such a Gift-love comes by Grace and should be called Charity, everyone will agree. But I have to add something which will not perhaps be so easily admitted. God, as it seems to me, bestows two other gifts; a supernatural Need-love of Himself and a supernatural Need-love of one another. By the first I do not mean the Appreciative love of Himself, the gift of adoration. What little I have to say on that higher—that highest—subject will come later. I mean a love which does not dream of disinterestedness, a bottomless indigence. Like a river making its own channel, like a magic wine which in being poured out should simultaneously create the glass that was to hold it, God turns our need of Him into Need-love of Him. What is stranger still is that He creates in us a more than natural receptivity of Charity from our fellow-men. Need is so near greed and we are so greedy already that it seems a strange grace. But I cannot get it out of my head that this is what happens.

Let us consider first this supernatural Need-love of Himself, bestowed by Grace. Of course the Grace does not create the need. That is there already; "given" (as the mathematicians say) in the mere fact of our being creatures, and incalculably increased by our being fallen creatures. What the Grace gives is the full recognition, the sensible awareness, the complete acceptance—even, with certain reservations, the glad acceptance—of this Need. For, without Grace, our wishes and our necessities are in conflict.

All those expressions of unworthiness which Christian practice puts into the believer's mouth seem to the outer world like the degraded and insincere grovellings of a sycophant before a tyrant, or at best a *façon de parler*[1] like the self-depreciation of a Chinese gentleman when he calls himself "this coarse and illiterate person." In reality, however, they express the continually renewed, because continually necessary, attempt to negate that misconception of ourselves and of our relation to God which nature, even while we pray, is always recommending to us. No sooner do we believe that God loves us than there is an impulse to believe that He does so, not because He is Love, but because we are intrinsically lovable. The Pagans obeyed this impulse unabashed; a good man was "dear to the gods" because he was good. We, being better taught, resort to subterfuge. Far be it from us to think that we have virtues for which God could love us. But then, how magnificently we have repented! As Bunyan says, describing his first and illusory conversion, "I thought there was no man in England that pleased God better than I." Beaten out of this, we next offer our own humility to God's admiration. Surely He'll like *that?* Or if not that, our clearsighted and humble recognition that we still lack humility. Thus, depth beneath depth and subtlety within subtlety, there remains some lingering idea of our own, our very own, attractiveness. It is easy to acknowledge, but almost impossible to realise for long, that we are mirrors whose brightness, if we are bright, is wholly derived from the sun that shines upon us. Surely we must have a little

1 [Way of speaking.]

—however little—native luminosity? Surely we can't be *quite* creatures?

For this tangled absurdity of a Need, even a Need-love, which never fully acknowledges its own neediness, Grace substitutes a full, childlike and delighted acceptance of our Need, a joy in total dependence. We become "jolly beggars." The good man is sorry for the sins which have increased his Need. He is not entirely sorry for the fresh Need they have produced. And he is not sorry at all for the innocent Need that is inherent in his creaturely condition. For all the time this illusion to which nature clings as her last treasure, this pretence that we have anything of our own or could for one hour retain by our own strength any goodness that God may pour into us, has kept us from being happy. We have been like bathers who want to keep their feet —or one foot—or one toe—on the bottom, when to lose that foothold would be to surrender themselves to a glorious tumble in the surf. The consequences of parting with our last claim to intrinsic freedom, power, or worth, are real freedom, power and worth, really ours just because God gives them and because we know them to be (in another sense) not "ours." Anodos has got rid of his shadow.

But God also transforms our Need-love for one another, and it requires equal transformation. In reality we all need at times, some of us at most times, that Charity from others which, being Love Himself in them, loves the unlovable. But this, though a sort of love we need, is not the sort we want. We want to be loved for our cleverness, beauty, generosity, fairness, usefulness. The first hint that anyone is offering us the highest love of all is a terrible shock. This is so well recognised that spiteful people will pretend to be loving us with Charity precisely because they know that it will wound us. To say to one who expects a renewal of Affection, Friendship, or Eros, "I forgive you as a Christian" is merely a way of continuing the quarrel. Those who say it are of course lying. But the thing would not be falsely said in order to wound unless, if it were true, it would be wounding.

How difficult it is to receive, and to go on receiving, from others a love that does not depend on our own attraction can be seen from an extreme case. Suppose yourself a man struck down shortly after marriage by an incurable disease which may not kill you for many years; useless, impotent, hideous, disgusting; dependent on your wife's earnings; impoverishing where you hoped to enrich; impaired even in intellect and shaken by gusts of uncontrollable temper, full of unavoidable demands. And suppose your wife's care and pity to be inexhaustible. The man who can take this sweetly, who can receive all and give nothing without resentment, who can abstain even from those tiresome self-depreciations which are really only a demand for petting and reassurance, is doing something which Need-love in its merely natural condition could not attain. (No doubt such a wife will also be doing something beyond the reach of a natural Gift-love, but that is not the point at present.) In such a case to receive is harder and perhaps more blessed than to give. But what the extreme example illustrates is universal. We are all receiving Charity. There is something in each of us that cannot be naturally loved. It is no one's fault if they do not so love it. Only the lovable can be naturally loved. You might as well ask people to like the taste of rotten bread or the sound of a mechanical drill. We can be forgiven, and pitied, and loved in spite of it, with Charity; no other way. All who have good parents, wives, husbands, or children, may be sure that at some times—and perhaps at all times in respect of some one particular trait or habit—they are receiving Charity, are loved not because they are lovable but because Love Himself is in those who love them.

Thus God, admitted to the human heart, transforms not only Gift-love but Need-love; not only our Need-love of Him, but our Need-love of one another. This is of course not the only thing that can happen. He may come on what seems to us a more dreadful mission and demand that a natural love be totally renounced. A high and terrible vocation, like Abraham's, may constrain a man to turn his back on his own people and his father's house. Eros, directed to a forbidden object, may have to be sacrificed. In such instances, the process, though hard to endure, is easy to understand. What we are more likely to overlook is the necessity for a transformation even when the natural love is allowed to continue.

In such a case the Divine Love does not *substitute* itself for the natural—as if we had to throw away our silver to make room for the gold. The natural loves are summoned to become modes of Charity while also remaining the natural loves they were.

One sees here at once a sort of echo or rhyme or corollary to the Incarnation itself. And this need not surprise us, for the Author of both is the same. As Christ is perfect God and perfect Man, the natural loves are called to become perfect Charity and also perfect natural loves. As God becomes Man "Not by conversion of the Godhead into flesh, but by taking of the Manhood into God," so here; Charity does not dwindle into merely natural love but natural love is taken up into, made the tuned and obedient instrument of, Love Himself.

How this can happen, most Christians know. All the activities (sins only excepted) of the natural loves can in favoured hour become works of the glad and shameless and grateful Need-love or of the selfless, unofficious Gift-love, which are both Charity. Nothing is either too trivial or too animal to be thus transformed. A game, a joke, a drink together, idle chat, a walk, the act of Venus—all these can be modes in which we forgive or accept forgiveness, in which we console or are reconciled, in which we "seek not our own." Thus in our very instincts, appetites and recreations, Love has prepared for Himself "a body."

But I said "in a favoured hour." Hours soon pass. The total and secure transformation of a natural love into a mode of Charity is a work so difficult that perhaps no fallen man has ever come within sight of doing it perfectly. Yet the law that loves must be so transformed is, I suppose, inexorable.

One difficulty is that here, as usual, we can take a wrong turn. A Christian—a somewhat too vocally Christian—circle or family, having grasped this principle, can make a show, in their overt behaviour and especially in their words, of having achieved the thing itself—an elaborate, fussy, embarrassing and intolerable show. Such people make every trifle a matter of explicitly spiritual importance—out loud and to one another (to God, on their knees, behind a closed door, it would be another matter). They are always unnecessarily asking, or insufferably offering, forgiveness. Who would not rather live with those ordinary people who get over their tantrums (and ours) unemphatically, letting a meal, a night's sleep, or a joke mend all? The real work must be, of all our works, the most secret. Even as far as possible secret from ourselves. Our right hand must not know what our left is doing. We have not got far enough if we play a game of cards with the children "merely" to amuse them or to show that they are forgiven. If this is the best we can do we are right to do it. But it would be better if a deeper, less conscious, Charity threw us into a frame of mind in which a little fun with the children was the thing we should at that moment like best.

We are, however, much helped in this necessary work by that very feature of our experience at which we most repine. The invitation to turn our natural loves into Charity is never lacking. It is provided by those frictions and frustrations that meet us in all of them; unmistakable evidence that (natural) love is not going to be "enough"—unmistakable, unless we are blinded by egotism. When we are, we use them absurdly. "If only I had been more fortunate in my children (that boy gets more like his father every day) I could have loved them perfectly." But every child is sometimes infuriating; most children are not infrequently odious. "If only my husband were more considerate, less lazy, less extravagant" . . . "If only my wife had fewer moods and more sense, and were less extravagant" . . . "If my father wasn't so infernally prosy and close-fisted." But in everyone, and of course in ourselves, there is that which requires forbearance, tolerance, forgiveness. The necessity of practising these virtues first sets us, forces us, upon the attempt to turn—more strictly, to let God turn—our love into Charity. These frets and rubs are beneficial. It may even be that where there are fewest of them the conversion of natural love is most difficult. When they are plentiful the necessity of rising above it is obvious. To rise above it when it is as fully satisfied and as little impeded as earthly conditions allow—to see that we must rise when all seems so well already—this may require a subtler conversion and a more delicate insight. In this way also it may be hard for "the rich" to enter the Kingdom.

And yet, I believe, the necessity for the conversion is inexorable; at least, if our natural loves are to enter the heavenly life. That they can enter it most of us in fact believe. We may hope that the resurrection of the body means also the resurrection of what may be called our "greater body"; the general fabric of our earthly life with its affections and relationships. But only on a condition; not a condition arbitrarily laid down by God, but one necessarily inherent in the character of Heaven: nothing can enter there which cannot become heavenly. "Flesh and blood," mere nature, cannot inherit that Kingdom. Man can ascend to Heaven only because the Christ, who died and ascended to Heaven, is "formed in him." Must we not suppose that the same is true of a man's loves? Only those into which Love Himself has entered will ascend to Love Himself. And these can be raised with Him only if they have, in some degree and fashion, shared His death; if the natural element in them has submitted—year after year, or in some sudden agony—to transmutation. The fashion of this world passes away. The very name of nature implies the transitory. Natural loves can hope for eternity only in so far as they have allowed themselves to be taken into the eternity of Charity; have at least allowed the process to begin here on earth, before the night comes when no man can work. And the process will always involve a kind of death. There is no escape. In my love for wife or friend the only eternal element is the transforming presence of Love Himself. By that presence, if at all, the other elements may hope, as our physical bodies hope, to be raised from the dead. For this only is holy in them, this only is the Lord.

Theologians have sometimes asked whether we shall "know one another" in Heaven, and whether the particular love-relations worked out on earth would then continue to have any significance. It seems reasonable to reply: "It may depend what kind of love it had become, or was becoming, on earth." For, surely, to meet in the eternal world someone for whom your love in this, however strong, had been merely natural, would not be (on that ground) even interesting. Would it not be like meeting in adult life someone who had seemed to be a great friend at your preparatory school solely because of common interests and occupations? If there was nothing more, if he was not a kindred soul, he will now be a total stranger. Neither of you now plays conkers. You no longer want to swop your help with his French exercise for his help with your arithmetic. In Heaven I suspect, a love that had never embodied Love Himself would be equally irrelevant. For Nature has passed away. All that is not eternal is eternally out of date.

But I must not end on this note, I dare not—and all the less because longings and terrors of my own prompt me to do so—leave any bereaved and desolate reader confirmed in the widespread illusion that reunion with the loved dead is the goal of the Christian life. The denial of this may sound harsh and unreal in the ears of the broken hearted, but it must be denied.

"Thou hast made us for thyself," said St. Augustine, "and our heart has no rest till it comes to Thee." This, so easy to believe for a brief moment before the altar or, perhaps, half-praying, half-meditating in an April wood, sounds like mockery beside a deathbed. But we shall be far more truly mocked if, casting this way, we pin our comfort on the hope—perhaps even with the aid of *séance* and necromancy—of some day, this time forever, enjoying the earthly Beloved again, and no more. It is hard not to imagine that such an endless prolongation of earthly happiness would be completely satisfying.

But, if I may trust my own experience, we get at once a sharp warning that there is something wrong. The moment we attempt to use our faith in the other world for this purpose, that faith weakens. The moments in my life when it was really strong have all been moments when God Himself was central in my thoughts. Believing in Him, I could then believe in Heaven as a corollary. But the reverse process—believing first in reunion with the Beloved, and then, for the sake of that reunion, believing in Heaven, and finally, for the sake of Heaven, believing in God—this will not work. One can of course imagine things. But a self-critical person will soon be increasingly aware that the imagination at work is his own; he knows he is only weaving a fantasy. And simpler souls will find the phantoms they try to feed on void of all comfort and nourishment, only to be stimulated into some semblance of reality by pitiful efforts of self-hypnotism, and perhaps by the aid of ignoble pictures and hymns and (what is worse) witches.

We find thus by experience that there is no good applying to Heaven for earthly comfort. Heaven can give heavenly comfort; no other kind. And earth cannot give earthly comfort either. There is no earthly comfort in the long run.

For the dream of finding our end, the thing we were made for, in a Heaven of purely human love could not be true unless our whole Faith were wrong. We were made for God. Only by being in some respect like Him, only by being a manifestation of His beauty, lovingkindness, wisdom or goodness, has any earthly Beloved excited our love. It is not that we have loved them too much, but that we did not quite understand what we were loving. It is not that we shall be asked to turn from them, so dearly familiar, to a Stranger. When we see the face of God we shall know that we have always known it. He has been a party to, has made, sustained and moved moment by moment within, all our earthly experiences of innocent love. All that was true love in them was, even on earth, far more His than ours, and ours only because His. In Heaven there will be no anguish and no duty of turning away from our earthly Beloveds. First, because we shall have turned already; from the portraits to the Original, from the rivulets to the Fountain, from the creatures He made lovable to Love Himself. But secondly, because we shall find them all in Him. By loving Him more than them we shall love them more than we now do.

But all that is far away in "the land of the Trinity," not here in exile, in the weeping valley. Down here it is all loss and renunciation. The very purpose of the bereavement (so far as it affects ourselves) may have been to force this upon us. We are then compelled to try to believe, what we cannot yet feel, that God is our true Beloved. That is why bereavement is in some ways easier for the unbeliever than for us. He can storm and rage and shake his fist at the universe, and (if he is a genius) write poems like Housman's or Hardy's. But we, at our lowest ebb, when the least effort seems too much for us, must begin to attempt what seem impossibilities.

"Is it easy to love God?" asks an old author. "It is easy," he replies, "to those who do it." I have included two Graces under the word Charity. But God can give a third. He can awake in man, towards Himself, a supernatural Appreciative love. This is of all gifts the most to be desired. Here, not in our natural loves, nor even in ethics, lies the true centre of all human and angelic life. With this all things are possible. . . .

POETRY

Edmund Spenser

MY LOVE IS LIKE TO ICE

My love is like to ice, and I to fire:
How comes it then that this her cold so great
Is not dissolved through my so hot desire,
But harder grows the more I her entreat?
Or how comes it that my exceeding heat
Is not allayed by her heart-frozen cold,
But that I burn much more in boiling sweat,
And feel my flames augmented manifold?
What more miraculous thing may be told,
That fire, which all things melts, should harden ice,
And ice, which is congeal'd with senseless cold,
Should kindle fire by wonderful device?
Such is the power of love in gentle mind,
That it can alter all the course of kind.

William Shakespeare

WHO IS SILVIA?

Who is Silvia? what is she,
That all our swains commend her?
Holy, fair, and wise is she;
The heaven such grace did lend her,
That she might admirèd be.

Is she kind as she is fair?
For beauty lives with kindness.
Love doth to her eyes repair,
To help him of his blindness;
And, being helped, inhabits there.

Then to Silvia let us sing,
That Silvia is excelling;
She excels each mortal thing
Upon the dull earth dwelling;
To her let us garlands bring.

William Shakespeare

SONNET 18

SHALL I compare thee to a summer's day?
Thou art more lovely and more temperate.
Rough winds do shake the darling buds of May,
And summer's lease hath all too short a date.
Sometime too hot the eye of heaven shines,
And often is his gold complexion dimmed.
And every fair from fair sometime declines,
By chance or nature's changing course untrimmed.
But thy eternal summer shall not fade,
Nor lose possession of that fair thou owest,
Nor shall Death brag thou wander'st in his shade
When in eternal lines to time thou grow'st.
So long as men can breathe, or eyes can see,
So long lives this, and this gives life to thee.

William Shakespeare

SONNET 116

LET ME not to the marriage of true minds
Admit impediments. Love is not love
Which alters when it alteration finds,
Or bends with the remover to remove.
Oh no! It is an ever-fixèd mark
That looks on tempests and is never shaken.
It is the star to every wandering bark,
Whose worth's unknown, although his height be taken.
Love's not Time's fool, though rosy lips and cheeks
Within his bending sickle's compass come.
Love alters not with his brief hours and weeks,
But bears it out even to the edge of doom.
If this be error and upon me proved
I never writ, nor no man ever loved.

Edmund Waller

SONG

GO, LOVELY rose,
Tell her that wastes her time and me
That now she knows,
When I resemble her to thee,
How sweet and fair she seems to be.

Tell her that's young,
And shuns to have her graces spied,
That hadst thou sprung
In deserts, where no men abide,
Thou must have uncommended died.

Small is the worth
Of beauty from the light retired;
Bid her come forth,
Suffer herself to be desired,
And not blush so to be admired.

Then die, that she
The common fate of all things rare
May read in thee;
How small a part of time they share
That are so wondrous sweet and fair.

Robert Burns

JOHN ANDERSON, MY JO

John Anderson, my jo, John,
When we were first acquent;
Your locks were like the raven,
Your bonny brow was brent,
But now your brow is beld, John,
Your locks are like the snaw;
But blessings on your frosty pow,
John Anderson, my jo.

John Anderson, my jo, John,
We clamb the hill thegither;
And mony a canty day, John,
We've had wi' ane anither.
Now we maun totter down, John,
But hand in hand we'll go;
And sleep thegither at the foot,
John Anderson, my jo.

William Wordsworth

SHE WAS A PHANTOM OF DELIGHT

She was a Phantom of delight
When first she gleamed upon my sight;
A lovely Apparition, sent
To be a moment's ornament;

Her eyes as stars of Twilight fair;
Like Twilight's, too, her dusky hair;
But all things else about her drawn
From May-time and the cheerful Dawn;
A dancing Shape, an Image gay,
To haunt, to startle, and way-lay.

I saw her upon nearer view,
A Spirit, yet a Woman too!
Her household motions light and free,
And steps of virgin-liberty;
A countenance in which did meet
Sweet records, promises as sweet;
A Creature not too bright or good
For human nature's daily food;
For transient sorrows, simple wiles,
Praise, blame, love, kisses, tears, and smiles.

And now I see with eye serene
The very pulse of the machine;
A Being breathing thoughtful breath,
A Traveller between life and death;
The reason firm, the temperate will,
Endurance, foresight, strength, and skill;
A perfect Woman, nobly planned,
To warn, to comfort, and command;
And yet a Spirit still, and bright
With something of angelic light.

John Keats

LA BELLE DAME SANS MERCI[1]

"O WHAT can ail thee, knight-at-arms,
Alone and palely loitering?
The sedge has wither'd from the lake,
And no birds sing.

"O what can ail thee, knight-at-arms,
So haggard and so woe-begone?
The squirrel's granary is full,
And the harvest's done.

"I see a lily on thy brow
With anguish moist and fever dew;
And on thy cheek a fading rose
Fast withereth too."

1 [The Fair Lady Without Pity.]

"I met a lady in the meads,
 Full beautiful—a faery's child,
Her hair was long, her foot was light,
 And her eyes were wild.

"I made a garland for her head,
 And bracelets too, and fragrant zone;
She look'd at me as she did love,
 And made sweet moan.

"I set her on my pacing steed
 And nothing else saw all day long,
For sidelong would she bend, and sing
 A faery's song.

"She found me roots of relish sweet,
 And honey wild, and manna dew,
And sure in language strange she said—
 'I love thee true.'

"She took me to her elfin grot,
 And there she wept, and sigh'd full sore;
And there I shut her wild wild eyes
 With kisses four.

"And there she lullèd me asleep,
 And there I dream'd—Ah! woe betide!
The latest dream I ever dream'd
 On the cold hill's side.

"I saw pale kings and princes too,
 Pale warriors, death-pale were they all;
They cried—'La Belle Dame sans Merci
 Hath thee in thrall!'

"I saw their starv'd lips in the gloom,
 With horrid warning gapèd wide,
And I awoke and found me here,
 On the cold hill's side.

"And this is why I sojourn here,
 Alone and palely loitering,
Though the sedge is wither'd from the lake,
 And no birds sing."

Alfred, Lord Tennyson

TITHONUS

THE WOODS decay, the woods decay and fall,
The vapors weep their burthen to the ground,
Man comes and tills the field and lies beneath,
And after many a summer dies the swan.
Me only cruel immortality
Consumes; I wither slowly in thine arms,
Here at the quiet limit of the world,
A white-hair'd shadow roaming like a dream
The ever-silent spaces of the East,
Far-folded mists, and gleaming halls of morn.
  Alas! for this gray shadow, once a man—
So glorious in his beauty and thy choice,
Who madest him thy chosen, that he seem'd
To his great heart none other than a God!
I ask'd thee, "Give me immortality."
Then didst thou grant mine asking with a smile,
Like wealthy men who care not how they give.
But thy strong Hours indignant work'd their wills,
And beat me down and marr'd and wasted me,
And tho' they could not end me, left me maim'd
To dwell in presence of immortal youth,
Immortal age beside immortal youth,
And all I was in ashes. Can thy love,
Thy beauty, make amends, tho' even now,
Close over us, the silver star, thy guide,
Shines in those tremulous eyes that fill with tears
To hear me? Let me go; take back thy gift.
Why should a man desire in any way
To vary from the kindly race of men,
Or pass beyond the goal of ordinance
Where all should pause, as is most meet for all?
  A soft air fans the cloud apart; there comes
A glimpse of that dark world where I was born.
Once more the old mysterious glimmer steals
From thy pure brows, and from thy shoulders pure,
And bosom beating with a heart renew'd.
Thy cheek begins to redden thro' the gloom,
Thy sweet eyes brighten slowly close to mine,
Ere yet they blind the stars, and the wild team
Which love thee, yearning for thy yoke, arise,
And shake the darkness from their loosen'd manes,
And beat the twilight into flakes of fire.
  Lo! ever thus thou growest beautiful

In silence, then before thine answer given
Departest, and thy tears are on my cheek.
Why wilt thou ever scare me with thy tears,
And make me tremble lest a saying learnt,
In days far-off, on that dark earth, be true?
"The God's themselves cannot recall their gifts."
Ay me! ay me! with what another heart
In days far-off, and with what other eyes
I used to watch—if I be he that watch'd—
The lucid outline forming round thee; saw
The dim curls kindle into sunny rings;
Changed with thy mystic change, and felt my blood
Glow with the glow that slowly crimson'd all
Thy presence and thy portals, while I lay,
Mouth, forehead, eyelids, growing dewy-warm
With kisses balmier than half-opening buds
Of April, and could hear the lips that kiss'd
Whispering I knew not what of wild and sweet,
Like that strange song I heard Apollo sing,
While Ilion like a mist rose into towers.
Yet hold me not for ever in thine East;
How can my nature longer mix with thine?
Coldly thy rosy shadows bathe me, cold
Are all thy lights, and cold my wrinkled feet
Upon thy glimmering thresholds, when the steam
Floats up from those dim fields about the homes
Of happy men that have the power to die,
And grassy barrows of the happier dead.
Release me, and restore me to the ground.
Thou seest all things, thou wilt see my grave;
Thou wilt renew thy beauty morn by morn,
I earth in earth forget these empty courts,
And thee returning on thy silver wheels.

Elizabeth Barrett Browning

SONNET 43

How do I love thee? Let me count the ways.
I love thee to the depth and breadth and height
My soul can reach, when feeling out of sight
For the ends of Being and ideal Grace.
I love thee to the level of everyday's
Most quiet need, by sun and candle-light.
I love thee freely, as men strive for Right;
I love thee purely, as they turn from Praise.

I love thee with the passion put to use
In my old griefs, and with my childhood's faith.
I love thee with a love I seemed to lose
With my lost saints—I love thee with the breath,
Smiles, tears, of all my life!—and, if God choose,
I shall but love thee better after death.

Robert Browning

TWO IN THE CAMPAGNA

I WONDER do you feel today
As I have felt since, hand in hand,
We sat down on the grass, to stray
In spirit better through the land,
This morn of Rome and May?

For me, I touched a thought, I know,
Has tantalized me many times,
(Like turns of thread the spiders throw
Mocking across our path) for rhymes
To catch at and let go.

Help me to hold it! First it left
The yellowing fennel, run to seed
There, branching from the brickwork's cleft,
Some old tomb's ruin; yonder weed
Took up the floating weft,

Where one small orange cup amassed
Five beetles—blind and green they grope
Among the honey-meal; and last,
Everywhere on the grassy slope
I traced it. Hold it fast!

The champaign with its endless fleece
Of feathery grasses everywhere;
Silence and passion, joy and peace,
An everlasting wash of air—
Rome's ghost since her decease.

Such life here, through such lengths of hours,
Such miracles performed in play,
Such primal naked forms of flowers,
Such letting nature have her way
While heaven looks from its towers!

How say you? Let us, O my dove,
Let us be unashamed of soul,
As earth lies bare to heaven above!
How is it under our control
To love or not to love?

I would that you were all to me,
You that are just so much, no more.
Nor yours nor mine, nor slave nor free!
Where does the fault lie? What the core
O' the wound, since wound must be?

I would I could adopt your will,
See with your eyes, and set my heart
Beating by yours, and drink my fill
At your soul's springs—your part my part
In life, for good and ill.

No. I yearn upward, touch you close,
Then stand away. I kiss your cheek,
Catch your soul's warmth—I pluck the rose
And love it more than tongue can speak—
Then the good minute goes.

Already how am I so far
Out of that minute? Must I go
Still like the thistle-ball, no bar,
Onward, whenever light winds blow,
Fixed by no friendly star?

Just when I seemed about to learn!
Where is the thread now? Off again!
The old trick! Only I discern—
Infinite passion, and the pain
Of finite hearts that yearn.

Matthew Arnold

TO MARGUERITE

YES! IN the sea of life enisled,
With echoing straits between us thrown,
Dotting the shoreless watery wild,
We mortal millions live *alone*.
The islands feel the enclasping flow,
And then their endless bounds they know.

But when the moon their hollows lights,
And they are swept by balms of spring,
And in their glens, on starry nights,
The nightingales divinely sing;
And lovely notes, from shore to shore,
Across the sounds and channels pour—

Oh! then a longing like despair
Is to their farthest caverns sent;
For surely once, they feel, we were
Parts of a single continent!
Now round us spreads the watery plain—
Oh might our marges meet again!

Who ordered, that their longing's fire
Should be, as soon as kindled, cooled?
Who renders vain their deep desire?—
A God, a God their severance ruled!
And bade betwixt their shores to be
The unplumbed, salt, estranging sea.

Matthew Arnold

ISOLATION

WE WERE apart; yet, day by day,
I bade my heart more constant be.
I bade it keep the world away,
And grow a home for only thee;
Nor feared but thy love likewise grew,
Like mine, each day, more tried, more true.

The fault was grave! I might have known,
What far too soon, alas! I learned—
The heart can bind itself alone,
And faith may oft be unreturned.
Self-swayed our feelings ebb and swell—
Thou lov'st no more;—Farewell! Farewell!

Farewell!—and thou, thou lonely heart,
Which never yet without remorse
Even for a moment didst depart
From thy remote and sphéred course
To haunt the place where passions reign—
Back to thy solitude again!

Back! with the conscious thrill of shame
Which Luna felt, that summer-night,
Flash through her pure immortal frame,
When she forsook the starry height
To hang over Endymion's sleep
Upon the pine-grown Latmian steep.

Yet she, chaste queen, had never proved
How vain a thing is mortal love,
Wandering in heaven, far removed.
But thou hast long had place to prove
This truth—to prove, and make thine own:
"Thou hast been, shalt be, art, alone."

Or, if not quite alone, yet they
Which touch thee are unmating things—
Ocean and clouds and night and day;
Lorn autumns and triumphant springs;
And life, and others' joy and pain,
And love, if love, of happier men.

Of happier men—for they, at least,
Have *dreamed* two human hearts might blend
In one, and were through faith released
From isolation without end
Prolonged; nor knew, although not less
Alone than thou, their loneliness.

Thomas Moore

THE TIME I'VE LOST IN WOOING

THE TIME I've lost in wooing
In watching and pursuing
The light, that lies
In woman's eyes,
Has been my heart's undoing.
Though Wisdom oft has sought me,
I scorned the lore she brought me,
My only books
Were woman's looks,
And folly's all they've taught me.

Her smile when Beauty granted,
I hung with gaze enchanted,
Like him the Sprite,
Whom maids by night

Oft meet in glen that's haunted.
Like him, too, Beauty won me,
But while her eyes were on me,
If once their ray
Was turned away,
O, winds could not outrun me.

And are those follies going?
And in my proud heart growing
Too cold or wise
For brilliant eyes
Again to set it glowing?
No, vain, alas! th' endeavor
From bonds so sweet to sever;—
Poor Wisdom's chance
Against a glance
Is now as weak as ever.

Ralph Waldo Emerson

GIVE ALL TO LOVE

Give all to love;
Obey thy heart;
Friends, kindred, days,
Estate, good-fame,
Plans, credit and the Muse,—
Nothing refuse.

'Tis a brave master;
Let it have scope:
Follow it utterly,
Hope beyond hope:
High and more high
It dives into noon,
With wing unspent,
Untold intent;
But it is a god,
Knows its own path
And the outlets of the sky.

It was never for the mean;
It requireth courage stout.
Souls above doubt,
Valor unbending,
It will reward,—
They shall return
More than they were,
And ever ascending.

Leave all for love;
Yet, hear me, yet,
One word more thy heart behoved,
One pulse more of firm endeavor,—
Keep thee today,
Tomorrow, forever,
Free as an Arab
Of thy beloved.

Cling with life to the maid;
But when the surprise,
First vague shadow of surmise
Flits across her bosom young,
Of a joy apart from thee,
Free be she, fancy-free;
Nor thou detain her vesture's hem,
Nor the palest rose she flung
From her summer diadem.

Though thou loved her as thyself,
As a self of purer clay,
Though her parting dims the day,
Stealing grace from all alive;
Heartily know,
When half-gods go,
The gods arrive.

Alice Meynell

RENOUNCEMENT

I MUST not think of thee; and, tired yet strong,
I shun the love that lurks in all delight—
The love of thee—and in the blue heaven's height,
And in the dearest passage of a song.
Oh, just beyond the sweetest thoughts that throng
This breast, the thought of thee waits hidden yet bright;
But it must never, never come in sight;
I must stop short of thee the whole day long.
But when sleep comes to close each difficult day,
When night gives pause to the long watch I keep,
And all my bonds I needs must loose apart,
Must doff my will as raiment laid away,—
With the first dream that comes with the first sleep
I run, I run, I am gather'd to thy heart.

William Butler Yeats

WHEN YOU ARE OLD

WHEN you are old and gray and full of sleep,
And nodding by the fire, take down this book,
And slowly read, and dream of the soft look
Your eyes had once, and of their shadows deep;

How many loved your moments of glad grace,
And loved your beauty with love false or true;
But one man loved the pilgrim soul in you,
And loved the sorrows of your changing face.

And bending down beside the glowing bars,
Murmur, a little sadly, how love fled
And paced upon the mountains overhead
And hid his face amid a crowd of stars.

Robert Frost

THE TUFT OF FLOWERS

I WENT to turn the grass once after one
Who mowed it in the dew before the sun,

The dew was gone that made his blade so keen
Before I came to view the leveled scene.

I looked for him behind an isle of trees;
I listened for his whetstone on the breeze.

But he had gone his way, the grass all mown,
And I must be, as he had been,—alone,

"As all must be," I said within my heart,
"Whether they work together or apart."

But as I said it, swift there passed me by
On noiseless wing a bewildered butterfly,

Seeking with memories grown dim over night
Some resting flower of yesterday's delight.

And once I marked his flight go round and round,
As where some flower lay withering on the ground.

And then he flew as far as eye could see,
And then on tremulous wing came back to me.

I thought of questions that have no reply,
And would have turned to toss the grass to dry;

But he turned first, and led my eye to look
At a tall tuft of flowers beside a brook,

A leaping tongue of bloom the scythe had spared
Beside a reedy brook the scythe had bared.

I left my place to know them by their name,
Finding them butterfly-weed when I came.

The mower in the dew had loved them thus,
By leaving them to flourish, not for us,

Nor yet to draw one thought of ours to him,
But from sheer morning gladness at the brim.

The butterfly and I had lit upon,
Nevertheless, a message from the dawn,

That made me hear the wakening birds around,
And hear his long scythe whispering to the ground,

And feel a spirit kindred to my own;
So that henceforth I worked no more alone;

But glad with him, I worked as with his aid,
And weary, sought at noon with him the shade;

And dreaming, as it were, held brotherly speech
With one whose thought I had not hoped to reach.

"Men work together," I told him from the heart,
"Whether they work together or apart."

Edwin Muir

IN LOVE FOR LONG

I'VE BEEN in love for long
With what I cannot tell
And will contrive a song
For the intangible
That has no mould or shape,
From which there's no escape.

It is not even a name,
Yet it is all constancy;
Tried or untried, the same,
It cannot part from me;
A breath, yet as still
As the established hill.

It is not any thing,
And yet all being is;
Being, being, being,
Its burden and its bliss.
How can I ever prove
What it is I love?

This happy happy love
Is sieged with crying sorrows,
Crushed beneath and above
Between to-days and morrows;
A little paradise
Held in the world's vice.

And there it is content
And careless as a child,
And in imprisonment
Flourishes sweet and wild;
In wrong, beyond wrong,
All the world's day long.

This love a moment known
For what I do not know
And in a moment gone
Is like the happy doe
That keeps its perfect laws
Between the tiger's paws
And vindicates its cause.

Jessica Powers

I WOULD DEFINE MY LOVE

HERE on the flyleaf of the garish day,
Here at the noonday of the long despair
I write the grave inconsequence of words.
When men stampede in panic-stricken herds
Down tangled roads of thought,
Speech dies without the seal of action there,
And even song, cast forth, must come to naught,
Lost in the blowing pockets of the air.

Shall I then sit apart in a sun stupor
Out of the rush of the bewildered feet
And fan my heart to keep it fresh and cool
And say "O beautiful . . ." and say "O sweet . . ."
Watching the butterflies that try to settle
On wet leaves in a water lily pool?

No, for my heart is on the road with these
Spiritual refugees,
And I would flee the grim inaction of words
And the paralysis of wish and dream.
How can a man in love sit still and stare?
O people of earth, if I am not with you, running and crying,
It is that I am paging hurriedly
Through wordless volumes of reality
To find what love has indicated there.
I would define my love in some incredible penance
Of which no impotent language is aware.

Robert P. Tristram Coffin

A FATHER IS A STRANGE THING

A FATHER is a strange thing, he will leap
Across a generation and will peep
Out of a grandson's eyes when unexpected
With all the secrets of him resurrected.

A man is taken by complete surprise
To see his father looking from the eyes
Of a little boy he thought his own
And thought he had the breeding of alone.

His father looks direct through eyes new blue,
His father moves on stout thighs quick and new,
He takes hold of things as once he did,
And none of his old handsomeness is hid.

The grace the father thought well hid away
Shines like the sun upon a boy at play,
The love he kept so close for none to see
Looks up naked at the father's knee.

All the proud, high ways his father had
Are lowered to his knee. A man is sad
To see them so, but then he catches breath
To see how one so loved has cheated death.

T. S. Eliot

THE LOVE SONG OF J. ALFRED PRUFROCK[1]

S'io credesse che mia risposta fosse
A persona che mai tornasse al mondo,
Questa fiamma staria senza piu scosse.
Ma perciocche giammai di questo fondo
Non torno vivo alcun, s'i'odo il vero,
Senza tema d'infamia ti rispondo.[2]

Let us go then, you and I,
When the evening is spread out against the sky
Like a patient etherized upon a table;
Let us go, through certain half-deserted streets,
The muttering retreats
Of restless nights in one-night cheap hotels
And sawdust restaurants with oyster-shells:
Streets that follow like a tedious argument

1 [The title is ironic. Prufrock, whose name suggests a prudish, frock-coated respectability, is incapable of love.]

2 [*S'io credesse, etc.*: From Dante, *The Divine Comedy, Inferno,* XXVII, 61-66: "If I thought my answer were to one who ever could return to the world, this flame [the soul of Guido da Montefeltro] should shake [speak] no more, but since none ever did return alive from this depth, if what I hear be true, without fear of infamy I answer thee." This epigraph suggests that a parallel between Prufrock and Guido will be developed in the poem.]

Of insidious intent
To lead you to an overwhelming question. . .
Oh, do not ask, "What is it?"
Let us go and make our visit.

In the room the women come and go
Talking of Michelangelo.

The yellow fog that rubs its back upon the window-panes,
The yellow smoke that rubs its muzzle on the window-panes,
Licked its tongue into the corners of the evening,
Lingered upon the pools that stand in drains,
Let fall upon its back the soot that falls from chimneys,
Slipped by the terrace, made a sudden leap,
And seeing that it was a soft October night,
Curled once about the house, and fell asleep.

And indeed there will be time
For the yellow smoke that slides along the street,
Rubbing its back upon the window-panes;
There will be time, there will be time
To prepare a face to meet the faces that you meet;
There will be time to murder and create,
And time for all the works and days[3] of hands
That lift and drop a question on your plate;
Time for you and time for me,
And time yet for a hundred indecisions,
And for a hundred visions and revisions,
Before the taking of a toast and tea.

In the room the women come and go
Talking of Michelangelo.

And indeed there will be time
To wonder, "Do I dare?" and, "Do I dare?"
Time to turn back and descend the stair,
With a bald spot in the middle of my hair—
(They will say: "How his hair is growing thin!")
My morning coat, my collar mounting firmly to the chin,
My necktie rich and modest, but asserted by a simple pin—
("They will say: "But how his arms and legs are thin!")

3 [*"Works and Days"* is the title of a poem by the Greek poet Hesiod (735 B.C.). It contains practical suggestions on farming. Eliot frequently echoes poems that present positive emotions and attitudes in order to stress the negative character of Prufrock. Thus Andrew Marvell's hearty "To His Coy Mistress" is echoed in ll. 23, 92; Shakespeare's *Twelfth Night* in l. 52; and *Hamlet* in ll. 111 ff. The epigraph from Dante (see preceding note) serves a similar purpose.]

Do I dare
Disturb the universe?
In a minute there is time
For decisions and revisions which a minute will reverse.

For I have known them all already, known them all:
Have known the evenings, mornings, afternoons,
I have measured out my life with coffee spoons;
I know the voices dying with a dying fall
Beneath the music from a farther room.
  So how should I presume?

And I have known the eyes already, known them all—
The eyes that fix you in a formulated phrase,
And when I am formulated, sprawling on a pin,
When I am pinned and wriggling on the wall,
Then how should I begin
To spit out all the butt-ends of my days and ways?
  And how should I presume?

And I have known the arms already, known them all—
Arms that are braceleted and white and bare
(But in the lamplight, downed with light brown hair!)
Is it perfume from a dress
That makes me so digress?

Arms that lie along a table, or wrap about a shawl,
  And should I then presume?
  And how should I begin?

. . . .

Shall I say, I have gone at dusk through narrow streets
And watched the smoke that rises from the pipes
Of lonely men in shirt-sleeves, leaning out of windows? . . .

I should have been a pair of ragged claws
Scuttling across the floors of silent seas.

. . . .

And the afternoon, the evening, sleeps so peacefully!
Smoothed by long fingers,
Asleep . . . tired . . . or it malingers,
Stretched on the floor, here beside you and me.
Should I, after tea and cakes and ices,
Have the strength to force the moment to its crisis?
But though I have wept and fasted, wept and prayed,

Though I have seen my head (grown slightly bald) brought in upon a platter,
I am no prophet[4]—and here's no great matter;
I have seen the moment of my greatness flicker,
And I have seen the eternal Footman[5] hold my coat, and snicker,
And in short, I was afraid.

And would it have been worth it, after all,
After the cups, the marmalade, the tea,
Among the porcelain, among some talk of you and me,
Would it have been worth while,
To have bitten off the matter with a smile,
To have squeezed the universe into a ball
To roll it toward some overwhelming question,
To say: "I am Lazarus, come from the dead,
Come back to tell you all, I shall tell you all"—
If one, settling a pillow by her head,
Should say: "That is not what I meant at all;
That is not it, at all."

And would it have been worth it, after all,
Would it have been worth while,
After the sunsets and the dooryards and the sprinkled streets,
After the novels, after the teacups, after the skirts that trail along the floor—
And this, and so much more?—
It is impossible to say just what I mean!
But as if a magic lantern threw the nerves in patterns on a screen:
Would it have been worth while
If one, settling a pillow or throwing off a shawl,
And turning toward the window, should say:
"That is not it at all,
That is not what I meant, at all."

. . . .

No! I am not Prince Hamlet, nor was meant to be;
Am an attendant lord, one that will do
To swell a progress, start a scene or two,
Advise the prince; no doubt, an easy tool.
Deferential, glad to be of use,
Politic, cautious, and meticulous;
Full of high sentence, but a bit obtuse;
At times, indeed, almost ridiculous—
Almost, at times, the Fool.

I grow old. . . . I grow old. . . .
I shall wear the bottoms of my trousers rolled.

4 [John the Baptist was beheaded by Herod at the request of his wife Herodias. Prufrock foresees a similar fate but does not expect to meet it with courage.]

5 [Death.]

Shall I part my hair behind? Do I dare to eat a peach?
I shall wear white flannel trousers, and walk upon the beach.
I have heard the mermaids singing, each to each.

I do not think that they will sing to me.
I have seen them riding seaward on the waves
Combing the white hair of the waves blown back
When the wind blows the water white and black.

We have lingered in the chambers of the sea
By sea-girls wreathed with seaweed red and brown
Till human voices wake us, and we drown.

William Shakespeare

from ROMEO AND JULIET

ACT II

SCENE II.°
CAPULET'S *orchard.*

[*Enter* ROMEO.]

ROM. He jests at scars that never felt a wound. [JULIET *appears above at a window.*]
But, soft! What light through yonder window breaks?
It is the east, and Juliet is the sun!
Arise, fair sun, and kill the envious moon,°
Who is already sick and pale with grief
That thou her maid art far more fair than she.
Be not her maid, since she is envious.
Her vestal° livery is but sick and green,
And none but fools do wear it. Cast it off.
It is my lady, oh, it is my love!
Oh, that she knew she were!
She speaks, yet she says nothing. What of that?
Her eye discourses, I will answer it.
I am too bold, 'tis not to me she speaks.
Two of the fairest stars in all the heaven,
Having some business, do entreat her eyes
To twinkle in their spheres till they return.
What if her eyes were there, they in her head?

Sc. ii: In the original quartos there is no change of locality; Romeo hides on the stage until the others have gone. 4. *envious moon*: the moon is also Diana, the virgin goddess. 8. *vestal*: virgin.

The brightness of her cheek would shame those stars
As daylight doth a lamp; her eyes in heaven
Would through the airy region stream so bright
That birds would sing and think it were not night.
See how she leans her cheek upon her hand!
Oh, that I were a glove upon that hand,
That I might touch that cheek!
JUL. Aye me!
ROM. She speaks.
Oh, speak again, bright angel! For thou art
As glorious to this night, being o'er my head,
As is a wingèd messenger of Heaven
Unto the white-upturnèd wondering eyes
Of mortals that fall back to gaze on him
When he bestrides the lazy-pacing clouds
And sails upon the bosom of the air.
JUL. O Romeo, Romeo, wherefore art thou Romeo?
Deny thy father and refuse thy name,
Of, if thou wilt not, be but sworn my love
And I'll no longer be a Capulet.
ROM. [*Aside*] Shall I hear more, or shall I speak at this?
JUL. 'Tis but thy name that is my enemy.
Thou art thyself, though not a Montague.
What's Montague? It is nor hand, nor foot,
Nor arm, nor face, nor any other part
Belonging to a man. Oh, be some other name!
What's in a name? That which we call a rose
By any other name would smell as sweet.
So Romeo would, were he not Romeo called,
Retain that dear perfection which he owes°
Without that title. Romeo, doff thy name,
And for thy name, which is no part of thee,
Take all myself.
ROM. I take thee at thy word.
Call me but love, and I'll be new baptized.
Henceforth I never will be Romeo.
JUL. What man art thou that, thus bescreened in night,
So stumblest on my counsel?
ROM. By a name
I know not how to tell thee who I am.
My name, dear saint, is hateful to myself
Because it is an enemy to thee.
Had I it written, I would tear the word.
JUL. My ears have yet not drunk a hundred words
Of thy tongue's uttering, yet I know the sound.
Art thou not Romeo, and a Montague?

46. *owes*: owns.

ROM. Neither, fair saint, if either thee dislike.°
JUL. How camest thou hither, tell me, and wherefore?
The orchard walls are high and hard to climb,
And the place death, considering who thou art,
If any of my kinsmen find thee here.
ROM. With love's light wings did I o'erperch° these walls,
For stony limits cannot hold love out.
And what love can do, that dares love attempt,
Therefore thy kinsmen are no let° to me.
JUL. If they do see thee, they will murder thee.
ROM. Alack, there lies more peril in thine eye
Than twenty of their swords. Look thou but sweet,
And I am proof° against their enmity.
JUL. I would not for the world they saw thee here.
ROM. I have night's cloak to hide me from their eyes,
And but° thou love me, let them find me here.
My life were better ended by their hate
Than death prorogued,° wanting of thy love.
JUL. By whose direction found'st thou out this place?
ROM. By love, that first did prompt me to inquire.
He lent me counsel, and I lent him eyes.
I am no pilot, yet wert thou as far
As that vast shore washed with the farthest sea,
I would adventure for such merchandise.
JUL. Thou know'st the mask of night is on my face,
Else would a maiden blush bepaint my cheek
For that which thou hast heard me speak tonight.
Fain would I dwell on form,° fain, fain deny
What I have spoke. But farewell compliment!°
Dost thou love me? I know thou wilt say "Aye,"
And I will take thy word. Yet if thou swear'st,
Thou mayst prove false. At lovers' perjuries
They say Jove laughs. O gentle Romeo,
If thou dost love, pronounce it faithfully.
Or if thou think'st I am too quickly won,
I'll frown and be perverse and say thee nay,
So thou wilt woo; but else, not for the world.
In truth, fair Montague, I am too fond,°
And therefore thou mayst think my 'havior light.
But trust me, gentleman, I'll prove more true
Than those that have more cunning to be strange,°
I should have been more strange, I must confess,
But that thou overheard'st, ere I was ware,

61. *dislike*: displease. 66. *o'erperch*: fly over. 69. *let*: hindrance. 73. *proof*: armored. 76. *And but*: if only. 78. *prorogued*: postponed. 88. *dwell on form*: behave according to convention. 89. *compliment*: polite behavior. 98. *fond*: foolishly affectionate. 101. *strange*: outwardly cold.

My true love's passion. Therefore pardon me,
And not impute this yielding to light love,
Which the dark night hath so discovered.
ROM. Lady, by yonder blessed moon I swear,
That tips with silver all these fruit-tree tops—
JUL. Oh, swear not by the moon, th' inconstant moon,
That monthly changes in her circled orb,
Lest that thy love prove likewise variable.
ROM. What shall I swear by?
JUL. Do not swear at all.
Or, if thou wilt, swear by thy gracious self,
Which is the god of my idolatry,
And I'll believe thee.
ROM. If my heart's dear love—
JUL. Well, do not swear. Although I joy in thee,
I have no joy of this contráct° tonight.
It is too rash, too unadvised, too sudden,
Too like the lightning, which doth cease to be
Ere one can say "It lightens." Sweet, good night!
This bud of love, by summer's ripening breath,
May prove a beauteous flower when next we meet.
Good night, good night! As sweet repose and rest
Come to thy heart as that within my breast!
ROM. Oh, wilt thou leave me so unsatisfied?
JUL. What satisfaction canst thou have tonight?
ROM. The exchange of thy love's faithful vow for mine.
JUL. I gave thee mine before thou didst request it,
And yet I would it were to give again.
ROM. Wouldst thou withdraw it? For what purpose, love?
JUL. But to be frank, and give it thee again.
And yet I wish but for the thing I have.
My bounty is as boundless as the sea,
My love as deep; the more I give to thee,
The more I have, for both are infinite.
I hear some noise within. Dear love, adieu! [NURSE *calls within.*°]
Anon,° good Nurse! Sweet Montague, be true.
Stay but a little, I will come again. [*Exit.*]
ROM. Oh, blessed, blessed night! I am afeard,
Being in night, all this is but a dream,
Too flattering-sweet to be substantial.

[*Re-enter* JULIET, *above.*]

JUL. Three words, dear Romeo, and good night indeed.
If that thy bent° of love be honorable,
Thy purpose marriage, send me word tomorrow
By one that I'll procure to come to thee,

117. *contract*: bethrothal. 136. [s.d.] *within*: off stage. 137. *Anon*: by and by, in a moment. 143. *bent*: intention.

Where and what time thou wilt perform the rite,
And all my fortunes at thy foot I'll lay,
And follow thee my lord throughout the world.
NURSE. [*Within*] Madam!
JUL. I come, anon.—But if thou mean'st not well, I do beseech thee——
NURSE. [*Within*] Madam!
JUL. By and by, I come—
To cease thy suit, and leave me to my grief.
Tomorrow will I send.
ROM. So thrive my soul——
JUL. A thousand times good night! [*Exit.*]
ROM. A thousand times the worse, to want thy light.
Love goes toward love as schoolboys from their books,
But love from love toward school with heavy looks.
[*Retiring slowly.*]

[*Re-enter* JULIET, *above.*]

JUL. Hist! Romeo, hist!—Oh, for a falconer's° voice,
To lure this tassel-gentle° back again!
Bondage is hoarse,° and may not speak aloud,
Else would I tear the cave where Echo lies
And make her airy tongue more hoarse than mine
With repetition of my Romeo's name.
ROM. It is my soul that calls upon my name.
How silver-sweet sounds lovers' tongues by night,
Like softest music to attending ears!
JUL. Romeo!
ROM. My dear?°
JUL. At what o'clock tomorrow
Shall I send to thee?
ROM. At the hour of nine.
JUL. I will not fail. 'Tis twenty years till then.
I have forgot why I did call thee back.
ROM. Let me stand here till thou remember it.
JUL. I shall forget, to have thee still stand there,
Remembering how I love thy company.
ROM. And I'll still stay, to have thee still forget,
Forgetting any other home but this.
JUL. 'Tis almost morning. I would have thee gone,
And yet no farther than a wanton's° bird,
Who lets it hop a little from her hand,
Like a poor prisoner in his twisted gyves,°
And with a silk thread plucks it back again,
So loving-jealous of his liberty.

159. *falconer*: keeper of hawks. 160. *tassel-gentle*: male peregrine falcon. 161. *Bondage is hoarse*: i.e., being under the control of my parents, I can only whisper. 168. *My dear*: In Elizabethan times this was a phrase of tenderest affection. 178. *wanton*: spoiled child. 180. *gyves*: fetters.

ROM. I would I were thy bird.
JUL. Sweet, so would I.
Yet I should kill thee with much cherishing.
Good night, good night! Parting is such sweet sorrow
That I shall say good night till it be morrow. [*Exit.*]
ROM. Sleep dwell upon thine eyes, peace in thy breast!
Would I were sleep and peace, so sweet to rest!
Hence will I to my ghostly° father's cell,
His help to crave and my dear hap° to tell. [*Exit.*]

ACT III

SCENE V.

CAPULET'S *orchard.*

[*Enter* ROMEO *and* JULIET, *above, at the window.*]

JUL. Wilt thou be gone? It is not yet near day.
It was the nightingale, and not the lark,
That pierced the fearful hollow of thine ear.
Nightly she sings on yond pomegranate tree.
Believe me, love, it was the nightingale.
ROM. It was the lark, the herald of the morn,
No nightingale. Look, love, what envious streaks
Do lace° the severing clouds in yonder east.
Night's candles are burnt out, and jocund day
Stands tiptoe on the misty mountaintops.
I must be gone and live, or stay and die.
JUL. Yond light is not daylight, I know it, I.
It is some meteor that the sun exhales,°
To be to thee this night a torchbearer
And light thee on thy way to Mantua.
Therefore stay yet—thou need'st not to be gone.
ROM. Let me be ta'en, let me be put to death,
I am content, so thou wilt have it so.
I'll say yon gray is not the morning's eye,
'Tis but the pale reflex° of Cynthia's° brow;
Nor that is not the lark whose notes do beat
The vaulty heaven so high above our heads.
I have more care to stay than will to go.
Come, death, and welcome! Juliet wills it so.
How is 't, my soul? Let's talk. It is not day.
JUL. It is, it is. Hie hence, be gone, away!
It is the lark that sings so out of tune,

189. *ghostly*: spiritual. 190. *hap*: luck.
Sc. v: 8. *lace*: cover with stripes. 13. *exhales*: draws out. Cf. *I Hen IV*, V.i.19.
20. *reflex*: reflection. *Cynthia's*: the moon's.

Straining harsh discords and unpleasing sharps.
Some say the lark makes sweet division.°
This doth not so, for she divideth us.
Some say the lark and loathèd toad change eyes.°
Oh, now I would they had changed voices too!
Since arm from arm that voice doth us affray,°
Hunting thee hence with hunt's-up° to the day.
Oh, now be gone, more light and light it grows.
ROM. More light and light. More dark and dark our woes!

[*Enter* NURSE, *to the chamber.*]

NURSE. Madam!
JUL. Nurse?
NURSE. Your lady mother is coming to your chamber.
The day is broke, be wary, look about. [*Exit.*]
JUL. Then, window, let day in, and let life out.
ROM. Farewell, farewell! One kiss, and I'll descend. [*Descends.*]
JUL. Art thou gone so? Love, lord, ay, husband, friend!
I must hear from thee every day in the hour,
For in a minute there are many days.
Oh, by this count I shall be much in years
Ere I again behold my Romeo!
ROM. Farewell!
I will omit no opportunity
That may convey my greetings, love, to thee.
JUL. Oh, think'st thou we shall ever meet again?
ROM. I doubt it not, and all these woes shall serve
For sweet discourses in our time to come.
JUL. Oh God! I have an ill-divining soul.
Methinks I see thee, now thou art below,
As one dead in the bottom of a tomb.
Either my eyesight fails or thou look'st pale.
ROM. And trust me, love, in my eye so do you.
Dry sorrow drinks our blood.° Adieu, adieu! [*Exit.*]
JUL. O Fortune, Fortune, all men call thee fickle.
If thou art fickle, what dost thou with him
That is renowned for faith? Be fickle, Fortune,
For then, I hope, thou wilt not keep him long,
But send him back.

29. *division*: melody. 31. *change eyes*: The toad has bright eyes and a harsh croak, the lark dull eyes but a lovely voice. 33. *affray*: frighten. 34. *hunt's-up*: song played or sung in the early morning to arouse the hunters. 59. *Dry . . . blood*: Sighing was supposed to consume the heart's blood, hence Juliet's pallor.

VIII

THE MEASURE OF JUSTICE

The Passionate Will to Give Each Man What Is Rightfully His

INTRODUCTION

I

THE WORD *justice* usually summons up the familiar image of *legal* justice—that is, of a blindfolded goddess holding a pair of scales in one hand and a sword in the other. Her blindfold symbolizes that she is no respecter of persons. Her scales symbolize her duty to balance one claim against another. Her sword symbolizes her right, based on men's faith in justice, to enforce her decisions. Justice, then, is closely linked with measure, with the balancing of conflicting rights and duties. It implies a norm according to which an action may be deemed just or unjust.

When we think of justice in connection with literature we naturally think first of the countless poems, plays, stories, and essays that center around the famous trials of famous men. Religious literature is replete with versions of the prophet Daniel's defense of Susanna against the elders, of Solomon's choice of the true mother, of Herod's judicial murder of John the Baptist, and of the paramount Christian theme, the trial and death of Christ.

Secular literature is not less concerned with the drama of the trial. Plato's account of the trial and death of Socrates, Sophocles' drama of Antigone's defiance of the authority of Creon, Lope de Vega's score of plays in which honor disputes power and authority, the social dramas of Henrik Ibsen and George Bernard Shaw—all treat the theme of justice. The courtroom scene itself has become a favorite theatrical and fictional device for representing the typical modern conflict between the authority of legal institutions and the rights of the individual. Shaw's *St. Joan,* Robert Bolt's *A Man for All Seasons,*

Arthur Koestler's *Darkness at Noon,* and Franz Kafka's *The Trial* are but a few examples of the contemporary preference for presenting the theme of justice in a legal or quasi-legal setting.

Literary men, however, are not usually concerned solely with the outcome of a particular trial. True, they are interested in the personal fate of Joan of Arc and Thomas More, of Rubashov and K. They care greatly about the validity of a particular law and the correctness of the legal process, but they are more concerned with the nature of justice itself and its effect on man in general. For most writers justice is less a matter of written prescription than of unwritten law. Indeed, it is less a law in the usual sense than an ennobling virtue of the human heart whereby man ardently, constantly, and unstintingly wills to give his fellow man what is rightfully his. Justice thus becomes, in Joubert's words, "truth in action." It directs the way we act toward each other; it is the complement of love and the fruition of intelligence.

It is hardly a paradox that writers who are concerned with justice are actually more aware of injustice. Aristotle begins his philosophical treatment of justice by remarking that "the many forms of injustice make the many forms of justice quite clear." Similarly, the imaginative writer clarifies his idea of justice by attacking injustice. Injustice is always man's most familiar and his most overwhelming experience. The cry for justice is particularly compelling in our own times, perhaps because there are so many more people to be unjust to. Sensitive writers have heard that cry and have responded to it in much of their work, despite the fact that modern literary convention discourages the direct appeal to justice that was both expected and applauded in the past.

II

JAMES JOYCE's "Counterparts" is one of a sequence of stories from his *Dubliners,* a book that aimed to depict the moral decay of a time and a city. In "Counterparts" the author shows how one injustice provokes another, and how one man's cruelty initiates a cycle of disasters. For instance, when Mr. Alleyne insults Farrington and threatens to sack him for turning in shoddy work, the clerk seeks "the dark snug of O'Neill's shop" and consoles himself with a drink. Upon his return, Alleyne insults him again, this time in the presence of a lady. Farrington, never slow to anger, becomes enraged, botches his work, and begins to long for violence. "He felt strong enough to clear out the whole office single-handed. His body ached to do something, to rush out and revel in violence. All the indignities of his life enraged him." In his third encounter with Mr. Alleyne, he is again stung to resentment, but this time he responds with a kind of psychic aggression—a witty answer that provokes his employer to demand an immediate apology on penalty of immediate dismissal.

In the next sequence of incidents the cycle is repeated. Farrington and his cronies reconstruct the afternoon's exchange as they make the rounds of the pubs of Dublin. But, during the evening, Farrington experiences further frustrations. The acrobat Weathers twice bests him at arm wrestling. At the end of the evening, Farrington, "full of smoldering anger and resentment," goes home and takes out his resentment on his young son Tom, treating the boy even more harshly than he himself had been treated by Alleyne.

"Counterparts" is not concerned with the technicalities of justice, but with the human effects of injustice. Human brutality begets brutality and eventually the whip lashes not the one who merits it but an innocent bystander. Injustice, Joyce seems to say, finally leads to the sacrifice of a scapegoat.

Franz Kafka's "The Bucket-Rider" attacks another form of injustice. Instead of Joyce's naturalistic technique, however, Kafka employs fantasy. In bare, brief declarations, the narrator tells us that he has reached the point of death. Since the coal-dealer "has already grown deaf to ordinary appeals," the bucket-rider decides to startle him into compassion. He rides to the coal-dealer's house on his bucket. If hardness of heart made the coal-dealer deaf to ordinary appeals, hardness of head makes his wife immune to even the most extraordinary ones. The coal-dealer's wife "sees nothing and hears nothing," and the bucket-rider flies off to perish in the mountains of ice.

Kafka's tale is an allegory of justice. The basis of the bucket-rider's need is his right to live. He is asking for more than compassion; he is asking for justice—for his life. His ultimate appeal is to the commandment, "Thou shalt not kill."

Joseph Conrad's "Amy Foster" relates a tragedy that need never have happened had the people of Colebrook been just enough to grant the stranger in their midst his elemental rights as a human being.

The narrator, a wise and intelligent doctor, tells us how Yanko Gooral was victimized by a bogus emigration agency. His family was swindled of their meager goods in return for his being shipped—or rather "exported"—to America as a contract laborer. The ship, the doctor tells us, sank as it lay at anchor in a haven off the west coast of England during a storm. Yanko, the sole survivor, was washed ashore. He wandered—sick, dazed, and starving— about the English countryside. Although he approached the inhabitants of Colebrook as a humble beggar, he found "all the men angry and all the women fierce." The children that he met threw stones at him, and it was only Amy Foster, the Smith's hired girl, who showed compassion for him when he was locked up as a madman in her employer's woodshed.

Yanko is never accepted by the villagers, even though he rescues a local child from drowning. After much resistance, he succeeds in marrying Amy Foster, but he is still "foreign" and therefore suspect. He recites the Lord's prayer in a different language, he walks differently, he sings as he works. "*They* wouldn't in their dinner hour lie flat on their backs in the grass to stare at the sky. . . . Ah! He was different; innocent of heart, and full of good will, which nobody wanted, this castaway." When he sings and dances in the local pub, the villagers black his eye and toss him out. Amy, in the end, fails him too. When their child is born, Yanko is exalted. "There was a man now . . . to whom he could sing and talk in the language of his country, and show how to dance by and by." But, the doctor goes on, when he sings to the child in his native language, Amy snatches the baby away, as if to prevent Yanko from doing the child harm. Later when Yanko grows ill and feverish and calls for water in his strange tongue, Amy abandons him in fear:

> "She had left him—sick—helpless—thirsty. The spear of the hunter had entered his very soul. 'Why?' he cried, in the penetrating and indignant voice of a man calling to a responsible Maker. A gush of wind and a swish of rain answered.
>
> "And as I turned away to shut the door he pronounced the word 'Merciful!' and expired."

Conrad's tale, like Kafka's, reminds us that the enemies of justice are not always the violent and the powerful. They are also the ignorant and the falsely prudent. Amy Foster and her fellow villagers are afraid of what they do not understand. They confuse their ignorance and fear with common sense and sagacity.

Albert Camus' "The Guest" explores a paradox similar to that which appears in "Amy Foster." The schoolmaster, Daru, is a man of compassion. He is devoted to his lonely mission on the high Algerian plateau where he "live[s] almost like a monk in his remote schoolhouse." When the gendarme Balducci delivers an Arab prisoner and hands Daru the order to conduct him to the nearest town, the schoolmaster is resentful. Although the Arab is a murderer and not a political prisoner, Daru refuses to hand him over.

> That man's stupid crime revolted him, but to hand him over was contrary to honor. Merely thinking of it made him smart with humiliation. And he cursed at one and the same time his own people who had sent him this Arab and the Arab too who had dared to kill and not managed to get away.

The next day Daru leads his prisoner to a high lonely spot. He points to the east where the police are waiting for the Arab, then to the south where he can find shelter and safety among nomad tribes. He gives the Arab food and money and tells him to decide his own fate. The Arab chooses to turn himself in.

When Daru returns home he finds a message scrawled on the blackboard by the prisoner's friends warning him that he will pay the price of handing over their "brother." They, like the people of Colebrook, reject a love that they cannot understand. Just as Dr. Kennedy sees Yanko's life as a "supreme disaster of loneliness and despair," so Camus sees Daru as an outcast of absurd injustice. "In this vast landscape he had loved so much, he was alone."

Alan Paton's "Life for a Life" has all the immediacy of a newsreel documentary. Its setting is South Africa. The opening incident tells us of the brutal murder of Flip, a wealthy white landowner. We witness the interrogation of Enoch Maarman, Flip's native head shepherd at Kroon, by Robbertse, the white detective. Robbertse is a clever, ruthless fanatic who foams at the mouth with lust at the prospect of taking a life for a life.

The cruelty of injustice is evident in its effects on Sara Maarman, on Sara's brother, and on the police themselves. When the police seize Enoch, Sara meditates on his blameless life. Enoch had never hurt anyone in his whole life. He was, "like the great Christ . . . a lover of sheep and of little children, and had been a good husband and father. . . ." When she learns that Enoch is dead, she insists on knowing how he died and why he was buried so quickly and stealthily. The equivocal answers anger and depress her. She wants to leave "this land of stone."

Injustice has more serious effects on the police themselves. One, Robbertse, is already mad. The others are ashamed, even craven, when confronted with their complicity in judicial murder. Their humanity has been tainted, if not wholly destroyed. And Solomon Koopman, Sara's brother, learns once again to smile, to dissemble, to apologize in order to retain his means of livelihood, but in his heart grows a cold and implacable hatred.

III

JUSTICE, as we have been using the term, is the passionate will to give each man what is rightfully his own. But what indeed does "rightfully his own" mean? Did Camus' Arab have a right to his freedom? Did Daru have a right to give it to him? To what extent was Kafka's coal-dealer obliged to give the bucket-rider his scuttle of coal? Did Yanko Gooral have a right to sympathetic treatment in a foreign land? Conversely, were the Englishmen of Colebrook obliged to extend their friendship to Yanko? When does justice end and charity begin? Does "rightfully his own" mean that which is granted man by authority or that which is his by nature? These are but a few of the questions asked by sober-minded men; it is just such questions that courts have attempted to adjudicate and essayists have attempted to explore.

Jonathan Swift's "A Modest Proposal" is commonly regarded as one of the most devastating satires in English literature on injustice to the poor. Swift wrote it in order to shock the consciences of those authorities responsible for the conditions of the poor, and of the wealthy land-owning classes that they represented.

Swift achieves his purpose indirectly. Instead of arguing, in the manner of a lawyer, that the people are starving and that starvation destroys the peace of civil society and deprives it of future prosperity, he pretends to approve of the situation. Thus, he shames his audience into the realization that letting the poor starve to death is essentially as unjust as raising and marketing the children of the poor for food. The landlords, he remarks, with macabre irony, "as they have already devoured most of the parents, seem to have the best title to the children."

At the same time the manner of his argument mocks the mode of thinking that the unjust have traditionally employed in rationalizing their injustice. His tone echoes the sweet complacency of the well-to-do in their mouthing of rotund platitudes about economy, projects, the state of the kingdom, and the good of the commonwealth. He satirizes the indifference of the rich to suffering by reducing persons to statistics, as one does cattle and swine. He marshals his arguments under the heading of expediency, and he details with horrifying calmness the "advantages" of his proposal: increase of wealth and decrease of population. By the end of "A Modest Proposal" we realize that Swift means by the term "what is rightfully his" man's inalienable right to be treated as a human being. No rights, he says, however "legal," antecede the rights to life, to the respect of others, and to the liberty to pursue these rights.

James Baldwin's "Notes of a Native Son" is another indictment of injustice. The essay opens with the death of the author's father. "As we drove him to the graveyard, the spoils of injustice, anarchy, discontent, and hatred were all around us." Baldwin sees in his father's bitter life and difficult death a warning of what he himself might expect of the future, indeed, of what he himself had already experienced. At nineteen he "had discovered the weight of white people in the world."

Baldwin's autobiographical narrative differs from Swift's in that Baldwin is concerned with the situation of the Negro in twentieth-century America, whereas Swift, for all his interest in the economic situation of Ireland in 1729, is chiefly concerned with human nature in general. Swift deals with principles, Baldwin with personalities. Baldwin tells us how it feels to lose a job or to be refused a hamburger in a diner, and how a race riot can erupt from the volcanoes of ancient frustrations.

Yet both Swift and Baldwin talk to a common point: They recognize injustice as commonplace. But, as Baldwin phrases it, they also recognize that "one must never, in one's own life, accept these injustices as commonplace but must fight them with all one's strength."

The theme of justice evokes in men of letters, whether they be story tellers, essayists, or poets, an attitude of anguish. Hamlet's heartfelt cry: "The time is out of joint; O cursèd spite/ That ever I was born to set it right!" might well be the motto of many writers. Few writers have ever been satisfied with the state of human justice. At best, they grant injustice its day on earth but prophesy as Edwin Markham does that the meek "shall rise to judge the world,/ After the silence of the centuries," or agree with Roy Campbell that it is the serf who "Ploughs down palaces, and thrones, and towers." At worst, they accept A. E. Housman's bleak stoicism:

> . . . I muse for why and never find the reason,
> I pace the earth, and drink the air, and feel the sun.
> Be still, be still, my soul; it is but for a season:
> Let us endure an hour and see injustice done.

If anguish is the attitude of most writers, then the question must be asked: Is justice a practical human ideal, a fixed star, or a thirst never to be slaked, or a mirage forever receding in the desert of human greed and apathy?

One of the most provocative plays of our times, Ugo Betti's *Corruption in the Palace of Justice*, addresses itself to this question. This play, set in the present (it was written in 1944), takes place in an imaginary foreign city. Although the palace itself is sumptuous, it is "a maze." There is a bad smell in the air, due "to a dead rat or something, under one of the floorboards." There is also a metaphorical dead rat: a scandal that Counsellor Erzi is investigating. The rich and powerful Ludvi-Pol has been found dead in the palace, and suspicion points to the malfeasance of one of the judges.

The plot revolves around the hunt for the false judge, "the leper in their midst." First Vanan, then Croz, then Cust, are implicated. Each has betrayed justice; one through vanity, a second through cynicism, a third through a false subtlety of intellect. All are guilty, and all come to make their confessions. Cust, who resists the longest, is finally overwhelmed by his feeling of complicity in the death of Elena—the one truly loving and lovable person in the play. The final scene shows Cust slowly ascending the stairs to give himself up to the Lord High Chancellor.

At first glance *Corruption* seems to be, indeed is, a ruthless exposure of the shortcomings of human justice. One judge is as fallible or venal as another. Nor does Betti extend any hope for improvement in a more perfect future. Corrupt human nature can only breed corruption. Yet, while the two instruments of justice, laws and men, are corrupt, Betti sees justice itself as holy and immaculate. Himself a judge in Italy for many years, Betti offers this commentary on justice:

> In the soul of the unjust man, and even in the soul of the judge who betrays justice, we will discover that, in the end, he, himself, cannot breathe or survive without justice. Underneath the hardened bitterness we will, at a certain point, discover in the cruel, selfish, lost souls, a need for mercy, harmony, solidarity, immortality, trust, and, above all, for love: a mercy and a love which are far greater than the pale imitations offered by this world.

Hence, as R. W. Corrigan says of this play in *The New Theatre of Europe*, "Betti does not discard the forms of human justice, inadequate as they may be, for he sees in reality man's quest for justice is a quest for God."

Justice, then, like love, is a necessity of the human spirit. We are meant to be just; it is a measure of our humanity.

STORIES

James Joyce

COUNTERPARTS

THE BELL rang furiously and, when Miss Parker went to the tube, a furious voice called out in a piercing North of Ireland accent:

"Send Farrington here!"

Miss Parker returned to her machine, saying to a man who was writing at a desk:

"Mr. Alleyne wants you upstairs."

The man muttered "*Blast* him!" under his breath and pushed back his chair to stand up. When he stood up he was tall and of great bulk. He had a hanging face, dark wine-coloured, with fair eyebrows and moustache: his eyes bulged forward slightly and the whites of them were dirty. He lifted up the counter and, passing by the clients, went out of the office with a heavy step.

He went heavily upstairs until he came to the second landing, where a door bore a brass plate with the inscription *Mr. Alleyne.* Here he halted, puffing with labour and vexation, and knocked. The shrill voice cried:

"Come in!"

The man entered Mr. Alleyne's room. Simultaneously Mr. Alleyne, a little man wearing gold-rimmed glasses on a clean-shaven face, shot his head up over a pile of documents. The head itself was so pink and hairless it seemed like a large egg reposing on the papers. Mr. Alleyne did not lose a moment:

"Farrington? What is the meaning of this? Why have I always to complain of you? May I ask you why you haven't made a copy of that contract between Bodley and Kirwan? I told you it must be ready by four o'clock."

"But Mr. Shelley said, sir——"

"*Mr. Shelley said, sir.* . . . Kindly attend to what I say and not to what *Mr. Shelley says, sir.* You have always some excuse or another for shirking work. Let me tell you that if the contract is not copied before this evening I'll lay the matter before Mr. Crosbie. . . . Do you hear me now?"

"Yes, sir."

"Do you hear me now? . . . Ay and another little matter! I might as well be talking to the wall as talking to you. Understand once for all that you get a half an hour for your lunch and not an hour and a half. How many courses do you want, I'd like to know. . . . Do you mind me now?"

"Yes, sir."

Mr. Alleyne bent his head again upon his pile of papers. The man stared fixedly at the polished skull which directed the affairs of Crosbie & Alleyne, gauging its fragility. A spasm of rage gripped his throat for a few moments and then passed, leaving after it a sharp sensation of thirst. The man recognised the sensation and felt that he must have a good night's drinking. The middle of the month was passed and, if he could get the copy done in time, Mr. Alleyne might give him an order on the cashier. He stood still, gazing fixedly at the head upon the pile of papers. Suddenly Mr. Alleyne began to upset all the papers, searching for something. Then, as if he had been unaware of the man's presence till that moment, he shot up his head again, saying:

"Eh? Are you going to stand there all day? Upon my word, Farrington, you take things easy!"

"I was waiting to see . . ."

"Very good, you needn't wait to see. Go downstairs and do your work."

The man walked heavily towards the door and, as he went out of the room, he heard Mr. Alleyne cry after him that if the contract was not copied by evening Mr. Crosbie would hear of the matter.

He returned to his desk in the lower office and counted the sheets which remained to be copied. He took up his pen and dipped it in the ink but he continued to stare stupidly at the last words he had written: *In no case shall the said Bernard Bodley be* . . . The evening was falling and in a few minutes they would be lighting the gas: then he could write. He felt that he must slake the thirst in his throat. He stood up from his desk and, lifting the counter as before, passed out of the office. As he was passing out the chief clerk looked at him inquiringly.

"It's all right, Mr. Shelley," said the man, pointing with his finger to indicate the objective of his journey.

The chief clerk glanced at the hat-rack, but, seeing the row complete, offered no remark. As soon as he was on the landing the man pulled a shepherd's plaid cap out of his pocket, put it on his head and ran quickly down the rickety stairs. From the street door he walked on furtively on the inner side of the path towards the corner and all at once dived into a doorway. He was now safe in the dark snug of O'Neill's shop, and, filling up the little window that looked into the bar with his inflamed face, the colour of dark wine or dark meat, he called out:

"Here, Pat, give us a g.p., like a good fellow."

The curate brought him a glass of plain porter. The man drank it at a gulp and asked for a caraway seed. He put his penny on the counter and, leaving the curate to grope for it in the gloom, retreated out of the snug as furtively as he had entered it.

Darkness, accompanied by a thick fog, was gaining upon the dusk of February and the lamps in Eustace Street had been lit. The man went up by the houses until he reached the door of the office, wondering whether he could finish his copy in time. On the stairs a moist pungent odour of perfumes saluted his nose: evidently Miss Delacour had come while he was out in O'Neill's. He crammed his cap back again into his pocket and re-entered the office, assuming an air of absent mindedness.

"Mr. Alleyne has been calling for you," said the chief clerk severely. "Where were you?"

The man glanced at the two clients who were standing at the counter as if to intimate that their presence prevented him from answering. As the clients were both male the chief clerk allowed himself a laugh.

"I know that game," he said. "Five times in one day is a little bit. . . . Well, you better look sharp and get a copy of our correspondence in the Delacour case for Mr. Alleyne."

This address in the presence of the public, his run upstairs and the porter he had gulped down so hastily confused the man and, as he sat down at his desk to get what was required, he realised how hopeless was the task of finishing his copy of the contract before half past five. The dark damp night was coming and he longed to spend it in the bars, drinking with his friends amid the glare of gas and the clatter of glasses. He got out the Delacour correspondence and passed out of the office. He hoped Mr. Alleyne would not discover that the last two letters were missing.

The moist pungent perfume lay all the way up to Mr. Alleyne's room. Miss Delacour was a middle-aged woman of Jewish appearance. Mr. Alleyne was said to be sweet on her or on her money. She came to the office often and stayed a long time when she came. She was sitting beside his desk now in an aroma of perfumes, smoothing the handle of her umbrella and nodding the great black feather in her hat. Mr. Alleyne had swivelled his chair round to face her and thrown his right foot jauntily upon his left knee. The man put the correspondence on the desk and bowed respectfully but neither Mr. Alleyne nor Miss Delacour took any notice of his bow. Mr. Alleyne tapped a finger on the correspondence and then flicked it towards him as if to say: *"That's all right: you can go."*

The man returned to the lower office and sat down again at his desk. He stared intently at the incomplete phrase: *In no case shall the said Bernard Bodley be* . . . and thought how strange it was that the last three words began with the same letter. The chief clerk began to hurry Miss Parker, saying she would never have the letters typed in time for post. The man listened to the clicking of the machine for a few minutes and then set to work to finish his copy. But his head was not clear and his mind wandered away to the glare and rattle of the public-house. It was a night for hot punches. He struggled on with his copy, but when the clock struck five he had still fourteen pages to write. Blast it! He couldn't finish it in time. He longed to execrate aloud, to bring his fist down on something violently. He was so enraged that he wrote *Bernard Bernard* instead of *Bernard Bodley* and had to begin again on a clean sheet.

He felt strong enough to clear out the whole office single-handed. His body ached to do something, to rush out and revel in violence. All the indignities of his life enraged him. . . . Could he ask the cashier privately for an advance? No, the cashier was no good, no damn good: he wouldn't give an advance. . . . He knew where he would meet the boys: Leonard and O'Halloran and Nosey Flynn. The barometer of his emotional nature was set for a spell of riot.

His imagination had so abstracted him that his name was called twice before he answered. Mr. Alleyne and Miss Delacour were standing outside the counter and all the clerks had turned round in anticipation of something. The man got up from his desk. Mr. Alleyne began a tirade of abuse, saying that two letters were missing. The man answered that he knew nothing about them, that he had made a faithful copy. The tirade continued: it was so bitter and violent that the man could hardly restrain his fist from descending upon the head of the manikin before him:

"I know nothing about any other two letters," he said stupidly.

"*You—know—nothing*. Of course you know nothing," said Mr. Alleyne. "Tell me," he added, glancing first for approval to the lady beside him, "do you take me for a fool? Do you think me an utter fool?"

The man glanced from the lady's face to the little egg-shaped head and back again; and, almost before he was aware of it, his tongue had found a felicitous moment:

"I don't think, sir," he said, "that that's a fair question to put to me."

There was a pause in the very breathing of the clerks. Everyone was astounded (the author of the witticism no less than his neighbours) and Miss Delacour, who was a stout amiable person, began to smile broadly. Mr. Alleyne flushed to the hue of a wild rose and his mouth twitched with a dwarf's passion. He shook his fist in the man's face till it seemed to vibrate like the knob of some electric machine:

"You impertinent ruffian! You impertinent ruffian! I'll make short work of you! Wait till you see! You'll apologise to me for your impertinence or you'll quit the office instanter! You'll quit this, I'm telling you, or you'll apologise to me!"

He stood in a doorway opposite the office watching to see if the cashier would come out alone. All the clerks passed out and finally the cashier came out with the chief clerk. It was no use trying to say a word to him when he was with the chief clerk. The man felt that his position was bad enough. He had been obliged to offer an abject apology to Mr. Alleyne for his impertinence but he knew what a hornet's nest the office would be for him. He could remember the way in which Mr. Alleyne had hounded little Peake out of the office in order to make room for his own nephew. He felt savage and thirsty and revengeful, annoyed with himself and with everyone else. Mr. Alleyne would never give him an hour's rest; his life would be a hell to him. He had made a proper fool of himself this time. Could he not keep his tongue in his cheek? But they had never pulled together from the first, he and Mr. Alleyne, ever since the day Mr. Alleyne had overheard him mimicking his North of Ireland accent to amuse Higgins and Miss Parker: that had been the beginning of it. He might have tried Higgins for the money, but sure Higgins never had anything for himself. A man with two establishments to keep up, of course he couldn't. . . .

He felt his great body again aching for the comfort of the public-house. The fog had begun to chill him and he wondered could he touch Pat in O'Neill's. He could not touch him for more than a bob —and a bob was no use. Yet he must get money somewhere or other: he had spent his last penny for the g.p. and soon it would be too late for getting money anywhere. Suddenly, as he was fingering his watch-chain, he thought of Terry Kelly's pawn-office in Fleet Street. That was the dart! Why didn't he think of it sooner?

He went through the narrow alley of Temple Bar quickly, muttering to himself that they could all go to hell because he was going to have a good night of it. The clerk in Terry Kelly's said A *crown!* but the consignor held out for six shillings; and in the end the six shillings was allowed him literally. He came out of the pawn-office joyfully, making a little cylinder of the coins between his thumb and fingers. In Westmoreland Street the footpaths were crowded with young men and women returning from business and ragged urchins ran here and there yelling out the names of the evening editions. The man passed through the crowd, looking on the spectacle generally with proud satisfaction and staring masterfully at the office-girls. His head was full of the noises of tram-gongs and swishing trolleys and his nose already sniffed the curling fumes of punch. As he walked on he preconsidered the terms in which he would narrate the incident to the boys:

"So, I just looked at him—coolly, you know, and looked at her. Then I looked back at him again—taking my time, you know. 'I don't think that that's a fair question to put to me,' says I."

Nosey Flynn was sitting up in his usual corner of Davy Byrne's and, when he heard the story, he stood Farrington a half-one, saying it was as smart a thing as ever he heard. Farrington stood a drink in his turn. After a while O'Halloran and Paddy Leonard came in and the story was repeated to them. O'Halloran stood tailors of malt, hot, all round and told the story of the retort he had made to the chief clerk when he was in Callan's of Fownes's Street; but, as the retort was after the manner of the liberal shepherds in the eclogues, he had to admit that it was not as clever as Farrington's retort. At this Farrington told the boys to polish off that and have another.

Just as they were naming their poisons who should come in but Higgins! Of course he had to join in with the others. The men asked him to give his version of it, and he did so with great vivacity for the sight of five small hot whiskies was very exhilarating. Everyone roared laughing when he showed the way in which Mr. Alleyne shook his fist in Farrington's face. Then he imitated Farrington, saying, "*And here was my nabs, as cool as you please,*" while Farrington looked at the company out of his heavy dirty eyes, smiling and at times drawing forth stray drops of liquor from his moustache with the aid of his lower lip.

When that round was over there was a pause. O'Halloran had money but neither of the other two seemed to have any; so the whole party left the shop somewhat regretfully. At the corner of Duke Street Higgins and Nosey Flynn bevelled off to the left while the other three turned back towards the city. Rain was drizzling down on the cold streets and, when they reached the Ballast Office, Farrington suggested the Scotch House. The bar was full of men and loud with the noise of tongues and glasses. The three men pushed past the whining match-sellers at the door and formed a little party at the corner of the counter. They began to exchange stories. Leonard introduced them to a young fellow named Weathers who was performing at the Tivoli as an acrobat and knockabout *artiste*. Farrington stood a drink all round. Weathers said he would take a small

Irish and Apollinaris. Farrington, who had definite notions of what was what, asked the boys would they have an Apollinaris too; but the boys told Tim to make theirs hot. The talk became theatrical. O'Halloran stood a round and then Farrington stood another round, Weathers protesting that the hospitality was too Irish. He promised to get them in behind the scenes and introduce them to some nice girls. O'Halloran said that he and Leonard would go, but that Farrington wouldn't go because he was a married man; and Farrington's heavy dirty eyes leered at the company in token that he understood he was being chaffed. Weathers made them all have just one little tincture at his expense and promised to meet them later on at Mulligan's in Poolbeg Street.

When the Scotch House closed they went round to Mulligan's. They went into the parlour at the back and O'Halloran ordered small hot specials all round. They were all beginning to feel mellow. Farrington was just standing another round when Weathers came back. Much to Farrington's relief he drank a glass of bitter this time. Funds were getting low but they had enough to keep them going. Presently two young women with big hats and a young man in a check suit came in and sat at a table close by. Weathers saluted them and told the company that they were out of the Tivoli. Farrington's eyes wandered at every moment in the direction of one of the young women. There was something striking in her appearance. An immense scarf of peacock-blue muslin was wound round her hat and knotted in a great bow under her chin; and she wore bright yellow gloves, reaching to the elbow. Farrington gazed admiringly at the plump arm which she moved very often and with much grace; and when, after a little time, she answered his gaze he admired still more her large dark brown eyes. The oblique staring expression in them fascinated him. She glanced at him once or twice and, when the party was leaving the room, she brushed against his chair and said "*O, pardon!*" in a London accent. He watched her leave the room in the hope that she would look back at him, but he was disappointed. He cursed his want of money and cursed all the rounds he had stood, particularly all the whiskies and Apollinaris which he had stood to Weathers. If there was one thing that he hated it was a sponge. He was so angry that he lost count of the conversation of his friends.

When Paddy Leonard called him he found that they were talking about feats of strength. Weathers was showing his biceps muscle to the company and boasting so much that the other two had called on Farrington to uphold the national honour. Farrington pulled up his sleeve accordingly and showed his biceps muscle to the company. The two arms were examined and compared and finally it was agreed to have a trial of strength. The table was cleared and the two men rested their elbows on it, clasping hands. When Paddy Leonard said "*Go!*" each was to try to bring down the other's hand on to the table. Farrington looked very serious and determined.

The trial began. After about thirty seconds Weathers brought his opponent's hand slowly down on to the table. Farrington's dark wine coloured face flushed darker still with anger and humiliation at having been defeated by such a stripling.

"You're not to put the weight of your body behind it. Play fair," he said.

"Who's not playing fair?" said the other.

"Come on again. The two best out of three."

The trial began again. The veins stood out on Farrington's forehead, and the pallor of Weathers' complexion changed to peony. Their hands and arms trembled under the stress. After a long struggle Weathers again brought his opponent's hand slowly on to the table. There was a murmur of applause from the spectators. The curate, who was standing beside the table, nodded his red head towards the victor and said with stupid familiarity:

"Ah! that's the knack!"

"What the hell do you know about it?" said Farrington fiercely, turning on the man. "What do you put in your gab for?"

"Sh, sh!" said O'Halloran, observing the violent expression of Farrington's face. "Pony up, boys. We'll have just one little smahan more and then we'll be off."

A very sullen-faced man stood at the corner of O'Connell Bridge waiting for the little Sandy-mount tram to take him home. He was full of smouldering anger and revengefulness. He felt humiliated and discontented; he did not even feel drunk; and he had only twopence in his pocket. He cursed everything. He had done for himself in the office, pawned his watch, spent all his money; and he had not even got drunk. He began to feel thirsty again and he longed to be back again in the hot reeking public-house. He had lost his reputation as a strong man, having been defeated twice by a mere boy. His heart swelled with fury and, when he thought of the woman in the big hat who had brushed against him and said *Pardon!* his fury nearly choked him.

His tram let him down at Shelbourne Road and he steered his great body along in the shadow of the wall of the barracks. He loathed returning to his home. When he went in by the side-door he found the kitchen empty and the kitchen fire nearly out. He bawled upstairs:

"Ada! Ada!"

His wife was a little sharp-faced woman who bullied her husband when he was sober and was bullied by him when he was drunk. They had five children. A little boy came running down the stairs.

"Who is that?" said the man, peering through the darkness.

"Me, pa."

"Who are you? Charlie?"

"No, pa. Tom."

"Where's your mother?"

"She's out at the chapel."

"That's right. . . . Did she think of leaving any dinner for me?"

"Yes, pa. I——"

"Light the lamp. What do you mean by having the place in darkness? Are the other children in bed?"

The man sat down heavily on one of the chairs while the little boy lit the lamp. He began to mimic his son's flat accent, saying half to himself: *"At the chapel. At the chapel, if you please!"* When the lamp was lit he banged his fist on the table and shouted:

"What's for my dinner?"

"I'm going . . . to cook it, pa," said the little boy.

The man jumped up furiously and pointed to the fire.

"On that fire! You let the fire out! By God, I'll teach you to do that again!"

He took a step to the door and seized the walking-stick which was standing behind it.

"I'll teach you to let the fire out!" he said, rolling up his sleeve in order to give his arm free play.

The little boy cried *"O, pa!"* and ran whimpering round the table, but the man followed him and caught him by the coat. The little boy looked about him wildly but, seeing no way of escape, fell upon his knees.

"Now, you'll let the fire out the next time!" said the man, striking at him vigorously with the stick. "Take that, you little whelp!"

The boy uttered a squeal of pain as the stick cut his thigh. He clasped his hands together in the air and his voice shook with fright.

"O, pa!" he cried. "Don't beat me, pa! And I'll . . . I'll say a *Hail Mary* for you. . . . I'll say a *Hail Mary* for you, pa, if you don't beat me. . . . I'll say a *Hail Mary*. . . ."

Franz Kafka

THE BUCKET-RIDER

COAL all spent; the bucket empty; the shovel useless; the stove breathing out cold; the room freezing; the leaves outside the window rigid, covered with rime; the sky a silver shield against any-one who looks for help from it. I must have coal; I cannot freeze to death; behind me is the pitiless stove, before me the pitiless sky, so I must ride out between them and on my journey seek aid from the coal-dealer. But he has already grown deaf to ordinary appeals; I must prove irrefutably to him that I have not a single grain of coal left, and that he means to me the very sun in the firmament. I must approach like a beggar who, with the death-rattle already in his throat, insists on dying on the doorstep, and to whom the grand people's cook accordingly decides to give the dregs of the coffee-pot; just so must the coal-dealer, filled with rage, but acknowledging the command, "Thou shalt not kill," fling a shovelful of coal into my bucket.

My mode of arrival must decide the matter; so I ride off on the bucket. Seated on the bucket, my hands on the handle, the simplest kind of bridle, I propel myself with difficulty down the stairs; but once down below my bucket ascends, superbly, superbly; camels humbly squatting on the ground do not rise with more dignity, shaking themselves under the sticks of their drivers. Through the hard frozen streets we go at a regular canter; often I am upraised as high as the first story of a house; never do I sink as low as the house doors. And at last I float at an extraordinary height above the vaulted cellar of the dealer, whom I see far below crouching over his table, where he is writing; he has opened the door to let out the excessive heat.

"Coal-dealer!" I cry in a voice burned hollow by the frost and muffled in the cloud made by my breath, "please, coal-dealer, give me a little coal. My bucket is so light that I can ride on it. Be kind. When I can I'll pay you."

The dealer puts his hand to his ear. "Do I hear rightly?" He throws the question over his shoulder to his wife."Do I hear rightly? A customer."

"I hear nothing," says his wife, breathing in and out peacefully while she knits on, her back pleasantly warmed by the heat.

"Oh, yes, you must hear," I cry. "It's me; an old customer; faithful and true; only without means at the moment."

THE BUCKET-RIDER: Reprinted by permission of Schocken Books, Inc., from *The Penal Colony* by Franz Kafka. Translated by Willa and Edwin Muir.

"Wife," says the dealer, "it's some one, it must be; my ears can't have deceived me so much as that; it must be an old, a very old customer, that can move me so deeply."

"What ails you, man?" says his wife, ceasing from her work for a moment and pressing her knitting to her bossom. "It's nobody, the street is empty, all our customers are provided for; we could close down the shop for several days and take a rest."

"But I'm sitting up here on the bucket," I cry, and unfeeling frozen tears dim my eyes, "please look up here, just once; you'll see me directly; I beg you, just a shovelful; and if you give me more it'll make me so happy that I won't know what to do. All the other customers are provided for. Oh, if I could only hear the coal clattering into the bucket!"

"I'm coming," says the coal-dealer, and on his short legs he makes to climb the steps of the cellar, but his wife is already beside him, holds him back by the arm and says: "You stay here; seeing you persist in your fancies I'll go myself. Think of the bad fit of coughing you had during the night. But for a piece of business, even if it's one you've only fancied in your head, you're prepared to forget your wife and child and sacrifice your lungs. I'll go."

"Then be sure to tell him all the kinds of coal we have in stock; I'll shout out the prices after you."

"Right," says his wife, climbing up to the street. Naturally she sees me at once. "Frau Coal-dealer," I cry, "my humblest greetings; just one shovelful of coal; here in my bucket; I'll carry it home myself. One shovelful of the worst you have. I'll pay you in full for it, of course, but not just now, not just now." What a knell-like sound the words "not just now" have, and how bewilderingly they mingle with the evening chimes that fall from the church steeple nearby!

"Well, what does he want?" shouts the dealer. "Nothing," his wife shouts back, "there's nothing here; I see nothing, I hear nothing; only six striking, and now we must shut up the shop. The cold is terrible; tomorrow we'll likely have lots to do again."

She sees nothing and hears nothing; but all the same she loosens her apron-strings and waves her apron to waft me away. She succeeds, unluckily. My bucket has all the virtues of a good steed except powers of resistance, which it has not; it is too light; a woman's apron can make it fly through the air.

"You bad woman!" I shout back, while she, turning into the shop, half-contemptuous, half-reassured, flourishes her fist in the air. "You bad woman! I begged you for a shovelful of the worst coal and you would not give me it." And with that I ascend into the regions of the ice mountains and am lost forever.

Joseph Conrad
AMY FOSTER

KENNEDY is a country doctor, and lives in Colebrook, on the shores of Eastbay. The high ground rising abruptly behind the red roofs of the little town crowds the quaint High Street against the wall which defends it from the sea. Beyond the sea wall there curves for miles in a vast and regular sweep the barren beach of shingle, with the village of Brenzett standing out darkly across the water, a spire in a clump of trees; and still farther out the perpendicular column of a lighthouse, looking in the distance no bigger than a lead pencil, marks the vanishing point of the land. The country at the back of Brenzett is low and flat; but the bay is fairly well sheltered from the seas, and occasionally a big ship, windbound or through stress of weather, makes use of the anchoring ground a mile and a half due north from you as you stand at the back door of the "Ship Inn" in Brenzett. A dilapidated windmill near by, lifting its shattered arms from a mound no loftier than a rubbish heap, and a Martello tower squatting at the water's edge half a mile to the south of the Coastguard cottages, are familiar to the skippers of small craft. These are the official seamarks for the patch of trustworthy bottom represented on the Admiralty charts by an irregular oval of dots enclosing several figure sixes, with a tiny anchor engraved among them, and the legend "mud and shells" over all.

The brow of the upland overtops the square tower of the Colebrook Church. The slope is green and looped by a white road. Ascending along this road, you open a valley broad and shallow, a wide green trough of pastures and hedges merging inland into a vista of purple tints and flowing lines closing the view.

In this valley down to Brenzett and Colebrook and up to Darnford, the market town fourteen miles away, lies the practice of my friend Kennedy. He had begun life as surgeon in the Navy, and afterwards had been the companion of a famous traveler, in the days when there were continents with unexplored interiors. His papers on the fauna and flora made him known to scientific societies. And now he had come to a country practice—from choice. The penetrating power of his mind, acting like a corrosive fluid, had destroyed his ambition, I fancy. His intelligence is of a scientific order, of an investigating

---

habit, and of that unappeasable curiosity which believes that there is a particle of a general truth in every mystery.

A good many years ago now, on my return from abroad, he invited me to stay with him. I came readily enough, and as he could not neglect his patients to keep me company, he took me on his rounds—thirty miles or so of an afternoon, sometimes. I waited for him on the roads; the horse reached after the leafy twigs, and, sitting high in the dogcart, I could hear Kennedy's laugh through the half-open door of some cottage. He had a big, hearty laugh that would have fitted a man twice his size, a brisk manner, a bronzed face, and a pair of gray, profoundly attentive eyes. He had the talent of making people talk to him freely, and an inexhaustible patience in listening to their tales.

One day, as we trotted out of a large village into a shady bit of road, I saw on our left hand a low, black cottage, with diamond panes in the windows, a creeper on the end wall, a roof of shingle, and some roses climbing on the rickety trelliswork of the tiny porch. Kennedy pulled up to a walk. A woman, in full sunlight, was throwing a dripping blanket over a line stretched between two old apple trees. And as the bobtailed, long-necked chestnut, trying to get his head, jerked the left hand, covered by a thick dogskin glove, the doctor raised his voice over the hedge: "How's your child, Amy?"

I had time to see her dull face, red, not with a mantling blush, but as if her flat cheeks had been vigorously slapped, and to take in the squat figure, the scanty, dusty brown hair drawn into a tight knot at the back of the head. She looked quite young. With a distinct catch in her breath, her voice sounded low and timid.

"He's well, thank you."

We trotted again. "A young patient of yours," I said; and the doctor, flicking the chestnut absently, muttered, "Her husband used to be."

"She seems a dull creature," I remarked, listlessly.

"Precisely," said Kennedy. "She is very passive. It's enough to look at the red hands hanging at the end of those short arms, at those slow, prominent brown eyes, to know the inertness of her mind—an inertness that one would think made it everlastingly safe from all the surprises of imagination. And yet which of us is safe? At any rate, such as you see her, she had enough imagination to fall in love. She's the daughter of one Isaac Foster, who from a small farmer has sunk into a shepherd; the beginning of his misfortunes dating from his runaway marriage with the cook of his widowed father—a well-to-do, apoplectic grazier, who passionately struck his name off his will, and had been heard to utter threats against his life. But this old affair, scandalous enough to serve as a motive for a Greek tragedy, arose from the similarity of their characters. There are other tragedies, less scandalous and of a subtler poignancy, arising from irreconcilable differences and from that fear of the Incomprehensible that hangs over all our heads—over all our heads. . . ."

The tired chestnut dropped into a walk; and the rim of the sun, all red in a speckless sky, touched familiarly the smooth top of a plowed rise near the road as I had seen it times innumerable touch the distant horizon of the sea. The uniform brownness of the harrowed field glowed with a rose tinge, as though the powdered clods had sweated out in minute pearls of blood the toil of uncounted plowmen. From the edge of a copse a wagon with two horses was rolling gently along the ridge. Raised above our heads upon the skyline, it loomed up against the red sun, triumphantly big, enormous, like a chariot of giants drawn by two slow-stepping steeds of legendary proportions. And the clumsy figure of the man plodding at the head of the leading horse projected itself on the background of the Infinite with a heroic uncouthness. The end of his carter's whip quivered high up in the blue. Kennedy discoursed.

"She's the eldest of a large family. At the age of fifteen they put her out to service at the New Barns Farm. I attended Mrs. Smith, the tenant's wife, and saw that girl there for the first time. Mrs. Smith, a genteel person with a sharp nose, made her put on a black dress every afternoon. I don't know what induced me to notice her at all. There are faces that call your attention by a curious want of definiteness in their whole aspect, as, walking in a mist, you peer attentively at a vague shape which, after all, may be nothing more curious or strange than a signpost. The only peculiarity I perceived in her was a slight hesitation in her utterance, a sort of preliminary stammer which passes away with the first word. When sharply spoken to, she was apt to lose her head at once; but her heart was of the kindest. She had never been heard to express a dislike for a single human being, and she was tender to every living creature. She was devoted to Mrs. Smith, to Mr. Smith, to their dogs, cats, canaries; and as to Mrs. Smith's gray parrot, its peculiarities exercised upon her a positive fascination. Nevertheless, when that outlandish bird, attacked by the cat, shrieked for help in human accents, she ran out into the yard stopping her ears, and did not prevent the crime. For Mrs. Smith this was another evidence of her stupidity; on the other hand, her want of charm, in view of Smith's well-known frivolousness, was a great recommendation. Her shortsighted eyes would swim with pity for a poor mouse in a trap, and she had been seen once by some boys on her knees in the wet grass helping a toad in difficulties. If it's true, as some German fellow has said, that without phosphorus there is no thought, it is still more true that there is no kindness of heart without a certain amount of imagination. She had some. She had even more than is necessary to understand suffering and to be moved by pity. She fell in love under circumstances that leave no room for doubt in the matter; for you need imagination to form a notion of beauty at all, and still more to discover your ideal in an unfamiliar shape.

"How this aptitude came to her, what it did feed upon, is an inscrutable mystery. She was born in the village, and had never been farther away from it than Colebrook or perhaps Darnford. She lived for four years with the Smiths. New Barns is an isolated farmhouse a mile away from the road, and she was content to look day after day at the same fields, hollows, rises; at the trees and the hedgerows; at the faces of the four men about the farm, always the same—day after day, month after month, year after year. She never showed a desire for conversation, and, as it seemed to me, she did not know how to smile. Sometimes of a fine Sunday afternoon she would put on her best dress, a pair of stout boots, a large gray hat trimmed with a black feather (I've seen her in that finery), seize an absurdly slender parasol, climb over two stiles, tramp over three fields and along two hundred yards of road—never farther. There stood Foster's cottage. She would help her mother to give their tea to the younger children, wash up the crockery, kiss the little ones, and go back to the farm. That was all. All the rest, all the change, all the relaxation. She never seemed to wish for anything more. And then she fell in love. She fell in love silently, obstinately—perhaps helplessly. It came slowly, but when it came it worked like a powerful spell; it was love as the ancients understood it: an irresistible and fateful impulse—a possession! Yes, it was in her to become haunted and possessed by a face, by a presence, fatally, as though she had been a pagan worshiper of form under a joyous sky—and to be awakened at last from that mysterious forgetfulness of self, from that enchantment, from that transport, by a fear resembling the unaccountable terror of a brute. . . ."

With the sun hanging low on its western limit, the expanse of the grasslands framed in the counterscarps of the rising ground took on a gorgeous and somber aspect. A sense of penetrating sadness, like that inspired by a grave strain of music, disengaged itself from the silence of the fields. The men we met walked past, slow, unsmiling, with downcast eyes, as if the melancholy of an overburdened earth had weighted their feet, bowed their shoulders, borne down their glances.

"Yes," said the doctor to my remark, "one would think the earth is under a curse, since of all her children these that cling to her the closest are uncouth in body and as leaden of gait as if their very hearts were loaded with chains. But here on this same road you might have seen amongst these heavy men a being lithe, supple and long-limbed, straight like a pine, with something striving upwards in his appearance as though the heart within him had been buoyant. Perhaps it was only the force of the contrast, but when he was passing one of these villagers here, the slopes of his feet did not seem to me to touch the dust of the road. He vaulted over the stiles, paced these slopes with a long elastic stride that made him noticeable at a great distance, and had lustrous black eyes. He was so different from the mankind around that, with his freedom of movement, his soft—a little startled—glance, his olive complexion and graceful bearing, his humanity suggested to me the nature of a woodland creature. He came from there."

The doctor pointed with his whip, and from the summit of the descent seen over the rolling tops of the trees in a park by the side of the road, appeared the level sea far below us, like the floor of an immense edifice inlaid with bands of dark ripple, with still trails of glitter, ending in a belt of glassy water at the foot of the sky. The light blur of smoke, from an invisible steamer, faded on the great clearness of the horizon like the mist of a breath on a mirror; and, inshore, the white sails of a coaster, with the appearance of disentangling themselves slowly from under the branches, floated clear of the foliage of the trees.

"Shipwrecked in the bay?" I said.

"Yes; he was a castaway. A poor emigrant from Central Europe bound to America and washed ashore here in a storm. And for him, who knew nothing of the earth, England was an undiscovered country. It was some time before he learned its name; and for all I know he might have expected to find wild beasts or wild men here, when, crawling in the dark over the sea wall, he rolled down the other side into a dyke, where it was another miracle he didn't get drowned. But he struggled instinctively like an animal under a net, and this blind struggle threw him out into a field. He must have been, indeed, of a tougher fiber than he looked to withstand without expiring such buffetings, the violence of his exertions, and so much fear. Later on, in his broken English that resembled curiously the speech of a young child, he told me himself that he put his trust in God, believing he was no longer in this world. And truly—he would add—how was he to know? He fought his way against the rain and the gale on all fours, and crawled at last among some sheep huddled close under the lee of a hedge. They ran off in all directions, bleating in the darkness, and he welcomed the first familiar sound he heard on these shores. It must have been two in the morning then. And this is all we know of the manner of his landing, though he did not arrive unattended by any means. Only his grisly company did not begin to come ashore till much later in the day. . . ."

The doctor gathered the reins, clicked his tongue; we trotted down the hill. Then turning, almost directly, a sharp corner into High Street, we rattled over the stones and were home.

Late in the evening Kennedy, breaking a spell of moodiness that had come over him, returned to the story. Smoking his pipe, he paced the long room from end to end. A reading lamp concentrated all its light upon the papers on his desk; and, sitting by the open window, I saw, after the windless, scorching day, the frigid splendor of a hazy sea lying motionless under the moon. Not a whisper, not a splash, not a stir of the shingle, not a footstep, not a sigh came up from the earth below—never a sign of life but the scent of climbing jasmine; and Kennedy's voice, speaking behind me, passed through the wide casement, to vanish outside in a chill and sumptuous stillness.

". . . The relations of shipwrecks in the olden times tell us of much suffering. Often the castaways were only saved from drowning to die miserably from starvation on a barren coast; others suffered violent death or else slavery, passing through years of precarious existence with people to whom their strangeness was an object of suspicion, dislike or fear. We read about these things, and they are very pitiful. It is indeed hard upon a man to find himself a lost stranger, helpless, incomprehensible, and of a mysterious origin, in some obscure corner of the earth. Yet amongst all the adventurers shipwrecked in all the wild parts of the world, there is not one, it seems to me, that ever had to suffer a fate so simply tragic as the man I am speaking of, the most innocent of adventurers cast out by the sea in the bight of this bay, almost within sight from this very window.

"He did not know the name of his ship. Indeed, in the course of time we discovered he did not even know that ships had names—'like Christian people'; and when, one day, from the top of Talfourd Hill, he beheld the sea lying open to his view, his eyes roamed afar, lost in an air of wild surprise, as though he had never seen such a sight before. And probably he had not. As far as I could make out, he had been hustled together with many others on board an emigrant ship at the mouth of the Elbe, too bewildered to take note of his surroundings, too weary to see anything, too anxious to care. They were driven below into the 'tween-deck and battened down from the very start. It was a low timber dwelling—he would say—with wooden beams overhead, like the houses in his country, but you went into it down a ladder. It was very large, very cold, damp and somber, with places in the manner of wooden boxes where people had to sleep one above another, and it kept on rocking all ways at once all the time. He crept into one of these boxes and lay down there in the clothes in which he had left his home many days before, keeping his bundle and his stick by his side. People groaned, children cried, water dripped, the lights went out, the walls of the place creaked, and everything was being shaken so that in one's little box one dared not lift one's head. He had lost touch with his only companion (a young man from the same valley, he said), and all the time a great noise of wind went on outside and heavy blows fell—boom! boom! An awful sickness overcame him, even to the point of making him neglect his prayers. Besides, one could not tell whether it was morning or evening. It seemed always to be night in that place.

"Before that he had been traveling a long, long time on the iron track. He looked out of the window, which had a wonderfully clear glass in it, and the trees, the houses, the fields, and the long roads seemed to fly round and round about him till his head swam. He gave me to understand that he had on his passage beheld uncounted multitudes of people—whole nations—all dressed in such clothes as the rich wear. Once he was made to get out of the carriage, and slept through a night on a bench in a house of bricks with his bundle under his head; and once for many hours he had to sit on a floor of flat stones, dozing, with his knees up and with his bundle between his feet. There was a roof over him, which seemed made of glass, and was so high that the tallest mountain pine he had ever seen would have had room to grow under it. Steam machines rolled in at one end and out at the other. People swarmed more than you can see on a feast day round the miraculous Holy Image in the yard of the Carmelite Convent down in the plains where, before he left his home, he drove his mother in a wooden cart—a pious old woman who wanted to offer prayers and make a vow for his safety. He could not give me an idea of how large and lofty and full of noise and smoke and gloom, and clang of iron, the place was, but someone had told him it was called Berlin. Then they rang a bell, and another steam machine came in, and again he was taken on and on through a land that wearied his eyes by its flatness without a single bit of a hill to be seen anywhere. One more night he spent shut up in a building like a good stable with a litter of straw on the floor, guarding his bundle amongst a lot of men, of whom not one could understand a single word he said. In the morning they were all led down to the stony shores of an extremely broad muddy river, flowing not between hills but between houses that seemed immense. There was a steam machine that went on the water, and they all stood upon it packed tight, only now there were with them many women and children who made much noise. A cold rain fell, the wind blew in his face; he was wet through, and his teeth chattered. He and the young man from the same valley took each other by the hand.

"They thought they were being taken to America straight away, but suddenly the steam machine bumped against the side of a thing like a great house on the water. The walls were smooth and black, and there uprose, growing from the roof as it were, bare trees in the shape of crosses, extremely high. That's how it appeared to him then, for he had never seen a ship before. This was the ship that was going to swim all the way to America. Voices shouted, everything swayed; there was a ladder dipping up and down. He went up on his hands and knees in mortal fear of falling into the water below, which made a great splashing. He got separated from his companion, and when he descended into the bottom of that ship his heart seemed to melt suddenly within him.

"It was then also, as he told me, that he lost contact for good and all with one of those three men who the summer before had been going about through all the little towns in the foothills of his country. They would arrive on market days driving in a peasant's cart, and would set up an office in an inn or some other Jew's house. There were three of them, of whom one with a long beard looked venerable; and they had red cloth collars round their necks and gold lace on their sleeves like Government officials. They sat proudly behind a long table; and in the next room, so that the common people shouldn't hear, they kept a cunning telegraph machine, through which they could talk to the Emperor of America. The fathers hung about the door, but the young men of the mountains would crowd up to the table asking many questions, for there was work to be got all the year round at three dollars a day in America, and no military service to do.

"But the American Kaiser would not take everybody. Oh, no! He himself had great difficulty in getting accepted, and the venerable man in uniform had to go out of the room several times to work the telegraph on his behalf. The American Kaiser engaged him at last at three dollars, he being young and strong. However, many able young men backed out, afraid of the great distance; besides, those only who had some money could be taken. There were some who sold their huts and their land because it cost a lot of money to get to America; but then, once there, you had three dollars a day, and if you were clever you could find places where true gold could be picked up on the ground. His father's house was getting over-full. Two of his brothers were married and had children. He promised to send money home from America by post twice a year. His father sold an old cow, a pair of piebald mountain ponies of his own raising, and a cleared plot of fair pasture land on the sunny slope of a pine-clad pass to a Jew innkeeper, in order to pay the people of the ship that took men to America to get rich in a short time.

"He must have been a real adventurer at heart, for how many of the greatest enterprises in the conquest of the earth had for their beginning just such a bargaining away of the paternal cow for the mirage or true gold far away! I have been telling you more or less in my own words what I learned fragmentarily in the course of two or three years, during which I seldom missed an opportunity of a friendly chat with him. He told me this story of his adventure with many flashes of white teeth and lively glances of black eyes, at first in a sort of anxious baby-talk, then, as he acquired the language, with great fluency, but always with that singing, soft, and at the same time vibrating intonation that instilled a strangely penetrating power into the sound of the most familiar English words, as if they had been the words of an unearthly language. And he always would come to an end, with many emphatic shakes of his head, upon that awful sensation of his heart melting within him directly he set foot on board that ship. Afterwards there seemed to come for him a period of blank ignorance, at any rate as to facts. No doubt he must have been abominably sea-sick and abominably unhappy—this soft and passionate adventurer, taken thus out of his knowledge, and feeling bitterly as he lay in his emigrant bunk his utter loneliness; for his was a highly sensitive nature. The next thing we know of him for certain is that he had been hiding in Hammond's pig-pound by the side of the road to Norton, six miles, as the crow flies, from the sea. Of these experiences he was unwilling to speak: they seemed to have seared into his soul a somber sort of wonder and indignation. Through the rumors of the country-side, which lasted for a good many days after his arrival, we know that the fishermen of West Colebrook had been disturbed and startled by heavy knocks against the walls of weatherboard cottages, and by a voice crying piercingly strange words in the night. Several of them turned out even, but, no doubt, he had fled in sudden alarm at their rough angry tones hailing each other in the darkness. A sort of frenzy must have helped him up the steep Norton hill. It was he, no doubt, who early the following morning had been seen lying (in a swoon, I should say) on the roadside grass by the Brenzett carrier, who actually got down to have a nearer look, but drew back, intimidated by the perfect immobility, and by something queer in the aspect of that tramp, sleeping so still under the showers. As the day advanced, some children came dashing into school at Norton in such a fright that the schoolmistress went out and spoke indignantly to a 'horrid-looking man' on the road. He edged away, hanging his head, for a few steps, and then suddenly ran off with extraordinary fleetness. The driver of

Mr. Bradley's milk cart made no secret of it that he had lashed with his whip at a hairy sort of gypsy fellow who, jumping up at a turn of the road by the Vents, made a snatch at the pony's bridle. And he caught him a good one, too, right over the face, he said, that made him drop down in the mud a jolly sight quicker than he had jumped up; but it was a good half a mile before he could stop the pony. Maybe that in his desperate endeavors to get help, and in his need to get in touch with someone, the poor devil had tried to stop the cart. Also three boys confessed afterwards to throwing stones at a funny tramp, knocking about all wet and muddy, and, it seemed, very drunk, in the narrow deep lane by the limekilns. All this was the talk of three villages for days; but we have Mrs. Finn's (the wife of Smith's wagoner) unimpeachable testimony that she saw him get over the low wall of Hammond's pig-pound and lurch straight at her, babbling aloud in a voice that was enough to make one die of fright. Having the baby with her in a perambulator, Mrs. Finn called out to him to go away, and as he persisted in coming nearer, she hit him courageously with her umbrella over the head, and, without once looking back, ran like the wind with the perambulator as far as the first house in the village. She stopped then, out of breath, and spoke to old Lewis, hammering there at a heap of stones; and the old chap, taking off his immense black wire goggles, got up on his shaky legs to look where she pointed. Together they followed with their eyes the figure of the man running over a field; they saw him fall down, pick himself up, and run on again, staggering and waving his long arms above his head, in the direction of the New Barns Farm. From that moment he is plainly in the toils of his obscure and touching destiny. There is no doubt after this of what happened to him. All is certain now: Mrs. Smith's intense terror; Amy Foster's stolid conviction held against the other's nervous attack, that the man 'meant no harm'; Smith's exasperation (on his return from Darnford Market) at finding the dog barking himself into a fit, the back door locked, his wife in hysterics; and all for an unfortunate dirty tramp, supposed to be even then lurking in his stackyard. Was he? He would teach him to frighten women.

"Smith is notoriously hot-tempered, but the sight of some nondescript and miry creature sitting cross-legged amongst a lot of loose straw, and swinging itself to and fro like a bear in a cage, made him pause. Then this tramp stood up silently before him, one mass of mud and filth from head to foot. Smith, alone amongst his stacks with this apparition, in the stormy twilight ringing with the infuriated barking of the dog, felt the dread of an inexplicable strangeness. But when that being, parting with his black hands the long matted locks that hung before his face, as you part the two halves of a curtain, looked out at him with glistening, wild, black-and-white eyes, the weirdness of this silent encounter fairly staggered him. He has admitted since (for the story has been a legitimate subject of conversation about here for years) that he made more than one step backwards. Then a sudden burst of rapid, senseless speech persuaded him at once that he had to do with an escaped lunatic. In fact, that impression never wore off completely. Smith has not in his heart given up his secret conviction of the man's essential insanity to this very day.

"As the creature approached him, jabbering in a most discomposing manner, Smith (unaware that he was being addressed as 'gracious lord,' and adjured in God's name to afford food and shelter) kept on speaking firmly but gently to it, and retreating all the time into the other yard. At last, watching his chance, by a sudden charge he bundled him headlong into the woodlodge, and instantly shot the bolt. Thereupon he wiped his brow, though the day was cold. He had done his duty to the community by shutting up a wandering and probably dangerous maniac. Smith isn't a hard man at all, but he had room in his brain only for that one idea of lunacy. He was not imaginative enough to ask himself whether the man might not be perishing with cold and hunger. Meantime, at first, the maniac made a great deal of noise in the lodge. Mrs. Smith was screaming upstairs, where she had locked herself in her bedroom; but Amy Foster sobbed piteously at the kitchen door, wringing her hands and muttering, 'Don't! don't!' I daresay Smith had a rough time of it that evening with one noise and another, and this insane, disturbing voice crying obstinately through the door only added to his irritation. He couldn't possibly have connected this troublesome lunatic with the sinking of a ship in Eastbay, of which there had been a rumor in the Darnford market place. And I dare say the man inside had been very near to insanity on that night. Before his excitement collapsed and he became unconscious he was throwing himself violently about in the dark, rolling on some dirty sacks, and biting his fists with rage, cold, hunger, amazement, and despair.

"He was a mountaineer of the eastern range of the Carpathians, and the vessel sunk the night before in Eastbay was the Hamburg emigrant ship *Herzogin*[1] *Sophia-Dorothea*, of appalling memory.

"A few months later we could read in the papers the accounts of the bogus 'Emigration Agencies' among the Slavic peasantry in the more remote provinces of Austria. The object of these scoundrels was to get hold of the poor ignorant people's homesteads, and they were in league with the local usurers. They exported their victims through Hamburg mostly. As to the ship, I had watched her out of

1 [Duchess.]

this very window, reaching close-hauled under short canvas into the bay on a dark, threatening afternoon. She came to an anchor, correctly by the chart, off the Brenzett Coastguard station. I remember before the night fell looking out again at the outlines of her spars and rigging that stood out dark and pointed on a background of ragged, slaty clouds like another and a slighter spire to the left of the Brenzett churchtower. In the evening the wind rose. At midnight I could hear in my bed the terrific gusts and the sounds of a driving deluge.

"About that time the Coastguardmen thought they saw the lights of a steamer over the anchoring ground. In a moment they vanished; but it is clear that another vessel of some sort had tried for shelter in the bay on that awful, blind night, had rammed the German ship amidships ('a breach'—as one of the divers told me afterwards—'that you could sail a Thames barge through'), and then had gone out either scatheless or damaged, who shall say; but had gone out, unknown, unseen, and fatal, to perish mysteriously at sea. Of her nothing ever came to light, and yet the hue and cry that was raised all over the world would have found her out if she had been in existence anywhere on the face of the waters.

"A completeness without a clue, and a stealthy silence as of a neatly executed crime, characterize this murderous disaster, which, as you may remember, had its gruesome celebrity. The wind would have prevented the loudest outcries from reaching the shore; there had been evidently no time for signals of distress. It was death without any sort of fuss. The Hamburg ship, filling all at once, capsized as she sank, and at daylight there was not even the end of a spar to be seen above water. She was missed, of course, and at first the Coastguardmen surmised that she had either dragged her anchor or parted her cable sometime during the night, and had been blown out to sea. Then, after the tide turned, the wreck must have shifted a little and released some of the bodies, because a child—a little fair-haired child in a red frock—came ashore abreast of the Martello tower. By the afternoon you could see along three miles of beach dark figures with bare legs dashing in and out of the tumbling foam, and rough-looking men, women with hard faces, children, mostly fair-haired, were being carried, stiff and dripping, on stretchers, on wattles, on ladders, in a long procession past the door of the 'Ship Inn,' to be laid out in a row under the north wall of the Brenzett Church.

"Officially, the body of the little girl in the red frock is the first thing that came ashore from that ship. But I have patients amongst the seafaring population of West Colebrook, and, unofficially, I am informed that very early that morning two brothers, who went down to look after their cobble hauled up on the beach, found a good way from Brenzett, an ordinary ship's hencoop, lying high and dry on the shore, with eleven drowned ducks inside. Their families ate the birds, and the hencoop was split into firewood with a hatchet. It is possible that a man (supposing he happened to be on deck at the time of the accident) might have floated ashore on that hencoop. He might. I admit it is improbable, but there was the man—and for days, nay, for weeks—it didn't enter our heads that we had amongst us the only living soul that had escaped from that disaster. The man himself, even when he learned to speak intelligibly, could tell us very little. He remembered he had felt better (after the ship had anchored, I suppose), and that the darkness, the wind, and the rain took his breath away. This looks as if he had been on deck sometime during that night. But we mustn't forget he had been taken out of his knowledge, that he had been seasick and battened down below for four days, that he had no general notion of a ship or of the sea, and therefore could have no definite idea of what was happening to him. The rain, the wind, the darkness he knew; he understood the bleating of the sheep, and he remembered the pain of his wretchedness and misery, his heartbroken astonishment that it was neither seen nor understood, his dismay at finding all the men angry and all the women fierce. He had approached them as a beggar, it is true, he said; but in his country, even if they gave nothing, they spoke gently to beggars. The children in his country were not taught to throw stones at those who asked for compassion. Smith's strategy overcame him completely. The wood-lodge presented the horrible aspect of a dungeon. What would be done to him next? . . . No wonder that Amy Foster appeared to his eyes with the aureole of an angel of light. The girl had not been able to sleep for thinking of the poor man, and in the morning, before the Smiths were up, she slipped out across the back yard. Holding the door of the woodlodge ajar, she looked in and extended to him half a loaf of white bread—'such bread as the rich eat in my country,' he used to say.

"At this he got up slowly from amongst all sorts of rubbish, stiff, hungry, trembling, miserable, and doubtful. 'Can you eat this?' she asked in her soft and timid voice. He must have taken her for a 'gracious lady.' He devoured ferociously, and tears were falling on the crust. Suddenly he dropped the bread, seized her wrist, and imprinted a kiss on her hand. She was not frightened. Through his forlorn condition she had observed that he was good-looking. She shut the door and walked back slowly to the kitchen. Much later on, she told Mrs. Smith, who shuddered at the bare idea of being touched by that creature.

"Through this act of impulsive pity he was brought back again within the pale of human relations with his new surroundings. He never forgot it—never.

"That very same morning old Mr. Swaffer (Smith's nearest neighbor) came over to give his advice, and ended by carrying him off. He stood, unsteady on his legs, meek, and caked over in half-dried mud, while the two men talked around him in an incomprehensible tongue. Mrs. Smith had refused to come downstairs till the madman was off the premises; Amy Foster, far from within the dark kitchen, watched through the open back door; and he obeyed the signs that were made to him to the best of his ability. But Smith was full of mistrust. 'Mind, sir! It may be all his cunning,' he cried repeatedly in a tone of warning. When Mr. Swaffer started the mare, the deplorable being sitting humbly by his side, through weakness, nearly fell out over the back of the high two-wheeled cart. Swaffer took him straight home. And it is then that I come upon the scene.

"I was called in by the simple process of the old man beckoning to me with his forefinger over the gate of his house as I happened to be driving past. I got down, of course.

" 'I've got something here,' he mumbled, leading the way to an outhouse at a little distance from his other farm buildings.

"It was there that I saw him first, in a long, low room taken upon the space of that sort of coach house. It was bare and whitewashed, with a small square aperture glazed with one cracked, dusty pane at its further end. He was lying on his back upon a straw pallet; they had given him a couple of horse blankets, and he seemed to have spent the remainder of his strength in the exertion of cleaning himself. He was almost speechless; his quick breathing under the blankets pulled up to his chin, his glittering, restless black eyes reminded me of a wild bird caught in a snare. While I was examing him, old Swaffer stood silently by the door, passing the tips of his fingers along his shaven upper lip. I gave some directions, promised to send a bottle of medicine, and naturally made some inquiries.

" 'Smith caught him in the stackyard at New Barns,' said the old chap in his deliberate, unmoved manner, and as if the other had been indeed a sort of wild animal. 'That's how I came by him. Quite a curiosity, isn't he? Now tell me, doctor—you've been all over the world—don't you think that's a bit of a Hindu we've got hold of here?'

"I was greatly surprised. His long black hair scattered over the straw bolster contrasted with the olive pallor of his face. It occurred to me he might be a Basque. It didn't necessarily follow that he should understand Spanish; but I tried him with the few words I know, and also with some French. The whispered sounds I caught by bending my ear to his lips puzzled me utterly. That afternoon the young ladies from the rectory (one of them read Goethe with a dictionary, and the other had struggled with Dante for years), coming to see Miss Swaffer, tried their German and Italian on him from the doorway. They retreated, just the least bit scared by the flood of passionate speech which, turning on his pallet, he let out at them. They admitted that the sound was pleasant, soft, musical—but, in conjunction with his looks perhaps, it was startling—so excitable, so utterly unlike anything one had ever heard. The village boys climbed up the bank to have a peep through the little square aperture. Everybody was wondering what Mr. Swaffer would do with him.

"He simply kept him.

"Swaffer would be called eccentric were he not so much respected. They will tell you that Mr. Swaffer sits up as late as ten o'clock at night to read books, and they will tell you also that he can write a check for two hundred pounds without thinking twice about it. He himself would tell you that the Swaffers had owned land between this and Darnford for these three hundred years. He must be eighty-five today, but he does not look a bit older than when I first came here. He is a great breeder of sheep, and deals extensively in cattle. He attends market days for miles around in every sort of weather, and drives sitting bowed low over the reins, his lank gray hair curling over the collar of his warm coat, and with a green plaid rug round his legs. The calmness of advanced age gives a solemnity to his manner. He is clean-shaved; his lips are thin and sensitive; something rigid and monachal in the set of his features lends a certain elevation to the character of his face. He has been known to drive miles in the rain to see a new kind of rose in somebody's garden, or a monstrous cabbage grown by a cottager. He loves to hear tell of or to be shown something what he calls 'outlandish.' Perhaps it was just that outlandishness of the man which influenced old Swaffer. Perhaps it was only an inexplicable caprice. All I know is that at the end of three weeks I caught sight of Smith's lunatic digging in Swaffer's kitchen garden. They had found out he could use a spade. He dug barefooted.

"His black hair flowed over his shoulders. I suppose it was Swaffer who had given him the striped old cotton shirt; but he wore still the national brown cloth trousers (in which he had been washed ashore) fitting to the leg almost like tights; was belted with a broad leather belt studded with little brass discs; and had never yet ventured into the village. The land he looked upon seemed to him kept neatly, like the grounds round a landowner's house; the size of the cart horses struck him with astonishment; the roads resembled garden walks, and the aspect of the people, especially on Sundays, spoke of opulence.

He wondered what made them so hardhearted and their children so bold. He got his food at the back door, carried it in both hands, carefully, to his outhouse, and, sitting alone on his pallet, would make the sign of the cross before he began. Beside the same pallet, kneeling in the early darkness of the short days, he recited aloud the Lord's Prayer before he slept. Whenever he saw old Swaffer he would bow with veneration from the waist, and stand erect while the old man, with his fingers over his upper lip, surveyed him silently. He bowed also to Miss Swaffer, who kept house frugally for her father—a broad-shouldered, big-boned woman of forty-five, with the pocket of her dress full of keys, and a gray, steady eye. She was Church—as people said (while her father was one of the trustees of the Baptist Chapel)—and wore a little steel cross at her waist. She dressed severely in black, in memory of one of the innumerable Bradleys of the neighborhood, to whom she had been engaged some twenty-five years ago—a young farmer who broke his neck out hunting on the eve of the wedding day. She had the unmoved countenance of the deaf, spoke very seldom, and her lips, thin like her father's, astonished one sometimes by a mysteriously ironic curl.

"These were the people to whom he owed allegiance, and an overwhelming loneliness seemed to fall from the leaden sky of that winter without sunshine. All the faces were sad. He could talk to no one, and had no hope of ever understanding anybody. It was as if these had been the faces of people from the other world—dead people—he used to tell me years afterwards. Upon my word, I wonder he did not go mad. He didn't know where he was. Somewhere very far from his mountains—somewhere over the water. Was this America, he wondered?

"If it hadn't been for the steel cross at Miss Swaffer's belt he would not, he confessed, have known whether he was in a Christian country at all. He used to cast stealthy glances at it, and feel comforted. There was nothing here the same as in his country! The earth and the water were different; there were no images of the Redeemer by the roadside. The very grass was different, and the trees. All the trees but the three old Norway pines on the bit of lawn before Swaffer's house, and these reminded him of his country. He had been detected once, after dusk, with his forehead against the trunk of one of them, sobbing, and talking to himself. They had been like brothers to him at that time, he affirmed. Everything else was strange. Conceive you the kind of an existence overshadowed, oppressed, by the everyday material appearances, as if by the visions of a nightmare. At night, when he could not sleep he kept on thinking of a girl who gave him the first piece of bread he had eaten in this foreign land. She had been neither fierce nor angry, nor frightened. Her face he remembered as the only comprehensible face amongst all these faces that were as closed, as mysterious, and as mute as the faces of the dead who are possessed of a knowledge beyond the comprehension of the living. I wonder whether the memory of her compassion prevented him from cutting his throat. But there! I suppose I am an old sentimentalist, and forget the instinctive love of life which it takes all the strength of an uncommon despair to overcome.

"He did the work which was given him with an intelligence which surprised old Swaffer. By and by it was discovered that he could help at the plowing, could milk the cows, feed the bullocks in the cattle-yard, and was of some use with the sheep. He began to pick up words, too, very fast; and suddenly, one fine morning in spring, he rescued from an untimely death a grandchild of old Swaffer.

"Swaffer's younger daughter is married to Willcox, a solicitor and the town clerk of Colebrook. Regularly twice a year they come to stay with the old man for a few days. Their only child, a little girl not three years old at the time, ran out of the house alone in her little white pinafore, and, toddling across the grass of a terraced garden, pitched herself over a low wall headfirst into the horsepond in the yard below.

"Our man was out with the wagoner and the plow in the field nearest to the house, and as he was leading the team round to begin a fresh furrow, he saw, through the gap of a gate, what for anybody else would have been a mere flutter of something white. But he had straight-glancing, quick, far-reaching eyes, that only seemed to flinch and lose their amazing power before the immensity of the sea. He was barefooted, and looking as outlandish as the heart of Swaffer could desire. Leaving the horses on the turn, to the inexpressible disgust of the wagoner he bounded off, going over the plowed ground in long leaps, and suddenly appeared before the mother, thrust the child into her arms, and strode away.

"The pond was not very deep; but still, if he had not had such good eyes, the child would have perished—miserably suffocated in the foot or so of sticky mud at the bottom. Old Swaffer walked out slowly into the field, waited till the plow came over to his side, had a good look at him, and without saying a word went back to the house. But from that time they laid out his meals on the kitchen table; and at first, Miss Swaffer, all in black and with an inscrutable face, would come and stand in the doorway of the living room to see him make a big sign of the cross before he fell to. I believe that from that day, too, Swaffer began to pay him regular wages.

"I can't follow step by step his development. He cut his hair short, was seen in the village and along the road going to and fro to his work like any other man. Children ceased to shout after him. He became aware of social differences, but remained for a long time surprised at the bare poverty of the churches among so much wealth. He couldn't understand either why they were kept shut up on weekdays. There was nothing to steal in them. Was it to keep people from praying too often? The rectory took much notice of him about that time, and I believe the young ladies attempted to prepare the ground for his conversion. They could not, however, break him of his habit of crossing himself, but he went so far as to take off the string with a couple of brass medals the size of a sixpence, a tiny metal cross, and a square sort of scapulary which he wore round his neck. He hung them on the wall by the side of his bed, and he was still to be heard every evening reciting the Lord's Prayer, in incomprehensible words and in a slow, fervent tone, as he had heard his old father do at the head of all the kneeling family, big and little, on every evening of his life. And though he wore corduroys at work, and a slop-made pepper-and-salt suit on Sundays, strangers would turn round to look after him on the road. His foreignness had a peculiar and indelible stamp. At last people became used to seeing him. But they never became used to him. His rapid, skimming walk; his swarthy complexion; his hat cocked on the left ear; his habit, on warm evenings, of wearing his coat over one shoulder, like a hussar's dolman; his manner of leaping over the stiles, not as a feat of agility, but in the ordinary course of progression—all these peculiarities were, as one may say, so many causes of scorn and offense to the inhabitants of the village. *They* wouldn't in their dinner hour lie flat on their backs on the grass to stare at the sky. Neither did they go about the fields screaming dismal tunes. Many times have I heard his high-pitched voice from behind the ridge of some sloping sheepwalk, a voice light and soaring, like a lark's, but with a melancholy human note, over our fields that hear only the song of birds. And I would be startled myself. Ah! He was different; innocent of heart, and full of good will, which nobody wanted, this castaway, that, like a man transplanted into another planet, was separated by an immense space from his past and by an immense ignorance from his future. His quick, fervent utterance positively shocked everybody. 'An excitable devil,' they called him. One evening, in the taproom of the Coach and Horses (having drunk some whisky), he upset them all by singing a love song of his country. They hooted him down, and he was pained; but Preble, the lame wheelwright, and Vincent, the fat blacksmith, and the other notables, too, wanted to drink their evening beer in peace. On another occasion he tried to show them how to dance. The dust rose in clouds from the sanded floor; he leaped straight up amongst the deal tables, struck his heels together, squatted on one heel in front of old Preble, shooting out the other leg, uttered wild and exulting cries, jumped up to whirl on one foot, snapping his fingers above his head—and a strange carter who was having a drink in there began to swear, and cleared out with his half-pint in his hand into the bar. But when suddenly he sprang upon a table and continued to dance among the glasses, the landlord interfered. He didn't want any 'acrobat tricks in the taproom.' They laid their hands on him. Having had a glass or two, Mr. Swaffer's foreigner tried to expostulate: was ejected forcibly: got a black eye.

"I believe he felt the hostility of his human surroundings. But he was tough—tough in spirit, too, as well as in body. Only the memory of the sea frightened him, with that vague terror that is left by a bad dream. His home was far away; and he did not want now to go to America. I had often explained to him that there is no place on earth where true gold can be found lying ready and to be got for the trouble of the picking up. How, then, he asked, could he ever return home with empty hands when there had been sold a cow, two ponies, and a bit of land to pay for his going? His eyes would fill with tears, and, averting them from the immense shimmer of the sea, he would throw himself face down on the grass. But sometimes, cocking his hat with a little conquering air, he would defy my wisdom. He had found his bit of true gold. That was Amy Foster's heart; which was 'a golden heart, and soft to people's misery,' he would say in the accents of overwhelming conviction.

"He was called Yanko. He had explained that this meant Little John; but as he would also repeat very often that he was a mountaineer (some word sounding in the dialect of his country like Goorall) he got it for his surname. And this is the only trace of him that the succeeding ages may find in the marriage register of the parish. There it stands—Yanko Goorall—in the rector's handwriting. The crooked cross made by the castaway, a cross whose tracing no doubt seemed to him the most solemn part of the whole ceremony, is all that remains now to perpetuate the memory of his name.

"His courtship had lasted some time—ever since he got his precarious footing in the community. It began by his buying for Amy Foster a green satin ribbon in Darnford. This was what you did in his country. You bought a ribbon at a Jew's stall on a fair-day. I don't suppose the girl knew what to do with it, but he seemed to think that his honorable intentions could not be mistaken.

"It was only when he declared his purpose to get married that I fully understood how, for a hundred futile and inappreciable reasons, how—shall I say odious?—he was to all the countryside. Every old woman in the village was up in arms. Smith, coming upon him near the farm, promised to break his head for him if he found him about again. But he twisted his little black mustache with such a bellicose air and rolled such big, black fierce eyes at Smith that this promise came to nothing. Smith, however, told the girl that she must be mad to take up with a man who was surely wrong in his head. All the same, when she heard him in the gloaming whistle from beyond the orchard a couple of bars of a weird and mournful tune, she would drop whatever she had in her hand—she would leave Mrs. Smith in the middle of a sentence—and she would run out to his call. Mrs. Smith called her a shameless hussy. She answered nothing. She said nothing at all to anybody, and went on her way as if she had been deaf. She and I alone in all the land, I fancy, could see his very real beauty. He was very good-looking, and most graceful in his bearing, with that something wild as of a woodland creature in his aspect. Her mother moaned over her dismally whenever the girl came to see her on her day out. The father was surly, but pretended not to know; and Mrs. Finn once told her plainly that 'this man, my dear, will do you some harm some day yet.' And so it went on. They could be seen on the roads, she tramping stolidly in her finery—gray dress, black feather, stout boots, prominent white cotton gloves that caught your eye a hundred yards away; and he, his coat slung picturesquely over one shoulder, pacing by her side, gallant of bearing and casting tender glances upon the girl with the golden heart. I wonder whether he saw how plain she was. Perhaps among types so different from what he had ever seen, he had not the power to judge; or perhaps he was seduced by the divine quality of her pity.

"Yanko was in great trouble meantime. In his country you get an old man for an ambassador in marriage affairs. He did not know how to proceed. However, one day in the midst of sheep in a field (he was now Swaffer's under-shepherd with Foster) he took off his hat to the father and declared himself humbly. 'I daresay she's fool enough to marry you,' was all Foster said. 'And then,' he used to relate, 'he puts his hat on his head, looks black at me as if he wanted to cut my throat, whistles the dog, and off he goes, leaving me to do the work.' The Fosters, of course, didn't like to lose the wages the girl earned: Amy used to give all her money to her mother. But there was in Foster a very genuine aversion to that match. He contended that the fellow was very good with sheep, but was not fit for any girl to marry. For one thing, he used to go along the hedges muttering to himself like a dam' fool; and then, these foreigners behave very queerly to women sometimes. And perhaps he would want to carry her off somewhere—or run off himself. It was not safe. He preached it to his daughter that the fellow might ill-use her in some way. She made no answer. It was, they said in the village, as if the man had done something to her. People discussed the matter. It was quite an excitement, and the two went on 'walking out' together in the face of opposition. Then something unexpected happened.

"I don't know whether old Swaffer ever understood how much he was regarded in the light of a father by his foreign retainer. Anyway the relation was curiously feudal. So when Yanko asked formally for an interview—'and the Miss, too' (he called the severe, deaf Miss Swaffer simply *Miss*)—it was to obtain their permission to marry. Swaffer heard him unmoved, dismissed him by a nod, and then shouted the intelligence into Miss Swaffer's best ear. She showed no surprise, and only remarked grimly, in a veiled blank voice, 'He certainly won't get any other girl to marry him.'

"It is Miss Swaffer who has all the credit for the munificence: but in a very few days it came out that Mr. Swaffer had presented Yanko with a cottage (the cottage you've seen this morning) and something like an acre of ground—had made it over to him in absolute property. Wilcox expedited the deed, and I remember him telling me he had a great pleasure in making it ready. It recited: 'In consideration of saving the life of my beloved grandchild, Bertha Wilcox.'

"Of course, after that no power on earth could prevent them from getting married.

"Her infatuation endured. People saw her going out to meet him in the evening. She stared with unblinking, fascinated eyes up the road where he was expected to appear, walking freely, with a swing from the hip, and humming one of the love tunes of his country. When the boy was born, he got elevated at the 'Coach and Horses,' essayed again a song and a dance, and was again ejected. People expressed their commiseration for a woman married to that jack-in-the-box. He didn't care. There was a man now (he told me boastfully) to whom he could sing and talk in the language of his country, and show how to dance by and by.

"But I don't know. To me he appeared to have grown less springy of step, heavier in body, less keen of eye. Imagination, no doubt; but it seems to me now as if the net of fate had been drawn closer round him already.

"One day I met him on the footpath over the Talfourd Hill. He told me that 'women were funny.' I had heard already of domestic differences. People were saying that Amy Foster was beginning to find out what sort of man she had married. He looked upon the sea with indifferent, unseeing eyes. His wife had snatched the child out of his arms one day as he sat on the doorstep crooning to it a song such as the mothers sing to babies in his mountains. She seemed to think he was doing it some harm. Women are funny. And she had objected to him praying aloud in the evening. Why? He expected the boy to repeat the prayer aloud after him by and by, as he used to do after his old father when he was a child—in his own country. And I discovered he longed for their boy to grow up so that he could have a man to talk with in that language that to our ears sounded so disturbing, so passionate, and so bizarre. Why his wife should dislike the idea he couldn't tell. But that would pass, he said. And tilting his head knowingly, he tapped his breastbone to indicate that she had a good heart: not hard, not fierce, open to compassion, charitable to the poor!

"I walked away thoughtfully; I wondered whether his difference, his strangeness, were not penetrating with repulsion that dull nature they had begun by irresistibly attracting. I wondered. . . ."

The doctor came to the window and looked out at the frigid splendor of the sea, immense in the haze, as if enclosing all the earth with all the hearts lost among the passions of love and fear.

"Physiologically, now," he said, turning away abruptly, "it was possible. It was possible."

He remained silent. Then went on—

"At all events, the next time I saw him he was ill—lung trouble. He was tough, but I dare say he was not acclimatized as well as I had supposed. It was a bad winter; and, of course, these mountaineers do get fits of homesickness; and a state of depression would make him vulnerable. He was lying half dressed on a couch downstairs.

"A table covered with a dark oilcloth took up all the middle of the little room. There was a wicker cradle on the floor, a kettle spouting steam on the hob, and some child's linen lay drying on the fender. The room was warm, but the door opens right into the garden, as you noticed perhaps.

"He was very feverish, and kept on muttering to himself. She sat on a chair and looked at him fixedly across the table with her brown, blurred eyes. 'Why don't you have him upstairs?' I asked. With a start and a confused stammer she said, 'Oh! ah! I couldn't sit with him upstairs, sir.'

"I gave her certain directions; and going outside, I said again that he ought to be in bed upstairs. She wrung her hands. 'I couldn't. I couldn't. He keeps on saying something—I don't know what.' With the memory of all the talk against the man that had been dinned into her ears, I looked at her narrowly. I looked into her shortsighted eyes, at her dumb eyes that once in her life had seen an enticing shape, but seemed, staring at me, to see nothing at all now. But I saw she was uneasy.

" 'What's the matter with him?' she asked in a sort of vacant trepidation. 'He doesn't look very ill. I never did see anybody look like this before. . . .'

" 'Do you think,' I asked indignantly, 'he is shamming?'

" 'I can't help it, sir,' she said, stolidly. And suddenly she clapped her hands and looked right and left. 'And there's the baby. I am so frightened. He wanted me just now to give him the baby. I can't understand what he says to it.'

" 'Can't you ask a neighbor to come in tonight?' I asked.

" 'Please, sir, nobody seems to care to come,' she muttered, dully resigned all at once.

"I impressed upon her the necessity of the greatest care, and then had to go. There was a good deal of sickness that winter. 'Oh, I hope he won't talk' she exclaimed softly just as I was going away.

"I don't know how it is I did not see—but I didn't. And yet, turning in my trap, I saw her lingering before the door, very still, and as if meditating a flight up the miry road.

"Towards the night his fever increased.

"He tossed, moaned, and now and then muttered a complaint. And she sat with the table between her and the couch, watching every movement and every sound, with the terror, the unreasonable terror, of that man she could not understand creeping over her. She had drawn the wicker cradle close to her feet. There was nothing in her now but the maternal instinct and that unaccountable fear.

"Suddenly coming to himself, parched, he demanded a drink of water. She did not move. She had not understood, though he may have thought he was speaking in English. He waited, looking at her, burning with fever, amazed at her silence and immobility, and then he shouted impatiently, 'Water! Give me water!'

"She jumped to her feet, snatched up the child, and stood still. He spoke to her, and his passionate remonstrances only increased her fear of that strange man. I believe he spoke to her for a long time, entreating, wondering, pleading, ordering, I suppose. She says she bore it as long as she could. And then a gust of rage came over him.

"He sat up and called out terribly one word—some word. Then he got up as though he hadn't been ill at all, she says. And as in fevered dismay, indignation, and wonder he tried to get to her round the table, she simply opened the door and ran out with the child in her arms. She heard him call twice after her down the road in a terrible voice—and fled. . . . Ah! but you should have seen stirring behind the dull, blurred glance of those eyes that the specter of the fear which had haunted her on that night three miles and a half to the door of Foster's cottage! I did the next day.

"And it was I who found him lying face down and his body in a puddle, just outside the little wicker gate.

"I had been called out that night to an urgent case in the village, and on my way home at daybreak passed by the cottage. The door stood open. My man helped me to carry him in. We laid him on the couch. The lamp smoked, the fire was out, the chill of the stormy night oozed from the cheerless yellow paper on the wall. 'Amy!' I called aloud, and my voice seemed to lose itself in the emptiness of this tiny house as if I had cried in a desert. He opened his eyes. 'Gone!' he said, distinctly. 'I had only asked for water—only for a little water. . . .'

"He was muddy. I covered him up and stood waiting in silence, catching a painfully gasped word now and then. They were no longer in his own language. The fever had left him, taking with it the heat of life. And with his panting breast and lustrous eyes he reminded me again of a wild creature under the net; of a bird caught in a snare. She had left him. She had left him—sick—helpless—thirsty. The spear of the hunter had entered his very soul. 'Why?' he cried, in the penetrating and indignant voice of a man calling to a responsible Maker. A gust of wind and a swish of rain answered.

"And as I turned away to shut the door he pronounced the word 'Merciful!' and expired.

"Eventually I certified heart failure as the immediate cause of death. His heart must have indeed failed him, or else he might have stood this night of storm and exposure, too. I closed his eyes and drove away. Not very far from the cottage I met Foster walking sturdily between the dripping hedges with his collie at his heels.

" 'Do you know where your daughter is?' I asked.

" 'Don't I!' he cried. 'I am going to talk to him a bit. Frightening a poor woman like this.'

" 'He won't frighten her any more,' I said. 'He is dead.'

"He struck with his stick at the mud.

" 'And there's the child.'

"Then, after thinking deeply for a while—

" 'I don't know that it isn't for the best.'

"That's what he said. And she says nothing at all now. Not a word of him. Never. Is his image as utterly gone from her mind as his lithe and striding figure, his caroling voice are gone from our fields? He is no longer before her eyes to excite her imagination into a passion of love or fear; and his memory seems to have vanished from her dull brain as a shadow passes away upon a white screen. She lives in the cottage and works for Miss Swaffer. She is Amy Foster for everybody, and the child is 'Amy Foster's boy.' She calls him Johnny—which means Little John.

"It is impossible to say whether this name recalls anything to her. Does she ever think of the past? I have seen her hanging over the boy's cot in a very passion of maternal tenderness. The little fellow was lying on his back, a little frightened at me, but very still, with his big black eyes, with his fluttered air of a bird in a snare. And looking at him I seemed to see again the other one—the father, cast out mysteriously by the sea to perish in the supreme disaster of loneliness and despair."

Albert Camus

THE GUEST

THE SCHOOLMASTER was watching the two men climb toward him. One was on horseback, the other on foot. They had not yet tackled the abrupt rise leading to the schoolhouse built on the hillside. They were toiling onward, making slow progress in the snow, among the stones, on the vast expanse of the high, deserted plateau. From time to time the horse stumbled. Without hearing anything yet, he could see the breath issuing from the horse's nostrils. One of the men, at least, knew the region. They were following the trail although it had disappeared days ago under a layer of dirty white snow. The schoolmaster calculated that it would take them half an hour to get onto the hill. It was cold; he went back into the school to get a sweater.

He crossed the empty, frigid classroom. On the blackboard the four rivers of France, drawn with four different colored chalks, had been flowing toward their estuaries for the past three days. Snow had suddenly fallen in mid-October after eight months of drought without the transition of rain, and the twenty pupils, more or less, who lived in the villages scattered over the plateau had stopped coming. With fair weather they would return. Daru now heated only the single room that was his lodging, adjoining the classroom and giving also onto the plateau to the east. Like the class windows, his window looked to the south too. On that side the school was a few kilometers from the point where the plateau began to slope toward the south. In clear weather could be seen the purple mass of the mountain range where the gap opened onto the desert.

Somewhat warmed, Daru returned to the window from which he had first seen the two men. They were no longer visible. Hence they must have tackled the rise. The sky was not so dark, for the snow had stopped falling during the night. The morning had opened with a dirty light which had scarcely become brighter as the ceiling of clouds lifted. At two in the afternoon it seemed as if the day were

---

merely beginning. But still this was better than those three days when the thick snow was falling amidst unbroken darkness with little gusts of wind that rattled the double door of the classroom. Then Daru had spent long hours in his room, leaving it only to go to the shed and feed the chickens or get some coal. Fortunately the delivery truck from Tadjid, the nearest village to the north, had brought his supplies two days before the blizzard. It would return in forty-eight hours.

Besides, he had enough to resist a siege, for the little room was cluttered with bags of wheat that the administration left as a stock to distribute to those of his pupils whose families had suffered from the drought. Actually they had all been victims because they were all poor. Every day Daru would distribute a ration to the children. They had missed it, he knew, during these bad days. Possibly one of the fathers or big brothers would come this afternoon and he could supply them with grain. It was just a matter of carrying them over to the next harvest. Now shiploads of wheat were arriving from France and the worst was over. But it would be hard to forget that poverty, that army of ragged ghosts wandering in the sunlight, the plateaus burned to a cinder month after month, the earth shriveled up little by little, literally scorched, every stone bursting into dust under one's foot. The sheep had died then by thousands and even a few men, here and there, sometimes without anyone's knowing.

In contrast with such poverty, he who lived almost like a monk in his remote schoolhouse, nonetheless satisfied with the little he had and with the rough life, had felt like a lord with his white-washed walls, his narrow couch, his unpainted shelves, his well, and his weekly provision of water and food. And suddenly this snow, without warning, without the foretaste of rain. This is the way the region was, cruel to live in, even without men—who didn't help matters either. But Daru had been born here. Everywhere else, he felt exiled.

He stepped out onto the terrace in front of the schoolhouse. The two men were now halfway up the slope. He recognized the horseman as Balducci, the old gendarme he had known for a long time. Balducci was holding on the end of a rope an Arab who was walking behind him with hands bound and head lowered. The gendarme waved a greeting to which Daru did not reply, lost as he was in contemplation of the Arab dressed in a faded blue jellaba, his feet in sandals but covered with socks of heavy raw wool, his head surmounted by a narrow, short *chèche*. They were approaching. Balducci was holding back his horse in order not to hurt the Arab, and the group was advancing slowly.

Within earshot, Balducci shouted: "One hour to do the three kilometers from El Ameur!" Daru did not answer. Short and square in his thick sweater, he watched them climb. Not once had the Arab raised his head. "Hello," said Daru when they got up onto the terrace. "Come in and warm up." Balducci painfully got down from his horse without letting go the rope. From under his bristling mustache he smiled at the schoolmaster. His little dark eyes, deep-set under a tanned forehead, and his mouth surrounded with wrinkles made him look attentive and studious. Daru took the bridle, led the horse to the shed, and came back to the two men, who were now waiting for him in the school. He led them into his room. "I am going to heat up the classroom," he said. "We'll be more comfortable there." When he entered the room again, Balducci was on the couch. He had undone the rope tying him to the Arab, who had squatted near the stove. His hands still bound, the *chèche* pushed back on his head, he was looking toward the window. At first Daru noticed only his huge lips, fat, smooth, almost Negroid; yet his nose was straight, his eyes were dark and full of fever. The *chèche* revealed an obstinate forehead and, under the weathered skin now rather discolored by the cold, the whole face had a restless and rebellious look that struck Daru when the Arab, turning his face toward him, looked him straight in the eyes. "Go into the other room," said the schoolmaster, "and I'll make you some mint tea." "Thanks," Balducci said. "What a chore! How I long for retirement." And addressing his prisoner in Arabic: "Come on, you." The Arab got up and, slowly, holding his bound wrists in front of him, went into the classroom.

With the tea, Daru brought a chair. But Balducci was already enthroned on the nearest pupil's desk and the Arab had squatted against the teacher's platform facing the stove, which stood between the desk and the window. When he held out the glass of tea to the prisoner, Daru hesitated at the sight of his bound hands. "He might perhaps be untied." "Sure," said Balducci. "That was for the trip." He started to get to his feet. But Daru, setting the glass on the floor, had knelt beside the Arab. Without saying anything, the Arab watched him with his feverish eyes. Once his hands were free, he rubbed his swollen wrists against each other, took the glass of tea, and sucked up the burning liquid in swift little sips.

"Good," said Daru. "And where are you headed?"

Balducci withdrew his mustache from the tea. "Here, son."

"Odd pupils! And you're spending the night?"

"No. I'm going back to El Ameur. And you will deliver this fellow to Tinguit. He is expected at police headquarters."

Balducci was looking at Daru with a friendly little smile.

"What's this story?" asked the schoolmaster. "Are you pulling my leg?"

"No, son. Those are the orders."

"The orders? I'm not . . ." Daru hesitated, not wanting to hurt the old Corsican. "I mean, that's not my job."

"What! What's the meaning of that? In wartime people do all kinds of jobs."

"Then I'll wait for the declaration of war!"

Balducci nodded.

"O.K. But the orders exist and they concern you too. Things are brewing, it appears. There is talk of a forthcoming revolt. We are mobilized, in a way."

Daru still had his obstinate look.

"Listen, son," Balducci said. "I like you and you must understand. There's only a dozen of us at El Ameur to patrol throughout the whole territory of a small department and I must get back in a hurry. I was told to hand this guy over to you and return without delay. He couldn't be kept there. His village was beginning to stir; they wanted to take him back. You must take him to Tinguit tomorrow before the day is over. Twenty kilometers shouldn't faze a husky fellow like you. After that, all will be over. You'll come back to your pupils and your comfortable life."

Behind the wall the horse could be heard snorting and pawing the earth. Daru was looking out the window. Decidedly, the weather was clearing and the light was increasing over the snowy plateau. When all the snow was melted, the sun would take over again and once more would burn the fields of stone. For days, still, the unchanging sky would shed its dry light on the solitary expanse where nothing had any connection with man.

"After all," he said, turning around toward Balducci, "what did he do?" And, before the gendarme had opened his mouth, he asked: "Does he speak French?"

"No, not a word. We had been looking for him for a month, but they were hiding him. He killed his cousin."

"Is he against us?"

"I don't think so. But you can never be sure."

"Why did he kill?"

"A family squabble, I think. One owed the other grain, it seems. It's not at all clear. In short, he killed his cousin with a billhook. You know, like a sheep, *kreezk*!"

Baldueci made the gesture of drawing a blade across his throat and the Arab, his attention attracted, watched him with a sort of anxiety. Daru felt a sudden wrath against the man, against all men with their rotten spite, their tireless hates, their blood lust.

But the kettle was singing on the stove. He served Balducci more tea, hesitated, then served the Arab again, who, a second time, drank avidly. His raised arms made the jellaba fall open and the schoolmaster saw his thin, muscular chest.

"Thanks, kid," Balducci said. "And now, I'm off."

He got up and went toward the Arab, taking a small rope from his pocket.

"What are you doing?" Daru asked dryly.

Balducci, disconcerted, showed him the rope.

"Don't bother."

The old gendarme hesitated. "It's up to you. Of course, you are armed?"

"I have my shotgun."

"Where?"

"In the trunk."

"You ought to have it near your bed."

"Why? I have nothing to fear."

"You're crazy, son. If there's an uprising, no one is safe, we're all in the same boat."

"I'll defend myself. I'll have time to see them coming."

Balducci began to laugh, then suddenly the mustache covered the white teeth.

"You'll have time? O.K. That's just what I was saying. You have always been a little cracked. That's why I like you, my son was like that."

At the same time he took out his revolver and put it on the desk.

"Keep it; I don't need two weapons from here to El Ameur."

The revolver shone against the black paint of the table. When the gendarme turned toward him, the schoolmaster caught the smell of leather and horseflesh.

"Listen, Balducci," Daru said suddenly, "every bit of this disgusts me, and first of all your fellow here. But I won't hand him over. Fight, yes, if I have to. But not that."

The old gendarme stood in front of him and looked at him severely.

"You're being a fool," he said slowly. "I don't like it either. You don't get used to putting a rope on a man even after years of it, and you're even ashamed—yes, ashamed. But you can't let them have their way."

"I won't hand him over," Daru said again.

"It's an order, son, and I repeat it."

"That's right. Repeat to them what I've said to you: I won't hand him over."

Balducci made a visible effort to reflect. He looked at the Arab and at Daru. At last he decided.

"No, I won't tell them anything. If you want to drop us, go ahead; I'll not denounce you. I have an order to deliver the prisoner and I'm doing so. And now you'll just sign this paper for me."

"There's no need. I'll not deny that you left him with me."

"Don't be mean with me. I know you'll tell the truth. You're from hereabouts and you are a man. But you must sign, that's the rule."

Daru opened his drawer, took out a little square bottle of purple ink, the red wooden penholder with the "sergeant-major" pen he used for making models of penmanship, and signed. The gendarme carefully folded the paper and put it into his wallet. Then he moved toward the door.

"I'll see you off," Daru said.

"No," said Balducci. "There's no use being polite. You insulted me."

He looked at the Arab, motionless in the same spot, sniffed peevishly, and turned away toward the door. "Good-by, son," he said. The door shut behind him. Balducci appeared suddenly outside the window and then disappeared. His footsteps were muffled by the snow. The horse stirred on the other side of the wall and several chickens fluttered in fright. A moment later Balducci reappeared outside the window leading the horse by the bridle. He walked toward the little rise without turning around and disappeared from sight with the horse following him. A big stone could be heard bouncing down. Daru walked back toward the prisoner, who, without stirring, never took his eyes off him. "Wait," the schoolmaster said in Arabic and went toward the bedroom. As he was going through the door, he had a second thought, went to the desk, took the revolver, and stuck it in his pocket. Then, without looking back, he went into his room.

For some time he lay on his couch watching the sky gradually close over, listening to the silence. It was this silence that had seemed painful to him during the first days here, after the war. He had requested a post in the little town at the base of the foothills separating the upper plateaus from the desert. There, rocky walls, green and black to the north, pink and lavender to the south, marked the frontier of eternal summer. He had been named to a post farther north, on the plateau itself. In the beginning, the solitude and the silence had been hard for him on these wastelands peopled only by stones. Occasionally, furrows suggested cultivation, but they had been dug to uncover a certain kind of stone good for building. The only plowing here was to harvest rocks. Elsewhere a thin layer of soil accumulated in the hollows would be scraped out to enrich paltry village gardens. This is the way it was: bare rock covered three quarters of the region. Towns sprang up, flourished, then disappeared; men came by, loved one another or fought bitterly, then died. No one in this desert, neither he nor his guest, mattered. And yet, outside this desert neither of them, Daru knew, could have really lived.

When he got up, no noise came from the classroom. He was amazed at the unmixed joy he derived from the mere thought that the Arab might have fled and that he would be alone with no decision to make. But the prisoner was there. He had merely stretched out between the stove and the desk. With eyes open, he was staring at the ceiling. In that position, his thick lips were particularly noticeable, giving him a pouting look. "Come," said Daru. The Arab got up and followed him. In the bedroom, the schoolmaster pointed to a chair near the table under the window. The Arab sat down without taking his eyes off Daru.

"Are you hungry?"

"Yes," the prisoner said.

Daru set the table for two. He took flour and oil, shaped a cake in a frying-pan, and lighted the little stove that functioned on bottled gas. While the cake was cooking, he went out to the shed to get cheese, eggs, dates, and condensed milk. When the cake was done he set it on the window sill to cool, heated some condensed milk diluted with water, and beat up the eggs into an omelette. In one of his motions he knocked against the revolver stuck in his right pocket. He set the bowl down, went into the classroom, and put the revolver in his desk drawer. When he came back to the room, night was falling. He put on the light and served the Arab. "Eat," he said. The Arab took a piece of the cake, lifted it eagerly to his mouth, and stopped short.

"And you?" he asked.

"After you. I'll eat too."

The thick lips opened slightly. The Arab hesitated, then bit into the cake determinedly.

The meal over, the Arab looked at the schoolmaster. "Are you the judge?"

"No, I'm simply keeping you until tomorrow."

"Why do you eat with me?"

"I'm hungry."

The Arab fell silent. Daru got up and went out. He brought back a folding bed from the shed, set it up between the table and the stove, perpendicular to his own bed. From a large suitcase which, upright in a corner, served as a shelf for papers, he took two blankets and arranged them on the camp bed. Then he stopped, felt useless, and sat down on his bed. There was nothing more to do or to get ready. He had to look at this man. He looked at him, therefore, trying to imagine his face bursting with rage. He couldn't do so. He could see nothing but the dark yet shining eyes and the animal mouth.

"Why did you kill him?" he asked in a voice whose hostile tone surprised him.

The Arab looked away.

"He ran away. I ran after him."

He raised his eyes to Daru again and they were full of a sort of woeful interrogation. "Now what will they do to me?"

"Are you afraid?"

He stiffened, turning his eyes away.

"Are you sorry?"

The Arab stared at him openmouthed. Obviously he did not understand. Daru's annoyance was growing. At the same time he felt awkward and self-conscious with his big body wedged between the two beds.

"Lie down there," he said impatiently. "That's your bed."

The Arab didn't move. He called to Daru:

"Tell me!"

The schoolmaster looked at him.

"Is the gendarme coming back tomorrow?"

"I don't know."

"Are you coming with us?"

"I don't know. Why?"

The prisoner got up and stretched out on top of the blankets, his feet toward the window. The light from the electric bulb shone straight into his eyes and he closed them at once.

"Why?" Daru repeated, standing beside the bed.

The Arab opened his eyes under the blinding light and looked at him, trying not to blink.

"Come with us," he said.

In the middle of the night, Daru was still not asleep. He had gone to bed after undressing completely; he generally slept naked. But when he suddenly realized that he had nothing on, he hesitated. He felt vulnerable and the temptation came to him to put his clothes back on. Then he shrugged his shoulders; after all, he wasn't a child and, if need be, he could break his adversary in two. From his bed he could observe him, lying on his back, still motionless with his eyes closed under the harsh light. When Daru turned out the light, the darkness seemed to coagulate all of a sudden. Little by little, the night came back to life in the window where the starless sky was stirring gently. The schoolmaster soon made out the body lying at his feet. The Arab still did not move, but his eyes seemed open. A faint wind was prowling around the schoolhouse. Perhaps it would drive away the clouds and the sun would reappear.

During the night the wind increased. The hens fluttered a little and then were silent. The Arab turned over on his side with his back to Daru, who thought he heard him moan. Then he listened for his guest's breathing, become heavier and more regular. He listened to that breath so close to him and mused without being able to go to sleep. In this room where he had been sleeping alone for a year, this presence bothered him. But it bothered him also by imposing on him a sort of brotherhood he knew well but refused to accept in the present circumstances. Men who share the same rooms, soldiers or prisoners, develop a strange alliance as if, having cast off their armor with their clothing, they fraternized every evening, over and above their differences, in the ancient community of dream and fatigue. But Daru shook himself; he didn't like such musings, and it was essential to sleep.

A little later, however, when the Arab stirred slightly, the schoolmaster was still not asleep. When the prisoner made a second move, he stiffened, on the alert. The Arab was lifting himself slowly on his arms with almost the motion of a sleepwalker. Seated upright in bed, he waited motionless without turning his head toward Daru, as if he were listening attentively. Daru did not stir; it had just occurred to him that the revolver was still in the drawer of his desk. It was better to act at once. Yet he continued to observe the prisoner, who, with the same slithery motion, put his feet on the ground, waited again, then began to stand up slowly. Daru was about to call out to him when the Arab began to walk, in a quite natural but extraordinarily silent way. He was heading toward the door at the end of the room that opened into the shed. He lifted the latch with precaution and went out, pushing the door behind him but without shutting it. Daru had not stirred. "He is running away," he merely thought. "Good riddance!" Yet he listened attentively. The hens were not fluttering; the guest must be on the plateau. A faint sound of water reached him, and he didn't know what it was until the Arab again stood framed in the doorway, closed the door carefully, and came back to bed without a sound. Then Daru turned his back on him and fell asleep. Still later he seemed, from the depths of his sleep, to hear furtive steps around the schoolhouse. "I'm dreaming! I'm dreaming!" he repeated to himself. And he went on sleeping.

When he awoke, the sky was clear; the loose window let in a cold, pure air. The Arab was asleep, hunched up under the blankets now, his mouth open, utterly relaxed. But when Daru shook him, he started dreadfully, staring at Daru with wild eyes as if he had never seen him and such a frightened expression that the schoolmaster stepped back. "Don't be afraid. It's me. You must eat." The Arab nodded his head and said yes. Calm had returned to his face, but his expression was vacant and listless.

The coffee was ready. They drank it seated together on the folding bed as they munched their pieces of the cake. Then Daru led the Arab under the shed and showed him the faucet where he washed. He went back into the room, folded the blankets and the bed, made his own bed and put the room in order. Then he went through the classroom and out onto the terrace. The sun was already rising in the blue sky; a soft, bright light was bathing the deserted plateau. On the ridge the snow was melting in spots. The stones were about to reappear. Crouched on the edge of the plateau, the schoolmaster looked at the deserted expanse. He thought of Balducci. He had hurt him, for he had sent him off in a way as if he didn't want to be associated with him. He could still hear the gendarme's farewell and, without knowing why, he felt strangely empty and vulnerable. At that moment, from the other side of the schoolhouse, the prisoner coughed. Daru listened to him almost despite himself and then, furious, threw a pebble that whistled through the air before sinking into the snow. That man's stupid crime revolted him, but to hand him over was contrary to honor. Merely thinking of it made him smart with humiliation. And he cursed at one and the same time his own people who had sent him this Arab and the Arab too who had dared to kill and not managed to get away. Daru got up, walked in a circle on the terrace, waited motionless, and then went back into the schoolhouse.

The Arab, leaning over the cement floor of the shed, was washing his teeth with two fingers. Daru looked at him and said: "Come." He went back into the room ahead of the prisoner. He slipped a hunting-jacket on over his sweater and put on walking-shoes. Standing, he waited until the Arab had put on his *chèche* and sandals. They went into the classroom and the schoolmaster pointed to the exit, saying: "Go ahead." The fellow didn't budge. "I'm coming," said Daru. The Arab went out. Daru went back into the room and made a package of pieces of rusk, dates, and sugar. In the classroom, before going out, he hesitated a second in front of his desk, then crossed the threshold and locked the door. "That's the way," he said. He started toward the east, followed by the prisoner. But, a short distance from the schoolhouse, he thought he heard a slight sound behind them. He retraced his steps and examined the surroundings of the house; there was no one there. The Arab watched him without seeming to understand. "Come on," said Daru.

They walked for an hour and rested beside a sharp peak of limestone. The snow was melting faster and faster and the sun was drinking up the puddles at once, rapidly cleaning the plateau, which gradually dried and vibrated like the air itself. When they resumed walking, the ground rang under their feet. From time to time a bird rent the space in front of them with a joyful cry. Daru breathed in deeply the fresh morning light. He felt a sort of rapture before the vast familiar expanse, now almost entirely yellow under its dome of blue sky. They walked an hour more, descending toward the south. They reached a level height made up of crumbly rocks. From there on, the plateau sloped down, eastward, toward a low plain where there were a few spindly trees and, to the south, toward outcroppings of rock that gave the landscape a chaotic look.

Daru surveyed the two directions. There was nothing but the sky on the horizon. Not a man could be seen. He turned toward the Arab, who was looking at him blankly. Daru held out the package to him. "Take it," he said. "There are dates, bread, and sugar. You can hold out for two days. Here are a thousand francs too." The Arab took the package and the money but kept his full hands at chest level as if he didn't know what to do with what was being given him. "Now look," the schoolmaster said as he pointed in the direction of the east, "there's the way to Tinguit. You have a two-hour walk. At Tinguit you'll find the administration and the police. They are expecting you." The Arab looked toward the east, still holding the package and the money against his chest. Daru took his elbow and turned him rather roughly toward the south. At the foot of the height on which they stood could be seen a faint path. "That's the trail across the plateau. In a day's walk from here you'll find pasture-lands and the first nomads. They'll take you in and shelter you according to their law." The Arab had now turned toward Daru and a sort of panic was visible in his expression. "Listen," he said. Daru shook his head: "No, be quiet. Now I'm leaving you." He turned his back on him, took two long steps in the direction of the school, looked hesitantly at the motionless Arab, and started off again. For a few minutes he heard nothing but his own step resounding on the cold ground and did not turn his head. A moment later, however, he turned around. The Arab was still there on the edge of the hill, his arms hanging now, and he was looking at the schoolmaster. Daru felt something rise in his throat. But he swore with impatience, waved vaguely, and started off again. He had already gone some distance when he again stopped and looked. There was no longer anyone on the hill.

Daru hesitated. The sun was now rather high in the sky and was beginning to beat down on his head. The schoolmaster retraced his steps, at first somewhat uncertainly, then with decision. When he reached the little hill, he was bathed in sweat. He climbed it as fast as he could and stopped, out of breath, at the top. The rock-fields to the south stood out sharply against the blue sky, but on the plain to the east a steamy heat was already rising. And in that slight haze, Daru, with heavy heart, made out the Arab walking slowly on the road to prison.

A little later, standing before the window of the classroom, the schoolmaster was watching the clear light bathing the whole surface of the plateau, but he hardly saw it. Behind him on the blackboard, among the winding French rivers, sprawled the clumsily chalked-up words he had just read: "You handed over our brother. You will pay for this." Daru looked at the sky, the plateau, and, beyond, the invisible lands stretching all the way to the sea. In this vast landscape he had loved so much, he was alone.

Alan Paton

LIFE FOR A LIFE

THE DOCTOR had closed up the ugly hole in Flip's skull so that his widow, and her brothers and sisters, and their wives and husbands and children, and Flip's own brothers and sisters and their wives and husbands and children, could come and stand for a minute and look down on the hard stony face of the master of Kroon, one of the richest farmers of the whole Karroo. The cars kept coming and going, the police, the doctor, the newspaper men, the neighbours from near and far.

All the white women were in the house, and all the white men outside. An event like this, the violent death of one of themselves, drew them together in an instant, so that all the world might see that they were one, and that they would not rest till justice had been done. It was this standing there, this drawing together, that kept the brown people in their small stone houses, talking in low voices; and their fear communicated itself to their children, so that there was no need to silence them. Now and then one of them would leave the houses to relieve his needs in the bushes, but otherwise there was no movement on this side of the valley. Each family sat in its house, at a little distance from each front door, watching with anxious fascination the goings and the comings of the white people standing in front of the big house.

Then the white predikant came from Poort, you could tell him by the black hat and the black clothes. He shook hands with Big Baas

---

Flip's sons, and said words of comfort to them. Then all the men followed him into the house, and after a while the sound of the slow determined singing was carried across the valley, to the small stone houses on the other side, to Enoch Maarman, head-shepherd of Kroon, and his wife Sara, sitting just inside the door of their own house. Maarman's anxiety showed itself in the movements of his face and hands, and his wife knew of his condition but kept her face averted from it. Guilt lay heavily upon them both, because they had hated Big Baas Flip, not with clenched fists and bared teeth, but, as befitted people in their station, with salutes and deference.

Sara suddenly sat erect.

—They are coming, she said.

They watched the four men leave the big stone house, and take the path that led to the small stone houses, and both could feel the fear rising in them. Their guilt weighed down on them all the more heavily because they felt no grief. They felt all the more afraid because the show of grief might have softened the harshness of the approaching ordeal. Someone must pay for so terrible a crime, and if not the one who did it, then who better than the one who could not grieve. That morning Maarman had stood hat in hand before Baas Gysbert, who was Big Baas Flip's eldest son, and had said to him, *my people are sorry to hear of this terrible thing*. And Baas Gysbert had given him the terrible answer, *that could be so*.

Then Sara said to him, Robbertse is one.

He nodded. He knew that Robbertse was one, the big detective with the temper that got out of hand, so that reddish foam would come out of his mouth, and he would hold a man by the throat till one of his colleagues would shout at him to let the man go. Sara's father, who was one of the wisest men in all the district of Poort, said that he could never be sure whether Robbertse was mad or only pretending to be, but that it didn't really matter, because whichever it was, it was dangerous.

Maarman and his wife stood up when two of the detectives came to the door of the small stone house. One was Robbertse, but both were big men and confident. They wore smart sports jackets and grey flannels, and grey felt hats on their heads. They came in and kept their hats on their heads, looking round the small house with the air of masters. They spoke to each other as though there were nobody standing there waiting to be spoken to.

Then Robbertse said, you are Enoch Maarman?

—Yes, baas.

—The head-shepherd?

—Yes, baas.

—Who are the other shepherds?

Enoch gave him the names, and Robbertse sat down on one of the chairs, and wrote the names in his book. Then he tilted his hat back on his head and said, has anyone of these men ever been in gaol?

Enoch moistened his lips. He wanted to say that the detective could easily find it out for himself, that he was the head-shepherd and would answer any question about the farm or the work. But he said instead, I don't know, baas.

—You don't know Kleinbooi was in gaol at Christmas?

—Yes, I know that, baas.

Suddenly Robbertse was on his feet, and his head almost touching the ceiling, and his body almost filling the small room, and he was shouting in a tremendous voice, then why did you lie?

Sara had shrunk back into the wall, and was looking at Robbertse out of terrified eyes, but Enoch did not move though he was deathly afraid.

He answered, I didn't mean to lie, baas. Kleinbooi was in gaol for drink, not killing.

Robbertse said, killing? Why do you mention killing?

Then when Enoch did not answer, the detective suddenly lifted his hand so that Enoch started back and knocked over the other chair. Down on his knees, and shielding his head with one hand, he set the chair straight again, saying, baas, we know that you are here because the master was killed.

But Robbertse's lifting his hand had been intended only to remove his hat from his head, and now with a grin he put his hat on the table.

—Why fall down, he asked, because I take off my hat? I like to take off my hat in another man's house.

He smiled at Sara, and looking at the chair now set upright, said to her, you can sit.

When she made no attempt to sit on it, the smile left his face, and he said to her coldly and menacingly, you can sit.

When she had sat down, he said to Maarman, don't knock over any more chairs. For if one gets broken, you'll tell the magistrate I broke it, won't you? That I lifted it up and threatened you?

—No, baas.

Robbertse sat down again, and studied his book as though something were written there, not the names of shepherds. Then he said suddenly, out of nothing, you hated him, didn't you?

And Enoch answered, no, baas.

—Where's your son Johannes?

—In Cape Town, baas.

—Why didn't he become a shepherd?

—I wouldn't let him, baas.

—You sent him to the white University?

—Yes, baas.

—So that he could play the white baas?

—No, baas.

—Why does he never come to see you?

—The Big Baas would not let him, baas.

—Because he wouldn't become a shepherd?

—Yes, baas.

—So you hated him, didn't you?

—No, baas.

Robbertse looked at him with contempt.

—A man keeps your own son away from your door, because you want a better life for him, and you don't hate him? God, what are you made of?

He continued to look at Maarman with contempt, then shrugged his shoulders as though it were a bad business; then he suddenly grew intimate, confidential, even friendly.

—Maarman, I have news for you, you may think it good, you may think it bad. But you have a right to know it, seeing it is about your son.

The shepherd was suddenly filled with a new apprehension. Robbertse was preparing some new blow. That was the kind of man he was, he hated to see any coloured man holding his head up, he hated to see any coloured man anywhere but on his knees or his stomach.

—Your son, said Robbertse, genially, you thought he was in Cape Town, didn't you?

—Yes, baas.

—Well, he isn't, said Robbertse, he's here in Poort, he was seen there yesterday.

He let it sink in, then he said to Maarman, he hated Big Baas Flip, didn't he?

Maarman cried out, no, baas.

For the second time Robbertse was on his feet, filling the room with his size, and his madness.

—He didn't hate him? he shouted. God Almighty, Big Baas Flip wouldn't let him come to his own home, and see his own father and mother, but he didn't hate him.

And you didn't hate him either, you creeping yellow bastard, what are you all made of?

He looked at the shepherd out of his mad red eyes. Then with contempt he said again, you creeping yellow Hottentot bastard.

—Baas, said Maarman.

—What?

—Baas, the baas can ask me what he likes, and I shall try to answer him, but I ask the baas not to insult me in my own house, before my own wife.

Robbertse appeared delighted, charmed. Some other white man might have been outraged that a coloured man should so advise him, but he was able to admire such manly pride.

—Insult you? he said. Didn't you see me take off my hat when I came into this house?

He turned to Sara and asked her, didn't you see me take off my hat when I came into this house?

—Yes, baas.

—Did you think I was insulting your husband?

—No, baas.

Robbertse smiled at her ingratiatingly. I only called him a creeping yellow Hottentot bastard, he said.

The cruel words destroyed the sense of piquancy for him, and now he was truly outraged. He took a step towards the shepherd, and his colleague, the other detective, the silent one, suddenly shouted at him, Robbertse!

Robbertse stopped. He looked vacantly at Maarman.

—Was someone calling me? he asked. Did you hear a voice calling me?

Maarman was terrified, fascinated, he could see the red foam. He was at a loss, not knowing whether this was madness, or madness affecting to be madness, or what it was.

—The other baas was calling you, baas.

Then it was suddenly all over. Robbertse sat down again on the chair to ask more questions.

—You knew there was money stolen?

—Yes, baas.

—Who told you?

—Mimi, the girl who works at the house.

—You knew the money was in an iron safe, and they took it away?

—Yes, baas.

—Where would they take it to?

—I don't know, baas.

—Where would you have taken it, if you had stolen it?

But Maarman didn't answer.

—You won't answer, eh?

All three of them watched Robbertse anxiously, lest the storm should return. But he smiled benevolently at Maarman, as though he knew that even a coloured man must have pride, as though he thought all the better of him for it, and said, all right, I won't ask that question. But I want you to think of the places where that safe could be. It must have been carried by at least two men, perhaps more. And they couldn't have got it off the farm in the time. So it's still on the farm. Now all I want you to do is to think where it could be. No one knows this farm better than you.

—I'll think, baas.

The other detective suddenly said, *the lieutenant's come*. The two of them stood just inside the door, looking over to the house on the other side of the valley. Then suddenly Robbertse rounded on Maarman, and catching him by the back of the neck, forced him to the door, so that he could look too.

—You see that, he said. They want to know who killed Big Baas Flip, and they want to know soon. Do you see them?

—Yes, baas.

—And you see that lieutenant. He rides round in a Chrysler, and by God, he wants to know too. And by God he'll ride me if I don't find out.

He pulled the shepherd back into the room, and put on his hat and went out, followed by the other.

—Don't think you've seen the last of me, he said to Maarman. You've got to show me where your friends hid that safe.

Then he and his companion joined the other two detectives, and all four of them turned back towards the big house. They talked animatedly, and more than once, all of them stood for a moment while one of them made some point or put forward some theory. No one would have known that one of them was mad.

Twelve hours since they had taken her husband away. Twelve hours since the mad detective had come for him, with those red tormented eyes, as though the lieutenant were riding him too hard. He had grinned at her husband. *Come and we'll look for the safe*, he said. The sun was sinking in the sky, over the hills of Kroon. It was no time to be looking for a safe.

She did not sleep that night. Her neighbours had come to sit with her, till midnight, till two o'clock, till four o'clock, but there was no sign. Why did he not come back? Were they still searching at this hour of the morning? Then the sun was rising, over the hills of Kroon.

On the other side of the valley the big house was awake, for this was the day that Big Baas Flip would be laid to rest, under the cypress trees of the graveyard in the stones. Leaderless, the shepherds had gone to Baas Gysbert to be given the day's work; and Hendrik Baadjies, second shepherd, speaking on behalf of Sara Maarman, wife of the head-shepherd, told Baas Gysbert that the police had taken Enoch Maarman at sunset, and now at dawn he had not yet returned, and that his wife was anxious. Would Baas Gysbert not please strike the telephone, not much only a little, not for long only a short time, to ask what had become of his father's head-shepherd?

And Baas Gysbert replied in a voice trembling with passion, do you not know it was my father who was killed?

So Hendrik Baadjies touched his hat, and said, Pardon me, baas, that I asked.

Then he went to stand with the other shepherds, a man shamed, a man shamed standing with other shamed men, who must teach their children to know forever their station.

Fifteen hours. But she would not eat. Her neighbours brought food, but she would not. She could see the red foam at the corners of the mouth, and see the tremendous form and hear the tremendous voice that filled her house with anger, and with feigned politeness, and with contempt, and with cruel smiling. Because one was a shepherd, because one had no certitude of home or work or life or favour, because one's back had to be bent though one's soul would be upright, because one had to speak the smiling craven words under any injustice, because one had to bear as a brand this dark sun-warmed colour of the skin, as good surely as any other, because of these things, this mad policeman could strike down, and hold by the neck, and call a creeping yellow Hottentot bastard, a man who had never hurt another in his long gentle life, a man who like the great Christ was a lover of sheep and of little children, and had been a good husband and father except for those occasional outbursts that any sensible woman will pass over, outbursts of the imprisoned manhood that has got tired of the chains that keep it down on its knees. Yes this mad policeman could take off his hat mockingly in one's house, and ask a dozen questions that he, for all that he was as big as a mountain, would never have dared to ask a white person.

But the anger went from her suddenly, leaving her spent, leaving her again full of anxiety for the safety of her husband, and for the safety of her son who had chosen to come to Poort at this dangerous hour. Just as a person sits in the cold, and by keeping motionless enjoys some illusion of warmth, so she sat inwardly motionless, lest by some interior movement she would disturb the numbness of her mind, and feel the pain of her condition. However she was not allowed to remain so, for at eleven o'clock a message came from Hendrik Baadjies to say that it was certain that neither detective nor head-shepherd was on the farm of Kroon. Then at noon a boy brought her a message that her brother Solomon Koopman had come with a taxi to the gate of the farm, and that she should come at once to him there, because he did not wish to come to her house. She tied a doek round her head, and as soon as she saw her brother, she cried out to him, *are they safe?* When he looked mystified, she said, *my man and my child,* and her brother told her it must have been Robbertse's joke, that her son was safe in Cape Town and had not been in Poort at all. He was glad to be able to tell her this piece of news, for his other news was terrible that Enoch her husband was dead. He had always been a little afraid of his sister, who had brought up the family when their mother had died, so he did not know how to comfort her. But she wept only a little, like one who is used to such events, and must not grieve but must prepare for the next.

Then she said, *how did he die?* So he told her the story that the police had told him of Enoch's death, how that the night was dark, and how they had gone searching down by the river, and how Enoch had slipped on one of the big stones there and had fallen on his head, and how they had not hesitated but had rushed him to Poort, but he had died in the car.

What can one say to a story like that? So they said nothing. He was ashamed to tell it, but he had to tell it so, because he had a butcher's licence in Poort, and he could not afford to doubt the police.

—This happened in the dark, Sara said. Why do they let me know now?

Alas, they could not give her her husband's body, it was buried already! Alas, she would know what it was like in the summer, how death began to smell because of the heat, that was why they had buried it! Alas, they wouldn't have done it had they only known who he was, and that his home was so near, at the well-known farm of Kroon!

Couldn't the body be lifted again, and be taken to Kroon, to be buried there in the hills where Enoch Maarman had worked so faithfully for nearly fifty years, tending the sheep of Big Baas Flip? Alas, no it couldn't be, for it is one thing to bury a man, and quite another thing to take him up again. To bury a man one only needs a doctor, and even that not always, but to take him up again you would have to go to Cape Town and get the permission of the Minister himself. And they do not permit that lightly, to disturb a man's bones when once he has been laid to rest in the earth.

Solomon Koopman would have gone away, with a smile on his lips, and cold hate in his heart. But she would not. For this surely was one thing that was her own, the body of the man she had lived with for so many years. She wanted the young white policeman behind the desk to show her the certificate of her husband's death, and she wanted to know by whose orders he had been buried, and who had hurried his body into the earth, so that she could tell for herself whether it was possible that such a person had not known that this was the body of Enoch Maarman, head-shepherd of the farm of Kroon, who had that very night been in the company of Detective Robbertse.

She put these questions, through her brother Solomon Koopman, who had a butcher's licence, and framed the questions apologetically, because he knew that they implied that something was very wrong somewhere, that something was being hidden. But although he put the questions as nicely as possible, he could see that the policeman behind the desk was becoming impatient with this importunity, and was beginning to think that grief was no excuse for this cross-examination of authority. Other policemen came in too, and listened to the questions of this woman who would not go away, and one of them said to the young constable behind the desk, *show her the death certificate.*

There it was, *death due to sub-cranial bleeding.*

—He fell on his head, explained the older policeman, and the blood inside finished him.

—I ask to see Detective Robbertse, she said.

The policemen smiled and looked at each other, not in any flagrant way, just knowingly.

—You can't see him, said the older policeman, he went away on holiday this very morning.

—Why does he go on holiday, she asked, when he is working on this case?

The policemen began to look at her impatiently. She was going too far, even though her husband was dead. Her own brother was growing restless, and he said to her, sister, let us go.

Her tears were coming now, made to flow by sorrow and anger. The policemen were uneasy, and drifted away, leaving only the young constable at the desk.

—What happened? she asked. How did my husband die? Why is Detective Robbertse not here to answer my questions?

The young policeman said to her angrily, we don't answer such questions here. If you want to ask such questions, get a lawyer.

—Good, she said, I shall get a lawyer.

She and her brother turned to leave, but the older policeman was there at the door, polite and reasonable.

—Why isn't your sister sensible? he asked Solomon Koopman. A lawyer will only stir up trouble between the police and the people.

Koopman looked from the policeman to his sister, for he feared them both.

—Ask him, Sara said to her brother, if it is not sensible to want to know about one's husband's death.

—Tell her, said the policeman to Koopman, that it was an accident.

—He knows who I am, Sara said. Why did he allow my husband to be buried here when he knew that he lived at Kroon?

Her voice was rising, and to compensate for it, the policeman's voice grew lower and lower.

—I did not have him buried, he said desperately. It was an order from a high person.

Outside in the street, Koopman said to his sister miserably, sister, I beg you, do not get a lawyer. For if you do, I shall lose the licence, and who will help you to keep your son at the university?

Sara Maarman got back to her house as the sun was sinking over the hills of Kroon, twenty-four hours from the time that her husband had left with Detective Robbertse to look for the safe. She lit the lamp and sat down, too weary to think of food. While she sat there, Hendrik Baadjies knocked at the door and came in and brought her the sympathy of all the brown people on the farm of Kroon. Then he stood before her, twisting his hat in his hand almost as though she were a white woman. He brought a message from Baas Gysbert, who now needed a new shepherd, and needed Enoch Maarman's house for him to live in. She would be given three days to pack all her possessions, and the loan of the cart and donkeys to take them and herself to Poort.

—Is three days enough? asked Baadjies. For if it is not, I could ask for more.

—Three days is enough, she said.

When Baadjies had gone, she thought to herself, three days is three days too many, to go on living in this land of stone, three days before she could leave it all for the Cape, where her son lived, where people lived, so he told her, softer and sweeter lives.

ESSAYS

Jonathan Swift

A MODEST PROPOSAL

It is a melancholy object to those who walk through this great town[1] or travel in the country, when they see the streets, the roads, and cabin doors, crowded with beggars of the female sex, followed by three, four, or six children, all in rags and importuning every passenger for an alms. These mothers, instead of being able to work for their honest livelihood, are forced to employ all their time in strolling to beg sustenance for their helpless infants: who as they grow up either turn thieves for want of work, or leave their dear native country to fight for the pretender in Spain, or sell themselves to the Barbadoes.

I think it is agreed by all parties that this prodigious number of children in the arms, or on the backs, or at the heels of their mothers, and frequently of their fathers, is in the present deplorable state of the kingdom a very great additional grievance; and, therefore, whoever could find out a fair, cheap, and easy method of making these children sound, useful members of the commonwealth, would deserve so well of the public as to have his statue set up for a preserver of the nation.

But my intention is very far from being confined to provide only for the children of professed beggars; it is of a much greater extent, and shall take in the whole number of infants at a certain age who are born of parents in effect as little able to support them as those who demand our charity in the streets.

As to my own part, having turned my thoughts for many years upon this important subject, and maturely weighed the several schemes of our projectors, I have always found them grossly mistaken in their computation. It is true, a child just dropped from its dam may be supported by her milk for a solar year, with little other nourishment; at most not above the value of 2s., which the mother may certainly get, or the value in scraps, by her lawful occupation of begging; and it is exactly at one year old that I propose to provide for them in such a manner as instead of being a charge upon their parents or the parish, or wanting food and raiment for the rest of their lives, they shall on the contrary contribute to the feeding, and partly to the clothing, of many thousands.

1 [Dublin.]

There is likewise another great advantage in my scheme, that it will prevent those voluntary abortions, and that horrid practice of women murdering their bastard children, alas! too frequent among us! sacrificing the poor innocent babes I doubt more to avoid the expense than the shame, which would move tears and pity in the most savage and inhuman breast.

The number of souls in this kingdom being usually reckoned one million and a half, of these I calculate there may be about 200,000 couple whose wives are breeders; from which number I subtract 30,000 couple who are able to maintain their own children (although I apprehend there cannot be so many, under the present distress of the kingdom); but this being granted, there will remain 170,000 breeders. I again subtract 50,000 for those women who miscarry, or whose children die by accident or disease within the year. There only remain 120,000 children of poor parents annually born. The question therefore is, how this number shall be reared and provided for? which, as I have already said, under the present situation of affairs, is utterly impossible by all the methods hitherto proposed. For we can neither employ them in handicraft or agriculture; we neither build houses (I mean in the country) nor cultivate land; they can very seldom pick up a livelihood by stealing, till they arrive at six years old, except where they are of towardly parts; although I confess they learn the rudiments much earlier; during which time they can, however, be properly looked upon only as probationers; as I have been informed by a principal gentleman in the county of Cavan, who protested to me that he never knew above one or two instances under the age of six, even in a part of the kingdom so renowned for the quickest proficiency in that art.

I am assured by our merchants, that a boy or a girl before twelve years old is no saleable commodity; and even when they come to this age they will not yield above 3*l.* or 3*l.* 2*s.* 6*d.* at most on the exchange; which cannot turn to account either to the parents or kingdom, the charge of nutriment and rags having been at least four times that value.

I shall now therefore humbly propose my own thoughts, which I hope will not be liable to the least objection.

I have been assured by a very knowing American of my acquaintance in London, that a young healthy child well nursed is at a year old a most delicious, nourishing, and wholesome food, whether stewed, roasted, baked, or broiled; and I make no doubt that it will equally serve in a fricassee or a ragout.

I do therefore humbly offer it to public consideration that of the 120,000 children already computed, 20,000 may be reserved for breed, whereof only one-fourth part to be males; which is more than we allow to sheep, black cattle, or swine; and my reason is, that these children are seldom the fruits of marriage, a circumstance not much regarded by our savages; therefore one male will be sufficient to serve four females. That the remaining 100,000 may, at a year old, be offered in sale to the persons of quality and fortune through the kingdom; always advising the mother to let them suck plentifully in the last month, so as to render them plump and fat for a good table. A child will make two dishes at an entertainment for friends; and when the family dines alone, the fore or hind quarter will make a reasonable dish, and seasoned with a little pepper or salt will be very good boiled on the fourth day, especially in winter.

I have reckoned upon a medium that a child just born will weigh 12 pounds, and in a solar year, if tolerably nursed, will increase to 28 pounds.

I grant this food will be somewhat dear, and therefore very proper for landlords, who, as they have already devoured most of the parents, seem to have the best title to the children.

Infant's flesh will be in season throughout the year, but more plentiful in March, and a little before and after: for we are told by a grave author, an eminent French physician, that fish being a prolific diet, there are more children born in Roman Catholic countries about nine months after Lent than at any other season; therefore, reckoning a year after Lent, the markets will be more glutted than usual, because the number of popish infants is at least three to one in this kingdom: and therefore it will have one other collateral advantage, by lessening the number of papists among us.

I have already computed the charge of nursing a beggar's child (in which list I reckon all cottagers, laborers, and four-fifths of the farmers) to be about 2*s.* per annum, rags included; and I believe no gentleman would repine to give 10*s.* for the carcass of a good fat child, which, as I have said, will make four dishes of excellent nutritive meat, when he has only some particular friend or his own family to dine with him. Thus the squire will learn to be a good landlord, and grow popular among the tenants; the mother will have 8*s.* net profit, and be fit for work till she produces another child.

Those who are more thrifty (as I must confess the times require) may flay the carcass; the skin of which artificially dressed will make admirable gloves for ladies, and summer boots for fine gentlemen.

As to our city of Dublin, shambles may be appointed for this purpose in the most convenient parts of it, and butchers we may be assured will not be wanting; although I rather recommend buying the child alive, and dressing them hot from the knife as we do roasting pigs.

A very worthy person, a true lover of his country, and whose virtues I highly esteem, was lately pleased in discoursing on this matter to offer a refinement upon my scheme. He said that many gentlemen of this kingdom, having of late destroyed their deer, he conceived that the want of venison might be well supplied by the bodies of young lads and maidens, not exceeding fourteen years of age nor under twelve; so great a number of both sexes in every country being now ready to starve for want of work and service; and these to be disposed of by their parents, if alive, or otherwise by their nearest relations. But with due deference to so excellent a friend and so deserving a patriot, I cannot be altogether in his sentiments; for as to the males, my American acquaintance assured me from frequent experience that their flesh was generally tough and lean, like that of our school-boys by continual exercise, and their taste disagreeable; and to fatten them would not answer the charge. Then as to the females, it would, I think, with humble submission be a loss to the public, because they soon would become breeders themselves: and besides, it is not improbable that some scrupulous people might be apt to censure such a practice (although indeed very unjustly), as a little bordering upon cruelty; which, I confess, has always been with me the strongest objection against any project, how well soever intended.

But in order to justify my friend, he confessed that this expedient was put into his head by the famous Psalmanazar, a native of the island Formosa, who came from thence to London about twenty years ago: and in conversation told my friend, that in his country when any young person happened to be put to death, the executioner sold the carcass to persons of quality as a prime dainty; and that in his time the body of a plump girl of fifteen, who was crucified for an attempt to poison the emperor, was sold to his imperial majesty's prime minister of state, and other great mandarins of the court, in joints from the gibbet, at 400 crowns. Neither indeed can I deny, that if the same use were made of several plump young girls in this town, who without one single groat to their fortunes cannot stir abroad without a chair, and appear at playhouse and assembles in foreign fineries which they never will pay for, the kingdom would not be the worse.

Some persons of a desponding spirit are in great concern about that vast number of poor people, who are aged, diseased, or maimed, and I have been desired to employ my thoughts what course may be taken to ease the nation of so grievous an encumbrance. But I am not in the least pain upon that matter, because it is very well known that they are every day dying and rotting by cold and famine, and filth and vermin, as fast as can be reasonably expected. And as to the young laborers, they are now in as hopeful a condition: they cannot get work, and consequently pine away for want of nourishment, to a degree that if at any time they are accidentally hired to common labor, they have not strength to perform it; and thus the country and themselves are happily delivered from the evils to come.

I have too long digressed, and therefore shall return to my subject. I think the advantages by the proposal which I have made are obvious and many, as well as of the highest importance.

For first, as I have already observed, it would greatly lessen the number of papists, with whom we are yearly overrun, being the principal breeders of the nation as well as our most dangerous enemies; and who stay at home on purpose to deliver the kingdom to the Pretender, hoping to take their advantage by the absence of so many good Protestants, who have chosen rather to leave their country than stay at home and pay tithes against their conscience to an Episcopal curate.

Secondly, The poor tenants will have something valuable of their own, which by law may be made liable to distress and help to pay their landlord's rent, their corn and cattle being already seized, and money a thing unknown.

Thirdly, Whereas the maintenance of 100,000 children from two years old and upward, cannot be computed at less than 10*s.* a-piece per annum, the nation's stock will be thereby increased £50,000 per annum, beside the profit of a new dish introduced to the tables of all gentlemen of fortune in the kingdom who have any refinement in taste. And the money will circulate among ourselves, the goods being entirely of our own growth and manufacture.

Fourthly, The constant breeders, beside the gain of 8*s.* sterling per annum by the sale of their children, will be rid of the charge of maintaining them after the first year.

Fifthly, This food would likewise bring great custom to taverns, where the vintners will certainly be so prudent as to procure the best receipts for dressing it to perfection, and consequently have their houses frequented by all the fine gentlemen, who justly value themselves upon their knowledge in good eating; and a skilful cook, who understands how to oblige his guests, will contrive to make it as expensive as they please.

Sixthly, This would be a great inducement to marriage, which all wise nations have either encouraged by rewards or enforced by laws and penalties. It would increase the care and tenderness of mothers toward their children, when they were sure of a settlement for life to the poor babes, provided in some sort by the public, to their annual profit instead of expense. We should see an honest emulation among the married women, which of them would bring the fattest child to the market. Men would become as fond of their wives during the time of their pregnancy as they are now of their mares in foal, their cows in calf, their sows when they are ready to farrow; nor offer to beat or kick them (as is too frequent a practice) for fear of a miscarriage.

Many other advantages might be enumerated. For instance, the addition of some thousand carcasses in our exportation of barreled beef, the propagation of swine's flesh, and improvement in the art of making good bacon, so much wanted among us by the great destruction of pigs, too frequent at our table; which are no way comparable in taste or magnificence to a well-grown, fat, yearling child, which roasted whole will make a considerable figure at a lord mayor's feast or any other public entertainment. But this and many others I omit, being studious of brevity.

Supposing that 1000 families in this city would be constant customers for infants' flesh, beside others who might have it at merry-meetings, particularly at weddings and christenings, I compute that Dublin would take off annually about 20,000 carcasses; and the rest of the kingdom (where probably they will be sold somewhat cheaper) the remaining 80,000.

I can think of no one objection that will possibly be raised against this proposal, unless it should be urged that the number of people will be thereby much lessened in the kingdom. This I freely own, and it was indeed one principal design in offering it to the world. I desire the reader will observe, that I calculate my remedy for this one individual kingdom of Ireland and for no other that ever was, is, or I think ever can be upon earth. Therefore let no man talk to me of other expedients: of taxing our absentees at 5*s*. a pound: of using neither clothes nor household furniture except what is of our own growth and manufacture: of utterly rejecting the materials and instruments that promote foreign luxury: of curing the expensiveness of pride, vanity, idleness, and gaming in our women: of introducing a vein of parsimony, prudence, and temperance: of learning to love our country, in the want of which we differ even from LAPLANDERS and the inhabitants of TOPINAMBOO[2]: of quitting our animosities and factions, nor acting any longer like the Jews, who were murdering one another at the very moment their city was taken: of being a little cautious not to sell our country and conscience for nothing: of teaching landlords to have at least one degree of mercy toward their tenants: lastly, of putting a spirit of honesty, industry, and skill into our shopkeepers; who, if a resolution could now be taken to buy only our native goods, would immediately unite to cheat and exact upon us in the price, the measure, and the goodness, nor

2 [In Brazil.]

could ever yet be brought to make one fair proposal of just dealing, though often and earnestly invited to it.

Therefore I repeat, let no man talk to me of these and the like expedients, till he has at least some glimpse of hope that there will be ever some hearty and sincere attempt to put them in practice.

But as to myself, having been wearied out for many years with offering vain, idle, visionary thoughts, and at length utterly despairing of success, I fortunately fell upon this proposal; which, as it is wholly new, so it has something solid and real, of no expense and little trouble, full in our own power, and whereby we can incur no danger in disobliging England. For this kind of commodity will not bear exportation, the flesh being of too tender a consistence to admit a long continuance in salt, although perhaps I could name a country which would be glad to eat up our whole nation without it.

After all, I am not so violently bent upon my own opinion as to reject any offer proposed by wise men, which shall be found equally innocent, cheap, easy, and effectual. But before something of that kind shall be advanced in contradiction to my scheme, and offering a better, I desire the author or authors will be pleased maturely to consider two points. First, as things now stand, how they will be able to find food and raiment for 100,000 useless mouths and backs. And secondly, there being a round million of creatures in human figure throughout this kingdom, whose whole subsistence put into a common stock would leave them in debt 2,000,000*l.* sterling, adding those who are beggars by profession to the bulk of farmers, cottagers, and laborers, with the wives and children who are beggars in effect; I desire those politicians who dislike my overture, and may perhaps be so bold as to attempt an answer, that they will first ask the parents of these mortals, whether they would not at this day think it a great happiness to have been sold for food at a year old in the manner I prescribe, and thereby have avoided such a perpetual scene of misfortunes as they have since gone through by the oppression of landlords, the impossibility of paying rent without money or trade, the want of common sustenance, with neither house nor clothes to cover them from the inclemencies of the weather, and the most inevitable prospect of entailing the like or greater miseries upon their breed for ever.

I profess, in the sincerity of my heart, that I have not the least personal interest in endeavoring to promote this necessary work, having no other motive than the public good of my country, by advancing our trade, providing for infants, relieving the poor, and giving some pleasure to the rich. I have no children by which I can propose to get a single penny; the youngest being nine years old, and my wife past child-bearing.

James Baldwin

NOTES OF A NATIVE SON

On the 29th of July, in 1943, my father died. On the same day, a few hours later, his last child was born. Over a month before this, while all our energies were concentrated in waiting for these events, there had been, in Detroit, one of the bloodiest race riots of the century. A few hours after my father's funeral, while he lay in state in the undertaker's chapel, a race riot broke out in Harlem. On the morning of the 3rd day of August, we drove my father to the graveyard through a wilderness of smashed plate glass.

The day of my father's funeral had also been my nineteenth birthday. As we drove him to the graveyard, the spoils of injustice, anarchy, discontent, and hatred were all around us. It seemed to me that God himself had devised, to mark my father's end, the most sustained and brutally dissonant of codas. And it seemed to me, too, that the violence which rose all about us as my father left the world had been devised as a corrective for the pride of his eldest son. I had declined to believe in that apocalypse which had been central to my father's vision; very well, life seemed to be saying, here is something that will certainly pass for an apocalypse until the real thing comes along. I had inclined to be contemptuous of my father for the conditions of his life, for the conditions of our lives. When his life had ended I began to wonder about that life and also, in a new way, to be apprehensive about my own.

I had not known my father very well. We had got on badly, partly because we shared, in our different fashions, the vice of stubborn pride. When he was dead I realized that I had hardly ever spoken to him. When he had been dead a long time I began to wish I had. It seems to be typical of life in America where opportunities, real and fancied, are thicker than anywhere else on the globe, that the second generation has no time to talk to the first. No one, including my father, seems to have known exactly how old he was, but his mother had been born during slavery. He was of the first generation of free men. He, along with thousands of other Negroes, came North after 1919 and I was part of that generation which had never seen the landscape of what Negroes sometimes call the Old Country.

He had been born in New Orleans and had been a quite young man there during the time that Louis Armstrong, a boy, was running errands for the dives and honky-tonks of what was always pre-

NOTES OF A NATIVE SON: From *Notes of a Native Son* by James Baldwin. Reprinted by permission of the Beacon Press.

sented to me as one of the most wicked of cities—to this day, whenever I think of New Orleans, I also helplessly think of Sodom and Gomorrah. My father never mentioned Louis Armstrong, except to forbid us to play his records; but there was a picture of him on our wall for a long time. One of my father's strong-willed female relatives had placed it there and forbade my father to take it down. He never did, but he eventually maneuvered her out of the house and when, some years later, she was in trouble and near death, he refused to do anything to help her.

He was, I think, very handsome. I gather this from photographs and from my own memories of him, dressed in his Sunday best and on his way to preach a sermon somewhere, when I was little. Handsome, proud, and ingrown, "like a toe-nail," somebody said. But he looked to me, as I grew older, like pictures I had seen of African tribal chieftains: he really should have been naked, with war-paint on and barbaric mementos, standing among spears. He could be chilling in the pulpit and indescribably cruel in his personal life and he was certainly the most bitter man I have ever met; yet it must be said that there was something else in him, buried in him, which lent him his tremendous power and, even, a rather crushing charm. It had something to do with his blackness, I think—he was very black—with his blackness and his beauty, and with the fact that he knew that he was black but did not know that he was beautiful. He claimed to be proud of his blackness but it had also been the cause of much humiliation and it had fixed bleak boundaries to his life. He was not a young man when we were growing up and he had already suffered many kinds of ruin; in his outrageously demanding and protective way he loved his children, who were black like him and menaced, like him; and all these things sometimes showed in his face when he tried, never to my knowledge with any success, to establish contact with any of us. When he took one of his children on his knee to play, the child always became fretful and began to cry; when he tried to help one of us with our homework the absolutely unabating tension which emanated from him caused our minds and our tongues to become paralyzed, so that he, scarcely knowing why flew into a rage and the child, not knowing why, was punished. If it ever entered his head to bring a surprise home for his children, it was, almost unfailingly, the wrong surprise and even the big watermelons he often brought home on his back in the summertime led to the most appalling scenes. I do not remember in all those years, that one of his children was ever glad to see him come home. From what I was able to gather of his early life, it seemed that this inability to establish contact with other people had always marked him and had been one of the things which had driven him out of New Orleans. There was something in him therefore, groping and tentative, which was never expressed and which was buried with him. One saw it most clearly when he was facing new people and hoping to impress them. But he never did, not for long. We went from church to smaller and more improbable church, he found himself in less and less demand as a minister, and by the time he died none of his friends had come to see him for a long time. He had lived and died in an intolerable bitterness of spirit and it frightened me, as we drove him to the graveyard through those unquiet, ruined streets, to see how powerful and overflowing this bitterness could be and to realize that this bitterness now was mine.

When he died I had been away from home for a little over a year. In that year I had had time to become aware of the meaning of all my father's bitter warnings, had discovered the secret of his proudly pursed lips and rigid carriage: I had discovered the weight of white people in the world. I saw that this had been for my ancestors and now would be for me an awful thing to live with and that the bitterness which had helped to kill my father could also kill me.

He had been ill a long time—in the mind, as we now realized, reliving instances of his fantastic intransigence in the new light of his affliction and endeavoring to feel a sorrow for him which never, quite, came true. We had not known that he was being eaten up by paranoia, and the discovery that his cruelty, to our bodies and our minds, had been one of the symptoms of his illness was not, then, enough to enable us to forgive him. The younger children felt, quite simply, relief that he would not be coming home anymore. My mother's observation that it was was he, after all, who had kept them alive all these years meant nothing because the problems of keeping children alive are not real for children. The older children felt, with my father gone, that they could invite their friends to the house without fear that their friends would be insulted or, as had sometimes happened with me, being told that their friends were in league with the devil and intended to rob our family of everything we owned. (I didn't fail to wonder, and it made me hate him, what on earth we owned that anybody else would want.)

His illness was beyond all hope of healing before anyone realized that he was ill. He had always been so strange and had lived, like a prophet, in such unimaginably close communion with the Lord that his long silences which were punctuated by moans and hallelujahs and snatches of old songs while he sat at the living-room window never seemed odd to us. It was not until he refused to eat because, he said, his family was trying to poison him that my mother was forced to accept as a fact what had, until then, been only an unwilling suspicion. When he was committed, it was discovered that he had tuberculosis and, as it turned out, the disease of his mind allowed the disease of his body to destroy him. For the doctors could not force him to eat, either, and, though he was fed intravenously, it was clear from the beginning that there was no hope for him.

In my mind's eye I could see him, sitting at the window, locked up in his terrors; hating and fearing every living soul including his children who had betrayed him, too, by reaching towards the world which had despised him. There were nine of us. I began to wonder what it could have felt like for such a man to have had nine children whom he could barely feed. He used to make little jokes about our poverty, which never, of course, seemed very funny to us; they could not have seemed very funny to him, either, or else our all too feeble response to them would never have caused such rages. He spent great energy and achieved, to our chagrin, no small amount of success in keeping us away from the people who surrounded us, people who had all-night rent parties to which we listened when we should have been sleeping, people who cursed and drank and flashed razor blades on Lenox Avenue. He could not understand why, if they had so much energy to spare, they could not use it to make their lives better. He treated almost everybody on our block with a most uncharitable asperity and neither they, nor, of course, their children were slow to reciprocate.

The only white people who came to our house were welfare workers and bill collectors. It was almost always my mother who dealt with them, for my father's temper, which was at the mercy of his pride, was never to be trusted. It was clear that he felt their very presence in his home to be a violation: this was conveyed by his carriage almost ludicrously stiff, and by his voice, harsh and vindictively polite. When I was around nine or ten I wrote a play which was directed by a young, white schoolteacher, a woman, who then took an interest in me, and gave me books to read and, in order to corroborate my theatrical bent, decided to take me to see what she somewhat tactlessly referred to as "real" plays. Theatergoing was forbidden in our house, but, with the really cruel intuitiveness of a child, I suspected that the color of this woman's skin would carry the day for me. When, at school, she suggested taking me to the theater, I did not, as I might have done if she had been a Negro, find a way of discouraging her, but agreed that she should pick me up at my house one evening. I then, very cleverly, left all the rest to my mother, who suggested to my father, as I knew she would, that it would not be very nice to let such a kind woman make the trip for nothing. Also, since it was a schoolteacher, I imagine that my mother countered the idea of sin with the idea of "education," which word, even with my father, carried a kind of bitter weight.

Before the teacher came my father took me aside to ask *why* she was coming, what *interest* she could possibly have in our house, in a boy like me. I said I didn't know but I, too, suggested that it had something to do with education. And I understood that my father was waiting for me to say something—I didn't quite know what; perhaps that I wanted his protection against this teacher and her "education." I said none of these things and the teacher came and we went out. It was clear, during the brief interview in our living room, that my father was agreeing very much against his will and that he would have refused permission if he had dared. The fact that he did not dare caused me to despise him: I had no way of knowing that he was facing in that living room a wholly unprecedented and frightening situation.

Later, when my father had been laid off from his job, this woman became very important to us. She was really a very sweet and generous woman and went to a great deal of trouble to be of help to us, particularly during one awful winter. My mother called her by the highest name she knew: she said she was a "christian." My father could scarcely disagree but during the four or five years of our relatively close association he never trusted her and was always trying to surprise in her open, Midwestern face the genuine, cunningly hidden, and hideous motivation. In later years, particularly when it began to be clear that this "education" of mine was going to lead me to perdition, he became more explicit and warned me that my white friends in high school were not really my friends and that I would see, when I was older, how white people would do anything to keep a Negro down. Some of them could be nice, he admitted, but none of them were to be trusted and most of them were not even nice. The best thing was to have as little to do with them as possible. I did not feel this way and I was certain, in my innocence, that I never would.

But the year which preceded my father's death had made a great change in my life. I had been living in New Jersey, working in defense plants, working and living among southerners, white and black. I knew about the south, of course, and about how southerners treated Negroes and how they expected them to behave, but it had never entered my mind that anyone would look at me and expect *me* to behave that way. I learned in New Jersey that to be a Negro meant, precisely, that one was never looked at but was simply at the mercy of the reflexes the color of one's skin caused in other people. I acted in New Jersey as I had always acted, that is as though I thought a great deal of myself—I had to *act* that way—with results that were, simply, unbelievable. I had scarcely arrived before I had earned the enmity, which was extraordinarily ingenious, of all my superiors and nearly all my co-workers. In the beginning, to make matters worse, I simply did not know what was happening. I did not know what I had done, and I shortly began to wonder what *anyone* could possibly do, to bring about such unanimous, active, and unbearably vocal hostility. I knew about jim-crow but I had never experienced it. I went to the same self-service restaurant three times and stood with all the Princeton boys before the counter, waiting for a hamburger and coffee; it was always an extraordinarily long time before anything was set before me; but it was not until the fourth visit that I learned that, in fact, nothing had ever been set before me: I had simply picked something up. Negroes were not served there, I was told, and they had been waiting for me to realize that I was always the only Negro present. Once I was told this, I determined to go there all the time. But now they were ready for me and, though some dreadful scenes were subsequently enacted in that restaurant, I never ate there again.

It was the same story all over New Jersey, in bars, bowling alleys, diners, places to live. I was always being forced to leave, silently, or with mutual imprecations. I very shortly became notorious and children giggled behind me when I passed and their elders whispered or shouted—they really believed that I was mad. And it did begin to work on my mind, of course; I began to be afraid to go anywhere and to compensate for this I went places to which I really should not have gone and where, God knows, I had no desire to be. My reputation in town naturally enhanced my reputation at work and my working day became one long series of acrobatics designed to keep me out of trouble. I cannot say that these acrobatics succeeded. It began to seem that the machinery of the organization I worked for was turning over, day and night, with but one aim: to eject me. I was fired once, and contrived, with the aid of a friend from New York, to get back on the payroll; was fired again, and bounced back again. It took a while to fire me for the third time, but the third time took. There were no loopholes anywhere. There was not even any way of getting back inside the gates.

That year in New Jersey lives in my mind as though it were the year during which, having an unsuspected predilection for it, I first contracted some dread, chronic disease, the unfailing symptom of which is a kind of blind fever, a pounding in the skull and fire in the bowels. Once this disease is contracted, one can never be really carefree again, for the fever, without an instant's warning, can recur at any moment. It can wreck more important things than race relations. There is not a Negro alive who does not have this rage in his blood—one has the choice, merely, of living with it consciously or surrendering to it. As for me, this fever has recurred in me, and does, and will until the day I die.

My last night in New Jersey, a white friend from New York took me to the nearest big town, Trenton, to go to the movies and have a few drinks. As it turned out, he also saved me from, at the very least, a violent whipping. Almost every detail of that night stands out very clearly in my memory. I even remember the name of the movie we saw because its title impressed me as being so patly ironical. It was a movie about the German occupation of France, starring Maureen O'Hara and Charles Laughton and called *This Land Is Mine*. I remember the name of the diner we walked into when the movie ended: it was the "American Diner." When we walked in the counterman asked what we wanted and I remember answering with the casual sharpness which had become my habit: "We want a hamburger and a cup of coffee, what do you think we want?" I do not know why, after a year of such rebuffs, I so completely failed to anticipate his answer, which was, of course, "We don't serve Negroes here." This reply failed to discompose me, at least for the moment. I made some sardonic comment about the name of the diner and we walked out into the streets.

This was the time of what was called the "brown-out," when the lights in all American cities were very dim. When we re-entered the streets something happened to me which had the force of an optical illusion, or a nightmare. The streets were very crowded and I was facing north. People were moving in every direction but it seemed to me, in that instant, that all of the people I could see, and many more than that, were moving toward me, against me, and that everyone was white. I remember how their faces gleamed. And I felt, like a physical sensation, a *click* at the nape of my neck as though some interior string connecting my head to my body had been cut. I began to walk. I heard my friend call after me, but I ignored him. Heaven only knows what was going on in his mind, but he had the good sense not to touch me—I don't know what would have happened if he had—and to keep me in sight. I don't know what was going on in my mind, either; I certainly had no conscious plan. I wanted to do something to crush these white faces, which were crushing me. I walked for perhaps a block or two until I came to an enormous, glittering, and fashionable restaurant in which I knew not even the intercession of the Virgin would cause me to be served. I pushed through the doors and took the first vacant seat I saw, at a table for two, and waited.

I do not know how long I waited and I rather wonder, until today, what I could possibly have looked like. Whatever I looked like, I frightened the waitress who shortly appeared, and the moment she appeared all of my fury flowed towards her. I hated her for her white face, and for her great, astounded, frightened eyes. I felt that if she found a black man so frightening I would make her fright worthwhile.

She did not ask me what I wanted, but repeated, as though she had learned it somewhere, "We don't serve Negroes here." She did not say it with the blunt, derisive hostility to which I had grown so accustomed, but, rather, with a note of apology in her voice, and fear. This made me colder and more murderous than ever. I felt I had to do something with my hands. I wanted her to come close enough for me to get her neck between my hands.

So I pretended not to have understood her, hoping to draw her closer. And she did step a very short step closer, with her pencil poised incongruously over her pad, and repeated the formula: "... don't serve Negroes here."

Somehow, with the repetition of that phrase, which was already ringing in my head like a thousand bells of a nightmare, I realized that she would never come any closer and that I would have to strike from a distance. There was nothing on the table but an ordinary watermug half full of water, and I picked this up and hurled it with all my strength at her. She ducked and it missed her and shattered against the mirror behind the bar. And, with that sound, my frozen blood abruptly thawed, I returned from wherever I had been, I *saw*, for the first time, the restaurant, the people with their mouths open, already, as it seemed to me, rising as one man, and I realized what I had done, and where I was, and I was frightened. I rose and began running for the door. A round, potbellied man grabbed me by the nape of the neck just as I reached the doors and began to beat me about the face. I kicked him and got loose and ran into the streets. My friend whispered, "*Run!*" and I ran.

My friend stayed outside the restaurant long enough to misdirect my pursuers and the police, who arrived, he told me, at once. I do not know what I said to him when he came to my room that night. I could not have said much. I felt, in the oddest, most awful way, that I had somehow betrayed him. I lived it over and over and over again, the way one relives an automobile accident after it has happened and one finds oneself alone and safe. I could not get over two facts, both equally difficult for the imagination to grasp, and one was that I could have been murdered. But the other was that I had been ready to commit murder. I saw nothing very clearly but I did see this: that my life, my *real* life, was in danger, and not from anything other people might do but from the hatred I carried in my own heart.

2

I HAD returned home around the second week in June—in great haste because it seemed that my father's death and my mother's confinement were both but a matter of hours. In the case of my mother, it soon became clear that she had simply made a miscalculation. This had always been her tendency and I don't believe that a single one of us arrived in the world, or has since arrived anywhere else, on time. But none of us dawdled so intolerably about the business of being born as did my baby sister. We sometimes amused ourselves, during those endless, stifling weeks, by picturing the baby sitting within in the safe, warm dark, bitterly regretting the necessity of becoming a part of our chaos and stubbornly putting it off as long as possible. I understood her perfectly and congratulated her on showing such good sense so soon. Death, however, sat as purposefully at my father's bedside as life stirred within my mother's womb and it was harder to understand why he so lingered in that long shadow. It seemed that he had bent, and for a long time, too, all of his energies towards dying. Now death was ready for him but my father held back.

All of Harlem, indeed, seemed to be infected by waiting. I had never before known it to be so violently still. Racial tensions throughout this country were exacerbated during the early years of the war, partly because the labor market brought together hundreds of thousands of ill-prepared people and partly because Negro soldiers, regardless of where they were born, received their military training in the south. What happened in defense plants and army camps had repercussions, naturally, in every Negro ghetto. The situation in Harlem had grown bad enough for clergymen, policemen, educators, politicians, and social workers to assert in one breath that there was no "crime wave" and to offer, in the very next breath, suggestions as to how to combat it. These suggestions always seemed to involve playgrounds, despite the fact that racial skirmishes were occurring in the playgrounds, too. Playground or not, crime wave or not, the Harlem police force had been augmented in March, and the unrest grew—perhaps, in fact, partly as a result of the ghetto's instinctive hatred of policemen. Perhaps the most revealing news item, out of the steady parade of reports of muggings, stabbings, shootings, assaults, gang wars, and accusations of police brutality, is the item concerning six Negro girls who set upon a white girl in the subway because, as they all too accurately put it, she was stepping on their toes. Indeed she was, all over the nation.

I had never before been so aware of policemen, on foot, on horseback, on corners, everywhere, always two by two. Nor had I ever been so aware of small knots of people. They were on stoops and on corners and in doorways, and what was striking about them, I think, was that they did not seem to be talking. Never, when I passed these groups, did the usual sound of a curse or a laugh ring out and neither did there seem to be any hum of gossip. There was certainly, on the other hand, occurring between them communication extraordinarily intense. Another thing that was striking was the unexpected diversity of the people who made up these groups. Usually, for example, one would see a group of sharpies standing on the street corner, jiving the passing chicks; or a group of older men, usually, for some reason, in the vicinity of a barber shop, discussing baseball scores, or the numbers, or making rather chilling observations about women they had known. Women, in a general way, tended to be seen less often together—unless they were church women, or very young girls, or prostitutes met together for an unprofessional instant. But that summer I saw the strangest combinations: large, respectable, churchly matrons standing on the stoops or the corners with their hair tied up, together with a girl in sleazy satin whose face bore the marks of gin and the razor, or heavy-set, abrupt, no-nonsense older men, in company with the most disreputable and fanatical "race" men, or these same "race" men with the sharpies, or these sharpies with the churchly women. Seventh Day Adventists and Methodists and Spiritualists seemed to be hobnobbing with Holyrollers and they were all, alike, entangled with the most flagrant disbelievers; something heavy in their stance seemed to indicate that they had all, incredibly, seen a common vision, and on each face there seemed to be the same strange, bitter shadow.

The churchly women and the matter-of-fact no-nonsense men had children in the Army. The sleazy girls they talked to had lovers there, the sharpies and the "race" men had friends and brothers there. It would have demanded an unquestioning patriotism, happily as uncommon in this country as it is undesirable, for these people not to have been disturbed by the bitter letters they received, by the newspaper stories they read, not to have been enraged by the posters, then to be found all over New York, which described the Japanese as "yellow-bellied Japs." It was only the "race" men, to be sure, who spoke ceaselessly of being revenged—how this vengeance was to be exacted was not clear—for the indignities and dangers suffered by Negro boys in uniform; but everybody felt a directionless, hopeless bitterness, as well as that panic which can scarcely be suppressed when one knows that a human being one loves is beyond one's reach, and in danger. This helplessness and this gnawing uneasiness does something, at length, to even the toughest mind. Perhaps the best way to sum all this up is to say that the people I knew felt, mainly, a peculiar kind of relief when they knew that their boys were being shipped out of the south, to do battle overseas. It was, perhaps, like feeling that the most dangerous part of a dangerous journey had been passed and that now, even if death should come, it would come with honor and without the complicity of their countrymen. Such a death would be, in short, a fact with which one could hope to live.

It was on the 28th of July, which I believe was a Wednesday, that I visited my father for the first time during his illness and for the last time in his life. The moment I saw him I knew why I had put off this visit so long. I had told my mother that I did not want to see him because I hated him. But this was not true. It was only that I *had* hated him and I wanted to hold on to this hatred. I did not want to look on him as a ruin: it was not a ruin I had hated. I imagine that one of the reasons people cling to their hates so stubbornly is because they sense, once hate is gone, that they will be forced to deal with pain.

We traveled out to him, his older sister and myself, to what seemed to be the very end of a very Long Island. It was hot and dusty and we wrangled, my aunt and I, all the way out, over the fact that I had recently begun to smoke and, as she said, to give myself airs. But I knew that she wrangled with me because she could not bear to face the fact of her brother's dying. Neither could I endure the reality of her despair, her unstated bafflement as to what had happened to her brother's life, and her own. So we wrangled and I smoked and from time to time she fell into a heavy reverie. Covertly, I watched her face, which was the face of an old woman; it had fallen in, the eyes were sunken and lightless; soon she would be dying, too.

In my childhood—it had not been so long ago—I had thought her beautiful. She had been quick-witted and quick-moving and very generous with all the children and each of her visits had been an event. At one time one of my brothers and myself had thought of running away to live with her. Now she could no longer produce out of her handbag some unexpected and yet familiar delight. She made me feel pity and revulsion and fear. It was awful to realize that she no longer caused me to feel affection. The closer we came to the hospital the more querulous she became and at the same time, naturally, grew more dependent on me. Between pity and guilt and fear I began to feel that there was another me trapped in my skull like a jack-in-the-box who might escape my control at any moment and fill the air with screaming.

She began to cry the moment we entered the room and she saw him lying there, all shriveled and still, like a little black monkey. The great, gleaming apparatus which fed him and would have compelled him to be still even if he had been able to move brought to mind, not beneficence, but torture; the tubes entering his arm made me think of pictures I had seen when a child, of Gulliver, tied down by the pygmies on that island. My aunt wept and wept, there was a whistling sound in my father's throat; nothing was said; he could not speak. I wanted to take his hand, to say something. But I do not know what I could have said, even if he could have heard me. He was not really in that room with us, he had at last really embarked on his journey; and though my aunt told me that he said he was going to meet Jesus, I did not hear anything except that whistling in his throat. The doctor came back and we left, into that unbearable train again, and home. In the morning came the telegram saying that he was dead. Then the house was suddenly full of relatives, friends, hysteria, and confusion and I quickly left my mother and the children to the care of those impressive women, who, in Negro communities at least, automatically appear at times of bereavement armed with lotions, proverbs, and patience, and an ability to cook. I went downtown. By the time I returned, later the same day, my mother had been carried to the hospital and the baby had been born.

3

FOR my father's funeral I had nothing black to wear and this posed a nagging problem all day long. It was one of those problems, simple, or impossible of solution, to which the mind insanely clings in order to avoid the mind's real trouble. I spent most of that day at the downtown apartment of a girl I knew, celebrating my birthday with whiskey and wondering what to wear that night. When planning a birthday celebration one naturally does not expect that it will be up against competition from a funeral and this girl had anticipated taking me out that night, for a big dinner and a night club afterwards. Sometime during the course of that long day we decided that we would go out anyway, when my father's funeral service was over. I imagine *I* decided it, since, as the funeral hour approached, it became clearer and clearer to me that I would not know what to do with myself when it was over. The girl, stifling her very lively concern as to the possible effects of the whiskey on one of my father's chief mourners, concentrated on being conciliatory and practically helpful. She found a black shirt for me somewhere and ironed it and, dressed in the darkest pants and jacket I owned, and slightly drunk, I made my way to my father's funeral.

The chapel was full, but not packed, and very quiet. There were, mainly, my father's relatives, and his children, and here and there I saw faces I had not seen since childhood, the faces of my father's one-time friends. They were very dark and solemn now, seeming somehow to suggest that they had known all along that something like this would happen. Chief among the mourners was my aunt, who had quarreled with my father all his life; by which I do not mean to suggest that her mourning was insincere or that she had not loved him. I suppose that she was one of the few people in the world who had, and their incessant quarreling proved precisely the strength of the tie that bound them. The only other person in the world, as far as I knew, whose relationship to my father rivaled my aunt's in depth was my mother, who was not there.

It seemed to me, of course, that it was a very long funeral. But it was, if anything, a rather shorter funeral than most, nor, since there were no overwhelming, uncontrollable expressions of grief, could it be called—if I dare to use the word—successful. The minister who preached my father's funeral sermon was one of the few my father had still been seeing as he neared his end. He presented to us in his sermon a man whom none of us had ever seen—a man thoughtful, patient, and forbearing, a Christian inspiration to all who knew him, and a model for his children. And no doubt the children, in their disturbed and guilty state, were almost ready to believe this; he had been remote enough to be anything and, anyway, the shock of the incontrovertible, that it was really our father lying up there in that casket, prepared the mind for anything. His sister moaned and this grief-stricken moaning was taken as corroboration. The other faces held a dark, non-committal thoughtfulness. This was not the man they had known, but they had scarcely expected to be confronted with *him*; this was, in a sense deeper than questions of fact, the man they had not known, and the man they had not known may have been the real one. The real man, whoever he had been, had suffered and now he was dead: this was all that was sure and all that mattered now. Every man in the chapel hoped that when his hour came he, too, would be eulogized, which is to say forgiven, and that all of his lapses, greeds, errors, and strayings from the truth would be invested with coherence and looked upon with charity. This was perhaps the last thing human beings could give each other and it was what they demanded, after all, of the Lord. Only the Lord saw the midnight tears, only He was present when one of His children, moaning and wringing hands, paced up and down the room. When one slapped one's child in anger the recoil in the heart reverberated through heaven and became part of the pain of the universe. And when the children were hungry and sullen and distrustful and one watched them, daily, growing wilder, and further away, and running headlong into danger, it was the Lord who knew what the charged heart endured as the strap was laid to the backside; the Lord alone who knew what one *would* have said if one had had, like the Lord, the gift of the living word. It was the Lord who knew of the impossibility every parent in that room faced: how to prepare the child for the day when the child would be despised and how to *create* in the child—by what means?—a stronger antidote to this poison than one had found for oneself. The avenues, side streets, bars, billiard halls, hospitals, police stations, and even the playgrounds of Harlem—not to mention the houses of correction, the jails, and the morgue—testified to the potency of the poison while remaining silent as to the efficacy of whatever antidote, irresistibly raising the question of whether or not such an antidote existed; raising, which was worse, the question of whether or not an antidote was desirable; perhaps poison should be fought with poison. With these several schisms in the mind and with more terrors in the heart than could be named, it was better not to judge the man who had gone down under an impossible burden. It was better to remember: *Thou knowest this man's fall; but thou knowest not his wrassling.*

While the preacher talked and I watched the children—years of changing their diapers, scrubbing them, slapping them, taking them to school, and scolding them had had the perhaps inevitable result of making me love them, though I am not sure I knew this then—my mind was busily breaking out with a rash of disconnected impressions. Snatches of popular songs, indecent jokes, bits of books I had read, movie sequences, faces, voices, political issues—I thought I was going mad; all these impressions suspended, as it were, in the solution of the faint nausea produced in me by the heat and liquor. For a moment I had the impression that my alcoholic breath, inefficiently disguised with chewing gum, filled the entire chapel. Then someone began singing one of my father's favorite songs and, abruptly, I was with him, sitting on his knee, in the hot, enormous, crowded church which was the first church we attended. It was the Abyssinia Baptist Church on 138th Street. We had not gone there long. With this image, a host of others came. I had forgotten, in the rage of my growing up, how proud my father had been of me when I was little. Apparently, I had had a voice and my father had liked to show me off before the members of the church. I had forgotten what he had looked like when he was pleased but now I remembered that he had always been grinning with pleasure when my solos ended. I even remembered certain expressions on his face when he teased my mother—had he loved her? I would never know. And when had it all begun to change? For now it seemed that he had not always been cruel. I remembered being taken for a haircut and scraping my knee on the footrest of the barber's chair and I remembered my father's face as he soothed my crying and applied the stinging iodine. Then I remembered our fights, fights which had been of the worst possible kind because my technique had been silence.

I remembered the one time in all our life together when we had really spoken to each other.

It was on a Sunday and it must have been shortly before I left home. We were walking, just the two of us, in our usual silence, to or from church. I was in high school and had been doing a lot of writing and I was, at about this time, the editor of the high school magazine. But I had also been a Young Minister and had been preaching from the pulpit. Lately, I had been taking fewer engagements and preached as rarely as possible. It was said in the church, quite truthfully, that I was "cooling off."

My father asked me abruptly, "You'd rather write than preach, wouldn't you?"

I was astonished at his question—because it was a real question. I answered, "Yes."

That was all we said. It was awful to remember that that was all we had *ever* said.

The casket now was opened and the mourners were being led up the aisle to look for the last time on the deceased. The assumption was that the family was too overcome with grief to be allowed to make this journey alone and I watched while my aunt was led to the casket and, muffled in black, and shaking, led back to her seat. I disapproved of forcing the children to look on their dead father, considering that the shock of his death, or, more truthfully, the shock of death as a reality, was already a little more than a child could bear, but my judgment in this matter had been overruled and there they were, bewildered and frightened and very small, being led, one by one, to the casket. But there is also something very gallant about children at such moments. It has something to do with their silence and gravity and with the fact that one cannot help them. Their legs, somehow, seem *exposed*, so that it is at once incredible and terribly clear that their legs are all they have to hold them up.

I had not wanted to go to the casket myself and I certainly had not wished to be led there, but there was no way of avoiding either of these forms. One of the deacons led me up and I looked on my father's face. I cannot say that it looked like him at all. His blackness had been equivocated by powder and there was no suggestion in that casket of what his power had or could have been. He was simply an old man dead, and it was hard to believe that he had ever given anyone either joy or pain. Yet, his life filled that room. Further up the avenue his wife was holding his newborn child. Life and death so close together, and love and hatred, and right and wrong, said something to me which I did not want to hear concerning man, concerning the life of man.

After the funeral, while I was downtown desperately celebrating my birthday, a Negro soldier, in the lobby of the Hotel Braddock, got into a fight with a white policeman over a Negro girl. Negro girls, white policemen, in or out of uniform, and Negro males—in or out of uniform—were part of the furniture of the lobby of the Hotel Braddock and this was certainly not the first time such an incident had occurred. It was destined, however, to receive an unprecedented publicity, for the fight between the policeman and the soldier ended with the shooting of the soldier. Rumor, flowing immediately to the streets outside, stated that the soldier had been shot in the back, an instantaneous and revealing invention, and that the soldier had died protecting a Negro woman. The facts were somewhat different—for example, the soldier had not been shot in the back, and was not dead, and the girl seems to have been as dubious a symbol of womanhood as her white counterpart in Georgia usually is, but no one was interested in the facts. They preferred the invention because this invention expressed and corroborated their hates and fears so perfectly. It is just as well to remember that people are always doing this. Perhaps many of those legends, including Christianity, to which the world clings began their conquest of the world with just some such concerted surrender to distortion. The effect, in Harlem, of this particular legend was like the effect of a lit match in a tin of gasoline. The mob gathered before the doors of the Hotel Braddock simply began to swell and to spread in every direction, and Harlem exploded.

The mob did not cross the ghetto lines. It would have been easy, for example, to have gone over Morningside Park on the west side or to have crossed the Grand Central railroad tracks at 125th Street on the east side, to wreak havoc in white neighborhoods. The mob seems to have been mainly interested in something more potent and real than the white face, that is, in white power, and the principal damage done during the riot of the summer of 1943 was to white business establishments in Harlem. It might have been a far bloodier story, of course, if, at the hour the riot began, these establishments had still been open. From the Hotel Braddock the mob fanned out, east and west along 125th Street, and for the entire length of Lenox, Seventh, and Eighth avenues. Along each of these avenues, and along each major side street—116th, 125th, 135th, and so on—bars, stores, pawnshops, restaurants, even little luncheonettes had been smashed open and entered and looted—looted, it might be added, with more haste than efficiency. The shelves really looked as though a bomb had struck them. Cans of beans and soup and dog food, along with toilet paper, corn flakes, sardines, and milk tumbled every which way, and abandoned cash registers and cases of beer leaned crazily out of the splintered windows and were strewn along the avenues. Sheets, blankets, and clothing of every description formed a kind of path, as though people had dropped them while running. I truly had not realized that Harlem *had* so many stores until I saw them all smashed open; the first time the word *wealth* ever entered my mind in relation to Harlem was when I saw it scattered in the streets. But one's first, incongruous impression of plenty was countered immediately by an impression of waste. None of this was doing anybody any good. It would have been better to have left the plate glass as it had been and the goods lying in the stores.

It would have been better, but it would also have been intolerable, for Harlem had needed something to smash. To smash something is the ghetto's chronic need. Most of the time it is the members of the ghetto who smash each other, and themselves. But as long as the ghetto walls are standing there will always come a moment when these outlets do not work. That summer, for example, it was not enough to get into a fight on Lenox Avenue, or curse out one's cronies in the barber shops. If ever, indeed, the violence which fills Harlem's churches, pool halls, and bars erupts outward in a more direct fashion, Harlem and its citizens are likely to vanish in an apocalyptic flood. That this is not likely to happen is due to a great many reasons, most hidden and powerful among them the Negro's real relation to the white American. This relation prohibits, simply, anything as uncomplicated and satisfactory as pure hatred. In order really to hate white people, one has to blot so much out of the mind—and the heart—that this hatred itself becomes an exhausting and self-destructive pose. But this does not mean, on the other hand, that love comes easily: the white world is too powerful, too complacent, too ready with gratuitous humiliation, and, above all, too ignorant and too innocent for that. One is absolutely forced to make perpetual qualifications and one's own reactions are always canceling each other out. It is this, really, which has driven so many people mad, both white and black. One is always in the position of having to decide between amputation and gangrene. Amputation is swift but time may prove that the amputation was not necessary—or one may delay the amputation too long. Gangrene is slow, but it is impossible to be sure that one is reading one's symptoms right. The idea of going through life as a cripple is more than one can bear, and equally unbearable is the risk of swelling up slowly, in agony, with poison. And the trouble, finally, is that the risks are real even if the choices do not exist.

"But as for me and my house," my father had said, "we will serve the Lord." I wondered, as we drove him to his resting place, what this line had meant for him. I had heard him preach it many times. I had preached it once myself, proudly giving it an interpretation different from my father's. Now the whole thing came back to me, as though my father and I were on our way to Sunday school and I were memorizing the golden text: *And if it seem evil unto you to serve the Lord, choose you this day whom you will serve; whether the gods which your fathers served that were on the other side of the flood, or the gods of the Amorites, in which land ye dwell: but as for me and my house, we will serve the Lord.* I suspected in these familiar lines a meaning which had never been there for me before. All of my father's texts and songs, which I had decided were meaningless, were arranged before me at his death like empty bottles, waiting to hold the meaning which life would give them for me. This was his legacy: nothing is ever escaped. That bleakly memorable morning I hated the unbelievable streets and the Negroes and whites who had, equally, made them that way. But I knew that it was folly, as my father would have said, this bitterness was folly. It was necessary to hold on to the things that mattered. The dead man mattered, the new life mattered; blackness and whiteness did not matter; to believe that they did was to acquiesce in one's own destruction. Hatred, which could destroy so much, never failed to destroy the man who hated and this was an immutable law.

It began to seem that one would have to hold in the mind forever two ideas which seemed to be in opposition. The first idea was acceptance, the acceptance, totally without rancor, of life as it is, and men as they are: in the light of this idea, it goes without saying that injustice is a commonplace. But this did not mean that one could be complacent, for the second idea was of equal power: that one must never, in one's own life, accept these injustices as commonplace but must fight them with all one's strength. This fight begins, however, in the heart and it now had been laid to my charge to keep my own heart free of hatred and despair. This intimation made my heart heavy and, now that my father was irrecoverable, I wished that he had been beside me so that I could have searched his face for the answers which only the future would give me now.

POETRY

William Blake

THE LITTLE BLACK BOY

My mother bore me in the southern wild,
And I am black, but O! my soul is white;
White as an angel is the English child,
But I am black, as if bereaved of light.

My mother taught me underneath a tree,
And sitting down before the heat of day,
She took me on her lap and kissèd me,
And pointing to the east, began to say:

"Look on the rising sun: there God does live,
And gives his light, and gives his heat away:
And flowers and trees and beasts and men receive
Comfort in morning, joy in the noonday.

"And we are put on earth a little space,
That we may learn to bear the beams of love;
And these black bodies and this sunburnt face
Is but a cloud, and like a shady grove.

"For when our souls have learned the heat to bear,
The cloud will vanish; we shall hear his voice,
Saying: 'Come out from the grove, my love and care,
And round my golden tent like lambs rejoice.'"

Thus did my mother say, and kissèd me;
And thus I say to little English boy.
When I from black and he from white cloud free,
And round the tent of God like lambs we joy,

I'll shade him from the heat, till he can bear
To lean in joy upon our father's knee;
And then I'll stand and stroke his silver hair,
And be like him, and he will then love me.

Roy Campbell

THE SERF

HIS NAKED skin clothed in the torrid mist
That puffs in smoke around the patient hooves,
The ploughman drives, a slow somnambulist,
And through the green his crimson furrow grooves.
His heart, more deeply than he wounds the plain,
Long by the rasping share of insult torn,
Red clod, to which the war-cry once was rain
And tribal spears the fatal sheaves of corn,
Lies fallow now. But as the turf divides
I see in the slow progress of his strides
Over the toppled clods and falling flowers,
The timeless, surly patience of the serf
That moves the nearest to the naked earth
And ploughs down palaces, and thrones, and towers.

Edwin Markham

THE MAN WITH THE HOE

(Written after seeing Millet's world-famous painting)

BOWED by the weight of centuries he leans
Upon his hoe and gazes on the ground,
The emptiness of ages in his face,
And on his back the burden of the world.
Who made him dead to rapture and despair,
A thing that grieves not and that never hopes,
Stolid and stunned, a brother to the ox?
Who loosened and let down this brutal jaw?
Whose was the hand that slanted back this brow?
Whose breath blew out the light within this brain?

Is this the Thing the Lord God made and gave
To have dominion over sea and land;
To trace the stars and search the heavens for power;
To feel the passion of Eternity?
Is this the dream He dreamed who shaped the suns
And marked their ways upon the ancient deep?
Down all the caverns of Hell to their last gulf

There is no shape more terrible than this—
More tongued with censure of the world's blind greed—
More filled with signs and portents for the soul—
More packt with danger to the universe.

What gulfs between him and the seraphim!
Slave of the wheel of labor, what to him
Are Plato and the swing of Pleiades?
What the long reaches of the peaks of song,
The rift of dawn, the reddening of the rose?
Through this dread shape the suffering ages look;
Time's tragedy is in that aching stoop;
Through this dread shape humanity betrayed,
Plundered, profaned, and disinherited,
Cries protest to the Judges of the World,
A protest that is also prophecy.

O masters, lords and rulers in all lands,
Is this the handiwork you give to God,
This monstrous thing distorted and soul-quenched?
How will you ever straighten up this shape;
Touch it again with immortality;
Give back the upward looking and the light;
Rebuild in it the music and the dream;
Make right the immemorial infamies,
Perfidious wrongs, immedicable woes?

O masters, lords and rulers in all lands,
How will the Future reckon with this man?
How answer his brute question in that hour
When whirlwinds of rebellion shake all shores?
How will it be with kingdoms and with kings—
With those who shaped him to the thing he is—
When this dumb terror shall rise to judge the world,
After the silence of the centuries?

A. E. Housman

BE STILL, MY SOUL

BE STILL, my soul, be still; the arms you bear are brittle,
  Earth and high heaven are fixt of old and founded strong.
Think rather,—call to thought, if now you grieve a little,
  The days when we had rest, O soul, for they were long.

Men loved unkindness then, but lightless in the quarry
I slept and saw not; tears fell down, I did not mourn;
Sweat ran and blood sprang out and I was never sorry:
Then it was well with me, in days ere I was born.

Now, and I muse for why and never find the reason,
I pace the earth, and drink the air, and feel the sun.
Be still, be still, my soul; it is but for a season:
Let us endure an hour and see injustice done.

Ay, look: high heaven and earth ail from the prime foundation;
All thoughts to rive the heart are here, and all are vain:
Horror and scorn and hate and fear and indignation—
Oh why did I awake? when shall I sleep again?

William Butler Yeats

THE LEADERS OF THE CROWD

THEY must to keep their certainty accuse
All that are different of a base intent;
Pull down established honor; hawk for news
Whatever their loose phantasy invent
And murmur it with bated breath, as though
The abounding gutter had been Helicon
Or calumny a song. How can they know
Truth flourishes where the student's lamp has shone,
And there alone, that have no solitude?
So the crowd come they care not what may come.
They have loud music, hope every day renewed
And heartier loves; that lamp is from the tomb.

Robert Frost

THE DEATH OF THE HIRED MAN

MARY sat musing on the lamp-flame at the table
Waiting for Warren. When she heard his step,
She ran on tip-toe down the darkened passage
To meet him in the doorway with the news
And put him on his guard. "Silas is back."

She pushed him outward with her through the door
And shut it after her. "Be kind," she said.
She took the market things from Warren's arms
And set them on the porch, then drew him down
To sit beside her on the wooden steps.
"When was I ever anything but kind to him?
But I'll not have the fellow back," he said.
"I told him so last haying, didn't I?
'If he left then,' I said, 'that ended it.'
What good is he? Who else will harbor him
At his age for the little he can do?
What help he is there's no depending on.
Off he goes always when I need him most.
'He thinks he ought to earn a little pay,
Enough at least to buy tobacco with,
So he won't have to beg and be beholden.'
'All right,' I say, 'I can't afford to pay
Any fixed wages, though I wish I could.'
'Someone else can.' 'Then someone else will have to.'
I shouldn't mind his bettering himself
If that was what it was. You can be certain,
When he begins like that, there's someone at him
Trying to coax him off with pocket-money,—
In haying time, when any help is scarce.
In winter he comes back to us. I'm done."

"Sh! not so loud: he'll hear you," Mary said.

"I want him to: he'll have to soon or late."

"He's worn out. He's asleep beside the stove.
When I came up from Rowe's I found him here,
Huddled against the barn-door fast asleep,
A miserable sight, and frightening, too—
You needn't smile—I didn't recognize him—
I wasn't looking for him—and he's changed.
Wait till you see."

"Where did you say he'd been?"

"He didn't say. I dragged him to the house,
And gave him tea and tried to make him smoke.
I tried to make him talk about his travels,
Nothing would do: he just kept nodding off."

"What did he say? Did he say anything?"

"But little."

"Anything? Mary, confess
He said he'd come to ditch the meadow for me."

"Warren!"

"But did he? I just want to know."

"Of course he did. What would you have him say?
Surely you wouldn't grudge the poor old man
Some humble way to save his self-respect.
He added, if you really care to know,
He meant to clear the upper pasture, too.
That sounds like something you have heard before?
Warren, I wish you could have heard the way
He jumbled everything. I stopped to look
Two or three times—he made me feel so queer—
To see if he was talking in his sleep.
He ran on Harold Wilson—you remember—
The boy you had in haying four years since.
He's finished school, and teaching in his college.
Silas declares you'll have to get him back.
He says they two will make a team for work:
Between them they will lay this farm as smooth!
The way he mixed that in with other things.
He thinks young Wilson a likely lad, though daft
On education—you know how they fought
All through July under the blazing sun,
Silas up on the cart to build the load,
Harold along beside to pitch it on."

"Yes, I took care to keep well out of earshot."

"Well, those days trouble Silas like a dream.
You wouldn't think they would. How some things linger!
Harold's young college boy's assurance piqued him.
After so many years he still keeps finding
Good arguments he sees he might have used.
I sympathize. I know just how it feels
To think of the right thing to say too late.
Harold's associated in his mind with Latin.
He asked me what I thought of Harold's saying
He studied Latin like the violin
Because he liked it—that an argument!
He said he couldn't make the boy believe
He could find water with a hazel prong—
Which showed how much good school had ever done him.
He wanted to go over that. But most of all

He thinks if he could have another chance
To teach him how to build a load of hay—"

"I know, that's Silas' one accomplishment.
He bundles every forkful in its place,
And tags and numbers it for future reference,
So he can find and easily dislodge it
In the unloading. Silas does that well.
He takes it out in bunches like birds' nests.
You never see him standing on the hay
He's trying to lift, straining to lift himself."

"He thinks if he could teach him that, he'd be
Some good perhaps to someone in the world.
He hates to see a boy the fool of books.
Poor Silas, so concerned for other folk,
And nothing to look backward to with pride,
And nothing to look forward to with hope,
So now and never any different."

Part of a moon was falling down the west,
Dragging the whole sky with it to the hills.
Its light poured softly in her lap. She saw
And spread her apron to it. She put out her hand
Among the harp-like morning-glory strings,
Taut with the dew from garden bed to eaves,
As if she played unheard the tenderness
That wrought on him beside her in the night.
"Warren," she said, "he has come home to die:
"You needn't be afraid he'll leave you this time."

"Home," he mocked gently.

"Yes, what else but home?
It all depends on what you mean by home.
Of course he's nothing to us, any more
Than was the hound that came a stranger to us
Out of the woods, worn out upon the trail."

"Home is the place where, when you have to go there,
They have to take you in."

"I should have called it
Something you somehow haven't to deserve."

Warren leaned out and took a step or two,
Picked up a little stick, and brought it back
And broke it in his hand and tossed it by.

"Silas has better claim on us, you think,
Than on his brother? Thirteen little miles
As the road winds would bring him to his door.
Silas has walked that far no doubt today.
Why didn't he go there? His brother's rich,
A somebody—director in the bank."

"He never told us that."

"We know it though."

"I think his brother ought to help, of course.
I'll see to that if there is need. He ought of right
To take him in, and might be willing to—
He may be better than appearances.
But have some pity on Silas. Do you think
If he'd had any pride in claiming kin
Or anything he looked for from his brother,
He'd keep so still about him all this time?"

"I wonder what's between them."

"I can tell you.
Silas is what he is—we wouldn't mind him—
But just the kind that kinsfolk can't abide.
He never did a thing so very bad.
He don't know why he isn't quite as good
As anyone. He won't be made ashamed
To please his brother, worthless though he is."

"I can't think Si ever hurt anyone."

"No, but he hurt my heart the way he lay
And rolled his old head on that sharp-edged chair-back.
He wouldn't let me put him on the lounge.
You must go in and see what you can do.
I made the bed up for him there tonight.
You'll be surprised at him—how much he's broken.
His working days are done; I'm sure of it."

"I'd not be in a hurry to say that."

"I haven't been. Go, look, see for yourself.
But, Warren, please remember how it is:
He's come to help you ditch the meadow.
He has a plan. You mustn't laugh at him.
He may not speak of it, and then he may.

I'll sit and see if that small sailing cloud
Will hit or miss the moon."

It hit the moon.
Then there were three there, making a dim row,
The moon, the little silver cloud, and she.

Warren returned—too soon, it seemed to her,
Slipped to her side, caught up her hand and waited.

"Warren?" she questioned.

"Dead," was all he answered.

DRAMA

Ugo Betti

CORRUPTION IN THE PALACE OF JUSTICE

PEOPLE IN THE PLAY

VANAN, *President of the Court*
ELENA, *his daughter*
ERZI, *Investigating Counsellor*
CROZ, *Chief Justice*
CUST, *a judge*
BATA, *a judge*
MAVERI, *a judge*
PERSIUS, *a judge*
MALGAI, *a record clerk*
A NURSE
And a number of officials, porters, bystanders.

The time is the present.

The action takes place in a foreign city. The scene is the same throughout: a large severe room in the Palace of Justice.

ACT I

The room is empty. MALGAI, *the record clerk, enters, pushing a wheeled basket. He goes round the tables, which are piled high with documents; some of these he selects and throws into the basket, after checking their dates against certain papers in his hand. He hums to himself.*

[A STRANGER *appears in the doorway.*]

STRANGER. I wonder if you could tell me where I can find Chief Justice Croz's office?

MALGAI. Will you ask the porter, sir? There's a porter for that purpose.

STRANGER. I'm sorry but I haven't been able to find any porters.

MALGAI. Well, you can't expect them to be here before they have to clock in, can you? Oh, it's no good looking at me; I'm one of the old brigade. What do you want to see Chief Justice Croz for?

STRANGER. I have to speak to him.

MALGAI. Well, that would be fine, sir, only unfortunately poor Mr.

Croz is dying. Has been for months. He doesn't come to the office any more. It has to be something very special to bring Mr. Croz here, and even then they almost have to carry him.

STRANGER. All the same I think he will come this morning.

MALGAI [*Glancing at him*]. Ah. [*Cautiously.*] Is there a judges' meeting perhaps?

STRANGER. I fancy we shall see them all here.

MALGAI. Ah. [*His tone has changed slightly.*] Well . . . If you want to get to Chief Justice Croz's office, you go down the corridor to the end, then to the right, then to the right again. . . . But if you don't mind my saying so, I think you'd do best to wait for him in here.

STRANGER. In here?

MALGAI. Yes, you'll hear his cane. You can always hear him when he comes up the corridor: he has to use a cane nowadays. If there *is* a sitting, they'll all have to come in here: this is the council chamber for the division. [*He points to a seat near the door.*] You can sit down if you wish.

STRANGER. Thank you. [*He sits.*]

MALGAI [*Throwing another glance at the visitor, as he goes on with his work*]. A huge building, this, isn't it? The place is just one great maze. We even get tourists in looking at it. In admiration. [*He drops his voice slightly.*] At the moment, unfortunately, the smell about the place isn't quite as sweet as it might be. I suppose it must be a dead rat or something, under one of the floorboards. What do you think about it all, sir? I don't know if you saw last night's papers?

STRANGER. Yes.

MALGAI. Well, it's no business of mine, of course, but I think there's something of a storm blowing up. There's thunder in the air.

STRANGER. Are you one of the clerks?

MALGAI. No, sir. I'm what you might call the gravedigger. This [*He smacks the side of the trolley.*] is the hearse; and these [*He waves the papers in his hand.*] are the death certificates; and these [*He taps the bundles of documents.*] are the bodies.

STRANGER. And the graveyard?

MALGAI [*Pointing to a door*]. Through there. The Archives. A quiet, shady little spot; I take all this stuff in there and see it gets decent burial.

STRANGER. Are you one of the record clerks?

MALGAI. The undertaker I always call myself. When I think of all the sweat, and all the money and tears, that have gone into even the silliest little bundle of these things here! Well, well . . . [*He drops a bundle into the trolley, and takes up another one.*] I stick a great big number on them, and register them in a great big book, so that people can pretend to believe they'll go on being important per secula et seculorum, and they can always take the thing up again . . .

STRANGER. While actually the only things really concerned about your graveyard are the mice and the grubs?

MALGAI. No, it's not the mice and the grubs, sir. It's the interested parties themselves: they get bored after a time, and turn their minds to other things. It's surprising how easily people *do* get bored and turn to other things.

[*A newcomer has entered, looking very worried.* MALGAI *turns to him solicitously.*]

MALGAI. Oh, good morning, Judge Bata.

BATA [*As he enters*]. Good morning, my dear fellow, good morning. [*Taking him aside, and whispering.*] Have you heard?

MALGAI [*Anxiously*]. What?

BATA. You didn't come past the secretary's office this morning?

MALGAI. No, I never go round that way.

BATA [*Cautiously*]. I came past the door a few moments ago; there's an official posted outside it: rather important-looking.

MALGAI. An official?

BATA. Yes, a sort of policeman. He politely told us we couldn't go in.

MALGAI. Not even the judges?

BATA. He was stopping everyone.

MALGAI. What . . . what for?

BATA. Well, I was wondering if *you* . . .

MALGAI. No, sir, I haven't the foggiest.

BATA. You've no idea . . . what it's all about . . . ?

MALGAI. Good gracious, no! They'd never tell *me*. I expect it's just some new piece of nonsense they've—.

BATA [*Trying to pooh-pooh the matter*]. Oh yes, yes, of course it is, but I do think they might have mentioned it to the magistrates.

MALGAI. Of course, sir! Naturally. I hear there's a special meeting of the division today.

BATA. Yes, it's all very odd. It's taken us all by surprise rather.

[*The other judges are entering:* PERSIUS, MAVERI, *and, shortly after,* CUST.]

PERSIUS [*As he approaches*]. Well, what is it all about?

BATA [*Pointing to the archivist, who backs respectfully away*]. He doesn't seem to know either.

MAVERI [*Cautiously*]. I think it's just a mistake; some order must have been misunderstood.

PERSIUS [*Unconvinced*]. Yes, quite. A mistake.

MAVERI. A misunderstanding. [*A brief silence.*]

BATA [*To* PERSIUS, *suddenly*]. My dear Persius, you yourself can bear me out, can't you? I've been saying it for months; there are a lot of things need clearing up in here, we need more light and air in the place. The air in these courts is becoming too thick to breathe. I've said that again and again, haven't I? Haven't I?

PERSIUS. My dear fellow, you don't think you're the only one, do you?

MAVERI. Lots of people have been saying so.

CUST. We've said so, too: all of us.

MAVERI. A man with a clear conscience has nothing to fear from the light; nothing at all.

BATA. It's important to realize of course that it may have all just blown up out of nothing. People thrive on scandal. The law courts are always a hive of discontented murmuring. Someone starts spreading scandal about the place, someone else joins in, and by the next day there are ten or twenty of them, buzz- buzz- buzzing their heads off. It's like gangrene spreading.

MAVERI. And the newspapers too: you can't trust any of them.

PERSIUS. And the politicians: party intrigues the whole time. I can't help feeling the whole thing is a deliberate plot.

BATA. But it's the city itself, more than anything, surely? This filthy, diseased city. I never thought people could be so evil, so nasty.

PERSIUS. Yes, just listen to them talking: there isn't a word of truth in anything they say.

MAVERI. Not to mention the women.

BATA. Yes, the place is just a dungheap. The odd thing is to find them screaming with indignation because right in the middle of their own stink there should be a building where the atmosphere isn't (shall I say?) quite as fragrant as it might be. In fact, the magistrates' crime . . . is simply that they're a little too like the man in the street.

PERSIUS [*Acidly*]. My dear friend and colleague, I never think one ought to generalize too readily. I don't think I personally bear the remotest resemblance to a dungheap.

BATA. Neither do I; the very idea.

PERSIUS. As far as I personally am concerned, I'm in the fortunate position of being able to say that I've never even *met* this man called Ludvi-Pol, never. I've never even seen him.

BATA. You sound rather as if your colleagues were less fortunate—what? As if some of us were in danger of being compromised in some way.

PERSIUS [*Diplomatically*]. *Did* I say that? Nonsense. I always aim at saying precisely what I mean. And if any of our colleagues *have* been off their feed lately, and *have* been having bad nights, well, I'm not one of them, that's all. There are times when every man has to look out for himself. This is one of them. Don't *you* think so, Cust?

BATA [*Spitefully*]. We all know that, my dear friend, we all know that. Some of our colleagues seem to have been very busy pulling strings and turning wheels these last few weeks. There seems to have been a good deal of angry fist-shaking about the place.

PERSIUS [*Sarcastically*]. Maybe, but the impression I have is that a lot of people in danger are trying to cling to one another as hard as they can. One notices that certain of one's colleagues have become very friendly all of a sudden. They keep trying to get into conversation with one the whole time. You find them waiting behind for you, so that you can leave the place together. They are all clutching at each other. Unfortunately, I'm always in a hurry. I'm always going in a different direction. I never know anything. I'm made of stone, dear friend. Oh, incidentally, Cust, I wanted to ask you something . . . [*Rather ostentatiously, he draws* CUST *apart.*]

BATA [*To* MAVERI]. Did you hear that? In any case, I don't quite see why it's suddenly become so very important whether people have or haven't known Ludvi-Pol. It rather looks—it rather *looks* now as if Ludvi-Pol had been put out of business. Though up to yesterday . . .

MAVERI. He was better respected than a cabinet minister!

BATA. One knows of course that these men are just like spiders; what keeps them going is precisely the web of relationships they so skilfully spin all round them. It stands to reason that a lot of people come into contact with them. It may be perfectly true that our dear friend Persius there has never met Ludvi-Pol; he still may have met one of his agents. [*He drops his voice.*] And considering what went on just before Persius was last promoted, he'd better not try being too self-righteous.

MAVERI [*Dropping his voice*]. Persius feels he's in a strong position.

BATA. Oh, does he? Why?

MAVERI. Important contacts.

BATA. Very likely; he's a born toady.

MAVERI. And now he's trying to suck up to Cust; as one might expect.

BATA. Oh. Why?

MAVERI. Cust! Our rising star.

BATA. Cust?

MAVERI. Cust. A very able man; and not overburdened with scruples, I imagine.

BATA. But what about the great Vanan?

MAVERI. Done for. A corpse.

BATA. Are you sure? Oh dear, it's very difficult trying to steer one's way, isn't it? One person's up and another's down, the whole time. You can never be sure what's going on. [*Looking thoughtfully at* CUST.] I've always been on very good terms with Cust, myself, of course.

MAVERI. Really? I thought he seemed rather offhand with you, just now.

BATA [*Disturbed*]. Cust? With me?

MAVERI. I expect it's only his way.

BATA. I've always said that he was really one of the best people in this place . . . [*Seeing that* MAVERI *is also about to join* CUST *and* PERSIUS.] Look, my dear Maveri, there's something I've been wanting to say to you for a long time. You *are* related to President Tomisco, aren't you?

MAVERI [*Warily*]. Well, it's a . . . very *distant* relationship. Why?

BATA [*Beaming sunnily*]. I was with President Tomisco for a time, you know, just when I was starting my career. A most admirable person. Influential. I'd so much like to meet him again sometime. Perhaps you'll be so good as to give him my kind regards, when next you . . .

MAVERI [*Evasively*]. I hardly ever see him, you know, hardly ever.

BATA [*Amiably*]. Dear colleague, please don't think that I'm trying to steal a march on you; please don't think that. On the contrary. If there's any way in which *I* can help *you*. . . . I have the greatest admiration for you, as you know.

MAVERI. So have I. For you, I mean.

BATA. Thank you. Sometimes . . . if two people are willing to stick together, they can . . . well, back each other up, stand by each other, as it were. It would be dreadful to have enemies at a time like this!

MAVERI [*Cautiously*]. Dreadful! But I hope . . .

BATA. One never knows, dear colleague. One can sometimes be betrayed by the very last person one expects it from. Well, of course, it's not for me to say.

MAVERI. What do you mean . . . ?

BATA. Well, you know how it is: one's colleagues . . . sometimes talk rather inconsiderately; I don't say they mean any harm, but . . .

MAVERI. Have you . . . heard anyone say anything about me?

BATA. Oh no, no. But the other night . . . Oh, it was just nonsense of course. But old Hill was in here, you know . . . [*He breaks off, and listens.*] Croz is coming.

[*A cane is heard in the corridor. This sound produces a rapid change in everyone present. The groups break up. Expressions change.*]

[CROZ *enters, leaning heavily on one side on his cane, and on the other on a manservant. His appearance reveals extreme physical prostration and at the same time a malignant energy: a quiver of the head gives him the appearance of continuously approving or disapproving of something. He advances half way across the room; here he halts for a few moments in order to draw breath, his eyes closed. He turns to the manservant without looking at him.*]

CROZ. Come back and fetch me later. That is, unless I die in the meantime. [*The manservant bows slightly and goes out.* CROZ *takes a few more steps forward.*] Is the great Vanan here yet?

BATA. No.

CROZ. Do any of you know if the old fool intends to come?

BATA. I don't really see why we should know any more than you do. With the wind blowing the way it is, I should think it's pretty unlikely.

CROZ. In that case, since the President is absent, it is my duty, as senior judge of the division, to deputize for him. [*Half-turning to* MALGAI.] You: get out. What are you doing here?

MALGAI. I'm just going, sir. [*He points to the* STRANGER, *who has just risen.*] I only wanted to tell your worship that there was a gentleman here waiting to see you. [*He goes out.*]

CROZ [*Turning to observe the newcomer*]. You wanted . . . to speak to me?

STRANGER. Yes, Justice Croz. I have a private communication for you.

CROZ [*To the other judges*]. He said private.

[*The other judges, half-curious, half-worried, withdraw to the other half of the room.* CROZ *walks a few steps towards the back. The* STRANGER *follows, speaking to him in a very low voice.* CROZ *listens, asking questions from time to time: finally he leads the* STRANGER *with great deference to an imposing armchair; then he once more approaches his colleagues.*]

Dear colleagues. [*He pauses and thinks.*] I have to tell you . . . [*Breaking off.*] Damn it, Persius, you *have* gone green in the face! You look scared to death.

PERSIUS. You can spare me your little jests, Croz. You'd do much better to think about yourself.

CROZ. You mean if anyone ought to be scared to death, it's me, eh? But, my dear Persius, I'm already dying in any case, am I not? *Moribundus.* So obviously—

PERSIUS. *Moribundus,* yes, you've been *moribundus* for a long time. It's an old trick, Croz; we're used to it, by now.

CROZ [*Grinning*]. Oh, such unkindness! Come, come. Well, dear colleagues, it appears that the Minister and the Lord High President are both very disturbed, very upset, poor dear things. Because of the lawcourts. The city is full of gossip. [*Satirically.*] Justice! Justice! *Justitia fondamentum regni.* [*He breaks off, coughing and gasping heavily.*]

BATA. Quite, my dear Croz, quite; the city is full, etc. etc. I don't quite see the point in coming here to tell *us* that; *we* can't shut the mouths of several million scandal-mongers. The only thing to do is to wait till they are tired of this subject and have found another. I don't see . . . [*He breaks off, under* CROZ's *stare.*]

CROZ. You very rarely do see. Anything. The Minister and the High President have issued orders for an inquiry.

[A *silence.*]

BATA [*Faintly*]. An inquiry?

CROZ. I think that's what I said. [*Teasing.*] But come, come, bless my soul, we mustn't let it frighten us.

MAVERI. We are not frightened, as a matter of fact.

CROZ. Good, good. It's nothing very serious, just a little something among ourselves. A little look round, that's all, a few inquiries, clear things up . . . That's all.

BATA [*Warmly*]. And naturally we all agree very heartily. We shall all be very glad to put our modest talents at the public disposal in order to . . . to investigate the matter and find out what's wrong. [*Murmurs of assent.*]

CROZ. Perhaps I didn't make myself clear. It is not ourselves who have to do the investigating.

BATA. No?

CROZ. No. Others will be doing the investigating.

BATA. But what about us?

CROZ. Well, we, if I might so put it, are the ones who have to be investigated. Which is slightly different. [*A silence.*]

PERSIUS [*Bitterly*]. I would like to know why respectable magistrates, after years and years of irreproachable service—I myself have been on the bench for twenty years—I'd like to know why we have to submit to—

CROZ. You are an ass, Persius! What about me? I'm on the eve of promotion. I've set great store by the thought of being buried with a President's cap on my head—always supposing of course that dear old brother Cust doesn't pop in ahead of me—eh, Cust? What do *you* think about all this nonsense? It *would* have to happen just now, of course, and endanger my promotion . . . My dear Persius, we are *all* respectable and irreproachable. I thought I'd made it quite, quite clear: all we have to do is to look into the matter, among ourselves. The magistrate who will carry out the inquiry is a friendly colleague of ours . . . [*He points to the* STRANGER, *who has risen.*] Councillor Erzi, from the Upper House; he himself was saying to me only a moment ago . . .

ERZI [*With great courtesy*]. Yes, all we need is a certain amount of discussion, in strict confidence, as between friends. My only reason for coming was to exchange a few preliminary words with you . . . and to shake hands with you all.

BATA [*Advancing with hand outstretched*]. But of course, of course. My dear Erzi, I am so glad to meet you.

PERSIUS [*Following suit, together with the others*]. Welcome into our midst!

MAVERI. My dear Erzi! I've heard a good deal about you. Surely we've met before somewhere?

BATA. Yes, you can understand, my dear friend, that we're the first people, the very first, to want to see the whole thing . . .

PERSIUS. . . . floodlit!

BATA. In strict confidence—that was your own expression—would you like to know my own humble opinion?

ERZI. That is what I'm here for.

BATA [*Pompously, to the others*]. We have to be quite frank about all this. The time for circumlocution is over. My dear Erzi, we're far from trying to pretend that there hasn't been a considerable amount of confusion piling up in these courts.

CUST. It's slackness, more than anything else; people have been a bit too easy-going.

PERSIUS. A bit too casual, too broad-minded perhaps. One can be too broad-minded, you know.

BATA. One might go even further, I think, and admit that there's been a certain lack of moral earnestness, a certain tolerance towards rogues.

CUST. The law courts have become almost a rogues' paradise.

MAVERI. There are certain forms of tolerance I'm afraid I've always disapproved of.

PERSIUS. Oh, we all have. We've all disapproved of them.

BATA. One might put it like this, I think: it is as if in this immense ramification of corridors and offices and stairs and—and so forth—it's as if there were odd nooks and corners here and there which have never been properly lit; and piles of dirt and dust and whatnot have accumulated in them. But who are the people scratching about in the middle of it all? Doormen, clerks, pen-pushers and other fusty old rubbish—

PERSIUS. The main trouble about this place is that out of every hole—

MAVERI. —an army of gnawing rats comes tumbling . . .

BATA. I'd be inclined to say myself that the whole thing has nothing to do with the magistrates at all.

ERZI. The Minister's opinion is that the staleness and poisonous air you speak of have actually produced something rather more: it might be called a poisonous plant. [A *silence*.]

BATA. I see. But think of ourselves for a moment: there are many hundreds of us here, all flapping our black gowns about the place and groaning out our prayers. It would be a little unnatural if so vast a monastery didn't harbor at least one or two wicked or negligent brethren.

ERZI. It is not about negligent brethren that the Minister is concerned. He is convinced that under one of the flapping gowns you speak of, securely hidden away, there must be somewhere a little red pustule of leprosy. Corruption.

BATA. Corruption?

ERZI. It is a leper we're looking for.

BATA. And why . . . why do you begin looking for your lepers in here, pray?

ERZI. You must regard that as an honor. Isn't this the division reserved for Major Causes?

CROZ. Hahaha! It's been a real pleasure to listen to you. What elegant conceits, what metaphors! I'm crazy about that sort of thing; I even try my hand at it myself sometimes. But the one you should really hear is Cust, he's an absolute artist. He's being very quiet today for some reason. I always think eloquence of expression adds so much to a magistrate—it's the sign of a highly developed brain, I think one can say. Well, perhaps you'll listen to a few of my own little similes? Do you know, my dear Erzi, what we poor devils really are?—we judges, in this division—yes,

yes, I know, the division for Major Causes. But each of us, every single one, is a little, lonely, insecure rock on which from every direction tremendous waves keep breaking; frightful; great foaming mountains. And those waves are the implacable interests, the boundless wealth, the iron blocks manipulated by dreadfully powerful men: genuine wild forces, whose blows—unhappily for us—are something savage, irresistible, ferocious . . .

ERZI [*Completing*]. . . . a species of telluric phenomenon.

CROZ. Telluric: exactly. Telluric.

ERZI. And it's very difficult to teach that phenomenon good manners.

CROZ. You take the words right out of my mouth. I'd like to see how the Minister would get on in our place.

ERZI. The pity of it is that amidst these iron blocks a fair number of very fragile shells are also tossed about on the waters; and they very easily get dashed to pieces. Take the case, for example, the day before yesterday, of that prostitute in Panama Street: a little smoke and burnt paper were sufficient to send her to her Maker. Was it not this division that had decided in complete secrecy to raid the house in Panama Street and confiscate certain documents?

CROZ. Yes.

ERZI. But when the police arrived, the place had been blazing for a good ten minutes; so had the documents, and so, unfortunately, had a harmless caretaker. The papers are still screaming about it.

CROZ. Do you mean—?

ERZI. I mean that someone from here had warned the interested parties. [*Pause.*] That is only one case among many: but it sums up the situation. [*A silence.*]

CROZ. Someone from here? One of us?

ERZI. One of you.

CROZ [*Laughing loudly*]. My dear friends, Just let's all take a close look at each other, shall we? You, for example, Bata: you have a look at me, while I of course have a look at you, eh? Can it be possible that not a tiny bead of sweat, not a single movement of the Adam's apple, not the slightest, smallest sign . . . should betray our ailing comrade? Our leper I mean. It could be myself; it could be you, Maveri; you've gone quite white. Or you, Cust.

CUST. No, no, Croz. That's not quite the way things work. There's an error in psychology there. If it were anybody, it would be the innocent man—if he had any imagination: he'd be the one who started to sweat, etc. Feel. [*He holds out his hand.*]

CROZ [*Touching it*]. Cold and clammy.

CUST. Yes. Once when I was a boy staying with friends, someone came and said a watch was missing. I . . . fainted.

CROZ. So you're the one with the imagination?

CUST. Obviously. And quite apart from that, I'd like to point out —simply in the interests of accuracy—that it isn't quite exact to say: one of us. It isn't true that *all* the men who took part in the decision you mentioned are here at this moment. Now, I don't want this to be taken as an insinuation, mind you. I am, after all, a referendary judge, and because of that I am always in very close contact with President Vanan; and no one knows better than I how completely above suspicion he is. I'm only saying this in order that we may maintain a certain precision, a certain strictness of method: President Vanan also took part in that decision. And he is not here at the moment.

CROZ [*Pointing to* CUST, *and speaking to* ERZI]. Cust. A very fine brain. My great enemy, my rival as successor to Vanan. A most worthy character; and gnawed by the most infernal ambition. We've hated each other from the minute we met.

CUST. That isn't true as far as I am concerned.

CROZ. Old humbug. He's like one of those iron safes. Absolutely impregnable.

BATA. Well, since Vanan's name's been mentioned—and as colleague Erzi has invited us to make a full and friendly disclosure . . . and also . . . out of a real wish for sincerity, mind you, and since all this will remain strictly among ourselves . . .

PERSIUS [*Slightly hysterical*]. Get *on*! Don't you see we've all got to defend ourselves!

BATA. I consider it my duty to state . . . at all events, it seems to me an affectation to deny that the responsibility of the disorder here, the . . . uneasiness we were talking of earlier, does, unfortunately, lie largely—well, not largely perhaps but partly—with the great Vanan himself.

CROZ [*To* ERZI]. You don't know the great Vanan?

ERZI. No.

CROZ. He has been a great man in his time; a very handsome one too. Very fond of the women. Well, well. It's horrible to grow old.

BATA. Like Cust, I would be very ashamed indeed to suggest that the great Vanan . . . had let himself be corrupted or bought up by Ludvi-Pol, or by anyone else for that matter. But he has great weaknesses: that I'm bound to say.

MAVERI. There are certain jobs he is no longer fitted for. He seems somehow . . . finished. That's the word, if the truth must be told.

MAVERI. One of those old wooden beams that if you go like that to them, your finger goes in.

BATA. Rotten.

CROZ. And terrific with the women, you understand? He himself must know where his strength's gone to, at any rate.

MAVERI. And it's still the same. Even now! One gathers that's the reason for his rapid disintegration, as you might call it. Poor old thing, it's very sad and terrible. He's been seen in the most frightful places.

BATA. In fact, when you talk to President Vanan, it's difficult to be sure if he really knows what he's saying and doing any longer. A thousand pities. A thousand pities.

MAVERI. These last few months, I almost think you could tell from the way he talks and moves about . . . well, he's in the final stages. It's become pathological by now.

CROZ [*To* MAVERI]. It's simply this, my dear fellow: he keeps himself going with drink. [*He laughs and coughs.*]

BATA. Naturally, I must repeat that I'm not saying I . . . believe that Vanan himself is the one . . . the man . . .

PERSIUS [*Suddenly and brutally*]. My dear colleagues, does this really seem to you the moment for delicacy? Do you understand or don't you, what a hell of a position we're in?

MAVERI [*Supporting him*]. The whole city's waiting. It wants somebody's head.

PERSIUS. It's a matter of life and death. Do we want to ruin ourselves, just for Vanan's sweet sake? Don't you think it's about time we all spoke out?

ERZI. Well?

PERSIUS. Look: if there was one man in this place who was absolutely *made* to be swallowed up by Ludvi-Pol, it was Vanan. If there was one man . . .

CUST [*Interrupting*]. One man. And why only one man? There's not the slightest evidence to show that our leper stands alone. We might all be infected. We might all have sold our souls to the devil, that is, to Ludvi-Pol.

CROZ. Perfect. Clever old Cust. [*To* ERZI.] Logic goes to old Cust's head at times, like drink. He's gleaming with sweat!

[*He breaks off. Some one has knocked on the door leading to the corridor. They all turn. A gloomy-looking stranger, possibly a* POLICE OFFICER, *comes in, and goes and speaks privately to* ERZI. ERZI *listens to him, then signs to him to wait, and stands for a moment, lost in thought.*]

ERZI. It's very unfortunate Vanan isn't here. Do you know where he could be found?

CUST. As a matter of fact, it's been rather difficult lately to know where you will or won't find Vanan. His habits have become rather uncertain.

ERZI. You've been very close to him?

CUST. Yes.

ERZI. Would you say that what we've heard about Vanan in here this morning is more or less the truth?

CUST [*After a silence*]. You put me in rather an embarrassing position; Vanan and I were fond of each other. There has perhaps been a certain amount of exaggeration.

ERZI. Go on.

CUST. The scale of human duties has become a little confused in

Vanan's mind. He's been sentencing people far too long. That can be rather dangerous after a time.

ERZI. Is there anything else?

CUST [*After a silence, looking down*]. Yes.

ERZI. Go on.

CUST. Vanan did know Ludvi-Pol. They had dealings. [*A silence.*] It's painful, for me, to speak of it. I think . . . I had the impression that Ludvi-Pol had passed a certain sum of money to President Vanan. [*His voice is low and calm.*] But look, Erzi, if what you said is true, surely Ludvi-Pol himeself is the one who could give you the name you're after—or names, as the case may be. Don't you think he'd talk?

ERZI. No. I don't.

BATA. Yes, but surely Ludvi-Pol's papers would talk!

CROZ [*Laughing*]. Do you think he's such a fool as to have put these things down on paper?

CUST. No, but perhaps under prolonged expert interrogation—

ERZI. No. We shan't get anything out of Ludvi-Pol.

CUST. Why not?

ERZI. Because he's dead. [A *silence.*] His body was discovered by accident in the early hours of this morning; do any of you know where?

CROZ. Where?

ERZI. Here. In this building, in a place where Ludvi-Pol had no reason whatever to be, least of all at night. He's lying there now.

CUST. So he was another fragile shell.

ERZI. It was suicide.

CUST. Are they sure of that?

ERZI. Yes.

CUST [*Almost imperceptibly excited*]. Forgive me, but that too could be a put-up job. The person you're looking for had a great interest in seeing that Ludvi-Pol kept his mouth shut, hadn't he? That person must be feeling very relieved at this moment. In any case, this Ludvi-Pol was a very contemptible creature, his death sentence is hardly likely to arouse much protest in the tribunal of any human soul I can think of. Or . . . look: the very things put there purposely to suggest murder, even those could be the results of a put-up job. For what purpose? To put you off the trail. To implicate some innocent person. There are so many possibilities, one can go on multiplying them as one chooses . . . always supposing we attribute a certain amount of subtlety to the man you're looking for. I advise you not to disregard any of those threads.

ERZI. Suicide. [*Pause.*] Are there many people in the building at night?

CUST. Oh, you can see quite a number of windows lit up till a very late hour. Industrious officials, all anxious to get on, losing their sleep over their papers. I myself, as a matter of fact, was here very late last night. [*As though recalling something.*] In fact . . . [*He breaks off.*]

ERZI. Go on.

CUST [*Lower*]. When I leave, I always have to go along the corridor that goes past the great Vanan's door. I may as well tell you the truth. As the corridor was in darkness . . . I saw a line of light under the door. I heard—[*He breaks off.*]

[MALGAI *enters excitedly: he clearly realizes what the situation is.*]

MALGAI. President Vanan.

[MALGAI *withdraws immediately. After a few moments* VANAN *appears; he is an old man, very tall and erect; his face is angry and inflamed, his hair like a mop of white cotton-wool; his tones are slightly stentorian. Sometimes he mutters to himself. He comes in, and looks round him.*]

VANAN. Quite. Quite . . . of course. Good morning to you all, my dear . . . friends. Here we are. [*To* BATA, *who is the nearest to him.*] Good morning, Bata; of course, yes . . . Give me a what-is-it, a match. [*His words drop into a great silence; everyone has risen.*]

BATA [*Backing away*]. I don't think I have any.

VANAN. What's the matter? What's the matter? Sit down. You could . . . surely, surely have waited for me too. Eh? Eh? Cust, I'm talking to you. Absolutely. Good morning, Erzi, I'm glad to see you. [*Shouting.*] Sit down! I'm perfectly aware of what's going on. You are here too, my clever Croz.

CROZ [*Shrugging his shoulders*]. Of course. What do you expect?

VANAN. Good. All of us. Absolutely. . . .

[*They are now all seated; only* VANAN *is standing.*]

ERZI [*With great courtesy*]. Mr. President, we were just waiting for you. There is a little information we need, if you would be so very kind as to give it to us.

VANAN. Absolutely. I know perfectly well what's going on. Fantastic, isn't it? Absolutely disgraceful.

ERZI. Mr. President, I have no doubt that you are acquainted with a person who has in recent years been at the center of the biggest concerns in the city, and who has consequently also been involved here in a number of very important law suits. I mean Ludvi-Pol. [*A silence.*]

VANAN [*Muttering*]. No . . . not that man . . . no, certainly not. Never. Listen, Erzi; I never knew him.

ERZI. You have, however, judged many cases in which he was involved.

VANAN. But . . . my dear Erzi, how . . . how can you possibly ask . . . [*Suddenly roaring.*] me, me, questions like this. It's fantastic . . . absolutely fantastic.

ERZI [*With extreme politeness*]. There was nothing in my question that could possibly offend you.

VANAN. Eh? What? That man . . .

ERZI. Yes. It would appear that you know him. That has been confirmed by several people here. [*A silence.*]

VANAN. Private. Private. An absolutely private matter. Absolutely. [*Dropping his voice slightly.*] In the lift. In the lift, Erzi, that's all! [*He laughs.*] In the lift in this building, that's all. What happens? A gentleman recognizes me and speaks to me. An acquaintance from long long ago, lost sight of. Boys . . . boys together, the family . . . ages ago, ages ago. In the lift. Ridiculous that I should have to . . . talk about that.

ERZI [*Gently*]. You received a sum of money from Ludvi-Pol? [*A silence.*]

VANAN [*His voice seems to diminish and he looks round him uncertainly*]. Croz . . . but why . . . why am I being asked all this? What's going on? Cust, you, say something. And the rest of you, you all know me, what do you think you're doing? [*A silence.*]

ERZI [*Quietly*]. Certainly, we all know you, Mr. President. You can speak with perfect frankness.

VANAN. Quite, quite, my dear Erzi, quite. There's no reason for me to hide anything . . . it's simple. The whole thing is absolutely . . . simple. It seems that Ludvi-Pol was slightly in debt to us, to my family I mean . . . nothing important, old liabilities, I'd quite forgotten them. But he . . . he remembered. Perfectly. He was very determined . . . to pay them back. That's the truth, that's the truth, Erzi. Absolutely . . . ridiculous, isn't it? He remembered it all perfectly.

ERZI. And did you remember?

VANAN. Well, actually I . . . yes, vaguely.

ERZI. Was it a large amount? Was it at a time when you happened to be in need?

VANAN [*Overcome with a kind of anguish*]. I don't . . . I don't . . . why . . . Cust! It's all so unexpected, so sudden. Ludvi-Pol himself will surely explain all this to you, won't he? You'll only have to ask him, won't you? He will tell you everything.

ERZI. Were you in this building last night?

VANAN. I? In this building? [*Roaring.*] But whatever do you . . . what does this mean . . . ?

ERZI. In your office, Mr. President: last night: were you alone?

VANAN. Absolutely. Absolutely. Alone. Absolutely.

ERZI. Cust.

CUST [*Slowly approaching*]. Yes. [*Affectionately, with regret.*] I had to tell him, Vanan. Last night . . . possibly you don't remember now . . .

VANAN [*With some fury*]. I? I don't remember? Shameful! Ridiculous! Absolutely grotesque! I don't remember, don't I? [*He breaks off; there is a moment of absolute silence; suddenly shouting and almost weeping.*] Do you think I don't understand what

. . . what you're all trying to do? You're trying to drag me down . . . trying to accuse me . . . aren't you? I understand perfectly! You blackguards! You filthy little pigmies! I'll crush you! I'll show you! I'll bring . . . I'll bring the whole court down! I'll tell them who's the guilty man, I'll tell them in the minutest detail! They don't know me yet. They don't know who Vanan is! I'll tear them to pieces, the whole lot of them. And after that . . . after . . . [*He stands there for a moment with his arm raised, breathing heavily: and then, as though his memory had suddenly given way, he drops slowly across the table, his face in his hands. A silence.*]

ERZI [*Politely, rising*]. Gentlemen, thank you all very much; I shan't need to take up any more of your time today. Though I shall have to ask for a little of yours, Croz, in a short while; and I also hope that you will all help me in the course of this inquiry. At the moment I am being waited for elsewhere. [*Thoughtfully, he turns to the police official who is still waiting.*] You. It's about time they removed Ludvi-Pol's body. I don't suppose they will be able to get it out of the building unnoticed. It's probably too late for that now. All the same, try to keep it covered up, if you possibly can, so that we shan't have to see his face in all the newspapers tomorrow, streaked with blood, with his eyes closed. He was a greatly respected man in his time. The city has all the rest of him to trample on now; let's leave his body for the worms alone—to whom all faces are the same. [*To the others.*] Good morning.

[*He goes out, followed by the official.* BATA, MAVERI, *and* PERSIUS, *one after another, go out cautiously and almost on tiptoe, so as not to attract the attention of* VANAN.]

[CROZ *and* CUST *are standing at some distance from him.*]

CROZ [*Observing his colleague*]. What's the matter, Cust?

CUST [*Looking at him before speaking*]. This is going to require a certain amount of courage.

CROZ. What do you mean?

CUST [*Drawing him away from* VANAN, *with a wan smile, and whispering*]. Croz, have you ever been out hunting?

CROZ. No.

CUST. Neither have I, but I've often been told about it. Do you know what it is the hunter always dreads most?

CROZ. No.

CUST. Finishing off the wounded quarry. Dying animals go on struggling; you have to take pity on them. Everyone'd be so very obliged to them, if only they'd die by themselves. But no, they struggle and fight for life; it's almost a point of honor with them. They almost make the hunter feel angry with them, because they actually in the end force one to . . . [*Dropping his voice still lower.*] smash their skulls in. It's horrible, isn't it? But it's something that has to be faced.

CROZ [*Looking at* VANAN]. Yes, yes, of course. The fool is going to ruin himself completely if he goes on like this. All those infantile lies! We shall have to . . . use a little persuasion.

CUST. It may not be difficult. A man who's just had a heavy blow on the head often behaves strangely docile. We are all of us fragile, but old men are like glass.

VANAN [*Has risen: his words are threatening, but his voice has completely changed*]. Croz, Cust. Eh? What do you say about all this? Why don't you say something, you filthy traitors! [CUST *and* CROZ *look at him in silence.*] What are you thinking? Tell me what to do . . . don't stand there looking at me . . .

CUST [*Quietly*]. My dear Vanan, do you know who it is *you* must talk to, now? Yourself.

VANAN. Myself?

CUST. Yes. You must explain to yourself the reason for all the lies you've been telling.

VANAN. Lies?

CUST. Lies, Vanan. What was the reason for them?

VANAN. Because . . . my God, actually . . . Cust, I was so confused . . .

CUST. Why were you confused? M'm? Reflect on that, my dear Vanan, and then you'll see for yourself the best way to go about things. Reflect on it, at great length.

VANAN. But oh, my God, I'm . . . an old man now.

CUST. Why ever did you deny that you talked to Ludvi-Pol last night?

VANAN. Cust, I swear to you . . . that man had come simply to plead with me . . . he thought I could still save him . . . he was a fool, a madman . . .

CUST. But why did he come to you? First he asked something from you; and then he asked something else, from death. You were the last door but one he knocked at. Why?

VANAN [*Shouting*]. I don't know, Cust! I don't know!

CUST. And why are you so frightened, even now? [*Very quietly.*] Oh no, Vanan, it's all too evident that your conscience is not untroubled. There is a doubt, in your conscience. They're saying that in this fine building of ours there is something rotten. But if you reflect on what you have been doing in here, yesterday, and every other day of your life, are you certain, quite certain, that you will be saved? What I advise you to do, my dear Vanan, is to make a long and minute examination of your conscience. Explore yourself, scrutinize yourself, go to bed with your doubt, carry it about with you by day. And only when one of the two, either you or it, has won, only then, and not before, must you come back here.

VANAN. Cust, what do you mean?

CUST. But of course, Vanan. You wouldn't want to insist on remaining here, in the courts, struggling, threatening, telling more bungling lies.

VANAN. You mean I ought to go away? Now?

CUST. For a few days.

VANAN. Never, never, never. I won't move from here, I'll defy them.

CUST. Good. And let them be even more vindictive against you in their inquiries, and lay more traps for you to fall into.

VANAN. No, Cust, I can't do it. To go away now would be . . .

CUST. . . . to put the matter in the hands of a very great doctor: time. Besides, would you really have the strength to face, day after day, the looks of contempt, the rudeness, the innuendoes? The very porters, the very walls are cruel to anyone who has fallen.

VANAN. My God.

CUST. Just be clever; let your enemies have a little rope. The important thing is simply to get through these next few days of suspicion and anger, and noise. Admit to some little thing or other, so as to give the fools, who are shouting so loudly, the illusion of victory. Throw a piece of flesh to the wolves who are following you . . .

VANAN. My God.

CUST. And very soon they'll all be thinking of something else; what you should do now is . . . [*He pauses.*]

VANAN. What?

CUST. My belief is that you ought to send the Investigating Councilor a note today; without saying too much, without giving your hand away; just telling him simply that in view of what has happened you don't feel that you ought, for the present—for the present—to remain in the building. For the present. Instead . . . [*He pauses again.*]

VANAN. . . . instead . . .

CUST. Very quietly, very, very quietly, just stay at home and think. Reflect. And in the meantime do you know what you can do as well? On your own account, silently. You can write.

VANAN. Write what?

CUST. A full statement, in which you explain everything. Just pass the time doing that. For the present.

VANAN. For the present. . . .

CUST. The important thing is the little note; and you must hurry: the note must arrive before they can decide anything disagreeable. It will restrain them. Write it now, straight away. [*Pointing to a desk.*] There.

VANAN. Cust, I don't want . . . Croz, what do you think?

CUST. Listen, Vanan, I've given you a piece of advice. I've probably gone too far in doing so.

VANAN [*Suddenly pleading*]. But, of course, I know, I am grateful, you must forgive me. And you too, Croz. Actually . . . you must understand my . . . [*He is gradually approaching the desk.*] Yes,

Cust, there's a good deal of sense in what you say. A full . . . precise statement, absolutely! Absolutely. And now, a note: yes, I must write it now. You know, Cust: you've been the only . . . [*Almost weeping.*] I've no friends: I've always been too proud. And now they'll all . . . be delighted, they all want to humiliate me. They've all become suddenly . . . wicked, treacherous. . . . [*He is fumbling at the desk; suddenly he breaks off, and listens intently; runs to the door, listens; and turns back to the other two men, his eyes widening in real fear.*] She's talking to the porter! My God! look; the only person I have in the world will be here in a minute! I beg you by whatever you hold most dear . . . [*Trying to control himself.*] Listen: it's my daughter. You don't know her. There's always been just the two of us; her mother died. She thinks I'm almost a king in here, she wouldn't understand anything of what's happened. I beg you, I beseech you not to let her suspect anything: pretend nothing has happened. It's a great favor. [*Changing his tone, speaking towards the door, which has just opened.*] Yes, Elena. Come in, my dear. I'm glad you stopped in, we can go home together. [*A radiant young girl, and at the moment looking rather surprised, is in the doorway. She comes shyly into the room.*] [*Breathlessly, to his two colleagues.*] This is my daughter. Elena. Fancy; she's never been here before. [ELENA *smiles at the two judges.*] [*Stammering, and fumbling about on the desk.*] Elena, these are two very clever . . . friends of mine who . . . are very fond of me, in spite of the fact that your father is the most exacting president there could possibly be. Yes, certainly . . . I'm an absolute . . . tyrant. Absolutely, quite, quite. [*Fumbling confusedly on the desk.*] Forgive me, Elena, I'm coming at once, I just have to finish a . . . a note; I'll finish it at once, my dear Cust. Tell me, Elena: I wonder whether you heard me in the corridor? I'm always shouting, I get angry over nothing, because . . . because everything falls on my shoulders, do you understand? The President. I'm the President. It's an honor, but it's also . . . a terrible responsibility.

[*He is already scribbling: there is a silence.* ELENA, *like someone in very great awe, smiles again at the two judges, who look at her attentively.*]

[VANAN *has finished. He goes over in silence to* CUST, *and places the letter in his hand, and then goes over to his daughter and lifts his hand, vaguely touching her hair, as if he wished to smoothe it.* ELENA *takes his hand and kisses it.*]

[VANAN *looks at the two judges with a flicker of sudden pride; slips his daughter's arm beneath his own, nods good-by, and goes out, very upright, in silence.*]

[CROZ *and* CUST *stand there for a moment as though lost in thought.* CROZ *gives a long glance at his companion, and then goes out, leaning heavily on his cane, without speaking.*]

[CUST, *after his departure, goes slowly across to a desk, sits at it, and suddenly seems overcome by a genuine prostration; he remains for a little while thus: with his head in his hands.*]

[MALGAI *enters and begins to put the room in order.*]

MALGAI [*At the door*]. Please sir, may I . . . ?

CUST [*Without raising his head*]. Yes.

MALGAI [*As he tidies up*]. That was the President's daughter, wasn't it, sir?

CUST [*As before*]. Yes.

MALGAI. A pretty girl. She's quite grown up . . . quite a young lady.

CUST [*As before*]. Yes. [*He looks up.*] She reminded me of something.

MALGAI. Sir, you're not looking very well.

CUST. I'm just tired, that's all. I feel rather upset. [*He pretends to unfold a roll of documents, and begins to hum to himself; thinking, quietly.*] My God, how horrible everything is. What a wasted life. Judge Cust. [*He hums again, and thinks idly.*] Yes, the girl reminded me of something. There was something about her. [*Lost in thought, as he goes on.*] Attilio, do you know who Vanan's daughter looked like? She looked like the figure on a box, a tin box we once had at home when I was a boy; a woman with flowing hair . . . and a crown . . . She was lifting a glass, it was an advertisement for something. I used to be tremendously fond of her. Tremendously. She looked like Vanan's daughter.

MALGAI [*As he goes out*]. Ah, Mr. Cust, sir . . . When I was a boy, I used to . . . [*He smiles.*] Oh, dear, the things that went through one's mind! Well, well . . . [*He goes.*]

CUST [*Almost singing the word*]. Tremendously. Tremendously. [*He begins to hum again; then, thinking.*] I might very well have had a daughter like that. "Elena, let's go out for a little shall we? Dear Elena." Judge Cust and his daughter . . . [*Hums.*] Or else my wife. "Come on, Elena, let's go home, shall we?" Judge Cust and his wife . . . [*Hums.*] Or my mother perhaps. I am a tiny little frog. She gives me milk. A young beloved mother, very young. [*He rises slowly to his feet.* ERZI *and* CROZ *have come in, and are walking across the room.* CUST *stares at them fixedly; just as they are about to go out, he calls:*] Councillor Erzi!

[ERZI *and* CROZ *stop.*]

CUST. How's it going?

ERZI. What?

CUST. The inquiry.

ERZI. Are you interested in it?

CUST. Can't stop thinking about it.

ERZI [*Dropping his voice a little*]. Cust, was there something you wanted to say to me?

CUST. I? I only wanted to tell you that . . . if I can help you at all . . . in any humble way . . . I'd of course be very pleased.

ERZI. Have you had any ideas?

CUST. Any ideas? Any ideas. [*He looks at* ERZI *for a moment, and then hands* VANAN's *letter to him.*] All the same, it would be a good thing, wouldn't it, if President Vanan were innocent, and the leper was somebody else.

ERZI [*Has glanced at the letter, and now turns and stares at* CUST]. Do you think so?

CUST [*Sighs*]. I'm just thinking. I wonder if it wouldn't after all be a good thing to abandon the inquiry . . .

ERZI. And who's suggested that we intend to abandon it? No. It will be pursued. Right to the end. And you will help me.

[*He shakes* CUST'S *hand warmly, and goes out with* CROZ.]

[CUST *stands looking after him.*]

Curtain

ACT II

Several days have passed. On one side of the stage, bored and impersonal, stands the gloomy police officer. BATA *and* PERSIUS, *wearing hats and overcoats, are wandering furtively about, rather as if they were spying. They meet, rapidly whisper something together, and part again with assumed indifference, as the door from the corridor opens.*

CUST *enters slowly.* BATA *and* PERSIUS, *torn between curiosity and the fear of compromising themselves by starting a conversation, make cautious nods of greeting towards him: prudence prevails however; and nodding once more to* CUST, *they both slip towards the door; here they throw a further long glance at him; and disappear.*

CUST *has followed them with his eyes. He hesitates; at last he removes his hat and overcoat, and approaches the police officer.*

CUST. I am Judge Cust. Councillor Erzi has sent for me. I don't know what he wants. Would you mind telling him I'm here?

[*The officer nods and goes out. After a few moments a door opens and* ERZI *enters.*]

ERZI. Ah thank you, my dear Cust, thank you; how good of you to come. Sit down. Well, now. It's always a pleasure to talk with a colleague like yourself. You've no idea, I suppose, why I asked you if you'd mind coming?

CUST. No.

ERZI [*After a pause*]. Did it really never occur to you to wonder?

CUST. No.

ERZI. Well . . . you did, after all, make me a promise. Yes, I asked you to help me in my investigation. I was greatly impressed by the acuteness of some of your observations. So I've always been expecting to see you. But you've been in very seldom, and then only fleetingly. I've been rather surprised at that.

CUST. I never thought you'd seriously need me.

ERZI. I needed someone who'd been breathing the air of this place for a long time. Besides, you're expecting a promotion which will be almost the goal of your whole career. It is in your own interest that this mess should be cleared up.

CUST. I'm not the only one with such an interest.

ERZI. Quite so. But Judge Croz will also be here in a short time. So will some of the others. [*A short pause; he smiles.*] My dear Cust, this evening I am expected to present my conclusions. The whole city is holding its breath. But before I go, as I shall do shortly, up to the office of the Lord High Chancellor, I wanted to call a few friends together again in here, and test the evidence once more.

CUST. I thought that the inquiry had already uncovered a great many facts and implicated a great number of people.

ERZI. Yes. But in the end everything must center on one particular fact. There must have been a beginning somewhere.

CUST. Has the inquiry broken down on that point?

ERZI. I'm not at all satisfied in my mind.

CUST. You had your eye on Vanan, or so I thought?

ERZI. Yes. Everything would seem to point to Vanan . . . if it were not that one authoritative voice had spoken in his favor.

[CUST *does not break the silence.*]

ERZI. Yours. It was you who told me that Vanan might in fact be innocent. Your observation showed me two things: first, that you had your own opinions, and secondly, that I must regard you yourself as above suspicion. Though in theory I might have suspected you also.

CUST. Yes.

ERZI. But I rather imagine that a guilty person would take great care not to call an investigator back off a false trail . . . and run the risk of having him at his own heels.

CUST. Unless he did so in order to *make* himself above suspicion.

ERZI. Quite so.

CUST [*Slowly*]. You have in fact sent for me in order to know what I really think of this matter.

ERZI. Precisely.

CUST. I think that if your leper really exists, and if it's not Vanan, then you're going to find it difficult to catch him.

ERZI. Not impossible, however. And why should it be difficult?

CUST. Because the thread of facts, which might have led you to him, has been snapped. Ludvi-Pol is dead: the mouth that could have talked has been shut.

ERZI. Then you think that, at this very moment, somewhere in one of the many rooms in this vast building, there is a person in whom by now, all fear has ceased.

CUST [*Thoughtfully*]. The rooms in this place are very quiet ones. Unhealthy-looking men sit in them; they have the faces of men who rarely see the sun. Over a period of many years, they have listened in silence to thousands of lies; they have examined human actions of the most extraordinary subtlety and wickedness. Their experience is immense. The people who have faced them across the table have seen merely a few polite, rather tired gentlemen. But in reality, especially among those who achieve very high office, there are wrestlers, dear colleague; despite the fact that their hardened veins burst so easily. As a rule they find it difficult to sleep at night. And as a result of that . . . [*He breaks off.*]

ERZI. Well?

CUST. As a result they have a great deal of time to brood over their thoughts. They're capable of listening very attentively; they're tough; and they are extremely careful.

ERZI. It would be difficult to catch them out, in that case.

CUST. Yes. And one of them is the man you're looking for.

ERZI. The leper.

CUST. Today that man is on the heights. The day you succeed in unmasking him, he will stand for a moment dumbfounded; millions of eyes will be on him; and then he will hurtle down into an abyss of darkness.

ERZI. And then?

CUST. Then he will begin to defend himself, dear colleague. I believe that his situation must give him a strange intoxicating feeling of liberty.

ERZI [*Looking hard at him*]. I imagine that one evening, at a very late hour, this man, this judge we're looking for, lifted his gaze from his desk. The person who had come in was very polite, the visit was a perfectly legitimate one. Then the conversation drifted, important friendships, secret powers, attractive enticements flickered about it . . . [CROZ *appears at the door of the clerk's office and stands listening, unseen by the others.*] [*Continuing without interruption.*] . . . The cautious visitor was trying to grope his way towards something already waiting there in the judge's mind: something called ambition; or greed perhaps; or envy; or hate. And at what exact point did that perfectly legitimate cordiality, those vague promises, become something more? When did that subtle bond between them become a leash, held in a master's hand?

CUST [*Sweating slightly*]. Yes: I think it's a very likely reconstruction.

ERZI [*With a barely perceptible increase of urgency*]. That is how this judge of ours came to place an acute and powerful intelligence at the disposal of a master, and in the service of injustice. He falsified decisions, he betrayed secrets, and he changed human destinies. He spread in here a trouble which rapidly defiled the entire Courts of Justice; he drove the iron wheel of the law over many innocent men and women. Even a murderer can sometimes regard himself as an executioner. But our man was well aware that he was falsifying the sacred scales of justice. For the sake of what? Why?

CROZ [*From the back, interrupting unexpectedly*]. Probably because he'd begun to have his doubts.

ERZI [*Turning*]. About what?

CROZ. Oh, about the sacred scales and so forth. [*He laughs, coughs, and goes on.*] The devil—Ludvi-Pol I mean—had come to get him that night, but that was probably just what our man had wanted, wasn't it, Cust! A judge is just like a priest in these matters: after officiating all his life in front of the holy altar, he conceives a terrible hatred of it and a great wish to see the devil himself appear in front of him for a change.

ERZI [*Staring now at* CROZ]. But hadn't so many years of being there made him wise, so many years of being outside the game?

CROZ [*Bursts out laughing*]. Outside the game? But one's never outside the game, my dear Erzi! My dear good fellow, just think for a minute of one of those nasty black insects, that sting. You excite one of them: and it stings. You cripple it: and it stings. You cut it in two: and it stings. You transfix it and smash its head in: and its sting goes on stinging, stinging, stinging. Just for nothing. That's what life is.

CUST [*Pointing a finger towards* CROZ]. A spite which amuses even the dying quarry. Doesn't it Croz?

ERZI [*Suddenly turning to* CUST]. But then, Cust, if the thread of facts is broken off, and if the person is so sure of himself, and so determined and cautious, why do you only say it will be *difficult* to find him, and not impossible? After all, that's what you said. What can possibly betray him?

CUST [*Speaking first with his eyes lowered, and eventually lifting them towards his questioner*]. This: that men are rather fragile; the very things that they themselves construct, their thoughts . . . their laws . . . their crimes . . . lie too heavy on their backs.

ERZI [*Slightly urging him on*]. You mean that the man who was guilty of this crime doesn't sleep very easily.

CUST. Yes.

ERZI. Why?

CUST. Because he thinks about it too much.

ERZI. Guilt?

CUST. No; he's beyond that.

ERZI. Why then?

CUST [*Smiling and staring at him*]. Because he doesn't want his little red spot to be discovered.

ERZI. Well?

CUST [*A little uneasily*]. Well, with extraordinary subtlety and patience, he calculates; he imagines that the slightest break in his voice, the quickest glance, may have left here and there traces, imperceptible signs . . .

ERZI. . . . which someone may find, and follow up . . .

CUST. Yes, and which he, with supreme caution, takes care to baffle and disperse.

ERZI. In what way?

CUST. He hastens to meet every tiny possible suspicion, even before it's born; sometimes indeed he even prompts the suspicion; and then he stares hard at it, and baffles it, makes it unsure of itself, dazed, destroyed by its own vagueness.

CROZ [*With a loud laugh*]. It's a big job, isn't it, Cust?

CUST. It is. If one's to discover the man, the secret is to *be* him.

ERZI. What do you mean?

CUST. . . . to feel that one *is* the man. [*His breathing thickens slightly.*] To feel the same chill here on the scalp, the same heavy pounding, not quite in the heart, but lower, almost in the belly. Boom . . . boom . . . boom . . . the same trembling at the knees . . . the same weariness. I hope you see what I mean?

ERZI. Perfectly. [*Very quietly.*] Then what exactly are his feelings, when he hears that we are at his heels? Fear, wouldn't you say?

CUST. You're wrong.

ERZI. Doesn't he know he's being pursued?

CUST. He's not a fool.

ERZI. You mean it doesn't alarm him?

CUST. Certainly not.

ERZI. Well?

CUST. He manages to control himself.

ERZI. What does he do?

CUST. We pretend to be him; he pretends to be us. He assumes we have a quite supernatural foresight. He dare not make a mistake.

CROZ [*Satirically*]. It really is a big job.

CUST [*Pointing a finger at* CROZ, *harshly and aggressively*]. Above all, he has to keep beginning over and over again.

ERZI. Why?

CROZ [*Staring at* CUST *in his turn*]. Because our eyes are always on him, our suspicions are always pursuing him . . .

CUST [*Counterattacking*]. . . . and he goes on arranging and constructing defenses ever more subtle and ingenious. [*Laughing, rather harshly.*] Today, for example, his hand . . . It occurred to me, watching your hand, Croz, lying idly there on the table . . . What I mean is that his hand, or even one finger of his hand, at the precise moment that someone utters the name of Ludvi-Pol . . . at that moment one finger of his hand . . . [*He is still pointing at* CROZ'S *hand.*] causes a tiny slackening of control; he is affected: for barely a second . . .

CROZ [*Nervously and jestingly moving his hand*]. Like that?

CUST. Like that. And what a mistake to make. Just because someone was staring at it . . . as we are staring at yours. And suppose someone had noticed that coincidence? And had thought about it? Was that imperceptible movement a confession? Yes, it's *that* that the guilty man thinks about all night long. And by daybreak: he has made up his mind.

ERZI. What to do?

CUST. An experiment. He will go back and face the other person . . . and name Ludvi-Pol again! And he'll put his hand there again, in the same position . . . just as Croz has done! And he'll repeat that imperceptible movement! But what matters this time is that the color of his cheeks, the sweat of his forehead, the sound of his voice, everything shall be beyond question. His hand will feel itself scorched by our look. He'd love to withdraw it . . .

CROZ. You describe it with great accuracy.

CUST. But he has to hold on. The moment has come . . . his heart turns to marble . . . Like this . . . [*He holds his breath for a moment, and then shakes himself and laughs.*] And then everything's all right, he can breathe again!

CROZ. A bit tired?

CUST. [*With a wan smile*]. Almost exhausted.

CROZ. Can I move my hand, now? These moments are rather overpowering.

ERZI [*Pointing his finger at* CUST]. But it would be incautious of him to rest for a moment, you said so yourself. . . .

CROZ [*Also urgently*]. There's not a moment that may not bring him some fresh danger . . .

CUST [*Suddenly, hoarsely, looking down*]. I believe the real dangers are inside himself.

ERZI. How?

CUST [*Painfully, and as though bewildered*]. He is at the end of his tether. He longs to run away . . . To run away . . . To be dead and buried. That's the most complete flight of all. But then . . .

ERZI. Go on.

CUST [*Almost to himself*]. Who would be left, to keep the thing snug and warm, the crime I mean, the danger, who would watch over it . . . ? Who would *live* it?

CROZ [*Bending over him*]. Do you know what I think, Cust, really? I believe his real wish, his most terrible need, is to talk about it. The whole thing. To talk about it. Am I right?

CUST [*Bewildered and lost in thought*]. Perhaps. He is alone. Everyone is a long way away from him. Alone. And so . . .

ERZI [*Returning to a previous question, almost cruelly*]. Guilt!

CUST [*As before*]. No. Astonishment. He is amazed. Amazed to see himself so busy, thinking and doing such strange, wild, ridiculous things . . . but he's forced on to them by the chain of consequences.

ERZI. And doesn't he feel a certain alarm?

CUST [*Whispering*]. Yes . . . he has the feeling one sometimes has in dreams: when one whispers to oneself: "But this isn't true! It's not true! It's not true! . . . I shall wake up in a minute." [*He breaks off. Someone has knocked at the door leading to the corridor. They all turn. The door opens. The* POLICE OFFICIAL *appears in the doorway; he looks at* ERZI *with a slight lift of the eyebrows and immediately withdraws.*] [*Coming up to the surface again, and laughing cheerfully to* ERZI.] There are times when I even fear you suspect him. [*He points to* CROZ.] . . . or me!

ERZI [*Also laughing*]. Oh please, please! I'm just looking for help.

Well, Cust, since you've penetrated so well into the psychology of our criminal, what would you say, now, are the moves which he expects us to make? What is the point that worries him, in the circle of his defense.

CUST [*Is still looking at the doorway where the* OFFICIAL *appeared; he thinks for a moment; then he turns and points to the archives; almost shouting*]. The papers! That's where I advise you to attack him!

ERZI. Explain what you mean exactly.

CUST [*Almost mildly*]. We're dealing with a judge, aren't we? Very well then; think of the vast number of words he uses to sustain the arguments in his statements, in pronouncing sentence, in discussions. All those words are now slumbering in there. The archives. Everyone of them was a weight thrown into the scales you spoke of: but a weight that had been falsified. The records in there, taken singly, page by page, would tell you nothing. But if you were to consider them all together, however tough and clever he had been, don't you feel there must be something there that is bound to betray him? The insistent recurrence of such and such an ambiguity or quibble: the flavor of corruption. That will be the flavor that will distinguish that judge's words from those of all the others. That is the one single thread. [*He points once more.*] The papers.

ERZI. My dear Cust, did you know that the record clerk was already outside in the corridor? It's just as though you'd been reading my thoughts. But you have gone deep down into them, thrown light on them. We are here to obey you, in a sense. But not only because of that, Cust. Your guilty man hasn't thought of everything.

CROZ [*Raising his voice slightly*]. Are you there, Malgai? Come in.

[*The door from the corridor opens and* MALGAI *appears. He crosses and opens the door of the archives, and goes inside.*]

ERZI. He calls it his graveyard. Well, we shall exhume from it whatever may be needed to put our man into our hands. [*Confidentially.*] It seems, among other things, that Ludvi-Pol himself was in the habit of suggesting certain specific and characteristic arguments in his own favor. We shall discover them all in there, shan't we? But with another signature attached to them. Eh? What do you think, Cust?

CROZ. Do you think our leper will be able to escape us?

CUST. It won't be easy. [*Suddenly, almost frightened, pointing towards the corridor.*] But who's that who's come as well? There was someone else besides the record clerk . . . I thought I heard . . .

ERZI. It's another of the people I needed to have here. [*Turning towards the corridor.*] Come in, come in, Vanan. We were expecting you.

[VANAN *enters. They look at him in surprise. He is extraordinarily wasted, and even shrunk in size. His daughter accompanies him, and almost pushes him forward as though he were a naughty child. She makes him advance to the middle of the room.*]

CROZ. Compassionate Antigone, gentle Cordelia, your father is among friends now, and doesn't need you any more.

[ELENA *is about to speak.*]

ERZI [*Preventing her*]. You may leave us. You would not be of any help to him.

[ELENA *strokes her father's arm, and goes out.*]

CROZ [*With cruel gaiety as soon as the door is shut*]. By God, Vanan, I believe you've actually shrunk. What's happened to you? I never thought you were so soft.

VANAN. Eh . . .

CROZ. You've crumpled right up, Vanan. It would be damned funny if you went before I did, wouldn't it? Now, you've got to listen to something. Our colleague Erzi, as you no doubt know, has a number of things to say to you.

ERZI [*In severe tones*]. Mr. President Vanan! The High Council had allowed you a deferment; that deferment is up today. You have been summoned here today to make your final statement. You promised to prepare your defense.

VANAN [*Uncertainly*]. I . . . yes . . . yes, sir.

ERZI. Have you done so? [*A silence.*]

CROZ [*Mutters*]. You even seem to have lost the power of speech.

ERZI. A number of very grave charges are being made against you. You declared that you could disprove and demolish them. How? [*A silence.*]

CROZ. He's lost his tongue.

ERZI [*His voice becoming steadily more stern as he speaks*]. Above all, you declared that if you were to reconsider certain remarks made by Ludvi-Pol, you would find yourself in a position to reveal the real criminal. Well? Vanan, who is it? [*A silence.*] Tell us the name, Vanan! [*A silence; he turns away and resumes his seat.*] Either from you, or in some other way, we shall know that name today. [*To the others.*] But perhaps this silence is itself an answer. Vanan, am I to assume that you are acknowledging yourself guilty? Is it true then? Is it you who are responsible for the fraud that has poisoned this bench, this whole building, and the city itself?

CUST [*Hoarsely*]. Do speak, Vanan; speak out.

VANAN [*Stammering, pleading, and oddly false in tone*]. I must . . . express my thanks.

ERZI [*Surprised*]. What?

VANAN [*As before*]. I have to say . . . that actually . . . the Administration has treated me . . . with very great kindness . . . [*Agitated.*] so that I have nothing to complain of.

ERZI [*Surprised*]. What are you talking about, Vanan?

VANAN [*As before*]. As an old . . . magistrate, I feel . . . it's my duty to express my . . . to kiss . . . the generous hand . . .

ERZI [*Suddenly shouting*]. What do you mean, Vanan!

VANAN [*Rather frightened*]. No, don't do that . . . Of course . . . I'm very old, and . . . sick now, as you know.

ERZI [*Quickly*]. Vanan, are you admitting that you are guilty?

VANAN [*Looks at him suspiciously; suddenly in a false oratorical voice*]. I am innocent, sir! Innocent and falsely accused. Nailed to the cross . . . like our innocent Savior . . . Gentlemen, these gray hairs have been . . . trampled on . . .

ERZI. Vanan, who is the guilty man?

VANAN [*As before*]. Oh, yes, sir, yes. There is, there *is* a guilty man. I swear before . . . before God's throne that someone is guilty! And I . . . and I can unmask him . . . The wicked shall be hurled to the dust . . . [*Suddenly becoming once more pitiful and pleading.*] I am innocent, sir, innocent. . . .

ERZI [*Sadly*]. Vanan, what has happened to you? You don't seem like the same man.

VANAN [*In the tones of a beggar*]. Sir . . . you must intercede . . . for this poor unfortunate judge . . . I don't deserve such . . . severity. [*With sincerity, almost whispering.*] I only want . . . a little quiet. Nothing else.

[*A silence.*]

ERZI [*Thoughtfully*]. My dear Croz, although the whole thing is really quite clear, it is rather disturbing when one thinks how fragile and delicate the human organism is. Man is far more perishable than even the most trivial object shaped by his own hands. Our colleague is indeed much changed.

CROZ [*Giggling*]. He'll be even more changed before long.

ERZI. But those cunning papers which he—and the others—blackened with their hurrying pens, those, we shall now find, though they're dead and buried, will be more alive than he is. [*Raising his voice, to* VANAN.] They will tell us the things which you wouldn't or couldn't tell us. You will wait for us here. [*To the others.*] Shall we go?

[ERZI *goes across to the archives and enters.* CROZ *follows him.* CUST *and* VANAN *remain behind.*]

VANAN [*Uneasily, his voice and attitude changing somewhat*]. What are they going to do? Why . . . did they tell me to wait for them? I hate those two, I don't trust them. Cust . . . [*He sees* CUST'S *face.*] Cust! For God's sake, what's the matter with you?

CUST [*Approaching him*]. Listen, Vanan. I am here to help you, I want you to trust me! It rather looks to me as if you're not being sincere in all this. Or am I wrong? Eh? [*He wipes his brow.*] Listen, Vanan, is it really true that you . . . have been reconsidering . . . certain remarks made by poor Ludvi-Pol . . . Is it true that you have actually discovered the man . . . we're looking for?

VANAN [*Moans*]. I don't remember anything any more . . .

CUST [*Dropping his voice*]. But I remember advising you to write a detailed, exact statement. . . .

VANAN. I . . . I . . . what?

CUST [*Harshly*]. A statement.

VANAN [*Moans*]. No, no . . .

CUST [*Urgently*]. Where is it?

VANAN. But I . . .

CUST. Have you written it?

VANAN. No . . . No . . . I couldn't do it. I only want . . . I don't want them to hurt me.

[*A silence.*]

CUST [*With sudden fierceness*]. My God, it's almost comic to think you can let yourself be buried so willingly. It's unnatural. [*Urgently and whispering.*] What's happened, Vanan? What is it? Tell me.

VANAN [*Suddenly whispering*]. Cust, I'll tell you the truth. I'm tired.

CUST. What of?

VANAN. The whole thing. You told me to think about it.

CUST. Well?

VANAN. People were cross with me, because I always kept saying the same things.

CUST. Well?

VANAN. Well, actually . . . I began to think about it by myself, at night.

CUST. Good. Well?

VANAN. The trouble was that I was alone; everyone believed that things had happened . . . that other way; and so—Cust, have you ever been bathing in a river, and suddenly seen the water all running the other way? You stand there, still, alone, by yourself, in the middle of the flowing water . . . and you feel a sort of giddiness . . . It was like that; I began to . . .

CUST. Yes?

VANAN. I began to feel weighed down, Cust, disheartened. There were times when I spoke out loud, all by myself, boldly, saying I was innocent . . . but even my own voice hadn't any conviction in it any longer . . . [*Suddenly.*] Do you know what it was? [*Whispering.*] I almost stopped believing in it myself.

CUST. In what?

VANAN. I stopped believing in it. I admit there may have been some little things, when I've been taking evidence, that I may have modified a little . . . Perhaps I've been responsible for a certain amount of confusion . . . I don't know: I may even have been a bit at fault myself; they all say so . . . [*Suddenly pointing towards the corridor.*] You know, Cust. *She's* my principal torment.

CUST. Who?

VANAN [*Still pointing*]. My daughter. It's she who drives me on.

CUST. What do you mean?

VANAN. Oh, yes, yes. She's become so naughty. She never leaves me in peace. Sometimes I pretend to be asleep, or feel unwell. But she has no pity, none at all.

CUST. Your daughter?

VANAN. Yes, yes.

CUST. What does she want you to do?

VANAN. She wants me . . . to . . . to write . . . to accuse somebody.

She knows I'm innocent, so she wants me to make them listen to me . . . But I'm old, Cust, I'm tired . . . And now everyone here is so rude and insolent to me the whole time. She can't understand that. She can't see that to insist on speaking out only means getting into worse trouble!

CUST. Was it she who brought you here?

VANAN. It was, yes. [*He laughs.*] You can't think how furious she must have been when they sent her away. She's out there now, waiting for me. But do you know what I'm going to do? I shall go out that way, through the clerk's office. [*Suddenly pushing* CUST *aside, with a loud cry and a strange unexpected energy.*] I hate all this! I hate you too, Cust. I could kill you. [*Moving almost solemnly towards the office door.*] Let me go away. I don't want to think about these things any more. [ELENA *slips in through the corridor door. She makes a sign to* CUST *not to say anything.*] [*In a completely different voice, stopping.*] Listen, Cust, I know I keep going about shouting that I am innocent, like Our Lord on the Cross; but suppose that was just a bit of hypocrisy? and suppose the Lord chastised me? [*Vaguely.*] A man needs peace, he can't stand against the whole world . . . sometimes I tell my daughter that I'm coming to the courts, but I actually go to a little public garden I know in the town, and just sit there a little. That's where I go. Goodbye, my dear Cust. Goodbye.

[*He moves towards the door of the clerk's office: there he nods goodbye to* CUST, *and disappears;* CUST *and* ELENA *remain alone.*]

ELENA. I'm his daughter.

CUST. I know.

ELENA [*In distress*]. He hasn't anyone else in the world. Neither have I. Don't you think it's sad he should run away from me like that? And silly that I should run after him?

CUST. It's never easy to understand what goes on inside us.

ELENA. Are you in charge of the inquiry?

CUST. Is there something you want to say?

ELENA. Yes, I came specially.

CUST. Well, you can speak. Is it about the inquiry?

ELENA. Yes. It's important, and private.

CUST. You'll have to be quick then. A decision has to be reached this evening.

ELENA. Sir, what my father told you wasn't the truth. I know he wasn't being sincere.

CUST [*Cautiously*]. When is a man being truly sincere? It's always difficult to be quite sure.

ELENA. Forgive me, sir. The earliest thing I can remember is when I used to sit on my father's knee. His hair wasn't gray in those days. He used to sit with his eyes closed, and I used to pretend I was drawing his face; I used to touch his eyes with my finger, like that, his nose, his mouth . . . it was one of our games; but we had so many games. I can't describe the happiness and delight we both had in those days! When I hear anyone talking of the people they love, I know that no one can ever be as we were, father and I. Whenever anyone said I looked like him I used to feel my cheeks go scarlet with pride. I would have refused to go to heaven, if my father wasn't to be there too. [*She is silent for a moment; then, without saying anything, she takes from her bag an envelope and shows it to him.*]

CUST. What is that?

ELENA. It's his defense, sir. The statement. They've only to read it, and I know my father will be acquitted. [A *silence.*]

CUST. But only a few moments ago your father said. . . .

ELENA. I know. He refuses to present it. I brought it myself, without telling him.

CUST. But he's definitely denied having written it.

ELENA. But he's spent night after night on it . . . I helped him.

CUST. Then why should he deny it now?

ELENA [*Sadly and anxiously*]. Because he's so bewildered and frightened. Someone has put the most dreadful doubts and fears into him; it's almost like an illness . . . He's like someone who has fallen down . . . and doesn't want to get up again; he just wants to shut his eyes.

CUST. Do you know the contents of this statement?

ELENA. Yes, of course. Father has remembered a thousand details . . . his innocence is quite plain. It throws light on everything.

CUST. And does this light help us to find who the other man is? The real culprit, I mean.

ELENA. Yes, sir, of course it does. As you read it, page by page, bit by bit, you can see who the real culprit is, you can guess.

CUST. Can you recall the name? Is it someone called Croz?

ELENA [*Uncertainly*]. No, that isn't the name. [*She puts the statement into* CUST'*s hand.*]

CUST. Good. [*He fingers the statement for a moment: suddenly he hums for a moment to himself.*] My dear child. Elena your name is, isn't it? Sit down. The friendship that binds me to your father . . . and also something that really shines in you yourself and . . . genuinely moves me . . . [*He breaks off.*] When I first saw you, I said to myself: this is true innocence; the radiance of justice herself entering into this sad place . . . [*Resuming.*] Well, all that, I was saying, compels me to make a request of you. You don't imagine, do you, that what you feel is really anything more than a mere hope? Or that the investigating magistrate [*Holding up the document.*] is likely to find anything more than that in here?

ELENA. I am certain, sir.

CUST. You will admit that the opinion of a judge may differ from that of a daughter?

ELENA. When you have read it you will run to my father and embrace him. You'll punish everyone who doubted him. You'll be so indignant; there's not a soul on earth who could be indifferent.

CUST. But your father, who is after all not inexperienced in these matters, must have had a reason for keeping silent about this document.

ELENA. But I've explained . . .

CUST. Yes, but you are probably not aware of all he said in here just now. He expressed a fear that any further light thrown on the facts might damage himself.

ELENA. Yes, exactly, he doesn't understand, it's what I was telling you.

CUST. He declares that the treatment given him by the Administration has been extremely indulgent; and that to insist might provoke great severity. Your father expressed his gratitude to us all.

ELENA. Sir, I have read that even people condemned to death—even when they've been innocent—at the last moment, they've begged forgiveness just as though they were guilty. I know that can happen. My father is a very tired man; but he is innocent.

CUST. Very well. [*He hums for a moment between his teeth, throws the statement down on the table, and goes on.*] Very well. You force me to this, my dear child. You are being very stubborn. Just now, while I was listening to you . . . [*He casts a glance towards the archives.*] I know time is very short and we haven't time to dawdle over all this . . . nevertheless, while I was listening to you, there were a lot of things I couldn't help thinking: rather silly things. For example: I'm old enough to be your father. Everything desirable that passes near us we would like in some way to make our own. [*Suddenly, in an almost anguished outburst.*] And I made you my daughter, I stole you from Vanan! I would have held my breath so as not to sully you in any way. I tell you that in a way I have known you ever since I was a boy, but that's too long to tell about now. There is a very simple word which to me expresses what you seem like: loyal. Loyal. But everyone of us runs on, tied to the indifferent ribbon of time; and that produces an infinite number of mistaken meetings, wrong relationships. One could have been father, brother, husband, son, receiving and giving . . . something. Instead . . . you don't even realize how absurd it is that I, at such a moment, should waste so much time telling you this. However. I wanted to tell you . . . [*With exaggerated anger, to force himself to stop talking.*] . . . a few moments ago, in here, your father explicity confessed himself guilty. [A *silence.*]

ELENA [*Almost to herself*]. I can't believe it.

CUST. You mean you don't want to believe it. Didn't you say your father avoided you? What does that mean? It means that it's you in particular he wants to hide something from.

ELENA [*Lost in her own thoughts*]. There will have been a reason. I will believe anything, but not that he could have disgraced himself.

[A *silence.*]

CUST [*Rather harshly*]. What a cruel word. Disgraced. Sad that you should use it, since it's your own father we're talking about. An inhuman word. [*Almost pleading.*] Can't you believe that one may make mistakes . . . which one only notices . . . after one's made them, and it's too late to turn back? One mistake is enough: the first one.

ELENA [*After reflecting for a moment*]. If I were to think that at some given moment—and that moment must come sooner or later, mustn't it, to people who commit these evil things—if I were to think of my father, at some given moment, doing something furtive, and secret, and looking round to see that no one was watching; or sitting there listening to a man whispering secret, wicked orders to him, and my father whispering back, hurriedly consenting . . . My father! My father, doing that! My father! [*She almost laughs.*]

CUST [*Agitated, pleading*]. Don't you think that everyone in the world, even your father, may at some time or other, need a little pity?

ELENA. But my father couldn't, couldn't possibly do anything he'd have to be ashamed or embarrassed about! You should see my father when he's really angry and outraged! There is nothing in my father but nobility and goodness and pride. People who disgrace themselves in such filthy ways have to be made of very different stuff from my father. You can tell at a glance when people are capable of such treachery: you feel a kind of contempt for them the minute you see them.

CUST. Yes, hideous toads leap from their mouths, and go hopping about these rooms. [*He hums for a moment.*] How cruel you are, my little angel. But it's only your age. The blank blue snow of childhood, smitten by the first incandescent ray of youth. [*With a gust of anger.*] Intoxicating dazzle of light! It leaves one melancholy, humiliated; oh, it's not your fault; you shine, literally, in the midst of this hell of ours. You remind one of the pure crystals of which, as you've perhaps been taught at school, inorganic matter is composed. Do you mean to hand in this statement?

ELENA [*A little disturbed*]. Yes.

CUST. Good. [*With a touch of harshness in his voice.*] I was saying that we were all crystals like you, once, my dear child; that's why it makes one sad to look at you. It seems that life comes into existence at a later stage, born on the icy geometric forms of the inorganic, like a kind of rash, a malignant growth . . . yes, a leprosy indeed. And on that day your voice will have lost this resonant light, and you won't talk any more about disgrace.

ELENA. My father . . .

CUST [*Interrupting*]. Your father. Why not let us be quite frank about him? He's a successful man, he's one of those who have got a great deal out of life. Are we to believe that life simply *gave* him what he got? Did he get it for nothing? Was it a gift from life? A birthday present? Did it cost him nothing? Not even cleverness? Cleverness: a name by which many kinds of villainy get past. It is unlikely that the statement refers to those.

ELENA. But my father . . .

CUST. Is after all rather like the unfortunate rest of us, isn't he? The only consolation is we're all made of the same stuff, my dear. Haven't you ever noticed . . . how shall I put it, haven't you ever caught a look on your father's face . . . something in his voice—yes, his voice would be enough to show you—something that worried you a little? That voice, so familiar to you, so dear to you: but did you never hear that voice talking to one of your father's superiors, someone high up: the Minister perhaps; and being very polite, and excited, and eager? And then suddenly did you never hear the same voice, sharp and impatient, speaking to a beggar? Well? Did that never happen? It happens with all of us. And then again . . . didn't you ever hear him pretending to be kind and gentle, from above, with the old man at the gate . . . well? Look at me: of course you remember. You're already a little tarnished, my fair crystal. Such a daily heap of hypocrisy and wickedness in the inflections of one single voice! After all that, shall we really be so very surprised if these pages [*He waves the document in the air.*] turn out to be a skillful selection of things which are true in themselves, but have been cunningly prised out of the whole. But if you really want to present it—

ELENA [*At a loss*]. I'd like . . .

CUST. And we haven't even got to the real thing yet, have we? We haven't mentioned the words, have we?—only the voice! Do you believe that these actions, just because no law book condemns them, are any less vile than those that you've called vile? Evil actions, hypocrisies, betrayals. Everywhere! Even here, in our own thoughts, which we falsify—yes, even those! As we formulate them inside us . . . not as they first tremble in our conscience, but as soon as certain cunning poisonous calculations occur to us; even in some of our highest impulses whose mysterious purity we contrive to cheat and twist and sully. [*Greatly agitated, but still with an attempt at sarcasm.*] Think, my dear, of the housewife who has carefully stored away her beautiful jars of jam for the winter: it's like that; one day we also decide to open our nice little boxes of fine ideas, and what do we find inside . . . [*He throws the statement on to the table.*] A swarming heap of maggots! And I can think of nothing, nothing on earth, that escapes that fate! [*He breaks off and turns round, as* MALGAI *enters.*] Have you found anything, Malgai?

MALGAI. Not yet; we're still working. [*He takes up a paper from the table and returns to the archives.*]

CUST [*Between his teeth*]. Good, so am I. [*He wipes his brow and goes on.*] No, my dear. I know of nothing that escapes. A single opaque mess asking one thing alone: to live. To live.

ELENA. But my father . . .

CUST [*Shouting*]. Your father was a man, and he was a man here in this ditch! And let me tell you that there was nothing on earth a man could do that he didn't know of!

ELENA [*Impetuously*]. But I am sure—

CUST. Of what? Sure of what?

ELENA. Whenever there's been any sort of injustice or mistake I've always thought of my father; I used to think of him here, in this building, in his ermine gown, looking very stern; and I used to feel calm again at once.

CUST. Well, you were wrong, my dear! Look at me! You know I'm not lying!

ELENA [*With a cry, and moving forward as though to retrieve the statement*]. You don't know my father! You're not his friend!

CUST [*Violently, breathing heavily, and seizing the statement again*]. My God! How stubborn you are! You only want to create havoc here! I want to tell you something. Perhaps it's not even connected with all this; I don't know. But once when I was only a boy, I remember an afternoon of atrocious, suffocating heat. It was during the siesta; everyone was asleep, soaked in sweat, naked. I must have heard a whisper somewhere in the house, perhaps that was it; or perhaps it was some vicious instinct calling me. I got up, and crept barefoot, furtively, through the shadowy house, towards that whisper, and at last, through a half-open door . . . What a silly disgusting commonplace story! Through the half-open door, that white-faced child saw a man and a woman . . . a man and a woman turned into animals by the stifling heat . . . unrecognizable faces, horrible gestures, choking, appalling words . . . It was my father and mother. My father, and my mother. Quite obvious, after all; what of it? Silly to make a tragedy of it; a door not closed properly, a nervous boy. [*Suddenly.*] But no, they weren't my father and mother any more! They were something confused, black, blind, insane! Before that moment I'd never really known them, never known my father and mother; nor myself; nor anyone else. I was horribly shocked. There always comes a day when a door opens a little way and we look through. And that day has come for you too, now, my dear. Look! Look at your father, for God's sake, look at him for the first time; and look at yourself too, my dear child! What do you think, do you think that this sweet flower of your body will never be sullied, that it too won't one day be filled with desire and frenzy, do you think that you'll never damage it, never contaminate it, your beautiful little body—and your voice as well, your angel's breath, your very mind? [*Still excited, but suddenly quiet.*] And did you really not know that the great Vanan was sick? Sick, sick, poor devil, that was what was making such a farcical muddle of everything he said. Life is very long, you know, it's very rare that towards the end a venerable white head is much more than to cover over a heap of nastiness; and nasty filthy sicknesses too, those are the things that make age weigh so heavily upon us. That wasn't written in the statement, I'm sure of it. Sad matters, aren't they? You know that I'm telling you the truth, the absolute truth, don't you? As a rule you blush very quickly. I've noticed. But now your color is slowly draining away from your cheeks. You are saying goodbye to the enchantment of youth. You are becoming a woman; it's a small disturbance, it has to come; like the first cigarette, we feel discomfort here. Yes, so it was I who didn't know the great Vanan! If you only realized how little *you* knew about him! And about the others! And about yourself. That is why you were unjust. You never even knew . . . [*With a sudden cry.*] that your father hates you! He hates you, yes, he said so in here! [*With a change of tone.*] You didn't even know about the slimy love affairs in which poor Vanan has got himself mixed up. The court itself, this very office, has had to look into it. No, that wasn't in the statement either. Slimy intrigues: the loves of old men. It's a sad and terrible thing, my poor angel; the loves of old men, horrible, unspeakable, tormenting! We all come to it. That's how we're made. They are things he never spoke to you about, aren't they? The man you used to kiss when he came back home at night! Suppose *you* look through the open door as well; it's a thing you have to get used to. You know it's the truth I'm telling you, don't you? Very well: you didn't even know that on the day when they first accused him, the great Vanan wrote a letter! And confessed! Yes, he confessed, my dear. He confessed right from the start. Do you want me to repeat the exact words of that letter! [*Striking his forehead.*] They're engraved here. [*Beginning.*] "My dear Lord Chief Justice . . . an aged magistrate writes to beg of you your extreme kindness . . ."

ELENA [*Signing to him not to go on*]. No. [*After a few moments, in a whisper.*] Poor father. [*A pause.*] And poor me.

[*A silence.*]

CUST. Do you want your statement back? [*He holds it out to her.*]

ELENA [*Shaking her head*]. It won't be any use now. [*She goes towards the door; and stops.*]

CUST. You'd better be quick, and go; no one has seen you.

ELENA [*Takes a few steps forward; whispers*]. I'm embarrassed, because now when I meet my father . . . I shan't know what to say to him. I'm afraid that when he looks at me, he'll see that I know. Poor father. I don't want to meet him. [*She moves still nearer to the door; and repeats, almost to herself.*] I don't want to meet him. [*She goes out.*]

[*Perturbed,* CUST *stands looking at the door through which she has departed; suddenly, he begins feverishly unwrapping the statement; a few pages fall to the floor, quickly he picks them up. He breaks off in order to listen for any noise from the archives. He looks once more at the door through which the girl has disappeared.*]

CUST. After all, she was no more than a child. Her gentleness will be enough to . . . She is too gentle almost . . . Tomorrow the color will have returned to her cheeks; and she will have forgotten. [*A pause.*] But I . . . Oh God, how tired I am! Tired to death. [*He covers his face with his hands; suddenly he hears steps approaching; he throws the statement down on the table, turns, and waits. The door of the archives opens, and* ERZI *comes out, followed by* CROZ.] [*Loudly, almost shouting.*] Well, dear friends, has any good come of your labors?

CROZ [*With a loud laugh*]. Haha. You're very cheerful, Cust. You've already guessed.

CUST [*As before*]. Haven't you found anything?

ERZI [*Casually laying a hand upon the statement*]. We find that in none of the suits have the documents survived.

CROZ [*Grinning*]. Cust! One of us has removed them.

CUST [*Excited and suspicious*]. Removed them? And then what?

ERZI [*Removing his hand, and moving away*]. Destroyed them.

CUST. Destroyed them? How? [*He laughs and almost shouts, excitedly, harshly.*] How! How! [*He gradually gets nearer the statement, takes it up, gesticulates with it, and then without disguising what he is doing, drops it into a basket.*] But, my dear friends, would it really have been as easy as all that? Do you think the criminal would have found it easy, or even possible, to burn or destroy, here, such a great number of documents?

ERZI. He could have . . .

CUST. . . . taken them away bit by bit, hidden about himself, do you think? That man, who doesn't want, [*Almost shouting.*] DOES NOT WANT to be found out, do you imagine he'd have gambled his whole position here, with the risk, however remote and theoretical, of being found with the papers on him in some accident or other, a fall, or a faint . . . ! My dear friends, you can't have the slightest idea what he must be really like! Why the very thought of it would have given him a fit!

ERZI [*Interrupting him almost with a cry*]. Cust. Where are those papers?

CUST [*Calmly, pointing to the archives*]. Still in there, in my opinion. But hidden away under mountains and mountains of other documents and papers. The man had patience, so we must have patience too . . . [*He breaks off.*] Did you hear that?

ERZI. What?

CUST. A noise. Not a noise exactly. Down there, somewhere in the building. It sounded to me like . . . [*Breaking off again.*] Yes, there must be something wrong. There's someone running up the corridor.

MALGAI [*Comes running out of the archives and hurries out of the door to the corridor*]. They say there's been an accident. [*He disappears.*]

BATA [*Comes running in from the corridor, crosses the room towards *the clerk's office*]. There's been an accident! Why are people always so careless? They go up and down, up and down, God knows what they're looking for. The gate up at the top must have been opened. Didn't you hear the shout? Yes, as she fell. A loud scream. [*He disappears.*]

[ERZI *runs out into the corridor.*]

CROZ [*Following him*]. This building: horrible things happening the whole time, blood on the ground, accidents. And it's no worse than they deserve, most of the people who come here. If you ask me . . . [*He disappears.*]

[CUST *is alone; he has stood perfectly still throughout; hurried footsteps and voices are heard outside.*]

A VOICE [*Outside the room*]. Let's have some light! Put the lights on!

ANOTHER. Call somebody! Tell somebody to come!

ANOTHER. Where's the porter? Porter!

MALGAI [*Re-entering, breathless*]. It was there, down at the bottom of the elevator shaft. It's so dark everywhere in this damned place, especially the stairs, and the passages. [*He is hastily clearing a divan of the documents on it.*]

CUST [*Without turning, almost tonelessly*]. Is she dead?

MALGAI. They don't think so, not yet. They say it's the daughter—

CUST [*Interrupts him with a gesture, turning round in sudden terror*]. What are you doing?

MALGAI. I'm getting this couch ready . . .

CUST [*Horrified*]. Here? Why . . . No. No. [*He childishly points towards the clerk's office.*] In there . . .

ERZI [*Rushing back in: to* MALGAI]. Yes, in there, that'll be better. We'll take her in there. Call somebody! Do call somebody! Telephone. [*He runs out again.*]

MALGAI. But who am I to call? There's no one there at this hour; everything's shut up. I ought to be at home too . . .

CUST [*Stopping him*]. Malgai, did you hear her cry out . . . ?

MALGAI. Yes, a loud cry—

CUST [*His teeth almost chattering*]. What . . . what do you think?

MALGAI. About what?

CUST. Do you think it's . . . an accident?

MALGAI. I think she must have tripped, people never look where they're going. She tried to dart back, but it was too late. [*He breaks off, and turns toward the corridor.*] Here she is.

[*A low murmur of voices is heard, and the scrape of footsteps approaching: finally the door on the corridor is thrown open wide. A big man enters carrying the girl in his arms, apparently unharmed and as though asleep, her hair flowing over her shoulders. A number of people follow. The man crosses the room, and disappears into the clerk's office: the door remains open. The others, except for* CUST, *follow him, talking in low tones, as though in church.*]

A VOICE. . . . yes, some strands of hair . . . in the iron work . . .

ANOTHER. . . . there was oil . . . there were traces of oil from the elevator shaft . . . They ought to . . .

ANOTHER. . . . clean it, of course, clean it . . .

ERZI [*Crossing the room with* MALGAI]. Anyway, send for somebody . . . send for a woman. Warn them . . . that they must send a car. And her father. Send for him . . . Make some excuse . . . Don't tell him . . .

CUST [*They have all gone into the clerk's office.* CUST *remains alone; he approaches the door of the office; stares at it: suddenly in a hushed voice, with an extraordinary note of pleading*]. Elena. [*A pause.*] Elena. Don't die. Try to live. [*A silence.*] Elena . . . [*He breaks off, as* MALGAI *hurries back in.*]

CUST. How is she, Malgai?

MALGAI. I don't think there's very much hope for her.

CUST [*With terror, almost with fury*]. Do you mean this girl is going to die?

MALGAI. It's a terrible accident, sir.

CUST [*Stammering*]. But that girl . . . she was in here a few moments ago . . . blushing, at a mere nothing . . . she was so young . . . I want to tell her . . . [*He breaks off.*]

MALGAI [*Alarmed*]. What's the matter, sir?

CUST [*Stands looking at one of his hands in real terror; suddenly with a suffocated cry*]. Malgai! I have her blood here on my hands! I've not touched her, Malgai! I've not touched her! [*He rubs his hand hysterically.*]

MALGAI. But . . . but there's nothing odd about that, sir. I touched her myself. You might easily have touched me, you might have brushed by me. Or you might have touched the others, there's nothing strange about that. [*He breaks off.*]

CROZ [*Rushes in from the corridor, in great distress*]. Oh my God, Cust; Her father's here! They sent for him. Who's going to tell him, what shall we do? Oh how dreadful it is, what a terrible mess, the whole thing is . . .

CUST [*With a fierce wild movement, runs to the door, throws it open and cries*]. Come in, Vanan! Come in. Quickly!

VANAN [*Letting himself be dragged in, suspicious and whimpering*]. But what more do you want of me? What is it? Leave me alone! Leave me in peace, why can't you?

CUST [*Shouting*]. You'll never be at peace any more, Vanan! [*Louder still.*] Never, never at peace, Vanan! You must do something! Something terrible! Your daughter. Your beautiful . . . dear Elena. [*Almost to himself alone.*] She's dead. She's dead.

Curtain

ACT III

Late in the evening; a single lamp is burning. MALGAI *is just coming from out of the archives. He puts on his hat and overcoat in preparation for leaving.* CUST *appears at the corridor door.*

MALGAI [*Noticing him*]. Good evening, sir. Did you want something?

[CUST *does not reply.*]

MALGAI. I'm really off duty now, but . . . never mind. We are always here when anybody wants us.

CUST [*Absently*]. No, you go along, Malgai. There's something I want to do, I shall be staying for a little while.

MALGAI. Ah yes, sir. You're another one who wears himself out, sir, working after hours!

CUST. Yes, I'm another. Are the archives open?

MALGAI. Yes sir, they're open. Mr. Justice Croz wanted to—

CUST. I'll see that they're locked up afterwards. Goodnight.

MALGAI [*Surprised*]. Then what shall I . . . very well, sir, very well.

[*He goes out, hesitatingly.*]

[CUST *waits until* MALGAI'S *footsteps have died away; then he goes to the door on tiptoe and turns the key; immediately afterwards he goes into the archives, and returns with an armful of documents which he throws on a table and begins to examine; very soon, however, something seems to distract him, and he stands there lost in thought; suddenly he starts: all the lamps have gone on.* CROZ *has risen slowly from a large armchair whose back has hidden him from sight; he has switched on the lights; now he gives way to a long burst of laughter mingled with coughing.* CUST *has turned round quickly; then he slowly returns to his previous attitude.*]

CROZ [*Frequently pausing for breath*]. Once upon a time there was a little mouse. And there was a trap. Instead of cheese, there were certain well-known papers hidden under mountains and mountains of other papers . . .

CUST [*Absently*]. What do you mean?

CROZ. You're losing your grip, Cust! For example, you just turned the key in the door there: excellent, but what about the other doors? A bit of a surprise, wasn't it, Cust, to find old Croz here?

CUST [*As before*]. We heard bad news about your health.

CROZ. Yes, I hardly managed to get up here, as a matter of fact. But if I've got to die, I wanted to die here. Besides, I know that spite is almost as good as oxygen. [*With a change of tone.*] Cust, it's all fixed for tonight, isn't it? The sentence on the guilty man; and the naming of the new president. [*He points towards the ceiling.*] The old men are already taking their seats up there. Cust, which of us two is going to walk off with it?

CUST [*As before*]. Do you think the Upper Council will definitely eliminate Vanan?

CROZ. Self-possessed, aren't you? You even indulge in the luxury of thinking about Vanan! . . . [*Sarcastically.*] Oh, he'll be sentenced all right . . . [*He pauses for breath.*] . . . and you or I will get the nomination. But you're not looking very well either, Cust. In fact, quite the opposite.

CUST [*In a monotone*]. It's just that my thoughts keep going over and over things which are already beyond the possibility of being changed.

CROZ. You must look after yourself.

CUST. I shall have to. Look at my hand: it costs me a great effort to stop trying to wipe it, though it's perfectly clean already. Like that, you see? [*He wipes his hand.*] I have done that so often that just here the skin has changed. I don't do it quite so much now.

CROZ. Cust, you've always interested me, you know. You've given me the creeps before now, often. You are very tough, aren't you? Stubborn. But now we're on the last lap.

CUST [*In a staccato monotone*]. Yes, I'm very stubborn. And Vanan's daughter showed that she too was pretty stubborn. She hasn't spoken since that day. They say she won't last until tomorrow morning.

CROZ. Cust, what are you doing in here?

CUST. Most of all, it was the cry she uttered as she fell which shocked me. I have tried to analyze it, these last few days; tried to reconstruct it.

CROZ [*Louder*]. Cust, what are you doing here?

CUST [*Quietly, and as though lost in thought*]. You can see; I am looking for something. It wasn't so much a fall into an elevator shaft—I keep getting the idea of her being sucked down into a funnel. Slowly at first, then quickly, then down, vertically, swallowed up. I think that cry expressed other things, besides fear. But what other things? A kind of reproach. But most of all—incredulity; surprise.

CROZ. Cust, you keep on talking to me about that girl. Has she some connection with our problem?

CUST [*As before*]. No real connection. What annoys me most of all is the fact of the interruption. That girl still had little round cheeks, almost like a baby's; and in fact she was very young: when you looked at her, it was like looking at a beautiful fresh leaf moving gently on the branch: one caught a hint of seasons, enchanting hours yet to come, long, long days drenched in sun . . . And where is all that now? Broken off. It's very strange. I don't think any logic in the whole world can explain that.

CROZ. Cust, I don't know if you've understood. This is the epilogue, Cust, the auditing. You've waited for the right moment to take me into your confidence.

CUST. Perhaps I've never really talked to anyone. Sometimes one begins to need to. Perhaps you'd understand me better than anyone else.

CROZ. Undoubtedly. I've always understood you. In a way, you've kept me company. I should have been bored without you. Cust, today you've made your first mistake.

CUST [*Still in the same indifferent, slightly surprised tones*]. Possibly. What was it?

CROZ. You were wrong to come here tonight! Those famous papers, eh? A feeling of fright lest they should still exist in there, subtle, slight, evil: they've drawn you here, like a rope. Right at the last moment, when everything was over, when the old men up aloft were actually dipping their pens into the ink, you had to stumble over this little pebble. [*Shouting.*] Cust, what are you doing here? What are you looking for?

CUST [*Almost wearily*]. The criminal.

CROZ. Well, help me then, because I'm looking for him too. And what is it that drives you on?

CUST. The idea that from tonight onwards he may begin to be calm again, that his footstep from tonight onwards may once more begin to be assured and authoritative in this place; as may his voice. I feel a sort of revulsion and stupefaction at the thought. It's like that girl's cry: I can't find a place for it anywhere in the world.

CROZ. Cust, you're a liar! You've sent the record clerk away by a trick! You've come here at this time of night, in secret! You've fallen into the trap; I have found you out!

CUST [*In a monotone*]. Croz. You too are here in secret. It's I who've found you out.

CROZ. Oh, is it really? Well, tell me then, [*Pointing to the documents.*] have you found nothing in those things there?

CUST. Nothing.

CROZ [*Gives a long laugh, and finds difficulty in getting his breath back*]. Nothing! Nothing! A fine result after all the risks you've taken. [*Mockingly.*] Do you know what I'm afraid of? That it's useless to go on looking any more; and that even in there [*Pointing to the archives.*] everything's vanished.

CUST. Nothing left. That too is strange.

CROZ. Why is it strange? Suppose the papers kept on going in through that door there, and never came out; suppose all the scoundrels in the city had to sign a piece of paper for every penny they ever stole, every lie they ever told; and suppose all the papers stayed in there: by this time there'd be nothing else left on the surface of the earth but papers; and the sea of papers would go on growing and growing till it reached the moon. Haha. Fortunately [*Pointing towards the door of the archives.*] so much goes in, and so much comes out. As in everything else. Here's a graveyard that's even more of a graveyard than that: it's called the pulping-mill. [*In satirically mysterious tones.*] Our friend has taken advantage of that. There's nothing left.

CUST [*In a monotone*]. Not a single trace. At this moment that girl too is perhaps gone without trace. Nothing. It's that that's strange.

CROZ. Nothing? No trace? [*He taps himself on the forehead.*] What about this? You don't count what's inside here? The papers have gone to the pulping-mill, but Croz will have to be sent there as well, because Croz knows who the criminal is. [*Shouting.*] He knows, he knows! Stay where you are, Cust. Don't you dare come near me. I know you're not a man of action, but you've good cause to send me to the pulping-mill too, haven't you? [*He goes over and unlocks the door.*] We don't quite know yet how this interview is going to finish. [*He pauses for breath.*] What a comfort it would be, wouldn't it, with me here, *moribundus*, almost at death's door, how very nice, when you come to think of it, if just one little vein, here inside me somewhere, were to burst and take your trouble away, now, here, at once, before Old Croz could get out of here and begin to chatter, eh?

CUST [*In a monotone*]. It's you whose real interest is that *I* don't get out of here; because the criminal, and I've known it for some time, is you, Croz. Possibly some of the others as well. But you, quite certainly. Not me.

CROZ. Cust, I've always admired you. That was really why I always hated you: and you have quite seriously shortened my life, did you know? You're made of steel. Good God, you're not tired yet: what are you still frightened of? It's done now; there's nothing left inside there. Even if I wanted to accuse you, now, my words would be no more than words. A rival's spite, to try and undermine you. Your words against me would be the same. You needn't hold your breath, Cust. You can speak. I know how much you want to; you're dying to.

CUST [*Rubbing his hand*]. But I'm not guilty. It's you.

CROZ [*Shouting*]. Yes! Yes! I too! I've also been a cheat! Bah. I've never even taken much trouble to hide it. I'd go on being one. Yes, it would have been worth it, wouldn't it, being honest among our dear fellow-citizens—a lot of filthy traitors in exactly the same way, but above all stupid, and villainous, all of them. And how they multiply! Not a drop of cleanliness in one of them; how disgusting! You too: you were quite right, Cust. They must be stamped out underfoot. Cust! I've spoken! You speak too!

CUST [*In a monotone*]. But I am not the criminal.

CROZ. Bah. [*He spits towards him: and stands there panting.*] What a swine you are. And you're a fool as well. It's stupid to care so much. [*He breathes heavily again.*] Who can tell how many men, century after century, must have stood . . . like us two, glaring at each other, quarrelling . . . their foreheads covered in sweat . . . and what a silly fuss to make of anything. It was all a lot of nonsense . . . because . . . [*He grips the table and sits down slowly in a strange way; and mutters.*] Damnation. [*He stays there gasping for breath.*]

CUST [*Without moving*]. Do you feel bad?

CROZ [*Almost speechless*]. Yes.

CUST. You've upset yourself. Do you want a drink of water?

CROZ [*Does not answer; after a moment*]. That'd be very nice. [*He gasps.*] Cust. You've always had the most outrageous luck. [*He slips to the floor.*]

CUST [*Without moving*]. Croz! [*Silence.*] Croz! [*Silence.*] Come on! [*Seeing that the other is trying to speak.*] What is it, do you want to tell me something?

CROZ [*In a whisper*]. I'm going, Cust.

CUST. Going? [*Calmly.*] Ah, one can never tell that.

CROZ [*As before*]. It's all over. [*He collapses onto the floor.*]

CUST [*After observing him for a moment*]. By God, Croz, I'm almost afraid you're right. Croz! Can you hear me? Where are you in pain? [*A silence.*] It's been the same with me these last few days: did you know? I've felt as if there were something at my back, I've felt like a boy going along a dark corridor and whistling. Mustn't turn round, must go straight on, Croz, stick it out. [*A silence.*] Is it your heart? I don't want to frighten you, but this time it does really look like it, doesn't it? These have been hard days for me too, Croz. I've tried to sleep as much as I possibly could. Even a man condemned to death is like a free man, when he's asleep. Sleep is the same for everyone. And let us hope death will be the same, Croz. You are going to sleep for a very long time now, I think. [*A silence.*] Listen, if it's really true that you're going, that it's all over, and there's no more danger, then . . . I may tell you . . . it's true, I *have* been a lucky man. Yes, Croz, I was the man we were all looking for, and I really needed, *needed*, to say so to somebody. I couldn't bear it any longer. *I* was the leper. You were looking for me, weren't you? But I'm still hopeful. I think I'm quite safe still. It's been a big job. I'd been frightened that I might not be able to carry it through, frightened I might suddenly begin to shout. We take far too much upon ourselves. Do you know, Croz, I've kept having the same dream over and over again, all these nights. I dreamt about a child, a boy. I've never had any children. And what an ugly child this was of mine! Naked, with an enormous belly, an evil face, and horrible, quick, crooked little legs, leaping about like a frog, yes, just like a frog; I would see it hiding in the record clerk's trolley, or disappearing among the bookshelves and the papers, in the most ridiculous places, and I would be after it . . . always after it . . . trying to grab hold of it; sometimes I managed to cut it, with a knife . . . cut it up in a hundred pieces . . . but every piece began to grow again with those little legs . . . and to leap about with me after it, I couldn't catch it. I was soaked in sweat, I had too many things to look out for, here, there, everywhere; it was too much, yes, it was too much! Nobody else could have borne it, I'm sure of that. [*In wild desperation.*] That girl's cry, Croz! I *studied* it! I pored over it! It's difficult to understand what she meant, one can make all sorts of guesses. "Aaaaah!" Like that, she cried! "Aaaaah!" The idea I've formed of it . . . is that it had somehow scratched something, made a scratch on a piece of glass. No, not quite, not on a glass . . . it was one of those scratches from which small drops of blood issue. Every now and then, a little drop. It all seems finished; but you look again; and there is another drop of blood. Yes, a scratch. Blood. They all believe it was an accident . . . But I . . . I'm mystified. I can't see . . . [*He breaks off.*]

CROZ [*Raises his head, gets up slowly from the ground; in an ordinary voice, quietly*]. To see ourselves clearly is a great privilege, Cust. You want to set too many things in order. [*Suddenly, wildly, and harshly, he begins to shout.*] Help! I'm dying! Help me, help me! Porter, porter! Hurry! [*He gasps for a moment.*] Quickly someone! Porter! Porter! [*He begins to beat his stick on the table.*] Help, help, help, help!

MALGAI [*Running in*]. What's the matter?

CROZ. It's me, I'm feeling bad, I am dying. Send for the Investigator, first . . . Councillor Erzi . . . tell him to come here at once. Then call the judges. All of them. Fetch as many people as you can, and Vanan as well, of course. Warn them . . . that I'm here, at the point of death, in the company of . . . him, my colleague Cust, look at him; tell them to hurry if they want . . . to find me alive. Hurry up, you fool. [MALGAI *runs out.*] [*Worn out by his efforts, speaks more slowly, breathing with difficulty.*] My poor Cust, I wish I could say that all this had only been . . . a charade for your benefit. Unfortunately . . . it's only too true . . . that I'm about to die; what a bloody disgrace. [*He pants slightly.*] My dear friend, the popular superstition about the words of the dying, strengthens . . . my credit. Strengthens it a great deal. I shall tell the truth; they will believe me; and you, at the very last minute, will have slipped up. You've spoken, you've told me. I could save you too, my dear fellow, I've always . . . liked a good joke . . . in that case I'd be the one who nominated you as president, I'd be the one who put the ermine gown on the back of the great leper; this filthy shell would have a snail inside worthy of it. A juicy sight! But I could never bring myself to help *you*, Cust. I don't like you. You're conceited. I want to punish you. [*He gasps for breath.*] The point of death makes me very powerful. I don't believe I have any duties. [*He gasps.*] I believe that things develop . . . according to a purely vegetable law. And it's not without . . . its comic side. I believe that if we . . . decided to think it was disgraceful to wear gray . . . [*He laughs.*] ha-ha, to wear gray stocking . . . anyone who actually had worn gray stockings . . . ha-ha-ha, would feel terrible guilt and shame. That's all it is. I don't believe that anything remains of us. We'd be in a real mess if . . . if anything could really be distilled from such a load of nonsense. [BATA *arrives, in haste, accompanied by* MAVERI.]

BATA. Croz, how are you?

CROZ. Much as you'd expect a man to be, who knows he'll be dead . . . in about ten minutes. Just stay over there, my dear fellow, there's something I have to say . . . to my colleague. [*To* CUST, *privately*.] All these judges . . . they've always turned my stomach. A lot of them are very upright and very worthy . . . and they'll live for a long time . . . They are made of wood. As for the rest . . . come a bit closer, Cust. They administer justice! Ha-ha-ha [*He laughs*.] Which means they express their opinion that certain actions are just, and certain others are not. Just as one sausage is hung on to another sausage, this opinion is hung on to the law books . . . beautifully bound of course . . . and these law books are hung on to other law books—and statutes and tables . . . older still. The trouble is, my dear fellow . . . [*He breaks off, and says to* PERSIUS, *who has just arrived*.] What's he doing?

PERSIUS. Who?

CROZ. Erzi. Silly old tortoise.

PERSIUS. They've sent for him. Everybody's on their way here.

CROZ [*Turning to* CUST]. . . . the trouble is that the main hook is missing, the original clasp . . . and without that . . . the whole string of sausages falls to the ground! But where, and how, and when! Who was it who decided one thing was right and another wasn't? We know perfectly well that things . . . are what they are, all equal. That's why we judges are all hypocrites, all of us stuffed with stale rancid sausage-meat. That's what the real corruption in these courts is, the whole place stinks terribly of it; I can't wait to be free of it. [*He breathes with difficulty: he points to the group of judges and winks*.] They all pretend. They don't really believe it, those chaps, they don't really believe in the resurrection after death, nor even in Lord Free-will; don't you see? [*He emits a soft scandalized whistle; suddenly thoughtful*.] And as a matter of fact, what reason on earth is there to expect that at some point in this chain, something autonomous will break out? The soul, I mean. I am speaking of the soul. But anyway, all that . . . is rapidly ceasing . . . to concern me. Naturally. [*He remains for a moment with drooping head*.] What about Erzi?

MALGAI [*Coming in*]. He's coming up from the offices.

CROZ. Good. Come here, Malgai. And you, Persius. [*The two men obey*.] Take hold of me firmly. You on that side, like that. You on this. That's right. [*He has made the two men take him firmly by the arms and lift him up*.] Now let's go and meet him. I've a number of disclosures to make to him. [*With a touch of pride*.] I don't want . . . to wait for him and death . . . in here . . . bent double . . . like a rat that . . . somebody's trampled on.

[*Supported by the two men, indeed almost carried by them,* CROZ *slowly crosses the room and goes out.* CUST, BATA *and* MAVERI *stand looking at each other.*]

BATA [*Excitedly to* CUST]. Poor Croz, the whole of his life, he's been nothing but an old tin of poison. What does he want to talk to Erzi about? Revelations at the point of death! What sort? Against whom?

MAVERI [*Distressed*]. Do you know anything about it, Cust? What was he saying to you just now?

CUST [*In a monotone*]. I ought in duty to warn everyone that our poor friend is no longer himself; I'm afraid he's raving . . . [*He breaks off.*]

MALGAI [*Appearing at the door, excited and jubilant*]. Croz is talking to Erzi! Big things! He has said—and he is dictating to the secretary also—that he, Croz, in solemn declaration, testifies that President Vanan . . .

BATA [*Taking the words out of his mouth*]. . . . is innocent!

MALGAI. . . . and that if he manages to live another five minutes, he intends to reveal . . .

BATA. . . . the name of the real criminal!

MALGAI. Exactly! [*He rushes out again.*]

CUST [*As before*]. Unfortunately the trust we can put in Croz's words is only relative. This crisis has produced a genuine disorder in him, and . . . [*He turns.*]

[VANAN *is entering, bent and terrified: a* NURSE *leads him in.* BATA *rushes up to him, making an overwhelming fuss of him.*]

BATA. Vanan! Vanan! Please allow someone who has never had a moment's doubt of you and your . . .

MAVERI [*In competition with* BATA]. . . . your absolute integrity, which now shines again in such a sudden, unexpected, even marvellous . . .

NURSE [*Stepping between the two judges and* VANAN, *who has timidly drawn back*]. Forgive me, he has to be treated and spoken to very gently. I always have to be with him.

CUST [*Who has stood staring at the* NURSE, *quietly, but in a voice slightly louder than necessary, almost solemnly*]. You have left Elena? [*Something in his voice makes the others turn and look at him.*]

NURSE. Didn't you know, sir? The poor child has no need of me or anyone else now.

CUST [*In the same tones*]. Is she dead?

NURSE. Two days ago, sir. What am I saying? Three. Her sufferings are over.

[*A silence.*]

CUST [*As before*]. What a very small coffin, she will have needed. They told me she was much changed.

NURSE. Just like a tiny little bird, sir. She weighed nothing at all.

CUST. She didn't say anything further?

NURSE. Nor even heard anything. Nor even looked at anything.

CUST. Did she complain at all?

NURSE. No, poor little thing. Only towards the end, she kept doing this with her poor little hand: as though to try and push something from her, or drive it away, a fly or something.

CUST. Was anyone at her side, when that gesture ceased?

NURSE [*Dropping her voice*]. You will hardly believe it, sir, but poor Mr. Vanan refused to go and see her again. He made the excuse that he was suffering too much. [*She shakes her head.*] At the end he made even stranger and more childish excuses. It isn't his fault.

CUST [*Thoughtfully, while they all look at him in some amazement*]. So no one will ever again meet the young girl I saw at that door. She stood there a little out of breath, as though after a race . . . No one ever said anything more to her, she never listened to anyone. [*To the woman almost threateningly.*] You: why didn't you make her listen to you, while there was time? Now no one will ever be able to do that. [*Almost to himself.*] I talked to her, I passed long nights with her, begging her not to die, all night through; but she didn't believe in me anymore.

NURSE. But that's not true, sir; you never once came.

CUST [*In a monotone, quietly, turning to* VANAN]. Vanan, I fear your daughter did not attribute enough importance to her own life. She ought to have been persuaded that in her there was . . . [*He pauses with his arm upraised.*]

PERSIUS [*Bursting in, greatly agitated*]. At this very moment Croz is revealing the criminal's name! They even sent *me* away. It appears it really is one of us!

CUST [*Who has listened without turning, goes on after a moment, in a louder voice*]. . . . that in her there was something which does not exist and will never again exist at any other point of eternity . . . [*Suddenly, almost with fury.*] Something immenser than the immensest star . . .

VANAN [*Retreating a little, to the woman*]. Take me away, I don't want to see that man.

CUST [*In amazed tones*]. Vanan, her cry split the crystal of the heavens in two, and was heard far, far away. You cannot have forgotten, for you were her father. It is your duty . . .

VANAN [*In a distant, almost childish voice*]. But it was all so long ago, and our Lord knows what He does. [*Fervently.*] I hope, hope, hope for heaven, and I don't want to know anything more. [*He makes the sign of the cross several times.*] Our Lord be praised forever. [*He mumbles a prayer; suddenly with a strange obstinacy and almost overbearingly.*] My daughter died when she was a little girl. It was years ago.

CUST [*Bewildered*]. What do you mean, Vanan?

VANAN [*With the same childish obstinacy and distrust*]. Yes, yes, my daughter died when she was a little girl. The Lord willed it so . . .

CUST. Vanan . . . [*He breaks off, they have all turned to the door.*]

MALGAI [*Has entered in haste, breathlessly*]. We know the criminal's name!

BATA. Come on, out with it, Malgai!

MALGAI [*Excitedly, enjoying the delay*]. I can imagine the outcry there's going to be!

MAVERI. Come on!

PERSIUS. What about Croz?

BATA. Is he dead?

MALGAI. No one will ever hear that fiendish old voice again. Even *I* couldn't tell you the impudent things the old devil invented before he was willing to give the real name of the criminal! He kept coughing, and winking the whole time. He kept letting out the most dreadful curses; he even pretended in the end to make Councillor Erzi play at guess-who, trying the names of this man and that! And suddenly Croz said: [*Imitating him.*] "No. It isn't any of them. The criminal's name is . . .

ERZI [*Who has already entered*]. His name *was* . . . Croz. [*Advancing with a certain detachment.*] Yes, gentlemen, your colleague Croz has disclosed at the point of death that the person responsible for the corruption in these courts was himself, and no one else; that Vanan is innocent; and that all the other judges are likewise innocent, mainly, he observed, because they hadn't the brains to be anything else; and that the best of the lot and the most deserving of being nominated for the Presidency . . . was you, Cust. He spoke of you in very respectful terms . . . though also, of course, satirically and sharply, as is his wont. He asked me to say to you . . . Wait a moment . . . [*He tries to remember.*] "That every man has to scratch his own scabs by himself."

BATA. Very fine. Anything else?

ERZI. He coughed, he blew a little, and he said: [*Imitating him.*] "Well, well, you've been a hell of a bore, Erzi." And died.

BATA [*Violently*]. And that filthy blackguard dared to pass judgment on his own colleagues!

MAVERI. Not only that, he still contrived to be smart and impudent right to the end.

BATA. Erzi, I'm not blaming you. But my God, dying or not, Croz ought to have been compelled—[*He points to the great doors at the back which have so far remained closed throughout the play.*] —to go out through there, through those doors; to drag himself at his last gasp up the great staircase and to knock at the door of the Lord High Chancellor, and humble himself there under the forms of law.

PERSIUS. And he could have died after that, if he wanted to!

BATA. And where, where, I should like to know are we to have any restitution for the offense against justice . . . ?

ERZI [*Almost smiling, absently*]. But it's Time, my dear friends, it is Time that repairs all insults, and obliterates all scars. And besides, in this case, since Nature has looked after Croz already, the only thing that remains for us to do is to compensate Vanan for our unjust suspicions by conferring some high distinction on him . . . and also to nominate a new President. And I have a fancy that at this minute the High Council is nominating . . . you, Cust. The news should be here any minute now. I congratulate you, Vanan. And you, Cust.

CUST [*Staring before him with wide-open eyes*]. The Council will nominate me President of this Court?

ERZI [*Lightly and genially*]. It's highly probable. The desk behind which, from now onwards, you will cultivate your penetrating thoughts will be very imposing and monumental.

CUST. Have you finished your inquiries?

ERZI. Their goal has been reached, and besides things are hurrying on, everything is moving forward. The stone drops to the bottom, the water becomes calm once more. Croz is dead, Ludvi-Pol is dead. And they're not the only ones. The town is already turning to other things. . . .

CUST [*Almost to himself, pointing to the archives*]. . . . Every trace of the crime gone . . .

ERZI [*Good-humoredly, jesting*]. . . . Our good Vanan is at peace with God, the tempest calmed . . . in a few moments workmen will lower a number of levers and the lights will be extinguished; and while dawn quickens over life's enchanting lake, now once more blue and peaceful, we shall go home to bed, certain that the affairs of this court . . . [*Turning to* CUST.] . . . are once more in good hands.

BATA [*Precipitating himself towards* CUST *with hand outstretched*]. Let me say, my dear Cust, that we're all proud and honored by this nomination. I am sure there can be no doubt about it! Are you glad?

CUST [*Absently, nodding*]. Very glad.

BATA. You'll be able to have a holiday now, won't you?

CUST. Yes, I could do with one. A holiday.

BATA. Well, goodbye for the present, my dear fellow. [*He goes out.*]

MAVERI [*Promptly*]. What is it, are you still a bit worried? No, no, don't worry, the nomination's certain. Well, so long. [*He goes out.*]

PERSIUS [*Promptly*]. Today you will reach the goal for which you have spent the best years of your life.

CUST. Yes, my whole life has been directed towards this moment.

PERSIUS [*Watching him*]. You will wait here for the news?

CUST [*Absently*]. Yes. Yes.

PERSIUS. Goodbye then. Till tomorrow. [*He goes out after colleagues.*]

CUST [*Suddenly*]. The stone dropping to the bottom . . . the lake becoming calm again . . . My God, Erzi! That image of yours . . .

ERZI. Is it that that's worrying you?

CUST. It's not that I'm worried . . . but I should like . . . [*With sudden anguish.*] . . . to be able to understand; otherwise . . . It's difficult to rest. [*Suddenly pleading.*] And God knows I have need of that . . .

MALGAI [*Coming forward in his turn*]. You're a bit exhausted, sir. A little rest and you'll be back in your old form again, quite recovered, Mr. . . . President! We can say that now, can't we? [*He goes out.*]

CUST [*In a low voice*]. But I *am* recovered. [*He raises his hand, and rubs it with the familiar gesture.*] Look, for some days past I've kept wanting to do this. *I* have. I like it, it keeps me company. But now I'm beginning to forget to. Hours go by and I forget to do it. [*To* ERZI, *breathing heavily.*] No, it's not that I'm worried, but certainly . . . there is something . . . that doesn't . . . [*With a cry.*] doesn't fit, do you understand? [*Suddenly turning round.*] Vanan! It's you who frighten me. When I look at you I feel that underneath this building, underneath you and me, a black gulf is opening!

ERZI [*His voice unexpectedly loud and severe*]. What's the matter, Cust? What's the matter?

CUST [*Frantically*]. Vanan, the matter is the blood-stained face of your daughter! I can't find a single explanation on earth for that.

VANAN. My daughter died when she was a little girl . . . my daughter died when she was a little girl . . . it's so very long ago now . . .

CUST [*As before*]. Vanan, suppose she . . . wanted to die . . . ? Suppose that was the terrible thing that happened? Suppose she threw herself down?

VANAN [*Muttering*]. You liar. You reptile. My poor Elena died when she was a little girl.

CUST [*With a cry*]. Vanan, I fear . . . that when she shouted . . . she was asking something! Is it possible that no one heard? That no one answered? That that has not been inscribed on any register? That such an enormous question should remain unsolved?

ERZI [*Suddenly, with sombre intensity*]. Cust, I don't think that a man should be more stubborn than his little powers allow him to be! Administration: that is a human fact, its task is to smooth things out, not to dig things up, and turn them upside down! Nature: she heals her wounds so rapidly that perhaps the real truth is something else: that she is unaware of them. [*Dropping his voice.*] And after all, if we want to talk about God . . .

VANAN [*Suddenly interrupting, and then slowly making his way to the door*]. . . . God is so good. He forgives. He forgets. And we too shall forget, in His blessedness. [*He goes out, supported by the* NURSE.]

ERZI. You are left alone to think about these things, Cust. You alone.

CUST [*Almost to himself*]. I alone. I alone. I alone. And when I too shall have turned my back and gone away . . .

ERZI. . . . what was done and what was left undone will all be the same.

[*The* POLICE OFFICIAL *enters and hands* ERZI *a paper.* ERZI *looks at it.*]

[*With a cry.*] Cust! The Council . . . has nominated you! You've won. [*Approaching him, with sombre pity.*] Poor Cust, you've almost changed in appearance during these last few days. In a short time you will have forgotten, exactly as Vanan has. The season granted to us is so brief, don't disturb it with your cries! Don't be stubborn. [*He points upwards.*] The Lord High Chancellor himself is happy that matters have been mended. He is very old; he is probably napping at the moment on his table. Pointless to go and disturb him. [*Moving towards the door.*] Good-by, Cust, let the world roll on. That is mankind's job.

[*He goes out followed by the* OFFICIAL. *A silence.* MALGAI *reappears and begins putting out the lights one by one, preparing to close the place up and go away.*]

MALGAI [*Moved by curiosity, and with rough kindliness*]. You are all alone, Mr. President. Aren't you going home?

CUST. Yes. I shall go now as well. [*He goes slowly towards the corridor entrance; and suddenly stops. The room is almost dark.*]

MALGAI [*Worried*]. What's the matter? What are you waiting for?

CUST [*His teeth are chattering slightly: he turns back*]. Because there is no argument on earth that would let me shut my eyes in peace tonight. I shall have to wake the Lord High Chancellor. I must confess the truth to him.

MALGAI. Shall I come with you, Mr. President?

CUST. No. I'm a bit frightened. But I know there is no one who can help me.

[*He makes his way to the door which leads to the office of the Lord High Chancellor, and which has hitherto remained unopened. He throws the door open. Beyond it a long staircase is revealed going upwards;* CUST *begins to make his way up the stairs, very slowly, as*

Curtain

IX

THE MEASURE OF WISDOM

Do You Suppose Wisdom To Be Anything Other Than Truth?

INTRODUCTION

I

WHY DOES man perpetually ask himself, "What is wisdom?" Many have tried to avoid the question either out of fear or out of scepticism. For instance, when a timid man reflects on the Wisdom books of the Bible—Job, Proverbs, Ecclesiastes—he may conclude that only God is wise and the wisdom of man is mere arrogance or folly. When a sceptic reflects on the history of human ignorance he may find, to paraphrase G. B. Shaw, that "if all the books ever written on wisdom were laid end to end, they would reach no conclusion." The sceptic's view is summed up with comparable wit in Thomas Moore's couplet

> Ask who is wise? You'll find the self-same man
> A sage in France, a madman in Japan.

On the other hand those who trust in man's ability to attain to some measure of wisdom are very cautious. Before man aspires to wisdom, warns John of Salisbury, he must consider "what he himself is; what is within him, what without, what below, what above, what opposite, what before, and what after." The lesson is plain. If wisdom is to be achieved, it will be at great expense of mind and heart and without any foolish expectation of humanly impossible perfection. Moreover, wisdom, in a sense, is a gift rather than an achievement. Cardinal Newman writes of wisdom that:

> [it] is the clear, calm, accurate vision and comprehension of the whole course, the whole work of God; and although there is none who has it in its fullness but *he who searcheth all things, yea, the deep things* of the Creator, yet *by the Spirit* they are in a measure revealed unto us.

Though wisdom is difficult to come by, every philosopher (the word means lover of wisdom) seeks it as the foundation of all knowledge. Every poet strives for it as the whole that gives coherence and delight to his particular impressions. It is important therefore to examine what men say of wisdom and how they have exhibited wisdom in literature.

II

THE FIVE essays in Section IX treat wisdom from varied points of view and in varied historical perspectives. Aristotle is concerned with the five ways in which man can perceive truth: scientific knowledge, art, practical wisdom, philosophic wisdom, and intuitive reason. First, he says, man perceives truth through scientific knowledge—that is, by way of the demonstrable laws of deduction and induction. Second, he perceives it through practical knowledge, or art, when he calculates correctly how to build a bridge or make a statue. Third, he perceives truth through practical wisdom, through his ability to choose the right means to attain some good for himself in the economic or political order. Fourth, he perceives truth through the ability to comprehend truth in the light of its first principles. And fifth, he perceives it through intuitive reason—through his power to perceive ultimates in both directions, that is, in particular facts and in general principles.

Wisdom in art, Aristotle concludes, is the production of an excellent work. Wisdom applied to human action "is the most finished of the forms of knowledge." Wisdom is "intuitive reason combined with scientific knowledge—scientific knowledge of the highest objects, which has received as it were its proper completion." Moreover, wisdom, united with virtue, or moral integrity, enables man to achieve that happiness which, according to Aristotle, is man's supreme desire and his ordained end.

Without presuming to summarize Aristotle's many-sinewed thoughts, we may venture to say that he teaches us to regard wisdom not as one way of knowing, but as a union of several ways of knowing. The distinctive characteristic of wisdom is its power to perceive the whole. Further, Aristotle shows how wisdom provides the light in which moral virtue, or character, can achieve its true goal. Wisdom, in short, is the most important of the intellectual virtues.

In a sense Sir Richard Livingstone's "The Rainbow Bridge" is a commentary on, an apology for, and a dialogue with the mind of Greece—that mind which is partly revealed in Aristotle's discussion of wisdom. Livingstone applies the key metaphor of the essay—that of the rainbow bridge made by the gods to let men cross from earth to heaven—to the Greek achievement in linking the human and the superhuman world:

> In Norse mythology the bridge is built by Odin and the Aesir; in history and fact it was built by the Greeks with a double-span, the bridge of goodness and the bridge of wisdom, by which men pass from barbarism to civilisation, if not from earth to heaven.

A brief history of Greek civilization is the prelude to an analysis of the qualities that explain its achievements. The three qualities Livingstone regards as outstanding—wonder or curiosity in the presence of the world, a calm, clear view of, and acceptance of, reality, and balance, poise, and soundness of mind, or temperance—are all aspects of wisdom. Indeed the third quality, *Sophrosyne,* is Aristotle's own expression for the virtue that preserves practical wisdom.

In effect, Livingstone is saying that Greek wisdom, which is invaluable for its ability to teach rational and scientific habits of mind, is even more valuable in our age for its ability to impart that comprehensive view of life which Matthew Arnold described as "seeing life steadily and seeing it whole." The Greeks, par excellence, espoused both particular knowledge and general or speculative knowledge. They respected empiricism and intuition, a knowledge of means and of ends.

In "The Idols of the Laboratory," Joseph Wood Krutch points out what he considers to be a serious defect of contemporary thought. Unlike the Greeks, many modern thinkers question whether "value judgments," that is, judgments based on conceptions of what is good, or true, or wise, are relevant in a scientific age. In the context of the dialogue initiated by Aristotle and continued by Livingstone, Krutch is suggesting that our contemporary thinkers restrict themselves unduly to the knowledge acquired through particular "sciences" such as anthropology, history, sociology, and psychology. They discard what Aristotle would call philosophical wisdom and intuitive reason in favor of pragmatic standards. They regard man not as an independent being, but as an object that can be made into a satisfactory social animal.

Krutch holds that this kind of thinking is confused. Substituting the terms "normality" for "norms of truth" and "satisfactory adjustment" for "pursuit of the good life," only *seems,* he says, to avoid difficulty:

> Such terms as "normality" and "satisfactory adjustment" have, of course, to be defined by somebody. The statistician can determine the meaning of the first, if it is assumed to mean "most usual." But the second will have to depend to some extent on the subjective preferences of some group.

In short, our failure to inquire into the nature of wisdom yields to "human engineers" a power to shape the world according to their will. They, the human engineers, not the philosophers or theologians or poets, "do not know what they are making us into and refuse to permit us even to ask. Moreover, in so far as their attempt to 'condition' the human beings on whom they practice their techniques are successful, they made it less and less probable that their fateful assumptions will ever be questioned."

Krutch shows how, in his opinion, scientific knowledge that ignores value or wisdom mistakes the true measure of man. In his "Being and Doing" Thomas Merton considers a similar problem: the attempt to measure man by his activities rather than by his true self. He poses this question: If, as all the sages have said, true wisdom begins in self-knowledge, then what is the real self that we attempt to know? And he gives this answer: "We must find our real selves not in the froth stirred up by the impact of our being upon the beings around us, but in our own soul which is the principle of all our acts."

Merton's essay is a subtly nuanced exploration of the distinction between activities that are merely reflections of the soul and the soul itself. While he regards activities as partial measures of the human soul, he keeps insisting that man's "being," understood in the light of a Christian philosophy, "is far greater than anything he feels or does." One's "being," that is, the true self, is a deep sea that is not to be confused with the fish that swim in it. Nor is man's happiness found in intense activity. Happiness, like music, is found in balance, order, rhythm, and harmony:

> Music is pleasing not only because of the sound but because of the silence that is in it: without the alternation of sound and silence there would be no rhythm. If we strive to be happy by filling all the silences of life with sound, productive by turning all life's leisure into work, and real by turning all our being into doing, we will only succeed in producing a hell on earth.

Merton is particularly rewarding, and consoling, in his insistence that we find our happiness within our own limitations. It has ever been a mark of wisdom, he says, to avoid the great folly of attempting "to be wise with an impossible wisdom." Francis Thompson also touches on this theme in his witty serio-comic essay, "The Way of Imperfection."

Opening his essay with Ovid's observation that a mole makes a face more comely, Thompson goes on to assail the cult of perfection, or "unendurable excellence," which, he says, "is the fruitful parent of unnumbered evils." First he attacks the spiritual perfectionists who distort nature by their religiosity, "as if the bird could not give glory to God, until it selected its airs from the diocesan hymnal!" His next targets are the faultless heroes and heroines of nineteenth-century fiction with whom he compares a typical Shakespearean heroine, Desdemona, whose very weakness makes her "more credible, more piteous, perhaps even more lovable, because more human." Finally he bickers amiably with advocates of a "pure" prose style, holding that mannerisms "are a season of style, and happily unavoidable."

At bottom Thompson is warning us against an impossible, and inhuman wisdom. "Order yourselves," he counsels, "to a wise conformity with that Nature who cannot for the life of her create a brain without making one half of it weaker than the other half, or even a fool without a flaw in his folly."

III

MAY WE properly look for the display of wisdom in the works of imaginative literature? We have just been warned not to. In Aristotle's essay the philosopher clearly distinguishes two orders of human action: that of making and that of doing. Art is in the order of making and wisdom in art is expressed in the perfection of the work. According to this point of view it may be argued that a wise artist is one who sees to it that he paints a good picture, chisels a good statue, composes a good sonata, or writes a good poem, play, or story. Art exists only in something that is beautifully made. Hence the wisdom of art is its very existence.

On the other hand it is difficult not to agree with Robert Frost's dictum that "poetry begins in delight and ends in wisdom." Nor can we restrict the term wisdom to the artistic habit alone. Some works of art depict clearly in some measure—in some cases in large measure—the kind of wisdom that has been described as a "clear, calm, accurate vision and comprehension of the whole. . . ." Certainly, the plays of Sophocles, Marlowe, Shakespeare, Molière, and Betti search out the deeper movements of the soul. These plays dazzle us by the practical wisdom of their skillful plotting, characterization, and diction, as well as by their compelling quest for ultimate values or philosophic wisdom. The resolutions of these plays, however ingenious, are less valuable than their power to stir in us a renewed, a renewable, an eternal wonder about the mystery of human life.

Many of the twenty-six stories in the previous sections of this book are, to use Livingstone's metaphor, rainbow bridges between a concrete human situation and some kind of ultimate truth. William Faulkner's "The Bear," Katherine Anne Porter's "Flowering Judas," Franz Kafka's "The Bucket-Rider," Joseph Conrad's "Amy Foster," and Alan Paton's "Life for a Life" are particularly vivid examples of stories that reflect, in tone and statement, the encounter with fundamental questions of man's destiny. The two stories in Section IX, Nathaniel Hawthorne's "Ethan Brand" and Robert Penn Warren's "Blackberry Winter," may also be taken as stories that describe the quest for wisdom.

"Ethan Brand" has long been regarded as one of Hawthorne's technically perfect tales. The frame supplied by Bartram and his son, the dramatized incidents of Ethan Brand's life, the parallel stories of Lawyer Giles, the doctor, old Humphrey and the wandering Jew, the imagery of light and darkness and fire and stone, and the concluding irony of the marble heart are all united in a symmetrical plot. This technical perfection, however, is itself merely the vehicle of the theme.

Ethan Brand is a figure of the gifted person who wishes to solve the mystery of man. His quest centers on the idea of the unpardonable sin. He wanders about the world for eighteen years during which time he has the opportunity to look "into many a human heart . . . hotter with sinful passions than yonder furnace is with fire." He makes Esther, "with . . . cold and remorseless purpose . . . the subject of [his] psychological experiment, and waste[s], absorb[s], and perhaps annihilate [s] her soul, in the process."

But in the end he finds the unpardonable sin not in others but in his own breast. The sin is "the sin of an intellect that triumphed over a sense of brotherhood with man and reverence for God, and sacrificed everything to its own mighty claims! The only sin that deserves a recompense of immortal agony!"

Ethan Brand's discovery of the unpardonable sin, however, is not the main theme of Hawthorne's story. The main theme is the effects of that discovery upon Brand himself. At first, Brand is bitterly proud of his discovery. He announces his finding "with a pride that distinguishes all enthusiasts of his stamp." He says he would do it again, and again incur the guilt. "Unshrinkingly I accept the retribution!" Yet, as his old acquaintances throng about him he becomes ashamed. Lawyer Giles' courage reproaches him; the doctor's scorn wilts him; old Humphrey's questions about his daughter Esther make him quail; the Jew of Nuremberg's conspiratorial smile brings home to him his own inner emptiness.

It is the appearance of the old dog, however, that gives Brand the final and most revolting shock of self-recognition. The dog began to chase his own tail "as if one end of the ridiculous brute's body were at deadly and most unforgivable enmity with the other." In like manner, Ethan Brand realizes, his own heart and head are in ridiculous enmity. He had cultivated his mind at the expense of his heart. "He had lost hold of the magnetic chain of humanity." He had become, in short, a fiend. By his suicide in the lime-kiln he condemns himself to a deserved torment. As Stallman and Watters have observed in *The Creative Reader*, "for Ethan Brand to search for the Unpardonable Sin was to commit the Unpardonable Sin; or conversely, to commit the Unpardonable Sin, he has but to search for it." May we not say too that to search for the meaning of things is in a sense to be wise, and, conversely, to be wise is to search for the meaning of things? The question is suggested by the second story in this section, Robert Penn Warren's "Blackberry Winter."

"Blackberry Winter" is a recollection of boyhood. The story is at once faithful to two points of view: that of the nine-year-old boy living through a summer day, and that of the mature man who, in looking backward, can see how that one day was seeded with future meaning.

Save for one incident, the boy's day is not unusual. He argues with his mother about going barefooted. After he meets the "mysterious stranger," to whom his mother gives a day's work, he joins his father and his neighbors at the bridge to watch the flood waters. He sees a drowned cow and listens to the men talk. He visits Dellie's cabin and plays with her son, young Jebb, and talks to old Jebb, the father. He gets back to the house in time to witness his father getting rid of the mysterious stranger. He follows the stranger down the road asking: "Where did you come from?" and "Where are you going?" The stranger curses at him and chases him away. That is the boy's day. But, as the author says in a comment on the story, what started out as

> an act of escape, of fleeing back into the simplicities of childhood, had turned, as it always must if we accept the logic of our lives, into an attempt to bring something meaningful out of that simple past into the complication of the present. And what started out as a personal indulgence had tried to be, in the end, an impersonal generalization about experience, as a story must always try to be if it accepts the logic of fiction.

The mature Seth realizes that the experiences of that day contained seeds of wisdom. He felt his own identity; he tested and verified his love for his self-reliant parents and their love for him; he began to learn the effects of poverty in his brief encounter with the poor whites at the flooded creek: "Son . . . you live long enough and you'll find a man will eat anything when the time comes. . . . Live long enough . . . and a man will settle fer what he kin git." One brief slap by Dellie prophesies the bad end in store for young Jebb, and in his conversation with old Jebb the boy senses the deep knowledge of a wise old man who was almost "too strong to die."

Warren analyzes the meaning of Seth's encounter with the tramp:

> In so far as later he had grown up, had really learned something of the meaning of life, he had been bound to follow the tramp all his life, in the imaginative recognition, with all the responsibility which such a recognition entails, of this lost, mean, defeated, cowardly, worthless, bitter being as somehow a man.

"Blackberry Winter," then, opens with a delighted recollection of particular events, and ends by establishing "the magnetic chain of humanity"—the wisdom that Ethan Brand had lost.

IV

IF ONE has doubts that poets are sometimes concerned with ultimate truths, or wisdom, the poems in this section may well dispel them. For here indeed are representative speculations on the meaning of reality, on man's state, on man's freedom, on his loneliness, on his relations to other men, on his relation to domestic animals, on death and the future life. That poets ask questions on these themes, even by implication, may surprise, and possibly offend those readers who have identified poetry exclusively with "the simple, sensuous, and passionate" expression of simple, sensuous, and passionate feelings.

Yet one of the oldest paradoxes of literary history is the fact that poets do meditate on "philosophic" themes. They convey thoughts at the same moment that they evoke feelings. Thus in Kathleen Raine's "Question and Answer"[1] we read:

> That which is, being the only answer
> The question is its measure.

Miss Raine here states the metaphysical axiom that the truth of being is the existence of a being. "The question is its measure" in that the question "What is a flower?" contains the answer: "The flower is. . . ."

> Ask the flower
> And the question unfolds in eloquent petals about the centre . . .
> Ask water, and the streams flow and dew falls . . .
> Earth answers fields and gardens and the grave.

Miss Raine's short hymn to being is at once accurate and profound; it communicates a vision of the truth and suggests her reverence and awe in its presence.

1 From *The Pythoness and Other Poems,* published by Hamish Hamilton Ltd., London.

In "Freedom" Charles Péguy presents the problem of human freedom. It is a difficult, a great problem, one with two faces. In the poem God explains:

Because if I am always holding them up, if I hold them up too often,
They will never learn how to swim by themselves.
But if I don't hold them up just at the right moment,
Perhaps these poor children will swallow more water than is healthy for them.

But if many poets search for ultimate truths they do not all, of course, arrive at the same conclusion. Even death, the ultimate fact of life, means one thing to one man, another to a second. For Wilfred Owen the thought of death is associated with a hopeless regret for things undone. D. H. Lawrence's meditation on "the long journey towards oblivion" is almost confident, even though the author subscribes to no belief in life after death. On the other hand Cardinal Newman's *The Dream of Gerontius,* solidly grounded on Christian hope, makes one shudder with the holy fear of judgment.

The wisdom of the poets, we remind ourselves again, often resides less in the structure of the thought or in explicit statements than in the tone of high seriousness or reverence in the face of destiny. T. S. Eliot's "Gerontion," for instance, shows us not how we should think but how we should regard ourselves in the light of man's history. "After such knowledge, what forgiveness?" The proper posture of man is humility, his wisest attitude that of a fear, which, we are told, is the beginning of wisdom. In "Without Ceremony," Vassar Miller describes that posture:

Except ourselves, we have no other prayer . . .
We fall, not on our knees, but on our hearts.

ESSAYS

Aristotle
KNOWLEDGE AND WISDOM

. . . .

THE FACULTIES by virtue of which the soul possesses truth by way of affirmation or denial are five in number, i.e. art, scientific knowledge, practical wisdom, philosophic wisdom, intuitive reason. . . .

Now what *scientific knowledge* is, if we are to speak exactly and not follow mere similarities, is plain from what follows. We all suppose that what we know is not even capable of being otherwise; of things capable of being otherwise we do not know, when they have passed outside our observation, whether they exist or not. Therefore the object of scientific knowledge is of necessity. Therefore it is eternal; for things that are of necessity in the unqualified sense are all eternal; and things that are eternal are ungenerated and imperishable. Again, every science is thought to be capable of being taught, and its object of being learned. And all teaching starts from what is already known, as we maintain in the *Analytics* also; for it proceeds sometimes through induction and sometimes by syllogism. Now induction is the starting-point which knowledge even of the universal presupposes, while syllogism proceeds *from* universals. There are therefore starting-points from which syllogism proceeds, which are not reached by syllogism; it is therefore by induction that they are acquired. Scientific knowledge is, then, a state of capacity to demonstrate, and has the other limiting characteristics which we specify in the *Analytics;* for it is when a man believes in a certain way and the starting-points are known to him that he has scientific knowledge, since if they are not better known to him than the conclusion, he will have his knowledge only incidentally.

Let this, then, be taken as our account of scientific knowledge.

In the variable are included both things made and things done; making and acting are different (for their nature we treat even the discussions outside our school as reliable); so that the reasoned state

KNOWLEDGE AND WISDOM: From Book VI of the Oxford edition of Aristotle's *Nichomachean Ethics,* translated by W. D. Ross. Used by permission of The Clarendon Press, Oxford.

of capacity to act is different from the reasoned state of capacity to make. Hence too they are not included one in the other; for neither is acting making nor is making acting. Now since architecture is an art and is essentially a reasoned state of capacity to make, and there is neither any art that is not such a state nor any such state that is not an art, *art* is identical with a state of capacity to make, involving a true course of reasoning. All art is concerned with coming into being, i.e. with contriving and considering how something may come into being which is capable of either being or not being, and whose origin is in the maker and not in the thing made; for art is concerned neither with things that are, or come into being, by necessity, nor with things that do so in accordance with nature (since these have their origin in themselves). Making and acting being different, art must be a matter of making, not of acting. And in a sense chance and art are concerned with the same objects; as Agathon says, "art loves chance and chance loves art." Art, then, as has been said, is a state concerned with making, involving a true course of reasoning, and lack of art on the contrary is a state concerned with making, involving a false course of reasoning; both are concerned with the variable.

Regarding *practical wisdom* we shall get at the truth by considering who are the persons we credit with it. Now it is thought to be the mark of a man of practical wisdom to be able to deliberate well about what is good and expedient for himself, not in some particular respect, e.g. about what sorts of thing conduce to health or to strength, but about what sorts of thing conduce to the good life in general. This is shown by the fact that we credit men with practical wisdom in some particular respect when they have calculated well with a view to some good end which is one of those that are not the object of any art. It follows that in the general sense also the man who is capable of deliberating has practical wisdom. Now no one deliberates about things that are invariable, nor about things that it is impossible for him to do. Therefore, since scientific knowledge involves demonstration, but there is no demonstration of things whose first principles are variable (for all such things might actually be otherwise), and since it is impossible to deliberate about things that are of necessity, practical wisdom cannot be scientific knowledge nor art; not science because that which can be done is capable of being otherwise, not art because action and making are different kinds of thing. The remaining alternative, then, is that it is a true and reasoned state of capacity to act with regard to the things that are good or bad for man. For while making has an end other than itself, action cannot; for good action itself is its end. It is for this reason that we think Pericles and men like him have practical wisdom, viz. because they can see what is good for themselves and what is good for men in general; we consider that those can do this who are good at managing households or states. (This is why we call temperance (*sophrosyne*) by this name; we imply that it preserves one's practical wisdom (*sodsousa ten phronesin*). Now what it preserves is a judgement of the kind we have described. For it is not any and every judgement that pleasant and painful objects destroy and pervert, e.g. the judgement that the triangle has or has not its angles equal to two right angles, but only judgements about what is to be done. For the originating causes of the things that are done consist in the end at which they are aimed; but the man who has been ruined by pleasure or pain forthwith fails to see any such originating cause—to see that for the sake of this or because of this he ought to choose and do whatever he chooses and does; for vice is destructive of the originating cause of action.)

Practical wisdom, then, must be a reasoned and true state of capacity to act with regard to human goods. But further, while there is such a thing as excellence in art, there is no such thing as excellence in practical wisdom; and in art he who errs willingly is preferable, but in practical wisdom, as in the virtues, he is the reverse. Plainly, then, practical wisdom is a virtue and not an art. There being two parts of the soul that can follow a course of reasoning, it must be the virtue of one of the two, i.e., of that part which forms opinions; for opinion is about the variable and so is practical wisdom. But yet it is not only a reasoned state; this is shown by the fact that a state of that sort may be forgotten but practical wisdom cannot.

Scientific knowledge is judgement about things that are universal and necessary, and the conclusions of demonstration, and all scientific knowledge, follow from first principles (for scientific knowledge involves apprehension of a rational ground). This being so, the first principle from which what is scientifically known follows cannot be an object of scientific knowledge, of art, or of practical wisdom; for that which can be scientifically known can be demonstrated, and art and practical wisdom deal with things that are variable. Nor are these first principles the objects of philosophic wisdom, for it is a mark of the philosopher to have *demonstration* about some things. If, then, the states of mind by which we have truth and are never deceived about things invariable or even variable are scientific knowledge, practical wisdom, philosophic wisdom, and intuitive reason, and it cannot be any of the three (i.e. practical wisdom, scientific knowledge, or philosophic wisdom), the remaining alternative is that it is *intuitive reason* that grasps the first principles.

Wisdom (1) in the arts we ascribe to their most finished exponents, e.g. to Phidias as a sculptor and to Polyclitus as a maker of portrait-statues, and here we mean nothing by wisdom except excellence in art; but (2) we think that some people are wise in general, not in some particular field or in any other limited respect, as Homer says in the *Margites,*

> Him did the gods make neither a digger nor yet a ploughman
> Nor wise in anything else.

Therefore wisdom must plainly be the most finished of the forms of knowledge. It follows that the wise man must not only know what follows from the first principles, but must also possess truth about the first principles. Therefore wisdom must be intuitive reason combined with scientific knowledge—scientific knowledge of the highest objects which has received as it were its proper completion.

Of the highest objects, we say; for it would be strange to think that the art of politics, or practical wisdom, is the best knowledge, since man is not the best thing in the world. Now if what is healthy or good is different for men and for fishes, but what is white or straight is always the same, any one would say that what is wise is the same but what is practically wise is different; for it is to that which observes well the various matters concerning itself that one ascribes practical wisdom, and it is to this that one will entrust such matters. This is why we say that some even of the lower animals have practical wisdom, viz. those which are found to have a power of foresight with regard to their own life. It is evident also that philosophic wisdom and the art of politics cannot be the same; for if the state of mind concerned with a man's own interests is to be called philosophic wisdom, there will be many philosophic wisdoms; there will not be one concerned with the good of all animals (any more than there is one art of medicine for all existing things), but a different philosophic wisdom about the good of each species.

But if the argument be that man is the best of the animals, this makes no difference; for there are other things much more divine in their nature even than man, e.g., most conspicuously, the bodies of which the heavens are framed. From what has been said it is plain, then, that philosophic wisdom is scientific knowledge, combined with intuitive reason, of the things that are highest by nature. This is why we say Anaxagoras, Thales, and men like them have philosophic but not practical wisdom, when we see them ignorant of what is to their own advantage, and why we say that they know things that are remarkable, admirable, difficult, and divine, but useless; viz. because it is not human goods that they seek.

Practical wisdom on the other hand is concerned with things

human and things about which it is possible to deliberate; for we say this is above all the work of the man of practical wisdom, to deliberate well, but no one deliberates about things invariable, nor about things which have not an end, and that a good that can be brought about by action. The man who is without qualification good at deliberating is the man who is capable of aiming in accordance with calculation at the best for man of things attainable by action. Nor is practical wisdom concerned with universals only—it must also recognize the particulars; for it is practical, and practice is concerned with particulars. This is why some who do not know, and especially those who have experience, are more practical than others who know; for if a man knew that light meats are digestible and wholesome, but did not know which sorts of meat are light, he would not produce health, but the man who knows that chicken is wholesome is more likely to produce health.

Now practical wisdom is concerned with action; therefore one should have both forms of it, or the latter in preference to the former. But of practical as of philosophic wisdom there must be a controlling kind.

Political wisdom and practical wisdom are the same state of mind, but their essence is not the same. Of the wisdom concerned with the city, the practical wisdom which plays a controlling part is legislative wisdom, while that which is related to this as particulars to their universal is known by the general name "political wisdom"; this has to do with action and deliberation, for a decree is a thing to be carried out in the form of an individual act. This is why the exponents of this art are alone said to "take part in politics"; for these alone "do things" as manual labourers "do things".

Practical wisdom also is identified especially with that form of it which is concerned with a man himself—with the individual; and this is known by the general name "practical wisdom"; of the other kinds one is called household management, another legislation, the third politics, and of the latter one part is called deliberative and the other judicial. Now knowing what is good for oneself will be one kind of knowledge, but it is very different from the other kinds; and the man who knows and concerns himself with his own interests is thought to have practical wisdom, while politicians are thought to be busybodies; hence the words of Euripides,

> But how could I be wise, who might at ease,
> Numbered among the army's multitude,
> Have had an equal share? . . .
> For those who aim too high and do too much. . . .

Those who think thus seek their own good, and consider that one ought to do so. From this opinion, then, has come the view that such men have practical wisdom; yet perhaps one's own good cannot exist without household management, nor without a form of government. Further, how one should order one's own affairs is not clear and needs inquiry.

What has been said is confirmed by the fact that while young men become geometricians and mathematicians and wise in matters like these, it is thought that a young man of practical wisdom cannot be found. The cause is that such wisdom is concerned not only with universals but with particulars, which become familiar from experience, but a young man has no experience, for it is length of time that gives experience; indeed one might ask this question too, why a boy may become a mathematician, but not a philosopher or a physicist. Is it because the objects of mathematics exist by abstraction, while the first principles of these other subjects come from experience, and because young men have no conviction about the latter but merely use the proper language, while the essence of mathematical objects is plain enough to them?

Further, error in deliberation may be either about the universal or about the particular; we may fail to know either that all water that weighs heavy is bad, or that this particular water weighs heavy.

That practical wisdom is not scientific knowledge is evident; for it is, as has been said, concerned with the ultimate particular fact, since the thing to be done is of this nature. It is opposed, then, to intuitive reason; for intuitive reason is of the limiting premisses, for which no reason can be given, while practical wisdom is concerned with the ultimate particular, which is the object not of scientific knowledge but of perception—not the perception of qualities peculiar to one sense but a perception akin to that by which we perceive that the particular figure before us is a triangle; for in that direction as well as in that of the major premiss there will be a limit. But this is rather perception than practical wisdom, though it is another kind of perception than that of the qualities peculiar to each sense.

There is a difference between inquiry and deliberation; for deliberation is inquiry into a particular kind of thing. We must grasp the nature of excellence in deliberation as well—whether it is a form of scientific knowledge, or opinion, or skill in conjecture, or some other kind of thing. *Scientific knowledge* it is not; for men do not inquire about the things they know about, but good deliberation is a kind of deliberation, and he who deliberates inquires and calculates. Nor is it *skill in conjecture*; for this both involves no reasoning and is something that is quick in its operation, while men deliberate a long time, and they say that one should carry out quickly the conclusions of one's deliberation, but should deliberate slowly. Again, *readiness of mind* is different from excellence in deliberation; it is a sort of skill in conjecture. Nor again is excellence in deliberation *opinion* of any sort. But since the man who deliberates badly makes a mistake, while he who deliberates well does so correctly, excellence in deliberation is clearly a kind of correctness, but neither of knowledge nor of opinion; for there is no such thing as correctness of knowledge (since there is no such thing as error of knowledge), and correctness of opinion is truth; and at the same time everything that is an object of opinion is already determined. But again excellence in deliberation involves reasoning. The remaining alternative, then, is that it is *correctness of thinking;* for this is not yet assertion, since, while even opinion is not inquiry but has reached the stage of assertion, the man who is deliberating, whether he does so well or ill, is searching for something and calculating.

But excellence in deliberation is a certain correctness of deliberation; hence we must first inquire what deliberation is and what it is about. And, there being more than one kind of correctness, plainly excellence in deliberation is not any and every kind; for (1) the incontinent man and the bad man, if he is clever, will reach as a result of his calculation what he sets before himself, so that he will have deliberated correctly, but he will have got for himself a great evil. Now to have deliberated well is thought to be a good thing; for it is this kind of correctness of deliberation that is excellence in deliberation, viz. that which tends to attain what is good. But (2) it is possible to attain even good by a false syllogism, and to attain what one ought to do but not by the right means, the middle term being false; so that this too is not yet excellence in deliberation—this state in virtue of which one attains what one ought but not by the right means. Again (3) it is possible to attain it by long deliberation while another man attains it quickly. Therefore in the former case we have not yet got excellence in deliberation, which is rightness with regard to the expedient—rightness in respect both of the end, the manner, and the time. (4) Further it is possible to have deliberated well either in the unqualified sense or with reference to a particular end. Excellence in deliberation in the unqualified sense, then, is that which succeeds with reference to what is the end in the unqualified sense, and excellence in deliberation in a particular sense is that which succeeds relatively to a particular end. If, then, it is characteristic of men of practical wisdom to have deliberated well, excellence in deliberation will be correctness with regard to what conduces to the end of which practical wisdom is the true apprehension.

Understanding, also, and goodness of understanding, in virtue of which men are said to be men of understanding or of good understanding, are neither entirely the same as opinion or scientific knowledge (for at that rate all men would have been men of understanding), nor are they one of the particular sciences, such as medicine, the science of things connected with health, or geometry, the science of spatial magnitudes. For understanding is neither about things that are always and are unchangeable, nor about any and every one of the things that come into being, but about things which may become subjects of questioning and deliberation. Hence it is about the same objects as practical wisdom; but understanding and practical wisdom are not the same. For practical wisdom issues commands, since its end is what ought to be done or not to be done; but understanding only judges. (Understanding is identical with goodness of understanding, men of understanding with men of good understanding.) Now understanding is neither the having nor the acquiring of practical wisdom; but as learning is called understanding when it means the exercise of the faculty of knowledge, so "understanding" is applicable to the exercise of the faculty of opinion for the purpose of judging of what some one else says about matters with which practical wisdom is concerned—and of judging soundly; for "well" and "soundly" are the same thing. And from this has come the use of the name "understanding" in virtue of which men are said to be "of good understanding," viz. from the application of the word to the grasping of scientific truth; for we often call such grasping understanding.

What is called judgement, in virtue of which men are said to "be sympathetic judges" and to "have judgement," is the right discrimination of the equitable. This is shown by the fact that we say the equitable man is above all others a man of sympathetic judgement, and identify equity with sympathetic judgement about certain facts. And sympathetic judgement is judgement which discriminates what is equitable and does so correctly; and correct judgement is that which judges what is true.

Now all the states we have considered converge, as might be expected, to the same point; for when we speak of judgement and understanding and practical wisdom and intuitive reason we credit the same people with possessing judgement and having reached years of reason and with having practical wisdom and understanding. For all these faculties deal with ultimates, i.e. with particulars; and being a man of understanding and of good or sympathetic judgement consists in being able to judge about the things with which practical wisdom is concerned; for the equities are common to all good men in relation to other men. Now all things which have to be done are included among particulars or ultimates; for not only must the man of practical wisdom know particular facts, but understanding and judgement are also concerned with things to be done, and these are ultimates. And intuitive reason is concerned with the ultimates in both directions; for both the first terms and the last are objects of intuitive reason and not of argument, and the intuitive reason which is presupposed by demonstrations grasps the unchangeable and first terms, while the intuitive reason involved in practical reasonings grasps the last and variable fact, i.e. the minor premiss. For these variable facts are the starting-points for the apprehension of the end, since the universals are reached from the particulars; of these therefore we must have perception, and this perception is intuitive reason.

This is why these states are thought to be natural endowments—why, while no one is thought to be a philosopher by nature, people are thought to have by nature judgement, understanding, and intuitive reason. This is shown by the fact that we think our powers correspond to our time of life, and that a particular age brings with it intuitive reason and judgement; this implies that nature is the cause. [Hence intuitive reason is both beginning and end; for demonstrations are from these and about these.] Therefore we ought to attend to the undemonstrated sayings and opinions of experienced and older people or of people of practical wisdom not less than to demonstrations; for because experience has given them an eye they see aright.

We have stated, then, what practical and philosophic wisdom are, and with what each of them is concerned, and we have said that each is the virtue of a different part of the soul.

Difficulties might be raised as to the utility of these qualities of mind. For (1) philosophic wisdom will contemplate none of the things that will make a man happy (for it is not concerned with any coming into being), and though practical wisdom has *this* merit, for what purpose do we need it? Practical wisdom is the quality of mind concerned with things just and noble and good for man, but these are the things which it is the mark of a *good* man to do, and we are none the more able to act for *knowing* them if the virtues are states of *character*, just as we are none the better able to act for knowing the things that are healthy and sound, in the sense not of producing but of issuing from the state of health; for we are none the more able to act for having the art of medicine or of gymnastics. But (2) if we are to say that a man should have practical wisdom not for the sake of knowing moral truths but for the sake of becoming good, practical wisdom will be of no use to those who *are* good; but again it is of no use to those who have *not* virtue; for it will make no difference whether they have practical wisdom themselves or obey others who have it, and it would be enough for us to do what we do in the case of health; though we wish to become healthy, yet we do not learn the art of medicine. (3) Besides this, it would be thought strange if practical wisdom, being inferior to philosophic wisdom, is to be put in authority over it, as seems to be implied by the fact that the art which produces anything rules and issues commands about that thing.

These, then, are the questions we must discuss; so far we have only stated the difficulties.

(1) Now first let us say that in themselves these states must be worthy of choice because they are the virtues of the two parts of the soul respectively, even if neither of them produce anything.

(2) Secondly, they do produce something, not as the art of medicine produces health, however, but as health produces health;[1] so does philosophic wisdom produce happiness; for, being a part of virtue entire, by being possessed and by actualizing itself it makes a man happy.

(3) Again, the work of man is achieved only in accordance with practical wisdom as well as with moral virtue; for virtue makes us aim at the right mark, and practical wisdom makes us take the right means. (Of the fourth part of the soul—the nutritive[2]—there is no such virtue; for there is nothing which it is in its power to do or not to do.)

(4) With regard to our being none the more able to do because of our practical wisdom what is noble and just, let us begin a little further back, starting with the following principle. As we say that some people who do just acts are not necessarily just, i.e. those who do the acts ordained by the laws either unwillingly or owing to ignorance or for some other reason and not for the sake of the acts themselves (though, to be sure, they do what they should and all the things that the good man ought), so is it, it seems, that in order to be good one must be in a certain state when one does the several acts, i.e. one must do them as a result of choice and for the sake of the acts themselves. Now virtue makes the choice right, but the question of the things which should naturally be done to carry out our choice belongs not to virtue but to another faculty. We must devote our attention to these matters and give a clearer statement about them. There is a faculty which is called cleverness; and this is such as to be able to do the things that tend towards the mark we have set before ourselves, and to hit it. Now if the mark be noble, the cleverness is laudable, but if the mark be bad, the cleverness is mere smartness; hence we call even men of practical wisdom clever

1 I.e. as health, as an inner state, produces the activities which we know as constituting health.

2 The other three being the scientific, the calculative, and the desiderative.

or smart. Practical wisdom is not the faculty, but it does not exist without this faculty. And this eye of the soul acquires its formed state not without the aid of virtue, as has been said and is plain; for the syllogisms which deal with acts to be done are things which involve a starting-point, viz. 'since the end, i.e. what is best, is of such and such a nature,' whatever it may be (let it for the sake of argument be what we please); and this is not evident except to the good man; for wickedness perverts us and causes us to be deceived about the starting-points of action. Therefore it is evident that it is impossible to be practically wise without being good.

We must therefore consider virtue also once more; for virtue too is similarly related; as practical wisdom is to cleverness—not the same, but like it—so is natural virtue to virtue in the strict sense. For all men think that each type of character belongs to its possessors in some sense by nature; for from the very moment of birth we are just or fitted for self-control or brave or have the other moral qualities; but yet we seek something else as that which is good in the strict sense—we seek for the presence of such qualities in another way. For both children and brutes have the natural dispositions to these qualities, but without reason these are evidently hurtful. Only we seem to see this much, that, while one may be led astray by them, as a strong body which moves without sight may stumble badly because of its lack of sight, still, if a man once acquires reason, that makes a difference in action; and his state, while still like what it was, will then be virtue in the strict sense. Therefore, as in the part of us which forms opinions there are two types, cleverness and practical wisdom, so too in the moral part there are two types, natural virtue and virtue in the strict sense, and of these the latter involves practical wisdom. This is why some say that all the virtues are forms of practical wisdom, and why Socrates in one respect was on the right track while in another he went astray; in thinking that all the virtues were forms of practical wisdom he was wrong, but in saying they implied practical wisdom he was right. This is confirmed by the fact that even now all men, when they define virtue, after naming the state of character and its objects add 'that (state) which is in accordance with the right rule'; now the right rule is that which is in accordance with practical wisdom. All men, then, seem somehow to divine that this kind of state is virtue, viz. that which is in accordance with practical wisdom. But we must go a little further. For it is not merely the state in accordance with the right rule, but the state that implies the *presence* of the right rule, that is virtue; and practical wisdom is a right rule about such matters. Socrates, then, thought the virtues were rules or rational principles (for he thought they were, all of them, forms of scientific knowledge), while we think they *involve* a rational principle.

It is clear, then, from what has been said, that it is not possible to be good in the strict sense without practical wisdom, nor practically wise without moral virtue. But in this way we may also refute the dialectical argument whereby it might be contended that the virtues exist in separation from each other; the same man, it might be said, is not best equipped by nature for all the virtues, so that he will have already acquired one when he has not yet acquired another. This is possible in respect of the natural virtues, but not in respect of those in respect of which a man is called without qualification good; for with the presence of the one quality, practical wisdom, will be given all the virtues. And it is plain that, even if it were of no practical value, we should have needed it because it is the virtue of the part of us in question; plain too that the choice will not be right without practical wisdom any more than without virtue; for the one determines the end and the other makes us do the things that lead to the end.

But again it is not *supreme* over philosophic wisdom, i.e. over the superior part of us, any more than the art of medicine is over health; for it does not use it but provides for its coming into being; it issues orders, then, for its sake, but not to it. Further, to maintain its supremacy would be like saying that the art of politics rules the gods because it issues orders about all the affairs of the state.

Sir Richard Livingstone

THE RAINBOW BRIDGE

THE CHIEF task of education is to make human beings, to develop the aptitudes and attitudes necessary for successful living. How can a classical education develop them? That is the subject of this article. "Of course, it cannot," is the obvious and, I would add, unthinking reply. "Why, these people are antiquated. Their civilisation, compared to ours, was primitive. They had no aeroplanes, automobiles, railroads, no atomic power or electricity, not even steam." All these things can also be said of the New Testament, of Shakespeare, of Molière, even of Goethe. But are they for that reason antiquated? The criticism of the classics which I have mentioned is

THE RAINBOW BRIDGE: From *The Cornhill Magazine,* Summer 1958. "The Rainbow Bridge" is published in book form by the Pall Mall Press, Ltd., of 2 Clements Inn, Strand, London W.C. 2, and by Clarke, Irwin & Co., Ltd., of Toronto. Reprinted by permission of the author's executors.

due to a failure to distinguish knowledge and wisdom. Knowledge gets out-of-date—often very quickly—especially scientific knowledge. But wisdom does not. Like gold, it keeps its value, however long ago some human mind dug it up.

"Still," it may be said, "a classical education is no equipment for the modern world. Perhaps it is suitable for a life of thought, of literature, of teaching; but not for politics, for a public career, and still less for business." Let me appeal to illustrations taken from life. At the annual meeting of the English Classical Association the presidential speech is given in alternate years by a scholar and by some public figure whose education was in the classics and who in his later life can give an address on them which will be suitable to a gathering of scholars. Among the presidents of the last fifty years have been two prime ministers, eight cabinet ministers, a lord chancellor, a lord chief justice, two masters of the rolls, a president of the Royal Society of Science, a president of the Royal Academy of Arts, the chairman of one of the five great British banks; and, to come to recent times, the education of Sir Oliver Franks, lately British ambassador in America and now chairman of Lloyds Bank, was in the classics both at school and university. No, one cannot argue that a good classical education is in fact a bad preparation for life in the world.

But what is the explanation of this paradox? How can the study of two long-dead peoples be any preparation for living in our modern age? This is an interesting problem, not only in itself but because it raises the general questions: What is a good education? What ought we to be seeking when we go to school or college or when we educate ourselves? What insights, what outlook, what training of the mind?

There are two types of teachers to whom we have reason to be grateful. There are those who teach us facts, who introduce us in a methodical way to a subject, lay solid foundations in it, and on these foundations raise the tower of knowledge, foursquare and firmly built. We owe much to them. But there is another, rarer type, to whom we owe more still—those teachers who have an attitude to life, an outlook on the world, that we have not met before, who open our eyes to a new point of view and teach us to see life in a new way. That is the most valuable education one ever gets; and one can recognise it not so much perhaps by the impression it makes at the moment as by the way in which the mind recurs with growing understanding and gratitude to an inspiration which the passage of time does nothing to dim. The Greeks belong to this rarer type of teachers. They give, or can give, two things which everyone needs, two things which education must give if it is to be education at all; first, a certain intellectual habit and attitude of mind; second, a view of life. If education can give these two things, a right view of life and the right mental habits, it will have given us the chief equipment which we need for our voyage through the world. My suggestion is that Greek can give these two things. If so, it has a very important connection with the modern world, and it is the connection between ancient Greece and modern civilisation with which this article deals—the mental habits and the attitude to life which can be learned from the Greeks. First their mental habits. What were they?

If we wish to know the nature and quality of a man's mind, we can discover it by studying his life and observing what he has achieved. So too with a nation. If we wish to know its quality, capacity, nature, genius, we have only to study what it has done, and then to ask what that nation must have been like to do this. What did the Greeks do?

In Norse mythology there is a legend of a rainbow bridge, made by the gods so that men who had earned the right could cross the deep and sundering gulf between Midgard, which is the earth, and Asgard, which is heaven. That legend reflects man's sense of the two worlds, human and superhuman, to both of which he belongs, and his instinct, often sleeping, never dead, to pass from the lower to the higher world. Earth and heaven, barbarism and civilisation; those are worlds between which a deep gulf lies. But the gulf can be bridged. In Norse mythology the bridge is built by Odin and the Aesir; in history and fact it was built by the Greeks with a double-span, the bridge of goodness and the bridge of wisdom, by which men pass from barbarism to civilisation, if not from earth to heaven.

It was not an easy bridge to build. Consider, very briefly, the Greek achievement—in the form of two contrasts. If we had lived in Greece in 650 B.C. we would have thought that the sun and moon were gods, that thunder and lightning were divine weapons, that the arrows of Apollo caused influenza, that corn was the gift of Demeter, that each mountain, tree, and river was the home of a spirit. Four hundred years later we would have known that the earth was a sphere rotating on its own axis and revolving round the sun; the circumference of the earth had been determined accurately within fifty miles; a recent astronomer had catalogued eight hundred fixed stars; and two hundred years earlier a scientist had argued that the universe was constructed of atoms in infinite space. There we have one of the great transformations of the world, one of the great steps forward in the history of man: the creation of a rational, scientific attitude to the universe. That is a bridge which the Greeks built between 600 and 300 B.C.

Human history shows nothing comparable. It is not of course the actual amount of knowledge achieved, of facts discovered. It is to have created, out of ignorance and superstition, the idea of science, the notion of a rational world. We have done infinitely more in detailed scientific discovery. But ours has been development; theirs was origination. Greek science—by which I mean the idea that the universe is rational and is capable of being explained and understood —was created in a world in which science, as we understand the word, did not exist; and to have originated science is greater than to have developed it.

That, to recur to my metaphor, is one span of the bridge leading from barbarism to civilisation which the Greeks built for us—the span of reason which leads to knowledge. Now let me turn to the other span. The fact that in the dark chaos of ignorance and superstition the Greeks conceived the idea of looking at the universe and life with the eye of reason shows that they must have had unique intellectual genius. But they created something else besides science and philosophy: they created a great human ideal; and from that fact we can divine that they had a rare spiritual genius too. We have seen the contrast between man's attitude to the universe before and after Greek thought, and how the Greeks built the bridge by which mankind crossed from a nonscientific view of the world to a scientific view. But they built an even more important bridge—the bridge by which it passed from barbarism to the life which caused Goethe to say that of all men the Greeks had dreamed the dream of life best.

Think of the early Greek world as we see it in the poems of Homer, a world with its splendid virtues, but also full of injustice, cruelty, and superstition, a world that knew human sacrifice and believed in gods who, even as men, would have been discreditable. And then contrast with it the Greek world of the fifth century B.C., and see how in the interval the Greeks had created out of a primitive society a great spiritual life. It may seem a surprising suggestion that Greece can help us in the field of conduct, of morals. People don't always think of her in that light; art, literature, thought—yes; morality—no. But Greece and Christianity are the two supreme masters of the ethical, the spiritual life. There and nowhere else in Western civilisation do we find what the modern world has largely lost—a clear philosophy of living.

Think, as I suggested, of the world of Homer; then look at two pictures: the first an ideal for the state, the second an ideal for the individual. The first, from the second book of Thucydides, is Pericles' political ideal for Athens:

> Our constitution is called a democracy because it is in the hands not of the few but of the many. But the laws secure equal justice for all in

their private disputes. As for social standing, our practice is that a citizen who has recognized ability in some field gets public preferment—it is a question of his abilities, not of his rank. As for poverty, our practice is that if any man can do good work for the community, humbleness of condition is no bar. . . . Open and friendly in our private intercourse, in our public conduct we keep strictly within the control of law . . . we are obedient to those in authority and to the laws, more especially to those which offer protection to the oppressed.

Has any finer definition of the democratic ideal ever been written? Has any nation gone beyond that? Or contrast with the ideals of the Homeric age this conception, from the *Theaetetus* of Plato, of what human life should be. "Evil, Theodorus, can never pass away, for there must always be an opposite to good. It has no place in heaven, so of necessity it haunts the mortal nature and this earthly sphere. Therefore we ought to escape from earth to heaven as quickly as we can; and the way to escape is to become like God, as far as this is possible; and the way to become like him is to become holy, good, and wise."

Between 700 and 400 B.C., besides the transformation of human outlook by the creation of the scientific spirit, came another of the great transformations of the world—the creation of a rational and worthy spiritual ideal for men. During those years a real civilisation emerged with incredible rapidity; amid heavy clouds a patch of the clearest sky appeared, in which of the three great lights of the human firmament—Goodness, Beauty, Truth—two at least, Beauty and Truth, shine as brightly as they have ever shone since. There is only one other movement in the spiritual history of Western civilisation in any degree comparable to it in importance—what was done in Palestine between the age of the Book of Judges and the age of the New Testament.

What qualities make the Greek achievement possible? How could a people pass, in a few centuries, from Homeric to Platonic morality, from primitive views about the universe to thinking that it was composed of atoms in infinite space?

Two qualities do much to explain this achievement; and they can be divined in some Greek sayings taken from the sixth and fifth centuries B.C., if we look behind the saying to the outlook of the man who said it. "I would rather discover one scientific fact than be King of Persia" (as we might say, a Rockefeller or a Ford). "Why are we born? To contemplate the works of Nature." What sort of men were the speakers of these words, Democritus and Anaxagoras? What do these phrases reveal? A passionate interest in the world and curiosity about it—their own word to describe their feeling, "wonder," is better. These men do not want money or fame or pleasure, but they find the world about them extraordinarily interesting, and it seems to them a sufficient occupation to contemplate and study it. People who felt like that were singularly well equipped to create science and philosophy. We recognise in those sayings the secret of perpetual youth, and feel in them the greatness of man—something divine and immortal emerging in this frail, sensuous, mundane, petty creature. The Greeks say in effect about the pursuit of knowledge what Antony in Shakespeare says about something very different: "The nobleness of life is to do thus." That attitude of wonder in the presence of the world is a continuous quality of Greek thought.

Then there is a second quality, which again is revealed in two sentences, if, as before, we look behind the words to the spirit of the man who uttered them. "The greatness of man consists in saying what is true, and in acting according to Nature, listening to her" (Heraclitus, sixth century B.C.). The second instance is a sentence from Plato:

> I am one of the people who would like to be proved wrong if they say anything which is not correct, and would like to prove others wrong if they are in error; and I should not find it more disagreeable to have my own errors pointed out than to prove others wrong, for it is a greater gain to be set free from the greatest of evils (error) than to set others free.

The speaker of these words was not a common type—how many of us think it an advantage to be shown wrong? In those two passages another secret of how the Greeks came to create science and philosophy and a rational view of life is apparent. They found the world and life intensely interesting, but they also desired to see both as they really are. That again is a continuous quality of Greek literature, the instinct to see things accurately—not to rest in prejudices and preconceptions. How difficult, how salutary, how liberating! Few things are more needed in politics, amid the cant of Party, in the work of education or administration—indeed everywhere—than this desire, without bitterness or cynicism, to see things as they are. There again we see the divine in man, something human and also superhuman.

These attitudes, curiosity, the capacity for intense interest, and the power

> To bear all naked truths,
> And to envisage circumstance, all calm,

are the essential qualities for achievement in science and philosophy. (But in what field of life are they not of supreme importance?) No people have ever used the eye of the mind so steadily and effectively as the Greeks. It meets us everywhere from Homer to Epictetus. Even the earliest Greek literature shows that instinct to see things without prejudice or prepossession, which is a forerunner of reason. Thus Homer writes of a war between Greeks and barbarians, but we could not tell from the *Iliad* whether he was Greek or Trojan. Thus Thucydides narrates the war in which his country was ruined; but it would be difficult to tell, except for the rare passages in which he speaks in the first person, whether he was an Athenian or a Spartan.

It is by the use of reason that the Ionians broke loose from a savage's views of the universe and argued their way through a series of hypotheses to the atomism of Democritus. It is by reason that the Greeks achieved the most difficult of all tasks, that of seeing further than the accepted conventions of their age; thus Plato, in a state where women had no education or share in public life, declared that they should have the same upbringing as men and follow the same pursuits and occupations; thus, in an age when slavery was universally accepted, Alcidamas (fifth century B.C.) wrote, "God has set all men free; nature has made no one a slave"; thus, two centuries later in a world divided by race, culture, and government, Diogenes, when asked what was his country, replied, "I am a citizen of the world"; and Zeno, the founder of Stoicism, said, "Let us look on all men as fellow countrymen and fellow citizens, and let there be unity in our life, like that of a flock feeding together in a common pasture."

The Greeks reached these truths—Plato, the emancipation of women; Alcidamas, the abolition of slavery; Zeno, the unity of mankind—not under the pressure of social or economic trends, but by the power of reason, breaking the thought barrier of their time. It has taken mankind a long time to see as far; even today we have not seen as far as Zeno.

A trinity of virtues shines throughout Greek literature. I have mentioned two; the Greek writers find the world intensely interesting, and they try to see it as it is. The third virtue is *Sophrosyne*. The word is untranslatable—the most interesting words in any language are always the words which cannot be translated, like *spirituel* in French, or "comfortable" and "gentleman" in English, for such words are characteristic of their creators and give a glimpse of their inner selves. We generally render it as "temperance"; "self-mastery" is better; but "balance" perhaps would come nearest to its meaning. It is the virtue which keeps men in the middle of the road, checks their waywardness and extravagance, saves them from the falsehood of extremes, and gives their life and thought the harmony of a fine piece of music. The literal meaning of the word is "soundness of mind": if you have *Sophrosyne*, you have health of spirit and intellect and character. Really it is reason in another aspect—the power to see things as a whole, each in its place and proportion. It is not a common virtue in human beings, as Shakespeare knew when he made Hamlet praise Horatio:

> A man that Fortune's buffets and rewards
> Hast ta'en with equal thanks; and blest are these
> Whose blood and judgment are so well commingled
> That they are not a pipe for Fortune's finger
> To sound what stop she please. Give me the man
> That is not passion's slave, and I will wear him
> In my heart's core.

That is a good description of *Sophrosyne*.

Nor is *Sophrosyne* a common virtue in peoples: witness the excesses of the French Revolution and the Nazi madness. But, apart from such spectacular instances of popular delirium, the history of most nations shows less destructive but equally irrational lapses from sanity. We can all think of such cases. There are plenty in Greek history, for the Greeks were a passionate people; *Sophrosyne*, supreme in their thought and literature, did not rule their political life. One would not recommend the study of Greek history to anyone who wished to know what *Sophrosyne* is in action. The British, in their better moments, can show this virtue. If anyone wishes to see *Sophrosyne* in a statesman, he could not find a better example than Abraham Lincoln.

Sophrosyne is as necessary a virtue in literature and in thought as in practical life. Can we see clearly if our eyes are bloodshot with prejudice or passion? If one of them is blind, are we likely to get things in focus? There is plenty of unbalance in the literature of the last hundred years. It is obvious in the sentimentality and facile optimism of the weaker Victorian writers; but in a different form it is quite as common in the generation which reacted against the Victorians, practised the Art of Debunking, and in a world often dreary and sordid was blind to the countervailing goodness.

The irony of it is that these modern writers of whom I am speaking profess to look at the world with clear eyes, to see things as they are. But no one's eyes are clear unless they see the good in life as well as the evil. To miss the good is unbalance too, unbalance of a more dangerous kind. It is not to be found in the great Greek writers. There is plenty of gloom in them, in Homer and Pindar or the tragic poets; but always, shining in the gloom, there is a sense of beauty and splendour in the world no less real than the tragedy and evil. It is best to see life as the Greeks saw it—for they saw it as it is—and to go into the world with eyes open indeed to its darker side, so that we may know what we have to face, but not to ignore the other aspect in which its growing good resides.

Yes, it may be said, but what exactly do we get by reading this literature and studying this civilisation? In what way does it prepare us to live in the modern world? No doubt the Greek achievement was remarkable, indeed unique. But how does it help us now?

My reply would be that the people who did these things must have been a very remarkable people, a people with extraordinary qualities of mind, the sort of people one likes to meet, the sort of people one cannot meet without learning something from them; and when one reflects that the Greeks brought into the world the idea of science and the ideal of democracy, and when one considers their achievement in philosophy, in political thought, in poetry, in sculpture, in architecture, in the creation of an ideal of life, are not the men who did these things worth meeting? Are they not likely to be able to teach us much, not in actual facts, but if we ask from them what Elisha asked Elijah—a portrait of their spirit? The most important thing in education is to live with the right people—in life, if we can find them; in the past, where they are easy to find. The Greeks, I think, stand highest among the right people.

No race has ever been so gifted, and taking them individually, some of its writers have no rivals. Can we think of anyone equal to Homer in epic, to Thucydides in history, to Aristophanes in his special field of comedy? There have been great philosophers since their time, but it would be difficult to maintain that any of them are equal to Aristotle and still less to Plato, of whom Whitehead said that "the safest general characterisation of the European philosophical tradition is that it consists of a series of footnotes to Plato." Shakespeare no doubt is supreme among dramatists, but each of the three great Greek tragic poets is his superior in a particular field.

Greek studies are a training of the eye of the mind to see rightly, and that is a sufficient reason for regarding them as a good training for life. Only a small minority of those who pass through school and college will learn Greek, though it might well be a larger minority than it is today. But any educated person can read at least some of the Greek masterpieces in English. He will of course lose much; poetry can never be transmuted from one tongue into another without change and loss. And he will not know the Greek language, "A language doubtless the most perfect that has been contrived by the art of man" (Gibbon).

If I had to prescribe a course of Greek literature in English, I should include at least Homer's *Odyssey* (the *Iliad* is greater but it has a less universal appeal); some Greek plays, including *Agamemnon* (in McNeice's translation, the best that I know of any Greek play); and in prose, Thucydides, the *Apology, Crito, Phaedo,* and *Republic* of Plato (the last of these in Cornford's translation). These are indispensables. Anyone interested in dramatic criticism will not omit Aristotle's *Poetics;* and one would like to add his *Ethics* and *Politics.* Neither of them is easy reading, but Sir Ernest Barker's translation, with notes, has smoothed the path in the case of *Politics.*

The prose works which I have mentioned should be read in translations with short notes; otherwise the reader who knows no Greek is liable to miss a good deal. If he plunges into a bare text of, for instance, the *Republic,* his head is not likely to be continuously above water. There are, however, editions with notes of all the prose works, except the *Ethics* and the *Poetics,* notably Cornford's brilliant translation of the *Republic;* and in Greek drama Gilbert Murray's short introduction and comments add greatly to the enjoyment and appreciation of the plays.

Joseph Wood Krutch

THE IDOLS OF THE LABORATORY

Of course "it" has not actually happened here. The convictions toward which we may seem to have been drifting and the techniques with which we have certainly been experimenting have not yet created the kind of society which these convictions, backed up by these techniques, may be capable of producing.

The most that can be said is what we have already said: namely that the means and methods we have developed are leading us on to other methods and ends which many neither criticize nor even recognize. We are drifting with a current of half-formulated preferences and judgments which conduct us we know not whither and sometimes in directions we might not want to take if we knew what the direction was.

Consider, for example, a simple situation somewhat different from that with which we have been concerned. Few of us would be willing to say that material goods are the only real goods and that increase in wealth and comfort is the only end worth pursuing. But just because we have learned effective methods of increasing both, we practice those methods with so much enthusiasm that we begin to act as though what they get us were the only things worth getting. And because we have not clearly formulated the other possible ends

---

which we may vaguely acknowledge as desirable, we have carelessly accepted a materialistic philosophy which makes any definition of these other ends difficult. Thus we act as though we believed what many of us would not confess to believing. In the very early days of the Second World War a popular writer on economic subjects warned us not to forget when we came to choose sides that contemporary Germany represented the highest stage which civilization had yet reached. And the proof offered was this: under Hitler production per man hour had reached a level never previously achieved!

Only by a criticism of the *ends* for which new powers may be used can the threat which they carry be minimized. And by "criticism" is meant not only that sort of public discussion which a given political situation may or may not permit, but also a genuine consideration of ends as well as means, a reopening of the question of what we want as possibly opposed to what it has now become possible to get: in a word, a renewed examination of our *value judgments.*

Yet criticism of this sort has now become extremely difficult if we attempt to apply it to the whole subject of the general intentions of those who claim to be acquiring a new power over men's thoughts. Such criticism inevitably becomes metaphysical, and the thesis of the positivists is that the metaphysical is essentially meaningless, or at least ineffectual. Even the general public which could not state its convictions so rigorously is at least committed to the belief that metaphysics is moonshine and that only "practical" matters are worth discussing. Yet we are finally thrown back upon the metaphysical question whether legitimate value judgments really are possible and whether, if they are not, dispensing with them necessarily opens the way to possibilities which seem to many of us no less revolting than they are disastrous.

Even the most moderate proponents of a "scientific" morality seem usually unaware of the closed circle around which they lead us when they consent to consider questions concerning value. They begin by saying—and it seems reasonable enough—that value judgments should be based on knowledge rather than on tradition or intuition; and they bid us, before we make them, to consult not merely the physical sciences but also such other bodies of available knowledge as history and anthropology. Unfortunately, however, it has usually turned out that when they follow their own advice the conclusion which they arrive at is not that a true value judgment has been scientifically justified but that the impossibility of making such a judgment has been demonstrated.

As far back as the nineteenth century this pattern was set by Lecky's great *History of European Morals* which undertook to study scientifically the ethical systems which had actually prevailed. The conclusion reached was summed up in Lecky's famous statement that there is no possible line of conduct which has not, at some time and place, been condemned, and which has not, at some other time and place, been enjoined as a duty. Thus what he arrived at was not a "scientific morality" but only the conviction that such a scientific morality is impossible; that, at least from the standpoint of science, "morals" are indistinguishable from "manners" or "mores" and that "the good" is nothing more than "the prevalent."

Anthropology—which is only history with an extended scope—has more recently been more fashionable as a body of knowledge to which the moralist may appeal. But one of the most prevalent, or at least the most popular, schools of anthropology has been that which defends a cultural relativism corresponding quite closely to the moral relativism of Lecky. In the United States Ruth Benedict's *Patterns of Culture* has probably been the most widely read of all anthropological works, and *Patterns of Culture* is devoted to the thesis that the scientist must concern himself, not with any attempt to define the characteristics of a *good* society, but only with the attempt to get an adequate understanding of the fact that the "patterns of culture" which have actually existed are almost infinitely varied and that any one of them may be "good" from the standpoint of those who live in accordance with it. Thus the final conclusion seems to be, not that anthropology can tell us objectively what a good society is, but rather that the question, when considered objectively, has no meaning.

It is true that Miss Benedict falls into the inconsistency to which all who deny that they are making value judgments usually fall. She is objective enough when she compares, say, the "Apollonian" culture of the Hopis with the "Dionysian" culture of some of the Plains Indians. But when she turns, as she does, to describe the Babbitt or Middletown culture—which she takes to be predominant in the United States at the moment of writing—nearly everything she says is loaded with an adverse judgment of that culture.

To be consistent she should say that Rotary Clubs and the ceremonies of the businessman's golf game cannot be objectively pronounced either good or bad since they are, like the Hopi snake dance, simply part of a pattern of culture. What actually happens is, of course, that her objectivity deserts her just as soon as she considers the culture of her own tribe and that she makes value judgments on it just as freely—but with much less awareness of what she is doing—as they are made by those ignorant of the science of anthropology but loyal to tradition, metaphysics, or intuition.

Moreover, and in so far as those who advocate a "scientific" morality actually do consistently follow the conclusions to which they are led, the practical result is to encourage the tendency, already strongly developed in our society, to make no distinction between what men do and what they "ought" to do; to turn the quest for scientific morality into nothing except a study of prevalent behavior.

To state that "whatever is is right" and to accept that statement fully or absolutely requires a metaphysical analysis of which most men are not capable and leads to conclusions which most men would probably hesitate to accept. But many if not most men are now pragmatically accepting it already when they propose to use studies of everything from the reading habits of adolescence to the sexual behavior of homosexuals as the bases for ordering the educational system or setting up standards of sexual morality. Thus though the assumption that the concept represented in the word "ought" is radically meaningless is one not usually consciously made it is nevertheless the assumption on which many "advanced thinkers" seem willing to proceed.

Hence it appears that when the advocates of the theory that value judgments should be based on knowledge actually follow consistently their principles, they end by admitting that the only thing which science can achieve is the discovery of what the most usual conduct is like. The only guidance they can offer is the suggestion that we should not expect anything other than what we find to be happening and this in turn comes down to little more than the statement "what has been has been, what will be will be."

No sociological determinist thoughtful enough to realize the implications of his position fails to recognize that questions concerning value must be answered somehow and he usually answers them by saying that though no value judgments arrived at by metaphysical processes are valid, there is something which serves the purpose which the so-called value judgments cannot really serve and takes their place in any functioning society. This something is provided for us by the contingencies of the natural world and, in the long run, would prevent the sustained development or continued existence of such perverse horrors as Nazism achieved or imagination may fear in a Walden Three.

Since Professor Skinner is one of the clearest and most persuasive exponents of this position we may again use him for the purpose of criticizing his statement of it both as implied in *Walden Two* and as explicitly defended elsewhere. Essentially his position is defined by the statement that there are certain "values" which are "self-evident" and that no human choice is necessarily involved in the acceptance of them. We do not "make" value judgments but they are imposed upon us.

And yet, as we shall see, this thesis breaks down as it always does when confronted by the fact that these "self-evident values" are not recognized as self-evident by everyone and therefore can be called self-evident only with the proviso that those to whom they do not seem so are declared to be not "normal" or "sane"—by the arbitrary standard set up by individuals who insist that they are not setting any arbitrary standards.

Anyone who believes in the all but unlimited effect of the conditioning to which every mind has been subjected ought logically to be the first to suspect that when a man calls something "self-evident" that means merely that he has been early and firmly conditioned to believe it; not at all that it would appear self-evident to those who happen to have been otherwise conditioned. Thus those who follow Mr. Skinner's line of argument may be hoisted very neatly on their own petards. While they profess to make no value judgment they are actually making one in the most absolute and unconditional way possible, namely, by saying "it is obviously true." And whatever dangers may be involved in accepting as absolutely true conclusions arrived at by the fallible processes of human reason it does not seem as though they could be avoided by refusing to think at all—which appears to be what Mr. Skinner is proposing when faced with an ultimate problem.

In his case the value judgment which he makes while insisting that it is not really a value judgment at all comes down to this: Whatever contributes to the health of an individual or the long-continued survival of the society of which he is a part is "good," or, as he put it in the course of a debate, "The one criterion that is thrust upon us is whether the group which observes a given practice will be here tomorrow." The implication is that, granted this premise, we can easily determine how a society should be planned and to what opinions, tastes, and activities an individual should be conditioned.

But what this, in its turn, really comes down to is, of course, only a rather fancy restatement of the doctrine implied in the phrase "survival of the fittest." And the semantic emptiness of the doctrine was long ago exposed by asking the simple question, "Fittest for what?" The only possible answer is "fittest to survive" which closes the circle and thereby reduces the statement to complete nonsense by making it read: "Those survive who survive."

For the moment the question is not whether the value judgment which declares "survival" and "health" to be goods is defensible either as one of those arbitrary choices which some declare all value judgments to be or as something at which reason can arrive. The question is simply whether or not they are "self-evident" goods in the sense that all men not certifiably insane have accepted them and that they therefore demonstrate how easily we may escape the necessity of making, for ourselves, any value judgments at all.

It is certainly not self-evident or universally admitted that if, as some believe, the intellectual acuteness and artistic genius of the ancient Athenians cut short the life of their state, then this acuteness and this genius were so far from being good that it would have been better if Greek thought and Greek art had never existed. Neither is it self-evident that the Egyptian civilization of the first and second dynasties—which historians have called the most enduring societies ever known—was also the most admirable and "right." May we not say instead that long survival is no more self-evidently the final measure of the worth of a society than it is of an individual and that by no means everyone agrees that the longest-lived men are the best, or that he who lives dully and viciously to the age of one hundred has demonstrated that his life was better than that of a man who dies at fifty after a full and fruitful career—or even, for that matter, after a short but merry one. Miss Edna Millay, as is well known, advised burning the candle at both ends, and though she may very well have been misguided, she was certainly not insane. Mr. Skinner's self-evident values were not self-evident to her.

One does not—to carry the argument a little further—need to accept Christian ethics to remember that the founder of Christianity is reported to have been so far from believing that "survival value" provided an ultimate test of the good that he said on one occasion, "He who loses his life shall gain it."

More than one biologist has remarked that the cockroach seems to be one of the most successful as well as one of the most stable of living organisms. Only a trained entomologist can distinguish any difference between those species living today and their fossilized ancestors who flourished some 250 million years ago. Throughout all these millennia their philosophy has worked. To Mr. Skinner's test question, "Will it be here tomorrow?" the members of the cockroach society can reply "Yes" with more justifiable confidence than could the members of any human society. Are we really forced to the conclusion that the cockroach's success is the only sort which can have any meaning? Are there no reasons why it is "better" to be a man than an insect? If there are, then some criterion other than the promise of continued survival must be applicable. For insects, for individuals, and for societies alike, there are ignoble as well as noble ways of surviving.

Once criticism or Mr. Skinner's first principles has been insisted on, it becomes obvious enough that "survival" and "health" are not actually ends at all but only means. Unless one survives *for* something, neither survival nor health has any value in itself. But the answer to the question what things are worth living for is not self-evident and thus the attempt to avoid value judgments leads back around the same circle to which every attempt to make a science do something of which it is incapable inevitably leads.

If we permit ourselves to develop methods or means which lead only to other methods and other means, not to any humanly valuable end, then both individual men and society must either live for the sake of their techniques—much as misers live for their money rather than for anything which it can buy—or they will pursue ends unacknowledged and unrecognized. Either the "self-evident" truths become a set of dogmas ferociously defended from criticism or we drift with a current of half-formulated preferences and judgments which conduct us we know not whither and sometimes in a direction contrary to that in which we would like to go.

In the totalitarian states the first of these possibilities has been more or less completely realized. In our own society—still protected by those "inner contradictions" which so distress the fanatical—we have not, so far at least, paid the full penalty for philosophizing badly. Perhaps that is partly because we have not fully accepted either the philosophy or the practice of totalitarianism and hence permit older ideals to temper somewhat the new. Perhaps it is also because the impossibility of not philosophizing at all manifests itself slowly and we have not yet reached the point of acquiescing in exclusive dogmas without knowing that we acquiesce in any dogmas at all.

What happens—and what is actually happening—is, that when critical awareness fades away, remoter and remoter deductions are made from the unexamined premises until conclusions are reached which even those who accept the premises might reject if they could follow the chain of unconscious and dubious logic by which they were led to them.

Take for example this matter of "health." Even before the meaning of the word is extended by metaphorical use to include the less easily definable "mental health" the value set on what the term implies soon goes beyond anything which could possibly be called self-evident. Not merely does "health" come to mean the absence of disease and a satisfactory physical fitness, but it begins to exalt a more and more perfect health and a more and more complete "fitness," regardless of the fact that health, like cleanliness, is not susceptible of an indefinitely useful increase. The ultimate absurdity is reached in those clubs of young men who spend the day displaying their tanned skins and muscles on the California beaches where this "fitness" has become an acknowledged "end in itself." One cannot ask "health for what?" or "fit for what?" without introducing value judgments which are not self-evident and which the tribe of logical positivists warns us against. We cannot even ask what a healthy race should do with itself unless we are willing to philosophize, and without philosophizing we must end content with a fitness which does not seem to be actually fit for anything.

"In what does *mental* health consist?" and "To what extent ought 'mental health' be valued above any other mental characteristic?" are questions to which it is even more obvious that no answer can be given by those who refuse to philosophize—unless indeed one is willing to take it as self-evident that a troubled Mozart who died at thirty-five or even a Shakespeare who died at fifty-two is to be counted a man less successful than those who lived longer and whose minds were more obviously "healthy" than the minds which produced the G Minor quintet and *King Lear*—neither of which is likely to be counted, in the most obvious meaning of the word, self-evidently "healthy." Nor will it do to object that to call "health" self-evidently good means only "other things being equal." Things never can be equal if we start with the premise about "health" without examining or criticizing the assumed meaning of the word.

Many who are little disposed to either masochism or even ascetic practices have nevertheless found it meaningful as well as convenient to recognize what they call "divine discontent," and there are those who see in some sort of "soul sickness" the indispensable condition of a fully developed humanity. How is it possible, without some kind of philosophizing, to accept or reject what such terms imply? Is it really self-evident at what point "aspiration" (which is admirable) becomes merely "maladjustment" (which is not); or that a man's reach should never exceed his grasp? What of the old problem of the pig who is contented and the Socrates who is not?

Such terms as "normality" and "satisfactory adjustment" have, of course, to be defined by somebody. The statistician can determine the meaning of the first, if it is assumed to mean "most usual." But the second will have to depend to some extent on the subjective preferences of some group. Fortunately, for them, that group is largely self-selecting in a society actively engaged in the attempt to mold the minds and characters of its members because the relatively aggressive, extraverted people are those who are temperamentally most likely to practice enthusiastically the available techniques for "conditioning." Thus it comes about that they are the ones who, in accord with their natures, provide the accepted definition.

Thus without the establishment of any totalitarian state or even the setting up of any Walden Two, merely by the rejection of all value judgments except those which a particular type of mind declares to be self-evident, we begin to evolve a mental climate with definitely recognizable characteristics. First it is "self-evident" that men ought to be healthy; then self-evident that "healthy" means "adjusted"; and then, finally, self-evident that "adjusted" means extraverted. "Doing" is therefore important and "thinking" can mean only "plans for doing" if it is to mean anything at all and to question any of the accepted values is to demonstrate "maladjustment" or "immaturity."

In "today's thinking" the two statements commonly made or implied come down to this: (1) Value judgments cannot validly be made by any metaphysical process. (2) Value judgments do not need to be made because they are entirely self-evident to every "normal" mind. But even if we accept the first of these statements the second is demonstrably false by simple historical evidence. Sane people have not in the past always made the same ones and neither for that matter do all sane people today. "Today's thinking" may have effectively put us into a dilemma but it has not, as it claims, then released us from it. If it has demonstrated that value judgments are never valid it has not demonstrated that we do not make them, arbitrarily and irrationally if not reasonably and defensibly. If we cannot think effectively on the subject, choices are still possible and for good or for ill we do make them.

As influence, power, and authority in our society pass, as they are passing, from philosophers and theologians into the hands of those who call themselves "human engineers" whether they happen to be functioning as lawmakers, publicists, teachers, psychologists, or even advertising managers, it is passing from those who were at least aware of what value judgments they were making to those who are not; passing into the hands of men who act on very inclusive and fateful judgments while believing that they are acting on self-evident principles immune to criticism. They do not know what they are making us into and refuse to permit us even to ask. Moreover, in so far as their attempt to "condition" the human beings on whom they practice their techniques are successful, they make it less and less probable that their fateful assumptions will ever be questioned.

From the situation in which they have placed us there seems no possible escape so long as we accept the premises which most thoughtful as well as most thoughtless men seem today inclined to accept. If man is only an animal and an animal is only some kind of machine, then both must be controlled by laws. The power of choice which we seem sometimes to exercise and the decisions which we seem sometimes to make must be illusory because the laws of cause and effect are inexorable. Once these assertions have been accepted as fact it becomes almost inevitable to agree that human nature and conduct will eventually become as predictable and as controllable as the other phenomena of the natural world now are. And since the controllers are themselves only the product of their own conditioning the control which they will exercise is itself already predetermined. There remains nothing which we can do except to close our eyes and to say, "Here we go—to become what and in what future we cannot even guess."

Even though we may think that we are moving in the direction of our desire, that desire was predetermined by the forces which conditioned us to want what we think we are wanting. Whether that will turn out to be something like Huxley's *Brave New World*, like Skinner's *Walden Two*, or something quite different from either, we cannot know. What we do know is only that what will be, will be.

> And what rough beast, its hour come round at last,
> Slouches towards Bethlehem to be born?

Thomas Merton

BEING AND DOING

WE ARE warmed by fire, not by the smoke of the fire. We are carried over the sea by a ship, not by the wake of a ship. So too, what we are is to be sought in the invisible depths of our own being, not in our outward reflection in our own acts. We must find our real selves not in the froth stirred up by the impact of our being upon the beings around us, but in our own soul which is the principle of all our acts.

But my soul is hidden and invisible. I cannot see it directly, for it is hidden even from myself. Nor can I see my own eyes. They are too close to me for me to see them. They are not meant to see themselves. I know I have eyes when I see other things with them.

I can see my eyes in a mirror. My soul can also reflect itself in the mirror of its own activity. But what is seen in the mirror is only the reflection of who I am, not my true being. The mirror of words and actions only partly manifests my being.

The words and acts that proceed from myself and are accomplished outside myself are dead things compared with the hidden life from which they spring. These acts are transient and superficial. They are

BEING AND DOING: From *No Man Is an Island* by Thomas Merton.

quickly gone, even though their effects may persist for a little while. But the soul itself remains. Much depends on how the soul sees itself in the mirror of its own activity.

My soul does not find itself unless it acts. Therefore it must act. Stagnation and inactivity bring spiritual death. But my soul must not project itself entirely into the outward effects of its activity. I do not need to *see* myself, I merely need to *be* myself. I must think and act like a living being, but I must not plunge my whole self into what I think and do, or seek always to find myself in the work I have done. The soul that projects itself entirely into activity, and seeks itself outside itself in the work of its own will is like a madman who sleeps on the sidewalk in front of his house instead of living inside where it is quiet and warm. The soul that throws itself outdoors in order to find itself in the effects of its own work is like a fire that has no desire to burn but seeks only to go up in smoke.

The reason why men are so anxious to see themselves, instead of being content to be themselves, is that they do not really believe in their own existence. And they do not fully believe that they exist because they do not believe in God. This is equally true of those who say they believe in God (without actually putting their faith into practice) and of those who do not even pretend to have any faith.

In either case, the loss of faith has involved at the same time a complete loss of all sense of reality. Being means nothing to those who hate and fear what they themselves are. Therefore they cannot have peace in their own reality (which reflects the reality of God). They must struggle to escape their true being, and verify a false existence by constantly viewing what they themselves do. They have to keep looking in the mirror for reassurance. What do they expect to see? Not themselves! They are hoping for some sign that they have become the god they hope to become by means of their own frantic activity—invulnerable, all powerful, infinitely wise, unbearably beautiful, unable to die!

When a man constantly looks and looks at himself in the mirror of his own acts, his spiritual double vision splits him into two people. And if he strains his eyes hard enough, he forgets which one is real. In fact, reality is no longer found either in himself or in his shadow. The substance has gone out of itself into the shadow, and he has become two shadows instead of one real person.

Then the battle begins. Whereas one shadow was meant to praise the other, now one shadow accuses the other. The activity that was meant to exalt him, reproaches and condemns him. It is never real enough. Never active enough. The less he is able to *be* the more he has to *do*. He becomes his own slave driver—a shadow whipping a shadow to death, because it cannot produce reality, infinitely substantial reality, out of his own nonentity.

Then comes fear. The shadow becomes afraid of the shadow. He who "is not" becomes terrified at the things he cannot do. Whereas for a while he had illusions of infinite power, miraculous sanctity (which he was able to guess at in the mirror of his virtuous actions), now it has all changed. Tidal waves of nonentity, of powerlessness, of hopelessness surge up within him at every action he attempts.

Then the shadow judges and hates the shadow who is not a god, and who can do absolutely nothing.

Self-contemplation leads to the most terrible despair: the despair of a god that hates himself to death. This is the ultimate perversion of man who was made in the image and likeness of the true God, who was made to love eternally and perfectly an infinite good—a good (note this well) which he was to find *dwelling within himself!*

In order to find God in ourselves, we must stop looking at ourselves, stop checking and verifying ourselves in the mirror of our own futility, and be content to *be* in Him and to do whatever He wills, according to our limitations, judging our acts not in the light of our own illusions, but in the light of His reality which is all around us in the things and people we live with.

All men seek peace first of all with themselves. That is necessary, because we do not naturally find rest even in our own being. We have to learn to commune with ourselves before we can communicate with other men and with God. A man who is not at peace with himself necessarily projects his interior fighting into the society of those he lives with, and spreads a contagion of conflict all around him. Even when he tries to do good to others his efforts are hopeless, since he does not know how to do good to himself. In moments of wildest idealism he may take it into his head to make other people happy: and in doing so he will overwhelm them with his own unhappiness. He seeks to find himself somehow in the work of making others happy. Therefore he throws himself into the work. As a result he gets out of the work all that he put into it: his own confusion, his own disintegration, his own unhappiness.

It is useless to try to make peace with ourselves by being pleased with everything we have done. In order to settle down in the quiet of our own being we must learn to be detached from the results of our own activity. We must withdraw ourselves, to some extent, from effects that are beyond our control and be content with the good will and the work that are the quiet expression of our inner life. We must be content to live without watching ourselves live, to work without expecting an immediate reward, to love without an instantaneous satisfaction, and to exist without any special recognition.

It is only when we are detached from ourselves that we can be at peace with ourselves. We cannot find happiness in our work if we are always extending ourselves beyond ourselves and beyond the sphere of our work in order to find ourselves greater than we are.

Our Christian destiny is, in fact, a great one: but we cannot achieve greatness unless we lose all interest in being great. For our own idea of greatness is illusory, and if we pay too much attention to it we will be lured out of the peace and stability of the being God gave us, and seek to live in a myth we have created for ourselves. It is, therefore, a very great thing to be little, which is to say: to be ourselves. And when we are truly ourselves we lose most of the futile self-consciousness that keeps us constantly comparing ourselves with others in order to see how big we are.

The fact that our being necessarily demands to be expressed in action should not lead us to believe that as soon as we stop acting we cease to exist. We do not live merely in order to "do something"—no matter what. Activity is just one of the normal expressions of life, and the life it expresses is all the more perfect when it sustains itself with an ordered economy of action. This order demands a wise alternation of activity and rest. We do not live more fully merely by doing more, seeing more, tasting more, and experiencing more than we ever have before. On the contrary, some of us need to discover that we will not begin to live more fully until we have the courage to do and see and taste and experience much less than usual.

A tourist may go through a museum with a Baedeker, looking conscientiously at everything important, and come out less alive than when he went in. He has looked at everything and seen nothing. He has done a great deal and it has only made him tired. If he had stopped for a moment to look at one picture he really liked and forgotten about all the others, he might console himself with the thought that he had not completely wasted his time. He would have discovered something not only outside himself but in himself. He would have become aware of a new level of being in himself and his life would have been increased by a new capacity for being and for doing.

Our being is not to be enriched merely by activity or experience as such. Everything depends on the *quality* of our acts and our experiences. A multitude of badly performed actions and of experiences only half-lived exhausts and depletes our being. By doing things badly we make ourselves less real. This growing unreality cannot help but make us unhappy and fill us with a sense of guilt. But the purity of our conscience has a natural proportion with the depth of our being and the quality of our acts: and when our activity is habitually disordered, our malformed conscience can think of nothing better to tell us than to multiply the *quantity* of our acts, without perfecting their quality. And so we go from bad to worse, exhaust ourselves, empty our whole life of all content, and fall into despair.

There are times, then, when in order to keep ourselves in existence at all we simply have to sit back for a while and do nothing. And for a man who has let himself be drawn completely out of himself by his activity, nothing is more difficult than to sit still and rest, doing nothing at all. The very act of resting is the hardest and most courageous act he can perform: and often it is quite beyond his power.

We must first recover the possession of our own being before we can act wisely or taste any experience in its human reality. As long as we are not in our own possession, all our activity is futile. If we let all our wine run out of the barrel and down the street, how will our thirst be quenched?

The value of our activity depends almost entirely on the humility to accept ourselves as we are. The reason why we do things so badly is that we are not content to do what we can.

We insist on doing what is not asked of us, because we want to taste the success that belongs to somebody else.

We never discover what it is like to make a success of our own work, because we do not want to undertake any work that is merely proportionate to our powers.

Who is willing to be satisfied with a job that expresses all his limitations? He will accept such work only as a "means of livelihood" while he waits to discover his "true vocation." The world is full of unsuccessful businessmen who still secretly believe they were meant to be artists or writers or actors in the movies.

The fruitfulness of our life depends in large measure on our ability to doubt our own words and to question the value of our own work. The man who completely trusts his own estimate of himself is doomed to sterility. All he asks of any act he performs is that it be *his* act. If it is performed by him, it must be good. All words spoken by him must be infallible. The car he has just bought is the best for its price, for no other reason than that he is the one who has bought it. He seeks no other fruit than this, and therefore he generally gets no other.

If we believe ourselves in part, we may be right about ourselves. If we are completely taken in by our own disguise, we cannot help being wrong.

The measure of our being is not to be sought in the violence of our experiences. Turbulence of spirit is a sign of spiritual weakness. When delights spring out of our depths like leopards we have nothing to be proud of: our soul's life is in danger. For when we are strong we are always much greater than the things that happen to us, and the soul of a man who has found himself is like a deep sea in which there may be many fish: but they never come up out of the sea, and not one of them is big enough to trouble its placid surface. His "being" is far greater than anything he feels or does.

The deep secrecy of my own being is often hidden from me by my own estimate of what I am. My idea of what I am is falsified by my admiration for what I do. And my illusions about myself are bred by contagion from the illusions of other men. We all seek to imitate one another's imagined greatness.

If I do not know who I am, it is because I think I am the sort of person everyone around me wants to be. Perhaps I have never asked myself whether I really wanted to become what everybody else seems to want to become. Perhaps if I only realized that I do not admire what everyone seems to admire, I would really begin to live after all. I would be liberated from the painful duty of saying what I really do not think and of acting in a way that betrays God's truth and the integrity of my own soul.

Why do we have to spend our lives striving to be something that we would never want to be, if we only knew what we wanted? Why do we waste our time doing things which, if we only stopped to think about them, are just the opposite of what we were made for?

We cannot be ourselves unless we know ourselves. But self-knowledge is impossible when thoughtless and automatic activity keeps our souls in confusion. In order to know ourselves it is not necessary to cease all activity in order to think about ourselves. That would be useless, and would probably do most of us a great deal of harm. But we have to cut down our activity to the point where we can think calmly and reasonably about our actions. We cannot begin to know ourselves until we can see the real reasons why we do the things we do, and we cannot be ourselves until our actions correspond to our intentions, and our intentions are appropriate to our own situation. But that is enough. It is not necessary that we succeed in everything. A man can be perfect and still reap no fruit from his work, and it may happen that a man who is able to accomplish very little is much more of a person than another who seems to accomplish very much.

A man who fails well is greater than one who succeeds badly.

One who is content with what he has, and who accepts the fact that he inevitably misses very much in life, is far better off than one who has much more but who worries about all he may be missing. For we cannot make the best of what we are, if our hearts are always divided between what we are and what we are not.

The lower our estimate of ourselves and the lower our expectations, the greater chance we have of using what we have. If we do not know how poor we are we will never be able to appreciate what we actually have. But, above all, we must learn our own weakness in order to awaken to a new order of action and of being—and experience God Himself accomplishing in us the things we find impossible.

We cannot be happy if we expect to live all the time at the highest peak of intensity. Happiness is not a matter of intensity but of balance and order and rhythm and harmony.

Music is pleasing not only because of the sound but because of the silence that is in it: without the alternation of sound and silence there would be no rhythm. If we strive to be happy by filling all the silences of life with sound, productive by turning all life's leisure into work, and real by turning all our being into doing, we will only succeed in producing a hell on earth.

If we have no silence, God is not heard in our music. If we have no rest, God does not bless our work. If we twist our lives out of shape in order to fill every corner of them with action and experience, God will silently withdraw from our hearts and leave us empty.

Let us, therefore, learn to pass from one imperfect activity to another without worrying too much about what we are missing. It is true that we make many mistakes. But the biggest of them all is to be surprised at them: as if we had some hope of never making any.

Mistakes are part of our life, and not the least important part. If we are humble, and if we believe in the Providence of God, we will see that our mistakes are not merely a necessary evil, something we must lament and count as lost: they enter into the very structure of our existence. It is by making mistakes that we gain experience, not only for ourselves but for others. And though our experience prevents neither ourselves nor others from making the same mistake many times, the repeated experience still has a positive value.

We cannot avoid missing the point of almost everything we do. But what of it? Life is not a matter of getting something out of everything. Life itself is imperfect. All created beings begin to die as soon as they begin to live, and no one expects any one of them to become absolutely perfect, still less to stay that way. Each individual thing is only a sketch of the specific perfection planned for its kind. Why should we ask it to be anything more?

If we are too anxious to find absolute perfection in created things we cease to look for perfection where alone it can be found: in God. The secret of the imperfection of all things, of their inconstancy, their fragility, their falling into nothingness, is that they are only a shadowy expression of the one Being from Whom they receive their being. If they were absolutely perfect and changeless in themselves, they would fail in their vocation, which is to give glory to God by their contingency.

It was the desire to "be as gods"—changelessly perfect in their own being—that led Adam and Eve to taste the fruit of the forbidden tree. What could be duller than an immutable man and an unchanging woman, eternally the same! As long as we are on earth our vocation is precisely to be imperfect, incomplete, insufficient in ourselves, changing, hapless, destitute, and weak, hastening toward the grave. But the power of God and His eternity and His peace and His completeness and His glory must somehow find their way into our lives, secretly, while we are here, in order that we may be found in Him eternally as He has meant us to be. And in Him, in our eternity, there will be no change in the sense of corruption, but there will be unending variety, newness of life, progression in His infinite depth. There, rest and action will not alternate, they will be one. Everything will be at once empty and full. But only if we have discovered how to combine emptiness and fullness, good will and indifferent results, mistakes and successes, work and rest, suffering and joy, in such a way that all things work together for our good and for the glory of God.

The relative perfection which we must attain to in this life if we are to live as sons of God is not the twenty-four-hour-a-day production of perfect acts of virtue, but a life from which practically all the obstacles to God's love have been removed or overcome.

One of the chief obstacles to this perfection of selfless charity is the selfish anxiety to get the most out of everything, to be a brilliant success in our own eyes and in the eyes of other men. We can only get rid of this anxiety by being content to miss something in almost everything we do. We cannot master everything, taste everything, understand everything, drain every experience to its last dregs. But if we have the courage to let almost everything else go, we will probably be able to retain the one thing necessary for us—whatever it may be. If we are too eager to have everything, we will almost certainly miss even the one thing we need.

Happiness consists in finding out precisely what the "one thing necessary" may be, in our lives, and in gladly relinquishing all the rest. For then, by a divine paradox, we find that everything else is given us together with the one thing we needed.

Francis Thompson

THE WAY OF IMPERFECTION

OVID, with the possible exception of Catullus, is the most modern-minded of Latin poets. It is therefore with delight that we first encounter his dictum, so essentially modern, so opposed to the aesthetic feeling of the ancient world, *decentiorem esse faciem in qua aliquis naevus esset.*[1] It was a dictum borne out by his own practice, a practice at heart essentially romantic rather than classic; and there can therefore be little wonder that the saying was scouted by his contemporaries as an eccentricity of genius. The dominant cult of classicism was the worship of perfection, and the Goth was its iconoclast. Then at length literature reposed in the beneficent and quickening shadow of imperfection, which gave us for consummate product Shakespeare, in whom greatness and imperfection reached their height. Since him, however, there has been a gradual decline from imperfection. Milton, at his most typical, was far too perfect; Pope was ruined by his quest for the quality; and if Dryden partially escaped, it was because of the rich faultiness with which Nature had endowed him. The stand made by the poets of the early part of this century was only temporarily successful; and now, we suppose, no thoughtful person can contemplate without alarm the hold which the renascent principle has gained over the contemporary mind. Unless some voice be raised in timely protest, we feel that English art (in its widest sense) must soon dwindle to the extinction of unendurable excellence.

The elementary truth of Ovid's maxim it is scarcely requisite to uphold. We have yet to see the perfect faces that are one half so attractive as the imperfect faces. Can any reader tolerate the novelistic heroine with the Greek features and the exquisitely chiselled nose? The hero invariably marries her instead of the other young lady (whose nose is perhaps a trifle *retroussé*),[2] in every respect more

1 [A mole, i.e., an imperfection, makes a face more comely.]
2 [Turned up.]

charming, who misses him simply through this essential note of a heroine.

Would, however, that the thing stopped here. This vicious taste for perfection is the fruitful parent of unnumbered evils. It is difficult to calculate the ravages caused by the insane passion. We will say this—that a man who once indulges in it never knows where he may end. At first, perhaps, he will content himself with spiritual perfection; but the fatal craving, once established, demands continually fresh gratification. He presently begins to find fault with Nature, and to desire an unimpeachably artistic house; insensibly he forms an addiction to the sonnet, and thence glides into the research of orbed perfection in his jokes; by degrees he even comes to admire the paintings of M. Bouguereau, and so to the final abomination of the camellia and the double dahlia. We would not be thought to denounce *ex cathedra* the wish for religious perfection. Abstractly it is harmless enough; but we should be careful how we allow ourselves even these innocent gratifications, they are often the first step on a course of unconscious declension which we shall regret all our after-lives. It is this which sometimes causes secular poets after a time to write distinctly inferior religious verse; under the impression, apparently, that secular poetry is an error of youth which must be expiated in maturity, and that only by direct consecration to religion can their art give glory to God. As if the flower could not give glory to God, until it abnegated its fragrance; as if the clouds of sunset could not give glory to God, until they had been passed through a bleaching-vat; as if the bird could not give glory to God, until it selected its airs from the diocesan hymnal! Over the whole contemporary mind is the trail of this serpent perfection. It even affects the realm of colour, where it begets cloying, enervating harmonies, destitute of those stimulating contrasts by which the great colourists threw into relief the general agreement of their hues. It leads in poetry to the love of miniature finish, and *that* in turn (because minute finish is most completely attainable in short poems) leads to the tyranny of sonnet, ballade, rondeau, triolet, and their kin. The principle leads again to aestheticism, which is simply the aspiration for a hot-house seclusion of beauty in a world which Nature has tempered by bracing gusts of ugliness. And yet again, by a peculiar refinement of perversity, it leads to the desire for perfect wives; though wherefore a man should desire a perfect wife it is indeed difficult to conceive—Why, he has to live with her! Now does any one seriously long to companion a "Treatise on Spiritual Perfection" bound in cloth—with the additional privilege of paying for the rebinding?

Returning to literature, however, let us consider more particularly the iniquity of this cult in generating the hero and heroine; who spring merely from the ambition to draw perfect characters—an ambition fatal to lifelike rendering. The most nobly conceived character in assuming *vraisemblance*[3] takes up a certain quantity of imperfection; it is its water of crystallization: expel this, and far from securing, as the artist fondly deems, a more perfect crystal, the character falls to powder. We by no means desire those improbable incongruities which, frequent enough in actual life, should in art be confined to comedy. But even incongruities may find their place in serious art, if they be artistic incongruities, not too glaring or suggestive of unlikelihood; incongruities which are felt by the reader to have a whimsical hidden keeping with the congruities of the character, which enhance the consent of the general qualities by an artistically modulated dissent; which just lend, and no more than lend, the ratifying seal of Nature to the dominating regularities of characterization. From the neglect of all this have come the hero and the heroine; and of these two the heroine is the worse. In most cases she is not a woman at all, but a male dream of a woman.

Among all prevalent types of heroine, *the* worst is one apparently founded on Pope's famous dictum,

> Most women have no characters at all—

a dictum which we should denounce with scorn, if so acute an observer as De Quincey did not stagger us by defending it. He defends it to attack Pope. Pope (says De Quincey) did not see that what he advances as a reproach against women constitutes the very beauty of them. It is the absence of any definite character which enables their character to be moulded by others; and it is this soft plasticity which renders them such charming companions as wives. It may be so. And it may be paradisaical bliss to have a wife whom you can cut out on a paper pattern. Personally, we should prefer to keep a dog; it would be less expensive. But possibly all these things are so; and we address our remarks to De Quincey, therefore, with diffidence. Nor do we mean them to have more than a generic application: we are by no means of that influential class who think that the Almighty creates men, but makes women—as they make sausages. Still, we are inclined to fancy that you take outward pliability and the absence of imperiousness for lack of essential character. Now to execute your determination by command you must have a position of command; the lever requires a fulcrum. Without this position you must either maintain an isolated, futile obstinacy, or be content to sway not by bending, but by manipulating, the will of others. It is, we think, the

3 [Probability.]

pleasanter way, and we are not sure that it is the less effectual way. Partly by nature, partly by the accumulative influence of heredity, partly perhaps by training, it is the way which instinctively commends itself to most women. But because in the majority of cases they accommodate themselves to male character and eschew direct opposition, it by no means follows, if our view be correct, that they forgo their own character. You might as well accuse the late Lord Beaconsfield of being wanting in character, because instead of hurling his ideas against an unstormable opposition he tactfully and patiently insinuated them. We should be inclined to say that the feminine characteristic which De Quincey considered plasticity was rather elasticity. Now the most elastic substance in Nature is probably ivory. What are the odds, you subtle, paradoxical, delightful ghost of delicate thought, what *are* the odds on your moulding a billiard ball? Watching the other day an insect which betrayed a scientific curiosity with regard to our lower extremities, we signified to it our inhospitable disposition by poking it with a stick. Never did we see such a plastic insect. Curling up into a little black-brown pellet, it lay so motionless that we thought it dead; but in a few moments it slowly uncurled, and after a period of cautious delay resumed its advance. Four times was this repeated, and on each occasion the advance was resumed as if never resisted. Then patience gave way. The insect was sent rolling into a little hole, where it lay curled up as before. For twenty minutes by the clock it remained still as death. Death, indeed, we thought had this time certainly overtaken it, and with a passing regret for our thoughtlessness we forgot the tiny being in thought. Tenderer were its recollections of us. When we awoke to consciousness it had resumed its crawling. If this be plasticity, then many women *are* plastic—very plastic.

An embodiment—or enshadowment—of the villainous saying which De Quincey thus approves, is that favourite creation of fiction which finds its most recognizable (because extremest) expression in Patient Grizzel and the Nut-brown Maid. Does any one believe in Patient Grizzel? Still more, does any one believe in the Nut-brown Maid? Their descendants infest literature, from Spenser to Dickens and Tennyson, from Una to Enid; made tolerable in the poem only by their ideal surroundings. The dream of "a perfect woman nobly planned" underlies the thing; albeit Wordsworth goes on to show that his "perfect woman" had her little failings. Shakespeare was not afraid to touch with such failings his finest heroines; he knew that these defects serve only to enhance the large nobilities of character, as the tender imperfections and wayward wilfulnesses of individual rose-petals enhance the prevalent symmetry of the rose. His most consummate woman, Imogen, possesses her little naturalizing traits.

Take the situation where she is confronted with her husband's order for her murder. What the Patient Grizzel heroine would have done we all know. She would have behaved with unimpeachable resignation, and prepared for death with a pathos ordered according to the best canons of art. What does this glorious Imogen do? Why (and we publicly thank Heaven for it), after the first paroxysm of weeping, which makes the blank verse sob, she bursts into a fit of thoroughly feminine and altogether charming jealousy. A perfect woman indeed, for she is imperfect! Imogen, however, it may be urged, is not a Patient Grizzel. Take, then, Desdemona, who is. That is to say, Desdemona represents the type in nature which Patient Grizzel misrepresents. Mark now the difference in treatment. Shakespeare knew that these gentle, affectionate, yielding, all-submissive and all-suffering dispositions are founded on weakness, and accordingly he gave Desdemona the defects of her qualities. He would have no perfection in *his* characters. Rather than face the anger of the man whom she so passionately loves, Desdemona will lie—a slight lie, but one to which the ideal distortion of her would never be allowed to yield. Yet the weakness but makes Shakespeare's lady more credible, more piteous, perhaps even more lovable, because more human. And Shakespeare's knowledge is borne out by the experience of those best qualified to speak. Woman is not, as a Shakespearian maxim belied by Shakespearian practice asserts, "a dish for the gods and the devil dress her not." She is a dish for men, and if she be imperfect the devil has little to do with it. Indeed we are sorry that Shakespeare stooped to this kind of thing. He might have left it to inferior men.

From the later developments of contemporary fiction the faultless hero and heroine have, we admit, relievingly disappeared. So much good has been wrought by the craze for "human documents." But alas! the disease expelled, who will expel the medicine? And the hydra perfection merely shoots up a new head. It is now a desire for the perfect reproduction of Nature, uninterfered with by the writer's ideals or sympathies; so that we have novelists who stand coldly aloof from their characters, and exhibit them with passionless countenance.[4] We all admire the representations which result: "How beautifully drawn! How exactly like Nature!" Yes, beautifully drawn; but they do not live. They resemble the mask in "Phaedrus" —a cunning semblance, *at animam non habet*.[5] The attitude of the novelist is fatal to artistic illusion: his personages do not move us because they do not move him. Partridge believed in the ghost because "the little man on the stage was more frightened than I"; and

4 We will not shield ourselves under generalities. We refer especially to Mr. Henry James.

5 [But it does not have a soul.]

in novel-reading we are all Partridges, we only believe in the novelist's creations when he shows us that he believes in them himself. Finally, this pestilence attacks in literature the form no less than the essence, the integuments even more than the vitals. Hence arises the dominant belief that mannerism is vicious; and accordingly critics have erected the ideal of a style stripped of everything special or peculiar, a style which should be to thought what light is to the sun. Now this pure white light of style is as impossible as undesirable; it *must* be splintered into colour by the refracting media of the individual mind, and humanity will always prefer the colour. Theoretically we ought to have no mannerisms; practically we cannot help having them, and without them style would be flavourless—"faultily faultless, icily regular, splendidly null." No man will drink distilled water; it is entirely pure and entirely insipid. The object of writing is to communicate individuality, the object of style to adequately embody that individuality; and since in every individuality worth anything there are characteristic peculiarities, these must needs be reproduced in the embodiment. So reproduced we call them mannerisms. They correspond to those little unconscious tricks of voice, manner, gesture in a friend which are to us the friend himself, and which we would not forgo. Conscious tricks of habit, it is true, a person must avoid, because they become exaggerations; similarly, conscious mannerisms must be pruned, lest *they* become exaggerations. It is affected to imitate another's tricks of demeanour: similarly, it is affected to imitate another's mannerisms. We should avoid as far as possible in conversation passing conventionalities of speech, because they are brainless; similarly, we should avoid as far as possible in writing the mannerisms of our age, because they corrupt originality. But in essence, mannerisms—individual mannerisms, are a season of style, and happily unavoidable. It is, for instance, stated in the lately completed *Encyclopaedia Britannica* that De Quincey is not a manneristic writer; and so put the assertion has much truth. Yet he is full of mannerisms, mannerisms which every student lovingly knows, and without which the essayist would not be our very own De Quincey.

We say, therefore: Be on your guard against this seductive principle of perfection. Order yourselves to a wise conformity with that Nature who cannot for the life of her create a brain without making one half of it weaker than the other half, or even a fool without a flaw in his folly; who cannot set a nose straight on a man's face, and whose geometrical drawing would be tittered at by half the young ladies of South Kensington. Consider who is the standing modern oracle of perfection, and what resulted from *his* interpretation of it. "Trifles make perfection, and perfection is no trifle." No; it is half a pound of muscle to the square inch—and *that* is no trifle. One satisfactory reflection we have in concluding. Wherever else the reader may be grieved by perfection, this article, at least, is sacred from the accursed thing.

Now, how much of all this do we mean?

Hearken, O reader, to an apologue. Once on a time there was a hypochondriac, who—though his digestion was excellent—believed that his delicate system required a most winnowed choice of viands. His physician, in order to humour him, prescribed a light and carefully varied diet. But the hypochondriac was not satisfied.

"I want to know, doctor," he said, "how much of this food really contributes to the building up of my system, and how much is waste material?"

"That," observed the sage physician, "I cannot possibly tell you without recondite analysis and nice calculation."

"Then," said the hypochondriac, in a rage, "I will not eat your food. You are an impostor, sir, and a charlatan, and I believe now your friends who told me that you were a homoeopath in disguise."

"My dear sir," replied the unmoved physician, "if you will eat nothing but what is entire nutriment, you will soon need to consult, not a doctor, but a chameleon. To what purpose are your digestive organs, unless to secrete what is nutritious, and excrete what is innutritious?"

And the moral is—no. On second thoughts our readers shall have a pleasure denied to them in their outraged childhood. They shall draw the moral themselves. He that hath understanding, let him understand.

STORIES

Nathaniel Hawthorne

ETHAN BRAND

A Chapter from an Abortive Romance

Bartram the lime-burner, a rough, heavy-looking man, begrimed with charcoal, sat watching his kiln at nightfall, while his little son played at building houses with the scattered fragments of marble, when, on the hill-side below them, they heard a roar of laughter, not mirthful, but slow, and even solemn, like a wind shaking the boughs of the forest.

"Father, what is that?" asked the little boy, leaving his play, and pressing betwixt his father's knees.

"Oh, some drunken man, I suppose," answered the lime-burner; "some merry fellow from the barroom in the village, who dared not laugh loud enough within doors lest he should blow the roof of the house off. So here he is, shaking his jolly sides at the foot of Graylock."

"But, father," said the child, more sensitive than the obtuse, middle-aged clown, "he does not laugh like a man that is glad. So the noise frightens me!"

"Don't be a fool, child!" cried his father, gruffly. "You will never make a man, I do believe; there is too much of your mother in you. I have known the rustling of a leaf startle you. Hark! Here comes the merry fellow now. You shall see that there is no harm in him."

Bartram and his little son, while they were talking thus, sat watching the same lime-kiln that had been the scene of Ethan Brand's solitary and meditative life, before he began his search for the Unpardonable Sin. Many years, as we have seen, had now elapsed, since that portentous night when the Idea was first developed. The kiln, however, on the mountain-side, stood unimpaired, and was in nothing changed since he had thrown his dark thoughts into the intense glow of its furnace, and melted them, as it were, into the one thought that took possession of his life. It was a rude, round, tower-like structure about twenty feet high, heavily built of rough stones, and with a hillock of earth heaped about the larger part of its circumference; so that the blocks and fragments of marble might be drawn by cartloads, and thrown in at the top. There was an opening at the bottom of the tower, like an oven-mouth, but large enough to admit a man in a stooping posture, and provided with a massive iron door. With the smoke and jets of flame issuing from the chinks and crevices of this door, which seemed to give admittance into the hill-side, it resembled nothing so much as the private entrance to the infernal regions, which the shepherds of the Delectable Mountains were accustomed to show to pilgrims.

There are many such lime-kilns in that tract of country, for the purpose of burning the white marble which composes a large part of the substance of the hills. Some of them, built years ago, and long deserted, with weeds growing in the vacant round of the interior, which is open to the sky, and grass and wildflowers rooting themselves into the chinks of the stones, look already like relics of antiquity, and may yet be overspread with the lichens of centuries to come. Others, where the lime-burner still feeds his daily and night-long fire, afford points of interest to the wanderer among the hills, who seats himself on a log of wood or a fragment of marble, to hold a chat with the solitary man. It is a lonesome, and, when the character is inclined to thought, may be an intensely thoughtful occupation; as it proved in the case of Ethan Brand, who had mused to such strange purpose, in days gone by, while the fire in this very kiln was burning.

The man who now watched the fire was of a different order, and troubled himself with no thoughts save the very few that were requisite to his business. At frequent intervals, he flung back the clashing weight of the iron door, and, turning his face from the insufferable glare, thrust in huge logs of oak, or stirred the immense brands with a long pole. Within the furnace were seen the curling and riotous flames, and the burning marble, almost molten with the intensity of heat; while without, the reflection of the fire quivered on the dark intricacy of the surrounding forest, and showed in the foreground a bright and ruddy little picture of the hut, the spring beside its door, the athletic and coal-begrimed figure of the lime-burner, and the half-frightened child, shrinking into the protection of his father's shadow. And when, again, the iron door was closed, then reappeared the tender light of the half-full moon, which vainly strove to trace out the indistinct shapes of the neighboring mountains; and, in the upper sky, there was a flitting congregation of clouds, still faintly tinged with the rosy sunset, though thus far down into the valley the sunshine had vanished long and long ago.

The little boy now crept still closer to his father, as footsteps were heard ascending the hillside, and a human form thrust aside the bushes that clustered beneath the trees.

"Halloo! who is it?" cried the lime-burner, vexed at his son's timidity, yet half infected by it. "Come forward, and show yourself, like a man, or I'll fling this chunk of marble at your head!"

"You offer me a rough welcome," said a gloomy voice, as the unknown man drew nigh. "Yet I neither claim nor desire a kinder one, even at my own fireside."

To obtain a distincter view, Bartram threw open the iron door of the kiln, whence immediately issued a gush of fierce light, that smote full upon the stranger's face and figure. To a careless eye there appeared nothing very remarkable in his aspect, which was that of a man in a coarse, brown, country-made suit of clothes, tall and thin, with the staff and heavy shoes of a wayfarer. As he advanced, he fixed his eyes—which were very bright—intently upon the brightness of the furnace, as if he beheld, or expected to behold, some object worthy of note within it.

"Good evening, stranger," said the lime-burner; "whence come you, so late in the day?"

"I come from my search," answered the wayfarer; "for, at last, it is finished."

"Drunk!—or crazy!" muttered Bartram to himself. "I shall have trouble with the fellow. The sooner I drive him away, the better."

The little boy, all in a tremble, whispered to his father, and begged him to shut the door of the kiln, so that there might not be so much light; for that there was something in the man's face which he was afraid to look at, yet could not look away from. And, indeed, even the lime-burner's dull and torpid sense began to be impressed by an indescribable something in that thin, rugged, thoughtful visage, with the grizzled hair hanging wildly about it, and those deeply sunken eyes, which gleamed like fires within the entrance of a mysterious cavern. But, as he closed the door, the stranger turned towards him, and spoke in a quiet, familiar way, that made Bartram feel as if he were a sane and sensible man, after all.

"Your task draws to an end, I see," said he. "This marble has already been burning three days. A few hours more will convert the stone to lime."

"Why, who are you?" exclaimed the lime-burner. "You seem as well acquainted with my business as I am myself."

"And well I may be," said the stranger; "for I followed the same craft many a long year, and here, too, on this very spot. But you are a newcomer in these parts. Did you never hear of Ethan Brand?"

"The man that went in search of the Unpardonable Sin?" asked Bartram, with a laugh.

"The same," answered the stranger. "He has found what he sought, and therefore he comes back again."

"What! then you are Ethan Brand himself?" cried the lime-burner, in amazement. "I am a newcomer here, as you say, and they call it eighteen years since you left the foot of Graylock. But, I can tell you, the good folks still talk about Ethan Brand, in the village yonder, and what a strange errand took him away from his lime-kiln. Well, and so you have found the Unpardonable Sin?"

"Even so!" said the stranger, calmly.

"If the question is a fair one," proceeded Bartram, "where might it be?"

Ethan Brand laid his finger on his own heart.

"Here!" replied he.

And then, without mirth in his countenance, but as if moved by an involuntary recognition of the infinite absurdity of seeking throughout the world for what was the closest of all things to himself, and looking into every heart, save his own, for what was hidden in no other breast, he broke into a laugh of scorn. It was the same slow, heavy laugh, that had almost appalled the lime-burner when it heralded the wayfarer's approach.

The solitary mountain-side was made dismal by it. Laughter, when out of place, mistimed, or bursting forth from a disordered state of feeling, may be the most terrible modulation of the human voice. The laughter of one asleep, even if it be a little child,—the madman's laugh,—the wild, screaming laugh of a born idiot,—are sounds that we sometimes tremble to hear, and would always willingly forget. Poets have imagined no utterance of fiends or hobgoblins so fearfully appropriate as a laugh. And even the obtuse lime-burner felt his nerves shaken, as this strange man looked inward at his own heart, and burst into laughter that rolled away into the night, and was indistinctly reverberated among the hills.

"Joe," said he to his little son, "scamper down to the tavern in the village, and tell the jolly fellows there that Ethan Brand has come back, and that he has found the Unpardonable Sin!"

The boy darted away on his errand, to which Ethan Brand made no objection, nor seemed hardly to notice it. He sat on a log of wood, looking steadfastly at the iron door of the kiln. When the child was out of sight, and his swift and light footsteps ceased to be heard treading first on the fallen leaves and then on the rocky mountain-path, the lime-burner began to regret his departure. He felt that the little fellow's presence had been a barrier between his guest and himself, and that he must now deal, heart to heart, with a man who, on his own confession, had committed the one only crime for which Heaven could afford no mercy. That crime, in its indistinct blackness, seemed to overshadow him. The lime-burner's own sins rose up within him, and made his memory riotous with a throng of evil shapes that asserted their kindred with the Master Sin, whatever it might be, which it was within the scope of man's corrupted nature to conceive and cherish. They were all of one family; they went to and fro between his breast and Ethan Brand's, and carried dark greetings from one to the other.

Then Bartram remembered the stories which had grown traditionally in reference to this strange man, who had come upon him like a shadow of the night, and was making himself at home in his old place, after so long absence, that the dead people, dead and buried for years, would have had more right to be at home, in any familiar spot, than he. Ethan Brand, it was said, had conversed with Satan himself in the lurid blaze of this very kiln. The legend had been matter of mirth heretofore, but looked grisly now. According to this tale, before Ethan Brand departed on his search, he had been accustomed to evoke a fiend from the hot furnace of the lime-kiln, night after night, in order to confer with him about the Unpardonable Sin; the man and the fiend each laboring to frame the image of some mode of guilt which could neither be atoned for nor forgiven. And, with the first gleam of light upon the mountain-top, the fiend crept in at the iron door, there to abide the intensest element of fire until again summoned forth to share in the dreadful task of extending man's possible guilt beyond the scope of Heaven's else infinite mercy.

While the lime-burner was struggling with the horror of these thoughts, Ethan Brand rose from the log, and flung open the door of the kiln. The action was in such accordance with the idea in Bartram's mind, that he almost expected to see the Evil One issue forth, red-hot, from the raging furnace.

"Hold! hold!" cried he, with a tremulous attempt to laugh; for he was ashamed of his fears, although they overmastered him. "Don't, for mercy's sake, bring out your Devil now!"

"Man!" sternly replied Ethan Brand, "what need have I of the Devil? I have left him behind me, on my track. It is with such half-way sinners as you that he busies himself. Fear not, because I open the door, I do but act by old custom, and am going to trim your fire, like a lime-burner, as I was once."

He stirred the vast coals, thrust in more wood, and bent forward to gaze into the hollow prison-house of the fire, regardless of the fierce glow that reddened upon his face. The lime-burner sat watching him, and half suspected this strange guest of a purpose, if not to evoke a fiend, at least to plunge bodily into the flames, and thus vanish from the sight of man. Ethan Brand, however, drew quietly back, and closed the door of the kiln.

"I have looked," said he, "into many a human heart that was seven times hotter with sinful passions than yonder furnace is with fire. But I found not there what I sought. No, not the Unpardonable Sin!"

"What is the Unpardonable Sin?" asked the lime-burner; and then he shrank farther from his companion, trembling lest his question should be answered.

"It is a sin that grew within my own breast," replied Ethan Brand, standing erect, with a pride that distinguishes all enthusiasts of his stamp. "A sin that grew nowhere else! The sin of an intellect that triumphed over the sense of brotherhood with man and reverence for God, and sacrificed everything to its own mighty claims! The only sin that deserves a recompense of immortal agony! Freely, were it to do again, would I incur the guilt. Unshrinkingly I accept the retribution!"

"The man's head is turned," muttered the lime-burner to himself. "He may be a sinner like the rest of us,—nothing more likely,—but, I'll be sworn, he is a madman too."

Nevertheless, he felt uncomfortable at his situation, alone with Ethan Brand on the wild mountain-side, and was right glad to hear the rough murmur of tongues, and the footsteps of what seemed a pretty numerous party, stumbling over the stones and rustling through the underbrush. Soon appeared the whole lazy regiment that was wont to infest the village tavern, comprehending three or four individuals who had drunk flip beside the bar-room fire through all the winters, and smoked their pipes beneath the stoop through all the summers, since Ethan Brand's departure. Laughing boisterously, and mingling all their voices together in unceremonious talk, they now burst into the moonshine and narrow streaks of firelight that illuminated the open space before the lime-kiln. Bartram set the door ajar again, flooding the spot with light, that the whole company might get a fair view of Ethan Brand, and he of them.

There, among other old acquaintances, was a once ubiquitous man, now almost extinct, but whom we were formerly sure to encounter at the hotel of every thriving village throughout the country. It was the stage-agent. The present specimen of the genus was a wilted and smoke-dried man, wrinkled and red-nosed, in a smartly cut, brown, bobtailed coat, with brass buttons, who, for a length of time unknown, had kept his desk and corner in the bar-room, and was still puffing what seemed to be the same cigar that he had lighted twenty years before. He had great fame as a dry joker, though, perhaps, less on account of any intrinsic humor than from a certain flavor of brandy-toddy and tobacco-smoke, which impregnated all his ideas and expressions, as well as his person. Another well-remembered, though strangely altered, face was that of Lawyer Giles, as people still called him in courtesy; an elderly ragamuffin, in his soiled shirt-sleeves and tow-cloth trousers. This poor fellow had been an attorney, in what he called his better days, a sharp practitioner, and in great vogue among the village litigants; but flip, and sling, and toddy, and cocktails, imbibed at all hours, morning, noon, and night, had caused him to slide from intellectual to various kinds and degrees of bodily labor, till at last, to adopt his own phrase, he slid into a soap-vat. In other words, Giles was now a soap-boiler, in a small way. He had come to be but the fragment of a human being, a part of one foot having been chopped off by an axe, and an entire hand torn away by the devilish grip of a steam-engine. Yet, though the corporeal hand was gone, a spiritual member remained; for, stretching forth the stump, Giles steadfastly averred that he felt an invisible thumb and fingers with as vivid a sensation as before the real ones were amputated. A maimed and miserable wretch he was; but one, nevertheless, whom the world could not trample on, and had no right to scorn, either in this or any previous stage of his misfortunes, since he had still kept up the courage and spirit of a man, asked nothing in charity, and with his one hand—and that the left one—fought a stern battle against want and hostile circumstances.

Among the throng, too, came another personage, who, with certain points of similarity to Lawyer Giles, had many more of difference. It was the village doctor; a man of some fifty years, whom, at an earlier period of his life, we introduced as paying a professional visit to Ethan Brand during the latter's supposed insanity. He was now a purple-visaged, rude, and brutal, yet half-gentlemanly figure, with something wild, ruined, and desperate in his talk, and in all the details of his gesture and manners. Brandy possessed this man like an evil spirit, and made him as surly and savage as a wild beast, and as miserable as a lost soul; but there was supposed to be in him such wonderful skill, such native gifts of healing, beyond any which medical science could impart, that society caught hold of him, and would not let him sink out of its reach. So, swaying to and fro upon his horse, and grumbling thick accents at the bedside, he visited all the sick-chambers for miles about among the mountain towns, and sometimes raised a dying man, as it were, by miracle, or quite as often, no doubt, sent his patient to a grave that was dug many a year too soon. The doctor had an everlasting pipe in his mouth, and, as somebody said, in allusion to his habit of swearing, it was always alight with hell-fire.

These three worthies pressed forward, and greeted Ethan Brand each after his own fashion, earnestly inviting him to partake of the contents of a certain black bottle, in which, as they averred, he would find something far better worth seeking for than the Unpardonable Sin. No mind, which has wrought itself by intense and solitary meditation into a high state of enthusiasm, can endure the kind of contact with low and vulgar modes of thought and feeling to which Ethan Brand was now subjected. It made him doubt—and, strange to say, it was a painful doubt—whether he had indeed found the Unpardonable Sin, and found it within himself. The whole question on which he had exhausted life, and more than life, looked like a delusion.

"Leave me," he said bitterly, "ye brute beasts, that have made yourselves so, shrivelling up your souls with fiery liquors! I have done with you. Years and years ago, I groped into your hearts and found nothing there for my purpose. Get ye gone!"

"Why, you uncivil scoundrel," cried the fierce doctor, "is that the way you respond to the kindness of your best friends? Then let me tell you the truth. You have no more found the Unpardonable Sin than yonder boy Joe has. You are but a crazy fellow,—I told you so twenty years ago,—neither better nor worse than a crazy fellow, and the fit companion of old Humphrey, here!"

He pointed to an old man, shabbily dressed, with long white hair, thin visage, and unsteady eyes. For some years past this aged person had been wandering about among the hills, inquiring of all travellers whom he met for his daughter. The girl, it seemed, had gone off with a company of circus-performers, and occasionally tidings of her came to the village, and fine stories were told of her glittering appearance as she rode on horseback in the ring, or performed marvellous feats on the tightrope.

The white-haired father now approached Ethan Brand, and gazed unsteadily into his face.

"They tell me you have been all over the earth," said he, wringing his hands with earnestness. "You must have seen my daughter, for she makes a grand figure in the world, and everybody goes to see her. Did she send any word to her old father, or say when she was coming back?"

Ethan Brand's eye quailed beneath the old man's. That daughter, from whom he so earnestly desired a word of greeting, was the Esther of our tale, the very girl whom, with such cold and remorseless purpose, Ethan Brand had made the subject of a psychological experiment, and wasted, absorbed, and perhaps annihilated her soul, in the process.

"Yes," murmured he, turning away from the hoary wanderer, "it is no delusion. There is an Unpardonable Sin!"

While these things were passing, a merry scene was going forward in the area of cheerful light, beside the spring and before the door of the hut. A number of the youth of the village, young men and girls, had hurried up the hill-side, impelled by curiosity to see Ethan Brand, the hero of so many a legend familiar to their childhood. Finding nothing, however, very remarkable in his aspect,—nothing but a sunburnt wayfarer, in plain garb and dusty shoes, who sat looking into the fire as if he fancied pictures among the coals,—these young people speedily grew tired of observing him. As it happened, there was other amusement at hand. An old German Jew travelling with a diorama on his back, was passing down the mountain-road towards the village just as the party turned aside from it, and, in hopes of eking out the profits of the day, the showman had kept them company to the lime-kiln.

"Come, old Dutchman," cried one of the young men, "let us see your pictures, if you can swear they are worth looking at!"

"Oh yes, Captain," answered the Jew,—whether as a matter of courtesy or craft, he styled everybody Captain,—"I shall show you, indeed, some very superb pictures!"

So, placing his box in a proper position, he invited the young men and girls to look through the glass orifices of the machine, and proceeded to exhibit a series of the most outrageous scratchings and daubings, as specimens of the fine arts, that ever an itinerant showman had the face to impose upon his circle of spectators. The pictures were worn out, moreover, tattered, full of cracks and wrinkles, dingy with tobacco-smoke, and otherwise in a most pitiable condition. Some purported to be cities, public edifices, and ruined castles in Europe; others represented Napoleon's battles and Nelson's sea-fights; and in the midst of these would be seen a gigantic, brown, hairy hand,—which might have been mistaken for the Hand of Destiny, though, in truth, it was only the showman's,—pointing its forefinger to various scenes of the conflict, while its owner gave historical illustrations. When, with much merriment at its abominable deficiency of merit, the exhibition was concluded, the German bade little Joe put his head into the box. Viewed through the magnifying-glasses, the boy's round, rosy visage assumed the strangest imaginable aspect of an immense Titanic child, the mouth grinning broadly, and the eyes and every other feature overflowing with fun at the joke. Suddenly, however, that merry face turned pale, and its expression changed to horror, for this easily impressed and excitable child had become sensible that the eye of Ethan Brand was fixed upon him through the glass.

"You make the little man to be afraid, Captain," said the German Jew, turning up the dark and strong outline of his visage from his stooping posture. "But look again, and, by chance, I shall cause you to see somewhat that is very fine, upon my word!"

Ethan Brand gazed into the box for an instant, and then starting back, looked fixedly at the German. What had he seen? Nothing, apparently; for a curious youth, who had peeked in almost at the same moment, beheld only a vacant space of canvas.

"I remember you now," muttered Ethan Brand to the showman.

"Ah, Captain," whispered the Jew of Nuremburg, with a dark smile, "I find it to be a heavy matter in my show-box,—this Unpardonable Sin! By my faith, Captain, it has wearied my shoulders, this long day, to carry it over the mountain."

"Peace," answered Ethan Brand, sternly, "or get thee into the furnace yonder!"

The Jew's exhibition had scarcely concluded, when a great, elderly dog—who seemed to be his own master, as no person in the company laid claim to him—saw fit to render himself the object of public notice. Hitherto, he had shown himself a very quiet, well-disposed old dog, going round from one to another, and, by way of being sociable, offering his rough head to be patted by any kindly hand that would take so much trouble. But now, all of a sudden, this grave and venerable quadruped, of his own mere motion, and without the slightest suggestion from anybody else, began to run round after his tail, which, to heighten the absurdity of the proceeding, was a great deal shorter than it should have been. Never was seen such headlong eagerness in pursuit of an object that could not possibly be attained; never was heard such a tremendous outbreak of growling, snarling, barking, and snapping,—as if one end of the ridiculous brute's body were at deadly and most unforgivable enmity with the other. Faster and faster, round about went the cur; and faster and still faster fled the unapproachable brevity of his tail; and louder and fiercer grew his yells of rage and animosity; until, utterly exhausted, and as far from the goal as ever, the foolish old dog ceased his performance as suddenly as he had begun it. The next moment he was as mild, quiet, sensible, and respectable in his deportment, as when he first scraped acquaintance with the company.

As may be supposed, the exhibition was greeted with universal laughter, clapping of hands, and shouts of encore, to which the canine performer responded by wagging all that there was to wag of his tail, but appeared totally unable to repeat his very successful effort to amuse the spectators.

Meanwhile, Ethan Brand had resumed his seat upon the log, and moved, it might be, by a perception of some remote analogy between his own case and that of this self-pursuing cur, he broke into the awful laugh, which, more than any other token, expressed the condition of his inward being. From that moment, the merriment of the party was at an end; they stood aghast, dreading lest the inauspicious sound should be reverberated around the horizon, and that mountain would thunder it to mountain, and so the horror be prolonged upon their ears. Then, whispering one to another that it was late,—that the moon was almost down,—that the August night was growing chill,—they hurried homewards, leaving the lime-burner and little Joe to deal as they might with their unwelcome guest. Save for these three human beings, the open space on the hill-side was a solitude, set in a vast gloom of forest. Beyond that darksome verge, the firelight glimmered on the stately trunks and almost black foliage of pines, intermixed with the lighter verdure of sapling oaks, maples, and poplars, while here and there lay the gigantic corpses of dead trees, decaying on the leaf-strewn soil. And it seemed to little Joe—a timorous and imaginative child—that the silent forest was holding its breath until some fearful thing should happen.

Ethan Brand thrust more wood into the fire, and closed the door of the kiln, then looking over his shoulder at the lime-burner and his son, he bade, rather than advised, them to retire to rest.

"For myself, I cannot sleep," said he. "I have matters that it concerns me to meditate upon. I will watch the fire, as I used to do in the old time."

"And call the Devil out of the furnace to keep you company, I suppose," muttered Bartram, who had been making intimate acquaintance with the black bottle above mentioned. "But watch, if you like, and call as many devils as you like! For my part, I shall be all the better for a snooze. Come, Joe!"

As the boy followed his father into the hut, he looked back at the wayfarer, and the tears came into his eyes, for his tender spirit had an intuition of the bleak and terrible loneliness in which this man had enveloped himself.

When they had gone, Ethan Brand sat listening to the crackling of the kindled wood, and looking at the little spirits of fire that issued through the chinks of the door. These trifles, however, once so familiar, had but the slightest hold of his attention, while deep within his mind he was reviewing the gradual but marvellous change that had been wrought upon him by the search to which he had devoted himself. He remembered how the night dew had fallen upon him,—how the dark forest had whispered to him,—how the stars had gleamed upon him,—a simple and loving man, watching his fire in the years gone by, and ever musing as it burned. He remembered with what tenderness, with what love and sympathy for mankind, and what pity for human guilt and woe, he had first begun to contemplate those ideas which afterwards became the inspiration of his life; with what reverence he had then looked into the heart of man, viewing it as a temple originally divine, and, however desecrated, still to be held sacred by a brother; with what awful fear he had deprecated the success of his pursuit, and prayed that the Unpardonable Sin might never be revealed to him. Then ensued that vast intellectual development, which, in its progress, disturbed the counterpoise between his mind and heart. The Idea that possessed his life had operated as a means of education; it had gone on cultivating his powers to the highest point of which they were susceptible; it had raised him from the level of an unlettered laborer to stand on a starlit eminence, whither the philosophers of the earth, laden with the lore of universities, might vainly strive to clamber after him. So much for the intellect! But where was the heart? That, indeed, had withered, —had contracted,—had hardened,—had perished! It had ceased to partake of the universal throb. He had lost his hold of the magnetic chain of humanity. He was no longer a brother-man, opening the chambers or the dungeons of our common nature by the key of holy sympathy, which gave him a right to share in all its secrets; he was now a cold observer, looking on mankind as the subject of his experiment, and, at length, converting man and woman to be his puppets, and pulling the wires that moved them to such degrees of crime as were demanded for his study.

Thus Ethan Brand became a fiend. He began to be so from the moment that his moral nature had ceased to keep the pace of improvement with his intellect. And now, as his highest effort and inevitable development,—as the bright and gorgeous flower, and rich, delicious fruit of his life's labor,—he had produced the Unpardonable Sin!

"What more have I to seek? what more to achieve?" said Ethan Brand to himself. "My task is done, and well done!"

Starting from the log with a certain alacrity in his gait and ascending the hillock of earth that was raised against the stone circumference of the lime-kiln, he thus reached the top of the structure. It was a space of perhaps ten feet across, from edge to edge, presenting a view of the upper surface of the immense mass of broken marble with which the kiln was heaped. All these innumerable blocks and fragments of marble were red-hot and vividly on fire, sending up great spouts of blue flame, which quivered aloft and danced madly, as within a magic circle, and sank and rose again, with continual and multitudinous activity. As the lonely man bent forward over this terrible body of fire, the blasting heat smote up against his person with a breath that, it might be supposed, would have scorched and shrivelled him up in a moment.

Ethan Brand stood erect, and raised his arms on high. The blue flames played upon his face, and imparted the wild and ghastly light which alone could have suited its expression; it was that of a fiend on the verge of plunging into his gulf of intensest torment.

"O Mother Earth," cried he, "who art no more my Mother, and into whose bosom this frame shall never be resolved! O mankind, whose brotherhood I have cast off, and trampled thy great heart beneath my feet! O stars of heaven, that shone on me of old, as if to light me onward and upward!—farewell all, and forever. Come, deadly element of Fire,—henceforth my familiar friend! Embrace me, as I do thee!"

That night the sound of a fearful peal of laughter rolled heavily through the sleep of the lime-burner and his little son; dim shapes of horror and anguish haunted their dreams, and seemed still present in the rude hovel, when they opened their eyes to the daylight.

"Up, boy, up!" cried the lime-burner, staring about him. "Thank Heaven, the night is gone, at last; and rather than pass such another, I would watch my lime-kiln, wide awake, for a twelve-month. This Ethan Brand, with his humbug of an Unpardonable Sin, has done me no such mighty favor, in taking my place!"

He issued from the hut, followed by little Joe, who kept fast hold of his father's hand. The early sunshine was already pouring its gold upon the mountaintops, and though the valleys were still in shadow, they smiled cheerfully in the promise of the bright day that was hastening onward. The village, completely shut in by hills, which swelled away gently about it, looked as if it had rested peacefully in the hollow of the great hand of providence. Every dwelling was distinctly visible; the little spires of the two churches pointed upwards, and caught a fore-glimmering of brightness from the sun-gilt skies upon their gilded weathercocks. The tavern was astir, and the figure of the old, smoke-dried stage-agent, cigar in mouth, was seen beneath the stoop. Old Graylock was glorified with a golden cloud upon his head. Scattered likewise over the breasts of the surrounding mountains, there were heaps of hoary mist, in fantastic shapes, some of them far down into the valley, others high up towards the summits, and still others, of the same family of mist or cloud, hovering in the gold radiance of the upper atmosphere. Stepping from one to another of the clouds that rested on the hills, and thence to the loftier brotherhood that sailed in air, it seemed almost as if a mortal man might thus ascend into the heavenly regions. Earth was so mingled with sky that it was a daydream to look at it.

To supply that charm of the familiar and homely, which Nature so readily adopts into a scene like this, the stage-coach was rattling down the mountain-road, and the driver sounded his horn, while Echo caught up the notes, and intertwined them into a rich and varied and elaborate harmony, of which the original performer could lay claim to little share. The great hills played a concert among themselves, each contributing a strain of airy sweetness.

Little Joe's face brightened at once.

"Dear father," cried he, skipping cheerily to and fro, "that strange man is gone, and the sky and the mountains all seem glad of it!"

"Yes," growled the lime-burner, with an oath, "but he had let the fire go down, and no thanks to him if five hundred bushels of lime are not spoiled. If I catch the fellow hereabouts again, I shall feel like tossing him into the furnace!"

With his long pole in his hand, he ascended to the top of the kiln. After a moment's pause, he called to his son.

"Come up here, Joe!" said he.

So little Joe ran up the hillock, and stood by his father's side. The marble was all burnt into perfect, snow-white lime. But on its surface, in the midst of the circle,—snow-white too, and thoroughly converted into lime,—lay a human skeleton, in the attitude of a person who, after long toil, lies down to long repose. Within the ribs—strange to say—was the shape of a human heart.

"Was the fellow's heart made of marble?" cried Bartram, in some perplexity at this phenomenon. "At any rate, it is burnt into what looks like special good lime, and, taking all the bones together, my kiln is half a bushel the richer for him."

So saying, the rude lime-burner lifted his pole, and, letting it fall upon the skeleton, the relics of Ethan Brand were crumbled into fragments.

Robert Penn Warren

BLACKBERRY WINTER

IT WAS getting into June and past eight o'clock in the morning, but there was a fire—even if it wasn't a big fire, just a fire of chunks—on the hearth of the big stone fireplace in the living room. I was standing on the hearth, almost into the chimney, hunched over the fire, working my bare toes slowly on the warm stone. I relished the heat which made the skin of my bare legs warp and creep and tingle, even as I called to my mother, who was somewhere back in the dining room or kitchen, and said: "But it's June, I don't have to put them on!"

"You put them on if you are going out," she called.

I tried to assess the degree of authority and conviction in the tone, but at that distance it was hard to decide. I tried to analyze the tone, and then I thought what a fool I had been to start out the back door and let her see that I was barefoot. If I had gone out the front door or the side door she would never have known, not till dinner time anyway, and by then the day would have been half gone and I would have been all over the farm to see what the storm had done and down to the creek to see the flood. But it had never crossed my mind that they would try to stop you from going barefoot in June, no matter if there had been a gully-washer and a cold spell.

Nobody had ever tried to stop me in June as long as I could remember, and when you are nine years old, what you remember seems forever; for you remember everything and everything is important and stands big and full and fills up Time and is so solid that you can walk around and around it like a tree and look at it. You are aware that time passes, that there is a movement in time, but that is not what Time is. Time is not a movement, a flowing, a wind then, but is, rather, a kind of climate in which things are, and when a thing happens it begins to live and keeps on living and stands solid in Time like the tree that you can walk around. And if there is a movement, the movement is not Time itself, any more than a breeze is climate, and all the breeze does is to shake a little the leaves on the tree which is alive and solid. When you are nine, you know that there are things that you don't know, but you know that when you know something you know it. You know how a thing has been and you know that you can go barefoot in June. You do not understand that voice from back in the kitchen which says that you cannot go barefoot outdoors and run to see what has happened and rub your feet over the wet shivery grass and make the perfect mark of your foot in the smooth, creamy, red mud and then muse upon it as though you had suddenly come upon that single mark on the glistening auroral beach of the world. You have never seen a beach, but you have read the book and how the footprint was there.

The voice had said what it had said, and I looked savagely at the black stockings and the strong, scuffed brown shoes which I had brought from my closet as far as the hearth rug. I called once more, "But it's June," and waited.

"It's June," the voice replied from far away, "but it's blackberry winter."

I had lifted my head to reply to that, to make one more test of what was in that tone, when I happened to see the man.

The fireplace in the living room was at the end; for the stone chimney was built, as in so many of the farmhouses in Tennessee, at the end of a gable, and there was a window on each side of the chimney. Out of the window on the north side of the fireplace I could see the man. When I saw the man I did not call out what I had intended, but, engrossed by the strangeness and the sight, watched him, still far off, come along the path by the edge of the woods.

What was strange was that there should be a man there at all. That path went along the yard fence, between the fence and the woods which came right down to the yard, and then on back past the chicken runs and on by the woods until it was lost to sight where the woods bulged out and cut off the back field. There the path disappeared into the woods. It led on back, I knew, through the woods and to the swamp, skirted the swamp where the big trees gave way to sycamores and water oaks and willows and tangled cane, and then led on to the river. Nobody ever went back there except people who wanted to gig frogs in the swamp or to fish in the river or to hunt in the woods, and those people, if they didn't have a standing permission from my father, always stopped to ask permission to cross the farm. But the man whom I now saw wasn't, I could tell even at that distance, a sportsman. And what would a sportsman have been doing down there after a storm? Besides, he was coming from the river, and nobody had gone down there that morning. I knew that for a fact, because if anybody had passed, certainly if a stranger had passed, the dogs would have made a racket and would have been out on him. But this man was coming up from the river and had come up through the woods. I suddenly had a vision of him moving up the grassy path in the woods, in the green twilight under the big trees, not making any sound on the path, while now and then, like drops off the eaves, a big drop of water would fall from a leaf or bough and strike a stiff oak leaf lower down with a small, hollow sound like a drop of water hitting tin. That sound, in the silence of the woods, would be very significant.

When you are a boy and stand in the stillness of woods, which can be so still that your heart almost stops beating and makes you want to stand there in the green twilight until you feel your very feet sinking into and clutching the earth like roots and your body breathing slow through its pores like the leaves—when you stand there and wait for the next drop to drop with its small, flat sound to a lower leaf, that sound seems to measure out something, to put an end to something, to begin something, and you cannot wait for it to happen and are afraid it will not happen, and then when it has happened, you are waiting again, almost afraid.

But the man whom I saw coming through the woods in my mind's eye did not pause and wait, growing into the ground and breathing with the enormous, soundless breathing of the leaves. Instead, I saw him moving in the green twilight inside my head as he was moving at that very moment along the path by the edge of the woods, coming toward the house. He was moving steadily, but not fast, with his shoulders hunched a little and his head thrust forward, like a man who has come a long way and has a long way to go. I shut my eyes for a couple of seconds, thinking that when I opened them he would not be there at all. There was no place for him to have come from, and there was no reason for him to come where he was coming, toward our house. But I opened my eyes, and there he was, and he was coming steadily along the side of the woods. He was not yet even with the back chicken yard.

"Mama," I called.

"You put them on," the voice said.

"There's a man coming," I called, "out back."

She did not reply to that, and I guessed that she had gone to the kitchen window to look. She would be looking at the man and wondering who he was and what he wanted, the way you always do in the country, and if I went back there now she would not notice right off whether or not I was barefoot. So I went back to the kitchen.

She was standing by the window. "I don't recognize him," she said, not looking around at me.

"Where could he be coming from?" I asked.

"I don't know," she said.

"What would he be doing down at the river? At night? In the storm?"

She studied the figure out the window, then said, "Oh, I reckon maybe he cut across from the Dunbar place."

That was, I realized, a perfectly rational explanation. He had not been down at the river in the storm, at night. He had come over this morning. You could cut across from the Dunbar place if you didn't mind breaking through a lot of elder and sassafras and blackberry bushes which had about taken over the old cross path, which nobody ever used any more. That satisfied me for a moment, but only for a moment. "Mama," I asked, "what would he be doing over at the Dunbar place last night?"

Then she looked at me, and I knew I had made a mistake, for she was looking at my bare feet. "You haven't got your shoes on," she said.

But I was saved by the dogs. That instant there was a bark which I recognized as Sam, the collie, and then a heavier, churning kind of bark which was Bully, and I saw a streak of white as Bully tore round the corner of the back porch and headed out for the man. Bully was a big, bone-white bull dog, the kind of dog that they used to call a farm bull dog but that you don't see any more, heavy chested and heavy headed, but with pretty long legs. He could take a fence as light as a hound. He had just cleared the white paling fence toward the woods when my mother ran out to the back porch and began calling, "Here you, Bully! Here you!"

Bully stopped in the path, waiting for the man, but he gave a few more of those deep, gargling, savage barks that reminded you of something down a stone-lined well. The red clay mud, I saw, was splashed up over his white chest and looked exciting, like blood.

The man, however, had not stopped walking even when Bully took the fence and started at him. He had kept right on coming. All he had done was to switch a little paper parcel which he carried from the right hand to the left, and then reach into his pants pocket to get something. Then I saw the glitter and knew that he had a knife in his hand, probably the kind of mean knife just made for devilment and nothing else, with a blade as long as the blade of a frog-sticker, which will snap out ready when you press a button in the handle. That knife must have had a button in the handle, or else how could he have had the blade out glittering so quick and with just one hand?

Pulling his knife against the dogs was a funny thing to do, for Bully was a big, powerful brute and fast, and Sam was all right. If those dogs had meant business, they might have knocked him down and ripped him before he got a stroke in. He ought to have picked up a heavy stick, something to take a swipe at them with and something which they could see and respect when they came at him. But he apparently did not know much about dogs. He just held the knife blade close against the right leg, low down, and kept on moving down the path.

Then my mother had called, and Bully had stopped. So the man let the blade of the knife snap back into the handle, and dropped it into his pocket, and kept on coming. Many women would have been afraid with the strange man who they knew had that knife in his pocket. That is, if they were alone in the house with nobody but a nine-year-old boy. And my mother was alone, for my father had gone off, and Dellie, the cook, was down at her cabin because she wasn't feeling well. But my mother wasn't afraid. She wasn't a big woman, but she was clear and brisk about everything she did and looked everybody and everything right in the eye from her own blue eyes in her tanned face. She had been the first woman in the county to ride a horse astride (that was back when she was a girl and long before I was born), and I have seen her snatch up a pump gun and go out and knock a chicken hawk out of the air like a busted skeet when he came over her chicken yard. She was a steady and self-reliant woman, and when I think of her now after all the years she has been dead, I think of her brown hands, not big, but somewhat square for a woman's hands, with square-cut nails. They looked, as a matter of fact, more like a young boy's hands than a grown woman's. But back then it never crossed my mind that she would ever be dead.

She stood on the back porch and watched the man enter the back gate, where the dogs (Bully had leaped back into the yard) were dancing and muttering and giving sidelong glances back to my mother to see if she meant what she had said. The man walked right by the dogs, almost brushing them, and didn't pay them any attention. I could see now that he wore old khaki pants, and a dark wool coat with stripes in it, and a gray felt hat. He had on a gray shirt with blue stripes in it, and no tie. But I could see a tie, blue and reddish, sticking in his side coat-pocket. Everything was wrong about what he wore. He ought to have been wearing blue jeans or overalls, and a straw hat or an old black felt hat, and the coat, granting that he might have been wearing a wool coat and not a jumper, ought not to have had those stripes. Those clothes, despite the fact that they were old enough and dirty enough for any tramp, didn't belong there in our back yard, coming down the path, in Middle Tennessee, miles away from any big town, and even a mile off the pike.

When he got almost to the steps, without having said anything, my mother, very matter-of-factly, said, "Good morning."

"Good morning," he said, and stopped and looked her over. He did not take off his hat, and under the brim you could see the perfectly unmemorable face, which wasn't old and wasn't young, or thick or thin. It was grayish and covered with about three days of stubble. The eyes were a kind of nondescript, muddy hazel, or something like that, rather bloodshot. His teeth, when he opened his mouth, showed yellow and uneven. A couple of them had been knocked out. You knew that they had been knocked out, because there was a scar, not very old, there on the lower lip just beneath the gap.

"Are you hunting work?" my mother asked him.

"Yes," he said—not "yes, mam"—and still did not take off his hat.

"I don't know about my husband for he isn't here," she said, and didn't mind a bit telling the tramp, or whoever he was, with the mean knife in his pocket, that no man was around, "but I can give you a few things to do. The storm has drowned a lot of my chicks. Three coops of them. You can gather them up and bury them. Bury them deep so the dogs won't get at them. In the woods. And fix the coops the wind blew over. And down yonder beyond that pen by the edge of the woods are some drowned poults. They got out and I couldn't get them in. Even after it started to rain hard. Poults haven't got any sense."

"What are them things—poults?" he demanded, and spat on the brick walk. He rubbed his foot over the spot, and I saw that he wore a black, pointed-toe low shoe, all cracked and broken. It was a crazy kind of shoe to be wearing in the country.

"Oh, they're young turkeys," my mother was saying. "And they haven't got any sense. I oughtn't to try to raise them around here with so many chickens, anyway. They don't thrive near chickens, even in separate pens. And I won't give up my chickens." Then she stopped herself and resumed briskly on the note of business. "When you finish that, you can fix my flower beds. A lot of trash and mud and gravel has washed down. Maybe you can save some of my flowers if you are careful."

"Flowers," the man said, in a low, impersonal voice which seemed to have a wealth of meaning, but a meaning which I could not fathom. As I think back on it, it probably was not pure contempt. Rather, it was a kind of impersonal and distant marveling that he should be on the verge of grubbing in a flower bed. He said the word, and then looked off across the yard.

"Yes, flowers," my mother replied with some asperity, as though she would have nothing said or implied against flowers. "And they were very fine this year." Then she stopped and looked at the man. "Are you hungry?" she demanded.

"Yeah," he said.

"I'll fix you something," she said, "before you get started." She turned to me. "Show him where he can wash up," she commanded, and went into the house.

I took the man to the end of the porch where a pump was and where a couple of wash pans sat on a low shelf for people to use before they went into the house. I stood there while he laid down his little parcel wrapped in newspaper and took off his hat and looked around for a nail to hang it on. He poured the water and plunged his hands into it. They were big hands, and strong looking, but they did not have the creases and the earth-color of the hands of men who work outdoors. But they were dirty, with black dirt ground into the skin and under the nails. After he had washed his hands, he poured another basin of water and washed his face. He dried his face, and with the towel still dangling in his grasp, stepped over to the mirror on the house wall. He rubbed one hand over the stubble on his face. Then he carefully inspected his face, turning first one side and then the other, and stepped back and settled his striped coat down on his shoulders. He had the movements of a man who has just dressed up to go to church or a party—the way he settled his coat and smoothed it and scanned himself in the mirror.

Then he caught my glance on him. He glared at me for a instant out of the bloodshot eyes, then demanded in a low, harsh voice, "What you looking at?"

"Nothing," I managed to say, and stepped back a step from him.

He flung the towel down, crumpled, on the shelf, and went toward the kitchen door and entered without knocking.

My mother said something to him which I could not catch. I started to go in again, then thought about my bare feet, and decided to go back of the chicken yard, where the man would have to come to pick up the dead chicks. I hung around behind the chicken house until he came out.

He moved across the chicken yard with a fastidious, not quite finicking motion, looking down at the curdled mud flecked with bits of chicken-droppings. The mud curled up over the soles of his black shoes. I stood back from him some six feet and watched him pick up the first of the drowned chicks. He held it up by one foot and inspected it.

There is nothing deader looking than a drowned chick. The feet curl in that feeble, empty way which back when I was a boy, even if I was a country boy who did not mind hog-killing or frog-gigging, made me feel hollow in the stomach. Instead of looking plump and fluffy, the body is stringy and limp with the fluff plastered to it, and the neck is long and loose like a little string of rag. And the eyes have that bluish membrane over them which makes you think of a very old man who is sick about to die.

The man stood there and inspected the chick. Then he looked all around as though he didn't know what to do with it.

"There's a great big old basket in the shed," I said, and pointed to the shed attached to the chicken house.

He inspected me as though he had just discovered my presence, and moved toward the shed.

"There's a spade there, too," I added.

He got the basket and began to pick up the other chicks, picking each one up slowly by a foot and then flinging it into the basket with a nasty, snapping motion. Now and then he would look at me out of the bloodshot eyes. Every time he seemed on the verge of saying something, but he did not. Perhaps he was building up to say something to me, but I did not wait that long. His way of looking at me made me so uncomfortable that I left the chicken yard.

Besides, I had just remembered that the creek was in flood, over the bridge, and that people were down there watching it. So I cut across the farm toward the creek. When I got to the big tobacco field I saw that it had not suffered much. The land lay right and not many tobacco plants had washed out of the ground. But I knew that a lot of tobacco round the country had been washed right out. My father had said so at breakfast.

My father was down at the bridge. When I came out of the gap in the osage hedge into the road, I saw him sitting on his mare over the heads of the other men who were standing around, admiring the flood. The creek was big here, even in low water; for only a couple of miles away it ran into the river, and when a real flood came, the red water got over the pike where it dipped down to the bridge, which was an iron bridge, and high over the floor and even the side railings of the bridge. Only the upper iron work would show, with the water boiling and frothing red and white around it. That creek rose so fast and so heavy because a few miles back it came down out of the hills, where the gorges filled up with water in no time when a rain came. The creek ran in a deep bed with limestone bluffs along both sides until it got within three quarters of a mile of the bridge, and when it came out from between those bluffs in flood it was boiling and hissing and steaming like water from a fire hose.

Whenever there was a flood, people from half the country would come down to see the sight. After a gully-washer there would not be any work to do anyway. If it didn't ruin your crop, you couldn't plow and you felt like taking a holiday to celebrate. If it did ruin your crop, there wasn't anything to do except to try to take your mind off the mortgage, if you were rich enough to have a mortgage, and if you couldn't afford a mortgage you needed something to take your mind off how hungry you would be by Christmas. So people would come down to the bridge and look at the flood. It made something different from the run of days.

There would not be much talking after the first few minutes of trying to guess how high the water was this time. The men and kids just stood around, or sat their horses or mules, as the case might be, or stood up in the wagon beds. They looked at the strangeness of the flood for an hour or two, and then somebody would say that he had better be getting on home to dinner and would start walking down the gray, puddled limestone pike, or would touch heel to his mount and start off. Everybody always knew what it would be like when he got down to the bridge, but people always came. It was like church or a funeral. They always came, that is, if it was summer and the flood unexpected. Nobody ever came down in winter to see high water.

When I came out of the gap in the bodock hedge, I saw the crowd, perhaps fifteen or twenty men and a lot of kids, and saw my father sitting his mare, Nellie Gray. He was a tall, limber man and carried himself well. I was always proud to see him sit a horse, he was so quiet and straight, and when I stepped through the gap of the hedge that morning, the first thing that happened was, I remember, the warm feeling I always had when I saw him up on a horse, just sitting. I did not go toward him, but skirted the crowd on the far side, to get a look at the creek. For one thing, I was not sure what he would say about the fact that I was barefoot. But the first thing I knew, I heard his voice calling, "Seth!"

I went toward him, moving apologetically past the men, who bent their large, red or thin, sallow faces above me. I knew some of the men, and knew their names, but because those I knew were there in a crowd, mixed with the strange faces, they seemed foreign to me, and not friendly. I did not look up at my father until I was almost within touching distance of his heel. Then I looked up and tried to read his face, to see if he was angry about my being barefoot. Before I could decide anything from that impassive, high-boned face, he had leaned over and reached a hand to me. "Grab on," he commanded.

I grabbed on and gave a little jump, and he said, "Up-see-daisy!" and whisked me, light as a feather, up to the pommel of his McClellan saddle.

"You can see better up here," he said, slid back on the cantle a little to make me more comfortable, and then, looking over my head at the swollen, tumbling water, seemed to forget all about me. But his right hand was laid on my side, just above my thigh, to steady me.

I was sitting there as quiet as I could, feeling the faint stir of my father's chest against my shoulders as it rose and fell with his breath, when I saw the cow. At first, looking up the creek, I thought it was just another big piece of driftwood steaming down the creek in the ruck of water, but all at once a pretty good-sized boy who had climbed part way up a telephone pole by the pike so that he could see better yelled out, "Golly-damn, look at that-air cow!"

Everybody looked. It was a cow all right, but it might just as well have been driftwood; for it was dead as a chunk, rolling and rolling down the creek, appearing and disappearing, feet up or head up, it didn't matter which.

The cow started up the talk again. Somebody wondered whether it would hit one of the clear places under the top girder of the bridge and get through or whether it would get tangled in the drift and trash that had piled against the upright girders and braces. Somebody remembered how about ten years before so much driftwood had piled up on the bridge that it was knocked off its foundations. Then the cow hit. It hit the edge of the drift against one of the girders, and hung there. For a few seconds it seemed as though it might tear loose, but then we saw that it was really caught. It bobbed and heaved on its side there in a slow, grinding, uneasy fashion. It had a yoke around its neck, the kind made out of a forked limb to keep a jumper behind fence.

"She shore jumped one fence," one of the men said.

And another: "Well, she done jumped her last one, fer a fack."

Then they began to wonder about whose cow it might be. They decided it must belong to Milt Alley. They said that he had a cow that was a jumper, and kept her in a fenced-in piece of ground up the creek. I had never seen Milt Alley, but I knew who he was. He was a squatter and lived up the hills a way, on a shirt-tail patch of set-on-edge land, in a cabin. He was pore white trash. He had lots of children. I had seen the children at school, when they came. They were thin-faced, with straight, sticky-looking, dough-colored hair, and they smelled something like old sour buttermilk, not because they drank so much buttermilk but because that is the sort of smell which children out of those cabins tend to have. The big Alley boy drew dirty pictures and showed them to the little boys at school.

That was Milt Alley's cow. It looked like the kind of cow he would have, a scrawny, old, sway-backed cow, with a yoke around her neck. I wondered if Milt Alley had another cow.

"Poppa," I said, "do you think Milt Alley has got another cow?"

"You say 'Mr. Alley,' " my father said quietly.

"Do you think he has?"

"No telling," my father said.

Then a big gangly boy, about fifteen, who was sitting on a scraggly little old mule with a piece of croker sack thrown across the saw-tooth spine, and who had been staring at the cow, suddenly said to nobody in particular, "Reckin anybody ever et drownt cow?"

He was the kind of boy who might just as well as not have been the son of Milt Alley, with his faded and patched overalls ragged at the bottom of the pants and the mud-stiff brogans hanging off his skinny, bare ankles at the level of the mule's belly. He had said what he did, and then looked embarrassed and sullen when all the eyes swung at him. He hadn't meant to say it, I am pretty sure now. He would have been too proud to say it, just as Milt Alley would have been too proud. He had just been thinking out loud, and the words had popped out.

There was an old man standing there on the pike, an old man with a white beard. "Son," he said to the embarrassed and sullen boy on the mule, "you live long enough and you'll find a man will eat anything when the time comes."

"Time gonna come fer some folks this year," another man said.

"Son," the old man said, "in my time I et things a man don't like to think on. I was a sojer and I rode with Gin'l Forrest, and them things we et when the time come. I tell you. I et meat what got up and run when you taken out yore knife to cut a slice to put on the fire. You had to knock it down with a carbeen butt, it was so active.

That-air meat would jump like a bullfrog, it was so full of skippers."

But nobody was listening to the old man. The boy on the mule turned his sullen sharp face from him, dug a heel into the side of the mule and went off up the pike with a motion which made you think that any second you would hear mule bones clashing inside that lank and scrofulous hide.

"Cy Dundee's boy," a man said, and nodded toward the figure going up the pike on the mule.

"Reckin Cy Dundee's young-uns seen times they'd settle fer drownt cow," another man said.

The old man with the beard peered at them both from his weak, slow eyes, first at one and then at the other. "Live long enough," he said, "and a man will settle fer what he kin git."

Then there was silence again, with the people looking at the red, foam-flecked water.

My father lifted the bridle rein in his left hand, and the mare turned and walked around the group and up the pike. We rode on up to our big gate, where my father dismounted to open it and let me myself ride Nellie Gray through. When he got to the lane that led off from the drive about two hundred yards from our house, my father said, "Grab on." I grabbed on, and he let me down to the ground. "I'm going to ride down and look at my corn," he said. "You go on." He took the lane, and I stood there on the drive and watched him ride off. He was wearing cowhide boots and an old hunting coat, and I thought that that made him look very military, like a picture. That and the way he rode.

I did not go to the house. Instead, I went by the vegetable garden and crossed behind the stables, and headed down for Dellie's cabin. I wanted to go down and play with Jebb, who was Dellie's little boy about two years older than I was. Besides, I was cold. I shivered as I walked, and I had gooseflesh. The mud which crawled up between my toes with every step I took was like ice. Dellie would have a fire, but she wouldn't make me put on shoes and stockings.

Dellie's cabin was of logs, with one side, because it was on a slope, set on limestone chunks, with a little porch attached to it, and had a little whitewashed fence around it and a gate with plow-points on a wire to clink when somebody came in, and had two big white oaks in the yard and some flowers and a nice privy in the back with some honeysuckle growing over it. Dellie and Old Jebb, who was Jebb's father and who lived with Dellie and had lived with her for twenty-five years even if they never had got married, were careful to keep everything nice around their cabin. They had the name all over the community for being clean and clever Negroes. Dellie and Jebb were what they used to call "white-folks' niggers." There was a big difference between their cabin and the other two cabins farther down where the other tenants lived. My father kept the other cabins weatherproof, but he couldn't undertake to go down and pick up after the litter they strewed. They didn't take the trouble to have a vegetable patch like Dellie and Jebb or to make preserves from wild plum, and jelly from crab apple the way Dellie did. They were shiftless, and my father was always threatening to get shed of them. But he never did. When they finally left, they just up and left on their own, for no reason, to go and be shiftless somewhere else. Then some more came. But meanwhile they lived down there, Matt Rawson and his family, and Sid Turner and his, and I played with their children all over the farm when they weren't working. But when I wasn't around they were mean sometimes to Little Jebb. That was because the other tenants down there were jealous of Dellie and Jebb.

I was so cold that I ran the last fifty yards to Dellie's gate. As soon as I had entered the yard, I saw that the storm had been hard on Dellie's flowers. The yard was, as I have said, on a slight slope, and the water running across had gutted the flower beds and washed out all the good black woods-earth which Dellie had brought in. What little grass there was in the yard was plastered sparsely down on the ground, the way the drainage water had left it. It reminded me of the way the fluff was plastered down on the skin of the drowned chicks that the strange man had been picking up, up in my mother's chicken yard.

I took a few steps up the path to the cabin, and then I saw that the drainage water had washed a lot of trash and filth out from under Dellie's house. Up toward the porch, the ground was not clean any more. Old pieces of rag, two or three rusted cans, pieces of rotten rope, some hunks of old dog dung, broken glass, old paper, and all sorts of things like that had washed out from under Dellie's house to foul her clean yard. It looked just as bad as the yards of the other cabins, or worse. It was worse, as a matter of fact, because it was a surprise. I had never thought of all that filth being under Dellie's house. It was not anything against Dellie that the stuff had been under the cabin. Trash will get under any house. But I did not think of that when I saw the foulness which had washed out on the ground which Dellie sometimes used to sweep with a twig broom to make nice and clean.

I picked my way past the filth, being careful not to get my bare feet on it, and mounted to Dellie's door. When I knocked, I heard her voice telling me to come in.

It was dark inside the cabin, after the daylight, but I could make out Dellie piled up in bed under a quilt, and Little Jebb crouched by the hearth, where a low fire simmered. "Howdy," I said to Dellie, "how you feeling?"

Her big eyes, the whites surprising and glaring in the black face, fixed on me as I stood there, but she did not reply. It did not look like Dellie, or act like Dellie, who would grumble and bustle around our kitchen, talking to herself, scolding me or Little Jebb, clanking pans, making all sorts of unnecessary noises and mutterings like an old-fashioned black steam thrasher engine when it has got up an extra head of steam and keeps popping the governor and rumbling and shaking on its wheels. But now Dellie just lay up there on the bed, under the patch-work quilt, and turned the black face, which I scarcely recognized, and the glaring white eyes to me.

"How you feeling?" I repeated.

"I'se sick," the voice said croakingly out of the strange black face which was not attached to Dellie's big, squat body, but stuck out from under a pile of tangled bedclothes. Then the voice added: "Mighty sick."

"I'm sorry," I managed to say.

The eyes remained fixed on me for a moment, then they left me and the head rolled back on the pillow. "Sorry," the voice said, in a flat way which wasn't question or statement of anything. It was just the empty word put into the air with no meaning or expression, to float off like a feather or a puff of smoke, while the big eyes, with the whites like the peeled white of hard-boiled eggs, stared at the ceiling.

"Dellie," I said after a minute, "there's a tramp up at the house. He's got a knife."

She was not listening. She closed her eyes.

I tiptoed over to the hearth where Jebb was and crouched beside him. We began to talk in low voices. I was asking him to get out his train and play train. Old Jebb had put spool wheels on three cigar boxes and put wire links between the boxes to make a train for Jebb. The box that was the locomotive had the top closed and a length of broom stick for a smoke stack. Jebb didn't want to get the train out, but I told him I would go home if he didn't. So he got out the train, and the colored rocks, and fossils of crinoid stems, and other junk he used for the load, and we began to push it around, talking the way we thought trainmen talked, making a chuck-chucking sound under the breath for the noise of the locomotive and now and then uttering low, cautious toots for the whistle. We got so interested in playing train that the toots got louder. Then, before he thought, Jebb gave a good, loud *toot-toot*, blowing for a crossing.

"Come here," the voice said from the bed.

Jebb got up slow from his hands and knees, giving me a sudden, naked, inimical look.

"Come here!" the voice said.

Jebb went to the bed. Dellie propped herself weakly up on one arm, muttering, "Come closer."

Jebb stood closer.

"Last thing I do, I'm gonna do it," Dellie said. "Done tole you to be quiet."

Then she slapped him. It was an awful slap, more awful for the kind of weakness which it came from and brought to focus. I had seen her slap Jebb before, but the slapping had always been the kind of easy slap you would expect from a good-natured, grumbling Negro woman like Dellie. But this was different. It was awful. It was so awful that Jebb didn't make a sound. The tears just popped out and ran down his face, and his breath came sharp, like gasps.

Dellie fell back. "Cain't even be sick," she said to the ceiling. "Git sick and they won't even let you lay. They tromp all over you. Cain't even be sick." Then she closed her eyes.

I went out of the room. I almost ran getting to the door, and I did run across the porch and down the steps and across the yard, not caring whether or not I stepped on the filth which had washed out from under the cabin. I ran almost all the way home. Then I thought about my mother catching me with the bare feet. So I went down to the stables.

I heard a noise in the crib, and opened the door. There was Big Jebb, sitting on an old nail keg, shelling corn into a bushel basket. I went in, pulling the door shut behind me, and crouched on the floor near him. I crouched there for a couple of minutes before either of us spoke, and watched him shelling the corn.

He had very big hands, knotted and grayish at the joints, with calloused palms which seemed to be streaked with rust with the rust coming up between the fingers to show from the back. His hands were so strong and tough that he could take a big ear of corn and rip the grains right off the cob with the palm of his hand, all in one motion, like a machine. "Work long as me," he would say, "and the good Lawd'll give you a hand lak cass-ion won't nuthin' hurt." And his hands did look like cast iron, old cast iron streaked with rust.

He was an old man, up in his seventies, thirty years or more older than Dellie, but he was strong as a bull. He was a squat sort of man, heavy in the shoulders, with remarkably long arms, the kind of build they say the river natives have on the Congo from paddling so much in their boats. He had a round bullet-head, set on powerful shoulders. His skin was very black, and the thin hair on his head was now grizzled like tufts of old cotton batting. He had small eyes and a flat nose, not big, and the kindest and wisest old face in the world, the blunt, sad, wise face of an old animal peering tolerantly out on the goings-on of the merely human creatures before him. He was a good man, and I loved him next to my mother and father. I crouched there on the floor of the crib and watched him shell corn with the rusty cast-iron hands, while he looked down at me out of the little eyes set in the blunt face.

"Dellie says she's might sick," I said.

"Yeah," he said.

"What's she sick from?"

"Woman-mizry," he said.

"What's woman-mizry?"

"Hit comes on 'em," he said. "Hit just comes on 'em when the time comes."

"What is it?"

"Hit is the change," he said. "Hit is the change of life and time."

"What changes?"

"You too young to know."

"Tell me."

"Time come and you find out everthing."

I knew that there was no use in asking him any more. When I asked him things and he said that, I always knew that he would not tell me. So I continued to crouch there and watch him. Now that I had sat there a little while, I was cold again.

"What you shiver fer?" he asked me.

"I'm cold. I'm cold because it's blackberry winter," I said.

"Maybe 'tis and maybe 'tain't," he said.

"My mother says it is."

"Ain't sayen Miss Sallie doan know and ain't sayen she do. But folks doan know everthing."

"Why isn't it blackberry winter?"

"Too late fer blackberry winter. Blackberries done bloomed."

"She said it was."

"Blackberry winter just a leetle cold spell. Hit come and then hit go away, and hit is growed summer of a sudden lak a gunshot. Ain't no tellen hit will go way this time."

"It's June," I said.

"June," he replied with great contempt. "That what folks say. What June mean? Maybe hit is come cold to stay."

"Why?"

" 'Cause this-here old yearth is tahrd. Hit is tahrd and ain't gonna perduce. Lawd let hit come rain one time forty days and forty nights, 'cause He wus tahrd of sinful folks. Maybe this-here old yearth say to the Lawd, Lawd, I done plum tahrd, Lawd, lemme rest. And Lawd say, Yearth, you done yore best, you give 'em cawn and you give 'em taters, and all they think on is they gut, and, Yearth, you kin take a rest."

"What will happen?"

"Folks will eat up everthing. The yearth won't perduce no more. Folks cut down all the trees and burn 'em 'cause they cold, and the yearth won't grow no more. I been tellen 'em. I been tellen folks. Sayen, maybe this year, hit is the time. But they doan listen to me, how the yearth is tahrd. Maybe this year they find out."

"Will everything die?"

"Everthing and everbody, hit will be so."

"This year?"

"Ain't no tellen. Maybe this year."

"My mother said it is blackberry winter," I said confidently, and got up.

"Ain't sayen nuthin' agin Miss Sallie," he said.

I went to the door of the crib. I was really cold now. Running, I had got up a sweat and now I was worse.

I hung on the door, looking at Jebb, who was shelling corn again.

"There's a tramp came to the house," I said. I had almost forgotten the tramp.

"Yeah."

"He came by the back way. What was he doing down there in the storm?"

"They comes and they goes," he said, "and ain't no tellen."

"He had a mean knife."

"The good ones and the bad ones, they comes and they goes. Storm or sun, light or dark. They is folks and they comes and they goes lak folks."

I hung on the door, shivering.

He studied me a moment, then said, "You git on to the house. You ketch yore death. Then what yore mammy say?"

I hesitated.

"You git," he said.

When I came to the back yard, I saw that my father was standing by the back porch and the tramp was walking toward him. They began talking before I reached them, but I got there just as my father was saying, "I'm sorry, but I haven't got any work. I got all the hands on the place I need now. I won't need any extra until wheat thrashing."

The stranger made no reply, just looked at my father.

My father took out his leather coin purse, and got out a half-dollar. He held it toward the man. "This is for half a day," he said.

The man looked at the coin, and then at my father, making no motion to take the money. But that was the right amount. A dollar a day was what you paid them back in 1910. And the man hadn't even worked half a day.

Then the man reached out and took the coin. He dropped it into the right side pocket of his coat. Then he said, very slowly and without feeling: "I didn't want to work on your —— farm."

He used the word which they would have frailed me to death for using.

I looked at my father's face and it was streaked white under the sunburn. Then he said, "Get off this place. Get off this place or I won't be responsible."

The man dropped his right hand into his pants pocket. It was the pocket where he kept the knife. I was just about to yell to my father about the knife when the hand came back out with nothing in it. The man gave a kind of twisted grin, showing where the teeth had been knocked out above the new scar. I thought that instant how maybe he had tried before to pull a knife on somebody else and had got his teeth knocked out.

So now he just gave that twisted, sickish grin out of the unmemorable, grayish face, and then spat on the brick path. The glob landed just about six inches from the toe of my father's right boot. My father looked down at it, and so did I. I thought that if the glob had hit my father's boot something would have happened. I looked down and saw the bright glob, and on one side of it my father's strong cowhide boots, with the brass eyelets and the leather thongs, heavy boots splashed with good red mud and set solid on the bricks, and on the other side the pointed-toe, broken, black shoes, on which the mud looked so sad and out of place. Then I saw one of the black shoes move a little, just a twitch first, then a real step backward.

The man moved in a quarter circle to the end of the porch, with my father's steady gaze upon him all the while. At the end of the porch, the man reached up to the shelf where the wash pans were to get his little newspaper-wrapped parcel. Then he disappeared around the corner of the house and my father mounted the porch and went into the kitchen without a word.

I followed around the house to see what the man would do. I wasn't afraid of him now, no matter if he did have the knife. When I got around in front, I saw him going out of the yard gate and starting up the drive toward the pike. So I ran to catch up with him. He was sixty yards or so up the drive before I caught up.

I did not walk right up even with him at first, but trailed him, the way a kid will, about seven or eight feet behind, now and then running two or three steps in order to hold my place against his longer stride. When I first came up behind him, he turned to give me a look, just a meaningless look, and then fixed his eyes up the drive and kept on walking.

When we had got around the bend in the drive which cut the house from sight, and were going along by the edge of the woods, I decided to come up even with him. I ran a few steps, and was by his side, or almost, but some feet off to the right. I walked along in this position for a while, and he never noticed me. I walked along until we got within sight of the big gate that let on the pike.

Then I said: "Where did you come from?"

He looked at me then with a look which seemed almost surprised that I was there. Then he said, "It ain't none of yore business."

We went on another fifty feet.

Then I said, "Where are you going?"

He stopped, studied me dispassionately for a moment, then suddenly took a step toward me and leaned his face down at me. The lips jerked back, but not in any grin, to show where the teeth were knocked out and to make the scar on the lower lip come white with the tension.

He said: "Stop following me. You don't stop following me and I cut yore throat, you little son-of-a-bitch."

Then he went on to the gate, and up the pike.

That was thirty-five years ago. Since that time my father and mother have died. I was still a boy, but a big boy, when my father got cut on the blade of a mowing machine and died of lockjaw. My mother sold the place and went to town to live with her sister. But she never took hold after my father's death, and she died within three years, right in middle life. My aunt always said, "Sallie just died of a broken heart, she was so devoted." Dellie is dead, too, but she died, I heard, quite a long time after we sold the farm.

As for Little Jebb, he grew up to be a mean and ficey Negro. He killed another Negro in a fight and got sent to the penitentiary, where he is yet, the last I heard tell. He probably grew up to be mean and ficey from just being picked on so much by the children of the other tenants, who were jealous of Jebb and Dellie for being thrifty and clever and being white-folks' niggers.

Old Jebb lived forever. I saw him ten years ago and he was about a hundred then, and not looking much different. He was living in town then, on relief—that was back in the Depression—when I went to see him. He said to me: "Too strong to die. When I was a young feller just comen on and seen how things wuz, I prayed the Lawd. I said, Oh, Lawd, gimme strength and meke me strong fer to do and to indure. The Lawd hearkened to my prayer. He give me strength. I was in-duren proud fer being strong and me much man. The Lawd give me my prayer and my strength. But now He done gone off and fergot me and left me alone with my strength. A man doan know what to pray fer, and him mortal."

Jebb is probably living yet, as far as I know.

That is what has happened since the morning when the tramp leaned his face down at me and showed his teeth and said: "Stop following me. You don't stop following me and I cut yore throat, you little son-of-a-bitch." That was what he said, for me not to follow him. But I did follow him, all the years.

POETRY

John Milton

SONNET 21
TO CYRIACK SKINNER

Cyriack, whose grandsire on the royal bench
  Of British Themis, with no mean applause
  Pronounced and in his volume taught our laws,
  Which others at their bar so often wrench;
To-day deep thoughts resolve with me to drench
  In mirth that after no repenting draws;
  Let Euclid rest and Archimedes pause,
  And what the Swede intend, and what the French.
To measure life learn thou betimes, and know
  Toward solid good what leads the nearest way;
  For other things mild Heaven a time ordains,
And disapproves that care, though wise in show,
  That with superfluous burden loads the day,
  And when God sends a cheerful hour, refrains.

Charles Péguy

FREEDOM

GOD SPEAKS:

WHEN you love someone, you love him as he is.
I alone am perfect.
It is probably for that reason
That I know what perfection is
And that I demand less perfection of those poor people.
I know how difficult it is.
And how often, when they are struggling in their trials,
How often do I wish and am I tempted to put my hand under their stomachs
In order to hold them up with my big hand
Just like a father teaching his son how to swim
In the current of the river

And who is divided between two ways of thinking.
For on the one hand, if he holds him up all the time and if he holds him up too much,
The child will depend on this and will never learn how to swim.
But if he doesn't hold him up just at the right moment
That child is bound to swallow more water than is healthy for him.
In the same way, when I teach them how to swim amid their trials
I too am divided by two ways of thinking.
Because if I am always holding them up, if I hold them up too often,
They will never learn how to swim by themselves.
But if I don't hold them up just at the right moment,
Perhaps those poor children will swallow more water than is healthy for them.
Such is the difficulty, and it is a great one.
And such is the doubleness itself, the two faces of the problem.
On the one hand, they must work out their salvation for themselves. That is the rule.
It allows of no exception. Otherwise it would not be interesting. They would not be men.
Now I want them to be manly, to be men, and to win by themselves
Their spurs of knighthood.
On the other hand, they must not swallow more water than is healthy for them,
Having made a dive into the ingratitude of sin.
Such is the mystery of man's freedom, says God,
And the mystery of my government towards him and towards his freedom.
If I hold him up too much, he is no longer free
And if I don't hold him up sufficiently, I am endangering his salvation.
Two goods in a sense almost equally precious.
For salvation is of infinite price.
But what kind of salvation would a salvation be that was not free?
What would you call it?
We want that salvation to be acquired by himself,
Himself, man. To be procured by himself.
To come, in a sense, from himself. Such is the secret.
Such is the mystery of man's freedom.
Such is the price we set on man's freedom.
Because I myself am free, says God, and I have created man in my own image and likeness.
Such is the mystery, such the secret, such the price
Of all freedom.
That freedom of that creature is the most beautiful reflection in this world
Of the Creator's freedom. That is why we are so attached to it,
And set a proper price on it.
A salvation that was not free, that was not, that did not come from

a free man could in no wise be attractive to us. What would it amount to?
What would it mean?
What interest would such a salvation have to offer?
A beatitude of slaves, a salvation of slaves, a slavish beatitude, how do you expect me to be interested in that kind of thing? Does one care to be loved by slaves?
If it were only a matter of proving my might, my might has no need of those slaves, my might is well enough known, it is sufficiently known that I am the Almighty.
My might is manifest enough in all matter and in all events.
My might is manifest enough in the sands of the sea and in the stars of heaven.
It is not questioned, it is known, it is manifest enough in inanimate creation.
It is manifest enough in the government,
In the very event that is man.
But in my creation which is endued with life, says God, I wanted something better, I wanted something more.
Infinitely better. Infinitely more. For I wanted that freedom.
I created that very freedom. There are several degrees to my throne.
When you once have known what it is to be loved freely, submission no longer has any taste.
All the prostrations in the world
Are not worth the beautiful upright attitude of a free man as he kneels. All the submission, all the dejection in the world
Are not equal in value to the soaring up point,
The beautiful straight soaring up of one single invocation
From a love that is free.

Stephen Crane

THE BOOK OF WISDOM

I MET a seer.
He held in his hands
The book of wisdom.
"Sir," I addressed him,
"Let me read."
"Child—" he began.
"Sir," I said.
"Think not that I am a child,
For already I know much
Of that which you hold;
Aye, much."

THE BOOK OF WISDOM: Reprinted from *Collected Poems of Stephen Crane* by permission of Alfred A. Knopf, Inc.

He smiled.
Then he opened the book
And held it before me.
Strange that I should have grown so suddenly blind.

D. H. Lawrence

SHIP OF DEATH

I SING of autumn and the falling fruit
and the long journey towards oblivion.

The apples falling like great drops of dew
to bruise themselves an exit from themselves.

Have you built your ship of death, oh, have you?
Build then your ship of death, for you will need it!

Can man his own quietus make
with a bare bodkin?

With daggers, bodkins, bullets, man can make
a bruise or break of exit for his life
but is that a quietus, oh tell me, is it quietus?

Quietus is the goal of the long journey
the longest journey towards oblivion.

Slips out the soul, invisible one, wrapped still
in the white shirt of the mind's experiences
and folded in the dark-red, unseen
mantle of the body's still mortal memories.

Frightened and alone, the soul slips out of the house
or is pushed out
to find himself on the crowded, arid margins of existence.

Oh, it is not so easy, I tell you it is not so easy
to set softly forth on the longest journey, the longest journey.

It is easy to be pushed out of the silvery city of the body
through any breach in the wall,
thrust out onto the grey grey beaches of shadow
the long marginal stretches of existence, crowded with lost souls
that intervene between our tower and the shaking sea of the beyond.

Oh build your ship of death, oh build it in time
and build it lovingly, and put it between the hands of your soul.

Once outside the gate of the walled silvery life of days
once outside, upon the grey marsh beaches, where lost souls moan
in millions, unable to depart
having no boat to launch upon the shaken, soundless
deepest and longest of seas,
once outside the gate
what will you do, if you have no ship of the soul?

Oh pity the dead that are dead, but cannot take
the journey, still they moan and beat
against the silvery adamant walls of this our exclusive existence.

They moan and beat, they gnash, they rage
they fall upon the new outcoming souls with rage
and they send arrows of anger, bullets and bombs of frustration
over the adamant walls of this, our by-no-means impregnable existence.

Pity, oh pity the poor dead that are only ousted from life
and crowd there on the grey mud beaches of the margins
gaunt and horrible
waiting, waiting till at last the ancient boatman with the common barge
shall take them abroad, towards the great goal of oblivion.

Pity the poor gaunt dead that cannot die
into the distance with receding oars
but must roam like outcast dogs on the margins of life,
and think of them, and with the soul's deep sigh
waft nearer to them the bark of delivery.

But for myself, but for my soul, dear soul
let me build a little ship with oars and food
and little dishes, and all accoutrements
dainty and ready for the departing soul.

And put it between the hands of the trembling soul.
So that when the hour comes, and the last door closes behind him
he shall slip down the shores invisible
between the half-visible hordes
to where the furthest and the longest sea
touches the margins of our life's existence
with wincing unwilling waves.

And launching there his little ship,
wrapped in the dark-red mantle of the body's memories
the little, slender soul sits swiftly down, and takes the oars
and draws away, away, away, towards the dark depths
fathomless deep ahead, far, far from the grey shores
that fringe with shadow all this world's existence.

Over the sea, over the farthest sea
on the longest journey
past the jutting rocks of shadow
past the lurking, octopus arms of agonised memory
past the strange whirlpools of remembered greed
through the dead weed of a life-time's falsity,
slow, slow my soul, in his little ship
on the most soundless of all seas
taking the longest journey.

Pulling the long oars of a life-time's courage,
drinking the confident water from the little jug
and eating the brave bread of a wholesome knowledge
row, little soul, row on
on the longest journey, towards the greatest goal

Neither straight nor crooked, neither here nor there
but shadows folded on deeper shadows
and deeper, to a core of sheer oblivion
like the convolutions of shadow-shell
or deeper, like the foldings and involvings of a womb.

Drift on, drift on, my soul, towards the most pure
most dark oblivion.
And at the penultimate porches, the dark-red mantle
of the body's memories slips and is absorbed
into the shell-like, womb-like convoluted shadow.

And round the great final bend of unbroken dark
the skirt of the spirit's experience has melted away
the oars have gone from the boat, and the little dishes
gone, gone, and the boat dissolves like pearl
as the soul at last slips perfect into the goal, the core
of sheer oblivion and of utter peace,
the womb of silence in the living night.

Ah peace, ah lovely peace, most lovely lapsing
of this my soul into the plasm of peace.

Oh lovely last, last lapse of death, into pure oblivion
at the end of the longest journey
peace, complete peace!
But can it be that also it is procreation?

Oh build your ship of death
oh, build it!
Oh, nothing matters but the longest journey.

John Henry Cardinal Newman

THE DREAM OF GERONTIUS

THE PRIEST

PROFICISCERE, *anima Christiana, de hoc mundo!*
Go forth upon thy journey, Christian soul!
Go from this world! Go, in the name of God,
The omnipotent Father, who created thee!
Go, in the name of Jesus Christ, our Lord,
Son of the living God, who bled for thee!
Go, in the name of the Holy Spirit, who
Hath been poured out on thee! Go, in the name
Of Angels and Archangels; in the name
Of Thrones and Dominations; in the name
Of Princedoms and of Powers; and in the name
Of Cherubim and Seraphim, go forth!
Go, in the name of Patriarchs and Prophets;
And of Apostles and Evangelists,
Of Martyrs and Confessors; in the name
Of Holy Monks and Hermits; in the name
Of Holy Virgins; and all Saints of God,
Both men and women, go! Go on thy course;
And may thy place to-day be found in peace,
And may the dwelling be the Holy Mount
Of Sion:—in the Name of Christ, our Lord....

ANGEL

We now have passed the gate, and are within
The House of Judgment; and whereas on earth
Temples and palaces are formed of parts
Costly and rare, but all material,
So in the world of spirits nought is found,
To mould withal and form into a whole,
But what is immaterial; and thus
The smallest portions of this edifice,
Cornice, or frieze, or balustrade, or stair,

The very pavement is made up of life—
Of holy, blessed, and immortal beings,
Who hymn their Maker's praise continually.

SECOND CHOIR OF ANGELICALS

Praise to the Holiest in the height,
  And in the depth be praise:
In all His words most wonderful;
  Most sure in all His ways!

Woe to thee, man! for he was found
  A recreant in the fight;
And lost his heritage of heaven,
  And fellowship with light.

Above him now the angry sky,
  Around the tempest's din;
Who once had angels for his friends,
  Had but the brutes for kin.

O man! a savage kindred they;
  To flee that monster brood
He scaled the seaside cave, and clomb
  The giants of the wood.

With now a fear, and now a hope,
  With aids which chance supplied,
From youth to eld, from sire to son,
  He lived, and toiled, and died.

He dreed his penance age by age;
  And step by step began
Slowly to doff his savage garb,
  And be again a man.

And quickened by the Almighty's breath,
  And chastened by His rod,
And taught by Angel-visitings,
  At length he sought his God:

And learned to call upon His name,
  And in His faith create
A household and a fatherland,
  A city and a state.

Glory to Him who from the mire,
  In patient length of days,
Elaborated into life
  A people to His praise!

SOUL

The sound is like the rushing of the wind—
The summer wind among the lofty pines;
Swelling and dying, echoing round about,
Now here, now distant, wild and beautiful;
While, scattered from the branches it has stirred,
Descend ecstatic odours.

THIRD CHOIR OF ANGELICALS

Praise to the Holiest in the height,
And in the depth be praise:
In all His words most wonderful;
Most sure in all His ways!

The Angels, as beseemingly
To spirit-kind was given,
At once were tried and perfected,
And took their seats in heaven.

For them no twilight or eclipse;
No growth and no decay;
'Twas hopeless, all-ingulfing night,
Or beatific day.

But to the younger race there rose
A hope upon its fall;
And slowly, surely, gracefully,
The morning dawned on all.

And ages, opening out, divide
The precious and the base,
And from the hard and sullen mass,
Mature the heirs of grace.

O man! albeit the quickening ray,
Lit from his second birth,
Makes him at length what once he was,
And heaven grows out of earth;

Yet still between that earth and heaven—
His journey and his goal—
A double agony awaits
His body and his soul.

A double debt he has to pay—
The forfeit of his sins,
The chill of death is past, and now
The penance-fire begins.

Glory to Him, who evermore
By truth and justice reigns;
Who tears the soul from out its case,
And burns away its stains!

ANGEL

They sing of thy approaching agony,
Which thou so eagerly didst question of:
It is the face of the Incarnate God
Shall smite thee with that keen and subtle pain;
And yet the memory which it leaves will be
A sovereign febrifuge to heal the wound;
And yet withal it will the wound provoke,
And aggravate and widen it the more.

SOUL

Thou speakest mysteries; still methinks I know
To disengage the tangle of thy words:
Yet rather would I hear thy angel voice,
Than for myself be thy interpreter.

ANGEL

When then—if such thy lot—thou seest thy Judge,
The sight of Him will kindle in thy heart,
All tender, gracious, reverential thoughts.
Thou wilt be sick with love, and yearn for Him,
And feel as though thou couldst but pity Him,
That one so sweet should e'er have placed Himself
At disadvantage such, as to be used
So vilely by a being so vile as thee.
There is a pleading in His pensive eyes
Will pierce thee to the quick, and trouble thee.
And thou wilt hate and loathe thyself; for, though
Now sinless, thou wilt feel that thou hast sinned,
As never thou didst feel; and wilt desire
To slink away, and hide thee from His sight
And yet wilt have a longing aye to dwell
Within the beauty of His countenance.
And these two pains, so counter and so keen,—
The longing for Him, when thou seest Him not;
The shame of self at thought of seeing Him,—
Will be thy veriest, sharpest purgatory.

SOUL

My soul is in my hand: I have no fear,—
In His dear might prepared for weal or woe.
But hark! a grand mysterious harmony:
It floods me, like the deep and solemn sound
Of many waters.

ANGEL

We have gained the stairs
Which rise towards the Presence-chamber; there
A band of mighty Angels keep the way
On either side, and hymn the Incarnate God.

ANGELS OF THE SACRED STAIR

Father, whose goodness none can know, but they
Who see Thee face to face,
By man hath come the infinite display
Of Thy victorious grace;
But fallen man—the creature of a day—
Skills not that love to trace.
It needs, to tell the triumph Thou has wrought,
An Angel's deathless fire, an Angel's reach of thought.

It needs that very Angel, who with awe,
Amid the garden shade,
The great Creator in His sickness saw,
Soothed by a creature's aid,
And agonised, as victim of the Law
Which He Himself had made;
For who can praise Him in His depth and height,
But he who saw Him reel amid that solitary fight?

SOUL

Hark! for the lintels of the presence-gate
Are vibrating and echoing back the strain.

FOURTH CHOIR OF ANGELICALS

Praise to the Holiest in the height,
And in the depth be praised:
In all His words most wonderful;
Most sure in all his ways!

The foe blasphemed the Holy Lord,
As if he reckoned ill,
In that he placed His puppet man
The frontier place to fill.

For even in his best estate,
With amplest gifts endued,
A sorry sentinel was he,
A being of flesh and blood.

As though a thing, who for his help
  Must needs possess a wife,
Could cope with those proud rebel hosts,
  Who had angelic life.

And when, by blandishment of Eve,
  That earth-born Adam fell,
He shrieked in triumph, and he cried,
  "A sorry sentinel;

The Maker by His word is bound,
  Escape or cure is none;
He must abandon to his doom,
  And slay His darling son."

ANGEL

And now the threshold, as we traverse it,
Utters aloud its glad responsive chant.

FIFTH CHOIR OF ANGELICALS

Praise to the Holiest in the height,
  And in the depth be praise:
In all His words most wonderful;
  Most sure in all His ways!

O loving wisdom of our God!
  When all was sin and shame,
A second Adam to the fight
  And to the rescue came.

O wisest love! that flesh and blood
  Which did in Adam fail,
Should strive afresh against the foe,
  Should strive and should prevail;

And that a higher gift than grace
  Should flesh and blood refine,
God's Presence and His very Self,
  And Essence all divine.

O generous love! that He who smote
  In man for man the foe,
The double agony in man
  For man should undergo;

And in the garden secretly,
  And on the cross on high,
Should teach his brethren and inspire
  To suffer and to die.

ANGEL

Thy judgment now is near, for we are come
Into the veiled presence of our God.

SOUL

I hear the voices that I left on earth.

ANGEL

It is the voice of friends around thy bed,
Who say the "Subvenite" with the priest.
Hither the echoes come; before the Throne
Stands the great Angel of the Agony,
The same who strengthened Him, what time He knelt
Lone in the garden shade, bedewed with blood.
That Angel best can plead with Him for all
Tormented souls, thy dying and the dead.

ANGEL OF THE AGONY

Jesu! by that shuddering dread which fell on Thee;
Jesu! by that cold dismay which sickened Thee;
Jesu! by that pang of heart which thrilled in Thee;
Jesu! by that mount of sins which crippled Thee;
Jesu! by that sense of guilt which stifled Thee;
Jesu! by that innocence which girdled Thee;
Jesu! by that sanctity which reigned in Thee;
Jesu! by that Godhead which was one with Thee;
Jesu! spare these souls which are so dear to Thee,
Who in prison, calm and patient, wait for Thee;
Hasten, Lord, their hour, and bid them come to Thee,
To that glorious Home, where they shall ever gaze on Thee.

SOUL

I go before my Judge. Ah! . . .

ANGEL

. . . Praise to His Name!
The eager spirit has darted from my hold,
And, with the intemperate energy of love,
Flies to the dear feet of Emmanuel;
But, ere it reach them, the keen sanctity,
Which with its effluence, like a glory, clothes
And circles round the Crucified, has seized,
And scorched, and shrivelled it; and now it lies
Passive and still before the awful Throne.
O happy, suffering soul! for it is safe,
Consumed, yet quickened, by the glance of God.

SOUL

Take me away, and in the lowest deep
There let me be,
And there in hope the lone night-watches keep,
Told out for me.
There, motionless and happy in my pain,
Lone, not forlorn,—
There will I sing my sad perpetual strain,
Until the morn.

There will I sing, and soothe my stricken breast,
Which ne'er can cease
To throb, and pine, and languish, till possest
Of its Sole Peace.
There will I sing my absent Lord and Love:—
Take me away,
That sooner I may rise, and go above,
And see Him in the truth of everlasting day.

ANGEL

Now let the golden prison ope its gates,
Making sweet music, as each fold revolves
Upon its ready hinge. And ye great powers,
Angels of Purgatory, receive from me
My charge, a precious soul, until the day,
When, from all bond and forfeiture released,
I shall reclaim it for the courts of light.

SOULS IN PURGATORY

1. Lord, Thou hast been our refuge: in every generation;
2. Before the hills were born, and the world was: from age to age Thou art God.
3. Bring us not, Lord, very low: for Thou has said, Come back again, ye sons of Adam.
4. A thousand years before Thine eyes are but as yesterday: and as a watch of the night which is come and gone.
5. The grass springs up in the morning: at evening-tide it shrivels up and dies.
6. So we fail in Thine anger: and in Thy wrath we are troubled.
7. Thou has set our sins in Thy sight: and our round of days in the light of Thy countenance.
8. Come back, O Lord! how long: and be entreated for Thy servants.
9. In Thy morning we shall be filled with Thy mercy: we shall rejoice and be in pleasure all our days.
10. We shall be glad according to the days of our humiliation: and the years in which we have seen evil.

11. Look, O Lord, upon Thy servants and on Thy work: and direct their children.
12. And let the beauty of the Lord our God be upon us: and the work of our hands, establish Thou it.

Glory be to the Father, and to the Son: and to the Holy Ghost.

As it was in the beginning, is now, and ever shall be: world without end. AMEN.

ANGEL

Softly and gently, dearly-ransomed soul,
  In my most loving arms I now enfold thee,
And, o'er the penal waters, as they roll,
  I poise thee, and I lower thee, and hold thee.

And carefully I dip thee in the lake,
  And thou, without a sob or a resistance,
Dost through the flood thy rapid passage take,
  Sinking deep, deeper into the dim distance.

Angels, to whom the willing task is given,
  Shall tend, and nurse, and lull thee, as thou liest;
And Masses on the earth, and prayers in heaven,
  Shall aid thee at the Throne of the Most Highest.

Farewell, but not for ever! brother dear,
  Be brave and patient on thy bed of sorrow;
Swiftly shall pass thy night of trial here,
  And I will come and wake thee on the morrow.

T. S. Eliot

GERONTION

Thou hast nor youth nor age
But as it were an after dinner sleep
Dreaming on both.[1]

HERE I am, an old man in a dry month,
  Being read to by a boy, waiting for rain.
I was neither at the hot gates
Nor fought in the warm rain
Nor knee deep in the salt marsh, heaving a cutlass,
Bitten by flies, fought.

1 [From *Measure for Measure,* Act 3, scene i.]

My house is a decayed house,
And the jew squats on the window sill, the owner,
Spawned in some estaminet of Antwerp,
Blistered in Brussels, patched and peeled in London.
The goat coughs at night in the field overhead;
Rocks, moss, stonecrop, iron, merds.
The woman keeps the kitchen, makes tea,
Sneezes at evening, poking the peevish gutter.
                                        I an old man,
A dull head among windy spaces.

Signs are taken for wonders. "We would see a sign!"
The word within a word, unable to speak a word,
Swaddled with darkness. In the juvescence of the year
Came Christ the tiger
In depraved May, dogwood and chestnut, flowering judas,
To be eaten, to be divided, to be drunk
Among whispers; by Mr. Silvero
With caressing hands, at Limoges
Who walked all night in the next room;
By Hakagawa, bowing among the Titians;
By Madame de Tornquist, in the dark room
Shifting the candles; Fräulein von Kulp
Who turned in the hall, one hand on the door. Vacant shuttles
Weave the wind. I have no ghosts,
An old man in a draughty house
Under a windy knob.

After such knowledge, what forgiveness? Think now
History has many cunning passages, contrived corridors
And issues, deceives with whispering ambitions,
Guides us by vanities. Think now
She gives when our attention is distracted
And what she gives, gives with such supple confusions
That the giving famishes the craving. Gives too late
What's not believed in, or if still believed,
In memory only, reconsidered passion. Gives too soon
Into weak hands, what's thought can be dispensed with
Till the refusal propagates a fear. Think
Neither fear nor courage saves us. Unnatural vices
Are fathered by our heroism. Virtues
Are forced upon us by our impudent crimes.
These tears are shaken from the wrath-bearing tree.

The tiger springs in the new year. Us he devours.
   Think at last
We have not reached conclusion, when I
Stiffen in a rented house. Think at last

I have not made this show purposelessly
And it is not by any concitation
Of the backward devils.
I would meet you upon this honestly.
I that was near your heart was removed therefrom
To lose beauty in terror, terror in inquisition.
I have lost my passion: why should I need to keep it
Since what is kept must be adulterated?
I have lost my sight, smell, hearing, taste, and touch:
How should I use them for your closer contact?

These with a thousand small deliberations
Protract the profit of their chilled delirium,
Excite the membrane, when the sense has cooled,
With pungent sauces, multiply variety
In a wilderness of mirrors. What will the spider do,
Suspend its operations, will the weevil
Delay? De Bailhache, Fresca, Mrs. Cammel, whirled
Beyond the circuit of the shuddering Bear
In fractured atoms. Gull against the wind, in the windy straits
Of Belle Isle, or running on the Horn,
White feathers in the snow, the Gulf claims,
And an old man driven by the Trades
To a sleepy corner.

Tenants of the house,
Thoughts of a dry brain in a dry season.

Edwin Muir

THE HORSES

BARELY a twelvemonth after
The seven days war that put the world to sleep,
Late in the evening the strange horses came.
By then we had made our covenant with silence,
But in the first few days it was so still
We listened to our breathing and were afraid.
On the second day
The radios failed; we turned the knobs; no answer.
On the third day a warship passed us, heading north,
Dead bodies piled on the deck. On the sixth day
A plane plunged over us into the sea. Thereafter
Nothing. The radios dumb;

THE HORSES: From *One Foot in Eden* by Edwin Muir, published by Grove Press, Inc.

And still they stand in corners of our kitchens,
And stand, perhaps, turned on, in a million rooms
All over the world. But now if they should speak,
If on a sudden they should speak again,
If on the stroke of noon a voice should speak,
We would not listen, we would not let it bring
That old bad world that swallowed its children quick
At one great gulp. We would not have it again.
Sometimes we think of the nations lying asleep,
Curled blindly in impenetrable sorrow,
And then the thought confounds us with its strangeness.
The tractors lie about our fields; at evening
They look like dank sea-monsters couched and waiting.
We leave them where they are and let them rust:
'They'll moulder away and be like other loam'.
We make our oxen drag our rusty ploughs,
Long laid aside. We have gone back
Far past our fathers' land.
                                        And then, that evening
Late in the summer the strange horses came.
We heard a distant tapping on the road,
A deepening drumming; it stopped, went on again
And at the corner changed to hollow thunder.
We saw the heads
Like a wild wave charging and were afraid.
We had sold our horses in our fathers' time
To buy new tractors. Now they were strange to us
As fabulous steeds set on an ancient shield
Or illustrations in a book of knights.
We did not dare go near them. Yet they waited,
Stubborn and shy, as if they had been sent
By an old command to find our whereabouts
And that long-lost archaic companionship.
In the first moment we had never a thought
That they were creatures to be owned and used.
Among them were some half-a-dozen colts
Dropped in some wilderness of the broken world,
Yet new as if they had come from their own Eden.
Since then they have pulled our ploughs and borne our loads,
But that free servitude still can pierce our hearts.
Our life is changed; their coming our beginning.

Wilfred Owen

STRANGE MEETING

IT SEEMED that out of the battle I escaped
Down some profound dull tunnel, long since scooped
Through granites which Titanic wars had groined.
Yet also there encumbered sleepers groaned,
Too fast in thought or death to be bestirred.
Then, as I probed them, one sprang up, and stared
With piteous recognition in fixed eyes,
Lifting distressful hands as if to bless.
And by his smile, I knew that sullen hall;
By his dead smile I knew I stood in Hell.
With a thousand fears that vision's face was grained;
Yet no blood reached there from the upper ground,
And no guns thumped, or down the flues made moan.
"Strange, friend," I said, "here is no cause to mourn."
"None," said the other, "save the undone years,
The hopelessness. Whatever hope is yours,
Was my life also; I went hunting wild
After the wildest beauty in the world,
Which lies not calm in eyes, or braided hair,
But mocks the steady running of the hour,
And if it grieves, grieves richlier than here.
For by my glee might many men have laughed,
And of my weeping something has been left,
Which must die now. I mean the truth untold,
The pity of war, the pity war distilled.
Now men will go content with what we spoiled,
Or, discontent, boil bloody, and be spilled.
They will be swift with swiftness of the tigress,
None will break ranks, though nations trek from progress.
Courage was mine, and I had mystery,
Wisdom was mine, and I had mastery;
To miss the march of this retreating world
Into vain citadels that are not walled.
Then when much blood had clogged their chariot-wheels
I would go up and wash them from sweet wells,
Even with truths that lie too deep for taint.
I would have poured my spirit without stint
But not through wounds; not on the cess of war.
Foreheads of men have bled where no wounds were.
I am the enemy you killed, my friend.
I knew you in this death; for so you frowned

STRANGE MEETING: From *Poems of Wilfred Owen*.

Yesterday through me as you jabbed and killed.
I parried; but my hands were loath and cold.
Let us sleep now. . . ."

Theodore Roethke

THE WAKING

I WAKE to sleep, and take my waking slow.
I feel my fate in what I cannot fear.
I learn by going where I have to go.

We think by feeling. What is there to know?
I hear my being dance from ear to ear.
I wake to sleep, and take my waking slow.

Of those so close beside me, which are you?
God bless the Ground! I shall walk softly there,
And learn by going where I have to go.

Light takes the Tree; but who can tell us how?
The lowly worm climbs up a winding stair;
I wake to sleep, and take my waking slow.

Great Nature has another thing to do
To you and me; so take the lively air,
And, lovely, learn by going where to go.

This shaking keeps me steady. I should know.
What falls away is always. And is near.
I wake to sleep, and take my waking slow.
I learn by going where I have to go.

Vassar Miller

WITHOUT CEREMONY

EXCEPT ourselves, we have no other prayer;
Our needs are sores upon our nakedness.
We do not have to name them; we are here.
And You who can make eyes can see no less.

We fall, not on our knees, but on our hearts,
A posture humbler far and more downcast;
While Father Pain instructs us in the arts
Of praying, hunger is the worthiest fast.
We find ourselves where tongues cannot wage war
On silence (farther, mystics never flew)
But on the common wings of what we are,
Borne on the wings of what we bear, toward You,
Oh Word, in whom our wordiness dissolves,
When we have not a prayer except ourselves.

Notes on Authors

A Glossary of Literary and Rhetorical Terms

Index

NOTES ON AUTHORS

THOMAS E. ADAMS (1924–) was born in Trenton, New Jersey. He was educated at La Salle College in Philadelphia, and at the University of Florida where he studied creative writing under Andrew Lytle. "Sled" is his first published story.

JAMES AGEE (1909–1955) was born in Knoxville, Tennessee. After attending Exeter Academy, he went to Harvard where he won the Poetry Prize and became an editor of the *Harvard Advocate*. Two years after his graduation in 1932 his first book of poetry, *Permit Me Voyage*, appeared in the Yale Series of Younger Poets. While he worked for *Fortune* Magazine he wrote *Let Us Now Praise Famous Men* (1941), a meditative essay-report on Alabama sharecroppers. His first novel, *The Morning Watch* (1954), tells of the life of a schoolboy. His second, *A Death in the Family* (1954), won the Pulitzer Prize; a dramatized version by Ted Mosel, *All the Way Home*, won the New York Drama Critics' Circle Award. Agee also wrote film reviews and screenplays; many of them are collected in *Agee on Film* (1958–60).

CONRAD ARENSBERG (1910–), a native of Pittsburgh, attended Harvard where he received a B.A. in 1931 and a Ph.D. in 1934. A well-known anthropologist and sociologist, he has taught at Harvard, M.I.T., Brooklyn College, and Columbia University. Among his books are *Irish Countryman* (1936), *Family and Community in Ireland* (1940), and *Trade and Money in Early Empires* (1957).

ARISTOTLE (384–322 B.C.) was born in the Greek colony of Stagira. He went to Athens at 18, became a pupil of Plato, and founded a school of rhetoric. In 342 Philip of Macedon asked him to be tutor to his son, the future Alexander the Great. His great work as physicist, scientist, and philosopher began when he returned to Athens in 335 to open his school, the Lyceum. Of his many books those that have had the greatest influence on students of literature are his *Rhetoric, Poetics,* and the *Nichomachean Ethics.* Aristotle barely escaped the fate of Socrates when, after Alexander's death, his enemies accused him of impiety. He fled to Chalcis in Euboea, where he died in 322.

MATTHEW ARNOLD (1822–1888) was educated at Winchester, Rugby, and Balliol College, Oxford. He was successively a Fellow of Oriel, a secretary to Lord Lansdowne, and Inspector of Schools. His literary career began with the publication of his *Poems* (1853–

1854), but he achieved an even greater reputation as a literary critic and as an interpreter of cultural history. In his later years Arnold devoted much of his effort to writings on religion, science, and education.

W. H. AUDEN (1907–) was educated at Gresham's in Holt and Christ Church, Oxford. He acquired an early reputation as a poet of social conscience and revolt with his *Poems* (1930). Shortly after his emigration to the United States in 1939, Auden's work began to reflect a more humanist and Christian orientation. His poetry, extremely varied in subject, form, and tone, ranges from lengthy philosophic and mystical meditations to brief lyrics and witty satires. His best work appears in *Collected Poems* (1945) and *Selected Poetry* (1960) and in a collection of essays, *The Dyer's Hand* (1963).

FRANCIS BACON (1561–1626), in addition to his active career as a lawyer and politician, was one of England's most influential philosophers, scholars, and essayists. His inductive philosophy is most completely revealed in his *Novum Organum* (*New Instrument*, 1620), his scholarship in his *The Advancement of Learning* (1605), and his great ability as an essayist in his *Essays* (1597, 1625). The *Essays* introduced a new style of writing that contributed greatly to the development of English prose.

JAMES BALDWIN (1924–) was born and raised in New York City. In his twenties, however, he went to Europe and remained there, mostly in Paris, for ten years. His first novel, *Go Tell It on the Mountain* (1954), is the story of Harlem Negroes in their search for true religious experience. *Notes of a Native Son* (1955) is a collection of autobiographical essays that describe the author's experiences as a Negro in the United States. A second novel, *Giovanni's Room*, appeared in 1956. A third novel, *Another Country*, and *Nobody Knows My Name* (a sequel to *Notes of a Native Son*) appeared in 1961. Mr. Baldwin's latest book, a study of the Black Muslim movement, is called *The Fire Next Time* (1963).

SIR MAX BEERBOHM (1872–1956) was born in London and was graduated from Charterhouse and Merton College, Oxford. Sir Max achieved the highest rank as a caricaturist, a writer of essays, a superb parodist, and a dramatic critic. His caricatures, as notable for their captions as for their lines, may be seen in *Poets' Corner* (1904). A good collection of his parodies appears in *The Happy Hypocrite* (1897) and *A Christmas Garland* (1912). Some of his best essays are contained in *And Even Now* (1920). Many connoisseurs of the inimitable Max regard his novel *Zuleika Dobson* (1902) as the richest and most subtle display of his genius for parody.

UGO BETTI (1892–1954) was born in Camerino, Italy. He was graduated from the University of Parma with a degree in law in 1914. After serving in World War I, he became a judge and eventually Chief Justice in the Italian Courts. He wrote poetry, three volumes of short stories, and more than a score of plays, of which *The Mistress* (1929) and *Corruption in the Palace of Justice* (1944) are the best known outside of Italy. Betti felt that few people in this age actually believe in the existence of good and evil. As a dramatist he felt his mission was to "try to convince them again." Betti is regarded by many as the equal and counterpart of Pirandello. But whereas Pirandello asked "What is truth?" Betti asks "What is justice?"

WILLIAM BLAKE (1757–1827), the son of a London hosier, was apprenticed at fourteen to an engraver. He studied painting at the Royal Academy School and began to achieve a reputation as an engraver and illustrator. Although his artistic work earned him a place in the history of art, he is perhaps best known as a lyrical poet whose intense love of freedom, both imaginative and personal, resulted in such exquisite lyrics as those in *Poetical Sketches* (1783), *Songs of Innocence* (1789), and *Songs of Experience* (1794). His "mystical" works, such as *The Book of Thel* (1789), are brilliant but often incomprehensible visions.

ELIZABETH BOWEN (1899–) was born in County Cork and considers Bowen's Court, her ancestral home, her permanent residence although she is equally at home in Dublin, London, Paris, Rome, and New York. Her first book of short stories, *Encounters* (1923), contains the germ of her fictional method in its title. Her later novels, particularly *The Death of the Heart* (1938), guaranteed her place among the best novelists in English. She is, in addition, a distinguished critic and a poetic interpreter of her favorite places. In *Bowen's Court* (1941) she evokes the quality and charm of Irish country life.

SIR CHARLES MAURICE BOWRA (1898–) was born in Kingkiang, China, and was educated at New College, Oxford. At present, he is the Warden of Wadham College, Oxford. In 1951 he added a knighthood to his many academic titles. He has been Professor of Poetry at both Oxford and Harvard and the President of the British Academy. Although he is a master of many languages, he has specialized in the classics, particularly in Greek. His *Tradition and Design in the Iliad* (1931), together with *Greek Lyric Poetry* (1936), *Sophoclean Tragedy* (1944), and *The Greek Experience* (1959) constitute an admirable review of the principal achievements of Hellenic culture.

Elizabeth Barrett Browning (1806–1861) was, if not a child prodigy, at least extremely precocious. At her father's estate in Herefordshire she learned to read Homer in the original at ten; at fourteen she composed an epic poem on the Battle of Marathon. Invalided by a childhood injury, she devoted herself to poetry. At nineteen she published her first book, *Essay on Mind, and Other Poems* and, at twenty-seven, a translation of *Prometheus Bound*. Shortly before her dramatic elopement with Robert Browning, she issued *Poems* (1844), which contained her celebrated "The Cry of the Children." Because Robert Browning's pet name for her was my little Portuguese, she entitled her love poems, of which "How Do I Love Thee" is a famous example, *Sonnets from the Portuguese*.

Robert Browning (1812–1889), one of the great Victorian poets, was self-educated, chiefly by reading at home and by travel. Before his marriage to Elizabeth Barrett he had written *Pauline* (1833) and *Paracelsus* (1835), both very difficult poems. But with the appearance of *Bells and Pomegranates* (1841–46) and *Men and Women* (1855) Browning became one of the most widely read poets of his time. His *The Ring and the Book* (1869), an intertwined series of dramatic monologues, crowned his career with an undoubted masterpiece. "Andrea del Sarto" (1855) is an early example of his mastery of the dramatic monologue.

Robert Burns (1759–1796) was born at Alloway near Ayr, Scotland, the son of a poor farmer. He had little formal schooling. From his father and his relatives, however, he came to know by heart the legends, songs, and ballads of the Scots peasants. He also read widely the eighteenth-century English writers. While working as a farmhand and later an exciseman, he began to write and, in 1786, published his *Poems: Chiefly in the Scottish Dialect*. Most of his other poems were contributed to two miscellanies, James Johnson's *Scots Musical Museum* (five volumes, 1787–1803), and George Thompson's *Select Collection of Original Scottish Airs for the Voice* (six volumes, 1793–1811). In 1793, just three years before his premature death, his *Poems* were reissued in two volumes. Burns reigns supreme among British poets in song, ballad, and tale.

Witter Bynner (1881–   ) was born in Brooklyn, New York, and was graduated from Harvard in 1902. The reception of his first book, *An Ode to Harvard* (1907), was so encouraging that he devoted himself to the writing of poetry. In 1917 he issued *Grenstone Poems* and in 1922 *A Book of Plays*. In addition to regular volumes of poetry, Bynner has translated and adapted Chinese classics and has written a memoir about his friendship with D. H. Lawrence, *Journey with Genius* (1951). In 1960 Bynner surprised his readers with *New Poems*, a collection that is as fresh and exciting as the best of his early work.

George Gordon, Lord Byron (1788–1824) attained his majority and claimed his seat in the House of Lords in 1809. As a child he had suffered neglect from a dissolute father and mistreatment from a neurotic mother. His first book, *Hours of Idleness* (1807), was pilloried by the *Edinburgh Review*. Yet in the next fifteen years he was to dominate the literary world with a dazzling series of poems and plays: *Childe Harold, Manfred, Beppo, Don Juan*, together with many shorter poems. His death at Missolonghi, while serving in the Greek war for independence, cut short a tragic life that, in his own words, "was half-mad, between metaphysics, mountains, lakes, love inextinguishable, and thoughts unutterable, and the nightmare of my own delinquencies."

Roy Campbell (1902–1957) was born in Durban, South Africa. His early poetry reflects his turbulent country and his equally turbulent personality. *The Flaming Terrapin* (1924) centers on a symbol of the life force that thrusts mankind on through storm and peril to a higher level of civilization. *The Wayzgoose* (1928) satirizes some South African follies that have since become more widely known. Campbell's *Collected Poems* appeared in 1949. His autobiography, notable for its strong loves and hates, is contained in *Broken Record* (1934) and *Light on a Dark Horse* (1951).

Albert Camus (1913–1959) was born in Mondovi, Algeria, the son of a farm laborer. He studied philosophy at the University of Algiers and then worked as a schoolteacher, actor, journalist, and playwright. During World War II he was an active resistance leader; after the war he was coeditor with Jean-Paul Sartre of *Le Combat*, a left-wing paper. He attracted international attention with his first novel, *The Stranger* (1946), an existentialist story that depicts man and his world as absurd. The meaninglessness of contemporary life is also the theme of his *The Plague* (1948) and his book of essays *The Myth of Sisyphus* (1955). He was awarded the Nobel Prize in 1957, and died two years later in an automobile accident.

Thomas Carlyle (1795–1881) tried divinity, teaching, and the law before he settled on a career as a writer. His first literary efforts were translations and studies of German literature. In 1837 his *French Revolution* became a national sensation by reason of its unusual vividness and poetic energy. *Sartor Resartus*, an autobiographical work that expressed his philosophy of life, was published in book form in 1839. His biographies *Oliver Cromwell* (1845) and *History of Frederick the Great* (1858–65) together with his many essays on heroes testify to his belief that history is the extended biography of the great man.

Willa Cather (1876?–1947) was born near Winchester, Virginia, but moved in her childhood to Nebraska where she studied at local schools and later at the University of Nebraska. A talent for writing was shown in verse in *April Twilights* (1903) and in short stories in "The Troll Garden" (1905) and "Youth and the Bright Medusa" (1920). Her early novels, *O Pioneers* (1913), *The Song of the Lark* (1915), *My Ántonia* (1918), and *A Lost Lady* (1923), depicted the stirrings of moral and aesthetic life among the immigrants on the midwestern frontier. With her novel *The Professor's House* (1925), Miss Cather turned for inspiration to the colonial era in the American southwest and French Canada. Her *Death Comes for the Archbishop* (1927) and *Shadows on the Rock* (1931) are marked by deep feeling, mellowness, and a faintly elegiac character. In a book of essays on writing, *Not Under Forty* (1936), she expressed an artistic creed that espoused the poetic as opposed to the journalistic novel.

LEWIS CARROLL (1832–1898), whose real name was Charles L. Dodgson, was educated at Rugby and Christ Church, Oxford, where he won first honors in mathematics. A professional mathematician, Carroll introduced in *Alice in Wonderland* (1865) and *Through the Looking Glass* (1872) logical problems that have since been widely quoted. *The Hunting of the Snark* appeared in 1876. He also published important mathematical and logical treatises.

MIGUEL DE CERVANTES SAAVEDRA (1547–1616) is one of the outstanding figures of world literature. He is first known to us by his verses on the death of Queen Isabel in 1569. In 1569 he went to Italy as secretary to Cardinal Acquaviva, but soon after joined the forces of Don Juan of Austria and served with valor at Lepanto, where he was badly wounded and maimed. In 1575, his homebound galley was captured and he and his brother spent five years in captivity in Algiers. After four unsuccessful attempts to escape (reflected in "The Captive's Story") Cervantes was ransomed by the Trinitarian fathers. He contributed to the then flourishing theater at Madrid some thirty plays of which *La Numancia* is a recognized masterpiece. *Don Quixote*, his greatest work, appeared in two parts in 1605 and 1615. During these years he brought out his superb *Exemplary Novels,* his *Voyage to Parnassus,* a long verse history of the poetry of his day, and his romance *Persiles and Segismunda.* He died in poverty, piety, and seclusion in Madrid.

GILBERT KEITH CHESTERTON (1874–1936), one of the most versatile writers of his time, was born in London and was educated at St. Paul's and the Slade School of Art. He was concurrently a poet, a literary journalist, a novelist, a detective-story writer, a biographer, a philosopher, and a religious thinker. Of his numerous published works his readers particularly cherish his *Collected Poems* (1927), his series of Father Brown stories, and his philosophical assessments of modern times in *Heretics* (1908), *Orthodoxy* (1908), and *The Everlasting*

Man (1925). His literary assessments, while marked by his strong personal views, are brilliant and provocative. Some of the best are *Charles Dickens* (1906), *George Bernard Shaw* (1909), *The Victorian Age in Literature* (1913), and *Chaucer* (1932). His play, *The Judgement of Dr. Johnson* (1927), is at once a study of one of his favorite Englishmen and a revelation of his own robust temperament.

Robert Peter Tristram Coffin (1892–1955) was born in Brunswick, Maine, and was graduated from Bowdoin and Oxford. Many of his poems reflect his Maine farm background. His *Strange Holiness* (1936) won the Pulitzer Prize for poetry. His *Collected Poems* appeared in 1948. Coffin was a distinctly affirmative poet who expressed his love of home, native state, and country with homely realism, colloquial diction, and simple, forceful rhythms. Besides writing much verse, Coffin was a successful college teacher, a popular lecturer, and a writer of prose. *Kennebec: Cradle of Americans* (1937) is an informal history of Maine.

Samuel Taylor Coleridge (1772–1834) was born in Devonshire, the son of the local vicar. He was educated at Christ's Hospital and Jesus College, Cambridge. After serving as a private in the dragoons, a journalist, and an itinerant Unitarian preacher, he encountered William Wordsworth and collaborated with him in writing the *Lyrical Ballads.* Although Coleridge wrote relatively few poems, they were immensely influential both for their literary value and their historical importance in the development of Romanticism. His "Ode to Dejection" (1802) marks a turning point in his career as a poet, and a repudiation of a theory of inspiration he had shared with Wordsworth. In his later life he turned to literary speculation and, in his *Biographia Literaria* (1817) and *Anima Poetae* (pub. 1895), he produced a body of literary criticism that has shaped much modern thinking on literature.

Joseph Conrad (1857–1924) was born in the Ukraine of Polish parents. He later Anglicized his name from Josef Teodor Konrad Korzeniowski. He was orphaned in his early youth. In 1874 he joined the French merchant marine and in 1878 the British merchant marine, where he rose to the rank of master. His seventeen years at sea took him to the Far East, the Belgian Congo, and the South Atlantic—places that provided the settings and sometimes the personalities of his stories. Conrad's literary career began with the publication of *Almayer's Folly* (1894). During the next ten years he wrote the bulk of his masterpieces, longer novels like *Lord Jim* (1900), *Romance* (1903), *Nostromo* (1904), *The Secret Agent* (1907), and *Chance* (1914), and novellas or tales like *The Nigger of the Narcissus* (1897), *Youth* (1902), *Typhoon and Other Stories* (1903), and *A Set of Six* (1908). "Amy Foster," included in *Typhoon,* is typical of Conrad's major interest not in the events or the setting but in "their effect on the persons in the tale."

STEPHEN CRANE (1871–1900) was born in Newark, New Jersey, the youngest child of a Methodist minister. He was educated at various public schools in New Jersey and New York before attending Lafayette College and Syracuse University. Crane, following a family tradition for authorship, began writing when he was eight years old. By 16 he was writing for newspapers. At 20 he wrote "in two days before Christmas" *Maggie: A Girl of the Streets*. At 21 he wrote *The Red Badge of Courage*, a sensational success that earned him numerous appointments as a correspondent for various syndicates. At 23 he toured the west for the Bachiller Syndicate to find material for articles, sketches, and stories. "The Blue Hotel" was partly the result of that trip although it was not written until 1898. Crane's subsequent career was one of hectic journalism that took him to Cuba, Greece, England, and Germany, where he died of tuberculosis.

JAMES VINCENT CUNNINGHAM (1911–   ) was born in Cumberland, Maryland. He was educated at Stanford University. His scholarly career has taken him to the University of Virginia, the University of Hawaii, and Brandeis University. He has written several books, one on Shakespearean tragedy: *Tradition and Poetic Structure*. His poems have been widely admired for their wit, elegance, and vigor. They are collected under the title *The Exclusions of a Rhyme: Poems and Epigrams* (1960).

DANTE ALIGHIERI (1265–1321) studied grammar with Franciscan friars, rhetoric with the philosopher-poet Brunetto Latini, and poetry with, or under the inspiration of, Guido Cavalcanti. His debt to Virgil and other Latin poets and to the medieval philosophy based on Aristotle's treatises suggests other mentors who cannot easily be identified. Dante's literary career is closely related to his ideal love for Beatrice Portinari. In his first book *La Vita Nuova* (*The New* [or Early] *Life*), 1292–94, he tells in thirty-one poems with prose commentary how he first met the nine-year-old Beatrice and how she inspired him to seek, through love of her, a higher life. What that life consists of is in part related in *Il Convivio* (*The Banquet*), 1304–1307, where Philosophy or Wisdom is personified as a gentle and compassionate lady. In his great work *Commedia* (*The Divine Comedy*), 1315–21, Beatrice is a figure of Wisdom who arranges for Virgil to guide Dante through Hell and Purgatory. She herself takes him to the heights of heaven (in the *Paradiso*) where St. Bernard's prayers gain for him a vision of the Trinity and with it the intuition of the whole scope and meaning of life here and hereafter.

EMILY DICKINSON (1830–1886) was born in Amherst, Massachusetts, and was educated at Mount Holyoke Seminary and Amherst

Institute. She led a retired life in the home of her father, a prominent lawyer. Although she published only three poems during her lifetime, she composed more than 2,000—almost all of them brief, aphoristic, and metaphysical. Her greatest gift was her realization of the presence of spiritual truth in natural objects and events. Because she wrote most of her verses in three drafts, her poetry, while admired for its extraordinary poignancy and delicacy, created many varied impressions. The appearance of a definitive three-volume *Poems of Emily Dickinson* in 1958 has inspired new efforts to understand her poetry.

FYODOR DOSTOEVSKY (1821–1881) was born in Moscow. He attended the College of Military Engineering in St. Petersburg and served his compulsory two years in the army before writing *Poor Folk* (1846), the success of which induced him to pursue a literary career. As a result of associating with political revolutionaries he was sentenced in 1849 to six years of hard labor in Siberia where he suffered some of the experiences set forth in his novel *The House of the Dead* (1862). His major novels, *Crime and Punishment* (1866), *The Possessed* (1871), and *The Brothers Karamazov* (1880), reflect his amazing ability to dramatize the conflict between good and evil in the individual soul.

MICHAEL DRAYTON (1563–1631) was born at Hartshill in Warwickshire. His first book of verse, *The Harmony of the Church*, was suppressed as offensive by ecclesiastical authorities. After writing an eclogue, "The Shepherd's Garland" (1593), he turned with great success to a series of historical poems. His long, immensely erudite *Poly-Olbion* (1613) is a versified geography of Britain full of interesting description and historical detail. "Agincourt" appears in *Poems Lyric and Heroic* (1606), which together with *Nymphidia* (1627) are most admired by modern readers.

RENÉ DUBOS (1901–) was born in St. Brice, France. He was educated in French schools and at Rutgers University and has studied and taught at Rochester, Harvard, and the Sorbonne. He is a prominent research scientist in the field of bacteriology and internal medicine, and is credited with the discovery of the antibiotic tyrothricin. He is a member of the Rockefeller Institute for Medical Research, and is the author of *Louis Pasteur: Free Lance of Science* (1950), *The White Plague: Tuberculosis, Man and Society* (1952), and numerous technical works on science.

THOMAS STERNS ELIOT (1888–) was born in St. Louis, Missouri. He was educated at Harvard and Merton College, Oxford, and has lived in England since 1914, where he has been an editor and publisher, and has achieved highest recognition as poet, playwright, and essayist. He became a British citizen in 1927. His *Prufrock and*

Other Observations (1917), *The Wasteland* (1922), and *The Hollow Men* (1925) marked a revolution in modern poetry with their emphasis on the theme of disillusion and their use of symbolism. Eliot's underlying Christian sensibility and his great indebtedness to Dante became more evident in *Ash Wednesday* (1930) and in *Four Quartets* (1943). His plays are even more unequivocally Christian in theme, setting, and tone. *The Rock* (1934) and *Murder in the Cathedral* (1935) are explicitly religious plays, while *The Family Reunion* (1939), *The Cocktail Party* (1950), *The Confidential Clerk* (1954), and *The Elder Statesmen* (1958) all contain conflicts arising from problems relating to Christian belief. Eliot's essays are partly a record of his literary affinities, as in *The Sacred Wood* (1920), *Elizabethan Essays* (1934), *After Strange Gods* (1936), and *Of Poetry and Poets* (1957), and partly a criticism of contemporary values, as in *Modern Education and the Classics* (1934), *The Idea of a Christian Society* (1939), and *Notes Towards the Definition of a Culture* (1948). He received the Nobel Prize in 1948.

Ralph Waldo Emerson (1803–1882) was graduated from the Boston Latin School and in 1821 from Harvard. In 1826 he was appointed a Unitarian pastor but left the ministry six years later. After a trip to England where he established a lifelong friendship with Carlyle, Emerson moved to Concord, Massachusetts. As lecturer, essayist, and poet he preached a transcendental doctrine that man's soul was divine, the same in all men, and in harmony with nature. His best-known essays appeared in *Representative Men* (1850) and *The Conduct of Life* (1860). Although known chiefly as a prose writer, Emerson's poetry contains some of his most effective writing.

William H. Faulkner (1897–1962) was born in New Albany, Mississippi. He served for a year in the Canadian Air Force, returning to Oxford, Mississippi, to attend the University, for two semesters. He held various odd jobs while he prepared himself to become a writer. In his early novels and short stories he tentatively explored the decay of traditional southern society, a theme he was later to develop in his major novels. These novels focus on the fortunes of various groups, chiefly on the Sartoris family in *Sartoris* (1929) and *The Unvanquished* (1938), in the Compsons in *The Sound and the Fury* (1929) and *Absalom, Absalom!* (1936), and on the Snopes family in *The Hamlet* (1940), *The Town* (1957), and *The Mansion* (1959). Other novels that round out his portrait of imaginary Yoknapa Tawpha County are *As I Lay Dying* (1930) and *Light in August* (1931). Faulkner received the Nobel Prize in 1949.

Francis Fergusson (1904–   ) was born in Albuquerque, New Mexico. He studied at Harvard for two years, then went on to Queen's College, Oxford, where he received his B.A. and M.A. degrees. He has been connected with the drama as a director, critic, and teacher since 1926. In addition to many articles and reviews, he has written three influential books: *The Idea of a Theater* (1949), *The Purgatorio: Dante's Drama of the Mind* (1953), and *The Human Image in Dramatic Literature* (1957). Fergusson is currently Professor of Literature at Rutgers.

ROBERT FROST (1875–1963) was born in San Francisco and was educated at Dartmouth and Harvard. His determination to become a poet led him to England where his first books, *A Boy's Will* (1913) and *North of Boston* (1914), were enthusiastically received. He returned to the United States and settled on a farm in New Hampshire. *Mountain Interval* (1916) and *New Hampshire* (1923) maintained the basic simplicity of theme and technique of his earlier volumes. With *A Further Range* (1936) Frost's poetry became more complex. His verse dramas, *A Masque of Reason* (1945) and *A Masque of Mercy* (1947), discussed large metaphysical questions that he had previously touched on only indirectly. His *Complete Poems* appeared in 1949. By the time of his death Frost was widely regarded as America's unofficial poet laureate.

CLAUDE M. FUESS (1885–) was educated at Amherst and Columbia. He was for many years headmaster of the Phillips Academy, at Andover, Massachusetts. He has written several outstanding biographies, including *Daniel Webster* (1930) and *Calvin Coolidge* (1940). His views on education may be found in his *Creed of a Schoolmaster* (1939) and *Independent Schoolmaster* (1952).

JOHN GARDNER (1912–) was educated at Stanford and the University of California. He has served as a Professor of Psychology at various United States universities and colleges. He is currently President of the Carnegie Foundation.

JOHN GAY (1685–1732) published *Wine*, his first poem, in 1708 and an essay entitled *The Present State of Wit* in 1711. While secretary to the Duchess of Monmouth he dedicated his *Rural Sports* (1713) to the poet Alexander Pope, who became his friend. Gay's chief successes were his witty and satirical *The Shepherd's Week* (1714) and *The Fables* (1727) and his celebrated parody of Italian opera, *The Beggar's Opera* (1728).

HERBERT GOLD (1924–) was born in Cleveland, Ohio, and was educated at Cornell, Columbia, and the Sorbonne. He has written numerous short stories, four novels, *Birth of a Hero* (1951), *The Prospect Before Us* (1954), *The Man Who Was Not With It* (1956), and *Therefore Be Bold* (1960). His latest novel, *Salt* (1963), is a satire on the aimlessness of twentieth-century man who lives without values. A collection of his essays, *The Age of Happy Problems*, appeared in 1962.

Robert Graves (1895–) was born in London and was educated at Charterhouse and St. John's College, Oxford. His autobiographies, *Goodbye to All That* (1929), *But It Still Goes On* (1930), and *Occupation Writer* (1950) recapitulate the history of his times. His historical novels, particularly *I, Claudius* (1934) and *Claudius the God* (1935), are extraordinary imaginative reconstructions of Roman life. His *Collected Poems* (1959) reveal him less as a modernist than as a reviver of traditional forms.

Graham Greene (1904–) was educated at Balliol College, Oxford. He started his career as a journalist and a critic of films. Both occupations are reflected in his early thrillers. *Orient Express* (1932), *It's a Battlefield* (1934), and *This Gun for Hire* (1936) are exciting adventure tales that seemed destined for the films. With the publication of *Brighton Rock* (1938) the police thriller took on deeper psychological and religious overtones. In *The Power and the Glory* (1940), *The Heart of the Matter* (1948), *The End of the Affair* (1951), and *A Burnt-Out Case* (1961), Greene explored the secret corruptions of the human soul, without, however, denying his characters the hope of regeneration and ultimate redemption. *The Lost Childhood and Other Essays* (1951) reveals Greene's talents as an essayist. He is also a successful playwright and a vivid reporter of his travels in Africa, Mexico, Indo-China, and other parts of the world.

Nathaniel Hawthorne (1804–1864) was born in Salem, Massachusetts, and was educated at Bowdoin College. From 1825 until 1837—the "twelve dark years," as he called them—he experimented with the writing of prose and verse. His first novel *Fanshawe* (1828) was unsuccessful, but *Twice-Told Tales* (1837) was enthusiastically received, and *The Scarlet Letter* (1850) was an immediate success. His ability to penetrate the consciences of his Puritan characters was sustained throughout *The House of the Seven Gables* (1851), the short stories that made up *The Snow-Image* (1851), and *The Blithedale Romance* (1852). When he wrote *The Marble Faun* in 1860 he was still investigating the unpardonable sin of pride that destroys the human soul. Since his death Hawthorne's *Notebooks* have aroused great interest because of their valuable insights into the creative process.

William Hazlitt (1778–1830), although trained for the Unitarian ministry, turned, under the influence of Samuel Coleridge, to a career of letters instead. He wrote extensively for many journals and on many topics, including philosophy, politics, painting, and literature. Many of his best essays are found in his *The Characters of Shakespeare's Plays* (1817), *Lectures on the English Poets* (1818), *English Comic Writers* (1819), and *Dramatic Literature of the Age of Elizabeth* (1820). These, together with *Table Talk* (1821–22) and *The*

Spirit of the Age (1825), are more interesting to modern readers than is his four-volume *Life of Napoleon* (1821–30).

WILLIAM ERNEST HENLEY (1849–1903) studied under the poet T. E. Brown at the Crypt Grammar School in Gloucester. A cripple from early childhood, he was alternately drawn to the themes of sickness and health. His best verses are found in *London Voluntaries* (1893) and *Hawthorn and Lavender* (1901). Henley was also a successful editor and dramatist.

SIR ALAN PATRICK HERBERT (1890–), a member of the bar and for fifteen years a Member of Parliament for Oxford, is best known as a humorist. He joined the staff of *Punch* in 1924, wrote the script of numerous comic reviews and operas, and published many volumes of verse and several amusing novels, among them *The Secret Battle* (1919), *The Water Gipsies* (1932), and *Holy Deadlock* (1934). His *What a Word!* (1935) is a witty attack on jargon.

GERARD MANLEY HOPKINS (1844–1889) gave great promise as a scholar while an undergraduate at Balliol College, Oxford. "The Star of Balliol" became a Catholic in 1866 and, in 1868, entered the Jesuit order where he performed pastoral duties up to his appointment in 1884 as Professor of Greek at the University of Dublin. Hopkins published no poetry during his lifetime. Robert Bridges, his friend and literary executor, released his *Poems* in 1918. A larger edition appeared in 1930. Publication of his *Letters to Robert Bridges* and *The Correspondence of Gerard Manley Hopkins and Richard Watson Dixon* in 1935 and his *Notebooks* in 1937 increased public understanding of his original aesthetic and literary principles. Hopkins is now regarded with Yeats and Eliot as one of the founders of modern poetry.

HORACE (65–8 B.C.) was born in Venusia in southern Italy. He studied grammar and rhetoric under Orbilius Pupillus at Rome and philosophy at Athens. In the Civil War following Julius Caesar's death he fought with the Republican forces under Brutus. After Brutus' defeat, Horace entered the Civil Service. His skill in poetry won him the attention of Virgil, who in turn presented him to Maecenas, the wealthy statesman and patron of the arts. Through Maecenas, Horace acquired a farm in the Sabine Hills that gave him a steady income and a peaceful retreat. Shortly afterwards he published his *Satires I* (35 B.C.) and *Satires II* and *Epodes* (30 B.C.). In about 19 B.C. his *Odes* and *Epistles* appeared. Horace ranks with his contemporary, Virgil, as one of Rome's best poets of the classical era.

A. E. HOUSMAN (1859–1936) was born near Bromsgrove and was educated at St. John's College, Oxford. He spent ten years as a clerk in the patent office before his learned articles won for him first a

Professorship in Latin at the University of London and then a chair at Cambridge. Although he was one of the greatest classical scholars of his day, Housman is best known for his poems: *A Shropshire Lad* (1896), *Last Poems* (1922), and a posthumous volume, *More Poems* (1936). His classical discipline gave order and shape to a profoundly romantic temperament.

EMMET JOHN HUGHES (1920–) has been, since his graduation from Princeton University in 1941, a press attaché in the United State Embassy in Madrid, a foreign correspondent for Time-Life, and an administrative assistant to President Dwight Eisenhower. He is currently an editor of Newsweek. He is the author of *The Church and the Liberal Society* (1943), *Report from Spain* (1947), and *The Ordeal of Power* (1963), the story of his participation in the Eisenhower administration.

THOMAS HENRY HUXLEY (1825–1895) studied medicine at Charing Cross Hospital. After a pioneering scientific expedition aboard H.M.S. Rattlesnake in 1846–50, he became a Professor of Natural History at the Royal School of Mines. He accepted Charles Darwin's theory of evolution and became, by virtue of his considerable literary skill, a leading apologist for the *Origin of Species*. Some of his popular scientific essays are found in *Man's Place in Nature* (1863). His conflicts with contemporaries on matters of theology and humanism are reflected in *Lay Sermons* (1870), and *Science and Education*, (1899).

SHIRLEY JACKSON (1919–) was educated in New York schools and at Syracuse University. Her short stories and novels concentrate on characters with a fantastic, or morbid, state of mind, often set in a paradoxically normal or realistic background. *The Lottery* (1949) is a representative collection of short stories, and *The Sundial* (1959), *The Haunting of Hill House* (1960), and *We Have Always Lived in the Castle* (1962) are typically fascinating novels. In a lighter mood are two autobiographical books about her domestic life with her husband and children, *Life Among the Savages* (1953) and *Raising Demons* (1957).

HENRY JAMES (1843–1916) was educated by tutors and at private schools; he also studied law for one year at Harvard. His literary career was long and varied. Up to 1890 his novels, especially *Roderick Hudson* (1875), *The American* (1877), *The Europeans* (1878), and *The Portrait of a Lady* (1881), were chiefly concerned with the encounter between Americans and Europeans. From *The Tragic Muse* (1890) to *The Awkward Age* (1899) James was concerned chiefly with English society. The works of his last period, *The Wings of the Dove* (1902), *The Ambassadors* (1903), and *The Golden Bowl* (1904), are masterpieces of psychological portraiture in which setting is manifested in and through the awareness of the principal characters. In addition to his success as a novelist, James was a superb essayist, a short-story writer, and an incomparable master of the novella. He also attempted the drama, but without success.

Ben Jonson (1572–1637) worked briefly at his stepfather's trade of bricklaying, then served as a soldier in Flanders. When he returned to England, he joined Henslowe's acting company. His first important play, *Every Man in His Humour*, appeared in 1598 with his close friend Shakespeare in the cast. A prolific dramatist, Jonson wrote four masterpieces: *Volpone* (1606), *The Silent Woman* (1609), *The Alchemist* (1610), and *Bartholomew Fair* (1614). Besides his plays he composed superb lyrics, verse letters, translations, and a book of short essays and notes on literary topics called *Timber, or Discoveries,* which appeared in 1640.

James Joyce (1882–1941) was educated at Jesuit schools and at Dublin University. After a brief career as a student of medicine and of music, he turned to literature. His first book was *Chamber Music* (1907), a collection of lyrics. *Dubliners* (1914) was a group of short stories that anticipated the major theme of his later work: the decay of Irish society and the mission of the artist to create in his own soul the "uncreated conscience of his race." *Exiles,* the drama that was published in 1915, reflects its author's role as a self-expatriated writer in Trieste, Zurich, and Paris. An autobiographical novel, *The Portrait of the Artist as a Young Man* (1916), introduces his experiments with the stream-of-consciousness technique. In *Ulysses* (1922) these experiments were extensively developed by combining logical expression with music and by suggesting a vast system of analogies and correspondences between man, society, history, and nature. *Finnegan's Wake* (1939) further extends his experiments up to the limits of consciousness.

Franz Kafka (1883–1924) studied law at the German University of Prague where he earned his doctorate in jurisprudence in 1906. From 1907 to 1923 he was an official in the workman's compensation bureau of the Austrian government; at the same time, however, he was encouraged by his friend Max Brod to continue to write. Only three books appeared during his lifetime, but after his death Brod edited and published his manuscripts in *Collected Works* (1935–37) and *Diaries: 1914–1939* (1949). Good English translations of *The Castle* (1930), *The Metamorphosis* (1937), *The Trial* (1937), *Amerika* (1938), and *The Penal Colony* (1948) made Kafka very well known in England and America where he has been read and studied as one of the most important writers of the twentieth century.

John Keats (1795–1821) was born in London. He studied at the Enfield school and for two years was a medical student at Edmonton.

Through Leigh Hunt, a Hampstead neighbor, Keats met Hazlitt, Shelley, and other young writers, and turned from medicine to poetry. His first books, *Poems* (1817) and *Endymion* (1818), contained some brilliant imagery, but their youthful sentimentality was savagely attacked. *Lamia and Other Poems* (1820), however, contained not only his best romances, but the odes that perfectly expressed his genius: "Ode to a Nightingale," "Ode on a Grecian Urn," "Ode to Autumn," "Ode to Psyche," and "Ode on Melancholy." Shelley lamented his early death in "Adonais." His complete letters were published posthumously. They reveal Keats as a sensitive thinker and critic of poetry as well as a warm-hearted friend, brother, and lover.

JOSEPH WOOD KRUTCH (1893–) was born in Knoxville, Tennessee. He was educated at the University of Tennessee and Columbia University, and was for twenty-six years drama critic of the *Nation.* In addition to writing several volumes of literary criticism, Krutch has written *Edgar Allen Poe: A Study in Genius* (1926), *Samuel Johnson* (1944), and *Henry David Thoreau* (1948). *The Modern Temper* (1929) signalized his growing concern for the predicament of men in a scientific age. *The Measure of Man* (1934) advances a humanistic philosophy of values that he further develops in *Is the Common Man Too Common?* (1954) and *Human Nature and the Human Condition* (1959). In recent years, too, Krutch has written extensively on man's relation to nature. *The Desert Year* (1952) and *The Great Chain of Life* (1956) are combinations of scientific observation and meditative wisdom.

SUSANNE LANGER (1895–) was born in New York and was educated at Radcliffe and in European universities. Her interest in philosophy and symbolic logic is best expressed in her influential *Philosophy in a New Key* (1942). More recently, she has stressed the importance of art not only as a necessity of the human spirit but also as a form of knowledge. Her *Feeling and Form* (1953), *Problems of Art* (1955), and *Reflections on Art* (1958) have influenced many contemporary attitudes in aesthetics and criticism.

LAURIE LEE (1914–), an English poet and musician, was born in the Cotswolds. He first attracted attention as a poet with his *The Sun My Monument* (1944), and *The Bloom of Candles* (1947). He has written two verse dramas as well as a travel book and a book of boyhood recollections, *The Edge of Day* (1959).

D. H. LAWRENCE (1885–1930) was born in Eastwood, Nottinghamshire, and was educated at the Nottingham High School. After teaching for several years at Croydon, a London suburb, Lawrence published his first novel, *The White Peacock*, in 1911. His first volume of poetry, *Love Poems and Others,* was published in 1913, the same year that the autobiographical *Sons and Lovers* appeared. From

1912 on, Lawrence was a constant traveler. Italy, Austria, Germany, Mexico, and New Mexico were the scenes of his search for health and tranquillity. *Sea and Sardinia* (1921) and *Mornings in Mexico* (1927), *Psychoanalysis and the Unconscious* (1921), and *Studies in Classic American Literature* (1923) alternated with a succession of poems, short stories, and novels that both attracted and repelled a large body of readers. Lawrence's emphasis on sex clearly invites contrary reactions. *The Rainbow* (1915) and *Women in Love* (1921), with their plea for a recognition of the interdependence of men and women, maintain a precarious balance between poetry and sentimentality; *Lady Chatterley's Lover*, on the other hand, is, for all its seriousness, inartistically explicit and frequently childish. Lawrence's vitality and his ability to convey it in literary terms, however, has rarely been questioned.

WALTER LEARNED (1847–1915) was born in New London, Connecticut. He is best known for his anthology *Treasury of Favorite American Poems* (1897). His own verses are collected in *Between Times* (1889).

CLIVE STAPLES LEWIS (1898–1963) was born in Belfast and was educated at University College, Oxford. A distinguished scholar, until shortly before his death Lewis held the Chair of Medieval and Renaissance English Literature at Cambridge University. Among his literary studies are *The Allegory of Love* (1936), *English Literature in the Sixteenth Century* (1954), and *A Preface to Paradise Lost* (revised edition, 1960). He was also the author of a number of allegorical novels, among them *Out of the Silent Planet* (1938) and *Perelandra* (1943). His books on religion, more especially on the role of the Christian in modern society, earned him the title "Apostle to the Sceptics." *The Problem of Pain* (1940) and *The Screwtape Letters* (1942) are two of these that have become world famous. Lewis also wrote many books for children and a candid autobiography, *Surprised by Joy* (1956).

SIR RICHARD LIVINGSTONE (1880–1960) was born in Liverpool and was educated at New College, Oxford. He has served as Vice-Chancellor of both Queen's University in Belfast and of Oxford University. A well-known Classical scholar Livingstone has written *The Greek Genius and Its Meaning to Us* (1912) and *A Defence of Classical Education* (1916). More general treatment of the problems of education appear in *Some Tasks for Education* (1947) and *Education and the Spirit of the Age* (1952).

KATHERINE MANSFIELD (1888–1923) was born in Wellington, New Zealand, and was educated at Queen's College, London. Inspired by the writings of Pater, Wilde, and Chekhov, she sought to live and to write at the highest pitch of intensity. She published her first volume of short stories, *In a German Pension*, in 1911. *Bliss* (1920), *The Garden Party* (1922), and *Something Childish* (1924) were enthusiastically received as models of the "new" short story that was to shape the fiction of the next three decades. After her death the publication of her *Journal* (1927), her *Letters* (1930), and her correspondence with her husband, *Letters to John Middleton Murry* (1951), stimulated wide discussion of both her tragic life and her technique of writing.

EDWIN MARKHAM (1852–1940) was born in Oregon City, Oregon, and spent his childhood and youth farming and ranching. He studied, when he could, in rural schools. At 18 he enrolled in San José State Normal School in California, and taught afterwards at various public schools. Privately, Markham had been writing verses that expressed his outrage at social injustice. Millet's famous painting "The Man with the Hoe" inspired Markham to write a poem, also called "The Man with the Hoe," which appeared in a San Francisco newspaper in 1899 and in the same year as the title poem of his first important book of verse. *Lincoln and Other Poems* (1901) repeated the success of his earlier volume and established Markham as a spokesman of democracy. Subsequent volumes were graceful but relatively ineffective repetitions of his earlier themes. His *Collected Poems* appeared in 1940.

CHRISTOPHER MARLOWE (1564–1593) was born at Canterbury and was educated at the King's School there and at Corpus Christi College, Cambridge. *Tamburlaine*, the story of an oriental despot, was first presented in 1587. In his tragedy, *Dr. Faustus* (1604), Marlowe adapted a well-known medieval legend to the Renaissance theme of power and intellectual rebellion. *Edward II* (produced in 1590) is perhaps Marlowe's best play in construction, characterization, and sustained verbal felicity. Although his next plays, *The Massacre at Paris* and *The Tragedy of Dido*, contributed little to his reputation, he remains second only to Shakespeare among the Elizabethans. Marlowe also wrote some inimitable short poems, translations of Ovid and Lucan, and a long narrative poem, *Hero and Leander*.

PHYLLIS MCGINLEY (1905–) was born in Ontario, Oregon, and was educated at convent schools and at the University of Utah. She taught for some time in public high schools. Soon, however, her verse, light in tone but incisively clever and often profoundly serious, began to appear in the *Atlantic Monthly*, the *New Yorker*, and other magazines. Her first book, a collection of verses called *On the Contrary*, was published in 1934. Since then she has brought forth more than a dozen volumes—of prose as well as poetry. She has written numerous books for children and, from time to time, essays no less witty than her verse. *Times Three: Selected Verse from Three Decades* appeared in 1960. *The Province of the Heart* (1960) contains the most recent selection of her prose.

HERBERT MARSHALL MCLUHAN (1911–) was educated at the University of Toronto where he is a professor of English and chairman of the Seminar on Culture and Communication. He is the author of *The Mechanical Bride: Folklore of Industrial Man* (1951), and a revolutionary book on language, *The Gutenberg Galaxy: The Making of Typographic Man* (1962).

THOMAS MERTON (1915–) was born in France. He attended French schools, Clare College, Cambridge, and Columbia University. He taught for a year at St. Bonaventure University, became a Roman Catholic, and shortly thereafter, in 1941, entered the Trappist monastery of Gethsemani. *The Seven Storey Mountain* (1948), his best-selling autobiography, was the effective beginning of a literary career that has witnessed the publication of over a dozen books on religion and theology as well as occasional volumes of poetry. A representative selection of his books is *Seeds of Contemplation* (1949), *Waters of Siloe* (1949), *The Sign of Jonas* (1953), and *The New Man* (1961). *A Thomas Merton Reader*, an anthology, appeared in 1963.

ALICE THOMPSON MEYNELL (1847–1922) was born in Surrey, England, but spent much of her early life in Italy. Her marriage to the critic and editor, Wilfrid Meynell, led her into active collaboration on the *Weekly Register* and the coeditorship of *Merry England*. Although the bulk of her writing—*The Rhythm of Life* (1893), *The Color of Life* (1896), and *Hearts of Controversy* (1917)—was prose, her poetry has a more permanent appeal to admirers. Among the early admirers of her work were John Ruskin, Coventry Patmore, George Meredith, and Francis Thompson. Her verses appeared at long intervals from *Preludes* in 1875 to *The Poems of Alice Meynell* in 1913. *Selected Poems*, with a memoir by Wilfrid Meynell, was published in 1931.

VASSAR MILLER (1924–) was born in Houston, Texas, and was educated at the University of Houston. Miss Miller, a victim of cerebral palsy, has espoused the tradition of George Herbert and Gerard Manley Hopkins in seeing poety "as akin to prayer, as an act of love." Her *Adam's Footprint* (1956) and *Wage War on Silence* (1960) have been greatly praised for their painstaking art and their compelling sincerity.

MOLIÈRE (1622–1673) was born in Paris, Jean Baptiste Poquelin. He studied for six years with the Jesuits at Clermont. Upon leaving

Clermont, Molière declined to enter his father's prosperous upholstery business and joined the Bigart family acting troupe instead. The troupe failed in Paris and toured the provinces for three years. Under the patronage of the king's brother, Molière organized his own company. Beginning with *Les Précieuses Ridicules* (*The Affected Ladies*, 1659), Molière wrote and produced a play each year. All of them bear testimony to his genius; those that have been widely admired are, in their English titles, *The School for Husbands* (1661), *The School for Wives* (1662), *Tartuffe* (1664), *Don Juan* (1665), *The Misanthrope* (1666), *The Would-Be Gentleman* (1670), *The Learned Ladies* (1672), and *The Imaginary Invalid* (1673). Molière is one of the world's greatest comic geniuses. His technical perfection in plot and style and his gallery of human types are matched by an uncommon clarity of purpose. His plays move relentlessly to the exposure of some vice or folly. His favorite targets are hypocrisy, injustice, and pretentiousness. *The Misanthrope* is called, not without reason, the "French *Hamlet*." It resembles *Hamlet* in that it portrays man's divided soul, although its uncompromising logic is more French than English.

THOMAS MOORE (1779–1852) was born in Dublin. He was educated at Trinity College there and at the Middle Temple in London. A translation of *Anacreon* (1800) won him an immediate reputation and the patronage of the Prince Regent. *Irish Melodies* (1807–35), consisting of 130 lyrics to accompany the music of Sir John Stevenson, were the most popular songs of the age. *Twopenny Post Bag* (1812) displayed a talent for satirical wit, as did the *Fudge Family in Paris* (1818). Moore's longest poem, *Lalla Rookh* (1817), was an oriental tale that rivaled Byron's *Childe Harold* and *Don Juan* in popularity. Moore wrote the first *Life of Byron* (1830) and several other biographies. His *Memoirs*, edited by Lord John Russell, appeared in 1853–56.

EDWIN MUIR (1887–1959) was born in Deerness, Orkney. When he was fourteen his family moved to Glasgow and there he worked as a clerk in a law office and educated himself privately. Between the two wars Muir lived abroad, writing, lecturing, and translating. Beginning with *First Poems* in 1925, he published eight volumes of verse. His *Collected Poems* appeared in 1952. Muir also wrote extensively on literature. His *Autobiography* (1954) is of distinct literary value.

JOHN HENRY, CARDINAL NEWMAN (1801–1890) was born in London and was educated at the Ealing School and Trinity College, Oxford. A fellow of Oriel College, Oxford, he was made Vicar of St. Mary's, the University Church, where his sermons won him an eminent reputation. In 1833, in association with Pusey, Keble, and others of the Anglican clergy, he led the Oxford Movement, which aimed to restore the Anglican Church to its Catholic orientation. After becoming a Catholic in 1845, Newman's writing began to reflect a twofold mission. To prepare Catholics for their role in modern society he wrote *Present Position of Catholics* (1851) and *The Idea of a University* (1852). To meet the objections of Anglicans and sceptics he wrote his celebrated autobiographical *Apologia pro Vita Sua* (1864) and *The Grammar of Assent* (1870). In 1879 Newman, the founder of the Oratorian community in England, was created a Cardinal. His collected writings (1868–81) consist of 40 volumes. *The Dream of Gerontius* appeared in 1865 and was republished in *Verses on Various Occasions* (1874).

JOHN NORRIS (1657–1711) was educated at Exeter College, Oxford. He entered the church and was appointed in 1692 to the rectory at Bemerton where George Herbert had been parson some sixty years before. He composed more than twenty-three works, most of them on religion and Cartesian philosophy. His poetry reflects a Platonic cast of mind and bears comparison with that of Herbert.

FRANK O'CONNOR (1903–) is the pen name of Michael O'Donovan. He was educated at the Christian Brothers Academy in Cork and worked as a librarian in County Cork and later in Dublin. He became a director of the Abbey Theatre. His first book of short stories, *Guests of the Nation* (1931), was followed over the years by many other collections. In addition, he has written stimulating literary criticism: *Art of the Theatre* (1947), *The Modern Novel* (1956), *The Mirror in the Roadway* (1956), and *The Lonely Voice* (1963). He now resides in the United States and continues to write short stories. He has lectured extensively in American universities.

LIAM O'FLAHERTY (1897–) was born in the Aran Islands, Galway, and was educated at Rockwell College, Blackrock College, and University College, Dublin. He served with the British Army in World War I and with the Republicans against the Free State in the Irish Civil War. He has written many novels of which *The Informer* (1926), *Famine* (1937), and *The Land* (1946) are representative. *Spring Sowing* (1924) is perhaps his best collection of short stories. His autobiographies, *Two Years* (1930) and *Shame the Devil* (1934), reflect his early revolutionary views.

IRIS ORIGO (1902–) was born in Birdlip, Gloucestershire, and was educated in Italy. She has written extensively on Renaissance history and literature. Her *Leopardi* (1935, rev. 1953) is one of the best studies of the Italian poet. *The Last Attachment* (1949) is the story of Byron's relations with Teresa Guiccioli; *The Merchant of Prato* (1957) is a study of a Renaissance merchant prince. Her latest book, *The World of San Bernardino* (1962), has been, as have her other books, widely acclaimed for both scholarship and style.

SHAEMAS O'SHEEL (1886–1954) was born in New York. His best-known work is contained in *The Blossomy Bough* (1911), *The Light Feet of Goats* (1915), and *Jealous of Dead Leaves* (1928).

WILFRED OWEN (1893–1918) was born at Oswestry, Shropshire, and was educated at the Birkenhead Institute in Liverpool. After serving as a tutor in Bordeaux for two years, he joined the British Army. He was invalided home but later returned to the Western front where he won the Military Cross for gallantry. He was killed in action in France a week before the Armistice. His friend and fellow poet, Siegfried Sassoon, gathered together his poetry in 1920. A new, enlarged edition, *The Poems of Wilfred Owen*, appeared in 1931.

ALAN PATON (1903–   ) was born and educated in Pietermaritzburg, South Africa. He taught in native schools there until his appointment in 1935 as principal of the Diepkloof Reformatory, where he was successful in substituting persuasion and understanding for some of the severe disciplinary methods. His knowledge of the character and problems of South Africa forms the background for *Cry, the Beloved Country* (1948), *Too Late the Phalarope* (1953), and his volume of short stories, *Tales from a Troubled Land* (1961).

CHARLES PÉGUY (1873–1914) was born at Orléans. He received his education at the École Normale Supérieure. In 1898 he started a Socialist bookshop, which failed, and then founded the *Cahiers de la Quinzaine* (*Fortnightly Notebooks*), in which he published his own views—a unique blend of socialism, nationalism, and religion—as well as those of many distinguished contemporaries. A prolific author, Péguy is best known in France for his *Le Mystère de la Charité de Jeanne d'Arc* (1910), *L'Argent* (1911) and *La Tapisserie de Nôtre Dame* (1912). Péguy was killed at Villeroy in 1914.

PLATO (*c.* 427–347 B.C.) was a pupil of Socrates. Plato witnessed Socrates' trial and death and reported it in three dialogues—the *Apology, Crito,* and *Phaedo.* He forever preserved Socrates' memory by making him his own powerful spokesman in other dialogues—namely, the *Republic, Symposium,* and *Timaeus.* Plato's dialogues, which are of the highest literary value, usually investigate some one point: self-knowledge, courage, virtue, love, wisdom. His most comprehensive work, the *Republic,* examines the nature of justice and the education of the philosopher-kings or guardians of the state. In 388 Plato founded his philosophical school, the Academy. Among his many outstanding pupils, Aristotle was the most brilliant and the most independent.

ALEXANDER POPE (1688–1744) was born in London and was educated privately. A precocious genius, he was quickly accepted by contemporary men of letters; his *Essay on Criticism* (1711) earned the praise of Addison. Continuously busy with many literary activities, including translations of Homer and an edition of Shakespeare, Pope achieved the highest technical perfection in the heroic couplet. He wrote the best mock epic in English literature, *The Rape of the Lock* (1712), a superb pastoral, *Windsor Forest* (1713), and the most stinging of satires, *The Dunciad* (1728, 1743). His *Moral Essays,* which contains "Epistle II. To a Lady," was an oblique attack on the Duchess of Marlborough and Lady Mary Wortley Montagu, both of whom had ridiculed him. Pope's *Letters* (1737, 1739) reveal both his complicated character and his excellent prose style.

KATHERINE ANNE PORTER (1890–) was born in Texas and was educated at convent schools. She has lived at various times in Louisiana, Texas, Mexico, and California. She began writing only after a long and patient study of her craft. *Flowering Judas* (1930), a collection of short tales, immediately established a reputation that grew with the publication of *Hacienda* (1934), *Pale Horse, Pale Rider* (1939), and *The Leaning Tower* (1944). A book of personal recollections, *The Days Before* (1952), expresses her artistic and personal philosophy. Her long-awaited novel, *Ship of Fools* (1962), was widely acclaimed.

JAMES F. POWERS (1917–) was born in Jacksonville, Illinois, and was educated at Quincy College. He has taught at Marquette University. Two collections of his short stories, *Prince of Darkness* (1947) and *The Presence of Grace* (1956), were widely praised. His novel *Morte D'Urban* (1962) won the National Book Award in that year.

JESSICA AGNES POWERS (1905–) was born in Manston, Wisconsin, and attended Marquette University. Since 1941 she has been a Carmelite nun in Milwaukee, Wisconsin. Her poems are collected in *The Lantern Burns* (1939) and *The Place of Splendor* (1946).

JOHN CROWE RANSOM (1888–) was born in Pulaski, Tennessee, and was educated at Vanderbilt University and Christ Church, Oxford. Ransom has exerted a deep and lasting influence on American thought by his contribution to the southern agrarian movement, by his influential books of literary criticism, *The World's Body* (1938) and *The New Criticism* (1941), and by his editorship of the *Kenyon Review,* which he founded in 1939. Ransom's poetry, however, promises to survive his prose. *Poems about God* (1919), *Chills and Fever* (1924), *Grace After Meat* (1924), and *Two Gentlemen in Bonds* (1927) established his place as one who could assimilate the tradition of poetry without resorting to pedantry, and experiment with new forms without becoming a mere technician. His most recent book is *Poems and Essays* (1951).

Sir Herbert Read (1893–) was born near Kirbymoorside, Yorkshire, and was educated at the University of Leeds. A critic of art and literature as well as a poet, he has served as a curator of the Victoria and Albert Museum, a Professor of Fine Art at the University of Edinburgh, and a lecturer at the universities of Cambridge, Harvard, London, and Liverpool. His principal books are *The Anatomy of Art* (1932), *Form in Modern Poetry* (1932), *Education Through Art* (1943), and *The Philosophy of Modern Art* (1952). *English Prose Style* (1928) was revised in 1952. His *Collected Poems* appeared in 1946.

Joseph N. Riddel (1931–) was educated at Glenville College, West Virginia, and the University of Wisconsin. He has written extensively on the poetry of Wallace Stevens, and is the coeditor of a bibliography of Stevens' writings. He has taught at Wisconsin and at Duke, where he is currently an assistant professor of American literature.

Theodore Roethke (1908–1963) was born in Saginaw, Michigan, and was educated at the University of Michigan and at Harvard. A consistently superior craftsman, Roethke showed his ability to write in a variety of modes on a great variety of topics. His verses are collected in *Open House* (1941), *The Lost Son* (1948), *Praise to the End* (1951), and *The Waking* (1953). *Words for the Wind* (1959) won three national awards. He was, until his death, Professor of English at the University of Washington.

St. Augustine (353–430) was born at Tagaste, North Africa. He was educated in the rhetorical schools in Carthage and later became a teacher himself. In his *Confessions* (397) he tells the story of his early life and his search for truth among the various philosophies and sects prior to his conversion by Ambrose, Bishop of Milan, at Easter in 387. As Bishop of Hippo, Augustine confronted the Donatist and Pelagian Heretics on the one hand and the pagans on the other. *The City of God* (413–426) is a masterly analysis of the role of Christians in secular society. Augustine's other writings, consisting of commentaries on the Bible, sermons, homilies, and exhortations, molded Christian thinking for centuries to come.

John Godfrey Saxe (1816–1887) was born in Highgate, Vermont, and was graduated from Middlebury College. During his varied career he was a superintendent of schools, an attorney, a newspaper editor, and the author of many volumes of humorous verse, which had a great vogue in the nineteenth century. Among his writings *Progress: A Satirical Poem* (1846), *Clever Stories of Many Nations Rendered in Rhyme* (1865), and *Leisure-Day Rhymes* (1875) were favorites.

Sir Walter Scott (1771–1832) was born at Edinburgh and was educated at the University of Edinburgh. A childhood illness allowed him to indulge his love of reading, particularly of Scots poetry, Percy's *Reliques,* and German ballads. His first major work was a three-volume edition of ballads called *Minstrelsy of the Scottish Border* (1802–1803). *The Lay of the Last Minstrel* (1805), *Marmion* (1808), and *The Lady of the Lake* (1810) marked a progressive development in his poetic talent and his popularity. *Waverley,* his first novel, appeared in 1814. Scott developed the historical novel around three themes: the Scottish theme, as in *The Heart of Midlothian* (1818) and *The Bride of Lammermoor* (1819); the English theme, as in *Ivanhoe* (1819) and *Kenilworth* (1821); and the European theme, as in *Quentin Durward* (1823) and *The Talisman* (1825). Scott also wrote several masterly short stories and a life of Napoleon, and compiled editions of Dryden and Swift.

William Shakespeare (1564–1616) was born in Stratford-on-Avon and was educated at the Stratford Grammar School. He left Stratford for London in 1585, where he joined a theatrical company. By 1592 he was a well-known actor and playwright with the Lord Chamberlain's company—one of the best in London. In 1593 the publication of his poem *Venus and Adonis* established his reputation as a poet. With the presentation of *Romeo and Juliet* (written about 1594) Shakespeare won even more fame as a playwright. During his "great" period between 1601 and 1608, Shakespeare, already England's leading playwright, composed *Hamlet, Twelfth Night, Othello, King Lear, Macbeth, Antony and Cleopatra,* and *Coriolanus. The Tempest,* his most poetic drama and probably his last play, is, fittingly, his best in the balance of story and meaning, of thought and style. G. B. Harrison's comment, "Beyond this the English language cannot reach," is richly deserved.

Percy Bysshe Shelley (1792–1822) was born in Sussex and was educated at Brentford, Eton, and University College, Oxford, from which he was expelled for writing and circulating a pamphlet called *The Necessity of Atheism.* His first important poem was "Queen Mab" (1813). With *Alastor* (1816), which set forth the character of the poet, Shelley began to explore the theme of personal freedom that was to appear, in various forms, in his most characteristic works, *The Cenci, Prometheus Unbound, Epipsychidion,* and *Hellas.* "Adonais," written in 1821, is not only a tribute to Keats but also Shelley's most eloquent description of his own sense of the poet's role as the unacknowledged legislator of the world. If Shelley's longer poems are excessively argumentative, many of his shorter lyrics are considered among the most perfect in the language.

Sophocles (c. 496–406 b.c.) was born at Colonus, near Athens. As a young man, Sophocles achieved public recognition for his excellence in singing, dancing, and gymnastics. At 27 he won first prize in tragedy at the Dionysian Festival, defeating Aeschylus, thirty years his senior. From that time on Sophocles was the first poet of Athens. He is said to have written over 120 poems, of which 100 are known by name. Seven of his tragedies survive; of these *Ajax*, *Philoctetes*, *Electra*, *Oedipus Tyrannus*, *Oedipus at Colonus*, and *Antigone* are all, each for different reasons, acclaimed as masterpieces. *Oedipus Tyrannus*, or *Oedipus the King*, is perhaps the most famous tragedy in the western world. Its unity of character and action, its coherent plot and integrated choral songs, commended it to Aristotle who, in his *Poetics*, refers to it frequently to exemplify the best practice in the writing of tragedy.

MURIEL SPARK (1918–) was born in Edinburgh and was educated at the Gillespie School for Girls. After a long residence in Central Africa she returned to England where she wrote poetry and literary criticism and edited several magazines. Her first novel, *The Comforters* (1957), was followed by *Robinson* (1958), *Memento Mori* (1959), *The Ballad of Peckham Rye* (1960), and *The Prime of Miss Jean Brodie* (1962). Her collection of short stories, *The Go-Away Bird*, appeared in 1960. Miss Spark has been cited both in England and in the United States as the outstanding comic writer of her generation, a judgment that has been confirmed by her most recent book, *The Girls of Slender Means* (1963).

EDMUND SPENSER (1552–1599) was born in London and was educated at the Merchant Taylors' School and Pembroke Hall, Cambridge. An erudite student of Renaissance poetry and philosophy, he made a name for himself with the publication of *The Shepherds Calendar* (1579), a collection of twelve eclogues. He entered government service and he was rewarded for his efforts in suppressing the Irish Revolt by the gift of a castle in Cork. There he began his greatest work, *The Faerie Queene*, which was designed as an allegorical epic on the virtues of an ideal courtier. Spenser completed six of the projected twelve books between 1586 and 1596. Despite its incomplete state, *The Faerie Queene* remains one of the great long poems in English. Spenser is also a masterly writer of sonnets, satires, hymns, and pastorals. As a sonnet writer he united English literature to the Continental tradition of Petrarch and Du Bellay.

WALLACE STEVENS (1879–1955) was born in Reading, Pennsylvania, and was educated at Harvard University and New York Law School. From 1916 until his death he was associated with the Hartford Accident and Indemnity Company; in 1934 he was made vice-President of the firm. From his *Harmonium* (1923) to *The Necessary Angel* (1951), a book of essays, his effort was directed toward developing the role of the imagination, "the supreme fiction," in creating order and beauty in a disintegrating world. His *Collected Poems* were issued in 1954; they won the Pulitzer Prize for poetry in 1955.

KEVIN SULLIVAN (1922–) was educated at Georgetown, Princeton, and Columbia. A scholar, critic, and poet, he is now an associate dean at Columbia University. His *Joyce Among the Jesuits* (1958) is an outstanding contribution to the biography of James Joyce.

JONATHAN SWIFT (1667–1745) was born in Dublin and was Graduated from Trinity College, Dublin. Strong-minded and temperamentally argumentative, Swift expressed himself vigorously on the three chief issues of his day: religion, literature, and politics. In *The Battle of the Books* (1704), a prose satire, he set the "ancients" against the "moderns" in a mock war. In *A Tale of a Tub* (1704), he satirized the religious controversialists of the three prominent faiths: Roman Catholicism, Anglicanism, and Nonconformism. In *Gulliver's Travels* (1726), he directed his criticism against follies in religion and politics and opposed to the current vogue of rationalistic science and "progress" his own orthodox Christianity and common sense. Although he was an unhappy exile in his native country, Swift espoused the cause of the Irish people in a series of letters directed against the government's attack upon their basic liberties. "A Modest Proposal" (1729) is the last and, by reason of its sustained irony, the most effective of his satires. Swift's tender side is evident in his *Journal to Stella,* begun in 1713 and published in 1766–68.

ALFRED, LORD TENNYSON (1809–1892) was born at Somersby in Lincolnshire and was educated at Louth Grammar School and Trinity College, Cambridge. His first two volumes, *Poems Chiefly Lyrical* (1830) and *Poems* (1833), contained much good work in a vein not popular at the time. He was disappointed at their reception and spent almost ten years revising them. *Poems* (1842) established his reputation. The death of his friend Arthur Henry Hallam inspired a series of elegiac lyrics, published as *In Memoriam* (1850). *In Memoriam* is considered his most representative work. *Idylls of the King,* the first installments of which were published in 1859 and the last in 1885, retold the Arthurian legend in the mood of Victorian England. Although temperamentally a "romantic" poet, Tennyson was attentive to social and intellectual change, as is evident in his *Maud* (1855) and *Locksley Hall Sixty Years After* (1866).

DYLAN THOMAS (1914–1953) was born in Swansea, Wales, and was largely self-educated. *Eighteen Poems* (1934) announced a new, vigorous, and highly original poetic talent. Subsequent volumes in 1936, 1939, 1943, and 1946 and his *Collected Poems* in 1953 celebrated, in explosive imagery and dynamic rhythms, a joy in life and nature. A frequent visitor to the United States, Thomas gave numerous recitals and lectures. One report of these experiences, "A Visit to

America," records his growing distaste for this kind of public exposure. Thomas' autobiographical *Portrait of the Artist as a Young Dog* (1940) and his posthumous *Quite Early One Morning* (1954) are other examples of his prose.

FRANCIS THOMPSON (1859–1907) was born in Ashton, Lancastershire, and was educated at Oscott and Owens Medical College, Manchester. A failure at medicine, he drifted to London where for four years he lived in extreme poverty and ill health. He was cared for by a streetwalker, and began to write poetry. Wilfrid and Alice Meynell, editors of *Merry England,* recognized his talent, befriended him, and encouraged him in his writing. The result was *Poems* (1893), *Sister Songs* (1895), and *New Poems* (1897). He was quickly recognized as a genuinely religious poet and his much anthologized "The Hound of Heaven" has achieved the status of a minor classic. Since his death *Literary Criticisms* (1948) and *The Real Robert Louis Stevenson and Other Critical Essays* (1959) have disclosed a previously unrecognized stature as a literary critic.

JAMES THURBER (1894–1961) was born in Columbus, Ohio. He was graduated from Ohio State University. In 1927 he joined the staff of the *New Yorker* to which he contributed essays, stories, and comic drawings. Representative collections of his essays are: *My Life and Hard Times* (1933), *Let Your Mind Alone* (1937), *Fables for Our Times* (1940–56), *Thurber Country* (1953), and *Alarms and Diversions* (1957). Thurber wrote several excellent children's books, including *The White Deer* (1945) and *The Thirteen Clocks* (1950), and was coauthor with Elliot Nugent of *The Male Animal* (1940), a successful play.

LEO TOLSTOY (1828–1910) was educated privately and at Kazan University. His early work, *Childhood* (1852), *Boyhood* (1854), and *Youth* (1856), as well as his tales and sketches based on his military experiences in the Crimean War, made him a favorite in Russian literary circles. *War and Peace,* his epic account of the Russian struggle with Napoleon, was published in 1866. *Anna Karenina* (1874–76) dealt with the moral problems of Russian aristocracy. In his later years Tolstoy's preoccupation with religious and ethical questions resulted in numerous tracts, and was reflected in *The Death of Ivan Ilyitch* (1886), *The Kreutzer Sonata* (1889), and *Resurrection* (1899).

FRANCIS G. TOWNSEND (1915–) was born in Maplewood, Missouri, and was educated at St. Louis University and Ohio State University. He has taught at the University of Illinois, Ohio State University, and Florida State University, where he is currently Chairman of the English Department. He has written on various phases of

Victorian literature. His *Ruskin and the Landscape Feeling* appeared in 1951.

JOHN UPDIKE (1932–) was born in Shillington, Pennsylvania, and was educated at Harvard and at the Ruskin School of Drawing and Fine Art. His book of poems, *The Carpentered Hen,* appeared in 1958. Two collections of short stories, *The Same Door* (1959) and *Pigeon Feathers* (1962), reflect his training as a *New Yorker* magazine contributor. His novels, *Poorhouse Fair* (1959), *Rabbit, Run* (1960), and *The Centaur* (1963), have established him as one of the outstanding young writers in America today.

VIRGIL (70–19 B.C.) was born at Andes, near Mantua. He studied at the rhetorical and philosophical schools in Rome. A fortunate encounter with Maecenas, first minister to Caesar Augustus, resulted in his appointment as a court poet. His *Eclogues* (37 B.C.) established his reputation as a pastoral poet. The *Georgics* (30 B.C.) expressed in a hitherto unknown richness of texture and harmony the rules of husbandry. Virgil's greatest work, the *Aeneid,* an epic poem on the founding of Rome, was written between 30 and 19 B.C. Virgil's fame, great even during his lifetime, was greater still afterwards when he became known as "the schoolmaster of Europe."

EDMUND WALLER (1606–1687) was educated at Eton and King's College, Cambridge. A member of Parliament at 16, he achieved great fame under the Protectorate of Oliver Cromwell. Later he became a Royalist and was arrested, fined, and banished in 1643 for plotting in favor of Charles I. In addition to his short lyrics, notable for their wit, grace, and charm, Waller wrote an epic poem, *The Summer Islands,* a sacred poem, *Of Divine Love,* and two panegyrics, one to Cromwell in 1655 and one to Charles II in 1660.

ROBERT PENN WARREN (1905–) was born in Guthrie, Kentucky, and was educated at Vanderbilt University, the University of California, Yale University, and Oxford. Warren is equally well known as a poet, fiction writer, and critic. His verses range from short lyrics, contained in *Selected Poems 1923–1943* (1944), to the long dramatic poem *Brother to Dragons* (1953). Warren's novels and short stories have brought him wide recognition because of their direct relevance to American history. *Night Rider* (1939) is about the tobacco war in his native Kentucky; *At Heaven's Gate* (1943) is about political corruption in Tennessee; *All the King's Men* (1946) is about a dictatorial southern governor reputed to be Louisiana's Huey Long. His short stories are collected in *Circus in the Attic* (1948) and his literary criticism in *Selected Essays* (1958).

EVELYN WAUGH (1903–) was born in London and read history at Hertford College, Oxford. His early novels were witty comedies.

Decline and Fall (1928), *Vile Bodies* (1930), *Black Mischief* (1932), and *Scoop* (1938) commented on the follies of society without attempting to prescribe a remedy. With *A Handful of Dust* (1934), however, his criticism of society began to take on a serious tone. *Brideshead Revisited* (1945) explored the role of religion in modern life. *The Loved One* (1948) satirized the modern attempt to avoid the fact of death. *Love Among the Ruins* (1953) protested against the dehumanization of man. His novels of World War II, *Men at Arms* (1952) and *Officers and Gentlemen* (1955), offer a vivid contrast between men with and men without a sense of tradition.

Eudora Welty (1909–) was born in Jackson, Mississippi, and was educated at Mississippi State College for Women and the University of Wisconsin. Her locale and her characters are drawn from her native Mississippi; her themes focus on both the humorous and the tragic aspects of seemingly ordinary people. *A Curtain of Green* (1941), *The Wide Net* (1943), and *The Golden Apples* (1949) are collections of short stories that have received almost unanimous approval from critics and readers. While a novella, *The Ponder Heart* (1954), and a novel, *Delta Wedding* (1946), are evidences of her ability to write longer fiction, her genius seems to find its normal expression in the short story.

Jessamyn West (1907–) was born in Indiana and was educated at Whittier College and the University of California. Her first book, *The Friendly Persuasion* (1945), is the story of a Quaker family in southern Indiana during the Civil War. *The Witch Diggers* (1951) is also set in Indiana but it describes life on a poor farm at the turn of the century. *Cress Delehanty* (1953) is an informal account of a young girl's growth into maturity. Miss West's short stories are collected in *Love, Death and the Ladies' Drill Team* (1959). Her novel about the Los Angeles area, *South of the Angels,* appeared in 1960.

E. B. White (1899–) was born at Mount Vernon, New York, and was educated at Cornell University. After a brief career as a reporter and advertising copywriter, White joined the staff of the *New Yorker* Magazine where he contributed regularly to the "Talk of the Town." Representative selections of his ironic essays on the wide variety of subjects that excite his interest are *One Man's Meat* (1942), *Here Is New York* (1949), and *The Second Tree from the Corner* (1953). White has also written two children's books, *Stuart Little* (1945) and *Charlotte's Web* (1952).

Alfred North Whitehead (1861–1947) was educated at Trinity College, Cambridge. Whitehead achieved great fame as a mathematician before extending his interests to philosophy. As a philosopher he is notable for his attention to the interdependent roles of concrete and abstract thinking and the interrelation of psychological, physical, and metaphysical knowledge. His essays all have distinct relevance to the education of modern man. His books of widest general interest are: *Science and the Modern World* (1925), *The Function of Reason* (1929), *Adventures of Ideas* (1933), *Modes of Thought* (1938), and *Essays in Science and Philosophy* (1947).

WALT WHITMAN (1819–1892) was born on Long Island, New York. He worked first as a printer's apprentice, then as an itinerant schoolteacher, and then as a reporter on various papers before becoming the editor of the Brooklyn *Daily Eagle* in 1846. His career as a poet began with the publication in 1855 of the first edition of *Leaves of Grass,* a book which was destined to grow from 94 pages to 500, and to create a revolution in poetry. Praised by Emerson and others, Whitman issued new and enlarged editions in 1856, 1860, and 1867. His Civil War service as a volunteer medical orderly is reflected in *Drum Taps* (1865) and *Sequel to Drum Taps* (1866), which contains Whitman's great dirge for Lincoln, "When Lilacs Last in the Dooryard Bloomed." A fifth enlarged edition of *Leaves of Grass* appeared in 1871. *Democratic Vistas,* an essay on the spirit of democratic freedom, also appeared in 1871. The final "deathbed" edition of *Leaves of Grass* was issued in 1892. As the self-styled "poet laureate" of spiritual democracy, Whitman has been apotheosized as a quasi-religious leader and ridiculed as a romantic idealist. Few, however, question his influence on the development of modern poetry.

EDMUND WILSON (1895–) was born in Red Bank, New Jersey, and was educated at the Hill School and at Princeton. During a long and active literary career, Wilson has written poetry, fiction, drama, travel books, political tracts, history, and studies of Biblical manuscripts. His authority is most widely accepted, however, in the field of literary criticism where he has interpreted new developments and reinterpreted the past with an expository skill unusual in modern writers. *Axel's Castle* (1931), *The Triple Thinkers* (1938), and *The Shores of Light* (1952), are outstanding contributions to American literary criticism. *The Shock of Recognition* (1943), a critical anthology, helped to reorient ideas on American literature.

WILLIAM WORDSWORTH (1770–1850) was born in Cumberland, in the English Lake District, and was educated at St. John's College, Cambridge. His first books, *An Evening Walk* and *Descriptive Sketches,* both published in 1793, attracted no attention. His intimate friendship with Samuel Coleridge resulted in their collaboration on *Lyrical Ballads* (1798), a collection of poems that ushered in the Romantic movement. Wordsworth's great work, *The Prelude,* an autobiographical record, was completed in 1805 and published, in a slightly altered form, in 1850. *Poems* (2 volumes, 1807) contain some of his best work, including the "Intimations" ode, which is perhaps his most impressive single poem. Wordsworth's later poetry is less vigorous than his early poems but his *The White Doe of Rylstone* (1815), *The River Duddon* (1820), *Ecclesiastical Sonnets* (1822), and *Yarrow Revisited* (1835) could, in their own right, have won their author a place in English literature.

WILLIAM BUTLER YEATS (1865–1939) was born in Dublin and was educated in Dublin schools and at the Royal Dublin Society of Art. During his long and varied career Yeats played many roles. He was a leader of the Celtic Renaissance by virtue of his collection of folklore and legends, his collection of essays, *The Celtic Twilight* (1893), and his collection of ballads and poems, *The Wanderings of Oisin* (1889). With Lady Gregory and others, he founded the Abbey Theatre to which he contributed a number of plays, including *Kathleen ni Houlihan* (1902) and *Deirdre* (1907). His interest in the occult is reflected in *A Vision* (1925) and in "The Second Coming" and "Byzantium." In his last years Yeats developed a spare, highly structured, and thoroughly modern style. He received the Nobel Prize in 1923. His *Collected Poems*, with his final revisions, appeared in 1956.

A GLOSSARY
OF LITERARY AND RHETORICAL TERMS

ABSTRACT and CONCRETE: *Abstract* applies to words or sentences that denote a class or the qualities of a class of persons, objects, or actions. The words POETRY and *rhetoric,* for example, denote classes of literature. The following sentences express general qualities of a class:

Poetry is the essence of man's thought.
Rhetoric is the art of effective writing.

Concrete applies to words or actions that can actually be perceived or imagined as physically present. The words *London* and *rain,* for example, denote concrete objects. The following sentences are concrete statements:

John Milton lived in London.
It rained heavily in London on Monday.

Although concreteness is often regarded as the unique characteristic of literature, general or abstract statements are just as necessary when a discourse aims to clarify ideas and relationships among ideas, as does Aristotle's essay, "Knowledge and Wisdom" (p. 1222). Imaginative literature also employs abstractions in the interest of wit, criticism of society, and so on. *See* Molière's *The Misanthrope* (p. 865).

ACCENT: *See* VERSIFICATION.

ACT and SCENE: *Act* is the name given to a major division of a play. The English play from the time of the Elizabethans to the late nineteenth century was normally divided into five acts. In recent times, most plays are divided into three acts. A *scene* is a subordinate unit of action within an act. It is announced by the entrance and exit of characters or, more frequently, by the dropping of the curtain.

The Greek tragedy (see *Oedipus,* p. 377) follows a different pattern. The *prologue* presents the situation or conflict of the drama; the *parodos,* or *parode,* is the opening commentary recited or sung by the chorus; a series of EPISODES, or scenes, each followed by an ODE, that is, a lyric song chanted or recited by the chorus, concludes in an *exodus,* or final scene, in which the CATASTROPHE is reported and the chorus comments on the meaning of the whole action. As drama developed, the choral commentary also appeared as an *epilogue,* or a summary of the action. *See* Shakespeare's *The Tempest* (p. 541). *See also* CHORUS.

ALLEGORY: *See* FIGURATIVE LANGUAGE.

ALLITERATION: *See* VERSIFICATION.

AMBIGUITY: In its ordinary sense, ambiguity is the confusion resulting when a word or phrase has a doubtful meaning; in other words, it designates a FALLACY. As a literary term, however, ambiguity refers to that device by which an author consciously gives a word or phrase more than one meaning. In order to grasp the whole significance of a passage where one suspects that the author has used this device, the reader must look for the other sense (or senses) in which the passage can be taken. Allegory, symbolism, and irony all employ ambiguity.

ANALOGY: A logical term that designates a mode of reasoning. It is based upon the probability that if *A* resembles *B* in several important particulars, it will resemble *B* in another particular. In literature, analogy is frequently found in the PARABLE, in which a story develops a point about one character or situation that is applicable to another character or situation. Thus "The Lottery" (p. 323) implies a similarity or analogy between the ritual murder described in the story and the persecutions and pogroms of recent history. *See also* DEDUCTION; FIGURATIVE LANGUAGE.

ANALYSIS: A term used in rhetoric to designate the various modes of investigating and explaining a subject. The principal modes are CAUSE and EFFECT, CLASSIFICATION and DIVISION, COMPARISON and CONTRAST, DEFINITION, and PROCESS.

ANAPEST: *See* VERSIFICATION.

ANAPHORA: *See* FIGURATIVE LANGUAGE.

ANTISTROPHE: *See* ODE.

ARGUMENT: A form of discourse in which the writer attempts to win assent to a belief or opinion. Formal argument advances a proposition, or statement to be proved, and adduces reasons clearly arranged in a deductive or inductive order, as, for example, in "The Retreat from Excellence" (p. 750). Informal argument advances a POINT OF VIEW in the course of a NARRATIVE, as in "Notes of a Native Son" (p. 1133), or as a corollary of EXPOSITION, as in "Being and Doing" (p. 1251), or ironically, as in "A Modest Proposal" (p. 1126). Argument is frequently used to designate the THEME or main problem of a play, an epic, or a novel.

ARTICLE: *See* ESSAY.

ASSONANCE: *See* VERSIFICATION.

ATMOSPHERE and SETTING: *Atmosphere* is the term used to describe the mental or emotional climate in which the action of a story takes place, while *setting* is a combination of the concrete time, place, and circumstances of the action. In "Ethan Brand" (p. 1266) the atmosphere is one of preternatural mystery, and the setting is that of a New England village. Atmosphere supplies the mood of a story and setting its realistic details.

BALLAD: A poem that tells a story and that is meant to be sung or recited. The *folk ballad,* for example, "Edward" (p. 344), is often built around a single episode whose action is developed swiftly, frequently by question and answer. Repetitions often supply a choral emphasis and foreshadow a final revelation.

The *literary ballad,* or *art ballad,* imitates the mood of the folk ballad but consciously employs devices of PLOT, CHARACTERIZATION, and STYLE to achieve a more sophisticated effect, as in "La Belle Dame sans Merci" (p. 1037) and "Lochinvar" (p. 231).

BIOGRAPHY: In general, the systematic account of a particular life characterized by the fair presentation of all the evidence. A biographical essay, for example, "La Giocosa: A School for Free Men" (p. 172), may deal with one feature of a man's life, or one that reveals a significant aspect of his total experience.

An *autobiography* is a life written by the subject himself. An example of an autobiographical essay is St. Augustine's "The Power of Memory" (p. 78). Much modern literature, while not formally autobiographical, is closely related to the writer's personal experiences, for example, Laurie Lee's "A Winter Treat" (p. 41).

BLANK VERSE: *See* VERSIFICATION.

BURLESQUE (parody, caricature): An imitation of human action or a style of action that aims by deliberate distortion to amuse. When the object of imitation is a literary style, burlesque is called *parody*; when the object is a person, it is *caricature*. "The Happy Hypocrite" (p. 966) is in part a parody of romantic style, while portions of "Epistle II. To a Lady" (p. 516) are caricatures of Lady Mary Wortley Montagu and the Duchess of Marlborough. Burlesque differs from SATIRE, which is more concerned with the correction of vice or folly.

CACOPHONY: *See* VERSIFICATION.

CAESURA: *See* VERSIFICATION.

CARICATURE: *See* BURLESQUE.

CATALEXIS: *See* Versification.

CATASTROPHE: *See* Plot.

CATHARSIS: *See* Tragedy.

CAUSE and EFFECT: Often called *causal analysis.* A mode of analyzing a subject either in terms of the elements that caused it or in terms of effects that the subject is calculated to produce. Normally, causal analysis stresses a complex of causes and effects rather than single ones. Thus in "The Retreat from Excellence" (p. 1133) the causes of academic deficiency are identified and analyzed as persons, programs, subjects studied, and a climate of opinion all acting together; in "La Giocosa" (p. 172) the effects of a humanistic education are seen as practical and theoretical, social and personal. Strict causal analysis distinguishes between elements that are the positive, immediate, and necessary factors that actually produce an effect, and those circumstances or conditions that favor the causal action of these factors.

CHARACTER and CHARACTERIZATION: A *character* is an invented person created in drama or fiction. The main character, or hero, is the protagonist; his opponent is the antagonist. Character is inseparable from action. The principal means of characterization (of developing character) is by presenting the character's conscious and deliberate actions, rendering his thoughts and motives, both in dialogue and by description, contrasting him with others, describing his appearances, and showing what other characters think of him. *See also* plot.

CHORUS: This term originally referred to a band of men who danced and sang during religious festivals in ancient Greece. As the Greek drama (see *Oedipus,* p. 377) developed, the chorus participated in the action, speculated on the meaning of fate, danced, sang, offered prayers to the Gods, composed lyrical and philosophical odes, and interpreted the meaning of the action. The chorus was adopted by the Roman playwrights and from them it passed into English drama. But here (see *Dr. Faustus,* p. 243) the Chorus was reduced to a single character who recited a prologue and an epilogue and occasionally spoke at the beginning of an act. In modern times, the chorus has been supplanted by the so-called choral character who, like Philinte in *The Misanthrope,* Steavens in "The Sculptor's Funeral," and Dr. Kennedy in "Amy Foster," stands at a distance from the action of the story and interprets it for the audience. The choral character is also called a confidant, spokesman for the author and the reflector.

CLASSICISM: *See* Romanticism.

CLASSIFICATION and DIVISION: Terms that refer to logical modes of analysis. In classifying, we place a subject in a class and that class into a higher class on the basis of a common trait or traits. Thus we classify *Romeo and Juliet* as a tragedy, tragedy as a species of drama, and drama as a species of literature. In dividing, we regard the subject as a class and then, on the basis of a principle, resolve the class into subclasses and various units. Thus the class LITERATURE may be divided into DRAMA, EPIC, and LYRIC, drama into TRAGEDY and COMEDY, and tragedy into classical tragedy, romantic tragedy, and so on. *Classification* and *division* are often interrelated and may be said to represent two aspects of the whole relationship. See the use of classification and division in "The Notion of an American Gentleman" (p. 196), and "Charity" (p. 1024).

CLIMAX: The moment of greatest intensity or interest in a narrative or play, normally found close to the turning point or coincidental with the catastrophe or final resolution of the plot. Climax also refers to that arrangement of sentences or larger units of composition which advances from the less interesting to the most interesting. *See also* PLOT.

COHERENCE: A characteristic of effective rhetorical expression. In the sentence, coherence contributes to *unity* by making evident the connection of the related parts of the sentence—that is, by maintaining a harmony of structure, a proper sequence of tenses, agreement in mood, voice, and person, and a consistent tone or style. In the paragraph, coherence is attained by relating each sentence to the next one, by a consistent order of logic, time, place, and climactic interest, by using appropriate linking expressions, and by the repetition of key words and parallel constructions. In a larger unit of composition, coherence is achieved by the natural or logical progression of beginning, middle, and end. Particularly useful models of coherent writing are found in "A Freshman in Lilliput" (p. 65) and "The Essentials of Education" (p. 769).

COMEDY: A term that is now generally applied to all works of literature that amuse and divert the audience without necessarily involving it emotionally. Its distinctive characteristics are: (1) the hero and/or the main characters are plunged into misfortune but in the end are brought if not to happiness, at least to safety; (2) the characters and the situation do not arouse deep feeling in the audience or a profound sense of identification; they appeal, rather, to the audience's intellectual sense; (3) the characters are presented as general types rather than as realistic individuals, and the situations are abstracted from their serious possibilities. Comedy, like tragedy, is based on incongruity. In tragedy, however, the incongruity between what is and what ought to be evokes sympathy and fear, whereas in comedy it evokes laughter.

Originally, comedy was associated with revels—that is, with the ritualistic release of tensions on festive occasions. When comedy became a dramatic form it divided into three main channels: *high comedy,* which is concerned with intellectual incongruities and is set in a sophisticated background, for example, Molière's *The Misanthrope* (p. 865); *romantic comedy,* which is concerned chiefly with the emotional incongruities displayed in the plight of lovers and is set in a purely imaginative background, for example, Shakespeare's *As You Like It* and the Ferdinand-Miranda episodes of *The Tempest* (p. 541); and *low comedy,* which is chiefly concerned with physical incongruities of appearance, speech, or action, for example, the nonsense interpolations in *Dr. Faustus* (p. 243), and the Caliban-Trinculo-Stephano episodes in *The Tempest.*

Comedy bears a close resemblance to satire (see p. 1379); in fact, most comedy is at least implicitly satirical. Its relevance to wit and humor is explored in the essays by Beerbohm (p. 499), Hazlitt (p. 502), and White (p. 509).

The term *comedy* has also been used to signify all that is not tragedy. This use of the term explains why Dante called his very serious work a "Comedy."

COMPARISON and CONTRAST: Modes of analyzing a subject. Strict, logical comparison and contrast point to similarities and differences between two subjects in the same class, for example, American democracy resembles British democracy in that both are based on representative government; they differ in that American democracy separates the executive, legislative, and judicial branches, whereas in England the executive branch is an agency of the legislative branch and the highest court is composed of legislators. In a rhetorical sense, the terms comparison and contrast are used to indicate the similarities and differences between subjects in different classes. The process of learning, for example, resembles an active journey of discovery and exploration as opposed to the passive storage of facts and ideas in a mental warehouse. See "On Wit and Humour" (p. 502) for a discussion of extended comparison and contrast.

Logical comparison, when extended and used as a basis of inference, is similar to ANALOGY.

Rhetorical comparison is similar to PARABLE, SIMILE, and other figures of speech. *See also* FIGURATIVE LANGUAGE.

COMPLICATION: *See* PLOT.

CONCRETE: *See* ABSTRACT.

CONFLICT: *See* PLOT.

CONNOTATION and DENOTATION: According to the common usage of literary critics, especially the "new" critics, the *denotation* of a word is the object or event the word actually stands for or points to. Thus the denotation of the word *home* is a human dwelling. The *connotation* of a word is what the word suggests or implies. Thus, *home* connotes not just a house, but a constellation of personal memories and a complex set of emotions. In a sense, denotative meaning is equivalent to an impersonal use of language, while connotative meaning is equivalent to its personal use. Words acquire connotative meaning by their history, by their current association, and by their context. Thus, the word *hell* arouses negative emotions because it is the traditional description of a place of torment; the term *status-seeker,* in itself neutral, is currently associated with indiscriminate ambition; the word *thum* simply denotes a sound but, in the context of the following sentence (by Edward L. Beach), it has a menacing connotation: "Now [the men in the submarine] can plainly hear the malignant *thum, thum, thum* [of the destroyer's propeller.]" Exact and highly charged connotative meaning blends into the FIGURATIVE LANGUAGE associated with poetry and imaginative literature.

CONTEXT: *See* FORM.

CRITICISM: The exposition of the meaning, form, and style of a literary work, and the judgment of its merit or value, usually in comparison with some other literary work and by reference to some standard, explicit or implied. The critic, in T. M. Greene's words, attempts "to re-create a work of art . . . to apprehend the content which its author actually expressed in it, i.e., to interpret it correctly as a vehicle of communication." Criticism of this kind is often called *formal* or *re-creative criticism.* See "Logic and Lyric" (p. 658). Formal criticism is closely related to the "new criticism," which emphasizes the literary aspects of a poem, as opposed to its moral tone, historical and social context, and intentions of its author. The new critics hold that a poem should be judged solely on its literary merit; thus, they advocate close textual analysis of imagery, rhythm, and structure. *Biographical* or *historical criticism* is concerned with the sources or background of the work, the language and conventions employed by the writer, and his literary models and influences. "Aeneas: The Roman Hero" (p. 161) exemplifies this type of criticism. Judgment of merit or value, called *judicial criticism,* estimates a work of art by certain standards or theories of value, as in "What is a Classic?" (p. 777). Much criticism cuts across these categories. Thus, "Oedipus Rex: The Tragic Rhythm of Action" (p. 416) is recreative, historical, and judicial.

DEDUCTION and INDUCTION: *Deduction* is a form of reasoning that leads from the truth of a general statement—that is, from a statement that pertains to a whole class—to the truth of a particular statement—that is, to the application of a general truth to a particular member of that class. The external form of deduction is the *syllo-*

gism, which consists of two propositions or statements so connected that a third necessarily follows.

All men are mortal. (general statement)
John is a man. (particular man placed in class)
John is mortal. (necessary conclusion)

Induction is a form of reasoning that leads from the truth of particular statements to the truth of a general statement. Huxley illustrates the use of induction and deduction in "The Methods of Scientific Investigation" (p. 644).

Both modes of reasoning (with ANALOGY) are normally employed in ARGUMENT. Informal use of these methods is found, however, in all rational communication and may frequently be found in poetry (see "Logic and Lyric," p. 658), and in the debates that take place in drama (see *The Misanthrope*, p. 865) and stories (see "The Crocodile," p. 462).

DEFINITION: A statement that answers the question, What is it? In a verbal definition, the defining statement explains what a word connotes and denotes (see CONNOTATION and DENOTATION). In real definition, that is, a definition of what a particular word stands for, the defining statement places an object in a class or genus, and differentiates it from the other members of that class. Thus, a real definition of man is: *Man is a rational animal. Animal* designates the class, and *rational* designates the characteristic that differentiates man from other animals. Informal methods of definition consist of DESCRIPTION of the appearances of an object, NARRATION of its origin and history, COMPARISON and CONTRAST with similar objects, CAUSAL ANALYSIS, and, in the case of dynamic objects, PROCESS. Essays containing many of these methods of definition are "The Notion of an American Gentleman" (p. 196), "The Essentials of Education" (p. 769), and "Knowledge and Wisdom" (p. 1222).

DENOUEMENT: *See* PLOT.

DESCRIPTION: A form of discourse which aims to present an object as it appears to the senses (*scientific description*), or to create an imaginative impression of a real or fictitious object (*artistic or impressionistic description*). Normally, description is integrated with other forms of discourse. Thus description is mingled with NARRATIVE in "Boyhood in the 1940's" (p. 48); with EXPOSITION in "La Giocosa" (p. 172) and "Countrymen at Work" (p. 630); and with narrative argument in "A Dog in Brooklyn" (p. 756). Most fiction employs description at least incidentally. The development of an effective description implies a consistent POINT OF VIEW, whether of a stationary or moving observer, a concern for a dominant and unifying impression, and a vivid, exact STYLE. Excellent examples of description may be found in "Ethan Brand" (p. 1266) and "Blackberry Winter" (p. 1279).

DIALOGUE: A form of literature in which two or more characters converse, usually on a serious subject. Plato's *Dialogues* are probably the first example of this genre. A dialogue may also be a type of dramatic poem developed largely by dialogue, for example, "The Death of the Hired Man" (p. 1154), or it may simply refer to the speech of characters in a play or story.

DICTION: In most literary discussion, diction is not simply acceptable usage, but the effective choice of words. Effective diction is described as clear, vigorous, and interesting. Words are clear when they are exact, vigorous when they are appropriate in tone and feeling, interesting when they are vivid and imaginative in quality. Effective diction avoids trite or worn-out expressions such as *mystical moment,* clichés such as *men of distinction,* and archaisms such as *anon I come* and *eftsoons*—except when, as in "Under Which Lyre" (p. 812), they are used consciously for a humorous or satirical effect. Good diction depends largely upon the context supplied by the purpose, occasion, and intended audience of the literary work, and hence must be considered as a subordinate unit in the structure of the whole discourse. *See also* ABSTRACT and CONCRETE, CONNOTATION and DENOTATION, and FIGURATIVE LANGUAGE.

DRAMA: A form of literature in which a story is acted out on a stage. Drama employs PLOT and CHARACTER, as do narrative poetry and prose fiction. Drama differs from them, however, in the use of living actors who convey the story by gesture, facial expression, pantomime, and DIALOGUE. In drama, dialogue is the principal means of developing both PLOT and CHARACTERIZATION; hence dramatic dialogue is generally more concise and purposeful than dialogue in prose fiction.

The principal kinds of drama are TRAGEDY and COMEDY. Other important kinds of drama are chronicle plays, such as Shakespeare's *Henry IV;* masques that combine poetry, music, dance, costuming, and spectacle, such as the masque in Act IV of *The Tempest* (p. 541); miracle and mystery plays based on Biblical episodes or on the lives of saints, such as those in the York mystery cycle; morality plays in which virtues and vices are personified, such as in *Everyman;* and PROBLEM PLAYS, such as *Corruption in the Palace of Justice* (p. 1160).

DRAMATIC MONOLOGUE: A form of poetry in which a single speaker addresses another person (or persons) whose presence is integral to the action, and thereby reveals his own character at a moment of crucial decision. The dramatic monologue is often identified with Robert Browning. (See "Andrea del Sarto," p. 806). It differs from the SOLILOQUY, in which the speaker voices his thoughts to himself, and from the monologue proper, in which the speaker addresses the audience directly. *See also* "Ulysses" (p. 223) and "The Love Song of J. Alfred Prufrock" (p. 1051).

ECLOGUE: *See* ELEGY.

ELEGY: A poem composed in elegiac meter, consisting of a dactylic hexameter couplet. *See* VERSIFICATION. In the second line of the couplet, the third and sixth feet normally contain one accented syllable. More commonly, elegy refers to a formal poem reflecting on some phase of death or lamenting a particular death. Any poem containing melancholy meditations on the vicissitudes of life may be loosely termed an elegy.

The pastoral elegy, a special form of the elegy derived from the Greek poet Theocritus and the Roman poet Virgil, employs numerous artificial conventions, one of which is that the speaker and the one he mourns are portrayed as shepherds. The background and setting are bucolic. The traditional pastoral elegy starts with the poet explaining that his grief is caused by the death of a dear friend. He invokes the Muses for aid in singing his lament. Then he recalls the happy days spent with his lost friend, and from there he goes on to express his deep grief at losing him. His grief turns to joy at the end of the poem, however, when the consoling thought occurs to him that his dead friend has found eternal happiness through death. See the elegies "Adonais" (p. 348) and "Tithonus" (p. 1039).

Eclogues and *idylls* are types of pastoral poetry in which shepherds and shepherdesses frolic in a bucolic setting. The subject, however, is usually in a lighter vein than that of an elegy.

EMPHASIS: A characteristic of effective arrangement of the sentence and larger units of composition. In the sentence *emphasis* is achieved by placing key words at the beginning or end; by witholding the key expression until the end (periodic structure); by placing contrasted ideas in a parallel structure or antithesis; by inverting the normal order; by arranging ideas or impressions in an order of climax; by the use of figurative language.

In larger units than the sentence emphasis is attained by the effective ordering of beginning, middle, and end; by a more intensive treatment of major ideas or incidents; by maintaining suspense and developing a climax; by the use of appropriate imagery and tone. *See also* DICTION.

EPIC: A long narrative poem that centers around the actions of an heroic character, and that aims to evoke admiration for this character as a figure of national importance. (See the discussion of the epic on pp. 104–05.) Primitive epics, such as *Beowulf* and the *Iliad*, derive from folk tales or lays transmitted orally until recorded by a poet. The literary epic, or artistic epic, a more sophisticated development of the primitive epic, follows certain conventions or traditions. Thus the *Aeneid* begins, after a formal invocation of the muse, in the middle rather than at the beginning of the action. The next two books recapitulate Aeneas' fate. In Book IV (p. 207) Aeneas encounters the first obstacle to his mission as the founder of Rome: his love for Dido. Succeeding books tell of his victories and adventures in founding Rome. The style of the epic is normally appropriate to noble heroes and their lofty emotions. Extended similes, frequent use of epithets, calculated digressions, set descriptions of storms, battles, funeral games, public meetings, dramatic hand-to-hand combats, and the hero's descent to the underworld for the purpose of his own education are all marks of the epic.

Derived from the epic are the *heroic poem* of a serious religious or patriotic character, such as Dante's *Divine Comedy* (p. 237); the *epyllion,* or little epic, sometimes called an *idyll,* which celebrates a single episode in the life of a hero, such as Tennyson's poem "Morte D'Arthur" (p. 225); and the *prose romance* which, in homely fashion, celebrates heroic adventure. *See* "The Captive's Story" (p. 112).

The *mock epic,* or *mock heroic* poem, is a satirical or comic use of the grand epic style to ridicule trivial personalities or events.

EPIGRAM: A short witty saying in verse or prose. Epigrams abound in "Under Which Lyre" (p. 812).

EPILOGUE: *See* ACT.

EPISODE: *See* ACT.

EPODE: See ODE.

ESSAY: In 1580, Michel de Montaigne published a collection of brief prose meditations on a variety of subjects. He called them *Essais,* which in French means "attempts." His title implies that he did not propose to develop specific ideas in the manner of the formal treatise or academic dissertation. His aim, rather, was to share his delight, dismay, doubts, and opinions with those who desired to speculate about the mysteries of human life. In a short time Montaigne had many imitators, Francis Bacon among them (pp. 331 and 1013).

With the rise of periodical literature in the seventeenth and eighteenth centuries the essay found its appropriate audience. In the meantime, however, prose writers in a tradition quite different from that of Montaigne and Bacon borrowed the word *essay.* John Locke, for instance, entitled a long formal study of philosophy *An Essay Concerning Human Understanding.* By the end of the nineteenth century, *essay* had become an umbrella term used to describe the intimate, lyrical pieces of Charles Lamb, the historical studies of Carlyle, the literary analyses of Matthew Arnold, and the expositions and arguments of Huxley. The essay had come to mean a moderately short prose composition that pleased the reader by virtue of the author's skill in presenting his subject.

It may be impossible to distinguish between the "essential" essay and the many types of prose, such as the *article,* that have come to be allied with it. It is difficult to determine exactly where autobiography ceases and the essay begins, or where a personal narrative such as "Boyhood in the 1940's" (p. 48) joins the reflective company of "The Lost Childhood" (p. 74). Literary compositions constantly cross lines from one genre to another.

If we cannot define the essay proper, we can distinguish between its two main varieties, the *informal* or *personal* essay and the *formal* essay. In the informal essay the personality of the author plays the larger role. A typical informal essayist—Max Beerbohm—attracts readers chiefly by the charm of his own character. We read Beerbohm's essays not for the sake of the subject but for the sake of Beerbohm.

In the formal essay, on the other hand, the writer is more committed to the needs of his purpose, his subject, and the conventions of prose discourse. His personality is still present, but it is channeled. His focus is on the subject rather than on his own personality and wit in discussing the subject. The formal essayist has sacrificed the liberty to pursue his personal impulse in order to do justice to the logical requirements of his argument. This is not to say that he has thereby abandoned his own passionate convictions; rather, he has disciplined his convictions the better to express them.

At bottom, then, the difference between the informal essay and the formal essay is a matter of emphasis. The informal essay tends toward the emphatic expression of personality, the formal essay toward the emphatic expression of subject and purpose. The informal essay is free in form, the formal essay abides by the logical requirements of expository and argumentative discourse. But the two types have much in common. Both are born of a deep attachment to an idea that compels the writer to find the precise shape and the precise words that will make the idea come alive.

EXPOSITION: A form of discourse that aims primarily to clarify an idea or an impression. Exposition avails itself of all the methods of ANALYSIS, and is frequently mingled with scientific DESCRIPTION, NARRATION, and ARGUMENT. Typical expository essays are "Unity" (p. 689), "The Essentials of Education" (p. 769), and "Knowledge and Wisdom" (p. 1222). In imaginative literature, *exposition* refers to introductory sections of stories or dramas where the facts necessary to understand future happenings are set forth. Act I in *The Tempest* is substantially an exposition of the history necessary to explain the subsequent action.

FALLACY: A mistake in the process of reasoning. Thus, a definition may be faulty (or fallacious) if the term being defined is used in the definition, as, for example, if goodness is defined as being good. A classification may be faulty if it includes details that are not actually in the class or if it excludes details that belong there.

Normally, however, fallacy refers to faulty processes of ANALOGY and DEDUCTION and INDUCTION. The principal fallacies are the *non sequitur,* in which a connection is asserted or implied where none in fact exists; the *hasty generalization,* in which a generalization is made on the basis of too few or unrepresentative particulars; *false analogy,* in which a conclusion based on a similarity between objects ignores significant differences; *equivocation,* in which a term is used in two different senses in the same argument; and *avoiding the question,* in which the point at issue is ignored, or an irrelevant issue is introduced.

Fallacies are distinguished from material errors—that is, from mistakes of fact. The serious or humorous correction or detection of fallacy is the staple of ARGUMENT, COMEDY, and SATIRE. Instances of detected fallacy occur in *Apology* (p. 332), "The Method of Scientific Investigation" (p. 644), "A Defence of Nonsense" (p. 670), and "The Idols of the Laboratory" (p. 1242).

John Ruskin's term "*pathetic fallacy*" refers to expressions such as "crawling foam" in which human capabilities are attributed to nonhuman objects. Most figurative language, however, makes uses of this type of "fallacy."

FIGURATIVE LANGUAGE: In poetry the term *image* is used to denote an expression that elicits a picture of a concrete object, such as "the rock of Gibraltar." The term *imagery* is used to indicate images taken collectively, or the total imaginative impression created by a poem, such as the impression of mastery conveyed in Hopkins' "The Windhover" (p. 805). An image appeals to sight, as in "blue sky of spring,/White clouds on the wing" (Allingham); to hearing, as in "roasted crabs hiss in the bowl" (Shakespeare); to the sense of taste, as in wine that tastes "of the warm South" (Keats); to the sense of touch as in "a drowsy numbness pains my sense" (Keats); to the sense of smell, as in "the fume of poppies" that sets the autumn reaper drowsing (Keats).

Thus the poet appeals to the senses by concrete language that refers directly to the *objects* we can see, hear, taste, touch, and smell. Sometimes, however, the poet uses figurative language to express an idea. A *figure* is a word or expression used to describe an object to which it is not *literally* applicable. For example, in common speech we often say that a very strong man is "as hard as iron," or that a ship "plows the sea." In these expressions, we transfer the word *hard* from iron, a literal application, to the strong man, a figurative application; and similarly we transfer the word *plows* from farming to a ship. Our language is figurative, then, when a word is "transferred to a sense different from its proper signification."

In poetry, figurative language may be used for expanded explanation, as in Jaques' famous comparison of man's life to drama ("All the world's a stage"); for ornament, as in certain descriptive stanzas of Spenser's *The Faerie Queene;* or for the expression of an idea that does not admit of literal statement. Some ideas or impressions require figurative statement because they are necessarily associated in the poet's mind with other ideas or impressions, as intellectual adventure is associated with putting out to sea in Tennyson's "Ulysses" (p. 223), or as "the lunatic, the lover, and the poet" are, in Shakespeare's imagination, "all compact." Figurative language is the means of expressing the unity of a complex impression; it is a fusion wrought in the heat of intense feeling and thought when the poet is simultaneously aware of several experiences.

Metaphor and Simile: Metaphor and simile are based on the perception of a likeness between two objects or acts. Both are species of analogy that express not an *exact* similarity, but a relation of likeness or proportion between things in *separate* classes. Thus, Burns does not say that his love is exactly like a red, red rose; rather, he says that his love is as fragrant in his life as the rose is fragrant in the month of June. Since metaphorical statement is often mistaken for strict logical parallel, it is important to realize its precise nature.

Metaphor and simile involve three main elements: (a) the main object or act and the secondary object or act with which it is to be compared, (b) the point of the comparison between the two objects or acts, and (c) the identification of the two objects or acts.

In metaphor this identification is implied; in simile, it is stated explicitly by the use of the terms *like, as,* or similar expressions, such as "When I *compare* thee to a summer's day" or "When I *resemble* her to thee." As in Waller's "Song" (p. 1035), the simile usually places the objects to be compared side by side, is somewhat longer than the metaphor, and tends to be more deliberately illustrative than the metaphor.

From the examples cited above it may readily be inferred that metaphor sometimes sacrifices logical clarity for vividness and emotional intensity. At bottom, metaphor is based upon the personal perceptions of the poet. Sometimes these perceptions are intimately linked with his own subconscious. Consequently, the point of the comparison will seem most effective to those readers who are in greatest rapport with the writer.

Allegory, Parable, and Symbol: An allegory is an extended metaphor; a parable, an extended simile. In an allegory the implied comparison is sustained throughout the entire narrative. Among the more extended allegories in English poetry are Edmund Spenser's *The Faerie Queene* and Samuel Taylor Coleridge's "The Rime of the Ancient Mariner."

A parable extends the simile by finding more than one point of comparison between two objects. Thus the details of the New Testament parable of the Good Shepherd—the loss of the sheep, the search, the recovery, the joyous return—illustrate point for point God's care of the sinner.

Allegory and parable are called symbolic because, like the symbol, they are signs that point to something beyond literal meaning. Strictly speaking, however, a symbol is an image that suggests a comparison or relation between two objects, but does not express one term of the comparison. Thus, for example, in "The Lottery" (p. 323), the lottery itself is a symbol of man's superstitious need for a scapegoat. It suggests, but does not develop, the comparison between the cruelty of the townspeople and the cruelties of pogroms, planned famines, and gas chamber executions.

Symbolism, like imagery in general, is founded on analogy, the relation of likeness or proportion that exists between two objects. All things are bound together in some relationship—man with nature, nature with man. Hence, as the lion is first in the animal kingdom, we may refer to a strong, natural leader as a "lion among men"; since thunder is a sign in nature of a storm, so in human life we may refer to "the thunder of human anger." All things not only exist in themselves but also point to or echo something other than themselves: the rain points back to its cause, the clouds and winds, and forward to its effects, the battering storm or the fertile fields; a house brings to mind people and town; and the plodding worker is inevitably associated with the patient ox. We shall see more of these analogies in the figures of speech described below.

Personification and Fable: Personification is a species of metaphor in which some *inanimate* object is identified with some aspect of human personality. Thus, in "Adonais" (p. 348), Shelley endows poetry and other intellectual virtues with the human power to think and feel. Similarly, in his sonnets, Shakespeare humanizes abstractions such as time, death, and love.

A fable, on the other hand, is an extended metaphor in which an animal character is identified with some aspect of human character. (A fable can also refer to a fictitious narrative, or to an animal story with a moral point, as in Aesop.) In "The Rat-Catcher" (p. 537) and "Macavity the Cat" (p. 538) the various animal characters think, speak, and act like human beings.

Synecdoche and Metonymy: Metaphor and simile, allegory and parable, personification and fable are figures of speech based on similarity; synecdoche and metonymy are figures of speech based on contiguity. Synecdoche and metonymy derive from the natural tendency, mentioned in our foregoing discussion of the symbol, to describe an object or action by the name of a second object or action with which the first is closely connected.

If the interchanged terms are connected intrinsically or essentially, that is, by a relation such as that of part to whole, species to genus, or material to thing made, the figure of contiguity is called *synec-*

doche (literally, *understood together*). Thus, for example, we refer to a sail (part) to designate a ship (whole), or to the Navy (whole) to describe a task force (part); or to science (genus) when we mean chemistry (species), or to metaphor (species) when we speak of figurative language (genus); or to brick and mortar (material) to characterize a building (the thing made).

If the interchanged terms are connected extrinsically, that is, by a relation such as that of cause to effect, container to the thing contained, or sign to the thing signified, the figure of contiguity is called *metonymy* (literally, *change of name*). Thus metonymy occurs when we state the cause (Shakespeare) for the effect (Hamlet, Lear), or the container (the theater) for the contained (the play and the cast), or the special characteristics of an office (crown and scepter) for the office itself (kingship). Metonymy, perhaps the most embracing of all figures, is a commonplace of popular speech.

Paradox and Irony: Paradox is a statement in which an apparent contradiction is true in some sense. Thus Keats's line, "Heard melodies are sweet, but those unheard are sweeter," seems absurd until we realize that the unheard melodies are those of the spirit. So, too, Wordsworth's line, "Our birth is but a sleep and a forgetting," seems contrary to sense. Only when the context of the ode (p. 98) supplies Wordsworth's Platonic frame of reference does its deeper, and truer, meaning become evident. By its very nature paradox is a challenging form of statement and is often employed by original thinkers (see "A Defence of Nonsense," p. 670) and by those advancing an unusual position (see "The Way of Imperfection," p. 1259).

Irony is a statement that implies its opposite, as in "War, the benefactor of mankind." In "A Modest Proposal," Swift (p. 1126) professes to aim, through the sale of children, to advance the welfare of the kingdom; he implies, however, that the present treatment of children of the poor is destructive of all justice. In addition to purely *verbal irony*, there is an *attitude of irony*, such as that Socrates displays toward his opponents in *Apology* (p. 332); *dramatic irony*, as in *Oedipus* (p. 377), when events move in an exactly opposite direction from the anticipations of Oedipus and the chorus; *irony of situation*, as in "The Crocodile" (p. 462), where normal values are reversed and the animal is more important than the man; and *pathetic irony*, as in "The Secret Life of Walter Mitty" (p. 447), where illusions and reality are counterposed.

Closely related to irony are *sarcasm*, or pretended praise, as in Waugh's remarks about the scientific elite in "Love Among the Ruins" (p. 989); and *invective*, or denunciation, evident in "Epistle II. To a Lady" (p. 516) and in some of Prospero's speeches to Caliban (pp. 552–55).

Hyperbole and Litotes: Hyperbole is a deliberate overstatement or exaggeration for the purpose of emphasis. Thus Virgil begins the Dido episode (p. 207) by saying that Dido, sick with love, had been "feeding the wound with her life-blood." Litotes, also called understatement, emphasizes a point by appearing to minimize it. Thus Marvell praises King Charles' courage in facing death by writing:

> He nothing common did, nor mean,
> Upon that memorable scene. . . .

Sustained hyperbole, a vein of understatement, as in "The Unknown Citizen" (p. 240), is an excellent support to irony.

When we reflect on figures of speech, we discover that all of them have two things in common: the perception of hidden connections between objects or actions in different classes, and the attempt to express these connections in a manner that will interest or arouse the reader. Figurative language is a thinking out in images, a dramatization of abstract thought. It reveals surprising similarities between nature and human life, between the world of matter and the world of spirit, between the familiar and the strange.

FORM and CONTENT: In literary criticism and rhetoric, *form* has a variety of meanings. In its most radical sense form is that which makes a thing the kind of thing it is. Form then is design, shape, or pattern by which we identify a work as drama, narrative, or lyric; as novel, short story; as argument, exposition, narrative, or description. Further, form is the individual structure of a particular work, the structure that distinguishes *Oedipus,* for instance, from *The Misanthrope,* or *The Tempest* from *A Midsummer Night's Dream.*

Content is that which is shaped, i.e., a body of ideas, impressions, or facts capable of being formed into comedy or tragedy, prose romance or poetic lyric. Before the actual writing there is a real difference between form and matter. After composition the two are fused, so that we are only aware of content insofar as it is formed, and of form only insofar as it has shaped a particular content.

Normally, however, form is used in two senses: to describe the principal kinds (*genres*) of literature in poetry and prose, and to describe the principal forms of discourse.

Poetry has three principal divisions: DRAMA, a story designed to be presented through action and dialogue before an audience; NARRATIVE, a story designed to be told or recited; LYRIC, a markedly personal, melodic, and personal expression of feeling.

Prose literature is usually divided into the NOVEL, the SHORT STORY, and the ESSAY. Of these, the ESSAY is by far the most comprehensive, ranging from formal scientific prose to expressions of personal attitudes or experiences.

The forms of discourse—ARGUMENT, DESCRIPTION, EXPOSITION, and NARRATION—are distinguished by their purpose or function. Argument aims to convince a reader by reasoning on evidence; description to report what is perceptible to the senses; exposition to clarify the meaning of things, events, or processes; narration to recount events that happen in time. As with the literary genres, the forms of discourse have much in common, yet each has its characteristic techniques.

Poetry, by virtue of its metrical regularity and its stanzaic patterns, and because of the conventions associated with its many varieties, is often identified by its external forms—ballad, sonnet, quatrain, and so on. More recently, form has been recognized as the shape imparted to the poem by its predominant image, metaphor, or myth.

In *prose,* form is frequently considered equivalent to arrangement and style. Thus the form of an essay is said to be determined by the order of the thoughts and their articulation in the sequence of sentences.

HEPTAMETER: *See* VERSIFICATION.

HEROIC COUPLET: *See* VERSIFICATION.

HUMOR: *See* COMEDY.

HYPERBOLE: *See* FIGURATIVE LANGUAGE.

HYPERMETER: *See* VERSIFICATION.

IDYLL: *See* ELEGY *and* EPIC.

IMAGERY: *See* FIGURATIVE LANGUAGE.

IMITATION: One of the oldest and most persistent theories of literature, that is, that art is an imitation (*mimesis*) of nature. The theory is derived from the Greek view, and best phrased by Aristotle. Since the rise of technology, the word *imitation* has suggested a shabby replica or a stereotyped reproduction. In its earlier and purer sense, however, *imitation* meant the re-presentation or the re-creation of objects or actions in accordance with a principle, and in the manner of nature itself. Hence to describe art as imitative is not to deny it originality, but to link the human process of thought with the creativity of nature. *See* "Oedipus Rex: The Tragic Rhythm of Action," p. 416.

INDUCTION: *See* DEDUCTION.

INTENTION: In literature *intention* has a twofold meaning, the intention of the writer and the intention of the work. Thus we know from history that Samuel Johnson wrote *Rasselas* in a very short time to pay for his mother's funeral. His immediate personal intention was to make money. But the work itself has its own end; as a didactic novel, *Rasselas* develops the theme that true happiness is impossible in this world. There is also a difference between professed intention and actual achievement. Thus *Don Quixote* is professedly written to show the dangerous effects of romantic tales of chivalry. It does so much more than this, that its professed intention seems misleading.

INVECTIVE: *See* FIGURATIVE LANGUAGE.

IRONY: *See* FIGURATIVE LANGUAGE.

LITERATURE: In current usage, the term *literature* is taken to mean that body of writing which, by virtue of excellent language, thought, and imagination, is read for its own sake rather than for the information it may convey. Literature is often divided into (1) imaginative or creative literature, which, in the form of fiction or poetry, appeals, as Joseph Conrad noted, "to our capacity for delight and wonder, to the sense of mystery surrounding our lives," and (2) the literature of knowledge which, in exceptional autobiographies, personal narrative, biography and history, and essays appeals primarily to our intelligence but contains elements of delight and wonder.

LITOTES: *See* FIGURATIVE LANGUAGE.

LYRIC: In general, the term *lyric* refers to poetry that is markedly personal, melodic, and emotional. The lyric includes a great variety of verse: the song (a brief, simple lyric that may be sung to a musical accompaniment), descriptive and reflective poetry of a personal nature, the sonnet, the ode, and the elegy. In Greek poetry the lyric, derived from *lyre,* designated the song of a single person as opposed to the collective choric song. Although this meaning of the term is rarely employed, the predominantly personal and emotional character of the lyric still distinguishes it from narrative, dramatic, satirical, and other types of poetry by a more objective nature. Some typical lyrics are: "Who is Silvia?" (p. 1034), Waller's "Song" (p. 1035), and "When You Are Old" (p. 1047).

METAPHOR: *See* FIGURATIVE LANGUAGE.

METONYMY: *See* FIGURATIVE LANGUAGE.

MYTH: A type of imaginative literature, such as the Greek myths, composed of legends about gods, deities, or superhuman heroes. A myth may also refer to an idea or theory offered as a symbolic interpretation of reality, such as the Platonic idea of pre-existence set forth in Wordsworth's "Ode: Intimations of Immortality" (p. 98), or it may refer to the basic story out of which a poet shapes a drama or poem. Myth is discussed in "Oedipus Rex: The Tragic Rhythm of Action" (p. 416) and "The Rainbow Bridge" (p. 1233).

NARRATION (or NARRATIVE): A form of discourse, common to verse and prose, that aims to tell a story—that is, to present a connected series of events that together make up a significant action. Its characteristics are a coherent order or chronology; a consistent POINT OF VIEW that identifies the narrator by the angle, physical or intellectual, from which he tells the story; and a STYLE that evokes a sense of movement. Fictional narrative is also distinguished by PLOT and CHARACTERIZATION.

NATURALISM: A style based upon the theory that literature should approximate science in its reliance on close observation and exact reporting. Naturalistic writers, like Zola in France or Theodore Dreiser in the United States, stress the influence of heredity and environment as the sole determinants of human character and conduct. Their style is keyed to this materialistic assumption. Unlike the realist, the naturalist admits imaginative, romantic, idealistic or humorous elements only as examples of illusion. In his "Love Among the Ruins" (p. 989), Evelyn Waugh attacks naturalistic assumptions and parodies the naturalistic style. Some traits of the naturalistic style may also be seen in "Counterparts" (p. 1070) and "The Guest" (p. 1105).

NOVEL: A long fictitious story in prose. Its name derives from the Italian *novella,* which is a short prose tale, for example, "The Captive's Story" (p. 112). The name is still used to describe short novels such as "The Blue Hotel" (p. 299) and "The Next Time" (p. 820). But the novel proper as it developed in England in the eighteenth century is more directly related to earlier romances such as Malory's *Morte D'Arthur,* and to the poetic epic, imaginative histories, journalism, and the drama. The principal elements of the novel are story (with or without PLOT), CHARACTER, ATMOSPHERE or setting, and STYLE.

Conventional divisions of the novel are based on mood, subject matter, emphasis, and technique. A novel may be, in mood, either realistic or romantic; its *subject matter* may be historical, contemporary, primarily social, or primarily concerned with the individual; its *emphasis* may be predominantly a tale, a plotted story, a character study, or a novel of atmosphere; and the author's *technique* may be dramatic, episodic, impressionistic, expressionistic, symbolic, or in the stream of consciousness or psychological mode.

The devices of fiction are many and perhaps unclassifiable for, as R. A. Scott-James remarked, "the critic who approaches an individual novel will always have before him a unique thing—this novel—and it will still remain for him to define its unique character, and study its *particular* technique." *See also* PLOT, CHARACTER, ATMOSPHERE, NARRATION, EPIC, DRAMA, and SHORT STORY.

ODE: A lyric poem that is formal in manner, lofty in tone, and dignified in its subject or theme. It is derived from the choral interlude in Greek dramatic poetry (see the choral odes in *Oedipus*), in which the chorus chanted its song, the STROPHE, as it moved up one side of the stage, the ANTISTROPHE as it returned, and the EPODE as it stood in its place. Eventually, the ode was developed as an independent lyric poem by the Greek poet Pindar. Although a few English poets (for instance, Thomas Gray in his "Progress of Poesy") wrote in the Pindaric tradition, the great majority have chosen either of two main ode forms—the regular monostrophic form, or the irregular form.

The regular form consists of a series of stanzas unvarying in number of lines, line lengths, and rhyme scheme. See Keats's ten-line stanza pattern in "Ode to a Nightingale." The irregular ode is extremely free in number and length of line and rhyme scheme. *See* Wordsworth's "Ode: Intimations of Immortality" (p. 98).

ONOMATOPOIEA: *See* VERSIFICATION.

PARABLE: *See* FIGURATIVE LANGUAGE.

PARADOX: *See* FIGURATIVE LANGUAGE.

PARALLELISM: *See* COHERENCE.

PARODY: *See* BURLESQUE.

PERIPETY: *See* PLOT.

PERSONIFICATION: *See* FIGURATIVE LANGUAGE.

PERSUASION: A mode of discourse characterized by the speaker's or writer's attempt not only to explain his subject (see EXPOSITION) or to convince his reader (see ARGUMENT), but also to induce a decision or a course of action. Sometimes the action is immediate and explicit, as in the case of Socrates' appeal to the jury to find him not guilty (p. 340). Sometimes the action is implicit, as in St. Augustine's suggestion that his reader might profitably follow his example (see p. 78). Many writers invite the reader to share their attitudes or emotions by the tone of their work rather than by argument.

PLOT: The conscious arrangement of incidents or details in a drama or story for the purpose of achieving the greatest artistic effect. In his *Poetics* Aristotle, using Sophocles' *Oedipus* as his most illustrious example, describes the characteristics of a good plot in terms of *complication, turning point* or *reversal,* and *resolution.* The resolution results in a *catastrophe* and *recognition* or *discovery.*

In a plotted drama or story, a main character or protagonist is presented in conflict with some opposing force—destiny, a personal antagonist, society, his own passions, or all four together. He wills, either consciously or unconsciously, a course of action that involves him in further action and decisions. These *complications* grow until that point when the hero's fortunes begin to change—to turn in his favor in the case of COMEDY, or against him in the case of TRAGEDY. Step by step the twisted skein of events unravels, and the mysterious questions raised in the complication are answered. The final solution, the catastrophe or denouement, leaves us with an answer to the main question. Faustus is damned; Oedipus is blinded and condemned to exile; Prospero is restored to his dukedom; Alceste abandons society; Cust voluntarily gives himself up to justice. Moreover, this change of fortune, whether for good or evil, is fully recognized by the protagonist. It does not merely happen to him, nor is it an accident. He realizes his own responsibility or role in creating or in cooperating with the event; often, as in *Oedipus,* he discovers a fact that was hitherto not known to himself or, as in *Corruption in the Palace of Justice,* a motive hitherto suppressed.

Plot is essentially interconnected with CHARACTER. Since plot involves meaningful human action, it involves characters who act consciously and deliberately. A plot is persuasive only insofar as those characters act in a manner that is reasonable, consistent, and natural. If we do not "believe" in the characters, we cannot "believe" in the action. Hence the motivation of the characters, whether they be protagonists or antagonists, must resemble the way men normally act.

Plot differs from *story,* as E. M. Forster suggests, in that story tells us what happened, whereas plot tells us why it happened. Hence an effective plot is one in which each incident is so connected that, save at the beginning, it is explained by what precedes and explains what follows. The mark of a strictly unified plot is that no incident can be deleted without in some way destroying the final meaning of the work. Poe expresses this view in another fashion: "In the whole composition there should be no word written, of which the tendency, direct or indirect, is not to the one pre-established design."

Plot is essentially the same in drama, the narrative poem, the novel, and the short story. It accommodates itself to the limitations of each form. Drama can depend upon the actor to create a more compelling illusion of reality, but it does not allow for the presence of the author in his own person or, as in *Don Juan,* in a fictitious representative. The novel permits the illusion of the passage of time and the presence of multitudes and thus favors multiple perspectives, while the short story, concentrating on a single main incident and a restricted point of view, often allows for a sharper focus on character and event. *See also* POINT OF VIEW.

POETRY: The art of literature, particularly in verse. VERSE is not essential to poetry, but is conventionally associated with it. *See* LITERATURE and VERSE AND VERSIFICATION.

POINT OF VIEW: A term used to describe the standpoint or mental attitude of the speaker or narrator in a poem, novel, short story, or in the various forms of discourse. The author may tell a story in his own person, as in "A Dog in Brooklyn" (p. 756), or as a fictitious I. This first person narrator may be simply a recorder like the I in "Amy Foster" (p. 1081), or the observer, like Dr. Kennedy in the same story. He may be both an observer and a participator in the action like the boy in "My Oedipus Complex" (p. 936). In a third-person narrative, the writer may identify one character as the main observer or agent in the action, as Katherine Anne Porter does in "Flowering Judas" (p. 150), or he may shift from the point of view of one character to that of another, as Tolstoy does in "Three Deaths" (p. 288). The omniscient point of view is sometimes adopted by a first-person narrator, sometimes presented in the third person. The use of the omniscient point of view assumes that the writer understands the minds of all the characters and that he has a complete knowledge of all the events. See "The Captive's Story" (p. 112).

There are specific advantages to each point of view. First-person narrative gives a greater illusion of immediacy and authority; the third-person point of view allows for greater detachment; the omniscient point of view permits a maximum of flexibility. But each point of view also has its limitations. The first-person story strains credibility, since no one person is likely to be aware of all the nuances of a complex action; the third-person story pretends to an objectivity that is sometimes violated by the appearance of a submerged I; the omniscient point of view advertises the fictitious nature of the events.

In realistic description and narration, the point of view of the speaker must be defined in terms of the exact angle from which he describes or narrates events and of the mental attitude he takes toward them. In a larger sense, point of view refers to the standard of values, explicit or implied, by which the author judges the actions of his characters.

PROBLEM PLAY: A conventional term used to describe many dramas, particularly those in the tradition of Ibsen, Shaw, and Pirandello, that present serious social, political, and religious problems. These plays are neither wholly tragic nor wholly comic. *Corruption in the Palace of Justice* (p. 1160) is serious and ends sadly, yet Cust's reconciliation of his inner struggle is in a sense a triumph. Another designation for the problem play is simply "serious" drama.

PROCESS: A mode of analysis that traces the development of a subject in the course of its operation. Process is called *historical* when it is chiefly concerned with temporal or chronological development, *natural* when it describes a psychological, biological, or physical development, *logical* when it describes the mode of thought employed in an argument or exposition. Often these various processes are combined. The essays by Conrad Arensberg, T. H. Huxley, James V. Cunningham, René Dubos, Edmund Wilson, and Joseph N. Riddell are predominantly analyses of various kinds of process.

PROLOGUE: *See* ACT.

PROSE: Language which is neither metrical nor rhymed. The word prose derives from the Latin term *oratio prorsus,* meaning speech that runs on ahead. The word verse derives from the Latin root *verto,* to turn, and signifies speech that returns to the same pattern. *See also* VERSE AND VERSIFICATION.

REALISM: A literary style antithetical to ROMANTICISM. The realist attempts to record life as it is, rather than as we would like it to be. The language that he uses approximates everyday speech, and the subject that he chooses is a familiar one, often even commonplace. The stories in this volume of William Faulkner, Stephen Crane, Eudora Welty, and Liam O'Flaherty are predominantly realistic.

RESOLUTION: *See* PLOT.

ROMANTICISM: As opposed to realism, romanticism refers to a style that presents life in a picturesque, fanciful, or exotic manner. A romantic writer tends to use elevated diction and intense strain of address. Kept within bounds, as in Shakespeare's *Romeo and Juliet,* or in Keats's "Ode on a Grecian Urn," the romantic style conveys a heightened sense of life in which the familiar seems strange and the strange suggests further mystery. Excessive romanticism on the other hand is marked by sentimentality, exaggeration and a straining after emotional or imaginative effects. Max Beerbohm parodies this kind of romanticism in "The Happy Hypocrite" (p. 966). Romanticism also refers to the traits of the literary period, circa 1772–1832, and of writers like Wordsworth, Coleridge, Keats, Shelley, and Byron. These writers often emphasized the experiences of childhood and youth as opposed to those of maturity, the activity of the imagination as opposed to that of reason, the subjective as opposed to the objective, the individual or personal as opposed to the general. Romanticism is also opposed to classicism, that is, a style often identified with the neo-classical period, circa 1660–1770. Classicism reflects a love of order, propriety, maturity, polished expression and respect for Greco-Roman literature written by and for men of learning and taste. At its best, as in the poetry of Pope (p. 516), the prose of Swift (p. 1126), and the criticism of T. S. Eliot (p. 777), the classical style pleases by its wit and lucidity. At its worst, it tends to be cold, unoriginal and abstract. T. S. Eliot explores the meaning of the classic in the essay cited above.

SARCASM: *See* FIGURATIVE LANGUAGE.

SATIRE: Like comedy, *satire* is primarily intellectual in character. A manner or mode of treating a subject, rather than a special type of literature, satire may be found in fiction, poetry, drama, and the essay and allied forms of prose.

In satire, a writer attacks vice, folly, or bad taste with a view toward their correction. The true satirist is not concerned with mere invective or abuse, or with sarcasm directed against individuals. Least of all is he attempting indirectly to assert his own moral, intellectual, or aesthetic superiority. His aim is to re-establish a virtue or truth that has been abandoned, or a manner of acting or thinking whose absence deprives life of its grace or charm.

The satirist's weapons are many. Sometimes he uses a combination of ARGUMENT and IRONY, as in Swift's "A Modest Proposal" (p. 1126). Occasionally he exposes or refutes a position by reducing it to an absurdity, as in "You Should Have Seen the Mess" (p. 145). Other means employed in satire are ridicule of a mental attitude, as in "Love Among the Ruins" (p. 989); wit, as in *The Misanthrope* (p. 865); and moral indignation as in "Notes of a Native Son" (p. 1133). *See also* BURLESQUE, COMEDY.

SCENE: *See* ACT.

SETTING: *See* ATMOSPHERE.

SHORT STORY: A type of fictitious narrative. It is brief, usually between 2,000 and 12,000 words; thus it may range in form from an anecdote to a narrative of events to a novella. Brevity, however, is not the essential characteristic of the short story. The essence of the short story is its unified treatment of a single action.

Usually a short story is carefully plotted. It normally has a definite beginning, middle, and end as well as a dramatic encounter in which a trait of character or a thematic point is clearly revealed. (See the commentary on the short stories in the introductions to the several sections.)

Many short stories avoid the appearance of a preconceived order of complication, turning point, and resolution in favor of an apparently artless narrative of an intensely personal experience. Close reading, however, reveals that, even when there is no marked climax or tidy resolution, the short story is usually the work of a skillful writer, who, as Poe described him, "having conceived with deliberate care, a certain unique or single effect to be wrought out . . . then invents such incidents—[and] combines such events as may best aid him in establishing this preconceived effect." *See also* NOVEL, PLOT.

SIMILE: *See* FIGURATIVE LANGUAGE.

SOLILOQUY: *See* DRAMATIC MONOLOGUE.

SONNET: *See* VERSIFICATION.

SPECTACLE: That aspect of drama which is concerned with the theatrical presentation. Spectacle may also refer to the presentation of pageant, dance, song and other visible displays, as, for example, in Act IV, *The Tempest.*

SPONDEE: *See* VERSIFICATION.

STANZA: *See* VERSIFICATION.

STORY: *See* PLOT.

STROPHE: *See* ODE.

STRUCTURE: *See* FORM.

STYLE: Style is the mode or manner of verbal expression. The three characteristics of good style are traditionally described as *clarity, vigor,* and *interest*. Style is *how* a writer uses words to form sentences and sentences to form paragraphs. (For a discussion of how writers use words, *see* DICTION, CONNOTATION and DENOTATION, and FIGURATIVE LANGUAGE.)

The clarity, vigor, and interest of sentences and larger compositional units are traditionally described under the headings UNITY, COHERENCE, and EMPHASIS. Sentence style is sometimes described as *periodic,* when the main idea is suspended until the end, or *loose,* when the main idea is stated first.

A paragraph in which a periodic and a loose sentence are used (in that order), is the following one by Samuel Johnson:

> If a madman were to come into this room with a stick in his hand, no doubt we should pity the state of his mind, but our primary consideration would be to take care of ourselves. We should knock him down first and pity him afterwards.

In a larger sense style refers to the expression in language of the writer's total personality as well as his ideas. In his famous apothegm, "Style is the man," Buffon undoubtedly meant that style conveys not only the writer's specific ideas on a given subject, but also his vision or general attitude toward life—the whole complex of sensibilities, intuitions, and reasonings that is sometimes called the writer's world view.

In his interpretation of Buffon's remark, Gorham Munson points out that a writer regards style as the substitute in print for his own person, a compensation for his absent qualities:

> I must somehow make words and phrases convey what I can ordinarily convey by posture and gesture, by dress and the given circumstances of a situation, by tone of voice and facial pantomime, by actions, and, in short, by my whole living personality. Hence, I must give much thought to tone and to rhythms, to preparatory scaffolding and connective tissues, to insure so far as I can that the reader will experience me as if I were indeed present.

Style may also refer to the literary manner that developed in certain epochs, for example, classical style, Renaissance style, or romantic style. Or it may refer to the manner associated with a particular writer, for example, Ciceronian style, Virgilian, Shakespearean, Baconian, or Tennysonian. Style may also be used to indicate levels of discourse, for example, grand or high style, which is appropriate when used by a speaker who commands respect on a formal occasion; middle style, which is appropriate to ordinary occasions and topics; and low style, which is appropriate to the rendering of the trivial, comic, or vulgar situation. *See also* TONE.

SYMBOL: *See* FIGURATIVE LANGUAGE.

SYNEDOCHE: *See* FIGURATIVE LANGUAGE.

THEME: The term theme, or thesis, refers (1) to the basic proposition or statement in an argument or exposition, and (2) to the underlying idea that unifies the structure of a drama, story, or poem.

THOUGHT: Refers to (1) the body of ideas contained in a work of literature, and (2) to the mode of reasoning employed by a writer speaking either in his own person or through his characters in a work of fiction.

TONE: A metaphorical expression, derived from music, that expresses a palpable but often undefinable aspect of style. Tone is the attitude of the writer toward the subject of his work. It may be sorrowful, as in "Notes of a Native Son" (p. 1133); ironic as in "A Modest Proposal" (p. 1126); sentimental as in "The Time I've Lost in Wooing" (p. 1044); or objective or impersonal as in "Countrymen at Work" (p. 630). *See* STYLE.

TRAGEDY: In Aristotle's *Poetics* tragedy is defined as "an imitation of an action that is serious, complete, and of a certain magnitude; in language embellished with each kind of artistic ornament, the several kinds being found in the separate parts of the play; in the mode of action, not of narrative; through pity and fear effecting the proper purgation (catharsis) of these emotions." Because of their identification with tragic drama, these and many other terms used by Aristotle are still part of our active critical vocabulary—for example, IMITATION, PLOT, CHARACTER, DICTION, THOUGHT, SONG, SPECTACLE. In the *Poetics* the terms directly applicable to tragedy are *hamartia, hubris,* and *catharsis.*

According to Aristotle, the tragic situation necessarily implies a human agent or character with "certain distinctive qualities both of character and thought." This person, Oedipus, for instance (p. 420), is at least partially responsible for his own destruction because of a *hamartia,* or flaw in his character. This flaw is not a grave defect but rather a weakness or the result of a mistake or the lack of a necessary virtue. If it were a defect that deserved serious punishment, then the death or defeat of the character would not elicit the degree of pity or fear regarded as essential to tragedy. In Oedipus' case the flaw is *hubris,* or a complacent pride in his own righteousness and wisdom. Hence when Oedipus is trapped in toils partly of his own making, he achieves the stature of a truly tragic character. (See pp. 284–85).

The emotional effect of tragedy is pity for the hero and a fear that what happened to him may indeed happen to any human being. These emotions are, at best, negative. But true tragedy, according to Aristotle, not only arouses these emotions but also effects their *catharsis.* The audience, in the aesthetic contemplation of the event on the stage, gives vent to feelings which, had they not been released, would have remained secret sources of embitterment and frustration.

The term *tragedy* has been extended in the course of time to include not only drama, but poetry and prose fiction that seriously represent action of high importance and end with the defeat of the hero. In many instances the tragic protagonist, like Marlowe's Dr. Faustus and Shakespeare's Macbeth, are not so much essentially good men or heroes as they are men of great possibilities who deserve their destruction. They command not so much our pity and fear as our astonishment at the magnitude of their crimes and follies.

Derivations of tragedy are *tragicomedy,* in which some events end happily and others do not, as in *Cymbeline,* or in which characters evade death but not unhappiness, and *melodrama,* which depends on suspenseful plot and exaggerated terror rather than on the development of a truly tragic character.

TROCHEE: *See* VERSIFICATION.

TURNING POINT: *See* PLOT.

UNDERSTATEMENT: *See* FIGURATIVE LANGUAGE.

UNITY and VARIETY: Unity is a characteristic of all effective writing. In rhetoric a sentence is said to be unified when all the parts contribute to a single main idea or impression. Such unity is achieved (1) by excluding the irrelevant, superfluous, or inappropriate elements, (2) by subordinating less important details, and (3) by giving coordinate rank to ideas of equal importance. The same principles apply, with due attention to proportion, to the larger elements of composition. In imaginative literature unity is equivalent to the FORM or total meaning of the work. Hence unity is often defined as the theme or underlying principle that relates the various parts to each other.

Variety is a necessary concomitant of unity, relieving it, so to speak, of monotony, repetition, or rigidity of development. Variety is attained by the right use of a rich vocabulary, by a pleasing alternation of the length and kind, the sound and rhythm of sentences, and in more lengthy compositions, by contrast, suspense, reversals, and controlled digressions. The greatest single source of variety is FIGURATIVE LANGUAGE.

VERSE and VERSIFICATION: A reader needs no special training to be able to distinguish between the music of poetry and the music of prose. Poetry has a more pronounced rhythm. It tends toward metrical regularity and a more emphatic melodic pattern of rhyme, assonance, and alliteration. Prose, on the other hand, avoids metrical regularity and rhyme. Yet the music of prose has its own rhythm, irregular perhaps, but definite. In prose the music is coincidental to the sense; in poetry the music is part of the sense itself. Without rhythm and melody, a poem hardly exists. A poem is what it is, not only in terms of the ideas or impressions conveyed by logical statement but also in terms of the mood evoked by the structure of the verse and the structure of the sound.

Essentially the rhythm and melody of a poem are as mysterious as the personality of the poet himself. No mechanical rules can completely explain how Tennyson sets his wild echoes flying, how Burns strikes the plaintive note in "A Red, Red Rose," or how A. E. Housman unites sound and sense in a line like, "With rue my heart is laden." Some harmonizing faculty, too deep for strict logical analysis, accomplishes this magic.

However, the music of poetry is not totally beyond comprehension. There are some rules of metrical and melodic arrangement that do more than name the mystery. These rules call attention to the usual practice of many great poets and provide, at the same time, a standard for noting their deviations. For, as T. S. Eliot has remarked, the ghost of some simple meter lurks "behind the arras in even the 'freest' verse. . . ."

Rhythm: Rhythm, the first of the two musical elements in poetry, is the regular rise and fall of stress. The rise and fall of stress is determined by the succession of accented (stressed) and unaccented (unstressed) syllables. The systematic measurement of the rhythm in terms of syllables or feet and in terms of lines or verses is called *meter*. Meter, the structure of rhythm, goes hand in hand with melody to produce the music of poetry. Meter and melody are not autonomous; their value in a given poem is determined by their consonance with each other and with the theme or mood of the poem.

Meter: Meter measures rhythm according to the *foot* and the *line*. A *foot* is a unit that consists of an accented syllable and one or more unaccented syllables.

In poetry, as in prose, every word and every syllable of a word is spoken with a greater or lesser degree of force. Accent is the greater degree of force placed on one syllable over another. Example: *póem̆*. In words of more than two syllables, such as: *exposítion*, there may be a secondary accent on a syllable one or two places removed from the principal accent.

The common feet in English poetry are:

The *iamb:* an unaccented syllable followed by an accented syllable:

˘ ´ as in dĕfénd

The *anapest:* two unaccented syllables followed by an accented syllable:

˘ ˘ ´ as in sŭpĕrséde

The *trochee:* an accented syllable followed by an unaccented syllable:

´ ˘ as in dóubtfŭl

The *dactyl:* an accented syllable followed by two unaccented syllables:

´ ˘ ˘ as in mércĭfŭl

Less frequently we find the *spondee,* an accented syllable followed by another accented syllable, as in *slów dówn;* and the *pyrrhic foot,* consisting of an unaccented syllable followed by another unaccented syllable, as in,

Tŏ thĕ | gréat háll cáme thĕ thróng.

Metrics of the Line: A line of verse consists of one or more feet. Lines are described according to the number and kind of feet they contain. Thus, when we describe verse according to the *number* of feet, a line consisting of one foot is called a *monometer*, of two feet a *dimeter*, of three feet a *trimeter,* of four feet a *tetrameter,* of five feet a *pentameter*, of six feet a *hexameter,* of seven feet a *heptameter,* and so on. Lines exceeding six feet are normally broken up into smaller segments.

We may also describe lines according to the *kind* of feet they contain—iambic, anapestic, and so on.

Thus a full description of the line, "When you are old and grey and full of sleep," is *iambic pentameter*.

Metrical Variations: A predominant metrical pattern in a poem establishes order or stability. Few poems, however, are metrically regular in every detail. To avoid the mechanical beat of the same rhythm, poets seek for variety in substitution, inversion, catalexis, hypermeter, pause, hovering accent, and elocutionary stress. By means of these and other variations, poets accelerate or retard the rhythm and thus increase or decrease the intensity of the poem.

Substitution is the interchange between an iamb and an anapest, or between a trochee and a dactyl:

Ĭ stúff | mў skín | sŏ fúll | wĭthín

Ŏf jól | lў góod ále | ănd óld

Lĭke thĕ léaves | ŏf thĕ fór | ĕst whĕn Áu | tŭmn hăth flówn

Thăt hóst | ŏn thĕ mór | rŏw lăy wíth | ĕred ănd strówn

Míne bĕ ă | hándfŭl ŏf | áshĕs

Inversion is the interchange between an iamb and a trochee, or between a dactyl and an anapest:

Bŭt whén | Ĭ grów | ăwáre | ŏf lóve
Swíftlў | Ĭ thínk | ŏn thée.

Catalexis is the omission (∧) of unaccented syllables from the beginning of an iambic or anapestic line, or from the end of a trochaic or dactylic line:

∧ Háil | tŏ thée | mў prínce | ănd fríend
Nóne wŏuld | Láunfăl | wíth hĭm | léad ∧
Sávĭng | Geoffrĕy, | ănd hĭs | stéed ∧

Hypermeter is the addition of unstressed syllables at the beginning of a trochaic line or at the end of an iambic line:

Thĕ án | gĕls kéep | thĕir án | cĭent plác | ĕs

A *pause* sometimes takes the place of an unstressed syllable in a line. Pause is a variation of meter when it does this.

Tréasŏn | hére ∧ | tréasŏn | thére ∧
Fídŏ | fóund ĭt | éverў | whére ∧

A *caesura* is a natural break (//) in the reading of a line. It is indicated by the punctuation, or demanded by the sense. It may occur at the end of a line or within the line. When the caesura occurs at the end of a line, a line is said to be *end-stopped.* Otherwise it is called a *run-on* line.

Maidens! // make a low music: // merely make
Silence a melody, // no more. // This day, //
She travels down a pale and lonely way: //

A *hovering accent* occurs (⌢) when the verse stress falls on the first syllable of a foot and the word accent on the second, or when two regularly accented syllables appear in the same foot. When the accent hovers, both syllables receive relatively equal stress. The hovering accent thus creates the same effect as a spondee, that is, a foot with two equally stressed syllables.

Ô nône, | ŭnléss | thĭs mír | ăclé | hâve mîght

Elocutionary stress. At times the stress demanded by the verse differs from the stress demanded by the meaning of the line. In such cases intelligent reading compels us to emphasize the words that are most meaningful, even if such an emphasis alters the regular rhythm. Thus, in Browning's "My Last Duchess" we have an elocutionary stress superimposed on the predominantly iambic verses:

Thát's my lást Dúchess paínted on the wáll
Lóoking as if she were alivé. I call
Thát piéce a wónder, now: . . .

In the first line the metrical stress falls on the words *my* and *on,* both relatively unemphatic words. In the second line the metrical stress falls on *were.* In all three cases, however, the words are relatively weak and unemphatic in comparison with the more important words marked by ´. Hence the meaning demands an alteration of the ordinary verse stress. Note that the first foot in each of the three lines is a variation. *That's my* in line 1 and *That piece* in line 3 illustrate a hovering accent. *Looking as* in line 2 is an inversion, that is, the use of a trochee in a predominantly iambic line.

Quantitative stress. Variation of metrical effect is also achieved by attention to the *quantity* of syllables, that is, to the duration or intensity of the accent. Thus in *immemorial* the second syllable is unstressed, yet it requires a longer time to pronounce than the unstressed syllable in a word like *tender*.

Melody: Melody is the regular and agreeable succession of tones or sounds. It produces a harmonious effect chiefly by rhyme, secondarily by assonance, alliteration, onomatopoeia, repetition, and euphony. Melody, like meter, contributes to the musical effect and helps to emphasize the meaning of words that are linked by similar sounds.

Rhyme may be divided into perfect and imperfect rhyme, end rhyme and internal rhyme, masculine and feminine rhyme.

Perfect rhyme consists in the agreement in two or more words of accented vowels and of the vowels and consonants that follow. The sounds preceding the accented vowel sound must be different:

maiden   laden
say   nay
stealing   wheeling
cherisheth   perisheth

Imperfect rhyme occurs when one or more of the requirements of a perfect rhyme are missing:

mother   father
lost   boast
powers   adores
steel   mill

End rhyme occurs at the end of a line, as in:

When I resemble her to *thee*
How sweet and fair she seems to *be.*

Internal rhyme occurs within the line, as in:

dapple-*dawn-drawn* Falcon
Fall, gall themselves
In a *land* of *sand* and ruin and gold

Masculine rhyme occurs when the final syllable of the rhyming words is accented:

perfúme   resúme
defeát   retreát

Feminine rhyme occurs when the rhymed syllables are followed by identical unaccented syllables, as in:

cheérful   eárful
ténderly   slénderly

Assonance is the repetition of the same or similar vowel sounds in a line or in successive lines:

So they *row*ed and there we landed
O venusta sirmi*o*

In X*a*n*a*du did Kubl*a* Kh*a*n

Alliteration is the repetition of the same consonant sound in a line or in successive lines of verse. Usually the repetition occurs at the beginning of words:

O *h*ark, O *h*ear, *h*ow thin and clear . . .

*F*ull *f*athom *f*ive thy *f*ather lies

Sometimes, however, it lies half buried in the midst of words:

. . . Melt me so
With thy del*ic*ious numbers
That being rav*ish*ed . . .

Onomatopoeia is the use of words whose sound suggests the object or action producing the sound. Some onomatopoeic words are *gong, thunder, hiss, screech, murmur, rumble, clink.*

Hark! now I hear them,—*Ding-dong,* bell

To reflect back her blushes
Or give *sigh for sigh*

Repetition is the use of the same word or phrase in several lines for the sake of emphasis:

Tears, idle *tears,* I know not what they mean,
Tears from the depth of some divine despair

Blow, bugle, *blow,* set the wild echoes flying,
Blow, bugle, answer, echoes, *dying, dying, dying.*

Euphony is a succession of light, harmonious syllables that contribute to the melody of a line. For example, the sibilants, liquids, and vowels in "Slowly, silently, now the morn" create a melodious effect.

Cacophony is a succession of heavy, harsh syllables. For example, the shaggy consonants and heavy vowels in "When Ajax strives some rocks' vast weight to throw" achieve a dissonant impression.

Both euphony and cacophony are frequently used to lend variety to a passage.

The Stanza: A stanza is a group of lines connected by a predominant meter and by a rhyme scheme. The stanza, like the prose paragraph, usually centers on a single thought or mood.

In English poetry, regular stanzaic patterns range from the couplet to the nineteen-line villanelle. Irregular stanzas are numerous and unclassifiable. The principal varieties of the stanza are:

The *rhymed couplet:* two lines with perfect end rhyme:

A sweet disorder in the dress
Kindles in clothes a wantonness.
—*Herrick*

The *heroic couplet:* two lines in iambic pentameter with perfect end rhyme:

Good and great God! can I not think of Thee
But it must straight my melancholy be?
—*Pope*

The *tercet:* a stanza of three lines. The rhyme scheme is either *aaa* or *aba:*

Whoe'er she be a
That not impossible she a
That shall command my heart and me a
—*Crashaw*

O wild West Wind, thou breath of Autumn's being a
Thou, from whose unseen presence the leaves dead b
Are driven, like ghosts from an enchanter fleeing, a
—*Shelley*

The tercet is frequently linked with other tercets in a rhyme scheme *aba-bcb-cdc*, etc., called *terza rima* (See *Paradiso* p. 237).

The *quatrain:* a stanza of four lines, in any length or meter, with a varied rhyme scheme. A few varieties of the quatrain are:

And can he who smiles on all a
Hear the wren with sorrows small, a
Hear the small bird's grief and care, b
Hear the woes that infants bear, b
—*Blake*

When at length he sat up and was able to speak, a
His sad story he offered to tell; b
And the Bellman cried "Silence! Not even a shriek!" a
And excitedly tingled his bell. b
—*Carroll*

Rhyme royal: a stanza of seven lines in iambic pentameter with the rhyme scheme *ababbcc*. A favorite measure of Chaucer, rhyme royal has also been used by John Masefield.

Ottava rima: a stanza of eight lines with the rhyme scheme *abababcc*. (See *Don Juan*, p. 523.)

The *Spenserian stanza:* eight lines in iambic pentameter followed by a ninth line in iambic hexameter (alexandrine), with the rhyme scheme *ababbcbcc*. Named for Edmund Spenser, who employed it in his *The Faerie Queene*.

The *sonnet:* a complete poem of fourteen lines in iambic pentameter. The *Italian sonnet* consists of two parts: the first part, composed of eight lines (octet), usually develops a set of particular problems; the second part, composed of six lines (sestet), frequently presents a solution to the problems or an emotional response to them. Although the usual rhyme scheme of the Italian sonnet is *abbaabbacdecde*, many variations are used.

The *Shakespearean sonnet* consists of three quatrains and a concluding couplet with a typical rhyme scheme *abab-cdcd-efef-gg*. In many instances, the first two quatrains of the Shakespearean sonnet perform the same function as the octet in the Italian sonnet, and the last quatrain and the couplet perform the functions of the sestet. More frequently the couplet states the conclusion in an epigram, that is, a short pointed statement of a general truth.

Some writers, Gerard Manley Hopkins among them, have written sonnets in irregular patterns.

Blank verse: unrhymed lines in iambic pentameter. Blank verse normally does not follow a stanzaic pattern but may be divided in the manner of prose into verse paragraphs.

Free verse avoids a fixed pattern of meter, melody, or stanza. Its rhythms are organized to suggest unemphatically the ebb and flow, the rise and fall, of the writer's mood or perception. Hence the rhythm of free verse is not independent of the emotional drive in the poem. (*See* "Freedom" [p. 1299] and "Ship of Death" [p. 1302].)

In concluding this note on verse and verification, we should recall once again that rhythm and melody are intimately related to the sense of the poem. Versification is the outer reflection of an inner meaning, not an arbitrary pattern that is imposed indifferently upon thoughts and emotions. Sound derives its value from its symbiotic life with sense. The great variety of meter, melody, and stanzaic pattern attests to the poet's need to express different purposes in different ways. Verse walks, stumbles, runs, skips, hops, pirouettes, glides, stops, starts again in reponse to the movement of thought and mood. It is grave or gay, sharp or muffled, dignified or frisky, confident or reticent at the direction of the inner voice or meaning of the poem. Thus verse is intimately linked with the diction and FIGURATIVE LANGUAGE.

WIT: *See* COMEDY, SATIRE.

AUTHOR INDEX

TITLE INDEX

A
B
C
D
E
F
G
H
I
J